DLA Piper UK LLP Leeds

HALSBURY'S
Laws of England

FIFTH EDITION
2017

Volume 1

This is volume 1 of the Fifth Edition of Halsbury's Laws of England, containing the titles AGENCY and AGRICULTURAL LAND AND ALLOTMENTS.

The titles AGENCY and AGRICULTURAL LAND AND ALLOTMENTS replace the titles AGENCY and AGRICULTURAL LAND contained in volume 1 (2008). The remaining title of volume 1 (2008), AGRICULTURAL PRODUCTION AND MARKETING, is replaced by the title of the same name contained in volume 1A (2017). Upon receipt of volume 1 (2017) and volume 1A (2017), volume 1 (2008) may be archived.

For a full list of volumes comprised in a current set of Halsbury's Laws of England please see overleaf.

Fifth Edition volumes:

1 (2017), 1A (2017), 2 (2017), 3 (2011), 4 (2011), 5 (2013), 6 (2011), 7 (2015), 8 (2015), 9 (2017), 10 (2017), 11 (2015), 12 (2015), 12A (2015), 13 (2017), 14 (2016), 15 (2016), 15A (2016), 16 (2017), 17 (2017), 18 (2009), 19 (2011), 20 (2014), 21 (2016), 22 (2012), 23 (2016), 24 (2010), 25 (2016), 26 (2016), 27 (2015), 28 (2015), 29 (2014), 30 (2012), 31 (2012), 32 (2012), 33 (2017), 34 (2011), 35 (2015), 36 (2015), 37 (2013), 38 (2013), 38A (2013), 39 (2014), 40 (2014), 41 (2014), 41A (2014), 42 (2011), 43 (2011), 44 (2011), 45 (2010), 46 (2010), 47 (2014), 47A (2014), 48 (2015), 49 (2015), 50 (2016), 50A (2016), 51 (2013), 52 (2014), 53 (2014), 54 (2017), 54A (2017), 55 (2012), 56 (2017), 57 (2012), 58 (2014), 58A (2014), 59 (2014), 59A (2014), 60 (2011), 61 (2010), 62 (2016), 63 (2016), 64 (2016), 65 (2015), 66 (2015), 67 (2016), 68 (2016), 69 (2009), 70 (2012), 71 (2013), 72 (2015), 73 (2015), 74 (2011), 75 (2013), 76 (2013), 77 (2016), 78 (2010), 79 (2014), 80 (2013), 81 (2010), 82 (2010), 83 (2010), 84 (2013), 84A (2013), 85 (2012), 86 (2017), 87 (2017), 88 (2012), 88A (2013), 89 (2011), 90 (2011), 91 (2012), 92 (2015), 93 (2017), 94 (2017), 95 (2017), 96 (2012), 97 (2015), 97A (2014), 98 (2013), 99 (2012), 100 (2009), 101 (2009), 102 (2016), 103 (2016), 104 (2014)

Consolidated Index and Tables:

2017 Consolidated Index (A–E), 2017 Consolidated Index (F–O), 2017 Consolidated Index (P–Z), 2018 Consolidated Table of Statutes, 2018 Consolidated Table of Statutory Instruments, 2018 Consolidated Table of Cases (A–G), 2018 Consolidated Table of Cases (H–Q), 2018 Consolidated Table of Cases (R–Z, ECJ Cases)

Updating and ancillary materials:

2017 annual Cumulative Supplement; monthly Noter-up; annual Abridgments 1974–2016

December 2017

HALSBURY'S
Laws of England

Volume 1

2017

Members of the LexisNexis Group worldwide

United Kingdom	RELX (UK) Ltd, trading as LexisNexis, 1–3 Strand, London WC2N 5JR and 9–10 St Andrew Square, Edinburgh EH2 2AF
Australia	Reed International Books Australia Pty Ltd trading as LexisNexis, Chatswood, New South Wales
Austria	LexisNexis Verlag ARD Orac GmbH & Co KG, Vienna
Benelux	LexisNexis Benelux, Amsterdam
Canada	LexisNexis Canada, Markham, Ontario
China	LexisNexis China, Beijing and Shanghai
France	LexisNexis SA, Paris
Germany	LexisNexis GmbH, Dusseldorf
Hong Kong	LexisNexis Hong Kong, Hong Kong
India	LexisNexis India, New Delhi
Italy	Giuffrè Editore, Milan
Japan	LexisNexis Japan, Tokyo
Malaysia	Malayan Law Journal Sdn Bhd, Kuala Lumpur
New Zealand	LexisNexis New Zealand Ltd, Wellington
Singapore	LexisNexis Singapore, Singapore
South Africa	LexisNexis, Durban
USA	LexisNexis, Dayton, Ohio

FIRST EDITION	*Published in 31 volumes between 1907 and 1917*
SECOND EDITION	*Published in 37 volumes between 1931 and 1942*
THIRD EDITION	*Published in 43 volumes between 1952 and 1964*
FOURTH EDITION	*Published in 56 volumes between 1973 and 1987, with reissues between 1988 and 2008*
FIFTH EDITION	*Published between 2008 and 2014, with reissues from 2014*

© 2017 RELX (UK) Ltd

A CIP Catalogue record for this book is available from the British Library.

ISBN 978-1-4743-0946-2

9 781474 309462

ISBN for the set: 9781405734394
ISBN for this volume: 9781474309462
Typeset by LexisNexis
Printed and bound by CPI Group (UK) Ltd, Croydon, CR0 4YY

Visit LexisNexis at www.lexisnexis.co.uk

AGENCY

Consultant Editor

RODERICK MUNDAY, MA, PhD,

Reader Emeritus in Law, University of Cambridge;
Fellow Emeritus of Peterhouse, Cambridge;
Bencher of Lincoln's Inn

AGRICULTURAL LAND AND ALLOTMENTS

Consultant Editor

CHRISTOPHER MCNALL, MA (Oxon), DPhil (Oxon),

Barrister-at-law of the Middle Temple;
Northern Circuit Deputy Chairman, Agricultural Lands Tribunal for Wales

The law stated in this volume is in general that in force on 1 November 2017, although subsequent changes have been included wherever possible.

Any future updating material will be found in the Noter-up and annual Cumulative Supplement to Halsbury's Laws of England.

TABLE OF CONTENTS

HOW TO USE HALSBURY'S LAWS OF ENGLAND

Volumes

Each text volume of Halsbury's Laws of England contains the law on the titles contained in it as at a date stated at the front of the volume (the operative date).

Information contained in Halsbury's Laws of England may be accessed in several ways.

First, by using the tables of contents.

Each volume contains both a general Table of Contents, and a specific Table of Contents for each title contained in it. From these tables you will be directed to the relevant part of the work.

Readers should note that the current arrangement of titles can be found in the Noter-up.

Secondly, by using tables of statutes, statutory instruments, cases or other materials.

If you know the name of the Act, statutory instrument or case with which your research is concerned, you should consult the Consolidated Tables of statutes, cases and so on (published as separate volumes) which will direct you to the relevant volume and paragraph.

(Each individual text volume also includes tables of those materials used as authority in that volume.)

Thirdly, by using the indexes.

If you are uncertain of the general subject area of your research, you should go to the Consolidated Index (published as separate volumes) for reference to the relevant volume(s) and paragraph(s).

(Each individual text volume also includes an index to the material contained therein.)

Updating publications

The text volumes of Halsbury's Laws should be used in conjunction with the annual Cumulative Supplement and the monthly Noter-up.

The annual Cumulative Supplement

The Supplement gives details of all changes between the operative date of the text volume and the operative date of the Supplement. It is arranged in the same volume, title and paragraph order as the text volumes. Developments affecting particular points of law are noted to the relevant paragraph(s) of the text volumes.

For narrative treatment of material noted in the Cumulative Supplement, go to the annual Abridgment volume for the relevant year.

Destination Tables

In certain titles in the annual *Cumulative Supplement*, reference is made to Destination Tables showing the destination of consolidated legislation. Those Destination Tables are to be found either at the end of the titles within the annual *Cumulative Supplement*, or in a separate *Destination Tables* booklet provided from time to time with the *Cumulative Supplement*.

The Noter-up

The Noter-up is issued monthly and notes changes since the publication of the annual Cumulative Supplement. Also arranged in the same volume, title and paragraph order as the text volumes, the Noter-up follows the style of the Cumulative Supplement.

For narrative treatment of material noted in the Noter-up, go to the annual Abridgment volume for the relevant year.

REFERENCES AND ABBREVIATIONS

ACT	Australian Capital Territory
A-G	Attorney General
Admin	Administrative Court
Admlty	Admiralty Court
Adv-Gen	Advocate General
affd	affirmed
affg	affirming
Alta	Alberta
App	Appendix
art	article
Aust	Australia
B	Baron
BC	British Columbia
C	Command Paper (of a series published before 1900)
c	chapter number of an Act
CA	Court of Appeal
CAC	Central Arbitration Committee
CA in Ch	Court of Appeal in Chancery
CB	Chief Baron
CCA	Court of Criminal Appeal
CCR	County Court Rules 1981 (as subsequently amended)
CCR	Court for Crown Cases Reserved
CJEU	Court of Justice of the European Union
C-MAC	Courts-Martial Appeal Court
CO	Crown Office
COD	Crown Office Digest
CPR	Civil Procedure Rules
Can	Canada
Cd	Command Paper (of the series published 1900–18)
Cf	compare
Ch	Chancery Division
ch	chapter
cl	clause
Cm	Command Paper (of the series published 1986 to date)
Cmd	Command Paper (of the series published 1919–56)
Cmnd	Command Paper (of the series published 1956–86)
Comm	Commercial Court

Comr	Commissioner
Court Forms (2nd Edn)	Atkin's Encyclopaedia of Court Forms in Civil Proceedings, 2nd Edn. See note 2 post.
CrimPR	Criminal Procedure Rules
DC	Divisional Court
DPP	Director of Public Prosecutions
EAT	Employment Appeal Tribunal
EC	European Community
ECJ	Court of Justice of the European Community (before the Treaty of Lisbon (OJ C306, 17.12.2007, p 1) came into force on 1 December 2009); European Court of Justice (after the Treaty of Lisbon (OJ C306, 17.12.2007, p 1) came into force on 1 December 2009)
EComHR	European Commission of Human Rights
ECSC	European Coal and Steel Community
ECtHR Rules of Court	Rules of Court of the European Court of Human Rights
EEC	European Economic Community
EFTA	European Free Trade Association
EGC	European General Court
EWCA Civ	Official neutral citation for judgments of the Court of Appeal (Civil Division)
EWCA Crim	Official neutral citation for judgments of the Court of Appeal (Criminal Division)
EWHC	Official neutral citation for judgments of the High Court
Edn	Edition
Euratom	European Atomic Energy Community
EU	European Union
Ex Ch	Court of Exchequer Chamber
ex p	ex parte
Fam	Family Division
Fed	Federal
Forms & Precedents (5th Edn)	Encyclopaedia of Forms and Precedents other than Court Forms, 5th Edn. See note 2 post
GLC	Greater London Council
HC	High Court
HC	House of Commons
HK	Hong Kong
HL	House of Lords
HMRC	Her Majesty's Revenue and Customs
IAT	Immigration Appeal Tribunal
ILM	International Legal Materials

INLR	Immigration and Nationality Law Reports
IRC	Inland Revenue Commissioners
Ind	India
Int Rels	International Relations
Ir	Ireland
J	Justice
JA	Judge of Appeal
Kan	Kansas
LA	Lord Advocate
LC	Lord Chancellor
LCC	London County Council
LCJ	Lord Chief Justice
LJ	Lord Justice of Appeal
LoN	League of Nations
MR	Master of the Rolls
Man	Manitoba
n.	note
NB	New Brunswick
NI	Northern Ireland
NS	Nova Scotia
NSW	New South Wales
NY	New York
NZ	New Zealand
OHIM	Office for Harmonisation in the Internal Market
OJ	The Official Journal of the European Union published by the Publications Office of the European Union
Ont	Ontario
P.	President
PC	Judicial Committee of the Privy Council
PEI	Prince Edward Island
Pat	Patents Court
q	question
QB	Queen's Bench Division
QBD	Queen's Bench Division of the High Court
Qld	Queensland
Que	Quebec
r	rule
RDC	Rural District Council
RPC	Restrictive Practices Court
RSC	Rules of the Supreme Court 1965 (as subsequently amended)
reg	regulation
Res	Resolution

revsd............................	reversed
Rly	Railway
s	section
SA	South Africa
S Aust	South Australia
SC	Supreme Court
SI	Statutory Instruments published by authority
SR & O	Statutory Rules and Orders published by authority
SR & O Rev 1904	Revised Edition comprising all Public and General Statutory Rules and Orders in force on 31 December 1903
SR & O Rev 1948	Revised Edition comprising all Public and General Statutory Rules and Orders and Statutory Instruments in force on 31 December 1948
SRNI	Statutory Rules of Northern Ireland
STI	Simon's Tax Intelligence (1973–1995); Simon's Weekly Tax Intelligence (1996-current)
Sask	Saskatchewan
Sch	Schedule
Sess	Session
Sing	Singapore
TCC	Technology and Construction Court
TS	Treaty Series
Tanz	Tanzania
Tas	Tasmania
UDC	Urban District Council
UKHL	Official neutral citation for judgments of the House of Lords
UKPC	Official neutral citation for judgments of the Privy Council
UN	United Nations
V-C	Vice-Chancellor
Vict	Victoria
W Aust	Western Australia
Zimb	Zimbabwe

NOTE 1. A general list of the abbreviations of law reports and other sources used in this work can be found at the beginning of the Consolidated Table of Cases.

NOTE 2. Where references are made to other publications, the volume number precedes and the page number follows the name of the publication; eg the reference '12 Forms & Precedents (5th Edn) 44' refers to volume 12 of the Encyclopaedia of Forms and Precedents, page 44.

NOTE 3. An English statute is cited by short title or, where there is no short title, by regnal year and chapter number together with the name by which it is commonly known or a description of its subject matter and date. In the case of a foreign statute, the mode of citation generally follows the style of citation in use in the country concerned with the addition, where necessary, of the name of the country in parentheses.

NOTE 4. A statutory instrument is cited by short title, if any, followed by the year and number, or, if unnumbered, the date.

TABLE OF STATUTES

TABLE OF STATUTORY INSTRUMENTS

TABLE OF CASES

C

G

M

N

Decisions of the European Court of Justice are listed below numerically. These decisions
are also included in the preceding alphabetical list.

AGENCY

1. NATURE AND FORMATION

(1) THE RELATION OF AGENCY

1. Nature of the relation of agency.
The terms 'agency' and 'agent' have in popular use a number of different meanings[1], but in law the word 'agency' is used to connote the relation which exists where one person has an authority or capacity to create legal relations between a person occupying the position of principal and third parties[2].

The relation of agency typically arises whenever one person, called the 'agent', has authority[3] to act on behalf of another, called the 'principal'[4], and consents so to act. Whether that relation exists in any situation depends not on the precise terminology employed by the parties to describe their relationship, but on the true nature of the agreement or the exact circumstances of the relationship between the alleged principal and agent[5]. If an agreement in substance contemplates the alleged agent acting on his own behalf, and not on behalf of a principal, then, although he may be described in the agreement as an agent, the relation of agency will not have arisen[6]. Conversely the relation of agency may arise despite a provision in the agreement that it shall not[7].

A servant or an independent contractor, though not necessarily the employer's agent, may often have authority to act as such when relations with third parties are involved[8]. Nevertheless an agent, as such, is not a servant. An agent, although bound to exercise his authority in accordance with all lawful instructions which may be given to him from time to time by his principal, is not, unless he is also the servant of the principal, subject in the exercise of his authority to the direct control or supervision of the principal[9].

The essence of the agent's position is that he is only an intermediary between two other parties, and it is therefore essential to an agency in this sense that a third party should be in existence or contemplated[10]. If a person who is employed as an agent to buy or sell property for another seeks to sell his own property to his principal or to buy the property of his principal, he violates the first condition of his employment, and changes the intrinsic nature of the contract between them[11].

1   For other uses of these terms see PARA 2. See also *Kennedy v De Trafford* [1897] AC 180 at 188, HL, per Lord Herschell ('No word is more commonly and constantly abused than the word 'agent'. A person may be spoken of as an 'agent' and no doubt in the popular sense of the word may properly be said to be an 'agent', although when it is attempted to suggest that he is an 'agent' under such circumstances as create the legal obligations attaching to agency that use of the word is only misleading').

2   *International Harvester Co of Australia Pty Ltd v Carrigan's Hazeldene Pastoral Co* (1958) 100 CLR 644, Aust HC; *Town of Timmins v Brewers' Warehousing Co Ltd* [1962] OR 536, Ont CA.
    An agent may be appointed who lacks authority to affect the legal relations of the principal. Although not an agent in the fullest sense, he can still owe fiduciary duties to his principal: *Hurstanger Ltd v Wilson* [2007] EWCA Civ 299, [2007] 4 All ER 1118, [2007] 1 WLR 2351 (loan broker); *McWilliam v Norton Finance (UK) Ltd* [2015] EWCA Civ 186, [2015] 1 All ER (Comm) 1026 at [32]–[56] per Tomlinson LJ; *Medsted Associates Ltd v Canaccord Genuity Wealth (International) Ltd* [2017] EWHC 1815 (Comm), [2017] All ER (D) 151 (Jul) at [89]–[95] per Teare J.

3   For the ways in which the agent's authority may be conferred or arise see PARA 29.

4   *Wolff v Horncastle* (1798) 1 Bos & P 316; *Pole v Leask* (1863) 33 LJ Ch 155; *Samson v Aitchison* [1912] AC 844, PC; *Atlantic Mutual Insurance Co v King* [1919] 1 KB 307; *Pratt v Patrick* [1924] 1 KB 488; *Brooke v Bool* [1928] 2 KB 578. Authority may be implied from the subsequent assent of the principal: see PARAS 58–71.

5   *Re Nevill, ex p White* (1871) 6 Ch App 397, CA; *Bennett v Smith* (1852) 16 Jur 421; *De Bussche v Alt* (1878) 8 ChD 286, CA; *Samuel Bros Ltd v Whetherley* [1908] 1 KB 184, CA; *National Bank*

of Scotland Ltd v Shaw 1913 SC 133; *Re Cotton, ex p Cooke* (1913) 108 LT 310, CA; *Gibson v O'Keeney* [1928] NI 66, CA; *Salsi v Jetspeed Air Services Ltd* [1977] 2 Lloyd's Rep 57.

A person appointed to carry on the business of a person incapable of managing his affairs or under a deed of arrangement for the benefit of creditors is an agent: *Plumpton v Burkinshaw* [1908] 2 KB 572, CA; *GB Nicholls & Co Ltd v Knapman* (1910) 102 LT 306, CA.

By the Consumer Credit Act 1974 s 56 antecedent negotiations are conducted by the negotiator as agent for the creditor under a regulated agreement: see CONSUMER PROTECTION vol 21 (2016) PARA 443.

There is no general rule that an insurance company when instructing repairs to be done to a policy-holder's vehicle is acting as agent for the policy-holder: *Godfrey Davis Ltd v Culling and Hecht* [1962] 2 Lloyd's Rep 349, CA; *Cooter and Green Ltd v Tyrrell* [1962] 2 Lloyd's Rep 377, CA; *Kirkland's Garage (Kinross) Ltd v Clark* 1967 SLT (Sh Ct) 60.

A sheriff's officer does not, merely by seeking and obtaining advice from a landlord's solicitor, become the landlord's agent: *Barclays Bank Ltd v Roberts* [1954] 3 All ER 107, [1954] 1 WLR 1212, CA.

For a consideration of the relationship between a bank and its client where the bank facilitates the transfer of money from abroad into the United Kingdom see *Thomson (Inspector of Taxes) v Moyse* [1961] AC 967, [1960] 3 All ER 684, HL.

As to the position of a confirming house see PARA 12 note 1.

6 See *Re Nevill, ex p White* (1871) 6 Ch App 397, CA (affd sub nom *John Towle & Co v White* (1873) 29 LT 78, HL); *Livingstone v Ross* [1901] AC 327, PC; *Michelin Tyre Co Ltd v Macfarlane (Glasgow) Ltd* 1917 55 SLR 35, HL (retailer described as agent but held to be buyer); *Kitson v PS King & Son Ltd* (1919) 36 TLR 162 (agency commission terms in publishing trade do not establish relation of principal and agent); *WT Lamb & Sons v Goring Brick Co Ltd* [1932] 1 KB 710, CA (merchants appointed 'sole selling agents' held to be purchasers from their alleged principal); *Dental Manufacturing Co Ltd v C De Trey & Co* [1912] 3 KB 76, CA (purchaser described as having an 'exclusive agency'). See also *Handley Page Ltd v Customs and Excise Comrs and Rockwell Machine Tool Co Ltd* [1971] 2 Lloyd's Rep 298, CA (person paying import deposit not an agent for purchaser for whom goods imported, even though purchaser's name entered on form as person making payment of deposit).

7 *Customs and Excise Comrs v Pools Finance (1937) Ltd* [1952] 1 All ER 775, CA.

8 See eg *Archer v Moss, Applegate v Moss* [1971] 1 QB 406, [1971] 1 All ER 747, CA (builder, an independent contractor, held to be agent of developer for purposes of the Limitation Act 1939 s 26(b) (repealed: see now the Limitation Act 1980 s 32; and LIMITATION PERIODS vol 68 (2016) PARA 1220 et seq)). As to whether the servant of A can simultaneously be the agent of B in respect of the same piece of work see *Sykes v Millington* [1953] 1 QB 770, [1953] 1 All ER 1098, DC.

9 *Wolff v Horncastle* (1798) 1 Bos & P 316; *Barnett v South London Tramways Co* (1887) 18 QBD 815, CA.

10 *Re Moline, ex p Dyster* (1816) 2 Rose 349; *Wilson v Short* (1848) 6 Hare 366.

11 *Robinson v Mollett* (1875) LR 7 HL 802; *De Bussche v Alt* (1878) 8 ChD 286, CA; *Re Moline, ex p Dyster* (1816) 2 Rose 349; *Armstrong v Jackson* [1917] 2 KB 822. See also PARA 90.

2. Other uses of the word 'agent'.

In addition to describing a person employed to create contractual relations between two parties[1], the word 'agent' is used in at least two other senses. Thus it is often used in business in a non-legal sense to refer to a distributor, as in the case of the appointment of a 'sole selling agent', 'exclusive agent', or 'authorised agent'[2]. The relation so established between the appointor and appointee is usually that of vendor and purchaser[3] and no contractual relationship is established between the appointor of the agent and third parties by the sale of goods by the so-called agent to those third parties. The word 'agent' is also frequently used to describe the position of a person who is employed by another to perform duties often of a technical or professional nature which he discharges as that other's alter ego and not merely as an intermediary between the principal and the third party[4]. Thus a solicitor may be his client's agent for the purpose of instituting or continuing legal proceedings on his behalf[5]. Similarly where a person other than a servant is permitted by the owner of a vehicle to drive it for the owner's purposes, the driver will be the owner's agent for the purpose of making the owner vicariously liable for the driver's negligence in driving[6].

1 See PARA 1.
2 See the cases cited in PARA 1 note 5.
3 See *WT Lamb & Sons v Goring Brick Co Ltd* [1932] 1 KB 710, CA.
4 The distinction between a professional man and his client and the usual case of principal and agent affects the client's rights to the ownership and possession of working papers, etc; see *London School Board v Northcroft* (1889) 2 Hudson's BC (4th Edn) 147, 11th Edn 230 (quantity surveyors); *Leicestershire County Council v Michael Faraday & Partners Ltd* [1941] 2 KB 205, [1941] 2 All ER 483, CA (valuers); *Chantrey Martin & Co v Martin* [1953] 2 QB 286, [1953] 2 All ER 691, CA (accountants); *Customs and Excise Comrs v Johnson* [1980] STC 624 (organiser of educational courses).
5 As to the limits of a solicitor's authority see LEGAL PROFESSIONS vol 66 (2015) PARA 584.
6 *Wheatley v Patrick* (1837) 2 M & W 650; *Samson v Aitchison* [1912] AC 844, PC; *Smith v Moss* [1940] 1 KB 424, [1940] 1 All ER 469; *Hewitt v Bonvin* [1940] 1 KB 188, CA; *Ormrod v Crosville Motor Services Ltd* [1953] 2 All ER 753, [1953] 1 WLR 1120, CA; *Vandyke v Fender (Sun Insurance Office Ltd, third party)* [1970] 2 QB 292, [1970] 2 All ER 335, CA; but see *Morgans v Launchbury* [1973] AC 127, [1972] 2 All ER 606, HL (permission by the owner coupled only with an 'interest or concern' on the owner's part in the object of the journey does not create an agency). As to torts committed by agents see generally PARA 151 et seq.

(2) COMPETENCY OF PARTIES

(i) Competency of Principals

3. General rule as to competency of principals.
It may be stated as a general proposition that whatever a person has power to do himself he may do by means of an agent[1]. The converse proposition similarly holds good; what a person cannot do himself he cannot do by means of an agent[2]. It is, in general, necessary to ascertain who is legally competent to act or contract[3] in order to know who is competent to be a principal.

There are, however, two exceptions to the general rule that a person may do by means of an agent whatever he has power to do himself, and these are:

(1)   where the transaction is required by statute[4] to be evidenced by the signature of the principal himself[5]; and

(2)   where the competency to do the act arises by virtue of the holding of some public office or by virtue of some power, authority or duty of a personal nature and requiring skill or discretion for its exercise[6], or where a statute imposes on a person a duty which he is not free to delegate[7].

There are also certain classes of persons who are legally incompetent, or have only a limited capacity, to contract or act as principals[8].

1 *Bevan v Webb* [1901] 2 Ch 59, CA; *Re Whitley Partners Ltd* (1886) 32 ChD 337, CA (memorandum of association of a company may be subscribed by an agent); *Compagnie Générale Trans-Atlantique v Thomas Law & Co, La Bourgogne* [1899] AC 431, HL; *Tharsis Sulphur and Copper Co v Société Industrielle et Commerciale des Métaux* (1889) 58 LJQB 435 (a foreign corporation may appoint an agent to accept service of writ); *Furnivall v Hudson* [1893] 1 Ch 335 (an agent may be appointed to execute a bill of sale); *R v Longnor (Inhabitants)* (1833) 1 Nev & MKB 576; *Foreman v Great Western Rly Co* (1878) 38 LT 851 (a principal who can read may appoint an agent who cannot read to sign a document); *Foster v Fyfe* [1896] 2 QB 104.
     The principle set out in the text to this note was cited with approval in *Lancashire County Council v Mason* [1998] ICR 907, EAT.
     A partner may employ an agent (to whom no reasonable objection can be taken, and on the agent undertaking not to use information) to examine partnership books under the Partnership Act

1890 s 24(9): see *Bevan v Webb*; and PARTNERSHIP vol 79 (2014) PARA 135; cf also the Limited Partnerships Act 1907 s 6(1); and PARTNERSHIP vol 79 (2014) PARA 225. An agent may be appointed to execute a deed of arrangement under the Deeds of Arrangement Act 1914: see *Re Wilson* [1916] 1 KB 382, CA (reversing the Divisional Court but without affecting this point); and BANKRUPTCY AND INDIVIDUAL INSOLVENCY vol 5 (2013) PARAS 853–854, 858–859. As to the concept of agency see PARA 1.

2   *Bateman v Mid-Wales Rly Co* (1866) LR 1 CP 499; *Poulton v London and South Western Rly Co* (1867) LR 2 QB 534; *Ashbury Railway Carriage and Iron Co Ltd v Riche* (1875) LR 7 HL 653; *Montreal Assurance Co v M'Gillivray* (1859) 13 Moo PCC 87. The principle set out in the text to this note was cited with approval in *Lancashire County Council v Mason* [1998] ICR 907, EAT.
      As regards creation of an agency, in *Dunhill v Burgin (Nos 1 and 2)* [2014] UKSC 18, [2014] 2 All ER 364, [2014] 1 WLR 933, the Supreme Court declined to comment upon whether a contract of agency could ever be created by a principal who was incapax.

3   As to capacity to contract see CONTRACT vol 22 (2012) PARA 232.

4   Eg by the Statute of Frauds Amendment Act 1828 s 6, which provides that a representation concerning character, credit, etc, is not actionable unless made in writing signed by the party to be charged.

5   *Williams v Mason* (1873) 28 LT 232; *Hirst v West Riding Union Banking Co Ltd* [1901] 2 KB 560, CA. Cf *Re Whitley Partners Ltd* (1886) 32 ChD 337, CA; *Swift v Jewsbury and Goddard* (1874) LR 9 QB 301; *Re Prince Blücher, ex p Debtor* [1931] 2 Ch 70, CA.
      A person cannot be added or substituted as a claimant to proceedings unless he has given his signed, written consent and such consent is filed with the court: see CPR 19.4(4); *Practice Direction—Addition and Substitution of Parties* PD19A paras 2.1, 2.2; and CIVIL PROCEDURE vol 11 (2015) PARA 484. Cf *Fricker v Van Grutten* [1896] 2 Ch 649, CA (decided under RSC Ord 16 r 11), requiring the signature of the plaintiff himself; and CIVIL PROCEDURE vol 12 (2015) PARA 1043. Particulars of claim signed by a solicitor's clerk, however, were held to be 'signed by the solicitor' within the County Court Rules 1889 (*France v Dutton* [1891] 2 QB 208; see now CPR Pt 19; *Practice Direction—Addition and Substitution of Parties* PD19A; and CIVIL PROCEDURE vol 11 (2015) PARA 480 et seq), and in general an agent may sign where the statute does not expressly or impliedly require personal signature of the principal: see eg *Dennison v Jeffs* [1896] 1 Ch 611; see also *LCC v Vitamins Ltd, LCC v Agricultural Food Products Ltd* [1955] 2 QB 218, [1955] 2 All ER 229, CA; *Tennant v LCC* (1957) 121 JP 428, CA (all cases of signatures by assistant to person authorised to sign notices to quit); *UBAF Ltd v European American Banking Corpn, The Pacific Colcotronis* [1984] QB 713, [1984] 2 All ER 226, CA (a representation signed on behalf of a limited company by its duly authorised agent acting within the scope of his authority constitutes a representation by the company for the purposes of the Statute of Frauds Amendment Act 1828 s 6).

6   *Re Great Southern Mysore Gold Mining Co* (1882) 48 LT 11, CA (the nomination of an official liquidator by a judge cannot be performed by an agent). Accordingly, a power of attorney does not empower the agent to swear an affidavit verifying a list of documents on behalf of his principal: *Clauss v Pir* [1988] Ch 267, [1987] 2 All ER 752.

7   *Omnibus Conveyance Co Ltd v Liverpool United Tramways and Omnibus Co* (1882) 26 Sol Jo 580 per Chitty J; *Corsellis v LCC* [1908] 1 Ch 13, CA; *Ticehurst and District Water and Gas Co Ltd v Gas and Waterworks Supply and Construction Co Ltd* (1911) 55 Sol Jo 459 per Warrington J. The principle does not apply to the performance of ministerial acts, eg by an independent contractor: see *Corsellis v LCC*. As to the nature of performance of duties by officers in government departments see PARA 49.

8   See PARAS 4–8. For the power of trustees and personal representatives to employ agents see the Trustee Act 2000 s 11; and TRUSTS AND POWERS vol 98 (2013) PARA 430.

4.   Competency of alien enemies as principals.

During the period of hostilities with the country of which he is a subject, an alien enemy is wholly incompetent to contract or act as a principal[1]. The outbreak of war dissolves a continuing agency agreement between a British subject[2] and an enemy alien which involves intercourse with the enemy[3], although an *administrateur-séquestre* appointed by the French court has been held to be entitled to receive dividends payable to an enemy alien resident in France[4] and a power of attorney given by a principal in an enemy-occupied territory is not abrogated on his leaving that territory and going to a country in alliance with Her Majesty, and thus temporarily dividing himself from his agent by the line of war[5].

1 *O'Mealey v Wilson* (1808) 1 Camp 482. As to the meaning of 'agent' and 'principal' see PARA 1.
2 As to the status of a British subject see BRITISH NATIONALITY vol 4 (2011) PARAS 407, 469–475.
3 *Hugh Stevenson & Sons Ltd v Aktiengesellschaft für Cartonnagen Industrie* [1918] AC 239, HL. See also *Nordisk Insulinlaboratorium v Gorgate Products Ltd (sued as CL Bencard (1934) Ltd)* [1953] Ch 430, [1953] 1 All ER 986, CA.
4 *Lepage v San Paulo Copper Estates Ltd* (1917) 33 TLR 457.
5 *Hangkam Kwingtong Woo v Liu Lan Fong (alias Liu Ah Lan)* [1951] AC 707, [1951] 2 All ER 567, PC.

5. Competency of minors as principals.

In general, where a minor[1] can lawfully do an act on his own behalf, so as to bind himself, he can appoint an agent to do it on his behalf[2]; where, however, a minor's contract is voidable at common law[3], it does not matter that he has appointed an agent to contract for him[4]. An agent can bind a minor in respect of necessaries[5], and also in respect of those contracts which at common law must be expressly renounced by the minor on attaining majority in order to be rendered void[6]. A power of attorney given by a minor, other than a married woman, is void[7]. A principal who is a minor is not liable for a tort committed by his agent, unless committed by his direct command[8], but a minor can authorise his agent to expel a trespasser, and the agent may plead such authority by way of defence in a claim by the trespasser[9].

1 A minor is a person who has not attained the age of 18: see the Family Law Reform Act 1969 s 1; and CHILDREN AND YOUNG PERSONS vol 9 (2017) PARA 3.
2 *G (A) v G (T)* [1970] 2 QB 643 at 652, [1970] 3 All ER 546 at 549, CA, per Lord Denning MR, explaining his judgment in *Re Shephard, Shephard v Cartwright* [1953] Ch 728, [1953] 2 All ER 608, CA; revsd on other grounds [1955] AC 431, [1954] 3 All ER 649, HL. See also the Minors' Contracts Act 1987, which disapplies and repeals the Infants Relief Act 1874; and CHILDREN AND YOUNG PERSONS vol 9 (2017) PARA 14. As to the concept of agency see PARA 1.
3 Or, if made before 9 June 1987 (ie the date on which the Minors' Contracts Act 1987 was brought into force by virtue of s 5(2)), void by virtue of the Infants Relief Act 1874 (repealed by the Minors' Contracts Act 1987). See note 2.
4 *Edwards v Carter* [1893] AC 360, HL; *G (A) v G (T)* [1970] 2 QB 643, [1970] 3 All ER 546, CA; *Chaplin v Leslie Frewin (Publishers) Ltd* [1966] Ch 71, [1965] 3 All ER 746, CA.
5 As to a minor's liability for necessaries and what are necessaries see CHILDREN AND YOUNG PERSONS vol 9 (2017) PARAS 18–19.
6 *Whittingham v Murdy* (1889) 60 LT 956.
7 *Zouch d Abbot and Hallet v Parsons* (1765) 3 Burr 1794.
8 *Burnard v Haggis* (1863) 14 CBNS 45.
9 *Ewer v Jones* (1846) 9 QB 623.

6. Competency of mentally disordered persons as principals.

A person suffering from a mental disorder has a restricted capacity to contract generally[1], and therefore to act via an agent[2], but he may be held liable on contracts made by an agent by virtue of an estoppel[3] or made during a lucid interval[4]. Statutory provision is made for the management of the affairs and dealings with the property of mentally disordered persons[5] and in connection with the creation and exercise of powers of attorney which are designed to survive the donor's subsequent mental incapacity[6].

1 See MENTAL HEALTH AND CAPACITY vol 75 (2013) PARA 614.
2 See MENTAL HEALTH AND CAPACITY vol 75 (2013) PARA 600. As to the meaning of 'agent' see PARA 1.

3 See PARA 25; and MENTAL HEALTH AND CAPACITY vol 75 (2013) PARA 600.
4 See *Drew v Nunn* (1879) 4 QBD 661, CA; and MENTAL HEALTH AND CAPACITY vol 75 (2013) PARAS 600, 614.
5 See the Mental Capacity Act 2005; and MENTAL HEALTH AND CAPACITY vol 75 (2013) PARA 558 et seq.
6 See PARA 195 et seq.

7. Competency of intoxicated persons as principals.

In order for agency to arise the person instructing the agent to act must have power to act himself[1]. A person may avoid a contract entered into by him while he was in such a state of intoxication as not to know what he was doing, but a person contracting with him may enforce the contract if he can prove that he had no knowledge of, and took no advantage of, the drunkenness[2]. A person who contracted when drunk may ratify his contract on becoming sober[3].

1 See PARA 3. As to the concept of agency see PARA 1.
2 See *Gore v Gibson* (1845) 13 M & W 623; *Matthews v Baxter* (1873) LR 8 Exch 132 (party allowed to ratify contract made whilst drunk); and CONTRACT vol 22 (2012) PARA 299.
3 *Matthews v Baxter* (1873) LR 8 Exch 132.

8. Competency of corporations as principals.

At common law it is an incident to a corporation created by Royal Charter[1] to use its common seal for the purpose of binding itself to anything to which a natural person could bind himself and to deal with its property as a natural person might deal with his own[2]. If the powers of the corporation are limited by the Charter, those limits are enforceable by a declaration of the court[3].

Corporations incorporated by statute[4] are subject to the common law doctrine of ultra vires, that is, what is not expressly or by implication authorised in the statute must be taken to have been forbidden[5]. This rule has been construed liberally, so that a company can do acts which it is not expressly authorised to do, provided that they are reasonably incidental to its main objects[6] provided those main objects are still being pursued[7].

In favour of a person dealing with a company in good faith, the power of the directors to bind the company, or to authorise others to do so[8], is deemed to be free of any limitation under the company's constitution[9]. A person is presumed to have acted in good faith unless the contrary is proved[10]. This is so even if that person has not inquired about the capacity of the company, or the powers of the directors[11]. Moreover, he is not to be regarded as acting in bad faith by reason only of his knowing that an act is beyond the powers of the directors under the company's constitution[12].

1 As to the creation of corporations by Royal Charter see CORPORATIONS vol 24 (2010) PARAS 329, 331 et seq.
2 *Sutton's Hospital Case* (1612) 10 Co Rep 1a, Ex Ch; *Hazell v Hammersmith and Fulham London Borough Council* [1992] 2 AC 1, [1991] 1 All ER 545, HL.
3 See generally *Pharmaceutical Society of Great Britain v Dickson* [1970] AC 403, [1968] 2 All ER 686, HL.
4 As to incorporation by statute see CORPORATIONS vol 24 (2010) PARAS 329, 344–346.
5 *Ashbury Railway Carriage and Iron Co Ltd v Riche* (1875) LR 7 HL 653.
6 *Foster v London, Chatham and Dover Rly Co* [1895] 1 QB 711, CA.
7 *Re Salisbury Railway and Market House Co Ltd* [1969] 1 Ch 349, [1967] 1 All ER 813.
8 As to the concept of agency see PARA 1.
9 See the Companies Act 2006 s 40(1); and COMPANIES vol 14 (2016) PARA 262. A person dealing with a company (ie where he is party to a transaction with a company) is not bound to inquire as

to any limitation on the powers of the directors to bind the company or authorise others to do so: s 40(2)(b)(i).

10 See the Companies Act 2006 s 40(2)(b)(ii); and COMPANIES vol 14 (2016) PARA 262.

11 See the Companies Act 2006 s 40(2)(b)(i); and COMPANIES vol 14 (2016) PARA 262.

12 See the Companies Act 2006 s 40(2)(b)(iii); and COMPANIES vol 14 (2016) PARA 262.

(ii) Competency of Agents

9. Capacity of agent to act.

An agent's competency to act or contract for his principal is not limited to his competency to contract for himself[1]. Thus a minor[2] may be an agent, and act and contract so as to bind the principal, although not personally liable on the contract of agency or on contracts with third parties, even in cases where an agent of full contractual capacity would have been personally liable[3]. A partner who is a minor can therefore bind the firm and partnership assets in respect of acts done in furtherance of the objects of the partnership[4].

1   *Kirby v Great Western Rly Co* (1868) 18 LT 658; *Re D'Angibau, Andrews v Andrews* (1880) 15 ChD 228, CA. An agent who cannot read may bind by his signature a principal who can read: *Foreman v Great Western Rly Co* (1878) 38 LT 851. As to the concept of agency see PARA 1.

2   A minor is a person who has not attained the age of 18: see the Family Law Reform Act 1969 s 1; and CHILDREN AND YOUNG PERSONS vol 9 (2017) PARA 3.

3   *Smally v Smally* (1700) 1 Eq Cas Abr 6.

4   *Goode and Bennion v Harrison* (1821) 5 B & Ald 147. As to minors as partners see PARTNERSHIP vol 79 (2014) PARA 28.

10. Special qualification or restriction on certain agents.

In the case of certain classes of agents, such as solicitors, the law requires a qualification before they can act[1]. Enforcement agents taking control of goods are required to have a certificate from a County Court judge before they may act[2].

No person who is contracting as a principal can act as agent to the other party to the contract for the purpose of signing a note or memorandum thereof so as to satisfy the provisions of the Statute of Frauds[3]. The same person may, however, act as agent of both parties for that purpose if so authorised by the other party[4].

1   A solicitor must be qualified before he can act and there are penalties for acting while unqualified (see the Solicitors Act 1974 ss 20, 21; and LEGAL PROFESSIONS vol 65 (2015) PARAS 428, 430). A solicitor must also take out an annual practising certificate (see LEGAL PROFESSIONS vol 65 (2015) PARA 466), and where he has no certificate his client cannot always recover costs from the other party, nor can the solicitor recover costs from the client: see s 25; and LEGAL PROFESSIONS vol 65 (2015) PARA 429. As to loss of right to remuneration see PARA 111.

2   See the Tribunals, Courts and Enforcement Act 2007 s 64; and CIVIL PROCEDURE vol 12A (2015) PARA 1336.

3   *Sharman v Brandt* (1871) LR 6 QB 720; *Wright v Dannah* (1809) 2 Camp 203; *Farebrother v Simmons* (1822) 5 B & Ald 333. The provisions mentioned in the text are contained in the Statute of Frauds (1677) s 4, which now relates only to contracts of guarantee (see further FINANCIAL INSTRUMENTS AND TRANSACTIONS vol 49 (2015) PARA 677 et seq); in so far as contracts for the sale of land are concerned see now the Law of Property (Miscellaneous Provisions) Act 1989 s 2; and CONVEYANCING vol 23 (2016) PARA 27.

4   *Hinde v Whitehouse* (1806) 7 East 558 (auctioneer); *Wilson & Sons v Pike* [1949] 1 KB 176, [1948] 2 All ER 267, CA (auctioneer); *Bird v Boulter* (1833) 1 Nev & MKB 313 (auctioneer's clerk); *Durrell v Evans* (1862) 1 H & C 174 (factor); *Thompson v Gardiner* (1876) 1 CPD 777 (broker). As to an auctioneer's authority to sign for a bidder at an auction see *Chaney v Maclow* [1929] 1 Ch 461, CA; and AUCTION vol 4 (2011) PARAS 7, 15.

(3) CLASSES OF AGENTS

11. Special agents and general agents.

The authorities draw a distinction between special agents and general agents[1]. A special agent is one who has authority to act for some special occasion or purpose which is not within the ordinary course of his business or profession[2], whereas a general agent is one who has authority, arising out of and in the ordinary course of his business or profession, to do some act or acts on behalf of his principal in relation thereto, or one who is authorised to act on behalf of the principal generally in transactions of a particular kind or incidental to a particular business[3]. Thus a factor, broker, auctioneer or estate agent who is authorised to do any act in the ordinary course of his business is a general agent in relation to that employment, as is a steward or manager of a business on an estate[4].

1   See eg *Smith v M'Guire* (1858) 3 H & N 554.
2   *Brady v Todd* (1861) 9 CBNS 592.
3   *Smith v M'Guire* (1858) 3 H & N 554; *Brady v Todd* (1861) 9 CBNS 592; *Barrett v Irvine* [1907] 2 IR 462, CA; *Kinahan & Co Ltd v Parry* [1910] 2 KB 389 (revsd on particular facts [1911] 1 KB 459, CA).
4   As to the agency of a partner for other partners see the Partnership Act 1890 s 5; and PARTNERSHIP vol 79 (2014) PARA 39. As to the agency of members of a limited liability partnership see PARA 22.

12. Mercantile agents under the Factors Act 1889.

A mercantile agent is one having, in the customary course of his business as such agent, authority either to sell goods, or to consign goods for the purpose of sale, or to buy goods, or to raise money on the security of goods[1]. An agent may be a mercantile agent although he has no general occupation as an agent or has only one customer[2], or although his general occupation is that of an independent dealer in the commodity entrusted to him[3], provided that he acts in the transaction in question in his capacity as mercantile agent[4]; but he must not be a mere servant or shopman[5]. An agent entrusted with goods on sale or return on terms that they were not to become his property and that his remuneration should be a share of the profits on sale is a mercantile agent[6]. An agent may still be a mercantile agent so as to transfer to a bona fide purchaser a title to goods which will be protected by the Factors Act 1889[7], although in accepting the agency the agent intends to disregard its terms and to act fraudulently for his own benefit, provided there is no error by the principal as to the identity of the agent and the principal intends to give the agent possession of the goods[8].

1   See the Factors Act 1889 s 1(1); the Sale of Goods Act 1979 s 26; *Inglis v Robertson and Baxter* [1898] AC 616, HL. An historical account of the law on this subject is to be found in *Official Assignee of Madras v Mercantile Bank of India Ltd* [1935] AC 53, PC. For a judicial definition of the term 'mercantile agent' see *Oppenheimer v Attenborough & Son* [1908] 1 KB 221, CA. See also *Lloyds Bank Ltd v Bank of America National Trust and Savings Association* [1938] 2 KB 147, [1938] 2 All ER 63, CA (pledgors of bills of lading entrusted with the bills to sell them are mercantile agents of the pledgees). The business of a confirming house is not that of a mercantile agent: *Rusholme and Bolton and Roberts Hadfield Ltd v S G Read & Co (London) Ltd* [1955] 1 All ER 180, [1955] 1 WLR 146; *Tellrite Ltd v London Confirmers Ltd* [1962] 1 Lloyd's Rep 236.
    As to the authority of a mercantile agent to dispose of goods in his possession see PARAS 149–150.
2   *Lowther v Harris* [1927] 1 KB 393.
3   *Weiner v Harris* [1910] 1 KB 285, CA.
4   *Oppenheimer v Frazer and Wyatt* [1907] 1 KB 519 (revsd on another point [1907] 2 KB 50, CA); *Staffs Motor Guarantee Ltd v British Wagon Co Ltd* [1934] 2 KB 305; *Budberg v Jerwood and Ward* (1934) 51 TLR 99.
5   *Lowther v Harris* [1927] 1 KB 393.

6   *Weiner v Harris* [1910] 1 KB 285, CA.
7   See PARA **149**.
8   *Pearson v Rose and Young Ltd* [1951] 1 KB 275, [1950] 2 All ER 1027, CA, following views
     expressed in *Folkes v King* [1923] 1 KB 282, CA, and disapproving the opinion expressed in
     Oppenheimer v Frazer and Wyatt [1907] 2 KB 50, CA; *Du Jardin v Beadman Bros Ltd* [1952] 2
     QB 712, [1952] 2 All ER 160; and see also *Turner v Sampson* (1911) 27 TLR 200; *Lake v
     Simmons* [1927] AC 487, HL; *Lloyds Bank Ltd v Bank of America National Trust and Savings
     Association* [1938] 2 KB 147, [1938] 2 All ER 63, CA.

13.   Factors and other classes of agents.

A 'factor' is a mercantile agent who in the ordinary course of business is entrusted with possession of goods or of the documents of title thereto[1], and a 'broker' is a mercantile agent who in the ordinary course of his business is employed to make contracts for the purchase or sale of property or goods of which he is not entrusted with the possession or documents of title[2].

A forwarding agent is one who undertakes the shipment or transmission of goods[3]. There is a custom of the trade that a forwarding agent incurs personal liability for freight charges whether transmission is by sea or by air; with the result that after paying cost of freight he can recover such payment even from a disclosed principal[4]. His duties in relation to goods do not cease once the goods have been dispatched but he has a duty to facilitate, or at least not to impede, their safe arrival[5]. His duty, generally, is to exercise reasonable care[6].

An insurance agent or insurance broker is employed to negotiate and effect policies of insurance[7].

A del credere agent is one who, usually for extra remuneration, undertakes to indemnify his employer against loss[8] arising from the failure of persons with whom he contracts to carry out their contracts[9]. A del credere agency may be inferred from facts showing that the agent was charging an additional commission for risk[10]. Such an agent need not be appointed in writing[11], the agreement not being an agreement to answer for the debt, default or miscarriage of another within the meaning of the Statute of Frauds[12].

An auctioneer is an agent who is employed to sell at a public auction. He may act as agent for both seller and buyer[13] and may or may not be entrusted with possession of the goods or property to be sold or of the documents of title thereto[14].

An estate agent is a person who, in connection with the acquisition or disposal of any land or other premises, brings together or takes steps to bring together the person wishing to dispose thereof and a person prepared to acquire it, or undertakes to do either of those things, or who acts or undertakes to act as auctioneer, or, in the case of a proposed transaction, negotiates or undertakes to negotiate as to the terms on behalf of either party[15].

A commercial agent is a self-employed intermediary who has continuing authority to negotiate the sale or purchase of goods on behalf of another person (the 'principal'), or to negotiate and conclude the sale or purchase of goods on behalf of and in the name of that principal[16].

1   *Baring v Corrie* (1818) 2 B & Ald 137; *Stevens v Biller* (1883) 25 ChD 31, CA. As to the implied
     authority of a factor see PARA 43.
2   *Milford v Hughes* (1846) 16 M & W 174; *Foster v Pearson* (1835) 1 Cr M & R 849; *Baring v
     Corrie* (1818) 2 B & Ald 137.
3   It is for this reason that they were known as forwarding agents. The nature of the operations
     carried out by a forwarder, and the contractual arrangements under which he does so, may render
     such a person a principal rather than an agent (see eg *Lee Cooper Ltd v CH Jeakins & Sons Ltd*
     [1967] 2 QB 1, [1965] 1 All ER 280, where it was held that a forwarding agent had incurred
     liability as a principal; *Mar-Train Heavy Haulage Ltd v Shipping.DK Chartering* [2014] EWHC

355 (Comm), [2014] All ER (D) 190 (Feb); cf *EW Taylor & Co (Forwarding) Ltd v Bell* [1968] 2 Lloyd's Rep 63, and the cases cited in notes 6, 7). This title is concerned only with the forwarder in the role of agent.

4   *Perishables Transport Co Ltd v N Spyropoulos (London) Ltd* [1964] 2 Lloyd's Rep 379. In *Cory Bros Shipping Ltd v Baldan Ltd* [1997] 2 Lloyd's Rep 58 the forwarding agents who gave no notice that they were acting as agents were held personally liable for unpaid freight.

5   *Langley Beldon & Gaunt Ltd v Morley* [1965] 1 Lloyd's Rep 297.

6   *Pringle of Scotland Ltd v Continental Express Ltd* [1962] 2 Lloyd's Rep 80.

7   See INSURANCE vol 60 (2011) PARA 75. The common practice of Lloyd's brokers whereby, having negotiated a policy for their client, they act in certain respects as agents for underwriters when the client makes a claim, was disapproved: see *Anglo-African Merchants Ltd v Bayley* [1970] 1 QB 311, [1969] 2 All ER 421; *North and South Trust Co v Berkeley, Berkeley v North and South Trust Co* [1971] 1 All ER 980, [1971] 1 WLR 470; and see PARA 90.

8   The mere signing of a deed of assignment does not establish a loss: *Montagu Stanley & Co v JC Solomon Ltd* [1932] 2 KB 287, CA. The loss must be quantified before the duty to indemnify arises: *Rusholme and Bolton and Roberts Hadfield Ltd v SG Read & Co (London) Ltd* [1955] 1 All ER 180, [1955] 1 WLR 146.

9   *Morris v Cleasby* (1816) 4 M & S 566; *Grove v Dubois* (1786) 1 Term Rep 112; *Hornby v Lacy* (1817) 6 M & S 166; *Churchill and Sim v Goddard* [1937] 1 KB 92, [1936] 1 All ER 675, CA. As to the distinction between the relationship of principal and del credere agent and that of buyer (retailer) and seller (manufacturer) see *Michelin Tyre Co Ltd v Macfarlane (Glasgow) Ltd* (1916) 54 SLR 1 (affd (1917) 55 SLR 35, HL); and as to the liability of a del credere agent in disputes between his principal and the other contracting party see *Thomas Gabriel & Sons v Churchill & Sim* [1914] 3 KB 1272, CA.

10   *Shaw v Woodcock* (1827) 7 B & C 73. Mere description in the contract as del credere agent does not make the agent a del credere agent of the other contracting party: *Nouvelles Huileries Anversoises SA v HC Mann & Co* (1924) 40 TLR 804.

11   *Couturier v Hastie* (1852) 8 Exch 40; *Sutton & Co v Grey* [1894] 1 QB 285, CA; *Wickham v Wickham* (1855) 2 K & J 478; *Harburg India Rubber Comb Co v Martin* [1902] 1 KB 778, CA. See also FINANCIAL INSTRUMENTS AND TRANSACTIONS vol 49 (2015) PARAS 688, 880.

12   See the Statute of Frauds (1677) s 4; and FINANCIAL INSTRUMENTS AND TRANSACTIONS vol 49 (2015) PARA 683 et seq.

13   See the cases cited in PARA 10 note 4.

14   See AUCTION vol 4 (2011) PARAS 1–2, 7.

15   This definition is based on that in the Restriction on Agreements (Estate Agents) Order 1970, SI 1970/1696, art 2(1) (revoked). That order rendered unlawful agreements and arrangements between estate agents relating to the charges, the advertising of the charges and the recommending of the charges for the supply of their services as estate agents in connection with the disposal of unfurnished dwellings. The Estate Agents Act 1979 (which imposes a degree of control on the activities of estate agents) does not define 'estate agent' but defines instead the term 'estate agency work': see PARA 255. Estate agents often also act as managing agents of residential leasehold property. As to the implied authority of an estate agent see PARA 41.

16   See the Commercial Agents (Council Directive) Regulations 1993, SI 1993/3053, reg 2(1); and PARA 73.

(4) FORMATION OF AGENCY

(i) Circumstances in which Agency may Arise

14. How agency is created.

The relation of agency is created by the express or implied agreement of principal and agent[1]. The relation can also be created by ratification by the principal of the agent's acts done on his behalf[2]. Express agency is created where the principal, or some person authorised by him, expressly appoints the agent, whether by deed, by writing under hand, or orally[3]. Implied agency[4] arises from the conduct or situation of the parties[5], or by operation of law, for example from necessity[6].

An agency may also be created by statute. For example, a dealer acting in respect of certain hire purchase agreements is by statute deemed to be the agent of the owner or the seller of the goods under the agreement for the purposes of service of notice of cancellation and other notices and in respect of representations made by the dealer with respect to the goods[7]. A statutory agency arises in respect of the unpaid seller of perishable goods exercising his right to resell[8].

1 *Pole v Leask* (1863) 33 LJ Ch 155; *Re Consort Deep Level Gold Mines Ltd, ex p Stark* [1897] 1 Ch 575, CA; *Love v Mack* (1905) 93 LT 352, CA; *Garnac Grain Co Inc v HMF Faure and Fairclough Ltd* [1968] AC 1130n, [1967] 2 All ER 353, HL; *Morgans v Launchbury* [1973] AC 127, [1972] 2 All ER 606, HL; *UBS AG (London Branch) v Kommunale Wasserwerke Leipzig GmbH* [2014] EWHC 3615 (Comm), [2014] All ER (D) 47 (Nov).

2 *Markwick v Hardingham* (1880) 15 ChD 339, CA; and see PARAS 58–71.

3 *Gosling v Gaskell* [1897] AC 575, HL; *Re Hale, Lilley v Foad* [1899] 2 Ch 107, CA; *Re Vimbos Ltd* [1900] 1 Ch 470.

4 Whereas the expression 'implied agency' is used in contradistinction to the expression 'express agency,' the expression 'implied authority' is used to describe an extension of an express authority which is necessary to give the express authority full business efficacy.

5 *Watson v Threlkeld* (1798) 2 Esp 637; *Ryan v Sams* (1848) 12 QB 460 (cohabitation as man and wife); *Trent v Hunt* (1853) 9 Exch 14 (mortgagor implied agent of mortgagee); *Vandyke v Fender (Sun Insurance Office Ltd, third party)* [1969] 2 QB 581, [1969] 3 All ER 1291 (on appeal [1970] 2 QB 292, [1970] 2 All ER 335, CA) (driving fellow employees to work on behalf of employer); *G (A) v G (T)* [1970] 2 QB 643, [1970] 3 All ER 546, CA (admissions of paternity made by parents of father who was a minor); *Townsends Carriers Ltd v Pfizer Ltd* (1977) 33 P & CR 361 (sister companies as agents of lessor and lessee); *Potter (t/a P & R Potter Wholesale) v Customs and Excise Comrs* [1985] STC 45, CA ('Tupperware' distributors sell as principals, not agents); *Cronin (t/a Cronin Driving School) v Customs & Excise Comrs* [1991] STC 333 (driving school supplying services to the public via agency of self-employed driving instructors); *Ringside Refreshments v Customs & Excise Comrs* [2003] EWHC 3043 (Ch), [2004] STC 426 (self-employed operators of vans selling cooked foods to public). See also *Redbank Schools Ltd v Abdullahzadeh* (1995) 95 LGR 176, CA (implied agency will not arise on a landowner's mere knowledge that his licensee is purporting to grant a tenancy in the land, where rent is being paid to, and kept by, the licensee); and *Lemmerbell Ltd v Britannia LAS Direct Ltd* [1998] 3 EGLR 67, [1998] 48 EG 188, CA (landlord demanding and accepting rent and insurance premiums from third party on tenant's instructions not enough to establish third party as tenant's agent). See also AUCTION vol 4 (2011) PARAS 7–8 (agency of auctioneer); MATRIMONIAL AND CIVIL PARTNERSHIP LAW vol 72 (2015) PARA 262 (agency of spouse); SHIPPING AND MARITIME LAW vol 93 (2017) PARA 427 et seq (agency of master); the cases cited in PARA 2 (relation of agency); PARA 25 (agency by estoppel); and PARAS 37–44 (implied authority of agents).

6 As to agency of necessity see PARA 24.

7 See the Consumer Credit Act 1974 s 57 (withdrawal), s 69 (cancellation), s 102 (rescission); and CONSUMER CREDIT vol 21 (2016) PARAS 163, 168, 242.

8 See the Sale of Goods Act 1979 s 48(3); and SALE OF GOODS AND SUPPLY OF SERVICES vol 91 (2012) PARA 280.

(ii) Agency by Agreement

15. When a deed is necessary.

Where an agent is given power to execute a deed, that power must itself be contained in a deed[1]. Certain acts are required, either by statute or common law, to be by deed, the chief of which include[2]:

(1) conveyances, including mortgages, charges, vesting declarations and vesting instruments, of land or any interest in land[3];

(2) certain leases of land[4];

(3)   instruments effecting certain dispositions of registered land[5];
(4)   transfers of shares in companies under the Companies Clauses Consolidation Act 1845[6];
(5)   bills of sale[7]; and
(6)   under the common law, a contract without consideration[8].

The necessity for appointment by deed of an agent for the purpose of executing an instrument as a deed does not, however, exist where the execution of the instrument is in the presence of the principal, when, at his request, someone signs on his behalf and in his name[9], and an agent who executes a deed, though not authorised by deed, may bind his principal if a deed was not required by law in such a case[10]. The authority to contract for, but not to execute, a lease of lands for a term exceeding three years may be given orally[11].

1   *Steiglitz v Egginton* (1815) Holt NP 141; *Berkeley v Hardy* (1826) 5 B & C 355. Where a deed has been executed in escrow, delivery of the escrow by an agent is ineffective unless the agent has been authorised under seal: *Windsor Refrigerator Co Ltd v Branch Nominees Ltd* [1961] Ch 88, [1960] 2 All ER 568; revsd on another point [1961] Ch 375, [1961] 1 All ER 277, CA.

2   As to the circumstances in which deeds are required see generally DEEDS AND OTHER INSTRUMENTS vol 32 (2012) PARA 210 et seq. A company may under the law of England and Wales, by instrument executed as a deed, empower a person, either generally or in respect of specified matters, as its attorney to execute deeds or other documents on its behalf: see the Companies Act 2006 s 47(1); and COMPANIES vol 14 (2016) PARA 288.

3   See the Law of Property Act 1925 s 52(1); and REAL PROPERTY AND REGISTRATION vol 87 (2017) PARA 244.

4   See the Law of Property Act 1925 ss 52(1), (2), 54(2); LANDLORD AND TENANT vol 62 (2016) PARAS 95–97; REAL PROPERTY AND REGISTRATION vol 87 (2017) PARA 244. See also DEEDS AND OTHER INSTRUMENTS vol 32 (2012) PARA 215.

5   The Land Registration Rules 2003, SI 2003/1417, specify which forms must be used: see rr 114, 161, 206, Sch 3 Form 6, Sch 4 Form C, Sch 7 paras 4, 6, 12, Sch 9; and REAL PROPERTY AND REGISTRATION vol 87 (2017) PARAS 409, 411, 417, 428, 476, 523, 572.

6   See the Companies Clauses Consolidation Act 1845 s 14; and COMPANIES vol 15A (2016) PARA 1908.

7   See the Bills of Sale Act (1878) Amendment Act 1882 s 9, Schedule; and FINANCIAL INSTRUMENTS AND TRANSACTIONS vol 49 (2015) PARA 494.

8   See CONTRACT vol 22 (2012) PARA 223; DEEDS AND OTHER INSTRUMENTS vol 32 (2012) PARA 210 et seq.

9   *Ball v Dunsterville* (1791) 4 Term Rep 313 (a deed executed for a partner in his presence); *R v Longnor (Inhabitants)* (1833) 4 B & Ad 647 (where the parties, who were unable to write, requested someone to execute the deed in their presence).

10 *Hunter v Parker* (1840) 7 M & W 322 (where the addition of a seal to the agent's contract of sale was not required for its validity). The requirement of a seal for the valid execution of a deed was abolished by the Law of Property (Miscellaneous Provisions) Act 1989 s 1(1).

11 *Callaghan v Pepper* (1840) 2 I Eq R 399; *Mortlock v Buller* (1804) 10 Ves 292.

16. Powers of attorney.

Where the authority of the agent is required to be conferred by a deed[1], or where in any other circumstances it is desired formally to appoint an agent to act for the principal in one transaction or a series of transactions or to manage the affairs of the principal generally, the necessary authority is conferred by an instrument known as a power of attorney[2]. Such powers are the subject of statutory provision, which specifies the method of execution[3], the proof of instruments creating such powers[4], the revocability[5] and the effect of revocation of powers[6]. Powers of attorney may also be created which will survive any subsequent mental incapacity of the donor[7].

Subject as stated below, an instrument creating a power of attorney must be executed as a deed by the donor of the power[8]. This requirement is, however, without prejudice to any requirement in, or having effect under, any other Act[9] as to the witnessing of instruments creating powers of attorney, and does not affect the rules relating to the execution of instruments by bodies corporate[10].

1   See PARA 15. As to the execution of deeds by the agent see PARA 45.
2   A general statutory form of power of attorney is provided by the Powers of Attorney Act 1971 s 10(1), Sch 1; and by the Powers of Attorney (Welsh Language Forms) Order 2000, SI 2000/215, art 3, Schedule Pt II. As to powers of attorney see further PARA 31 et seq.
3   See the Powers of Attorney Act 1971 s 1; and the text and notes 8–10.
4   See the Evidence and Powers of Attorney Act 1940 s 4; the Powers of Attorney Act 1971 s 3; and PARA 17.
5   See the Powers of Attorney Act 1971 s 4; and PARA 176.
6   See the Powers of Attorney Act 1971 ss 5–7; and PARAS 45, 194.
7   As to lasting and enduring powers of attorney see PARA 195 et seq. As to the effect of the Enduring Powers of Attorney Act 1985 on existing grants of a power of attorney see *Practice Direction* [1986] 2 All ER 42.
8   Powers of Attorney Act 1971 s 1(1) (amended by the Law of Property (Miscellaneous Provisions) Act 1989 s 1(8), Sch 1 para 6).
9   See eg the Trustee Act 1925 s 25; and TRUSTS AND POWERS vol 98 (2013) PARA 425.
10 Powers of Attorney Act 1971 s 1(3). As to execution by bodies corporate see PARAS 20–23.

17.   Proof of instruments creating powers of attorney.

The contents of an instrument creating a power of attorney may be proved[1] by means of a copy which is a reproduction of the original made with a photographic or other device for reproducing documents in facsimile[2], and contains a certificate or certificates signed by the donor of the power or by a solicitor, authorised person[3] or stockbroker[4] that the copy is a true and complete copy of the original[5], and, where the original consists of two or more pages, that each page is a true and complete copy of the corresponding page of the original[6]. The certificate must appear at the end of a single page document or at the end of each page where the document consists of more than one page[7]. Where a copy has been made in compliance with these requirements the contents of such an instrument may also be proved by means of a copy of that copy if the further copy has, mutatis mutandis, also been made in compliance with those requirements[8]. Special provision is made in connection with instruments creating powers of attorney which were deposited before 1 October 1971[9].

1   This provision is without prejudice to the Evidence and Powers of Attorney Act 1940 s 4 (amended by the Statute Law Revision Act 1950; and the Supreme Court Act 1981 s 154, Sch 7) (which provides for certain documents or instruments creating powers of attorney registered or deposited in Scotland or Northern Ireland to be sufficient evidence without further proof of their contents, deposition or registration) or to any other method of proof authorised by law: Powers of Attorney Act 1971 s 3(4). As to methods of proving the contents of documents see generally CIVIL PROCEDURE vol 12 (2015) PARA 934 et seq.
2   Powers of Attorney Act 1971 s 3(1)(a).
3   Ie a person (other than a solicitor) who, for the purposes of the Legal Services Act 2007, is an authorised person in relation to any activity which constitutes a notarial activity (within the meaning of that Act): Powers of Attorney Act 1971 s 3(3) (amended by the Legal Services Act 2007 Sch 21 para 26). As to persons authorised under the Legal Services Act 2007 see LEGAL PROFESSIONS vol 65 (2015) PARA 356.
4   'Stockbroker' means a member of any stock exchange within the meaning of the Stock Transfer Act 1963 (see s 4(1); and COMPANIES vol 14 (2016) PARA 411) or the Stock Transfer Act (Northern Ireland) 1963: Powers of Attorney Act 1971 s 3(3).
5   Powers of Attorney Act 1971 s 3(1)(b)(i) (s 3(1)(b) amended by the Legal Services Act 2007 Sch 21 para 26).

6   Powers of Attorney Act 1971 s 3(1)(b)(ii) (as amended: see note 5).
7   Powers of Attorney Act 1971 s 3(1)(b)(i), (ii) (as amended: see note 5).
8   Powers of Attorney Act 1971 s 3(2).
9   See the Senior Courts Act 1981 s 134 (amended by the Courts Act 2003 s 109(1), Sch 8 para 262(c); and the Constitutional Reform Act 2005 s 59(5), Sch 11 para 26).

18. Agent for the purchase of land.

Writing is not necessary in the case of an appointment of an agent to purchase land, although contracts for the sale or other disposition of an interest in land can only be made in writing[1].

Subject to what is said in the following paragraph[2], an agreement relating to land may be signed by or on behalf of each party to the contract[3], that is by the principal or by his lawfully authorised agent, whether the authority is given orally or otherwise[4]; and the principal may prove the oral creation of an agency and enforce the contract against both the agent and the other party to the contract[5]. The rule that declarations of trust in land must be proved by writing[6] does not invalidate the oral appointment of an agent to purchase land, as such an agent is not a trustee unless and until the land has been conveyed to him, but an intermediary, whose contract vests the equitable estate in the principal[7]; and, further, as the court did not allow the Statute of Frauds[8] to be made an instrument of fraud, an agent to whom land purchased on behalf of his principal has been conveyed is not permitted to plead the present statute against the principal, for whom he is a trustee[9].

1   See *Cave v Mackenzie* (1877) 46 LJ Ch 564; *McLaughlin v Duffill* [2008] EWCA Civ 1627, [2010] Ch 1, CA (sale of property executed by agent under oral authority specifically enforced); the Law of Property (Miscellaneous Provisions) Act 1989 s 2(1); and CONVEYANCING vol 23 (2016) PARA 27.
2   See PARA 19.
3   See the Law of Property (Miscellaneous Provisions) Act 1989 s 2(3); and CONVEYANCING vol 23 (2016) PARA 27.
4   See *Clinan v Cooke* (1802) 1 Sch & Lef 22; *Brooks v Billingham* (1912) 56 Sol Jo 503; *North v Loomes* [1919] 1 Ch 378; and CONVEYANCING vol 23 (2016) PARAS 42–43.
5   *Heard v Pilley* (1869) 4 Ch App 548; *Cave v Mackenzie* (1877) 46 LJ Ch 564.
6   See the Law of Property Act 1925 s 53(1)(b); and DEEDS AND OTHER INSTRUMENTS vol 32 (2012) PARA 224. However, there is no such requirement in respect of an agreement under which a party executes such declaration of trust: see *Rollerteam Ltd v Riley* [2016] EWCA Civ 1291, [2017] Ch 109.
7   *Cave v Mackenzie* (1877) 46 LJ Ch 564.
8   Ie the Statute of Frauds (1677) ss 3, 7–9 (repealed) which were replaced by the Law of Property Act 1925 s 53 (see DEEDS AND OTHER INSTRUMENTS vol 32 (2012) PARA 224).
9   The rule thus stated was accepted in *Longfield Parish Council v Robson* (1913) 29 TLR 357. The contrary view was once held (*Bartlett v Pickersgill* (1760) 1 Cox Eq Cas 15), and was recognised as still law in *James v Smith* [1891] 1 Ch 384, CA, but very grave doubt has been cast upon it: see *Booth v Turle* (1873) LR 16 Eq 182; *Davies v Otty (No 2)* (1865) 35 Beav 208; *Haigh v Kaye* (1872) 7 Ch App 469; and *Rochefoucauld v Boustead* [1897] 1 Ch 196, CA, in which *James v Smith* was adversely criticised by the Court of Appeal.

19. Agent to sign written contract.

Even in cases where the signature of a principal is required by statute, an agent may be appointed orally or in any other informal manner to sign for him, unless the statute expressly requires the agent, if any, to be authorised by writing[1], or expressly or impliedly requires a personal signature, and so renders an agent incompetent to sign at all[2]. Thus an agent informally appointed may sign a memorandum of association[3], or a consent to a dissolution of a building society[4].

Subject, therefore, to the requirements already mentioned, an agent's authority may be conferred orally, but the agency agreement itself must be evidenced by writing[5].

1   See eg the Law of Property Act 1925 s 53; and DEEDS AND OTHER INSTRUMENTS vol 32 (2012) PARA 224.
2   *Fricker v Van Grutten* [1896] 2 Ch 649, CA; and see PARA 3 note 5.
3   *Re Whitley Partners Ltd* (1886) 32 ChD 337, CA. As to a company's memorandum and articles of association see COMPANIES vol 14 (2016) PARA 226 et seq.
4   See the Building Societies Act 1986 s 87; *Dennison v Jeffs* [1896] 1 Ch 611; and FINANCIAL INSTITUTIONS vol 48 (2015) PARAS 539–542.
5   *Mortlock v Buller* (1804) 10 Ves 292; *Coles v Trecothick* (1804) 9 Ves 234; *Deverell v Lord Bolton* (1812) 18 Ves 505. The common law rule, *qui facit per alium facit per se* (he who acts through another is deemed to act in person) will not be restricted except where a statute requires personal signature: see eg PARA 3.

20.   Agents of corporations generally.

Where an act is required to be by deed[1] in order to be effective, the requirement applies to corporations and other persons equally, and so an authority to an agent in such a case must be conferred by deed[2]. By statute, a corporation may, however, also contract through its officers either in writing or orally, and the authority to an agent to enter into such contracts may be conferred informally[3]. This power is in addition to and largely replaces the earlier general statutory power of the governing body of a corporation to appoint by resolution or otherwise an agent to execute instruments which are not deeds[4].

1   For examples of acts which are required to be by deed see PARA 15.
2   As to the appointment of agents by corporations generally see CORPORATIONS vol 24 (2010) PARA 475.
3   See the Corporate Bodies' Contracts Act 1960 s 1(1); and CORPORATIONS vol 24 (2010) PARA 474. These provisions do not apply to companies registered under the Companies Act 2006, or to a company incorporated outside the United Kingdom or to a limited liability partnership: see the Corporate Bodies' Contracts Act 1960 s 2 (substituted by SI 2009/1941); and CORPORATIONS vol 24 (2010) PARA 463. As to agents of companies under the Companies Act 2006 see PARA 21.
       As to provisions applicable to joint stock companies incorporated by special Act see the Companies Clauses Consolidation Act 1845 s 97; and COMPANIES vol 15A (2016) PARA 1965. As to the provisions applicable to limited liability partnerships see PARA 22. As to contracts by industrial and provident societies see the Industrial and Provident Societies Act 1965 s 29; and FINANCIAL INSTITUTIONS vol 48 (2015) PARA 977.
4   See the Law of Property Act 1925 s 74(2); and CORPORATIONS vol 24 (2010) PARA 475. As to the execution of conveyances by an agent appointed by a corporation or by a corporate agent see the Law of Property Act 1925 s 74(3), (4); PARA 45; and CORPORATIONS vol 24 (2010) PARA 469.

21.   Companies subject to the Companies Act 2006.

The Companies Act 2006 makes provision for the contractual formalities to be observed by companies[1]. A contract may be made on behalf of a company by a person acting under its authority, express or implied[2]. Any formalities required by law in the case of a contract made by an individual also apply, unless a contrary intention appears, to a contract made by or on behalf of a company[3].

1   See the Companies Act 2006 ss 43–47; and COMPANIES vol 14 (2016) PARAS 281–285. Companies were specifically excluded from the provisions of the Corporate Bodies' Contracts Act 1960 (see PARA 20), but the two sets of provisions are nevertheless very similar in effect. Prior to the enactment of the Corporate Bodies' Contracts Act 1960, it was not contemplated that there

should be any difference in effect between the two sets of provisions: see the Eighth Report of the Law Reform Committee (Cmnd 622); 223 HL Official Report (5th series) col 1296; and 623 HC Official Report (6th series) col 838.

2 See the Companies Act 2006 s 43(1); and COMPANIES vol 14 (2016) PARA 281.
3 See the Companies Act 2006 s 43(2); and COMPANIES vol 14 (2016) PARA 281.

22. Limited liability partnerships.

As in the case of ordinary partnerships[1], every member of a limited liability partnership[2] is the agent of the partnership[3]. However, a limited liability partnership is not bound by anything done by a member in dealing with a person if the member in fact has no authority to act for the partnership by doing that thing, and the person knows that he has no authority or does not know or believe him to be a member of the partnership[4].

Where a person has ceased to be a member of a limited liability partnership, he is to be regarded (in relation to any person dealing with the partnership) as still being a member of the partnership unless the person has notice that the former member has ceased to be a member of the partnership, or notice that the former member has ceased to be a member of the partnership has been delivered to the Registrar of Companies[5].

Where a member of a limited liability partnership is liable to any person (other than another member of the partnership) as a result of a wrongful act or omission of his in the course of the business of the partnership or with its authority, the partnership is liable to the same extent as the member[6].

1 See PARTNERSHIP vol 79 (2014) PARA 39.
2 As to the meaning of 'limited liability partnership' see the Limited Liability Partnerships Act 2000 s 1; and PARTNERSHIP vol 79 (2014) PARA 233.
3 Limited Liability Partnerships Act 2000 s 6(1).
4 Limited Liability Partnerships Act 2000 s 6(2).
5 Limited Liability Partnerships Act 2000 ss 6(3), 18. As to the registrar see COMPANIES vol 14 (2016) PARA 126 et seq.
6 Limited Liability Partnerships Act 2000 s 6(4).

23. Local authorities.

The contracts of every local authority[1] and therefore contracts appointing an agent of a local authority must comply with its standing orders[2], but a person contracting with a local authority need not inquire whether the standing orders applicable to the particular contract have been complied with in any case where, apart from such standing orders, the contract would have been valid[3].

1 As to the meaning of 'local authority' for these purposes see LOCAL GOVERNMENT vol 69 (2009) PARA 23. The Local Government Act 1972 s 135 also applies to National Park authorities (see the Environment Act 1995 s 65(7), Sch 8 para 3(1); and OPEN SPACES AND COUNTRYSIDE vol 78 (2010) PARA 642), and to joint authorities, economic prosperity boards, combined authorities, the Broads Authority and the London Fire and Emergency Planning Authority (see the Local Government Act 1972 ss 146A(1)(a), 265A(1)(f); and LOCAL GOVERNMENT). As from a day to be appointed the reference to the London Fire and Emergency Planning Authority is replaced by a reference to the London Fire Commissioner: see the Policing and Crime Act 2017 s 9(3)(c), Sch 2 Pt 2 paras 35, 43(1), (2)(b). At the date at which this volume states the law no such day had been appointed.
2 See *R v Hereford Corpn, ex p Harrower* [1970] 3 All ER 460, [1970] 1 WLR 1424, DC (a decision under the Local Government Act 1933 s 266 (repealed)). The replacing provision in the Local Government Act 1972 s 135(2), (3) (see LOCAL GOVERNMENT vol 69 (2009) PARA 492) does not, except in the case of contracts for the supply of goods or materials or for the execution of works,

require the making of or compliance with standing orders. Power is, however, given to make standing orders (see s 135(1)), but contracts made without compliance with any orders are not invalidated (see s 135(4)).

3   See the Local Government Act 1972 s 135(4); and LOCAL GOVERNMENT vol 69 (2009) PARA 492.

(iii) Agency of Necessity

24. Agency of necessity.

Agency of necessity is said to arise in a limited number of cases[1] where, by reason of an emergency either the relation of principal and agent is deemed to exist between persons not otherwise in contractual relations[2] or authority to act on behalf of another is implied as between persons already in contractual relations[3]. The term was formerly used to describe the right of a deserted wife who was in need to pledge her husband's credit for necessaries[4]. Most of the cases have reference to sea or land carriage, when, to prevent destruction of the ship, cargo or goods, the shipmaster or carrier has to take prompt action in excess of his instructions[5]. The occurrence of exceptional circumstances during the carrying out of the act of agency, from the nature of the contract itself, necessitates its extension in the interests of both principal and agent; of the principal because otherwise his property or interests might be sacrificed, and of the agent so that he will have the necessary authority to preserve them and acquire rights against third parties for his principal and against the principal in respect of his own remuneration or indemnity. The authority arises only under urgent necessity[6]; and, if questioned, it will lie upon the party contracting with the agent to show that such was the nature of the circumstances[7]. Thus the bailee of non-perishable goods, which he has undertaken to store until demanded, is not an agent of necessity to sell them simply because their continued storage has become inconvenient for him and he is temporarily unable to obtain instructions from the bailor as to their disposal[8].

The conditions which entitle an agent to exceed his authority under the doctrine of necessity are:

(1)   that he could not communicate with his principal[9];

(2)   that the course he took was necessary in the sense that it was in the circumstances the only reasonable and prudent course to take[10]; and

(3)   that he acted bona fide in the interest of the parties concerned[11].

At the same time, though a strong case is required, it is not essential that any other course should be an impossibility[12].

1   It has been suggested that the doctrine could extend to vendor and purchaser (*Prager v Blatspiel, Stamp and Heacock Ltd* [1924] 1 KB 566) and to bailor and gratuitous bailee (*Sachs v Miklos* [1948] 2 KB 23, [1948] 1 All ER 67, CA), though in neither case did an agency of necessity arise on the facts; but see the criticism by Scrutton LJ in *Jebara v Ottoman Bank* [1927] 2 KB 254 at 271, CA (revsd (without dealing with this criticism) sub nom *Ottoman Bank v Jebara* [1928] AC 269, HL). See also *Dimurro v Charles Caplin & Co* (1969) 211 Estates Gazette 31 (solicitor stakeholder paid rent out of deposit to salvage lease: no agency of necessity); and *Croskery v Gee* [1957] NZLR 586, where a relative who paid the funeral expenses of a deceased person whose widow and family lived in China was held entitled to recover from the tortfeasor who caused the death.

2   This includes eg an acceptor of a bill of exchange for honour of the drawer or a shipmaster: *Hawtayne v Bourne* (1841) 7 M & W 595.

3   See eg *Walker v Great Western Rly Co* (1867) LR 2 Exch 228; *Langan v Great Western Rly Co* (1873) 30 LT 173, Ex Ch (general manager and railway police inspector held to have authority to bind railway company for cost of aid to injured passengers); cf *Cox v Midland Counties Rly Co* (1849) 3 Exch 268 (surgeon operating on injured passenger of railway not entitled to recover cost

from railway company although surgeon acting at request of doctor normally employed on railway); see also *Great Northern Rly Co v Swaffield* (1874) LR 9 Exch 132 (carriers of a horse, finding no one to receive it at the destination, maintained it from 'common humanity' and could recover cost of doing so).

4　See eg *Bazeley v Forder* (1868) LR 3 QB 559; *JN Nabarro & Sons v Kennedy* [1955] 1 QB 575, [1954] 2 All ER 605. This right was abrogated by the Matrimonial Proceedings and Property Act 1970 s 41(1) (repealed by the Matrimonial Causes Act 1973 but without reviving the former agency of necessity). Where a husband and wife live together, this used to give rise to a presumption that the wife had authority to pledge her husband's credit (*Debenham v Mellon* (1860) 6 App Cas 24, HL), although it is doubtful whether this is so at the present day. As to a wife's authority to contract on behalf of her husband or to pledge his credit see further MATRIMONIAL AND CIVIL PARTNERSHIP LAW vol 72 (2015) PARA 262.

5　*Sims & Co v Midland Rly Co* [1913] 1 KB 103; *Springer v Great Western Rly Co* [1921] 1 KB 257, CA. As to the authority of a shipmaster to sell the ship or cargo see SHIPPING AND MARITIME LAW vol 93 (2017) PARA 438 et seq. See also *John Koch Ltd v C and H Products Ltd* [1956] 2 Lloyd's Rep 59, CA, where the possibility of communication with the principal precluded an agency of necessity in respect of perishables.

6　See *Surrey Breakdown Ltd v Knight* [1999] RTR 84, CA (the removal of a stolen car from a pond on the instruction of the police was not a pressing emergency compelling intervention without the owner's authority).

7　*The Bonita, The Charlotte* (1861) 5 LT 141 (sale of ship by master); *The Gratitudine* (1801) 3 Ch Rob 240; *Benson v Duncan* (1849) 3 Exch 644; *Gibbs v Grey* (1857) 2 H & N 22 (payment of freight by master on reshipment of cargo); and see SHIPPING AND MARITIME LAW vol 93 (2017) PARA 438 et seq.

8　*Sachs v Miklos* [1948] 2 KB 23, [1948] 1 All ER 67, CA; *Munro v Willmott* [1949] 1 KB 295, [1948] 2 All ER 983. There is, however, a statutory right of sale in certain circumstances after the service of notice: see BAILMENT AND PLEDGE vol 4 (2011) PARA 173.

9　*Springer v Great Western Rly Co* [1921] 1 KB 257, CA; *Prager v Blatspiel, Stamp and Heacock Ltd* [1924] 1 KB 566; *John Koch Ltd v C and H Products Ltd* [1956] 2 Lloyd's Rep 59, CA; *Dimurro v Charles Caplin & Co* (1969) 211 Estates Gazette 31.

10　*Sims & Co v Midland Rly Co* [1913] 1 KB 103; *Atlantic Mutual Insurance Co Ltd v Huth* (1880) 16 ChD 474, CA; and see the cases cited in note 9.

11　*Tronson v Dent* (1853) 8 Moo PCC 419; *Prager v Blatspiel, Stamp and Heacock Ltd* [1924] 1 KB 566.

12　*The Australia* (1859) 13 Moo PCC 132. It is not necessary that the ship should be absolutely beyond repair to entitle a master to sell, the question being whether it was prudent to incur so large an expense; cf *The Mariposa* [1896] P 273 (as to whether the shipmaster was acting as agent for the ship or the passengers).

(iv) Agency by Estoppel

25. Apparent authority.

The doctrine of 'holding out', also known as apparent or ostensible authority, is based on estoppel[1]. Such agency by estoppel arises where one person has acted[2] so as to lead another to believe that he has authorised a third person to act on his behalf, and that other in such belief[3] enters into transactions with the third person within the scope of such ostensible authority[4]. In this case the first-mentioned person is estopped from denying the fact of the third person's agency under the general law of estoppel, and it is immaterial whether the ostensible agent had no authority whatever in fact[5], or merely acted in excess of his actual authority[6]. The principal cannot set up a private limitation upon the agent's actual authority so as to reduce the ostensible authority[7], for, so far as third persons are concerned, the ostensible authority is the sole test of his liability[8]. If, however, the agent is held out as having only a limited authority to do, on behalf of his principal, acts of a particular class, the principal is not bound by an act outside that authority even though it is an act of that particular class[9]. The onus lies upon the person dealing with the agent to prove either real or ostensible authority[10], and it is a matter of fact in each case whether ostensible authority existed for the particular act for which it is sought to make the principal liable[11]. Holding out is something more than estoppel by negligence; it is necessary to prove affirmatively conduct amounting to holding out[12]. No representation made solely by the agent as to the extent of his authority can amount to a holding out by the principal[13].

A person who assumes to act as an agent is estopped, as between himself and the person on whose behalf he professed to act, from denying the agency[14].

1 *Rama Corpn Ltd v Proved Tin and General Investments Ltd* [1952] 2 QB 147, [1952] 1 All ER 554; *Freeman and Lockyer (a firm) v Buckhurst Park Properties (Mangal) Ltd* [1964] 2 QB 480, [1964] 1 All ER 630, CA (applied in *Acute Property Developments Ltd v Apostolou* [2013] EWHC 200 (Ch), [2013] All ER (D) 231 (Feb)). Where, however, a good title to goods is passed under an apparent authority, the rule is not based on estoppel but on apparent authority as an exception, evolved by the courts for mercantile convenience, to the rule *nemo dat quod non habet*: see *Eastern Distributors Ltd v Goldring (Murphy, third party)* [1957] 2 QB 600, [1957] 2 All ER 525, CA; and SALE OF GOODS AND SUPPLY OF SERVICES vol 91 (2012) PARAS 149, 155. As to estoppel generally see ESTOPPEL vol 47 (2014) PARA 301 et seq.

2 The holding out may be by acts of the principal (see *Hazard v Treadwell* (1722) 1 Stra 506; *Summers v Solomon* (1857) 26 LJQB 301; *Jetley v Hill* (1884) Cab & El 239; *Filmer v Lynn* (1835) 4 Nev & MKB 559; *Mahony v East Holyford Mining Co* (1875) LR 7 HL 869; *Barrett v Deere* (1828) Mood & M 200; *Trueman v Loder* (1840) 11 Ad & El 589; *Barrett v Irvine* [1907] 2 IR 462, CA; *F Mildner & Sons v Noble* (1956) Times, 8 March, CA), or by the principal allowing the agent to hold himself out as having authority (see *Re Henry Bentley & Co and Yorkshire Breweries Ltd, ex p Harrison* (1893) 69 LT 204, CA; *Re International Contract Co, Levita's Case* (1870) 5 Ch App 489; *London Freehold and Leasehold Property Co v Suffield* [1897] 2 Ch 608, CA; *Fuller v Glyn, Mills, Currie & Co* [1914] 2 KB 168; *Wood v Clydesdale Bank Ltd* 1914 SC 397, Ct of Sess; *Bailey and Whites Ltd v House* (1915) 31 TLR 583, DC; *Soanes v London and South Western Rly Co* (1919) 88 LJKB 524, CA; *Australian Bank of Commerce Ltd v Perel* [1926] AC 737, PC; *Ashford Shire Council v Dependable Motors Pty Ltd* [1961] AC 336, [1961] 1 All ER 96, PC). Cf *Discount Kitchens v Crawford* (1988) Times, 5 December, CA; *Hector v Lyons* (1988) 58 P & CR, (1988) Times, 19 December, CA; *Charrington Fuel Oil Ltd v Parvant Co Ltd* (1988) Times, 28 December.

   A mere failure by a principal to detect irregularities in transactions by the agent will not by itself amount to a holding out for future transactions even where the failure is caused by negligence: see *Lloyds Bank Ltd v Chartered Bank of India, Australia and China* [1929] 1 KB 40, CA; *Bank of Ireland v Evans' Charities Trustees in Ireland* (1885) 5 HL Cas 389; *Swan v North British Australasian Co* (1863) 2 H & C 175. Cf *Morison v London County and Westminster Bank Ltd* [1914] 3 KB 356, CA.

3 *MacFisheries Ltd v Harrison* (1924) 93 LJKB 811.

4 *Summers v Solomon* (1857) 26 LJQB 301; and see *Biggs v Evans* [1894] 1 QB 88; *Dickinson v Valpy* (1829) 10 B & C 128; *Farquharson Bros & Co v C King & Co* [1902] AC 325, HL; *St Margaret's Trust Ltd v Byrne* (1976) Times, 23 January, CA. A thief who shows a stolen indorsed receipt to a bank and thereon receives payment of money which a customer had directed the bank to pay to the customer's brother on showing the receipt is not an agent by estoppel although the brother was not known to the bank: *Wood v Clydesdale Bank Ltd* 1914 SC 397, Ct of Sess. An agreement between two persons that one should occupy a position that could only be lawfully occupied by the other does not create an agency by estoppel: *MacFisheries Ltd v Harrison* (1924) 93 LJKB 811.

5 *Pickard v Sears* (1837) 6 Ad & El 469; *Freeman v Cooke* (1848) 2 Exch 654; *Muir's Executors v Craig's Trustees* 1913 SC 349, Ct of Sess; *Povey v Taylor* (1966) 116 NLJ 1656, CA.

6 *Union Credit Bank Ltd v Mersey Docks and Harbour Board* [1899] 2 QB 205; *King v Smith* [1900] 2 Ch 425; *Little v Spreadbury* [1910] 2 KB 658, DC; *Eastern Distributors Ltd v Goldring (Murphy, third party)* [1957] 2 QB 600, [1957] 2 All ER 525, CA.

7 *Hawken v Bourne* (1841) 8 M & W 703; and see *Maddick v Marshall* (1864) 17 CBNS 829, Ex Ch; *Riley v Packington* (1867) LR 2 CP 536; *Robinson v Mollett* (1875) LR 7 HL 802.

8 *Pickering v Busk* (1812) 15 East 38. This applies even where the agent is acting for his own benefit and in fraud of the principal: *Hambro v Burnand* [1904] 2 KB 10, CA.

9 *Grant v Norway* (1851) 10 CB 665; *Chapleo v Brunswick Permanent Benefit Building Society* (1881) 6 QBD 696, CA; *George Whitechurch Ltd v Cavanagh* [1902] AC 117, HL; *Ruben v Great Fingall Consolidated* [1906] AC 439, HL; *Russo-Chinese Bank v Li Yau Sam* [1910] AC 174, PC;

A-G for Ceylon v Silva [1953] AC 461, [1953] 2 WLR 1185, PC; *Armagas Ltd v Mundogas SA, The Ocean Frost* [1986] AC 717, [1986] 2 All ER 385, HL.

10 *Pole v Leask* (1863) 33 LJ Ch 155, HL. See also *Rimpacific Navigation Inc v Daehan Shipbuilding Co Ltd* [2011] EWHC 2618 (Comm), [2011] All ER (D) 119 (Oct).

11 *Brazier v Camp* (1894) 63 LJQB 257, CA; *Dyer v Pearson* (1824) 4 Dow & Ry KB 648; *Young v Cole* (1837) 3 Bing NC 724. See also *Soanes v London and South Western Rly Co* (1919) 88 LJKB 524, CA (authority of railway porter in uniform); *Leckenby v Wolman* [1921] WN 100 (authority of furniture salesman to take back furniture); *Bocking Garage v Mazurk* (1954) Times, 4 February, CA (authority of man behind counter to take money); *Cleveland Manufacturing Co Ltd v Muslim Commercial Bank Ltd* [1981] 2 Lloyd's Rep 646 (lack of authority of forwarding agent to indorse sight draft).

12 *Bailey and Whites Ltd v House* (1915) 31 TLR 583, DC; *Howard v Carline* (1956) 7 DLR (2d) 324, BC CA. The borderline between negligence and conduct amounting to holding out is narrow: *F Mildner & Sons v Noble* (1956) Times, 8 March, CA; *Povey v Taylor* (1966) 116 NLJ 1656, CA.

13 *A-G for Ceylon v Silva* [1953] AC 461, [1953] 2 WLR 1185, PC.

14 *Moore v Peachey* (1891) 7 TLR 748; *Roberts v Ogilby* (1821) 9 Price 269; *V/O Rasnoimport v Guthrie & Co Ltd* [1966] 1 Lloyd's Rep 1. As to the personal liability of one who purports to contract on behalf of a company not yet formed see the Companies Act 2006 s 51; and COMPANIES vol 14 (2016) PARA 59.

26. Equitable agency.

The circumstances in which a creditor is answerable for inequitable conduct on the part of a debtor are not limited to those when the debtor is the creditor's agent in the common law sense[1]. The creditor can be visited with the consequences of the debtor's conduct even where the debtor was neither actually nor ostensibly authorised to act as he did, thus giving rise to what may be termed an 'equitable agency'[2].

1 See *Barclays Bank v O'Brien* [1993] QB 109, [1992] 4 All ER 983, CA (affd on other grounds [1994] 1 AC 180, [1993] 4 All ER 417, HL) (the bank agreed an overdraft facility with its customer on condition, inter alia, that a legal charge over the matrimonial home was provided by his wife as well as himself; no warning was given to the wife that she should take independent legal advice before signing, and the husband misrepresented to her the extent of the charge).

2 See *Barclays Bank v O'Brien* [1993] QB 109, [1992] 4 All ER 983, CA (affd on other grounds [1994] 1 AC 180, [1993] 4 All ER 417, HL). See also *Bank of Credit & Commerce International SA v Aboody* [1990] 1 QB 923, [1992] 4 All ER 955, CA (overruled on other grounds by *CIBC Mortgages plc v Pitt* [1994] 1 AC 200, [1993] 4 All ER 433, HL).

(v) Co-principals and Co-agents

27. Co-principals.

Co-principals may jointly appoint an agent to act for them, and in such case become jointly liable to him[1], and may jointly sue him[2]. The agent is not bound to account separately to one of several co-principals[3], and, if he has done so, is not, apart from special stipulation, thereby discharged from liability to the other or others[4] unless the co-principals are also partners[5].

1 *Keay v Fenwick* (1876) 1 CPD 745, CA. One co-principal may ratify the acts of an agent, for example a sale, without ratifying the appointment of the agent, and may therefore not be liable for a share of the commission payable to the agent: see *Hughes v Hughes* (1971) 115 Sol Jo 911, CA.

2 *Skinner v Stocks* (1821) 4 B & Ald 437; *Cothay v Fennell* (1830) 10 B & C 671; *Jones v Cuthbertson* (1873) LR 8 QB 504.

3 *Hatsall v Griffith* (1834) 2 Cr & M 679.

4 *Innes v Stephenson* (1831) 1 Mood & R 145; *Lee v Sankey* (1873) LR 15 Eq 204.

5 *Innes v Stephenson* (1831) 1 Mood & R 145; and see *Heath v Chilton* (1844) 12 M & W 632. As to the implied authority of a partner to release debts owed to a firm see eg *Furnival v Weston* (1822) 7 Moore CP 356; and PARTNERSHIP vol 79 (2014) PARA 49.

28. Co-agents.

A principal may give authority to co-agents to act for him, either jointly, or jointly and severally. A mere authority to act, without further specification, is a joint authority[1], and can be acted upon only by the co-agents jointly[2]; but an authority given jointly and severally may be acted upon by all or any of the co-agents so as to bind the principal[3].

A principal may also appoint co-agents, giving power to a quorum to act on his behalf. This is normally the position as between a registered company and its directors[4]. In such case the principal will not be bound by the act of any number less than the appointed quorum[5].

Where a power of a public nature is committed to several persons, in the absence of statutory provision or implication to the contrary the act of the majority is binding upon the minority[6].

One co-agent is not liable for the act of another unless he has expressly authorised or tacitly permitted it[7], or the co-agents are partners[8].

1 *Brown v Andrew* (1849) 18 LJQB 153.
2 *Brown v Andrew* (1849) 18 LJQB 153; and see also *Boyd v Durand* (1809) 2 Taunt 161 (warrant issued to four bailiffs jointly and not severally held not to authorise an arrest by one); *Bell v Nixon* (1832) 9 Bing 393 (two persons filling office of clerk to turnpike trustees must both join in executing a contract on behalf of the trustees).
3 *Guthrie v Armstrong* (1822) 5 B & Ald 628. For the statutory form of power of attorney, which provides for joint and several authority, see PARA 30.
4 See eg *Ridley v Plymouth Grinding and Baking Co* (1848) 2 Exch 711; and see the Companies (Tables A to F) Regulations 1985, SI 1985/805, Schedule Table A, regs 70, 89; and COMPANIES vol 14 (2016) PARAS 569, 581.
5 *Kirk v Bell* (1851) 16 QBD 290; *D'Arcy v Tamar, Kit Hill and Callington Rly Co* (1867) LR 2 Exch 158; and see *Re Liverpool Household Stores Association Ltd* (1890) 59 LJ Ch 616; *Brown v Andrew* (1849) 18 LJQB 153. The principal would, however, be bound if it were to be held, in construing what is now the Companies Act 2006 s 40 (see PARA 8; and COMPANIES vol 14 (2016) PARA 262), that a matter decided on by less than a quorum is nonetheless 'decided on by the directors' within the meaning of that provision.
6 *Grindley v Barker* (1798) 1 Bos & P 229. See the Report of the Judicial Committee of the Privy Council on questions submitted in connection with the Irish Boundary Commission (1924) 59 LJo 517. See also *Atkinson v Brown* [1963] NZLR 755, NZ CA; *Picea Holdings Ltd v London Rent Assessment Panel* [1971] 2 QB 216, [1971] 2 All ER 805, DC.
7 This rule is chiefly exemplified in the case of the acts of one or more directors of a company without the knowledge of the others, and extends to fraudulent acts: *Cargill v Bower* (1878) 10 ChD 502; *Re Denham & Co* (1883) 25 ChD 752; *Re Montrotier Asphalte Co, Perry's Case* (1876) 34 LT 716; *Lucas v Fitzgerald* (1903) 20 TLR 16; *Bear v Stevenson* (1874) 30 LT 177, PC; *Land Credit Co of Ireland v Lord Fermoy* (1870) 5 Ch App 763; *Weir v Bell* (1878) 3 ExD 238, CA; *Cullerne v London and Suburban General Permanent Building Society* (1890) 25 QBD 485, CA.
8 See the Partnership Act 1890 s 6; and PARTNERSHIP vol 79 (2014) PARA 52.

2. AUTHORITY OF THE AGENT

(1) DERIVATION AND EXTENT

29. Derivation of agent's authority.

As has been previously stated[1], the authority of the agent may be derived expressly from an instrument, either a deed or simply in writing, or may be conferred orally. Authority may also be implied from the conduct of the parties or from the nature of the employment[2]. It may in certain cases be due to the necessity of circumstances[3], and in others be conferred by a valid ratification subsequent to the actual performance[4]. In addition, a person may appear to have given authority to another, and acts within such apparent authority may effectively bind him to the third party[5]. There would also, in certain circumstances, appear to be the possibility that the court will imply an equitable agency where no agency exists at common law[6].

An agent cannot be said to have authority solely on the basis that he holds himself out as having it[7].

1 See PARA 14 et seq.
2 See PARAS 37–44.
3 See PARA 24.
4 See PARAS 58–71.
5 Such authority may create an agency relationship where none already exists, or it may extend an existing relationship: *Swiss Air Transport Co Ltd v Palmer* [1976] 2 Lloyd's Rep 604; see further, as to the doctrine of ostensible authority PARA 25.

   'This type of apparent authority is often described as the usual authority of an agent. But it is important to remember that the idea of usual authority is used in two senses. First, it sometimes means that the agent had implied actual authority to perform acts necessarily incidental to the performance of the agency. Secondly, it sometimes means that the principal's conduct in clothing the agent with the trappings of authority was such as to induce a third party to rely on the existence of the agency': *First Energy (UK) Ltd v Hungarian International Bank Ltd* [1993] BCLC 1409 at 1417, [1993] 2 Lloyd's Rep 194 at 201, CA, per Steyn LJ. See also *Kelly v Fraser* [2012] UKPC 25, [2013] 1 AC 450, [2013] 1 All ER (Comm) 296 (pension plan trustees delegated administration of the plan to the employee benefits division of the company whose acts were therefore binding on the trustees).

6 See PARA 26.
7 See *Kelly v Fraser* [2012] UKPC 25 at [15], [2013] 1 AC 450, [2013] 1 All ER (Comm) 296 (discussing *Armagas v Mundogas* [1986] AC 717, [1986] 2 All ER 385, HL; and *First Energy (UK) Ltd v Hungarian International Bank Ltd* [1993] BCLC 1409, [1993] 2 Lloyd's Rep 194). See PARA 25. 'I find it very hard indeed to conceive of any circumstances in which an alleged agent, who does not have actual or apparent authority to bind the principal, can nevertheless acquire apparent authority to do so, simply by representing to the third party that he has such authority. . . . [B]efore any representation by the agent could be relied on to assist the contention that he had apparent authority, the court would have to be satisfied that the principal had given the alleged agent apparent authority to make the representation in question. Furthermore, any such representation would have to be clear and unequivocal': *Thanakharn Kasikorn Thai Chamkat (Mahachon) v Akai Holdings Ltd (in liquidation)* [2010] HKEC 927 at [70]–[71] per Lord Neuberger NPJ, HKCFA. However, it is possible for a principal to organise its affairs in such a way that subordinates who would not have authority to approve a transaction are nevertheless held out by the principal as the persons who are to communicate to outsiders the fact that it had been approved by those who were authorised to approve it or that some particular agent had been duly authorised to approve it: see *Kelly v Fraser* at [15].

30. Extent of agent's authority.

The authority of an agent may be confined to a particular act or be general[1] in its character. It will extend not only to acts expressly authorised but also to subordinate acts which are necessary or ordinarily incidental to the exercise of the express authority[2] and to acts within the agent's ostensible authority[3]. In no case, however, can the authority of the agent exceed the power of the principal to act on his own behalf[4]. As between the agent and his principal, an agent's authority may be limited by agreement or special instructions, but, as regards third persons, the authority which the agent has is that which he is reasonably believed to have, having regard to all the circumstances, and which is reasonably to be gathered from the nature of his employment and duties[5].

Where the agency is created by a general power of attorney in statutory form[6], however, the power will operate to confer upon the agent or agents authority to do anything which the donor can lawfully do by an attorney[7], other than functions which the donor has as a trustee, personal representative, tenant for life or statutory owner[8].

1 See PARA 11.
2 See PARA 33.
3 See PARA 25.
4 *Shrewsbury and Birmingham Rly Co v North Western Rly Co* (1857) 6 HL Cas 113; *Montreal Assurance Co v M'Gillivray* (1859) 13 Moo PCC 87; *Ashbury Railway Carriage and Iron Co v Riche* (1875) LR 7 HL 653.
   Corporations and incorporated companies can only enter into contracts within the powers of their charter, memorandum of association or Act of Parliament (see COMPANIES vol 14 (2016) PARAS 251 et seq, 255 et seq), but the validity of an act done by a company must not be called into question on the ground of lack of capacity by reason of anything in the company's constitution: see the Companies Act 2006 s 39(1); and COMPANIES vol 14 (2016) PARA 264. However, this does not apply to acts of a company that is a charity except in certain circumstances: see s 42(1); and COMPANIES vol 14 (2016) PARA 264 A person dealing with a company is not bound to inquire as to any limitation on the powers of the directors to bind the company or authorise others to do so: see s 40(2)(b); PARA 8; and COMPANIES vol 14 (2016) PARA 262.
5 *Brady v Todd* (1861) 9 CBNS 592 (a servant sent to deliver a horse has no implied authority to warrant it, and the person to whom it is delivered takes it at the risk that the servant had no authority in fact). As to the apparent and implied authority of the agent see PARAS 25, 37–44.
6 See the Powers of Attorney Act 1971 s 10(1), Sch 1. The statutory form provides for the appointment of either one or two attorneys, jointly or jointly and severally. Any form to the like effect but expressed to be made under the Powers of Attorney Act 1971 will confer the same authority as the statutory form: see s 10(1). A general power under s 10 does not empower its donee to transfer trust property: *Walia v Michael Naughton Ltd* [1985] 3 All ER 673, [1985] 1 WLR 1115. A Welsh language form is prescribed by the Powers of Attorney (Welsh Language Forms) Order 2000, SI 2000/215, art 3, Schedule Pt II.
7 Powers of Attorney Act 1971 s 10(1). This does not confer a right to conduct litigation where the attorney would not otherwise have that right: see *Gregory v Turner; R (on the application of Morris) v North Somerset Council* [2003] EWCA Civ 183, [2003] 2 All ER 1114, [2003] 1 WLR 1149. As to the acts a donor of a power may lawfully do by an attorney see PARA 15.
8 Powers of Attorney Act 1971 s 10(2). This is now subject to the Trustee Delegation Act 1999 s 1 (see TRUSTS AND POWERS vol 98 (2013) PARA 426): Powers of Attorney Act 1971 s 10(2) (amended by the Trustee Delegation Act 1999 s 3)).

(2) CONSTRUCTION OF AUTHORITY

(i) Powers of Attorney

31. Strict construction of instrument conferring authority.
An instrument conferring authority by deed is termed a power of attorney[1]. The person conferring the authority is termed the donor of the power, and the recipient of the authority, the donee. A power of attorney is construed strictly by the courts,

according to well-recognised rules[2], regard first being had to any recitals which, showing the general object, control the general terms in the operative part of the deed[3].

General words used in conferring the power are construed as limited by reference to the special powers conferred[4], but incidental powers necessary for carrying out the authority will be implied[5]. Thus a power granted to the donee to manage certain property, followed by general words giving him full power to do all lawful acts relating to the donor's business and affairs, of what nature or kind soever, does not necessarily include authority to indorse bills, for the general words are construed as having reference to managing the donor's property, for which indorsing bills may not be incidental or necessary[6]. A power to complete all contracts which the donee may deem necessary for a specific object, however, includes authority to obtain money for payment in respect of such contracts, where the payment is necessary and incidental to the completion[7].

1 See PARA 16.
2 *Bryant, Powis and Bryant Ltd v La Banque du Peuple* [1893] AC 170, PC; *Howard v Baillie* (1796) 2 Hy Bl 618; *Withington v Herring* (1829) 5 Bing 442.
3 *Rooke v Lord Kensington* (1856) 2 K & J 753; *Danby v Coutts & Co* (1885) 29 ChD 500.
4 *Attwood v Munnings* (1827) 7 B & C 278; *Perry v Holl* (1860) 2 De GF & J 38; *Lewis v Ramsdale* (1886) 55 LT 179.
5 *Re Wallace, ex p Wallace* (1884) 14 QBD 22, CA, where a solicitor authorised to conduct legal proceedings was held justified in presenting a bankruptcy petition; but he is not justified in assenting to the execution by the defendant of a deed of assignment for the benefit of his creditors: *Re A Debtor (No 1 of 1914), ex p Debtor v Petitioning Creditor* [1914] 2 KB 758.
6 *Esdaile v La Nauze* (1835) 1 Y & C Ex 394; cf *Harper v Godsell* (1870) LR 5 QB 422 (general words limited to exercise of privileges under a partnership); and see *Lewis v Ramsdale* (1886) 55 LT 179. See generally *Brown v InnovatorOne plc* [2012] EWHC 1321 (Comm) at [808]–[809] per Hamblen J.
7 *Withington v Herring* (1829) 5 Bing 442; and see *Henley v Soper* (1828) 8 B & C 16 (authority to dissolve partnership and appoint any other person the donee might see fit includes authority to submit the accounts to arbitration).

32. Limits of authority to be observed.

There must be strict adherence to the authority conferred by power of attorney[1]. If the agent in the pretended exercise of his authority acts in excess of and outside the reasonable scope of its special powers, the third party will be unable to make the principal liable[2]. Thus, where an instrument gives authority to sign contracts, acceptances and other documents, it gives power to sell or purchase negotiable instruments, but it does not give power to pledge them[3]. Similarly, a power to draw cheques extends only to drawing cheques in relation to the principal's affairs[4]. A signature by procuration to a negotiable instrument operates as notice that the agent has only a limited authority to sign and the principal is bound by such signature only if the agent in so signing was in fact acting within the limits of his authority[5]. Such notice operates as and when the document is negotiated or delivered[6].

1 See PARAS 16, 31.
2 *Jacobs v Morris* [1902] 1 Ch 816, CA, where a loan to the agent was made without inquiry, and, as he had no general borrowing powers, it was held not within his authority to bind his principal.
3 *Jonmenjoy Coondoo v Watson* (1884) 9 App Cas 561, PC; *De Bouchout v Goldsmid* (1800) 5 Ves 211.
4 *Reckitt v Barnett, Pembroke and Slater Ltd* [1929] AC 176, HL (payee, aware that cheque had been drawn in payment of attorney's private debt, was obliged to refund).
5 See the Bills of Exchange Act 1882 s 25; and FINANCIAL INSTRUMENTS AND TRANSACTIONS vol 49 (2015) PARA 258.
6 *Midland Bank Ltd v Reckitt* [1933] AC 1, HL.

33. Examples of incidental powers implied.

The construction of authorities given by powers of attorney[1] has given rise to a multiplicity of cases, of which the following are examples, which serve to indicate the extent to which the court, following its strict rules of construction, will allow actual expressions to imply incidental powers.

A power to deal with land gives authority to sell, the conditions of sale depending on the wording of the authority[2], but not to sell that portion included in a voluntary settlement[3]. A general power gives authority to instruct a solicitor[4], to sue[5], and to submit to arbitration[6]; but, when given to act in partnership matters, it does not give authority to dissolve the partnership[7]. A power to sell land belonging to the donor does not give authority to exercise a power of sale vested in the donor as a mortgagee[8]; a general power to mortgage, sell, or otherwise deal with an estate does not authorise the donee to execute a deed as a voluntary gift[9]; and a power to mortgage does not enable an attorney to execute a mortgage of the principal's property to secure an existing debt of the principal[10].

A power given by an executrix to receive debts due to her as executrix does not authorise the donee to bind the donor by accepting bills of exchange on her account[11]; a power to sue for debts and conduct the business of the principal does not give authority to indorse bills of exchange in his name[12], nor does a power to demand, sue for, recover and receive moneys by all lawful ways and means whatsoever give such an authority[13]; but the words 'to sell, indorse and assign' authorise the indorsement of bills of exchange in the name of the donor[14]. A power to draw cheques 'without restriction' does not give the donee authority to draw cheques for the payment of his private debts[15]. An authority to discount a bill includes authority to warrant it[16]. A shipmaster's authority may be sufficient to empower him to assign the passage money of the ship[17] or to enter into a charterparty[18]; and a ship agent's authority may enable him to dismiss the captain[19]. A clause by which the principal ratifies 'whatsoever the attorney shall do or purports to do' under the instrument does not extend the actual authority given by the power of attorney[20].

1   See PARAS **16, 31.**
2   *Hawksley v Outram* [1892] 3 Ch 359, CA.
3   *General Meat Supply Association Ltd v Bouffler* (1879) 41 LT 719, CA.
4   *Re Frampton, ex p Frampton* (1859) 1 De GF & J 263, CA.
5   *Gray v Pearson* (1870) LR 5 CP 568.
6   *Henley v Soper* (1828) 8 B & C 16; and see *Goodson v Brooke* (1815) 4 Camp 163.
7   *Harper v Godsell* (1870) LR 5 QB 422.
8   *Re Dowson and Jenkins's Contract* [1904] 2 Ch 219, CA. As to land vested in the donor as trustee for sale upon the statutory trusts see *Green v Whitehead* [1930] 1 Ch 38, CA.
9   *Re Bowles' Mortgage Trust* (1874) 31 LT 365, CA.
10 *Re Bowles' Mortgage Trust* (1874) 31 LT 365, CA.
11 *Gardner v Baillie* (1796) 6 Term Rep 591; cf *Howard v Baillie* (1796) 2 Hy Bl 618.
12 *Esdaile v La Nauze* (1835) 1 Y & C Ex 394; *Murray v East India Co* (1821) 5 B & Ald 204; *Hogg v Snaith* (1808) 1 Taunt 347.
13 *Murray v East India Co* (1821) 5 B & Ald 204.
14 *Bank of Bengal v Macleod* (1849) 5 Moo Ind App 1, PC; *Bank of Bengal v Fagan* (1849) 5 Moo Ind App 27, PC.
15 *Reckitt v Barnett, Pembroke and Slater Ltd* [1929] AC 176, HL.
16 *Fenn v Harrison* (1791) 4 Term Rep 177.
17 *Willis v Palmer* (1859) 7 CBNS 340.
18 *Routh v Macmillan* (1863) 2 H & C 750.
19 *Berwick v Horsfall* (1858) 4 CBNS 450.
20 *Midland Bank Ltd v Reckitt* [1933] AC 1, HL.

(ii) Written Authority

34. Interpretation of authority under hand.

Where the principal gives the agent authority in writing this is capable of extension either orally or by conduct[1]. Such an authority is not so strictly construed as one by deed, and regard is had to all the circumstances of the agency business[2]. The ordinary full authority given in one part of the instrument will not be cut down because there are ambiguous and uncertain expressions elsewhere[3]; but the document will be considered as a whole for the interpretation of particular words or directions[4]. When once an authority has been reduced into writing, the interpretation of the written document is, in general, a matter of law and not a question of fact[5].

1 *Pole v Leask* (1860) 28 Beav 562; affd (1863) 33 LJ Ch 155, HL.
2 *Pole v Leask* (1860) 28 Beav 562; affd (1863) 33 LJ Ch 155, HL; *Foxtons Ltd v Puri* [2010] EWCA Civ 925 ('sale of the property', known by both principal and agent to be sole asset of offshore company, held to include transfer of shares in said company).
3 *Pariente v Lubbock* (1856) 8 De GM & G 5.
4 See eg *Entwisle v Dent* (1848) 1 Exch 812, where 'may' was interpreted as being directory.
5 See eg *Re L Sutro & Co and Heilbut Symons & Co* [1917] 2 KB 348, CA; and DEEDS AND OTHER INSTRUMENTS vol 32 (2012) PARA 385.

35. Agent's discretion.

In the absence of express directions, the agent may exercise his discretion so as to act in the best manner possible for his principal[1]. An agent whose instructions are in ambiguous terms may be justified if he acts in good faith and places a reasonable construction on his authority[2], but where the limits imposed are definite, he has no right to exercise a discretion[3] even if he judges the principal's instructions commercially imprudent[4].

1 *Wolff v Horncastle* (1798) 1 Bos & P 316; *Pariente v Lubbock* (1856) 8 De GM & G 5. See also *Tallentire v Ayre* (1884) 1 TLR 143, CA.
2 *Ireland v Livingston* (1872) LR 5 HL 395; *Boden v French* (1851) 10 CB 886; *Johnston v Kershaw* (1867) LR 2 Exch 82; *Miles v Haslehurst & Co* (1906) 23 TLR 142; *Cobridge Steamship Co Ltd v Bucknall Steamship Lines Ltd* (1910) 15 Com Cas 138, CA; *S Weigall & Co v Runciman & Co* (1916) 85 LJKB 1187, CA; *Gould v South Eastern and Chatham Rly Co* [1920] 2 KB 186, DC; *James Vale & Co v Van Oppen & Co Ltd* (1921) 37 TLR 367; *Finn v Shelton Iron, Steel and Coal Co Ltd* (1924) 131 LT 213, CA; *Westminster Bank Ltd v Hilton* (1926) 136 LT 315. Where, because of modern communications, an agent can easily resolve a patent ambiguity by communicating with his principal, it may be that he has a duty to do so, and early cases should probably be considered in this light: *European Asian Bank AG v Punjab and Sind Bank (No 2)* [1983] 2 All ER 508 at 516–517, [1983] 1 WLR 642 at 656 per Robert Goff LJ. Quaere if an agent acting in good faith fails to spot ambiguity. As to the authority for an estate agent to make a contract for the sale of land see PARA 41.
3 *Bertram, Armstrong & Co v Godfray* (1830) 1 Knapp 381, PC.
4 *Overend & Gurney Co v Gibb* (1871–72) LR 5 HL 480; *Redmayne Bentley Stockbrokers v Isaacs* [2010] EWHC 1504 (Comm), [2010] All ER (D) 233 (Jun); *Luffeorm Ltd v Kitsons LLP* [2015] EWHC B10 (QB), [2015] Lexis Citation 137, [2015] PNLR 30.

(iii) Oral Authority

36. Oral authority given in general terms.

When authority is given orally to the agent, its terms and extent are questions of fact, depending on the circumstances of the particular case and the usages of the profession, trade or business[1]. An authority conferred in general terms gives an agent power to act in the ordinary way in reference to the particular business, and to do subordinate acts[2], and all reasonable acts in relation to the business[3], but does not, in the absence of special conditions, give authority to take more than the usual risks or employ extraordinary means[4].

1   As to custom and usage see generally PARA 44; and CUSTOM AND USAGE.
2   *Collen v Gardner* (1856) 21 Beav 540.
3   *Wiltshire v Sims* (1808) 1 Camp 258; *East India Co v Hensley* (1794) 1 Esp 111; *Howard v Braithwaite* (1812) 1 Ves & B 202.
4   *Papé v Westacott* [1894] 1 QB 272, CA; *Hine Bros v Steamship Insurance Syndicate Ltd, The Netherholme, Glen Holme and Rydal Holme* (1895) 72 LT 79; *Underwood v Nicholls* (1855) 17 CB 239; *Re Williams, ex p Howell* (1865) 12 LT 785, CA; *Blumberg v Life Interests and Reversionary Securities Corpn Ltd* [1897] 1 Ch 171 (affd [1898] 1 Ch 27, CA). The authority to receive money is to receive in cash and not by set-off, nor, in the absence of special custom, by bill of exchange or cheque: see PARA 38.

(3) IMPLIED AUTHORITY

37. Necessary and incidental acts.

The implied authority of an agent extends to all subordinate acts which are necessary or ordinarily incidental to the exercise of his express authority[1]. It does not, however, extend to acts which are outside the ordinary course of his business, or which are neither necessary nor incidental to his express authority[2].

The manager of a business has authority to do all acts necessary to the regular conduct of the business[3], but he has no implied authority to borrow money[4]. A servant has not, merely from the fact of service, authority to pledge his master's credit[5], but an agent has been held, in particular instances, to have implied authority to pledge his principal's credit[6].

Authority to act generally (whether conferred by writing or orally) includes authority to instruct a solicitor[7].

1   *Bayley v Wilkins* (1849) 7 CB 886; *Collen v Gardner* (1856) 21 Beav 540; *Montaignac v Shitta* (1890) 15 App Cas 357, PC; *Financings Ltd v Stimson* [1962] 3 All ER 386, [1962] 1 WLR 1184, CA (implied authority of dealer when acting as agent for hire purchase finance company); *Benmag v Barda* [1955] 2 Lloyd's Rep 354 (implied authority of agent to warrant quality of goods); *Blandy Bros & Co Lda v Nello Simoni Ltd* [1963] 2 Lloyd's Rep 393, CA (authority of ship's agent to incur loading expenses on charterers' accounts). See also *Wright v Pepin* [1954] 2 All ER 52, [1954] 1 WLR 635 (implied authority of solicitor, instructed to 'clear up' client's affairs, to acknowledge debt for the purposes of the Limitation Act 1939 (repealed: see now the Limitation Act 1980)); *Gavaghan v Edwards* [1961] 2 QB 220, [1961] 2 All ER 477, CA (solicitors acting for both parties already in agreement may have implied authority to make additional memorandum for the purpose of recording a final term agreed by the parties); and *Heatons Transport (St Helens) Ltd v Transport and General Workers Union* [1973] AC 15, [1972] 3 All ER 101, HL (implied authority of shop stewards to act in the interests of members including by industrial action provided acts are not outside union rules or policy).
2   An agent authorised to deliver a horse has no authority to give a warranty (*Woodin v Burford* (1834) 2 Cr & M 391); nor has an agent authorised to sell a horse privately (*Brady v Todd* (1861) 9 CBNS 592), unless he is the agent of a horse dealer (*Howard v Sheward* (1866) LR 2 CP 148; *Bank of Scotland v Watson* (1813) 1 Dow 40; *Baldry v Bates* (1885) 1 TLR 558, DC); but an agent authorised to sell at a fair may give such a warranty (*Brooks v Hassall* (1883) 49 LT 569). An agent to sell a car may have implied authority to give warranties concerning its insurance: *Abrahams v Spitz* (1963) 107 Sol Jo 113, CA. An agent authorised to get a bill discounted may warrant it good, but not indorse it in the principal's name: *Fenn v Harrison* (1790) 3 Term Rep 757; and see *Dingle v Hare* (1859) 7 CBNS 145. The depositary of a policy of insurance on a ship at sea has no implied authority to give notice to the underwriter of abandonment as for a total loss: *Jardine v Leathley* (1863) 3 B & S 700. As to the extent of implied authority of a bank manager to advise a customer see *Banbury v Bank of Montreal* [1918] AC 626, HL; and of a solicitor to sign a contract for sale of land see *Blackburn v Walker* (1920) 150 LT Jo 73. A person employed merely to deliver milk has no implied authority to sell (*Whittaker v Forshaw* [1919] 2 KB 419), nor a furniture salesman to cancel a sale (*Leckenby v Wolman* [1921] WN 100), nor, in general, an agent for sale of goods

to receive payment (*Butwick v Grant* [1924] 2 KB 483; see further PARA 38). Similarly, a mercantile agent has no authority, implied or statutory, to give goods of his principal to another to pledge for him, even though he may have authority to pledge them himself: see *De Gorter v Attenborough & Son* (1904) 21 TLR 19. As to the statutory protection of third parties dealing with mercantile agents see PARAS 149–150. A managing director of a theatre company has implied authority to refuse admission (*Said v Butt* [1920] 3 KB 497), and an agent for the sale of property has implied authority to sign an open contract (*Keen v Mear* [1920] 2 Ch 574), but not to make conditions as to title (*Keen v Mear*; and see also PARA 41). It is only in very special circumstances that an agent has implied authority to pay his principal's cheques into his own account: *Australia and New Zealand Bank Ltd v Ateliers de Construction Electrique de Charleroi* [1967] 1 AC 86, [1966] 2 WLR 1216, PC.

3   *Hawken v Bourne* (1841) 8 M & W 703. Cf *Rutherford v Ounan* [1913] 2 IR 265. Such acts include the accepting of a bill in the name in which the business is carried on where drawing and accepting bills is incident to the ordinary course of the business: *Edmunds v Bushell and Jones* (1865) LR 1 QB 97; *Watteau v Fenwick* [1893] 1 QB 346; and see PARA 126 note 6. As to the authority of the manager of a public house see *Daun v Simmins* (1879) 41 LT 783, CA. A fraudulent preference of a creditor by the agent entrusted with the financial affairs of a principal who becomes insolvent is the act of the principal: *Re Drabble Bros* [1930] 2 Ch 211, CA. As to the authority of the 'European sales manager' of a property development company see *Kabel v Ronald Lyon Espanola SA* (1968) 208 Estates Gazette 265.

4   *Hawtayne v Bourne* (1841) 7 M & W 595; and see *Dickinson v Valpy* (1829) 10 B & C 128; *Burmester v Norris* (1851) 6 Exch 796. The directors of a banking or trading company, however, have been held to be entitled to borrow for the business of the company: *Re Hamilton's Windsor Ironworks, ex p Pitman and Edwards* (1879) 12 ChD 707; *Maclae v Sutherland* (1854) 3 E & B 1; *Royal British Bank v Turquand* (1855) 5 E & B 248 (affd (1856) 6 E & B 327, Ex Ch).

5   See eg *Wright v Glyn* [1902] 1 KB 745, CA (coachman held not to be an agent to pledge his master's credit for forage).

6   Thus the general manager of a railway company has been held to have authority for credit for medical attendance to a servant of the company: see *Walker v Great Western Rly Co* (1867) LR 2 Exch 228. The position has been held to be otherwise in the case of a stationmaster for medical attendance to an injured passenger: *Cox v Midland Counties Rly Co* (1849) 3 Exch 268. A hospital matron was held to have implied authority to pledge the credit of the managing committee for meat supplied to the hospital: see *Real and Personal Advance Co v Phalempin* (1893) 9 TLR 569, CA.

7   *Re Frampton, ex p Frampton* (1859) 1 De GF & J 263, CA (agent held to have authority to instruct solicitor to appear on behalf of overseas principal to dispute an adjudication of bankruptcy made against latter).

38. Authority of agent to receive payment.

Payment made in the ordinary course of business to the agent of the creditor discharges the debt if the agent is authorised or held out as having authority to receive payment[1]. An agent authorised to sell, however, does not necessarily have implied authority to receive payment for his principal[2]. Where it is in the ordinary course of business for the agent to receive payment for his principal, such payment should, generally speaking, be received in cash[3]. Where, however, a cheque taken by the agent has been paid the transaction is equivalent to payment in cash[4]. To restrict the authority of an agent authorised to receive payment to a particular form of payment other than cash, for example by a crossed cheque payable to the principal, there must be plain intimation to the third party[5]. In general, an agent has no implied authority to receive payment by cheque[6], by bill[7], by other goods[8], or before it becomes due[9], nor may he give credit[10]. A reasonable custom to receive payment in any particular mode may, however, be proved[11].

An authority given to an agent to receive payment does not authorise a settlement of accounts between him and the third party by setting off a debt due from the agent to the third party[12], unless this can be justified by a known usage which is binding on the principal[13].

1   See eg *Bridges v Garrett* (1870) LR 5 CP 451, Ex Ch. See also *Bocking Garage v Mazurk* (1954) Times, 4 February, CA. As to the discharge of the third party generally see PARA 134.

2   *Drakeford v Piercy* (1866) 7 B & S 515; *Butwick v Grant* [1924] 2 KB 483. As to the discharge by the third party of his obligation to the principal by payment to an agent having apparent authority see eg *Townsend v Inglis* (1816) Holt NP 278; and PARA 134. As to the authority to receive payment where a solicitor produces a deed containing or indorsed with a receipt by the principal see the Law of Property Act 1925 s 69; CONVEYANCING vol 23 (2016) PARA 228; LEGAL PROFESSIONS vol 66 (2015) PARA 585.

3   *Legge v Byas, Mosley & Co* (1901) 7 Com Cas 16; *Williams v Evans* (1866) LR 1 QB 352; *Sykes v Giles* (1839) 5 M & W 645; *Hogarth v Wherley* (1875) LR 10 CP 630; *Charles v Blackwell* (1877) 2 CPD 151, CA; and see the cases cited in PARA 86 note 6.

4   *Bridges v Garrett* (1870) LR 5 CP 451, Ex Ch; *Walker v Barker* (1900) 16 TLR 393.

5   *International Sponge Importers Ltd v Andrew Watt & Sons* [1911] AC 279, HL; *Bradford & Sons v Price Bros* (1923) 92 LJKB 871.

6   *Blumberg v Life Interests and Reversionary Securities Corpn* [1897] 1 Ch 171; affd [1898] 1 Ch 27, CA.

7   *Hine Bros v Steamship Insurance Syndicate Ltd, The Netherholme, Glen Holme and Rydal Holme* (1895) 72 LT 79, CA; *Boothman v Byrne* (1923) 57 ILT 36.

8   *Howard v Chapman* (1831) 4 C & P 508.

9   *Breming v Mackie* (1862) 3 F & F 197.

10   *Wiltshire v Sims* (1808) 1 Camp 258.

11   See *Bridges v Garrett* (1870) LR 5 CP 451, Ex Ch (payment by cheque); *Hine Bros v Steamship Insurance Syndicate Ltd, The Netherholme, Glen Holme and Rydal Holme* (1895) 72 LT 79, CA (by bill); *Pelham v Hilder* (1841) 1 Y & C Ch Cas 3 (giving credit); and see PARA 44. Where the principal authorises the agent to receive payment, intending that he pay himself from the sum received a debt due from his principal, the agent may receive payment in any manner: *Barker v Greenwood* (1837) 2 Y & C Ex 414. An agent appointed, on the dissolution of a partnership, by a retiring partner to liquidate the partnership affairs, has no authority to accept bills in the name of his principal: *Odell v Cormack Bros* (1887) 19 QBD 223.

12   *Bartlett v Pentland* (1830) 10 B & C 760; *Barker v Greenwood* (1837) 2 Y & C Ex 414; *Pearson v Scott* (1878) 9 ChD 198; *Anderson v Sutherland* (1897) 13 TLR 163.

13   *Stewart v Aberdein* (1838) 4 M & W 211; *Catterall v Hindle* (1867) LR 2 CP 368, Ex Ch.

39.   Authority of agent to give into custody.

Whether an agent or servant has implied authority to give persons into custody has been considered in many cases; the test is whether in so doing he is acting within the scope of his ordinary duties, and also within the scope of the employer's powers[1]. If he is, he has implied authority[2]; if he is not, he or his employer or both will be liable in tort to the third party[3]; and it is for the person asserting the existence of the authority to prove it[4].

To be within the scope of an agent's implied authority, an act must be apparently necessary, arising out of the ordinary discharge of his duties[5], or to protect the principal's property[6].

A distinction must be observed between those acts of an agent which are of a reasonable nature and those which are of an excessive or improper character, which latter would not fall within an implied authority[7]. The manager of a restaurant has no implied authority to give a customer into custody on a dispute over the bill[8], but a person in a similar capacity is justified in giving persons into custody on a charge of creating disorder on the premises[9].

1   As to arrest generally see POLICE AND INVESTIGATORY POWERS vol 84A (2013) PARA 485 et seq.

2   *Lowe v Great Northern Rly Co* (1893) 62 LJQB 524; *Percy v Glasgow Corpn* [1922] 2 AC 299, HL.

3   *Walker v South Eastern Rly Co* (1870) LR 5 CP 640; *Moore v Metropolitan Rly Co* (1872) LR 8 QB 36. As to actions for false imprisonment arising out of this class of act see *Knight v North Metropolitan Tramways Co* (1898) 78 LT 227; *Charleston v London Tramways Co Ltd* (1888) 4 TLR 629, CA; *Ormiston v Great Western Rly Co* [1917] 1 KB 598; *Tims v John Lewis & Co Ltd* [1951] 2 KB 459, [1951] 1 All ER 814, CA (revsd on other grounds sub nom *John Lewis & Co Ltd v Tims* [1952] AC 676, [1952] 1 All ER 1203, HL).

4   *Goff v Great Northern Rly Co* (1861) 30 LJQB 148.

5   *Lord Bolingbroke v Swindon New Town Local Board* (1874) LR 9 CP 575. There is no implied
    authority in a servant to do unlawful acts, nor in a solicitor to exceed his necessary duties, eg where
    issuing fieri facias to direct the sheriff to seize certain goods: *Smith v Keal* (1882) 9 QBD 340, CA.
6   *Hanson v Waller* [1901] 1 KB 390; *Allen v London and South Western Rly Co* (1870) LR 6 QB
    65; *Abrahams v Deakin* [1891] 1 QB 516, CA (a railway clerk or manager of a business has no
    implied authority to give into custody except for the purpose of protecting the property of his
    employer).
7   *Bank of New South Wales v Owston* (1879) 4 App Cas 270, PC.
8   *Stedman v Baker & Co* (1896) 12 TLR 451, CA.
9   *Ashton v Spiers and Pond* (1893) 9 TLR 606.

40. No authority to commit illegal acts.

By virtue of general rules of the common law, an agent cannot be given
authority to do an illegal act, and no agent can recover remuneration or indemnity
against a principal for the performance of an act known by him to be illegal[1].
Powers of attorney given for illegal purposes, for example in general restraint of
trade[2], or to prevent penal legal proceedings[3], are void.

1   *Collins v Blantern* (1767) 2 Wils 341; *Holman v Johnson* (1775) 1 Cowp 341. See further as to the
    loss of right to remuneration or indemnity PARAS **111–114**.
2   *Mitchel v Reynolds* (1711) 1 P Wms 181.
3   *Kirwan v Goodman* (1841) 9 Dowl 330.

41. Estate agents.

The making of a contract for the sale of land is no part of an estate agent's
business[1] and authority to make such a contract is not to be lightly inferred from
vague or ambiguous language[2]. Accordingly, an estate agent authorised to procure
a purchaser has no implied authority to enter into a contract of sale[3] or to give a
warranty[4]; nor has an agent who is merely authorised to treat with people and
permit them to view the property[5]. Similarly an agent authorised to act 'in and
about' a purchase has no implied authority to purchase[6]; but, where definite and
unequivocal instructions are given to sell at a stated price, it may be inferred that
the agent has authority to enter into an open contract[7]. This, however, does not
imply authority either to make conditions as to title[8] or to receive the purchase
money[9].

When a vendor engages an estate agent, he does not thereby confer on the
estate agent any implied or ostensible authority to receive as his agent a
pre-contract deposit. Where a pre-contract deposit is paid to the estate agent the
purchaser is the only person with a right or claim to the deposit money until
contract, the vendor has no claim to or control over the deposit money and
consequently is under no liability to the purchaser to repay it in the event of
default by the estate agent[10]. An estate agent who claims to be a sole agent has no
implied authority to appoint a sub-agent[11]. Where the agent employs a sub-agent
without authority, the principal will not be liable to refund a deposit paid to the
sub-agent should the latter default; the agent only will be so liable[12].

1   As to the regulation of the activities of estate agents under the Estate Agents Act 1979 see PARA
    254 et seq.
2   *Wragg v Lovett* [1948] 2 All ER 968, CA, per Lord Greene MR.
3   *Hamer v Sharp* (1874) LR 19 Eq 108; *Chadburn v Moore* (1892) 61 LJ Ch 674; *Prior v Moore*
    (1887) 3 TLR 624; *Wilde v Watson* (1878) 1 LR Ir 402; *Thuman v Best* (1907) 97 LT 239; *Carney
    v Fair* (1902) 54 ILT 61; *Lewcock v Bromley* (1920) 127 LT 116; and see *Yallop v Fosh* (1953)
    161 Estates Gazette 603 (no implied authority to grant new lease to existing tenant). He has,
    however, authority to describe the property and state facts affecting its value: *Mullens v Miller*
    (1882) 22 ChD 194.
4   *Hill v Harris* [1965] 2 QB 601, [1965] 2 All ER 358, CA.
5   *Godwin v Brind* (1868) 17 WR 29.

6 *Vale of Neath Colliery Co v Furness* (1876) 45 LJ Ch 276.
7 *Rosenbaum v Belson* [1900] 2 Ch 267; *Keen v Mear* [1920] 2 Ch 574. There is a substantial
   difference between 'to sell' and 'to find a purchaser': see *Lewcock v Bromley* (1920) 127 LT 116;
   and cf *Carney v Fair* (1920) 54 ILT 61; *AH Allen & Co Ltd v Whiteman* (1920) 89 LJ Ch 534;
   Wragg v Lovett [1948] 2 All ER 968, CA; and see *Davies v Sweet* [1962] 2 QB 300, [1962] 1 All
   ER 92, CA.
8 *Keen v Mear* [1920] 2 Ch 574.
9 *Mynn v Joliffe* (1834) 1 Mood & R 326. Cf *Butwick v Grant* [1924] 2 KB 483, DC.
10 *Sorrell v Finch* [1977] AC 728, [1976] 2 All ER 371, HL, which overruled *Goding v Frazer* [1966]
   3 All ER 234, [1967] 1 WLR 286 and *Burt v Claude Cousins & Co Ltd* [1971] 2 QB 426, [1971]
   2 All ER 611, CA, and doubted *Ryan v Pilkington* [1959] 1 All ER 689, [1959] 1 WLR 403, CA.
   As to pre-contract deposits see PARA 263.
11 *John McCann & Co v Pow* [1975] 1 All ER 129, [1974] 1 WLR 1643, CA; and see *Robert Bruce
   & Partners v Winyard Developments* [1987] 1 EGLR 20.
12 See *Maloney v Hardy and Moorshed* [1971] 2 QB 442n, [1971] 2 All ER 630n, CA. As to
   delegation to sub-agents generally see PARAS 51–57.

42. Bailiffs, enforcement agents and stewards.

Prior to the abolition of the common law right to distrain for arrears of rent
and the introduction of commercial rent arrears recovery[1] under which landlords
of commercial premises may take control of a tenant's goods to recover rent
payable under the lease[2], a bailiff authorised to distrain had implied authority to
receive the rent, although a man left in possession by the bailiff had no such
implied authority[3]. It is likely that an enforcement agent performing commercial
rent arrears recovery, to whom a debtor pays the amount outstanding in full after
the enforcement agent has taken control of goods, and before they are sold or
abandoned[4], enjoys similar authority.

A steward has implied authority to give or receive notices to quit[5], but a mere
rent collector has not[6]; nor has a steward implied authority to bind his principal
by signing bills of exchange[7], or by a contract to grant a lease for a term of years[8].
A steward appointed for a particular occasion has a more limited implied
authority than one appointed to act generally, and when appointed only for the
purpose of maintaining order on a special occasion, has no authority to commit
an assault[9].

1 See the Tribunals, Courts and Enforcement Act 2007 s 71; and LANDLORD AND TENANT vol 62
   (2016) PARA 282.
2 See the Tribunals, Courts and Enforcement Act 2007 Pt 3; the Taking Control of Goods
   Regulations 2013, SI 2013/1894; and LANDLORD AND TENANT vol 62 (2016) PARA 282 et seq.
   A landlord under a lease of commercial premises may now use the procedure set out in the
   Tribunals, Courts and Enforcement Act 2007 Sch 12 for taking control of goods to recover from
   a tenant rent payable under the lease ('commercial rent arrears recovery' or 'CRAR'): see
   LANDLORD AND TENANT vol 62 (2016) PARA 282. As to CRAR see LANDLORD AND TENANT vol
   62 (2016) PARA 283 et seq.
3 *Hatch v Hale* (1850) 15 QB 10; *Boulton v Reynolds* (1859) 2 E & E 369. An agent authorised to
   receive rents for his own benefit had no authority to distrain therefor: *Ward v Shew* (1833) 9 Bing
   608.
4 Tribunals, Courts and Enforcement Act 2007, Schedule 12, para 58.
5 *Roe d Dean and Chapter of Rochester v Pierce* (1809) 2 Camp 96; *Papillon v Brunton* (1860) 5
   H & N 518; *Jones v Phipps* (1868) LR 3 QB 567. See also *Harmond Properties Ltd v Gajdzis*
   [1968] 3 All ER 263, [1968] 1 WLR 1858, CA (authority of director of property company to give
   notice to quit).
6 *Pearse v Boulter* (1860) 2 F & F 133. Cf *Barker v Levinson* [1951] 1 KB 342, [1950] 2 All ER 825
   (rent collector has no authority to take illegal premium).
7 *Davidson v Stanley* (1841) 3 Scott NR 49.
8 *Collen v Gardner* (1856) 21 Beav 540, on the ground that a steward is employed to manage
   property, which does not involve a right to contract with tenants, nor is any such custom

established, although he may contract for the usual and customary leases: *Peers v Sneyd* (1853) 17 Beav 151. Cf *Barker v Levinson* [1951] 1 KB 342, [1950] 2 All ER 825.
9   *Lucas v Mason* (1875) LR 10 Exch 251.

43. Factors.

The implied authority of a factor[1] includes, subject to special instructions, authority:

(1)   to sell in his own name[2];

(2)   to sell on reasonable credit[3], and at such time and price as he may think best for his principal[4];

(3)   to warrant[5]; and

(4)   to receive payment when he has sold in his own name[6].

It does not include authority to barter[7] or pledge[8] the principal's goods, or the bill of lading therefor[9], or to delegate his authority[10], save as to purely ministerial acts[11].

1   As to the meaning of 'factor' see PARA **13**.
2   *Baring v Corrie* (1818) 2 B & Ald 137; *Re Henley, ex p Dixon* (1876) 4 ChD 133, CA. As to dispositions by mercantile agents under the Factors Act 1889, see generally PARAS **149–150**.
3   *Houghton v Matthews* (1803) 3 Bos & P 485; *Scott v Surman* (1742) Willes 400.
4   *Smart v Sandars* (1846) 3 CB 380.
5   *Pickering v Busk* (1812) 15 East 38. This authority apparently arises only where there exists a custom to warrant the class of article sold: *Dingle v Hare* (1859) 7 CBNS 145.
6   *Drinkwater v Goodwin* (1775) 1 Cowp 251. This authority relates only to payment by the usual mode of payment: *Underwood v Nicholls* (1855) 17 CB 239; and see further PARA **38**.
7   *Guerreiro v Peile* (1820) 3 B & Ald 616.
8   *Fielding v Kymer* (1821) 2 Brod & Bing 639, sub nom *Gill v Kymer* (1821) 5 Moore CP 503; *Martini v Coles* (1813) 1 M & S 140; *Paterson v Tash* (1743) 2 Stra 1178; *Guichard v Morgan* (1819) 4 Moore CP 36. As to the law of pledge see further BAILMENT AND PLEDGE.
9   *Newsom v Thornton* (1805) 6 East 17.
10 *Cockran v Irlam* (1814) 2 M & S 301; *Solly v Rathbone* (1814) 2 M & S 298.
11 See PARAS **51–54**.

44. Custom and usage.

An agent also has implied authority to act in accordance with the customs and usages of the place where[1], or the business in respect of which[2], his express authority permits him to act, subject to the condition that such customs and usages must not be unreasonable, or change the essential nature of the contract of agency[3]. Where the agent is a professional person, a contract made in the ordinary course of his profession and as agent is deemed to incorporate all reasonable[4] usages, rules and regulations of that profession[5].

To be recognised as such, a usage must be certain (meaning, its practice can be clearly established), notorious (meaning, so well-known in the relevant market that those operating in that market contract with the usage as an implied term), and reasonable[6].

Provided that the custom or usage is reasonable, the agent's implied authority to act in accordance with it is not affected by the fact that the principal may have been unaware of its existence[7]; and the agent is entitled to indemnity from his principal against losses caused by acting in accordance with it[8]. Reliance will not, however, be permitted on a custom which is in direct conflict with the express terms of the contract of agency[9].

What is a reasonable custom or usage is a question of law[10]. It must be a generally recognised custom or usage, and not merely a course of business between the agent and the third party[11].

An agent has, however, no implied authority to act in accordance with an unreasonable custom or usage unless the principal has notice of the custom or usage and agrees to be bound by it[12]; the burden of proving that the principal had notice of it lies on the person alleging the existence of the authority[13]. Nor is it necessarily any practice that happens to be observed by those operating within a particular business or market[14].

1 *Foster v Pearson* (1835) 1 Cr M & R 849; *Bayliffe v Butterworth* (1847) 1 Exch 425; *Pollock v Stables* (1848) 12 QB 765.

2 *Lienard v Dresslar* (1862) 3 F & F 212.

3 *Robinson v Mollett* (1875) LR 7 HL 802; *Bostock v Jardine* (1865) 3 H & C 700.

4 As to reasonableness see note 10.

5 *Graves v Legg* (1857) 2 H & N 210; *Stray v Russell* (1859) 1 E & E 888 (affd (1860) 1 E & E 916, Ex Ch); *London Founders' Association Ltd and Palmer v Clarke* (1888) 20 QBD 576, CA.

6 See *Cunliffe-Owen v Teather and Greenwood* [1967] 3 All ER 561 at 572, [1967] 1 WLR 1421 at 1439 per Ungoed-Thomas J; and CUSTOM AND USAGE vol 32 (2012) PARA 50.

7 *Scott and Horton v Godfrey* [1901] 2 KB 726; *Consolidated Goldfields of South Africa v E Spiegel & Co* (1909) 100 LT 351; see also *Beckhuson and Gibbs v Hamblet* [1901] 2 KB 73, CA; *Cropper v Cook* (1868) LR 3 CP 194; *Sutton v Tatham* (1839) 10 Ad & El 27; *Fal Bunkering of Sharjah v Grecale Inc of Panama* [1990] 1 Lloyd's Rep 369. As to usages of the stock exchange see *Maxted v Paine* (1869) LR 4 Exch 203 (affd (1871) LR 6 Exch 132); *Robinson v Mollett* (1875) LR 7 HL 802.

8 *Harker v Edwards* (1887) 57 LJQB 147, CA.

9 See *Bower v Jones* (1831) 8 Bing 65; *Cruse v Paine* (1869) 4 Ch App 441; *Grissell v Bristowe* (1868) LR 4 CP 36; *Robinson v Mollett* (1875) LR 7 HL 802; see also *Laskin v Bache & Co Inc* [1972] 1 OR 465, 23 DLR (3d) 385, Ont CA.

10 See *Bradburn v Foley* (1878) 3 CPD 129; and CUSTOM AND USAGE vol 32 (2012) PARA 51.

11 *Coles v Bristowe* (1868) 4 Ch App 3; *Re Williams, ex p Howell* (1865) 12 LT 785, CA. For examples of usages which have been held to be reasonable see *Bridges v Garrett* (1870) LR 5 CP 451 (receipt of payment by cheque); *Walker v Barker* (1900) 16 TLR 393, DC (payment by cheque made out to agent); *Cropper v Cook* (1868) LR 3 CP 194 (agent incurring personal liability on the contract); *Pelham v Hilder* (1841) 1 Y & C Ch Cas 3 (sale on credit); *Scott and Horton v Godfrey* [1901] 2 KB 726 (consolidation of orders); *Produce Brokers Co Ltd v Olympia Oil and Cake Co Ltd* [1917] 1 KB 320, CA (buyers to accept shippers' appropriation); *Anglo Overseas Transport Co Ltd v Titan Industrial Corpn (United Kingdom) Ltd* [1959] 2 Lloyd's Rep 152 (personal liability of forwarding agents for cost of freight space).

For examples of customs which have been held to be unreasonable see *Sweeting v Pearce* (1859) 7 CBNS 449 (affd (1861) 9 CBNS 534, Ex Ch); *Matveieff & Co v Crossfield* (1903) 51 WR 365; *McCowin Lumber and Export Co Inc v Pacific Marine Insurance Co Ltd* (1922) 38 TLR 901 (all cases of set-off by insurers against insurance brokers); *Robinson v Mollett* (1875) LR 7 HL 802 (tallow market: agent acting as principal); *Marsh v Jelf* (1862) 3 F & F 234 (auctioneer selling by private contract); *Blackburn v Mason* (1893) 68 LT 510, CA (set-off by stockbroker); *Thuman v Best* (1907) 97 LT 239 (contract for lease by estate agent); *Fullwood v Hurley* [1928] 1 KB 498, CA (commission from vendor and purchaser); *Anglo-African Merchants Ltd v Bayley* [1970] 1 QB 311, [1969] 2 All ER 421; *North and South Trust Co v Berkeley, Berkeley v North and South Trust Co* [1971] 1 All ER 980, [1971] 1 WLR 470 (both cases of insurance broker acting as agent for insurers for certain purposes). See further CUSTOM AND USAGE vol 32 (2012) PARA 59.

12 *Blackburn v Mason* (1893) 68 LT 510, CA; *Hamilton v Young* (1881) LR 7 Ir 289; *Stewart v Aberdein* (1838) 4 M & W 211; *Sweeting v Pearce* (1861) 9 CBNS 534; *Bartlett v Pentland* (1830) 10 B & C 760; *Perry v Barnett* (1885) 15 QBD 388, CA; *Robinson v Mollett* (1875) LR 7 HL 802 (in which the opinions of the judges were taken); *Bostock v Jardine* (1865) 3 H & C 700; *Scott v Irving* (1830) 1 B & Ad 605. The principal may be precluded from denying the usage, for example by not being permitted to revoke an authority under which the agent, by usage, has incurred a personal liability: *Seymour v Bridge* (1885) 14 QBD 460.

13 *Matveieff & Co v Crossfield* (1903) 51 WR 365.

14 *Drexel Burnham Lambert International NV v Nasr* [1986] 1 Lloyd's Rep 356 at 365 per Devlin J.

(4) EXERCISE OF AUTHORITY

45. Exercise of authority under deed.

An agent acting under a power of attorney should, as a general rule, act in the name of the principal[1]. If he is authorised to sue on the principal's behalf, the claim should be brought in the principal's name[2]. A deed executed in pursuance of such a power is properly executed in the name of the principal or with words to show that the agent is signing for him[3], but if the donee of the power is an individual he may, if he thinks fit and where so authorised by the donor of the power, execute any instrument with his own signature[4], and act in his own name[5]. This provision for execution and action by the donee in his own name exists as an alternative to the statutory procedure for the execution of a conveyance by the attorney of a corporation[6]. Any instrument executed or thing done under this provision[7] is as effective as if executed by the donee in any manner which would constitute due execution of that instrument by the donor or, as the case may be, as if done by the donee in the name of the donor[8] (except in the case of an instrument executed by the donee as a deed, in which case it is as effective as if executed by the donee in a manner which would constitute due execution of it as a deed by the donor only if it is executed in accordance with the appropriate statutory requirements[9]).

The attorney of a corporation sole or aggregate may execute a conveyance by signing the name of the corporation in the presence of at least one witness who attests the signature[10]. A corporation aggregate, appointed the attorney of any person or corporation to convey any property, may execute instruments by signing them in the name of such person or corporation by an officer duly appointed for such purpose[11].

1 As to the effect of acts by an agent where the principal is undisclosed see PARAS 47, 158. As to powers of attorney see PARAS 16, 31 et seq.
2 *Jones and Saldanha v Gurney* [1913] WN 72.
3 *White v Cuyler* (1795) 6 Term Rep 176; *Wilks v Back* (1802) 2 East 142; *Berkeley v Hardy* (1826) 8 Dow & Ry KB 102; *M'Ardle v Irish Iodine and Marine Salts Manufacturing Co* (1864) 15 ICLR 146.
4 Powers of Attorney Act 1971 s 7(1)(a) (amended by the Law of Property (Miscellaneous Provisions) Act 1989 s 1(8), Sch 1 para 7(1)).
5 Powers of Attorney Act 1971 s 7(1)(b). This provision does not enlarge the scope of things which may be done by the donee of a power of attorney; it is merely procedural: *Clauss v Pir* [1988] Ch 267, [1987] 2 All ER 752.
6 Powers of Attorney Act 1971 s 7(2) (amended by the Law of Property (Miscellaneous Provisions) Act 1989 ss 1(8), 4, Sch 1 para 7(2), Sch 2). The statutory procedure referred to is that under the Law of Property Act 1925 s 74(3) (see the text and note 10).
7 Ie under the Powers of Attorney Act 1971 s 7(1) (see the text and notes 3–5).
8 Powers of Attorney Act 1971 s 7(1) (amended by SI 2005/1906). This provision applies whenever the power of attorney was created: Powers of Attorney Act 1971 s 7(4).
9 Powers of Attorney Act 1971 s 7(1A) (added by SI 2005/1906). 'The appropriate statutory requirements' are the Law of Property (Miscellaneous Provisions) Act 1989 s 1(3)(a) (see DEEDS AND OTHER INSTRUMENTS vol 32 (2012) PARA 233): Powers of Attorney Act 1971 s 7(1A) (as so added).
10 Law of Property Act 1925 s 74(3) (amended by the Law of Property (Miscellaneous Provisions) Act 1989 s 4, Sch 2; and by SI 2005/1906).
11 Law of Property Act 1925 s 74(4) (amended by SI 2005/1906). If the instrument is to be a deed it must be signed in the presence of a witness who attests the signature: Law of Property Act 1925 s 74(4) (as so amended). This applies to powers conferred or agents appointed before or since 1926 (s 74(5)), and is in addition to any other powers which may be exercised by or on behalf of corporations (see s 74(6) (amended by SI 2009/1941). Instruments to which the Law of Property Act 1925 s 74(4) applies may not be executed under the alternative procedure prescribed in the Powers of Attorney Act 1971 s 7(1) (see the text and notes 1–8): s 7(2) (as amended: see note 6). As to the making of contracts by corporations generally see PARAS 20–23.

An instrument is validly executed by a corporation aggregate as a deed for the purposes of the Law of Property (Miscellaneous Provisions) Act 1989 s 1(2)(b) (see DEEDS AND OTHER INSTRUMENTS vol 32 (2012) PARA 208) if and only if, it is duly executed by the corporation and it is delivered as a deed: Law of Property Act 1925 s 74A(1) (s 74A added by SI 2005/1906). An instrument is presumed to be delivered for these purposes upon its being executed, unless a contrary intention is proved: Law of Property Act 1925 s 74A(2) (as so added).

46.   Signature of documents by agent.

At common law the general rule[1] is that a person sufficiently signs a document if it is signed in his name and with his authority by someone else; and in such case the agent's signature is treated as that of his principal[2]. Although it is usual and the better practice to indicate on the document that the signature the agent has written is not that of the principal, omission so to do, though misleading and undesirable, does not necessarily invalidate the document[3].

1   Personal signature may be required by statute: cf PARA 3.
2   See *R v Kent Justices* (1873) LR 8 QB 305; *R v Cowper* (1890) 24 QBD 533, CA; *France v Dutton* [1891] 2 QB 208, DC; *LCC v Agricultural Food Products Ltd* [1955] 2 QB 218, [1955] 2 All ER 229, CA; *Tennant v LCC* (1957) 121 JP 428, CA; and see DEEDS AND OTHER INSTRUMENTS vol 32 (2012) PARA 213.
3   *LCC v Agricultural Food Products Ltd* [1955] 2 QB 218, sub nom *LCC v Vitamins Ltd* [1955] 2 All ER 229, CA.

47.   Effect of agent not disclosing principal.

An agent having authority to sign a bill of exchange cannot render his principal liable thereon by signing in his own name[1]. Subject to this rule and to any personal liability which the agent may incur by reason of acting in his own name[2], an agent may exercise his authority, whether orally or by writing, without disclosing the name or existence of his principal[3].

1   *Leadbitter v Farrow* (1816) 5 M & S 345; and see *Bult v Morrell* (1840) 12 Ad & El 745; *Elliott v Bax-Ironside* [1925] 2 KB 301, CA; *Kettle v Dunster and Wakefield* (1927) 138 LT 158; but see *Lindus v Bradwell* (1848) 5 CB 583 (where, however, the agent was a married woman, who, as such, could at that time only sign as agent).
2   See PARAS 157–160.
3   *Calder v Dobell* (1871) LR 6 CP 486; *Wilson v Hart* (1817) 1 Moore CP 45; *Weidner v Hoggett* (1876) 1 CPD 533. As to the effect of non-disclosure of the principal as between the principal and the third party see PARA 126.

3. DELEGATION

(1) GENERAL RULE AGAINST DELEGATION

48. Agent's powers not generally delegable.

Delegation by an agent, that is the entrusting to another person by an agent of the exercise of a power or duty entrusted to him by his principal, is in general prohibited, under the maxim *delegatus non potest delegare*, without the express authority of the principal[1], or authority derived from statute[2].

Where there is personal confidence reposed in or skill required from the agent[3] there normally may be no delegation however general the nature of the duties[4] (unless urgent necessity compels the handing over of the responsibility to another[5]). However, where there is no personal confidence reposed or skill required and the duties are capable of being equally well discharged by any person, an authority to delegate will in some cases be implied[6].

1 *Sims v Brittain* (1832) 1 Nev & MKB 594.
2 Certain powers of delegation are conferred by statute on trustees and personal representatives: see eg the Trustee Act 1925 s 25; the Trustee Act 2000 Pt IV (ss 11–27); and TRUSTS AND POWERS vol 98 (2013) PARA 425 et seq. There is no power to delegate a judicial function (*Barnard v National Dock Labour Board* [1953] 2 QB 18, [1953] 1 All ER 1113, CA), or other statutory disciplinary functions (*Vine v National Dock Labour Board* [1957] AC 488, [1956] 3 All ER 939, HL). As to delegation by directors see PARA 50.
3 *Cockran v Irlam* (1814) 2 M & S 301; *Catlin v Bell* (1815) 4 Camp 183; *Henderson v Barnewall* (1827) 1 Y & J 387; *Re County Palatine Loan and Discount Co, Cartmell's Case* (1874) 9 Ch App 691; *Tarry v Ashton* (1876) 1 QBD 314; *Doe d Rhodes v Robinson* (1837) 3 Bing NC 677. In the absence of express authority, an estate agent may not delegate his duties which require personal skill and competence: *John McCann & Co v Pow* [1975] 1 All ER 129, [1974] 1 WLR 1643, CA, considered in *Robert Bruce & Partners v Winyard Developments* [1987] 1 EGLR 20.
4 *St Margaret, Rochester, Burial Board v Thompson* (1871) LR 6 CP 445.
5 *De Bussche v Alt* (1878) 8 ChD 286, CA; *Gwilliam v Twist* [1895] 2 QB 84, CA.
6 See PARA 51.

49. Delegation by ministers of the Crown and local authorities.

Where functions entrusted to a minister are performed by an official employed in the minister's department there is in law no delegation because constitutionally the act or decision of the official is that of the minister[1]. Similarly, where a local authority appoints a committee for the discharge of certain of its functions[2], the committee is merely machinery for the discharge by the authority of the business entrusted to the committee, all of whose acts are subject to the authority's approval[3].

1 *Carltona Ltd v Works Comrs* [1943] 2 All ER 560; *Lewisham Metropolitan Borough and Town Clerk v Roberts* [1949] 2 KB 608, [1949] 1 All ER 815, CA; and see CONSTITUTIONAL AND ADMINISTRATIVE LAW vol 20 (2014) PARA 365.
2 Ie under the powers in the Local Government Act 1972 ss 101, 102: see LOCAL GOVERNMENT vol 69 (2009) PARAS 370, 371 et seq.
3 *R v Sunderland Corpn* [1911] 2 KB 458, DC; *Osgood v Nelson* (1872) LR 5 HL 636; *Huth v Clarke* (1890) 25 QBD 391, DC; *Manton v Brighton Corpn* [1951] 2 KB 393, [1951] 2 All ER 101.

50. Delegation by directors of companies.

The powers and duties of directors cannot be delegated except in accordance with the articles of association of the company[1]. Where, however, there has been a purported or apparent delegation in favour of a sub-agent and such delegation if duly made would have been within the scope of a power in the articles, any internal management irregularity will be disregarded in relation to those who deal bona fide with the sub-agent and without knowledge of such irregularity[2].

1   *Re County Palatine Loan and Discount Co, Cartmell's Case* (1874) 9 Ch App 691; *Re Leeds Banking Co, Howard's Case* (1866) 1 Ch App 561; *Totterdell v Fareham Blue Brick and Tile Co Ltd* (1866) LR 1 CP 674.
2   See *Mahony v East Holyford Mining Co* (1875) LR 7 HL 869; *Biggerstaff v Rowatt's Wharf Ltd, Howard v Rowatt's Wharf Ltd* [1896] 2 Ch 93, CA; *Freeman and Lockyer (a firm) v Buckhurst Park Properties (Mangal) Ltd* [1964] 2 QB 480, [1964] 1 All ER 630, CA.

(2) IMPLIED AUTHORITY TO DELEGATE

51. Permissible delegation by agent.

An authority to delegate will in some cases be implied, generally on the ground that there is no personal confidence reposed or skill required, and that the duties are capable of being equally well discharged by any person[1].

Authority to delegate will be implied in the case of purely ministerial acts, where no special discretion or skill is required[2], and in the case of acts subsidiary to the main purpose[3]. Thus authority to sign may in general be delegated[4]; but, in cases where an agent has implied authority to sign a contract for both parties, for example where the agent is an auctioneer or broker, the signature of his clerk will not suffice[5]; nor was the signature of the clerk of an authorised agent sufficient for the purposes of a memorandum in order to satisfy the requirements of the Statute of Frauds[6].

1   As to the usual rule against delegation see PARA **48**.
2   *St Margaret, Rochester, Burial Board v Thompson* (1871) LR 6 CP 445 (delegation by sexton); *Parker v Kett* (1701) 1 Ld Raym 658 (delegation by steward of manor); *Allam & Co Ltd v Europa Poster Services Ltd* [1968] 1 All ER 826, [1968] 1 WLR 638 (service of notices terminating licences); *The Berkshire* [1974] 1 Lloyd's Rep 185 at 188 (signing bill of lading on behalf of shipowner).
3   *Re London and Mediterranean Bank, ex p Birmingham Banking Co* (1868) 3 Ch App 651; *Re Marshall, ex p Sutton* (1788) 2 Cox Eq Cas 84, where an agent was authorised to draw bills in the common course of business, and it was held that he could do this by means of his clerk; see also *Henderson v Barnewall* (1827) 1 Y & J 387; *Murphy v Boese* (1875) LR 10 Exch 126; *LCC v Hobbis* (1896) 75 LT 687; *Coles v Trecothick* (1804) 9 Ves 234; *Hemming v Hale* (1859) 7 CBNS 487; *Rossiter v Trafalgar Life Assurance Association* (1859) 27 Beav 377.
4   *Mason v Joseph* (1804) 1 Smith KB 406; *Lord v Hall* (1849) 2 Car & Kir 698; *Brown v Tombs* [1891] 1 QB 253; *Allam & Co Ltd v Europa Poster Services Ltd* [1968] 1 All ER 826, [1968] 1 WLR 638.
5   *Peirce v Corf* (1874) LR 9 QB 210; *Bell v Balls* [1897] 1 Ch 663.
6   See the Statute of Frauds (1677) s 4 (now relating only to contracts of guarantee: see further FINANCIAL INSTRUMENTS AND TRANSACTIONS vol 49 (2015) PARA 677 et seq). See also *Blore v Sutton* (1817) 3 Mer 237; *Doe d Rhodes v Robinson* (1837) 3 Bing NC 677; *Peirce v Corf* (1874) LR 9 QB 210; *Bell v Balls* [1897] 1 Ch 663.

52. Delegation in accordance with custom or usage.

Delegation of an agent's authority is also permissible[1] if it is in accordance with a reasonable custom or usage of trade[2]. Thus a master of a foreign ship may be justified in delegating the signing of a charterparty to a shipbroker[3], and a country solicitor may employ his town agent, who has power to bind the client in the ordinary course[4].

1   As to the usual rule against delegation see PARA **48**.
2   *De Bussche v Alt* (1878) 8 ChD 286, CA. See also CUSTOM AND USAGE vol 32 (2012) PARA 90.

3 *The Fanny, The Matilda* (1883) 5 Asp MLC 75, CA. See also *Moon v Witney Union Guardians* (1837) 3 Bing NC 814.
4 See eg *Griffiths v Williams* (1787) 1 Term Rep 710; *Solley v Wood* (1852) 16 Beav 370; *Re Newen* [1903] 1 Ch 812; and LEGAL PROFESSIONS vol 66 (2015) PARA 802.

53. Acquiescence of principal in agent's delegation of authority.

Where the principal knows of the agent's intention at the time of his employment to delegate, or subsequently acquiesces in the delegation, the rule prohibiting delegation can have no application[1]. Where there is a ratification by the principal of the acts of the sub-agent, the sub-agent becomes jointly liable with the agent to the principal[2]. Ratification or adoption of the delegation may be evident from the conduct of the parties[3].

1 Thus an English contractor for a railway in Canada, known not to be personally undertaking the work, was entitled to engage a sub-agent: *Quebec and Richmond Rly Co v Quinn* (1858) 12 Moo PCC 232. As to the usual rule against delegation see PARA 48.
2 *Keay v Fenwick* (1876) 1 CPD 745, CA; *Dew v Metropolitan Rly Co* (1885) 1 TLR 358, CA.
3 *De Bussche v Alt* (1878) 8 ChD 286, CA.

54. Delegation of agent's authority due to necessity of the case.

Where the very nature of the employment necessitates a partial or total delegation of the agent's authority, the rule prohibiting delegation can have no application[1]. Similarly, where unforeseen circumstances arise, the necessity of the case may make it imperative to delegate, and authority so to do will be implied[2]. That authority will not be implied, however, unless the exigencies of the situation preclude communication at the material time between the agent and his principal[3].

1 As to the usual rule against delegation see PARA 48.
2 See *De Bussche v Alt* (1878) 8 ChD 286, CA.
3 *Gwilliam v Twist* [1895] 2 QB 84, CA. See also *Harris v Fiat Motors Ltd* (1906) 22 TLR 556.

(3) POSITION OF SUB-AGENT

55. Privity between principal and sub-agent.

As a general rule there is no privity of contract[1] between the principal and a sub-agent (as distinct from a co-agent); the sub-agent being liable only to his employer, the agent[2]. The rule will not apply where the principal was a party to the appointment of the sub-agent, or has subsequently adopted his acts, and it was the intention of the parties that privity of contract should be established between them[3].

1 As to the doctrine of privity see CONTRACT vol 22 (2012) PARA 327 et seq.
2 *Mackersy v Ramsays, Bonars & Co* (1843) 9 Cl & Fin 818, HL; *Schmaling v Thomlinson* (1815) 6 Taunt 147; *Cobb v Becke* (1845) 6 QB 930; *A-G v Earl of Chesterfield* (1854) 18 Beav 596; *New Zealand and Australian Land Co v Watson* (1881) 7 QBD 374, CA; *Dunlop & Sons v De Murrieta & Co* (1886) 3 TLR 166, CA; *Lockwood v Abdy* (1845) 14 Sim 437; *Montagu v Forwood* [1893] 2 QB 350, CA; *Pinto v Santos* (1814) 1 Marsh 132; *Calico Printers' Association Ltd v Barclays Bank Ltd* (1931) 145 LT 51, CA.
3 *De Bussche v Alt* (1878) 8 ChD 286, CA; discussed in *Velos Group Ltd v Harbour Insurance Services Ltd* [1997] 2 Lloyd's Rep 461; *Prentis Donegan & Partners Ltd v Leeds & Leeds Co Inc* [1998] 2 Lloyd's Rep 326.

56. Classes of sub-agents.

There may be said to be three classes of sub-agents:
(1) those employed without the authority, express or implied, of the principal, by whose acts the principal is not bound[1];

(2)   those employed with the express or implied authority of the principal, but between whom and the principal there is no privity of contract[2]; and

(3)   those employed with the principal's authority, between whom and the principal there is privity of contract, and a direct relationship of principal and agent is, accordingly, established[3].

For the acts and defaults of the first two classes the agent is responsible to the principal[4]; in the third case the sub-agent has both the rights and the liabilities of an agent vis-à-vis the principal[5].

1   *Blore v Sutton* (1817) 3 Mer 237; *Wray v Kemp* (1884) 26 ChD 169; *Dunlop & Sons v De Murrieta & Co* (1886) 3 TLR 166, CA; *Re Becket, Purnell v Paine* [1918] 2 Ch 72, CA.
2   See PARA 55.
3   See PARA 55.
4   *Mackersy v Ramsays, Bonars & Co* (1843) 9 Cl & Fin 818, HL (where an agent employed to obtain payment employed a sub-agent in India and payment was made to the sub-agent but not credited to the agent, the agent was liable for the sub-agent's failure on the ground that the principal should not suffer loss through a sub-agent with whom he had no privity); see also *Swire v Francis* (1877) 3 App Cas 106, PC; *Skinner & Co v Weguelin, Eddowes & Co* (1882) 1 Cab & El 12; *Re Mitchell, Mitchell v Mitchell* (1884) 54 LJ Ch 342; *Ecossaise Steamship Co Ltd v Lloyd, Low & Co* (1890) 7 TLR 76; *Meyerstein v Eastern Agency Co Ltd* (1885) 1 TLR 595. See further PARA 99.
5   *De Bussche v Alt* (1878) 8 ChD 286, CA.

57.   Remuneration and liability of sub-agent.

The sub-agent, not as a rule being brought into contractual relationship with the principal[1], must look to the agent for his remuneration and indemnity[2]. Thus, where an agent for the transport of goods without authority delegated his entire duties, it was held that the person performing them was not entitled to recover for his services against the principal[3].

Similarly, as a general rule, a sub-agent is accountable only to the agent who employs him, and that agent in turn to his principal[4], so that a sub-agent taking over the conduct of the principal's business is not liable to render an account to the principal[5] and even if the sub-agent is negligent, he cannot be sued directly by the principal[6]. Where, however, there is privity between the principal and the sub-agent[7], or sufficient knowledge by the sub-agent concerning the true position of the parties for some fiduciary obligation to be implied[8], the sub-agent may be held liable to the principal for money had and received to the principal's use from third parties[9].

1   See PARA 55.
2   *Solly v Rathbone* (1814) 2 M & S 298; *Mason v Clifton* (1863) 3 F & F 899. Cf *Hampton v Glamorgan County Council* [1917] AC 13, HL. See, however, the Contracts (Rights of Third Parties) Act 1999 (which sets out the circumstances under which a person who is not a party to a contract may nevertheless enforce its terms); and CONTRACT vol 20 (2012) PARA 342 et seq.
3   *Schmaling v Thomlinson* (1815) 6 Taunt 147.
      This rule is unaffected by the Commercial Agents (Council Directive) Regulations 1993, SI 1993/3053. A 'commercial agent' is defined for those purposes as a self-employed intermediary who has continuing authority to negotiate the sale or purchase of goods on behalf of another person (the 'principal') or to negotiate and conclude the sale or purchase of goods on behalf of and in the name of that principal (see reg 2(1); and PARA 73): if a sub-agent has no authority to negotiate, it follows that he is not entitled to look to the principal for remuneration.
4   *Stephens v Badcock* (1832) 3 B & Ad 354; *Sims v Brittain* (1832) 1 Nev & MKB 594.
5   *Lockwood v Abdy* (1845) 14 Sim 437; *Cartwright v Hateley* (1791) 1 Ves 292.
6   *Balsamo v Medici* [1984] 2 All ER 304, [1984] 1 WLR 951.
7   See PARA 55.
8   See *Powell and Thomas v Evan Jones & Co* [1905] 1 KB 11, CA; and PARA 74.
9   See *Moody v Spencer* (1822) 2 Dow & Ry KB 6; *Robbins v Heath* (1848) 11 QB 257; *Ex p Edwards* (1881) 8 QBD 262, CA; *Powell and Thomas v Evan Jones & Co* [1905] 1 KB 11, CA

(overruled on a different point by *FHR European Ventures LLP v Mankarious* [2014] UKSC 45, [2015] AC 250, [2014] 4 All ER 79: see PARA 94). For a consideration of the right of the principal to recover money paid through an agent to a sub-agent for the purpose of paying a third party, where the sub-agent appropriated the money to a debt owed by the agent to the sub-agent, see *Cobb v Becke* (1845) 6 QB 930.

4. RATIFICATION

(1) GENERAL PRINCIPLE OF RATIFICATION

58. Principal's retrospective ratification of agent's acts.

Under certain conditions an act which, at the time it was entered into or done by an agent, lacked the authority, express or implied, of a principal, may by the subsequent conduct of the principal become ratified by him and made as effectively his own as if he had previously authorised it.

Where the act has been done by a person not assuming to act on his own behalf[1], but for another, though without his precedent authority[2] or knowledge[3], and is subsequently ratified by that other person, the relation of principal and agent is constituted retrospectively, and the principal is bound by the act whether it is to his advantage or detriment, and whether liability therefor is founded in contract or in tort, to the same extent and with all the same consequences as if it had been done by his previous authority[4].

A ratification may be of one act or a series of acts; and as a general rule every act, other than one which is void at its inception[5], may be ratified, whether legal or illegal, provided that it was capable of being done by the principal himself[6].

The act of a public officer performed in his public capacity, is not capable of ratification by a private person[7], but, where that officer professes and intends to act on behalf of a private individual, or a corporation, the private individual or corporation can ratify his act[8].

1   See PARA **61**.
2   *Simpson v Eggington* (1855) 10 Exch 845; *Webb v Ipswich Borough Council* (1989) 21 HLR 325, CA.
3   *Ancona v Marks* (1862) 7 H & N 686.
4   *Wilson v Tumman* (1843) 6 Man & G 236; *Maclean v Dunn* (1828) 1 Moo & P 761. The agent is similarly bound: see *Foster v Bates* (1843) 12 M & W 226; *Lawson (Inspector of Taxes) v Hosemaster Machine Co Ltd* [1966] 2 All ER 944, [1966] 1 WLR 1300, CA. As to the effect of ratification see PARA **70**.
5   See *Spackman v Evans* (1868) LR 3 HL 171 (act ultra vires a company).
6   See *Firth v Staines* [1897] 2 QB 70; *Boston Deep Sea Fishing and Ice Co Ltd v Farnham (Inspector of Taxes)* [1957] 3 All ER 204, [1957] 1 WLR 1051 (principal, incapable of doing act by virtue of being an enemy alien, cannot ratify the act after cessation of enemy status). See further, as to acts capable of ratification PARAS **58–59**.
7   *Wilson v Tumman* (1843) 6 Man & G 236; *Woollen v Wright* (1862) 1 H & C 554, Ex Ch.
8   *Walker v Hunter* (1845) 2 CB 324; *Carter v St Mary Abbot's, Kensington Vestry* (1900) 64 JP 548, CA.

(2) ACTS CAPABLE OF RATIFICATION

59. Ratification of contract.

A contract may be ratified by the principal even though the circumstances have altered, as by a loss occurring under an unauthorised marine insurance policy[1], or even when the third party has given notice of repudiation[2], provided that it is ratified within a reasonable time[3]. It is immaterial that the contract was made by the agent in fraud of the principal[4]. Where, however, the agent and third party are able to rescind their transaction so that there remains nothing to ratify, ratification by the principal is inoperative[5]. If the third party knows that the transaction is subject to ratification there will be no contract until ratification is communicated to him[6].

The holder of a bill of exchange may avail himself of notice of dishonour by ratification of the act of another person[7].

1 See the Marine Insurance Act 1906 s 86; *Hagedorn v Oliverson* (1814) 2 M & S 485; *Williams v North China Insurance Co* (1876) 1 CPD 757, CA; and INSURANCE vol 60 (2011) PARA 379. In *Grover & Grover Ltd v Mathews* [1910] 2 KB 401, it was held that in the case of non-marine insurance there could be no ratification after loss had occurred, but the point cannot be regarded as settled. See also *Byas v Miller* (1897) 3 Com Cas 39; and *Yangtsze Insurance Association v Lukmanjee* [1918] AC 585, PC.
2 *Bolton Partners v Lambert* (1889) 41 ChD 295, CA. This decision has been much criticised, and Lord Lindley in *Fleming v Bank of New Zealand* [1900] AC 577, PC, expressly reserved the right of the Privy Council to consider the point: see further PARA 64. Ratification does not relate back when parties other than the co-contracting party have acquired rights before ratification: *Re Gloucester Municipal Election Petition, 1900, Ford v Newth* [1901] 1 KB 683. As to the general principle of ratification see PARA 58.
3 *Re Portuguese Consolidated Copper Mines Ltd* (1890) 45 ChD 16, CA; *Re Tiedemann and Ledermann Frères* [1899] 2 QB 66.
4 *Re Tiedemann and Ledermann Frères* [1899] 2 QB 66.
5 *Walter v James* (1871) LR 6 Exch 124 (payment to third party followed by repayment to agent by mutual agreement); *Watson v Davies* [1931] 1 Ch 455 (offer accepted by agent subject to ratification withdrawn before ratification); but see also *Hooper v Kerr, Stuart & Co* (1900) 83 LT 729 (validation by directors' meeting of issue of notice convening company meeting although directors' meeting, which was condition precedent to issue of notice, not held until after issue).
6 *Warehousing and Forwarding Co of East Africa Ltd v Jafferali & Sons Ltd* [1964] AC 1, [1963] 3 All ER 571, PC.
7 See the Bills of Exchange Act 1882 s 49(1), (2); *Chapman v Keane* (1835) 3 Ad & El 193; and FINANCIAL INSTRUMENTS AND TRANSACTIONS vol 49 (2015) PARA 308 et seq.

60. Ratification of unlawful acts.

The illegality of an act will not of itself prevent its ratification[1]. Where the act of the agent is tortious, for example a trespass or an assault[2], the principal may ratify and become liable but only to the extent of the acts to which the ratification relates[3]. The act of ratification may in itself constitute a tort by the principal; for example where the tort of conversion has been committed by the agent, any act by the principal inconsistent with the title of the third party will also amount to a conversion[4]. Some degree of knowledge by the principal of the unlawfulness may be required; thus the receipt of money produced by an illegal distress was not a sufficient ratification of the illegal acts of the agent levying the distress, unless the principal had knowledge of the illegality[5].

A principal cannot ratify a contract made by an agent if at the time it was made the principal had no power to make it himself[6]. A forgery is probably, being void in its inception, incapable of ratification by the person whose name is forged[7]. Such a person may, however, be estopped by his conduct from denying the validity of an instrument forged in his name, if he fails to disclose that the instrument is a forgery[8] or instructs the third party to act upon the instrument[9].

The unauthorised institution of legal proceedings may also be ratified[10].

1 *Hull v Pickersgill* (1819) 1 Brod & Bing 282. As to a principal's retrospective ratification of an agent's acts see PARA 58.
2 *Eastern Counties Rly Co v Broom* (1851) 6 Exch 314.
3 *Haseler v Lemoyne* (1858) 5 CBNS 530; *Lewis v Read* (1845) 13 M & W 834; *Knight v North Metropolitan Tramways Co* (1898) 78 LT 227.
4 *Hilbery v Hatton* (1864) 2 H & C 822; see also *Barns v St Mary, Islington, Guardians* (1911) 76 JP 11 (knowledge of principal of acts of agent amounting to conversion; principal liable because of delay in denying authority of agent).
5 *Freeman v Rosher* (1849) 13 QB 780.
6 *Ashbury Railway Carriage and Iron Co v Riche* (1875) LR 7 HL 653; *Newborne v Sensolid (Great Britain) Ltd* [1954] 1 QB 45, [1953] 1 All ER 708, CA; *Boston Deep Sea Fishing and Ice Co Ltd*

v Farnham (Inspector of Taxes) [1957] 3 All ER 204, [1957] 1 WLR 1051. As to the time at which capacity is needed see PARA 64. As to the effect of contracts purporting to be made on behalf of companies but void as being ultra vires such companies see *Ashbury Rly Carriage and Iron Co v Riche.* The ultra vires rules is modified by the Companies Act 2006 ss 39, 51: see COMPANIES vol 14 (2016) PARAS 59, 264.

As to the effect of forged bills of exchange see the Bills of Exchange Act 1882 s 24; and FINANCIAL INSTRUMENTS AND TRANSACTIONS vol 49 (2015) PARA 209.

7 *Brook v Hook* (1871) LR 6 Exch 89; but see contra *M'Kenzie v British Linen Co* (1881) 6 App Cas 82, HL. See also *Muir's Executors v Craig's Trustees* 1913 SC 349; *Morison v London County and Westminster Bank Ltd* [1914] 3 KB 356, CA; *Fung Kai Sun v Chan Fui Hing* [1951] AC 489, 95 Sol Jo 431, PC.

8 *Greenwood v Martins Bank Ltd* [1933] AC 51, HL. See also *Morison v London County and Westminster Bank Ltd* [1914] 3 KB 356, CA (estoppel of principal where no action taken by him in respect of cheques returned to him after payment into personal account of agent; bank therefore not liable to principal despite the Bills of Exchange Act 1882 s 25 (see FINANCIAL INSTRUMENTS AND TRANSACTIONS vol 49 (2015) PARA 258)). There can be no estoppel of the principal unless the third party has relied on the conduct of the principal, for example the non-disclosure that an instrument is a forgery, to his detriment: see *McKenzie v British Linen Co* (1881) 6 App Cas 82, HL (no reliance and no contractual relationship between principal and third party); *Muir's Executors v Craig's Trustees* 1913 SC 349 (detriment caused by delay in notifying third party of irregularity). If the principal merely delays in notifying the third party that an instrument is a forgery, the third party can only recover under estoppel of the principal if the chance of recovering from the agent or elsewhere has been materially prejudiced by the delay: see *Fung Kai Sun v Chan Fui Hing* [1951] AC 489, [1951] 2 TLR 47, PC.

9 See *Welch v Bank of England (Francis and Praed, third parties)* [1955] Ch 508, [1955] 1 All ER 811 (trustee accepted explanation given by co-trustee for forging signature on a cheque and authorised the bank, which had queried the signature, to pay the cheque; trustee estopped from claiming rectification on Bank of England registers of stock transferred under other forged instruments).

10 *Ancona v Marks* (1862) 7 H & N 686; *Danish Mercantile Co Ltd v Beaumont* [1951] Ch 680, [1951] 1 All ER 925, CA (action instituted without authority in name of company ratified by liquidator).

(3) CONDITIONS OF RATIFICATION

61. Act must be on behalf of principal.

As the whole hypothesis upon which ratification is based is that the person ratifying is already in appearance the contractor[1], the agent must not be purporting to act for himself, but must profess to be acting on behalf of a named or ascertainable principal, and one who is actually in existence at the time when the act subsequently ratified is done[2].

A contract made by one professing to act on his own behalf, though at that time he has the undeclared intention of acting on behalf of another person, cannot be ratified by that other person so as to confer on himself the status of principal and the right to sue and the liability to be sued on the contract[3].

Where one person not purporting to act for another wrongfully takes property, that other cannot ratify the act so as to make himself liable in tort[4].

1 See *Keighley, Maxsted & Co v Durant* [1901] AC 240, HL. As to the general principle of ratification see PARA 58.

2 *Wilson v Tumman* (1843) 6 Man & G 236; *Royal Albert Hall Corpn v Lady Winchelsea* (1891) 7 TLR 362; *Marsh v Joseph* [1897] 1 Ch 213, CA; *Keighley, Maxsted & Co v Durant* [1901] AC 240, HL; *Imperial Bank of Canada v Begley* [1936] 2 All ER 367, PC. See PARA 62.

3 *Heath v Chilton* (1844) 12 M & W 632; *Keighley Maxsted & Co v Durant* [1901] AC 240, HL; *Dunlop Pneumatic Tyre Co Ltd v Selfridge & Co Ltd* [1915] AC 847, HL. Cf *Jones v Hope* (1880)

3 TLR 247, CA; and *Saunderson v Griffiths* (1826) 5 B & C 909. As to the general right to sue
and the liability to be sued see PARA **126.**

4   See *Wilson v Barker* (1833) 4 B & Ad 614. See also *Eastern Construction Co Ltd v National Trust
Co Ltd and Schmidt* [1914] AC 197, HL (principal not liable where agents cut trees from wrong
land, where no knowledge or adoptive acts by principal).

62. Principal must be in existence and capable.

In order that the intended principal may be able effectively to ratify a contract,
he must be in existence and ascertainable at the time of the act of the agent to be
ratified, and be himself capable of entering into it[1]. If there is no such principal
there can be no ratification, and the so-called agent may himself be liable on the
contract[2], and if so may, therefore, sue upon it[3].

Contracts made in furtherance of the projects of an intended company, not
actually formed, cannot be ratified by the company when it comes into existence,
as the company could not have given actual authority to the agent. At common
law, where the purported agent makes the agreement as agent for an intended
company which has not at the time been formed, the agreement will be personally
binding upon the purported agent as his own agreement[4] on a presumption that
he must have intended to bind himself if the contract would otherwise be
inoperative[5]; the purported agent may then sue and be sued on the agreement[6].
Where, however, the purported agent does not make the agreement as agent, but
the unformed company purports to be the contracting party whose contract is
merely authenticated by the signature of an agent[7], such as a director, there is no
contract in existence at common law upon which either party can sue[8].

However, by statute a contract that purports to be made by or on behalf of a
company at a time when the company has not been formed has effect, subject to
any agreement to the contrary, as one made with the person purporting to act for
the company or as agent for it, and he is personally liable on the contract
accordingly[9]. The effect of this is to allow the agent to enforce the contract against
the third party, unless such enforcement is precluded by ordinary common law
principles[10]. There may, however, always be evidence that the company after
formation has entered into a new contract[11].

1   *Watson v Swann* (1862) 11 CBNS 756; *Foster v Bates* (1843) 12 M & W 226; *Boston Deep Sea
Fishing and Ice Co Ltd v Farnham (Inspector of Taxes)* [1957] 3 All ER 204, [1957] 1 WLR 1051.
As to the position with regard to children's contracts see PARA 5; the Minors' Contracts Act 1987;
and CHILDREN AND YOUNG PERSONS VOL 9 (2017) PARA 14.

2   If the agent is not personally liable on the contract, he may be liable in damages on a breach of
warranty of authority: see further PARAS **161–162.**

3   *Harper & Co v Vigers Bros* [1909] 2 KB 549.

4   *Kelner v Baxter* (1866) LR 2 CP 174; *Re Empress Engineering Co* (1880) 16 ChD 125, CA; *Re
Northumberland Avenue Hotel Co Ltd* (1885) 33 ChD 16 (affd (1886) 33 ChD 16, CA); *Star Corn
Millers' Society v W Moore & Co* (1886) 2 TLR 751, CA; *North Sydney Investment and Tramway
Co v Higgins* [1899] AC 263, PC; *Natal Land and Colonization Co Ltd v Pauline Colliery and
Development Syndicate Ltd* [1904] AC 120, PC. As to the liability, apart from ratification, of a
company which has benefited under the contract of its promoters, see *Touche v Metropolitan
Railway Warehousing Co* (1871) 6 Ch App 671; *Preston v Liverpool, Manchester, etc Rly Co
(Proprietors)* (1856) 5 HL Cas 605; *Re English and Colonial Produce Co Ltd* [1906] 2 Ch 435,
CA; *Earl of Shrewsbury v North Staffordshire Rly Co* (1865) LR 1 Eq 593. As to the position of
a company in relation to contracts made before formation, and as to the liability of a company to
its promoters and of the promoters to third parties, see further COMPANIES VOL 14 (2016)
PARAS 278–280.

5   *Kelner v Baxter* (1866) LR 2 CP 174.

6   *Kelner v Baxter* (1866) LR 2 CP 174. See also *Newborne v Sensolid (Great Britain) Ltd* [1954] 1
QB 45, [1953] 1 All ER 708, CA.

7   See *Newborne v Sensolid (Great Britain) Ltd* [1954] 1 QB 45, [1953] 1 All ER 708, CA.

8   *Newborne v Sensolid (Great Britain) Ltd* [1954] 1 QB 45, [1953] 1 All ER 708, CA.

9   See the Companies Act 2006 s 51(1); and COMPANIES vol 14 (2016) PARA 59. This is so even if
    both parties to the contract knew that the company had not been formed: *Phonogram Ltd v Lane*
    [1982] QB 938, [1981] 3 All ER 182, CA. As to contracts made before incorporation see
    COMPANIES vol 14 (2016) PARA 278 et seq. As to the ratification of agents' acts see COMPANIES
    vol 14 (2016) PARA 277.
10 *Braymist Ltd v Wise Finance Co Ltd* [2002] EWCA Civ 127, [2002] Ch 273, [2002] 2 All ER 333;
    Gibson v Imperial Homes and Developments Ltd [2002] All ER (D) 367 (Feb).
11 See *Howard v Patent Ivory Manufacturing* Co (1888) 38 ChD 156; *Bridgetown Co-operative
    Society v Whelan* [1917] 2 IR 39.

63.   Principal must have been ascertainable.

In order to be effective, the retrospective ratification of an agent's act[1] must be
made by the person for whom the act was professedly done or his personal
representative[2]. The person ratifying need not necessarily have been a named
individual at the time when the act was done, but must have been ascertainable[3].
A person entitled to the reversion of an estate may ratify the agency of one who
has been professedly receiving the rents for the rightful owner[4].

1   As to the general principle of ratification see PARA 58.
2   *Whitehead v Taylor* (1839) 10 Ad & El 210; *Foster v Bates* (1843) 12 M & W 226.
3   *Hagedorn v Oliverson* (1814) 2 M & S 485; *Boston Fruit Co v British and Foreign Marine
    Insurance Co* [1906] AC 336, HL; see *Purcell v Henderson* (1885) 16 LR Ir 213, 466. See also
    Lawson (Inspector of Taxes) v Hosemaster Machine Co Ltd [1966] 2 All ER 944, [1966] 1 WLR
    1300, CA (ratification by subsequent receiver under debentures effective in respect of acts during
    management by first receiver).
4   *Lyell v Kennedy* (1889) 14 App Cas 437, HL.

64.   Time for ratification.

Because ratification[1] enables a principal to so extend his rights by seeking an
advantage for himself beyond any that he would have in the absence of
ratification[2], the courts will not allow ratification to operate in such manner as to
cause undue prejudice to a third party[3]. Thus, in order to be effective, the
retrospective ratification of an agent's act must be made either within a period
fixed by the nature of the particular case, or within a reasonable time, after which
an act cannot be ratified to the prejudice of a third person[4]. Ratification cannot be
made so as to divest persons not parties to the contract ratified of their rights or
otherwise prejudicially to affect those rights, where such rights have vested prior
to the purported ratification[5], or so as prejudicially to affect the rights of persons
such as assignees in bankruptcy claiming through parties to the contract[6]. Thus an
unauthorised notice to quit can only be ratified by the landlord within the period
for giving notice[7]; the payment of a debt to a creditor of another cannot be ratified
after the money has been returned to the unauthorised agent[8]; an unauthorised
stoppage in transit cannot be ratified after the transit is ended[9]; and the exercise
of an option must be ratified within the time for which the option was open[10].

An unauthorised demand for payment of a debt by the creditor's agent cannot,
after tender by the debtor, be ratified so as to defeat the plea of tender, unless the
agent had implied authority to receive the debt and give a discharge[11]. An
ineffectual notice of abandonment of a ship given by a mere pledgee by way of
deposit of a policy of insurance on the ship is not validated by ratification by the
owner[12].

1   As to the general principle of ratification see PARA 58.
2   See eg *Kaupthing Singer & Friedlander Ltd (in administration) v USB AG* [2014] EWHC 2450
    (Comm), [2014] All ER (D) 200 (Jul).

3 *Smith v Henniker-Major & Co (a firm)* [2002] EWCA Civ 762, [2003] Ch 182; *Kilcarne Holdings Ltd v Targetfellow (Birmingham) Ltd* [2004] EWHC 2547 (Ch), [2005] 2 P & CR 105 (affd [2005] EWCA Civ 1355, [2006] 1 P & CR D55).

4 Ratification has, however, been held effective after a purported revocation of an offer by the third party: see *Bolton Partners v Lambert* (1889) 41 ChD 295, CA. The court decided the case on the basis that ratification is retrospective and could, in general, be valid in all cases where it did not involve divesting a vested estate; as to vested estates see the text to note 5. Ratification was not permitted so as to entitle the principal to sue, however, in *Kidderminster Corpn v Hardwick* (1873) LR 9 Exch 13, where the third party failed to meet a condition as to sureties, required for the making of the contract, and eventually withdrew from the agreement before the purported ratification. This case was not considered in *Bolton Partners v Lambert*, but might there have been distinguishable on the ground that the condition as to the sureties was a condition precedent to any agreement and that there was therefore nothing capable of ratification until the condition had been met. As to criticism of *Bolton Partners v Lambert* see PARA 59 note 2.

The limitations of this principle were extensively discussed in *Presentaciones Musicales SA v Secunda* [1994] Ch 271, [1994] 2 All ER 737, CA, though there are significant differences between the judgments of Dillon LJ (with whom Nolan LJ agreed) and that of Roch LJ. As to ratification of writ issued without authority, after expiry of limitation period, see *Presentaciones Musicales SA v Secunda* (applied in *Adams v Ford* [2012] EWCA Civ 544, [2012] 3 All ER 247). As to ratification of an insurance policy after a loss has occurred see PARA 59. As to the retrospective effect of a valid ratification see further PARA 70.

In *Johnson Matthey & Co Ltd v Constantine Terminals Ltd* [1976] 2 Lloyd's Rep 215 it was held that in certain circumstances a sub-bailee could invoke protective terms in the sub-bailment against the principal bailor. In *KH Enterprises (Cargo Owners) v Pioneer Container (Owners), The Pioneer Container* [1994] 2 AC 324, [1994] 2 All ER 250, PC, Lord Goff held that the doctrine of ratification was not an appropriate way of rationalising this decision. If the principal bailor were to be bound, there had to be actual or ostensible authority to sub-bail on the terms in question.

5 *Donelly v Popham* (1807) 1 Taunt 1; *Re Gloucester Municipal Election Petition (1900), Ford v Newth* [1901] 1 KB 683; and see *Presentaciones Musicales SA v Secunda* [1994] Ch 271, [1994] 2 All ER 737, CA.

6 *Bird v Brown* (1850) 4 Exch 786.

7 *Doe d Mann v Walters* (1830) 10 B & C 626; and see *Right d Fisher, Nash and Hyrons v Cuthell* (1804) 5 East 491; *Doe d Lyster v Goldwin* (1841) 2 QB 143.

8 *Walter v James* (1871) LR 6 Exch 124; *Lucas v Wilkinson* (1856) 1 H & N 420.

9 *Bird v Brown* (1850) 4 Exch 786. See also *Lord Audley v Pollard* (1597) Cro Eliz 561.

10 *Dibbins v Dibbins* [1896] 2 Ch 348. See also *Holland v King* (1848) 6 CB 727; *Managers of the Metropolitan Asylums Board v Kingham & Sons* (1890) 6 TLR 217; *Morrell v Studd and Millington* [1913] 2 Ch 648.

11 *Coles v Bell* (1808) 1 Camp 478n; *Coore v Callaway* (1794) 1 Esp 115.

12 *Jardine v Leathley* (1863) 3 B & S 700. As to ratification of contracts of marine insurance, however, see PARA 59 note 1.

65. Ratification must not be partial.

A contract cannot be ratified in part and repudiated in part; if ratified, the whole contract must be ratified, and the agency accepted with all its obligations[1]. Ratification of one of a series of acts constituting one transaction operates as a ratification of the entire transaction[2].

1 *Hovil v Pack* (1806) 7 East 164 per Lord Ellenborough; *Wilson v Poulter* (1730) 2 Stra 859. See also *Union Bank of Australia Ltd v McClintock* [1922] 1 AC 240, PC (ratification of unauthorised obtaining of bank drafts by manager of business must include ratification of subsequent dealings with drafts), applied in *Commercial Banking Co of Sydney Ltd v Mann* [1961] AC 1, [1960] 3 All ER 482, PC; *Re Mawcon Ltd* [1969] 1 All ER 188, [1969] 1 WLR 78 (liquidator held to have ratified a debt by adopting the transaction in which it was incurred); *Smith v Henniker-Major & Co (a firm)* [2002] EWCA Civ 762 at [56], [2003] Ch 182. As to the general principle of ratification see PARA 58.

2 *Rodmell v Eden* (1859) 1 F & F 542; *Walter v James* (1871) LR 6 Exch 124. Cf, however, *Harrisons and Crossfield Ltd v London and North Western Rly Co* [1917] 2 KB 755, where carriers who had prosecuted for larceny a servant who had by a false pretence obtained goods and

disposed of them, laying the property in the goods in themselves, were held to have ratified only a bare bailment and not possession of the goods for purposes of carriage.

(4) MANNER OF RATIFICATION

66. Form of ratification.

A ratification may be express, whether in writing or oral, or may be implied from conduct[1]. A claim by a principal on a voidable contract entered into by an agent without authority[2] or a pleading relying on the efficacy of an unauthorised act[3] is an adoption of the agency. The execution of a deed by an agent without authority, however, can only be ratified by deed or by matter of record[4].

1 *Maclean v Dunn* (1828) 1 Moo & P 761; *Fitzmaurice v Bayley* (1860) 9 HL Cas 78; *Soames v Spencer* (1822) 1 Dow & Ry KB 32. Even where a contract was unenforceable unless evidenced by a note or memorandum in writing, it was not necessary that the ratification should be in writing. As to ratification by acquiescence see further PARA 69.
2 *Lacey v Walrond* (1837) 6 LJCP 290.
3 *Belshaw v Bush* (1851) 11 CB 191.
4 *Hunter v Parker* (1840) 7 M & W 322; *Tupper v Foulkes* (1861) 9 CBNS 797; *Oxford Corpn v Crow* [1893] 3 Ch 535.

67. Essentials of ratification.

Ratification is an unilateral act of will. The principal does not need to inform the agent, or indeed any other person, that ratification has taken place[1]. Nevertheless, ratification must be evidenced either by clear adoptive acts[2], or by acquiescence equivalent thereto[3]. The act or acts of adoption or acquiescence must be accompanied by full knowledge of all the essential facts[4], and must relate to a transaction to which effect can be given[5], unless the principal shows an intention to take all risks[6], but it is not necessary that he should know the legal effect of the act ratified[7]. A mere act of repudiation of the act of the intended agent by the principal does not in itself, and apart from any conduct which it may have induced in any third person, estop the principal from subsequently adopting or ratifying the agent's act[8].

1 *Yona International Ltd v La Réunion Française SA* [1996] 2 Lloyd's Rep 84, 106, Moore-Bick J.
2 *Lythgoe v Vernon* (1860) 5 H & N 180; *Smith v Baker* (1873) LR 8 CP 350. As to what will amount to such an adoptive act see *Brewer and Gregory v Sparrow* (1827) 7 B & C 310; *Valpy v Sanders* (1848) 5 CB 886; *Moon v Towers* (1860) 8 CBNS 611; and PARA 68. A principal cannot be said to adopt an act when he cannot help himself; see *Re Becket, Purnell v Paine* [1918] 2 Ch 72, CA; *Barrett v Irvine* [1907] 2 IR 462, CA (where negotiation for settlement by the parent of a minor who in purchasing a horse had misrepresented himself as the parent's agent was held not to be ratification); and see *Forman & Co Pty Ltd v The Liddesdale* [1900] AC 190, PC; and PARA 69. In *Morison v London County and Westminster Bank Ltd* [1914] 3 KB 356, CA, continuance of employment of a dishonest servant after discovery of his dishonesty and conversion of his discovered defalcations into an ordinary debt were held to be adoptive acts; but on this point the decision has been questioned as inconsistent with *Bank of Ireland v Evans' Charities Trustees in Ireland* (1855) 5 HL Cas 389; and *Swan v North British Australasian Co* (1863) 2 H & C 175; see *Lloyds Bank Ltd v Chartered Bank of India, Australia and China* [1929] 1 KB 40, CA.
3 See PARA 69.
4 *Savery v King* (1856) 5 HL Cas 627; *Haseler v Lemoyne* (1858) 5 CBNS 530; *Gunn v Roberts* (1874) LR 9 CP 331; *Suncorp Insurance and Finance v Milano Assicurazioni SpA* [1993] 2 Lloyd's Rep 225 at 234; and see *Marsh v Joseph* [1897] 1 Ch 213, CA; *Morison v London County and Westminster Bank Ltd* [1914] 3 KB 356, CA (knowledge of auditors employed to examine principal's business books held to be knowledge of principal); *Deveney v Crampsey* [1969] SCR 267, Can SC (silence and inactivity by some joint tenants during negotiations for sale by other joint tenants, evidence rather of ignorance of rights than of approval; no ratification; joint tenant not in any event purporting to act as agent).

5   *Banque Jacques-Cartier v Banque d'Epargne de Montréal* (1887) 13 App Cas 111, PC; *Foligno v Martin* (1852) 22 LJ Ch 502; *Jackson v Jacob* (1837) 3 Bing NC 869; *Munnings v Bury* (1829) Taml 147.

6   *Brewer and Gregory v Sparrow* (1827) 7 B & C 310 (where the assignees of a bankrupt affirmed the acts of a person wrongfully selling property, they could not afterwards treat him as a wrongdoer and claim in conversion against him); *Haseler v Lemoyne* (1858) 5 CBNS 530. Cf *Valpy v Sanders* (1848) 5 CB 886 (assignees in bankruptcy could make affirmation of wrongful sale conditional on payment by buyer of price, and on buyer's refusal to pay could repudiate the unauthorised acts and sue in trover).

7   *Powell v Smith* (1872) LR 14 Eq 85; *Lewis v Read* (1845) 13 M & W 834; *Fitzmaurice v Bayley* (1856) 6 E & B 868 (revsd on another point (1860) 9 HL Cas 78); *Hilbery v Hatton* (1864) 2 H & C 822.

8   *Simpson v Eggington* (1855) 10 Exch 845; *Soames v Spencer* (1822) 1 Dow & Ry KB 32.

68.   Evidence of ratification.

The receipt of purchase money is generally sufficient evidence of ratification of a sale, but not if it is received in ignorance of the true facts[1]. If the act alleged to be ratified is a fraudulent act, full knowledge and unequivocal adoption thereafter must be proved, or the circumstances of the alleged ratification must be such as to warrant the clear inference that the principal was adopting the agent's acts whatever they were and however culpable[2]. In a case of alleged false imprisonment where a servant of a railway company took a passenger into custody for an alleged breach of a byelaw, the fact that the company's solicitor attended to prosecute before the magistrate was not a ratification of the servant's acts[3]. The assignment by the principal of the benefit of a contract entered into by the agent without authority is a ratification of that contract[4].

1   *The Bonita, The Charlotte* (1861) 5 LT 141; *Freeman v Rosher* (1849) 13 QB 780. See also *Cornwal v Wilson* (1750) 1 Ves Sen 509.

2   *Marsh v Joseph* [1897] 1 Ch 213, CA.

3   *Eastern Counties Rly Co v Broom* (1851) 6 Exch 314; but see *Carter v St Mary Abbotts, Kensington Vestry* (1900) 64 JP 548, CA. A corporation will be liable, however, if its officials, purporting to act under a byelaw, make a mistake either of fact or of law which leads them to arrest wrongfully: *Percy v Glasgow Corpn* [1922] 2 AC 299, HL; *Moore v Metropolitan Rly Co* (1872) LR 8 QB 36; *Goff v Great Northern Rly Co* (1861) 30 LJQB 148.

4   *Thompson v Hickman* [1907] 1 Ch 550.

69.   Ratification by acquiescence.

Although a ratification must be clear and must bear distinct reference to the facts of the particular case, it need not necessarily be proved by positive acts of adoption. In certain cases it is sufficient evidence of ratification that the intended principal, having all material facts brought to his knowledge and knowing that he is being regarded as having accepted the position of principal, takes no steps to disown that character within a reasonable time, or adopts no means of asserting his rights at the earliest time possible[1].

Like acts of adoption, acquiescence cannot avail when the contract or act is made or done before the alleged principal came into existence[2], even where such principal has derived advantage from the services rendered[3].

The acquiescence must be acquiescence in the particular facts and be incapable of referring to another set of facts[4]. Acts which the principal has no choice but to perform will not of themselves amount to ratification[5].

Acquiescence is stronger evidence of ratification where the relationship of principal and agent previously existed between the parties, and the act to be ratified was rather one in excess of the agent's authority than one which was totally unauthorised[6]. Thus, where a shipmaster who was entrusted with the sale of goods, the proceeds to be devoted to particular purchases, devoted the proceeds to other purchases and advised his employer thereof, it was held that the fact that there was no repudiation by the employer within a reasonable time was evidence that he assented to and ratified the shipmaster's conduct[7].

1   *The Australia* (1859) 13 Moo PCC 132; *Jackson v Jacob* (1837) 3 Bing NC 869; *Banque Jacques-Cartier v Banque d'Epargne de Montreal* (1887) 13 App Cas 111, PC; *Robinson v Gleadow* (1835) 2 Bing NC 156; *Hall v Laver* (1842) 1 Hare 571. The burden of proving such ratification rests on the person alleging it, who must also prove full knowledge of facts: *Wall v Cockerell* (1863) 10 HL Cas 229. See also *Morison v London County and Westminster Bank Ltd* [1914] 3 KB 356, CA. Whether ratification by acquiescence has occurred will be judged objectively: *Suncorp Insurance and Finance v Milano Assicurazioni SpA* [1993] 2 Lloyd's Rep 225 at 235, 241.

2   See PARA **62**.

3   *Re Rotherham Alum and Chemical Co* (1883) 25 ChD 103, CA.

4   *De Bussche v Alt* (1878) 8 ChD 286, CA; *SEB Trygg Holding Aktiebolag v Manches Sprecher Grier Halberstam* [2005] EWHC 35 (Comm) at [162], [2005] 2 Lloyd's Rep 129; *Sea Emerald SA v Prominvestbank-Joint Stockpoint Commercial Industrial and Investment Bank* [2008] EWHC 1979 (Comm), [2008] All ER (D) 75 (Aug).

5   Thus, where the agent of a shipowner contracted for repairs in excess of his authority, the fact that the owner took his own ship as repaired and sold it did not amount to acquiescence: *Forman & Co Pty Ltd v The Liddesdale* [1900] AC 190, PC.

6   *Sentance v Hawley* (1863) 13 CBNS 458; *Benham v Batty* (1865) 6 New Rep 42; *Waithman v Wakefield* (1807) 1 Camp 120; *The Australia* (1859) 13 Moo PCC 132; *Allard v Bourne* (1863) 15 CBNS 468; *Smith v Hull Glass Co* (1852) 11 CB 897; *Pott v Bevan* (1844) 1 Car & Kir 335; *Bank Melli Iran v Barclays Bank (Dominion, Colonial and Overseas)* [1951] 2 TLR 1057, [1951] 2 Lloyd's Rep 367.

7   *Prince v Clark* (1823) 1 B & C 186; *Sentance v Hawley* (1863) 13 CBNS 458 (principal found to have acquiesced in a reasonable custom of brokers); *Fothergill v Phillips* (1871) 6 Ch App 770 (where one tenant in common entered into negotiations for sale, and the other, who allowed them to go on for three years without dissenting, knowing that the mortgagee was threatening to foreclose unless the sale took place, was held too late to allege absence of authority). See also *Bigg v Strong* (1858) 32 LTOS 98, CA (agreement for sale of land by son on behalf of self and father: father who had full knowledge of agreement within a few days of signing held to have ratified, so that agreement specifically enforceable against father and son).

(5) EFFECT OF RATIFICATION

70. General effect of principal's ratification of agent's unauthorised act.
An effective ratification places all the parties in a position similar to that which they would have occupied at the material time if the agent had had actual authority to perform the acts ratified. This is expressed by the maxim *omnis ratihabitio retrotrahitur et mandato priori aequiparatur*[1].

Where a contract is ratified, provided that ratification can also be seen to constitute a waiver by the principal of his rights against the agent for his breach of duty[2], the agent is relieved from personal liability to his principal for acting in excess of his authority[3], and may recover his commission and expenses[4]. The principal must perform the contract made by the agent in its entirety[5]; and provided that the contracting party has suffered no actionable damage by reason of the agent's breach of warranty, the agent is relieved from personal liability to the other contracting party for breach of warranty of authority, the only remedy of that party being against the principal, unless the agent so contracted as to make himself additionally liable[6].

Where the act ratified is tortious, the agent remains liable for the tort, but the principal will also become liable[7], unless the act is only wrongful because of lack of authority, in which case it will be justified by the ratification[8]. It is no justification for the commission of a tortious act that the wrongdoer is acting under another's authority, unless that other can justify the alleged wrong[9].

Ratification by a principal of one act done by an agent in excess of his authority does not extend the agent's authority so as to authorise him to do similar acts in future[10].

1   Ie 'Every ratification of an act already done has a retrospective effect, and is equivalent to a previous request to do it': Co Litt 207a; *Maclean v Dunn* (1828) 1 Moo & P 761; *Bolton Partners v Lambert* (1889) 41 ChD 295 at 302, CA; *Firth v Staines* [1897] 2 QB 70; *R v Chapman, ex p Arlidge* [1918] 2 KB 298; *Koenigsblatt v Sweet* [1923] 2 Ch 314, CA; *Lawson (Inspector of Taxes) v Hosemaster Machine Co Ltd* [1966] 2 All ER 944, [1966] 1 WLR 1300, CA. This principle has been used by the courts to permit a ratification after the third party has purported to revoke his offer: see *Bolton Partners v Lambert*; and PARA 64.

2   *Great Atlantic Insurance Co v Home Insurance Co* [1981] 2 All ER 485, [1981] 1 WLR 529; *Suncorp Insurance and Finance v Milano Assicurazioni SpA* [1993] 2 Lloyd's Rep 225 at 235.

3   *Smith v Cologan* (1788) 2 Term Rep 188n; *Risbourg v Bruckner* (1858) 3 CBNS 812 (foreign principal); *Hartas v Ribbons* (1889) 22 QBD 254, CA; *Clarke v Perrier* (1679) Freem Ch 48.

4   *Keay v Fenwick* (1876) 1 CPD 745, CA; *Mason v Clifton* (1863) 3 F & F 899; *Cornwal v Wilson* (1750) 1 Ves Sen 509; *Frixione v Tagliaferro & Sons* (1856) 10 Moo PCC 175; *Gleadow v Hull Glass Co* (1849) 19 LJ Ch 44 (directors of a company entitled to indemnity).

5   *Bristow v Whitmore* (1861) 9 HL Cas 391.

6   *Spittle v Lavender* (1821) 2 Brod & Bing 452.

7   *Stephens v Elwall* (1815) 4 M & S 259; *Hilbery v Hatton* (1864) 2 H & C 822; *Perkins v Smith* (1752) 1 Wils 328; *Heugh v Earl of Abergavenny and Delves* (1874) 23 WR 40.

8   *Anon* (1406) YB 7 Hen 4 fol 34 pl 1; *Anon* (1586) Godb 109. See also *Whitehead v Taylor* (1839) 10 Ad & El 210.

9   *Stephens v Elwall* (1815) 4 M & S 259.

10 *Irvine v Union Bank of Australia* (1877) 2 App Cas 366, PC.

71. Ratification by the Crown.

The ratification by the Crown of a purported exercise of sovereign power abroad against an alien by a public official in excess of his authority makes the act of such official an act of state in respect of which there is no legal remedy against either the official or the Crown[1]. However, the protection afforded by the Crown to those within the realm who owe allegiance (and who therefore could be guilty of acts of treason), means that such conduct committed against an alien[2] resident in British territory, who is a subject of a friendly state, or who is a British subject[3], cannot by purported ratification be justified as an act of state[4].

1   *Buron v Denman* (1848) 2 Exch 167; *Secretary of State in Council for India v Kamachee Boye Sahaba* (1859) 7 Moo Ind App 476, PC; *Salaman v Secretary of State for India* [1906] 1 KB 613, CA. As to state responsibility see INTERNATIONAL RELATIONS LAW vol 61 (2010) PARA 327 et seq.

2   As to the status of aliens see BRITISH NATIONALITY vol 4 (2011) PARA 411.

3   As to the status of a British subject see BRITISH NATIONALITY vol 4 (2011) PARAS 407, 469–475.

4   See *Johnstone v Pedler* [1921] 2 AC 262, HL.

5. RELATIONS BETWEEN PRINCIPAL AND AGENT

(1) NATURE OF THE RELATIONSHIP

72. Rights and duties.

At common law the rights and duties arising out of the relation of principal and agent are to be ascertained by reference to the contract, express or implied, which subsists between them[1]. This statement must, however, be modified in relation to those cases where the Commercial Agents (Council Directive) Regulations 1993[2] apply. Those regulations appreciably restrict the parties' freedom of contract[3].

The mere existence of the relation raises the implication of a contract involving certain rights and duties, the nature and extent of which depend upon the circumstances of the particular case[4], and the parties, in entering upon the relation, may leave the incidents arising out of it to be determined wholly by reference to the rights and duties so implied[5].

Where, however, the parties have defined their position by an express contract (subject to the Commercial Agents (Council Directive) Regulations 1993)[6], the incidents of their relation depend upon their contract, as legally construed[7], subject nevertheless to such of the rights and duties implied by law as are not clearly excluded by express words or by necessary implication[8]. A term will not be implied merely because it is reasonable; it must necessarily be implied in the nature of the contract[9].

A contract of agency, being in the nature of a contract for personal services, will not be specifically enforced at the suit of either party[10], but an injunction may be granted to restrain a breach of such a contract[11].

1   *Love v Mack* (1905) 93 LT 352, CA; *Pole v Leask* (1863) 33 LJ Ch 155, HL.
2   Ie the Commercial Agents (Council Directive) Regulations 1993, SI 1993/3053. As to the cases where those Regulations apply see PARA 73.
3   See PARA 73.
4   See PARA 75 et seq; and see *Shaw v Woodcock* (1827) 7 B & C 73, where the facts raised an inference of a del credere agency (as to which see PARA 13).
5   As to agency by necessity see PARA 24. As to the implication of reasonable usages see PARA 44.
6   See note 2.
7   *Bull v Price* (1831) 7 Bing 237; *Kofi Sunkersette Obu v A Strauss & Co Ltd* [1951] AC 243, PC.
8   See *Graham v Ackroyd* (1852) 10 Hare 192, where a del credere agent was held not to be entitled to reimbursement in respect of matters covered by his agency; and cf *Hooper v Treffry* (1847) 1 Exch 17, where the reimbursement claimed and upheld was outside the del credere agency. As to the implication of reasonable usages where not inconsistent with the contract see PARA 44.
9   *Lazarus v Cairn Line of Steamships Ltd* (1912) 106 LT 378; *Shackleton Aviation Ltd v Maitland Drewery Aviation Ltd* [1964] 1 Lloyd's Rep 293. See generally *AG of Belize v Belize Telecom Ltd* [2009] UKPC 10, [2009] 2 All ER 1127, [2009] 1 WLR 1988; *Marks and Spencer plc v BNP Paribas Securities Services Trust Company (Jersey) Ltd* [2015] UKSC 72, [2016] AC 742, [2016] 4 All ER 441.
10   *White v Boby* (1877) 37 LT 652, CA. The rule that a contract for personal services will not be the subject of a decree of specific performance is not an absolute one, which is not subject to exceptions, but there are instances, for example, where a single act is required to be procured, as in the case of the execution of a document, where such an order would be made: *CH Giles & Co Ltd v Morris* [1972] 1 All ER 960, [1972] 1 WLR 307. See also SPECIFIC PERFORMANCE vol 95 (2017) PARAS 507–508, 512.
11   *Mutual Reserve Fund Life Association v New York Life Insurance Co* (1896) 75 LT 528, CA. Cf *Chapman v Westerby* [1913] WN 277.

73. Commercial agents under the Commercial Agents (Council Directive) Regulations 1993.

The freedom of contract as between principal and agent is restricted in the case of commercial agents[1]. For this purpose a 'commercial agent' is a self-employed intermediary[2] who has continuing authority[3] to negotiate[4] the sale or purchase of goods on behalf of another person (the 'principal')[5], or to negotiate the sale and purchase of goods on behalf of and in the name of that principal[6]. This definition does not, however, include:

(1)   a person who, in his capacity as an officer of a company or association, is empowered to enter into commitments binding on that company or association[7];

(2)   a partner who is lawfully authorised to enter into commitments binding on his partners[8]; or

(3)   a person who acts as an insolvency practitioner[9] or the equivalent in any other jurisdiction[10].

The Regulations also do not apply to persons whose activities as commercial agents are to be considered secondary[11] or to:

(a)   commercial agents whose activities are unpaid[12];

(b)   commercial agents when they operate on commodity exchanges or in the commodity market[13]; and

(c)   the Crown Agents for Overseas Governments and Administrations[14] or its subsidiaries[15].

The Regulations, like the European Directive they implement[16], apply where an agent's operations take effect within the European Union on behalf of a principal situated outside the European Union[17]. This cannot be overridden by a choice of law clause purporting to choose the law of a non-EU jurisdiction[18].

Even if their relationship does not necessarily fall within the definition of commercial agent within the European Directive, principal and agent may choose to incorporate the Regulations into their contract[19].

1   Ie by virtue of the Commercial Agents (Council Directive) Regulations 1993, SI 1993/3053 (implementing Council Directive (EC) 86/653 (OJ L382, 31.12.86, p 17), on the co-ordination of the laws of the member states relating to self-employed commercial agents).

2   This term includes both legal and natural persons: *Bell Electric Ltd v Aweco Appliance Systems GmbH* [2002] EWHC 872 (QB), [2002] CLC 1246; affd on other grounds [2002] EWCA Civ 1501, [2003] 1 All ER 344.

3   The authority to negotiate successive extensions to a contract amounts to 'continuing authority': see Case C-3/04 *Poseidon Chartering BV v Marianne Zeeschipp VOF* [2006] 2 Lloyd's Rep 105, ECJ. In determining whether an agent has continuing authority a court may inquire into whether a single transaction is likely to lead to further transactions with the same customer or to customers in the same geographical area. From this it follows that whether that authority comes to be exercised less frequently (or even not at all) as the agency continues and customer relationships are established and then cemented, is neither here nor there, unless the continuing authority is withdrawn: *Tamarind International Ltd v Eastern Natural Gas (Retail) Ltd* (2000) Times, 27 June, [2000] CLC 1397, [2000] All ER (D) 787; *Invicta UK v International Brands Ltd* [2013] EWHC 1564 (QB), [2013] ECC 30. Whether an agent has continuing authority is to be determined by reference to the terms of the contract with the principal, not by the extent or frequency of the exercise of that authority: *Edwards v International Connection (UK) Ltd* [2006] EWCA Civ 662 at [19]; *W Nagel (a firm) v Pluczenik Diamond Company NV* [2017] EWHC 1750 (Comm) at [44].

4   See *PJ Pipe & Valve CO v Audco India Ltd* [2005] EWHC 1904 (QB), [2006] Eu LR 368; *Nigel Fryer Joiner Services Ltd v Ian Firth Hardware Ltd* [2008] 2 Lloyd's Rep 108.

5   Thus, a person who buys and sells himself as principal falls outside the Commercial Agents (Council Directive) Regulations 1993, SI 1993/3053: see *AMB Imballaggi Plastici SRL v Pacflex Ltd* [1999] 2 All ER (Comm) 249 at 252; *Raoul Sagal (t/a Bunz UK) v Atelier Bunz GmBH* [2009] EWCA Civ 700, [2009] 4 All ER 1253.

6   Commercial Agents (Council Directive) Regulations 1993, SI 1993/3053, reg 2(1). See *Mercantile International Group plc v Chuan Soon Huat Industrial Group plc* [2001] 2 All ER (Comm) 632; affd [2002] EWCA Civ 288, [2002] 1 All ER (Comm) 788. Although there is no express reference to a contract in the Commercial Agents (Council Directive) Regulations 1993, SI 1993/3053, art 2(1), there is nothing to suggest that a contract is not required in order to qualify as a commercial agent for these purposes: see *Light v Ty Europe Ltd* [2003] EWCA Civ, [2004] 1 Lloyd's Rep 693.

For the purposes of the definition of 'commercial agent', the sale or supply of software counts as the 'sale of goods': *The Software Incubator Ltd v Computer Associates UK Ltd* [2016] EWHC 1587 (QB), [2016] All ER (D) 13 (Jul).

An agent with authority to contract, as opposed to authority to negotiate, is only a commercial agent for the purpose of Directive 86/653 if he has authority to contract, and does contract, in the name of the principal as well as on its behalf: *Sagal (t/a Bunz UK) v Atelier Bunz GmbH* [2009] EWCA Civ 700, [2009] 4 All ER 1253; considered in *Rossetti Marketing Ltd v Diamond Sofa Co Ltd* [2011] EWHC 2482 (QB), [2012] Bus LR 571.

7   Commercial Agents (Council Directive) Regulations 1993, SI 1993/3053, reg 2(1)(i).

8   Commercial Agents (Council Directive) Regulations 1993, SI 1993/3053, reg 2(1)(ii).

9   Ie as that expression is defined in the Insolvency Act 1986 s 388 (see BANKRUPTCY AND INDIVIDUAL INSOLVENCY vol 5 (2013) PARA 40): Commercial Agents (Council Directive) Regulations 1993, SI 1993/3053, reg 2(1)(iii).

10 Commercial Agents (Council Directive) Regulations 1993, SI 1993/3053, reg 2(1)(iii). See also *AMB Imballaggi Plastici SRL v Pacflex Ltd* [1999] 2 All ER (Comm) 249.

11 Commercial Agents (Council Directive) Regulations 1993, SI 1993/3053, reg 2(4). The activities of a person as a commercial agent are to be considered 'secondary' where it may reasonably be taken that the primary purpose of the arrangement is other than:

    (1)   that the business of the principal is the sale, or as the case may be purchase, of goods of a particular kind (reg 2(3), Schedule paras 1, 2(a)); and

    (2)   that the goods concerned are such that transactions are normally individually negotiated and concluded on a commercial basis and procuring a transaction on one occasion is likely to lead to further transactions in those goods with that customer on future occasions, or to transactions in those goods with other customers in the same geographical area or among the same group of customers, and that accordingly it is in the commercial interests of the principal in developing the market in those goods to appoint a representative to such customers with a view to the representative devoting effort, skill and expenditure from his own resources to that end (Schedule para 2(b)).

The effect of this is that estate agents are thus excluded, because they do not deal in goods, though they are subject to their own specific regulation (see PARA 254 et seq).

The following are indications that an arrangement falls within the scope of heads (1) and (2) above, and the absence of any of them is an indication to the contrary:

    (a)   the principal is the manufacturer, importer or distributor of goods (Schedule para 3(a));

    (b)   the goods are specifically identified with the principal in the market in question rather than, or to a greater extent than, with any other person (Schedule para 3(b));

    (c)   the agent devotes substantially the whole of his time to representative activities (whether for one principal or for a number of principals whose interests are not conflicting) (Schedule para 3(c));

    (d)   the goods are not normally available in the market in question other than by means of the agent (Schedule para 3(d)); and

    (e)   the arrangement is one described as one of commercial agency (Schedule para 3(e)).

The following are indications that an arrangement does not fall within the scope of heads (1) and (2) above:

    (i)   promotional material is supplied direct to potential customers (Schedule para 4(a));

    (ii)   persons are granted agencies without reference to existing agents in a particular area or in relation to a particular group (Schedule para 4(b)); and

    (iii)   customers normally select goods for themselves and merely place their orders through the agent (Schedule para 4(c)).

The activities of mail order catalogue agents for consumer goods, and consumer credit agents, are presumed not to fall within the scope of heads (1) and (2) above, unless the contrary is established: Schedule para 5.

As to the legitimacy of reg 2(3), (4) in implementing Council Directive (EC) 86/653 (OJ L382, 31.12.86, p 17), and as to the interpretation of these provisions generally, see *Crane v Sky In-Home Service Ltd* [2007] EWHC 66 (Ch), [2007] 2 All ER (Comm) 599. See also *Tamarind International Ltd v Eastern Natural Gas (Retail) Ltd* [2000] 26 LS Gaz R 35, (2000) Times, 27 June.

12 Commercial Agents (Council Directive) Regulations 1993, SI 1993/3053, reg 2(2)(a). Payment by commission is not essential: see *Mercantile International Group plc v Chuan Soon Huat Industrial Group plc* [2001] 2 All ER (Comm) 632; affd [2002] EWCA Civ 288, [2002] 1 All ER (Comm) 788.

13 Commercial Agents (Council Directive) Regulations 1993, SI 1993/3053, reg 2(2)(b). See *W Nagel (a firm) v Pluczenik Diamond Company NV* [2017] EWHC 1750 (Comm).

14 The Crown Agents for Overseas Governments and Administrations became a statutory corporation under the Crown Agents Act 1979. The body has undergone a series of administrative reorganisations and is now a private limited company (Crown Agents Ltd): see the Crown Agents Act 1995; the Crown Agents Act 1995 (Appointed Day) Order 1997, SI 1997/1139; the Crown Agents Act 1995 (Successor Company) Order 1997, SI 1997/1140; Crown Agents Holding and Realisation Board (Prescribed Day) Order 2008, SI 2008/921; and the Crown Agents Holding and Realisation Board (Dissolution) Order 2009, SI 2014/1366.

15 Commercial Agents (Council Directive) Regulations 1993, SI 1993/3053, reg 2(2)(c).

16 See note 1.

17 See Case C–381/98 *Ingmar GB Ltd v Eaton Leonard Technologies Ltd* [2001] 1 All ER (Comm) 329, [2001] 2 All ER (EC) 57, ECJ.

18 See Case C–381/98 *Ingmar GB Ltd v Eaton Leonard Technologies Ltd* [2001] 1 All ER (Comm) 329, [2001] 2 All ER (EC) 57, ECJ.

19 See eg *McQuillan v McCormick* [2010] EWHC 1112 (QB), [2011] ECC 18.

74. Fiduciary nature of relation.

The relationship of agency is of a fiduciary nature[1]. In some cases, commonly where property or money has been placed in the hands of the agent for a specific purpose, the agent becomes a trustee for his principal[2]. In all cases the agent[3] owes duties of a fiduciary character to the principal, for example to keep accounts[4], to disclose any conflict of interest[5] and not to receive any secret commission or bribe[6].

In performing his activities a commercial agent[7] must look after the interests of his principal, and act dutifully and in good faith[8]. Similarly, in his relations with his commercial agent a principal must act dutifully and in good faith[9]. No derogation from these requirements is permissible[10].

1 See eg *Parker v McKenna* (1874) 10 Ch App 96.

2 See eg *Burdick v Garrick* (1870) 5 Ch App 233; *Brown v IRC* [1965] AC 244, [1964] 3 All ER 119, HL; cf *Henry v Hammond* [1913] 2 KB 515, where a shipping agent holding the proceeds of sale of a wreck was held not to be bound to keep such proceeds as a separate fund on behalf of his principal and was a mere debtor as to the sum, and not a trustee.

3 A sub-agent may also owe such duties even where there is no privity of contract between him and the principal if the sub-agent knows that the agent is acting for a principal and the principal assents to the employment of the sub-agent: *Powell and Thomas v Evan Jones & Co* [1905] 1 KB 11, CA, where, however, it was considered that the relation of principal and agent in fact existed between the principal and the sub-agent. As to privity of contract between sub-agents and principals see also PARA 55. Note that *Powell and Thomas v Evan Jones & Co* [1905] 1 KB 11, CA, was overruled on the issue of how the agent was to account for the secret commission by *FHR European Ventures LLP v Mankarious* [2014] UKSC 45, [2015] AC 250, [2014] 4 All ER 79: see PARA 94.

4 See PARA 83.

5 See PARA 90.

6 See PARAS 92–95. An agent has a duty to give a principal continued access to records relating to acts done in the principal's name unless that duty is expressly excluded by any contract made between the parties: see *Yasuda Fire and Marine Insurance Co of Europe Ltd v Orion Marine Insurance Underwriting Agency Ltd* [1995] QB 174, [1995] 3 All ER 211; and PARA 83.

7 As to the meaning of 'commercial agent' see PARA 73.

8 Commercial Agents (Council Directive) Regulations 1993, SI 1993/3053, reg 3(1). As to the cases to which those Regulations apply see PARA 73. This obligation has variously been likened to fiduciary duties in English law (*Rossetti Marketing Ltd v Diamond Sofa Co Ltd* [2012] EWHC 354 (QB), [2013] 1 All ER (Comm) 308) or to the implied obligation of trust in the relations between master and servant (*Crocs Europe BV v Anderson* [2012] EWCA Civ 1400, [2013] 1 Lloyd's Rep 1).

9 Commercial Agents (Council Directive) Regulations 1993, SI 1993/3053, reg 4(1).

10 Commercial Agents (Council Directive) Regulations 1993, SI 1993/3053, reg 5(1). The consequence of breach is governed by the law applicable to the contract: reg 5(2).

(2) DUTIES OF AGENT TO PRINCIPAL

(i) General Duties of Agent

75. Agent to perform business undertaken.

The primary duty of an agent is to carry out, generally in person[1], the business he has undertaken[2], or to inform his principal promptly if it is impossible to do so[3].

If the agent is given definite instructions from his principal as to the manner in which the business is to be carried out, he must follow them strictly[4], provided that they are lawful[5]; and, if he does so, he will not be liable to his principal merely because the consequences differ from those which the principal had expected[6]. He has, however, no discretion to disregard them, even though he acts in good faith in the interests of his principal[7].

A commercial agent[8] must:

(1)   make proper efforts to negotiate and where appropriate conclude the transactions of which he is instructed to take care[9];

(2)   communicate to his principal[10] all the necessary information available to him[11]; and

(3)   comply with reasonable instructions given by his principal[12].

No derogation from the requirements so imposed on a commercial agent is permissible[13].

1 *Catlin v Bell* (1815) 4 Camp 183; *Cook v Ward* (1877) 2 CPD 255, CA; *Henderson v Barnewall* (1827) 1 Y & J 387. As to delegation by the agent see further PARAS 48–57.

2 *Turpin v Bilton* (1843) 5 Man & G 455. Thus the duty of an agent employed to sell land does not terminate on submitting an offer which is accepted 'subject to contract'. As the matter is still open to negotiation he is bound to continue submitting any higher offer received until a binding contract has been signed: *Keppel v Wheeler* [1927] 1 KB 577, CA. The contract between a vendor and an estate agent does not usually, however, require the agent to disclose confidential information to the vendor about other vendors of comparable properties on whose behalf he may be acting or preclude the agent from seeking to earn a commission on the sale of the property of a rival vendor: *Kelly v Cooper* [1993] AC 205, PC. This principle in likelihood applies only in the case of estate agents, and is certainly inapplicable to commercial agents under the European Directive: *Rossetti Marketing Ltd v Diamond Sofa Co Ltd* [2012] EWHC 354 (QB), [2013] 1 All ER (Comm) 308. If, however, the business is unlawful (*Webster v De Tastet* (1797) 7 Term Rep 157) or the agency is gratuitous (*Balfe v West* (1853) 13 CB 466), the agent incurs no liability through his failure to carry out the business. See also *Lothian v Jenolite Ltd* 1969 SC 111, Ct of Sess (no duty on agent to devote himself exclusively to business of principal and not to act on behalf of competitors of principal, in absence of express or implied term in the contract to that effect). See also *Bailey v Barclays Bank plc* [2014] EWHC 2882 (QB), [2014] All ER (D) 151 (Aug) (bank's business relations manager as the bank's employee and agent was not a third party carrying on regulated activity in contravention of general prohibition).

3 *Cassaboglou v Gibb* (1883) 11 QBD 797, CA; *Callander v Oelrichs* (1838) 5 Bing NC 58. An estate agent into whose hands property is placed for sale on commission terms is not, in the absence of specific provisions, under any obligation to do anything (see *Luxor (Eastbourne) Ltd v Cooper* [1941] AC 108, [1941] 1 All ER 33, HL), unless he is appointed a sole agent, in which case there may be implied a condition that he will use his best endeavours (*Mendoza & Co v Bell* (1952) 159 Estates Gazette 372). As to the nature of the contract with an estate agent and his right to commission generally see PARA 104. As to the statutory regulation of estate agents see PARA 254 et seq.

4 *Lilley v Doubleday* (1881) 7 QBD 510; *Smith v Lascelles* (1788) 2 Term Rep 187; *Catlin v Bell* (1815) 4 Camp 183; *Barber v Taylor* (1839) 5 M & W 527; *Dufresne v Hutchinson* (1810) 3 Taunt 117.

5 *Bexwell v Christie* (1776) 1 Cowp 395. Thus failure to comply with instructions as to effecting a ppi ('policy proof of interest') insurance policy is not a breach of duty for which damages will be awarded: *Thomas Cheshire & Co v Vaughan Bros & Co* [1920] 3 KB 240, CA.

6 *Overend and Gurney Co v Gibb and Gibb* (1872) LR 5 HL 480; and see *Commonwealth Portland Cement Co Ltd v Weber Lohmann & Co Ltd* [1905] AC 66, PC.

7 *Bertram, Armstrong & Co v Godfray* (1830) 1 Knapp 381, PC; *Fray v Voules* (1859) 1 E & E 839, where a solicitor compromised an action on the advice of counsel against the express instructions of his client; and contrast *Chown v Parrott* (1863) 14 CBNS 74 (where the client had given no express instructions).

8 As to the meaning of 'commercial agent' see PARA 73.

9 Commercial Agents (Council Directive) Regulations 1993, SI 1993/3053, reg 3(2)(a). As to the cases to which those Regulations apply see PARA 73.

10 As to the meaning of 'principal' see PARA 73. For the principal's corresponding responsibilities see reg 4(2); and PARA 82.

11 Commercial Agents (Council Directive) Regulations 1993, SI 1993/3053, reg 3(2)(b).

12 Commercial Agents (Council Directive) Regulations 1993, SI 1993/3053, reg 3(2)(c).

13 Commercial Agents (Council Directive) Regulations 1993, SI 1993/3053, reg 5(1). The consequence of breach is governed by the law applicable to the contract: reg 5(2).

76. Agent's exercise of discretion.

Where no definite instructions have been given to the agent, or where his instructions leave him a discretion, the agent must be guided by the honest exercise of his own judgment and the interests of his principal[1]. If his instructions leave two alternative courses open to him, he incurs no liability merely because he chooses that course which proves in the event less favourable to his principal[2]. Where he is a professional agent, he must follow the ordinary course of such a business[3], which includes the ordinary course of any previous business as between the principal and the agent[4], and any special usages applicable to the particular case[5].

1 *Chown v Parrott* (1863) 14 CBNS 74; see also *Lagunas Nitrate Co v Lagunas Syndicate* [1899] 2 Ch 392, CA.

2 *Comber v Anderson* (1808) 1 Camp 523; *Moore v Mourgue* (1776) 2 Cowp 479; *Ireland v Livingston* (1872) LR 5 HL 395; *S Weigall & Co v Runciman & Co* (1916) 85 LJKB 1187, CA; *Gould v South Eastern and Chatham Rly Co* [1920] 2 KB 186, DC. See also PARA 35, and the suggestion made there as to the potential effect of the development of modern communications on this rule.

3 *Russell v Hankey* (1794) 6 Term Rep 12; *Mallough v Barber* (1815) 4 Camp 150; *Papé v Westacott* [1894] 1 QB 272, CA.

4 See *World Transport Agency Ltd v Royte (England) Ltd* [1957] 1 Lloyd's Rep 381, where the ordinary course of business between the parties was for the shipping agents not to enter goods for customs without specific instructions, and the agents had been given express prohibition to this effect; the agents were held not to be negligent in not making an entry of goods where such entry would have saved the principal paying increased duties.

5 *Farrer v Lacy, Hartland & Co* (1885) 31 ChD 42, CA; *Solomon v Barker* (1862) 2 F & F 726.

77. Use of information, etc acquired in agency.

It is the duty of an agent to employ the materials and information obtained by reason of his agency solely for the purposes of the agency[1], and not to use any materials or information so acquired, whether his agency has come to an end or not, in any manner inconsistent with good faith, as by divulging them to third parties[2], or by using them himself in unfair competition with his principal[3]. In the case of alleged misuse of information by competition with the principal, the agent will be liable to account for profits made unless the business in which use is made of the information is outside the scope of the business of the principal and does not compete with it[4]. When called upon to account for profits acquired by reason of his fiduciary position and of information obtained in that position, the agent can only defeat the claim by showing that he made the profits with the knowledge and assent of the principal[5]. It is no defence that the principal would not in fact have the capacity or the desire to carry out the transactions out of which the profits arose, or that the agent acted in good faith[6].

An agent will not be made to account to a principal or former principal for profits made by the use of such information or knowledge acquired in the course of the agency as is not secret or confidential[7]. Where an agent in breach of duty to his principal acts for a second principal and in the course of so acting acquires information which is confidential to the second principal, he must not disclose that information to the first principal[8]. The agent may, however, be liable to compensate the first principal for any loss caused by the resultant conflict of duties[9].

1 *Lamb v Evans* [1893] 1 Ch 218, CA, per Bowen LJ; *Merryweather v Moore* [1892] 2 Ch 518; *Louis v Smellie* (1895) 73 LT 226, CA.
2 *Merryweather v Moore* [1892] 2 Ch 518; *Lamb v Evans* [1893] 1 Ch 218, CA, where Bowen LJ disapproved *Reuter's Telegram Co v Byron* (1874) 43 LJ Ch 661; *Taylor v Blacklow* (1836) 3 Scott 614; *Davies v Clough* (1837) 8 Sim 262; *Kirchner & Co v Gruban* [1909] 1 Ch 413; *LS Harris Trustees Ltd (t/a LS Harris & Co) v Power Packing Services (Hermit Road) Ltd* [1970] 2 Lloyd's Rep 65; *Fogg v Gaulter and Blanc* (1960) 110 L Jo 718. Third parties here include a second principal of the agent: see *North and South Trust Co v Berkeley, Berkeley v North and South Trust Co* [1971] 1 All ER 980, [1971] 1 WLR 470. There is no requirement for an agent to be able to bind a principal regarding third parties before a fiduciary duty will arise: see *Società Esplosivi Industriali SpA v Ordnance Technologies (UK) Ltd (formerly SEI (UK) Ltd)* [2004] EWHC 48 (Ch), [2004] 1 All ER (Comm) 619.
3 *Robb v Green* [1895] 2 QB 315, CA; *Yovatt v Winyard* (1820) 1 Jac & W 394; *Amber Size and Chemical Co Ltd v Menzel* [1913] 2 Ch 239; *Measures Bros Ltd v Measures* [1910] 1 Ch 336. As to the position in the case of employees see *Louis v Smellie* (1895) 73 LT 226, CA; *Faccenda Chicken Ltd v Fowler* [1987] Ch 117, [1986] 1 All ER 617, CA. As a general rule a former employee must be free to use the skills and knowledge acquired while working for the ex-employer subject to the law protecting the employer's trade secrets: see EMPLOYMENT vol 39 (2014) PARA 71.
4 *Aas v Benham* [1891] 2 Ch 244, CA.
5 *Regal (Hastings) Ltd v Gulliver* [1967] 2 AC 134n, [1942] 1 All ER 378, HL; *Phipps v Boardman* [1964] 2 All ER 187, [1964] 1 WLR 993 (affd [1965] Ch 992, [1965] 1 All ER 849, CA, sub nom *Boardman v Phipps* [1967] 2 AC 46, [1966] 3 All ER 721, HL); *English v Dedham Vale Properties Ltd* [1978] 1 All ER 382, [1978] 1 WLR 93.
6 *Boardman v Phipps* [1967] 2 AC 46, [1966] 3 All ER 721, HL.
7 *Nordisk Insulinlaboratorium v Gorgate Products Ltd (sued as CL Bencard (1934) Ltd)* [1953] Ch 430, [1953] 1 All ER 986, CA.
8 See *North and South Trust Co v Berkeley, Berkeley v North and South Trust Co* [1971] 1 All ER 980, [1971] 1 WLR 470.
9 See *North and South Trust Co v Berkeley, Berkeley v North and South Trust Co* [1971] 1 All ER 980, [1971] 1 WLR 470.

78. Contracts made by agent.

In the absence of authority to do so, an agent must not purport to bind his principal by contract[1]. Where he possesses authority so to do, he must contract in his principal's name and not in his own, unless the terms of his employment permit it[2]. If he purchases property in his own name on behalf of his principal, and has the legal estate transferred to himself, he is a trustee for his principal in respect of the property[3].

No agent, however, is under any personal liability to his principal upon any contracts made by him on the latter's behalf[4], unless he is made personally liable by usage, or unless he is acting as a del credere agent[5], or unless he otherwise contracts to be so liable.

1   Cf *Chadburn v Moore* (1892) 61 LJ Ch 674 with *Rosenbaum v Belson* [1900] 2 Ch 267; and see *Hamer v Sharp* (1874) LR 19 Eq 108; *Lewcock v Bromley* (1920) 127 LT 116. The principal may, however, be liable on such contracts to the third party: see PARAS **124, 146**.
2   A factor has implied authority to contract in his own name; a broker, in the absence of usage, has not: *Baring v Corrie* (1818) 2 B & Ald 137; *Cropper v Cook* (1868) LR 3 CP 194. See also as to factors PARA **43**.
3   *Lees v Nuttall* (1834) 2 My & K 819; and see PARA **97**; cf *James v Smith* [1891] 1 Ch 384, CA.
4   *Alsop v Silvester* (1823) 1 C & P 107; *Risbourg v Bruckner* (1858) 3 CBNS 812; *Castrique v Buttigieg* (1855) 10 Moo PCC 94. As to the agent's liability to his principal as holder of a bill of exchange signed by the agent without qualification see FINANCIAL INSTRUMENTS AND TRANSACTIONS vol 49 (2015) PARAS 260, 261.
5   See PARA **13**.

(ii) Care, Skill and Diligence

79. Agent's ordinary duty to use care and skill.

Every agent[1], including a gratuitous agent[2], is responsible to his principal for any loss occasioned by his want of proper care, skill or diligence, in the carrying out of his undertaking[3], even though the principal has himself been negligent in not discovering the agent's breach of duty[4]. No absolute standard can be laid down as to what constitutes proper care, skill or diligence, and each particular case must be judged by its own circumstances[5].

In the case of a gratuitous agent this duty is founded on the law of tort[6]. In the case of a contractual agent the duty arises only from contract where the duty would not have arisen apart from contract[7]. The duty may be based on both contract and tort in cases where, apart from the contract, the law would regard the mere status of the parties as giving rise to a duty of care[8].

1   This does not generally include advocates: see *Fell v Brown* (1791) 1 Peake 131; *Mulligan v McDonagh* (1860) 2 LT 136; *Perring v Rebutter* (1842) 2 Mood & R 429; *Kelley v Corston* [1998] QB 686, [1997] 4 All ER 466, CA; *Richardson v Morton* [2002] EWCA Civ 124. As to a barrister's duty of care see LEGAL PROFESSIONS vol 66 (2015) PARA 876.
2   *Chaudhry v Prabhakar* [1988] 3 All ER 718, [1989] 1 WLR 29, CA. As to gratuitous agents see PARA **80**.
3   *Beal v South Devon Rly Co* (1864) 3 H & C 337, Ex Ch.
4   *Becker v Medd* (1897) 13 TLR 313, CA.
5   The question will turn on the specific facts of the case: see *Beauchamp v Powley* (1831) 1 Mood & R 38; *Doorman v Jenkins* (1834) 2 Ad & El 256; *Faruk v Wyse* [1988] 2 EGLR 26 (failure of estate agent to make proper inquiries as to status of tenant).
6   See eg *Gomer v Pitt and Scott* (1922) 12 Ll L Rep 115; *Chaudhry v Prabhakar* [1988] 3 All ER 718, [1989] 1 WLR 29, CA. As to the extent of a gratuitous agent's duty see PARA **80**. See also *Glasgow West Housing Association Ltd v Siddique* 1998 SLT 1081, Ct of Sess (agreement conferred absolute discretion on agent; term not implied obliging agent to carry out work to a particular standard).
7   See eg *Jarvis v Moy, Davies, Smith, Vandervell & Co* [1936] 1 KB 399, CA (stockbroker); *Groom v Crocker* [1939] 1 KB 194, [1938] 2 All ER 394, CA (solicitor); *Bagot v Stevens Scanlan & Co Ltd* [1966] 1 QB 197, [1964] 3 All ER 577 (architect); *Redmayne Bentley Stockbrokers v Isaacs* [2010] EWHC 1504 (Comm), [2010] All ER (D) 233 (Jun) (stockbroker).
8   Persons owing such duty include common carriers, common innkeepers, bailees and employers: see *Bagot v Stevens Scanlan & Co Ltd* [1966] 1 QB 197, [1964] 3 All ER 577.

80. Degree of skill and care of gratuitous agents.

Where an agent acts without reward he is only bound to use such skill as he has[1], except where he has represented himself as possessing skill, in which case the amount of skill requisite is such as may reasonably be expected under the circumstances[2]. The care and diligence required are such as persons ordinarily use in their own affairs[3].

1   *Beal v South Devon Rly Co* (1864) 3 H & C 337, Ex Ch; *Wilson v Brett* (1843) 11 M & W 113; *Moffatt v Bateman* (1869) LR 3 PC 115.
2   *Chaudhry v Prabhakar* [1988] 3 All ER 718, [1989] 1 WLR 29, CA. Such representation may be express (*Whitehead v Greetham* (1825) 2 Bing 464) or implied (*Donaldson v Haldane* (1840) 7 Cl & Fin 762).
3   *Beal v South Devon Rly Co* (1864) 3 H & C 337, Ex Ch; *Shiells and Thorne v Blackburne* (1789) 1 Hy Bl 159; *Doorman v Jenkins* (1834) 2 Ad & El 256; *Giblin v McMullen* (1868) LR 2 PC 317; *Bullen v Swan Electric Engraving Co* (1907) 23 TLR 258, CA. See also PARA 79.

81.   Degree of skill and care where agent acts for reward.

Where an agent acts for reward, a higher standard is exacted than in the case of an agent acting without reward[1]. The care, skill or diligence required is not merely that which the agent in fact possesses, but such as is reasonably necessary for the due performance of his undertaking[2]. He must show at least such diligence in conducting his principal's business as the principal would reasonably have been able to display if the principal had undertaken the business himself[3]. If he is an agent following a particular trade or profession, and holding himself out to the world for employment as such, he represents himself as reasonably competent to carry out any business which he undertakes in the course of such trade or profession[4]. He must then show such care and diligence as are exercised in the ordinary and proper course, and such skill as is usual and requisite, in the business for which he receives payment[5]. In considering the question regard must be had to the nature of the business[6], and such special usages as may be binding on the principal[7].

The agent is not responsible for failure to go beyond his reasonable duty, even though a loss is occasioned thereby, which might have been avoided by extra care, skill or diligence[8]. Nor does he incur liability in respect of matters which are not within the scope of his employment[9], nor in respect of failure to enter on behalf of his principal into contracts which, if made, would be void[10]. If the agent, according to the instructions of his principal, makes a contract which is void for illegality, the agent is not liable if the contract is also unenforceable owing to negligence on the part of the agent[11].

1   *Grill v General Iron Screw Collier Co* (1866) LR 1 CP 600. As to a member's agent's duty of care to a Lloyd's name in relation to high-risk syndicates, see *Brown v KMR Services Ltd* [1995] 4 All ER 598, CA. As to the extent of a gratuitous agent's duty see PARA 80.
2   *Beal v South Devon Rly Co* (1864) 3 H & C 337, Ex Ch. See also *Brown v KMR Services Ltd* [1995] 4 All ER 598, CA.
3   *B Davis Ltd v Tooth & Co Ltd* [1937] 4 All ER 118, PC.
4   *Harmer v Cornelius* (1858) 5 CBNS 236; *Jenkins v Betham* (1855) 15 CB 168. See also *Tenenbaum v Garrod* [1988] 2 EGLR 178, CA (estate agent's valuations).
5   *Beal v South Devon Rly Co* (1864) 3 H & C 337, Ex Ch, per Crompton J; *Smith v Barton* (1866) 15 LT 294; *Lee v Walker* (1872) LR 7 CP 121; *Solomon v Barker* (1862) 2 F & F 726; *Weld-Blundell v Stephens* [1920] AC 956, HL; *Jones v European and General Express Co Ltd* (1920) 25 Com Cas 296; *Keppel v Wheeler* [1927] 1 KB 577, CA; *Club Speciality (Overseas) Inc v United Marine* (1939) Ltd [1971] 1 Lloyd's Rep 482 (forwarding agents); *Youell v Bland Welch & Co Ltd (No 2)* [1990] 2 Lloyd's Rep 431 (brokers).
6   *Heys v Tindall* (1861) 1 B & S 296.
7   *Russell v Hankey* (1794) 6 Term Rep 12; *Mallough v Barber* (1815) 4 Camp 150; *Papé v Westacott* [1894] 1 QB 272, CA; *Farrer v Lacy, Hartland & Co* (1885) 31 ChD 42, CA; *Wilts and Dorset Bank v Cook* (1889) 5 TLR 703; *Pelham v Hilder* (1841) 1 Y & C Ch Cas 3. See further PARA 44.
8   *Commonwealth Portland Cement Co Ltd v Weber, Lohmann & Co Ltd* [1905] AC 66, PC; *World Transport Agency Ltd v Royte (England) Ltd* [1957] 1 Lloyd's Rep 381.

9   *Zwilchenbart v Alexander* (1860) 1 B & S 234; *Jenkins v Betham* (1855) 15 CB 168; and see *Lee v Walker* (1872) LR 7 CP 121; *Lamert v Heath* (1846) 15 M & W 486; *Pappa v Rose* (1871) LR 7 CP 32; affd (1872) LR 7 CP 525, Ex Ch.
10   *Cohen v Kittell* (1889) 22 QBD 680, DC.
11   *Thomas Cheshire & Co v Vaughan Bros & Co* [1920] 3 KB 240, CA (ppi (policy proof of interest) policy repudiated by insurers for non-disclosure).

82.   Agent's duties in negotiating contracts.

Both where the Commercial Agents (Council Directive) Regulations 1993 apply[1], and at common law, the agent must make proper efforts to negotiate and conclude transactions[2]. In the negotiation of a contract the agent must take all reasonable precautions that may be requisite for the protection of his principal[3]. Any contract made by him must be in accordance with his instructions[4] or with usage[5]. Its form must be such that it is capable of being enforced by the principal[6]. If the contract is once completed, the agent cannot rescind it[7] or vary its terms[8], unless he is expressly authorised to do so.

The agent must not be guilty of unreasonable delay in carrying out his instructions[9], or in communicating to his principal any material information[10], including any shortcomings in the performance of his instructions[11].

In the case of a commercial agent a principal must inform his commercial agent within a reasonable period of his acceptance or refusal of, and of any non-execution by him of, a commercial transaction which the commercial agent has procured for him[12].

1   Ie the Commercial Agents (Council Directive) Regulations 1993, SI 1993/3053. As to where those Regulations apply see PARA 73.
2   See the Commercial Agents (Council Directive) Regulations 1993, SI 1993/3053, reg 3(2)(a); PARA 75. In the case of a commercial agent a principal is obliged to provide his agent with the necessary documentation for the goods concerned, and information necessary for the performance of the agency contract, and must give his agent reasonable notice if he anticipates that the volume of commercial transactions will be significantly lower than that which the commercial agent could normally have expected: reg 4(2). As to the meaning of 'commercial agent' see PARA 73.
3   *Heys v Tindall* (1861) 1 B & S 296; *Smith v Barton* (1866) 15 LT 294; *Solomon v Barker* (1862) 2 F & F 726.
4   *Park v Hammond* (1816) 6 Taunt 495; and see *Dickson & Co v Devitt* (1916) 86 LJKB 315.
5   *Mallough v Barber* (1815) 4 Camp 150. As to usage see PARA 44.
6   *McManus v Fortescue* [1907] 2 KB 1, CA; *Rainbow v Howkins* [1904] 2 KB 322; *Scott and Horton v Godfrey* [1901] 2 KB 726; *May and Hart v Angeli* (1898) 14 TLR 551, HL; *Neilson v James* (1882) 9 QBD 546, CA. A broker must make the contract binding on both parties: *Grant v Fletcher* (1826) 5 B & C 436.
7   *Xenos v Wickham* (1866) LR 2 HL 296; *Thomas v Lewis* (1878) 4 ExD 18; *Nelson v Aldridge* (1818) 2 Stark 435.
8   *Hibbert v Bayley* (1860) 2 F & F 48.
9   *Turpin v Bilton* (1843) 5 Man & G 455.
10   *Proudfoot v Montefiore* (1867) LR 2 QB 511. As to the duty of disclosure see further PARAS 90–91.
11   *Youell v Bland Welch & Co Ltd (No 2)* [1990] 2 Lloyd's Rep 431 at 446–447 per Phillips J.
12   Commercial Agents (Council Directive) Regulations 1993, SI 1993/3053, regs 4(3), 5.

(iii)   Accounts: Money Received on Behalf of Principal

83.   Agent's duty to keep accounts.

It is the duty of an agent to keep accurate accounts of all his transactions[1] and to be prepared at all times to produce them to his principal[2]. If he fails to keep proper accounts every presumption consistent with the facts will weigh in favour of the principal[3]. Thus, if he improperly mixes the principal's property with his own, all that he cannot show to be his own will be presumed to belong to the principal[4]. Further, all books and documents relating to the principal's business must on demand be produced to the principal, or to some person named by him[5], provided that such person is not one against whom the agent may have reasonable grounds of objection[6]. The principal's right to be informed of the state of his contractual relationships with both third parties, and with the agent, is inherent in the agency mandate, and accordingly the right can exist both in the case of a gratuitous agency, and in the case of a contractual agency that has been terminated[7].

1   *Gray v Haig* (1855) 20 Beav 219; *Lord Chedworth v Edwards* (1802) 8 Ves 46; *White v Lady Lincoln* (1803) 8 Ves 363; *Yasuda Fire and Marine Insurance of Europe Ltd v Orion Marine Insurance Underwriting Agency Ltd* [1995] QB 174, [1995] 3 All ER 211. The rule does not, however, apply where the agency is only to receive moneys in respect of separate transactions known to the principal in detail at the time: *Re Lee, ex p Neville* (1868) 4 Ch App 43, CA.
2   *Pearse v Green* (1819) 1 Jac & W 135. Investigation of an agent's accounts is not an imputation of dishonesty: *Drysdale v Earl of Rosebery* 1909 SC 1121.
3   *Gray v Haig* (1855) 20 Beav 219; *Clarke v Tipping* (1846) 9 Beav 284.
4   *Lupton v White* (1808) 15 Ves 432. As to keeping the principal's property separate see also PARA 85.
5   *Bevan v Webb* [1901] 2 Ch 59, CA. As to the position where an agent owes a duty to more than one principal see PARA 77.
6   *Dadswell v Jacobs* (1887) 34 ChD 278, CA.
7   *Yasuda Fire and Marine Insurance of Europe Ltd v Orion Marine Insurance Underwriting Agency Ltd* [1995] QB 174, [1995] 3 All ER 211.

84. Sale of horticultural produce on commission.

Provided that the owner or consignor sends to the salesman before the sale an advice note specifying the nature and description of the packages consigned and the contents thereof, an agent employed to sell on commission horticultural produce (vegetables, fruit, flowers and plants) is under a statutory duty to keep a special form of accounts, and to render specified particulars of sales to his principal as soon after the sales as is practicable[1].

1   See the Horticultural Produce (Sales on Commission) Act 1926; and AGRICULTURAL PRODUCTION AND MARKETING vol 1A (2017) PARAS 215–217.

85. Keeping principal's property separate.

Where money is entrusted to an agent by his principal or received by him on his principal's behalf, it depends upon the terms of the agency whether the agent is bound to keep the money separate or is entitled to mix it with his own. In the former case the agent will be a trustee, in the latter a debtor[1].

1   *Burdick v Garrick* (1870) 5 Ch App 233, CA; *Lyell v Kennedy* (1889) 14 App Cas 437, HL; *Henry v Hammond* [1913] 2 KB 515.

86. Payments made to agent for principal.

When an agent is employed to carry out any transaction which involves a payment to him on his principal's behalf[1], he must not compromise his principal's rights[2] or part with his property[3], until he has received payment, unless authorised by his instructions or by usage to do so[4]; but, in the absence of negligence on the part of the agent, he is not liable merely because the debtor, being insolvent, does not pay the debt in full: in such circumstances his duty is to collect all he can[5]. In the absence of instructions or usage, payment must be received in cash, and not otherwise[6].

All moneys received on the principal's behalf[7] must be paid over[8] or accounted for[9] to the principal upon request[10], unless the agent has for some lawful reason repaid them to the person from whom he received them[11]. It is immaterial that the transaction in respect of which the moneys are received is void[12] or illegal[13], provided that the agency itself is not illegal[14]. Nor can the agent retain such moneys against the principal in respect of a debt due to himself from the person paying them, or because of some claim made to them by some third person[15]. Failure to pay renders the agent liable to a claim for money had and received[16].

Where the moneys are received on behalf of joint principals, the agent is liable to account to them jointly, and is not discharged by payment to one or more of them only, unless by authority of all[17].

1 As to the agent's authority to receive payment and whether payment to the agent discharges the debt see PARAS 38, 134.
2 As in *Papé v Westacott* [1894] 1 QB 272, CA.
3 As in *Brown v Boorman, Boorman and Wild* (1844) 11 Cl & Fin 1, HL; *Kidd v Horne* (1885) 2 TLR 141.
4 *Wiltshire v Sims* (1808) 1 Camp 258; *Earl Ferrers v Robins* (1835) 2 Cr M & R 152. A factor (*Houghton v Matthews* (1803) 3 Bos & P 485) and a broker (*Brown v Boorman, Boorman and Wild* (1844) 11 Cl & Fin 1, HL) have an implied authority to sell on credit. As to usage see further PARA 44.
5 *Gokal Chand-Jagan Nath v Nand Ram Das-Atma Ram* [1939] AC 106, [1938] 4 All ER 407, PC, following *Russell v Palmer* (1767) 2 Wils 325.
6 Thus it may not normally be received by a negotiable instrument (*Papé v Westacott* [1894] 1 QB 272, CA; *Wiltshire v Sims* (1808) 1 Camp 258; *Earl Ferrers v Robins* (1835) 2 Cr M & R 152; *Hine Bros v Steamship Insurance Syndicate Ltd, The Netherholme, Glen Holme, and Rydal Holme* (1895) 72 LT 79, CA), unless authorised by usage (*Farrer v Lacy Hartland & Co* (1885) 31 ChD 42, CA); or by set-off or settlement of accounts (*Sweeting v Pearce* (1859) 7 CBNS 449 (affd (1861) 9 CBNS 534, Ex Ch); *Legge v Byas, Mosley & Co* (1901) 7 Com Cas 16), any usage to that effect being unreasonable (*Matveieff & Co v Crossfield* (1903) 51 WR 365; *Sweeting v Pearce*; *Legge v Byas, Mosley & Co*); or by taking other goods (*Howard v Chapman* (1831) 4 C & P 508). See also *Catterall v Hindle* (1866) LR 1 CP 187; on appeal (1867) LR 2 CP 368, Ex Ch; *International Sponge Importers Ltd v Andrew Watt & Sons* [1911] AC 279, HL; *Bradford & Sons v Price Bros* (1923) 92 LJKB 871; and PARA 38.
7 As to what may amount to a receipt see *Gillard v Wise* (1826) 5 B & C 134.
8 *Wilkinson v North Suburban Properties Ltd* (1959) 174 Estates Gazette 213, CA (whole of deposit paid to sub-agent 'subject to contract' payable by sub-agent to estate agent).
9 As to the claim for account see PARA 88.
10 *Harsant v Blaine, Macdonald & Co* (1887) 56 LJQB 511, CA.
11 *Murray v Mann* (1848) 2 Exch 538.
12 *Bridger v Savage* (1885) 15 QBD 363, CA; *De Mattos v Benjamin* (1894) 63 LJQB 248, DC.
13 *Bousfield v Wilson* (1846) 16 M & W 185; *Tenant v Elliott* (1797) 1 Bos & P 3; *Farmer v Russell* (1798) 1 Bos & P 296; *Sharp v Taylor* (1849) 2 Ph 801; and see *Sykes v Beadon* (1879) 11 ChD 170.
14 See *Booth v Hodgson* (1795) 6 Term Rep 405; *Catlin v Bell* (1815) 4 Camp 183; *Knowles v Haughton* (1805) 11 Ves 168; *Battersby v Smyth* (1818) 3 Madd 110, with which cf *Davenport v Whitmore* (1836) 2 My & Cr 177.
15 *Roberts v Ogilby* (1821) 9 Price 269; *Dixon v Hammond* (1819) 2 B & Ald 310. As to the cases in which he may make a stakeholder application see PARA 121.
16 See *Blaustein v Maltz Mitchell & Co* [1937] 2 KB 142, [1937] 1 All ER 497, CA.
17 *Lee v Sankey* (1873) LR 15 Eq 204; *Heath v Chilton* (1844) 12 M & W 632.

(iv) Remedies for Default of Agent

87. Principal's claim for damages.

Upon an agent's breach of duty the principal's remedy is, as a rule, to claim damages for breach of contract[1], and the period of limitation[2] runs in the agent's favour from the date of the breach[3].

Where an agent is sued by his principal for breach of contract, the measure of damages is the measure recoverable under the general law of contract, which is the full amount of the loss actually sustained[4], and no more[5], provided that such loss is the natural and probable consequence[6] of the breach of duty, or such as was within the contemplation of the parties[7]. This may include profit which has actually been lost, but not merely expected profits which might have been made if the agent had performed his duty[8]. Where the agency is gratuitous, the claim by the principal for damages will be in tort[9].

Where, owing to the negligence of the agent, the principal has been convicted of a criminal offence, whether or not the principal can recover by way of damages for that negligence any penalty imposed on him upon his conviction is the subject of conflicting authorities, but, where the liability for the offence is absolute, and the principal has not himself been guilty of any fault, negligence or dishonesty, but he has been grossly misled by his agent, he has been held entitled to recover the amount of the penalty from the agent[10].

1   Where the agent has accepted a bribe, the principal may alternatively claim the amount of the bribe as money had and received: *Mahesan v Malaysia Government Officers' Co-operative Housing Society Ltd* [1979] AC 374, [1978] 2 All ER 405, PC. As to damages for breach of contract see DAMAGES vol 29 (2014) PARA 499 et seq.

2   See the Limitation Act 1980 s 5; and LIMITATION PERIODS vol 68 (2016) PARA 952.

3   *Wood v Jones* (1889) 61 LT 551; *Metropolitan Bank v Heiron* (1880) 5 ExD 319, CA (fraud) (overruled on a different point by *FHR European Ventures LLP v Mankarious* [2014] UKSC 45, [2015] AC 250, [2014] 4 All ER 79: see PARAS 92–95). This is so even where the agent acted in a fiduciary capacity, unless he has been guilty of fraud, or unless the claim is for property entrusted to him, or for the proceeds or value of such property: see the Limitation Act 1980 ss 21, 32; *North American Land and Timber Co Ltd v Watkins* [1904] 1 Ch 242; affd [1904] 2 Ch 233, CA; *Re Lands Allotment Co* [1894] 1 Ch 616, CA; and LIMITATION PERIODS vol 68 (2016) PARAS 1138 et seq, 1220 et seq. As to whether a claim lies in tort or in contract see PARA 79.

4   *Smith v Price* (1862) 2 F & F 748; *Maydew v Forrester* (1814) 5 Taunt 615; *Neilson v James* (1882) 9 QBD 546, CA. If there has been no actual loss, the principal is entitled to nominal damages (*Van Wart v Woolley* (1830) Mood & M 520). As to the measure of damages where an agent to sell land signs a contract in excess of authority and the principal is sued for specific performance see *Lewcock v Bromley* (1920) 127 LT 116; and as to the measure where an agent to sell land fails to disclose a higher offer see *Keppel v Wheeler* [1927] 1 KB 577, CA. As to the right of the principal to an indemnity where an agent has abused powers of which he is a trustee see *Eastern Shipping Co Ltd v Quah Beng Kee* [1924] AC 177, PC.

5   *Waddell v Blockey* (1879) 4 QBD 678, CA; *Cassaboglou v Gibb* (1883) 11 QBD 797, CA; and see *Michael v Hart & Co* [1902] 1 KB 482, CA (affd sub nom *Hart & Co v Michael* (1903) 89 LT 422, HL); *Johnston v Braham and Campbell* [1917] 1 KB 586, CA. Nominal damages only will be awarded where the principal is unable to show that any damage has been suffered: *Carreras Ltd v Levy* (1970) 215 Estates Gazette 707 (misrepresentation as to amount of office space in building to be taken in sub-lease; no damages proved since rent paid might equally represent the market value of the smaller space actually available).

6   Cf *Mainwaring v Brandon* (1818) 2 Moore CP 125, with *Re United Service Co, Johnston's Claim* (1871) 6 Ch App 212.

7   *Hadley v Baxendale* (1854) 9 Exch 341; *Boyd v Fitt* (1864) 11 LT 280. As to the measure of damages see DAMAGES vol 29 (2014) PARA 318 et seq.

8   *Salvesen & Co v Rederi Aktiebolaget Nordstjernan* [1905] AC 302, HL; *Cassaboglou v Gibb* (1883) 11 QBD 797, CA; *Johnston v Braham and Campbell* [1917] 1 KB 586, CA. See also *Laskin v Bache & Co Inc* [1972] 1 OR 465, Ont CA (damages recovered in respect of loss of opportunity to sell stock certificates in a declining market where broker failed to obtain possession of certificates).

9   See PARA 79. As to damages in tort see DAMAGES vol 29 (2014) PARA 408 et seq.

10   See *Osman v J Ralph Moss Ltd* [1970] 1 Lloyd's Rep 313, CA, where insurance brokers had grossly misled the principal as to the financial standing of an insurance company, with the result that the principal became uninsured and was convicted for driving while uninsured. Cf *R Leslie Ltd v Reliable Advertising and Addressing Agency Ltd* [1915] 1 KB 652; see also *Askey v Golden Wine Co Ltd* [1948] 2 All ER 35. Cf, as to the right of the agent to an indemnity in respect of payments made under illegal transactions, PARA 114.

88. Principal's claim for account.

Where an agent fails to pay over to his principal on demand money received by him, the principal may bring a claim for money had and received[1], and may also claim an account[2].

The relationship of principal and agent ordinarily being fiduciary in character[3], proceedings for an account lay in the Court of Chancery[4] and are now brought, particularly if the accounts are complicated[5], by a claim in the Chancery Division[6]. Where the accounts are of a simple nature, they can be taken in an ordinary claim in the Queen's Bench Division[7]. The principal may seek an account of the profits made by an agent from his use of confidential information[8]. It would appear that the court will determine the appropriate remedy in such cases, rather than permitting the principal to elect[9].

On the taking of an account the agent is entitled to deduct, in addition to all authorised expenses, any sums due from the principal to the agent[10], but deductions may not be made until such sums are due[11]. An agent is not entitled to an indemnity in respect of money which, even with the authority of his principal, he has expended for an unlawful purpose[12]; but where the money has already been paid over to the agent the principal cannot recover it[13], even though the unlawful purpose has not been carried out, unless the principal had withdrawn from the carrying out of the purpose by reason of repentance[14]. Ordinarily, a claim for an account is barred after the expiration of any time limit applicable to the claim which is the basis of the duty to account[15].

Where an account has been agreed the principal may sue the agent on an account stated[16]. This may take the form of an oral or written acknowledgment from which a debt may be inferred, but the agent may prove that there is no such sum in fact due to his principal[17]. If the account takes the form of items on both sides of a written account and a balance is struck, however, the agent can only dispute such items debited against him in the account as, if paid by him, could have been recovered as on a total failure of consideration[18].

Settled accounts cannot, as a rule, be reopened[19], but the principal may obtain leave to surcharge and falsify[20] them[21]. An account does not come within this principle as a settled account unless there is mutuality: that is, two or more parties accounting to each other[22]. On proof of fraud[23] or undue influence[24], however, the principal is entitled to have settled accounts reopened from the beginning of the agency[25].

1 See eg *Harsant v Blaine, Macdonald & Co* (1887) 56 LJQB 511, CA; *Mahesan v Malaysia Government Officers' Co-operative Housing Society Ltd* [1979] AC 374, [1978] 2 All ER 405, PC; and PARA 86.

2 The account must not, however, include damages for breach of duty: *Great Western Insurance Co of New York v Cunliffe* (1874) 9 Ch App 525; *Trans Barwil Agencies (UK) Ltd v John S Braid & Co Ltd* 1989 SLT 73, Ct of Sess. It is doubtful whether a court has power to award damages in lieu of an account: see *English v Dedham Vale Properties Ltd* [1978] 1 All ER 382, [1978] 1 WLR 93.

3 See *Makepeace v Rogers* (1865) 4 De GJ & Sm 649, CA; *Padwick v Stanley* (1852) 9 Hare 627; and PARA 74.

4 *Foley v Hill* (1848) 2 HL Cas 28.

5 See *Harrington v Churchward* (1860) 29 LJ Ch 521.

6 See *Leslie v Clifford* (1884) 50 LT 590, DC. As to claims regarding accounts generally see CPR PD 40A—*Accounts, Inquiries, etc*; and CIVIL PROCEDURE vol 12A (2015) PARAS 1250–1255.

7 *Foley v Hill* (1848) 2 HL Cas 28; *Barry v Stevens* (1862) 31 Beav 258; *Blyth v Whiffin* (1872) 27 LT 330; *York v Stowers* (1883) Bitt Rep in Ch 2. As to the referral of cases to the Technology and Construction Court see CIVIL PROCEDURE vol 11 (2015) PARA 180.

8 *Peter Pan Manufacturing Corpn v Corsettes Silhouette Ltd* [1963] 3 All ER 402, [1964] 1 WLR 96.

9   *English v Dedham Vale Properties Ltd* [1978] 1 All ER 382, [1978] 1 WLR 93.
10 *Dale v Sollet* (1767) 4 Burr 2133. As to the right of the agent to claim expenses after accounts between him and his principal have been settled see *Struthers v Smith* 1913 2 SLT 155.
11 *Wilkinson v North Suburban Properties Ltd* (1959) 174 Estates Gazette 213, CA.
12 *Re Parker* (1882) 21 ChD 408, CA (agent unable to recover illegal election expenses); see also PARA 114.
13 *Bayntun v Cattle* (1833) 1 Mood & R 265.
14 *Harry Parker Ltd v Mason* [1940] 2 KB 590, [1940] 4 All ER 199, CA (conspiracy to make sham bets); *Bigos v Bousted* [1951] 1 All ER 92 (share certificate deposited in breach of exchange control legislation).
15 See the Limitation Act 1980 s 23; and LIMITATION PERIODS vol 68 (2016) PARA 1008. See also ss 21(1), 32; and LIMITATION PERIODS vol 68 (2016) PARAS 1138 et seq, 1220 et seq. No lapse of time, however, bars the right of a principal to an account of property which the agent holds in a fiduciary capacity for the principal during the continuance of the fiduciary relationship, and where the agent has been guilty of fraud time does not begin to run until after the discovery of the fraud: see ss 21, 32; *North American Land and Timber Co Ltd v Watkins* [1904] 1 Ch 242; affd [1904] 2 Ch 233, CA; and LIMITATION PERIODS vol 68 (2016) PARAS 1138 et seq, 1220 et seq.
16 For the right to sue on an account stated see CONTRACT vol 22 (2012) PARAS 611–612.
17 *Siqueira v Noronha* [1934] AC 332, PC.
18 *Camillo Tank Steamship Co Ltd v Alexandria Engineering Works* (1921) 38 TLR 134, HL; *Siqueira v Noronha* [1934] AC 332, PC.
19 *Parkinson v Hanbury* (1867) LR 2 HL 1. As to the reopening of settled accounts see EQUITABLE JURISDICTION vol 47 (2014) PARA 53.
20 'Falsify' is here used with its meaning of 'show to be false'.
21 *Mozeley v Cowie* (1877) 47 LJ Ch 271; *Cheese v Keen* [1908] 1 Ch 245; and see *Shaw v Picton* (1825) 4 B & C 715; *Cave v Mills* (1862) 7 H & N 913.
22 *Anglo-American Asphalt Co Ltd v Crowley Russell & Co Ltd* [1945] 2 All ER 324; and distinguish *Hunter v Belcher* (1864) 2 De GJ & Sm 194, CA.
23 *Clarke v Tipping* (1846) 9 Beav 284; *Walsham v Stainton* (1863) 1 De GJ & Sm 678.
24 *Watson v Rodwell* (1879) 11 ChD 150, CA.
25 *Stainton v Carron Co* (1857) 24 Beav 346; *Williamson v Barbour* (1877) 9 ChD 529.

89.   Interest payable by agent.

Interest is payable by an agent in respect of money received by him on his principal's behalf[1], under a contract express or implied, or where there has been some default on his part[2], such as a dealing with the money in breach of duty[3], or a failure to pay it over at the principal's request[4], in which cases interest is payable from the date of default[5]. The agent must also pay interest in all cases of fraud[6], and on all bribes[7] and secret profits[8] received by him during his agency. The court has a wide statutory discretion to award interest in proceedings for the recovery of any debt[9].

1   If money is received by him as a stakeholder, however, he is not liable to pay interest on it: see *Harington v Hoggart* (1830) 1 B & Ad 577. Where an estate agent received a pre-contract deposit, which he held as stakeholder, and which, when he believed the contract had ceased to be conditional, he placed on deposit, he was entitled to retain the interest earned on the purchaser's money before the time when the intending purchaser withdrew from the contract: see *Potters v Loppart* [1973] Ch 399, [1973] 1 All ER 658, where Pennycuick V-C justified the retention as a reward for the estate agent's trouble and also as recompense for loss of prospect of earning commission on sale during the period concerned. As to stakeholders see further AUCTION vol 4 (2011) PARA 58.
2   *Webster v British Empire Mutual Life Assurance Co* (1880) 15 ChD 169, CA.
3   As by employing it in his own business (*Rogers v Boehm* (1799) 2 Esp 702; *Burdick v Garrick* (1870) 5 Ch App 233); but contrast *Lord Chedworth v Edwards* (1802) 8 Ves 46.
4   *Edgell v Day* (1865) LR 1 CP 80; *Harsant v Blaine, Macdonald & Co* (1887) 56 LJQB 511, CA (decided under the Civil Procedure Act 1833 s 28 (repealed)). Merely retaining money which the agent ought to pay over, but which he has never been required to pay, is not sufficient to entitle the principal to interest, in the absence of fraud: *Turner v Burkinshaw* (1867) LR 2 Ch App 488.
5   *Edgell v Day* (1865) LR 1 CP 80; *Barclay v Harris and Cross* (1915) 85 LJKB 115.

6 *Earl Hardwicke v Vernon* (1808) 14 Ves 504.
7 *Boston Deep Sea Fishing and Ice Co v Ansell* (1888) 39 ChD 339, CA. See further PARA 95.
8 *Nant-y-glo and Blaina Ironworks Co v Grave* (1878) 12 ChD 738. See further PARA 92 et seq.
9 See the Senior Courts Act 1981 s 35A; and DAMAGES vol 29 (2014) PARA 635.

(v) Disclosure by Agent

90. Agent to avoid or declare conflict of interest.

An agent will not be allowed to put his duty in conflict with his interest[1], and therefore he must not enter into any transaction likely to produce that result[2], unless he has first made to his principal the fullest disclosure of the exact nature of his interest, and the principal has assented[3]. An agent does not discharge his duty in this behalf merely by disclosing that he has an interest[4], or by making statements which might put the principal on inquiry[5]. In particular, notwithstanding any usage to the contrary[6], he must not sell his own property to the principal[7], nor buy the principal's property[8], nor, by acting as agent for the principal and the other contracting party, obtain remuneration from both, without the knowledge of the principal[9]: to act as agent for both principals without the knowledge and consent of the first principal will amount to a breach of duty to that principal[10].

To the rule that an agent may not buy his principal's property there is an apparent exception in the case of a broker who has a right, or is under a duty, to close his principal's outstanding account of transactions entered into by him on his principal's behalf. The broker may ascertain (and realise) the value of the shares or commodity by a simultaneous sale and repurchase on his own account, provided that the transactions are bona fide, at fair market price and he makes no secret profit[11].

1 *Bank of Upper Canada v Bradshaw* (1867) LR 1 PC 479; *Parker v McKenna* (1874) 10 Ch App 96; *Tiessen v Henderson* [1899] 1 Ch 861; *King, Viall and Benson v Howell* (1910) 27 TLR 114, CA. This rule will not prohibit the agent from canvassing, after notice has been given terminating the agency agreement, for custom in respect of a period after termination, where such canvassing is not in itself a breach of the agreement: *Julien Praet et Cie SA v HG Poland Ltd, Poland v Julien Praet et Cie SA* [1962] 1 Lloyd's Rep 566.
2 For cases where the transaction is entered into with a person with whom he is dealing on his principal's behalf see PARA 94.
3 *Gwatkin v Campbell* (1854) 1 Jur NS 131; *Glasgow Assurance Corpn Ltd v William Symondson & Co* (1911) 104 LT 254; *Ellis & Co's Trustee v Watsham* (1923) 155 LT Jo 363; *Thornton Hall & Partners v Wembley Electrical Appliances Ltd* [1947] 2 All ER 630, CA. The rule applies equally to persons who purport to act as agents and subsequently profit by use of information obtained during the purported agency: see *Boardman v Phipps* [1967] 2 AC 46, [1966] 3 All ER 721, HL; and PARA 77.
4 *Imperial Mercantile Credit Association v Coleman* (1873) LR 6 HL 189; *Alexander v Automatic Telephone Co* [1900] 2 Ch 56, CA; *Gluckstein v Barnes* [1900] AC 240, HL; *Costa Rica Rly Co v Forwood* [1901] 1 Ch 746, CA. As to the statutory duty of a company director to disclose his interest in contracts with the company see the Companies Act 2006 ss 182–187; and COMPANIES vol 14 (2016) PARAS 590, 595 et seq.
5 *Dunne v English* (1874) LR 18 Eq 524; and see *Swale v Ipswich Tannery Ltd* (1906) 11 Com Cas 88.
6 *Robinson v Mollett* (1875) LR 7 HL 802; *Hamilton v Young* (1881) LR 7 Ir 289.
7 *Gillett v Peppercorne* (1840) 3 Beav 78; *Rothschild v Brookman* (1831) 2 Dow & Cl 188, HL; *Skelton v Wood* (1894) 71 LT 616, DC; *King, Viall and Benson v Howell* (1910) 27 TLR 114, CA; *Kuhlirz v Lambert Bros Ltd* (1913) 108 LT 565; *Armstrong v Jackson* [1917] 2 KB 822; and see PARA 1.
8 *McPherson v Watt* (1877) 3 App Cas 254, HL; *Re Pemberton, ex p Huth* (1840) 4 Deac 294; *Lowther v Lord Lowther* (1806) 13 Ves 95; *Livingstone v Ross* [1901] AC 327, PC; *Patten v*

Hamilton [1911] 1 IR 46, CA; *Coats' Trustees* 1914 SC 723, Ct of Sess. An agent who is also given an option may purchase: *Kelly v Enderton* [1913] AC 191, PC.

9　*Fullwood v Hurley* [1928] 1 KB 498, CA; *Harrods Ltd v Lemon* [1931] 2 KB 157, CA.

10　The usage whereby insurance brokers, who are the agents of the insured, act for certain purposes, including the appointment of assessors of claims and the receipt of assessors' reports with strict instructions not to disclose the contents to the insured, as the agents of the underwriters, has been the subject of disapproval by the courts: see *Anglo-African Merchants Ltd v Bayley* [1970] 1 QB 311, [1969] 2 All ER 421; *North and South Trust Co v Berkeley, Berkeley v North and South Trust Co* [1971] 1 All ER 980, [1971] 1 WLR 470 (although to act as agents for the insurer is a breach of duty to the principal, the principal is not thereby entitled to documents confidential to the insurers which come into the hands of the agents in the course of such breach).

11　*Macoun v Erskine, Oxenford & Co* [1901] 2 KB 493, CA; *Erskine, Oxenford & Co v Sachs* [1901] 2 KB 504, CA; *Re Finlay, C S Wilson & Co v Finlay* [1913] 1 Ch 247; affd [1913] 1 Ch 565, CA; *Christoforides v Terry* [1924] AC 566, HL.

91.　Effect of agent's non-disclosure of conflict of interest.

In all other transactions[1] with the principal, the agent must disclose every material fact which is or ought to be known by him, if it would be likely to operate upon the principal's judgment[2]. If this is not done, the fairness of the transaction is immaterial[3], and it is voidable at the principal's option[4], and the principal may obtain rescission of the transaction after it has been completely executed without the necessity of establishing fraud on the part of the agent[5].

The principal's remedies in cases of fraudulent concealment, fraud or mistake do not become statute barred until six years after he has discovered, or could with reasonable diligence have discovered, the relevant circumstances upon which his claim is based[6].

1　*Lord Selsey v Rhoades* (1824) 2 Sim & St 41. The rule applies to gifts: see *Hunter v Atkins* (1834) 3 My & K 113; as to gifts between solicitor and client see LEGAL PROFESSIONS vol 66 (2015) PARAS 599–601.

2　*Dunne v English* (1874) LR 18 Eq 524; *Charter v Trevelyan* (1844) 11 Cl & Fin 714; *Savery v King* (1856) 5 HL Cas 627; *Luddy's Trustee v Peard* (1886) 33 ChD 500; *Imeson v Lister* (1920) 149 LT Jo 446; *Demerara Bauxite Co v Hubbard* [1923] AC 673, PC; *Heath v Parkinson* (1926) 136 LT 128. The test is what a reasonable man would consider material in the ordinary course of business: *Payne v Lewis and Peat* [1917] WN 195. There is no duty on an agent to communicate an offer which the principal had previously told him would not be accepted: *Burchell v Gowrie and Blockhouse Collieries Ltd* [1910] AC 614, PC.

3　*Gillett v Peppercorne* (1840) 3 Beav 78; *Aberdeen Rly Co v Blaikie Bros* (1854) 2 Eq Rep 1281, HL; *Transvaal Lands Co v New Belgium (Transvaal) Land and Development Co* [1914] 2 Ch 488, CA; *Imeson v Lister* (1920) 149 LT Jo 446.

4　*Houldsworth v City of Glasgow Bank* (1880) 5 App Cas 317, HL, per Lord Cairns; *Re Cape Breton Co* (1885) 29 ChD 795, CA; *Gillett v Peppercorne* (1840) 3 Beav 78; *Oliver v Court* (1820) Dan 301; *Great Luxembourg Rly Co v Magnay (No 2)* (1858) 25 Beav 586; *Moody v Cox and Hatt* [1917] 2 Ch 71, CA.

5　*Armstrong v Jackson* [1917] 2 KB 822. The remedy of rescission is available in respect of all contracts induced by misrepresentation, whether or not the misrepresentation has become a term of the contract or the contract has been performed, without proof of fraud: see the Misrepresentation Act 1967 s 1; and MISREPRESENTATION vol 76 (2013) PARAS 703, 816. Where rescission is inappropriate, however, or where additional loss has been suffered, damages may be awarded, without proof of fraud: see s 2; CONTRACT vol 22 (2012) PARAS 352–353; MISREPRESENTATION vol 76 (2013) PARA 832.

6　*Oelkers v Ellis* [1914] 2 KB 139; Limitation Act 1980 s 32. The title of innocent purchasers for value is, however, protected: see s 32(3), (4); and LIMITATION PERIODS vol 68 (2016) PARA 1220 et seq.

(vi) Secret Profits and Bribes

92. General rule prohibiting agent from acquiring secret profit.

An agent must not, without the knowledge of his principal[1], acquire any profit[2] or benefit[3] from his agency[4] other than that contemplated by the principal at the time of making the contract of agency[5]. The agent owes a duty of undivided loyalty to the principal, unless the latter has given informed consent to a less demanding standard of duty. The principal, therefore, is entitled to the entire benefit of the agent's acts in the course of his agency[6].

This rule may apply even though at the time of the transaction itself the agency has ceased[7]. The rule applies in spite of the fact that the agent has done his best under the circumstances[8] or incurred a possibility of loss[9], or that the principal has in fact received the benefit he himself contemplated from the transaction[10].

All such profits and the value of such benefits must be paid over to the principal[11]. The agent's duty is to deliver up to his principal the benefit which he has obtained and not simply to pay compensation for having obtained it in excess of his authority[12]. All unauthorised benefits received by an agent as a result of his agency and in breach of his fiduciary duty to his principal should be treated as the property of the principal and should therefore be held on trust for him[13].

1   *Re Haslam and Hier-Evans* [1902] 1 Ch 765, CA; *Ritchie v Couper* (1860) 28 Beav 344; *Jordy v Vanderpump* (1920) 64 Sol Jo 324; see also *Darvell v Basildon Development Corpn* (1969) 211 Estates Gazette 33 (full knowledge by principal of sale to estate agent's daughter; good title held to pass to enable daughter to obtain specific performance of later sale).

2   *Thompson v Meade* (1891) 7 TLR 698.

3   *Fawcett v Whitehouse* (1829) 1 Russ & M 132; *Tarkwa Main Reef Ltd v Merton* (1903) 19 TLR 367. See *FHR European Ventures LLP v Mankarious* [2014] UKSC 45, [2015] AC 250, [2014] 4 All ER 79, where agent received a secret commission from brokering a deal between the principal and the hotel vendors.

4   *Erskine, Oxenford & Co v Sachs* [1901] 2 KB 504, CA; cf *Kirkham v Peel* (1881) 44 LT 195, CA; and see *Williamson v Hine Bros* [1891] 1 Ch 390; *Re Finlay, C S Wilson & Co v Finlay* [1913] 1 Ch 247 (affd [1913] 1 Ch 565, CA); *Kitson v P S King & Son Ltd* (1919) 36 TLR 162; *Grinsted v Hadrill* [1953] 1 All ER 1188, [1953] 1 WLR 696, CA.

5   See the cases cited in notes 2–4. This rule applies even though the agency is gratuitous: *Turnbull v Garden* (1869) 38 LJ Ch 331. The same rule applies to sub-agents where a fiduciary relation is established: *Powell and Thomas v Evan Jones & Co* [1905] 1 KB 11, CA (overruled on a different point by *FHR European Ventures LLP v Mankarious* [2014] UKSC 45, [2015] AC 250, [2014] 4 All ER 79: see PARA 94).

    For the application of the rule to house agents acting as repairers see *Sherrard v Barron* [1923] 1 IR 21, CA; and to directors of a company, see *Bath v Standard Land Co Ltd* [1911] 1 Ch 618, CA; and COMPANIES vol 14 (2016) PARA 635; as to its application to agents acting for a trust and persons in a similar position see *Boardman v Phipps* [1967] 2 AC 46, [1966] 3 All ER 721, HL; and TRUSTS AND POWERS vol 98 (2013) PARA 100.

    See also *Stubbs v Slater* [1910] 1 Ch 632, CA (sums deducted by broker under usage of stock exchange for carrying over although not justifiable as contractual remuneration could be retained as reasonable remuneration on quantum meruit).

6   *FHR European Ventures LLP v Mankarious* [2014] UKSC 45 at [33], [2015] AC 250, [2014] 4 All ER 79.

7   *Carter v Palmer* (1842) 8 Cl & Fin 657, HL; *Regier v Campbell-Stuart* [1939] Ch 766, [1939] 3 All ER 235. Where, however, the profit is made after the termination of the agency by means of information obtained during the agency but not secret or confidential, there will be no liability to account for the profit: *Nordisk Insulinlaboratorium v Gorgate Products Ltd (sued as C L Bencard (1934) Ltd)* [1953] Ch 430, [1953] 1 All ER 986, CA.

8   *Shallcross v Oldham* (1862) 2 John & H 609.

9   *Williams v Stevens* (1866) LR 1 PC 352.

10 *De Bussche v Alt* (1878) 8 ChD 286, CA.

11 *Thompson v Meade* (1891) 7 TLR 698; *Regier v Campbell-Stuart* [1939] Ch 766, [1939] 3 All ER 235; see also *Brown v IRC* [1965] AC 244, [1964] 3 All ER 119, HL. The agent, however, may

still be entitled to retain the normal commission, in the absence of fraud: see *Hippisley v Knee Bros* [1905] 1 KB 1; *Nitedals Taendstikfabrik v Bruster* [1906] 2 Ch 671. A fiduciary who acts dishonestly will normally forfeit his right to fees, but fees may not be forfeit if the betrayal of trust has not been in respect of the entire subject matter of the fiduciary relationship and forfeiture would be disproportionate and inequitable: see *Imageview Management Ltd v Jack* [2009] EWCA Civ 63 at [50], [2009] 2 All ER 666 ('cases of harmless collaterality'); *Stupples v Stupples & Co (High Wycombe) Ltd* [2012] EWHC 1226 (Ch), [2013] 1 BCLC 729.
12 *FHR European Ventures LLP v Mankarious* [2014] UKSC 45 at [33], [2015] AC 250, [2014] 4 All ER 79.
13 *FHR European Ventures LLP v Mankarious* [2014] UKSC 45 at [35], [46], [2015] AC 250, [2014] 4 All ER 79.

93. Agent to purchase.

Where an agent who is employed to buy property on his principal's behalf sells his own to the principal, and thereby makes a profit, the principal, in lieu of rescinding the sale, may affirm it[1]. If rescission is no longer possible, the contract remains in existence[2]. In either case he may then recover from the agent the full amount of the profit received by the latter, together with interest[3].

Where the agent is employed to buy a particular property[4] in which he in fact had an interest before accepting the agency, and sells it to his principal during the agency without disclosing his interest, the principal may affirm or rescind the contract, but, if he affirms it, he cannot also claim the profits[5] in the absence of any underhand dealing[6].

1 The onus of maintaining that the sale has been affirmed lies on the agent: *Cavendish-Bentinck v Fenn* (1887) 12 App Cas 652, HL.
2 See *Re Leeds and Hanley Theatres of Varieties Ltd* [1902] 2 Ch 809, CA (rescission impossible because property sold by mortgagees to third party); and see *Re Cape Breton Co* (1885) 29 ChD 795, CA (property sold by company to third party); affd on other grounds sub nom *Cavendish-Bentinck v Fenn* (1887) 12 App Cas 652, HL.
3 *Bentley v Craven* (1853) 18 Beav 75; *Tyrrell v Bank of London* (1862) 10 HL Cas 26; *Benson v Heathorn* (1842) 1 Y & C Ch Cas 326; *Massey v Davies* (1794) 2 Ves 317.
4 Quaere whether the same rule applies where no particular property is indicated: see *Re Cape Breton Co* (1885) 29 ChD 795, CA; affd on other grounds sub nom *Cavendish-Bentinck v Fenn* (1887) 12 App Cas 652, HL.
5 *Re Cape Breton Co* (1885) 29 ChD 795, CA (affd on another ground sub nom *Cavendish-Bentinck v Fenn* (1887) 12 App Cas 652, HL), approved in *Burland v Earle* [1902] AC 83, PC. Cf *Cook v Deeks* [1916] 1 AC 554, PC.
6 *Kimber v Barber* (1872) 8 Ch App 56.

94. Bribe or secret commission.

A bribe or secret commission is a profit or benefit received by the agent from the third person with whom the agent is dealing on his principal's behalf without the knowledge or consent of the principal, or which was not contemplated by the principal at the creation of the agency[1]. The receipt of a bribe, whether in money[2] or otherwise[3], is a breach of duty[4]. The motive of the donor is immaterial since there is an irrebuttable presumption that the gift was made with the intention that the agent should be influenced by it[5], and the court will not inquire whether the agent was influenced by the bribe in a way prejudicial to his principal's interest[6]. It is immaterial that the principal's interest is not involved[7].

Where, however, the principal leaves the agent to look to the third party for his remuneration, or knows that he will receive something from the third party, the agent is entitled to receive and retain such commissions as are usual and customary, and the principal cannot object merely on the ground that he was unaware of the actual amount thereof[8].

1 An undisclosed but realistic possibility of a conflict of interest is a breach of the agent's duty of good faith to his principal. All the agent has to do to avoid being in breach of duty is to make full

disclosure: see *Imageview Management Ltd v Jack* [2009] EWCA Civ 63 at [6]–[7], [2009] 2 All ER 666 (player's agent failed to disclose side deal with football club).

2 *Re Canadian Oil Works Corpn, Hay's Case* (1875) 10 Ch App 593; *Boston Deep Sea Fishing and Ice Co v Ansell* (1888) 39 ChD 339, CA; *Fyffes Group Ltd v Templeman* [2000] 2 Lloyd's Rep 643.

3 *Nant-y-glo and Blaina Ironworks Co v Grave* (1878) 12 ChD 738; *Re Morvah Consols Tin Mining Co, McKay's Case* (1875) 2 ChD 1, CA.

4 The agent owes a duty of undivided loyalty to the principal (unless the latter has given his informed consent to some less demanding standard of duty): *European Ventures LLP v Mankarious* [2014] UKSC 45 at [33], [2015] AC 250, [2014] 4 All ER 79. The whole reason the agent should not have accepted the bribe or commission is that it puts him in conflict with his duty to his principal: *European Ventures LLP v Mankarious* at [37].

5 *Hovenden & Sons v Millhoff* (1900) 83 LT 41, CA; *Re A Debtor (No 229 of 1927)* [1927] 2 Ch 367, CA; *Industries and General Mortgage Co Ltd v Lewis* [1949] 2 All ER 573, [1949] WN 333; *Taylor v Walker* [1958] 1 Lloyd's Rep 490.

6 *Harrington v Victoria Graving Dock Co* (1878) 3 QBD 549.

7 *A-G v Goddard* (1929) 98 LJKB 743; *Reading v A-G* [1951] AC 507, [1951] 1 All ER 617, HL.

8 *Great Western Insurance Co of New York v Cunliffe* (1874) 9 Ch App 525; *Baring v Stanton* (1876) 3 ChD 502, CA; *Lord Norreys v Hodgson* (1897) 13 TLR 421; *Bow's Emporium Ltd v A R Brett & Co* (1927) 44 TLR 194, HL. Cf *E Green & Son Ltd v G Tughan & Co* (1913) 30 TLR 64; and see *Fyffes Group Ltd v Templeman* [2000] 2 Lloyd's Rep 643.

95. Effect of receipt of bribe by agent.

On discovering the receipt of a bribe the principal may instantly dismiss the agent[1], and, if he has already been dismissed, may justify the dismissal on that ground, even though the bribery was not discovered till after the dismissal[2]. The agent's duty is to deliver up to his principal the benefit which he has obtained and not simply to pay compensation for having obtained it in excess of his authority[3]. Any benefit acquired by an agent as a result of his agency and in breach of his fiduciary duty is held on trust for the principal[4].

Once a conflict of interest is shown, the agent invariably loses his right to remuneration, notwithstanding that the principal may have received a benefit from the agent[5]. The agent forfeits any commission in respect of the transaction[6], and becomes liable to his principal for the amount of the bribe, if in money[7], or for the value of the property so received by him[8], such value being measured by the highest value which the property might have fetched whilst in his possession[9]. Interest also is payable from the date when the bribe was received[10]. In addition, the agent is liable, jointly and severally with the briber, for any loss actually sustained by the principal in consequence of any breach of duty on the agent's part[11]; and both he and the briber may be subject to criminal proceedings[12]. The principal is entitled to treat the transaction entered into as void ab initio[13].

1 See *Swale v Ipswich Tannery Ltd* (1906) 11 Com Cas 88; *Temperley v Blackrod Manufacturing Co Ltd* (1907) 71 JP Jo 341. Where the agent is also an employee, the statutory provisions as to notice periods do not affect the right to terminate the contract by reason of conduct which would apart from that Act entitle the other party to terminate: see the Employment Rights Act 1996 ss 86, 210, 211; and EMPLOYMENT vol 39 (2014) PARA 130; EMPLOYMENT vol 41 (2014) PARAS 735–736. The principal also has the right to avoid any contract or transaction entered into by the agent in consequence of, or in connection with the bribe: see PARA 140.

2 *Boston Deep Sea Fishing and Ice Co v Ansell* (1888) 39 ChD 339, CA; *Swale v Ipswich Tannery Co* (1906) 11 Com Cas 88. To accept a denial of guilt from an agent who has in fact accepted a bribe is not condonation: *Federal Supply and Cold Storage Co of South Africa v Angehrn and Piel* (1910) 80 LJPC 1. The proposition set out in the text to this note must presumably be taken not to apply where the agent is an employee of the principal, in which case the law relating to termination of employment (see EMPLOYMENT vol 41 (2014) PARA 722 et seq) applies.

3 *European Ventures LLP v Mankarious* [2014] UKSC 45 at [33], [2015] AC 250, [2014] 4 All ER 79.

4 *European Ventures LLP v Mankarious* [2014] UKSC 45 at [35], [46], [50], [2015] AC 250, [2014] 4 All ER 79 (overruling *Tyrrell v Bank of London* (1862) 10 HL Cas 26; *Metropolitan Bank v Heiron* (1880) 5 ExD 319, CA; *Lister & Co v Stubbs* (1890) 45 ChD 1, CA; *Powell and Thomas v Evan Jones & Co* [1905] 1 KB 11, CA; *Sinclair Investments (UK) Ltd v Versailles Trade Finance Ltd* [2011] EWCA Civ 347, [2012] Ch 453, [2011] 4 All ER 335).

5 *Imageview Management Ltd v Jack* [2009] EWCA Civ 63, [2009] 2 All ER 666 (player's agent profited from undisclosed side deal with football club). In such circumstances, one was concerned not merely with damages such as those for tort or breach contract, but with what the remedy should be when the agent had betrayed the trust reposed in him: *Imageview Management Ltd v Jack* at [50].

6 *Andrews v Ramsay & Co* [1903] 2 KB 635; *Price v Metropolitan House Investment and Agency Co Ltd* (1907) 23 TLR 630, CA. See also *E Green & Son Ltd v G Tughan & Co* (1913) 30 TLR 64.

7 *Salford Corpn v Lever* [1891] 1 QB 168, CA; *Re Canadian Oil Works Corpn, Hay's Case* (1875) 10 Ch App 593; *A-G v Goddard* (1929) 98 LJKB 743; *Reading v A-G* [1951] AC 507, [1951] 1 All ER 617, HL; *Mahesan v Malaysia Government Officers' Co-operative Housing Society Ltd* [1979] AC 374, [1978] 2 All ER 405, PC.

8 *Re Morvah Consols Tin Mining Co, McKay's Case* (1875) 2 ChD 1, CA; *Nant-y-glo and Blaina Ironworks Co v Grave* (1878) 12 ChD 738; *Re Caerphilly Colliery Co, Pearson's Case* (1877) 5 ChD 336, CA.

9 *Re Morvah Consols Tin Mining Co, McKay's Case* (1875) 2 ChD 1, CA.

10 *Boston Deep Sea Fishing and Ice Co v Ansell* (1888) 39 ChD 339, CA (at 5%); *Nant-y-glo and Blaina Ironworks Co v Grave* (1878) 12 ChD 738 (4%). Outside the field of agency the modern cases show a higher trend: *De Maurier (Jewels) Ltd v Bastian Insurance Co Ltd and Coronet Insurance Co* [1967] 2 Lloyd's Rep 550 (7%); *The Mecca* [1968] P 665, [1968] 2 All ER 731 (5½%); *Jefford v Gee* [1970] 2 QB 130, [1970] 1 All ER 1202, CA (6%). It is submitted that an award of interest against an unscrupulous agent would be at not less than a 'realistic rate' (see *Jefford v Gee*) for the time being.

11 *Salford Corpn v Lever* [1891] 1 QB 168, CA; *Morgan v Elford* (1876) 4 ChD 352, CA. The agent is not, however, liable for both the amount of the bribe and the loss sustained: *Mahesan v Malaysia Government Officer's Co-operative Housing Society Ltd* [1979] AC 374, [1978] 2 All ER 405, PC.

12 Ie for conspiracy to defraud (*R v Barber* (1887) 3 TLR 491), or under the Bribery Act 2010 (see CRIMINAL LAW vol 25 (2016) PARA 369 et seq).

13 *Logicrose Ltd v Southend United Football Club Ltd* [1988] 1 WLR 1256.

(vii) Estoppel in Respect of Rights and Title of Principal

96. Agent estopped from denying principal's rights.

Where a person has admittedly acted as agent on a principal's behalf[1] in any transaction, he is estopped from denying the rights which have accrued to his principal in consequence thereof, and from setting up any claims adverse thereto, whether in himself[2] or third parties[3].

This rule applies in particular in the case of goods which have been entrusted to him[4], or in respect of which he has acknowledged the title of his principal, whether in actual possession of them or not[5]. Where, however, the adverse claim is made by a third person, the agent may set up the latter's title, if he has actually handed over the goods to him or is acting by his authority and on his behalf[6], provided that he had no knowledge of the claim when he received the goods or attorned to his principal[7]. If he is acting as agent for both parties, he may elect between them[8].

1 *Sheridan v New Quay Co* (1858) 4 CBNS 618; *A-G v London Corpn* (1850) 2 Mac & G 247.
2 *Lyell v Kennedy* (1889) 14 App Cas 437, HL; *Williams v Pott* (1871) LR 12 Eq 149; *Moore v Peachey* (1891) 7 TLR 748.
3 *Eames v Hacon* (1881) 18 ChD 347, CA; *Dixon v Hammond* (1819) 2 B & Ald 310; *Blaustein v Maltz, Mitchell & Co* [1937] 2 KB 142, [1937] 1 All ER 497, CA.
4 *Zulueta v Vinent* (1852) 1 De GM & G 315.
5 *Henderson & Co v Williams* [1895] 1 QB 521, CA; *Evans and Evans v Nichol and Nichol* (1841) 4 Scott NR 43.

6   *Biddle v Bond* (1865) 6 B & S 225; *Rogers, Sons & Co v Lambert & Co* [1891] 1 QB 318, CA.
    The principle of these cases does not extend to money due on an account: see *Blaustein v Maltz,*
    Mitchell & Co [1937] 2 KB 142, [1937] 1 All ER 497, CA.
7   *Biddle v Bond* (1865) 6 B & S 225; *Re Sadler, ex p Davies* (1881) 19 ChD 86, CA.
8   *Shee v Clarkson* (1810) 12 East 507.

97. Agent cannot acquire title against principal.

An agent in possession of property as agent will not be permitted to deny that
his possession is that of his principal[1]. He is therefore estopped from setting up a
statutory title against the principal[2], or maintaining his own title as true owner
against the statutory title acquired by his principal through him[3]. If he purchases
land and has the legal estate conveyed to him, he will not be permitted to plead
the absence of a written declaration of trust[4], and, if he refuses to reconvey the
land to his principal, he will be considered to hold it in trust for his principal[5].
Similarly, if money is paid to him by a third person, he will not be permitted to set
up the illegality or nullity of the contract under which he received it[6].

1   The possession must be as agent: *White v Bayley* (1861) 10 CBNS 227; cf *Bell v Marsh* [1903] 1
    Ch 528, CA; *Markwick v Hardingham* (1880) 15 ChD 339, CA.
2   *Lyell v Kennedy* (1889) 14 App Cas 437, HL; and cf *Ward v Carttar* (1865) LR 1 Eq 29.
3   *Williams v Pott* (1871) LR 12 Eq 149.
4   A written declaration is normally required by the Law of Property Act 1925 s 53(1)(b) (see DEEDS
    AND OTHER INSTRUMENTS vol 32 (2012) PARAS 224, 347–348; TRUSTS AND POWERS vol 98
    (2013) PARAS 59, 532), although that requirement may not be used as an instrument of fraud
    (see *Rochefoucauld v Boustead* [1897] 1 Ch 196, CA; see also *Hodgson v Marks* [1971] Ch 892,
    [1970] 3 All ER 513; revsd on another point [1971] Ch 892, [1971] 2 All ER 684, CA).
5   *Longfield Parish Council v Robson* (1913) 29 TLR 357; and see PARA 78.
6   See PARA 86.

(viii) Committal of Defaulting Agent

98. Committal of defaulting agent.

Whenever an agent, who has received money on behalf of his principal in a
fiduciary capacity, fails to comply with an order of the court to pay over the
money, he becomes liable to committal, even though he has parted with the money
or become bankrupt or insolvent[1].

1   See the Debtors Act 1869 s 4; *Crowther v Elgood* (1887) 34 ChD 691, CA; and CONTEMPT OF
    COURT vol 22 (2012) PARA 88. Although not formally abolished, the remedy of attachment
    (referred to in the Debtors Act 1869) is now obsolete and all cases of criminal contempt are
    punishable by committal (as to which see CONTEMPT OF COURT vol 22 (2012) PARA 93 et seq).
    As to the criminal liability of an agent who misappropriates his principal's money or property see
    the Theft Act 1968 ss 1–7; and CRIMINAL LAW vol 25 (2016) PARA 315 et seq.

(ix) Co-agents and Sub-agents

99. Co-agents and sub-agents.

An agent is under no responsibility to his principal for the acts or defaults[1] of
his co-agents (except where they are his partners[2]) unless he expressly or tacitly
authorised such acts or defaults[3].

An agent is, however, liable for the acts[4] and defaults[5] of his sub-agents even though their employment was authorised by his principal[6], and he must account to his principal for all money received by them[7].

1   *Lucas v Fitzgerald* (1903) 20 TLR 16; *Land Credit Co of Ireland v Lord Fermoy* (1870) 5 Ch App 763; *Cullerne v London and Suburban General Permanent Building Society* (1890) 25 QBD 485, CA.
2   See *Hamlyn v John Houston & Co* [1903] 1 KB 81, CA. As to relations between partners see PARTNERSHIP vol 79 (2014) PARA 105 et seq.
3   *Cargill v Bower* (1878) 10 ChD 502.
4   *Re Mutual Aid Permanent Benefit Building Society, ex p James* (1883) 49 LT 530; *Swire v Francis* (1877) 3 App Cas 106, PC; but see the doubt expressed by Atkin LJ in *Thomas Cheshire & Co v Vaughan Bros & Co* [1920] 3 KB 240 at 259, CA.
5   *Collins v Griffin* (1734) Barnes 37; *Mackersy v Ramsays, Bonars & Co* (1843) 9 Cl & Fin 818, HL.
6   *Skinner & Co v Weguelin, Eddowes & Co* (1882) 1 Cab & El 12. This does not apply when there is privity of contract between the sub-agent and the principal: see PARAS 55–57.
7   *Matthews v Haydon* (1796) 2 Esp 509; *Mackersy v Ramsays, Bonars & Co* (1843) 9 Cl & Fin 818, HL; *Re Mitchell, Mitchell v Mitchell* (1884) 54 LJ Ch 342.

(3) RIGHTS OF AGENT AGAINST PRINCIPAL

(i) Basic Principles

100. Derivation of agent's rights against principal.

The rights of an agent against his principal flow from the principles:

(1)   that an agent, as the representative of his principal and acting wholly on his behalf, is entitled to be indemnified for such liabilities incurred and losses suffered as were in contemplation when the agency was undertaken, or as were stipulated by the contract of agency[1]; and

(2)   that, where he is an agent for reward, his principal must not wrongfully hinder his opportunity of earning the reward[2].

In the light of these main principles the agent's rights are to be discovered by reference to the terms, express or implied, of the contract between him and his principal[3]. The rights of an agent are also now varied and supplemented in relation to certain commercial agents[4].

1   See PARAS 112–113.
2   See PARA 109.
3   See generally PARA 100 et seq.
4   Ie where the Commercial Agents (Council Directive) Regulations 1993, SI 1993/3053, apply. As to the meaning of 'commercial agent', and as to where those Regulations apply, see PARA 73. As to their effect on the rights of agents see PARA 102 et seq.

101. Agent's right to account.

An agent has a right to have an account taken, and where the accounts are of a simple nature they can be taken in an ordinary claim in the Queen's Bench Division[1]. Where the accounts are more complicated, the claim will generally proceed in the Chancery Division[2].

1   *Padwick v Hurst* (1854) 18 Beav 575. As to claims regarding accounts generally see CPR PD 40A—*Accounts, Inquiries, etc*; and CIVIL PROCEDURE vol 12A (2015) PARAS 1250–1055. For the right to sue on an account stated see CONTRACT vol 22 (2012) PARAS 611–612. As to the

reopening of settled accounts see EQUITABLE JURISDICTION vol 47 (2014) PARA 53. For a consideration of the principal's right to an account against the agent see PARA 88.
2   See PARA 88.

(ii) Agent's Remuneration

102. Contractual basis of right.
An agent has no right to receive remuneration from his principal unless there is a contract, express or implied, to that effect[1]. Where the parties have made an express contract for remuneration, the amount of remuneration and the conditions under which it will become payable must be ascertained by reference to the terms of that contract; no terms may be implied which would be inconsistent with such express agreement[2]. If money has been advanced against commission but the commission falls short of the advance, the difference must be repaid[3].

In the absence of an express contract on the subject, a contract to pay reasonable remuneration may be implied from the circumstances of the case[4]. In awarding such remuneration the court may have regard to previous negotiations between the parties[5] or trade custom[6]; but, where the commission is left to the discretion of the principal, the court cannot determine either the basis or the rate of commission and therefore in the absence of payment by the principal, no commission will be recoverable[7].

In the case of a commercial agent[8], in the absence of agreement as to remuneration between the parties, the agent is entitled to the remuneration that commercial agents appointed for the goods forming the subject of his agency contract are customarily allowed in the place where he carried on his activities and, if there is no such customary practice, to reasonable remuneration taking into account all the aspects of the transaction[9].

The mere fact of employment of a professional agent itself raises the presumption of a contract to remunerate him[10], the amount of the remuneration and the conditions of its payment being ascertainable from the usages of his profession[11]. He is not, however, entitled to any further or other remuneration than the usages of the profession justify, unless he does work not strictly ancillary to the agency, in which case, as in the case of a non-professional agent, the implied contract is to pay reasonable remuneration, having regard to the circumstances of the particular case[12]. Thus, where an estate agent is employed to sell property subject to a mortgage, the agent's commission is calculated not only on the value of the equity of redemption but also on the amount of the mortgage, as the agent is employed to find someone who will take over the equity of redemption and indemnify his principal in respect of his liabilities under the mortgage[13].

1   *Reeve v Reeve* (1858) 1 F & F 280; *Roberts v Smith* (1859) 4 H & N 315; and cf *Taylor v Brewer* (1813) 1 M & S 290 with *Bryant v Flight* (1839) 5 M & W 114. No barrister can make a binding contract for remuneration in respect of professional services: see *Kennedy v Broun* (1863) 13 CBNS 677; and LEGAL PROFESSIONS vol 66 (2015) PARA 927.
2   *Barnett v Isaacson* (1888) 4 TLR 645; *Green v Mules* (1861) 30 LJCP 343; *Alder v Boyle* (1847) 4 CB 635; *Lott v Outhwaite* (1893) 10 TLR 76, CA; *Broad v Thomas* (1830) 7 Bing 99; *Read v Rann* (1830) 10 B & C 438; *Howard, Houlder & Partners Ltd v Manx Isles Steamship Co Ltd* [1923] 1 KB 110; *Harley & Co v Nagata* (1917) 34 TLR 124; *Moor Line Ltd v Louis Dreyfus & Co* [1918] 1 KB 89, CA; *Burrough's Adding Machine Ltd v Aspinall* (1925) 41 TLR 276, CA; *Jones v Lowe* [1945] KB 73, [1945] 1 All ER 194. The contract may, however, be interpreted by reference to usages which are not inconsistent with it: see PARA 44.
3   *Rivoli Hats Ltd v Gooch* [1953] 2 All ER 823, [1953] 1 WLR 1190; cf *Clayton Newbury Ltd v Findlay* [1953] 2 All ER 826n [1953] 1 WLR 1195n.

4 *Bryant v Flight* (1839) 5 M & W 114. See also the Commercial Agents (Council Directive) Regulations 1993, SI 1993/3053, reg 6; and the text and notes 8, 9.
5 *Way v Latilla* [1937] 3 All ER 759, HL, applying *Scarisbrick v Parkinson* (1869) 20 LT 175.
6 *Bower v Jones* (1831) 8 Bing 65.
7 *Kofi Sunkersette Obu v A Strauss & Co Ltd* [1951] AC 243, PC. This does not apply where there is a binding promise to pay a reasonable sum: *Powell v Braun* [1954] 1 All ER 484, [1954] 1 WLR 401, CA. See also *Re Wolfe, Heller v Wolfe* [1952] 2 All ER 545 (assessment by court of fees for auctioneers acting in sale by court where no scale fees applicable). Scales of charges laid down by professional bodies if not expressly or impliedly incorporated into the contract may indicate what a reasonable sum would be. In *Withey Robinson (a firm) v Edwards* [1986] 1 EGLR 32, CA, a firm of surveyors was held to be entitled to remuneration on a quantum meruit basis even though it had sought initially to apply the scale fees of the relevant professional body.
8 Ie a commercial agent to whom the Commercial Agents (Council Directive) Regulations 1993, SI 1993/3053, apply: see PARA 73. As to the meaning of 'commercial agent' for these purposes see PARA 73. As to the form and amount of remuneration see regs 7–12; and PARA 106 et seq.
9 Commercial Agents (Council Directive) Regulations 1993, SI 1993/3053, reg 6(1). This is without prejudice to the application of any enactment or rule of law concerning the level of remuneration: reg 6(2).
10 *Miller v Beal* (1879) 27 WR 403; *Manson v Baillie* (1855) 2 Macq 80, HL; *Turner v Reeve* (1901) 17 TLR 592. Cf *Corbin v Stewart* (1911) 28 TLR 99 (where the general rule was displaced).
11 *Broad v Thomas* (1830) 7 Bing 99; *Read v Rann* (1830) 10 B & C 438; *Moor Line v Louis Dreyfus & Co* [1918] 1 KB 89, CA; *Harley & Co v Nagata* (1917) 34 TLR 124; and see the cases cited in note 10.
12 *Williamson v Hine Bros* [1891] 1 Ch 390; *Marshall v Parsons* (1841) 9 C & P 656.
13 See *Way and Walker Ltd v Ryde* [1944] 1 All ER 9, CA.

103. Remuneration must be earned.

The following rules, derived from common law, must be read as being subject to legislative provision relating to commercial agents[1], where such provision applies[2].

In order to entitle the agent to receive his remuneration, he must have carried out that which he bargained to do[3], and all conditions imposed by the contract must have been fulfilled[4], unless the principal by his conduct estops himself from relying on them[5]. He is not, however, deprived of his right to remuneration, where he has done all he undertook to do[6], by the fact that the transaction is not beneficial to the principal[7], or that it has subsequently fallen through[8], whether by some act[9] or default[10] of the principal, or otherwise[11], unless there is a provision of the contract, express[12] or implied[13], to that effect, or unless the agent was himself the cause of his services being abortive[14]; nor does he necessarily lose his right to remuneration through making a bona fide mistake even if it amounts to a breach of duty entitling the principal to compensation against him[15].

An agent employed to achieve a particular purpose will not be entitled to commission unless he is the effective cause of the purpose being achieved[16]. An agent employed to sell property on commission who fails to do so but agrees to buy from his principal, does not earn his commission in the absence of express agreement[17]. To be an effective cause the agent need not necessarily complete or take part in the negotiations[18]. An agent who is to be remunerated by a commission on the price paid by the purchaser does not lose his right to remuneration if the vendor varies the contract by selling at a price lower than the lowest price stated to the agent[19]. Where, however, an agent is to be paid a commission upon a sum obtained or paid or earned for the principal, the agent is not entitled to remuneration until the principal has received the money[20]. Similarly, an agent cannot recover as upon quantum meruit for work or labour when he has failed to comply with the terms imposed upon him[21].

1 Ie the Commercial Agents (Council Directive) Regulations 1993, SI 1993/3053. As to the meaning of 'commercial agent' for these purposes see PARA 73.

2 As to where the Commercial Agents (Council Directive) Regulations 1993, SI 1993/3053, apply see PARA 73.

3 *Bull v Price* (1831) 7 Bing 237; *Martin v Perry and Daw* [1931] 2 KB 310 (commission payable 'on sale being effected'). Auctioneers may be entitled to their commission on an abortive sale: see *Skinner v Andrews and Hall* (1910) 26 TLR 340, CA (AUCTION vol 4 (2011) PARA 24), not following *Peacock v Freeman* (1888) 4 TLR 541, CA; cf *John Meacock & Co v Abrahams* [1956] 3 All ER 660, [1956] 1 WLR 1463, CA; and the cases cited in notes 17, 20. The original bargain may of course be varied: see *Harrods Ltd v Geneen* [1938] 4 All ER 493, CA (where agent instructed to find tenant to pay rent in advance, and principal accepted, initially, tenant to pay in arrear, agent still entitled to commission after principal later rejected tenant). See also *Bell Houses Ltd v City Wall Properties Ltd* (1967) 205 Estates Gazette 535, CA (no stage reached in negotiations for loan at which procuration fee payable under terms of agreement and no sufficient evidence of variation of terms of agreement).

4 *Chapman v Winson* (1904) 91 LT 17, CA; *Kirk v Evans* (1889) 6 TLR 9 (conditions imposed by usage of trade). See also the cases cited in notes 20, 21.

5 *Norwegian American Cruises A/S v Paul Mundy, The Vistafjord* [1988] 2 Lloyd's Rep 343, CA.

6 *Skinner v Andrews and Hall* (1910) 26 TLR 340, CA; *Price, Davies & Co v Smith* (1929) 141 LT 490, CA; cf *Howard, Houlder & Partners Ltd v Manx Isles Steamship Co Ltd* [1923] 1 KB 110.

7 *Green v Lucas* (1875) 33 LT 584, CA; *Moir v Marten* (1891) 7 TLR 330.

8 *Fuller v Eames* (1892) 8 TLR 278; *Harris v Petherick* (1878) 39 LT 543.

9 *Horford v Wilson* (1807) 1 Taunt 12; *Platt v Depree* (1893) 9 TLR 194; *Passingham v King* (1898) 14 TLR 392, CA.

10 *Fisher v Drewett* (1878) 48 LJQB 32, CA; *Roberts v Barnard* (1884) Cab & El 336; *Lockwood v Levick* (1860) 8 CBNS 603; *Vulcan Car Agency v Fiat Motors Ltd* (1915) 32 TLR 73. See also *Blake & Co v Sohn* [1969] 3 All ER 123, [1969] 1 WLR 1412 (default means wilful refusal or deceit and not mere inability to complete).

11 *Fuller v Eames* (1892) 8 TLR 278; cf *Re Sovereign Life Assurance Co, Salter's Claim* (1891) 7 TLR 602.

12 *Alder v Boyle* (1847) 4 CB 635; *Bull v Price* (1831) 7 Bing 237; *Clack v Wood* (1882) 9 QBD 276, CA; and cf *Lara v Hill* (1863) 15 CBNS 45.

13 *Read v Rann* (1830) 10 B & C 438; *Berthoud v Schweder & Co* (1915) 31 TLR 404.

14 *Dalton v Irwin* (1830) 4 C & P 289; *Hill v Featherstonhaugh* (1831) 7 Bing 569.

15 *Keppel v Wheeler* [1927] 1 KB 577, CA; *Harrods Ltd v Lemon* [1931] 2 KB 157, CA.

16 *Wilkinson v Martin* (1837) 8 C & P 1; *Gillow & Co v Lord Aberdare* (1892) 9 TLR 12; *Chamberlain and Willows v HBS (Trust) Ltd* (1962) 184 Estates Gazette 849, CA. See further PARA 105.

17 *Hocker v Waller* (1924) 29 Com Cas 296. A sole agency for sale does not prohibit the principal from selling directly, and if the principal does so sell the agent will not be entitled to damages for lost commission: *Sadler v Whittaker* (1953) 162 Estates Gazette 404, CA; cf *Snelgrove v Ellringham Colliery Co* (1881) 45 JP 408. As to estate agents' commission see generally PARA 104.

18 *Thompson, Rippon & Co v Thomas* (1895) 11 TLR 304, CA.

19 *Price, Davies & Co v Smith* (1929) 141 LT 490, CA; and see *Allan v Leo Lines Ltd* [1957] 1 Lloyd's Rep 127.

20 *Bull v Price* (1831) 7 Bing 237; *White v Turnbull, Martin & Co* (1898) 3 Com Cas 183, CA; *Foster's Agency Ltd v Romaine* [1916] WN 231, CA; *L French & Co Ltd v Leeston Shipping Co Ltd* [1922] 1 AC 451, HL; *Knight, Frank and Rutley v Gordon* (1923) 39 TLR 399; *Howard, Houlder & Partners Ltd v Manx Isles Steamship Co Ltd* [1923] 1 KB 110; *Price, Davies & Co v Smith* (1929) 141 LT 490, CA; but cf *Vulcan Car Agency v Fiat Motors Ltd* (1915) 32 TLR 73.

21 *Martin v Tucker* (1885) 1 TLR 655; *Barnett v Isaacson* (1888) 4 TLR 645; *Lott v Outhwaite* (1893) 10 TLR 76, CA; *Howard, Houlder & Partners Ltd v Manx Isles Steamship Co Ltd* [1923] 1 KB 110; *Bartlett v Farmer and Jelley* (1965) 194 Estates Gazette 279.

104. Estate agent's commission.

A contract by which an owner of property puts it into the hands of an agent for letting or sale amounts to a promise binding upon the principal to pay a sum of money upon the happening of a specified event through the instrumentality of the agent[1]. It is not a contract of employment in the ordinary meaning of those words for, except where he is appointed as sole agent[2], the agent is under no obligation to do anything, and consequently no term can be implied in such a contract that the principal will not so act as to prevent the agent from earning his commission, as by disposing of the property himself or through another agent or by breaking off negotiations before the happening of the specified event[3]. Once, however, an agent undertakes work and enters upon it, he has a duty to take reasonable care in connection with it[4]. What the event is, on the happening of which the money is payable, must depend upon the construction of the contract[5] and the clarity with which the event is defined by the contract[6] and there are no special rules of construction applicable to estate agency contracts. Normally, when that event is the finding of a purchaser, no claim for commission can arise until the purchase price has been received or would have been received but for the default of the principal[7]. Commission is payable upon completion of a sale to a purchaser introduced by the agent notwithstanding the fact that instructions were withdrawn beforehand[8]. If the principal enters into a binding contract[9] with the purchaser, and the latter is able and willing to complete, a fact which the agent must establish[10], and the principal refuses to complete, the commission is payable[11]. If, however, the sale is not completed owing to the default of the purchaser, no commission is payable[12], even though the deposit has been paid and forfeited[13], for the principal is not bound to bring a claim against the defaulting purchaser[14]. No commission is payable where estate agents offer the property at a sum below the price agreed with the vendor[15]. In the event of the principal succeeding on a claim for specific performance or damages, commission will be payable[16].

If the agent desires to bind the principal to pay commission, not only on sale but on the introduction of a person who makes an offer to purchase, as contrasted with one who actually buys, he must use clear and unequivocal language to that effect[17]. In those cases the offer must be a firm offer, which by acceptance will give rise to a contractual relationship[18]. An offer made subject to contract[19], or subject to a condition of whose fulfilment the offeror is the sole arbiter[20], or subject to some uncertain event[21], will not suffice. In this case also the offeror must be ready, able and willing to complete[22], and if before acceptance of the offer he withdraws, no commission is payable. If the principal withdraws his instructions at a time when the agent has found a person who is able and willing, and such ability and willingness are unequivocally clear, commission may be payable[23]. An agent cannot, however, secure such commission by registration of a charge on the deposit and purchase money as a land charge, for his right relates only to the money[24].

1   *Luxor (Eastbourne) Ltd v Cooper* [1941] AC 108, [1941] 1 All ER 33, HL.
2   Where the appointment is as a sole agent, the agent is under an implied obligation to use his best endeavours to sell the property, and this is sufficient consideration to support the contract, and the agent would be in breach of his contract if he did not do something, although he might not be successful: see *E Christopher & Co v Essig* [1948] WN 461; *Mendoza & Co v Bell* (1952) 159 Estates Gazette 372.
3   *Luxor (Eastbourne) Ltd v Cooper* [1941] AC 108, [1941] 1 All ER 33, HL, approving the dissenting judgment of Scrutton LJ in *George Trollope & Sons v Martyn Bros* [1934] 2 KB 436, CA, and overruling *George Trollope & Sons v Caplan* [1936] 2 KB 382, [1936] 2 All ER 842, CA. See also *Sadler v Whittaker* (1953) 162 Estates Gazette 404, CA ('sole agency' agreement construed contra proferentem); and PARA 109 note 10.
4   *PG Prebble & Co v West* (1969) 113 Sol Jo 657, CA (duty to communicate a reasonable offer to the client); *John D Wood & Co (Residential & Agricultural Land) Ltd v Knatchbull* [2002] EWHC 2822 (QB), [2003] 1 EGLR 33, [2002] All ER (D) 232 (Dec) (duty to communicate to client vendor information as to selling price of neighbouring property).
5   *James v Smith* (1921) [1931] 2 KB 317n, CA; *Luxor (Eastbourne) Ltd v Cooper* [1941] AC 108, [1941] 1 All ER 33, HL; *Chamberlain and Willows v HBS (Trust) Ltd* (1962) 184 Estates Gazette 849, CA; *FP Rolfe & Co v George* (1969) 210 Estates Gazette 455, CA (agent called in to negotiate

entitled to commission). See also *McCulloch Co of Canada v Lloyd G Howe Industrial Real Estate Ltd* [1960] OWN 224, 24 DLR (2d) 57, Ont HC (commission payable 'on transaction'; transaction held to mean mutually enforceable agreement, so no commission payable by purchaser where agreement binding on vendor only); *Christie, Owen and Davies Ltd v Rapacioli* [1974] QB 781, [1974] 2 All ER 311, CA; *Harwood (t/a RSBS Group) v Smith* [1998] 1 EGLR 5, [1998] 11 EG 178, CA (whether transaction arranged by the seller fell within the parameters of the sole selling agreement which had been terminated by the seller) (doubted in *G and S Properties v Francis* 2001 SLT 934, Ct of Sess); *Estafnous v London & Leeds Business Centres Ltd* [2011] EWCA Civ 1157, [2012] 1 P & CR DG4 (sale of property did not cover acquisition of shares in holding company that owned the property).

6   *Midgley Estates Ltd v Hand* [1952] 2 QB 432, [1952] 1 All ER 1394, CA; *Sheggia v Gradwell* [1963] 3 All ER 114, [1963] 1 WLR 1049, CA; *Foxtons Ltd v Thesleff* [2005] EWCA Civ 514, [2005] 2 EGLR 29. If the parties have failed to specify the 'trigger event' upon which commission will become payable, they may not have concluded a binding contract at all. In the absence of a valid contract, the court cannot decide what additional terms, if any, require to be implied: *Wells v Devani* [2016] EWCA Civ 1106, [2017] 2 WLR 1391 (applying *Marks & Spencer plc v BNP Paribas Securities Services Trust Co (Jersey) Ltd* [2015] UKSC 72, [2016] AC 742, [2016] 4 All ER 441).

7   *Jones v Lowe* [1945] KB 73, [1945] 1 All ER 194; *Fowler v Bratt* [1950] 2 KB 96, [1950] 1 All ER 662, CA; *McCallum v Hicks* [1950] 2 KB 271, [1950] 1 All ER 864, CA; *Dennis Reed Ltd v Goody* [1950] 2 KB 277, [1950] 1 All ER 919, CA; *Jaques v Lloyd D George & Partners Ltd* [1968] 2 All ER 187, [1968] 1 WLR 625, CA; *Blake & Co v Sohn* [1969] 3 All ER 123, [1969] 1 WLR 1412 (commission is normally payable from the purchase price so in the absence of agreement or default a sale is a condition precedent to payment); cf *Brodie Marshall & Co (Hotel Division) Ltd v Sharer* [1988] 1 EGLR 21 (example of such an agreement); *Marcan Shipping (London) v Polish Steamship Co, The Manifest Lipkowy* [1988] 2 Lloyd's Rep 171; *WA Ellis Services Ltd v Wood* [1993] 2 EGLR 24, [1993] 31 EG 78 (no implied term that commission payable directly out of proceeds of sale held by vendor's solicitors); *Connell Estate Agents (a firm) v Begej* [1993] 2 EGLR 35, [1993] 39 EG 123, CA (property sold partly for cash and partly in part exchange for another property; commission payable on total value of property sold).

8   *Robinson Scammell & Co v Ansell* [1985] 2 EGLR 41, CA (instructions withdrawn because agent, acting in good faith, failed to consult principals before communicating with purchasers). Where two agents send particulars to the eventual purchaser, the effective cause of the sale is the agent who had succeeded in awakening the purchaser's interest at the opportune moment: *Bentleys Estate Agents Ltd v Granix Ltd* [1989] 2 EGLR 21. See also *Chesterfield & Co Ltd v Zahid* [1989] 2 EGLR 24; and *Brodie Marshall & Co (Hotel Division) Ltd v Sharer* [1988] 1 EGLR 21. See further *Peter Yates & Co v Bullock* [1990] 2 EGLR 24, [1990] 37 EG 75, CA (property sold through second agent to purchaser introduced by first agent); *Day Morris Associates v Voyce* [2003] EWCA Civ 189, [2003] All ER (D) 368 (Feb) (property sold directly by husband, after divorce proceedings, to purchaser previously introduced by estate agent in dealings with wife; commission payable); *Fleurets Ltd v Dashwood* [2007] EWHC 1610 (QB), [2007] 28 EG 120 (property sold through second agency following withdrawal of instructions); *Foxtons Ltd v Pelkey Bicknell* [2008] EWCA Civ 419, [2008] 17 EG 163 (CS) (first agent introduced purchaser to property but second agent held to be the effective cause of sale).

9   A contract unenforceable for lack of appropriate formalities is not a binding contract (*Bavin v Bunney* [1950] WN 181), nor is a contract which the intending purchaser is entitled to rescind on the grounds of innocent misrepresentation (*Gregory v Fearn* [1953] 2 All ER 559, [1953] 1 WLR 974, CA; *Peter Long & Partners v Burns* [1956] 3 All ER 207, [1956] 1 WLR 1083, CA). Commission may, however, be payable even though the contract is not specifically enforceable, if a claim for damages will lie: *Sheggia v Gradwell* [1963] 3 All ER 114, [1963] 1 WLR 1049, CA.

10   *Martin v Perry and Daw* [1931] 2 KB 310; *James v Smith* (1921) [1931] 2 KB 317n, CA; *Dennis Reed Ltd v Nicholls* [1948] 2 All ER 914.

11   *Luxor (Eastbourne) Ltd v Cooper* [1941] AC 108, [1941] 1 All ER 33, HL; *Fowler v Bratt* [1950] 2 KB 96, [1950] 1 All ER 662; *Dennis Reed Ltd v Goody* [1950] 2 KB 277, [1950] 1 All ER 919, CA; *John E Trinder & Partners v Haggis* [1951] WN 416, CA.

12   *Martin v Perry and Daw* [1931] 2 KB 310; *James v Smith* (1921) [1931] 2 KB 317n, CA; *Musson v Moxley* [1936] 1 All ER 64; *Poole v Clarke & Co* [1945] 2 All ER 445.

13   *Boots v E Christopher & Co* [1952] 1 KB 89, [1951] 2 All ER 1045, CA.

14   *Dennis Reed Ltd v Goody* [1950] 2 KB 277, [1950] 1 All ER 919, CA; *Boots v E Christopher & Co* [1952] 1 KB 89, [1951] 2 All ER 1045, CA.

15   *Spiers v Taylor* (1984) 271 Estates Gazette 196, CA.

16 *Boots v E Christopher & Co* [1952] 1 KB 89, [1951] 2 All ER 1045, CA. Where, however, the agent is also in breach, for example by failure to take a deposit from the prospective purchaser, he will not be entitled to commission: see *Columbus v Williamson & Co Ltd* [1969] NZLR 708, NZ CA.

17 *Luxor (Eastbourne) Ltd v Cooper* [1941] AC 108, [1941] 1 All ER 33, HL; *Jones v Lowe* [1945] KB 73, [1945] 1 All ER 194; *Dennis Reed Ltd v Goody* [1950] 2 KB 277, [1950] 1 All ER 919, CA. For cases where it was held that this was the effect of the contract see *Giddys v Horsfall* [1947] 1 All ER 460; *Dennis Reed Ltd v Nicholls* [1948] 2 All ER 914; *Bennett & Partners v Millett* [1949] 1 KB 362, [1948] 2 All ER 929. In *EP Nelson & Co v Rolfe* [1950] 1 KB 139, [1949] 2 All ER 584, CA, it was assumed that this was the effect of the contract; see the explanation in *Graham and Scott (Southgate) Ltd v Oxlade* [1950] 2 KB 257, [1950] 1 All ER 856, CA; *Dennis Reed Ltd v Goody*; and *Midgley Estates Ltd v Hand* [1952] 2 QB 432, [1952] 1 All ER 1394, CA. See also *Ackroyd & Sons v Hasan* [1960] 2 QB 144, [1960] 2 All ER 254, CA; *Lucas & Sons v Mayne* (1954) 164 Estates Gazette 441; *Drewery v Ware-Lane* [1960] 3 All ER 529, [1960] 1 WLR 1204, CA; *Foxtons Ltd v Thesleff* [2005] EWCA Civ 514, [2005] 2 EGLR 29. Cf *Sheggia v Gradwell* [1963] 3 All ER 114, [1963] 1 WLR 1049, CA; *Bartlett v Farmer and Jelley* (1965) 194 Estates Gazette 279. See also *Jaques v Lloyd D George & Partners Ltd* [1968] 2 All ER 187, [1968] 1 WLR 625, CA, where the meaning of a clause relating to commission was misrepresented to the principal and was so uncertain that it was held unenforceable. See also *Lordsgate Properties Ltd v Balcombe* [1985] 1 EGLR 20 (vendor held liable for commission to two different agents on different bases).

18 *Bennett, Walden & Co v Wood* [1950] 2 All ER 134, CA. See also *Ackroyd & Sons v Hasan* [1960] 2 QB 144, [1960] 2 All ER 254, CA; *Bartlett v Farmer and Jelley* (1965) 194 Estates Gazette 279. It is not necessary, however, for the vendor to bring a claim for specific performance for the agent to be entitled to commission: *Boots v E Christopher & Co* [1952] 1 KB 89, [1951] 2 All ER 1045, CA.

19 See *Graham and Scott (Southgate) Ltd v Oxlade* [1950] 2 KB 257, [1950] 1 All ER 856, CA; *Dennis Reed Ltd v Goody* [1950] 2 KB 277, [1950] 1 All ER 919, CA; *Christie, Owen and Davies Ltd v Stockton* [1953] 2 All ER 1149, [1953] 1 WLR 1353. Cf *Ackroyd & Sons v Hasan* [1960] 2 QB 144, [1960] 2 All ER 254, CA (offer originally made subject to contract had become unconditional, but no commission allowed because vendor did not accept offer). See also *George A Woodman & Sons v Linden* [1957] 1 All ER 365n, (1956) 167 Estates Gazette 384, CA; *Martin Gale and Wright v Buswell* (1961) 105 Sol Jo 466, CA; *Beresford (St James) Ltd v Howard (Kensington) Ltd* (1965) 193 Estates Gazette 439.

20 *Graham and Scott (Southgate) Ltd v Oxlade* [1950] 2 KB 257, [1950] 1 All ER 856, CA (subject to a satisfactory survey).

21 *Murdoch Lownie Ltd v Newman* [1949] 2 All ER 783 (subject to mortgage being obtained).

22 *Dennis Reed Ltd v Goody* [1950] 2 KB 277, [1950] 1 All ER 919, CA. Ability to complete is not confined to financial ability: *Dellafiora v Lester* [1962] 3 All ER 393, [1962] 1 WLR 1208, CA (where after contract the landlord's consent to assignment was refused). Whether a purchaser is willing and able is a question of fact: *AL Atkinson Ltd v O'Neil and Bland & Co (Investments) Ltd* (1961) 105 Sol Jo 1067, CA. See also *AL Wilkinson Ltd v Brown* [1966] 1 All ER 509, [1966] 1 WLR 194, CA (offer conditional on purchaser selling own house); cf *Sheggia v Gradwell* [1963] 3 All ER 114, [1963] 1 WLR 1049, CA; *Martin Gale and Wright v Buswell* (1961) 105 Sol Jo 466, CA.

23 *EP Nelson & Co v Rolfe* [1950] 1 KB 139, [1949] 2 All ER 584, CA; *John E Trinder & Partners v Haggis* [1951] WN 416, CA. This does not apply where the commission is only payable on the acceptance of an offer by a willing and able purchaser: see *Christie, Owen and Davies Ltd v Stockton* [1953] 2 All ER 1149, [1953] 1 WLR 1353; *Christie, Owen and Davies Ltd v Rapacioli* [1974] QB 781, [1974] 2 All ER 311, CA (commission payable on introduction of person ready, able and willing to purchase at acceptable price; price agreed but vendor withdrew before contract; vendor liable).

24 *Georgiades v Edward Wolfe & Co Ltd* [1965] Ch 487, [1964] 3 All ER 433, CA.

105. Transactions in respect of which the agent may claim remuneration.

The following rules, derived from common law, must be read as being subject to legislative provision relating to commercial agents[1], where such provision applies[2].

Remuneration can be claimed by the agent only on transactions which are the direct consequence of the agency[3]. It is not necessary that the agent should actually complete the transaction[4], but he must show that it was brought about as the direct result of his intervention[5]. It is not sufficient to show that it would not have been entered into but for his services, if it resulted from them only as a casual or remote consequence[6]. It follows therefore that, where several agents are concerned in negotiating a transaction between the principal and a particular third party, the agent entitled to remuneration is not necessarily the agent who first introduces the business to him, but the agent who is the effective cause of the transaction being completed[7]. An agent who introduces a property to a prospective lessee who then negotiates the lease through the lessor's agent may claim commission in respect of the work he has done on a quantum meruit basis[8].

The rule that an agent is entitled to remuneration when his intervention was the effective cause in bringing about the transaction between the principal and the third party is exemplified in cases where an agent has been held entitled to a commission upon sale to a purchaser introduced by him, or through him by other agents[9], although the sale was effected directly between the principal and the third party[10], at a lower price than the minimum stated to the agent[11], or on terms which the agent had advised the principal not to accept[12]. The rule that the agent must be the effective cause can be negated by the express words of the contract[13].

If the agent is only an agent to let, a subsequent sale to the tenant does not entitle the agent to a commission[14]; but it is otherwise if an agent, instructed to sell or let, has let with an option to purchase and the option is exercised[15].

1 Ie the Commercial Agents (Council Directive) Regulations 1993, SI 1993/3053. As to the meaning of 'commercial agent' for these purposes see PARA 73.

2 See PARA 106. As to where the Commercial Agents (Council Directive) Regulations 1993, SI 1993/3053, apply see PARA 73.

3 *Tribe v Taylor* (1876) 1 CPD 505; *Gibson v Crick* (1862) 1 H & C 142; *Toulmin v Millar* (1887) 12 App Cas 746, HL; *Curtis v Nixon* (1871) 24 LT 706; *Thompson v British Berna Motor Lorries Ltd* (1917) 33 TLR 187; *Coles v Enoch* [1939] 3 All ER 327, CA. The Commercial Agents (Council Directive) Regulations 1993, SI 1993/3053, impose analogous requirements concerning the commercial agent's entitlement to commission on transactions concluded both during (see reg 7(1)(a)) and following the termination (see reg 8(a)) of the agency contract, and also provide for the time at which payment is due and the extinction of the right to commission: see regs 7–11; and PARA 106. Notably, reg 8(a) demands that after termination a transaction resulting from the commercial agent's intervention must have been 'mainly attributable' to his efforts. In *Monk v Largo Foods Ltd* [2016] EWHC 1837 (Comm) at [112] it was suggested that 'mainly attributable' imposes a heightened causation requirement. See also *Tigana Ltd v Decoro Ltd* [2003] EWHC 23 (QB) at [54], [2003] All ER (D) 09 (Feb); cf *PJ Pipe & Valve Co Ltd v Audco India Ltd* [2005] EWHC 1904 (QB) at [120], [2005] All ER (D) 18 (Sep).

4 *Mansell v Clements* (1874) LR 9 CP 139; *Green v Bartlett* (1863) 14 CBNS 681; *Walker, Fraser and Steele v Fraser's Trustees* 1909 2 SLT 453; *Burchell v Gowrie and Blockhouse Collieries Ltd* [1910] AC 614, PC; *Bow's Emporium Ltd v AR Brett & Co Ltd* (1927) 44 TLR 194, HL. See also *Allen v Anderson* [1969] NZLR 951, NZ CA, where an agent, employed to sell a business owned by a company, which sale was ultimately effected by a sale of shares in the company, was held nevertheless entitled to his commission, although he was not a sharebroker and so did not complete the transaction.

5 *Wilkinson v Martin* (1837) 8 C & P 1; *Burton v Hughes* (1885) 1 TLR 207; *Howard, Houlder & Partners Ltd v Manx Isles Steamship Co Ltd* [1923] 1 KB 110; *Thompson, Rippon & Co v Thomas* (1895) 11 TLR 304, CA; *Jack Windle Ltd v Brierly* [1952] 1 All ER 398; *Stewarts and Lloyds Ltd v Zoes* (1955) Times, 5 July, HL; and see the cases in note 4.

6 *Tribe v Taylor* (1876) 1 CPD 505; *Lumley v Nicholson* (1886) 34 WR 716; *Antrobus v Wickens* (1865) 4 F & F 291; *Millar, Son & Co v Radford* (1903) 19 TLR 575, CA; *County Homesearch Co (Thames & Chilterns) Ltd v Cowham* [2008] EWCA Civ 26, [2008] 1 WLR 909, [2008] All ER (D) 281 (Jan). See also *Nightingale v Parsons* [1914] 2 KB 621, CA.

7 *Taplin v Barrett* (1889) 6 TLR 30; *Barnett v Brown & Co* (1890) 6 TLR 463; *Millar, Son & Co v Radford* (1903) 19 TLR 575, CA; *Bartlett v Cole* (1963) 188 Estates Gazette 397, CA; *Allan v Leo Lines Ltd* [1957] 1 Lloyd's Rep 127; *Robinson v Tuck* (1957) 107 LJo 683 (County Court); *John D Wood & Co v Dantata* [1987] 2 EGLR 23, CA; *Bentleys Estate Agents Ltd v Granix Ltd* [1989] 2 EGLR 21; *Chesterfield & Co Ltd v Zahid* [1989] 2 EGLR 24; *Peter Yates & Co v Bullock*

[1990] 2 EGLR 24, [1990] 37 EG 75, CA; *Chasen Ryder & Co v Hedges* [1993] 1 EGLR 47, [1993] 08 EG 119, CA; *Harding Maughan Hambly Ltd v Cie Européenne de Courtage d'Assurances et de Réassurances SA* [2000] 1 All ER (Comm) 225; *County Homesearch Co (Thames & Chilterns) Ltd v Cowham* [2008] EWCA Civ 26, [2008] 1 WLR 909, [2008] All ER (D) 281 (Jan); *MSM Consulting Ltd v Tanzania* [2009] EWHC 121 (QB), 123 Con LR 154. See further PARA 104. The principal cannot interplead if several agents claim commission upon the same transaction: *Greatorex & Co v Shackle* [1895] 2 QB 249.

8 *Sinclair Goldsmith v Minero Pinero Commercial* (1978) 248 Estates Gazette 1015. See also *Lordsgate Properties Ltd v Balcombe* [1985] 1 EGLR 20.

9 *Price, Davies & Co v Smith* (1929) 141 LT 490, CA; *Nahum v Royal Holloway and Bedford New College* [1999] EMLR 252, CA (introduction by art dealer of a purchaser to the seller principal via the seller's agent was the effective cause of sale).

10 *Burchell v Gowrie and Blockhouse Colleries Ltd* [1910] AC 614, PC; contrast *Davis v George Trollope & Sons* [1943] 1 All ER 501, CA. See also *Foxtons Ltd v Pelkey Bicknell* [2008] EWCA Civ 419, [2008] 17 EG 163 (CS).

11 *Price, Davies & Co v Smith* (1929) 141 LT 490, CA; cf *Howard, Houlder & Partners Ltd v Manx Isles Steamship Co Ltd* [1923] 1 KB 110.

12 *Burchell v Gowrie and Blockhouse Colleries Ltd* [1910] AC 614, PC.

13 *Brian Cooper & Co v Fairview Estates (Investments) Ltd* [1987] 1 EGLR 18, CA.

14 *Nightingale v Parsons* [1914] 2 KB 621, CA.

15 *Cox & Son v Starley* (1913) 48 LJo 705.

106. Remuneration of commercial agents.

A commercial agent[1] who is remunerated wholly or partly by commission[2] is entitled to commission on commercial transactions concluded during the period covered by the agency contract where:

(1)   the transaction has been concluded as a result of his action[3];

(2)   the transaction is concluded with a third party whom he has previously acquired as a customer for transactions of the same kind[4]; or

(3)   he has an exclusive right to a specific geographical area or to a specific group of customers and the transaction has been entered into with a customer belonging to that area or group[5];

and the commission must be paid not later than on the last day of the month following the quarter[6] in which it became due[7]. The right to commission can be extinguished only if and to the extent that it is established that the contract between the third party and the principal will not be executed due to a reason for which the principal is not to blame[8]. A commercial agent is not entitled to commission as described above if that commission is payable to a previous commercial agent of the principal[9], unless it is equitable because of the circumstances for the commission to be shared between the commercial agents[10].

Any agreement to derogate from these provisions to the detriment of the commercial agent is void[11].

1 Ie a commercial agent to whom the Commercial Agents (Council Directive) Regulations 1993, SI 1993/3053, apply: see PARA 73. As to the meaning of 'commercial agent' see PARA 73.

2 Commercial Agents (Council Directive) Regulations 1993, SI 1993/3053, reg 6(3). 'Commission' means any part of the remuneration of a commercial agent which varies with the number or value of business transactions: reg 2(1). A mark-up is not a 'commission' within this definition: see *Mercantile International Group plc v Chuan Soon Huat Industrial Group plc* [2001] 2 All ER (Comm) 632; on appeal [2002] EWCA Civ 288, [2002] 1 All ER (Comm) 788. These provisions (ie the Commercial Agents (Council Directive) Regulations 1993, SI 1993/3053, regs 7–12 (see the text and notes 3–11) do not apply where a commercial agent is not remunerated (wholly or in part) by commission: reg 6(3).

3 Commercial Agents (Council Directive) Regulations 1993, SI 1993/3053, reg 7(1)(a).

4 Commercial Agents (Council Directive) Regulations 1993, SI 1993/3053, reg 7(1)(b).

5 Commercial Agents (Council Directive) Regulations 1993, SI 1993/3053, reg 7(2). A commercial agent entrusted with a specific geographical area does not have the right to a commission for transactions concluded by customers belonging to that area without any action, direct or indirect, on the part of the principal: *Chevassus-Marche (Heirs of) v Groupe Danone* C-19/07 [2008] ECR

I-159, [2008] 2 All ER (Comm) 1093. The commercial agent's right to commission arises either when the principal has or should have carried out his obligation, or when the third party to the agency contract, namely, the customer, has executed the transaction or should have done, had the principal executed his part of the transaction: see *Chevassus-Marche (Heirs of) v Groupe Danone*; and the Commercial Agents (Council Directive) Regulations 1993, SI 1993/3053, reg 10.

6 For these purposes, unless otherwise agreed between the parties, the first quarter period runs from the date the agency contract takes effect, and subsequent periods run from that date in the third month thereafter or the beginning of the fourth month, whichever is sooner: Commercial Agents (Council Directive) Regulations 1993, SI 1993/3053, reg 10(3).

7 Commercial Agents (Council Directive) Regulations 1993, SI 1993/3053, reg 10(3). Commission becomes due as soon as, and to the extent that, one of the following circumstances occurs:
   (1) the principal has executed the transaction (reg 10(1)(a));
   (2) the principal should, according to his agreement with the third party, have executed the transaction (reg 10(1)(b)); or
   (3) the third party has executed the transaction (reg 10(1)(c)),
and becomes due at the latest when the third party has executed his part of the transaction or should have done so if the principal had executed his part of the transaction, as he should have (reg 10(2)).

8 Commercial Agents (Council Directive) Regulations 1993, SI 1993/3053, reg 11(1). Any commission which the commercial agent has already received must be refunded if the right to it is extinguished: reg 11(2).

9 Ie payable to a commercial agent who is entitled to commission by virtue of the Commercial Agents (Council Directive) Regulations 1993, SI 1993/3053, reg 8 (see PARA 108).

10 Commercial Agents (Council Directive) Regulations 1993, SI 1993/3053, reg 9(1). The principal is liable for any sum due under reg 9(1) to the person entitled to it in accordance therewith, and any sum which the other commercial agent receives to which he is not entitled must be refunded to the principal: reg 9(2).

11 Commercial Agents (Council Directive) Regulations 1993, SI 1993/3053, regs 10(4), 11(3).

107. Transactions beyond scope of agent's authority.

An agent is not entitled to receive any remuneration in respect of a transaction resulting from the agency which differs substantially from that which he was employed to procure[1], nor, generally, in respect of a transaction in which he is at the same time the remunerated agent of the other party[2], or where he becomes himself the purchaser[3].

1 *Toulmin v Millar* (1887) 12 App Cas 746, HL; *Barnett v Isaacson* (1888) 4 TLR 645; *Johnson v Kearley* [1908] 2 KB 514, CA; *Henderson and Boal v Martin* (1911) 46 ILT 13; *Blaker v Hawes and Brown* (1913) 109 LT 320; *Aston v Kelsey* [1913] 3 KB 314, CA; *Mote v Gould* (1935) 152 LT 347; *GT Hodges & Sons v Hackbridge Park Residential Hotel Ltd* [1940] 1 KB 404, [1939] 4 All ER 347, CA (compulsory acquisition at less than vendor's price).
2 *Fullwood v Hurley* [1928] 1 KB 498, CA; see also *Foster v Reaume* [1924] 2 DLR 951, Can SC.
3 *Hocker v Waller* (1924) 29 Com Cas 296.

108. Transactions after termination of authority.

At common law, as a rule, no remuneration is payable upon transactions between the principal and third persons introduced to him by the agent arising after the termination of the authority[1], whether such transactions are due to the agent's introduction[2] or not[3]. Remuneration may, however, be payable in respect of such later transactions if they are in fact part of a transaction in which the agent was employed[4], or if there was an express term in the contract to that effect, or a clear intention to continue such remuneration after determination of the agent's employment can be discovered from the construction of the contract of agency[5]. Such a construction may more readily be found where the agent is an independent contractor and not an employee[6], and in these cases commission will be payable even though the agent was dismissed[7], and may be so though he was not the effective cause of the transaction[8].

At common law a commission agent, whose contract entitles him to commission on repeat orders, may, after termination of the agency, recover from the principal compensation based on the then existing value of the repeat orders likely to be received, adjusted in respect of expenses the agent would save and the principal would incur as a consequence of the termination; the agent is not, in general, entitled to a declaration or an account for the future in relation to such repeat orders[9].

These rules are significantly modified in relation to commercial agents to whom certain statutory provisions apply[10]. Such a commercial agent is entitled to commission on commercial transactions concluded after the agency contract has terminated if the transaction is mainly attributable to his efforts during the period covered by the agency contract and was entered into within a reasonable period after that contract terminated[11]. He is also so entitled where the order of the third party reached the principal or the commercial agent before the agency contract terminated[12] pursuant to a transaction which has been concluded as a result of his action[13] or concluded with a third party whom he has previously acquired as a customer for transactions of the same kind[14] or where he has an exclusive right to a specific geographical area or to a specific group of customers and the transaction was entered into with a customer belonging to that area or group[15]. A commercial agent is not entitled to commission[16] if that commission is payable to a previous commercial agent by virtue of the principle as described above[17], unless it is equitable because of the circumstances for the commission to be shared between the commercial agents[18].

1   *Tribe v Taylor* (1876) 1 CPD 505; *Ward v Spivak* [1957] IR 40. See also *Sales v Crispi* (1913) 29 TLR 491. As to temporary suspension of the agent's activities see *Nordman v Rayner and Sturges* (1916) 33 TLR 87.
2   *Barrett v Gilmour & Co* (1901) 6 Com Cas 72; *Hilton v Helliwell* [1894] 2 IR 94; *Nayler v Yearsley* (1860) 2 F & F 41; *Crocker Horlock Ltd v B Lang & Co Ltd* [1949] 1 All ER 526; *Jack Windle Ltd v Brierley* [1952] 1 All ER 398.
3   *Boyd v Tovil Paper Co Ltd* (1888) 4 TLR 332, CA.
4   *Wilkinson v Martin* (1837) 8 C & P 1. See also *Christie, Owen and Davies (t/a Christie & Co) v Jones* (1966) 198 Estates Gazette 1093, where estate agents were held entitled to their commission on sale to a purchaser, originally introduced by them, which took place after the agents ceased to act, as their introduction was, on the facts, the effective cause of the sale (see PARAS 103–104).
5   Such intention was discovered in *Bilbee v Hasse & Co* (1889) 5 TLR 677; *Salomon v Brownfield and Brownfield Guild Pottery Society Ltd* (1896) 12 TLR 239; *Faulkner v Cooper & Co Ltd* (1899) 4 Com Cas 213; *Wilson v Harper, Son & Co* [1908] 2 Ch 370; *British Bank for Foreign Trade Ltd v Novinex Ltd* [1949] 1 KB 623, [1949] 1 All ER 155, CA. However it was not so found in *Weare v Brimsdown Lead Co Ltd* (1910) 103 LT 429; *Bickley v Browning, Todd & Co* (1913) 30 TLR 134; *Marshall v Glanvill* [1917] 2 KB 87; *Cramb v Godwin* (1919) 35 TLR 477, CA; *Crocker Horlock Ltd v B Lang & Co Ltd* [1949] 1 All ER 526 (repeat orders). See also *Roberts v Elwells Engineers Ltd* [1972] 2 QB 586, [1972] 2 All ER 890, CA (entitlement by agreement, as supplemented by course of dealing, to commission on orders and repeat orders attributable to salesman's original introduction); *Marshall v NM Financial Management Ltd* [1995] 4 All ER 785, [1995] 1 WLR 1461 (affd [1997] 1 WLR 1527, [1997] ICR 1065, CA).
6   *Sellers v London Counties Newspapers* [1951] 1 KB 784, [1951] 1 All ER 544, CA.
7   *Salomon v Brownfield and Brownfield Guild Pottery Society Ltd* (1896) 12 TLR 239; *Bilbee v Hasse & Co* (1889) 5 TLR 677. See also *Levy v Goldhill & Co* [1917] 2 Ch 297; *Roberts v Elwells Engineers Ltd* [1972] 2 QB 586, [1972] 2 All ER 890, CA; and cf *Cramb v Godwin* (1919) 35 TLR 477, CA.
8   *Robey v Arnold* (1898) 14 TLR 220, CA; *Walker, Fraser and Steele v Fraser's Trustees* 1909 2 SLT 453; *Brandon v Hanna* [1907] 2 IR 212, CA.
9   *Roberts v Elwells Engineers Ltd* [1972] 2 QB 586, [1972] 2 All ER 890, CA.
10 Ie where the Commercial Agents (Council Directive) Regulations 1993, SI 1993/3053, apply. As to the meaning of 'commercial agent', and as to the cases to which those Regulations apply, see PARA 73. In addition to the provisions set out in the text and notes 11–18, reg 10 (when

commission becomes due, and date for payment), reg 11 (extinction of right to commission), an reg 12 (information as to commission due) apply: see PARAS 106, 110.

11 Commercial Agents (Council Directive) Regulations 1993, SI 1993/3053, reg 8(a). See *Monk v Largo Foods Ltd* [2016] EWHC 1837 (Comm) at [112] ('mainly attributable' impose heightened causation requirement beyond simply being an effective cause).

12 Commercial Agents (Council Directive) Regulations 1993, SI 1993/3053, reg 8(b).

13 Commercial Agents (Council Directive) Regulations 1993, SI 1993/3053, regs 7(1)(a), 8(b).

14 Commercial Agents (Council Directive) Regulations 1993, SI 1993/3053, reg 7(1)(b).

15 Commercial Agents (Council Directive) Regulations 1993, SI 1993/3053, reg 7(2).

16 Ie under the Commercial Agents (Council Directive) Regulations 1993, SI 1993/3053, reg 7 (see PARA 106).

17 Ie under the Commercial Agents (Council Directive) Regulations 1993, SI 1993/3053, reg 8 (see the text and notes 10–12).

18 Commercial Agents (Council Directive) Regulations 1993, SI 1993/3053, reg 9(1). The principal is liable for any sum due under reg 9(1) to the person entitled to it in accordance with that provision, and any sum which the other commercial agent receives to which he is not entitled must be refunded to the principal: reg 9(2).

109. Agent wrongfully prevented from earning remuneration.

Subject to the operation of statutory provisions relating to commercial agents[1], an agent who is prevented from earning his remuneration by the conduct of the principal is entitled to recover damages only if he can show some term of the contract of which the principal is in breach[2]. If an implied term is asserted, the agent must show that the term is necessary to give business efficacy to the contract[3]. Where the agent has done everything to entitle him to receive his remuneration, the measure of damages is the full amount of remuneration which he would have received if the transaction in respect of which it was to be payable had been completed, less expenses and any sum earned in substitution[4]. Where the agent has not done everything to entitle him to remuneration, but has been prevented by an act or default of his principal from being able to earn a remuneration to which he might have been entitled under the terms of his agreement, the measure of damages will be the amount of remuneration which the agent might reasonably have earned in accordance with the terms and duration of the agreement[5].

If a contract of agency can be performed only with the co-operation of the principal, a term will be implied, to give the contract efficacy, that such co-operation will be forthcoming[6]. Where the principal prevents an agent from earning or continuing to earn commission by disposing of his business or ceasing to trade, this will be wrongful if it constitutes a breach of the agency contract[7], but a term will not be implied that the principal will not part with his business so as to deprive the agent of commission[8]. Where an estate agent is appointed sole agent for a limited period, it will be a breach of the principal's undertaking for him to appoint a second agent[9], but it is not a breach of contract if the principal sells the property himself during such period, for such an appointment does not impliedly prohibit the principal from so acting[10]. In other classes of agency, however, the appointment of a sole agent may preclude sale by the principal himself unless the contract otherwise provides[11]. An agent employed to procure a purchaser of property, whether or not the agent is by profession an estate agent, is not wrongfully prevented from earning commission because his principal decides not to proceed with the transaction before a binding contract has been made[12].

1 Ie subject to the application of the Commercial Agents (Council Directive) Regulations 1993, SI 1993/3053. As to the meaning of 'commercial agent', and as to the cases to which those regulations apply, see PARA 73. As to the transactions in respect of which an agent is entitled to remuneration see PARAS 105–106.

2 *Luxor (Eastbourne) Ltd v Cooper* [1941] AC 108, [1941] 1 All ER 33, HL. See also *Turner v Goldsmith* [1891] 1 QB 544, CA; *Reigate v Union Manufacturing Co (Ramsbottom) Ltd* [1918] 1 KB 592, CA; *Warren & Co v Agdeshman* (1922) 38 TLR 588; *Bauman v Hulton Press Ltd* [1952] 2 All ER 1121.

3 *Hamlyn & Co v Wood & Co* [1891] 2 QB 488, CA; *L French & Co Ltd v Leeston Shipping Co Ltd* [1922] 1 AC 451, HL; *Shackleton Aviation Ltd v Maitland Drewery Aviation Ltd* [1964] 1 Lloyd's Rep 293; *Alpha Trading Ltd v Dunnshaw-Patten Ltd* [1981] QB 290, [1981] 1 All ER 482, CA. The effect of these cases gives rise to doubt as to the extent of the authority of *Prickett v Badger* (1856) 1 CBNS 296 (term providing for remuneration, at least on quantum meruit, implied by law rather than as question of fact). For a case where the express term was held to exclude an implied term, see *Rhodes v Forwood* (1876) 1 App Cas 256, HL. Where the agent has done only part of the work he was employed to do, he will recover, if at all, on a quantum meruit basis: see *Inchbald v Western Neilgherry Coffee, Tea and Cinchona Plantation Co Ltd* (1864) 17 CBNS 733; *Luxor (Eastbourne) Ltd v Cooper* [1941] AC 108, [1941] 1 All ER 33, HL.

4 *Prickett v Badger* (1856) 1 CBNS 296; *Roberts v Barnard* (1884) Cab & El 336. See also *Nahum v Royal Holloway and Bedford New College* [1999] EMLR 252, CA (art dealer wrongfully prevented from assisting with sale of painting due to interference from buyer's agent entitled to a commission from the sale).

5 *Reigate v Union Manufacturing Co (Ramsbottom) Ltd* [1918] 1 KB 592, CA; *Hampton & Sons Ltd v George* [1939] 3 All ER 627.

6 *Mona Oil Equipment and Supply Co Ltd v Rhodesia Railways Ltd* [1949] 2 All ER 1014.

7 *Turner v Goldsmith* [1891] 1 QB 544, CA; *Reigate v Union Manufacturing Co (Ramsbottom) Ltd* [1918] 1 KB 592, CA; *Warren & Co v Agdeshman* (1922) 38 TLR 588; *Nolan v Watson & Co* (1965) 109 Sol Jo 288, CA. The contract cannot be enforced by means of an injunction if this would involve specific performance of an agreement by the principal for personal services: *Page One Records Ltd v Britton (t/a The Troggs)* [1967] 3 All ER 822, [1968] 1 WLR 157. As to when a right to damages arises on termination of the principal's business see PARA 184.

8 *Rhodes v Forwood* (1876) 1 App Cas 256, HL; *Lazarus v Cairn Line of Steamships Ltd* (1912) 106 LT 378; *L French & Co Ltd v Leeston Shipping Co Ltd* [1922] 1 AC 451, HL; *Howard, Houlder & Partners Ltd v Manx Isles Steamship Co Ltd* [1923] 1 KB 110.

9 *Mendoza & Co v Bell* (1952) 159 Estates Gazette 372; *E Christopher & Co v Essig* [1948] WN 461. See also *Simpson v Lamb* (1856) 17 CB 603 (agent appointed to sell advowson).

10 *Bentall, Horsley and Baldry v Vicary* [1931] 1 KB 253; *Sadler v Whittaker* (1953) 162 Estates Gazette 404, CA; *Ronald Preston and Partners v Markheath Securities plc* [1988] 2 EGLR 23. It is, however, a breach if he sells through other agents: *Newton v Erickson* (1951) 157 Estates Gazette 414.

11 *Snelgrove v Ellringham Colliery Co* (1881) 45 JP 408, considered in *WT Lamb & Sons v Goring Brick Co Ltd* [1932] 1 KB 710, CA, where the case was decided on the basis that the transaction was one of vendor and purchaser and not principal and agent. In modern business terminology 'sole' is generally understood to mean that the principal may undertake sales in the agent's territory, whilst 'exclusive' means that the principal is not allowed to compete with the agent in the allotted territory; see PARA 103 note 17. See also *Chinnock v Sainsbury* (1860) 30 LJ Ch 409; *Ronald Preston and Partners v Markheath Securities plc* [1988] 2 EGLR 23.

12 *Luxor (Eastbourne) Ltd v Cooper* [1941] AC 108, [1941] 1 All ER 33, HL; *Raymond v Wooten* (1931) 47 TLR 606, DC.

110. Commercial agent's right to information.

A principal must supply his commercial agent[1] with a statement of the commission due[2], not later than the last day of the month following the quarter in which the commission has become due, and that statement must set out the main components used in calculating the amount of the commission[3]. Further, a commercial agent is entitled to demand that he be provided with all the information (and in particular an extract from the books) which is available to his principal and which he needs in order to check the amount of the commission due to him[4]. Any agreement to derogate from these provisions is void[5], although these rules do not prevent reliance on any enactment or rule of law that recognises the right of the agent to inspect the books of the principal[6].

Both the commercial agent and the principal are entitled to receive from the other on request a signed written document setting out the terms of the agency contract including any terms subsequently agreed[7].

1   As to the meaning of 'commercial agent', and as to the cases to which these provisions apply, see PARA 73.
2   As to the meaning of 'commission' see PARA 106 note 2. As to when commission becomes due see PARA 106 note 7.
3   Commercial Agents (Council Directive) Regulations 1993, SI 1993/3053, reg 12(1).
4   Commercial Agents (Council Directive) Regulations 1993, SI 1993/3053, reg 12(2).
5   Commercial Agents (Council Directive) Regulations 1993, SI 1993/3053, reg 12(3).
6   Commercial Agents (Council Directive) Regulations 1993, SI 1993/3053, reg 12(4).
7   Commercial Agents (Council Directive) Regulations 1993, SI 1993/3053, reg 13(1). Any purported waiver of this right is void: reg 13(2).

111. Agent's loss of right to remuneration.

An agent who is required by law to possess a particular qualification to enable him to act as such is not entitled to any remuneration if at the time when he rendered the services in respect of which the remuneration is claimed he was not so qualified[1]; nor is an agent entitled to any remuneration in respect of transactions in the course of which he has been guilty of wilful misconduct[2] or breach of faith, whether his principal has been damnified thereby or not[3], or where the receipt of money for the services he has provided is illegal[4], or in respect of transactions which were unauthorised by his principal and not subsequently ratified[5], or which were or must have been known by the agent to be unlawful[6], or in respect of any services which were rendered abortive by reason of his negligence or other breach of duty[7]. An agent guilty of a breach of duty due to a bona fide mistake may, however, still be entitled to his remuneration[8].

1   *Palk v Force* (1848) 12 QB 666; *Cope v Rowlands* (1836) 2 M & W 149. Statutory provision is made precluding the recovery of remuneration by persons acting as solicitors who are not qualified or do not have a practising certificate: see the Solicitors Act 1974 s 25; and LEGAL PROFESSIONS vol 65 (2015) PARA 429.
2   *Andrews v Ramsay & Co* [1903] 2 KB 635; *Price v Metropolitan House Investment Agency Co Ltd* (1907) 23 TLR 630, CA; *Stubbs v Slater* [1910] 1 Ch 632, CA; *E Green & Son Ltd v G Tughan & Co* (1913) 30 TLR 64; *Rhodes v Macalister* (1923) 29 Com Cas 19, CA; cf *The Macleod* (1880) 5 PD 254. However the agent is entitled to his remuneration in other transactions where he has acted properly (*Hippisley v Knee Bros* [1905] 1 KB 1; *Nitedals Taendstikfabrik v Bruster* [1906] 2 Ch 671), and if he is remunerated by commission, he is entitled to commission for the period prior to his breach of contract (*Graham & Co v United Turkey Red Co Ltd* 1922 SC 533, Ct of Sess).
3   *Salomons v Pender* (1865) 3 H & C 639; *Columbus v Williamson & Co Ltd* [1969] NZLR 708, NZ CA (estate agent in breach of contract not entitled to commission even where principal has successfully sued purchaser).
4   See the Accommodation Agencies Act 1953 s 1; *McInnes v Clarke* [1955] 1 All ER 346, [1955] 1 WLR 102, DC, distinguished in *Saunders v Soper* [1975] AC 239, [1974] 3 All ER 1025, HL; and PARA 304.
5   *Marsh v Jelf* (1862) 3 F & F 234; *Campanari v Woodburn* (1854) 15 CB 400.
6   *Stackpole v Earle* (1761) 2 Wils KB 133; *Josephs v Pebrer* (1825) 3 B & C 639; *Allkins v Jupe* (1877) 2 CPD 375, DC; *Harrington v Victoria Graving Dock Co* (1878) 3 QBD 549.
7   *Denew v Daverell* (1813) 3 Camp 451; *Bracey v Carter* (1840) 12 Ad & El 373; *Dalton v Irwin* (1830) 4 C & P 289; *Hamond v Holiday* (1824) 1 C & P 384. See also *John D Wood & Co (Residential & Agricultural Land) Ltd v Knatchbull* [2002] EWHC 2822 (QB), [2003] 1 EGLR 33, [2002] All ER (D) 232 (Dec) (failure of estate agent to communicate to client vendor the higher selling price of neighbouring property).
8   *Keppel v Wheeler* [1927] 1 KB 577, CA; *Harrods Ltd v Lemon* [1931] 2 KB 157, CA; *Robinson Scammell & Co v Ansell* [1985] 2 EGLR 41, CA (estate agent acting in good faith entitled to commission although he failed to consult the vendors before communicating with the purchasers).

(iii) Reimbursement and Indemnity

112. Agent's rights to be reimbursed and indemnified.

The relation of principal and agent raises by implication a contract on the part of the principal to reimburse the agent in respect of all expenses, and to indemnify him against all liabilities, incurred in the reasonable performance of the agency[1], provided that such implication is not excluded by the express terms of the contract between them[2], and provided that such expenses and liabilities are in fact occasioned by his employment[3]. The right is not affected by the fact that the payment in respect of which the agent seeks to be indemnified is not a payment for which the principal could be made liable[4].

The agent may enforce his rights of reimbursement and indemnity by claim, or by the exercise of his lien[5], and, if he is sued by the principal[6], he may assert them by way of set-off[7] or counterclaim[8].

1 *Adamson v Jarvis* (1827) 4 Bing 66; *Frixione v Tagliaferro & Sons* (1856) 10 Moo PCC 175. This includes liabilities arising out of a premature revocation of his authority: *Warlow v Harrison* (1859) 1 E & E 309, Ex Ch. See also *Lazarus v Cairn Line of Steamships Ltd* (1912) 106 LT 378; *Reigate v Union Manufacturing Co (Ramsbottom)* [1918] 1 KB 592, CA; *Wilson v Avec Audio-Visual Equipment Ltd* [1974] 1 Lloyd's Rep 81, CA; *SCF Finance Co Ltd v Masri (No 2)* [1986] 1 All ER 40 (affd [1987] QB 1002, [1987] 1 All ER 175, CA). As to liabilities to which the right of indemnity does not extend see PARA **114**.
2 This will be so in the case of a del credere agent: *Morris v Cleasby* (1816) 4 M & S 566; a del credere agent is, however, entitled to indemnity against losses outside the scope of the del credere commission: *Hooper v Treffry* (1847) 1 Exch 17. As to a del credere agent see PARA **13**.
3 *Williams v Lister & Co* (1913) 109 LT 699, CA; and contrast *Halbronn v International Horse Agency and Exchange Ltd* [1903] 1 KB 270; *Tomlinson v Scottish Amalgamated Silks Ltd (Liquidators)* 1935 SC (HL) 1. Liability is not confined to legal liability: *Rhodes v Fielder, Jones and Harrison* (1919) 89 LJKB 15, DC (barrister's fees).
4 *Brittain v Lloyd* (1845) 14 M & W 762; *Adams v Morgan & Co Ltd* [1924] 1 KB 751, CA. The right to indemnity does not, however, apply in respect of liability, such as to income tax, incurred in respect of profit made by the agent acting as principal: *Re Hollebone's Agreement, Hollebone v WJ Hollebone & Sons Ltd* [1959] 2 All ER 152, [1959] 1 WLR 536, CA.
     Where an agent was entitled to be indemnified in respect of the expenses of litigation and was ordered to pay costs on the standard basis, the court might in its discretion order that costs between him and the principal be allowed on the indemnity basis, the costs of proceedings by the agent to recover his indemnity from the principal normally being payable on the standard basis: see *The James Seddon* (1866) LR 1 A & E 62; *Williams v Lister & Co* (1913) 109 LT 699, CA; *Simpson and Miller v British Industries Trust Ltd* (1923) 39 TLR 286. As a consequence of the agent's right to indemnity, it might follow that, where he succeeded in the litigation but only recovered costs on the standard basis, he was entitled to be reimbursed the difference between those costs and costs on the indemnity basis: see *Re Famatina Development Corpn Ltd* [1914] 2 Ch 271, CA.
5 As to lien see PARAS **115–119**.
6 Or by any person claiming through the principal: *Cropper v Cook* (1868) LR 3 CP 194.
7 *Curtis v Barclay* (1826) 5 B & C 141.
8 As to counterclaims generally see CIVIL PROCEDURE vol 11 (2015) PARA 367 et seq.

113. Extent of indemnity.

The right of indemnity covers not merely the losses actually sustained by the agent, but also, in accordance with the principles of equity, the full amount of the liabilities incurred by him, even though they may never in fact be enforced[1], and extends to cases where they were incurred under an honest mistake of judgment[2]. It is immaterial whether or not the agent professed to be acting on his principal's behalf, if he was in fact so acting[3].

Where an agent is employed to deal in a particular market or at a particular place, he may acquire rights of reimbursement and indemnity, which he would not otherwise have, in consequence of the usages of the particular market or place[4]. Such usages are binding on the principal, even though unknown to him, if they are reasonable[5], but not if they are unreasonable[6], unless his knowledge of them is proved[7].

1   *Lacey v Hill, Crowley's Claim* (1874) LR 18 Eq 182. See also *British Union and National Insurance Co v Rawson* [1916] 2 Ch 476, CA. A possibility of a future claim is not, however, enough: *Dyson v Peat* [1917] 1 Ch 99. As to liabilities to which the right of indemnity does not extend see PARA **114**.
2   *Broom v Hall* (1859) 7 CBNS 503; *Pettman v Keble* (1850) 9 CB 701.
3   *Re Fox, Walker & Co, ex p Bishop* (1880) 15 ChD 400, CA; *Re Rogers, ex p Rogers* (1880) 15 ChD 207, CA.
4   *Bayliffe v Butterworth* (1847) 1 Exch 425; *Anglo Overseas Transport Ltd v Titan Industrial Corpn (United Kingdom) Ltd* [1959] 2 Lloyd's Rep 152 (London freight market); *Perishables Transport Co Ltd v N Spyropoulos (London) Ltd* [1964] 2 Lloyd's Rep 379. As to post-termination indemnity under the Commercial Agents (Council Directive) Regulations 1993, SI 1993/3053, see reg 17; and PARA **179**. As to the effect of usages generally see PARA **44**.
5   *Reynolds v Smith* (1893) 9 TLR 494, HL; *Chapman v Shepherd* (1867) LR 2 CP 228.
6   *Perry v Barnett* (1885) 15 QBD 388, CA.
7   *Seymour v Bridge* (1885) 14 QBD 460. As to custom and usage see further PARA **44**.

114. Liabilities to which right of reimbursement or indemnity does not extend.

An agent is not entitled to reimbursement or indemnity in respect of expenses or liabilities incurred in consequence of his own default[1] or breach of duty[2], or transactions which are outside the scope of his authority and have not been ratified by his principal[3]. There is no right of indemnity in respect of the consequences of transactions involving a breach of the criminal law where the party performing them knows that they are unlawful[4], or where, being ignorant of their illegality, he knows the circumstances which render them unlawful[5], or where the transaction is contrary to public policy[6]. Consequently an agent who makes a contract which is prohibited by statute[7], or makes payments which it is criminally illegal for him to make[8], is not only debarred from recovering any remuneration but is also not entitled to any indemnity against his expenses in such transaction[9].

Where the agent's conduct amounts to a tort, but not a crime, he is at common law entitled to be indemnified against expenses and liabilities if the transaction was not manifestly tortious or tortious to his knowledge[10]. Where an agent incurs liability to a third party in respect of a tort committed with the authority of his principal, he is entitled to such contribution from his principal as the court considers to be just and equitable having regard to the extent of their respective responsibility for the damage[11]. Such contribution may take the form of a complete indemnity[12], but where the principal is entitled to be indemnified by the agent against such damage, the agent will not be entitled to any contribution[13].

Where a principal desiring to speculate in shares or commodities employs an agent to buy or sell on his behalf on the recognised stock exchanges or commodity or produce exchanges or markets, the principal intending throughout only to pay or receive differences, the agent will be entitled to be indemnified against losses incurred in these transactions in so far as he has entered into genuine contracts with third parties who are not parties to an agreement or tacit understanding that there shall be no obligation on either party to take or deliver but that differences only shall be payable[14]. The agent's right is not affected by knowledge that his principal does not expect to be called upon to settle the transaction except by payment of differences[15]. The fact that the contract effected through the agent is made subject to the rules of the stock or other exchange, or contains a term that one party or other can require delivery, does not preclude evidence that it was in fact a gaming or wagering transaction[16].

1   *Lewis v Samuel* (1846) 8 QB 685; *Duncan v Hill* (1873) LR 8 Exch 242. See also *Goulandris Bros Ltd v B Goldman & Sons Ltd* [1958] 1 QB 74, [1957] 3 All ER 100.
2   *Ellis v Pond* [1898] 1 QB 426, CA; *Thomas v Atherton* (1878) 10 ChD 185, CA; *Solloway v Mclaughlin* [1938] AC 247, [1937] 4 All ER 328, PC.
3   *Bowlby v Bell* (1846) 3 CB 284; and contrast *Hartas v Ribbons* (1889) 22 QBD 254, CA; *Colonial Bank of Australasia v Marshall* [1906] AC 559, PC; *Johnson v Kearley* [1908] 2 KB 514, CA; and cf *Aston v Kelsey* [1913] 3 KB 314, CA; *Blaker v Hawes and Brown* (1913) 109 LT 320.
4   *Smith v White* (1866) LR 1 Eq 626. Cf *R Leslie Ltd v Reliable Advertising and Addressing Agency Ltd* [1915] 1 KB 652.
5   See *Burrows v Rhodes* [1899] 1 QB 816; *Haseldine v Hosken* [1933] 1 KB 822, CA; and CONTRACT vol 22 (2012) PARA 427 et seq.
6   *Herman v Jeuchner* (1885) 15 QBD 561, CA; and see CONTRACT vol 22 (2012) PARA 429 et seq.
7   *Ex p Mather* (1797) 3 Ves 373; *Warwick v Slade* (1811) 3 Camp 127.
8   *Josephs v Pebrer* (1825) 3 B & C 639; *Re Parker* (1882) 21 ChD 408, CA (unlawful payments by election agent).
9   See the cases cited in notes 7, 8. It is otherwise where the indemnity is sought in respect of expenses which are distinct from the illegal transaction: *Lindo v Smith* (1858) 5 CBNS 587, Ex Ch. See the Accommodation Agencies Act 1953 s 1; *McInnes v Clarke* [1955] 1 All ER 346, [1955] 1 WLR 102, DC, distinguished in *Saunders v Soper* [1975] AC 239, [1974] 3 All ER 1025, HL; and PARA 304.
10   *Adamson v Jarvis* (1827) 4 Bing 66; *Betts and Drewe v Gibbins* (1834) 2 Ad & El 57; *W Cory & Son Ltd v Lambton and Hetton Collieries Ltd* (1916) 86 LJKB 401, CA.
11   See the Civil Liability (Contribution) Act 1978 ss 1, 2; DAMAGES vol 29 (2014) PARA 620 et seq; TORT vol 97 (2015) PARA 450 et seq.
12   See the Civil Liability (Contribution) Act 1978 s 2(2); DAMAGES vol 29 (2014) PARA 622; TORT vol 97 (2015) PARA 453.
13   See the Civil Liability (Contribution) Act 1978 s 2(2), (3); DAMAGES vol 29 (2014) PARA 622; TORT vol 97 (2015) PARA 453. See also *Lister v Romford Ice and Cold Storage Co Ltd* [1957] AC 555, [1957] 1 All ER 125, HL (employer and employee).
14   *Thacker v Hardy* (1878) 4 QBD 685, CA; *Forget v Ostigny* [1895] AC 318, PC; *Ironmonger & Co v Dyne* (1928) 44 TLR 497, CA; *Barnett v Sanker* (1925) 41 TLR 660; *Weddle, Beck & Co v Hackett* [1929] 1 KB 321; *Cunliffe-Owen v Teather and Greenwood* [1967] 3 All ER 561, [1967] 1 WLR 1421.
15   *Thacker v Hardy* (1878) 4 QBD 685, CA; *Forget v Ostigny* [1895] AC 318, PC; *Re Rogers, ex p Rogers* (1880) 15 ChD 207, CA; *Barnett v Sanker* (1925) 41 TLR 660; *H W Franklin & Co Ltd v Dawson* (1913) 29 TLR 479.
16   *Universal Stock Exchange v Strachan* [1896] AC 166, HL; *Re Gieve* [1899] 1 QB 794, CA; *Weddle, Beck & Co v Hackett* [1929] 1 KB 321.

(iv) Lien

115. For what claims agent has lien.

Every agent has a lien on the goods and chattels of his principal in respect of all claims against the principal[1] arising out of his employment, whether for remuneration earned, or for expenses or liabilities incurred, except where the right of lien is inconsistent with the contract between the parties[2], or with the special purpose for which the goods or chattels were entrusted to him[3].

The lien of an agent is, as a rule, a particular lien, confined to such claims as arise in connection with the goods and chattels in respect of which the right is claimed[4]. He may, however, be given a general lien, extending to all claims arising out of the agency, either by express contract or by usage[5].

1   Including those claims that are statute-barred (*Spears v Hartly* (1800) 3 Esp 81), but not in respect of a mere possibility of liability (*Dyson v Peat* [1917] 1 Ch 99).

2   *Re Bowes, Earl of Strathmore v Vane* (1886) 33 ChD 586; *Wolstenholm v Sheffield Union Banking Co Ltd* (1886) 54 LT 746, CA. The inconsistency must be clear: *Fisher v Smith* (1868) 4 App Cas 1, HL; *Rolls Razor Ltd v Cox* [1967] 1 QB 552, [1967] 1 All ER 397, CA.

3   *Brandao v Barnett* (1846) 3 CB 519; *Burn v Brown* (1817) 2 Stark 272; *Skinner v Reed's Trustee* [1967] Ch 1194, [1967] 2 All ER 1286 (auctioneer has lien only on so much of deposit as becomes the property of the vendor).

4   *Bock v Gorrissen* (1861) 30 LJ Ch 39, CA; see also *Williams v Millington* (1788) 1 Hy Bl 81. As to particular liens see LIEN vol 68 (2016) PARAS 838–845.

5   There is no lien in respect of claims accruing before the agency began: *Houghton v Matthews* (1803) 3 Bos & P 485. A general lien is possessed by factors (*Baring v Corrie* (1818) 2 B & Ald 137; *Hammonds v Barclay* (1802) 2 East 227), bankers (*London Chartered Bank of Australia v White* (1879) 4 App Cas 413, PC), insurance brokers (*Mann v Forrester* (1814) 4 Camp 60), solicitors (*Re Broomhead* (1847) 5 Dow & L 52; Solicitors Act 1974 s 73), stockbrokers (*Re London and Globe Finance Corpn* [1902] 2 Ch 416), wharfingers (*Spears v Hartly* (1800) 3 Esp 81), and packers (*Re Witt, ex p Shubrook* (1876) 2 ChD 489, CA); see LIEN vol 68 (2016) PARAS 828–837. As to the lien of a ship's master see the Merchant Shipping Act 1995 s 41; and SHIPPING AND MARITIME LAW vol 93 (2008) PARA 477.

116.   Possession necessary for lien to be exercised.

To enable an agent to exercise his lien, the goods must be in his possession, actual[1] or constructive[2]. The possession must have been acquired without breach of duty[3], and the agent must hold the goods by virtue of the same agency as that under which he claims the lien[4].

1   *Ridgway v Lees* (1856) 25 LJ Ch 584; *Kinloch v Craig* (1790) 3 Term Rep 783, HL.

2   *Bryans v Nix* (1839) 4 M & W 775. See also *Langley, Beldon and Gaunt Ltd v Morley* [1965] 1 Lloyd's Rep 297 (forwarding agents who had parted with possession held not to have a general lien).

3   *Walshe v Provan* (1853) 8 Exch 843; *Madden v Kempster* (1807) 1 Camp 12; and cf *Barratt v Gough-Thomas* [1951] Ch 242, [1950] 2 All ER 1048, CA (solicitor cannot set up lien if thereby he asserts right inconsistent with his legal obligations).

4   *Misa v Currie* (1876) 1 App Cas 554, HL; *Dixon v Stansfield* (1850) 10 CB 398; *Barratt v Gough-Thomas* [1951] Ch 242, [1950] 2 All ER 1048, CA.

117.   Lien affecting third parties.

As against third persons, the agent cannot, by the exercise of his lien, deprive them of their existing rights in respect of the goods, except in so far as the principal could have done so[1] or statute so provides[2]. An agent's lien on negotiable instruments and money entrusted to him is absolute, notwithstanding any defects in the title of the principal[3], provided that, when the lien attached, the agent had no notice of any such defects[4].

1   Cf *Brunton v Electrical Engineering Corpn* [1892] 1 Ch 434 with *Re Capital Fire Insurance Association* (1883) 24 ChD 408, CA (a winding-up order cannot defeat a valid lien existing at the time when the winding-up petition is presented); *Re Rapid Road Transit Co* [1909] 1 Ch 96; and see *Turner v Letts* (1855) 20 Beav 185; *Barry v Longmore* (1840) 12 Ad & El 639; *Copland v Stein* (1799) 8 Term Rep 199. See also the Insolvency Act 1986 s 284(4); and BANKRUPTCY AND INDIVIDUAL INSOLVENCY vol 5 (2013) PARA 213.

2   See eg the Factors Act 1889 ss 8, 9; the Sale of Goods Act 1979 ss 24–26; and SALE OF GOODS AND SUPPLY OF SERVICES vol 91 (2012) PARAS 155–156.

3   *Brandao v Barnett* (1846) 3 CB 519; *Bank of New South Wales v Goulburn Valley Butter Co Pty Ltd* [1902] AC 543, PC; *Jones v Peppercorne* (1858) John 430; and cf *London Joint Stock Bank v Simmons* [1892] AC 201, HL; *Bechuanaland Exploration Co v London Trading Bank Ltd* [1898] 2 QB 658.

4   *Solomons v Bank of England* (1791) 13 East 135n; *Jeffryes v Agra and Masterman's Bank* (1866) LR 2 Eq 674.

118. Loss of lien.

An agent loses his lien by parting with the possession of the goods[1], unless at the time of parting with them he reserves expressly or by implication his right of lien[2], or they are obtained from him by fraud or other unlawful means[3]. He may also, whilst remaining in possession of the goods, lose his lien by dealing with them in any way which is inconsistent with its continuance[4], or by entering into any agreement[5], or doing any act[6] which necessarily implies its abandonment, or if the character and legal basis of his possession is changed[7]. The lien is not affected by the subsequent bankruptcy of the principal[8].

1   *Sweet v Pym* (1800) 1 East 4; *Langley, Beldon and Gaunt Ltd v Morley* [1965] 1 Lloyd's Rep 297.
2   *Watson v Lyon* (1855) 7 De GM & G 288; *North Western Bank Ltd v Poynter, Son and Macdonalds* [1895] AC 56, HL; *Albermarle Supply Co Ltd v Hind & Co* [1928] 1 KB 307, CA; *Caldwell v Sumpters (a firm)* [1972] Ch 478, [1972] 1 All ER 567, CA.
3   *Dicas v Stockley* (1836) 7 C & P 587; *Wallace v Woodgate* (1824) Ry & M 193.
4   *Weeks v Goode* (1859) 6 CBNS 367; *Jacobs v Latour* (1828) 5 Bing 130.
5   *The Rainbow* (1885) 53 LT 91.
6   *Re Taylor, Stileman and Underwood, ex p Payne Collier* [1891] 1 Ch 590, CA. The mere taking of security is not by itself sufficient (*Angus v McLachlan* (1883) 23 ChD 330).
7   *Barratt v Gough-Thomas* [1951] Ch 242, [1950] 2 All ER 1048, CA.
8   *Robson v Kemp* (1802) 4 Esp 233; *Re Capital Fire Insurance Association* (1883) 24 ChD 408, CA.

119. Lien of sub-agent.

A sub-agent has, in general, no right of lien against the principal as such[1]. If, however, he is employed with the authority of the principal, and at the time when the right attaches he is unaware of the existence of a principal, he has the same right of lien against him as he would have had if the agent employing him had been the principal[2]; and although he may be aware of the principal's existence, he has a similar right of lien against the principal in respect of claims arising out of the transaction in which he was employed as sub-agent, notwithstanding any settlement between the principal and the agent[3]; but his general lien, if any, is co-extensive with the actual rights of the agent in that behalf, and no wider[4].

1   *Solly v Rathbone* (1814) 2 M & S 298. As to the power of a bailee to subject to an artificer's lien the goods bailed to him see *Tappenden (t/a English and American Autos) v Artus* [1964] 2 QB 185, [1963] 3 All ER 213, CA. As to the lien of a marine insurance broker see the Marine Insurance Act 1906 s 53(2); *Near East Relief v King, Chausseur & Co Ltd* [1930] 2 KB 40; *Eide Insurance UK Ltd v Lowndes Lambert Group Ltd* [1999] QB 199, [1998] 1 All ER 946; and INSURANCE vol 60 (2011) PARA 278 et seq.
2   *Taylor v Kymer* (1832) 3 B & Ad 320; *Mann v Forrester* (1814) 4 Camp 60; *New Zealand and Australian Land Co v Watson* (1881) 7 QBD 374, CA.
3   *Fisher v Smith* (1878) 4 App Cas 1, HL.
4   *Mildred, Goyeneche & Co v Maspons Y Hermano* (1883) 8 App Cas 874, HL; *Ex p Edwards* (1881) 8 QBD 262, CA.

(v) Stoppage in Transit

120. Stoppage in transit.

If an agent has bought goods on behalf of his principal, either with his own money[1], or under such circumstances as to incur a personal liability towards the seller for the price[2], he stands towards his principal in the position of an unpaid seller[3], and on delivery to a carrier for transmission to the principal, possesses the same rights of stoppage in transit[4].

1   *Jenkyns v Brown* (1849) 14 QB 496.
2   As to the circumstances in which a personal liability is incurred see PARA 159.

3   See the Sale of Goods Act 1979 s 38(2); and SALE OF GOODS AND SUPPLY OF SERVICES vol 91 (2012)
    PARA 239. See also *Feise v Wray* (1802) 3 East 93; *Falk v Fletcher* (1865) 18 CBNS 403; and see
    Cassaboglou v Gibb (1883) 11 QBD 797, CA.
4   *Ireland v Livingston* (1872) LR 5 HL 395; *Imperial Bank v London and St Katharine Docks Co*
    (1877) 5 ChD 195. As to the unpaid seller's right to stoppage in transit see CARRIAGE AND CARRIERS
    vol 7 (2015) PARA 496; SALE OF GOODS AND SUPPLY OF SERVICES vol 91 (2012) PARA 254 et
    seq.

(vi) Competing Claims by Principal and Third Party

121.   Agent's right to make a stakeholder application.

Where, by virtue of his agency, an agent is in possession of any money, goods
or chattels[1], to which conflicting claims are made by his principal and a third
person, he may make a stakeholder application to the court[2] notwithstanding his
agency[3], even though he has expressly attorned to his principal[4]. If, at the time of
so attorning, the agent had notice of the claim of the third party, he may be
estopped, as against his principal, from denying the latter's title, and so be unable
to bring the stakeholder application[5].

The agent must, however, stand in a position of real impartiality between the
claimants[6], and therefore he must not collude with either[7], nor claim any interest
in the subject matter except for his costs and charges[8]. A claim of lien in respect
of the latter does not oust him from his right[9]. He cannot bring a stakeholder
claim if he claims any further lien or interest[10], nor where one of the claimants
seeks unliquidated damages[11].

1   This includes choses in action: *Robinson v Jenkins* (1890) 24 QBD 275, CA.
2   See CPR Pt 86; and CIVIL PROCEDURE vol 12A (2015) PARAS 1404–1405. The principles
    underlying the following cases decided under RSC Ord 17 and CCR Ord 33 (both now repealed)
    appear to be equally applicable under CPR Pt 86.
3   *Ex p Mersey Docks and Harbour Board* [1899] 1 QB 546; *Attenborough v London and St
    Katherine's Dock Co* (1878) 3 CPD 450, CA; *Tanner v European Bank* (1866) LR 1 Exch 261.
4   *Ex p Mersey Docks and Harbour Board* [1899] 1 QB 546.
5   Cf *Re Sadler, ex p Davies* (1881) 19 ChD 86, CA; and see PARA 96.
6   *Murietta v South American, etc, Co Ltd* (1893) 62 LJQB 396.
7   See CPR 86.2(4)(b); and CIVIL PROCEDURE vol 12A (2015) PARA 1404. It is collusion to agree
    with one claimant to do what the agent legally can to defeat the other (*Murietta v South American,
    etc, Co Ltd* (1893) 62 LJQB 396), or to take an indemnity from one of them (*Tucker v Morris*
    (1832) 1 Cr & M 73), though the party giving the indemnity cannot raise this objection
    (*Thompson v Wright* (1884) 13 QBD 632).
8   CPR 86.2(4)(a); *Best v Hayes* (1863) 1 H & C 718; and CIVIL PROCEDURE vol 12A (2015)
    PARA 1404.
9   *Cotter v Bank of England* (1833) 3 Moo & S 180; *Attenborough v London and St Katharine's
    Dock Co* (1878) 3 CPD 450, CA.
10 *Mitchell v Hayne* (1824) 2 Sim & St 63.
11 *Ingham v Walker* (1887) 3 TLR 448, CA.

6. RELATIONS BETWEEN PRINCIPAL AND THIRD PERSONS

(1) PRINCIPAL'S LIABILITY FOR AGENT'S ACTS

122. General rule: principal responsible for acts of agent.

As a general rule, a principal is responsible for all acts of his agent within the authority of the agent, whether the responsibility is contractual[1] or tortious[2]. Similarly the principal will be bound by many dispositions of property made by the agent[3]. In some exceptional instances, a principal may be criminally liable even where he does not himself take part in, authorise or connive at the act or default of the agent[4].

1   See PARAS 126–141.
2   See PARAS 151–155.
3   See PARAS 145–150.
4   See PARA 156.

123. Fraudulent motive of agent immaterial.

A principal is not exempt, where he would otherwise be liable in respect of an act done or bound by a contract made by his agent, by reason of the fact that the agent in doing it was acting in fraud of the principal[1], or otherwise to his detriment[2]. A third party dealing in good faith with an agent, who acts within the apparent scope of his authority, and purports to act as agent[3], is not prejudiced by the fact that the agent is using his authority for his own benefit and not that of his principal[4].

1   *Hambro v Burnand* [1904] 2 KB 10, CA; *Montague v Perkins* (1853) 22 LJCP 187; *Summers v Solomon* (1857) 7 E & B 879; *Meyer & Co Ltd v Sze Hai Tong Banking and Insurance Co Ltd* [1913] AC 847, PC; *Navarro v Moregrand Ltd* [1951] WN 335, CA.
2   *Hawken v Bourne* (1841) 8 M & W 703; *Howard v Sheward* (1866) LR 2 CP 148; *Wing v Harvey* (1854) 5 De GM & G 265.
3   *AL Underwood Ltd v Bank of Liverpool and Martins* [1924] 1 KB 775, CA.
4   *Lloyd v Grace, Smith & Co* [1912] AC 716, HL; *Lloyds Bank Ltd v Chartered Bank of India, Australia and China* [1929] 1 KB 40, CA; *Uxbridge Permanent Benefit Building Society v Pickard* [1939] 2 KB 248, [1939] 2 All ER 344, CA. The fact that the agent is acting in his own interests may negative actual authority and put the third party on notice as regards apparent authority: *Biggar v Rock Life Assurance Co* [1902] 1 KB 516; *Midland Bank Ltd v Reckitt* [1933] AC 1, HL.

124. Effect of limitation of authority.

Where a principal, in conferring authority upon his agent to act on his behalf, imposes conditions[1] or limitations[2] on its exercise, no act done by the agent in excess of the conditional or limited authority is treated as the act of the principal as regards such persons as have[3] or ought to have[4] notice of such excess of authority, or have had notice of an irregularity placing them upon inquiry as to whether the agent's authority was being exceeded[5]. In the absence of notice, however, the principal cannot escape liability for acts done by the agent which fall within the apparent scope of his authority, by any particular instructions to his agent limiting his authority[6].

1   *Jordan v Norton* (1838) 4 M & W 155.
2   *Jacobs v Morris* [1902] 1 Ch 816, CA; *Balfour v Ernest* (1859) 5 CBNS 601.
3   *Evans v Kymer* (1830) 1 B & Ad 528; *Bodenham v Hoskyns* (1852) 2 De GM & G 903; *Cuthbert v Robarts, Lubbock & Co* [1909] 2 Ch 226, CA; *Forman & Co Pty v The Liddesdale* [1900] AC 190, PC; *Russo-Chinese Bank v Li Yau Sam* [1910] AC 174, PC; *Doey v London and North Western Rly Co* [1919] 1 KB 623, DC; *Reckitt v Barnett, Pembroke and Slater Ltd* [1929] AC 176,

HL. Cf *A-G for Ceylon v Silva* [1953] AC 461, [1953] 2 WLR 1185, PC (representation as to the extent of the authority made solely by the agent did not bind principal); *Armagas Ltd v Mundogas SA, The Ocean Frost* [1986] AC 717, [1986] 2 All ER 385, [1986] 2 Lloyd's Rep 109, HL. See also *Hudson Bay Apparel Brands LLC v Umbro International Ltd* [2010] EWCA Civ 949, [2011] 1 BCLC 259.

4 *Hatch v Searles* (1854) 2 Sm & G 147; *Flight v Provident Association of London Ltd* (1895) 12 TLR 51, CA; *Cuthbert v Robarts, Lubbock & Co* [1909] 2 Ch 226, CA; *Morison v Kemp* (1912) 29 TLR 70; *Morison v London County and Westminster Bank Ltd* [1914] 3 KB 356, CA; *Lloyds Bank Ltd v Chartered Bank of India, Australia and China* [1929] 1 KB 40, CA; *Reckitt v Barnett, Pembroke and Slater Ltd* [1929] AC 176, HL. As to limitation usual in a particular business see *Baines v Ewing* (1866) LR 1 Exch 320; *Daun v Simmins* (1879) 41 LT 783, CA. As to the effect of limitations under the memorandum or articles of association of a company see PARA 8. For the effect of signatures by procuration and analogous signatures on bills of exchange etc see *Midland Bank Ltd v Reckitt* [1933] AC 1, HL; the Bills of Exchange Act 1882 s 25; and FINANCIAL INSTRUMENTS AND TRANSACTIONS vol 49 (2015) PARA 258.

5 *AL Underwood Ltd v Bank of Liverpool and Martins* [1924] 1 KB 775, CA; *Lloyds Bank Ltd v Chartered Bank of India, Australia and China* [1929] 1 KB 40, CA; *Navarro v Moregrand Ltd* [1951] WN 335, CA.

6 *National Bolivian Navigation Co v Wilson* (1880) 5 App Cas 176, HL; *Trickett v Tomlinson* (1863) 13 CBNS 663; *Duke of Beaufort v Neeld* (1845) 12 Cl & Fin 248, HL; *Davy v Waller* (1899) 81 LT 107; *Edmunds v Bushell and Jones* (1865) LR 1 QB 97; *Limpus v London General Omnibus Co Ltd* (1862) 1 H & C 526, Ex Ch; *Roper v SS Fort Lamy (Managers)* (1943) 36 BWCC 255, CA; *Pharmed Medicare Private Ltd v Univar Ltd* [2002] EWCA Civ 1569, [2003] 1 All ER (Comm) 321. As to implied authority see further PARAS 37–44.

125. Act beyond actual or apparent scope of authority.

Where an act done by an agent is not within the scope of his express or implied authority[1], or falls outside the apparent scope of his authority[2], the principal is not bound by, or liable for, that act[3], even if the opportunity to do it arose out of the agency[4], and it was purported to be done on his behalf[5], unless he expressly adopted it by taking the benefit of it[6] or otherwise[7].

Where the agent obtains the money or property of a third person by means of any act beyond the actual or apparent scope of his authority, the principal is not responsible unless the money[8] or property[9] or the proceeds thereof[10] have been received by him[11], or have been applied for his benefit[12], in which case he becomes liable to the extent of the benefit received[13].

When a principal has mistakenly paid money to a third party in respect of unauthorised contracts by which he is not bound, he may recover the money as money paid by mistake[14].

1 *McGowan & Co v Dyer* (1873) LR 8 QB 141; *Re Cunningham & Co Ltd, Simpson's Claim* (1887) 36 ChD 532; *Watkin v Lamb* (1901) 85 LT 483; *Biggar v Rock Life Assurance Co* [1902] 1 KB 516; *Barnett v South London Tramways Co* (1887) 18 QBD 815, CA; *George Whitechurch Ltd v Cavanagh* [1902] AC 117, HL; *M'Millan v Accident Insurance Co* 1907 SC 484; *Connors v London and Provincial Assurance Co* (1913) 6 BWCC 146; *Thornton-Smith v Motor Union Insurance Co Ltd* (1913) 30 TLR 139; *Newsholme Bros v Road Transport and General Insurance Co Ltd* [1929] 2 KB 356, CA; *Dunn v Ocean Accident and Guarantee Corpn Ltd* (1933) 50 TLR 32; *Re Transplanters (Holding Co) Ltd* [1958] 2 All ER 711, [1958] 1 WLR 822; *Armagas Ltd v Mundogas SA* [1986] AC 717, [1986] 2 All ER 385, HL.

2 *Linford v Provincial Horse and Cattle Insurance Co* (1864) 34 Beav 291; *Newlands v National Employers' Accident Association Ltd* (1885) 54 LJQB 428, CA; *Re Southport and West Lancashire Banking Co* (1885) 1 TLR 204, CA; *Xenos v Wickham* (1866) LR 2 HL 296; *Spooner v Browning* [1898] 1 QB 528, CA; *Levy v Scottish Employers' Insurance Co* (1901) 17 TLR 229, DC; *Wright v Glyn* [1902] 1 KB 745, CA; *Comerford v Britannic Assurance Co* (1908) 24 TLR 593.

3 Nor can it amount to an act of bankruptcy by the principal: *Re Sawers, ex p Blain* (1879) 12 ChD 522, CA. Statute may, however, impose responsibility for the acts of an agent: see eg the Equality Act 2010 ss 109(2), (3), 110(2), (3); and DISCRIMINATION vol 33 (2017) PARA 120.

4   *Ruben v Great Fingall Consolidated* [1906] AC 439, HL; *Truman v Attenborough* (1910) 103 LT 218.
5   See the cases cited in notes 1, 4.
6   *Jacobs v Morris* [1902] 1 Ch 816, CA.
7   As to ratification see PARAS 58–71.
8   *Bannatyne v MacIver* [1906] 1 KB 103, CA; *Reid v Rigby & Co* [1894] 2 QB 40.
9   *Glyn v Baker* (1811) 13 East 509.
10   *Marsh v Keating* (1834) 1 Bing NC 198, HL.
11   *Glyn v Baker* (1811) 13 East 509; *Marsh v Keating* (1834) 1 Bing NC 198, HL. See also *Kettlewell v Refuge Assurance Co* [1908] 1 KB 545, CA (affd sub nom *Refuge Assurance Co Ltd v Kettlewell* [1909] AC 243, HL); *Holdsworth v Lancashire and Yorkshire Insurance Co* (1907) 23 TLR 521; *Murfitt v Royal Insurance* Co (1922) 38 TLR 334.
12   *Bannatyne v MacIver* [1906] 1 KB 103, CA; *Reid v Rigby & Co* [1894] 2 QB 40; *Re Japanese Curtains and Patent Fabric Co Ltd, ex p Shoolbred* (1880) 28 WR 339; *Blackburn Building Society v Cunliffe Brooks & Co* (1882) 22 ChD 61, CA (affd sub nom *Cunliffe Brooks & Co v Blackburn and District Benefit Building Society* (1884) 9 App Cas 857, HL); *Reversion Fund and Insurance Co Ltd v Maison Cosway Ltd* [1913] 1 KB 364, CA; *B Liggett (Liverpool) Ltd v Barclays Bank Ltd* [1928] 1 KB 48. See also *Re Cleadon Trust Ltd* [1939] Ch 286, [1938] 4 All ER 518, CA.
13   If, however, the third person was indebted to the principal, and the unauthorised act relates to the mode of enforcing payment, the principal is entitled to keep the benefit without being liable for the agent's act: *Freeman v Rosher* (1849) 13 QB 780; *Lewis v Read* (1845) 13 M & W 834; but contrast *Haseler v Lemoyne* (1858) 5 CBNS 530, where there was in fact a ratification (all cases of distress for rent).
14   *Bailey and Whites Ltd v House* (1915) 31 TLR 583, DC. As to the recovery of payments made under a mistake see MISTAKE vol 77 (2016) PARA 64. As to contracts on which the principal will be bound see PARA 126.

(2) CONTRACTUAL RELATIONS

(i) Enforcement Generally

126. Rights and liabilities of principal.

As a general rule[1], any contract made by an agent with the authority[2] of his principal may be enforced by[3] or against[4] the principal where his name or existence was disclosed to the other contracting party at the time when the contract was made[5].

Where the principal is undisclosed, the authorised contract of the agent may also as a general rule be enforced by or against the principal[6]. If, however, the agent contracts in such terms as to imply that he is the real and only principal, evidence to contradict the terms of the contract will not be admitted[7]. Whether he has contracted in such terms or not depends upon the construction of the particular contract[8]. Where an agent contracts in his own name but not in terms which are consistent only with his having done so as principal, oral evidence may be admitted to prove the identity of the principal[9].

If a person contracts with an agent honestly believing[10] him to be the principal and makes the contract with the agent for reasons personal to the agent, the real principal cannot sue upon the contract[11]. If, however, the agent's contract related to the principal's goods, the principal may have a right to claim against the other contracting party for conversion[12] or upon an implied contract to pay for the goods[13].

Where a contract is made without the actual or ostensible authority[14] of the principal, it cannot be enforced by or against the principal, unless it is a contract which purports to be made on behalf of a principal[15] and is capable of being, and has been, ratified by the principal in question[16].

1 For the exceptions to this rule see PARAS **128–132**.

2 'Authority' means all types of authority and not merely express authority: see generally PARA **122**.

3 If the agent has begun a claim against the other contracting party, the principal may intervene: *Sadler v Leigh* (1815) 4 Camp 195.

4 Ie including the Crown: see *Thomas v R* (1874) LR 10 QB 31. See also *Camillo Tank Steamship Co Ltd v Alexandria Engineering Works* (1921) 38 TLR 134, HL.

5 *Skinner v Stocks* (1821) 4 B & Ald 437; *Hornby v Lacy* (1817) 6 M & S 166; *Sadler v Leigh* (1815) 4 Camp 195; *Duke of Norfolk v Worthy* (1808) 1 Camp 337; *Petty v Anderson* (1825) 3 Bing 170; *Bateman v Phillips* (1812) 15 East 272; *Higgins v Senior* (1841) 8 M & W 834. As to the personal liability of the agent see PARAS **157–160**.

6 *Edmunds v Bushell and Jones* (1865) LR 1 QB 97; *Watteau v Fenwick* [1893] 1 QB 346; *Boyter v Thompson* [1995] 2 AC 628, [1995] 3 All ER 135, HL (undisclosed principal liable for breach of implied condition of merchantable quality and fitness for purpose contained in the Sale of Goods Act 1979 s 14(2), (3) (see SALE OF GOODS AND SUPPLY OF SERVICES vol 91 (2012) PARAS 79, 81)). In the case of an undisclosed principal there will be no apparent authority of the agent, since authority relates to a known agency situation; the agent will, however, bind the principal and the third party where he acts within the powers usually possessed by the class of person to which the principal has allowed the agent to appear to belong: *Watteau v Fenwick*. But see the remarks of Bingham J in *Rhodian River Shipping Co and Rhodian Sailor Shipping Co SA v Halla Maritime Corpn, The Rhodian River and Rhodian Sailor* [1984] 1 Lloyd's Rep 373 at 379; *Sign-O-Lite Plastics Ltd v Metropolitan Life Insurance Co* (1990) 73 DLR (4th) 541. The undisclosed principal may sue even if he is bankrupt, if personal qualifications are not material: *Dyster v Randall & Sons* [1926] Ch 932, CA. A contract for insurance is an ordinary commercial contract and an undisclosed principal can sue unless the insurance company only intended to contract with the agent: *Siu Yin Kwan v Eastern Insurance Co Ltd* [1994] 2 AC 199, [1994] 1 All ER 213, PC (applied in *Novasen SA v Alimenta SA* [2011] EWHC 49 (Comm), [2011] 2 All ER (Comm) 555 (nothing to suggest that seller of groundnut oil was not willing to treat as a party to the contract anyone on whose behalf the intermediary might have been authorised to contract)).

7 *Humble v Hunter* (1848) 12 QB 310 (agent describing himself as 'owner' of a ship, the subject matter of a charterparty); *Formby Bros v Formby* [1910] WN 48, CA (agent describing himself as 'proprietor' in a building contract); *Dunlop Pneumatic Tyre Co Ltd v Selfridge & Co Ltd* [1915] AC 847, HL; *Rederiaktiebolaget Argonaut v Hani* [1918] 2 KB 247.

8 *Fred Drughorn Ltd v Rederiaktiebolaget Trans-Atlantic* [1919] AC 203, HL (agent signing as 'charterer'), in which *Rederiaktiebolaget Argonaut v Hani* [1918] 2 KB 247, was doubted; *Danziger v Thompson* [1944] KB 654, [1944] 2 All ER 151 (agent signing as 'tenant'). See also *Murphy v Rae* [1967] NZLR 103, NZ CA (description of husband, acting for self and wife and with full authority, as 'vendor'; evidence admissible of identity of true owners, and fact that husband contracted as 'vendor' no ground for repudiation by purchaser).

9 See *Danziger v Thompson* [1944] KB 654, [1944] 2 All ER 151; and DEEDS AND OTHER INSTRUMENTS vol 32 (2012) PARA 386.

10 The fact that such person had constructive notice is insufficient because the doctrine of constructive notice does not extend to commercial contracts (*Manchester Trust Ltd v Furness* [1895] 2 QB 539, CA; *Greer v Downs Supply Co* [1927] 2 KB 28, CA).

11 *Said v Butt* [1920] 3 KB 497; *Greer v Downs Supply Co* [1927] 2 KB 28, CA; *Collins v Associated Greyhound Racecourses Ltd* [1930] 1 Ch 1, CA.

12 *Cundy v Lindsay* (1878) 3 App Cas 459, HL; *Greer v Downs Supply Co* [1927] 2 KB 28, CA.

13 *Ramazotti v Bowring* (1859) 7 CBNS 851; *Boulton v Jones* (1857) 2 H & N 564; *Farquharson Bros & Co v King & Co* [1902] AC 325, HL; *Greer v Downs Supply Co* [1927] 2 KB 28, CA. As to dispositions of goods by the agent see PARAS **145–150**.

14 As to ostensible authority see PARA **25**.

15 *Keighley, Maxsted & Co v Durant* [1901] AC 240, HL.

16 *Kelner v Baxter* (1866) LR 2 CP 174; *Newborne v Sensolid (Great Britain) Ltd* [1954] 1 QB 45, [1953] 1 All ER 708, CA. See further PARAS **58–71**.

127. Where signed memorandum necessary.

Where the enforcement of the contract depends upon the existence of a signed memorandum[1], a memorandum signed by the agent is sufficient[2], provided that the agent has authority, express or implied, to sign it[3], and the principal is sufficiently described[4].

1   As to the contracts requiring such memoranda see the Statute of Frauds (1677) s 4 (which now relates only to contracts of guarantee: see FINANCIAL INSTRUMENTS AND TRANSACTIONS vol 49 (2015) PARA 677 et seq); and the Law of Property (Miscellaneous Provisions) Act 1989 s 2 (see CONVEYANCING vol 23 (2016) PARA 27). As to the informal appointment of an agent where he will be required to sign a memorandum see PARAS 18–19. As to agents for the purchase of land see PARA 18.

2   Except where the signature of the party himself is essential, as in representations as to credit under the Statute of Frauds Amendment Act 1828 s 6: see *Williams v Mason* (1873) 28 LT 232. See also *Re Whitley Partners Ltd* (1886) 32 ChD 337, CA; and PARA 19. The signature of the agent is sufficient to revive a statute-barred debt: see the Limitation Act 1980 s 30; and LIMITATION PERIODS vol 68 (2016) PARA 1182. See also *Gavaghan v Edwards* [1961] 2 QB 220, [1961] 2 All ER 477, CA.

3   *Sims v Landray* [1894] 2 Ch 318; cf *Bell v Balls* [1897] 1 Ch 663; *Durrell v Evans* (1862) 1 H & C 174, Ex Ch; *Rosenbaum v Belson* [1900] 2 Ch 267; *North v Loomes* [1919] 1 Ch 378; *Thirkell v Cambi* [1919] 2 KB 590, CA; *Blackburn v Walker* (1920) 150 LT Jo 73. See also *Ramsay v Love* [2015] EWHC 65 (Ch), [2015] All ER (D) 130 (Jan) (principal held liable on guarantee which had been signed by agent using a machine which automatically signed the principal's signature because agent he had been acting within the wide general authority conferred on him by the principal). As to brokers' bought and sold notes see SALE OF GOODS AND SUPPLY OF SERVICES vol 91 (2012) PARA 46.

4   *Grainger v Moseley* (1961) 179 Estates Gazette 221. If the principal is insufficiently described, evidence will not be admissible to identify the principal, at least from other documents which are not in themselves a memorandum of the agreement: *Lovesy v Palmer* [1916] 2 Ch 233.

(ii) Limitations on Rights and Liabilities

128. Deed executed in name of agent.

At common law, a contract by deed executed by an agent in his own name cannot be enforced by[1] or against[2] the principal, even though it is expressly stated that the agent is contracting on behalf of the principal[3], but where the agent executes a deed and is trustee for his principal of the rights conferred by the deed, the principal is entitled to enforce the contract[4]. The claim should be in the name of the trustee; but, if he refuses to sue, the beneficiary may do so, joining the trustee as a defendant[5]. By statute, any instrument executed in pursuance of a power of attorney by the donee in his own name is as effective as if executed by the donor of the power, thus entitling the donor to enforce the instrument directly[6].

1   *Schack v Anthony* (1813) 1 M & S 573.
2   *Re International Contract Co, Pickering's Claim* (1871) 6 Ch App 525; *Viscount Torrington v Lowe* (1868) LR 4 CP 26.
3   *Berkeley v Hardy* (1826) 8 Dow & Ry KB 102; *Chesterfield and Midland Silkstone Colliery Co Ltd v Hawkins* (1865) 3 H & C 677. As to the execution of a conveyance under seal by a corporate agent or by an attorney for a corporation see PARA 45. As to the statutory modification of the common law rule in the case of powers of attorney see the text and note 6.
4   *Harmer v Armstrong* [1934] Ch 65, CA.
5   See *Vandepitte v Preferred Accident Insurance Corpn of New York* [1933] AC 70, PC.
6   See the Powers of Attorney Act 1971 s 7(1); and PARA 45.

129. Bills of exchange, etc.

A principal is not liable upon any bill of exchange, cheque or promissory note unless his name appears thereon[1], but his signature may be written by the hand of an agent[2]. In determining whether any signature is that of the principal, or of the agent in his personal capacity, the construction most favourable to the validity of the instrument is adopted[3].

Where the agent signs the instrument in his principal's name, the principal is liable[4], except in the case of a bill drawn upon the agent, in which case the principal cannot be liable as acceptor[5], even if the agent accepts it in the principal's name and by his authority[6].

Where the agent signs the instrument in his own name, the agent is not relieved from personal liability and the principal is not liable on the instrument[7] unless the agent's signature purports to be made on the principal's behalf[8]. In the case of a bill drawn upon the principal, however, the principal is liable, though the agent accepts in his own name[9].

Where the principal carries on a trade or business in the agent's name, he is liable as acceptor[10] or otherwise[11], as the case may be, on all instruments signed by the agent in his own name in the course of such trade or business.

1 See the Bills of Exchange Act 1882 s 23; and FINANCIAL INSTRUMENTS AND TRANSACTIONS vol 49 (2015) PARAS 251–252.
2 See the Bills of Exchange Act 1882 ss 25, 26, 91(1); and FINANCIAL INSTRUMENTS AND TRANSACTIONS vol 49 (2015) PARAS 257–261.
3 See the Bills of Exchange Act 1882 s 26(2); and FINANCIAL INSTRUMENTS AND TRANSACTIONS vol 49 (2015) PARA 259.
4 See the Bills of Exchange Act 1882 ss 25, 26; and FINANCIAL INSTRUMENTS AND TRANSACTIONS vol 49 (2015) PARAS 258–260.
5 As to acceptance see the Bills of Exchange Act 1882 s 17; and FINANCIAL INSTRUMENTS AND TRANSACTIONS vol 49 (2015) PARAS 235, 245–248.
6 Cf *Polhill v Walter* (1832) 3 B & Ad 114; *Steele v M'Kinlay* (1880) 5 App Cas 754, HL.
7 Bills of Exchange Act 1882 s 26(1); *Ducarrey v Gill* (1830) Mood & M 450; *Formby Bros v Formby* [1910] WN 48, CA.
8 Bills of Exchange Act 1882 s 26(1); *Alexander v Sizer* (1869) LR 4 Exch 102.
9 *Lindus v Bradwell* (1848) 5 CB 583; *Jenkins v Morris* (1847) 16 M & W 877; *Okell v Charles* (1876) 34 LT 822, CA.
10 *Edmunds v Bushell and Jones* (1865) LR 1 QB 97.
11 *Furze v Sharwood* (1841) 2 QB 388.

130. Contract on behalf of foreign principal.

Where a contract is made by an agent on behalf of a foreign principal there is no presumption that the agent necessarily incurs personal liability and has no authority to establish privity of contract between the principal and the third party[1]. Where the intention of the parties is not clear or the terms of the contract are in dispute, the fact that the principal is a foreigner is a factor to be taken into account in determining whether in the circumstances the contract is enforceable by or against the foreign principal or whether the agent is personally liable[2].

1 *Teheran-Europe Co Ltd v ST Belton (Tractors) Ltd* [1968] 2 QB 545, [1968] 2 All ER 886, CA. As to an agent's personal liability see generally PARAS 157–160.
2 *HO Brandt & Co v HN Morris & Co Ltd* [1917] 2 KB 784, CA; *JS Holt and Moseley (London) Ltd v Sir Charles Cunningham & Partners* (1949) 83 Ll L Rep 141; *Anglo-African Shipping Co of New York Inc v J Mortner Ltd* [1962] 1 Lloyd's Rep 610, CA; *Maritime Stores v HP Marshall & Co* [1963] 1 Lloyd's Rep 602; *Teheran-Europe Co Ltd v ST Belton (Tractors) Ltd* [1968] 2 QB 545, [1968] 2 All ER 886, CA.

131. Exclusion of principal's rights and liabilities.

The rights and liabilities of a principal under his agent's contracts may be excluded by the express terms of the contract[1], but in no case can the principal be deprived of his right to enforce the contract in his own name, or be exempted from his liability thereunder, notwithstanding that a usage, rule or regulation of a professional body purporting to have that effect was known to him at the time when the contract was made[2]. The mere fact that the agent is himself liable on the contract, and that credit has been given him[3], is not sufficient to exclude the principal's liability.

1   *Montgomerie v United Kingdom Mutual Steamship Association* [1891] 1 QB 370; *United Kingdom Mutual Steamship Assurance Association v Nevill* (1887) 19 QBD 110, CA; and contrast *Great Britain 100 A1 Steamship Insurance Association v Wyllie* (1889) 22 QBD 710, CA; *Humble v Hunter* (1848) 12 QB 310; *Formby Bros v Formby* [1910] WN 48, CA; *Dunlop Pneumatic Tyre Co Ltd v Selfridge & Co Ltd* [1915] AC 847, HL; *Rederiaktiebolaget Argonaut v Hani* [1918] 2 KB 247; *Collins v Associated Greyhound Racecourses Ltd* [1930] 1 Ch 1, CA; *Fred Drughorn Ltd v Rederiaktiebolaget Trans-Atlantic* [1919] AC 203, HL.
2   *Langton v Waite* (1868) LR 6 Eq 165; *Levitt v Hamblet* [1901] 2 KB 53, CA; *Allen v F O'Hearn & Co* [1937] AC 213, [1936] 3 All ER 828, PC (stock exchange usage that members act as principals).
3   *Paterson v Gandasequi* (1812) 15 East 62; *Thomson v Davenport* (1829) 9 B & C 78. As to the personal liability of the agent see generally PARAS **157–160**.

132. Election to treat agent as principal.

Where the other contracting party, whether in ignorance of the principal's existence or not[1], obtains a judgment against the agent[2], or, though he knows[3] at the time when the contract is made[4], or discovers afterwards[5], who the real principal is, elects to look to the agent to the exclusion of the principal, the principal is discharged from liability to the third party and his liability cannot be revived[6]. Such election is conclusively proved by obtaining judgment against the agent[7], even for part of the claim[8], unless the part for which judgment has been obtained constitutes a separate cause of action[9]. Otherwise the question of election is one of fact[10], and depends on the circumstances of the particular case[11].

1   If the other contracting party sues the agent he will not be allowed to interrogate the agent as to the existence or identity of an undisclosed principal for the purpose of making such principal a party to the claim: *Thöl v Leask* (1855) 10 Exch 704; *Sebright v Hanbury* [1916] 2 Ch 245.
2   This applies even where the judgment is unsatisfied: *Kendall v Hamilton* (1879) 4 App Cas 504, HL. The principal's liability revives if the judgment is set aside on the merits (*Partington v Hawthorne* (1888) 52 JP 807); but not where it is merely with the agent's consent (*Cross & Co v Matthews and Wallace* (1904) 91 LT 500; *Hammond v Schofield* [1891] 1 QB 453). See also *Sullivan v Sullivan* [1912] 2 IR 116, CA; *Firm of RMKRM v Firm of MRMVL* [1926] AC 761, PC.
3   Actual knowledge must be proved in order to show an election: *Dunn v Newton* (1884) Cab & El 278.
4   *Paterson v Gandasequi* (1812) 15 East 62; *Addison v Gandassequi* (1812) 4 Taunt 574.
5   *Priestly v Fernie* (1865) 3 H & C 977.
6   *Paterson v Gandasequi* (1812) 15 East 62. The same principle applies where the principal is sued first instead of the agent: *London General Omnibus Co Ltd v Pope* (1922) 38 TLR 270. As to the common law principle of election and as to estoppel where judgment is obtained against one of two who are alternatively liable see ESTOPPEL vol 47 (2014) PARAS **312, 363**. See *LC Fowler & Sons Ltd v St Stephen's College Board of Governors* [1991] 3 NZLR 304 (referred to in *Nueva Fortuna Corpn v Tata Ltd, The Nea Tyhi* [1999] 2 Lloyd's Rep 497).
7   *Morel Bros & Co Ltd v Earl of Westmorland* [1904] AC 11, HL; *Priestly v Fernie* (1865) 3 H & C 977; *Moore v Flanagan* [1920] 1 KB 919, CA. Cf *Goldrei, Foucard & Son v Sinclair and Russian Chamber of Commerce in London* [1918] 1 KB 180, CA; but see *Ingram Clothing Manufacturing Co (Glasgow) v Lewis* 1961 SLT (Sh Ct) 18.
8   *French v Howie* [1906] 2 KB 674, CA.
9   *Debenham's Ltd v Perkins* (1925) 133 LT 252.

10 *Clarkson, Booker Ltd v Andjel* [1964] 2 QB 775, [1964] 3 All ER 260, CA; *Cyril Lord Carpet Sales v Browne* (1966) 111 Sol Jo 51, CA.

11 *Calder v Dobell* (1871) LR 6 CP 486: *Curtis v Williamson* (1874) LR 10 QB 57; *Robinson v Read* (1829) 9 B & C 449; *Stoneham and Messenger v Wyman* (1901) 17 TLR 562 174; *Ex p Pitt* (1923) 40 TLR 5, CA.

(iii) Settlement with Agent

133. Payments by principal.

Where a principal is indebted to a third person on a contract made by his agent, he is not discharged from his liability to pay the debt by any payment to or settlement by him with the agent[1], unless such payment or settlement takes place bona fide and at a time when the third person is unaware of the existence of the principal and is extending credit only to the agent[2], or unless the third person by his conduct leads the principal reasonably to believe that the debt has been paid by the agent[3] or that the third person has elected[4] to look to the agent alone for payment[5], and the principal in consequence alters his position as regards the agent to his prejudice[6]. Mere delay on the part of the creditor is not, of itself, sufficient to discharge the principal[7].

1 *Irvine & Co v Watson & Sons* (1880) 5 QBD 414, CA; *Davison v Donaldson* (1882) 9 QBD 623, CA; *Heald v Kenworthy* (1855) 10 Exch 739; *Smyth v Anderson* (1849) 7 CB 21.

2 *Armstrong v Stokes* (1872) LR 7 QB 598, doubted in *Irvine & Co v Watson & Sons* (1880) 5 QBD 414, CA.

3 *Wyatt v Marquis of Hertford* (1802) 3 East 147; *MacClure v Schemeil* (1871) 20 WR 168.

4 See PARA 132.

5 *Priestly v Fernie* (1865) 3 H & C 977; and cf *Harvey v Norton* (1840) 4 Jur 42.

6 *Hopkins v Ware* (1869) LR 4 Exch 268; *Smith v Ferrand* (1827) 7 B & C 19.

7 *Davison v Donaldson* (1882) 9 QBD 623, CA; *Irvine & Co v Watson & Sons* (1880) 5 QBD 414, CA; and contrast *Hopkins v Ware* (1869) LR 4 Exch 268.

134. Payments by third party.

The third party is not discharged from his liability to the principal by any payment to or settlement with the agent[1], unless such payment or settlement is ratified by the principal or is made in the ordinary course of business, or in accordance with the agent's authority[2], express, implied or apparent[3]. If, however, the principal has allowed the agent to appear as principal in the transaction in respect of which the payment or settlement is made, the third person is discharged by any payment to or settlement with the agent which would have discharged him if the agent had been in fact the principal[4]. The third party is also entitled to set off[5] any debts due to him from the agent personally, provided that the payment or settlement was made or the debt incurred before the third party knew of the existence of the principal[6].

1 *Crossley v Magniac* [1893] 1 Ch 594; *Linck, Moeller & Co v Jameson & Co* (1885) 2 TLR 206, CA; *Catterall v Hindle* (1867) LR 2 CP 368, Ex Ch; *Dorf v Neumann, Luebeck & Co* (1924) 40 TLR 405.

2 *Hogarth v Wherley* (1875) LR 10 CP 630; *Catterall v Hindle* (1867) LR 2 CP 368, Ex Ch; *Legge v Byas, Mosley & Co* (1901) 7 Com Cas 16. As to the agent's authority to receive payment see generally PARA 38.

3 The third party is not, in the absence of express authority, discharged by payment by a negotiable instrument (*Williams v Evans* (1866) LR 1 QB 352; *Hine Bros v Steamship Insurance Syndicate Ltd, The Netherholme, Glen Holme, and Rydal Holme* (1895) 72 LT 79, CA), unless justified by usage, such usage being a reasonable one and binding on the principal without notice (*Bridges v Garrett* (1870) LR 5 CP 451). A settlement of accounts with the agent does not bind the principal (*Pearson v Scott* (1878) 9 ChD 198), notwithstanding any usage to that effect, unless the principal has notice of it (*Sweeting v Pearce* (1861) 9 CBNS 534). As to the effect of usage see further PARA

44. See also *Boothman v Byrne* (1923) 57 ILT 36; *Bradford & Sons v Price Bros* (1923) 92 LJKB 871; *Clay Hill Brick and Tile Co Ltd v Rawlings* [1938] 4 All ER 100, 159 LT 482. As to apparent authority see *Townsend v Inglis* (1816) Holt NP 278. See also PARA 25.

4   *Ramazotti v Bowring* (1859) 7 CBNS 851; *Borries v Imperial Ottoman Bank* (1873) LR 9 CP 38; *George v Clagett* (1797) 7 Term Rep 359; and see PARA 38. Similarly, where an agent is authorised to retain part of a debt paid to him for his own account, he may settle with the third party as he pleases in respect of such part: *Barker v Greenwood* (1837) 2 Y & C Ex 414.

5   *Borries v Imperial Ottoman Bank* (1873) LR 9 CP 38; *Montagu v Forwood* [1893] 2 QB 350, CA.

6   *Kaltenbach v Lewis* (1885) 10 App Cas 617, HL; *Mildred, Goyeneche & Co v Maspons Y Hermano* (1883) 8 App Cas 874, HL; *Dresser v Norwood* (1864) 17 CBNS 466, Ex Ch; *Semenza v Brinsley* (1865) 18 CBNS 467; and see *Isaac Cooke & Sons v Eshelby* (1887) 12 App Cas 271, HL.

135. Purchaser from agent having lien.

Where an agent sells in his own name goods belonging to his principal over which he has a lien against the principal, the purchaser is discharged to the extent of the value of the agent's lien by any payment to, or settlement with, or set-off against the agent[1], even though the purchaser knew of the existence of the principal at the time of the contract[2], or has had a demand for payment from the principal[3].

1   *Hudson v Granger* (1821) 5 B & Ald 27.

2   *Warner v McKay* (1836) 1 M & W 591.

3   Or from his trustee in bankruptcy: *Drinkwater v Goodwin* (1775) 1 Cowp 251.

(iv) Fraud, Misrepresentation or Concealment

136. Fraud etc of principal or agent.

Where, in the negotiation of any contract[1] by an agent, the agent while acting within the scope of his authority[2] is guilty, whether or not the principal is privy thereto[3], of fraud[4], undue influence[5] or innocent misrepresentation[6], or of concealment of essential facts which ought to be disclosed to the other contracting party[7], the contract is voidable, and the other party thereto may rescind it[8] and recover any benefit which has passed thereunder to the principal[9]. If sued, the other party may successfully resist any claim brought upon the contract whether for specific performance[10] or otherwise[11]. Where the other party elects to affirm the contract or has lost the right to rescind[12], he may bring a claim for deceit if the agent has induced the contract by fraud[13], or sue for breach of warranty if the representation constituted a warranty[14]. On the other hand, where in a contract of insurance the insurer learns that an agent of the insured has acted in breach of his duty as an agent of his principal in an earlier transaction, such misconduct will not entitle the insurer to repudiate the contract; further, despite the duty *uberrimae fidei* in insurance matters, the insurer has no duty of care to warn the insured and is not liable for any misconduct of the agent towards his principal thereafter[15].

If the third party has suffered loss through a misrepresentation which was not made fraudulently he may be entitled to sue for damages, and, where he would be entitled to rescind the contract for such a representation, the court may, if it considers it equitable so to do, declare the contract subsisting and award damages in lieu of rescission[16].

Where a misrepresentation is made by an agent acting within his express or ostensible authority, he is not personally liable under the Misrepresentation Act 1967[17] to the person who has entered into the contract with the principal on the strength of the misrepresentation[18].

An insurance broker may be liable to his client for loss sustained through being uninsured owing to the broker's misrepresentation[19].

1   The knowledge of the agent is not imputable to the principal in reference to the negotiation of another contract through another agent. Contrast *Blackburn, Low & Co v Haslam* (1888) 21 QBD 144, CA, with *Blackburn, Low & Co v Vigors* (1887) 12 App Cas 531, HL.

2   See *Overbrooke Estates Ltd v Glencombe Properties Ltd* [1974] 3 All ER 511, [1974] 1 WLR 1335, where limits were placed on the agent's ostensible authority, preventing any statement by the agent from becoming a binding representation or warranty. As to ostensible authority see PARA 25.

3   *Biggs v Lawrence* (1789) 3 Term Rep 454. For a consideration of the position where fraud is also practised on the principal see *Kwei Tek Chao (t/a Zung Fu Co) v British Traders and Shippers Ltd* [1954] 2 QB 459, [1954] 1 All ER 779.

4   *Lloyd v Grace, Smith & Co* [1912] AC 716, HL; *Barwick v English Joint Stock Bank* (1867) LR 2 Exch 259; *S Pearson & Son Ltd v Dublin Corpn* [1907] AC 351, HL; *Mair v Rio Grande Rubber Estates Ltd* [1913] AC 853, HL.

5   *Barclays Bank plc v Kennedy and Kennedy* (1988) 58 P & CR 221, [1989] 1 FLR 356, CA.

6   *Mullens v Miller* (1882) 22 ChD 194. As to the right of rescission for innocent misrepresentation or to damages in lieu of rescission see the Misrepresentation Act 1967 ss 1, 2; and CONTRACT vol 22 (2012) PARAS 352–353; MISREPRESENTATION vol 76 (2013) PARAS 703, 816, 832.

7   *Morrison v Universal Marine Insurance Co* (1873) LR 8 Exch 197; *Blackburn, Low & Co v Haslam* (1888) 21 QBD 144, CA.

8   *Reese River Silver Mining Co v Smith* (1869) LR 4 HL 64. As to the requirements for an effective rescission so as to prevent the acquisition of title to goods by an innocent third party see *Car and Universal Finance Co Ltd v Caldwell* [1965] 1 QB 525, [1964] 1 All ER 290, CA; and PARA 146. As to the right to rescind contracts see generally MISREPRESENTATION vol 76 (2013) PARA 811 et seq. The third party may possibly rescind where the contract is brought about by the fraud of an undisclosed principal where such fraud is unknown to the agent: see *Garnac Grain Co Inc v HMF Faure and Fairclough Ltd and Bunge Corpn* [1966] 1 QB 650, [1965] 1 All ER 47n; revsd on another point [1966] 1 QB 650, [1965] 3 All ER 273, CA; affd [1968] AC 1130n, [1967] 2 All ER 353, HL.

9   *Refuge Assurance Co Ltd v Kettlewell* [1909] AC 243, HL; *Hughes v Liverpool Victoria Legal Friendly Society* [1916] 2 KB 482, CA.

10 *Mullens v Miller* (1882) 22 ChD 194.

11 *Blackburn, Low & Co v Haslam* (1888) 21 QBD 144, CA.

12 Certain bars to the right to rescind were removed by the Misrepresentation Act 1967 s 1 (see MISREPRESENTATION vol 76 (2013) PARAS 703, 816).

13 *Udell v Atherton* (1861) 7 H & N 172. As to the liability of the principal in respect of misrepresentations made by the agent see PARAS 153–154; and MISREPRESENTATION vol 76 (2013) PARA 725.

14 *Brown v Sheen and Richmond Car Sales Ltd* [1950] 1 All ER 1102. The court will not readily infer that a representation constitutes a warranty: *Heilbut, Symons & Co v Buckleton* [1913] AC 30, HL; and see CONTRACT vol 22 (2012) PARA 352 et seq. Where the third party has been induced to contract on the basis of a negligent misrepresentation for which the principal is not liable because of lack of authority of the agent, the third party may also have a separate cause of action against the agent where the third party relied on a special skill and knowledge of the agent in the making of the misrepresentation: see *Hedley Byrne & Co Ltd v Heller & Partners Ltd* [1964] AC 465, [1963] 2 All ER 575, HL; *Dodds v Millman, Warwicker, Lister and Merlin M Lister Ltd* (1964) 47 WWR 690, 45 DLR (2d) 472, BC CA. The skill or knowledge must, however, be special skill or specialist knowledge: *Jones v Still* [1965] NZLR 1071, NZ CA. As to the liability of the agent generally see PARAS 151–155 (tortious liability), PARAS 161–162 (warranty of authority).

15 *Banque Financière de la Cité SA (formerly Banque Keyser Ullmann SA) v Westgate Insurance Co Ltd (formerly Hodge General & Mercantile Co Ltd)* [1991] 2 AC 249, [1990] 2 All ER 947, HL.

16 See the Misrepresentation Act 1967 s 2; and CONTRACT vol 22 (2012) PARAS 352–353; MISREPRESENTATION vol 76 (2013) PARA 832. As to an agent's duty of care to a purchaser in respect of a negligent misstatement see *McCullagh v Lane Fox & Partners Ltd* [1996] 1 EGLR 35, [1996] 18 EG 104, CA.

17 Ie under the Misrepresentation Act 1967 s 2 (see CONTRACT vol 22 (2012) PARAS 352–353; MISREPRESENTATION vol 76 (2013) PARA 832).

18 *Resolute Maritime Inc v Nippon Kaiji Kyokai, The Skopas* [1983] 2 All ER 1, [1983] 1 WLR 857.
19 *Warren v Henry Sutton & Co* [1976] 2 Lloyd's Rep 276, CA.

(v) Admissions by Agent

137. When and how far principal bound.

Where a principal gives authority to his agent to make admissions on his behalf, the principal is bound, as regards third persons, by any admission so made[1], provided that the admission is within that authority[2]. Where, however, the agent makes any admission without, or in excess of, his authority, the principal is not bound by it[3], although if the agent, at the time when he made the admission[4], was acting on his principal's behalf[5] in the transaction to which the admission referred[6], and made it in the ordinary course of his duty as such agent, the principal would be bound by the admission[7].

An admission by an agent is not receivable in evidence against the principal unless made in the exercise of actual authority, express or implied[8], and unless made in the course of and with reference to a transaction on behalf of the principal[9]. No statement made by an agent to the principal can be used against the principal by a third party as an admission[10].

Where the admission made by an agent binds the principal, it binds him to the same extent as it would have done if the principal had made it himself[11].

1 *Welsbach Incandescent Gas Lighting Co v New Sunlight Incandescent Co* [1900] 2 Ch 1, CA; *Williams v Innes* (1808) 1 Camp 364.
2 *Linsell v Bonsor* (1835) 2 Bing NC 241; *Meredith v Footner* (1843) 11 M & W 202; *Tustin v Arnold & Sons* (1915) 84 LJKB 2214.
3 *Barnett v South London Tramways Co* (1887) 18 QBD 815, CA; *Petch v Lyon* (1846) 9 QB 147; *Young v Wright* (1807) 1 Camp 139; *Watson v King* (1846) 3 CB 608; *Blackstone v Wilson* (1857) 26 LJ Ex 229.
4 *Great Western Rly Co v Willis* (1865) 18 CBNS 748.
5 *Petch v Lyon* (1846) 9 QB 147; *Young v Wright* (1807) 1 Camp 139.
6 *Blackstone v Wilson* (1857) 26 LJ Ex 229.
7 *Kirkstall Brewery Co v Furness Rly Co* (1874) LR 9 QB 468; *Biggs v Lawrence* (1789) 3 Term Rep 454; *Richardson v Peto* (1840) 1 Man & G 896; *Edwards v Brookes (Milk) Ltd* [1963] 3 All ER 62, [1963] 1 WLR 795, DC.
8 *Wright v Pepin* [1954] 2 All ER 52, [1954] 1 WLR 635; *Re Transplanters (Holding Co) Ltd* [1958] 2 All ER 711, [1958] 1 WLR 822.
9 *Blackstone v Wilson* (1857) 26 LJ Ex 229. As to the admissibility in evidence of admissions see CIVIL PROCEDURE vol 12 (2015) PARAS 709–711, 871.
10 *Re Devala Provident Gold Mining Co* (1883) 22 ChD 593; *Langhorn v Allnutt* (1812) 4 Taunt 511; *Kahl v Jansen* (1812) 4 Taunt 565; *Reyner v Pearson* (1812) 4 Taunt 662; *Swan v Miller* [1919] 1 IR 151, CA. There are exceptions to this principle in Admiralty jurisdiction: see *The Solway* (1885) 10 PD 137. The principle is in any court subject to the general rules as to what can be an admission (see eg *Wiedemann v Walpole* [1891] 2 QB 534, CA (silence after an accusation does not necessarily amount to an admission)) but the rule against the admissibility of such statements may often be circumvented by means of the provisions as to the admissibility of hearsay evidence (see CIVIL PROCEDURE vol 12 (2015) PARA 859 et seq).
11 As, for instance, if in writing, in preventing the running of time (Limitation Act 1980 s 30 (see LIMITATION PERIODS vol 68 (2016) PARA 1182); *Anderson v Sanderson* (1817) 2 Stark 204; *Burt v Palmer* (1804) 5 Esp 145; *Gregory v Parker* (1808) 1 Camp 394; *Re Transplanters (Holding Co) Ltd* [1958] 2 All ER 711, [1958] 1 WLR 822), and similarly in cases of part payment (*Re Hale, Lilley v Foad* [1899] 2 Ch 107, CA).

(vi) Notice to Agent

138. When notice to agent is imputed to principal.

Where in the course of any transaction[1] in which he is employed on his principal's behalf[2], an agent receives notice[3] or acquires knowledge[4] of any fact material to such transaction[5], under such circumstances that it is his duty to communicate it to the principal[6], the principal is precluded, as regards the persons who are parties to such transaction[7], from relying upon his own ignorance of that fact[8], and is taken to have received notice of it from the agent[9] at the time when he should have received it if the agent had performed his duty with due diligence[10]. There is also a presumption of fact that, where an agent in a commercial transaction receives a notice intended for his principal in the ordinary course of business, he will send or hand on the notice to his principal even though he has no authority to accept the notice on his principal's behalf[11].

1 Notice to purchasers is superseded in certain cases by the requirement of registration: see the Law of Property Act 1925 s 199(1)(i); and REAL PROPERTY AND REGISTRATION vol 87 (2017) PARA 656. As to the doctrine of constructive notice to a purchaser of property see EQUITABLE JURISDICTION vol 47 (2014) PARAS 134–137.

2 *Wilson v Salamandra Assurance Co of St Petersburg* (1903) 88 LT 96; *Hiern v Mill* (1806) 13 Ves 114; and contrast *Bawden v London, Edinburgh and Glasgow Assurance Co* [1892] 2 QB 534, CA, with *Biggar v Rock Life Assurance Co* [1902] 1 KB 516; and *Kelling v Pearl Assurance Co Ltd* (1923) 129 LT 573 with *Newsholme Bros v Road Transport and General Insurance Co Ltd* [1929] 2 KB 356, CA. See also *Thornton-Smith v Motor Union Insurance Co Ltd* (1913) 30 TLR 139; *Ayrey v British Legal and United Provident Assurance Co Ltd* [1918] 1 KB 136. The rule applies to sub-agents employed with the principal's consent: *Re Ashton, ex p McGowan* (1891) 64 LT 28; *Re Brewery Assets Corpn, Truman's Case* [1894] 3 Ch 272.

3 *Gladman v Johnson* (1867) 36 LJCP 153; *Tanham v Nicholson* (1872) LR 5 HL 561; *Golding v Royal London Auxiliary Insurance Co Ltd* (1914) 30 TLR 350; *Wilbraham v Colclough* [1952] 1 All ER 979.

4 *Baldwin v Casella* (1872) LR 7 Exch 325. The knowledge may have been acquired before the transaction, if it is in fact present in the agent's mind at the material time: *Fuller v Benett* (1843) 2 Hare 394; *Rolland v Hart* (1871) 6 Ch App 678; *Bradley v Riches* (1878) 9 ChD 189. Knowledge acquired by the agent prior to the creation of the relationship of principal and agent is not in general imputable to the principal: see PARA 139.

5 *Wyllie v Pollen* (1863) 3 De GJ & Sm 596, CA.

6 *Blackburn, Low & Co v Vigors* (1887) 12 App Cas 531, HL; *Bradley v Riches* (1878) 9 ChD 189.

7 Unless they are aware of the agent's intention not to communicate it: *Sharpe v Foy* (1868) 4 Ch App 35.

8 *Bawden v London, Edinburgh and Glasgow Assurance Co* [1892] 2 QB 534, CA; *Dresser v Norwood* (1864) 17 CBNS 466; *Holdsworth v Lancashire and Yorkshire Insurance Co* (1907) 23 TLR 521; *Apthorp v Neville & Co* (1907) 23 TLR 575; *Thornton-Smith v Motor Union Insurance Co Ltd* (1913) 30 TLR 139; *Taylor v Yorkshire Insurance Co* [1913] 2 IR 1; *Golding v Royal London Auxiliary Insurance Co Ltd* (1914) 30 TLR 350; *Ayrey v British Legal and United Provident Assurance Co Ltd* [1918] 1 KB 136; *Wells v Smith* [1914] 3 KB 722; *Newsholme Bros v Road Transport and General Insurance Co Ltd* [1929] 2 KB 356, CA.

9 *Gladstone v King* (1813) 1 M & S 35.

10 As, for example, by telegram instead of by letter: *Proudfoot v Montefiore* (1867) LR 2 QB 511.

11 *Rendal, A/S v Arcos Ltd* [1937] 3 All ER 577, 106 LJKB 756, HL. A car dealer may be the agent of the finance company for which he acts to receive notification of revocation of an offer from the prospective hirer: *Financings Ltd v Stimson* [1962] 3 All ER 386, [1962] 1 WLR 1184, CA. A dealer is, by statute, deemed to be the agent of the finance company to receive notice of withdrawal, cancellation or rescission: see the Consumer Credit Act 1974 ss 57, 69, 102; and CONSUMER CREDIT vol 21 (2016) PARAS 163, 168, 242.

139. When principal not bound by notice to agent.

Absent any duty to communicate the agent's knowledge to the principal, the principal is not bound by any notice given to, or any knowledge acquired by, the agent, if at the time when the agent received such notice or acquired such knowledge he was not acting as agent on the principal's behalf[1], or was not so acting in respect of the transaction in which the notice or knowledge is material[2].

Where the agent, though acting on his principal's behalf in some transaction in which his knowledge would otherwise be imputed to his principal, takes part in any fraud[3] or misfeasance[4] against the principal, the principal is not bound by the agent's knowledge of such fraud or misfeasance[5].

1 *Société Générale de Paris v Tramways Union Co* (1884) 14 QBD 424, CA (affd sub nom *Société Générale de Paris v Walker* (1885) 11 App Cas 20, HL); *Saffron Walden Second Benefit Building Society v Rayner* (1880) 14 ChD 406, CA; *Bolckow v Fisher* (1882) 10 QBD 161, CA; *Welsbach Incandescent Gas Lighting Co v New Sunlight Incandescent Co* [1900] 2 Ch 1, CA; *Taylor v Yorkshire Insurance Co* [1913] 2 IR 1; *Wells v Smith* [1914] 3 KB 722; *Newsholme Bros v Road Transport and General Insurance Co Ltd* [1929] 2 KB 356, CA; *O'Keefe v London and Edinburgh Insurance Co* [1928] NI 85, CA; *The Hayle* [1929] P 275 (harbour master; no duty to inform shipowner of defective state of berth); *Bottomley v Harrison* [1952] 1 All ER 368, (1952) 116 JP 113, DC (secretary of landlord not agent to receive abatement notice); *Dunn v Ocean Accident and Guarantee Corpn Ltd* (1933) 50 TLR 32, CA; *Stoneleigh Finance Ltd v Phillips* [1965] 2 QB 537, [1965] 1 All ER 513, CA; *Wilkinson v General Accident, Fire and Life Assurance Corpn Ltd* [1967] 2 Lloyd's Rep 182. As to the duty or absence of duty to communicate to the principal, where the principal is a company, see *Re Fenwick, Stobart & Co, Deep Sea Fishery Co's (Ltd) Claim* [1902] 1 Ch 507 (secretary of two companies; no notice where he is under duty not to communicate to one information acquired when acting for the other); and COMPANIES vol 14 (2016) PARA 122.

2 *Wyllie v Pollen* (1863) 3 De GJ & Sm 596, CA; *Tate v Hyslop* (1885) 15 QBD 368, CA; *Re Holland, ex p Warren* (1885) 15 QBD 48, CA; *Cawood, Wharton & Co Ltd v Samuel Williams & Sons Ltd, The Cawood III* [1951] P 270, [1951] 1 Lloyd's Rep 350.

3 *Cave v Cave* (1880) 15 ChD 639; *Williams v Preston* (1882) 20 ChD 672. See also *Kwei Tek Chao (t/a Zung Fu Co) v British Traders and Shippers Ltd* [1954] 2 QB 459, [1954] 1 All ER 779. Aliter, if the fraud is not against the principal: *Dixon v Winch* [1900] 1 Ch 736, CA; *Boursot v Savage* (1866) LR 2 Eq 134.

4 *Re Fitzroy Bessemer Steel Co Ltd* (1884) 50 LT 144.

5 *Wells v Smith* [1914] 3 KB 722. It is not sufficient to show merely that it was to the agent's interest to withhold from his principal the knowledge which he should have communicated: *Bradley v Riches* (1878) 9 ChD 189; but see *Re David Payne & Co Ltd, Young v David Payne & Co Ltd* [1904] 2 Ch 608, CA.

(vii) Corruption of Agent

140. Principal's remedies.

Where a principal has entered into any contract either through the mediation of an agent[1], or directly by himself on the faith of representations made by an agent[2], and it afterwards appears[3] that the other contracting party had made to the agent[4] a payment or promise of payment in the nature of a bribe[5], the principal has two courses open to him[6]. He may repudiate the contract and have it set aside[7], or he may affirm it and obtain such relief as the court may think right to give him[8].

There is an irrebuttable presumption that the payment was made with the intention that the agent should be influenced by it[9]; consequently it is immaterial to inquire whether or not the agent was in fact influenced by such payment or promise of payment to disregard his duty towards his principal[10].

The rule extends to cases where the payment or promise was not made directly with reference to the particular contract, but generally with a view to influencing the agent in his dealings with the other contracting party[11].

1 *Panama and South Pacific Telegraph Co v India Rubber, Gutta Percha and Telegraph Works Co* (1875) 10 Ch App 515; *Salford Corpn v Lever* [1891] 1 QB 168, CA. See also *Ross River Ltd v*

Cambridge City Football Club Ltd [2007] EWHC 2115 (Ch), [2007] All ER (D) 113 (Sep) (explaining *Panama and South Pacific Telegraph Co v India Rubber, Gutta Percha and Telegraph Works Co* above).

2 *Shipway v Broadwood* [1899] 1 QB 369, CA; *Re A Debtor (No 229 of 1927)* [1927] 2 Ch 367, CA.

3 *Alexander v Webber* [1922] 1 KB 642. This rule applies even where the giving or offering of a bribe to the agent first becomes known during the trial of a claim on the contract: *Shipway v Broadwood* [1899] 1 QB 369, CA; *Hough v Bolton* (1885) 1 TLR 606. The agent is required to disclose the payment to his principal: see *Ross River Ltd v Cambridge City Football Club Ltd* [2007] EWHC 2115 (Ch), [2007] All ER (D) 113 (Sep).

4 If the other contracting party discovers after his promise, but before payment, that the agent is in fact acting as agent for the principal, the payment will apparently be a bribe, but not if he does not discover it till after payment: *Grant v Gold Exploration and Development Syndicate Ltd* [1900] 1 QB 233, CA.

5 See further PARAS 94–95.

6 *Panama and South Pacific Telegraph Co v India Rubber, Gutta Percha and Telegraph Works Co* (1875) 10 Ch App 515; *Alexander v Webber* [1922] 1 KB 642.

7 As in *Shipway v Broadwood* [1899] 1 QB 369, CA; *Panama and South Pacific Telegraph Co v India Rubber, Gutta Percha and Telegraph Works Co* (1875) 10 Ch App 515; *Smith v Sorby* (1875) 3 QBD 552n; *Bartram & Sons v Lloyd* (1904) 90 LT 357, CA; *Re A Debtor (No 229 of 1927)* [1927] 2 Ch 367, CA; *Logicrose Ltd v Southend United Football Club Ltd* [1988] 1 WLR 1256. Even if a principal wrongfully repudiates the contract, being ignorant of a corrupt payment or agreement, he is entitled to relief upon discovery of the fraud: *Alexander v Webber* [1922] 1 KB 642.

8 As in *Salford Corpn v Lever* [1891] 1 QB 168, CA; *Grant v Gold Exploration and Development Syndicate Ltd* [1900] 1 QB 233, CA. Relief is available against the briber of an agent: *Fyffes Group Ltd v Templeman* [2000] 2 Lloyd's Rep 643.

9 *Hovenden & Sons v Millhoff* (1900) 83 LT 41, CA; *Re A Debtor (No 229 of 1927)* [1927] 2 Ch 367, CA; *Industries and General Mortgage Co Ltd v Lewis* [1949] 2 All ER 573, [1949] WN 333. It is also presumed that the payer had a corrupt motive: see *Taylor v Walker* [1958] 1 Lloyd's Rep 490. The whole reason that the agent should not accept a bribe or commission is that it puts him in conflict with his duty to his principal. Further, in terms of elementary economics, there must be a strong possibility that the bribe has disadvantaged the principal: *FHR European Ventures LLP v Mankarious* [2014] UKSC 45 at [37], [2015] AC 250, [2014] 4 All ER 79.

10 *Shipway v Broadwood* [1899] 1 QB 369, CA; *Hovenden & Sons v Millhoff* (1900) 83 LT 41, CA; and see *Harrington v Victoria Graving Dock Co* (1878) 3 QBD 549; but see *Rowland v Chapman* (1901) 17 TLR 669, where the agent's duty and interest were not in conflict.

11 *Smith v Sorby* (1875) 3 QBD 552n.

141. Principal's remedies when contract not repudiated.

Where the principal elects to affirm the contract, or does not discover the corruption of his agent until it is too late to rescind it[1], he may recover from the person who has paid or promised the bribe, jointly or severally with the agent[2], damages for any loss which he has sustained by reason of entering into the contract[3]. The measure of damages prima facie includes the amount of the bribe, without any deduction in respect of such portion of the bribe as may already have been recovered from the agent[4].

The person giving or promising any bribe to an agent is also liable to criminal proceedings[5].

1 He may lose the right to rescind by acquiescing in the receipt of the bribe by his agent, provided that there is full disclosure: *Bartram & Sons v Lloyd* (1904) 90 LT 357, CA.

2 As to the position of the agent see PARA 95.

3 The claim may be framed either for money had and received (*Hovenden & Sons v Millhoff* (1900) 83 LT 41, CA), where the amount of damages is a liquidated sum, or for damages for deceit (*Grant v Gold Exploration and Development Syndicate Ltd* [1900] 1 QB 233, CA; see also *Salford Corpn v Lever* [1891] 1 QB 168, CA). The giver of the bribe cannot escape liability on the ground that he thought the agent would disclose its receipt to his principal: *Panama and South Pacific Telegraph Co v India Rubber, Gutta Percha and Telegraph Works Co* (1875) 10 Ch App 515; *Grant v Gold Exploration and Development Syndicate Ltd*; *Ross River Ltd v Cambridge City Football Club Ltd* [2007] EWHC 2115 (Ch), [2008] All ER 1004.

4   *Salford Corpn v Lever* [1891] 1 QB 168, CA. An unconditional release of the agent, however, operates as a release to the third person: *Salford Corpn v Lever*.
5   He may be indicted for conspiracy (*R v De Kromme* (1892) 66 LT 301), or may be proceeded against under the Bribery Act 2010 (see CRIMINAL LAW vol 25 (2016) PARA 369 et seq). As to corruption of election agents see ELECTIONS AND REFERENDUMS vol 38A (2013) PARA 896.

(3) DISPOSITIONS OF PROPERTY

142.   Principal's right on agent's bankruptcy.

Where the agent becomes bankrupt[1], the general rule that the agent's unauthorised dispositions are not binding on the principal[2] applies in favour of the principal against the agent's trustee in bankruptcy and creditors, and entitles the principal to follow and recover any goods of his in the possession of the agent[3], together with any debts which may be due to him in his capacity as agent of the principal[4]. This right of the principal is, however, subject to any lien which the agent may have in respect of the goods or debts[5].

Where the agent has mixed his principal's money or property with his own, the principal has a first charge, as against the agent's trustee in bankruptcy and creditors, on the mixed fund[6] or property[7], if still in specie, or on their proceeds[8], as the case may be, provided that the money, property or proceeds can be clearly identified.

1   For the general law of bankruptcy see BANKRUPTCY AND INDIVIDUAL INSOLVENCY vol 5 (2013) PARA 1 et seq.
2   See PARA 145.
3   *Ex p Sayers* (1800) 5 Ves 169; *Whitfield v Brand* (1847) 16 M & W 282; *Re Thickbroom, ex p Greenwood* (1862) 6 LT 558; *Giles v Perkins* (1807) 9 East 12. See also *Re Chaplin, Milne, Grenfell & Co* (1914) 59 Sol Jo 250.
4   *Scott v Surman* (1742) Willes 400; *Re Tyre and Lightfoot, ex p Pauli* (1838) 3 Deac 169; *Re Smith, ex p Bright* (1879) 10 ChD 566, CA.
5   See *Giles v Perkins* (1807) 9 East 12. As to the lien of an agent see PARAS 115–119.
6   *Hancock v Smith* (1889) 41 ChD 456, CA; *Re Hallett & Co, ex p Blane* [1894] 2 QB 237, CA; *Re Hallett's Estate, Knatchbull v Hallett* (1880) 13 ChD 696, CA; but see *Wilsons and Furness-Leyland Line Ltd v British and Continental Shipping Co Ltd* (1907) 23 TLR 397.
7   *Harris v Truman* (1882) 9 QBD 264, CA.
8   *Frith v Cartland* (1865) 2 Hem & M 417.

143.   Misappropriation by agent.

Where the agent has misappropriated his principal's money or property, as against the agent's trustee in bankruptcy and creditors, the principal is entitled to follow the proceeds of such money or property, and take them in their existing form, provided that it is possible to trace them[1].

1   *Taylor v Plumer* (1815) 3 M & S 562. As to the extent to which money may be followed see *Banque Belge pour l'Etranger v Hambrouck* [1921] 1 KB 321, CA. As to the following of assets see further EQUITABLE JURISDICTION vol 47 (2014) PARA 238 et seq.

144.   Privilege from commercial rent arrears recovery.

Before the abolition of the common law right to levy distress for arrears of rent[1], when a principal entrusted goods to an agent, the goods were not, as a general rule, privileged from seizure in respect of the premises on which they were at the time[2]. This principle, however, may no longer apply in respect of commercial rent arrears recovery under the Tribunals, Courts and Enforcement

Act 2007, which stipulates that an enforcement agent may take control of goods only if they are goods of the debtor[3].

1 The common law right to distrain for arrears of rent was abolished and replaced by the regime for commercial rent arrears recovery by the Tribunals, Courts and Enforcement Act 2007 Pt 3 Ch 2 (ss 71–87) (see LANDLORD AND TENANT vol 62 (2016) PARA 282 et seq).
2 *Tapling & Co v Weston* (1883) Cab & El 99, CA.
3 See the Tribunals, Courts and Enforcement Act 2007 Sch 12 para 10; and CIVIL PROCEDURE vol 12A (2015) PARA 1345.

145. Unauthorised dispositions not binding on principal.

Where an agent is entrusted with any money, goods, or other property belonging to his principal, as a general rule[1], no disposition of such property made by the agent without the authority of the principal is binding upon the principal[2]; and, notwithstanding any such disposition, the principal is entitled to follow the property into the hands of third persons and recover it[3] or its value[4].

Where an agent is entrusted by his principal with property to be applied for the purposes of the principal, and to be accounted for on that footing, he is in a fiduciary position, and a third person taking from the agent a transfer of the property, with knowledge of a breach of duty committed, or of excess of authority exercised by him, in making the transfer, holds what has been transferred to him under a transmitted fiduciary obligation to account for it to the principal[5].

1 For the exceptions to the rule see PARAS 146–150.
2 *Farquharson Bros & Co v King & Co* [1902] AC 325, HL; *Cole v North Western Bank* (1875) LR 10 CP 354, Ex Ch.
3 *Fox v Martin* (1895) 64 LJ Ch 473; *Bodenham v Hoskyns* (1852) 2 De GM & G 903; *M'Combie v Davies* (1805) 7 East 5; *Solomons v Bank of England* (1791) 13 East 135n; *Société Coloniale Anversoise v London and Brazilian Bank Ltd* [1911] 2 KB 1024 (affd on other grounds [1911] 2 KB 1031n, CA). As to the right in equity to follow assets see EQUITABLE JURISDICTION vol 47 (2014) PARA 238 et seq.
4 *Farquharson Bros & Co v C King & Co* [1902] AC 325, HL; *Midland Bank Ltd v Reckitt* [1933] AC 1, HL.
5 *John v Dodwell & Co* [1918] AC 563, PC; *Corporation Agencies Ltd v Home Bank of Canada* [1927] AC 318, PC; *Reckitt v Barnett, Pembroke and Slater Ltd* [1929] AC 176, HL; *Reckitt v Nunburnholme* (1929) 45 TLR 629.

146. Dispositions by apparent owner.

Where a principal by any conduct on his part allows or enables his agent to appear as owner of any property belonging to the principal, the principal is bound by any sale, pledge[1] or other disposition of that property by the agent to the extent of the disposition, as regards all persons dealing for valuable consideration with the agent, provided that at the time of the disposition they had no notice of the principal's title and believed the agent to be the owner[2]. It is not, however, sufficient for the principal merely to have been guilty of negligence, however gross[3], in the care of his property, whereby the agent obtained the opportunity of making the unauthorised disposition[4]. The principal must himself have done some act which was calculated to mislead, and did in fact mislead, the person dealing with the agent, or omitted some precaution against such misleading which he was bound to take[5].

In the case of money[6] or negotiable instruments[7], the principal will be bound even though the persons dealing with the agent knew him to be an agent, unless they knew, or ought to have known him[8] to be acting without authority[9] or in breach of faith[10], or unless they had been put upon inquiry as to the extent of his authority[11].

1 *Callow v Kelson* (1862) 10 WR 193; *M'Combie v Davies* (1805) 7 East 5; *Wood v Clydesdale Bank Ltd* 1914 SC 397, Ct of Sess. See BAILMENT AND PLEDGE; SALE OF GOODS AND SUPPLY OF SERVICES.

2 *Pickering v Busk* (1812) 15 East 38; *Marshall v National Provincial Bank of England* (1892) 61 LJ Ch 465; *Eastern Distributors Ltd v Goldring (Murphy, third party)* [1957] 2 QB 600, [1957] 2 All ER 525, CA; *Lloyds and Scottish Finance Ltd v Williamson* [1965] 1 All ER 641, [1965] 1 WLR 404, CA. The rule has been applied where there is no agency, but where the true owner allows another person to appear to be the owner (see eg *Commonwealth Trust v Akotey* [1926] AC 72, PC), but will not apply where there has been no positive conduct on the part of the owner to enable that other person to appear to be the owner (see eg *Farquharson Bros & Co v C King & Co* [1902] AC 325, HL; *Jerome v Bentley & Co* [1952] 2 All ER 114, [1952] 2 TLR 58). In the case of the sale of goods, this rule operates as an exception to the general principle *nemo dat quod non habet*, and is preserved by statute: see the Sale of Goods Act 1979 s 21(1); and SALE OF GOODS AND SUPPLY OF SERVICES vol 91 (2012) PARA 148. In other cases, the agent is regarded as having apparent authority to make the disposition and the principal as being estopped from denying the authority: see ss 21(1), 62(2); SALE OF GOODS AND SUPPLY OF SERVICES vol 91 (2012) PARA 10; *Eastern Distributors Ltd v Goldring (Murphy, third party)*; and PARA 25. Nothing in the Sale of Goods Act 1979 affects the provisions of the Factors Act 1889, or any enactment enabling the apparent owner of goods to dispose of them as if he were the true owner of the goods: see the Sale of Goods Act 1979 s 21(2)(a); and SALE OF GOODS AND SUPPLY OF SERVICES vol 91 (2012) PARA 148. As to dispositions under the Factors Act 1889 see PARAS 149–150.
   The giving of documents of title to the agent will enable the agent to appear as owner, but documents such as the registration document of a car (which is not a document of title: see PARA 148 note 1) will not alone give an agent sufficient authority to pass good title: *Central Newbury Car Auctions Ltd v Unity Finance Ltd (Mercury Motors, third parties)* [1957] 1 QB 371, [1956] 3 All ER 905, CA. As to dealings with documents of title see further PARA 148.
   As to dispositions by sellers or buyers in possession of goods see the Factors Act 1889 ss 8, 9; the Sale of Goods Act 1979 ss 24, 25; and SALE OF GOODS AND SUPPLY OF SERVICES vol 91 (2012) PARAS 155–156.
   The knowledge of a dealer of a defect in title will not of itself fix a finance company purchasing from the dealer with that knowledge: *Car and Universal Finance Co Ltd v Caldwell* [1965] 1 QB 525, [1964] 1 All ER 290, CA; see further SALE OF GOODS AND SUPPLY OF SERVICES vol 91 (2012) PARA 152. The dealer will not generally be the agent of the finance company for this purpose: see *Car and Universal Finance Co Ltd v Caldwell*; and CONTRACT vol 22 (2012) PARA 207.

3 *Lloyds Bank Ltd v Chartered Bank of India, Australia and China* [1929] 1 KB 40, CA; but see *Fox v Martin* (1895) 64 LJ Ch 473; *Isaac Cooke & Sons v Eshelby* (1887) 12 App Cas 271, HL.

4 See *Mercantile Credit Co Ltd v Hamblin* [1965] 2 QB 242, [1964] 3 All ER 592, CA.

5 *Bank of Ireland v Evans' Charities Trustees in Ireland* (1855) 5 HL Cas 389; *Scholfield v Earl of Londesborough* [1896] AC 514, HL; *Heap v Motorists' Advisory Agency Ltd* [1923] 1 KB 577; *Morison v London County and Westminster Bank Ltd* [1914] 3 KB 356, CA; but see *Lloyds Bank Ltd v Chartered Bank of India, Australia and China* [1929] 1 KB 40, CA.

6 *Marten v Rocke, Eyton & Co* (1885) 53 LT 946; *Union Bank of Australia Ltd v Murray-Aynsley* [1898] AC 693, PC.

7 *London Joint Stock Bank v Simmons* [1892] AC 201, HL; *Goodwin v Robarts* (1876) 1 App Cas 476, HL; *Rumball v Metropolitan Bank* (1877) 2 QBD 194; *Jameson v Union Bank of Scotland* (1913) 109 LT 850; *Lloyds Bank Ltd v Chartered Bank of India, Australia and China* [1929] 1 KB 40, CA.

8 *Lloyds Bank Ltd v Chartered Bank of India, Australia and China* [1929] 1 KB 40, CA; *Reckitt v Barnett, Pembroke and Slater Ltd* [1929] AC 176, HL.

9 *Earl of Sheffield v London Joint Stock Bank* (1888) 13 App Cas 333, HL.

10 *Bodenham v Hoskyns* (1852) 2 De GM & G 903; and cf *Shields v Governor of Bank of Ireland* [1901] 1 IR 222; *Bank of New South Wales v Goulburn Valley Butter Co Pty Ltd* [1902] AC 543, PC; *Lloyds Bank Ltd v Swiss Bankverein, Union of London and Smiths Bank Ltd v Swiss Bankverein* (1913) 108 LT 143, CA; *Paine v Bevan and Bevan* [1914] WN 147, CA; *Fuller v Glyn, Mills, Currie & Co* [1914] 2 KB 168.

11 *AL Underwood Ltd v Bank of Liverpool and Martins* [1924] 1 KB 775, CA; *B Liggett (Liverpool) v Barclays Bank Ltd* [1928] 1 KB 48.

147. Uncompleted negotiable instruments given by principal to agent.

If a principal signs a piece of paper and hands it to his agent with the intention that it be converted into a negotiable instrument, the principal will be estopped, as against a bona fide purchaser for value without notice, from showing any limitation upon the authority of his agent which is not obvious upon the face of the instrument[1]. A principal is not, however, estopped from relying upon a limitation of the agent's authority where the uncompleted instrument has been handed to the agent for safe custody[2].

1 *Lloyds Bank Ltd v Cooke* [1907] 1 KB 794, CA; contrast *Wilson and Meeson v Pickering* [1946] KB 422, [1946] 1 All ER 394, CA (cheque marked 'not negotiable'). As to negotiable instruments see further FINANCIAL INSTRUMENTS AND TRANSACTIONS vol 49 (2015) PARAS 184 et seq, 393 et seq.

2 *Smith v Prosser* [1907] 2 KB 735, CA. As to the general liability of a principal under bills of exchange see PARA 129.

148. Documents of title entrusted to agent.

Where a principal entrusts his agent with documents of title[1], and gives him authority to raise a loan by means of them, he is bound, as regards any person who has dealt with the agent in good faith, by any security given by the agent to the full amount advanced by that person to the agent on the faith of the security, notwithstanding the fact that the agent exceeded his authority in borrowing such amount[2].

No disposition which depends for its validity upon a forged instrument is, however, binding upon the principal[3].

1 Documents of title do not include the registration document of a car, although such documents have frequently been used by sellers as evidence of title: see *Central Newbury Car Auctions Ltd v Unity Finance Ltd (Mercury Motors, third parties)* [1957] 1 QB 371, [1956] 3 All ER 905, CA (a case concerning a registration book, the predecessor of a vehicle registration document). As to dispositions by apparent owners of goods together with documents evidencing title see PARA 146.

2 *Brocklesby v Temperance Permanent Building Society* [1895] AC 173, HL; *Robinson v Montgomeryshire Brewery Co* [1896] 2 Ch 841; *Gordon v James* (1885) 30 ChD 249, CA; *Rimmer v Webster* [1902] 2 Ch 163; *France v Clark* (1884) 26 ChD 257, CA; *Hambro v Burnand* [1904] 2 KB 10, CA; *Cuthbert v Robarts, Lubbock & Co* [1909] 2 Ch 226, CA; *Fry and Mason v Smellie and Taylor* [1912] 3 KB 282, CA. The owner of shares in a ship does not hold out another as his agent merely by transferring the shares to him so that they stand in his name: *Burgis v Constantine* [1908] 2 KB 484, CA.

3 *Mayor, etc of Merchants of Staple of England v Bank of England* (1887) 21 QBD 160, CA; *Bank of Ireland v Evans' Charities Trustees in Ireland* (1855) 5 HL Cas 389; *Painter v Abel* (1863) 2 H & C 113. See also *Morison v London County and Westminster Bank Ltd* [1914] 3 KB 356, CA. There may be a duty to prevent forgery: see *London Joint Stock Bank Ltd v MacMillan and Arthur* [1918] AC 777, HL. See also PARA 60.

149. Dispositions under the Factors Act 1889.

Where a mercantile agent[1] is with the consent[2] of the owner[3] (that is his principal) in possession[4] (when acting in the capacity of a mercantile agent[5]) of goods[6] or of the documents of title[7] to goods, the owner is bound by any sale, pledge[8] or other disposition[9] of the goods made by the agent[10] for valuable consideration[11] when acting in the ordinary course of business[12] of a mercantile agent[13]. The owner is bound notwithstanding that the transaction is one which by custom of the trade the agent has no implied authority to carry out[14]. In all such cases, the person taking under the disposition must act in good faith, and have no notice at the time of the disposition that the agent had no authority to make it, otherwise the principal is not bound[15]. The onus of proving that he acted in good faith and without notice of the agent's want of authority is upon the person taking under the disposition[16].

If the agent has been in possession with his principal's consent, the determination of the consent is immaterial unless the person taking under the disposition had notice of the determination at the time of the disposition[17], and the consent of the principal is presumed in the absence of evidence to the contrary[18].

1 As to the meaning of 'mercantile agent' see PARA 12.
2 The agent can give a good title even if the consent was obtained by fraud (*Whitehorn Bros v Davison* [1911] 1 KB 463, CA; *Pearson v Rose and Young Ltd* [1951] 1 KB 275, [1950] 2 All ER 1027, CA), unless the owner did not intend the agent to have possession at all (*Stadium Finance Ltd v Robbins* [1962] 2 QB 664, [1962] 2 All ER 633, CA). Illegality may preclude consent being proved: see *Belvoir Finance Co Ltd v Harold G Cole & Co Ltd* [1969] 2 All ER 904, [1969] 1 WLR 1877.
3 The owner is the person who can give express authority with regard to dealing with the goods or documents of title: *Lloyds Bank Ltd v Bank of America National Trust and Savings Association* [1938] 2 KB 147, [1938] 2 All ER 63 at 70, CA.
4 The agent is in possession when the goods or documents are in his actual custody or are held by any other person subject to his control, or for him, or on his behalf: Factors Act 1889 s 1(2).
5 He must be acting in relation to the goods in his possession: *Lowther v Harris* [1927] 1 KB 393; *Staffs Motor Guarantee Ltd v British Wagon Co Ltd* [1934] 2 KB 305; *Pearson v Rose and Young Ltd* [1951] 1 KB 275, [1950] 2 All ER 1027, CA; *Stadium Finance Ltd v Robbins* [1962] 2 QB 664, [1962] 2 All ER 633, CA; *Astley Industrial Trust Ltd v Miller* [1968] 2 All ER 36; *Belvoir Finance Co Ltd v Harold G Cole & Co Ltd* [1969] 2 All ER 904, [1969] 1 WLR 1877. Cf *Gray v Smith* [2013] EWHC 4136 (Comm) at [124], [2014] All ER (Comm) 359 (mercantile agent in fact owner of the goods).
6 It was suggested in *Pearson v Rose and Young Ltd* [1951] 1 KB 275, [1950] 2 All ER 1027, CA, that a person who obtained possession of a car with consent but of the registration book without consent was not in possession of the 'goods'. The reasoning was rejected in *Stadium Finance Ltd v Robbins* [1962] 2 QB 664, [1962] 2 All ER 633, CA; it was held, however, in that case that the sale of a car without an ignition key or registration book was not in the ordinary course of business of a mercantile agent.
7 'Documents of title' include any bill of lading, dock warrant, warehouse-keeper's certificate, and warrant or order for the delivery of goods, and any other document used in the ordinary course of business as proof of the possession or control of goods, or authorising or purporting to authorise, either by indorsement or by delivery, the possessor of the document to transfer or receive goods thereby represented: Factors Act 1889 s 1(4). If the agent obtains possession of any documents of title by reason of being or having been, with the consent of his principal, in possession of goods or other documents of title, his possession of the first-mentioned documents of title is deemed to be with the consent of the principal: s 2(3).
   A delivery order may be a valid document of title even though it does not relate to specific goods: *Ant Jurgens Margarinefabrieken v Louis Dreyfus & Co* [1914] 3 KB 40.
   A motor vehicle registration document is not a document of title: *Joblin v Watkins and Roseveare (Motors) Ltd* [1949] 1 All ER 47, 64 TLR 464; *Bishopsgate Motor Finance Corpn Ltd v Transport Brakes Ltd* [1949] 1 KB 322, [1949] 1 All ER 37, CA; *Central Newbury Car Auctions Ltd v Unity Finance Ltd (Mercury Motors, third parties)* [1957] 1 QB 371, [1956] 3 All ER 905, CA.
8 'Pledge' includes any contract pledging, or giving a lien or security on, goods, whether in consideration of an original advance, or of any further or continuing advance, or of any pecuniary liability: Factors Act 1889 s 1(5). A pledge of the documents of title to goods is deemed to be a pledge of the goods: s 3. See *Dublin City Distillery Ltd v Doherty* [1914] AC 823, HL.
9 Handing goods for sale to an auctioneer who advances money upon them is not a 'sale, pledge, or other disposition': *Waddington & Sons v Neale & Sons* (1907) 96 LT 786.
10 Or by his clerk or other person authorised in the ordinary course of business: see the Factors Act 1889 s 6. The Act does not, however, protect dispositions by persons who are not mercantile agents within its meaning: *Lamb v Attenborough* (1862) 1 B & S 831; *Wood v Rowcliffe* (1846) 6 Hare 183.
11 In general the consideration necessary to validate a disposition by a mercantile agent may be either a payment in cash, or the delivery or transfer of other goods or of a document of title to goods or of a negotiable security, or any other valuable consideration: Factors Act 1889 s 5.

12 The agent must not only be in possession as a mercantile agent but also act in the ordinary course of business as one: *Oppenheimer v Attenborough & Son* [1908] 1 KB 221, CA (outside business hours and outside business premises; see also *Heap v Motorists' Advisory Agency Ltd* [1923] 1 KB 577; *Pearson v Rose and Young Ltd* [1951] 1 KB 275, [1950] 2 All ER 1027, CA; *Stadium Finance Ltd v Robbins* [1962] 2 QB 664, [1962] 2 All ER 633, CA). Title to goods will also pass where the seller is a buyer in possession of the goods, if the sale is one which would be in the ordinary course of business of a mercantile agent if the seller had been such an agent: see the Factors Act 1889 s 9; *Newtons of Wembley Ltd v Williams* [1965] 1 QB 560, [1964] 3 All ER 532, CA; and SALE OF GOODS AND SUPPLY OF SERVICES vol 91 (2012) PARA 156.

13 Factors Act 1889 s 2(1).

14 A pledge by a diamond broker entrusted with diamonds has been held valid, although it is contrary to the custom of the diamond trade for brokers to have implied authority to pledge: *Oppenheimer v Attenborough & Son* [1908] 1 KB 221, CA; *Janesich v George Attenborough & Son* (1910) 102 LT 605.

15 See the Factors Act 1889 s 2(1); and SALE OF GOODS AND SUPPLY OF SERVICES vol 91 (2012) PARA 156.

16 *Heap v Motorists' Advisory Agency Ltd* [1923] 1 KB 577.

17 Factors Act 1889 s 2(2); and see *Moody v Pall Mall Deposit and Forwarding Co Ltd* (1917) 33 TLR 306.

18 Factors Act 1889 s 2(4); and see *Pearson v Rose and Young Ltd* [1951] 1 KB 275, [1950] 2 All ER 1027, CA; *Stadium Finance Ltd v Robbins* [1962] 2 QB 664, [1962] 2 All ER 633, CA.

150. Rights acquired by pledgee.

In the case of a pledge of goods by a mercantile agent[1], the pledgee acquires a right to hold the goods against the principal for the full value of the consideration if the advance has been made in cash[2]. If the goods are pledged to secure a debt due from the agent to the pledgee before the time of the pledge, the pledgee acquires no right to the goods beyond that which could have been enforced by the agent at the time of the pledge[3]. Where, however, the goods are pledged in exchange for other goods, documents of title or negotiable securities, the pledgee acquires no right or interest in the goods so pledged in excess of the value of the other goods, documents of title or negotiable securities at the time of the exchange[4].

1 As to the meaning of 'mercantile agent' see PARA 12. As to pledges see also PARA 149 note 8.

2 See the Factors Act 1889 s 5; and SALE OF GOODS AND SUPPLY OF SERVICES vol 91 (2012) PARAS 156, 158.

3 Factors Act 1889 s 4.

4 See the Factors Act 1889 s 5; and SALE OF GOODS AND SUPPLY OF SERVICES vol 91 (2012) PARAS 156, 158.

(4) TORTIOUS LIABILITY

151. Agent's act expressly authorised by principal.

Where a principal gives his agent express authority to do a particular act which is wrongful in itself[1], or which necessarily results in a wrongful act[2], the principal is responsible, jointly and severally with the agent[3], to third persons for any loss or damage occasioned thereby.

1 *Schuster v McKellar* (1857) 7 E & B 704; *Parkes v Prescott* (1869) LR 4 Exch 169.

2 *Glynn v Houston* (1841) 2 Man & G 337.

3 As to the effect of joint liability and the rights of the principal and agent inter se see PARA 152. As to tortious liability generally see TORT.

152. Agent's act not expressly authorised by principal.

Where the act complained of is not expressly authorised by the principal, the principal is, while the agent is acting within the scope of his implied authority or within the scope of his apparent or ostensible authority[1], jointly and severally responsible with the agent[2], however improper[3] or imperfect[4] the manner in which the authority is carried out. It is immaterial that actual malice is an essential ingredient of the wrongful act[5], that the wrongful act is also a crime[6], or that the act in question has been expressly prohibited by the principal[7].

Where the act done by the agent falls entirely outside the scope of his authority, the principal will not be responsible[8].

The rights of the injured party against the principal and agent as joint tortfeasors and their rights and liabilities inter se are regulated by the provisions of the Civil Liability (Contribution) Act 1978[9].

1   *Uxbridge Permanent Benefit Building Society v Pickard* [1939] 2 KB 248, [1939] 2 All ER 344, CA; *Morris v CW Martin & Sons Ltd* [1966] 1 QB 716, [1965] 2 All ER 725, CA. See also *Abraham v Bullock* (1902) 86 LT 796, CA; *Lloyd v Grace, Smith & Co* [1912] AC 716, HL; *United Africa Co Ltd v Saka Owoade* [1955] AC 130, [1957] 3 All ER 216, PC; *Kooragang Investments Pty Ltd v Richardson & Wrench Ltd* [1982] AC 462, [1981] 3 All ER 65, PC. In many cases the courts have not found it necessary to decide whether the person committing the tort was an agent or an employee under a contract of service, and have used the terminology of either relationship interchangeably; in such cases the 'scope of authority' of an agent will be much the same as the 'course of employment' of an employee: see eg *Lloyd v Grace, Smith & Co.* The Supreme Court has extended the scope of vicarious liability to relationships that can be claimed to wear many of the elements of a relationship of employer and his employee: see *Various Claimants v Institute of the Brothers of the Christian Schools* [2012] UKSC 56, [2013] 2 AC 1, [2013] 1 All ER 670; *Cox v Ministry of Justice* [2016] UKSC 10, [2016] AC 660, [2017] 1 All ER 1; *A v Trustees of the Watchtower Bible and Tract Society* [2015] EWHC 1722 (QB), [2015] All ER (D) 249 (Jun); *Various Claimants v Barclays Bank plc* [2017] EWHC 1929 (QB), [2017] All ER (D) 112 (Aug).

      For consideration of the liability of an employer see generally *Morris v CW Martin & Sons Ltd*; and EMPLOYMENT vol 39 (2014) PARA 149 et seq. As to ostensible authority see PARA 25.

2   The agent will not, however, be liable personally if the act arises out of negligence of the principal: *WB Anderson & Sons Ltd v Rhodes (Liverpool) Ltd* [1967] 2 All ER 850. As to the rights of the principal and agent inter se see the text and note 9. As to the personal liability of the agent to the third party see PARAS 165–166.

3   The following are examples of particular torts, but the list should not be taken to be exhaustive:
      (1)   assault: *Smith v North Metropolitan Tramways Co* (1891) 7 TLR 459, CA; *Bayley v Manchester, Sheffield and Lincolnshire Rly Co* (1873) LR 8 CP 148; *Hutchins v LCC* (1915) 85 LJKB 1177; *Whittaker v LCC* [1915] 2 KB 676;
      (2)   conversion: *Giles v Taff Vale Rly Co* (1853) 2 E & B 822, Ex Ch; *Ewbank v Nutting* (1849) 7 CB 797; *Morris v C W Martin & Sons Ltd* [1966] 1 QB 716, [1965] 2 All ER 725, CA;
      (3)   false imprisonment: *Moore v Metropolitan Rly Co* (1872) LR 8 QB 36; *Poulton v London and South Western Rly Co* (1867) LR 2 QB 534; *Percy v Glasgow Corpn* [1922] 2 AC 299; *Lambert v Great Eastern Rly Co* [1909] 2 KB 776, CA; *Fisher v Oldham Corpn* [1930] 2 KB 364 (as to giving into custody see PARA 39);
      (4)   fraud: *Udell v Atherton* (1861) 7 H & N 172; *British Mutual Bank Co Ltd v Charnwood Forest Rly Co* (1887) 18 QBD 714, CA; *Lloyd v Grace, Smith & Co* [1912] AC 716, HL; cf *Terrill v Parker and Thomas* (1915) 32 TLR 48; see also *Russo-Chinese Bank v Li Yau Sam* [1910] AC 174, PC; *Uxbridge Permanent Benefit Building Society v Pickard* [1939] 2 KB 248, [1939] 2 All ER 344, CA (solicitor liable for clerk's fraud although person defrauded not a client); *British Railway Traffic and Electric Co Ltd v Roper* (1939) 162 LT 217 (fraudulent completion of hire purchase forms by dealer on behalf of intending hirer); *Briess v Woolley* [1954] AC 333, [1954] 1 All ER 909, HL;
      (5)   infringement of copyright: *Monaghan v Taylor* (1866) 2 TLR 685;
      (6)   infringement of patent: *Betts v De Vitre* (1868) 3 Ch App 429, varied sub nom *Nielson v Betts* (1871) LR 5 HL 1;

(7) negligence: *Thelma (Owners) v University College School* [1953] 2 Lloyd's Rep 613, where a pupil acting as cox for a school eight was held to be the school's agent and the governors were liable for his negligence;

(8) negligence on highway: *Whatman v Pearson* (1868) LR 3 CP 422; *Engelhart v Farrant & Co* [1897] 1 QB 240, CA; *Aitchison v Page Motors Ltd* (1935) 154 LT 128; *Ormrod v Crosville Motor Services Ltd* [1953] 2 All ER 753, [1953] 1 WLR 1120, CA; *Scarsbrook v Mason* [1961] 3 All ER 767, 105 Sol Jo 889; *Klein v Caluori* [1971] 2 All ER 701, [1971] 1 WLR 619; *Nottingham v Aldridge* [1971] 2 QB 739, [1971] 2 All ER 751; see also *Morgans v Launchbury* [1973] AC 127, [1972] 2 All ER 606, HL (where driver in question held not to be an agent of the owner);

(9) nuisance to highway: *Whiteley v Pepper* (1877) 2 QBD 276;

(10) slander: *Ormiston v Great Western Rly Co* [1917] 1 KB 598;

(11) threats causing nervous shock: *Janvier v Sweeney* [1919] 2 KB 316, CA;

(12) trespass: *Gregory v Piper* (1829) 9 B & C 591; *Stewart v Adams* 1920 SC 129, Ct of Sess;

(13) wrongful distress: *Hatch v Hale* (1850) 15 QB 10; *Richards v West Middlesex Waterworks Co* (1885) 15 QBD 660;

(14) wrongful execution: *Smith v Keal* (1882) 9 QBD 340, CA; *Morris v Salberg* (1889) 22 QBD 614, CA; and see *Clissold v Cratchley* [1910] 2 KB 244, CA.

4 Cf *Whatman v Pearson* (1868) LR 3 CP 422, with *Storey v Ashton* (1869) LR 4 QB 476; *Engelhart v Farrant & Co* [1897] 1 QB 240, CA, with *Beard v London General Omnibus Co* [1900] 2 QB 530, CA.

5 *Cornford v Carlton Bank* [1900] 1 QB 22, CA; *Citizens' Life Assurance Co v Brown* [1904] AC 423, PC; *Aiken v Caledonian Rly Co* 1913 SC 66, Ct of Sess. This does not apply where malice must be proved in order to defeat a plea of privilege: *Egger v Viscount Chelmsford* [1965] 1 QB 248, [1964] 3 All ER 406, CA.

6 *Morris v CW Martin & Sons Ltd* [1966] 1 QB 716, [1965] 2 All ER 725, CA; *Osborn v Gillett* (1873) LR 8 Exch 88. This is so even if the agent has been convicted: *Dyer v Munday* [1895] 1 QB 742, CA. A forgery, like any other fraudulent act, if within the ostensible scope of the agent's authority, imposes liability on the principal: *Uxbridge Permanent Benefit Building Society v Pickard* [1939] 2 KB 248, [1939] 2 All ER 344, CA, disagreeing with statements in *Slingsby v District Bank Ltd* [1932] 1 KB 544, CA.

7 *Limpus v London General Omnibus Co Ltd* (1862) 1 H & C 526; *Gregory v Piper* (1829) 9 B & C 591; *Lloyd v Grace, Smith & Co* [1912] AC 716, HL; *Warrington v Windhill Industrial Co-operative Society* (1918) 88 LJKB 280.

8 *Sanderson v Collins* [1904] 1 KB 628, CA; *Poulton v London and South Western Rly Co* (1867) LR 2 QB 534; *Whatman v Pearson* (1868) LR 3 CP 422; *Engelhart v Farrant & Co* [1897] 1 QB 240, CA; *Rand v Craig* [1919] 1 Ch 1, CA; *Warren v Henlys Ltd* [1948] 2 All ER 935, 92 Sol Jo 706 (assault).

9 See the Civil Liability (Contribution) Act 1978 (especially s 1); the Law Reform (Husband and Wife) Act 1962 s 1; MATRIMONIAL AND CIVIL PARTNERSHIP LAW vol 72 (2015) PARA 258; TORT vol 97 (2015) PARA 447 et seq.

153. Fraudulent misrepresentation by agent.

Where an agent is personally guilty of fraudulent misrepresentation[1] and has actual or apparent authority to make the representation, the principal is responsible as for any other tort, and a claim of deceit lies against him[2]. It is irrelevant that the fraudulent misrepresentation was made before the agent's authority was granted if the misrepresentation is not corrected before the third party acts upon it[3]. Where the agent makes a representation which he honestly believes to be true, but which the principal knows to be false, the principal is responsible for fraudulent misrepresentation if there was actual fraud or dishonesty on his part[4], as where he employs the agent in order that the misrepresentation might be made[5]. If, however, there is no actual fraud or dishonesty on the part of the principal, he will not be liable on a claim for deceit if the agent made the representation innocently without the knowledge of the principal, although the principal knew the facts which rendered the representation false[6].

1   As to the effect of such misrepresentation upon contracts made by the agent see PARA 136.
2   *Barwick v English Joint Stock Bank* (1867) LR 2 Exch 259; *Lloyd v Grace, Smith & Co* [1912] AC 716, HL; *Byrne v Rudd* [1920] 2 IR 12, CA. Cf *Armagas Ltd v Mundogas SA, The Ocean Frost* [1986] AC 717, [1986] 2 All ER 385, [1986] 2 Lloyd's Rep 109, HL. See also *Barclays Bank plc v Kalamohan* [2010] EWHC 1383 (Ch), [2010] All ER (D) 59 (Jun). This does not apply where the fraud is primarily practised on the principal: *Kwei Tek Chao (t/a Zung Fu Co) v British Traders and Shippers Ltd* [1954] 2 QB 459, [1954] 1 All ER 779. As to the requirement of writing where the fraudulent misrepresentation is as to character or credit see PARA 155. As to the liability of the agent to the third party see PARAS 161–162 (warranty of authority), PARAS 165–166 (tortious liability). As to the liability of the principal where the third party has relied on a particular skill of the agent see eg *Bango v Holt (AE Austin & Co Ltd, third parties)* [1971] 5 WWR 522, 21 DLR (3d) 66, BC SC.
3   *Briess v Woolley* [1954] AC 333, [1954] 1 All ER 909, HL.
4   *Armstrong v Strain* [1952] 1 KB 232, [1952] 1 All ER 139, CA. See also *Cornfoot v Fowke* (1840) 6 M & W 358; *National Exchange Co of Glasgow v Drew* (1855) 2 Macq 103, HL; *Ludgater v Love* (1881) 44 LT 694, CA; *Gordon Hill Trust Ltd v Segall* [1941] 2 All ER 379, 85 Sol Jo 191, CA; *London County Freehold and Leasehold Properties Ltd v Berkeley Property and Investment Co Ltd* [1936] 2 All ER 1039, 155 LT 190, CA; *Anglo-Scottish Beet Sugar Corpn Ltd v Spalding UDC* [1937] 2 KB 607, [1937] 3 All ER 335; *Turvey v Dentons (1923) Ltd* [1953] 1 QB 218, [1952] 2 All ER 1025.
5   *Ludgater v Love* (1881) 44 LT 694, CA. See also *Garnac Grain Co Inc v HMF Faure and Fairclough Ltd and Bunge Corpn* [1966] 1 QB 650, [1965] 1 All ER 47n (revsd on another point [1966] 1 QB 650, [1965] 3 All ER 273, CA; affd [1968] AC 1130n, [1967] 2 All ER 353, HL); *Gosling v Anderson* (1972) 122 NLJ 152, CA. As to rescission of contracts in addition to damages for misrepresentation see further PARA 136.
6   See *Armstrong v Strain* [1952] 1 KB 232, [1952] 1 All ER 139, CA, where *S Pearson & Son Ltd v Dublin Corpn* [1907] AC 351, HL, and *Anglo-Scottish Beet Sugar Corpn Ltd v Spalding UDC* [1937] 2 KB 607, [1937] 3 All ER 335, are discussed.

154.   Negligent misrepresentation by agent.

The principal may be vicariously liable in negligence for the negligent misrepresentation of the agent and also liable in respect of the supply of false information to the agent which results in misrepresentation by the agent to persons to whom the principal owes a duty of care[1].

1   *WB Anderson & Sons Ltd v Rhodes (Liverpool) Ltd* [1967] 2 All ER 850. See also *Hedley Byrne & Co Ltd v Heller & Partners* [1964] AC 465, [1963] 2 All ER 575, HL; the Misrepresentation Act 1967 s 2; CONTRACT vol 22 (2012) PARAS 352–353; MISREPRESENTATION vol 76 (2013) PARA 832. There is no reason in principle why the professional agent of an employer cannot become liable to a contractor for negligent misstatements made to induce him to tender if the contractor relies on those statements: *J Jarvis and Sons Ltd v Castle Wharf Developments Ltd* [2001] EWCA Civ 19, [2001] Lloyd's Rep PN 328, (2001) Times, 28 February. As to employers' vicarious liability generally see TORT vol 97 (2015) PARA 767 et seq.

155.   Representation by agent as to credit.

The principal is not liable on a claim for deceit[1] for any representation as to the character or credit[2] of another person made by his agent, unless such representation is in writing signed by the principal himself[3]. A signature by the agent is not sufficient[4], even though expressly authorised or adopted by the principal[5].

1   The Statute of Frauds Amendment Act 1828 (see note 3) applies only to actions for deceit: see *Banbury v Bank of Montreal* [1918] AC 626, HL; *WB Anderson & Sons Ltd v Rhodes (Liverpool) Ltd* [1967] 2 All ER 850. As to liability for negligent misrepresentation see PARA 154.
2   As to the meaning of 'representation as to credit' see *Bishop v Balkis Consolidated Co* (1890) 25 QBD 512, CA. See also *Banbury v Bank of Montreal* [1918] AC 626, HL.

3 See the Statute of Frauds Amendment Act 1828 s 6; *Swift v Jewsbury and Goddard* (1874) LR 9 QB 301, Ex Ch.
4 This applies even though the principal is a corporation: *Hirst v West Riding Union Banking Co Ltd* [1901] 2 KB 560, CA.
5 *Williams v Mason* (1873) 28 LT 232.

(5) CRIMINAL LIABILITY

156. Criminal liability.

As a general rule, no act or default on the part of an agent imposes any criminal liability on the principal in respect thereof, unless the principal himself takes part in or authorises the commission of such act or default[1].

The general rule is, however, subject to two exceptions. First, the principal may be criminally liable at common law for a public nuisance[2] committed by him through the instrumentality of his agent[3]. Secondly, a particular statute may, by its express terms or by implication, impose a criminal liability upon the principal in respect of the acts or defaults of his agent by imposing a liability which can exist without proof of any criminal intent[4].

These exceptions do not apply where negligence is an essential ingredient in the offence; in this case the principal is not criminally responsible for the negligence of his agent[5].

1 *R v Stephens* (1866) LR 1 QB 702; *Hardcastle v Bielby* [1892] 1 QB 709.
2 Such proceedings, though criminal in form, are civil in substance: *R v Stephens* (1866) LR 1 QB 702. As to public nuisance see NUISANCE vol 78 (2010) PARAS 105, 187 et seq; TORT vol 97 (2015) PARA 499.
3 *R v Stephens* (1866) LR 1 QB 702; but see *Chisholm v Doulton* (1889) 22 QBD 736. Cf *Barnes v Akroyd* (1872) LR 7 QB 474.
4 *Sykes v Millington* [1953] 1 QB 770, [1953] 1 All ER 1098, DC; *Hardcastle v Bielby* [1892] 1 QB 709; *Pearks, Gunston and Tee Ltd v Ward, Hennen v Southern Counties Dairies Co Ltd* [1902] 2 KB 1; *Mousell Bros Ltd v London and North-Western Rly Co* [1917] 2 KB 836, DC; *Quality Dairies (York) Ltd v Pedley* [1952] 1 KB 275, [1952] 1 All ER 380, DC (regulations under the Food and Drugs Acts (now the Food Safety Act 1990)).
5 *Chisholm v Doulton* (1889) 22 QBD 736.

7. RELATIONS BETWEEN AGENT AND THIRD PERSONS

(1) LIABILITIES OF AGENT

(i) On Contracts

157. Fact of agency not disclosed.

Where a person makes a contract in his own name without disclosing either the name or the existence of a principal, he is personally liable on the contract to the other contracting party, though he may be in fact acting on a principal's behalf[1]. He will continue to be liable even after the discovery of the agency by the other party, unless and until there has been an unequivocal election by the other contracting party to look to the principal alone[2]. The agent will also be liable where he holds himself out as agent for a named person, but is in fact acting as agent for an unnamed person[3]. Where the contract is not written but oral, the question whether the agent is personally liable must be determined in the context of the background against which the contract was made[4].

1 *Saxon v Blake* (1861) 29 Beav 438; *Re Southampton, Isle of Wight and Portsmouth Improved Steam Boat Co Ltd, Bird's Case* (1864) 4 De GJ & Sm 200; *Seaber v Hawkes* (1831) 5 Moo & P 549. See also *Collins v Associated Greyhound Racecourses Ltd* [1930] 1 Ch 1, CA; *Ernest Scragg & Sons Ltd v Perseverance Banking and Trust Co Ltd* [1973] 2 Lloyd's Rep 101, CA (order form signed 'for and on behalf of' the agents: agents liable). As to the liability of the principal see PARAS 126–141.
2 *Dramburg v Pollitzer* (1873) 28 LT 470; cf *Basma v Weekes* [1950] AC 441, [1950] 2 All ER 146, PC. For a consideration of the position where the third party elects to look only to the agent see PARA 132.
3 *Savills v Scott* [1988] 1 EGLR 20, [1988] 12 EG 115, DC.
4 *N & J Vlassopulos Ltd v Ney Shipping Ltd, The Santa Carina* [1977] 1 Lloyd's Rep 478, CA (contract made by telephone; although fact of agency not specifically mentioned, the circumstances were such that it must have been presumed).

158. Identity of principal not disclosed.

Where an agent in making a contract discloses the existence, but not the name, of a principal on whose behalf he is acting, he is not made liable by the mere fact of not disclosing the name, for that is only a relevant factor in deciding whether the agent contracted personally or not[1], although he may become liable, for example, by trade usage[2]. The issue of liability depends upon the terms in which the agent contracted, and the fact of non-disclosure of the identity of the principal will not be conclusive either way[3].

Prima facie a party is personally liable on a contract if he puts his unqualified signature to it[4]. In order, therefore, to exonerate the agent from liability, the contract must show, when construed as a whole, that he contracted as agent only, and did not undertake any personal liability[5]. It is not sufficient that he should have described himself in the contract as an agent[6], for the contract and the surrounding circumstances may indicate that he is liable[7]. If he states in the contract[8], or indicates by an addition to his signature[9], that he is contracting as agent only on behalf of a principal, he is not liable, unless the rest of the contract clearly involves his personal liability[10], or unless he is shown to be the real principal[11].

The words 'as agents', 'on account of', 'on behalf of', and 'for' are conclusive when qualifying the signature to negative responsibility of the signatory as principal[12] whether the identity of the actual principal is disclosed or not[13], and notwithstanding that the contract may impose active obligations upon the agent towards the other contracting party[14]. If the addition to the signature is merely 'agent' the effect will depend on whether the term is used as a description or as a qualification[15]. The mere addition of the words 'secretary' or 'director' to the signature of a company's agent will not be sufficient to avoid his personal responsibility[16].

When, on the construction of a written contract, the agent is held not to have contracted personally, evidence of usage may be admissible to make him liable[17], unless the usage is inconsistent with the express contract[18]. No oral evidence of intention is, however, admissible to exonerate him from liability contrary to the terms of the contract[19], except that by way of defence he may set up an express agreement between himself and the other contracting party to that effect[20].

An employer's liability policy is not a personal contract of the type which excludes rights of an undisclosed principal[21].

1 *Hutchinson v Tatham* (1873) LR 8 CP 482; *Southwell v Bowditch* (1876) 1 CPD 374, CA. See also *Hobhouse v Hamilton* (1826) 1 Hog 401; *Franklyn v Lamond* (1847) 4 CB 637; *Wakefield v Duckworth & Co* [1915] 1 KB 218, CA. See also PARA 168. The agent is not a trustee for his principal vis-à-vis the third party: *Pople v Evans* [1969] 2 Ch 255, [1968] 2 All ER 743.

2 *Anglo Overseas Transport Ltd v Titan Industrial Corpn (United Kingdom) Ltd* [1959] 2 Lloyd's Rep 152; *Perishables Transport Co Ltd v N Spyropoulos (London) Ltd* [1964] 2 Lloyd's Rep 379.

3 *Jones v Littledale* (1837) 6 Ad & El 486; *Southwell v Bowditch* (1876) 1 CPD 374, CA; *Associated Portland Cement Manufacturers (1910) Ltd v Ashton* [1915] 2 KB 1, CA. Cf *Chidley v Norris* (1862) 3 F & F 228; *Wakefield v Duckworth & Co* [1915] 1 KB 218, CA; *Benton v Campbell, Parker & Co Ltd* [1925] 2 KB 410; *Hichens, Harrison, Woolston & Co v Jackson & Sons* [1943] AC 266, [1943] 1 All ER 128, HL. As to the liability of the principal, and his rights to sue, on a contract to which he is not party see PARAS 126–141.

4 See CONTRACT vol 22 (2012) PARA 284. As to the position with regard to an oral contract see *N & J Vlassopulos Ltd v Ney Shipping Ltd, The Santa Carina* [1977] 1 Lloyd's Rep 478, CA.

5 *Thomson v Davenport* (1829) 9 B & C 78; *Hutcheson v Eaton* (1884) 13 QBD 861, CA; *Samuel Bros Ltd v Whetherly* [1908] 1 KB 184, CA; *Bridges and Salmon Ltd v The Swan (Owner), The Swan* [1968] 1 Lloyd's Rep 5; *Freimuller (Ships Stores) Ltd v Ocean Carriers (London) Ltd* [1961] 2 Lloyd's Rep 309; cf *Henry Browne & Sons Ltd v Smith* [1964] 2 Lloyd's Rep 476; *Tudor Marine Ltd v Tradex Export SA, The Virgo* [1976] 2 Lloyd's Rep 135, CA. The agent will be exonerated if he shows that he stipulated that his personal liability should cease in events which have happened: *Oglesby v Yglesias* (1858) EB & E 930.

6 *Parker v Winlow* (1857) 7 E & B 942; *Oglesby v Yglesias* (1858) EB & E 930. See also *Hutcheson v Eaton* (1884) 13 QBD 861, CA; *Landes v Marcus and Davids* (1909) 25 TLR 478.

7 *Rusholme and Bolton and Roberts Hadfield Ltd v SG Read & Co (London) Ltd* [1955] 1 All ER 180, [1955] 1 WLR 146 (assumption of liability of principal buyers as between selves and sellers by confirming house on confirmation). A confirming house guarantees that orders will be carried out: *Sobell Industries Ltd v Cory Bros & Co Ltd* [1955] 2 Lloyd's Rep 82.

8 *Gadd v Houghton* (1876) 1 ExD 357, CA; *Ogden v Hall* (1879) 40 LT 751; *Southwell v Bowditch* (1876) 1 CPD 374, CA. *Gadd v Houghton* has been extensively followed and is regarded in the more recent decisions on this topic as the leading case.

9 *Hutcheson v Eaton* (1884) 13 QBD 861, CA; *Fleet v Murton* (1871) LR 7 QB 126. See also the cases cited in note 12. As to the signature of documents by the agent in his own name see PARA 160.

10 This has been said to be 'a highly improbable and conjectural case'; see *Universal Steam Navigation Co Ltd v James McKelvie & Co* [1923] AC 492 at 499, HL, per Lord Shaw. See also *Weidner v Hoggett* (1876) 1 CPD 533.

11 *Carr v Jackson* (1852) 7 Exch 382; *Gardiner v Heading* [1928] 2 KB 284, CA. If, however, the agent is unable to show who is the real principal, he may be held liable on the contract: *Owen v Gooch* (1797) 2 Esp 567; *Hersom v Bernett* [1955] 1 QB 98, [1954] 3 All ER 370 (where evidence of agent disbelieved with respect to alleged principal; agent not permitted to escape liability by alleging existence of another unnamed principal).

12 *Gadd v Houghton* (1876) 1 ExD 357, CA; *W and T Avery Ltd v Charlesworth* (1914) 31 TLR 52, CA; *Ariadne Steamship Co v James McKelvie & Co* [1922] 1 KB 518, CA (affd sub nom *Universal Steam Navigation Co Ltd v James McKelvie & Co* [1923] AC 492, HL); *Kimber Coal Co v Stone*

and Rolfe Ltd [1926] AC 414, HL. See also *Flatau, Dick & Co v Keeping* (1931) 36 Com Cas 243, CA; *North Eastern Timber Importers Ltd v Ch Arendt & Sons and Impresa Cerrito* [1952] 2 Lloyd's Rep 513; *Lester v Balfour Williamson Merchant Shippers Ltd* [1953] 2 QB 168, [1953] 1 All ER 1146, DC; following *Gadd v Houghton*.

13 *Ariadne Steamship Co v James McKelvie & Co* [1922] 1 KB 518, CA (affd sub nom *Universal Steam Navigation Co Ltd v James McKelvie & Co* [1923] AC 492, HL); *Lovesy v Palmer* [1916] 2 Ch 233.

14 As in *Universal Steam Navigation Co Ltd v James McKelvie & Co* [1923] AC 492, HL, and *Kimber Coal Co v Stone and Rolfe Ltd* [1926] AC 414, HL.

15 See *Gadd v Houghton* (1876) 1 ExD 357, CA; and *Universal Steam Navigation Co Ltd v James McKelvie & Co* [1923] AC 492, HL.

16 *Brebner v Henderson* 1925 SC 643, Ct of Sess. See also notes 9, 12. Cf *Sika Contracts Ltd v BL Gill and Closeglen Properties Ltd* (1978) 9 BLR 11 (chartered civil engineer).

17 *Hutchinson v Tatham* (1873) LR 8 CP 482; *Fleet v Murton* (1871) LR 7 QB 126; *Pike v Ongley* (1887) 18 QBD 708, CA; *Dale v Humfrey* (1858) EB & E 1004, Ex Ch; *Imperial Bank v London and St Katharine Docks Co* (1877) 5 ChD 195; *Bacmeister v Fenton, Levy & Co* (1883) Cab & El 121; *Benton v Campbell, Parker & Co Ltd* [1925] 2 KB 410.

18 *Robinson v Mollett* (1875) LR 7 HL 802; *Barrow & Bros v Dyster, Nalder & Co* (1884) 13 QBD 635, DC; and see *Miller, Gibb & Co v Smith and Tyrer Ltd* [1917] 2 KB 141, CA. As to the incorporation of usages in contracts made by the agent see generally PARA 44.

19 *Higgins v Senior* (1841) 8 M & W 834; *Jones v Littledale* (1837) 6 Ad & El 486; *Lindsay v Craig* 1919 SC 139.

20 *Wake v Harrop* (1862) 1 H & C 202, Ex Ch.

21 *Siu Yin Kwan v Eastern Insurance Co Ltd* [1994] 2 AC 199, [1994] 1 All ER 213, PC.

159. Identity of principal disclosed.

Where an agent in making a contract discloses both the existence and the name of a principal on whose behalf he purports to make it, the agent is not, as a general rule, liable on the contract to the other contracting party[1], whether he had in fact authority to make it or not[2]; but a personal liability may be imposed upon him by the express terms of the contract[3], by the ordinary course of business[4], or by usage[5], and he will be liable for breach of warranty of authority in cases where he had no authority[6].

Further, the agent is personally liable on the contract if it is shown that he is the real principal[7], or that the principal named by him is non-existent[8] or incapable of making the contract in question[9], or is not the real principal although there might be another principal in existence[10]. The agent is also liable if he holds himself out as agent for a named person, but is in fact agent for an unnamed person[11].

1 *Jenkins v Hutchinson* (1849) 13 QB 744; *Paquin Ltd v Beauclerk* [1906] AC 148, HL; *Stewart v Engel* [2000] 3 All ER 518 (liquidators relied on a contractual term which stated they were agents of the company in liquidation and were not personally liable for negligently performing the contract). The same rule applies to public agents contracting on behalf of the Crown (*Macbeath v Haldimand* (1786) 1 Term Rep 172; *O'Grady v Cardwell* (1872) 20 WR 342; *Hosier Bros v Earl of Derby* [1918] 2 KB 671, CA); see CONSTITUTIONAL AND ADMINISTRATIVE LAW vol 20 (2014) PARA 197.

2 *Lewis v Nicholson* (1852) 18 QB 503. He may, however, be made liable in tort in respect of fraud or the obtaining of money: see *TD Keegan Ltd v Palmer* [1961] 2 Lloyd's Rep 449 (money recoverable from agent where obtained by agent by duress and paid into company account). As to the liability of an unauthorised agent for breach of warranty of authority see PARAS 161–162.

3 *Hall v Ashurst* (1833) 1 Cr & M 714; *McCollin v Gilpin* (1881) 6 QBD 516, CA; *Woolfe v Horne* (1877) 2 QBD 355; *Burrell v Jones* (1819) 3 B & Ald 47; *Parker v Winlow* (1857) 7 E & B 942; and contrast *Redpath v Wigg* (1866) LR 1 Exch 335. A public agent may bind himself personally. See also *Clutterbuck v Coffin* (1842) 3 Man & G 842; *Graham v Public Works Comrs* [1901] 2 KB 781; and CONSTITUTIONAL AND ADMINISTRATIVE LAW vol 20 (2014) PARA 190. Whether or not an agent has so bound himself is a question of fact: *Auty v Hutchinson* (1848) 6 CB 266. See, however, *Foalquest Ltd v Roberts* [1990] 1 EGLR 50, [1990] 21 EG 156, CA (intention to make agent personally liable may be inferred).

4 *Warlow v Harrison* (1859) 1 E & E 309, Ex Ch; *Newton v Chambers* (1844) 1 Dow & L 869.

5   One example of such a usage is in the case of confirming houses: see *Sobell Industries v Cory Bros & Co Ltd* [1955] 2 Lloyd's Rep 82; *Anglo-African Shipping Co of New York Inc v J Mortner Ltd* [1962] 1 Lloyd's Rep 610, CA. For a consideration of stock exchange usages, see eg *Bayliffe v Butterworth* (1847) 1 Exch 425; *Hodgkinson v Kelly* (1868) LR 6 Eq 496. As to contracts made on behalf of foreign principals see PARA 130.

6   See PARAS 161–162.

7   *Jenkins v Hutchinson* (1849) 13 QB 744. This is so even though temporary credit has been mistakenly given to the supposed principal: *Gardiner v Heading* [1928] 2 KB 284, CA. See also *Wood v Baxter* (1883) 49 LT 45, DC; *Murphy v Jonathan Howlett (a firm)* (1960) 176 Estates Gazette 311.

8   *Kelner v Baxter* (1866) LR 2 CP 174; *Scott v Lord Ebury* (1867) LR 2 CP 255; *Wilson & Co v Baker, Lees & Co* (1901) 17 TLR 473. This is so unless the other contracting party did not intend to accept the agent's liability: *Jones v Hope* (1880) 3 TLR 247, CA; *Steele v Gourley and Davis* (1887) 3 TLR 772, CA; and see *Bailey v Macaulay* (1849) 13 QB 815. See also *Newborne v Sensolid (Great Britain) Ltd* [1954] 1 QB 45, [1953] 1 All ER 708, CA; *Black v Smallwood* (1966) 117 CLR 52, [1966] ALR 744, Aust HC; *Wickberg v Shatsky* (1969) 4 DLR (3d) 540, BC CA; see also the cases cited in PARA 158 note 5. By statute, the agent may incur personal liability where he purports to contract for an unformed company: see the Companies Act 1985 s 51; PARA 62; and COMPANIES vol 14 (2016) PARA 59.

9   *Queensland Investment and Land Co Ltd v O'Connell and Palmer* (1896) 12 TLR 502.

10 *Hersom v Bernett* [1955] 1 QB 98, [1954] 3 All ER 370.

11 *Savills v Scott* [1988] 1 EGLR 20.

160. Documents executed or signed in agent's name.

An agent who executes a deed in his own name is personally liable upon it, whether he discloses the name and existence of his principal or not[1].

In respect of bills of exchange, cheques and promissory notes signed by an agent on his principal's behalf, the agent is not liable unless he signs his own name[2], in which case he is personally liable even though he adds to his signature words describing him as an agent[3], unless he makes it perfectly clear that he is signing only on his principal's behalf[4]. He is not liable upon any acceptance in his own name[5], unless the bill was in fact drawn upon him[6], in which case he is liable although he purports to accept merely as agent[7].

In the case of any other written contract signed by the agent in his own name, but purporting to be made on behalf of a named principal, the agent will not be personally liable, unless from the terms of the contract it appears that such was the intention of the parties[8]. Where the principal is a registered company, the requirements of the Companies Act 2006 as to the appearance of the company's name in its correspondence etc must be complied with[9]. Failure to mention the company's name may lay the agent open to a fine[10], and possibly expose him to personal liability[11].

1   *Appleton v Binks* (1804) 5 East 148; *Hancock v Hodgson* (1827) 4 Bing 269; *Cass v Rudele* (1692) 2 Vern 280; *Chapman v Smith* [1907] 2 Ch 97. As to the liability of a public agent on a contract under seal made on behalf of the Crown see *Unwin v Wolseley* (1787) 1 Term Rep 674; *Cunningham v Collier* (1785) 4 Doug KB 233.

2   See the Bills of Exchange Act 1882 ss 23, 29; and FINANCIAL INSTRUMENTS AND TRANSACTIONS vol 49 (2015) PARAS 251–252, 269–270.

3   See the Bills of Exchange Act 1882 s 26(1); *Leadbitter v Farrow* (1816) 5 M & S 345; *The Elmville* [1904] P 319; *Landes v Marcus and Davids* (1909) 25 TLR 478.

4   See the Bills of Exchange Act 1882 s 26(1); *Aggs v Nicholson* (1856) 1 H & N 165; *Alexander v Sizer* (1869) LR 4 Exch 102; *Lindus v Melrose* (1857) 3 H & N 177; *Chapman v Smethurst* [1909] 1 KB 927, CA; *Brebner v Henderson* 1925 SC 643, Ct of Sess; *Elliott v Bax-Ironside* [1925] 2 KB 301, CA; *Kettle v Dunster and Wakefield* (1927) 138 LT 158; and FINANCIAL INSTRUMENTS AND TRANSACTIONS vol 49 (2015) PARA 260. Cf *Dutton v Marsh* (1871) LR 6 QB 361.

5   *F Stacey & Co Ltd v Wallis* (1912) 106 LT 544.

6   *Okell v Charles* (1876) 34 LT 822, CA; *Dermatine Co Ltd v Ashworth* (1905) 21 TLR 510.

7   *Jones v Jackson* (1870) 22 LT 828; *Mare v Charles* (1856) 5 E & B 978.

8   *Norton v Herron* (1825) 1 C & P 648; *W and T Avery Ltd v Charlesworth* (1914) 31 TLR 52, CA;
    and contrast *McCollin v Gilpin* (1881) 6 QBD 516, CA, with *Downman v Williams* (1845) 7 QB
    103, Ex Ch.
9   See the Company, Limited Liability Partnership and Business (Names and Trading Disclosures)
    Regulations 2015, SI 2015/17; and COMPANIES vol 14 (2016) PARA 220.
10 As to the fine see COMPANIES vol 14 (2016) PARA 220. Where a company fails, without
    reasonable excuse, to comply with any requirement in the Company, Limited Liability Partnership
    and Business (Names and Trading Disclosures) Regulations 2015, SI 2015/17, regs 20 to 27
    (trading disclosures), an offence is committed by the company and every officer of the company
    who is in default: reg 28(1). A person guilty of such an offence is liable on summary conviction to
    a fine not exceeding level 3 on the standard scale; and for continued contravention, a daily default
    fine not exceeding one-tenth of level 3 on the standard scale: reg 28(2). As to the powers of
    magistrates' courts to issue fines on summary conviction see SENTENCING vol 92 (2015)
    PARA 176.
11 See COMPANIES vol 14 (2016) PARA 220.

(ii) Warranty of Authority

161. Warranty of authority implied.

Where any person purports to do any act[1] or make any contract as agent on
behalf of a principal, he is deemed to warrant[2] that he has in fact authority from
such principal to do the act[3] or make the contract[4] in question. If, therefore, he has
no such authority[5], he is liable to be sued for breach of warranty of authority by
any third person who was induced by his conduct in purporting to act as agent to
believe that he had authority to do the act or make the contract, and who, by
acting upon such belief, has suffered loss in consequence of the absence of
authority[6].

The agent's belief in the existence of his authority is immaterial[7], whether the
belief extends to an authority which the agent believed that he had but in fact
never had, or to an authority which the agent originally had but which has ceased
without his knowledge or means of knowledge[8]. He will not, however, be liable if
at the time of doing the act or making the contract he expressly disclaims any
present authority[9], or if the other party knows that he has no authority[10], or is
fully acquainted with the facts from which the inference of authority is drawn[11].

1   Ie such as the issue and preparation of a bill of lading: *Heskell v Continental Express Ltd* [1950]
    1 All ER 1033, (1950) 94 Sol Jo 339; *V/O Rasnoimport v Guthrie & Co Ltd* [1966] 1 Lloyd's Rep
    1.
2   Unless he is a public agent making a contract terminable at the pleasure of the Crown: *Dunn v
    Macdonald* [1897] 1 QB 555, CA. As to agents of the Crown see CONSTITUTIONAL AND
    ADMINISTRATIVE LAW vol 20 (2014) PARA 197.
3   *Starkey v Bank of England* [1903] AC 114, HL; *Yonge v Toynbee* [1910] 1 KB 215, CA; *Cherry
    and M'Dougall v Colonial Bank of Australasia* (1869) LR 3 PC 24; *Richardson v Williamson and
    Lawson* (1871) LR 6 QB 276; *Weeks v Propert* (1873) LR 8 CP 427. If the agent merely
    misrepresents the name of the party for whom he is acting, he will not be held in breach of
    warranty of authority provided that he did not warrant the accuracy of the name given: *SEB Trygg
    Liv Holding AB v Manches* [2005] EWCA Civ 1237, [2006] 1 All ER 437, [2006] 1 WLR 2276
    (solicitors wrongly stated name of company they were representing in litigation); *Knight Frank
    LLP v du Haney* [2011] EWCA Civ 404, [2011] EG78 (CS) (estate agent mis-spelled client's
    corporate name); *P&P Property Ltd v Owen White and Catlin LLP* [2016] EWHC 2276 (Ch),
    [2017] PNLR 3 (estate agent and solicitors selling property on behalf of supposititious seller). Cf
    Nelson v Nelson [1997] 1 All ER 970, [1997] 1 WLR 233.
4   *Collen v Wright* (1857) 8 E & B 647; *Simons v Patchett* (1857) 7 E & B 568; *Re National Coffee
    Palace Co, ex p Panmure* (1883) 24 ChD 367, CA; *Anderson v John Croall & Sons Ltd* (1903) 6
    F 153, Ct of Sess; *Hughes v Graeme* (1863) 3 F & F 885; *British Russian Gazette and Trade
    Outlook Ltd v Associated Newspapers Ltd* [1933] 2 KB 616, CA.

5 He is not liable for exceeding his real authority, if his apparent or ostensible authority would be sufficient to bind his principal: *Rainbow v Howkins* [1904] 2 KB 322; *Re Sherlock Holmes International Society (Costs)* [2016] EWHC 1392 (Ch), [2016] 4 WLR 173, [2017] 2 BCLC 38. If the principal disputes the authority on a claim brought by the third person, the agent may be joined as defendant, and relief claimed against him in the alternative: *Honduras Inter-Oceanic Rly Co v Lefevre and Tucker* (1877) 2 ExD 301, CA; and see *Massey v Heynes & Co* (1888) 21 QBD 330, CA; *Bennetts & Co v McIlwraith* [1896] 2 QB 464, CA.

6 See *Collen v Wright* (1857) 8 E & B 647, Ex Ch; *Starkey v Bank of England* [1903] AC 114, HL; and notes 3, 4. See also *Salvesen & Co v Rederi Aktiebolaget Nordstjernan* [1905] AC 302, HL. A warranty of authority may be implied even in the absence of any apparent or ostensible authority: see *V/O Rasnoimport v Guthrie & Co Ltd* [1966] 1 Lloyd's Rep 1.

7 *Starkey v Bank of England* [1903] AC 114, HL; *Firbank's Executors v Humphreys* (1886) 18 QBD 54, CA; *Chapleo v Brunswick Permanent Benefit Building Society* (1881) 6 QBD 696, CA. See also *Penn v Bristol and West Building Society* [1997] 3 All ER 470, [1997] 1 WLR 1356, CA (solicitor who mistakenly believed he had authority for a vendor and negotiated with the purchaser and the purchaser's building society's solicitor, gave a warranty of authority to both the purchaser and the building society); *Habton Farms v Nimmo* [2003] EWCA Civ 68, [2004] QB 1, sub nom *Nimmo v Habton Farms* [2003] 1 All ER 1136, applying *Suleman v Shahsavari* [1989] 2 All ER 460, [1988] 1 WLR 1181. If the agent is aware of the absence of authority, he may be sued either for breach of warranty of authority, or, if there was fraud, for deceit: *Polhill v Walter* (1832) 3 B & Ad 114.

8 *Yonge v Toynbee* [1910] 1 KB 215, CA; *Simmons v Liberal Opinion Ltd, Re Dunn* [1911] 1 KB 966, CA.

9 *Halbot v Lens* [1901] 1 Ch 344; *Yonge v Toynbee* [1910] 1 KB 215, CA.

10 *Halbot v Lens* [1901] 1 Ch 344.

11 *Smout v Ilbery* (1842) 10 M & W 1, may still be an authority for this proposition, but in so far as it decides that an agent innocently continuing to act without knowledge of revocation of his authority is not liable to the third party, and as interpreted in *Salton v New Beeston Cycle Co* [1900] 1 Ch 43, it has been overruled by *Yonge v Toynbee* [1910] 1 KB 215, CA. See also *McManus v Fortescue* [1907] 2 KB 1, CA; and contrast *Lilly, Wilson & Co v Smales, Eeles & Co* [1892] 1 QB 456, with *Suart v Haigh* (1893) 9 TLR 488, HL; and cf *West London Commercial Bank Ltd v Kitson* (1884) 13 QBD 360, CA. When the evidence of the agency is an inference of law, the agent is not liable, provided that the facts are equally within the knowledge of both parties: *Eaglesfield v Marquis of Londonderry* (1878) 38 LT 303; *Jones v Hope* (1880) 3 TLR 247, CA; *Rashdall v Ford* (1866) LR 2 Eq 750.

162. Measure of damages for breach of warranty of authority.

The measure of damages for a breach of warranty of authority is the measure normally applicable in contract, namely loss actually sustained by the third person as the natural and probable consequence of the non-existence of the authority or such as both parties might reasonably expect to result as a probable consequence of the breach of warranty[1]. In the case of a contract made without authority and repudiated by the principal, the loss will be the amount that could have been recovered from the principal on a claim for breach of the contract if it had in fact been made with his authority[2], together with the costs of any claim upon the contract reasonably brought by the third person against him[3]. In principle, a claim for breach of warranty cannot put a claimant in a better position than if the warranty had been true[4].

1 *Collen v Wright* (1857) 8 E & B 647; *Starkey v Bank of England* [1903] AC 114, HL; *Firbank's Executors v Humphreys* (1886) 18 QBD 54, CA; *Richardson v Williamson and Lawson* (1871) LR 6 QB 276; *Meek v Wendt & Co* (1888) 21 QBD 126 (affd [1889] WN 14, CA); *Hubbart v Phillips* (1845) 2 Dow & L 707; *Salvesen & Co v Rederi Aktiebolaget Nordstjernan* [1905] AC 302, HL; and see *Salton v New Beeston Cycle Co* [1900] 1 Ch 43. Thus, in the case of a solicitor who continues proceedings without authority the measure of damages is the amount of costs thrown away by the other party to the proceedings: *Yonge v Toynbee* [1910] 1 KB 215, CA; *Fernée v Gorlitz* [1915] 1 Ch 177. As to damages for breach of contract generally see DAMAGES vol 29 (2014) PARA 499 et seq.

2 *Simons v Patchett* (1857) 7 E & B 568; *Richardson v Williamson and Lawson* (1871) LR 6 QB 276; *Suart v Haigh* (1893) 9 TLR 488, HL; *Heskell v Continental Express Ltd* [1950] 1 All ER

1033. The contract must not have been one which would have been unenforceable against the principal owing to the absence of some formality: *Warr v Jones* (1876) 24 WR 695; and see *Rainbow v Howkins* [1904] 2 KB 322.

3   *Hughes v Graeme* (1864) 4 New Rep 190; *Spedding v Nevell* (1869) LR 4 CP 212; *Godwin v Francis* (1870) LR 5 CP 295; *D'Almeida Araujo Lda v Becker & Co Ltd* [1953] 2 QB 329, [1953] 2 All ER 288; and contrast *Pow v Davis* (1861) 1 B & S 220. See also *Osman v J Ralph Moss Ltd* [1970] 1 Lloyd's Rep 313, CA, for the measure of damages where the principal sues the agent.

4   *Skylight Maritime SA v Ascot Underwriting Ltd* [2005] EWHC 15 (Comm) at [20], [2005] PNLR 25.

(iii) Money Received by Agent

163. Liability to repay to third person.

The receipt of money from a third person by an agent on his principal's behalf does not in itself render the agent personally liable to repay it when the third person becomes entitled as against the principal to repayment, whether the money remains in the agent's hands or not[1]. If, however, a third person pays money to an agent under a mistake of fact[2], or in consequence of some wrongful act[3], the agent is personally liable to repay it[4], unless, before the claim for repayment was made upon him, he has paid it to the principal or done something equivalent to payment to his principal[5], or where the principal is a foreign sovereign immune from suit[6]. Where, however, the agent has been a party to the wrongful act[7], or has acted as a principal in the transaction[8], in consequence of which the money has been paid to him, he is not discharged from his liability to make repayment by any payment over to his principal[9].

1   *Ellis v Goulton* [1893] 1 QB 350, CA; *Bamford v Shuttleworth* (1840) 11 Ad & El 926; *Steam Saw Mills Co Ltd v Baring Bros & Co Ltd, Archangel Saw Mills Co v Baring Bros & Co Ltd* [1922] 1 Ch 244, CA; see also *Hindle v Brown* (1908) 98 LT 791, CA.

2   *Cox v Prentice* (1815) 3 M & S 344; *Taylor v Metropolitan Rly Co* [1906] 2 KB 55. Note that since the decision of the House of Lords in *Kleinwort Benson Ltd v Lincoln City Council* [1999] 2 AC 349, [1998] 4 All ER 513, the remedy is no longer restricted to mistakes of fact: see MISTAKE vol 77 (2016) PARA 11.

3   *Holland v Russell* (1863) 4 B & S 14; *Galland v Hall* (1888) 4 TLR 761, CA; *East India Co v Tritton* (1824) 5 Dow & Ry KB 214; *Re Bourne, ex p Bird* (1851) 4 De G & Sm 273.

4   It is not necessary to make the principal, who has knowledge of the payment, a party to the proceedings: *Cary v Webster* (1721) 1 Stra 480; *Admiralty Comrs v National Provincial and Union Bank of England Ltd* (1922) 127 LT 452. A bank is in the same position as any other agent: *Admiralty Comrs v National Provincial and Union Bank of England Ltd*; *Kerrison v Glyn, Mills, Currie & Co* (1911) 81 LJKB 465, HL.

5   *Pollard v Bank of England* (1871) LR 6 QB 623; *Kleinwort, Sons & Co v Dunlop Rubber Co* (1907) 97 LT 263, HL; *Gowers v Lloyds and National Provincial Foreign Bank Ltd* [1938] 1 All ER 766, 158 LT 467, CA; *Cox v Prentice* (1815) 3 M & S 344; *Baylis v Bishop of London* [1913] 1 Ch 127, CA. Merely crediting the principal with the amount without there being any change of circumstances rendering it inequitable for the agent to refund the money is not sufficient: *Buller v Harrison* (1777) 2 Cowp 565; *Cox v Prentice*; *Continental Caoutchouc and Gutta Percha Co v Kleinwort, Sons & Co* (1904) 90 LT 474, CA; *Scottish Metropolitan Assurance Co Ltd v P Samuel & Co Ltd* [1923] 1 KB 348.

6   *Rahimtoola v Nizam of Hyderabad* [1958] AC 379, [1957] 3 All ER 441, HL. The doctrine of sovereign immunity is modified by the State Immunity Act 1978: see generally INTERNATIONAL RELATIONS LAW vol 61 (2010) PARA 244 et seq.

7   *Close v Phipps* (1844) 7 Man & G 586; *Snowdon v Davis* (1808) 1 Taunt 359; *Re Chapman, ex p Edwards* (1884) 13 QBD 747, CA; *Wakefield v Newbon* (1844) 6 QB 276. This is so unless both parties are *in pari delicto*: *Goodall v Lowndes* (1844) 6 QB 464.

8   *Newall v Tomlinson* (1871) LR 6 CP 405; *Kleinwort, Sons & Co v Dunlop Rubber Co* (1907) 97 LT 263, HL.

9   *Citizens' Bank of Louisiana and New Orleans Canal and Banking Co v First National Bank of New Orleans* (1873) LR 6 HL 352; *Stewart v Fry and Chapman* (1817) 7 Taunt 339. The same

rule applies to public agents, whether of the British Crown (*Gidley v Lord Palmerston* (1822) 3 Brod & Bing 275; *R v Secretary of State for War* [1891] 2 QB 326, CA; *Kinloch v Secretary of State for India in Council* (1882) 7 App Cas 619, HL; *Salaman v Secretary of State for India* [1906] 1 KB 613, CA), or of foreign governments (*Henderson v Rothschild & Sons* (1887) 56 LJ Ch 471, CA; *Twycross v Dreyfus* (1877) 5 ChD 605, CA).

164. Direction from principal to pay to third person.

Where an agent is directed by his principal to pay to a third person any money which he has received or is about to receive on his principal's behalf, he is not in general responsible to the third person if he fails to do so[1], notwithstanding the fact that the money is received by him from the principal for the express purpose of paying it over to the third person[2], or that his failure to comply with the direction is a breach of duty towards his principal[3]. The agent renders himself personally liable, however, if he assents to the direction, and the assent is communicated to the third person[4], or if he enters into an unconditional undertaking[5] to pay the money to the third person or to hold it on his behalf[6]. In this case he is not discharged from liability by the subsequent bankruptcy of the principal[7], or the purported revocation of his authority to pay[8].

If the direction is not a mere authority to make the payment[9], but amounts to an assignment of a specific fund, or a charge upon it[10], the agent, upon receiving notice of the assignment or charge, becomes liable to the third person for the amount due to him thereunder. The agent will not, however, be deprived thereby of any right of lien or set-off which accrued before he received such notice[11].

1 *Citizens' Bank of Louisiana and New Orleans Canal and Banking Co v First National Bank of New Orleans* (1873) LR 6 HL 352; *Stewart v Fry and Chapman* (1817) 7 Taunt 339. The same rule applies to public agents, whether of the British Crown (*Gidley v Lord Palmerston* (1822) 3 Brod & Bing 275; *R v Secretary of State for War* [1891] 2 QB 326, CA; *Kinloch v Secretary of State for India in Council* (1882) 7 App Cas 619, HL; *Salaman v Secretary of State for India* [1906] 1 KB 613, CA), or of foreign governments (*Henderson v Rothschild & Sons* (1887) 56 LJ Ch 471, CA; *Twycross v Dreyfus* (1877) 5 ChD 605, CA).

2 *Moore v Bushell* (1857) 27 LJ Ex 3.

3 *Schroeder v Central Bank of London Ltd* (1876) 34 LT 735.

4 *Walker v Rostron* (1842) 9 M & W 411; *Noble v National Discount Co* (1860) 5 H & N 225; *Lilly v Hays* (1836) 5 Ad & El 548; *Griffin v Weatherby* (1868) LR 3 QB 753. This rule applies in other situations: see eg *Shamia v Joory* [1958] 1 QB 448, [1958] 1 All ER 111 (money owed by principal to agent; direction by agent to principal to pay third party).

5 *Brind v Hampshire* (1836) 1 M & W 365; *Malcolm v Scott* (1850) 5 Exch 601.

6 *Crowfoot v Gurney* (1832) 9 Bing 372; *Williams v Everett* (1811) 14 East 582; *Scott v Porcher* (1817) 3 Mer 652. If the undertaking to pay was subject to a condition, the condition must have been accepted by the third person (*Baron v Husband* (1833) 4 B & Ad 611), and must have been fulfilled (*Stevens v Hill* (1805) 5 Esp 247). If the condition is to pay when the money is received from the principal, the agent is only liable for the amount which he actually receives: *Langston v Corney* (1815) 4 Camp 176.

7 *Crowfoot v Gurney* (1832) 9 Bing 372; *Walker v Rostron* (1842) 9 M & W 411.

8 *Robertson v Fauntleroy* (1823) 8 Moore CP 10.

9 *Re Whitting, ex p Hall* (1878) 10 ChD 615; affd 10 ChD 619, CA.

10 *William Brandt's Sons & Co v Dunlop Rubber Co Ltd* [1905] AC 454, HL; *Rodick v Gandell* (1851) 1 De GM & G 763; for a consideration of the assignment of debts, and the meaning to be given to assignment from a 'fund', see *Shamia v Joory* [1958] 1 QB 448, [1958] 1 All ER 111. As to assignment of debts see further CHOSES IN ACTION vol 13 (2017) PARA 13 et seq.

11 *Webb v Smith* (1885) 30 ChD 192, CA; *Roxburghe v Cox* (1881) 17 ChD 520, CA. See further CHOSES IN ACTION vol 13 (2009) PARA 63.

(iv) Tortious Liability; Breach of Trust

165. General liability of agent for wrongful act.

Any agent, including a public agent[1], who commits a wrongful act[2] in the course of his employment, is personally liable[3] to any third person who suffers loss or damage thereby[4], notwithstanding that the act was expressly authorised or ratified by the principal[5], unless it was thereby deprived of its wrongful character[6]. It is immaterial that the agent did the act innocently and without knowledge that it was wrongful[7], except in cases where actual malice is essential to constitute the wrong[8]. An agent cannot rely upon an exclusion clause contained in the contract between the principal and the third party[9], unless on the wording of the contract the principal has contracted not only on his own behalf, but also on behalf of his agent[10].

1 *Entick v Carrington* (1765) 19 State Tr 1029; *Sinclair v Broughton and Government of India* (1882) 47 LT 170, PC; *Hamilton v Clancy* [1914] 2 IR 514; *Roper v Public Works Comrs* [1915] 1 KB 45; and see *Dixon v London Small Arms Co* (1876) 1 App Cas 632, HL. At common law a public agent could not be sued in his official capacity: *Raleigh v Goschen* [1898] 1 Ch 73; *Bainbridge v Postmaster-General* [1906] 1 KB 178, CA; *Roper v Public Works Comrs*. As to proceedings against government departments and the liability of Crown servants see CONSTITUTIONAL AND ADMINISTRATIVE LAW vol 20 (2014) PARAS 190 et seq, 197. As to the immunity from legal process of diplomatic agents of foreign governments see INTERNATIONAL RELATIONS LAW vol 61 (2010) PARA 274.

2 As to what acts of the agent are sufficient to impose liability, contrast *Adair v Young* (1879) 12 ChD 13, CA, with *Nobel's Explosive Co Ltd v Jones, Scott & Co* (1882) 8 App Cas 5, HL; see also *TD Keegan Ltd v Palmer* [1961] 2 Lloyd's Rep 449. The act must be his personal act, and he is not liable for the acts of his co-agents (*Re Denham & Co* (1883) 25 ChD 752) or sub-agents (*Stone v Cartwright* (1795) 6 Term Rep 411), unless he is a partner (*Weir v Bell* (1878) 3 ExD 238, CA), or has otherwise made himself a principal in the transaction (*Cargill v Bower* (1878) 10 ChD 502; *Weir v Bell*), or unless he is made liable by statute.

3 The agent can be sued notwithstanding that judgment has been obtained against the principal: see the Civil Liability (Contribution) Act 1978 s 1; and TORT vol 97 (2015) PARA 450 et seq.

4 *Bennett v Bayes, Pennington and Harrison* (1860) 5 H & N 391; *Arnot v Biscoe* (1748) 1 Ves Sen 95; *Swift v Jewsbury and Goddard* (1874) LR 9 QB 301, Ex Ch; *Lowe v Dorling & Son* [1906] 2 KB 772, CA; *Re National Funds Assurance Co* (1878) 10 ChD 118; *Cullen v Thomson's Trustees* (1862) 4 Macq 424, HL; *Cope v Sharpe (No 2)* [1912] 1 KB 496, CA.

5 *Johnson v Emerson and Sparrow* (1871) LR 6 Exch 329. As to the liability of the principal see generally PARAS 151–155. As to the right of the third party to rescission of contracts made as a result of a misrepresentation by the agent see PARA 136; and see also PARAS 153–154. For a consideration of the tort of conversion by an agent see PARA 166.

6 *Hull v Pickersgill* (1819) 1 Brod & Bing 282; *Anderson v Watson* (1827) 3 C & P 214; *Sykes v Sykes* (1870) LR 5 CP 113; and contrast *Sharland v Mildon* (1846) 5 Hare 469; *Padget v Priest* (1787) 2 Term Rep 97; see also *Egger v Viscount Chelmsford* [1965] 1 QB 248, [1964] 3 All ER 406, CA (agent relying on qualified privilege was held not to be affected by malice of principal). As to ratification of acts of agents of the Crown see PARA 71.

7 *Baschet v London Illustrated Standard Co* [1900] 1 Ch 73.

8 *Eaglesfield v Marquis of Londonderry* (1878) 38 LT 303; *Tims v John Lewis & Co Ltd* [1951] 2 KB 459, [1951] 1 All ER 814, CA (revsd sub nom *John Lewis & Co Ltd v Tims* [1952] AC 676, [1952] 1 All ER 1203, HL, but approved on this point).

9 *Adler v Dickson* [1955] 1 QB 158, [1954] 3 All ER 397, CA; *Scruttons Ltd v Midland Silicones Ltd* [1962] AC 446, [1962] 1 All ER 1, HL; *Canadian General Electric Co Ltd v The Lake Bosomtwe and Pickford and Black Ltd* [1970] 2 Lloyd's Rep 81. A contract expressly providing that it is made for the benefit of another person points strongly to the conclusion that it has been made on his behalf, especially if he will not be entitled to the benefit of the contract unless it was so made: see *Borvigilant (Owners) v Romina G (Owners)* [2003] EWCA Civ 935, [2003] 2 All ER (Comm) 736.

10 *Pyrene Co v Scindia Navigation Co* [1954] 2 QB 402, [1954] 2 All ER 158; *Alsey Steam Fishing Co Ltd v Hillman (Owners), The Kirknes* [1957] P 51, [1957] 1 All ER 97. The limitations on liability of shipowners and carriers by air conferred by statute extend also to their servants and

agents acting in the course of their employment: see the Merchant Shipping Act 1995 ss 185, 186; and SHIPPING AND MARITIME LAW vol 94 (2017) PARA 992 et seq; and see the various versions of the Carriage by Air Act 1961 s 1, Sch 1 art 25A; the Carriage by Air (Supplementary Provisions) Act 1962 s 1, Schedule art V; and CARRIAGE AND CARRIERS vol 7 (2015) PARAS 121 et seq, 155 et seq. See also the Contracts (Rights of Third Parties) Act 1999; and CONTRACT vol 22 (2012) PARA 341 et seq. Subject to the exceptions in s 6 (see CONTRACT vol 22 (2012) PARA 346), where a term of a contract excludes or limits liability in relation to any matter references in the Act to the third party enforcing the term is to be construed as references to his availing himself of the exclusion or limitation: see s 1(6); and CONTRACT vol 22 (2012) PARA 343.

166. Conversion by agent.

Any agent who, while acting on his principal's behalf, acquires the actual or constructive[1] possession of goods[2] or securities[3] which are not in fact the property of his principal, and deals with them in any manner which is obviously wrongful if his principal is not their owner[4] or duly authorised by their owner, as by selling and delivering them to a stranger[5], or otherwise purporting to dispose of the property in them[6], is guilty of a conversion[7], and is liable to their true owner for their value. His liability is not affected by the fact that he received them in good faith as the property of his principal, and dealt with them in accordance with his principal's instructions and in ignorance of the true owner's claim[8], unless the true owner is estopped from denying the principal's authority to dispose of them[9], or unless the agent is a banker receiving payment[10] of a cheque on behalf of a customer[11].

No agent is guilty of a conversion, however, who, not being in possession of the goods or securities, merely negotiates a contract of sale between his principal and a third person[12], or who, though being in possession of them, does not do any act which is obviously wrongful if the principal is not the true owner, but deals only with the possession of them as directed by his principal without purporting to dispose of the property in them[13]. Nevertheless, any dealings whatsoever with the goods or securities against the will of the true owner will amount to a conversion if done with notice of his claim[14].

1 *Union Credit Bank Ltd v Mersey Docks and Harbour Board* [1899] 2 QB 205.
2 *Consolidated Co v Curtis & Son* [1892] 1 QB 495; *Cochrane v Rymill* (1879) 40 LT 744, CA; *Hollins v Fowler* (1875) LR 7 HL 757; *Stephens v Elwall* (1815) 4 M & S 259.
3 *Great Western Rly Co v London and County Banking Co Ltd* [1901] AC 414, HL; *Arnold v Cheque Bank* (1876) 1 CPD 578; *Fine Art Society Ltd v Union Bank of London Ltd* (1886) 17 QBD 705, CA.
4 *McEntire v Potter & Co* (1889) 22 QBD 438.
5 *Consolidated Co v Curtis & Son* [1892] 1 QB 495; *Cochrane v Rymill* (1879) 40 LT 744, CA; *Hollins v Fowler* (1875) LR 7 HL 757.
6 *McEntire v Potter & Co* (1889) 22 QBD 438; *Stephens v Elwall* (1815) 4 M & S 259; *Pearson v Graham* (1837) 6 Ad & El 899.
7 As to conversion generally see TORT vol 97 (2015) PARA 604 et seq.
8 See the cases cited in notes 1–6.
9 As to where the principal is a mercantile agent, or buyer or seller in possession of goods or the documents of title thereto with the consent of the true owner, see the Factors Act 1889 ss 2, 8, 9; the Sale of Goods Act 1979 ss 24, 25; PARAS 149–150; and SALE OF GOODS AND SUPPLY OF SERVICES vol 91 (2012) PARAS 155–156.
10 This does not apply to any other instrument: *Bavins, Junr, and Sims v London and South Western Bank Ltd* [1900] 1 QB 270, CA.
11 See the Cheques Act 1957 s 4; *Orbit Mining and Trading Co Ltd v Westminster Bank Ltd* [1963] 1 QB 794, [1962] 3 All ER 565, CA; and FINANCIAL INSTITUTIONS vol 48 (2015) PARA 202.
12 *Cochrane v Rymill* (1879) 40 LT 744, CA; *Barker v Furlong* [1891] 2 Ch 172.
13 *National Mercantile Bank v Rymill* (1881) 44 LT 767, CA; *Union Credit Bank Ltd v Mersey Docks and Harbour Board* [1899] 2 QB 205; *Barker v Furlong* [1891] 2 Ch 172.

14 *Davis v Artingstall* (1880) 49 LJ Ch 609. A refusal to deliver up the goods without an order from the principal, or a request for a reasonable time for inquiry, will not of itself amount to conversion: *Alexander v Southey* (1821) 5 B & Ald 247; *Pillott v Wilkinson* (1864) 3 H & C 345, Ex Ch.

167. Breach of trust by agent.

No agent, who is in possession of property which his principal holds in trust for another[1] and who makes, on the instructions of his principal, any disposition of such property which is inconsistent with the trust, is guilty of a breach of trust[2], unless he had notice of the trust at the time[3] and was aware that the disposition made by him was in breach of trust[4].

1   As to the exercise of trust functions by agents generally see the Trustee Act 2000 Pt IV (ss 11–27); and TRUSTS AND POWERS vol 98 (2013) PARA 430 et seq.
2   *Gray v Johnston* (1868) LR 3 HL 1; *Bank of New South Wales v Goulburn Valley Butter Co Pty Ltd* [1902] AC 543, PC; and see *Union Bank of Australia Ltd v Murray-Aynsley* [1898] AC 693, HL. As to breach of trust generally see TRUSTS AND POWERS vol 98 (2013) PARAS 665–722.
3   *Williams v Williams* (1881) 17 ChD 437; *Re Gross, ex p Kingston* (1871) 6 Ch App 632. A fortiori, knowledge of a trust is not to be imputed to an agent such as a solicitor merely because it is claimed against his client that there is a trust: *Carl Zeiss Stiftung v Herbert Smith & Co (a firm) (No 2)* [1969] 2 Ch 276, [1969] 2 All ER 367, CA.
4   *Magnus v Queensland National Bank* (1888) 37 ChD 466, CA; and contrast *Coleman v Bucks and Oxon Union Bank* [1897] 2 Ch 243. The fact that a personal benefit to the agent is designed or stipulated for is strong evidence that the agent is privy to the breach of trust: *Gray v Johnston* (1868) LR 3 HL 1. See further TRUSTS AND POWERS vol 98 (2013) PARA 129.

(2) RIGHTS OF AGENT

(i) Enforcement of Contract

168. Agent's right to enforce contract.

Any person who makes a contract in his own name without disclosing the existence of a principal[1], or who, though disclosing the fact that he is acting as an agent on behalf of a principal, renders himself personally liable on the contract[2], is entitled to enforce it against the other contracting party[3], notwithstanding that the principal has renounced the contract[4]. A similar right appears to exist where the agent purports to contract as agent only for an unnamed principal who in fact is non-existent[5]. But where he names his principal and makes the contract expressly as agent[6] on his behalf, he cannot enforce it[7], even though he is the real principal[8], unless the other party has affirmed the contract with knowledge of the fact[9]. Where an agent signatory seeks to add himself to the existing named principals as a party to the contract, he can do so if he was one of the principals at the relevant time[10].

An agent cannot sue for a promised bribe, even though he was not influenced thereby in the discharge of his duty to his principal[11].

In a claim brought by an agent on his principal's contract, the defendant is entitled to disclosure from the principal as fully as if he were the claimant on the record, even though he is a foreign principal[12].

1   *Sims v Bond* (1833) 5 B & Ad 389. See eg *Craig & Co v Blackater* 1923 SC 472, Ct of Sess.
2   *Short v Spackman* (1831) 2 B & Ad 962; *Cooke v Wilson* (1856) 1 CBNS 153; *Agacio v Forbes* (1861) 14 Moo PCC 160; *Sargent v Morris* (1820) 3 B & Ald 277. See also *Harper & Co v Vigers Bros* [1909] 2 KB 549; *H O Brandt & Co v H N Morris & Co Ltd* [1917] 2 KB 784, CA; cf *N and J Vlassopulos Ltd v Ney Shipping Ltd, The Santa Carina* [1977] 1 Lloyd's Rep 478, CA. See also PARA 158.

3 *Fisher v Marsh* (1865) 6 B & S 411. He must sue on his own behalf and he will have no claim in the alleged capacity of trustee for his principals: *Allen v F O'Hearn & Co* [1937] AC 213, [1936] 3 All ER 828, PC. See also *Braymist Ltd v Wise Finance Co Ltd* [2002] EWCA Civ 127, [2002] Ch 273, [2002] 2 All ER 333.
4 *Short v Spackman* (1831) 2 B & Ad 962.
5 *Schmalz v Avery* (1851) 16 QB 655; *Harper & Co v Vigers Bros* [1909] 2 KB 549. These decisions are criticised in *Hill Steam Shipping Co v Hugo Stinnes Ltd* 1941 SC 324, Ct of Sess; but cf *Chapman v Smith* [1907] 2 Ch 97 at 103, where the fact that the person making a lease was therein described 'as agent, hereinafter called the landlord', was held not to prevent the lease operating as a demise of the estate vested in him as mortgagee. It must be clear that the person seeking to enforce the contract was, when entering into the contract, purporting to contract as agent, for example intending to bind a non-existent company and not merely applying his signature as that of the company: *Newborne v Sensolid (Great Britain) Ltd* [1954] 1 QB 45, [1953] 1 All ER 708, CA. See also *Black v Smallwood* (1966) 117 CLR 52, [1966] ALR 744, Aust HC. See further PARA 159.
6 The rules apply to a del credere agent: *Bramwell v Spiller* (1870) 21 LT 672. As to this class of agency see PARA 13.
7 *Fairlie v Fenton* (1870) LR 5 Exch 169; *Bowen v Morris* (1810) 2 Taunt 374, Ex Ch; *Evans v Hooper* (1875) 1 QBD 45, CA; *TP Jordeson & Co and Kahn v London Hardwood Co Ltd* (1913) 110 LT 666. Aliter, where he is an insurance broker (*Provincial Insurance Co of Canada v Leduc* (1874) LR 6 PC 224), or an agent with a special interest in the subject matter of the contract (see PARA 169).
8 *Bickerton v Burrell* (1816) 5 M & S 383.
9 *Rayner v Grote* (1846) 15 M & W 359.
10 *Fraser v Thames Television Ltd* [1984] QB 44, [1983] 2 All ER 101.
11 *Harrington v Victoria Graving Dock Co* (1878) 3 QBD 549.
12 *Willis & Co v Baddeley* [1892] 2 QB 324, CA; *James Nelson & Sons Ltd v Nelson Line (Liverpool) Ltd* [1906] 2 KB 217, CA; but see *Queen of Portugal v Glyn* (1840) 7 Cl & Fin 466, HL.

169. Loss of right to enforce contract.

Where an agent is entitled to sue upon a contract made by him, his right is lost by the intervention of his principal[1], and is subject to any settlement with the principal[2]. An agent who has a special interest in the subject matter of the contract[3] may enforce it[4], notwithstanding any settlement with the principal[5], unless the agent has not been prejudiced by the settlement[6], or unless he is estopped from setting up his interest against the other contracting party[7].

1 *Atkinson v Cotesworth* (1825) 3 B & C 647; *Sadler v Leigh* (1815) 4 Camp 195.
2 *Rogers v Hadley* (1863) 2 H & C 227; *Thornton v Maynard* (1875) LR 10 CP 695.
3 Ie as a factor or auctioneer (*Gray v Pearson* (1870) LR 5 CP 568), but not a broker (*Fairlie v Fenton* (1870) LR 5 Exch 169), nor an agent to whom a principal has indorsed a bill of lading in respect of goods comprised therein (*Burgos v Nascimento* (1908) 100 LT 71).
4 *Williams v Millington* (1788) 1 Hy Bl 81; *Drinkwater v Goodwin* (1775) 1 Cowp 251.
5 *Robinson v Rutter* (1855) 4 E & B 954; *Atkyns and Batten v Amber* (1796) 2 Esp 491; *Isberg v Bowden* (1853) 8 Exch 852; *Manley & Sons Ltd v Berkett* [1912] 2 KB 329.
6 *Grice v Kenrick* (1870) LR 5 QB 340; *Holmes v Tutton* (1855) 5 E & B 65; cf *Manley & Sons Ltd v Berkett* [1912] 2 KB 329.
7 *Coppin v Walker* (1816) 7 Taunt 237.

(ii) Recovery of Money Paid

170. Agent's claim for money had and received.

An agent who has paid money on behalf of his principal to a third person under such circumstances[1] that the principal, if the payment had been made by him, would have been entitled to recover the money, may bring a claim in his own name for money had and received against the third person[2].

1 Eg as mistake of fact (*Colonial Bank v Exchange Bank of Yarmouth, Nova Scotia* (1885) 11 App Cas 84, PC), or fraud (*Holt v Ely* (1853) 1 E & B 795), or extortion (*Stevenson v Mortimer* (1778)

2 Cowp 805). See also *Royal Securities Corpn Ltd v Montreal Trust Co* [1967] 1 OR 137, 59 DLR (2d) 666 (affd [1967] 2 OR 200, 63 DLR (2d) 15, Ont CA). It is immaterial whether the principal authorised the payment or not: see *Holt v Ely*.

2 The claim may be brought either by the principal or by the agent: *Holt v Ely* (1853) 1 E & B 795. Note that since the decision of the House of Lords in *Kleinwort Benson Ltd v Lincoln City Council* [1999] 2 AC 349, [1998] 4 All ER 513, the remedy is no longer restricted to mistakes of fact: see MISTAKE vol 77 (2016) PARA 11.

8. TERMINATION OF AGENCY

(1) MEANS OF TERMINATION

171. Ways in which agency may be terminated.

Agency may be terminated either by the act of the parties or by operation of law. The act of the parties may be an agreement between them or acts amounting to a revocation by the principal or a renunciation by the agent[1].

The law terminates the agency:

(1) on the expiration of the time, if any, agreed upon[2];
(2) on complete performance of the undertaking[3];
(3) on frustration of the contract or the happening of an event rendering the continuance of the agency unlawful[4]; or
(4) where either party becomes incapable of continuing the contract by reason of death, bankruptcy or unsoundness of mind[5].

The termination of agency by these various events is, however, subject to qualifications either defined by law, or due to the facts of the particular case[6].

Where an agent goes into administrative receivership, the cessation of its business does not automatically bring its agency agreement with its principal to an end[7].

1 See PARAS 178–183, 186.
2 See PARA 187.
3 See PARA 188.
4 See PARA 188.
5 See PARAS 189–192.
6 As to irrevocable authorities see PARAS 172–177.
7 *Triffit Nurseries (a firm) v Salads Etcetera Ltd* [2000] 1 All ER (Comm) 737, CA.

(2) IRREVOCABLE AUTHORITY

172. Authority coupled with interest.

Where the agency is created by deed, or for valuable consideration, and the authority is given to effectuate a security or to secure the interest of the agent, the authority cannot be revoked[1]. Thus, if an agreement is entered into on a sufficient consideration whereby an authority is given for the purpose of securing some benefit to the donee of the authority, the authority is irrevocable on the ground that it is coupled with an interest[2]. So an authority to sell in consideration of forbearance to sue for previous advances[3], an authority to apply for shares to be allotted on an underwriting agreement, a commission being paid for the underwriting[4], and an authority to receive rents until the principal and interest of a loan have been paid off[5] or to receive money from a third party in payment of a debt[6], have been held to be irrevocable. On the other hand, an authority is not irrevocable merely because the agent has a special property in or a lien upon goods to which the authority relates, the authority not being given for the purpose of securing the claims of the agent[7].

1 As to what will amount to an authority coupled with an interest so as to be irrevocable see *Smart v Sandars* (1848) 5 CB 895; *Angove's Pty Ltd v Bailey* [2016] UKSC 47 at [7], [2017] 1 All ER 773, [2016] 1 WLR 3179 per Lord Sumption. As to irrevocable powers of attorney see PARA 176.
2 *Smart v Sandars* (1848) 5 CB 895 per Wilde CJ. See also *Walsh v Whitcomb* (1797) 2 Esp 565; *Gaussen v Morton* (1830) 10 B & C 731; *De Comas v Prost and Kohler* (1865) 3 Moo PCCNS

158; *Kiddill v Farnell* (1857) 3 Sm & G 428; *Angove's Pty Ltd v Bailey* [2016] UKSC 47, [2017]
   1 All ER 773, [2016] 1 WLR 3179; but see *Watson v King* (1815) 4 Camp 272.
3 *Raleigh v Atkinson* (1840) 6 M & W 670.
4 *Re Hannan's Empress Gold Mining and Development Co, Carmichael's Case* [1896] 2 Ch 643,
   CA; *Re Olympic Fire and General Reinsurance Co* [1920] 2 Ch 341, CA; but cf *Re Consort Deep
   Level Gold Mines Ltd, ex p Stark* [1897] 1 Ch 575, CA.
5 *Abbott v Stratton* (1846) 9 I Eq R 233; *Spooner v Sandilands* (1842) 1 Y & C Ch Cas 390.
6 *Alley v Hotson* (1815) 4 Camp 325. See also *Re Rose, ex p Hasluck and Garrard* (1894) 1 Mans
   218, DC; *Gurnell v Gardner* (1863) 4 Giff 626; *Lepard v Vernon* (1813) 2 Ves & B 51; and *Re
   Bultfontein Sun Diamond Mine Ltd, ex p Cox, Hughes and Norman* (1897) 75 LT 669, CA.
7 *Taplin v Florence* (1851) 10 CB 744; *Chinnock v Sainsbury* (1860) 30 LJ Ch 409; and see *Frith
   v Frith* [1906] AC 254, PC.

173. Agent becoming personally liable.

Where, in pursuance of his authority, the agent has contracted a personal
liability, the principal cannot revoke the authority so as to destroy the agent's right
of indemnity in respect of such liability, nor can the trustee in bankruptcy of the
principal do so[1]. Similarly, where the agent has incurred a contractual liability to
pay money to a third party and the principal subsequently forbids the payment,
the agent is entitled to be indemnified in respect of any payments he makes[2].

1 *Crowfoot v Gurney* (1832) 9 Bing 372; *Walker v Rostron* (1842) 9 M & W 411; *Hutchinson v
   Heyworth* (1838) 9 Ad & El 375; *Dickinson v Marrow* (1845) 14 M & W 713; *Griffin v
   Weatherby* (1868) LR 3 QB 753.
2 *Hodgson v Anderson* (1825) 3 B & C 842; *Hamilton v Spottiswoode* (1849) 4 Exch 200; *Metcalf
   v Clough* (1828) 6 LJOS KB 281; *Yates v Hoppe* (1850) 9 CB 541; *Chappell v Bray* (1860) 6 H
   & N 145.

174. Agent liable to personal loss.

Where liability to personal loss, though not amounting to a legal liability, has
been incurred by the agent in the exercise of his authority (as, for example, by the
operation of the rules of the Stock Exchange which are binding upon the
members, or by a solicitor incurring liability for barrister's fees[1]) the principal
cannot revoke the authority after the liability has been incurred[2].

Illustrations of this rule are to be found in the case of betting transactions[3].

1 *Rhodes v Fielder, Jones and Harrison* (1919) 89 LJKB 15, DC.
2 *Seymour v Bridge* (1885) 14 QBD 460.
3 *Read v Anderson* (1884) 13 QBD 779, CA (decision reversed by statute: see the Gaming Act 1892
   s 1 (now repealed) barring recovery under any promise to repay a payment made 'in respect of' a
   wagering contract: see eg *Tatam v Reeve* [1893] 1 QB 44). As to the operation of gambling
   contracts see LEISURE AND ENTERTAINMENT vol 67 (2016) PARA 603 et seq. In *Temple Legal
   Protection Ltd v QBE Insurance (Europe) Ltd* [2009] EWCA Civ 453, [2010] 1 All ER (Comm)
   703, it has been suggested that agencies such as in *Read v Anderson* are 'irrevocable' in a highly
   peculiar sense, essentially involving cases that recognise that, despite the principal's purported
   revocation of the agency, the agent retains a contractual (or, possibly, a restitutionary) claim for
   sums due from the principal owing to the fact the obligations were incurred during the currency
   of the parties' agreement.

175. Agent acquiring rights in subject matter.

Where the agent is entitled to sue on a contract and to a lien on the subject
matter, the right to sue is not revocable by the act of bankruptcy of the principal
until the claim secured by the lien is satisfied[1].

A factor's authority to sell, however, is not irrevocable merely because he has
made advances on the goods to his principal. The making of advances may,
however, be a good consideration for an irrevocable authority to sell, provided

that there is an agreement to that effect; such an agreement may be inferred from the circumstances[2].

1 *Drinkwater v Goodwin* (1775) 1 Cowp 251; *Robson v Kemp* (1802) 4 Esp 233.
2 *De Comas v Prost and Kohler* (1865) 3 Moo PCCNS 158; *Smart v Sandars* (1848) 5 CB 895.

176. Irrevocable powers of attorney.

Where a power of attorney is expressed to be irrevocable and is given to secure a proprietary interest of the donee or the performance of an obligation owed to the donee, the power is irrevocable either by the donor without the consent of the donee or by the death, incapacity, bankruptcy, winding up or dissolution of the donor, so long as the donee has the interest or the obligation remains undischarged[1]. A power of attorney given to secure a proprietary interest may be given to the person entitled to the interest and persons deriving title under him to that interest, and those persons will be the duly constituted donees of the power for all the purposes of the power, without prejudice to any right to appoint substitutes given by the power[2].

Provision is also made enabling a person to appoint an attorney whose authority will not be revoked by the donor's mental incapacity[3].

1 Powers of Attorney Act 1971 s 4(1). Section 4 applies to powers of attorney whenever created: s 4(3).
2 Powers of Attorney Act 1971 s 4(2); and see note 1. As to the protection of persons dealing with the donee of a power expressed to be irrevocable and given by way of security see PARA 194.
3 As to enduring and lasting powers of attorney see PARA 195 et seq.

177. Agency for fixed time.

Where an agency is created for a fixed time, any right of the principal, as between himself and the agent, to terminate it before the expiration of the time agreed upon must be ascertained from the terms of the agreement[1] and the facts of the particular case[2]. The taking of a bribe has been held to be good ground for termination of the agency[3], as has a breach of confidence by the disclosure of confidential information[4]. The common defences of incompetence or negligence may avail on a claim for wrongful dismissal[5].

1 *Lazarus v Cairn Line of Steamships Ltd* (1912) 106 LT 378; *Re An Indenture, Sir Herbert Marshall & Sons Ltd v John Brinsmead & Sons Ltd* (1912) 106 LT 460; *Reigate v Union Manufacturing Co (Ramsbottom) Ltd* [1918] 1 KB 592, CA; *Monk v Largo Foods Ltd* [2016] EWHC 1837 (Comm). As to remuneration in respect of transactions after termination see PARA 108; and as to the effect of termination of the business of the principal see PARA 184.
2 *Burton v Great Northern Rly Co* (1854) 9 Exch 507; *Aspdin v Austin* (1844) 5 QB 671; *Dunn v Sayles* (1844) 5 QB 685; *Williamson v Taylor* (1843) 5 QB 175; *Emmens v Elderton* (1853) 4 HL Cas 624; *Eley v Positive Government Security Life Assurance Co Ltd* (1875) 1 ExD 20 (where a solicitor was appointed by articles of association, and it was held that the articles were an agreement *inter socios* and not a contract with third parties). See also *Lothian v Jenolite Ltd* 1969 SC 111 (termination not justifiable on grounds of agent acting for competitors, in absence of implied term prohibiting such action).
3 *Boston Deep Sea Fishing and Ice Co v Ansell* (1888) 39 ChD 339, CA; *Bulfield v Fournier* (1894) 11 TLR 62 (affd (1895) 11 TLR 282, CA).
4 *LS Harris Trustees Ltd v Power Packing Services (Hermit Road) Ltd* [1970] 2 Lloyd's Rep 65 (agency for single transaction).
5 For a discussion of these defences see EMPLOYMENT vol 41 (2014) PARA 744.

(3) TERMINATION BY ACT OF PARTIES

178. Modes of termination of agencies for an indefinite term.

As in the case of any other contract, subject to the cases of irrevocable authority previously mentioned[1], agency could, in principle, be freely terminated at common law by the parties either by agreement, or by revocation by the principal on notice or summarily[2], or by the agent renouncing his authority[3]. In relation to free termination it is necessary to distinguish between fixed term and indefinite term contracts. Fixed term agencies[4] end with the expiry of the term specified. If an agency is entered into for the performance of a specific task by the agent, it will expire on performance of that task. In such cases, no notice need be given by either party. A principal can also terminate an agency contract for breach on the part of the agent. However, the courts will be reluctant to hold that trivial breaches on the part of the agent justify termination, so the contract should spell out clearly events which entitle the principal to terminate[5]. Similarly, the agent may be entitled to terminate for breach on the part of the principal.

In relation to commercial agents[6], where a fixed term contract is continued by both parties after the expiry of the term, it is deemed to be converted into an agency contract for an indefinite term[7]. An indefinite term agency contract[8] can only be terminated by notice[9] for the specified period[10]. Specific provision is also made regarding the entitlement of commercial agents to compensation or indemnity where the agency is brought to an end[11].

1 See PARAS 172–177.
2 See PARAS 182–183, 185.
3 See PARA 186. For a discussion of methods of termination at common law see *Crean v Deane* [1959] IR 347.
4 The period of time may be specified, or implied by trade usage: see *Dickinson v Lilwal* (1815) 4 Camp 279.
5 See *Schuler AG v Wickman Machine Tool Sales Ltd* [1974] AC 235, [1973] 2 All ER 39, HL.
6 Ie commercial agents to whom the Commercial Agents (Council Directive) Regulations 1993, SI 1993/3053, apply. As to the meaning of 'commercial agent', and as to the cases to which the Regulations apply, see PARA 73.

    The Regulations do not affect the application of any enactment or rule of law (see the text and notes 1–5) which provides for the immediate termination of the agency contract because of the failure of one party to carry out all or part of his obligations under that contract, or where exceptional circumstances arise: reg 16. See *Crane v Sky In-Home Ltd* [2007] EWHC 66 (Ch), [2007] All ER (Comm) 599; *Nigel Fryer Joinery Services Ltd v Ian Firth Hardware Ltd* [2008] EWHC 767 (Ch), [2008] 2 Lloyd's Rep 108; *Anderson (t/a Spectrum Agencies) v Crocs Europe BV v* [2012] EWCA Civ 1400, [2013] 1 Lloyd's Rep 1.
7 Commercial Agents (Council Directive) Regulations 1993, SI 1993/3053, reg 14.
8 This applies also to fixed period agency contracts that are converted into agency contracts of an indefinite period under the Commercial Agents (Council Directive) Regulations 1993, SI 1993/3053, reg 14 (see the text and notes 6–7): reg 15(5).
9 Notice can be served by either party on the other by delivery, leaving it at his proper address addressed to him, by post addressed to his registered address or to the address of his registered or principal office, or by any other means provided for in the agency contract: Commercial Agents (Council Directive) Regulations 1993, SI 1993/3053, reg 22(1). In the case of a corporation it can be served on the secretary or clerk, and in the case of a partnership, on any partner having control over the management of the partnership: reg 22(2).
10 Commercial Agents (Council Directive) Regulations 1993, SI 1993/3053, reg 15(1). These periods are: one month for the first year of the contract (reg 15(2)(a)); two months for the second year commenced (reg 15(2)(b)); and, three months for the third year commenced and for subsequent years (reg 15(2)(c)). The parties may agree longer periods, but not shorter ones, and where a longer period is agreed, the period of notice to be observed by the principal must not be shorter than that to be observed by the commercial agent: reg 15(2), (3). Unless otherwise agreed by the parties, the period of notice must coincide with the end of a calendar month: reg 15(4).
11 See PARA 179.

179. Entitlement of commercial agent to compensation or indemnity on termination of agency.

After termination of an agency contract[1], a commercial agent[2] is entitled to indemnity or compensation, as described below[3]. The parties are free to agree which compensation right applies, but in the absence of agreement, the agent is entitled to be compensated rather than indemnified[4].

Irrespective of a breach on the part of the principal[5], the commercial agent is entitled to an indemnity if and to the extent that:

(1)   he has brought the principal new customers[6] or has significantly increased the volume of business with existing customers and the principal continues to derive substantial benefits from the business with such customers[7]; and

(2)   the payment of this indemnity is equitable having regard to all the circumstances and, in particular, the commission lost by the commercial agent on the business transacted with such customers[8].

The amount of the indemnity must not exceed a figure equivalent to an indemnity for one year calculated from the commercial agent's average annual remuneration over the preceding five years and if the contract goes back less than five years the indemnity must be calculated on the average for the period in question[9].

The grant of an indemnity does not prevent the commercial agent from seeking damages[10], but payment of compensation or indemnity is excluded if:

(a)   the principal has terminated the agency contract because of default attributable to the agent which would justify immediate termination[11];

(b)   the commercial agent has himself terminated the contract[12]; or

(c)   the commercial agent with the agreement of the principal assigns his rights and duties under the contract to another person[13].

The right to compensation or indemnity will also be lost if the agent fails to claim it within one year[14]. The parties may not derogate from these rights to the detriment of the commercial agent before the agency contract expires[15].

1   In *Moore v Piretta PTA Ltd* [1999] 1 All ER 174, 'agency contract' was held to mean the whole agency relationship. The Commercial Agents (Council Directive) Regulations 1993, SI 1993/3053, reg 17 (see the text and notes 2–15) applies to a contract which has expired by effluxion of time: *Tigana Ltd v Decoro Ltd* [2003] EWHC 23 (QB), [2003] All ER (D) 09 (Feb). Entitlement to indemnity or compensation under these provisions also arises where the agency contract is terminated as a result of the death of the commercial agent: Commercial Agents (Council Directive) Regulations 1993, SI 1993/3053, reg 17(8).

2   Ie commercial agents to whom the Commercial Agents (Council Directive) Regulations 1993, SI 1993/3053, apply. As to the meaning of 'commercial agent', and as to the cases to which the Regulations apply, see PARA 73.

3   See the Commercial Agents (Council Directive) Regulations 1993, SI 1993/3053, reg 17(1); the text and notes 4–15; and PARA 180. Council Directive (EC) 86/653 (OJ L382, 31.12.86, p 17) on the coordination of the laws of the member states relating to self-employed commercial agents, which is implemented by the Commercial Agents (Council Directive) Regulations 1993, SI 1993/3053, requires member states to confer either a right of compensation or a right of indemnity in cases of termination (see art 17): however the Commercial Agents (Council Directive) Regulations 1993, SI 1993/3053, confer both rights, leaving the parties free to agree which right will apply (although in the absence of agreement the right to compensation takes precedence) (see reg 17). Because the right of compensation is based on the French system (which does not exactly correspond to the English notion of damages for loss) and the right of indemnity is based on the German system, the courts used to have regard to French and German law in applying the concepts of compensation (see *AMB Imballaggi Plastici SRL v Pacflex Ltd* [1999] 2 All ER (Comm) 249, CA; *Roy v MR Pearlman Ltd* [1999] 2 CMLR 1155, Ct of Sess; *King v T Tunnock Ltd* [2000] IRLR 569, Ct of Sess; *Moore v Piretta PTA Ltd* [1999] 1 All ER 174). This approach was questioned in *Bell Electric Ltd v Aweco Appliance Systems GmbH & Co KG* [2002] EWHC 872 (QB), [2002] CLC 1246, and rejected by Lord Hoffmann in *Lonsdale (t/a Lonsdale Agencies Ltd) v Howard & Hallam Ltd* [2007] UKHL 32, [2007] 4 All ER 1, [2007] 1 WLR 2055.

4   Commercial Agents (Council Directive) Regulations 1993, SI 1993/3053, reg 17(2) (amended by SI 1998/2868). As to the determination of the level of compensation payable see *Lonsdale (t/a Lonsdale Agencies) v Howard & Hallam Ltd* [2007] UKHL 32, [2007] 4 All ER 1, [2007] 1 WLR 2055.

5   See *Moore v Piretta PTA Ltd* [1999] 1 All ER 174. It is unclear whether or not the right to compensation or indemnity arises in the case of closure or liquidation of the principal's business. At common law, this would depend on whether cessation of the principal's business is a repudiation of the contract (see eg cases on employees, such as *Thomas Marshall (Exports) Ltd v Guinle* [1979] Ch 227, [1978] 3 All ER 193; *Gunton v Richmond-upon-Thames London Borough Council* [1981] Ch 448, [1980] 3 All ER 577). In the case of an involuntary liquidation the matter is likely to be of largely academic interest: *Lonsdale (t/a Lonsdale Agencies Ltd) v Howard & Hallam Ltd* [2007] UKHL 32 at [20], [2007] 4 All ER 1, [2007] 1 WLR 2055. In *Page v Combined Shipping and Trading Co Ltd* [1997] 3 All ER 656, CA, it was held that the agent was entitled to compensation or indemnity where the principal closed down a healthy business; this was regarded as circumstances attributable to the principal within head (1) in the text. See also *King v T Tunnock Ltd* [2000] IRLR 569, Ct of Sess.

6   See *Moore v Piretta PTA Ltd* [1999] 1 All ER 174, where the court declined to interpret this as meaning that the agent must have introduced new customers; rather it was equivalent to a requirement that the agent should have been instrumental in obtaining new customers, and that indemnity should be calculated by reference to whether the commercial agent has significantly increased the volume of business of the principal.

7   Commercial Agents (Council Directive) Regulations 1993, SI 1993/3053, reg 17(3)(a).

8   Commercial Agents (Council Directive) Regulations 1993, SI 1993/3053, reg 17(3)(b). The requirement that the indemnity must be equitable is not equivalent to the duty to mitigate that applies in wrongful dismissal cases; this requirement is only relevant in relation to the goodwill received and no parallel with employment law should be drawn: *Moore v Piretta PTA Ltd* [1999] 1 All ER 174.

      Directive 86/653 art 17(2)(a) (implemented by the Commercial Agents (Council Directive) Regulations 1993, SI 1993/3053, reg 17(3)) precludes the automatic limitation of the indemnity to which a commercial agent is entitled by the amount of commission lost as a result of the termination of the agency contract, even though the benefits which the principal continues to derive have to be given a higher monetary value: Case C-348/07 *Semen v Deutsche Tamoil GmbH* [2009] 2 All ER (Comm) 243, ECJ.

9   Commercial Agents (Council Directive) Regulations 1993, SI 1993/3053, reg 17(4). This does not require that indemnity be assessed by reference to the year following termination: *Moore v Piretta PTA Ltd* [1999] 1 All ER 174. Indemnity should be calculated with reference to the agency relationship as a whole (see note 1): *Moore v Piretta PTA Ltd*. National legislation providing that a commercial agent is entitled, on termination of the agency contract, both to an indemnity for customers limited to a maximum of one year's remuneration and, if that indemnity does not cover all of the loss actually incurred, to the award of additional damages, is not precluded, provided that such legislation does not result in the agent being compensated twice for the loss of commission following termination of the contract: Case C-338/14 *Quenon K SPRL v Beobank SA* ECLI:EU:C:2015:795, [2015] All ER (D) 74 (Dec), ECJ.

10 See the Commercial Agents (Council Directive) Regulations 1993, SI 1993/3053, reg 17(5); and PARA 180. The award of damages is not conditional on demonstration of the existence of a fault attributable to the principal which has caused the alleged harm, but does require the alleged harm to be distinct from that compensated for by the indemnity for clients: see Case C-338/14 *Quenon K SPRL v Beobank SA* ECLI:EU:C:2015:795, [2015] All ER (D) 74 (Dec), ECJ.

11 Commercial Agents (Council Directive) Regulations 1993, SI 1993/3053, regs 17(3), 18(a) (amended by SI 1993/3173) (which refers to immediate termination under the Commercial Agents (Council Directive) Regulations 1993, SI 1993/3053, reg 16, as to which see PARA 178 note 6). See *Bell Electric Ltd v Aweco Appliance Systems GmbH* [2002] EWHC 872 (QB), [2002] CLC 1246 (where it was suggested that this provision and the circumstances provided for by the Commercial Agents (Council Directive) Regulations 1993, SI 1993/3053, reg 18(b)(i) (see note 12) were the reverse sides of the same coin (affd on other grounds [2002] EWCA Civ 1501, [2003] 1 All ER 344)), and *Cooper v Pure Fishing (UK) Ltd* [2003] EWCA Civ 375, [2004] 2 Lloyd's Rep 518 (a principal cannot be said to have terminated a contract within the meaning of the Commercial Agents (Council Directive) Regulations 1993, SI 1993/3053, reg 18(a) where the contract comes to an end simply by the effluxion of time).

12 Commercial Agents (Council Directive) Regulations 1993, SI 1993/3053, reg 18(b). Payment of compensation or indemnity is not excluded on these grounds if the termination is justified by

circumstances attributable to the principal (reg 18(b)(i)) or on grounds of the age, infirmity or illness of the commercial agent in consequence of which he cannot reasonably be required to continue his activities (reg 18(b)(ii)).

13 Commercial Agents (Council Directive) Regulations 1993, SI 1993/3053, reg 18(c).

14 Commercial Agents (Council Directive) Regulations 1993, SI 1993/3053, reg 17(9). See also *Claramoda Ltd v Zoomphase Ltd (t/a Jenny Packham)* [2009] EWHC 2857 (Comm), [2010] 1 All ER (Comm) 830 (difficulty in fixing exact date of termination). As to the question of effective notice of intention to pursue see *Hackett v Advanced Medical Computer Systems Ltd* [1999] CLC 160 (letter sent by plaintiff's solicitor failed to state expressly that the plaintiff actually intended to pursue a claim; the court held that it should avoid any requirements of formality as such; the test to be applied is whether a particular communication conveys to the objectively reasonable reader that the agent intends to pursue claims under the Commercial Agents (Council Directive) Regulations 1993, SI 1993/3053). Similarly, the agent need not specify whether the claim is for compensation or indemnity: *Hackett v Advanced Medical Computer Systems*.

15 Commercial Agents (Council Directive) Regulations 1993, SI 1993/3053, reg 19.

180. Entitlement of commercial agent to damages on termination of agency.

A commercial agent[1] is entitled to compensation for the damage he suffers as a result of the termination of his relations with his principal[2]. For this purpose such damage is deemed to occur particularly when the termination takes place in either or both of the following circumstances[3], namely circumstances which:

(1) deprive the commercial agent of the commission which proper performance of the agency contract would have procured for him whilst providing his principal with substantial benefits linked to the activities of the commercial agent[4]; or

(2) have not enabled the commercial agent to amortise the costs and expenses that he had incurred in the performance of the agency contract on the advice of his principal[5].

The agent will only be compensated either if lost commission flows from transactions from which substantial benefits would have accrued to the principal or if the principal has effectively warranted to the commercial agent that he would amortise the costs which the agent was advised to incur[6]. In calculating lost commission, the court's task is to value the agency and the connections that have been established by the agent at the time of or immediately before termination, and then to compensate the agent for the value of that agency in the open market[7]. The value of an agency will depend upon the circumstances actually obtaining at the time of termination, and the damage for which the agent is to be compensated consists in the loss of the value or goodwill he can be said to have possessed in the agency. Since the commercial value of an agency is what, if anything, a hypothetical purchaser would be prepared to pay for it[8], expert valuation evidence may be required[9], although the court is not bound to accept such valuation evidence[10].

Compensation will not be payable if:

(a) the principal has terminated the agency contract because of default attributable to the agent which would justify immediate termination[11];

(b) the commercial agent has himself terminated the contract[12]; or

(c) the commercial agent with the agreement of the principal assigns his rights and duties under the contract to another person[13].

The right to compensation cannot be derogated from[14], but it will be lost if the agent fails to claim it within one year[15].

1 Ie a commercial agent to whom the Commercial Agents (Council Directive) Regulations 1993, SI 1993/3053, apply. As to the meaning of 'commercial agent', and as to the cases to which the Regulations apply, see PARA 73. Regulation 17 (see the text and notes 2–5) applies to a contract which has expired by effluxion of time: *Tigana Ltd v Decoro Ltd* [2003] EWHC 23 (QB), [2003] All ER (D) 09 (Feb). Entitlement to indemnity or compensation under these provisions also arises

where the agency contract is terminated as a result of the death of the commercial agent: Commercial Agents (Council Directive) Regulations 1993, SI 1993/3053, reg 17(8). As to a commercial agent's entitlement to compensation and indemnity on the termination of the agency see PARA 179.

2   Commercial Agents (Council Directive) Regulations 1993, SI 1993/3053, reg 17(6). As to the courts' approach in applying this principle see *AMB Imballaggi Plastici SRL v Pacflex Ltd* [1999] 2 All ER (Comm) 249, CA; *Moore v Piretta PTA Ltd* [1999] 1 All ER 174; *Roy v MR Pearlman Ltd* [1999] 2 CMLR 1155, Ct of Sess; and *King v T Tunnock Ltd* [2000] IRLR 569, Ct of Sess.

   In *Duffen v FRA BO SpA* (1998) 17 Tr LR 460, the Court of Appeal upheld a payment in respect of unpaid commission, but disallowed a claim under a liquidated damages clause. Otton LJ observed that since the commercial agent could not rely on the liquidated damages clause, he was entitled to rely on the Commercial Agents (Council Directive) Regulations 1993, SI 1993/3053, to augment his common law entitlement. However, this appears to be inconsistent with the rule that the Regulations are mandatory, and cannot be derogated from (see the text and note 14).

   See also the observations of Hallgarten J in the consequent proceedings between the parties in the county court ([2000] 1 Lloyd's Rep 180 at 190): compensation must be paid up to the earliest date when the agreement might have expired. The right approach to the evaluation of compensation is to look at the earnings which might have accrued to the claimant during the period to that date.

   See also *Barrett McKenzie & Co Ltd v Escada (UK) Ltd* [2001] All ER (D) 78 (Jun), (2001) Times, 15 May. The award of damages is not conditional on demonstration of the existence of a fault attributable to the principal which has caused the alleged harm, but does require the alleged harm to be distinct from that compensated for by the indemnity for clients: see Case C-338/14 *Quenon K SPRL v Beobank SA* ECLI:EU:C:2015:795, [2015] All ER (D) 74 (Dec), ECJ.

3   Commercial Agents (Council Directive) Regulations 1993, SI 1993/3053, reg 17(7). These provisions do not limit the amount of compensation payable; cf the position with regard to indemnity (see reg 17(4); PARA 179).

4   Commercial Agents (Council Directive) Regulations 1993, SI 1993/3053, reg 17(7)(a).

5   Commercial Agents (Council Directive) Regulations 1993, SI 1993/3053, reg 17(7)(b). See *Vick v Vogle-Gapes Ltd* [2006] EWHC 1665 (QB) at [124]–[125], [2006] All ER (D) 365 (Jun).

6   See *Vick v Vogle-Gapes Ltd* [2006] EWHC 1665 (QB) at [124]–[125], [2006] All ER (D) 365 (Jun).

7   *Lonsdale (t/a Lonsdale Agencies Ltd) v Howard & Hallam Ltd* [2007] UKHL 32, [2007] 4 All ER 1, [2007] 1 WLR 2055.

8   See eg *Warren (t/a On-Line Cartons and Print) v Drukkerij Flack BV* [2014] EWCA Civ 993, [2015] 1 Lloyd's Rep 111; *Alan Ramsay Sales & Marketing Ltd v Typhoo Tea Ltd* [2016] EWHC 486 (Comm), [2016] 4 WLR 59, [2016] All ER (D) 72 (Mar).

9   *Lonsdale (t/a Lonsdale Agencies Ltd) v Howard & Hallam Ltd* [2007] UKHL 32 at [35], [2007] 4 All ER 1, [2007] 1 WLR 2055.

10 *McQuillan v McCormick* [2010] EWHC 1112 (QB), [2011] ECC 18.

11 Commercial Agents (Council Directive) Regulations 1993, SI 1993/3053, reg 18(a) (amended by SI 1993/3173) (which refers to immediate termination under the Commercial Agents (Council Directive) Regulations 1993, SI 1993/3053, reg 16, as to which see PARA 178 note 6). See further PARA 179 note 11.

12 Commercial Agents (Council Directive) Regulations 1993, SI 1993/3053, reg 18(b). Payment of compensation is not excluded on these grounds if the termination is justified by circumstances attributable to the principal (reg 18(b)(i)) or on grounds of the age, infirmity or illness of the commercial agent in consequence of which he cannot reasonably be required to continue his activities (reg 18(b)(ii)).

13 Commercial Agents (Council Directive) Regulations 1993, SI 1993/3053, reg 18(c).

14 Commercial Agents (Council Directive) Regulations 1993, SI 1993/3053, reg 19.

15 Commercial Agents (Council Directive) Regulations 1993, SI 1993/3053, reg 17(9). See further PARA 179 note 14.

181. Restraint of trade clauses in commercial agency contracts.

An agreement restricting the business activities of a commercial agent[1] following termination of the agency contract[2] is valid only if and to the extent that it is concluded in writing and relates to the geographical area or the group of customers and the geographical area entrusted to the commercial agent and to the kind of goods covered by his agency under the contract[3]. A restraint of trade clause may be valid for not more than two years after termination of the agency contract[4].

1   Ie a commercial agent to whom the Commercial Agents (Council Directive) Regulations 1993, SI 1993/3053, apply. As to the meaning of 'commercial agent', and as to the cases to which the Regulations apply, see PARA 73.

2   Ie a 'restraint of trade clause': Commercial Agents (Council Directive) Regulations 1993, SI 1993/3053, reg 2(1). As to restraint of trade generally see COMPETITION vol 18 (2009) PARA 377 et seq. Nothing in reg 20 (see the text and notes 3–4) affects any enactment or rule of law which imposes other restrictions on the validity or enforceability of restraint of trade clauses or which enables a court to reduce the obligations on the parties resulting from such clauses: reg 20(3). For an example of a clause in an agency contract held to be in restraint of trade, and consequently severable, see *Marshall v NM Financial Management Ltd* [1995] 4 All ER 785, [1995] 1 WLR 1461 (affd [1997] 1 WLR 1527, [1997] ICR 1065, CA).
     In *Moore v Piretta PTA Ltd* [1999] 1 All ER 174, 'agency contract' was held to mean the whole agency relationship.

3   Commercial Agents (Council Directive) Regulations 1993, SI 1993/3053, reg 20(1).

4   Commercial Agents (Council Directive) Regulations 1993, SI 1993/3053, reg 20(2).

182. Revocation by notice.

Except in relation to certain commercial agents[1], notice of revocation may be given at any time before the authority is wholly exercised[2], subject to any right to damages on the part of the agent for breach of contract[3].

An authority is not deemed to be exercised, so as to prevent revocation, merely because a preliminary step has been taken which does not bind either principal or agent; for example, where an insurance broker has given instructions for a marine insurance policy, the presentation of the slip by the broker merely constitutes an offer which an underwriter accepts by 'writing a line'. Up to that point, the agent's authority would, in principle, be revocable[4]. A revocation after partial exercise of the authority will be ineffective[5] unless the authority is severable into parts, so that the unexecuted parts may be countermanded[6]. An estate agent, not being a sole agent, normally contracts on the footing that at any time before earning his commission his principal may refuse to continue with the transaction or may dispose of the property through other agents[7], and may in some cases do so without notice of revocation[8].

Money paid to an agent by his principal, under authority to devote it to a specific purpose, is recoverable at any time before that purpose has been carried out[9], even though paid to abide the event of a wager[10]. Where, however, the principal has given the agent authority to make a payment of money, and a sum has been appropriated under an agreement with the payee[11], or where the circumstances are such that the payee has obtained an equitable assignment of such sum[12], the principal cannot afterwards revoke the authority to make such payment.

Where the agency agreement involves a continuing relationship between the parties any express provision in the agreement for termination will prevail[13]. Where the agreement contains no such provision, it is not normally presumed that the parties intended the relationship to endure in perpetuity and a provision for termination by reasonable notice will be implied in cases where the relationship is analogous to that between employer and employee[14], but, in other cases, the agency agreement may be terminable summarily[15].

In the case of a commercial agent, termination of an agency contract for an indefinite period is subject to prescribed periods of notice[16].

1 Ie commercial agents to whom the Commercial Agents (Council Directive) Regulations 1993, SI 1993/3053, apply. As to the meaning of 'commercial agent', and as to the cases to which the Regulations apply, see PARA 73. As to termination of contracts of agency to which the Regulations apply see PARA 178; and the text and notes 13–16.

2 *Warlow v Harrison* (1859) 1 E & E 309 (auctioneer's authority may be revoked at any time before the fall of the hammer); *Crean v Deane* [1959] IR 347 (recovery of stake money of backers of contest where game uncompleted); *Farmer v Robinson* (1805) 2 Camp 339n; *Freeman v Fairlie* (1838) 8 LJ Ch 44; *Manser v Back* (1848) 6 Hare 443; *Doward, Dickson & Co v Williams & Co* (1890) 6 TLR 316; *Alexander v Davis & Co* (1885) 2 TLR 142; *Bovine Ltd v Dent and Wilkinson* (1904) 21 TLR 82; *Barrett v Gilmour & Co* (1901) 6 Com Cas 72; *Re Hare and O'More's Contract* [1901] 1 Ch 93.

3 *Toppin v Healey* (1863) 1 New Rep 326; *Turner v Goldsmith* [1891] 1 QB 544, CA.

4 *General Reinsurance Corpn v Forsakringsaktiebolaget Fennia Patria* [1983] QB 856, [1983] 3 WLR 318, CA.

5 *Day v Wells* (1861) 30 Beav 220; *Rhodes v Fielder, Jones and Harrison* (1919) 89 LJKB 15, DC.

6 *Bristow and Porter v Taylor* (1817) 2 Stark 50.

7 *Luxor (Eastbourne) Ltd v Cooper* [1941] AC 108, [1941] 1 All ER 33, HL; see further PARA 104.

8 *EP Nelson & Co v Rolfe* [1950] 1 KB 139, [1949] 2 All ER 584, CA; see also *Jerome v Bentley & Co* [1952] 2 All ER 114 (agent for sale of jewellery).

9 *Taylor v Lendey* (1807) 9 East 49; *Brummell v M'Pherson* (1828) 5 Russ 263; *Gibson v Minet* (1824) 9 Moore CP 31; *Edgar v Fowler* (1803) 3 East 222; and see *Taylor v Bowers* (1876) 1 QBD 291, CA.

10 *Smith v Bickmore* (1812) 4 Taunt 474; *Hastelow v Jackson* (1828) 8 B & C 221; *Varney v Hickman* (1847) 5 CB 271; *Diggle v Higgs* (1877) 2 ExD 422, CA; *Trimble v Hill* (1879) 5 App Cas 342, PC; *Gatty v Field* (1846) 9 QB 431; *Hampden v Walsh* (1876) 1 QBD 189.

11 *Burn v Carvalho* (1839) 4 My & Cr 690; *Dickinson v Marrow* (1845) 14 M & W 713; *Crowfoot v Gurney* (1832) 9 Bing 372.

12 *Robertson v Fauntleroy* (1823) 8 Moore CP 10; *Fisher v Miller* (1823) 7 Moore CP 527; *Walker v Rostron* (1842) 9 M & W 411; *Hutchinson v Heyworth* (1838) 9 Ad & El 375; *Chartered Bank of India, Australia and China v Evans* (1869) 21 LT 407, PC.

13 Cf, as to the minimum periods of notice applicable to employees under contracts of service, the Employment Rights Act 1996 ss 86, 210, 211; EMPLOYMENT vol 39 (2014) PARA 130; EMPLOYMENT vol 41 (2014) PARAS 735–736.

14 See *Llanelly Rly and Dock Co v London and North Western Rly Co* (1873) 8 Ch App 942; affd (1875) LR 7 HL 550. See also *Martin-Baker Aircraft Co Ltd v Canadian Flight Equipment Ltd, Martin-Baker Aircraft Co Ltd v Murison* [1955] 2 QB 556, [1955] 2 All ER 722.

15 See PARA 185.

16 See PARA 178.

183. Mode of revocation of authority.

Revocation need not necessarily be by formal instrument. A deed may be revoked by word of mouth[1], or the principal may intervene in the course of negotiations[2], but until some such action of the principal is taken the agent is justified in assuming the continuance of the agency[3]. Once the agency has been terminated the agent must cease to act for the principal. However, if for some reason it was intended that the agent would continue to act on the principal's behalf once the relationship had broken down, then clear language would be required to effect this[4].

1 *The Margaret Mitchell* (1858) 4 Jur NS 1193; *R v Wait* (1823) 11 Price 518.

2 *Atkinson v Cotesworth* (1825) 3 B & C 647.

3 *Re Oriental Bank Corpn, ex p Guillemin* (1884) 28 ChD 634. The agent may, however, incur personal liability to the third party for breach of warranty of authority where he continues to act after a revocation by operation of law, on the death or mental incapacity of the principal (see PARA 189), or bankruptcy of the principal (see PARA 191). As to warranty of authority see PARAS 161–162. As to revocation by termination of the business of the principal see PARA 184.

4 *Temple Legal Protection Ltd v QBE Insurance (Europe) Ltd* [2009] EWCA Civ 453, [2010] 1 All ER (Comm) 703 (agent's claim that it had authority to manage cases without principal's permission after the date of termination failed). It would be unusual and uncommercial for any principal who had employed an agent to manage some aspect of his business to be obliged to allow that agent to continue to act on his behalf once the necessary degree of trust and confidence had, for whatever reason, been lost: *Temple Legal Protection Ltd v QBE Insurance (Europe) Ltd* at [65] per Moore-Bick LJ.

184. Termination of principal's business.

Where an agency has been created for a fixed period, the question whether the agent is entitled to claim damages on cessation of the principal's business before the end of that period for wrongful revocation of the agency depends upon whether there was any obligation, express or implied, on the part of the principal to continue his business to the end of that period[1]. This can only be determined from the circumstances of each particular case[2], and the express words of the particular agency agreement; a term will only be implied if it is strictly necessary to give business efficacy to the contract, and it will not be implied merely because the court thinks it is a reasonable term[3].

An agreement, for a definite time, by an agent to act as agent and by a principal to remunerate the agent by a commission on business effected by the agent in connection with the principal's business, does not impose a necessary implication that the principal's business must be continued during that period[4]. This implication may, however, arise where there is an active obligation upon the principal to do something to enable the agent to earn his commission[5]. There may also be an implication that the principal must not by terminating the agreement deprive the agent of the fruits of his labour[6].

When there is an express term which casts upon the principal an obligation to continue the business, no term will be implied that the agent's rights are to cease upon events for which no provision has been made[7]. Where there is such an obligation, liability will not be avoided by the voluntary winding up of a company[8], or the dissolution of a partnership firm[9], constituting the principal; but, if there was no such obligation, then the winding up of a company or dissolution of a partnership firm constituting the principal will put an end to the contract of agency[10], unless (in the case of a partnership) the contract was not of a personal character[11].

Where there is an agreement for a fixed period, it will not lawfully be terminated, so as to exclude the right to damages, by the principal discontinuing the business on the ground of its unprofitable character[12], or in consequence of the principal ceasing to carry on business under agreement with competitors[13].

The application of the rules described above to commercial agents[14] is unclear[15].

1 As to termination of the contract by impossibility of performance other than as a result of the act of the parties, where the law treats the contract as frustrated, see PARA 188.

2 *Shackleton Aviation Ltd v Maitland Drewery Aviation Ltd* [1964] 1 Lloyd's Rep 293; *Hamlyn & Co v Wood & Co* [1891] 2 QB 488, CA; *M'Intyre v Belcher* (1863) 14 CBNS 654; *Turner v Goldsmith* [1891] 1 QB 544, CA. See *Page v Combined Shipping and Trading Co Ltd* [1997] 3 All ER 656, CA (damages under the Commercial Agents (Council Directive) Regulations 1993, SI 1993/3053, reg 17 (see PARAS 179–180) may reflect level of commission agent would have earned if principal had not terminated contract prematurely).

3 *Hamlyn & Co v Wood & Co* [1891] 2 QB 488, CA; *The Moorcock* (1889) 14 PD 64, CA; *Lazarus v Cairn Line of Steamships Ltd* (1912) 106 LT 378; *L French & Co Ltd v Leeston Shipping Co Ltd* [1922] 1 AC 451, HL. As to damages for the loss of opportunity to earn remuneration see generally PARA 109.

4   *Rhodes v Forwood* (1876) 1 App Cas 256, HL; *Re English and Scottish Marine Insurance Co, ex p Maclure* (1870) 5 Ch App 737, CA; *White v Turnbull, Martin & Co* (1898) 3 Com Cas 183, CA; *Re R S Newman Ltd, Raphael's Claim* [1916] 2 Ch 309, CA; and the cases cited in note 3.

5   *Warren & Co v Agdeshman* (1922) 38 TLR 588; and see *Dowling v Methven, Sons & Co Ltd* 1921 SC 948, Ct of Sess.

6   *Re Patent Floor Cloth Co, Dean and Gilbert's Claim* (1872) 41 LJ Ch 476; *Dowling v Methven, Sons & Co Ltd* 1921 SC 948, Ct of Sess; *L French & Co Ltd v Leeston Shipping Co Ltd* [1922] 1 AC 451, HL.

7   *Turner v Goldsmith* [1891] 1 QB 544, CA; *Ogdens Ltd v Nelson* [1905] AC 109, HL; *Lazarus v Cairn Line of Steamships Ltd* (1912) 106 LT 378.

8   *Re Patent Floor Cloth Co, Dean and Gilbert's Claim* (1872) 41 LJ Ch 476; *Re Imperial Wine Co, Shirreff's Case* (1872) LR 14 Eq 417; *Re London and Scottish Bank, ex p Logan* (1870) LR 9 Eq 149; *Re English and Scottish Marine Insurance Co, ex p Maclure* (1870) 5 Ch App 737, CA; *Reigate v Union Manufacturing Co (Ramsbottom) Ltd* [1918] 1 KB 592, CA.

9   *Rhodes v Forwood* (1876) 1 App Cas 256, HL (agreement for agency for sale of coals for fixed time implied no undertaking to pay damages on sale of the colliery); *Stirling v Maitland* (1864) 5 B & S 840 (the dissolution of an insurance company dissolved the agency agreement); *Northey v Trevillion* (1902) 7 Com Cas 201.

10 *Tasker v Shepherd* (1861) 6 H & N 575; *Salton v New Beeston Cycle Co* [1900] 1 Ch 43; *Friend v Young* [1897] 2 Ch 421.

11 *Phillips v Alhambra Palace Co* [1901] 1 KB 59, DC.

12 *Nielans v Cuthbertson* (1891) 7 TLR 516.

13 *Ogdens Ltd v Nelson* [1905] AC 109, HL; but see *Lazarus v Cairn Line of Steamships Ltd* (1912) 106 LT 378.

14 Ie commercial agents to whom the Commercial Agents (Council Directive) Regulations 1993, SI 1993/3053, apply. As to the meaning of 'commercial agent', and as to the cases to which the Regulations apply, see PARA 73. As to termination of contracts of agency to which the Regulations apply see PARAS 178–180.

15 If the principal dismisses the agent, the normal termination rights under the Commercial Agents (Council Directive) Regulations 1993, SI 1993/3053, reg 18(b)(i) (see PARAS 179–180) can be claimed by the agent. As seen above, cessation of the principal's business does not necessarily terminate the contract of agency. However, if in connection with the cessation, the principal failed to satisfy an order, or pay the agent commission, or the like, that would seem to amount to a repudiation on the part of the principal. The agent could accept this repudiation, in which case the agency contract would be terminated, and termination payments could then be claimed under reg 18(b).

185. Summary termination of agency.

An agency created by power of attorney may prima facie be terminated at will[1]. In the case of an agent who is a mere commission agent with no obligation to seek orders for the principal and who is in no other sense 'employed' by the principal, the agency may be terminated summarily[2].

1   *Bromley v Holland* (1802) 7 Ves 3; *Re Gowett and Leigh, ex p Smither* (1836) 1 Deac 413, Ct of R. As to powers of attorney expressed to be irrevocable and given by way of security, however, see PARA 176. As to the protection of third parties where a power of attorney is revoked see PARA 194.

2   *Motion v Michaud* (1892) 8 TLR 253 (affd 8 TLR 447, CA); *Joynson v Hunt & Son* (1905) 93 LT 470, CA; *Clerk v Laurie* (1857) 2 H & N 199 (as to what amounts to a revocation); *Levy v Goldhill & Co* [1917] 2 Ch 297; *Hampton & Sons Ltd v George* [1939] 3 All ER 627 (termination on appointment of another agent); cf *Barrett v Gilmour & Co* (1901) 6 Com Cas 72; *Sellers v London Counties Newspapers* [1951] 1 KB 784, [1951] 1 All ER 544, CA; and *Martin-Baker Aircraft Co Ltd v Canadian Flight Equipment Ltd, Martin-Baker Aircraft Co Ltd v Murison* [1955] 2 QB 556, [1955] 2 All ER 722 (reasonable notice required where the relationship is analogous to master and servant).

186. Renunciation of authority by agent.

An agent may renounce his authority at any time before completion of the agency, but subject to any claim of his principal for damages for breach of the contract of agency[1].

1 *Hochster v De la Tour* (1853) 2 E & B 678; *Balfe v West* (1853) 13 CB 466; *Elsee v Gatward* (1793) 5 Term Rep 143. As to breach of contract see CONTRACT vol 22 (2012) PARA 553 et seq. As to damages for breach of contract see DAMAGES vol 29 (2014) PARA 499 et seq.

(4) TERMINATION BY OPERATION OF LAW

187. Agency terminated by effluxion of time.

Termination by operation of law may take place by effluxion of the time which may be fixed for the continuance of the agency by the parties or by custom or usage of the particular trade or business[1]. It is not necessary that the time for the continuance of the agency should be expressly stated. It may be presumed from the nature of the authority; for example, when a power of attorney recited the fact that the donor was about to go abroad, it was held to be impliedly revoked on his return home[2].

1 *Dickinson v Lilwall* (1815) 4 Camp 279 (custom for broker's authority to expire with the day); *Seton v Slade* (1802) 7 Ves 265.
2 *Danby v Coutts & Co* (1885) 29 ChD 500; *Lawford & Co v Harris* (1896) 12 TLR 275 (as to stockbroker's authority); and see *Graham v Manders* (1918) 53 ILT 5.

188. Agency terminated by performance, impossibility or illegality of continuance.

The agency may also be terminated by the conclusion of the agency by performance[1], by frustration of the contract[2], or by the happening of an event rendering the continuance of the agency unlawful[3]. On completion of the agency by performance the agent is functus officio, and has no further authority to bind the principal[4].

1 *Bell v Balls* [1897] 1 Ch 663 (the performance of the particular duty ends the authority; where an auctioneer signed a memorandum a week after the auction he was held to have no authority). The relationship between a principal and an agent employed to sell property does not end with the introduction of a person willing to buy: *Toulmin v Millar* (1887) 12 App Cas 746, HL; *Keppel v Wheeler* [1927] 1 KB 577, CA; and see *Nightingale v Parsons* [1914] 2 KB 621, CA.
2 As to the discharge of contracts on the ground of impossibility of performance or frustration, and the adjustment of rights and liabilities on frustration, see CONTRACT vol 22 (2012) PARA 467 et seq. As to termination of the business of the principal in circumstances where this does not amount to frustration see PARA 184.
3 *Esposito v Bowden* (1857) 7 E & B 763, Ex Ch (where the outbreak of war avoided a charterparty); *Hugh Stevenson & Sons v Aktiengesellschaft für Cartonnagen-Industrie* [1918] AC 239, HL (where continuance of an agency agreement necessarily involved property of the enemy); *Marshall v Glanvill* [1917] 2 KB 87; *Tingley v Müller* [1917] 2 Ch 144, CA. An agency agreement is not avoided or rendered impossible of performance by the agent being a subject of an enemy state while he is allowed to dwell in Great Britain and exempted from internment (*Schostall v Johnson* (1919) 36 TLR 75), or by the temporary internment of the agent (*Nordman v Rayner and Sturges* (1916) 33 TLR 87), or by the agent being in territory under enemy administration (*Hangkam Kwingtong Woo v Liu Lan Fong (alias Lui Ah Lan)* [1951] AC 707, [1951] 2 All ER 567, PC), unless the performance of the agency would involve dealings between persons in this country and the enemy during war; cf *V/O Sovfracht v Van Udens Scheepvaart en Agentuur Maatschappij (NV Gebr)* [1943] AC 203, [1943] 1 All ER 76, HL (termination of solicitor's authority).

4 *Blackburn v Scholes* (1810) 2 Camp 341; *Macbeath v Ellis* (1828) 4 Bing 578; *Gillow & Co v Lord Aberdare* (1892) 9 TLR 12, CA; *Seton v Slade* (1802) 7 Ves 265; *Bell v Balls* [1897] 1 Ch 663; *Nightingale v Parsons* [1914] 2 KB 621, CA; and see *Butler v Knight* (1867) LR 2 Exch 109; and *R v Leitrim Justices* [1900] 2 IR 397.

189. Agency terminated by death or mental illness of principal.

Except as already stated with regard to irrevocable authorities[1], the authority of an agent is terminated by the principal's death[2], or by the principal becoming incapable by reason of mental illness of managing his affairs[3]. The representatives of a deceased principal may, however, ratify a contract made by the agent subsequent to his principal's death if they think fit, though, in the absence of a ratification, they are not bound by it[4].

Although, if the principal becomes incapable by reason of mental illness, the agency as between the principal and agent is terminated, the agent may continue to bind his principal vis-à-vis a third person dealing with the agent without knowledge of the condition of the principal[5].

1 See PARAS 172–177. As to lasting and enduring powers of attorney see PARA 195 et seq.
2 *Blades v Free* (1829) 9 B & C 167 (death of husband determining the implied authority of wife to bind his estate for necessaries; as to abolition of a wife's agency of necessity see PARA 24 note 4); *Lepard v Vernon* (1813) 2 Ves & B 51; *Wallace v Cook* (1804) 5 Esp 117; *Whitehead v Lord* (1852) 7 Exch 691; *Pool v Pool* (1889) 58 LJP 67; *Farrow v Wilson* (1869) LR 4 CP 744; *Campanari v Woodburn* (1854) 15 CB 400; *Houstoun v Robertson* (1816) 6 Taunt 448; *Cottle v Aldrich* (1815) 4 M & S 175; *Phillips v Jones* (1888) 4 TLR 401; *Re Overweg, Haas v Durant* [1900] 1 Ch 209; *Graham v Jackson* (1845) 6 QB 811; *Bailey v Collett* (1854) 18 Beav 179; *Watson v King* (1815) 1 Stark 121 (even if the authority is coupled with an interest); *Kennedy v Thomassen* [1929] 1 Ch 426; but see *Spooner v Sandilands* (1842) 1 Y & C Ch Cas 390; and see *Carter v White* (1883) 25 ChD 666, CA (distinction between authority and contract).
3 *Drew v Nunn* (1879) 4 QBD 661, CA; *Yonge v Toynbee* [1910] 1 KB 215, CA. See also *Blankley v Central Manchester and Manchester Children's University Hospitals NHS Trust* [2015] EWCA Civ 18, [2016] 3 All ER 382, [2015] 1 WLR 4307 (a solicitor's conditional fee agreement was not terminated by the client's intervening incapacity). The estate of a person of unsound mind may be liable for necessaries: see *Re Weaver* (1882) 21 ChD 615, CA; and the Sale of Goods Act 1979 s 3 (see SALE OF GOODS AND SUPPLY OF SERVICES vol 91 (2012) PARA 38). For Baroness Hale's general comment on the present state of the law, see *Dunhill v Burgin (Nos 1 and 2)* [2014] UKSC 18 at [31], [2014] 2 All ER 364, [2014] 1 WLR 933. As to the statutory protection to the donee of a revoked power of attorney where he has no notice of the revocation see PARA 194. A power of attorney may, however, be created which will survive the subsequent mental incapacity of the donor (ie a lasting power of attorney or an enduring power of attorney): see PARA 195 et seq.
4 *Foster v Bates* (1843) 12 M & W 226; *Campanari v Woodburn* (1854) 15 CB 400.
5 *Drew v Nunn* (1879) 4 QBD 661, CA; *Platt v Depree* (1893) 9 TLR 194, where the principal released the representative of the purchaser, who had become insane, and the agent was held entitled to commission. The doctrine of apparent authority would appear to apply. See also *Re Walden, ex p Bradbury* (1839) Mont & Ch 625; *Duke of Beaufort v Glynn* (1856) 3 Sm & G 213 (affd 3 WR 502, CA).

190. Agency terminated by death or mental illness of agent.

The death or, apparently, the incapacity for managing his affairs by reason of mental illness of an agent terminates the agency, which rests on personal relationship[1]. A joint agency is terminated by the death of any one of the joint agents[2].

1 *Friend v Young* [1897] 2 Ch 421; *Pool v Pool* (1889) 58 LJP 67.
2 *Friend v Young* [1897] 2 Ch 421; *Pool v Pool* (1889) 58 LJP 67.

191. Agency terminated by bankruptcy of principal.

Except as stated above with regard to irrevocable authorities[1], the authority of an agent is, as a general rule, terminated by the bankruptcy of the principal[2].

Mere formal acts in completion of a transaction already binding on the principal may, however, be performed by the agent under his authority after the principal's bankruptcy[3]. Additionally, the agent and third parties are protected in respect of any property[4] or payment received before the commencement of the bankruptcy[5] but after the presentation of the petition, in good faith, for value and without notice[6] that the petition has been presented; and in respect of any interest in property which derives from an interest thus protected[7].

In relation to transactions after the bankruptcy order is made, an agent is only protected to a limited extent. If, after the commencement of his bankruptcy, the bankrupt has incurred a debt to a banker or other person by reason of the making of a void payment[8], that debt is deemed to have been incurred before the commencement of the bankruptcy (and is therefore a valid bankruptcy debt which may be proved in the bankruptcy[9]), unless the banker or other person had notice of the bankruptcy before the debt was incurred or it is not reasonably practicable for the amount of the payment to be recovered from the person to whom it was made[10].

If the agent has a right of lien on goods of the principal or their proceeds, such right is not affected by the principal's bankruptcy[11]. If there have been mutual credits or dealings between the principal and agent, the agent is entitled to a right of set-off against all money of the principal received before the date of the bankruptcy order provided that no notice of the bankruptcy petition has been given[12].

1 See PARAS 172–177.
2 *Dawson v Sexton* (1823) 1 LJOS Ch 185. This was the rule under the previous law of bankruptcy, and it is likely that the same principle applies under the Insolvency Act 1986. As to bankruptcy see generally BANKRUPTCY AND INDIVIDUAL INSOLVENCY vol 5 (2013) PARA 1 et seq.
3 *Dixon v Ewart* (1817) Buck 94; *Markwick v Hardingham* (1880) 15 ChD 339, CA.
4 As to the meaning of 'property' for these purposes see the Insolvency Act 1986 s 436; and BANKRUPTCY AND INDIVIDUAL INSOLVENCY vol 5 (2013) PARA 412.
5 Ie normally the day on which the bankruptcy order is made: see the Insolvency Act 1986 s 278; and BANKRUPTCY AND INDIVIDUAL INSOLVENCY vol 5 (2013) PARA 209.
6 The onus of proving want of notice rests on the person relying thereon: *Pearson v Graham* (1837) 6 Ad & El 899.
7 See the Insolvency Act 1986 s 284(4); and BANKRUPTCY AND INDIVIDUAL INSOLVENCY vol 5 (2013) PARA 213. This is an exception to the rule that any disposition of property by the bankrupt between the day of presentation of the petition and the vesting of the bankrupt's estate in a trustee, which was not made with the consent of the court or subsequently ratified by the court, is void: see s 284(1)–(3); and BANKRUPTCY AND INDIVIDUAL INSOLVENCY vol 5 (2013) PARA 213. See also *Re MacDonnell, ex p MacDonnell* (1819) Buck 399; *Re Douglas, ex p Snowball* (1872) 7 Ch App 534. The same exception applies in the compulsory winding up of a company where the company's agent has no notice of winding-up proceedings: *Re Oriental Bank Corpn, ex p Guillemin* (1884) 28 ChD 634. As to provisions for notice by advertisement of winding up see COMPANY AND PARTNERSHIP INSOLVENCY vol 16 (2011) PARA 437. It is submitted that the cases cited above, although decided in relation to acts of bankruptcy (now abolished), are still relevant to the position of an agent in relation to a principal who becomes bankrupt under the Insolvency Act 1986. Most of the cases arising under the previous law related to the authority of solicitors (acting as agents). Quaere whether an agent who continues to act after he has had notice that a bankruptcy petition has been presented takes the risk of being held personally liable; cf *Kynaston v Crouch* (1845) 14 M & W 266; *Re Lamb, ex p Gibson and Bolland* (1886) 55 LT 817.
8 Ie a payment not made with the consent of the court or subsequently ratified by the court: see the Insolvency Act 1986 s 284(1), (2); and BANKRUPTCY AND INDIVIDUAL INSOLVENCY vol 5 (2013) PARA 213. If the payment is void, the person paid holds the sum paid for the bankrupt as part of his estate: see s 284(2); and BANKRUPTCY AND INDIVIDUAL INSOLVENCY vol 5 (2013) PARA 213.

9 As to bankruptcy debts and proving in the bankruptcy see BANKRUPTCY AND INDIVIDUAL INSOLVENCY vol 5 (2013) PARA 507 et seq.

10 See the Insolvency Act 1986 s 284(5); and BANKRUPTCY AND INDIVIDUAL INSOLVENCY vol 5 (2013) PARA 213.

11 *Drinkwater v Goodwin* (1775) 1 Cowp 251.

12 See the Insolvency Act 1986 s 323; and BANKRUPTCY AND INDIVIDUAL INSOLVENCY vol 5 (2013) PARA 561. See also *Elliott v Turquand* (1881) 7 App Cas 79, PC. It is submitted that this case, although decided in relation to acts of bankruptcy, is still relevant; see note 7. As to what constitutes 'mutual credits' see *Palmer v Day & Sons* [1895] 2 QB 618. The rule does not apply to the case of a sum paid to an agent for a specific purpose: *Re Pollitt, ex p Minor* [1893] 1 QB 455, CA. As to the meaning of 'mutual credits' see BANKRUPTCY AND INDIVIDUAL INSOLVENCY vol 5 (2013) PARA 561.

192. When bankruptcy of agent terminates agency.

The bankruptcy of an agent will not as a matter of law terminate the authority of the agent; whether it does so terminate is a question of fact which will depend upon the construction of the agreement[1]. It will not do so where the bankruptcy does not make the agent less fit and competent for the proper performance of his duties[2], or where the act he is authorised to do is merely a formal one[3]. The effect of the agent ceasing to trade is not to bring the agency to an automatic end, nor to convert the relationship between principal and agent to one of trustee and beneficiary; accordingly, sums received by the agent are available to the agent's creditors[4].

1 *McCall v Australian Meat Co Ltd* (1870) 19 WR 188; *Hudson v Granger* (1821) 5 B & Ald 27; *Bailey v Thurston & Co Ltd* [1903] 1 KB 137, CA. Similarly where an agent goes into administrative receivership, the cessation of its business does not automatically bring its agency agreement with its principal to an end: *Triffit Nurseries (a firm) v Salads Etcetera Ltd* [2000] 1 All ER (Comm) 737, CA.

2 *McCall v Australian Meat Co Ltd* (1870) 19 WR 188; *Hudson v Granger* (1821) 5 B & Ald 27; *Bailey v Thurston & Co Ltd* [1903] 1 KB 137, CA.

3 *Dixon v Ewart* (1817) 3 Mer 322.

4 *Triffit Nurseries (a firm) v Salads Etcetera Ltd* [2000] 1 All ER (Comm) 737, CA.

(5) NOTICE TO THIRD PERSONS

193. Third person led to believe in authority.

The cases in which notice of termination has been held to be necessary are, in general, cases in which a third person had been induced to believe through the act of the principal that the agent had authority, and therefore depend on the principle of apparent authority[1]. The belief may have been induced through the principal giving the agent express authority to do certain acts[2], or through his having ratified the agent's acts[3]. In such cases, in the absence of actual notice, or of constructive notice by lapse of time or other indications[4], the principal will remain liable to those dealing in good faith with the agent on the assumption that his authority still continues[5].

An exception to this rule arises where the agency is determined by the death of the principal[6], and also in the case of a termination of an implied agency[7]; and no notice of termination of an agency is required after a bankruptcy order against the principal has been made[8].

1 *Trueman v Loder* (1840) 11 Ad & El 589; *Scarf v Jardine* (1882) 7 App Cas 345, HL; *Drew v Nunn* (1879) 4 QBD 661, CA; *Willis, Faber & Co Ltd v Joyce* (1911) 104 LT 576.

2 *— v Harrison* (1699) 12 Mod Rep 346; *Curlewis v Birkbeck* (1863) 3 F & F 894; *Pole v Leask* (1863) 33 LJ Ch 155, HL.

3 *Ryan v Sams* (1848) 12 QB 460.
4 *Staveley v Uzielli* (1800) 2 F & F 30; *Aste v Montague* (1858) 1 F & F 264; *Marsden v City and County Assurance Co* (1865) LR 1 CP 232.
5 *Trueman v Loder* (1840) 11 Ad & El 589; and see the cases cited in note 1.
6 By his death the principal necessarily becomes unable to give notice of its termination (*Blades v Free* (1829) 9 B & C 167); but see the dictum of Brett LJ in *Drew v Nunn* (1879) 4 QBD 661 at 668, CA, that the estate of the deceased remains liable.
7 *Debenham v Mellon* (1880) 6 App Cas 24, HL.
8 See the Insolvency Act 1986 s 284; and BANKRUPTCY AND INDIVIDUAL INSOLVENCY vol 5 (2013) PARA 213. The reason why no notice of termination of agency is required is that any disposition of property after the commencement of bankruptcy is void. As to the limited protection of the agent see PARA 191.

194. Protection where power of attorney revoked.

A donee of a power of attorney, who acts in pursuance of the power after it has been revoked, does not, by reason of the revocation, incur any liability either to the donor of the power or to any other person, if at the time of so acting he did not know of the revocation[1]. Where any person, without knowledge[2] of the revocation of the power, deals with the donee of the power after its revocation, the transaction between them is, in favour of that person, as valid as if the power had then been in existence[3]. Where the power is expressed to be irrevocable and to be given by way of security then, unless the person dealing with the donee knows that it was not in fact so given, he is entitled to assume that the power is incapable of revocation except by the donor acting with the consent of the donee, and he is to be treated for the purposes of the foregoing provision as having knowledge of the revocation only if he knows that the power has been revoked in that manner[4]. Where the interest of a purchaser[5] depends on whether a transaction between the donee of a power and another person was valid by virtue of that provision[6], it must be conclusively presumed in favour of the purchaser that that other person did not at the material time know of the revocation of the power if either the transaction was completed within 12 months of the date on which the power came into operation, or that other person makes a statutory declaration, before or within three months after the completion of the purchase[7], that he did not at the material time know of the revocation of the power[8].

Without prejudice to the foregoing protection afforded to a purchaser, where the donee of a power of attorney executes, as transferor, an instrument transferring registered securities[9] and the instrument is executed for the purposes of a stock exchange transaction[10], it must be conclusively presumed in favour of the transferee that the power had not been revoked at the date of the instrument if a statutory declaration is made to that effect by the donee on or within three months after that date[11].

1 Powers of Attorney Act 1971 s 5(1). These provisions apply whenever the power of attorney was created but only to acts and transactions after 1 October 1971 (ie the date on which the Powers of Attorney Act 1971 was brought into force by virtue of s 11(4) (repealed)).
   For these purposes knowledge of the revocation of a power includes knowledge of the occurrence of any event, such as the death of the donor, which has the effect of revoking the power: s 5(5). As to the events which operate to revoke powers see PARAS 187–191. In its application to a lasting power of attorney under the Mental Capacity Act 2005 (see s 9; and PARAS 218–219) which relates to matters in addition to the donor's property and affairs, the Powers of Attorney Act 1971 s 5 (see the text and notes 2–8) has effect as if references to 'revocation' included the cessation of the power in relation to the donor's property and affairs: Mental Capacity Act 2005 s 14(5). As to lasting powers of attorney and enduring powers of attorney generally see PARA 195 et seq.
2 As to knowledge see note 1.
3 Powers of Attorney Act 1971 s 5(2).

4　Powers of Attorney Act 1971 s 5(3). As to powers expressed to be irrevocable and given by way of security see PARA 176.

5　As to the meanings of 'purchaser' and 'purchase' see the Law of Property Act 1925 s 205(1) (see LANDLORD AND TENANT vol 62 (2016) PARA 83; REAL PROPERTY AND REGISTRATION vol 87 (2012) PARA 708); definition applied by the Powers of Attorney Act 1971 s 5(6).

6　Ie the Powers of Attorney Act 1971 s 5(2): see the text and note 3.

7　See note 5.

8　Powers of Attorney Act 1971 s 5(4).

9　As to the meaning of 'registered securities' see the Stock Transfer Act 1963 s 4 (see COMPANIES vol 14 (2016) PARA 411); definition applied by the Powers of Attorney Act 1971 s 6(2).

10　As to the meaning of 'stock exchange transaction' see the Stock Transfer Act 1963 s 4 (see COMPANIES vol 14 (2016) PARA 411); definition applied by the Powers of Attorney Act 1971 s 6(2).

11　Powers of Attorney Act 1971 s 6(1).

9. LASTING AND ENDURING POWERS OF ATTORNEY

(1) LASTING AND ENDURING POWERS: INTRODUCTION

195. Enduring and lasting powers.

Enduring powers of attorney and lasting powers of attorney are powers of attorney which are intended to survive the subsequent mental incapacity of the donor[1].

Enduring powers were introduced by the Enduring Powers of Attorney Act 1985[2] and could be created until 1 October 2007[3], on which date that Act was repealed[4] and a new and expanded power called a 'lasting power of attorney' was introduced[5]. Enduring powers created before 1 October 2007 continue to have effect under modified statutory provisions[6], but no new enduring power can be created after that date[7]. All powers created after 1 October 2007 are lasting powers governed by the Mental Capacity Act 2005[8].

1   See the Enduring Powers of Attorney Act 1985 s 1 (repealed); the Mental Capacity Act 2005 s 9; and PARAS **196, 218**.

2   The Enduring Powers of Attorney Act 1985 was brought into force on 10 March 1986 by the Enduring Powers of Attorney Act 1985 (Commencement) Order 1986, SI 1986/125.

3   Ie the date appointed by the Mental Capacity Act 2005 (Commencement No 2) Order 2007, SI 2007/1897, for the purposes of the repeal of the Enduring Powers of Attorney Act 1985 (see note 4) and the coming into force of the Mental Capacity Act 2005 ss 9–14, 22, 23, Schs 1, 4, Sch 5 Pt 2 (which make provision for lasting powers of attorney and for the continuing operation of enduring powers of attorney created before that date).

4   Ie by the Mental Capacity Act 2005 ss 66(1)(b), 67(2), Sch 7.

5   See the Mental Capacity Act 2005 ss 9–14, 22, 23, Sch 1; and PARA **218** et seq.

6   See the Mental Capacity Act 2005 Sch 4; and PARA **196** et seq. Schedule 4 is a modified version of the Enduring Powers of Attorney Act 1985, having effect in relation to enduring powers after 1 October 2007 in place of the corresponding provisions of the 1985 Act (repealed). Any order or determination made, or other thing done, under the Enduring Powers of Attorney Act 1985 which had effect immediately before 1 October 2007 continues to have effect despite the repeal of that Act (Mental Capacity Act 2005 s 66(4), Sch 5 para 11(1)) and in so far as any such order, determination or thing could have been made or done under Sch 4 if it had then been in force it is to be treated as made or done thereunder and the powers of variation and discharge exercisable by the court apply accordingly (Sch 5 para 11(2)). This is without prejudice to the Interpretation Act 1978 s 16 (general savings on repeal: see STATUTES AND LEGISLATIVE PROCESS vol 96 (2012) PARA 1021). An application for the exercise of a power under the Enduring Powers of Attorney Act 1985 which was pending immediately before 1 October 2007 is to be treated, in so far as a corresponding power is exercisable under the Mental Capacity Act 2005 Sch 4, as an application for the exercise of that power: Sch 5 para 12(1). See further PARAS **201** note 4, **207** note 8, **212** note 3.

7   Mental Capacity Act 2005 s 66(2).

8   See the Mental Capacity Act 2005 ss 9–14, 22, 23, Sch 1; and PARA **218** et seq.

(2) ENDURING POWERS OF ATTORNEY

(i) Nature and Effect of Power

196. Effect of enduring power.

An enduring power of attorney[1] disapplies in respect of the donor of the power, upon his mental incapacity[2], the statutory provisions governing mental capacity and the ability to make decisions[3], and empowers the donee to act in accordance with the enduring power to make and implement decisions regarding the donor's property and affairs[4].

An attorney under an enduring power expressed[5] to confer general authority on the attorney may, following registration of the instrument creating the power[6], do on behalf of the donor anything which the donor could lawfully do by an attorney at the time when the donor executed the instrument[7], provided that the thing done is not unreasonable having regard to all the circumstances and in particular the size of the donor's estate[8]. An attorney under an enduring power, whether general or limited, may following registration act under the power so as to benefit himself or other persons than the donor to the following extent (but no further):

(1)   he may so act in relation to himself or in relation to any other person if the donor might be expected to provide for his or that person's needs respectively[9]; and

(2)   he may do whatever the donor might be expected to do to meet those needs[10],

and, without prejudice to the foregoing, may dispose of the property[11] of the donor by way of gift to the following extent but no further:

(a)   he may make gifts of a seasonal nature or at a time, or on an anniversary, of a birth, a marriage or the formation of a civil partnership, to persons (including himself) who are related to or connected with the donor[12]; and

(b)   he may make gifts to any charity to whom the donor made or might be expected to make gifts[13],

provided that the value of each such gift is not unreasonable having regard to all the circumstances and in particular the size of the donor's estate[14].

These powers are exercisable without the attorney obtaining any consent[15] but are subject to any conditions or restrictions contained in the instrument creating the power[16]. The exercise of trustee functions under an enduring power of attorney is subject to the Trustee Delegation Act 1999[17]. The grant of an enduring power of attorney does not confer a right on the attorney to conduct litigation in court, if he would not otherwise have had a right of audience[18].

1   Ie an 'enduring power' for the purposes of the Mental Capacity Act 2005 s 66(3), Sch 4 (see the text and notes 2–4; and PARAS 197–217). As to the characteristics and procedural requirements for enduring powers see PARAS 197–199. Schedule 4 governs the continuing operation of enduring powers of attorney created under and formerly governed by the Enduring Powers of Attorney Act 1985 (repealed). The power to create enduring powers of attorney under the Enduring Powers of Attorney Act 1985 ceased on 1 October 2007, but powers created before that date continue to have effect: see PARA 195.
    The provisions of the Mental Capacity Act 2005 Sch 4 referred to in this paragraph make provision for the operation of enduring powers of attorney after 1 October 2007 corresponding to the provision made in respect of the operation of those powers before that date by the Enduring Powers of Attorney Act 1985 ss 1(1)(a), 3, 13(2) (repealed).

2   'Mentally incapable' or 'mental incapacity', except where it refers to revocation at common law, means in relation to any person, that he is incapable by reason of mental disorder of managing and administering his property and affairs; and 'mentally capable' and 'mental capacity' are construed accordingly: Mental Capacity Act 2005 Sch 4 para 23(1) (definition amended by the Mental Health Act 2007 ss 1(4), 55, Sch 1 para 23, Sch 11 Pt 1). 'Mental disorder', for the purposes of this definition, means mental disorder within the meaning of the Mental Health Act 1983 (as to which see s 1; and MENTAL HEALTH AND CAPACITY vol 75 (2013) PARA 761) disregarding the amendments made to that provision by the Mental Health Act 2007: see the Mental Capacity Act 2005 Sch 4 para 23(1A) (added by the Mental Health Act 2007 ss 1(4), 55, Sch 1 para 23, Sch 11 Pt 1).

3 Ie the Mental Capacity Act 2005 s 1 (see MENTAL HEALTH AND CAPACITY vol 75 (2013) PARA 601): those provisions accordingly do not apply in respect of an individual who has created an enduring power of attorney (see Sch 4 para 1(1)).

4 See PARA 197 et seq. An enduring power of attorney is accordingly not revoked by any subsequent mental incapacity of the donor: Mental Capacity Act 2005 Sch 4 para 1(1)(a).

5 Ie expressed by means of the instrument creating the power: Mental Capacity Act 2005 Sch 4 para 3(1). As to the creation of enduring powers see PARAS 197–199.

6 As to the requirement for, and effect of, registration see PARAS 200–211.

7 Mental Capacity Act 2005 Sch 4 para 3(1).

8 Mental Capacity Act 2005 Sch 4 para 3(1)(a), (3).

9 Mental Capacity Act 2005 Sch 4 para 3(2)(a). Any question arising under or for the purposes of Sch 4 as to what the donor of an enduring power might at any time be expected to do is determined by assuming that he had full mental capacity at the time but otherwise by reference to the circumstances existing at that time: Sch 4 para 23(2). The education of a child was a 'need' within the meaning of the Enduring Powers of Attorney Act 1985 s 3(4) (ie the provision (repealed) to which the Mental Capacity Act 2005 Sch 4 para 3(2)(a) corresponds): *Re Cameron; Phillips v Cameron* [1999] Ch 386, [1999] 2 All ER 924.

10 Mental Capacity Act 2005 Sch 4 para 3(2)(b).

11 'Property' includes any thing in action and any interest in real or personal property: Mental Capacity Act 2005 s 64(1).

12 Mental Capacity Act 2005 Sch 4 para 3(3)(a). Marriage includes marriage of a same sex couple: see Marriage (Same Sex Couples) Act 2013 Sch 3 para 1(1)(a), (2), (3); and MATRIMONIAL AND CIVIL PARTNERSHIP LAW vol 72 (2015) PARA 1 et seq.

13 Mental Capacity Act 2005 Sch 4 para 3(3)(b).

14 Mental Capacity Act 2005 Sch 4 para 3(3).

15 Mental Capacity Act 2005 Sch 4 para 3(2), (3).

16 Mental Capacity Act 2005 Sch 4 para 3(1)(b), (2), (3).

17 See the Trustee Delegation Act 1999 s 1; and TRUSTS AND POWERS vol 98 (2013) PARA 426.

18 *Gregory v Turner; R (on the application of Morris) v North Somerset Council* [2003] EWCA Civ 183, [2003] 2 All ER 1114, [2003] 1 WLR 1149.

197. Characteristics of an enduring power.

A power of attorney cannot be an enduring power[1] unless, when he executed the instrument creating it[2], the attorney was:

(1) an individual who had attained 18 years and was not bankrupt or subject to a debt relief order[3]; or

(2) a trust corporation[4].

A power of attorney also cannot be an enduring power if it gives the attorney a right to appoint a substitute or successor[5], and an instrument which appoints more than one person to be an attorney cannot create an enduring power unless the attorneys are appointed to act jointly or jointly and severally[6].

Certain older powers of attorney delegating trustee powers[7] also could not be enduring powers[8].

1 Ie for the purposes of the Mental Capacity Act 2005 Sch 4: see PARA 196 note 1. The provisions of Sch 4 referred to in this paragraph make provision for the operation of enduring powers of attorney after 1 October 2007 corresponding to the provision made in respect of the operation of those powers before that date by the Enduring Powers of Attorney Act 1985 ss 2(7), (9), 11(1)–(4), (8), Sch 3 paras 1, 2 (repealed). The power to create enduring powers of attorney under the Enduring Powers of Attorney Act 1985 ceased on 1 October 2007, but powers created before that date continue to have effect: see PARA 195.

2 For the purposes of joint attorneys the reference to the time when the attorney executed the instrument is read as a reference to the time when the second or last attorney executed the instrument: Mental Capacity Act 2005 Sch 4 para 21(1).

3 Mental Capacity Act 2005 Sch 4 paras 2(5)(a), 23(1) (amended by SI 2012/2404). References in the Mental Capacity Act 2005 to the 'bankruptcy' of an individual include a case where a bankruptcy restrictions order (or, as the case may be, an interim bankruptcy restrictions order) under the Insolvency Act 1986 (see BANKRUPTCY AND INDIVIDUAL INSOLVENCY) has effect in respect of him: Mental Capacity Act 2005 s 64(3), (4). References in the Mental Capacity Act 2005 to a

debt relief order (under the Insolvency Act 1986 Pt 7A) being made in relation to an individual include a case where a debt relief restrictions order (or, as the case may be, an interim debt relief restrictions order) under the Insolvency Act 1986 has effect in respect of him: Mental Capacity Act 2005 s 64(3A), (4A) (both added by SI 2012/2404). As to bankruptcy restrictions orders and interim bankruptcy restrictions orders see the Insolvency Act 1986 Sch 4A; and BANKRUPTCY AND INDIVIDUAL INSOLVENCY vol 5 (2013) PARA 657 et seq. As to debt relief orders under the Insolvency Act 1986 Pt 7A (ss 251A–251X) see BANKRUPTCY AND INDIVIDUAL INSOLVENCY vol 5 (2013) PARA 101 et seq.

4   Mental Capacity Act 2005 Sch 4 para 2(5)(b). As to the meaning of 'trust corporation' see the Trustee Act 1925 s 68(1) (TRUSTS AND POWERS vol 98 (2013) PARA 238); definition applied by the Mental Capacity Act 2005 s 64(1).

5   Mental Capacity Act 2005 Sch 4 para 2(6). In the case of joint attorneys the reference to the attorney is to be read as a reference to any attorney under the power: Sch 4 para 21(2).

6   Mental Capacity Act 2005 Sch 4 para 20(1)–(3). In the case of joint and several attorneys a failure, as respects any one attorney, to comply with the requirements for the creation of enduring powers (ie Sch 4 para 2(1)–(7), (10) (as to which see also PARAS 198–199) and the regulations cited in PARA 198) prevents the instrument from creating such a power in his case without affecting either its efficacy for that purpose as respects the other or others or its efficacy in his case for the purpose of creating a power of attorney which is not an enduring power: Sch 4 para 20(4), (8).

A valid enduring power of attorney can, however, appoint successive attorneys where the power contemplates that the attorney may begin to act before subsequently ceasing to act, to be replaced by the second attorney: *Re J* [2009] EWCOP 436.

7   Ie a power of attorney created before 1 March 2000 (see note 8) under which a trustee may delegate the execution of trusts pursuant to the Trustee Act 1925 s 25 as that provision had effect before its substitution by the Trustee Delegation Act 1999 s 5(1), (2).

8   See the Enduring Powers of Attorney Act 1985 s 2(8) (repealed). Section 2(8) does not apply to powers of attorney created pursuant to the Trustee Act 1925 s 25 as substituted (see note 7; and TRUSTS AND POWERS vol 98 (2013) PARA 425) after 1 March 2000 (ie the date on which the substitution of the Trustee Act 1925 s 25 was brought into force by the Trustee Delegation Act 1999 (Commencement) Order 2000, SI 2000/216): see the Trustee Delegation Act 1999 s 6.

(ii)   Creation, Revocation and Disclaimer of Power

198.   Procedural requirements for creation of enduring power.

A power of attorney is an enduring power[1] if the instrument which creates the power:

(1)   is in the prescribed form[2];
(2)   was executed in the prescribed manner by the donor and the attorney[3]; and
(3)   incorporated at the time of execution by the donor the prescribed explanatory information[4].

An instrument in the prescribed form purporting to have been executed in the prescribed manner is to be taken, in the absence of evidence to the contrary, to be a document which incorporated at the time of execution by the donor the prescribed explanatory information[5], and an instrument that differs in an immaterial respect in form or mode of expression from the prescribed form is treated as sufficient in point of form and expression[6].

The donor of an enduring power of attorney must possess sufficient capacity at the time of its creation; the ability to understand the nature and effect of the power, not the ability to perform all acts authorised under the power[7].

1   Ie for the purposes of the Mental Capacity Act 2005 Sch 4: see PARA 196 note 1. The provisions of Sch 4 referred to in this paragraph make provision for the operation of enduring powers of attorney after 1 October 2007 corresponding to the provision made in respect of the operation of those powers before that date by the Enduring Powers of Attorney Act 1985 ss 2(1), (5), (6), (13),

11(1), (4), (8) (repealed). The power to create enduring powers of attorney under the Enduring Powers of Attorney Act 1985 ceased on 1 October 2007, but powers created before that date continue to have effect: see PARA 195.

2 Mental Capacity Act 2005 Sch 4 para 2(1)(a). The prescribed form is the form prescribed at the time the instrument was executed: Sch 4 para 2(2). For the prescribed form for an instrument executed between 10 March 1986 and 30 October 1987 see the Enduring Powers of Attorney (Prescribed Form) Regulations 1986, SI 1986/126, reg 3, Schedule (revoked); for the prescribed form for an instrument executed between 1 November 1987 and 30 July 1990 see the Enduring Powers of Attorney (Prescribed Form) Regulations 1987, SI 1987/1612, reg 2, Schedule (revoked); and for the prescribed form for an instrument executed between 31 July 1990 and 30 September 2007 see the Enduring Powers of Attorney (Prescribed Form) Regulations 1990, SI 1990/1376, reg 2, Schedule (substituted by SI 2005/3116 with savings (see below)). Note also that by virtue of the Enduring Powers of Attorney (Prescribed Form) Regulations 1987, SI 1987/1612, reg 4 (revoked), a power executed in the form prescribed by the Enduring Powers of Attorney (Prescribed Form) Regulations 1986, SI 1986/126, and executed before 1 July 1988, was capable of being a valid enduring power of attorney; that by virtue of the Enduring Powers of Attorney (Prescribed Form) Regulations 1990, SI 1990/1376, reg 5(a), a power executed in the form prescribed by the Enduring Powers of Attorney (Prescribed Form) Regulations 1987, SI 1987/1612, and executed by the donor before 31 July 1991 was capable (whether or not seals were affixed to it) of being a valid enduring power of attorney; and that by virtue of the Enduring Powers of Attorney (Prescribed Form) (Amendment) Regulations 2005, SI 2005/3116, reg 3 (amended by SI 2007/548), a power executed in the form prescribed in the Enduring Powers of Attorney (Prescribed Form) Regulations 1990, SI 1990/1376, as though it had not been substituted as noted above and executed by the donor before 1 October 2007 was capable (whether or not seals were affixed to it) of being a valid enduring power of attorney. Provision was also made for the use of a Welsh language form instead of the form prescribed by the Enduring Powers of Attorney (Prescribed Form) Regulations 1990, SI 1990/1376: see the Enduring Powers of Attorney (Welsh Language Prescribed Form) Regulations 2005, SI 2005/3125, reg 2, Sch 1 (replacing the form provided for in the Enduring Powers of Attorney (Welsh Language Prescribed Form) Regulations 2000, SI 2000/289, reg 2, Schedule, subject to the proviso that a power executed in that form and executed by the donor before 1 October 2007 was capable (whether or not seals were affixed to it) of being a valid enduring power of attorney (Powers of Attorney (Welsh Language Prescribed Form) Regulations 2005, SI 2005/3125, reg 3 (amended by SI 2007/549))).

These regulations were made under and in accordance with the Enduring Powers of Attorney Act 1985 s 2(2)–(4) (repealed).

3 Mental Capacity Act 2005 Sch 4 para 2(1)(b). The prescribed manner is the manner prescribed at the time the instrument was executed: Sch 4 para 2(2). For the prescribed manner of execution for an instrument executed between 10 March 1986 and 30 October 1987 see the Enduring Powers of Attorney (Prescribed Form) Regulations 1986, SI 1986/126, reg 4 (revoked); for the prescribed manner of execution for an instrument executed between 1 November 1987 and 30 July 1990 see the Enduring Powers of Attorney (Prescribed Form) Regulations 1987, SI 1987/1612, reg 3 (revoked); and for the prescribed manner of execution for an instrument executed between 31 July 1990 and 30 September 2007 see the Enduring Powers of Attorney (Prescribed Form) Regulations 1990, SI 1990/1376, regs 3, 4. As to the form of execution see note 2.

These regulations were made under and in accordance with the Enduring Powers of Attorney Act 1985 s 2(2)–(4) (repealed).

In the case of joint and several attorneys (see PARA 197) a failure, as respects any one attorney, to comply with the requirements for the creation of enduring powers (ie the Mental Capacity Act 2005 Sch 4 para 2(1)–(7), (10) (as to which see also PARAS 197, 199) and the regulations cited herein) prevents the instrument from creating such a power without affecting either its efficacy for that purpose as respects the other or others or its efficacy in his case for the purpose of creating a power of attorney which is not an enduring power: Sch 4 para 20(4), (8).

4 Mental Capacity Act 2005 Sch 4 para 2(1)(c). The prescribed explanatory information is the explanatory information prescribed at the time the instrument was executed: Sch 4 para 2(2). For the prescribed explanatory information for an instrument executed between 10 March 1986 and 30 October 1987 see the Enduring Powers of Attorney (Prescribed Form) Regulations 1986, SI 1986/126, reg 5, Schedule (revoked); for the prescribed explanatory information for an instrument executed between 1 November 1987 and 30 July 1990 see the Enduring Powers of Attorney (Prescribed Form) Regulations 1987, SI 1987/1612, reg 2, Schedule (revoked); and for the prescribed explanatory information for an instrument executed between 31 July 1990 and 30 September 2007 see the Enduring Powers of Attorney (Prescribed Form) Regulations 1990, SI 1990/1376, reg 2, Schedule (substituted by SI 2005/3116 with savings (see note 2)).

These regulations were made under and in accordance with the Enduring Powers of Attorney Act 1985 s 2(2)–(4) (repealed).

5   Mental Capacity Act 2005 Sch 4 para 2(3).
6   Mental Capacity Act 2005 Sch 4 para 2(4). See, however, *Practice Direction* [1989] 2 All ER 64, [1989] 1 WLR 311 (which states that marginal notes in the prescribed form may be omitted only if they are irrelevant, correspond to the omitted or deleted one of a pair of alternatives, or constitute an immaterial difference from the prescribed form); and the Enduring Powers of Attorney (Prescribed Form) Regulations 1990, SI 1990/1376, reg 2(1), (2).
7   *Re K; Re F* [1988] Ch 310, [1988] 1 All ER 358, [1988] 2 WLR 781, COP.

199.   Revocation, suspension and disclaimer of enduring powers.

An enduring power of attorney[1] is revoked by the bankruptcy[2] of the donor or the attorney or the making of a debt relief order[3] (although if the donor or attorney is bankrupt merely because an interim bankruptcy restrictions order[4] has effect in respect of him or where the donor or attorney is subject to an interim debt relief restrictions order, the power is only suspended for so long as the order has effect[5]). An enduring power is also revoked if the court[6] so directs on exercising a power[7] to make decisions or appoint a deputy to make such decisions in relation to the donor[8].

No disclaimer of an enduring power, whether by deed or otherwise, is valid unless and until the attorney gives notice[9] of it to the donor or, in certain circumstances[10], to the court[11].

1   Ie an enduring power of attorney for the purposes of the Mental Capacity Act 2005 Sch 4: see PARA 196 note 1. The provisions of Sch 4 referred to in this paragraph make provision for the operation of enduring powers of attorney after 1 October 2007 corresponding to the provision made in respect of the operation of those powers before that date by the Enduring Powers of Attorney Act 1985 ss 2(10)–(12), 8(4)(b), Sch 3 paras 2, 7 (repealed). The power to create enduring powers of attorney under the Enduring Powers of Attorney Act 1985 ceased on 1 October 2007, but powers created before that date continue to have effect: see PARA 195.
2   As to the meaning of 'bankruptcy' see PARA 197 note 3.
3   Mental Capacity Act 2005 Sch 4 para 2(7) (amended by SI 2012/2404). In the case of joint attorneys (see PARA 197) the reference in the Mental Capacity Act 2005 Sch 4 para 2(7) to the attorney is to be read as a reference to any attorney under the power (Sch 4 para 21(2)), and in the case of joint and several attorneys (see PARA 197), the reference to the bankruptcy of the attorney is to be read as a reference to the bankruptcy of the last remaining attorney under the power (with the bankruptcy of any other attorney under the power causing that person to cease to be an attorney under the power) (Sch 4 para 22(1)). Similarly, in the case of joint and several attorneys, the reference to the making of a debt relief order in respect of the attorney is to be read as a reference to the making of a debt relief order in respect of the last remaining attorney under the power; and the making of a debt relief order in respect of any other attorney under the power causes that person to cease to be an attorney under the power: Sch 4 para 22(1A) (added by SI 2012/2404). As to debt relief orders under the Insolvency Act 1986 Pt 7A (ss 251A–251X) see BANKRUPTCY AND INDIVIDUAL INSOLVENCY vol 5 (2013) PARA 101 et seq.
    The Public Guardian must cancel the registration of an instrument creating an enduring power if satisfied that the power has been revoked by the bankruptcy of the donor or attorney (or, if the attorney is a body corporate, by its winding up or dissolution): see Sch 4 para 17(b); and PARA 211. As to the Public Guardian see ss 57–60; and MENTAL HEALTH AND CAPACITY vol 75 (2013) PARA 751 et seq.
4   As to bankruptcy restrictions orders and interim bankruptcy restrictions orders see the Insolvency Act 1986 Sch 4A; and BANKRUPTCY AND INDIVIDUAL INSOLVENCY vol 5 (2013) PARA 657 et seq.
5   Mental Capacity Act 2005 Sch 4 para 2(8) (amended by SI 2012/2404). In the case of joint attorneys the reference in the Mental Capacity Act 2005 Sch 4 para 2(8) to the attorney is to be read as a reference to any attorney under the power (Sch 4 para 21(2)), and in the case of joint and several attorneys the reference to the suspension of the power is to be read as a reference to its suspension in so far as it relates to the attorney in respect of whom the interim bankruptcy restrictions order has effect (Sch 4 para 22(2)). Similarly, in the case of joint and several attorneys,

the reference to the suspension of the power is to be read as a reference to its suspension in so far as it relates to the attorney in respect of whom the interim debt relief restrictions order has effect: Sch 4 para 22(2A) (added by SI 2012/2404).

6   Ie the Court of Protection established by the Mental Capacity Act 2005 s 45: see s 64(1); and MENTAL HEALTH AND CAPACITY vol 75 (2013) PARA 720 et seq. For specific procedural provision in connection with these matters see the Court of Protection Rules 2017, SI 2017/1035, r 9.8.

7   Ie under the Mental Capacity Act 2005 ss 16–20 (see MENTAL HEALTH AND CAPACITY vol 75 (2013) PARAS 724, 726, 727, 734, 735–738). See eg *Re AB (Revocation of Enduring Power of Attorney)* [2014] EWCOP 12, [2014] WTLR 1303, [2014] All ER (D) 87 (Jul); cf *Re DT* [2015] EWCOP 10, [2015] All ER (D) 48 (Mar).

8   Mental Capacity Act 2005 Sch 4 para 2(9). Prior to 1 October 2007 (see note 1) an enduring power would be revoked if the court so directed on the exercise of any of its powers relating to the management of a person's property and affairs under the Mental Health Act 1983 Pt VII (ss 93–113) (repealed): see the Enduring Powers of Attorney Act 1985 s 2(11) (repealed).

The court must direct the Public Guardian to cancel the registration of an instrument creating an enduring power on giving a direction under this provision that the power is to be revoked: see the Mental Capacity Act 2005 Sch 4 para 16(4)(b); and PARA 214.

9   Ie notice in writing: Mental Capacity Act 2005 Sch 4 para 23(1).

10 Ie where the Mental Capacity Act 2005 Sch 4 para 4(6) (notification of disclaimer on actual or impending incapacity of donor: see PARA 201) or Sch 4 para 15(1) (disclaimer after registration: see PARA 210) applies.

11 Mental Capacity Act 2005 Sch 4 para 2(10). The Public Guardian must cancel the registration of an instrument creating an enduring power on receipt of a disclaimer signed by the attorney: see Sch 4 para 17(a); and PARA 211.

(iii) Activation and Operation of Power

200. Requirement for registration.

The donee of an enduring power[1] may not, upon the donor's mental incapacity[2] supervening, do anything under the authority of the power unless or until the instrument creating the power is registered[3]. This prohibition on activating the power before registration is not, however, absolute: the attorney may take action under the power to maintain the donor or prevent loss to his estate[4] or to maintain himself or other persons to the extent that the donor might be expected to provide for his or the other person's needs[5], provided he has made an application for registration of the instrument[6]. Provision is also made for protecting the attorney from liability during the period when his authority to act is suspended pending registration[7].

1   Ie an enduring power of attorney for the purposes of the Mental Capacity Act 2005 Sch 4: see PARA 196 note 1. The provisions of Sch 4 referred to in this paragraph make provision for the operation of enduring powers of attorney after 1 October 2007 corresponding to the provision made in respect of the operation of those powers before that date by the Enduring Powers of Attorney Act 1985 ss 1(1)(b), (c), (2), (3), 3(4), 11(5)(a) (repealed). The power to create enduring powers of attorney under the Enduring Powers of Attorney Act 1985 ceased on 1 October 2007, but powers created before that date continue to have effect: see PARA 195.

2   As to the meaning of 'mentally incapable' and cognate expressions see PARA 196 note 2.

3   Mental Capacity Act 2005 Sch 4 para 1(1)(b). As to registration see PARA 207.

4   Mental Capacity Act 2005 Sch 4 para 1(2)(a).

5   Mental Capacity Act 2005 Sch 4 paras 1(2)(b), 3(2)(a). In these circumstances the attorney may do whatever the donor might be expected to do to meet the needs referred to: Sch 4 para 3(2)(b). The education of a child was a 'need' within the meaning of the Enduring Powers of Attorney Act 1985 s 3(4) (ie the provision (now repealed) to which the Mental Capacity Act 2005 Sch 4 para 3(2)(a) corresponds): *Re Cameron (deceased); Phillips v Cameron* [1999] Ch 386, [1999] 2 All ER 924.

6   Mental Capacity Act 2005 Sch 4 para 1(2). Where the attorney purports to act as provided by Sch 4 para 1(2) then, in favour of a person who deals with him without knowledge that the

attorney is acting otherwise than in accordance with Sch 4 para 1(2)(a) or (b), the transaction between them is as valid as if the attorney were acting in accordance with Sch 4 para 1(2)(a) or (b): Sch 4 para 1(3).

In the case of joint and joint and several attorneys (see PARA 197), where one or more but not both or all of the attorneys make or join in making an application for registration of the instrument then an attorney who is not an applicant as well as one who is may act pending the initial determination of the application: Sch 4 para 20(5)(a). As to applications prior to registration see also *Practice Direction* [1986] 2 All ER 42.

7　See the Mental Capacity Act 2005 Sch 4 para 1(1)(c), which provides that if and so long as Sch 4 para 1(1)(b) (see the text and notes 1–3) operates to suspend the donee's authority to act under the enduring power, the Powers of Attorney Act 1971 s 5 (protection of donee and third persons: see PARA 194), so far as applicable, applies as if the power had been revoked by the donor's mental incapacity.

201. Matters preceding registration.

If the attorney under an enduring power[1] has reason to believe that the donor is or is becoming mentally incapable[2] he must as soon as practicable make an application to the Public Guardian[3] for registration of the instrument creating the power[4]. Before making such application, the attorney must comply with the provisions as to notice[5] and may refer to the court[6] for its determination any question as to the validity of the power[7] and must comply with any direction given to him by the court on that determination[8]. No disclaimer of the power is valid unless and until the attorney gives notice[9] of it to the Public Guardian[10].

1　Ie an enduring power of attorney for the purposes of the Mental Capacity Act 2005 Sch 4: see PARA 196 note 1. The provisions of Sch 4 referred to in this paragraph make provision for the operation of enduring powers of attorney after 1 October 2007 corresponding to the provision made in respect of the operation of those powers before that date by the Enduring Powers of Attorney Act 1985 s 4(1)–(3), (5), (6), Sch 3 para 8 (repealed). The power to create enduring powers of attorney under the Enduring Powers of Attorney Act 1985 ceased on 1 October 2007, but powers created before that date continue to have effect: see PARA 195.
2　As to the meaning of 'mentally incapable' and cognate expressions see PARA 196 note 2.
3　As to the Public Guardian see the Mental Capacity Act 2005 ss 57–60; and MENTAL HEALTH AND CAPACITY vol 75 (2013) PARA 724 et seq.
4　Mental Capacity Act 2005 Sch 4 para 4(1), (2). As to registration see further PARA 207. An application for the exercise of a power under the Enduring Powers of Attorney Act 1985 (repealed) which is pending immediately before 1 October 2007 (see note 1; and PARA 195) is to be treated, in so far as a corresponding power is exercisable under the Mental Capacity Act 2005 Sch 4, as an application for the exercise of that power, and accordingly a pending application under the Enduring Powers of Attorney Act 1985 s 4(2) (repealed) for the registration of an instrument is to be treated as an application to the Public Guardian under the Mental Capacity Act 2005 Sch 4 para 4, and any notice given in connection with that application under the Enduring Powers of Attorney Act 1985 Sch 1 (repealed) is to be treated as given under the Mental Capacity Act 2005 Sch 4 paras 5–12 (as the case may be): Sch 5 para 12(1), (2)(a).
5　Mental Capacity Act 2005 Sch 4 para 4(3). As to the notification requirements see PARA 202. Provision is made for the registration of an instrument in certain circumstances notwithstanding the failure to give notice: see Sch 4 para 13(3); and PARA 208.
6　Ie the Court of Protection: see PARA 199 note 6. For specific procedural provision in connection with these matters see the Court of Protection Rules 2017, SI 2017/1035, r 9.8.
7　Mental Capacity Act 2005 Sch 4 para 4(5)(a).
8　Mental Capacity Act 2005 Sch 4 para 4(5)(b).
9　As to the giving of notices see PARA 199 note 9. As to the duty to give notice of disclaimer to the donor see the Mental Capacity Act 2005 Sch 4 para 2(10); and PARA 199.
10　Mental Capacity Act 2005 Sch 4 para 4(6). For the purpose of joint and several attorneys (see PARA 197), the restriction on disclaimer imposed by Sch 4 para 4(6) applies only to those attorneys who have reason to believe that the donor is or is becoming mentally incapable: Sch 4 para 22(3).

The Public Guardian must notify the donor if he receives a notice under Sch 4 para 4(6) (Sch 4 para 4(6)), and must cancel the registration of an instrument creating an enduring power on receipt of a disclaimer signed by the attorney (see Sch 4 para 17(a); and PARA 211).

202. Who should be notified of intended registration.

Before making an application to register[1] an instrument creating an enduring power[2] the attorney must give notice[3] of his intention to do so to the donor[4] and no more than three[5] (in this order of preference[6]) of:

(1)   the donor's spouse or civil partner[7];
(2)   the donor's children[8];
(3)   the donor's parents[9];
(4)   the donor's brothers and sisters, whether of the whole or half blood[10];
(5)   the widow, widower or surviving civil partner of a child of the donor[11];
(6)   the donor's grandchildren[12];
(7)   the children of the donor's brothers and sisters of the whole blood[13];
(8)   the children of the donor's brothers and sisters of the half blood[14];
(9)   the donor's uncles and aunts of the whole blood[15]; and
(10) the children of the donor's uncles and aunts of the whole blood[16].

An attorney is not required to give notice to himself or any other attorney under the power who is joining in making the application (even though he or the other attorney is entitled to receive notice by virtue of being a prescribed relative)[17], unless the application for registration is being made under a joint and several power[18], in which case the attorney must give notice of his intention to apply to any other attorney under the power who is not joining in making the application[19].

Before applying for registration the attorney may make an application to the court[20] to be dispensed from the requirement to give notice to any of these persons (including the donor and any other attorney), and the court must grant the application if it is satisfied that it would be undesirable or impracticable for the attorney to give the relevant person notice[21] or that no useful purpose is likely to be served by giving him notice[22]. Moreover, a person (other than the donor) is not entitled to receive notice under these provisions if his name or address is not known to the applying attorney and cannot be reasonably ascertained by him[23] or the applying attorney has reason to believe that he has not reached 18 or is mentally incapable[24].

1   For the duty to register an enduring power see PARA 200. As to registration see further PARA 207.
2   Ie an enduring power of attorney for the purposes of the Mental Capacity Act 2005 Sch 4: see PARA 196 note 1. The provisions of Sch 4 referred to in this paragraph make provision for the operation of enduring powers of attorney after 1 October 2007 corresponding to the provision made in respect of the operation of those powers before that date by the Enduring Powers of Attorney Act 1985 Sch 1 paras 1–4, 7, 8(2) (repealed). The power to create enduring powers of attorney under the Enduring Powers of Attorney Act 1985 ceased on 1 October 2007, but powers created before that date continue to have effect: see PARA 195.
3   As to the giving of notices see PARA 199 note 9. For these purposes a notice given by post is regarded as given on the date on which it was posted, notwithstanding anything in the Interpretation Act 1978 s 7 (construction of references to service by post: see STATUTES AND LEGISLATIVE PROCESS vol 96 (2012) PARA 1219): Mental Capacity Act 2005 Sch 4 para 12. Any pending notice given in connection with an application under the Enduring Powers of Attorney Act 1985 Sch 1 (repealed) is to be treated as given under these provisions: see the Mental Capacity Act 2005 Sch 5 para 12(1), (2)(a); and PARA 201 note 4.
4   Mental Capacity Act 2005 Sch 4 para 8(1).
5   Mental Capacity Act 2005 Sch 4 para 6(3)(a). Notwithstanding the specified limit of three persons, if there is more than one person falling within any of classes listed in heads (1)–(9) in the text, and at least one of those persons would be entitled to receive notice under these provisions, then (subject to Sch 4 para 6(2) (see the text and notes 23–24)), all the persons falling within that class are entitled to receive notice: Sch 4 para 6(4).
6   Mental Capacity Act 2005 Sch 4 para 6(3)(b).

7   Mental Capacity Act 2005 Sch 4 paras 5, 6(1)(a). Spouse includes a person who is married to a person of the same sex: see Marriage (Same Sex Couples) Act 2013 Sch 3 para 1(1)(c), (2), (3); and MATRIMONIAL AND CIVIL PARTNERSHIP LAW vol 72 (2015) PARA 1 et seq.

8   Mental Capacity Act 2005 Sch 4 para 6(1)(b).

9   Mental Capacity Act 2005 Sch 4 para 6(1)(c).

10   Mental Capacity Act 2005 Sch 4 para 6(1)(d).

11   Mental Capacity Act 2005 Sch 4 para 6(1)(e).

12   Mental Capacity Act 2005 Sch 4 para 6(1)(f).

13   Mental Capacity Act 2005 Sch 4 para 6(1)(g).

14   Mental Capacity Act 2005 Sch 4 para 6(1)(h).

15   Mental Capacity Act 2005 Sch 4 para 6(1)(i).

16   Mental Capacity Act 2005 Sch 4 para 6(1)(j).

17   Mental Capacity Act 2005 Sch 4 para 7(1). The 'prescribed relatives' are those persons entitled to be given notice under Sch 4 paras 5, 6 (see the text and notes 1–16).

18   As to joint and several powers of attorney see PARA 197.

19   Mental Capacity Act 2005 Sch 4 para 11(1). In the case of joint and joint and several attorneys, where one or more but not both or all of the attorneys makes or joins in making an application for registration of the instrument then notice of the application must also be given to the other attorney or attorneys: Sch 4 para 20(5)(b).

20   Ie the Court of Protection: see PARA 199 note 6. For specific procedural provision in connection with these matters see the Court of Protection Rules 2017, SI 2017/1035, r 9.8.

21   Mental Capacity Act 2005 Sch 4 paras 7(2)(a), 8(2), 11(1).

22   Mental Capacity Act 2005 Sch 4 para 7(2)(b).

23   Mental Capacity Act 2005 Sch 4 paras 6(2)(a), 11(2)(a).

24   Mental Capacity Act 2005 Sch 4 paras 6(2)(b), 11(2)(b). As to the meaning of 'mentally incapable' and cognate expressions see PARA 196 note 2.

203. Form and content of notices of intended registration.

A notice to relatives[1] or to the donor of the intended registration[2] of an enduring power of attorney[3] must be in the prescribed form[4] and state that the attorney proposes to make an application to the Public Guardian for the registration of the instrument creating the enduring power in question[5]. In addition, a notice to relatives must inform the person to whom it is given of the right to object[6] to the proposed registration[7] and specify the grounds on which an objection to registration may be made[8], and a notice to the donor must also provide (or arrange for the provision of) an explanation to the donor of the notice and its effect and why it is being brought to his attention[9] and inform him that, while the instrument creating the enduring power remains registered, any revocation of the power by him will be ineffective unless and until the revocation is confirmed by the court[10].

1   Ie the persons listed in PARA 202. As to the giving of notices see PARA 199 note 9.

2   For the duty to register an enduring power see PARA 200. As to registration see further PARAS 202, 207.

3   Ie an enduring power of attorney for the purposes of the Mental Capacity Act 2005 Sch 4: see PARA 196 note 1. The provisions of Sch 4 referred to in this paragraph make provision for the operation of enduring powers of attorney after 1 October 2007 corresponding to the provision made in respect of the operation of those powers before that date by the Enduring Powers of Attorney Act 1985 Sch 1 paras 5, 6 (repealed). The power to create enduring powers of attorney under the Enduring Powers of Attorney Act 1985 ceased on 1 October 2007, but powers created before that date continue to have effect: see PARA 195.

4   Mental Capacity Act 2005 Sch 4 paras 9(a), 10(a). 'Prescribed' means prescribed by regulations under the Mental Capacity Act 2005: s 64(1). For the prescribed form see the Lasting Powers of Attorney, Enduring Powers of Attorney and Public Guardian Regulations 2007, SI 2007/1253, reg 23(1), Sch 7 (substituted by SI 2010/1063). Provision is also made for the use of Welsh language forms (reg 3(1)(a)); forms which differ in an immaterial respect in form or mode of expression from the specified form, forms to the same effect but with such variations as the circumstances may require or the court or Public Guardian may approve, and Welsh versions of such forms, are also acceptable (reg 3(1)(b)).

5 Mental Capacity Act 2005 Sch 4 paras 9(b), 10(b). Any pending notice given in connection with an application under the Enduring Powers of Attorney Act 1985 Sch 1 (repealed) is to be treated as given under these provisions: see the Mental Capacity Act 2005 Sch 5 para 12(1), (2)(a); and PARA 201. As to the Public Guardian see the Mental Capacity Act 2005 ss 57–60; and MENTAL HEALTH AND CAPACITY vol 75 (2013) PARA 751 et seq.

6 Ie under the Mental Capacity Act 2005 Sch 4 para 13(4) (see PARA 207).

7 Mental Capacity Act 2005 Sch 4 para 9(c).

8 Mental Capacity Act 2005 Sch 4 para 9(d). These are the grounds set out in Sch 4 para 13(9) (see PARA 205).

9 Lasting Powers of Attorney, Enduring Powers of Attorney and Public Guardian Regulations 2007, SI 2007/1253, reg 23(2). This information must be provided to the donor personally and in a way that is appropriate to the donor's circumstances (for example using simple language, visual aids or other appropriate means): reg 23(3).

10 Mental Capacity Act 2005 Sch 4 para 10(c). 'The court' is the Court of Protection: see PARA 199 note 6. For specific procedural provision in connection with these matters see the Court of Protection Rules 2017, SI 2017/1035, r 9.8.

204. Form and content of applications for registration.

An application for the registration of an enduring power[1] must be made in the prescribed form[2]. The Public Guardian must not register an instrument where only a certified copy of the instrument is sent with the application, unless the applicant verifies that he cannot produce the original instrument because it has been lost or, as the case may be, destroyed[3].

Any person who, in an application for registration, makes a statement which he knows to be false in a material particular is guilty of an offence[4].

1 Ie an enduring power of attorney for the purposes of the Mental Capacity Act 2005 Sch 4: see PARA 196 note 1. Applications are made to the Public Guardian: see PARA 203. For the duty to register an enduring power see PARA 200. As to registration see further PARAS 202, 207.

   The provisions of Sch 4 referred to in this paragraph make provision for the operation of enduring powers of attorney after 1 October 2007 corresponding to the provision made in respect of the operation of those powers before that date by the Enduring Powers of Attorney Act 1985 s 4(4), (7), (8) (repealed). The power to create enduring powers of attorney under the Enduring Powers of Attorney Act 1985 ceased on 1 October 2007, but powers created before that date continue to have effect: see PARA 195.

2 Mental Capacity Act 2005 Sch 4 para 4(4)(a). For the prescribed form see the Lasting Powers of Attorney, Enduring Powers of Attorney and Public Guardian Regulations 2007, SI 2007/1253, reg 24(1), Sch 8 (substituted by SI 2010/1063). The Mental Capacity Act 2005 Sch 4 para 4(4)(b) also requires that an application for the registration of an enduring power must contain such statements as may be prescribed: however at the date at which this volume states the law no such statements had been prescribed. Provision is also made for the administration of applications where the instrument to be registered is neither the original instrument creating the power nor a certified copy thereof: see the Lasting Powers of Attorney, Enduring Powers of Attorney and Public Guardian Regulations 2007, SI 2007/1253, reg 24(2), (3); and PARA 207. A fee is payable: see the Public Guardian (Fees, etc) Regulations 2007, SI 2007/2051, reg 4 (amended by SI 2011/2189), Public Guardian (Fees, etc) Regulations 2007, SI 2007/2051, Schedule (amended by SI 2009/514; SI 2011/2189; SI 2013/1748; SI 2017/503).

3 Lasting Powers of Attorney, Enduring Powers of Attorney and Public Guardian Regulations 2007, SI 2007/1253, reg 24(1A) (added by SI 2010/1063).

4 Mental Capacity Act 2005 Sch 4 para 4(7). A person who is found guilty of this offence is liable on conviction on indictment to imprisonment for a term not exceeding two years, or a fine, or both, and on summary conviction to imprisonment for a term not exceeding six months, or a fine not exceeding the statutory maximum, or both: Sch 4 para 4(7). As to the powers of magistrates' courts to issue fines on summary conviction see SENTENCING vol 92 (2015) PARA 176.

205. Objections to registration.

A notice of objection to the registration of an instrument creating an enduring power[1] is valid if the objection is made on one or more of the following grounds:

(1)   that the power purported to have been created by the instrument was not valid as an enduring power of attorney[2];

(2)   that the power created by the instrument no longer subsists[3];

(3)   that the application is premature because the donor is not yet becoming mentally incapable[4];

(4)   that fraud or undue pressure was used to induce the donor to create the power[5]; and

(5)   that the attorney is unsuitable to be the donor's attorney, having regard to all the circumstances and in particular the attorney's relationship to or connection with the donor[6].

If any of these grounds is established to the satisfaction of the court[7] it must direct the Public Guardian not to register the instrument[8], but if not so satisfied it must direct its registration[9].

1   Ie an enduring power of attorney for the purposes of the Mental Capacity Act 2005 Sch 4: see PARA 196 note 1. For the duty to register an enduring power see PARA 200 et seq. As to the giving of notices see PARA 199 note 9.

The provisions of Sch 4 referred to in this paragraph make provision for the operation of enduring powers of attorney after 1 October 2007 corresponding to the provision made in respect of the operation of those powers before that date by the Enduring Powers of Attorney Act 1985 ss 6(5), (7), (8), 11(5)(c), (6), Sch 3 para 4 (repealed). The power to create enduring powers of attorney under the Enduring Powers of Attorney Act 1985 ceased on 1 October 2007, but powers created before that date continue to have effect: see PARA 195.

2   Mental Capacity Act 2005 Sch 4 para 13(9)(a). The test as to whether or not a power is validly created is not the same as the test for whether it has ceased to be exercisable; the test of validity is whether at the time of execution the donor understood the nature and effect of the power and not whether he would have been able to perform all the acts which the power authorised: *Re K* [1988] Ch 310, [1988] 1 All ER 358. See *Re W (Enduring Power of Attorney)* [2001] Ch 609, [2001] 4 All ER 88, CA (the onus is on the objector to show that the donor lacked the capacity to execute the power of attorney); *C v S* [2008] EWHC 1869 (Ch), [2008] WTLR 1159 (the judge must consider the totality of the evidence, and if there is compelling medical evidence of incapacity, the burden may shift to those seeking to register the enduring power of attorney).

3   Mental Capacity Act 2005 Sch 4 para 13(9)(b). Where an objection is made on the ground that the power in respect of which registration is sought has already been revoked, the onus is on the objector to show that the donor, by his or her conduct, must have intended such revocation: *Re E (Enduring Power of Attorney)* [2001] Ch 364, sub nom *Re E, X v Y* [2000] 3 All ER 1004.

4   Mental Capacity Act 2005 Sch 4 para 13(9)(c). As to the meaning of 'mentally incapable' and cognate expressions see PARA 196 note 2.

5   Mental Capacity Act 2005 Sch 4 para 13(9)(d).

6   Mental Capacity Act 2005 Sch 4 para 13(9)(e). See *Re W (Enduring Power of Attorney)* [2000] Ch 343, [1999] 2 FLR 1163 (hostility between siblings does not necessarily mean that one of them is an unsuitable attorney for a parent, provided the estate is simple). See also *Re E (Enduring Power of Attorney)* [2001] Ch 364, sub nom *Re E, X v Y* [2000] 3 All ER 1004. As to intervention by the Public Guardian on grounds of unsuitability see PARA 215. For the purposes of joint attorneys (see PARA 197), the Mental Capacity Act 2005 Sch 4 para 13 has effect as if the ground of objection specified in Sch 4 para 13(9)(e) applied to any attorney under the power: Sch 4 para 21(3). For the purposes of joint and several attorneys, where one or more but not both or all of the attorneys make or join in making an application for registration of the instrument, objection may validly be taken on a ground relating to an attorney or to the power of an attorney who is not an applicant as well as to one or the power of one who is an applicant: Sch 4 para 20(5)(c). As to the Public Guardian see the Mental Capacity Act 2005 ss 57–60; and MENTAL HEALTH AND CAPACITY vol 75 (2013) PARA 751 et seq.

7   Ie the Court of Protection: see PARA 199 note 6. For specific procedural provision in connection with these matters see the Court of Protection Rules 2017, SI 2017/1035, r 9.8.

8   If the court directs the Public Guardian not to register an instrument because it is satisfied that the ground in the Mental Capacity Act 2005 Sch 4 para 13(9)(d) or (e) (see the text and notes 5–6) is established, it must by order revoke the power created by the instrument (Sch 4 para 13(11)); and if the court directs the Public Guardian not to register an instrument because it is satisfied that any

ground in Sch 4 para 13(9)(a), (b), (d) or (e) (see the text and notes 1–3, 5–6) is established, the instrument must be delivered up to be cancelled unless the court otherwise directs (Sch 4 para 13(12)).
9   Mental Capacity Act 2005 Sch 4 para 13(10). As to the role of objections in the registration process see further PARA 206.

206. Dealing with objections.

If, in the case of an application for the registration of an instrument creating an enduring power[1], the Public Guardian[2] has reason to believe that appropriate inquiries might bring to light evidence on which he could be satisfied that one of the grounds of objection[3] was established, he must not register the instrument[4] and must undertake such inquiries as he thinks appropriate in all the circumstances[5]. If having complied with these requirements the Public Guardian is satisfied that one of the grounds of objection is established the attorney may apply to the court[6] for directions[7] and the Public Guardian must not register the instrument except in accordance with the court's directions[8].

In the case of joint and several attorneys the Public Guardian is not precluded by these provisions from registering an instrument and the court must not direct him not to do so[9] if an enduring power subsists as respects some attorney who is not affected by the ground or grounds of the objection in question; and where the Public Guardian registers an instrument in that case, he must make against the registration an entry in the prescribed form[10].

1   Ie an enduring power of attorney for the purposes of the Mental Capacity Act 2005 Sch 4: see PARA 196 note 1. For the duty to register an enduring power see PARA 200 et seq.
    The provisions of Sch 4 referred to in this paragraph make provision for the operation of enduring powers of attorney after 1 October 2007 corresponding to the provision made in respect of the operation of those powers before that date by the Enduring Powers of Attorney Act 1985 s 6(4), (6) (repealed). The power to create enduring powers of attorney under the Enduring Powers of Attorney Act 1985 ceased on 1 October 2007, but powers created before that date continue to have effect: see PARA 195.
2   Applications are made to the Public Guardian: see PARA 203. As to the Public Guardian see the Mental Capacity Act 2005 ss 57–60; and MENTAL HEALTH AND CAPACITY vol 75 (2013) PARA 751 et seq.
3   As to the making of objections to registration see the Mental Capacity Act 2005 Sch 4 para 13(9); and PARA 205.
4   Mental Capacity Act 2005 Sch 4 para 13(7)(a). Where the Public Guardian is prevented by virtue of Sch 4 para 13(7) from registering an instrument creating an enduring power of attorney he must notify the person (or persons) who applied for registration of that fact: Lasting Powers of Attorney, Enduring Powers of Attorney and Public Guardian Regulations 2007, SI 2007/1253, reg 26(c).
5   Mental Capacity Act 2005 Sch 4 para 13(7)(b).
6   Ie the Court of Protection: see PARA 199 note 6. For specific procedural provision in connection with these matters see the Court of Protection Rules 2017, SI 2017/1035, r 9.8.
7   Mental Capacity Act 2005 Sch 4 para 13(8)(a).
8   Mental Capacity Act 2005 Sch 4 para 13(8)(b). For a case where the question of inquiries on objections came before the court see *Re C (Power of Attorney)* [2000] 2 FLR 1, CA.
9   Ie under the Mental Capacity Act 2005 Sch 4 para 13(10) (see PARA 205).
10 Mental Capacity Act 2005 Sch 4 para 20(6). This does not, however, preclude the court from revoking a power in so far as it confers a power on any other attorney in respect of whom the ground in Sch 4 para 13(9)(d) or (e) (see PARA 205) is established; and where any ground in Sch 4 para 13(9) affecting any other attorney is established the court must direct the Public Guardian to make against the registration an entry in the prescribed form: Sch 4 para 20(7). In a case within Sch 4 para 20(6) or (7) the form of the entry to be made in the register of enduring powers (see PARA 207) in respect of an instrument creating the enduring power of attorney is a stamp bearing the following words (inserting the information indicated, as appropriate): 'THE REGISTRATION OF THIS ENDURING POWER OF ATTORNEY IS QUALIFIED AND EXTENDS TO THE APPOINTMENT OF [insert name of attorney(s) not affected by ground(s) of objection or

revocation] ONLY AS THE ATTORNEY(S) OF [insert name of donor]': Lasting Powers of Attorney, Enduring Powers of Attorney and Public Guardian Regulations 2007, SI 2007/1253, reg 28.

207. Registering the instrument.

If an application for the registration of an instrument creating an enduring power[1] is made in accordance with the requirements concerning the giving of notification to the donor and family members[2] and complying with the statutory requirements as to the form and content of application[3], the Public Guardian[4] must register the instrument to which the application relates[5]. This is, however, subject to specific additional requirements if:

(1)   there is a person already appointed to make decisions on behalf of the donor[6];

(2)   there is no-one to whom notice of intended registration has been given[7];

(3)   the Public Guardian receives[8] a valid notice of objection to the registration[9] from a person entitled to notice of the application[10]; or

(4)   the Public Guardian has reason to believe that there may be grounds for objection[11]; or

(5)   the instrument to be registered which is sent with the application is neither the original instrument creating the power nor a certified copy[12].

Where the Public Guardian registers an instrument creating an enduring power of attorney he must retain a copy of the instrument[13] and return to the person (or persons) who applied for registration the original instrument, or the certified copy[14] of it, which accompanied the application[15]. The Public Guardian also has the function of establishing and maintaining a register of enduring powers for these purposes[16].

1   Ie an enduring power of attorney for the purposes of the Mental Capacity Act 2005 Sch 4: see PARA 196 note 1. Applications are made to the Public Guardian: see PARA 203. For the duty to register an enduring power see PARA 200 et seq.
      The provisions of Sch 4 referred to in this paragraph make provision for the operation of enduring powers of attorney after 1 October 2007 corresponding to the provision made in respect of the operation of those powers before that date by the Enduring Powers of Attorney Act 1985 s 6(1), (2), (7), (8) (repealed). The power to create enduring powers of attorney under the Enduring Powers of Attorney Act 1985 ceased on 1 October 2007, but powers created before that date continue to have effect: see PARA 195.
2   Ie the requirements of the Mental Capacity Act 2005 Sch 4 para 4(3) (see PARAS 201–202). Provision is made for the registration of an instrument where it appears from the application that there is no one to whom notice of intended registration has been given (see the text and note 7) and, in certain circumstances, notwithstanding the failure to give such notice (see Sch 4 para 13(3); and PARA 208).
3   Ie the requirements of the Mental Capacity Act 2005 Sch 4 para 4(4) (see PARA 204).
4   As to the Public Guardian see the Mental Capacity Act 2005 ss 57–60; and MENTAL HEALTH AND CAPACITY vol 75 (2013) PARA 751 et seq.
5   Mental Capacity Act 2005 Sch 4 para 13(1).
6   If it appears to the Public Guardian that there is a person already appointed to make decisions on behalf of the donor of the power created by the instrument (a 'deputy') and the powers conferred on the deputy would, if the instrument were registered, to any extent conflict with the powers conferred on the attorney, the Public Guardian must not register the instrument except in accordance with the court's directions: Sch 4 para 13(2). 'Court' means the Court of Protection: see PARA 199 note 6. For specific procedural provision in connection with these matters see the Court of Protection Rules 2017, SI 2017/1035, r 9.8. As to deputies see the Mental Capacity Act 2005 s 16 et seq; and MENTAL HEALTH AND CAPACITY vol 75 (2013) PARAS 724, 734. Where the Public Guardian is prevented by virtue of Sch 4 para 13(2) from registering an instrument creating an enduring power of attorney he must notify the person (or persons) who applied for registration of that fact: Lasting Powers of Attorney, Enduring Powers of Attorney and Public Guardian Regulations 2007, SI 2007/1253, reg 26(a).

7   Ie if, in the case of an application for registration, it appears from the application that there is no one to whom notice has been given under the Mental Capacity Act 2005 Sch 4 para 5 (see PARA 202) (Sch 4 para 13(6)(a)), the Public Guardian must not register the instrument (Sch 4 para 13(7)(a)) and must undertake such inquiries as he thinks appropriate in all the circumstances (Sch 4 para 13(7)(b)). If having complied with this requirement the Public Guardian is satisfied that one of the grounds of objection (see Sch 4 para 13(9); and PARA 205) is established the attorney may apply to the court for directions (Sch 4 para 13(8)(a)) and the Public Guardian must not register the instrument except in accordance with the court's directions (Sch 4 para 13(8)(b)). As to the giving of notices see PARA 199 note 9.

8   Ie within the applicable time limits, that is, before the end of the period of five weeks beginning with the date (or the latest date) on which the attorney gave notice under the Mental Capacity Act 2005 Sch 4 para 5 (see PARA 202) of an application for registration: Sch 4 para 13(4). A notice of objection under this provision must be given in writing, setting out the name and address of the objector, the name and address of the donor of the power (if different), the name and address of the attorney (or attorneys) (if known) and the ground for making the objection: Lasting Powers of Attorney, Enduring Powers of Attorney and Public Guardian Regulations 2007, SI 2007/1253, reg 25.

An application for the exercise of a power under the Enduring Powers of Attorney Act 1985 (repealed) which is pending immediately before 1 October 2007 (see note 1; and PARA 195) is to be treated, in so far as a corresponding power is exercisable under the Mental Capacity Act 2005 Sch 4, as an application for the exercise of that power, and accordingly a notice of objection to the registration of an instrument is to be treated as a notice of objection under these provisions: Sch 5 para 12(1), (2)(b).

9   As to the circumstances in which a notice of objection to registration is valid see PARA 205.

10 In these circumstances the Public Guardian must not register the instrument except in accordance with the court's directions: Mental Capacity Act 2005 Sch 4 para 13(5). In connection with this see also the Court of Protection Rules 2017, SI 2017/1035, r 24.4. Where the Public Guardian is prevented by virtue of Sch 4 para 13(5) from registering an instrument creating an enduring power of attorney he must notify the person (or persons) who applied for registration of that fact: Lasting Powers of Attorney, Enduring Powers of Attorney and Public Guardian Regulations 2007, SI 2007/1253, reg 26(b).

11 As to the registration of instruments where objections have been made see PARA 206.

12 The Public Guardian must not register an instrument where only a certified copy of the instrument is sent with the application, unless the applicant verifies that he cannot produce the original instrument because it has been lost or, as the case may be, destroyed: Lasting Powers of Attorney, Enduring Powers of Attorney and Public Guardian Regulations 2007, SI 2007/1253, reg 24(1A) (added by SI 2010/1063). Where the instrument to be registered which is sent with the application is neither the original instrument creating the power, nor a certified copy of it in relation to which the Lasting Powers of Attorney, Enduring Powers of Attorney and Public Guardian Regulations 2007, SI 2007/1253, reg 24(1A) has been complied with, the Public Guardian must not register the instrument unless the court directs him to do so: reg 24(2) (amended by SI 2010/1063). 'Certified copy', in relation to an enduring power of attorney, means a copy certified in accordance with the Powers of Attorney Act 1971 s 3 (see PARA 17): Lasting Powers of Attorney, Enduring Powers of Attorney and Public Guardian Regulations 2007, SI 2007/1253, regs 24(3), 27(2). Where the Public Guardian is prevented by virtue of reg 24(2) from registering an instrument creating an enduring power of attorney he must notify the person (or persons) who applied for registration of that fact: reg 26(d).

13 Lasting Powers of Attorney, Enduring Powers of Attorney and Public Guardian Regulations 2007, SI 2007/1253, reg 27(1)(a).

14 See note 12.

15 Lasting Powers of Attorney, Enduring Powers of Attorney and Public Guardian Regulations 2007, SI 2007/1253, reg 27(1)(b).

16 Mental Capacity Act 2005 Sch 4 para 14. As to the administration of the register by the Public Guardian see the Lasting Powers of Attorney, Enduring Powers of Attorney and Public Guardian Regulations 2007, SI 2007/1253, regs 30–32; and MENTAL HEALTH AND CAPACITY vol 75 (2013) PARA 753.

208. Registration notwithstanding failure to give notice.

If an application for the registration of an instrument creating an enduring power[1] is made[2] but the statutory requirements concerning the giving of notification of intended registration to the donor and family members[3] have not been complied with, the court[4] may, on the application of the attorney, direct the Public Guardian to register the instrument[5] if the court is satisfied that it was undesirable or impracticable for the attorney to give notice to that person[6] or that no useful purpose is likely to be served by giving him notice[7]. Provision is made for the registration of an instrument where it appears from the application that there is no one to whom notice of intended registration has been given[8].

1 Ie an enduring power of attorney for the purposes of the Mental Capacity Act 2005 Sch 4: see PARA 196 note 1. For the duty to register an enduring power see PARA 200 et seq.
  The provisions of Sch 4 referred to in this paragraph make provision for the operation of enduring powers of attorney after 1 October 2007 corresponding to the provision made in respect of the operation of those powers before that date by the Enduring Powers of Attorney Act 1985 s 6(3) (repealed). The power to create enduring powers of attorney under the Enduring Powers of Attorney Act 1985 ceased on 1 October 2007, but powers created before that date continue to have effect: see PARA 195.
2 Applications are made to the Public Guardian: see PARA 203. As to the Public Guardian see the Mental Capacity Act 2005 ss 57–60; and MENTAL HEALTH AND CAPACITY vol 75 (2013) PARA 751 et seq.
3 Ie the requirements of the Mental Capacity Act 2005 Sch 4 paras 4(3), 5–12 (see PARAS 201–203). As to the giving of notices see PARA 199 note 9.
4 Ie the Court of Protection: see PARA 199 note 6. For specific procedural provision in connection with these matters see the Court of Protection Rules 2017, SI 2017/1035, r 9.8.
5 Ie notwithstanding the non-compliance referred to in the text and specified as a prerequisite for registration by the Mental Capacity Act 2005 Sch 4 para 13(1) (see PARA 207).
6 Mental Capacity Act 2005 Sch 4 para 13(3)(a).
7 Mental Capacity Act 2005 Sch 4 para 13(3)(b).
8 See the Mental Capacity Act 2005 Sch 4 para 13(6)(a), (7); and PARA 207.

209. Proof of registration.

A document purporting to be an office copy of a registered instrument creating an enduring power[1] is evidence of the contents of the instrument and of the fact that it has been so registered[2]. A person requesting an office copy must pay the appropriate fee at the time the request is made[3].

1 Ie an enduring power of attorney for the purposes of the Mental Capacity Act 2005 Sch 4: see PARA 196 note 1. As to registration see Sch 4 para 13; and PARAS 207–208.
  The provisions of Sch 4 referred to in this paragraph make provision for the operation of enduring powers of attorney after 1 October 2007 corresponding to the provision made in respect of the operation of those powers before that date by the Enduring Powers of Attorney Act 1985 s 7(3), (4) (repealed). The power to create enduring powers of attorney under the Enduring Powers of Attorney Act 1985 ceased on 1 October 2007, but powers created before that date continue to have effect: see PARA 195.
2 Mental Capacity Act 2005 Sch 4 para 15(3). This is without prejudice to the Powers of Attorney Act 1971 s 3 (proof by certified copies; see PARA 17): Mental Capacity Act 2005 Sch 4 para 15(4).
3 See the Public Guardian (Fees etc) Regulations 2007, SI 2007/2051, reg 4A (added by SI 2009/514). The fees are set out in the Public Guardian (Fees etc) Regulations 2007, SI 2007/2051, Schedule (amended by SI 2009/514; SI 2011/2189; SI 2013/1748; SI 2017/503). 'Office copy' means a true copy of the original marked by the Public Guardian as being an office copy: Public Guardian (Fees etc) Regulations 2007, SI 2007/2051, reg 2 (definition added by SI 2009/514).

210. Effect of registration.

The effect of the registration of an instrument creating an enduring power[1] is that:

(1)   no revocation of the power by the donor is valid unless and until the court[2] confirms[3] the revocation[4];

(2)   no disclaimer of the power is valid unless and until the attorney gives notice[5] of it to the court[6]; and

(3)   the donor may not extend or restrict the scope of the authority conferred by the instrument and no instruction or consent given by him after registration may confer any right on, impose or confer any obligation on or create any liability of the attorney or other persons having notice of the instruction or consent[7].

These provisions apply for so long as the instrument is registered[8] whether or not the donor is for the time being mentally incapable[9].

1   Ie an enduring power of attorney for the purposes of the Mental Capacity Act 2005 Sch 4: see PARA 196 note 1. For the duty to register an enduring power see PARA 200 et seq.
        The provisions of Sch 4 referred to in this paragraph make provision for the operation of enduring powers of attorney after 1 October 2007 corresponding to the provision made in respect of the operation of those powers before that date by the Enduring Powers of Attorney Act 1985 ss 7(1), (2), 9(5) (repealed). The power to create enduring powers of attorney under the Enduring Powers of Attorney Act 1985 ceased on 1 October 2007, but powers created before that date continue to have effect: see PARA 195.
2   Ie the Court of Protection: see PARA 199 note 6.
3   Ie under the Mental Capacity Act 2005 Sch 4 para 16(3) (see PARA 212). For specific procedural provision in connection with these matters see the Court of Protection Rules 2017, SI 2017/1035, r 9.8.
4   Mental Capacity Act 2005 Sch 4 para 15(1)(a). For the purposes of the Powers of Attorney Act 1971 s 5 (protection where power is revoked: see PARA 194) in its application to an enduring power the revocation of which by the donor is by virtue of these provisions invalid unless and until confirmed by the court (ie under the Mental Capacity Act 2005 Sch 4 para 16), knowledge of the confirmation of the revocation is knowledge of the revocation of the power but knowledge of the unconfirmed revocation is not: Sch 4 para 18(5).
5   As to the giving of notices see PARA 199 note 9. As to the duty to give notice of disclaimer to the donor where the Mental Capacity Act 2005 Sch 4 para 15(1) and Sch 4 para 4(6) (see PARA 201) do not apply, see Sch 4 para 2(10); and PARA 199.
6   Mental Capacity Act 2005 Sch 4 para 15(1)(b).
7   Mental Capacity Act 2005 Sch 4 para 15(1)(c).
8   Ie under the Mental Capacity Act 2005 Sch 4 para 13 (see PARAS 207–208).
9   Mental Capacity Act 2005 Sch 4 para 15(2). As to the meaning of 'mentally incapable' and cognate expressions see PARA 196 note 2.

211. Cancellation of registration.

The Public Guardian[1] must cancel the registration of an instrument creating an enduring power[2]:

(1)   on receipt of a disclaimer signed by the attorney[3];
(2)   if satisfied that the power has been revoked by the death or bankruptcy of the donor or attorney or the making of a debt relief order or, if the attorney is a body corporate, by its winding up or dissolution[4];
(3)   on receipt of notification from the court[5] that the court has revoked the power[6];
(4)   on confirmation from the court that the donor has revoked the power[7].

1   As to the Public Guardian see the Mental Capacity Act 2005 ss 57–60; and MENTAL HEALTH AND CAPACITY vol 75 (2013) PARA 751 et seq.
2   Ie an enduring power of attorney for the purposes of the Mental Capacity Act 2005 Sch 4: see PARA 196 note 1.
        The provisions of Sch 4 referred to in this paragraph make provision for the operation of enduring powers of attorney after 1 October 2007; no corresponding provisions applied under the Enduring Powers of Attorney Act 1985 (repealed) in respect of the operation of those powers before that date. The power to create enduring powers of attorney under the Enduring Powers of Attorney Act 1985 ceased on 1 October 2007, but powers created before that date continue to have effect: see PARA 195.

3 Mental Capacity Act 2005 Sch 4 para 17(a). As to the revocation, suspension and disclaimer of enduring powers see PARA 199. In the case of joint attorneys, references in these provisions to 'the attorney' include references to any attorney under the power: Sch 4 para 21(6).
4 Mental Capacity Act 2005 Sch 4 para 17(b) (amended by SI 2012/2404). As to revocation following the bankruptcy of the donor or attorney see PARA 199. As to the meaning of 'bankruptcy' see PARA 197 note 3. As to debt relief orders under the Insolvency Act 1986 Pt 7A (ss 251A–251X) see BANKRUPTCY AND INDIVIDUAL INSOLVENCY vol 5 (2013) PARA 101 et seq.
5 Ie the Court of Protection: see PARA 199 note 6.
6 Mental Capacity Act 2005 Sch 4 para 17(c). For the court's power of revocation see PARA 213.
7 Mental Capacity Act 2005 Sch 4 para 17(d). For the donor's power of revocation see PARA 213.

(iv) Administration of Power and Protection of Parties

212. Interpretation and administration of enduring power.

Where an instrument creating an enduring power[1] has been registered[2] the court[3] may[4]:

(1)   determine any question as to the meaning or effect of the instrument[5];
(2)   give directions with respect to the management or disposal by the attorney[6] of the property and affairs of the donor[7];
(3)   give directions with respect to the rendering of accounts by the attorney and the production of records kept by him for accounting purposes[8];
(4)   give directions with respect to the remuneration or expenses of the attorney[9];
(5)   require the attorney to supply information or produce documents or things in his possession as attorney[10];
(6)   give any consent or authorisation to act which the attorney would have to obtain from a mentally capable[11] donor[12];
(7)   authorise the attorney to act so as to benefit himself or persons other than the donor, otherwise than in accordance with the statutory provisions[13] relating to the attorney's authority under the power[14]; and
(8)   relieve the attorney wholly or partly from any liability which he has or may have incurred on account of a breach of his duties as attorney[15].

1 Ie an enduring power of attorney for the purposes of the Mental Capacity Act 2005 Sch 4: see PARA 196 note 1.
   The provisions of Sch 4 referred to in this paragraph make provision for the operation of enduring powers of attorney after 1 October 2007 corresponding to the provision made in respect of the operation of those powers before that date by the Enduring Powers of Attorney Act 1985 s 8(1), (2), Sch 3 para 5 (repealed). The power to create enduring powers of attorney under the Enduring Powers of Attorney Act 1985 ceased on 1 October 2007, but powers created before that date continue to have effect: see PARA 195.
2 Ie under the Mental Capacity Act 2005 Sch 4 para 13 (see PARAS 207–208).
3 Ie the Court of Protection: see PARA 199 note 6. For specific procedural provision in connection with these matters see the Court of Protection Rules 2017, SI 2017/1035, r 9.8.
   An application for the exercise of a power under the Enduring Powers of Attorney Act 1985 (repealed) which is pending immediately before 1 October 2007 (see note 1; and PARA 195) is to be treated, in so far as a corresponding power is exercisable under the Mental Capacity Act 2005 Sch 4, as an application for the exercise of that power, and accordingly pending proceedings under the Enduring Powers of Attorney Act 1985 s 5 (repealed) are to be treated as proceedings on an application for the exercise by the court of a power which would become exercisable in relation to an instrument under these provisions on its registration: Mental Capacity Act 2005 Sch 5 para 12(1), (2)(c).
4 Mental Capacity Act 2005 Sch 4 para 16(1).
5 Mental Capacity Act 2005 Sch 4 para 16(2)(a).

6 For the purposes of joint attorneys (see PARA **197**), the references in the Mental Capacity Act 2005 Sch 4 para 16(2) to the attorney include references to any attorney under the power: Sch 4 para 21(4).
7 Mental Capacity Act 2005 Sch 4 para 16(2)(b)(i). This does not give the court power to direct the disposal of property of the donor by way of gift or in recognition of a moral obligation unaccompanied by any legal obligation: *Re R (Enduring Power of Attorney)* [1990] Ch 647, [1990] 2 All ER 893.
8 Mental Capacity Act 2005 Sch 4 para 16(2)(b)(ii).
9 Mental Capacity Act 2005 Sch 4 para 16(2)(b)(iii). Such directions may be given whether or not in default of or in accordance with any provision made by the instrument, and may include directions for the repayment of excessive remuneration or the payment of additional remuneration: Sch 4 para 16(2)(b)(iii).
10 Mental Capacity Act 2005 Sch 4 para 16(2)(c).
11 As to the meaning of 'mentally capable' and cognate expressions see PARA **196** note 2.
12 Mental Capacity Act 2005 Sch 4 para 16(2)(d).
13 Ie the Mental Capacity Act 2005 Sch 4 para 3(2), (3) (see PARA **196**).
14 Mental Capacity Act 2005 Sch 4 para 16(2)(e). The exercise of this power is subject to any conditions or restrictions contained in the instrument: Sch 4 para 16(2)(e).
15 Mental Capacity Act 2005 Sch 4 para 16(2)(f).

213. Revocation of the power at request of donor.

Where an instrument creating an enduring power[1] has been registered[2] and the court[3] is satisfied that the donor has done whatever is necessary in law to effect an express revocation of the power[4] and was mentally capable[5] of revoking a power of attorney when he did so (whether or not he is so when the court considers the application)[6], the court must, on an application made for the purpose by or on behalf of the donor, confirm the revocation of the power[7].

1 Ie an enduring power of attorney for the purposes of the Mental Capacity Act 2005 Sch 4: see PARA **196** note 1.
   The provisions of Sch 4 referred to in this paragraph make provision for the operation of enduring powers of attorney after 1 October 2007 corresponding to the provision made in respect of the operation of those powers before that date by the Enduring Powers of Attorney Act 1985 ss 8(1), (3), (4)(a) (repealed). The power to create enduring powers of attorney under the Enduring Powers of Attorney Act 1985 ceased on 1 October 2007, but powers created before that date continue to have effect: see PARA **195**.
2 Ie under the Mental Capacity Act 2005 Sch 4 para 13 (see PARAS **207–208**).
3 Ie the Court of Protection: see PARA **199** note 6. For specific procedural provision in connection with these matters see the Court of Protection Rules 2017, SI 2017/1035, r 9.8.
4 Mental Capacity Act 2005 Sch 4 para 16(3)(a).
5 As to the meaning of 'mentally capable' and cognate expressions see PARA **196** note 2. See also *Re KJP* [2016] EWCOP 6, [2016] WTLR 687.
6 Mental Capacity Act 2005 Sch 4 para 16(3)(b).
7 Mental Capacity Act 2005 Sch 4 para 16(3). The court must direct the Public Guardian to cancel the registration of an instrument creating an enduring power on confirming the revocation of the power under these provisions: see Sch 4 para 16(4)(a); and PARA **214**. The Public Guardian must cancel the registration of an instrument creating an enduring power on receipt of notification from the court that the court or the donor has revoked the power: see Sch 4 para 17(c), (d); and PARA **211**. As to the protection of the attorney and third persons in respect of acts done pursuant to a power so revoked see PARA **217**. As to the Public Guardian see ss 57–60; and MENTAL HEALTH AND CAPACITY vol 75 (2013) PARA 751 et seq.

214. Cancellation of the power.

The court[1] must direct the Public Guardian[2] to cancel the registration of an instrument creating an enduring power[3]:

(1)   on confirming[4] the revocation of the power[5];
(2)   on giving a direction[6] that the power is to be revoked[7];
(3)   on being satisfied that the donor is and is likely to remain mentally capable[8];

(4)   on being satisfied that the power has expired or has been revoked by the mental incapacity of the attorney[9];

(5)   on being satisfied that the power was not a valid and subsisting enduring power when registration was effected[10];

(6)   on being satisfied that fraud or undue pressure was used to induce the donor to create the power[11]; or

(7)   on being satisfied that, having regard to all the circumstances and in particular the attorney's relationship to or connection with the donor, the attorney is unsuitable to be the donor's attorney[12].

If the court directs the cancellation of the registration of an instrument in any of the circumstances described above (other than on being satisfied that the donor is and is likely to remain mentally capable[13]) the instrument must, unless the court otherwise directs, be delivered up to the Public Guardian to be cancelled[14]. If the court directs the Public Guardian to cancel the registration of an instrument on being satisfied that fraud or undue pressure was used to induce the donor to create the power[15] or that the attorney is unsuitable[16], it must by order revoke the power created by the instrument[17].

1 Ie the Court of Protection: see PARA 199 note 6. For specific procedural provision in connection with these matters see the Court of Protection Rules 2017, SI 2017/1035, r 9.8.

2 As to the Public Guardian see the Mental Capacity Act 2005 ss 57–60; and MENTAL HEALTH AND CAPACITY vol 75 (2013) PARA 751 et seq.

3 Ie an enduring power of attorney for the purposes of the Mental Capacity Act 2005 Sch 4: see PARA 196 note 1. For the duty to register an enduring power see PARA 200 et seq.

    The provisions of Sch 4 referred to in this paragraph make provision for the operation of enduring powers of attorney after 1 October 2007 corresponding to the provision made in respect of the operation of those powers before that date by the Enduring Powers of Attorney Act 1985 s 8(1), (4)–(6), Sch 3 para 6 (repealed). The power to create enduring powers of attorney under the Enduring Powers of Attorney Act 1985 ceased on 1 October 2007, but powers created before that date continue to have effect: see PARA 195.

4 Ie under the Mental Capacity Act 2005 Sch 4 para 16(3) (see PARA 213).

5 Mental Capacity Act 2005 Sch 4 para 16(4)(a).

6 Ie under the Mental Capacity Act 2005 Sch 4 para 2(9) (see PARA 199).

7 Mental Capacity Act 2005 Sch 4 para 16(4)(b). See eg *Public Guardian v JD* [2015] EWCOP 26, sub nom *Re ED* [2015] All ER (D) 147 (Apr) (attorneys unsuitable because of mutual hostility and dishonesty).

8 Mental Capacity Act 2005 Sch 4 para 16(4)(c). As to the meaning of 'mentally capable' and cognate expressions see PARA 196 note 2.

9 Mental Capacity Act 2005 Sch 4 para 16(4)(d). For the purposes of joint attorneys (see PARA 197) the references in Sch 4 para 16(4) to 'the attorney' include references to any attorney under the power: Sch 4 para 21(5).

10 Mental Capacity Act 2005 Sch 4 para 16(4)(e). As to the characteristics of a valid enduring power see PARAS 197–198.

11 Mental Capacity Act 2005 Sch 4 para 16(4)(f).

12 Mental Capacity Act 2005 Sch 4 para 16(4)(g). As to 'unsuitability' see *Re W (Enduring Power of Attorney)* [2000] Ch 343, [2000] 1 All ER 175, [2000] 3 WLR 45; *Re E (Enduring Power of Attorney)* [2001] Ch 364, [2000] 3 All ER 1004, [2000] 3 WLR 1974; *Re F (Enduring Power of Attorney)* [2004] EWHC 725 (Ch), [2004] 3 All ER 277; *Re RG* [2015] EWCOP 2, [2015] All ER (D) 27 (Feb). For a case where the question of the power to cancel registration on the grounds of unsuitability came before the court see *Re C (Power of Attorney)* [2000] 2 FLR 1, CA. As to intervention by the Public Guardian on grounds of unsuitability see PARA 215.

13 Ie under the Mental Capacity Act 2005 Sch 4 para 16(4)(c) (see the text and note 8).

14 Mental Capacity Act 2005 Sch 4 para 16(6). Where a person is required by or under the Mental Capacity Act 2005 to deliver up to the Public Guardian an instrument registered as an enduring power of attorney, an office copy of that registered instrument or a certified copy of that registered instrument, and the document has been lost or destroyed (Lasting Powers of Attorney, Enduring Powers of Attorney and Public Guardian Regulations 2007, SI 2007/1253, reg 29(1)), the person required to deliver up the document must provide to the Public Guardian in writing either the date

of the loss or destruction and the circumstances in which it occurred (if known) or a statement of when he last had the document in his possession (reg 29(2)).

15 Ie under the matters referred to in the Mental Capacity Act 2005 Sch 4 para 16(4)(f) (see the text and note 11).

16 Ie under the matters referred to in the Mental Capacity Act 2005 Sch 4 para 16(4)(g) (see the text and note 12).

17 Mental Capacity Act 2005 Sch 4 para 16(5).

215. Intervention by Public Guardian.

Where it appears to the Public Guardian[1] that there are circumstances suggesting that, having regard to all the circumstances (and in particular the attorney's relationship to or connection with the donor) the attorney under a registered enduring power of attorney[2] may be unsuitable to be the donor's attorney, he may require the attorney:

(1)   to provide specified information or information of a specified description[3]; or

(2)   to produce specified documents or documents of a specified description[4],

and may require any information so provided to be verified, and any document so produced to be authenticated, in such manner as he may reasonably require[5].

The Public Guardian may also direct a Court of Protection Visitor[6] to visit an attorney under a registered enduring power of attorney, or to visit the donor of such a power, and to make a report to the Public Guardian on such matters as he may direct[7], and also has power to deal with representations (including complaints) about the way in which an attorney under a registered enduring power is exercising his powers[8].

1 As to the Public Guardian see the Mental Capacity Act 2005 ss 57–60; and MENTAL HEALTH AND CAPACITY vol 75 (2013) PARA 751 et seq.

2 Ie an enduring power of attorney for the purposes of the Mental Capacity Act 2005 Sch 4: see PARA 196 note 1. For the duty to register an enduring power see PARA 200 et seq. The power to create enduring powers of attorney under the Enduring Powers of Attorney Act 1985 ceased on 1 October 2007, but powers created before that date continue to have effect: see PARA 195.

3 Lasting Powers of Attorney, Enduring Powers of Attorney and Public Guardian Regulations 2007, SI 2007/1253, reg 47(1), (2)(a). 'Specified' means specified in a notice in writing given to the attorney by the Public Guardian: reg 47(5). The information or documents must be provided or produced before the end of such reasonable period as may be specified (reg 47(3)(a)) and at such place as may be specified (reg 47(3)(b)).

4 Lasting Powers of Attorney, Enduring Powers of Attorney and Public Guardian Regulations 2007, SI 2007/1253, reg 47(2)(b). See note 3.

5 Lasting Powers of Attorney, Enduring Powers of Attorney and Public Guardian Regulations 2007, SI 2007/1253, reg 47(4).

6 As to Court of Protection Visitors see the Mental Capacity Act 2005 s 61; and MENTAL HEALTH AND CAPACITY vol 75 (2013) PARA 748.

7 Lasting Powers of Attorney, Enduring Powers of Attorney and Public Guardian Regulations 2007, SI 2007/1253, reg 48(1)(a) (reg 48(1) renumbered by SI 2010/1063). The functions conferred by the Lasting Powers of Attorney, Enduring Powers of Attorney and Public Guardian Regulations 2007, SI 2007/1253SI 2007/1253, reg 48(1) may be discharged in co-operation with any other person who has functions in relation to the care or treatment of the donor: reg 48(2) (added by SI 2010/1063).

8 Lasting Powers of Attorney, Enduring Powers of Attorney and Public Guardian Regulations 2007, SI 2007/1253, reg 48(1)(b) (as renumbered: see note 7). See note 7.

216. Acts done in pursuance of invalid power.

Where an instrument which did not create a valid enduring power of attorney[1] has been registered[2], an attorney who acts in pursuance of the power does not incur any liability, either to the donor or to any other person, by reason of the non-existence of the power unless at the time of acting he knows that:

(1)   the instrument did not create a valid enduring power[3];

(2)   an event has occurred which, if the instrument had created a valid enduring power, would have had the effect of revoking the power[4]; or

(3)   if the instrument had created a valid enduring power, the power would have expired before the time of acting[5];

and any transaction between the attorney and another person is valid in favour of that person as if the power had then been in existence, unless at the time of the transaction that person had knowledge of any of the matters previously mentioned above[6].

1   Ie an enduring power of attorney for the purposes of the Mental Capacity Act 2005 Sch 4: see PARA 196 note 1. As to the characteristics of a valid enduring power see PARAS 197–198.
        The provisions of Sch 4 referred to in this paragraph make provision for the operation of enduring powers of attorney after 1 October 2007 corresponding to the provision made in respect of the operation of those powers before that date by the Enduring Powers of Attorney Act 1985 s 9(1)–(4), (7) (repealed). The power to create enduring powers of attorney under the Enduring Powers of Attorney Act 1985 ceased on 1 October 2007, but powers created before that date continue to have effect: see PARA 195.
2   Ie under the Mental Capacity Act 2005 Sch 4 para 13 (see PARA 207): Sch 4 para 18(1). These provisions apply whether or not the registration has been cancelled at the time of the act or transaction in question: Sch 4 para 18(1).
3   Mental Capacity Act 2005 Sch 4 para 18(2)(a).
4   Mental Capacity Act 2005 Sch 4 para 18(2)(b).
5   Mental Capacity Act 2005 Sch 4 para 18(2)(c).
6   Mental Capacity Act 2005 Sch 4 para 18(3). Where the interest of a purchaser depends on whether a transaction between the attorney and another person was valid by virtue of Sch 4 para 18(3), it is conclusively presumed in favour of the purchaser that the transaction was valid if the transaction between that person and the attorney was completed within 12 months of the date on which the instrument was registered (Sch 4 para 18(4)(a)) and that person makes a statutory declaration, before or within three months after the completion of the purchase, that he had no reason at the time of the transaction to doubt that the attorney had authority to dispose of the property which was the subject of the transaction (Sch 4 para 18(4)(b)). As to the meanings of 'purchaser' and 'purchase' see the Law of Property Act 1925 s 205(1); and LANDLORD AND TENANT vol 62 (2016) PARA 83; REAL PROPERTY AND REGISTRATION vol 87 (2017) PARA 656; definition applied by the Mental Capacity Act 2005 s 64(1).

217.   Acts done in pursuance of revoked power.

Where an instrument in the prescribed form[1] creates a power which is not a valid enduring power[2] and the power is revoked by the donor's mental incapacity[3], then, whether or not the instrument has been registered[4]:

(1)   an attorney who acts in pursuance of the power does not, by reason of the revocation, incur any liability either to the donor or to any other person[5]; and

(2)   any transaction between the attorney and another person is valid in favour of that person as if the power had then been in existence[6],

unless at the time of acting or, as the case may be, the time of the transaction the attorney or the other person knows that the instrument did not create a valid enduring power and that the donor had become mentally incapable[7].

1   As to the prescribed form for these purposes see PARA 198 note 2.
2   Ie a valid enduring power of attorney for the purposes of the Mental Capacity Act 2005 Sch 4: see PARA 196 note 1. As to the characteristics of a valid enduring power see PARAS 197–198.
        The provisions of Sch 4 referred to in this paragraph make provision for the operation of enduring powers of attorney after 1 October 2007 corresponding to the provision made in respect of the operation of those powers before that date by the Enduring Powers of Attorney Act 1985

Sch 2 (repealed). The power to create enduring powers of attorney under the Enduring Powers of Attorney Act 1985 ceased on 1 October 2007, but powers created before that date continue to have effect: see PARA 195.

3 As to the meaning of 'mental incapacity' and cognate expressions see PARA 196 note 2. As to revocation on these grounds see PARA 213.

4 Mental Capacity Act 2005 Sch 4 para 19(1).

5 Mental Capacity Act 2005 Sch 4 para 19(2).

6 Mental Capacity Act 2005 Sch 4 para 19(3).

7 Mental Capacity Act 2005 Sch 4 para 19(2), (3). Where the interest of a purchaser depends on whether a transaction between the attorney and another person was valid by virtue of Sch 4 para 19(3), it is conclusively presumed in favour of the purchaser that the transaction was valid if the transaction between that person and the attorney was completed within 12 months of the date on which the instrument was registered (Sch 4 paras 18(4)(a), 19(4)) and that person makes a statutory declaration, before or within three months after the completion of the purchase, that he had no reason at the time of the transaction to doubt that the attorney had authority to dispose of the property which was the subject of the transaction (Sch 4 para 18(4)(b)). As to the meanings of 'purchaser' and 'purchase' see the Law of Property Act 1925 s 205(1); and REAL PROPERTY AND REGISTRATION vol 87 (2017) PARA 656; definition applied by the Mental Capacity Act 2005 s 64(1).

(3) LASTING POWERS OF ATTORNEY

(i) Nature and Effect of Power

218. Effect of lasting power.

A lasting power of attorney[1] is a power of attorney under which the donor confers on the donee or donees authority to make decisions[2] about all or any of the donor's personal welfare, property[3] and affairs or specified matters concerning his personal welfare, property and affairs, and which includes authority to make such decisions in circumstances where the donor no longer has capacity[4].

Where a lasting power authorises the donee[5] to make decisions about the donor's personal welfare, the authority:

(1)   does not extend to making such decisions in circumstances other than those where the donor lacks, or the donee reasonably believes that the donor lacks, capacity[6];

(2)   is subject to the statutory provisions concerning advance decisions to refuse treatment[7]; and

(3)   extends to giving or refusing consent to the carrying out or continuation of a treatment[8] by a person providing health care for the donor[9].

A lasting power also does not authorise the donee[10] to do an act that is intended to restrain the donor[11] unless:

(a)   the donor lacks, or the donee reasonably believes that he lacks, capacity in relation to the matter in question[12];

(b)   the donee reasonably believes that it is necessary to do the act in order to prevent harm to the donor[13]; and

(c)   the act is a proportionate response to the likelihood of the donor suffering harm[14] and the seriousness of that harm[15].

Where a lasting power confers authority to make decisions about the donor's property and affairs, it does not authorise a donee[16] to dispose of the donor's property by making gifts[17] other than:

(i)   on customary occasions[18] to persons (including himself) who are related to or connected with the donor[19]; or

(ii)   to any charity to whom the donor made or might have been expected to make gifts[20],

provided that the value of any such gift is not unreasonable having regard to all the circumstances and, in particular, the size of the donor's estate[21].

An instrument which purports to create a lasting power of attorney but does not comply with the requirements concerning the authority and appointment of the donee[22] or the making and registration of instruments[23] confers no authority[24]. Moreover, the authority conferred by a lasting power is subject to the statutory provisions relating to persons who lack capacity[25] (with particular regard to the principles of that legislation[26] and the provisions concerned with the determination of a person's best interests[27]) and any conditions or restrictions in the instrument conferring the power[28].

1   The power to confer lasting powers of attorney under the Mental Capacity Act 2005 ss 9–14, Sch 1 (see the text and notes 2–28; and PARA 219 et seq) came into effect on 1 October 2007: see the Mental Capacity Act 2005 (Commencement No 2) Order 2007, SI 2007/1897. It replaced the power to confer enduring powers of attorney under the Enduring Powers of Attorney Act 1985 (repealed), which ceased on that date: see further PARA 195. Although no new enduring powers of attorney could be created under the Enduring Powers of Attorney Act 1985 after 1 October 2007, enduring powers created before that date continue to have effect: see PARA 195.

2   References to 'making decisions', in relation to a donee of a lasting power of attorney, include, where appropriate, acting on decisions made: Mental Capacity Act 2005 s 64(2).

3   As to the meaning of 'property' see PARA 196 note 11.

4   Mental Capacity Act 2005 s 9(1). As to the meaning of 'capacity' and cognate expressions see PARA 196 note 2.

     When making investments, an attorney acting for an incapacitated donor, has fiduciary obligations. Although the Trustee Act 2000 s 4 (see TRUSTS AND POWERS vol 98 (2013) PARA 454) does not expressly apply to attorneys, it is recommended that attorneys have regard to the standard investment criteria and the requirement to seek proper financial advice. They should also have regard to the guidance issued by the Office of the Public Guardian. All investments must be made in the donor's name, unless that is not possible, in which case there ought to be a declaration of trust or some other formal record acknowledging the donor's beneficial interest. The donor's money and property must be kept separate from the attorney's and from anyone else's: *Public Guardian v C* [2013] EWHC 2965 (COP), sub nom *Re Buckley* [2013] WTLR 373.

5   Or, if more than one, any of them: Mental Capacity Act 2005 s 11(7).

6   Mental Capacity Act 2005 s 11(7)(a).

7   Mental Capacity Act 2005 s 11(7)(b). The statutory provisions concerning advance decisions to refuse treatment are ss 24–26 (see MENTAL HEALTH AND CAPACITY vol 75 (2013) PARAS 624–626 et seq).

8   'Treatment' includes a diagnostic or other procedure: Mental Capacity Act 2005 s 64(1).

9   Mental Capacity Act 2005 s 11(7)(c). This does not, however, authorise the giving or refusing of consent to the carrying out or continuation of life-sustaining treatment, unless the instrument contains express provision to that effect (s 11(8)(a)) and is subject to any conditions or restrictions in the instrument (s 11(8)(b)). 'Life-sustaining treatment' means treatment which in the view of a person providing health care for the person concerned is necessary to sustain life: ss 4(10), 64(1).

10 Or, if more than one, any of them: Mental Capacity Act 2005 s 11(1).

11 For these purposes the donee restrains the donor if he uses, or threatens to use, force to secure the doing of an act which the donor resists (Mental Capacity Act 2005 s 11(5)(a)) or restricts the donor's liberty of movement, whether or not the donor resists (s 11(5)(b)), or if he authorises another person to do any of those things. For controls on deprivation of liberty see the Mental Capacity Act 2005 ss 4A, 4B, 16A; and MENTAL HEALTH AND CAPACITY vol 75 (2013) PARAS 648, 650, 726.

12 Mental Capacity Act 2005 s 11(2).

13 Mental Capacity Act 2005 s 11(3).

14 Mental Capacity Act 2005 s 11(4)(a).

15 Mental Capacity Act 2005 s 11(4)(b).

16 Or, if more than one, any of them: Mental Capacity Act 2005 s 12(1).

17 Mental Capacity Act 2005 s 12(1).
18 'Customary occasion' means the occasion or anniversary of a birth, a marriage or the formation of a civil partnership or any other occasion on which presents are customarily given within families or among friends or associates: Mental Capacity Act 2005 s 12(3). Marriage includes marriage of a same-sex couple: see Marriage (Same Sex Couples) Act 2013 Sch 3 para 1(1)(a), (2), (3); and MATRIMONIAL AND CIVIL PARTNERSHIP LAW vol 72 (2015) PARA 1 et seq.
19 Mental Capacity Act 2005 s 12(2)(a). The power to make limited gifts conferred by s 12(2) is subject to any conditions or restrictions in the instrument conferring the lasting power: s 12(4). The court (ie the Court of Protection: see PARA 199 note 6) may authorise the making of gifts which are not within s 12(2): see s 23(4); and PARA 236.
20 Mental Capacity Act 2005 s 12(2)(b). See note 19.
21 Mental Capacity Act 2005 s 12(2). See eg *Re PC* [2014] EWCOP 41, [2015] WTLR 465, [2014] All ER (D) 64 (Nov) (attorneys made excessive gifts to themselves).
22 Ie the provisions of the Mental Capacity Act 2005 s 9 (see the text and notes 1–4, 23–28) and s 10 (see PARA 219).
23 Ie the Mental Capacity Act 2005 Sch 1 paras 1–3 (making instruments) (see PARAS 220–223), Sch 1 paras 4–16 (registration) (see PARAS 226–234).
24 Mental Capacity Act 2005 s 9(3).
25 Ie the provisions of the Mental Capacity Act 2005 (see MENTAL HEALTH AND CAPACITY vol 75 (2013) PARA 601 et seq).
26 Ie the Mental Capacity Act 2005 s 1 (see MENTAL HEALTH AND CAPACITY vol 75 (2013) PARA 601).
27 Ie the Mental Capacity Act 2005 s 4 (see MENTAL HEALTH AND CAPACITY vol 75 (2013) PARA 606).
28 Mental Capacity Act 2005 s 9(4).

219. Characteristics of a lasting power.

A donee of a lasting power of attorney[1] must be an individual who has reached the age of 18[2], unless the power relates only to the donor's property[3] and affairs, in which case the donee may be either such an individual or a trust corporation[4]. An individual who is bankrupt or is a person in relation to whom a debt relief order is made[5] may not be appointed as donee of a lasting power of attorney in relation to the donor's property and affairs[6].

An instrument used to create a lasting power of attorney cannot give the donee[7] power to appoint a substitute or successor[8], although that instrument may itself appoint a person to replace the donee[9] where disclaimer, death, bankruptcy, partnership break-up or incapacity[10] has the effect of terminating the donee's appointment[11]. Provision is also made for circumstances where two or more persons are appointed to act as donees: an instrument appointing two or more persons may appoint them to act jointly, jointly and severally or jointly in respect of some matters and jointly and severally in respect of others[12]. If the donees are to act jointly, a failure as respects one of them to comply with the requirements as to the status of the donee[13] or the making and registration of instruments[14] prevents a lasting power of attorney from being created[15]. If they are to act jointly and severally, such a failure as respects one of them prevents the appointment taking effect in his case[16] but does not prevent a lasting power of attorney from being created in the case of the other or others[17].

A lasting power is not created unless these provisions[18] and the statutory requirements as to the making and registration of instruments[19] are complied with[20] and at the time when the donor executes the instrument he has reached the age of 18 and has capacity[21] to execute it[22]. The court[23] may determine any question relating to whether one or more of the requirements for the creation of a lasting power of attorney have been met[24].

1 As to the meaning of 'lasting power of attorney' see PARA 218.

2　Mental Capacity Act 2005 s 10(1)(a).
3　As to the meaning of 'property' see PARA **196** note 11.
4　Mental Capacity Act 2005 s 10(1)(b). As to the meaning of 'trust corporation' see PARA **197** note 4.
5　As to references in the Mental Capacity Act 2005 to the 'bankruptcy' of an individual see PARA **197** note 3. As to debt relief orders under the Insolvency Act 1986 Pt 7A (ss 251A–251X) see BANKRUPTCY AND INDIVIDUAL INSOLVENCY vol 5 (2013) PARA 101 et seq.
6　Mental Capacity Act 2005 s 10(2) (amended by SI 2012/2404).
7　Or, if more than one, any of them: Mental Capacity Act 2005 s 10(8)(a).
8　Mental Capacity Act 2005 s 10(8)(a).
9　Or, if more than one, any of them: Mental Capacity Act 2005 s 10(8)(b).
10　Ie an event mentioned in the Mental Capacity Act 2005 s 13(6)(a)–(d) (see PARA **235**).
11　Mental Capacity Act 2005 s 10(8)(b). A replacement attorney can only replace an original attorney in accordance with s 10(8)(b) and cannot replace a replacement attorney: *Public Guardian v Boff* [2013] WTLR 1349, Ct of Protection.
12　Mental Capacity Act 2005 s 10(3), (4). To the extent to which it does not specify whether they are to act jointly or jointly and severally, the instrument is to be assumed to appoint them to act jointly: s 10(5).
13　Ie the Mental Capacity Act 2005 s 10(1), (2) (see the text and notes 1–6).
14　Ie the Mental Capacity Act 2005 Sch 1 paras 1–3 (making instruments) (see PARAS **220–223**), Sch 1 paras 4–16 (registration) (see PARAS **226–234**).
15　Mental Capacity Act 2005 s 10(6).
16　Mental Capacity Act 2005 s 10(7)(a).
17　Mental Capacity Act 2005 s 10(7)(b).
18　Ie the Mental Capacity Act 2005 s 10 (see the text and notes 1–17).
19　Ie the Mental Capacity Act 2005 Sch 1 paras 1–3 (making instruments) (see PARAS **220–223**), Sch 1 paras 4–16 (registration) (see PARAS **226–234**).
20　Mental Capacity Act 2005 s 9(2)(a), (b).
21　As to the meaning of 'capacity' and cognate expressions see PARA **196** note 2.
22　Mental Capacity Act 2005 s 9(2)(c).
23　Ie the Court of Protection: see PARA **199** note 6.
24　See PARA **237**.

(ii)　Creation, Revocation and Disclaimer of Power

220.　Form of instrument.

An instrument conferring a lasting power of attorney[1] must be in the form prescribed by regulations[2]. Two different forms are prescribed as the forms which, in the circumstances to which they apply, are to be used for instruments intended to create a lasting power[3], one to be used for an instrument intended to create a property and affairs power[4] and the other for an instrument intended to create a personal welfare power[5]. The instrument must include the information contained in the form which appears under the heading 'Your legal rights and responsibilities' and concerns the purpose of the instrument and the effect of a lasting power[6].

If an instrument differs in an immaterial respect in form from the prescribed form, it is to be treated by the Public Guardian[7] as sufficient in point of form and expression[8]; moreover the court[9] may declare that an instrument which is not in the prescribed form is to be treated as if it were, if it is satisfied that the persons executing the instrument intended it to create a lasting power of attorney[10]. Provision is also made for the use of Welsh language forms[11].

An instrument which does not comply with these provisions does not create a lasting power of attorney[12].

1　As to the meaning of 'lasting power of attorney' see PARA **218**.
2　Mental Capacity Act 2005 Sch 1 para 1(1)(a), (3).

3   Mental Capacity Act 2005 Sch 1 para 1(2)(a); Lasting Powers of Attorney, Enduring Powers of Attorney and Public Guardian Regulations 2007, SI 2007/1253, reg 5.
4   See the Lasting Powers of Attorney, Enduring Powers of Attorney and Public Guardian Regulations 2007, SI 2007/1253, Sch 1 Pt 1 (substituted by SI 2015/899).
5   See the Lasting Powers of Attorney, Enduring Powers of Attorney and Public Guardian Regulations 2007, SI 2007/1253, Sch 1 Pt 2 (substituted by SI 2015/899).
6   Mental Capacity Act 2005 Sch 1 paras 1(1)(b), 2(1)(a); Lasting Powers of Attorney, Enduring Powers of Attorney and Public Guardian Regulations 2007, SI 2007/1253, reg 2(1) (amended by SI 2015/899).
7   As to the Public Guardian see the Mental Capacity Act 2005 ss 57–60; and MENTAL HEALTH AND CAPACITY vol 75 (2013) PARA 751 et seq.
8   Mental Capacity Act 2005 Sch 1 para 3(1). See eg *Re Lane* [2012] MHLO 15 (LPA) COP (old forms differed in immaterial way from new ones).
9   Ie the Court of Protection: see PARA 199 note 6.
10 Mental Capacity Act 2005 Sch 1 para 3(2). See eg *Re Gunn* [2012] MHLO 97 (LPA), COP; *Re Helmsley* (2009) COP 30/11/09; *Re Ker* (2009) COP 21/9/09; *Re Nazran* (2008) COP 27/6/08; but see *Re Murdoch* (2009) COP 30/10/09 (errors in execution too fundamental to enable registration of instrument).
11 See the Lasting Powers of Attorney, Enduring Powers of Attorney and Public Guardian Regulations 2007, SI 2007/1253, reg 3(1)(a).
12 See the Mental Capacity Act 2005 s 9(2)(b); and PARA 219.

221. Statements to be included in instrument.

An instrument conferring a lasting power of attorney[1] must include, in addition to the prescribed information[2], two statements by the donor:

(1)   to the effect that he has read the prescribed information or a prescribed part of it (or has had it read to him)[3] and intends the authority conferred under the instrument to include authority to make decisions[4] on his behalf in circumstances where he no longer has capacity[5]; and

(2)   either naming a person or persons whom the donor wishes to be notified of any application for the registration of the instrument[6] or stating that there are no persons whom he wishes to be notified of any such application[7].

The instrument must also include a statement by the donee[8] to the effect that he has read the prescribed information or a prescribed part of it (or has had it read to him)[9] and understands the duties imposed on a donee of a lasting power by the principles of the legislation relating to persons who lack capacity[10] and under the provisions concerned with the determination of a person's best interests[11].

An instrument which does not comply with these provisions does not create a lasting power of attorney[12].

1   As to the meaning of 'lasting power of attorney' see PARA 218.
2   As to the prescribed information see PARA 220.
3   Mental Capacity Act 2005 Sch 1 paras 1(1)(b), 2(1)(b)(i). See *Re JL (Revocation of Lasting Power of Attorney)* [2014] EWCOP 36, [2014] All ER (D) 131 (Oct).
4   As to references to the making of decisions see PARA 218 note 2.
5   Mental Capacity Act 2005 Sch 1 para 2(1)(b)(ii). As to the meaning of 'capacity' and cognate expressions see PARA 196 note 2.
6   Mental Capacity Act 2005 Sch 1 para 2(1)(c)(i). As to registration see PARA 226 et seq. The persons who may be named persons do not include a person who is appointed as donee under the instrument (Sch 1 para 2(3)), and the maximum number of people to notify that the donor of a lasting power of attorney may specify in the instrument intended to create the power is five (Sch 1 para 2(2)(a); Lasting Powers of Attorney, Enduring Powers of Attorney and Public Guardian Regulations 2007, SI 2007/1253, reg 6 (amended by SI 2015/899)).
7   Mental Capacity Act 2005 Sch 1 para 2(1)(c)(ii).
8   Or, if more than one, each of them: Mental Capacity Act 2005 Sch 1 para 2(1)(d).
9   Mental Capacity Act 2005 Sch 1 para 2(1)(d)(i).

10 Ie by the Mental Capacity Act 2005 s 1 (see MENTAL HEALTH AND CAPACITY vol 75 (2013) PARA 601).

11 Mental Capacity Act 2005 Sch 1 para 2(1)(d)(ii). For the provisions concerned with the determination of such a person's best interests see s 4; and MENTAL HEALTH AND CAPACITY vol 75 (2013) PARA 606.

12 See the Mental Capacity Act 2005 s 9(2)(b); and PARA 219.

222. Certificate to be included in instrument.

An instrument conferring a lasting power of attorney[1] must include, in addition to the prescribed information[2] and the donor's and donee's statements[3], an 'LPA certificate'[4], that is, a certificate that, in the opinion of the person making the certificate, at the time when the donor executes the instrument:

(1)   the donor understands the purpose of the instrument and the scope of the authority conferred under it[5];

(2)   no fraud or undue pressure is being used to induce the donor to create a lasting power of attorney[6]; and

(3)   there is nothing else which would prevent a lasting power of attorney from being created by the instrument[7].

An LPA certificate may be given by a person chosen by the donor as being someone who has known him personally for the period of at least two years which ends immediately before the date on which that person signs the certificate[8] or a person so chosen who, on account of his professional skills and expertise, reasonably considers that he is competent to make the judgments necessary to certify the matters set out above[9]. The certificate may not be given by a person appointed as donee under the instrument[10] or any other similar power[11] or by specified family members and persons professionally associated with the donor[12].

An instrument which does not comply with these provisions does not create a lasting power of attorney[13].

1   As to the meaning of 'lasting power of attorney' see PARA 218.
2   As to the prescribed information see PARA 220.
3   As to the required statements see PARA 221.
4   Provision is made requiring an LPA certificate to be made in the form, and to include information, prescribed by regulations: Mental Capacity Act 2005 Sch 1 para 2(5). At the date at which the law no such form or information had been prescribed.
5   Mental Capacity Act 2005 Sch 1 para 2(1)(e)(i).
6   Mental Capacity Act 2005 Sch 1 para 2(1)(e)(ii).
7   Mental Capacity Act 2005 Sch 1 para 2(1)(e)(iii).
8   Lasting Powers of Attorney, Enduring Powers of Attorney and Public Guardian Regulations 2007, SI 2007/1253, reg 8(1)(a).
9   Lasting Powers of Attorney, Enduring Powers of Attorney and Public Guardian Regulations 2007, SI 2007/1253, reg 8(1)(b). Examples of such a person are a registered health care professional, a barrister, solicitor or advocate called or admitted in any part of the United Kingdom, a registered social worker or an independent mental capacity advocate: reg 8(2). 'Registered health care professional' means a person who is a member of a profession regulated by a body mentioned in the National Health Service Reform and Health Care Professions Act 2002 s 25(3) (see MEDICAL PROFESSIONS vol 74 (2011) PARA 48); and 'registered social worker' means a person registered as a social worker in a register maintained by the Health and Care Professions Council, Social Care Wales, the Scottish Social Services Council or the Northern Ireland Social Care Council (see SOCIAL SERVICES vol 95 (2017) PARA 152 et seq): Lasting Powers of Attorney, Enduring Powers of Attorney and Public Guardian Regulations 2007, SI 2007/1253, reg 8(4) (definition amended by SI 2012/1479; SI 2017/52).

10 Mental Capacity Act 2005 Sch 1 para 2(6); Lasting Powers of Attorney, Enduring Powers of Attorney and Public Guardian Regulations 2007, SI 2007/1253, reg 8(3)(b).

11 Ie a donee of any other lasting power of attorney or an enduring power of attorney (see PARA 196 et seq) which has been executed by the donor (whether or not it has been revoked): Lasting Powers of Attorney, Enduring Powers of Attorney and Public Guardian Regulations 2007, SI 2007/1253, reg 8(3)(c).

12 Ie the certificate may not be given by:

(1) a family member of the donor (Lasting Powers of Attorney, Enduring Powers of Attorney and Public Guardian Regulations 2007, SI 2007/1253, reg 8(3)(a));

(2) a family member of the donee (reg 8(3)(d));

(3) a director or employee of a trust corporation acting as a donee under the power (reg 8(3)(e));

(4) a business partner or employee of the donor or a donee under the power (reg 8(3)(f)); and

(5) an owner, director, manager or employee of any care home in which the donor is living when the instrument is executed or a family member of any such person (reg 8(3)(g), (h)).

See eg *Re Kittle* (2009) COP 1/12/2009 (first cousin not a family member under the Lasting Powers of Attorney, Enduring Powers of Attorney and Public Guardian Regulations 2007, SI 2007/1253, reg 8(3)(a)); *Re Phillips* [2012] MHLO 60 (LPA) (unmarried partner of an attorney not eligible to be certificate provider); *Re Putt* (2011) COP 22/3/11 (two partners in a limited liability partnership appointed as attorneys; associate in same firm not eligible to be certificate provider).

13 See the Mental Capacity Act 2005 s 9(2)(b); and PARA 219.

223. Execution of instrument.

The procedure for the execution of an instrument intending to create a lasting power of attorney[1] is:

(1) the donor must read (or have read to him) all the prescribed information[2];

(2) the donor must complete the provisions of the instrument[3] that apply to him (or direct another person to do so[4]) and sign[5] the relevant part[6] in the presence of a witness[7];

(3) the person or persons giving an LPA certificate[8] must complete[9] and sign it[10];

(4) the donee[11] must read (or have read to him) all the prescribed information[12]; and

(5) the donee[13] must complete the provisions of the instrument[14] that apply to him (or direct another person to do so)[15] and must sign the relevant part[16] in the presence of a witness[17].

Each of these steps must be taken as soon as reasonably practicable after the previously required step has been taken[18]. An instrument which does not comply with these provisions does not create a lasting power of attorney[19].

1 As to the meaning of 'lasting power of attorney' see PARA 218.

2 Mental Capacity Act 2005 Sch 1 para 1(1)(c); Lasting Powers of Attorney, Enduring Powers of Attorney and Public Guardian Regulations 2007, SI 2007/1253, reg 9(1), (2). As to the prescribed information see PARA 220.

3 Ie the provisions of Sections 1 to 7 of the instrument: Lasting Powers of Attorney, Enduring Powers of Attorney and Public Guardian Regulations 2007, SI 2007/1253, reg 9(3)(a) (amended by SI 2015/899).

4 Lasting Powers of Attorney, Enduring Powers of Attorney and Public Guardian Regulations 2007, SI 2007/1253, reg 9(3)(a).

5 Any reference in these provisions to a person 'signing' an instrument (however expressed) includes his signing it by means of a mark made on the instrument at the appropriate place: Lasting Powers of Attorney, Enduring Powers of Attorney and Public Guardian Regulations 2007, SI 2007/1253, reg 9(10).

6 He must sign Section 9 of the instrument if the instrument is intended to create a lasting power of attorney for property and financial affairs (Form LP1F); or he must sign Sections 5 and 9 of the instrument if the instrument is intended to create a lasting power of attorney for health and welfare

(Form LP1H): Enduring Powers of Attorney and Public Guardian Regulations 2007, SI 2007/1253, reg 9(3)(b) (substituted by SI 2015/899).

7   Lasting Powers of Attorney, Enduring Powers of Attorney and Public Guardian Regulations 2007, SI 2007/1253, reg 9(3)(b). The donor may not witness any signature required for the power, and a donee may not witness any signature required for the power apart from that of another donee: reg 9(8). A person witnessing a signature must sign the instrument and give his full name and address: reg 9(9). If the instrument is to be signed by any person at the direction of the donor or any donee the signature must be done in the presence of two witnesses: reg 9(7). See *Re Clarke* (2011) COP 19/9/11 (witness not in the same room as the signing donor, but could see donor through glass doors; instrument held properly witnessed).

8   As to the meaning of 'LPA certificate' see PARA 222.

9   Ie at Section 10 of the instrument: Lasting Powers of Attorney, Enduring Powers of Attorney and Public Guardian Regulations 2007, SI 2007/1253, reg 9(4) (amended by SI 2015/899).

10   Lasting Powers of Attorney, Enduring Powers of Attorney and Public Guardian Regulations 2007, SI 2007/1253, reg 9(4).

11   Or if more than one, each of the donees: Lasting Powers of Attorney, Enduring Powers of Attorney and Public Guardian Regulations 2007, SI 2007/1253, reg 9(5)(b).

12   Lasting Powers of Attorney, Enduring Powers of Attorney and Public Guardian Regulations 2007, SI 2007/1253, reg 9(5)(a).

13   Or if more than one, each of the donees: Lasting Powers of Attorney, Enduring Powers of Attorney and Public Guardian Regulations 2007, SI 2007/1253, reg 9(6).

14   Ie the provisions of Section 11 of the instrument: Lasting Powers of Attorney, Enduring Powers of Attorney and Public Guardian Regulations 2007, SI 2007/1253, reg 9(6)(a) (amended by SI 2015/899).

15   Lasting Powers of Attorney, Enduring Powers of Attorney and Public Guardian Regulations 2007, SI 2007/1253, reg 9(6)(a).

16   Ie Section 11 of the instrument: Lasting Powers of Attorney, Enduring Powers of Attorney and Public Guardian Regulations 2007, SI 2007/1253, reg 9(6)(b) (amended by SI 2015/899).

17   Lasting Powers of Attorney, Enduring Powers of Attorney and Public Guardian Regulations 2007, SI 2007/1253, reg 9(6)(b). See reg 9(7)–(9); and note 7. See eg *Re Smith* [2012] MHLO 63 (LPA) (one attorney's signature had not been properly witnessed; LPA not validly registered).

18   Lasting Powers of Attorney, Enduring Powers of Attorney and Public Guardian Regulations 2007, SI 2007/1253, reg 9(3)–(6).

19   See the Mental Capacity Act 2005 s 9(2)(b); and PARA 219.

224. Revocation of lasting power by donor or court.

The donor may, at any time when he has capacity[1] to do so, revoke an instrument executed with a view to creating a lasting power of attorney[2]. The donor's bankruptcy or the making of a debt relief order[3] also revokes the instrument so far as it relates to his property[4] and affairs[5].

The court[6] may revoke an instrument purporting to create a lasting power of attorney, if the donor lacks capacity to do so[7], if it is satisfied either:

(1)   that fraud or undue pressure was used to induce the donor to execute an instrument for the purpose of creating a lasting power or to create a lasting power[8]; or

(2)   that the donee[9] of a lasting power has behaved, or is behaving, in a way that contravenes his authority or is not in the donor's best interests or proposes to behave in such a way[10].

The court may also on these grounds direct that an instrument purporting to create a lasting power is not to be registered[11], and may determine any question relating to whether a power has been revoked or has otherwise come to an end[12].

1   As to the meaning of 'capacity' and cognate expressions see PARA 196 note 2.

2   Mental Capacity Act 2005 s 13(1)(a), (2). As to the meaning of 'lasting power of attorney' see PARA 218. As to the execution of instruments with a view to creating lasting powers see PARA 223.

     A donor who revokes a lasting power of attorney must notify the Public Guardian that he has done so (Lasting Powers of Attorney, Enduring Powers of Attorney and Public Guardian Regulations 2007, SI 2007/1253, reg 21(1)(a)) and notify the donee (or, if more than one, each of them) of the revocation (reg 21(1)(b)). The Public Guardian may also require the donor to provide such further information, or produce such documents, as he reasonably considers necessary to enable him to determine whether the steps necessary for revocation have been taken: reg 21(3). As to the Public Guardian see the Mental Capacity Act 2005 ss 57–60; and MENTAL HEALTH AND CAPACITY vol 75 (2013) PARA 751 et seq.

3   As to references in the Mental Capacity Act 2005 to the 'bankruptcy' of an individual see PARA 197 note 3. As to debt relief orders under the Insolvency Act 1986 Pt 7A (ss 251A–251X) see BANKRUPTCY AND INDIVIDUAL INSOLVENCY vol 5 (2013) PARA 101 et seq.

4   As to the meaning of 'property' see PARA 196 note 11.

5   Mental Capacity Act 2005 s 13(3) (amended by SI 2012/2404). If the donor is bankrupt merely because an interim bankruptcy restrictions order under the Insolvency Act 1986 (see BANKRUPTCY AND INDIVIDUAL INSOLVENCY) has effect in respect of him, or where he is subject to an interim debt relief restrictions order under the Insolvency Act 1986 Sch 4ZB, the power is suspended, so far as it relates to the donor's property and affairs, for so long as the order has effect: Mental Capacity Act 2005 s 13(4) (amended by SI 2012/2404).

6   Ie the Court of Protection: see PARA 199 note 6. For specific procedural provision in connection with these matters see the Court of Protection Rules 2017, SI 2017/1035, r 9.7.

7   Mental Capacity Act 2005 s 22(4)(b). If there is more than one donee, the court may under this provision revoke the instrument or the lasting power so far as it relates to any of them: s 22(5). 'Donee' includes an intended donee: s 22(6).

8   Mental Capacity Act 2005 s 22(3)(a).

9   Or, if more than one, any of them: Mental Capacity Act 2005 s 22(3)(b). See note 7.

10 Mental Capacity Act 2005 s 22(3)(b). See eg *Re DP (Revocation of Lasting Power of Attorney* [2014] EWCOP B4, [2014] COPLR 188, [2014] MHLO 8. As to intervention by the Public Guardian for the purpose of safeguarding the donor's best interests and monitoring the donee's behaviour see PARA 238.

11 See PARA 231.

12 See PARA 237.

225.   Termination of donee's appointment.

The donee's appointment is terminated[1] if:

(1)   he disclaims it[2];

(2)   he dies or is bankrupt or a debt relief order is made in respect of him[3];

(3)   the donee is a trust corporation[4] and is wound up or dissolved[5];

(4)   a marriage or civil partnership between the donor and the donee is dissolved or annulled[6]; or

(5)   the donee lacks capacity[7].

The occurrence in relation to a donee of any of these events will also revoke an instrument creating a lasting power of attorney[8] unless the donee is replaced under the terms of the instrument[9] or he is one of two or more persons appointed to act as donees jointly and severally in respect of any matter and, after the event, there is at least one remaining donee[10]. Additionally:

(a)   the donee's bankruptcy or the making of a debt relief order in respect of him neither terminates his appointment nor revokes the instrument in so far as his authority relates to the donor's personal welfare[11];

(b)   where the donee is bankrupt merely because an interim bankruptcy restrictions order has effect in respect of him, or where he is subject to an interim debt relief restrictions order his appointment and the instrument are suspended, so far as they relate to the donor's property and affairs, for so long as the order has effect[12]; and

(c)   the dissolution or annulment of a marriage or civil partnership does not terminate the appointment of a donee, or revoke the instrument, if the instrument provided that it was not to do so[13].

1   Mental Capacity Act 2005 s 13(5)(a).

2   Mental Capacity Act 2005 s 13(6)(a). For the prescribed form which a donee must use to disclaim his appointment as donee see the Lasting Powers of Attorney, Enduring Powers of Attorney and

Public Guardian Regulations 2007, SI 2007/1253, reg 20(1), Sch 6 (Sch 6 substituted by SI 2015/899). The donee must send the completed form to the donor and a copy of it to the Public Guardian and any other donee who, for the time being, is appointed under the power (reg 20(2)). Provision is also made for the use of Welsh language forms: see reg 3(1)(a). Forms which differ in an immaterial respect in form or mode of expression from the specified form, forms to the same effect but with such variations as the circumstances may require or the court (ie the Court of Protection: see PARA 199 note 6) or Public Guardian may approve, and Welsh versions of such forms, are also acceptable: see reg 3(1)(b). As to the Public Guardian see the Mental Capacity Act 2005 ss 57–60; and MENTAL HEALTH AND CAPACITY vol 75 (2013) PARA 751 et seq.

3 Mental Capacity Act 2005 s 13(6)(b) (amended by SI 2012/2404). As to references in the Mental Capacity Act 2005 to the 'bankruptcy' of an individual see PARA 197 note 3. In connection with the donee's bankruptcy see also s 13(8), (9); and the text and notes 11–12. As to debt relief orders under the Insolvency Act 1986 Pt 7A (ss 251A–251X) see BANKRUPTCY AND INDIVIDUAL INSOLVENCY vol 5 (2013) PARA 101 et seq.

4 As to the meaning of 'trust corporation' see PARA 197 note 4.

5 Mental Capacity Act 2005 s 13(6)(b).

6 Mental Capacity Act 2005 s 13(6)(c). Marriage includes marriage of a same sex couple: see Marriage (Same Sex Couples) Act 2013 Sch 3 para 1(1)(a), (2), (3); and MATRIMONIAL AND CIVIL PARTNERSHIP LAW vol 72 (2015) PARA 1 et seq.

7 Mental Capacity Act 2005 s 13(6)(d). As to the meaning of 'capacity' and cognate expressions see PARA 196 note 2.

8 Mental Capacity Act 2005 s 13(5)(b). As to the meaning of 'lasting power of attorney' see PARA 218. As to the execution of instruments with a view to creating lasting powers see PARA 223.

9 Mental Capacity Act 2005 s 13(7)(a).

10 Mental Capacity Act 2005 s 13(7)(b).

11 Mental Capacity Act 2005 s 13(8) (amended by SI 2012/2404).

12 Mental Capacity Act 2005 s 13(9) (amended by SI 2012/2404). Where the donee is one of two or more appointed to act jointly and severally under the power in respect of any matter, the reference in s 13(9) to the suspension of the power is to its suspension in so far as it relates to that donee: s 13(10).

13 Mental Capacity Act 2005 s 13(11).

(iii) Activation and Operation of Power

226. Requirement for, and notification of, registration.

A lasting power of attorney[1] is not created unless the instrument conferring the appropriate authority[2] is properly registered[3]. Either the donor or the donee may apply for registration[4], but may not do so unless they have first notified their intention to the named persons[5] or satisfied the court[6] that no useful purpose would be served by giving such notification[7]. The form of notice which must be given by a donor or donee who is about to make an application for the registration of an instrument intended to create a lasting power of attorney is prescribed by regulations[8].

If these requirements are not complied with the instrument in question will not create a lasting power of attorney[9].

1 As to the meaning of 'lasting power of attorney' see PARA 218.

2 As to authority under a lasting power of attorney see the Mental Capacity Act 2005 s 9(1); and PARA 218.

3 Mental Capacity Act 2005 s 9(2)(b).

4 Mental Capacity Act 2005 Sch 1 para 4(2)(a), (b). If the instrument appoints two or more donees to act jointly and severally in respect of any matter, any of the donees may apply for registration: Sch 1 para 4(2)(c).

5 Mental Capacity Act 2005 Sch 1 para 6. 'Named person' means a person named under Sch 1 para 2(1)(c) (see PARA 221): Sch 1 para 2(4).

6 Ie the Court of Protection: see PARA 199 note 6.

7 See the Mental Capacity Act 2005 Sch 1 para 10, which provides that the court may on the application of the donor, donee or donees concerned dispense with the requirement to notify under Sch 1 para 6, if satisfied that no useful purpose would be served by giving the notice.

8 Mental Capacity Act 2005 Sch 1 para 9(1); Lasting Powers of Attorney, Enduring Powers of Attorney and Public Guardian Regulations 2007, SI 2007/1253, reg 10, Sch 2 (reg 10 amended, and Sch 2 substituted by SI 2015/899). It is also provided that a notice under the Mental Capacity Act 2005 Sch 1 para 6 must include such information, if any, as may be prescribed: see Sch 1 para 9(2). At the date at which this volume states the law no such information had been prescribed.

   Provision is also made for the use of Welsh language forms (see the Lasting Powers of Attorney, Enduring Powers of Attorney and Public Guardian Regulations 2007, SI 2007/1253, reg 3(1)(a)). Forms which differ in an immaterial respect in form or mode of expression from the specified form, forms to the same effect but with such variations as the circumstances may require or the court or Public Guardian may approve, and Welsh versions of such forms, are also acceptable: see reg 3(1)(b).

9 See the Mental Capacity Act 2005 s 9(2)(b); and PARA **219**.

227. Form and content of applications for registration.

The form which must be used for making an application to the Public Guardian[1] for the registration of an instrument intended to create a lasting power of attorney[2] is prescribed by regulations[3]. The application must be accompanied by the instrument intended to be registered[4] and the applicable fee[5], and the Public Guardian must notify receipt of the application to the donor or donee, as the case may be[6]. Any person who, in an application for registration, makes a statement which he knows to be false in a material particular is guilty of an offence[7].

If these requirements are not complied with the instrument in question will not create a lasting power of attorney[8].

1 As to the Public Guardian see the Mental Capacity Act 2005 ss 57–60; and MENTAL HEALTH AND CAPACITY vol 75 (2013) PARA 751 et seq.

2 As to the meaning of 'lasting power of attorney' see PARA **218**. Either the donor or the donee (or any of the donees) of a lasting power may apply for it to be registered: see the Mental Capacity Act 2005 Sch 1 para 4(2); and PARA **226**.

3 Mental Capacity Act 2005 Sch 1 para 4(1)(a); Lasting Powers of Attorney, Enduring Powers of Attorney and Public Guardian Regulations 2007, SI 2007/1253, reg 11(1)–(5), (7), Sch 3 (reg 11 and Sch 3 both substituted by SI 2015/899). It is also provided that an application for registration must include such information as may be prescribed (Lasting Powers of Attorney, Enduring Powers of Attorney and Public Guardian Regulations 2007, SI 2007/1253, Sch 1 para 4(1)(b)). At the date at which this volume states the law no such information had been prescribed.

   Provision is also made for the use of Welsh language forms (see the Lasting Powers of Attorney, Enduring Powers of Attorney and Public Guardian Regulations 2007, SI 2007/1253, reg 3(1)(a)). Forms which differ in an immaterial respect in form or mode of expression from the specified form, forms to the same effect but with such variations as the circumstances may require or the court or Public Guardian may approve, and Welsh versions of such forms, are also acceptable: see reg 3(1)(b).

4 Mental Capacity Act 2005 Sch 1 para 4(3)(a). Where the instrument to be registered which is sent with the application is neither the original instrument intended to create the power nor a certified copy of it, the Public Guardian must not register the instrument unless the court (ie the Court of Protection: see PARA **199** note 6) directs him to do so: see the Lasting Powers of Attorney, Enduring Powers of Attorney and Public Guardian Regulations 2007, SI 2007/1253, reg 11(6) (as substituted: see note 3); and PARA **232**. A 'certified copy' is a photographic or other facsimile copy which is certified as an accurate copy by the donor or a solicitor or notary: reg 11(7) (as so substituted), reg 17(5). Where the Public Guardian is prevented by this provision from registering an instrument as a lasting power of attorney he must notify the person (or persons) who applied for registration of that fact: reg 16(e).

5 Mental Capacity Act 2005 Sch 1 para 4(3)(b). For the applicable fee see the Public Guardian (Fees, etc) Regulations 2007, SI 2007/2051, reg 5, Schedule (both amended by SI 2011/2189). As to the fee payable on requesting an office copy of a lasting power of attorney see the Public Guardian (Fees, etc) Regulations 2007, SI 2007/2051, reg 5A, Schedule (reg 5A added, and the Schedule amended by SI 2009/514).

6   Notification that an application has been received must be made as soon as is practicable after receiving the application, and the means of notification depends on the identity of the applicant:

     (1)   if the application is made by the donor under the Mental Capacity Act 2005 Sch 1 para 4(2)(a) (see PARA 226), the Public Guardian must notify the donee (or donees) in the form set out in the Lasting Powers of Attorney, Enduring Powers of Attorney and Public Guardian Regulations 2007, SI 2007/1253, Sch 4 Pt 1 (substituted by SI 2015/899) (see the Mental Capacity Act 2005 Sch 1 para 7; Lasting Powers of Attorney, Enduring Powers of Attorney and Public Guardian Regulations 2007, SI 2007/1253, reg 13(1));

     (2)   if the application is made by a donee (or donees) under the Mental Capacity Act 2005 Sch 1 para 4(2)(b) (see PARA 226), the Public Guardian must notify the donor in the form set out in the Lasting Powers of Attorney, Enduring Powers of Attorney and Public Guardian Regulations 2007, SI 2007/1253, Sch 4 Pt 2 (substituted by SI 2015/899) (see the Mental Capacity Act 2005 Sch 1 para 8(1); Lasting Powers of Attorney, Enduring Powers of Attorney and Public Guardian Regulations 2007, SI 2007/1253, reg 13(2)); and

     (3)   if the application is made by a donee under the Mental Capacity Act 2005 Sch 1 para 4(2)(c) (see PARA 226), the Public Guardian must notify both the donor (in the form set out in the Lasting Powers of Attorney, Enduring Powers of Attorney and Public Guardian Regulations 2007, SI 2007/1253, Sch 4 Pt 2) and the donees that did not join in the making of the application (in the form set out in the Lasting Powers of Attorney, Enduring Powers of Attorney and Public Guardian Regulations 2007, SI 2007/1253, Sch 4 Pt 1) (see the Mental Capacity Act 2005 Sch 1 para 8(2); Lasting Powers of Attorney, Enduring Powers of Attorney and Public Guardian Regulations 2007, SI 2007/1253, reg 13(1), (2)).

If the application is made by the donee and it appears to the Public Guardian that there is good reason to do so, the Public Guardian must also provide (or arrange for the provision of) an explanation to the donor of the notice referred to in reg 13(2) and what the effect of it is, and why it is being brought to his attention: Mental Capacity Act 2005 Sch 1 para 9(2); Lasting Powers of Attorney, Enduring Powers of Attorney and Public Guardian Regulations 2007, SI 2007/1253, reg 13(3). Any information so provided must be provided to the donor personally and in a way that is appropriate to the donor's circumstances (for example using simple language, visual aids or other appropriate means): reg 13(4). Provision is also made for the use of Welsh language forms (see reg 3(1)(a)). Forms which differ in an immaterial respect in form or mode of expression from the specified form, forms to the same effect but with such variations as the circumstances may require or the court or Public Guardian may approve, and Welsh versions of such forms, are also acceptable: see reg 3(1)(b).

7   Mental Capacity Act 2005 Sch 1 para 4(4). A person who is found guilty of this offence is liable on conviction on indictment to imprisonment for a term not exceeding two years, or a fine, or both, and on summary conviction to imprisonment for a term not exceeding 12 months, or a fine not exceeding the statutory maximum, or both: Sch 1 para 4(4). As to the powers of magistrates' courts to issue fines on summary conviction see SENTENCING vol 92 (2015) PARA 176.

8   See the Mental Capacity Act 2005 s 9(2)(b); and PARA 219.

228. Objections to registration.

The donee of a lasting power of attorney[1], or a person named for the purposes of such power[2], may give notice to the Public Guardian[3], or make an application to the court[4], objecting to the registration of the instrument creating the power[5].

The grounds on which the donee or a named person may notify his objection to the Public Guardian are that the instrument has been revoked by:

     (1)   the donor's bankruptcy[6];

     (2)   the disclaimer of the appointment by the donee[7];

     (3)   the death or bankruptcy of the donee or, if the donee is a trust corporation[8], its winding-up or dissolution[9];

     (4)   the dissolution or annulment of a marriage or civil partnership between the donor and the donee[10]; or

     (5)   the lack of capacity[11] of the donee[12].

The grounds on which the donee or a named person may apply to the court objecting to the registration of an instrument as a lasting power of attorney are:

(a)   that one or more of the requirements for the creation of a lasting power of attorney has not been met[13];

(b)   that the power has been revoked[14], or has otherwise come to an end, on a ground other than one of the grounds on which an objection to registration may be made to the Public Guardian[15]; and

(c)   any of the specified grounds on which the court may intervene to direct that a lasting power not be registered or to revoke such a power[16].

The donor of a lasting power may also object to registration by giving notice of his objection to the Public Guardian[17].

Where an objection is established, the instrument will not be registered unless the court so directs[18].

1   As to the meaning of 'lasting power of attorney' see PARA 218.

2   Ie a 'named person': see PARA 226 note 5. As to such persons see PARA 221.

3   Mental Capacity Act 2005 Sch 1 para 13(1)(b). As to the Public Guardian see the Mental Capacity Act 2005 ss 57–60; and MENTAL HEALTH AND CAPACITY vol 75 (2013) PARA 751 et seq. Notice must be given in writing, setting out the name and address of the objector, the name and address of the donor of the power (if different), the name and address of the donee (or donees) (if known) and the ground for making the objection: Lasting Powers of Attorney, Enduring Powers of Attorney and Public Guardian Regulations 2007, SI 2007/1253, reg 14(3) (amended by SI 2007/2161).

4   Mental Capacity Act 2005 Sch 1 para 13(3)(b)(i). The court is the Court of Protection: see PARA 199 note 6. If the donee or named person makes an application to the court under this provision he must notify the Public Guardian in writing of the application: Sch 1 para 13(3)(b)(ii); Lasting Powers of Attorney, Enduring Powers of Attorney and Public Guardian Regulations 2007, SI 2007/1253, reg 15(4).

5   Mental Capacity Act 2005 Sch 1 para 13(1)(b), (3)(b)(i). The procedure for making objections differs depending on whether the objection is being made to the Public Guardian or to the court: see PARA 229. Nothing in the Lasting Powers of Attorney, Enduring Powers of Attorney and Public Guardian Regulations 2007, SI 2007/1253, reg 14 (see the text and notes 1–3; and PARA 229 et seq) prevents an objector from making a further objection under the Mental Capacity Act 2005 Sch 1 para 13 where the notice under the Lasting Powers of Attorney, Enduring Powers of Attorney and Public Guardian Regulations 2007, SI 2007/1253, reg 14(4) (see PARA 230) indicates that the Public Guardian is not satisfied that the particular ground of objection to which that notice relates is established and the period specified in reg 14(2) (see PARA 229) has not expired: reg 14(7). There are time limits and other procedural matters relating to the making of objections which must be observed: see reg 14A (added by SI 2007/2161; and amended by SI 2013/506).

6   Mental Capacity Act 2005 s 13(3), Sch 1 para 13(1)(b). As to references in the Mental Capacity Act 2005 to the 'bankruptcy' of an individual see PARA 197 note 3. As to the revocation of an instrument on these grounds see s 13(3); and PARA 234.

7   Mental Capacity Act 2005 s 13(6)(a), Sch 1 para 13(1)(b). As to the revocation of an instrument on these grounds see s 13(6)(a); and PARA 235.

8   As to the meaning of 'trust corporation' see PARA 197 note 4.

9   Mental Capacity Act 2005 s 13(6)(b), Sch 1 para 13(1)(b). As to the revocation of an instrument on these grounds see s 13(6)(b); and PARA 235.

10 Mental Capacity Act 2005 s 13(6)(c), Sch 1 para 13(1)(b). As to the revocation of an instrument on these grounds see s 13(6)(c); and PARA 235. Marriage includes marriage of a same sex couple: see Marriage (Same Sex Couples) Act 2013 Sch 3 para 1(1)(a), (2), (3); and MATRIMONIAL AND CIVIL PARTNERSHIP LAW vol 72 (2015) PARA 1 et seq.

11 As to the meaning of 'capacity' and cognate expressions see PARA 196 note 2.

12 Mental Capacity Act 2005 s 13(6)(d), Sch 1 para 13(1)(b). As to the revocation of an instrument on these grounds see s 13(6)(d); and PARA 235.

13 Mental Capacity Act 2005 Sch 1 para 13(3)(b)(i); Lasting Powers of Attorney, Enduring Powers of Attorney and Public Guardian Regulations 2007, SI 2007/1253, reg 15(1), (2)(a). As to the requirements for the creation of a lasting power of attorney see PARA 219 et seq.

14 As to the revocation of powers see PARA 234.

15 Lasting Powers of Attorney, Enduring Powers of Attorney and Public Guardian Regulations 2007, SI 2007/1253, reg 15(2)(b). As to the grounds on which an objection to registration may be made to the Public Guardian see the Mental Capacity Act 2005 Sch 1 para 13(1); and the text and notes 6–12.
16 Lasting Powers of Attorney, Enduring Powers of Attorney and Public Guardian Regulations 2007, SI 2007/1253, reg 15(2)(c). As to the specified grounds on which the court may intervene see the Mental Capacity Act 2005 s 22(3); and PARA 234.
17 Mental Capacity Act 2005 Sch 1 para 14(1)(b). Notice must be given in writing, setting out the name and address of the objector, the name and address of the donor of the power (if different), the name and address of the donee (or donees) (if known) and the ground for making the objection: Lasting Powers of Attorney, Enduring Powers of Attorney and Public Guardian Regulations 2007, SI 2007/1253, reg 14(3) (amended by SI 2007/2161).
18 See PARA 230.

229. Procedure for making objections.

Objections to applications for the registration of an instrument as a lasting power of attorney[1] may be made only after the person objecting to the registration has been notified[2] of the application[3].

A donee of the power or person to notify[4] who:

(1)   is entitled to receive notice[5] of an application for the registration of an instrument as a lasting power of attorney[6]; and

(2)   wishes to give notice to the Public Guardian[7] that he objects to the registration on a specified ground[8],

must do so before the end of the period of three weeks beginning with the date on which the notification of application for registration is given[9]. At any time after receiving the notice of objection and before notifying the objector as to whether or not he is satisfied that the ground of the objection is established[10], the Public Guardian may require the objector to provide such further information, or produce such documents, as the Public Guardian reasonably considers necessary to enable him to determine whether the ground for making the objection is established[11].

A donor who wishes to give notice to the Public Guardian that he objects to registration must do so before the end of the period of three weeks beginning with the date on which the notification of application for registration is given[12].

Any person who:

(a)   is entitled to receive notice[13] of an application for the registration of an instrument as a lasting power[14]; and

(b)   wishes to make an application to the court[15] objecting[16] to the registration[17],

must make the application before the end of the period of three weeks beginning with the date on which the notice is given[18].

1 As to the meaning of 'lasting power of attorney' see PARA 218. As to the grounds on which objections may be made see PARA 228.
2 Ie under the Mental Capacity Act 2005 Sch 1 para 6, 7 or 8 (see PARAS 226, 227).
3 Mental Capacity Act 2005 Sch 1 paras 13(1)(a), (3)(a), 14(1)(a).
4 Lasting Powers of Attorney, Enduring Powers of Attorney and Public Guardian Regulations 2007, SI 2007/1253, reg 14(2) (amended by SI 2007/2161; SI 2015/899). As to the persons to notify see PARA 221; and PARA 226 note 5.
5 See note 2.
6 Lasting Powers of Attorney, Enduring Powers of Attorney and Public Guardian Regulations 2007, SI 2007/1253, reg 14(2)(a).
7 As to the Public Guardian see the Mental Capacity Act 2005 ss 57–60; and MENTAL HEALTH AND CAPACITY vol 75 (2013) PARA 751 et seq. As to the making of objections to the Public Guardian see PARA 228.

8 Lasting Powers of Attorney, Enduring Powers of Attorney and Public Guardian Regulations 2007, SI 2007/1253, reg 14(1), (2)(b). For the 'specified grounds' for an objection under these provisions see the Mental Capacity Act 2005 Sch 1 para 13(1); and PARA 228.

9 Mental Capacity Act 2005 Sch 1 para 13(1)(b), (3)(b); Lasting Powers of Attorney, Enduring Powers of Attorney and Public Guardian Regulations 2007, SI 2007/1253, reg 14(2) (amended by SI 2013/506). Any period of time specified in the Lasting Powers of Attorney, Enduring Powers of Attorney and Public Guardian Regulations 2007, SI 2007/1253, which is expressed as a number of days must be computed as clear days (reg 4(1), (2)); 'clear days' means that in computing the number of days the day on which the period begins and, if the end of the period is defined by reference to an event, the day on which that event occurs, are not included (reg 4(5)). Where the specified period is seven days or less, and would include a day which is not a business day, that day does not count (reg 4(3)); 'business day' means a day other than a Saturday, Sunday, Christmas Day or Good Friday or a bank holiday under the Banking and Financial Dealings Act 1971 (see TIME vol 97 (2015) PARA 321), in England and Wales (reg 4(5)). When the specified period for doing any act at the office of the Public Guardian ends on a day on which the office is closed, that act will be done in time if done on the next day on which the office is open: reg 4(4).

10 Ie before giving the notice required by the Lasting Powers of Attorney, Enduring Powers of Attorney and Public Guardian Regulations 2007, SI 2007/1253, reg 14(4) (see PARA 230).

11 Lasting Powers of Attorney, Enduring Powers of Attorney and Public Guardian Regulations 2007, SI 2007/1253, reg 14(5).

12 Mental Capacity Act 2005 Sch 1 para 14(1)(b); Lasting Powers of Attorney, Enduring Powers of Attorney and Public Guardian Regulations 2007, SI 2007/1253, reg 14(2) (amended by SI 2013/506).

13 See note 2.

14 Lasting Powers of Attorney, Enduring Powers of Attorney and Public Guardian Regulations 2007, SI 2007/1253, reg 15(3)(a).

15 The court is the Court of Protection: see PARA 199 note 6. As to applications to the court objecting to registration see PARA 228.

16 Ie on one or more of the grounds set out in the Lasting Powers of Attorney, Enduring Powers of Attorney and Public Guardian Regulations 2007, SI 2007/1253, reg 15(2) (see PARA 228).

17 Lasting Powers of Attorney, Enduring Powers of Attorney and Public Guardian Regulations 2007, SI 2007/1253, reg 15(3)(b).

18 Lasting Powers of Attorney, Enduring Powers of Attorney and Public Guardian Regulations 2007, SI 2007/1253, reg 15(3) (amended by SI 2013/506). As to the computation of time limits see note 9.

230. Dealing with objections.

If the Public Guardian[1] is satisfied, on an objection to the registration of an instrument as a lasting power of attorney[2] being made to him by the donee or a named person[3], that a ground for making the objection is established[4], he must not register the instrument unless the court[5], on the application of the person applying for the registration, is satisfied that the ground is not established and directs the Public Guardian to register the instrument[6]. If the donee or a named person applies to the court objecting to registration[7], the Public Guardian must not register the instrument unless the court directs him to do so[8]. If the donor gives notice to the Public Guardian of an objection to the registration[9], the Public Guardian must not register the instrument unless the court, on the application of the donee or, if more than one, any of them, is satisfied that the donor lacks capacity[10] to object to the registration and directs the Public Guardian to register the instrument[11].

Where the Public Guardian is prevented by these provisions from registering an instrument as a lasting power of attorney he must notify the person (or persons) who applied for registration of that fact[12].

1 As to the Public Guardian see the Mental Capacity Act 2005 ss 57–60; and MENTAL HEALTH AND CAPACITY vol 75 (2013) PARA 751 et seq.

2 As to the meaning of 'lasting power of attorney' see PARA 218. As to the grounds on which objections may be made, and the procedure for making objections, see PARAS 228–229.

3   Ie under the Mental Capacity Act 2005 Sch 1 para 13(1) (see PARAS 228–229). As to the meaning
    of 'named person' see PARA 226 note 5.
4   Where an objection has been notified to the Public Guardian he must notify the objector as to
    whether or not he is satisfied that the ground of the objection is established (Lasting Powers of
    Attorney, Enduring Powers of Attorney and Public Guardian Regulations 2007, SI 2007/1253, reg
    14(4)), although if he is so satisfied but by virtue of the Mental Capacity Act 2005 s 13(7) (see
    PARA 235) the instrument is not revoked, such notice must contain a statement to that effect
    (Lasting Powers of Attorney, Enduring Powers of Attorney and Public Guardian Regulations
    2007, SI 2007/1253, reg 14(6)).
5   Ie the Court of Protection: see PARA 199 note 6. As to applications to the court objecting to
    registration see PARA 228.
6   Mental Capacity Act 2005 Sch 1 para 13(2).
7   Ie under the Mental Capacity Act 2005 Sch 1 para 13(3) (see PARAS 228–229).
8   Mental Capacity Act 2005 Sch 1 para 13(4).
9   Ie under the Mental Capacity Act 2005 Sch 1 para 14(1) (see PARAS 228–229).
10 As to the meaning of 'capacity' and cognate expressions see PARA 196 note 2.
11 Mental Capacity Act 2005 Sch 1 para 14(2).
12 Lasting Powers of Attorney, Enduring Powers of Attorney and Public Guardian Regulations 2007,
    SI 2007/1253, reg 16(c), (d).

231.   Intervention by the Court of Protection.

The court[1] may direct that an instrument purporting to create a lasting power
of attorney[2] is not to be registered[3] if it is satisfied either:

(1)   that fraud or undue pressure was used to induce the donor to execute
        the relevant instrument or to create the lasting power[4]; or

(2)   that the donee[5] of a lasting power has behaved, or is behaving, in a way
        that contravenes his authority or is not in the donor's best interests or
        proposes to behave in such a way[6].

If the donor lacks capacity[7] to do so, the court may also revoke the instrument or
the lasting power[8].

1   Ie the Court of Protection: see PARA 199 note 6. For specific procedural provision in connection
    with these matters see the Court of Protection Rules 2017, SI 2017/1035, r 9.7.
2   Ie where a person has executed or purported to execute an instrument with a view to creating a
    lasting power of attorney: Mental Capacity Act 2005 s 22(1)(a).
3   Mental Capacity Act 2005 s 22(4)(a).
4   Mental Capacity Act 2005 s 22(3)(a).
5   Or, if more than one, any of them: Mental Capacity Act 2005 s 22(3)(b).
6   Mental Capacity Act 2005 s 22(3)(b). As to intervention by the Public Guardian for the purpose
    of safeguarding the donor's best interests and monitoring the donee's behaviour see PARA 238. As
    to the Public Guardian see ss 57–60; and MENTAL HEALTH AND CAPACITY vol 75 (2013) PARA 751
    et seq.
7   As to the meaning of 'capacity' and cognate expressions see PARA 196 note 2.
8   Mental Capacity Act 2005 s 22(4)(b). If there is more than one donee, the court may under s
    22(4)(b) revoke the instrument or the lasting power of attorney so far as it relates to any of them:
    s 22(5). 'Donee' includes an intended donee: s 22(6).

232.   Registering the instrument.

If the Public Guardian[1] is able to register an instrument as a lasting power of
attorney[2] he must do so by the end of the period of four weeks beginning with the
date on which he gave the notice or notices[3] of receipt of an application for
registration[4]. Registration is, however, subject to the discretion of the court[5] if:

(1)   the instrument accompanying an application for registration is not
        properly made[6];

(2)   the instrument contains a provision which would be ineffective as part
        of a lasting power of attorney or would prevent the instrument from
        operating as such[7];

(3)   there is a person already appointed to make decisions on behalf of the donor[8];

(4)   grounds for objection are established[9];

(5)   the court is satisfied that it should intervene in the interests of the donor[10]; or

(6)   the instrument which is sent with the registration application is neither the original instrument intended to create the power nor a certified copy of it[11].

Where the Public Guardian registers an instrument as a lasting power of attorney he must give notice of the fact to the donor and donee[12]. He must also retain a copy of the instrument[13] and return to the person (or persons) who applied for registration the original instrument, or the certified copy[14] of it, which accompanied the application for registration[15]. The Public Guardian also has the function of establishing and maintaining a register of lasting powers for these purposes[16].

1   As to the Public Guardian see the Mental Capacity Act 2005 ss 57–60; and MENTAL HEALTH AND CAPACITY vol 75 (2013) PARA 751 et seq.

2   As to the meaning of 'lasting power of attorney' see PARA 218. As to applications for registration see PARA 226 et seq.

3   Ie the notice or notices under the Mental Capacity Act 2005 Sch 1 para 7 or 8: see PARA 227 note 6.

4   Mental Capacity Act 2005 Sch 1 para 5; Lasting Powers of Attorney, Enduring Powers of Attorney and Public Guardian Regulations 2007, SI 2007/1253, reg 12(a) (reg 12 amended by SI 2013/506). If notices were given on more than one date, the six-week period runs from the latest of those dates: reg 12(b).

5   Ie the Court of Protection: see PARA 199 note 6.

6   See the Mental Capacity Act 2005 Sch 1 para 11(1) (if it appears to the Public Guardian that an instrument accompanying an application under Sch 1 para 4 (see PARAS 226–227) is not made in accordance with this Sch 1, he must not register the instrument unless the court directs him to do so). Where the Public Guardian is prevented by this provision from registering an instrument as a lasting power of attorney he must notify the person (or persons) who applied for registration of that fact: Lasting Powers of Attorney, Enduring Powers of Attorney and Public Guardian Regulations 2007, SI 2007/1253, reg 16(a).

7   Mental Capacity Act 2005 Sch 1 para 11(2), (4). If it appears to the Public Guardian that the instrument contains a provision which would be ineffective as part of a lasting power of attorney or would prevent the instrument from operating as a valid lasting power of attorney, he must apply to the court for it to determine the matter under s 23(1) (see PARA 236) and, pending the determination by the court, must not register the instrument: Sch 1 para 11(3). If the court determines under s 23(1) (whether or not on an application by the Public Guardian) that the instrument contains a provision which would be ineffective as part of a lasting power of attorney, or would prevent the instrument from operating as a valid lasting power of attorney, it must notify the Public Guardian that it has severed the provision, or direct him not to register the instrument: Sch 1 para 11(5). Where the court notifies the Public Guardian that it has severed a provision, he must register the instrument with a note to that effect attached to it: Sch 1 para 11(6). The Public Guardian must register a lasting power of attorney which has legal effect, even if it is subject to restrictions causing practical difficulties for its operation: *XZ v Public Guardian* [2015] EWCOP 35, [2015] WTLR 1657, sub nom *Re XZ* [2015] All ER (D) 189 (May).

8   If it appears to the Public Guardian that there is a deputy appointed by the court for the donor and the powers conferred on the deputy would, if the instrument were registered, to any extent conflict with the powers conferred on the attorney, the Public Guardian must not register the instrument unless the court directs him to do so: Mental Capacity Act 2005 Sch 1 para 12. Where the Public Guardian is prevented by this provision from registering an instrument as a lasting power of attorney he must notify the person (or persons) who applied for registration of that fact: Lasting Powers of Attorney, Enduring Powers of Attorney and Public Guardian Regulations 2007, SI 2007/1253, reg 16(b). As to deputies see MENTAL HEALTH AND CAPACITY vol 75 (2013) PARA 724.

9   As to the court's discretion concerning the registration of instruments where objections have been made see PARA 230.

10   For the court's power to intervene in cases of fraud or undue influence or abuse of authority see PARA 231.

11   Where the instrument to be registered which is sent with the application is neither the original instrument intended to create the power nor a certified copy of it, the Public Guardian must not register the instrument unless the court directs him to do so: see the Lasting Powers of Attorney, Enduring Powers of Attorney and Public Guardian Regulations 2007, SI 2007/1253, reg 11(2); and PARA 227. As to the meaning of 'certified copy' see PARA 227 note 4.

12   Mental Capacity Act 2005 Sch 1 para 15. If there is more than one donee, notice must be given to each of them: Sch 1 para 15. For the prescribed form of notice see the Lasting Powers of Attorney, Enduring Powers of Attorney and Public Guardian Regulations 2007, SI 2007/1253, reg 17(2), Sch 5. Provision is also made for the use of Welsh language forms (reg 3(1)(a)). Forms which differ in an immaterial respect in form or mode of expression from the specified form, forms to the same effect but with such variations as the circumstances may require or the court or Public Guardian may approve, and Welsh versions of such forms, are also acceptable: see reg 3(1)(b). Where it appears to the Public Guardian that there is good reason to do so, he must also provide (or arrange for the provision of) an explanation to the donor of such notice and its effect and why it is being brought to his attention: reg 17(3). Any information so provided must be provided to the donor personally and in a way that is appropriate to the donor's circumstances (for example using simple language, visual aids or other appropriate means): reg 17(4).

13   Lasting Powers of Attorney, Enduring Powers of Attorney and Public Guardian Regulations 2007, SI 2007/1253, reg 17(1)(a).

14   As to the meaning of 'certified copy' see PARA 227 note 4.

15   Lasting Powers of Attorney, Enduring Powers of Attorney and Public Guardian Regulations 2007, SI 2007/1253, reg 17(1)(b).

16   Mental Capacity Act 2005 s 58(1)(a). As to the duties of the Public Guardian see further MENTAL HEALTH AND CAPACITY vol 75 (2013) PARA 752. As to the administration of the register by the Public Guardian see the Lasting Powers of Attorney, Enduring Powers of Attorney and Public Guardian Regulations 2007, SI 2007/1253, regs 30–32; and MENTAL HEALTH AND CAPACITY vol 75 (2013) PARA 753.

233.   Proof of registration.

A document purporting to be an office copy of a registered instrument creating a lasting power of attorney[1] is evidence of the contents of the instrument and of the fact that it has been so registered[2]. A person requesting an office copy must pay the appropriate fee at the time the request is made[3].

1   As to the meaning of 'lasting power of attorney' see PARA 218. As to applications for registration see PARA 226 et seq.

2   Mental Capacity Act 2005 Sch 1 para 16(1). This is without prejudice to the Powers of Attorney Act 1971 s 3 (proof by certified copies: see PARA 17): Mental Capacity Act 2005 Sch 1 para 16(2).

3   See the Public Guardian (Fees etc) Regulations 2007, SI 2007/2051, reg 5A (added by SI 2009/514). The fees are set out in the Public Guardian (Fees etc) Regulations 2007, SI 2007/2051, Schedule (amended by SI 2009/514; SI 2011/2189; SI 2013/1748; SI 2017/513). As to the meaning of 'office copy' see PARA 209 note 3.

234.   Revocation of registered power by donor or court.

The donor may, at any time when he has capacity[1] to do so, revoke a registered instrument creating a lasting power of attorney[2]. The donor's bankruptcy or the making of a debt relief order[3] also revokes the instrument and power so far as it relates to his property[4] and affairs[5], and the Public Guardian must cancel the registration of an instrument as a lasting power of attorney on being satisfied that the power has been so revoked[6].

The court[7] may revoke a registered power, if the donor lacks capacity to do so[8], if it is satisfied either:

(1)   that fraud or undue pressure was used to induce the donor to execute an instrument for the purpose of creating a lasting power or to create a lasting power[9]; or

(2)   that the donee[10] of a lasting power has behaved, or is behaving, in a way that contravenes his authority or is not in the donor's best interests or proposes to behave in such a way[11],

and must direct the Public Guardian to cancel the registration of an instrument as a lasting power of attorney accordingly[12].

The court may also determine any question relating to whether a power has been revoked or has otherwise come to an end[13].

1   As to the meaning of 'capacity' and cognate expressions see PARA **196** note 2.
2   Mental Capacity Act 2005 s 13(1)(b), (2). As to the meaning of 'lasting power of attorney' see PARA **218**. As to registration see PARA **226** et seq. References in these provisions to revoking the power include revoking the instrument: s 13(1).
       A donor who revokes a lasting power of attorney must notify the Public Guardian that he has done so (Lasting Powers of Attorney, Enduring Powers of Attorney and Public Guardian Regulations 2007, SI 2007/1253, reg 21(1)(a)) and notify the donee (or, if more than one, each of them) of the revocation (reg 21(1)(b)). The Public Guardian may also require the donor to provide such further information, or produce such documents, as he reasonably considers necessary to enable him to determine whether the steps necessary for revocation have been taken: reg 21(3). Where the Public Guardian receives such a notice he must cancel the registration of the instrument creating the power if he is satisfied that the donor has taken such steps as are necessary in law to revoke it: reg 21(2). Where the Public Guardian cancels the registration of the instrument he must notify the donor and the donee (or, if more than one, each of them): reg 21(4).
       As to the Public Guardian see the Mental Capacity Act 2005 ss 57–60; and MENTAL HEALTH AND CAPACITY vol 75 (2013) PARA 751 et seq.
3   As to references in the Mental Capacity Act 2005 to the 'bankruptcy' of an individual see PARA **197** note 3.
4   As to the meaning of 'property' see PARA **196** note 11.
5   Mental Capacity Act 2005 s 13(3) (amended by SI 2012/2404). If the donor is bankrupt merely because an interim bankruptcy restrictions order under the Insolvency Act 1986 (see BANKRUPTCY AND INDIVIDUAL INSOLVENCY) has effect in respect of him, or if he is subject to an interim debt relief restrictions order under Sch 4ZB (see BANKRUPTCY AND INDIVIDUAL INSOLVENCY), the power is suspended, so far as it relates to the donor's property and affairs, for so long as the order has effect: Mental Capacity Act 2005 s 13(4) (amended by SI 2012/2404). As to debt relief orders under the Insolvency Act 1986 Pt 7A (ss 251A–251X) see BANKRUPTCY AND INDIVIDUAL INSOLVENCY vol 5 (2013) PARA 101 et seq.
       If in the case of a registered instrument it appears to the Public Guardian that under the Mental Capacity Act 2005 s 13 a lasting power of attorney is revoked in relation to the donor's property and affairs (but not in relation to other matters), the Public Guardian must attach to the instrument a note to that effect: Sch 1 para 21. In any case where any of Sch 1 paras 21–24 (see PARAS 235–236) requires the Public Guardian to attach a note to an instrument registered as a lasting power of attorney (Lasting Powers of Attorney, Enduring Powers of Attorney and Public Guardian Regulations 2007, SI 2007/1253, reg 18(1)), the Public Guardian must give a notice to the donor and the donee (or, if more than one, each of them) requiring him to deliver to the Public Guardian the original instrument which was sent to the Public Guardian for registration, any office copy of that registered instrument and any certified copy of that registered instrument (reg 18(2) (amended by SI 2009/1884) and on receipt of the document the Public Guardian must attach the required note and return the document to the person from whom it was obtained (Lasting Powers of Attorney, Enduring Powers of Attorney and Public Guardian Regulations 2007, SI 2007/1253, reg 18(3)). If the Public Guardian attaches a note to an instrument under the Mental Capacity Act 2005 Sch 1 paras 21–24 he must give notice of the note to the donee or donees of the power (or, as the case may be, to the other donee or donees of the power): Sch 1 para 25.
       Where a person is required by or under the Mental Capacity Act 2005 to deliver up to the Public Guardian an instrument registered as a lasting power of attorney, an office copy of that registered instrument or a certified copy of that registered instrument, and the document has been lost or destroyed (Lasting Powers of Attorney, Enduring Powers of Attorney and Public Guardian Regulations 2007, SI 2007/1253, reg 19(1)), the person required to deliver up the document must

provide to the Public Guardian in writing either the date of the loss or destruction and the circumstances in which it occurred (if known) or a statement of when he last had the document in his possession (reg 19(2)).

6   Mental Capacity Act 2005 Sch 1 para 17(1)(a) (amended by SI 2012/2404). If the Public Guardian cancels the registration of an instrument he must notify the donor and the donee or, if more than one, each of them: Mental Capacity Act 2005 Sch 1 para 17(2). On the cancellation of the registration of an instrument, the instrument and any office copies of it must be delivered up to the Public Guardian to be cancelled: Sch 1 para 20. See note 5.

7   Ie the Court of Protection: see PARA 199 note 6. For specific procedural provision in connection with these matters see the Court of Protection Rules 2017, SI 2017/1035, r 9.7.

8   Mental Capacity Act 2005 s 22(1), (4)(b). If there is more than one donee, the court may under this provision revoke the instrument or the lasting power so far as it relates to any of them: s 22(5). 'Donee' includes an intended donee: s 22(6).

9   Mental Capacity Act 2005 s 22(3)(a).

10 Or, if more than one, any of them: Mental Capacity Act 2005 s 22(3)(b). See note 6.

11 Mental Capacity Act 2005 s 22(3)(b). As to intervention by the Public Guardian for the purpose of safeguarding the donor's best interests and monitoring the donee's behaviour see PARA 238. See eg *Public Guardian v CS and PL* [2015] EWCOP 30, sub nom *Re EL* [2015] All ER (D) 71 (May); *Public Guardian v SR and NC* [2015] EWCOP 32 sub nom *Re MC* [2015] All ER (D) 78 (May).

12 Mental Capacity Act 2005 Sch 1 para 18(c).

13 See PARA 237.

235. Termination of donee's appointment.

The donee's appointment is terminated[1] if:

(1)   he disclaims it[2];

(2)   he dies[3] or becomes bankrupt or has a debt relief order made in respect of him[4];

(3)   the donee is a trust corporation[5] and is wound up or dissolved[6];

(4)   a marriage or civil partnership between the donor and the donee is dissolved or annulled[7]; or

(5)   the donee lacks capacity[8].

The occurrence in relation to a donee of any of these events will also revoke the registered power[9] (unless the donee is replaced under the terms of the instrument[10] or he is one of two or more persons appointed to act as donees jointly and severally in respect of any matter and, after the event, there is at least one remaining donee[11]) and the Public Guardian must cancel the registration accordingly[12]. However:

(a)   the donee's bankruptcy or the making of a debt relief order in respect of him neither terminates his appointment nor revokes the registered power in so far as his authority relates to the donor's personal welfare[13];

(b)   where the donee is bankrupt merely because an interim bankruptcy restrictions order has effect in respect of him, or where the donee is subject to an interim debt relief restrictions order, his appointment and the registered power are suspended, so far as they relate to the donor's property and affairs, for so long as the order has effect[14]; and

(c)   the dissolution or annulment of a marriage or civil partnership does not terminate the appointment of a donee, or revoke the registered power, if the instrument provided that it was not to do so[15].

1   Mental Capacity Act 2005 s 13(5)(a).

2   Mental Capacity Act 2005 s 13(6)(a). For the prescribed form which a donee must use to disclaim his appointment as donee see the Lasting Powers of Attorney, Enduring Powers of Attorney and Public Guardian Regulations 2007, SI 2007/1253, reg 20(1), Sch 6 (substituted by SI 2015/899). The donee must send the completed form to the donor and a copy of it to the Public Guardian and any other donee who, for the time being, is appointed under the power (Lasting Powers of Attorney, Enduring Powers of Attorney and Public Guardian Regulations 2007, SI 2007/1253, reg

20(2)). Forms which differ in an immaterial respect in form or mode of expression from the specified form, forms to the same effect but with such variations as the circumstances may require or the court (ie the Court of Protection: see PARA 199 note 6) or Public Guardian may approve, and Welsh versions of such forms, are also acceptable: reg 3(1)(b). As to the Public Guardian see the Mental Capacity Act 2005 ss 57–60; and MENTAL HEALTH AND CAPACITY vol 75 (2013) PARA 751 et seq.

3 The Public Guardian must cancel the registration of an instrument as a lasting power of attorney if he is satisfied that the power has been revoked as a result of the donor's death: Lasting Powers of Attorney, Enduring Powers of Attorney and Public Guardian Regulations 2007, SI 2007/1253, reg 22(1). Where the Public Guardian cancels the registration of an instrument he must notify the donee or, if more than one, each of them: reg 22(2).

4 Mental Capacity Act 2005 s 13(6)(b) (amended by SI 2012/2024). As to references in the Mental Capacity Act 2005 to the 'bankruptcy' of an individual see PARA 197 note 3. As to debt relief orders under the Insolvency Act 1986 Pt 7A (ss 251A–251X) see BANKRUPTCY AND INDIVIDUAL INSOLVENCY vol 5 (2013) PARA 101 et seq.

5 As to the meaning of 'trust corporation' see PARA 197 note 4.

6 Mental Capacity Act 2005 s 13(6)(b).

7 Mental Capacity Act 2005 s 13(6)(c). Marriage includes marriage of a same sex couple: see Marriage (Same Sex Couples) Act 2013 Sch 3 para 1(1)(a), (2), (3); and MATRIMONIAL AND CIVIL PARTNERSHIP LAW vol 72 (2015) PARA 1 et seq.

8 Mental Capacity Act 2005 s 13(6)(d).

9 Mental Capacity Act 2005 s 13(5)(b).

10 Mental Capacity Act 2005 s 13(7)(a). If in the case of a registered instrument it appears to the Public Guardian that the donee has been replaced under the terms of the instrument the Public Guardian must attach to the instrument a note to that effect: Sch 1 para 23. See also note 11. For procedural provisions relating to the attachment of notes see PARA 234 note 5.

11 Mental Capacity Act 2005 s 13(7)(b). If in the case of a registered instrument it appears to the Public Guardian that an event has occurred which has terminated the appointment of the donee but which has not revoked the instrument, the Public Guardian must attach to the instrument a note to that effect: Sch 1 para 22. See also note 10.

12 Mental Capacity Act 2005 Sch 1 para 17(1)(b). If the Public Guardian cancels the registration of an instrument he must notify the donor and the donee or, if more than one, each of them: Sch 1 para 17(2). On the cancellation of the registration of an instrument, the instrument and any office copies of it must be delivered up to the Public Guardian to be cancelled: Sch 1 para 20. As to the delivery up of documents see PARA 234 note 5.

13 Mental Capacity Act 2005 s 13(8) (amended by SI 2012/2404).

14 Mental Capacity Act 2005 s 13(9) (amended by SI 2012/2404). Where the donee is one of two or more appointed to act jointly and severally under the registered power in respect of any matter, the reference in the Mental Capacity Act 2005 s 13(9) to the suspension of the power is to its suspension in so far as it relates to that donee: s 13(10). If in the case of a registered instrument it appears to the Public Guardian that under s 13 a lasting power of attorney is suspended in relation to the donor's property and affairs (but not in relation to other matters), the Public Guardian must attach to the instrument a note to that effect: Sch 1 para 21. For procedural provisions relating to such notes see PARA 234 note 5.

15 Mental Capacity Act 2005 s 13(11).

(iv) Administration of Power and Protection of Parties

236. Interpretation and administration of lasting power.

Where a person has executed or purported to execute an instrument with a view to creating a lasting power of attorney[1], or an instrument has been registered as a lasting power of attorney[2] conferred by that person[3], the court[4] may determine any question as to the meaning or effect of the power or an instrument purporting to create one[5], and if the court determines that a lasting power contains a provision which is ineffective as part of a lasting power or prevents the instrument from operating as a valid lasting power it must either notify the Public Guardian[6] that it has severed the provision[7] or direct him to cancel the registration of the instrument as a lasting power[8].

The court may also give directions with respect to decisions which the donee[9] has authority to make and the donor lacks capacity[10] to make[11] and give any consent or authorisation to act which the donee would have to obtain from the donor if the donor had capacity to give it[12]. Moreover the court may, if the donor lacks capacity to do so:

(1)   give directions to the donee with respect to the rendering by him of reports or accounts and the production of records kept by him for that purpose[13];

(2)   require the donee to supply information or produce documents or things in his possession as donee[14];

(3)   give directions with respect to the remuneration or expenses of the donee[15];

(4)   relieve the donee wholly or partly from any liability which he has or may have incurred on account of a breach of his duties as donee[16].

The court may authorise the making of gifts which are not permitted gifts[17].

1   Mental Capacity Act 2005 s 22(1)(a). As to the meaning of 'lasting power of attorney' see PARA 218. As to execution see PARA 223.

2   As to registration see PARA 226 et seq.

3   Mental Capacity Act 2005 s 22(1)(b).

4   Ie the Court of Protection: see PARA 199 note 6. For specific procedural provision in connection with these matters see the Court of Protection Rules 2017, SI 2017/1035, r 9.7.

5   Mental Capacity Act 2005 s 23(1).

6   As to the Public Guardian see the Mental Capacity Act 2005 ss 57–60; and MENTAL HEALTH AND CAPACITY vol 75 (2013) PARA 751 et seq.

7   Mental Capacity Act 2005 Sch 1 para 19(1), (2)(a). If in the case of a registered instrument the court notifies the Public Guardian under Sch 1 para 19(2)(a) that it has severed a provision of the instrument, the Public Guardian must attach to it a note to that effect: Sch 1 para 24. For procedural provisions relating to the attachment of notes see PARA 234 note 5.

8   Mental Capacity Act 2005 Sch 1 para 19(2)(b). If the Public Guardian cancels the registration of an instrument he must notify the donor and the donee or, if more than one, each of them: Sch 1 para 17(2). On the cancellation of the registration of an instrument, the instrument and any office copies of it must be delivered up to the Public Guardian to be cancelled: Sch 1 para 20. As to the delivery up of documents see PARA 234 note 5.

9   Where two or more donees are appointed under a lasting power of attorney, these provisions apply as if references to the donee were to all or any of them: Mental Capacity Act 2005 s 23(5).

10   As to the meaning of 'capacity' and cognate expressions see PARA 196 note 2.

11   Mental Capacity Act 2005 s 23(2)(a).

12   Mental Capacity Act 2005 s 23(2)(b).

13   Mental Capacity Act 2005 s 23(3)(a).

14   Mental Capacity Act 2005 s 23(3)(b).

15   Mental Capacity Act 2005 s 23(3)(c).

16   Mental Capacity Act 2005 s 23(3)(d).

17   Mental Capacity Act 2005 s 23(4). Gifts which are not permitted gifts are gifts that are not within s 12(2) (see PARA 218). Where the potential infringement is so minor that it would be disproportionate to make a formal application to the court, an application must be made to the court for an order under the Mental Capacity Act 2005 s 23 in any of the following cases:

    (1)   gifts that exceed the limited scope of the authority conferred on attorneys by the Mental Capacity Act 2005 s 12;

    (2)   loans to the attorney or to members of the attorney's family;

    (3)   any investment in the attorney's own business;

    (4)   sales or purchases at an undervalue; and

    (5)   any other transactions in which there is a conflict between the interests of the donor and the interests of the attorney: see *Public Guardian v C* [2013] EWHC 2965 (COP) at [43], sub nom *Re Buckley* [2013] WTLR 373.

237. Power to cancel lasting power.

Where a person has executed or purported to execute an instrument with a view to creating a lasting power of attorney[1], or an instrument has been registered as a lasting power of attorney[2] conferred by that person[3], the court[4] may:

(1) determine any question relating to whether one or more of the requirements for the creation of a lasting power of attorney have been met[5]; and

(2) determine any question relating to whether the power has been revoked or has otherwise come to an end[6],

and must direct the Public Guardian[7] to cancel the registration of an instrument as a lasting power of attorney if it determines[8] either that a requirement for creating the power was not met[9] or that the power has been revoked or has otherwise come to an end[10]. The court may also intervene in the process of creating, executing or registering a lasting power where it is appropriate to do so in the interests of the donor[11].

1 Mental Capacity Act 2005 s 22(1)(a). As to the meaning of 'lasting power of attorney' see PARA 218. As to execution see PARA 223.
2 As to registration see PARA 226 et seq.
3 Mental Capacity Act 2005 s 22(1)(b).
4 Ie the Court of Protection: see PARA 199 note 6. For specific procedural provision in connection with these matters see the Court of Protection Rules 2017, SI 2017/1035, r 9.7.
5 Mental Capacity Act 2005 s 22(2)(a). As to the requirements for the creation of a lasting power of attorney see PARA 220 et seq.
6 Mental Capacity Act 2005 s 22(2)(b). As to revocation and termination see PARAPARAS 234–235 (revocation and termination of registered power).
7 As to the Public Guardian see the Mental Capacity Act 2005 ss 57–60; and MENTAL HEALTH AND CAPACITY vol 75 (2013) PARA 751 et seq.
8 Ie under either the Mental Capacity Act 2005 s 22(2)(a) or s 22(2)(b) (see the text and notes 5, 6).
9 Mental Capacity Act 2005 Sch 1 para 18(a).
10 Mental Capacity Act 2005 Sch 1 para 18(b). If the Public Guardian cancels the registration of an instrument he must notify the donor and the donee or, if more than one, each of them: Sch 1 para 17(2). On the cancellation of the registration of an instrument, the instrument and any office copies of it must be delivered up to the Public Guardian to be cancelled: Sch 1 para 20. As to the delivery up of documents see PARA 234 note 5.
11 Ie where fraud or undue pressure is being used to induce the donor to execute an instrument for the purpose of creating a lasting power or to create a lasting power or where the donee has behaved, or is behaving, in a way that contravenes his authority or is not in the donor's best interests or proposes to behave in such a way: see the Mental Capacity Act 2005 s 22(3)–(6), Sch 1 para 18(c); and PARAS 225, 232, 234. As to intervention by the Public Guardian for the purpose of safeguarding the donor's best interests and monitoring the donee's behaviour see PARA 238.

238. Intervention by Public Guardian.

Where it appears to the Public Guardian[1] that there are circumstances suggesting that the donee of a lasting power of attorney[2] may:

(1) have behaved, or may be behaving, in a way that contravenes his authority or is not in the best interests of the donor of the power[3];

(2) be proposing to behave in a way that would contravene that authority or would not be in the donor's best interests[4]; or

(3) have failed to comply with the requirements of an order made, or directions given, by the court[5],

the Public Guardian may require the donee:

(a) to provide specified information or information of a specified description[6]; or

(b)   to produce specified documents or documents of a specified description[7],

and may require any information so provided to be verified, and any document so produced to be authenticated, in such manner as he may reasonably require[8].

1   As to the Public Guardian see the Mental Capacity Act 2005 ss 57–60; and MENTAL HEALTH AND CAPACITY vol 75 (2013) PARA 751 et seq.
2   As to the meaning of 'lasting power of attorney' see PARA 218.
3   Lasting Powers of Attorney, Enduring Powers of Attorney and Public Guardian Regulations 2007, SI 2007/1253, reg 46(1)(a).
4   Lasting Powers of Attorney, Enduring Powers of Attorney and Public Guardian Regulations 2007, SI 2007/1253, reg 46(1)(b).
5   Lasting Powers of Attorney, Enduring Powers of Attorney and Public Guardian Regulations 2007, SI 2007/1253, reg 46(1)(c). The court is the Court of Protection: see PARA 199 note 6.
6   Lasting Powers of Attorney, Enduring Powers of Attorney and Public Guardian Regulations 2007, SI 2007/1253, reg 46(2)(a). 'Specified' means specified in a notice in writing given to the donee by the Public Guardian: reg 46(5). The information or documents must be provided or produced before the end of such reasonable period as may be specified (reg 46(3)(a)) and at such place as may be specified (reg 46(3)(b)).
7   Lasting Powers of Attorney, Enduring Powers of Attorney and Public Guardian Regulations 2007, SI 2007/1253, reg 46(2)(b). See note 6.
8   Lasting Powers of Attorney, Enduring Powers of Attorney and Public Guardian Regulations 2007, SI 2007/1253, reg 46(4).

239. Acts done in pursuance of invalid power.

If an instrument has been registered[1] as a lasting power of attorney[2] but a lasting power of attorney was not created[3] a donee[4] who acts in purported exercise of the power does not incur any liability[5] because of the non-existence of the power[6] and any transaction between the donee and another person is, in favour of that person, as valid as if the power had been in existence[7]. This applies whether or not the registration has been cancelled at the time of the act or transaction in question[8], unless at the time of acting the donee knows that a lasting power was not created[9] or is aware of circumstances which, if a lasting power had been created, would have terminated his authority to act as a donee[10] or at the time of the transaction the other person has knowledge of any such matter[11].

1   Ie under the Mental Capacity Act 2005 Sch 1 (see PARA 226 et seq).
2   Mental Capacity Act 2005 s 14(1)(a). As to the meaning of 'lasting power of attorney' see PARA 218.
3   Mental Capacity Act 2005 s 14(1)(b).
4   Where two or more donees are appointed under a lasting power of attorney, these provisions apply as if references to the donee were to all or any of them: Mental Capacity Act 2005 s 14(6).
5   Ie to the donor or any other person: Mental Capacity Act 2005 s 14(2).
6   Mental Capacity Act 2005 s 14(2).
7   Mental Capacity Act 2005 s 14(3).
8   Mental Capacity Act 2005 s 14(1).
9   Mental Capacity Act 2005 s 14(2)(a).
10 Mental Capacity Act 2005 s 14(2)(b).
11 Mental Capacity Act 2005 s 14(3). Where the interest of a purchaser depends on whether a transaction between the donee and another person was valid by virtue of s 14(3), it is conclusively presumed in favour of the purchaser that the transaction was valid if the transaction between that person and the donee was completed within 12 months of the date on which the instrument was registered (s 14(4)(a)) and that person makes a statutory declaration, before or within three months after the completion of the purchase, that he had no reason at the time of the transaction to doubt that the donee had authority to dispose of the property which was the subject of the transaction (s 14(4)(b)). As to the meanings of 'purchaser' and 'purchase' see the Law of Property Act 1925 s 205(1); and LANDLORD AND TENANT vol 62 (2016) PARA 83; REAL PROPERTY AND

REGISTRATION vol 87 (2017) PARA 656; definition applied by the Mental Capacity Act 2005 s 64(1). As to the meaning of 'property' see PARA **196** note 11.

10. GUARDIANSHIP ORDERS

240. Provision for managing the property and affairs of missing persons.

The Guardianship (Missing Persons) Act 2017[1] makes provision for managing the property and affairs of missing persons. For the purposes of the Act, a person is 'missing'[2] if:

(1)   he is absent from his usual place of residence[3];

(2)   he is absent from his usual day-to-day activities[4]; and

(3)   the first or second condition is met[5].

The first condition is met if the person's whereabouts are either not known at all, or are not known with sufficient precision to enable the person to be contacted for the purposes of decisions relating to his property and financial affairs[6]. The second condition is met if:

(a)   the person is unable to make decisions relating to his property and financial affairs or to communicate such decisions with a view to their implementation (or both)[7]; and

(b)   the reason for that is something beyond the person's control, other than illness, injury or lack of capacity[8] in relation to a matter[9].

A guardianship order may be made appointing a guardian to exercise certain rights of the missing person in relation to their property and financial affairs[10].

1   At the date at which this volume states the law the Guardianship (Missing Persons) Act 2017 was not fully in force. The following provisions came into force on 27 April 2017 (ie the day on which the Act was passed): s 16(5)–(7), s 17 (so far as it confers power to make regulations), s 18(6)–(8) (see PARA 244), s 24, s 25: see s 25(1), (2), (5). The remaining provisions come into force on such day as the Secretary of State may appoint by regulations made by statutory instrument: s 25(3), (4).

    In any enactment, 'Secretary of State' means one of Her Majesty's principal Secretaries of State: see the Interpretation Act 1978 Sch 1; and STATUTES AND LEGISLATIVE PROCESS vol 96 (2012) PARA 1209. The office of Secretary of State is a unified office, and in law each Secretary of State is generally capable of performing the functions of all or any of them: see CONSTITUTIONAL AND ADMINISTRATIVE LAW vol 20 (2014) PARA 153.

2   In relation to an application or order under the Guardianship (Missing Persons) Act 2017, 'the missing person' means the missing person whose property or financial affairs are or would be the subject of the application or order; and in relation to a guardian, the missing person in respect of whose property or financial affairs the guardian is appointed: s 24(1) (not yet in force). References in ss 8, 9, 11, 14(1), 15(1) and 18, and in ss 19 and 21 (so far as they apply to applications or proceedings in connection with such a person) to a missing person include a person whose property or financial affairs are or were the subject of a guardianship order but who is no longer missing: s 24(2) (not yet in force). As to guardianship orders see PARA 241 et seq.

3   Guardianship (Missing Persons) Act 2017 ss 1(1)(a), 24(1) (not yet in force). See note 4.

4   Guardianship (Missing Persons) Act 2017 s 1(1)(b) (not yet in force). A person who is detained, whether in a prison or another place, is to be treated for these purposes as absent from his or her usual place of residence and usual day-to-day activities: s 1(4) (not yet in force).

5   Guardianship (Missing Persons) Act 2017 s 1(1)(c) (not yet in force).

6   Guardianship (Missing Persons) Act 2017 s 1(2) (not yet in force).

7   Guardianship (Missing Persons) Act 2017 s 1(3)(a) (not yet in force).

8   Ie within the meaning of the Mental Capacity Act 2005: see MENTAL HEALTH AND CAPACITY.

9   Guardianship (Missing Persons) Act 2017 s 1(3)(b) (not yet in force).

10 See the Guardianship (Missing Persons) Act 2017 ss 2–17; and PARA 241 et seq.

241. Applying for a guardianship order.

As from a day to be appointed, the following provisions have effect[1].

A person may apply to the court[2] for an order appointing a guardian in respect of some or all of a missing person's property and financial affairs[3]. For a guardianship order to be made, the applicant must have a sufficient interest in relation to the missing person's property or financial affairs[4]. For these purposes, the following applicants are treated as having a sufficient interest[5]:

(1)   the missing person and the missing person's personal representatives[6];
(2)   the missing person's spouse, civil partner, parent, child or sibling[7];
(3)   a person who was the guardian in respect of some or all of the missing person's property and financial affairs at any time during the period of one year ending with the day on which the application is made[8].

The applicant must send notice of the application to the persons specified by rules of court, and the application must also be advertised in the required manner[9], otherwise the court will refuse to hear the application[10].

1   At the date at which this volume states the law the Guardianship (Missing Persons) Act 2017 was not fully in force: see PARA 240 note 1.
2   As to the making of a guardianship order see PARA 242.
3   Guardianship (Missing Persons) Act 2017 s 2(1) (not yet in force). As to the meaning of 'missing person' see PARA 240. 'Property' includes any thing in action and any interest in real or personal property: s 24(1) (not yet in force).
4   Guardianship (Missing Persons) Act 2017 s 19(1), (2)(a) (not yet in force).
5   The Guardianship (Missing Persons) Act 2017 s 19, which lists those persons with a sufficient interest, applies also for the purposes of s 9 (applications in respect of accounts and information: see PARA 247), s 10 (directions to guardians: see PARA 245), s 11 (actions outside the guardian's authority: see PARA 245), s 12 (variation of a guardianship order: see PARA 248), s 13 (revocation of a guardianship order: see PARA 249). In relation to an application under s 10, 12 or 13, the guardian is treated as having sufficient interest: see s 19(3)(d) (not yet in force).
6   Guardianship (Missing Persons) Act 2017 s 19(3)(a) (not yet in force). 'Personal representative', in relation to a person who has died, means a person responsible for administering the person's estate under the law of England and Wales, or a person who, under the law of another country or territory, has functions equivalent to those of administering the person's estate under the law of England and Wales: s 24(1) (not yet in force).
7   Guardianship (Missing Persons) Act 2017 s 19(3)(b) (not yet in force).
8   Guardianship (Missing Persons) Act 2017 s 19(3)(c) (not yet in force).
9   See the Guardianship (Missing Persons) Act 2017 s 20(1), (2)(a) (not yet in force). Further provision imposing obligations to send notice to persons specified in the rules and to advertise may be made by rules of court: see s 20(5) (not yet in force). Section 20 also applies to applications to vary a guardianship order (see s 12; and PARA 248) and applications to revoke a guardianship order (see s 13; and PARA 249).
10 See the Guardianship (Missing Persons) Act 2017 s 20(3) (not yet in force). If the court makes an order on an application in circumstances in which a notice or advertisement requirement has not been met, this failure to meet the requirement does not invalidate the order, but where the court considers varying or revoking a guardianship order which it knows was made or varied in such circumstances, it must consider the effect of the failure: s 20(4) (not yet in force). See note 5.

242.   Making a guardianship order.

As from a day to be appointed, the following provisions have effect[1].

The court[2] has jurisdiction to hear and determine an application for a guardianship order[3] in relation to property or financial affairs of a missing person[4] only if:

(1)   the person was domiciled in England and Wales on the day before he or she was first known to be missing[5];
(2)   the person had been habitually resident in England and Wales throughout the period of one year ending with that day[6]; or
(3)   the application is made by the person's spouse or civil partner and the applicant is either domiciled in England and Wales on the day on which the application is made, or has been habitually resident in England and Wales throughout the period of one year ending with that day[7].

The court may make the guardianship order if it is satisfied that:

(a) the person whose property or financial affairs are the subject of the application is missing[8];

(b) the person was missing throughout the period of 90 days ending with the day on which the application was made (this is called the 'absence condition')[9];

(c) in all the circumstances, the appointment of a guardian in respect of property or financial affairs of the missing person is in the missing person's best interests[10]; and

(d) there is a person who could be appointed as guardian[11].

If the absence condition is not met[12], but a decision is needed, or is likely to be needed, in relation to property or financial affairs of the missing person before the day on which that condition would be met, then the court may nevertheless make the guardianship order[13]. This is referred to as 'the urgency condition'[14].

The court must send a copy of a guardianship order to the Public Guardian[15].

The guardianship order specifies the period for which the guardian is appointed[16] and this must be no longer than four years from the date the order is made[17]. However, the court may make further guardianship orders in respect of some or all of the missing person's property and financial affairs, including orders re-appointing a person as a guardian[18].

The court has power to appoint two or more guardians in respect of some or all of a missing person's property and financial affairs[19], and it may do so whether or not the appointment of multiple guardians is proposed in the application for the guardianship order[20].

1 At the date at which this volume states the law the Guardianship (Missing Persons) Act 2017 was not fully in force: see PARA 240 note 1.

2 After making the required consultations, the Lord Chancellor must by regulations made by statutory instrument designate the High Court or the Court of Protection to have the functions of the court under the Guardianship (Missing Persons) Act 2017: see s 23 (not yet in force).

3 The court must refuse to hear an application for a guardianship order if it considers that the applicant does not have a sufficient interest in relation to the missing person's property or financial affairs: Guardianship (Missing Persons) Act 2017 s 19(1) (not yet in force).

4 As to the meaning of 'missing person' see PARA 240.

5 Guardianship (Missing Persons) Act 2017 s 2(2)(a) (not yet in force). If a person is missing for two or more separate periods, the reference in s 2(2)(a) to the day before he was first known to be missing is to be read as a reference to the day before the latest period began: s 2(3) (not yet in force).

6 Guardianship (Missing Persons) Act 2017 s 2(2)(b) (not yet in force).

7 Guardianship (Missing Persons) Act 2017 s 2(2)(c)(i), (ii) (not yet in force).

8 Guardianship (Missing Persons) Act 2017 s 3(1), (2)(a) (not yet in force).

9 Guardianship (Missing Persons) Act 2017 s 3(1), (2)(b) (not yet in force). The Secretary of State may issue regulations to increase or reduce the period for the time being specified in s 3(2)(b): see s 3(5), (6), (7) (not yet in force).

10 Guardianship (Missing Persons) Act 2017 s 3(1), (2)(c). As to the missing person's best interests see PARA 244.

11 Guardianship (Missing Persons) Act 2017 s 3(1), (2)(d) (not yet in force). As to the role of guardian see PARA 243.

12 Ie if the court is satisfied that the Guardianship (Missing Persons) Act 2017 s 3(2) does not apply because (and only because) the absence condition in s 3(2)(b) is not met: see s 3(3)(a) (not yet in force).

13 Guardianship (Missing Persons) Act 2017 s 3(3)(b) (not yet in force).

14 Guardianship (Missing Persons) Act 2017 s 3(3) (not yet in force).

15 Guardianship (Missing Persons) Act 2017 s 3(4) (not yet in force). As to the role of the Public Guardian in relation to guardians and guardianship orders see PARA 253.

16 Guardianship (Missing Persons) Act 2017 s 7(1) (not yet in force).

17 Guardianship (Missing Persons) Act 2017 s 7(2) (not yet in force).

18 Guardianship (Missing Persons) Act 2017 s 7(3) (not yet in force).

19 Guardianship (Missing Persons) Act 2017 s 16(1) (not yet in force).

20 Guardianship (Missing Persons) Act 2017 s 16(3) (not yet in force). The court may appoint
additional guardians at the same time or at different times, and may do so either by means of the
same guardianship order or separate guardianship orders: s 16(2) (not yet in force). Provision is
made concerning the powers of the court when appointing two or more guardians: see s 16(4),
Schedule paras 1–5 (not yet in force). The court may remove one or more of the guardians without
appointing a replacement, but may not remove them all without replacing any: see Schedule para
2 (not yet in force). Where the guardians are appointed to act jointly they must act unanimously
in relation to the missing person's property or financial affairs: see Schedule para 3 (not yet in
force). Where a guardianship order appoints two or more guardians, and one of the guardians dies,
the guardianship order is not revoked on the guardian's death unless no other guardian appointed
under the order remains alive, or the only other guardian remaining alive is appointed only to act
jointly with the deceased guardian: see Schedule para 4 (not yet in force). Where the order appoints
two or more guardians, and a guardian's period of appointment expires, the order is not revoked
if the period of appointment of another guardian appointed under the order has not expired: see
Schedule para 5 (not yet in force).

　　The Secretary of State may by regulations make further provision about the appointment of
two or more guardians: see s 16(5), (6), (7). At the date at which this volume states the law, no such
regulations had been made.

243. The role of guardian.

As from a day to be appointed, the following provisions have effect[1].

A guardianship order[2] either appoints the guardian in relation to all of the
missing person's[3] property and financial affairs, or appoints him in relation to
only specified property or financial affairs of the missing person[4]. Similarly, the
order either appoints the guardian to exercise on behalf of the missing person all
of the missing person's rights and powers in relation to the property or financial
affairs to which the order relates[5], or it appoints the guardian to exercise only
specified rights and powers in relation to them[6]. A guardianship order does not
affect any rights, powers or other interests of third parties in relation to the
missing person's property or financial affairs[7].

The order may impose duties on the guardian and include conditions and
restrictions[8]. The rights and powers that a guardian may be appointed to exercise
include: selling, letting or mortgaging the missing person's property[9]; making
investments[10]; executing deeds and other documents[11]; recovering money owed to
the missing person[12]; discharging debts and other obligations of the missing
person (whether legally enforceable or not)[13]; resigning trusteeships held by the
missing person[14]; bringing or conducting legal proceedings[15]; and making a gift
out of the missing person's property[16]. However, a guardian may not execute a will
for the missing person, or exercise a power vested in the missing person as a
trustee in relation to another person's property[17].

A guardian must act in what the guardian reasonably believes to be the missing
person's best interests[18]. He is to be treated as the missing person's agent with the
authority conferred by the guardianship order and the Guardianship (Missing
Persons) Act 2017[19]. Before taking a decision in relation to which it would be
reasonable to expect the missing person to consult a particular person, the
guardian must consult that person unless it is not reasonably practicable to do
so[20].

1　At the date at which this volume states the law the Guardianship (Missing Persons) Act 2017 was
　not fully in force: see PARA 240 note 1.
2　As to applications for guardianship orders see PARA 241. As to the making of such orders see PARA
　242.
3　As to the meaning of 'missing person' see PARA 240.
4　Guardianship (Missing Persons) Act 2017 s 5(1) (not yet in force). A guardianship order may be
　made in respect of any property or financial affairs of the missing person, whether or not
　mentioned in the application: s 5(3) (not yet in force). However, a guardianship order may be made
　only in respect of property or financial affairs in respect of which the court is satisfied that, in all

the circumstances, the appointment of a guardian is in the missing person's best interests and that there is a person who could be appointed as guardian: ss 3(2)(c), (d), 5(4)(a) (not yet in force). Where the order is made in reliance on s 3(3) (see PARA 242), the order may only be made in relation to property or financial affairs in respect of which the court is satisfied that the urgency condition is met: s 5(4)(b) (not yet in force). The order may not relate to the property and financial affairs of more than one person: s 5(2) (not yet in force).

5   Guardianship (Missing Persons) Act 2017 s 6(1)(a) (not yet in force).
6   Guardianship (Missing Persons) Act 2017 s 6(1)(b) (not yet in force).
7   Guardianship (Missing Persons) Act 2017 s 8(4) (not yet in force).
8   Guardianship (Missing Persons) Act 2017 s 6(2) (not yet in force). The court has power to require the guardian to give the Public Guardian security for the exercise of the guardian's functions (s 6(3)(a) (not yet in force)), to require the guardian to submit to the Public Guardian such reports at such times or intervals as the court may direct (s 6(3)(b) (not yet in force)), and to make provision suspending the guardian's authority to exercise rights and powers for a period (s 6(3)(c) (not yet in force)).
9   Guardianship (Missing Persons) Act 2017 s 6(4)(a) (not yet in force).
10 Guardianship (Missing Persons) Act 2017 s 6(4)(b) (not yet in force).
11 Guardianship (Missing Persons) Act 2017 s 6(4)(c) (not yet in force).
12 Guardianship (Missing Persons) Act 2017 s 6(4)(d) (not yet in force).
13 Guardianship (Missing Persons) Act 2017 s 6(4)(e) (not yet in force).
14 Guardianship (Missing Persons) Act 2017 s 6(4)(f) (not yet in force).
15 Guardianship (Missing Persons) Act 2017 s 6(4)(g) (not yet in force).
16 Guardianship (Missing Persons) Act 2017 s 6(4)(h) (not yet in force). A guardian may only make a gift out of the missing person's property if the guardianship order expressly authorises the making of the gift, the making of gifts of a description which includes the gift or the making of gifts generally: s 6(7) (not yet in force). However, this does not apply in relation to a gift made for the maintenance of, or otherwise for the benefit of, a dependant of the missing person: s 6(8) (not yet in force). 'Dependant', in relation to a missing person, means an individual who, if the missing person were not missing, would reasonably rely on the missing person to provide for his or her maintenance: s 6(9) (not yet in force).
17 Guardianship (Missing Persons) Act 2017 s 6(5), (6) (not yet in force). For these purposes, 'will' includes codicil: s 24(1) (not yet in force).
18 See the Guardianship (Missing Persons) Act 2017 s 8(1) (not yet in force); and PARA 244. References in the Act to action by a guardian (however expressed) include inaction: s 24(3) (not yet in force).
19 Guardianship (Missing Persons) Act 2017 s 8(2) (not yet in force).
20 Guardianship (Missing Persons) Act 2017 s 8(3) (not yet in force).

244. Guardian to act in missing person's best interests.

As from a day to be appointed, the following provisions have effect[1].

A guardian must act in what he reasonably believes to be the missing person's best interests[2]. In determining what is in a missing person's best interests, the court or a guardian must consider all the relevant circumstances of which the court or guardian is aware, and must, among other things, take the following steps[3].

First, the court or guardian must consider, so far as is reasonably ascertainable:

(1)   any relevant wishes and feelings expressed by the missing person at any time, including any relevant written statement made by the missing person[4];

(2)   the beliefs and values that would be likely to influence the missing person[5]; and

(3)   any other factors that the missing person would be likely to consider[6].

Secondly, the court or guardian must take into account the views of any persons of whom the court or guardian (as appropriate) is aware with a relevant interest in relation to the missing person's property or financial affairs, where it is reasonably practicable and appropriate to do so[7]. Thirdly, the court or guardian must consider the consequences of taking a proposed action[8].

Neither the court nor the guardian is required to decide a matter by reference to the decision the missing person is likely to have taken in relation to the matter[9], nor are they required to consider any question as to whether or when the missing person might cease to be missing[10].

The Secretary of State may by regulations provide that doing something specified or described in the regulations, or doing it in circumstances specified or described in the regulations, is or is not to be treated as being in a missing person's best interests[11].

1 At the date at which this volume states the law the Guardianship (Missing Persons) Act 2017 was not fully in force: see PARA 240 note 1.

2 Guardianship (Missing Persons) Act 2017 s 8(1) (not yet in force). As to the meaning of 'missing person' see PARA 240.

3 Guardianship (Missing Persons) Act 2017 s 18(1) (not yet in force). As to the court see PARA 242 note 2.

4 Guardianship (Missing Persons) Act 2017 s 18(2)(a) (not yet in force).

5 Guardianship (Missing Persons) Act 2017 s 18(2)(b) (not yet in force).

6 Guardianship (Missing Persons) Act 2017 s 18(2)(c) (not yet in force).

7 Guardianship (Missing Persons) Act 2017 s 18(3) (not yet in force).

8 Guardianship (Missing Persons) Act 2017 s 18(4) (not yet in force).

9 Guardianship (Missing Persons) Act 2017 s 18(5)(a) (not yet in force).

10 Guardianship (Missing Persons) Act 2017 s 18(5)(b) (not yet in force).

11 See the Guardianship (Missing Persons) Act 2017 s 18(6), (7), (8). At the date at which this volume states the law, no such regulations had been made.

245. Directions concerning the scope of the guardian's authority.

As from a day to be appointed, the following provisions have effect[1].

The court[2] may give a direction to a guardian about whether or how to act in a particular case[3], or about the scope of the guardian's authority under the guardianship order and the Guardianship (Missing Persons) Act 2017[4].

The court may make a declaration that action taken by a guardian, when purporting to exercise functions as a guardian, was within or outside the scope of the guardian's authority under the guardianship order and the Act[5]. The court may also make a declaration that a guardian performed or failed to perform a duty under the guardianship order, the Act or regulations under the Mental Capacity Act 2005[6] or a duty owed to the missing person under a rule of law[7]. If the court makes a declaration[8] that a guardian acted outside the scope of the guardian's authority or failed to perform a duty, it may:

(1) make an order disallowing expenses incurred by the guardian or remuneration to which the guardian would otherwise be entitled[9];

(2) make an order requiring the guardian to make a payment of an amount determined by the court to the missing person or the missing person's estate[10];

(3) make such other order as the court considers appropriate for the purpose of compensating the missing person or the missing person's estate for any loss resulting from the action or failure[11].

If the court makes a declaration[12], or otherwise determines, that a guardian acted outside the scope of the guardian's authority or failed to perform a duty as described above but:

(a) the guardian shows that the guardian behaved honestly and reasonably in doing so; and

(b) the court considers that, having regard to all the circumstances, the guardian ought to be relieved of personal liability, the court may relieve the guardian, either entirely or partly, of personal liability in respect of the action or failure[13]. In considering whether to relieve a guardian of personal liability, the court must have regard to the care and skill that it is reasonable to expect the guardian to have exercised in the circumstances[14], and in the case of a person acting as a guardian in the course of a business or profession, it must have regard to any special knowledge or experience that it is reasonable to expect of a person acting in the course of that kind of business or profession[15].

1 At the date at which this volume states the law the Guardianship (Missing Persons) Act 2017 was not fully in force: see PARA 240 note 1.
2 As to the court see PARA 242 note 2.
3 Guardianship (Missing Persons) Act 2017 s 10(1)(a) (not yet in force). The court may make such a declaration on an application (see PARA 241) or without an application being made: s 10(2) (not yet in force).
   The court must refuse to hear an application under s 10 if it considers that the applicant does not have a sufficient interest in relation to the missing person's property or financial affairs: s 19(1), (2)(c) (not yet in force). As to persons having a sufficient interest see PARA 241.
4 Guardianship (Missing Persons) Act 2017 s 10(1)(b) (not yet in force). See note 3.
5 Guardianship (Missing Persons) Act 2017 s 11(1)(a) (not yet in force). The court may make such a declaration on an application (see PARA 241) or without an application being made: s 11(2) (not yet in force).
   The court must refuse to hear an application under s 11 if it considers that the applicant does not have a sufficient interest in relation to the missing person's property or financial affairs: s 19(1), (2)(d) (not yet in force). As to persons having a sufficient interest see PARA 241.
6 Ie regulations under the Mental Capacity Act 2005 s 58.
7 Guardianship (Missing Persons) Act 2017 s 11(1)(b) (not yet in force). See note 5.
8 Ie under the Guardianship (Missing Persons) Act 2017 s 11(1) (not yet in force).
9 Guardianship (Missing Persons) Act 2017 s 11(3)(a) (not yet in force). This does not prevent the court from exercising powers otherwise available to it: s 11(4) (not yet in force).
10 Guardianship (Missing Persons) Act 2017 s 11(3)(b) (not yet in force). See note 9.
11 Guardianship (Missing Persons) Act 2017 s 11(3)(c) (not yet in force). See note 9.
12 Ie under the Guardianship (Missing Persons) Act 2017 s 11(1) (not yet in force).
13 Guardianship (Missing Persons) Act 2017 s 11(5) (not yet in force).
14 Guardianship (Missing Persons) Act 2017 s 11(6)(a) (not yet in force).
15 Guardianship (Missing Persons) Act 2017 s 11(6)(b) (not yet in force).

246. Who may be appointed as guardian.

As from a day to be appointed, the following provisions have effect[1].

The court[2] may only appoint a person as a guardian in respect of property or financial affairs of a missing person[3] if it is satisfied that the person:

(1)   is an individual aged at least 18 or a trust corporation[4];
(2)   consents to the appointment[5];
(3)   is suitable to act as the guardian of the property or financial affairs[6]; and
(4)   if appointed, will act in the missing person's best interests[7].

For the purposes of determining whether the proposed guardian is suitable to act as the guardian of property or financial affairs, the court must, among other things, have regard to:

(a)   the proposed guardian's relationship with the missing person[8];
(b)   the missing person's views on the proposed guardian, so far as they are known to, or reasonably ascertainable by, the court[9];
(c)   whether the proposed guardian has the skills and knowledge necessary to carry out the functions proposed to be conferred on the proposed guardian by the guardianship order[10];
(d)   any conflict between the proposed guardian's interests and the missing person's interests[11].

For the purposes of determining whether there is a conflict between the proposed guardian's interests and the missing person's interests, the court must, among other things, consider any connection between the proposed guardian's property and financial affairs and the missing person's property and financial affairs[12], and how any such connection might affect the taking of decisions by the proposed guardian if appointed[13]. There is not a conflict between the proposed guardian's interests and the missing person's interests merely because the proposed guardian is the missing person's spouse, civil partner, parent, child, sibling or other relative[14], or was living with the missing person immediately before he became a missing person[15], or may benefit from being appointed as guardian, whether directly or indirectly[16].

The court may make a guardianship order appointing a person as a guardian whether or not the person is proposed in the application for the order[17].

1 At the date at which this volume states the law the Guardianship (Missing Persons) Act 2017 was not fully in force: see PARA 240 note 1.
2 As to the court see PARA 242 note 2.
3 As to the meaning of 'missing person' see PARA 240.
4 Guardianship (Missing Persons) Act 2017 s 4(1)(a) (not yet in force). As to trust corporations see the Trustee Act 1925 s 68; and TRUSTS AND POWERS vol 98 (2013) PARA 238 et seq.
5 Guardianship (Missing Persons) Act 2017 s 4(1)(b) (not yet in force).
6 Guardianship (Missing Persons) Act 2017 s 4(1)(c) (not yet in force).
7 Guardianship (Missing Persons) Act 2017 s 4(1)(d) (not yet in force). As to the missing person's best interests see PARA 244.
8 Guardianship (Missing Persons) Act 2017 s 4(2)(a) (not yet in force).
9 Guardianship (Missing Persons) Act 2017 s 4(2)(b) (not yet in force).
10 Guardianship (Missing Persons) Act 2017 s 4(2)(c) (not yet in force). As to the making of a guardianship order see PARA 242.
11 Guardianship (Missing Persons) Act 2017 s 4(2)(d) (not yet in force).
12 Guardianship (Missing Persons) Act 2017 s 4(3)(a) (not yet in force).
13 Guardianship (Missing Persons) Act 2017 s 4(3)(b) (not yet in force).
14 Guardianship (Missing Persons) Act 2017 s 4(4)(a) (not yet in force).
15 Guardianship (Missing Persons) Act 2017 s 4(4)(b) (not yet in force).
16 Guardianship (Missing Persons) Act 2017 s 4(4)(c) (not yet in force).
17 Guardianship (Missing Persons) Act 2017 s 4(5) (not yet in force). As to applications for a guardianship order see PARA 241.

247. Guardian's records, accounts and expenses.

As from a day to be appointed, the following provisions have effect[1].

A guardian appointed under the Guardianship (Missing Persons) Act 2017 must keep records of the exercise of functions as a guardian, including accounts relating to the exercise of those functions[2]. On ceasing to be a guardian, he must give a copy of the records to such persons as the court directs[3]. The court may, on an application, order a person to provide the applicant with accounts or other information relating to the person's exercise of functions as a guardian in the form and manner specified in the order[4].

A guardian is entitled to be reimbursed out of the missing person's property for reasonable expenses incurred in connection with the exercise of functions as a guardian[5]. The court may direct that a guardian is also entitled to remuneration payable out of the missing person's property for exercising those functions[6].

1 At the date at which this volume states the law the Guardianship (Missing Persons) Act 2017 was not fully in force: see PARA 240 note 1.
2 Guardianship (Missing Persons) Act 2017 s 9(3)(a) (not yet in force). As to the role of guardian see PARA 243.
3 Guardianship (Missing Persons) Act 2017 s 9(3)(b) (not yet in force). When giving a direction under s 9(3), the court must have regard to the need to keep the missing person's affairs

confidential, and the need to impose only such requirements as are reasonable in all the circumstances: s 9(5) (not yet in force). Such directions may include conditions and restrictions: s 9(6) (not yet in force).

4   Guardianship (Missing Persons) Act 2017 s 9(4) (not yet in force). When considering an application under s 9(4), the court must have regard to the need to keep the missing person's affairs confidential, and the need to impose only such requirements as are reasonable in all the circumstances: s 9(5) (not yet in force). Such directions may include conditions and restrictions: s 9(6) (not yet in force).

The court must refuse to hear an application under s 9 if it considers that the applicant does not have a sufficient interest in relation to the missing person's property or financial affairs: s 19(1), (2)(b) (not yet in force). As to persons having a sufficient interest see PARA 241.

5   Guardianship (Missing Persons) Act 2017 s 9(1) (not yet in force).
6   Guardianship (Missing Persons) Act 2017 s 9(2) (not yet in force).

248. Variation of guardianship order.

As from a day to be appointed, the following provisions have effect[1].

The court[2] may make an order varying a guardianship order either with or without an application being made[3]. It may do so only if it is satisfied that:

(1)   the person whose property or financial affairs are the subject of the guardianship order is missing[4];
(2)   the absence condition or the urgency condition is met[5]; and
(3)   in all the circumstances, the proposed variation is in the missing person's best interests[6].

The court may appoint a different person to be the guardian[7], add or remove property or financial affairs[8], add, remove or alter conditions or restrictions contained in the order[9], or alter the period for which the guardian is appointed[10]. In fact it may do anything else that it could do on making a guardianship order[11].

The court must send a copy of an order varying a guardianship order to the Public Guardian[12].

Where an application to vary a guardianship order is made, the applicant must send notice of the application and any other specified information to the persons specified by rules of court, and the application must be appropriately advertised[13], otherwise the court must refuse to hear the application[14].

1   At the date at which this volume states the law the Guardianship (Missing Persons) Act 2017 was not fully in force: see PARA 240 note 1.
2   As to the court see PARA 242 note 2.
3   Guardianship (Missing Persons) Act 2017 s 12(1) (not yet in force). The court must refuse to hear an application under s 12 if it considers that the applicant does not have a sufficient interest in relation to the missing person's property or financial affairs: s 19(1), (2)(e) (not yet in force). As to persons having a sufficient interest see PARA 241.
4   Guardianship (Missing Persons) Act 2017 s 12(2)(a) (not yet in force). As to missing persons see PARA 240.
5   Guardianship (Missing Persons) Act 2017 s 12(2)(b) (not yet in force). As to the absence condition and the urgency condition see PARA 242.
6   Guardianship (Missing Persons) Act 2017 s 12(2)(c) (not yet in force). As to the missing person's best interests see PARA 244.
7   Guardianship (Missing Persons) Act 2017 s 12(3)(a) (not yet in force).
8   Guardianship (Missing Persons) Act 2017 s 12(3)(b) (not yet in force). However, where the court varies a guardianship order in circumstances in which the urgency condition (but not the absence condition) is met, it may only make provision in respect of property or financial affairs in respect of which it is satisfied that the urgency condition is met: s 12(4) (not yet in force).
9   Guardianship (Missing Persons) Act 2017 s 12(3)(c) (not yet in force).
10 Guardianship (Missing Persons) Act 2017 s 12(3)(d) (not yet in force). However, the court may not vary a guardianship order so that the period for which the guardian is appointed ends after the last day of the four year period specified in s 7(2) (see PARA 242): s 12(5) (not yet in force).
11 Guardianship (Missing Persons) Act 2017 s 12(3)(e) (not yet in force).

12 Guardianship (Missing Persons) Act 2017 s 12(6) (not yet in force). As to the role of the Public Guardian see PARA 253.

13 See the Guardianship (Missing Persons) Act 2017 s 20(1), (2)(b) (not yet in force); and PARA 241.

14 See the Guardianship (Missing Persons) Act 2017 s 20(3) (not yet in force); and PARA 241.

249. Revocation of guardianship order.

As from a day to be appointed, the following provisions have effect[1].

The court[2] may make an order revoking a guardianship order either with or without an application being made[3]. If a guardian has reasonable grounds to believe that the person whose property or financial affairs are the subject of the guardianship order is no longer missing[4], the guardian must apply to the court as soon as reasonably practicable for the revocation of the order[5].

Where an application to revoke a guardianship order is made, the applicant must send notice of the application and any other information specified by rules of court to the persons specified by rules of court, and the application must be appropriately advertised[6], otherwise the court will refuse to hear the application[7].

The court may revoke a guardianship order only if it is satisfied that the person whose property or financial affairs are the subject of the guardianship order is no longer missing[8], or it is satisfied that in all the circumstances, revocation is in the missing person's best interests[9]. The court must send a copy of an order revoking a guardianship order to the Public Guardian[10].

A guardianship order is automatically revoked in the following circumstances:

(1)   on the death of the missing person[11];

(2)   on the making of a declaration of presumed death in respect of the missing person[12];

(3)   on the death of the guardian[13];

(4)   on the expiry of the guardian's period of appointment[14].

Where a person becomes aware that a guardianship order appointing the person as guardian has been revoked under head (1) or (2), the person must inform the Public Guardian as soon as reasonably practicable[15].

1   At the date at which this volume states the law the Guardianship (Missing Persons) Act 2017 was not fully in force: see PARA 240 note 1.

2   As to the court see PARA 242 note 2.

3   Guardianship (Missing Persons) Act 2017 s 13(1) (not in force). The court must refuse to hear an application under s 13 if it considers that the applicant does not have a sufficient interest in relation to the missing person's property or financial affairs: s 19(1), (2)(f) (not yet in force). As to persons having a sufficient interest see PARA 241.

4   As to missing persons see PARA 240.

5   Guardianship (Missing Persons) Act 2017 s 13(2) (not yet in force).

6   See the Guardianship (Missing Persons) Act 2017 s 20(1), (2)(c) (not yet in force); and PARA 241.

7   See the Guardianship (Missing Persons) Act 2017 s 20(3) (not yet in force); and PARA 241.

8   Guardianship (Missing Persons) Act 2017 s 13(3)(a) (not yet in force).

9   Guardianship (Missing Persons) Act 2017 s 13(3)(b) (not yet in force). As to the missing person's best interests see PARA 244.

10 Guardianship (Missing Persons) Act 2017 s 13(4) (not yet in force). As to the role of the Public Guardian see PARA 253.

11 Guardianship (Missing Persons) Act 2017 s 14(1)(a) (not yet in force). A guardianship order made after the death of the missing person is to be treated as having been immediately revoked under s 14(1)(a): see s 14(2) (not yet in force).

12 Guardianship (Missing Persons) Act 2017 s 14(1)(b) (not yet in force). As to declarations of presumed death under the Presumption of Death Act 2013 s 2 see CIVIL PROCEDURE vol 11 (2015) PARA 162 et seq.

13 Guardianship (Missing Persons) Act 2017 s 14(1)(c) (not yet in force). As to the appointment of two or more guardians see PARA 242.

14 Guardianship (Missing Persons) Act 2017 s 14(1)(d) (not yet in force). As to the guardian's period
    of appointment see PARA 242.
15 Guardianship (Missing Persons) Act 2017 s 14(3) (not yet in force).

250. Acts of guardian after variation or revocation of guardianship order.

As from a day to be appointed, the following provisions have effect[1].

Where a guardian acts within the scope of the authority conferred by the guardianship order and the Guardianship (Missing Persons) Act 2017 at a time when the guardianship order has been revoked[2], but the guardian does not know that, the guardian does not incur any personal liability (either to the missing person or any other person) because of the revocation[3].

Where a person deals with a guardian at a time when the guardianship order has been varied[4] or revoked, but the person does not know that, then the transaction between them is, in favour of that person, as valid as if the guardianship order had not been varied or revoked[5].

Where the interest of a purchaser[6] depends on whether a transaction between a guardian and another person was valid[7], it is to be conclusively presumed in favour of the purchaser that the other person did not at the material time know of the variation or revocation of the guardianship order if:

(1)   the transaction between the guardian and the other person was completed within the period of 12 months beginning with the day on which the guardianship order was made[8]; or

(2)   before the completion of the purchase, or within the period of 3 months beginning with the day of its completion, the other person makes a statutory declaration that the person did not at the material time know of the variation or revocation of the guardianship order[9].

1 At the date at which this volume states the law the Guardianship (Missing Persons) Act 2017 was
   not fully in force: see PARA 240 note 1.
2 Ie under the Guardianship (Missing Persons) Act 2017 s 14: see PARA 249.
3 Guardianship (Missing Persons) Act 2017 s 15(1) (not yet in force). Knowledge that a
   guardianship order has been revoked includes knowledge of the occurrence of an event which
   caused it to be revoked under s 14 (see PARA 249): s 15(4)(a) (not yet in force).
4 As to variation of a guardianship order see PARA 248.
5 Guardianship (Missing Persons) Act 2017 s 15(2) (not yet in force).
6 For these purposes, 'purchaser' and 'purchase' have the meaning given in the Law of Property Act
   1925 s 205(1) (see REAL PROPERTY AND REGISTRATION vol 87 (2017) PARA 656): Guardianship
   (Missing Persons) Act 2017 s 15(4)(b) (not yet in force).
7 Ie by virtue of the Guardianship (Missing Persons) Act 2017 s 15(2): see the text and note 5.
8 Guardianship (Missing Persons) Act 2017 s 15(3)(a) (not yet in force).
9 Guardianship (Missing Persons) Act 2017 s 15(3)(b) (not yet in force).

251. Right to intervene in proceedings under the Guardianship (Missing Persons) Act 2017.

As from a day to be appointed the following provisions have effect[1].

The missing person's[2] spouse, civil partner, parent, child or sibling[3] may intervene in proceedings[4] on an application for a guardianship order[5], or proceedings relating to the variation or revocation of a guardianship order[6], or any other proceedings relating to the exercise of functions by a guardian[7]. Other persons may intervene in such proceedings only with the permission of the court[8].

The court must refuse permission to intervene if it considers that the applicant does not have a sufficient interest in relation to the missing person's property or financial affairs[9].

1   At the date at which this volume states the law the Guardianship (Missing Persons) Act 2017 was not fully in force: see PARA 240 note 1.
2   As to the meaning of 'missing person' see PARA 240.
3   'Sibling' means a sibling of the full blood or the half blood: Guardianship (Missing Persons) Act 2017 s 24(1) (not yet in force).
4   This includes arguing before the court any question which the court considers it necessary to have fully argued for the purposes of the proceedings: Guardianship (Missing Persons) Act 2017 s 21(4) (not yet in force).
5   Guardianship (Missing Persons) Act 2017 s 21(1)(a) (not yet in force). As to applications for guardianship orders see PARA 241.
6   Guardianship (Missing Persons) Act 2017 s 21(1)(b) (not yet in force). As to variation of a guardianship order see PARA 248. As to revocation of a guardianship order see PARA 249.
7   Guardianship (Missing Persons) Act 2017 s 21(1)(c) (not yet in force).
8   Guardianship (Missing Persons) Act 2017 s 21(2) (not yet in force).
9   Guardianship (Missing Persons) Act 2017 s 21(3) (not yet in force).

252.   Guidance to supplement the Guardianship (Missing Persons) Act 2017.

As from a day to be appointed the following provisions have effect[1].

A guardian appointed under the Guardianship (Missing Persons) Act 2017 must have regard to any relevant code issued by the Lord Chancellor[2]. If it appears to a court or tribunal conducting legal proceedings that a provision of a code of practice or a failure to comply with such a code, is relevant to a question arising in the proceedings, the provision or failure must be taken into account in deciding the question[3].

1   At the date at which this volume states the law the Guardianship (Missing Persons) Act 2017 was not fully in force: see PARA 240 note 1.
2   Guardianship (Missing Persons) Act 2017 s 22(1), (2) (not yet in force). The Lord Chancellor must prepare and issue codes of practice for the guidance of guardians, and persons making applications under the Act, and with respect to such other matters concerned with the Act as he thinks fit, in accordance with s 22: see s 22(1)–(10). At the date at which this volume states the law no such codes of practice had been issued.
3   Guardianship (Missing Persons) Act 2017 s 22(3).

253.   Role of the Public Guardian.

As from a day to be appointed the following provisions have effect[1].

The Public Guardian[2] is responsible for establishing and maintaining a register of guardianship orders[3], and for supervising guardians[4]. He is required to report to the court on such matters relating to proceedings under the Guardianship (Missing Persons) Act 2017 as the court requires[5].

His functions also include dealing with representations (including complaints) about the way in which a guardian is exercising the guardian's functions[6], and publishing information about the exercise of his functions in connection with guardians and guardianship orders[7].

1   At the date at which this volume states the law the Guardianship (Missing Persons) Act 2017 was not fully in force: see PARA 240 note 1.
2   As to the Public Guardian see MENTAL HEALTH AND CAPACITY vol 75 (2013) PARAS 751–756.
3   Mental Capacity Act 2005 s 58(2A)(a) (prospectively added by the Guardianship (Missing Persons) Act 2017 s 17(1), (2)).
4   Mental Capacity Act 2005 s 58(2A)(b) (prospectively added: see note 3). He also receives reports from guardians (see s 58(2A)(d) (as so prospectively added)) and receives security which the court requires a guardian to give for the exercise of the guardian's functions (see s 58(2A)(c) (as so prospectively added)).
5   Mental Capacity Act 2005 s 58(2A)(e) (prospectively added: see note 3).

6   Mental Capacity Act 2005 s 58(2A)(f) (prospectively added: see note 3).
7   Mental Capacity Act 2005 s 58(2A)(g) (prospectively added: see note 3).

11. ESTATE AGENCIES AND ACCOMMODATION AGENCIES

(1) ESTATE AGENCIES

(i) Scope of Regulation

254. Regulation of estate agency work under the Estate Agents Act 1979.
The Estate Agents Act 1979[1] imposes controls in respect of persons engaged in estate agency work[2]. The following paragraphs[3] outline the extent of these controls, which relate to standards of competence[4], dealings with clients and third parties[5], and clients' money[6] and the prohibition of unfit persons from engaging in estate agency work[7].

1   As to the enforcement of the Estate Agents Act 1979 see PARA 291; and CONSUMER PROTECTION vol 21 (2016) PARA 686 et seq.
2   As to what does and does not amount to 'estate agency work' see PARAS 255–256.
3   See PARA 255 et seq.
4   See the Estate Agents Act 1979 ss 22, 23; and PARAS 258–259.
5   See PARA 260 et seq. As to the duties of service providers generally see SALE OF GOODS AND SUPPLY OF SERVICES vol 91 (2012) PARA 321 et seq. As to the regulation of unfair commercial practices (eg the misleading descriptions of property details) see CONSUMER PROTECTION vol 21 (2016) PARA 422 et seq.
6   See the Estate Agents Act 1979 ss 12–21A; and PARA 266 et seq.
7   See the Estate Agents Act 1979 ss 3, 4; and PARAS 281, 287.

255. Estate agency work.
For the purpose of the statutory regulation of estate agents[1], 'estate agency work' is defined as things done by any person in the course of a business[2] pursuant to instructions received from another person (the 'client') who wishes to dispose of or acquire an interest in land[3]:

(1)   for the purpose of, or with a view to, effecting the introduction to the client of a third person who wishes to acquire or, as the case may be, dispose of such an interest[4]; and

(2)   after such an introduction has been effected in the course of that business, for the purpose of securing the disposal or, as the case may be, the acquisition of that interest[5].

Things done in a professional capacity by associated persons, and things which are incidental to estate agency work, are not regulated under these provisions[6].

1   Ie for the purposes of the Estate Agents Act 1979.
2   Ie including a business in which the person in question is employed: Estate Agents Act 1979 s 1(1). Any reference in s 1 to 'employment' is a reference to employment under a contract of employment: s 1(5)(c). As to contracts of employment see EMPLOYMENT vol 39 (2014) PARA 1 et seq.
3   Any reference in the Estate Agents Act 1979 to 'disposing' of an interest in land is a reference to transferring a legal estate in fee simple absolute in possession or transferring or creating (elsewhere than in Scotland) a lease which, by reason of the level of the rent, the length of the term or both, has a capital value which may be lawfully realised on the open market, and any reference to acquiring an interest in land must be construed accordingly: s 2(1)(a), (b). 'Lease' includes the rights and obligations arising under an agreement to grant a lease: s 2(2). However, references to 'disposing' of an interest in land do not extend to disposing of the interest of a creditor whose debt is secured by way of a mortgage or charge of any kind over land or an agreement for any such mortgage or charge: s 2(3)(a).

4 Estate Agents Act 1979 s 1(1)(a); Estate Agents (Provision of Information) Regulations 1991, SI 1991/859, reg 1(2); Estate Agents (Undesirable Practices) (No 2) Order 1991, SI 1991/1032, art 1(2).
5 Estate Agents Act 1979 s 1(1)(b).
6 See the Estate Agents Act 1979 s 1(2)–(5); and PARA 256.

256. Excluded activities.

The statutory regulation of estate agents[1] does not apply to things done:

(1)   in the course of his profession by a practising solicitor[2] or a person employed[3] by him[4];

(2)   in the course of credit brokerage[5];

(3)   in the course of carrying out any survey or valuation pursuant to a contract which is distinct from that under which estate agency work[6] is done[7];

(4)   in connection with specified planning matters[8],

or to things done by any person:

(a)   pursuant to instructions received by him in the course of his employment in relation to an interest in land if his employer is the person who, on his own behalf, wishes to dispose of or acquire that interest[9];

(b)   in relation to any interest in any property if the property is subject to a mortgage[10] and he is the receiver of the income of it[11]; or

(c)   in relation to a present, prospective or former employee of his or of any person by whom he also is employed if the things are done by reason of the employment (whether past, present or future)[12].

The statutory regulation of estate agents[13] also does not apply to the following things when done by a person who does no other things which amount to estate agency work:

(i)   publishing advertisements or disseminating information;

(ii)   providing a means by which:

(A)   a person who wishes to acquire or dispose of an interest in land can, in response to such an advertisement or dissemination of information, make direct contact with a person who wishes to dispose of or, as the case may be, acquire an interest in land;

(B)   the persons mentioned in head (A) can continue to communicate directly with each other[14].

1 Ie by the Estate Agents Act 1979. As to the matters to which the legislation does apply see PARA 255.
2 'Practising solicitor' means a solicitor who is qualified to act as such under the Solicitors Act 1974 s 1 (see LEGAL PROFESSIONS vol 65 (2015) PARA 466) or corresponding Northern Irish legislation: Estate Agents Act 1979 s 1(5)(a).
3 As to the meaning of 'employment' see PARA 255 note 2.
4 Estate Agents Act 1979 s 1(2)(a).
5 Estate Agents Act 1979 s 1(2)(b). 'Credit brokerage' means credit brokerage within the meaning of the Consumer Credit Act 1974 (see s 145(2)–(4); and CONSUMER CREDIT vol 21 (2016) PARA 260): Estate Agents Act 1979 s 1(2)(b).
6 Ie the things falling within the Estate Agents Act 1979 s 1(1) (see PARA 255).
7 Estate Agents Act 1979 s 1(2)(d).
8 Estate Agents Act 1979 s 1(2)(e) (amended by the Planning (Consequential Provisions) Act 1990 s 4, Sch 2 para 42). The 'specified planning matters' are things done in connection with applications and other matters arising under the Town and Country Planning Act 1990, the Planning (Listed Buildings and Conservation Areas) Act 1990, the Planning (Hazardous Substances) Act 1990 or corresponding Scottish and Northern Irish legislation: Estate Agents Act 1979 s 1(2)(e) (as so amended).

9 Estate Agents Act 1979 s 1(3)(a). As to 'acquiring' and 'disposing of' an interest in land see PARA 255 note 3.
10 'Mortgage' includes a debenture and any other charge on property for securing money or money's worth: Estate Agents Act 1979 s 1(5)(b).
11 Estate Agents Act 1979 s 1(3)(b).
12 Estate Agents Act 1979 s 1(3)(c).
13 See note 1.
14 Estate Agents Act 1979 s 1(4) (substituted by the Enterprise and Regulatory Reform Act 2013 s 70). As to what amounts to 'estate agency work' see PARA 255.

257. Business relationships and other associates.

For the purposes of the statutory regulation of estate agents[1] a person is an 'associate' of another if he is the spouse[2] or civil partner[3] or a relative[4] of that other or of a business associate of that other[5]. A body corporate can be an 'associate' of another body corporate[6], an unincorporated association can be an 'associate' of another unincorporated association[7] and a partnership can be an 'associate' of another partnership[8].

'Associate' also encompasses a business associate[9] and a spouse, civil partner or a relative thereof[10]. Every director and controller[11] of a body corporate is a 'business associate' of that body as respects acts done in the course of a business carried on by it[12]. Members of partnerships are 'business associates' of the other partners and of the partnership itself[13], and officers of unincorporated associations are 'business associates' of their fellow officers[14].

Where an offence committed by a body corporate is proved to have been committed with the consent or connivance of, or to be attributable to any neglect on the part of, any director, manager, secretary or other similar officer of the body corporate, or any person who was purporting to act in any such capacity, he as well as the body corporate is guilty of that offence and liable to be proceeded against and punished accordingly[15].

1 Ie the Estate Agents Act 1979.
2 For this purpose references to a 'spouse' include a former spouse and a reputed spouse: Estate Agents Act 1979 s 32(3) (s 32(2), (3) amended by the Civil Partnership Act 2004 s 261(1), (4), Sch 27 para 63, Sch 30). Marriage includes marriage of a same sex couple: see Marriage (Same Sex Couples) Act 2013 Sch 3 para 1(1)(a), (2), (3); and MATRIMONIAL AND CIVIL PARTNERSHIP LAW vol 72 (2015) PARA 1 et seq.
3 For this purpose references to a 'civil partner' include a former civil partner and a reputed civil partner: Estate Agents Act 1979 s 32(3) (as amended (see note 2); further amended by SI 2005/3129).
4 For this purpose 'relative' means brother, sister, uncle, aunt, nephew, niece, lineal ancestor or linear descendant: Estate Agents Act 1979 s 32(3) (as amended: see note 2). A relationship is established as if an illegitimate child or stepchild of a person were the legitimate child of the relationship in question: s 32(3) (as so amended).
5 Estate Agents Act 1979 s 32(2) (as amended: see note 2); Estate Agents (Provision of Information) Regulations 1991, SI 1991/859, reg 1(2).
6 A body corporate is an associate of another body corporate if the same person is a controller of both, or a person is a controller of one and persons who are his associates, or he and persons who are his associates, are controllers of the other (Estate Agents Act 1979 s 32(4)(a)) or if a group of two or more persons is a controller of each company, and the groups either consist of the same persons or could be regarded as consisting of the same persons by treating (in one or more cases) a member of either group as replaced by a person of whom he is an associate (s 32(4)(b)).
7 An unincorporated association is an associate of another unincorporated association if any person is an officer of both associations (Estate Agents Act 1979 s 32(5)(a)), has the management or control of the activities of both associations (s 32(5)(b)) or is an officer of one association and has the management or control of the activities of the other association (s 32(5)(c)).
8 A partnership is an associate of another partnership if any person is a member of both partnerships (Estate Agents Act 1979 s 32(6)(a)), a person who is a member of one partnership is an associate

of a member of the other partnership (s 32(6)(b)) or a member of one partnership has an associate who is also an associate of a member of the other partnership (s 32(6)(c)).

9 Estate Agents Act 1979 s 32(1); Estate Agents (Undesirable Practices) (No 2) Order 1991, SI 1991/1032, art 1(2).

10 Estate Agents Act 1979 s 32(2) (as amended: see note 2).

11 In relation to a body corporate, 'controller' means a person in accordance with whose directions or instructions the directors of the body or of any other body corporate which is its controller (or any of them) are accustomed to act (Estate Agents Act 1979 s 31(5)(a)) or a person who, either alone or with any associate or associates, is entitled to exercise, or control the exercise of, one third or more of the voting power at any general meeting of the body corporate or of another body corporate which is its controller (s 31(5)(b)).

12 Estate Agents Act 1979 s 31(1), (2).

13 As respects acts done in the course of a business carried on by a partnership, each partner is a business associate of every other member of the partnership and also of the partnership itself and, in the case of a partner which is a body corporate, every person who is a business associate of that body (ie by virtue of the Estate Agents Act 1979 s 31(2) (see the text and note 12)) is also a business associate of every other member of the partnership: s 31(3).

14 As respects acts done in the course of a business carried on by an unincorporated association, every officer of the association and any other person who has the management or control of its activities is a business associate of that association: s 31(4).

15 Estate Agents Act 1979 s 28(2).

(ii) Competence to Act as Estate Agent

258. Standards of competence required of estate agents.

As from a day to be appointed[1] the Secretary of State may by regulations[2] make provision to ensure that estate agents[3] satisfy minimum standards of competence[4]. Such regulations must prescribe a degree of practical experience which is to be taken as evidence of competence and may make provision for professional or academic qualifications[5], and after the appointed day persons may not engage in estate agency work without having attained the required standard[6]: any who do will commit an offence[7].

1 At the date at which this volume states the law the Estate Agents Act 1979 s 22 (see the text and notes 2–7) had not been brought into force.

2 As to the making of such regulations see the Estate Agents Act 1979 s 22(5) (not yet in force).
   Before making any order or regulations under s 3(1)(a)(iii), (d), 14–16, 18, 19, 22, the Secretary of State must consult the lead enforcement authority, such bodies representative of persons carrying on estate agency work, such bodies representative of consumers and such other persons as he thinks fit: s 30(1), (2) (s 30(1) amended by the Enterprise Act 2002 s 278(1), Sch 25 para 9(1), (14)(b)); SI 2014/631. As to the Secretary of State see PARA 240 note 1. As to the lead enforcement authority see PARA 291. As from a day to be appointed these requirements also apply in respect of regulations under the Estate Agents Act 1979 s 21A (see PARA 265) (s 30(2) (prospectively amended by the Consumers, Estate Agents and Redress Act 2007 Sch 7 para 3). At the date at which this volume states the law no such day had been appointed.
   Any power of the Secretary of State to make orders or regulations under the Estate Agents Act 1979 may be so exercised as to make different provision in relation to different cases or classes of cases and to exclude certain cases or classes of cases and includes power to make such supplemental, incidental and transitional provisions as he thinks fit: s 30(3). As to the meaning of 'estate agency work' see PARA 255; for activities not amounting to 'estate agency work' for these purposes see PARA 256.

3 Ie persons engaging in estate agency work as defined in the Estate Agents Act 1979 s 1(1) (see PARA 255).

4 Estate Agents Act 1979 s 22(1) (not yet in force). References in s 22 to a person who has attained the required standard of competence are references to a person who has that degree of practical experience which, in accordance with the regulations (see note 5), is to be taken as evidence of competence or, where the regulations so provide, holds such qualifications or otherwise fulfils such conditions as, in accordance with the regulations, are to be taken to be evidence of competence: s 22(2) (not yet in force).

5   See Estate Agents Act 1979 s 22(2) (not yet in force), which provides that if the Secretary of State exercises his power to make regulations under s 2(1) he must in those regulations prescribe a degree of practical experience which is to be taken as evidence of competence. Without prejudice to the generality of this requirement, the regulations may also:

    (1)   prescribe professional or academic qualifications which are also be taken to be evidence of competence (s 22(2)(a) (not yet in force));

    (2)   designate any body of persons as a body which may itself specify professional qualifications the holding of which is to be taken as evidence of competence (s 22(2)(b) (not yet in force));

    (3)   make provision for and in connection with the establishment of a body having power to examine and inquire into the competence of persons engaged or professing to engage in estate agency work (s 22(2)(c) (not yet in force)); and

    (4)   delegate to a body established as mentioned above powers of the Secretary of State with respect of the matters referred to under head (1) above (s 22(2)(d) (not yet in force)).

At the date at which this volume states the law no such regulations had been made.

6   See the Estate Agents Act 1979 s 22(3) (not yet in force), which provides that after the day appointed for the coming into force of s 22 no individual may engage in estate agency work on his own account unless he has attained the required standard of competence, no member of a partnership may engage in estate agency work on the partnership's behalf unless a prescribed number of the partners have attained the required standard of competence, and no body corporate or unincorporated association may engage in estate agency work unless a prescribed number and prescribed description of the officers, members or employees of the body have attained the required standard of competence. The prescribed number of partners for these purposes, and the prescribed number and description of officers, members or employees of a corporate body or unincorporated association, are to be specified by order of the Secretary of State (s 22(4) (not yet in force)). At the date at which this volume states the law no such order had been made. 'Unincorporated association' does not include a partnership: s 33(1). Any such order will be made by statutory instrument, which is subject to annulment in pursuance of a resolution of either House of Parliament: s 22(4) (not yet in force).

7   Estate Agents Act 1979 s 22(3) (not yet in force). Any person who contravenes s 22(3) is liable on conviction on indictment or on summary conviction to a fine which, on summary conviction, may not exceed the statutory maximum: s 22(3) (not yet in force). As to the powers of magistrates' courts to issue fines on summary conviction see SENTENCING vol 92 (2015) PARA 176.

In any proceedings for an offence under the Estate Agents Act 1979 it is a defence for the person charged to prove that he took all reasonable precautions and exercised all due diligence to avoid the commission of an offence by himself or any person under his control: s 28(1).

259. Bankrupts not permitted to do estate agency work.

An individual who is made bankrupt or in respect of whom a debt relief order is made[1] may not engage in any form of estate agency work[2] except as an employee of another[3]. If he does engage in estate agency work in contravention of this restriction, he commits an offence[4].

This prohibition ceases to have effect when:

    (1)   the bankruptcy order made against the individual is annulled[5]; or

    (2)   the person in question is discharged from bankruptcy[6]; or

    (3)   the debt relief order is revoked on the ground that any information supplied by the debtor was incomplete, incorrect or otherwise misleading[7];

    (4)   the debt relief order is revoked on the ground that a bankruptcy order has been made in relation to the debtor[8]; or

    (5)   the individual is discharged from all the qualifying debts specified under the debt relief order at the end of the moratorium period applicable to the order[9]; or

    (6)   the debt relief order is revoked and a period of one year has elapsed beginning with the effective date for the order[10].

The lead enforcement authority has power under the Estate Agents Act 1979 to make orders prohibiting unfit persons doing estate agency work[11].

1   As to debt relief orders under the Insolvency Act 1986 Pt 7A (ss 251A–251X) see BANKRUPTCY AND INDIVIDUAL INSOLVENCY vol 5 (2013) PARA 101 et seq. As to bankruptcy generally see BANKRUPTCY AND INDIVIDUAL INSOLVENCY.

2   As to the meaning of 'estate agency work' see PARA 255. For activities not amounting to 'estate agency work' for these purposes see PARA 256.

3   Estate Agents Act 1979 s 23(1) (amended by SI 2016/481); Estate Agents Act 1979 s 23(1A) (added by SI 2012/2404). 'Employment' in this context does not include employment by a body corporate of which the person concerned is a director or controller: s 23(3) (amended by SI 2012/2404). As to the meaning of 'controller' see PARA 257 note 11.

4   Estate Agents Act 1979 s 23(4) (amended by SI 2012/2404). A person who commits this offence is liable on conviction on indictment or on summary conviction to a fine which, on summary conviction, is not to exceed the statutory maximum: Estate Agents Act 1979 s 23(4). As to the powers of magistrates' courts to issue fines on summary conviction see SENTENCING vol 92 (2015) PARA 176. As to offences by bodies corporate see PARA 257. As to defences see PARA 258 note 7.

5   Estate Agents Act 1979 s 23(2)(a) (amended SI 2016/481). As to annulment and discharge see BANKRUPTCY AND INDIVIDUAL INSOLVENCY vol 5 (2013) PARAS 620–653.

6   Estate Agents Act 1979 s 23(2)(b) (substituted by the Insolvency Act 1985 s 235, Sch 8 para 33; the Insolvency Act 1986 s 437, Sch 11).

7   Estate Agents Act 1979 s 23(2A)(a) (s 23(2A) added by SI 2012/2404); Insolvency Act 1986 s 251L(2)(a) (s 251L added by the Tribunals, Courts and Enforcement Act 2007 s 108(1), Sch 17).

8   Estate Agents Act 1979 s 23(2A)(a) (as added: see note 7); Insolvency Act 1986 s 251L(2)(c) (as added: see note 7).

9   Estate Agents Act 1979 s 23(2A)(b) (as added: see note 7).

10   Estate Agents Act 1979 s 23(2A)(c) (as added: see note 7).

11   See PARA 281 et seq. This includes persons with certain criminal convictions (see PARA 282), persons who have committed discrimination in the course of estate agency work (see PARA 283), persons who have failed to comply with statutory requirements relating to clients and their money (see PARA 284), persons who have engaged in undesirable practices (see PARA 285) and persons who have breached compliance requirements under the Estate Agents Act 1979 (see PARA 286). As to the lead enforcement authority see PARA 291.

(iii) Dealing with Clients and Clients' Money

A. RELATIONSHIP WITH CLIENTS GENERALLY

260. Provision of information as to services.

Prior to entering into a contract to undertake estate agency work[1] for a client[2] an estate agent[3] must provide the client with information regarding the services[4] being offered, that is information as to the services:

(1)   which the agent is himself offering, or intends to offer, to any prospective purchaser of an interest in the land[5]; or

(2)   which he knows a connected person[6] or (in a case where he or a connected person would derive a financial benefit from the provision of the service) another person is offering, or intends to offer, to any prospective purchaser of an interest in the land[7].

The agent is required to give this information (as well as the information he is required to give as to remuneration[8]) at the time when communication commences between the agent and the client or as soon as is reasonably practicable thereafter provided it is a time before the client is committed to any liability towards the agent[9]. All such information must be given in writing[10].

Failure to comply with any of these provisions renders the agency contract unenforceable[11] other than by order of the court[12].

1   As to the meaning of 'estate agency work' see PARA 255. For activities not amounting to 'estate agency work' for these purposes see PARA 256.

2   For the purposes of the Estate Agents (Provision of Information) Regulations 1991, SI 1991/859, 'client' means a person on whose behalf an estate agent acts: reg 1(2).

3   For the purposes of the Estate Agents (Provision of Information) Regulations 1991, SI 1991/859, 'estate agent' means any person who in the course of a business (including one in which he is employed) engages in estate agency work and includes cases where he is negotiating on his own behalf: reg 1(2).

4   'Services' means any services to a prospective purchaser for consideration, being services which are such as would ordinarily be made available to a prospective purchaser in connection with his acquisition of an interest in land or his use or enjoyment of it (including the provision to that purchaser of banking and insurance services and financial assistance and securing the disposal for that purchaser of an interest in land if that disposal is one which has to be made in order for him to be able to make the acquisition he is proposing or is one which is a result of that acquisition); 'purchaser' means a person to whom an interest in land is transferred or in whose favour it is created; 'interest in land' means any of the interests referred to in the Estate Agents Act 1979 s 2 (see PARA 255); references in the Estate Agents (Provision of Information) Regulations 1991, SI 1991/859, to an 'interest in the land' are references to the particular interest in land of which the estate agent is engaged to secure the disposal or acquisition; and 'financial benefit' includes commission and any performance related benefit: reg 1(2).

5   Estate Agents Act 1979 s 18(1)(b), (4)(a); Estate Agents (Provision of Information) Regulations 1991, SI 1991/859, reg 2(1)(a). As to the making of regulations generally see PARA 258 note 2. As to the information the agent is required to give the client see *Great Estates Group Ltd v Digby* [2011] EWCA Civ 1120, [2012] 2 All ER (Comm) 361, [2011] 3 EGLR 101; and PARA 261.

6   In relation to an estate agent 'connected person' means his employer or principal, any employee or agent of his or any associate of his or of any such person: Estate Agents (Provision of Information) Regulations 1991, SI 1991/859, reg 1(2). As to the meaning of 'associate' see PARA 257.

7   Estate Agents (Provision of Information) Regulations 1991, SI 1991/859, reg 2(1)(b).

8   Ie the information specified for the purposes of the Estate Agents Act 1979 s 18(2) (see PARA 261).

9   Estate Agents Act 1979 s 18(4)(b); Estate Agents (Provision of Information) Regulations 1991, SI 1991/859, regs 2(2), 3(1).

10   Estate Agents (Provision of Information) Regulations 1991, SI 1991/859, reg 4.

11   References to the enforcement of a contract or variation include the withholding of money in pursuance of a lien for money alleged to be due under the contract or as a result of the variation: Estate Agents Act 1979 s 18(7)(a).

12   See the Estate Agents Act 1979 s 18(5), which provides that if any person either fails to comply with the obligation under s 18(1) with respect to a contract or with any provision of the Estate Agents (Provision of Information) Regulations 1991, SI 1991/859, relating to that obligation (see the text and notes 1–10; and PARA 261) or fails to comply with the obligation under the Estate Agents Act 1979 s 18(3) with respect to any variation of a contract or with any provision of the Estate Agents (Provision of Information) Regulations 1991, SI 1991/859, relating to that obligation (see PARA 262) the contract or, as the case may be, the variation of it is not enforceable by him except pursuant to an order of the court. If in such a case the agent concerned makes an application to the court (ie any court having jurisdiction to hear and determine matters arising out of the contract) for the enforcement of the contract or, as the case may be, of a contract as varied by the variation, the court must dismiss the application if, but only if, it considers it just to do so having regard to prejudice caused to the client by the agent's failure to comply with his obligation and the degree of culpability for the failure; and where the court does not dismiss the application, it may nevertheless order that any sum payable by the client under the contract or, as the case may be, under the contract as varied is to be reduced or discharged so as to compensate the client for prejudice suffered as a result of the agent's failure to comply with his obligation (s 18(6), (7)(b)). See *Wells v Devani* [2016] EWCA Civ 1106, [2017] 2 WLR 1391.

261. Provision of information as to remuneration.

Prior to entering into a contract to undertake estate agency work[1] for a client[2], an estate agent[3] must provide the client with information regarding remuneration for the work[4], including:

(1)   particulars of the circumstances in which the client will become liable to pay remuneration to the agent for carrying out estate agency work[5];

(2)   particulars of the amount of the agent's remuneration for carrying out such work or, if that amount is not ascertainable at the time the information is given, particulars of the manner in which it will be calculated[6];

(3)   particulars of any payments which do not form part of the agent's remuneration for carrying out estate agency work or a contract or pre-contract deposit[7] but which, under the contract for estate agency work, will or may in certain circumstances be payable by the client to the agent or any other person and particulars of the circumstances in which any such payments will become payable[8]; and

(4)   particulars of the amount of any payment falling within head (3) above or, if that amount is not ascertainable at the time the information is given, an estimate of that amount together with particulars of the manner in which it will be calculated[9].

An estate agent must also explain to the client the meanings of the terms 'sole selling rights', 'sole agency' and 'ready, willing and able purchaser', or terms having similar purport or effect, if those terms are used by him in the course of carrying out estate agency work[10].

Provision is made for the means of giving this information and the time when it must be given[11]. Failure to comply with any of these provisions renders the agency contract unenforceable other than by order of the court[12].

1   As to the meaning of 'estate agency work' see PARA 255. For activities not amounting to 'estate agency work' for these purposes see PARA 256.
2   As to the meaning of 'client' see PARA 260 note 2.
3   As to the meaning of 'estate agent' see PARA 260 note 3.
4   Estate Agents Act 1979 s 18(1)(a).
5   Estate Agents Act 1979 s 18(2)(a).
6   Estate Agents Act 1979 s 18(2)(b).
7   'Contract deposit' means any sum paid by a purchaser which in whole or in part is, or is intended to form part of, the consideration for acquiring such an interest as is referred to in the Estate Agents Act 1979 s 12(1)(a) (see PARA 266) or for a connected contract; and which is paid by him at or after the time at which he acquires the interest or enters into an enforceable contract to acquire it (s 12(2)); and 'pre-contract deposit' means any sum paid by any person in whole or in part as an earnest of his intention to acquire such an interest as is referred to in s 12(1)(a), or in whole or in part towards meeting any liability of his in respect of the consideration for the acquisition of such an interest which will arise if he acquires or enters into an enforceable contract to acquire the interest, or in respect of a connected contract, and which is paid by him at a time before he either acquires the interest or enters into an enforceable contract to acquire it (s 12(3)). 'Connected contract', in relation to the acquisition of an interest in land, means a contract which is conditional upon such an acquisition or upon entering into an enforceable contract for such an acquisition (whether or not it is also conditional on other matters): s 12(4).
8   Estate Agents Act 1979 s 18(2)(c).
9   Estate Agents Act 1979 s 18(2)(d).
10 Estate Agents Act 1979 s 18(1)(b), (4)(a); Estate Agents (Provision of Information) Regulations 1991, SI 1991/859, reg 5(1), (2). As to the making of regulations see PARAS 258 note 2, 260 note 5. Where an agency contract used the expression 'sole agency', the effect of the Estate Agents Act 1979 s 18, together with the Estate Agents (Provision of Information) Regulations 1991, SI 1991/859, reg 5, Schedule para (b), was to place an obligation on the agent to inform his client what 'sole agency' meant: *Great Estates Group Ltd v Digby* [2011] EWCA Civ 1120, [2012] 2 All ER (Comm) 361, [2011] 3 EGLR 101.
11 See the Estate Agents (Provision of Information) Regulations 1991, SI 1991/859, regs 2(2), 3(1), 4; and PARA 260. Where the information concerns the meaning of 'sole selling rights', 'sole agency' and 'ready, willing and able purchaser', the written explanation must have the form and content of the statement set out in the applicable part of the Schedule, provided that if, by reason of the

provisions of the contract in which those terms appear, the respective explanations are in any way misleading, the content of the explanation must be altered so as accurately to describe the liability of the client to pay remuneration in accordance with those provisions: reg 5(1). The explanation of the terms must be given by the agent to his client in a document setting out the terms of the contract between them (whether that document be a written or printed agreement, a letter, terms of engagement or a form, and whether or not such document is signed by any of the parties): reg 5(3).

Subject to the proviso to reg 5(1), the explanations set out in the Schedule must be reproduced in the documents embodying them in the same form as they appear in that Schedule and without any material alterations or additions to the text, and must be shown prominently, clearly and legibly: reg 6(1). The wording of such explanations must be given no less prominence than that given to any other information in the document setting out the terms of the contract (as more particularly described in reg 5(3)) between the estate agent and his client apart from the heading thereto, trade names, names of the parties and numbers or lettering subsequently inserted therein in handwriting or in type: reg 6(2).

12 See the Estate Agents Act 1979 s 18(5)–(7); and PARA 260.

262. Provision of information as to contractual variations.

If at any time after an estate agent[1] and a client[2] have entered into a contract they are agreed that the terms of the contract should be varied so far as they relate to the carrying out of estate agency work[3] or any payment[4], the agent must give the client details of any changes which, at the time the statement is given, fall to be made in the information which was given to the client before the contract was entered into[5]. Such information must be given, in writing[6], at the time when, or as soon as is reasonably practicable after, the changes are agreed[7].

1 As to the meaning of 'estate agent' see PARA 260 note 3.
2 As to the meaning of 'client' see PARA 260 note 2.
3 As to the meaning of 'estate agency work' see PARA 255. For activities not amounting to 'estate agency work' for these purposes see PARA 256.
4 Ie any payment falling within the Estate Agents Act 1979 s 18(2)(c) (see PARA 261).
5 Estate Agents Act 1979 s 18(3). As to the information which must be given to a client before a contract is entered into see PARAS 260–261.
6 Estate Agents (Provision of Information) Regulations 1991, SI 1991/859, reg 4. As to the making of regulations see PARAS 258 note 2, 260 note 5.
7 Estate Agents (Provision of Information) Regulations 1991, SI 1991/859, regs 2(2), 3(2).

263. Pre-contract deposits.

As from a day to be appointed[1] no person may, in the course of estate agency work[2], seek from any prospective purchaser[3] a payment which, if made, would constitute a pre-contract deposit[4] in excess of a prescribed limit[5] and if in the course of such work any person receives from a prospective purchaser a pre-contract deposit which exceeds such a limit, so much of that deposit as exceeds the limit must forthwith be either repaid to the prospective purchaser or paid to such other person as the prospective purchaser may direct[6]. Failure to comply with these requirements does not render any person liable to any criminal penalty nor constitute a ground for any civil claim[7], but it may be taken into account[8] for the purpose of determining whether a person is unfit to carry out estate agency work[9].

It is now settled that, unless otherwise agreed, an agent, including an estate agent, receives a deposit as a 'stakeholder'[10] and not as agent for the seller[11]. Thus, at any time until contract the purchaser has a right to demand the return of the deposit from the agent, and if the agent becomes insolvent or otherwise defaults the seller is not liable to the purchaser[12].

1 At the date at which this volume states the law the Estate Agents Act 1979 s 19 (see the text and notes 2–9) had not been brought into force.

2   As to the meaning of 'estate agency work' see PARA 255. For activities not amounting to 'estate agency work' for these purposes see PARA 256.
3   Ie a prospective purchaser who wishes to acquire an interest in land in the United Kingdom: Estate Agents Act 1979 s 19(1) (not yet in force). As to 'acquiring' and 'disposing of' an interest in land see PARA 255 note 3.
4   As to the meaning of 'pre-contract deposit' see PARA 261 note 7. In relation to a prospective purchaser, references in the Estate Agents Act 1979 s 19(1), (2) to a 'pre-contract deposit' are to be treated as references to the aggregate of all the payments which constitute pre-contract deposits in relation to his proposed acquisition of a particular interest in land in the United Kingdom: s 19(3) (not yet in force).
5   Estate Agents Act 1979 s 19(1) (not yet in force). The limit may be prescribed by the Secretary of State by regulations made by statutory instrument subject to annulment in pursuance of a resolution of either House of Parliament (s 19(4), (5) (not yet in force)): it may be so prescribed as either a specific amount or a percentage or fraction of a price or other amount determined in any particular case in accordance with the regulations (s 19(4)). At the date at which this volume states the law no such regulations had been made. As to the making of regulations generally see PARA 258 note 2.
6   Estate Agents Act 1979 s 19(2) (not yet in force).
7   Ie other than a claim for the recovery of such an excess as is referred to in the Estate Agents Act 1979 s 19(2) (not yet in force) (see the text and note 6).
8   Ie in accordance with the Estate Agents Act 1979 s 3(1)(c) (see PARA 284).
9   Estate Agents Act 1979 s 19(6) (not yet in force) (amended by the Enterprise Act 2002 s 278, Sch 25 para 9(1), (11)(a)).
10 The term is used here in the loose sense of a person who holds money for two persons pending the happening of a particular event. An agent who receives a deposit is not, strictly speaking, a stakeholder because there has been no contract at that stage: see *Maloney v Hardy and Moorshead* [1971] 2 QB 442n, [1971] 2 All ER 630n, CA, per Russell LJ.
11 *Sorrell v Finch* [1977] AC 728, [1976] 2 All ER 371, HL. There are suggestions in that case that the deposit may be received on the seller's behalf if the seller expressly authorises the agent to accept deposits and the agent signs the receipt 'as agent for the seller'. However, quaere whether that is consistent with the purchaser's right to demand the return of the deposit at any time until the contract has been concluded.
12 *Sorrell v Finch* [1977] AC 728, [1976] 2 All ER 371, HL. Once the contract has been completed the agent is liable to the seller for the deposit subject to his right to deduct commission and expenses. Where both the seller and purchaser claim the deposit, the agent should interplead. As to an estate agent's commission see PARA 104.

264.   Land in which the agent has an interest.

An estate agent[1] may not enter into negotiations with any person with respect to the acquisition or disposal by that person of any land[2] in which the agent has a personal interest[3], unless he has first disclosed the nature and extent of that interest[4], and in any case where the result of a proposed disposal of an interest in land or of such a proposed disposal and other transactions would be that an estate agent would have a personal interest in that land, the agent may not enter into negotiations with any person with respect to the proposed disposal until he has disclosed to that person the nature and extent of that interest[5]. These restrictions apply where an estate agent is negotiating on his own behalf as well as where he is negotiating in the course of estate agency work[6].

An estate agent may not seek or receive a contract deposit[7] or pre-contract deposit[8] in respect of the acquisition or proposed acquisition of a personal interest of his in land in the United Kingdom or of any other interest in any such land in which he has a personal interest[9].

Failure to comply with these requirements does not render any person liable to any criminal penalty nor constitute a ground for any civil claim, but it may be taken into account[10] for the purpose of determining whether a person is unfit to carry out estate agency work[11].

1 Ie a person who is engaged in estate agency work: Estate Agents Act 1979 s 21(1). As to the meaning of 'estate agency work' see PARA 255. For activities not amounting to 'estate agency work' for these purposes see PARA 256.
2 As to 'acquiring' and 'disposing of' an interest in land see PARA 255 note 3.
3 For these purposes, an estate agent has a personal interest in land if he has a beneficial interest in the land or in the proceeds of sale of any interest in it, or he knows or might reasonably be expected to know that his employer or principal, any employee or agent of his, or any associate of his or of any such person, has such a beneficial interest: Estate Agents Act 1979 s 21(5). As to the meaning of 'associate' see PARA 257.
4 Estate Agents Act 1979 s 21(1).
5 Estate Agents Act 1979 s 21(2).
6 Estate Agents Act 1979 s 21(3).
7 As to the meaning of 'contract deposit' see PARA 261 note 7.
8 As to the meaning of 'pre-contract deposit' see PARA 261 note 7.
9 Estate Agents Act 1979 s 21(4).
10 Ie taken into account by the lead enforcement agency in accordance with the Estate Agents Act 1979 s 3(1)(c) (see PARA 284). As to the lead enforcement agency see PARA 291.
11 Estate Agents Act 1979 s 21(6) (amended by SI 2014/631).

265. Keeping of permanent records.

As from a day to be appointed[1] a person engaged in estate agency work[2] is required to keep permanent records[3], and must ensure that there is included in those records[4]:

(1)   information given relating to the services to be provided, remuneration and agreed contractual variations[5];

(2)   information given concerning the nature and extent of the agent's personal interest, if any, in a transaction[6];

(3)   any offer of a prescribed description received by the person concerned and any prescribed information relating to the making of the offer[7];

(4)   any action of a prescribed description taken by the person concerned in relation to such an offer and any prescribed information relating to that action[8]; and

(5)   any other information or event of a prescribed description[9].

The Secretary of State may by regulations[10] make provision as to the manner in which the permanent records are to be kept[11] and the place or places at which they are to be kept[12]. At the date at which this volume states the law no such regulations had been made.

1 The Estate Agents Act 1979 s 21A (see the text and notes 2–12) is added by the Consumers, Estate Agents and Redress Act 2007 s 54(1), as from a day to be appointed. At the date at which this volume states the law no such day had been appointed.
2 As to the meaning of 'estate agency work' see PARA 255. For activities not amounting to 'estate agency work' for these purposes see PARA 256. In the case of a person engaged in estate agency work in the course of employment the duties under the Estate Agents Act 1979 s 21A(1) are duties of the employer and not the employee: s 21A(2) (prospectively added: see note 1). If the person concerned is acting in the course of employment, it is also the duty of the employer to ensure that the record of the information or event referred to in heads (1)–(5) in the text is included in the permanent records; but the employer is not to be regarded as having breached his duty if he shows that he took such steps as were reasonably practicable to ensure that the duty to record such information or events (ie the duty under s 21A(3)) was complied with by his employees: s 21A(5) (as so prospectively added).
3 Estate Agents Act 1979 s 21A(1)(a) (prospectively added: see note 1).
4 Ie for a period of at least six years beginning with the day on which it is included: Estate Agents Act 1979 s 21A(1)(b) (prospectively added: see note 1).

5   Estate Agents Act 1979 s 21A(3), (4)(a) (prospectively added: see note 1). This is the information that the person concerned is required to give by s 18(1) or (3) and any prescribed information relating to the giving of that information (see PARAS 260–262).

6   Estate Agents Act 1979 s 21A(4)(b) (prospectively added: see note 1). This is the information that the person concerned is required to disclose by s 21(1) or s 21(2) and any prescribed information relating to the disclosure of that information (see PARA 264).

7   Estate Agents Act 1979 s 21A(4)(c) (prospectively added: see note 1). 'Prescribed' means prescribed by regulations made by the Secretary of State: s 21A(7) (as so prospectively added). Any power to make regulations under s 21A is exercisable by statutory instrument which is be subject to annulment in pursuance of a resolution of either House of Parliament: s 21A(8) (as so prospectively added). At the date at which this volume states the law no such regulations had been made. As to the making of regulations generally see PARA 258 note 2.

8   Estate Agents Act 1979 s 21A(4)(d) (prospectively added: see note 1). See note 7.

9   Estate Agents Act 1979 s 21A(4)(e) (prospectively added: see note 1). See note 7.

10 Any power to make regulations under the Estate Agents Act 1979 s 21A is exercisable by statutory instrument subject to annulment in pursuance of a resolution of either House of Parliament: s 21A(8) (prospectively added: see note 1). As to the making of regulations generally see PARA 258 note 2.

11 Estate Agents Act 1979 s 21A(6)(a) (prospectively added: see note 1).

12 Estate Agents Act 1979 s 21A(6)(b) (prospectively added: see note 1).

B. CLIENTS' MONEY

266. Clients' money and client accounts.

'Clients' money', in relation to a person engaged in estate agency work[1], means any money received by him in the course of that work which is a contract[2] or pre-contract deposit[3] in respect of the acquisition of an interest in land in the United Kingdom, or in respect of a connected contract[4]. Any clients' money received by any person in the course of estate agency work is held by him on trust for the person entitled to call for it to be paid over to him or to be paid on his direction or to have it otherwise credited to him[5].

A 'client account' is a current or deposit account which is with an institution authorised for the purpose[6], is in the name of a person who is or has been engaged in estate agency work[7] and contains in its title the word 'client'[8].

1   As to the meaning of 'estate agency work' see PARA 255. For activities not amounting to 'estate agency work' for these purposes see PARA 256.

2   As to the meaning of 'contract deposit' see PARA 261 note 7.

3   As to the meaning of 'pre-contract deposit' see PARA 261 note 7.

4   Estate Agents Act 1979 s 12(1). As to the meaning of 'connected contract' see PARA 261 note 7.

5   Estate Agents Act 1979 s 13(1)(a). If money is received by the estate agent as stakeholder, it is held by him on trust for the person who may become so entitled on the occurrence of the event against which the money is held: s 13(1)(b). As to the estate agent as stakeholder see further PARA 263.

6   Estate Agents Act 1979 s 14(2)(a). For a list of the financial institutions authorised for this purpose see the Estate Agents (Accounts) Regulations 1981, SI 1981/1520, reg 2, Schedule (amended by SI 2001/1149).

    These regulations were made under the Estate Agents Act 1979 s 14(3)–(7), which provides that the Secretary of State may make provision by regulations ('accounts regulations') as to the opening and keeping of client accounts, the keeping of accounts and records relating to clients' money and the auditing of those accounts; in relation to the opening and keeping of client accounts the regulations may in particular specify the institutions authorised for the purpose (s 14(3), (4)(a)). As to the making of regulations generally see PARA 258 note 2. As to client money and client accounts see PARAS 267 et seq.

    A person who contravenes any provision of the Estate Agents Act 1979 or of accounts regulations as to the manner in which clients' money is to be dealt with or accounts and records relating to such money are to be kept commits an offence and is liable on summary conviction to a fine not exceeding level 4 on the standard scale: Estate Agents Act 1979 s 14(8)(a) (amended by virtue of the Criminal Justice Act 1982 ss 37, 46). As to the powers of magistrates' courts to issue fines on summary conviction see SENTENCING vol 92 (2015) PARA 176. As to offences by bodies corporate see PARA 257. As to defences see PARA 258 note 7.

The provisions of the Estate Agents Act 1979 ss 14, 15 (see the text and notes 7–8; and PARAS 267–269) as to the investment of clients' money, the keeping of accounts and records and accounting for interest have effect in place of the corresponding duties which would be owed by a person holding clients' money as trustee under the general law: s 13(3).

7   Estate Agents Act 1979 s 14(2)(b).
8   Estate Agents Act 1979 s 14(2)(c).

267. Duty to pay clients' money into client accounts.

Every person[1] who receives clients' money[2] in the course of estate agency work[3] must, without delay, pay the money into a client account[4] maintained by him or by a person in whose employment he is[5]. The sole exception to this rule concerns certain deposits not forming part of the consideration for the acquisition of an interest in land[6].

Money other than clients' money may be paid into a client account only if it is the minimum required for the purpose of opening or maintaining the account or to restore in whole or part any money paid out of the account in contravention of accounts regulations[7].

1   Ie every person other than the financial institutions specified in the Estate Agents (Accounts) Regulations 1981, SI 1981/1520, reg 2, Schedule (amended by SI 2001/1149): Estate Agents (Accounts) Regulations 1981, SI 1981/1520, reg 3. As to the making of accounts regulations see PARA 266 note 6. Such regulations may in particular specify any persons or classes of persons to whom, or any circumstances in which, the obligation imposed by the Estate Agents Act 1979 s 14(1) (see the text and notes 2–5) does not apply (s 14(4)(b)) and any circumstances in which money other than clients' money may be paid into a client account (see the text and note 6) (s 14(4)(c)).
2   As to the meaning of 'clients' money' see PARA 266.
3   As to the meaning of 'estate agency work' see PARA 255. For activities not amounting to 'estate agency work' for these purposes see PARA 256.
4   As to the meaning of 'client account' see PARA 266.
5   Estate Agents Act 1979 s 14(1).
6   Where part of a contract deposit paid by a purchaser is not, or is not intended to form part of, the consideration for acquiring an interest in land in the United Kingdom or for a connected contract, or part of a pre-contract deposit either is paid as an earnest of the payer's intention to acquire an interest in land in the United Kingdom or is not paid towards meeting any liability of the payer in respect of the consideration for the acquisition of such an interest which will arise if he acquires or enters into an enforceable contract to acquire the interest, and the money is received in cash or in any other form which it is practicable and lawful to split, then part of the contract deposit referred to above, or any of the part of the pre-contract deposit referred to above which is not paid in respect of a connected contract, must not be paid into a client account: Estate Agents (Accounts) Regulations 1981, SI 1981/1520, reg 4(2).
7   Estate Agents (Accounts) Regulations 1981, SI 1981/1520, reg 4(1). See note 1.

268. Payments out of client accounts.

The occasions on which, and the persons to whom, money held in a client account[1] may be paid out are:

(1)   in the case of money other than clients' money[2], where it is no longer required for the specified purpose and is paid to the person entitled to it[3];

(2)   in the case of money paid into the account in contravention of accounts regulations[4], where it is paid to the person entitled to it[5];

(3)   in the case of clients' money, where it is paid to the person who is entitled to call for it to be paid over to him or to be paid on his direction or to have it otherwise credited to him[6];

(4)   in the case of clients' money, in payment of any remuneration for, or in reimbursement of money expended in, carrying out estate agency work[7] to which the person in question is entitled, with the agreement of the person for whom the money is held[8];

(5)   in the case of clients' money, in the exercise of any lien on the money which is entitled to be exercised[9]; and

(6)   in the case of clients' money, where it is transferred to another client account maintained by the person who received the money or by his employer[10].

1   As to the meaning of 'client account' see PARA 266.
2   Ie money paid into the account by virtue of the Estate Agents (Accounts) Regulations 1981, SI 1981/1520, reg 4(1) (see PARA 267). As to the meaning of 'clients' money' see PARA 266.
3   Estate Agents (Accounts) Regulations 1981, SI 1981/1520, reg 5(a). As to the making of accounts regulations see PARA 266 note 6. Such regulations may in particular specify the occasions on which, and the persons to whom, money held in a client account may be paid out: Estate Agents Act 1979 14(4)(d).
4   Ie money paid into the account in contravention of the Estate Agents (Accounts) Regulations 1981, SI 1981/1520, reg 4 (see PARA 267).
5   Estate Agents (Accounts) Regulations 1981, SI 1981/1520, reg 5(b).
6   Estate Agents (Accounts) Regulations 1981, SI 1981/1520, reg 5(c)(i).
7   As to the meaning of 'estate agency work' see PARA 255. For activities not amounting to 'estate agency work' for these purposes see PARA 256.
8   Estate Agents (Accounts) Regulations 1981, SI 1981/1520, reg 5(c)(ii).
9   Estate Agents (Accounts) Regulations 1981, SI 1981/1520, reg 5(c)(iii). The fact that any person has or may have a lien on clients' money held by him does not affect the operation of the Estate Agents Act 1979 s 13 (clients' money held on trust or as agent: see PARA 266) and nothing in s 13 prevents such a lien from being given effect: s 13(5).
10 Estate Agents (Accounts) Regulations 1981, SI 1981/1520, reg 5(c)(iv). 'Employee' means a person engaged in estate agency work under a contract of employment, and 'employer' means his employer under that contract: reg 1(2). As to contracts of employment see EMPLOYMENT vol 39 (2014) PARA 1 et seq.

269.   Interest on clients' money.

A person engaged in estate agency work[1] who has received any clients' money[2] and does not hold it as stakeholder on trust for the person who may become entitled to it on the occurrence of the event against which it is held[3] must account to any other person who is for the time being entitled to that money for the interest earned or potentially earned on it[4].

If money is held in a client account[5] which is a separate deposit account[6], a client account which is not a separate deposit account[7], or in circumstances where the money is required[8] to be held in a client account but is not so held[9], the agent is required to account for interest or potential interest on that money if the amount of the sum held exceeds £500 and the interest which is, or, as the case may be, could have been, earned on the money for the person in question during the period for which it is held for him by keeping it in a separate deposit account at the institution concerned is at least £10[10]. If the person who has received any clients' money is a specified institution[11] or an employee of such an institution, and accordingly[12] does not pay it into a client account[13], he is required to account for interest in any case in which interest is not credited to the person for the time being entitled to the money in the normal course of business and the amount of the sum held exceeds £500 and the interest which could have been earned on the money during the period for which it is held if it had been kept in a separate deposit account at the institution is at least £10[14].

Failure to comply with these requirements does not render any person liable to any criminal penalty, but it may form the basis of a civil claim for interest which was or should have been earned on clients' money and may be taken into account[15] for the purpose of determining whether a person is unfit to carry out estate agency work[16].

1   As to the meaning of 'estate agency work' see PARA 255. For activities not amounting to 'estate agency work' for these purposes see PARA 256.
2   As to the meaning of 'clients' money' see PARA 266.
3   As to the holding of clients' money generally see PARA 266.
4   See the Estate Agents (Accounts) Regulations 1981, SI 1981/1520, reg 7; and the text and notes 5–14. Regulation 7 is made pursuant to the Estate Agents Act 1979 s 15, under which it is provided that accounts regulations (see PARA 266 note 6) may make provision for requiring a person who has received any clients' money to account, in such cases as may be prescribed by the regulations, to the person who is or becomes entitled to the money for the interest which was, or could have been, earned by putting the money in a separate deposit account at an institution authorised for the purposes of s 14: s 15(1), (6). The cases in which a person may be required by accounts regulations so to account for interest may be defined, amongst other things, by reference to the amount of the sum held or received by him or the period for which it is likely to be retained, or both: s 15(2). A person who maintains a client account in which he keeps clients' money generally is not otherwise liable to account to any person for interest received by him on money in that account (subject to the operation of any arrangement in writing, whenever made, between a person engaged in estate agency work and any other person as to the application of, or of any interest on, money in which that other person has or may have an interest): s 15(3), (4).
5   As to the meaning of 'client account' see PARA 266.
6   Estate Agents (Accounts) Regulations 1981, SI 1981/1520, reg 7(1)(a). The interest earned on the money must be accounted for: reg 7(1)(a).
7   Estate Agents (Accounts) Regulations 1981, SI 1981/1520, reg 7(1)(b). The interest which could have been earned on the money if it had been kept in a separate deposit account at the institution concerned must be accounted for: reg 7(1)(b).
8   Ie under the Estate Agents Act 1979 and the Estate Agents (Accounts) Regulations 1981, SI 1981/1520.
9   Estate Agents (Accounts) Regulations 1981, SI 1981/1520, reg 7(1)(c). The interest which could have been earned on the money if it had been kept in a separate deposit account at whichever of the specified institutions listed in the Schedule (amended by SI 2001/1149) in which a current or deposit account is held by the person on whom this is imposed was, on the day when it could first have been put in such an account, offering the highest rate of interest offered by any of those institutions on money kept in such an account, or if no such account is so held, at whichever of the said institutions was on the day in question offering the highest rate of interest offered by any of the institutions on money kept in such an account, must be accounted for: Estate Agents (Accounts) Regulations 1981, SI 1981/1520, reg 7(1)(c).
10 Estate Agents (Accounts) Regulations 1981, SI 1981/1520, reg 7(2).
11 Ie an institution listed in the Estate Agents (Accounts) Regulations 1981, SI 1981/1520, reg 2, Schedule (amended by SI 2001/1149).
12 Ie under the Estate Agents (Accounts) Regulations 1981, SI 1981/1520, reg 3 (see PARA 267).
13 Estate Agents (Accounts) Regulations 1981, SI 1981/1520, reg 7(1)(d). The interest which could have been earned on the money if it had been kept in a separate deposit account at the specified institution must be accounted for: reg 7(1)(d).
14 Estate Agents (Accounts) Regulations 1981, SI 1981/1520, reg 7(3).
15 Ie taken into account by the lead enforcement authority in accordance with the Estate Agents Act 1979 s 3(1)(c) (see PARA 284). As to the lead enforcement authority see PARA 291.
16 Estate Agents Act 1979 s 15(5) (amended by SI 2014/631).

270. Insurance cover for clients' money.

As from a day to be appointed[1] a person may not accept clients' money[2] in the course of estate agency work[3] unless there are in force authorised arrangements under which, in the event of his failing to account for such money to the person entitled to it, his liability will be made good by another[4], and no person carrying on estate agency work will be permitted to use the description 'estate agent' or so use any name or in any way hold himself out as to indicate or reasonably be understood to indicate that he is carrying on a business in the course of which he is prepared to act as a broker in the acquisition or disposal of interests in land unless information relating to authorised arrangements is displayed at his place of business[5] and included in any relevant document[6] issued or displayed in connection with his business[7].

Failure to comply with these requirements[8] is an offence[9]. However, the lead enforcement authority[10] may, on an application made to it in that behalf[11], exempt a person engaged in estate agency work from all or any of the requirements relating to the making of insurance arrangements[12] if it considers that such an exemption may be made without loss of adequate protection to consumers, and may issue to such a person a certificate of exemption[13]. Failure to comply with any condition of exemption specified in a current certificate of exemption is an offence[14]. Persons may also be excluded from the insurance requirements by regulations[15].

1   At the date at which this volume states the law the Estate Agents Act 1979 ss 16, 17 (see the text and notes 2–15) had not been brought into force.
2   As to the meaning of 'clients' money' see PARA 266.
3   As to the meaning of 'estate agency work' see PARA 255; for activities not amounting to 'estate agency work' for these purposes see PARA 256.
4   Estate Agents Act 1979 s 16(1) (not yet in force). Every guarantee entered into by a person (the 'insurer') who provides authorised arrangements covering another person (the 'agent') carrying on estate agency work enures for the benefit of every person from whom the agent has received clients' money as if the guarantee were contained in a contract made by the insurer with every such person, and, where the guarantee is given by two or more insurers, they had bound themselves jointly and severally: s 16(3) (not yet in force).
       Regulations may be made specifying arrangements which are authorised: s 16(2)(b) (not yet in force). Regulations may also specify the terms and conditions upon which any payment is to be made under such arrangements and any circumstances in which the right to any such payment may be excluded or modified (s 16(2)(c) (not yet in force)); and provide that any limit on the amount of any such payment is to be not less than a specified amount (s 16(2)(d) (not yet in force)). Regulations under s 16 are made by statutory instrument subject to annulment in pursuance of a resolution of either House of Parliament: s 16(2). As to the making of regulations generally see PARA 258 note 2. At the date at which this volume states the law no such regulations had been made.
5   For these purposes any business premises at which a person carries on estate agency work and to which the public has access is a place of business of his: Estate Agents Act 1979 s 16(5)(a) (not yet in force).
6   For these purposes 'relevant document' means any advertisement, notice or other written material which might reasonably induce any person to use the services of another in connection with the acquisition or disposal of an interest in land: Estate Agents Act 1979 s 16(5)(b) (not yet in force).
7   Estate Agents Act 1979 s 16(4) (not yet in force). Regulations may be made requiring a person providing authorised arrangements covering any person carrying on estate agency work to issue a certificate in a form specified in the regulations certifying that arrangements complying with the regulations have been made with respect to that person (s 16(2)(e) (not yet in force)), and prescribing any matter required to be prescribed for the purposes of s 16(4) (s 16(2)(f) (not yet in force)). At the date at which this volume states the law no such regulations had been made.
8   Ie the requirements of the Estate Agents Act 1979 s 16(1) or (4) or regulations under s 16(2) (see the text and notes 1–7).
9   Estate Agents Act 1979 s 16(6) (not yet in force). A person guilty of this offence is liable on conviction on indictment or summary conviction to a fine which, on summary conviction, is not to exceed the statutory maximum: s 16(6) (not yet in force). As to the powers of magistrates' courts to issue fines on summary conviction see SENTENCING vol 92 (2015) PARA 176. As to offences by bodies corporate see PARA 257. As to defences see PARA 258 note 7.
10 As to the lead enforcement authority see PARA 291.
11 An application for an exemption must state the reasons why the applicant considers that he should be granted a certificate of exemption, and must be accompanied by the prescribed fee: Estate Agents Act 1979 s 17(2) (not yet in force). If the lead enforcement authority decides to refuse such an application it must give the applicant notice of its decision and of the reasons for it, including

any facts which in its opinion justify the decision: s 17(5) (not yet in force) (s 17(1), (5), (6) amended by the Enterprise Act 2002 s 278(1), Sch 25 para 9(1), (10); and SI 2014/631).

If a person who made an application under the Estate Agents Act 1979 s 17(1) is aggrieved by a decision of the lead enforcement authority either to refuse his application or to grant him a certificate of exemption subject to conditions, he may appeal against the decision to the Secretary of State: s 17(6) (not yet in force). Provision is made for the procedure for appeals: see s 7(2)–(6); and PARA 289.

Any notice which is to be given under the Estate Agents Act 1979 to any person by the lead enforcement authority, any penalty charge notice which is to be given under s 23B(1) (see PARA 278) by a duly authorised officer of an enforcement authority other than the lead enforcement authority, and any notice which is to be given by such an authority under Sch 4 para 5(1)(c) (see PARA 279), may be so given by delivering it to the person, leaving it at his proper address, or sending it by post to him at that address: s 29(1) (amended by SI 2014/631); Estate Agents Act 1979 Sch 4 para 10 (added by the Consumers, Estate Agents and Redress Act 2007 Sch 6, paras 1, 4). In the case of a body corporate or unincorporated association, the notice may be given to the secretary or clerk of that body or association, and in the case of a partnership, it must be given to a partner or a person having the control or management of the partnership business: Estate Agents Act 1979 s 29(2). The proper address of any person to whom a notice is to be given is his last-known address, except that in the case of a body corporate or its secretary or clerk, it is the address of the registered or principal office of that body, in the case of an unincorporated association or its secretary or clerk, it is that of the principal office of that association, and in the case of a partnership or a person having the control or management of the partnership business, it is that of the principal office of the partnership (s 29(4)); for these purposes the principal office of a company registered outside the United Kingdom or of an unincorporated association or partnership carrying on business outside the United Kingdom is its principal office within the United Kingdom (s 29(4)). If the person to be given the notice has specified an address within the United Kingdom other than his proper address (within the meaning of s 29(4)) as the one at which he or someone on his behalf will accept notices under the Estate Agents Act 1979, that address is also treated for the purposes of s 29(4) as his proper address: s 29(5). Any application or other document which may be made or given to the lead enforcement authority may be so made or given by sending it by post to the lead enforcement authority at such address as may be specified for the purposes of the Act by a general notice: s 29(3) (amended by SI 2014/631). 'General notice' means a notice published by the lead enforcement authority at a time and in a manner appearing to it suitable for securing that the notice is seen within a reasonable time by persons likely to be affected by it: Estate Agents Act 1979 s 33(1) (definition amended by SI 2014/631).

12 Ie all or any of the provisions of the Estate Agents Act 1979 s 16(1) or of regulations under s 16(2) (see the text and notes 1–4).

13 Estate Agents Act 1979 s 17(1) (not yet in force) (as amended: see note 11). A certificate of exemption may impose conditions of exemption on the person to whom it is issued, and may be issued to have effect for a period specified in the certificate or without limit of time: s 17(3) (not yet in force). If and so long as a certificate of exemption has effect and the person to whom it is issued complies with any conditions of exemption specified in the certificate, that person remains exempt, to the extent so specified, from the provisions of s 16(1) and of any regulations made under s 16(2): see s 17(4) (not yet in force).

Particular duties are imposed on the Commission for Equality and Human Rights to furnish to the lead enforcement authority such information relating to any finding, notice, injunction or order falling within Sch 1 para 2 (see PARA 283) as is in its possession and appears to the Commission to be relevant to the functions of the lead enforcement authority under the Estate Agents Act 1979: see s 9(6) (amended by the Equality Act 2006 ss 40, 91, Sch 3, paras 36, 37, Sch 4; and SI 2014/631).

14 Estate Agents Act 1979 s 17(7) (not yet in force). A person guilty of this offence is liable on conviction on indictment or on summary conviction to a fine which, on summary conviction, must not exceed the statutory maximum: s 17(7) (not yet in force).

15 Estate Agents Act 1979 s 16(2)(a) (not yet in force). At the date at which this volume states the law no such regulations had been made.

271. Estate agents' accounts and records.

Any person who receives client's money[1] in the course of estate agency work[2] is under a duty to keep such accounts and records relating to clients' money received, held or paid out as are sufficient to show that he has discharged the duty[3] to keep client accounts[4] and to show and explain readily at any time all dealings with the money to which such accounts relate[5]. Any accounts and records so kept must be retained for six years after the end of the accounting period[6] to which they relate[7].

If a person ceases to be engaged in the estate agency work in which he has been engaged and the accounts and records relating to clients' money received by him are handed over to another person, that person is required to keep the accounts and records required to be kept under these provisions in place of the first person[8].

Failure to comply with these requirements is an offence[9].

1   As to the meaning of 'clients' money' see PARA 266.
2   Ie including an employer in the case of money received by his employee (Estate Agents (Accounts) Regulations 1981, SI 1981/1520, reg 6(1)), but not including an employee who pays clients' money received by him without delay into a client account maintained by his employer (reg 6(2)(b)) or any of the persons listed in the Schedule (amended by SI 2001/1149) or to an employee of any such person (Estate Agents (Accounts) Regulations 1981, SI 1981/1520, reg 6(2)(a)). As to the meanings of 'employer' and 'employee' see PARA 268 note 10. As to the meaning of 'client account' see PARA 266. As to the meaning of 'estate agency work' see PARA 255. For activities not amounting to 'estate agency work' for these purposes see PARA 256.

     As to the making of accounts regulations see PARA 266 note 6. Such regulations may in particular make provision requiring accounts to be drawn up in respect of specified accounting periods and to be audited by a qualified auditor within a specified time after the end of each such period (Estate Agents Act 1979 s 14(5)(a)); requiring the auditor to report whether in his opinion the requirements of the Estate Agents Act 1979 and of the accounts regulations have been complied with or have been substantially complied with (s 14(5)(b)); as to the matters to which such a report is to relate and the circumstances in which a report of substantial compliance may be given (s 14(5)(c)); and requiring a person who maintains a client account to produce on demand to a duly authorised officer of an enforcement authority the latest auditor's report (s 14(5)(d)). As to enforcement authorities see PARA 291. 'Qualified auditor' in s 14(5)(a) means a person who is eligible for appointment as a statutory auditor under the Companies Act 2006 Pt 42 (ss 1209–1264) (see COMPANIES vol 15 (2016) PARAS 1059 et seq, 1086): Estate Agents Act 1979 s 14(6) (substituted by SI 1991/1997; and amended by SI 2008/948). However a person is not a qualified auditor for the purposes of the Estate Agents Act 1979 s 14(5)(a) if, in the case of a client account maintained by a company, he is prohibited from acting as a statutory auditor of the company by virtue of the Companies Act 2006 s 1214 (see COMPANIES vol 15 (2016) PARA 1088): Estate Agents Act 1979 s 14(7) (substituted by SI 1991/1997; and amended by SI 2008/948).

3   Ie the duty imposed by the Estate Agents Act 1979 s 14 (see PARAS 266–268).
4   Such accounts and records must be such as to show, in the case of clients' money received:

     (1)   the amount (Estate Agents (Accounts) Regulations 1981, SI 1981/1520, reg 6(3)(a)(i));
     (2)   the name and address of the payer (reg 6(3)(a)(ii));
     (3)   whether the sum paid is a contract or a pre-contract deposit and, in either case, whether it is or includes any sum in respect of a connected contract (reg 6(3)(a)(iii));
     (4)   if the sum paid includes any such money as is referred to in reg 4(2) (see PARA 267), for what purposes and in what form it is received (reg 6(3)(a)(iv));
     (5)   the interest in land to which the money relates (reg 6(3)(a)(v));
     (6)   the person wishing to dispose of such an interest (reg 6(3)(a)(vi));
     (7)   the capacity in which the money is received and (where known by the person upon whom the duty is imposed) is from time to time held (whether as agent, bailee, stakeholder or in any other capacity) (reg 6(3)(a)(vii));
     (8)   the identity of the person for whom the money has been received and (where known) is from time to time held (reg 6(3)(a)(viii)); and
     (9)   the date of its receipt (reg 6(3)(a)(ix)).

     As to the meanings of 'contract deposit', 'pre-contract deposit' and 'connected contract' see PARA 261 note 7.

     The records must:
     (a)   be kept in such manner as to show separately all clients' money held by reference to the interest in land to which it relates (reg 6(3)(b));
     (b)   in the case of any payment out of a client account, be such as to show the amount, the identity of the payee, the date of the payment, any interest in land to which the money

relates and such other information as may be necessary to show the corresponding payment into the account, the occasion on which the payment is made and, where the payment is made in accordance with reg 5(c)(ii) or (iii) (see PARA 268), such particulars as may be necessary to enable any information (and changes therein) required to be given to clients under the Estate Agents Act 1979 s 18 (see PARAS 260–262) and regulations made thereunder to be identified (Estate Agents (Accounts) Regulations 1981, SI 1981/1520, reg 6(3)(c));

(c) include counterfoils kept or duplicate copies of all receipts issued in respect of clients' money received which must contain the particulars required to be shown in the accounts and records under reg 6(3)(a)(i)–(v), (ix) (see above) (reg 6(3)(d)); and

(d) in the case of any sum transferred from one client account to another, be such as to show the occasion for the transfer and to enable the corresponding payment into the account from which the transfer is made to be identified, except sums transferred between a specified client current account and a specified client deposit account in both of which clients' money is kept generally (reg 6(3)(e)).

Where under reg 6 accounts and records are required to be kept so as to show the interest in land to which any clients' money relates, or by reference to such an interest, the requirement is taken to be complied with only if the land as well as the nature of the interest therein are identified: reg 6(5).

5 Estate Agents (Accounts) Regulations 1981, SI 1981/1520, reg 6(1). This includes the title of the client account into which the money is paid, the date of such payment and the identity of the institution with which that account is held, any payments out (other than those mentioned in the exception to reg 6(3)(e) (see note 4)) and all dealings with any other money which may have been dealt with through that account: reg 6(1).

6 'Accounting period' means a period of not more than 12 months in respect of which accounts required to be kept under the Estate Agents (Accounts) Regulations 1981, SI 1981/1520, reg 6 are drawn up; provided that an accounting period may end on a date not more than seven days after the end of a period of 12 months: reg 1(2).

7 Estate Agents (Accounts) Regulations 1981, SI 1981/1520, reg 6(4).

8 Estate Agents (Accounts) Regulations 1981, SI 1981/1520, reg 6(6).

9 Estate Agents Act 1979 s 14(8)(a). A person who commits this offence is liable on summary conviction to a fine not exceeding level 4 on the standard scale: s 14(8) (amended by virtue of the Criminal Justice Act 1982 s 46). As to the powers of magistrates' courts to issue fines on summary conviction see SENTENCING vol 92 (2015) PARA 176. As to offences by bodies corporate see PARA 257. As to defences see PARA 258 note 7.

272. Audit of estate agents' accounts.

Any person who is required to keep accounts in respect of estate agency work[1] must draw them up in respect of consecutive accounting periods[2] and have them audited by a qualified auditor[3] within six months after the end of each accounting period[4]. The auditor must report to such persons whether in his opinion the statutory requirements as to the manner in which clients' money is to be dealt with[5] have been complied with or have been substantially complied with[6]. If he reports that in his opinion those requirements have not been complied with or substantially complied with he must specify in his report the matters in respect of which it appears to him that the said requirements have not been complied with or substantially complied with[7]; and if he is unable to form an opinion as to whether or not the said requirements have been complied with or substantially complied with, he must specify in his report the matters in respect of which he has been unable to satisfy himself and the reasons therefor[8].

A person who maintains a client account[9] must produce on demand to a duly authorised officer of an enforcement authority[10] the latest auditor's report relating to the account[11]: failure to do so is an offence[12].

1 Ie under the Estate Agents (Accounts) Regulations 1981, SI 1981/1520, reg 6 (see PARA 271). As to the making of accounts regulations see PARA 266 note 6; and see also, with regard to the auditing of accounts, PARA 271 note 2. As to the meaning of 'estate agency work' see PARA 255. For activities not amounting to 'estate agency work' for these purposes see PARA 256.

2 As to the meaning of 'accounting period' see PARA 271 note 6. An employee who is required to keep accounts under the Estate Agents (Accounts) Regulations 1981, SI 1981/1520, reg 6 must adopt the same accounting period in respect of those accounts as his employer: reg 8(2). As to the meanings of 'employer' and 'employee' see PARA 268 note 10.

3 As to the meaning of 'qualified auditor' for these purposes see PARA 271 note 2.

4 Estate Agents (Accounts) Regulations 1981, SI 1981/1520, reg 8(1).

5 Ie the requirements of the Estate Agents Act 1979 and the Estate Agents (Accounts) Regulations 1981, SI 1981/1520.

6 Estate Agents (Accounts) Regulations 1981, SI 1981/1520, reg 8(3). The auditor may report that the said requirements have been substantially complied with if in his opinion they have been complied with except so far as concerns certain trivial breaches due to clerical errors or mistakes in book-keeping, all of which were rectified on discovery, and none of which in his opinion resulted in any loss to any person entitled to the clients' money: reg 8(4). As to the meaning of 'clients' money' see PARA 266.

   For the purpose of making his report under reg 8(3) the auditor must ascertain from the person to whom he is reporting particulars of all bank accounts kept, maintained or operated by him or his employee in the course of estate agency work at any time during the accounting period to which the report relates and so examine the accounts and records of that person as to enable him to verify whether they comply with the requirements of reg 6, for which purpose he may ask for such further information and explanations as he may consider necessary (reg 8(7)) (although nothing in reg 8(7) requires the auditor either to extend his inquiries beyond the information contained in the relevant documents produced to him, supplemented by such information and explanations as he may obtain from the person to whom he is making his report or to consider whether the accounts and records have been properly kept in accordance with reg 6 at any time other than the time at which his examination of those accounts and records takes place (reg 8(8))).

7 Estate Agents (Accounts) Regulations 1981, SI 1981/1520, reg 8(5).

8 Estate Agents (Accounts) Regulations 1981, SI 1981/1520, reg 8(6).

9 As to the meaning of 'client account' see PARA 266.

10 As to enforcement authorities see PARA 291.

11 Estate Agents (Accounts) Regulations 1981, SI 1981/1520, reg 8(9).

12 Estate Agents Act 1979 s 14(8)(b). A person who commits this offence is liable on summary conviction to a fine not exceeding level 4 on the standard scale: s 14(8) (amended by virtue of the Criminal Justice Act 1982 s 46). As to the powers of magistrates' courts to issue fines on summary conviction see SENTENCING vol 92 (2015) PARA 176. As to offences by bodies corporate see PARA 257. As to defences see PARA 258 note 7.

(iv) Redress Schemes

273. Redress schemes for residential estate agents.

Provision is made for the establishment of schemes, known as 'redress schemes', providing for the investigation and determination of complaints[1] against persons who engage in estate agency work[2] in relation to residential property[3]. 'Residential property' means any land that consists of or includes a building or part of a building[4] the whole or part of which is used as a dwelling or as more than one dwelling[5] or that is (or is to be) offered for sale on the basis that the whole or part of it is suitable for such use or is intended to be so suitable by the time the seller disposes of his interest in it[6]. The Secretary of State may by order exclude land of a specified description from these provisions, and any land of a description so specified will not be 'residential property' for these purposes[7].

Complaints under a redress scheme are investigated and determined by an independent person know as the 'ombudsman'[8].

1 A 'complaint' is a complaint made by a person by virtue of his being or having been a seller or buyer of residential property; 'seller', in relation to residential property, means a person who claims that he is or may become interested in disposing of an interest in land in respect of that property (and includes a person who disposes of such an interest); and 'buyer', in relation to residential property, means a person who claims that he is or may become interested in acquiring an interest in land in respect of that property (and includes a person who acquires such an interest):

Estate Agents Act 1979 s 23A(8)(c)–(e), (10), Sch 3 para 16 (ss 23A, 23C, Sch 3 added by the Consumers, Estate Agents and Redress Act 2007 Sch 6 paras 1–3; and the Estate Agents Act 1979 Sch 3 amended by SI 2014/631). As to references to the 'disposal' of an interest in land see PARA 255 note 3.

2 As to the meaning of 'estate agency work' see PARA 255. For activities not amounting to 'estate agency work' for these purposes see PARA 256.

3 Estate Agents Act 1979 s 23A(1), (8)(a) (as added: see note 1).

4 This reference to a building or part of a building (so far as relating to the Estate Agents Act 1979 s 23C(2)(b) (see the text and note 6)) includes a reference to a building or part that is being or is to be constructed: s 23C(3) (as so added).

5 Estate Agents Act 1979 s 23C(1)(a), (2)(a) (as added: see note 1).

6 Estate Agents Act 1979 s 23C(2)(b) (as added: see note 1).

7 Estate Agents Act 1979 s 23C(1)(b) (as added: see note 1). A description of land specified by order under s 23C(1)(b) may be framed by reference to the purpose or purposes for which the land (or part of it) is or is intended to be used: s 23C(4) (as so added). The power to make an order under s 23C(1)(b) is exercisable by statutory instrument subject to annulment in pursuance of a resolution of either House of Parliament: s 23C(5) (as so added). As to the making of orders generally see PARA 258 note 2. At the date at which this volume states the law no such orders had been made.

8 Estate Agents Act 1979 s 23A(8)(a) (as added: see note 1). For the purposes of the law relating to defamation, proceedings under an approved redress scheme (see PARA 274 et seq) in relation to the investigation and determination of a complaint are treated in the same way as proceedings before a court: Sch 3 para 15 (as so added; and amended by SI 2014/631).

274. Approval of redress schemes by lead enforcement authority.

The lead enforcement authority[1] may approve redress schemes[2] for residential estate agents[3] if it considers that the provisions of the scheme[4] and the manner in which it will be operated (so far as can be judged from facts known to the authority)[5] are satisfactory[6]. The lead enforcement authority must not, however, approve a scheme unless it considers that it makes satisfactory provision about:

(1) the complaints[7] which may be made under the scheme[8];

(2) the ombudsman's duties and powers in relation to the investigation and determination of complaints[9];

(3) the redress which the ombudsman may require members to provide to complainants[10];

(4) the enforcement of any requirement to provide redress imposed on a member in accordance with the scheme[11]; and

(5) the provision of information by the ombudsman or the scheme administrator[12] to persons exercising functions under other approved schemes, persons exercising functions under other consumer redress schemes, and the lead enforcement authority or any other person exercising regulatory functions in relation to the activities of persons engaging in estate agency work[13],

or if it considers that the scheme provides for membership to be revoked on any unfair grounds[14].

Where the lead enforcement authority is proposing, or has decided, to refuse an application for approval it must notify the applicant[15]. The scheme administrator of an approved scheme must notify the lead enforcement authority of any change to the scheme[16].

1 As to the lead enforcement authority see PARA 291.

2 Ie for the purposes of the Estate Agents Act 1979 s 23A (see PARAS 273, 277). As to the meaning of 'redress scheme' see PARA 273. An application for approval of a redress scheme must be made in such manner as the lead enforcement authority may determine and be accompanied by such information as the lead enforcement authority may require: s 23A(10), Sch 3 para 6 (s 23A, Sch 3 added by the Consumers, Estate Agents and Redress Act 2007 Sch 6 paras 1–3; and amended by SI 2014/631).

3   Estate Agents Act 1979 s 23A(8)(b)(i), Sch 3 para 1 (as added and amended: see note 2).
4   Estate Agents Act 1979 Sch 3 para 2(1)(a) (as added and amended: see note 2).
5   Estate Agents Act 1979 Sch 3 para 2(1)(b) (as added and amended: see note 2).
6   Estate Agents Act 1979 Sch 3 para 2. Ie for the purposes of the Estate Agents Act 1979 s 23A (see PARAS 273, 277). In determining whether a scheme, or any provisions mentioned in Sch 3 para 2(2) (see the text and notes 7–11), are satisfactory the lead enforcement authority must have regard to the interests of members of the scheme and of sellers and buyers of residential properties and such principles as in the opinion of the lead enforcement authority constitute generally accepted principles of best practice in relation to consumer redress schemes and it is reasonable to regard as applicable to the scheme: Sch 3 para 3(1) (as added and amended: see note 2). In considering the interests of members of the scheme and of sellers and buyers of residential properties the lead enforcement authority may have regard to the number of other redress schemes which are (or are likely to become) approved redress schemes: Sch 3 para 3(2) (as so added and amended). As to the meanings of 'buyer' and 'seller' see PARA 273 note 1.
7   As to the meaning of 'complaint' see PARA 273 note 1. Such complaints may include complaints about non-compliance with the provisions of a code of practice or other document: Estate Agents Act 1979 Sch 3 para 2(2)(a) (as added: see note 2).
8   Estate Agents Act 1979 Sch 3 para 2(2)(a) (as added: see note 2).
9   Estate Agents Act 1979 Sch 3 para 2(2)(b) (as added: see note 2). These powers may include power to decide not to investigate or determine a particular complaint: Sch 3 para 2(2)(b) (as so added). 'Ombudsman' means the independent person mentioned in s 23A(8)(a) (see PARA 273): Sch 3 para 16 (as so added).
10 Estate Agents Act 1979 Sch 3 para 2(2)(c) (as added: see note 2). Such types of redress must include providing an apology or explanation, paying compensation and taking such other actions in the interests of the complainant as the ombudsman may specify: Sch 3 para 2(3) (as so added).
11 Estate Agents Act 1979 Sch 3 para 2(2)(d) (as added: see note 2).
12 'Scheme administrator', in relation to a redress scheme, means the person who administers the scheme: Estate Agents Act 1979 Sch 3 para 16 (as added: see note 2).
13 Estate Agents Act 1979 Sch 3 para 4 (as added and amended: see note 2). As to the meaning of 'estate agency work' see PARA 255. For activities not amounting to 'estate agency work' for these purposes see PARA 256.
14 Estate Agents Act 1979 Sch 3 para 5 (as added and amended: see note 2).
15 Where the lead enforcement authority is proposing to refuse an application for approval it must give the applicant a notice stating that it is proposing to refuse the application, the grounds for the proposed refusal and that representations about the proposed refusal may be made within such period of not less than 30 days as is specified in the notice: Estate Agents Act 1979 Sch 3 para 7 (as added and amended: see note 2). If the lead enforcement authority decides to refuse an application for approval, it must give the applicant a notice stating its decision to refuse the application and the reasons for the decision: Sch 3 para 8 (as so added and amended). As to the giving of notices see PARA 270 note 11.
16 Estate Agents Act 1979 Sch 3 para 9 (as added and amended: see note 2). Notification must be given before the end of the period of 14 days beginning with the day on which the change is made: Sch 3 para 9 (as so added).

275. Withdrawal of approval by the lead enforcement authority.

The lead enforcement authority[1] may withdraw approval of a redress scheme[2] which is for the time being approved by it[3]. Before withdrawing its approval the lead enforcement authority must give the scheme administrator[4] a notice stating that it proposes to withdraw its approval and the grounds for the proposed withdrawal, and giving the administrator an opportunity to make representations on the matter[5]. The lead enforcement authority must also notify the scheme administrator about its decision on a proposal to withdraw approval and the reasons for its decision[6].

1   As to the lead enforcement authority see PARA 291.
2   As to the meaning of 'redress scheme' see PARA 273.
3   Estate Agents Act 1979 Sch 3 para 10 (Sch 3 added by the Consumers, Estate Agents and Redress Act 2007 Sch 6 paras 1, 3; and amended by SI 2014/631).
4   As to the meaning of 'scheme administrator' see PARA 274 note 12.

5   Estate Agents Act 1979 Sch 3 para 11 (as added and amended: see note 3). As to the giving of
     notices see PARA 270 note 11. The notice must inform the scheme administrator that
     representations about the proposed withdrawal may be made within such period of not less than
     30 days as is specified in the notice: Sch 3 para 11(c) (as so added).
6   Estate Agents Act 1979 Sch 3 para 12 (as added and amended: see note 3). If the lead enforcement
     authority decides to withdraw approval of a scheme the withdrawal has effect from such date as
     may be specified in the notice under Sch 3 para 12 (Sch 3 para 13(a) (as so added and amended))
     and the scheme administrator must give a copy of the notice under Sch 3 para 12 to every member
     of the scheme (Sch 3 para 13(b) (as so added and amended)).

276. Approval of redress schemes by Secretary of State.

A redress scheme[1] is also 'approved' if it is administered by or on behalf of the
Secretary of State and designated by him[2] as an approved redress scheme[3]. The
Secretary of State may not designate a scheme as an approved redress scheme for
these purposes unless he is satisfied that the scheme is one which could be
approved[4] by the lead enforcement authority[5]. The Secretary of State may also
decide to revoke a designation, and where he makes such a decision he must give
every member of the scheme a notice stating that he has so decided, the reasons
for his decision and the date from which the revocation has effect[6].

1   As to the meaning of 'redress scheme' see PARA 273.
2   Ie for the purposes of the Estate Agents Act 1979 s 23A (see PARAS 273, 277).
3   Estate Agents Act 1979 s 23A(8)(b)(ii) (s 23A, Sch 3 added by the Consumers, Estate Agents and
     Redress Act 2007 Sch 6 paras 1–3; and amended by SI 2014/631).
4   Ie in accordance with the Estate Agents Act 1979 Sch 3 paras 2–5 (see PARA 274).
5   Estate Agents Act 1979 s 23A(9) (as added and amended: see note 3). As to the lead enforcement
     authority see PARA 291.
6   Estate Agents Act 1979 Sch 3 para 14 (as added: see note 3).

277. Compulsory and voluntary redress scheme membership.

Every person who engages in relevant estate agency work (that is estate agency
work in relation to residential property[1]) is required to be a member of an
approved redress scheme for dealing with complaints[2] in connection with that
work[3]. Membership of an approved redress scheme is also open to persons who
are not subject to the statutory duty[4] to be members of such a scheme[5].

An approved redress scheme may also provide for the investigation and
determination of any complaints in relation to which the duty to be a member of
a scheme does not apply if the members concerned have voluntarily accepted the
jurisdiction of the scheme over those complaints[6], and for the exclusion from
investigation and determination under the scheme of any complaint in such cases
or circumstances as may be specified in or determined under the scheme[7].

1   For these purposes the reference to persons who engage in estate agency work does not include a
     reference to persons who engage in that work in the course of their employment: Estate Agents Act
     1979 s 23A(4) (s 23A added by the Consumers, Estate Agents and Redress Act 2007 Sch 6 paras
     1). As to the meaning of 'estate agency work' see PARA 255. For activities not amounting to 'estate
     agency work' for these purposes see PARA 256. As to the meaning of 'residential property' see
     PARA 273.
2   As to the meaning of 'complaint' see PARA 273 note 1.
3   Estate Agents Act 1979 s 23A(1), (2), (3), (5), (6) (as added: see note 1); Estate Agents (Redress
     Scheme) Order 2008, SI 2008/1712, arts 1, 2. As to the meaning of 'redress scheme' see PARA 273.
     As to the approval of redress schemes see PARAS 274 et seq.
4   Ie the duty under the Estate Agents Act 1979 s 23A(1).
5   Estate Agents Act 1979 s 23A(7)(a) (as added: see note 1).
6   Estate Agents Act 1979 s 23A(7)(b) (as added: see note 1).
7   Estate Agents Act 1979 s 23A(7)(c) (as added: see note 1).

278. Penalty charge notice for breach of duty to belong to approved redress scheme.

If an enforcement authority[1] other than the lead enforcement authority[2] believes that a person has engaged (or is engaging) in estate agency work[3] in relation to residential property[4] in breach of the duty to be a member of an approved redress scheme[5], it must notify the lead enforcement authority[6]. If a duly authorised officer of an enforcement authority believes that a person has engaged (or is engaging) in estate agency work in relation to residential property in breach of the statutory duty, he may give to the person in question a penalty charge notice[7] which:

(1)   states his belief that that person has committed a breach of the duty[8];

(2)   gives such other particulars of the circumstances as may be necessary to give reasonable notice of the breach[9];

(3)   requires the person[10] either to pay a penalty charge specified in the notice (not exceeding £1,000[11]) or to give notice to the enforcement authority that he wishes to review the notice[12];

(4)   sets out the arrangements for the institution of proceedings, if necessary, for the recovery of the charge[13];

(5)   specifies the person to whom and the address at which the charge may be paid and the method or methods by which payment may be made[14]; and

(6)   specifies the person to whom and the address at which a notice requesting a review may be sent (and to which any representations relating to the review may be addressed)[15].

A penalty charge notice may not be given after the end of the period of six months beginning with the day (or in the case of a continuing breach the last day) on which the breach of duty was committed[16]. The enforcement authority may, if it considers that the penalty charge notice ought not to have been given, give the recipient a notice withdrawing the penalty charge notice[17].

1   As to enforcement authorities see PARA 291.

2   As to the lead enforcement authority see PARA 291.

3   As to the meaning of 'estate agency work' see PARA 255. For activities not amounting to 'estate agency work' for these purposes see PARA 256.

4   As to the meaning of 'residential property' see PARA 273.

5   Ie the duty imposed by an order under the Estate Agents Act 1979 s 23A(1) (see PARA 277). As to the meaning of 'redress scheme' see PARA 273. As to the approval of redress schemes see PARA 274 et seq.

6   Estate Agents Act 1979 s 23B(4) (s 23B, Sch 4 added by the Consumers, Estate Agents and Redress Act 2007 Sch 6 paras 1, 2, 4; and amended by SI 2014/631).

7   Estate Agents Act 1979 s 23B(1) (as added and amended: see note 6). As to the giving of penalty charge notices see PARA 270 note 11.
        The Secretary of State may by regulations prescribe the form of penalty charge notices and any other notice to be given under Sch 4, and the circumstances in which penalty charge notices may not be given: Sch 4 para 11(a), (b) (as so added). At the date at which this volume states the law no such regulations had been made. Any power to make regulations under Sch 4 is exercisable by statutory instrument subject to annulment in pursuance of a resolution of either House of Parliament: Sch 4 para 12 (as so added).

8   Estate Agents Act 1979 s 23B(3), Sch 4 para 1(a) (Sch 4 para 1 as added and amended: see note 6).

9   Estate Agents Act 1979 Sch 4 para 1(b) (as added: see note 6).

10 Ie within a period specified in the notice: Estate Agents Act 1979 Sch 4 para 1(c) (as added: see note 6). The specified period must not be less than 28 days beginning with the day after that on which the penalty charge notice was given, although the enforcement authority may extend the period for

complying with the requirement either to pay the charge or ask for a review in any particular case if it considers it appropriate to do so: Sch 4 para 3 (as so added). As to reviews see PARA **279**. As to enforcement authorities see PARA **291**.

11 The amount of the penalty charge specified in a notice is £1000: Estate Agents Act 1979 Sch 4 para 2 (as added: see note 6); Estate Agents (Redress Scheme) (Penalty Charge) Regulations 2008, SI 2008/1713, regs 1, 2.

12 Estate Agents Act 1979 Sch 4 para 1(c) (as added: see note 6).

13 Estate Agents Act 1979 Sch 4 para 1(d) (as added: see note 6). This involves stating the effect of Sch 4 para 8 (see PARA **280**).

14 Estate Agents Act 1979 Sch 4 para 1(e) (as added: see note 6).

15 Estate Agents Act 1979 Sch 4 para 1(f) (as added: see note 6).

16 Estate Agents Act 1979 s 23B(2) (as added: see note 6).

17 Estate Agents Act 1979 Sch 4 para 4 (as added: see note 6). A notice may also be withdrawn or quashed on review or appeal (see PARA **279**). If a penalty charge notice is withdrawn or quashed the authority must repay any amount previously paid as a penalty charge in pursuance of the notice: Sch 4 para 7 (as so added).

279. Reviews of, and appeals against, penalty charge notices.

The recipient of a penalty charge notice[1] may give notice[2] to the enforcement authority[3] requesting a review, and the authority must consider any representations made by the recipient and all other circumstances of the case[4] and decide whether to confirm or withdraw the notice[5]. The authority must withdraw the penalty charge notice if it is not satisfied that the recipient committed the breach of duty specified in the notice[6] and that in the circumstances of the case it was appropriate for a penalty charge notice to be given to the recipient[7]. If, however, the authority confirms the notice the recipient may appeal against the notice to the County Court[8] on the ground that he did not commit the breach of duty specified in the notice[9], that the notice was not given within the time allowed[10] or the procedural requirements[11] were not complied with[12], or that in the circumstances of the case it was inappropriate for the notice to be given[13], and the county court must either uphold the notice or quash it[14].

If a penalty charge notice is withdrawn or quashed the authority must repay any amount previously paid as a penalty charge in pursuance of the notice[15].

1 As to penalty charge notices for failure to belong to an approved redress scheme see PARA **278**. As to the meaning of 'redress scheme' see PARA **273**. As to the approval of redress schemes see PARA **274** et seq.

2 Ie within the period specified under the Estate Agents Act 1979 Sch 4 para 1(c) (see PARA **278**) or that period as extended under Sch 4 para 3 (see PARA **278**): Sch 4 para 5(1) (Sch 4 added by the Consumers, Estate Agents and Redress Act 2007 Sch 6 paras 1, 4). As to the form of notices see PARA **278** note 7. As to the giving of notices see PARA **270** note 11.

3 As to enforcement authorities see PARA **291**.

4 Estate Agents Act 1979 Sch 4 para 5(1)(a) (as added: see note 2).

5 Estate Agents Act 1979 Sch 4 para 5(1)(b) (as added: see note 2). Notice of this decision must be given to the recipient: Sch 4 para 5(1)(c) (as so added). A notice under Sch 4 para 5(1)(c) which confirms the penalty charge notice must also state the effect of Sch 4 para 6(1)–(3) (see the text and notes 8–13) and Sch 4 para 8(1), (3) (see PARA **280**). As to the giving of notices see PARA **270** note 11.

   A notice may also be withdrawn at any time at the behest of the enforcement authority (see PARA **278**).

6 Estate Agents Act 1979 Sch 4 para 5(3)(a) (as added: see note 2).

7 Estate Agents Act 1979 Sch 4 para 5(3)(c) (as added: see note 2). The authority must also be satisfied that the notice was given within the time allowed by s 23B(2) (see PARA **278**) and complies with the other specified requirements imposed by or under Sch 4: Sch 4 para 5(3)(b) (as so added).

8 Estate Agents Act 1979 Sch 4 para 6(1) (as added (see note 2); and amended by the Crime and Courts Act 2013 s 17(5), Sch 9 para 82). An appeal against a penalty charge notice is by way of a rehearing: Estate Agents Act 1979 Sch 4 para 6(4) (as so added). Such an appeal must be brought

within the period of 28 days beginning with the day after that on which the notice under Sch 4 para 5(1)(c) (see note 5) is given (Sch 4 para 6(1) (as so added)), although the County Court may extend this period (Sch 4 para 6(2) (as so added)).

9   Estate Agents Act 1979 Sch 4 para 6(3)(a) (as added: see note 2).
10 Ie the time allowed by the Estate Agents Act 1979 s 23B(2) (see PARA 278).
11 Ie the requirements of the Estate Agents Act 1979 Sch 4.
12 Estate Agents Act 1979 Sch 4 para 6(3)(b) (as added: see note 2).
13 Estate Agents Act 1979 Sch 4 para 6(3)(c) (as added: see note 2).
14 Estate Agents Act 1979 Sch 4 para 6(4) (as added: see note 2).
15 Estate Agents Act 1979 Sch 4 para 7 (as added: see note 2).

280.   Recovery of the penalty charge.

Unless a penalty charge is paid[1] or the penalty charge notice has been withdrawn or quashed[2], the amount of the charge is recoverable from the recipient of the notice as a debt owed to the enforcement authority[3]. Proceedings for the recovery of the charge may not be commenced before the end of the period within which the recipient of the notice may request a review[4], and if within that period the recipient of the notice gives notice[5] to the authority that he wishes the authority to review the notice, proceedings may not be commenced before the end of the period within which the recipient may appeal to the county court against a confirmed notice[6] and, where the recipient appeals against the notice, before the end of the period of 28 days beginning with the day on which the appeal is withdrawn or determined[7].

The Secretary of State may by regulations prescribe the method or methods by which penalty charges may be paid[8].

1   Estate Agents Act 1979 Sch 4 para 8(1)(b) (Sch 4 added by the Consumers, Estate Agents and Redress Act 2007 Sch 6 paras 1, 4). As to penalty charges and penalty charge notices see PARA 278. In proceedings for recovery a certificate which purports to be signed by or on behalf of the person having responsibility for the financial affairs of the enforcement authority and states that payment of the penalty charge was or was not received by a date specified in the certificate is evidence of the facts stated: Sch 4 para 9 (as so added).
2   Estate Agents Act 1979 Sch 4 para 8(1)(a) (as added: see note 1). A penalty charge notice may be withdrawn at any time at the behest of the enforcement authority (see PARA 278) and may also be withdrawn or quashed on review or appeal (see PARA 279).
3   Estate Agents Act 1979 Sch 4 para 8(1) (as added: see note 1). As to enforcement authorities see PARA 291.
4   Estate Agents Act 1979 Sch 4 para 8(2) (as added: see note 1). This is the period referred to in Sch 4 para 5(1) (see PARA 279).
5   As to the form of notices see PARA 278 note 7. As to the giving of notices see PARA 270 note 11.
6   Estate Agents Act 1979 Sch 4 para 8(3)(a) (as added: see note 1). This is the period referred to in Sch 4 para 6(1) (see PARA 279).
7   Estate Agents Act 1979 Sch 4 para 8(3)(b) (as added: see note 1).
8   Estate Agents Act 1979 Sch 4 para 11(c) (as added: see note 1). At the date at which this volume states the law no such regulations had been made. As to the making of regulations generally see PARAS 258 note 2, 278 note 7.

(v) Prohibition of Unfit Persons

281.   Power to make orders prohibiting unfit persons doing estate agency work.

Where the lead enforcement authority[1] is satisfied that a person is unfit to carry on estate agency work[2], either generally or in relation to a specific activity, it may make an order prohibiting that person from carrying on estate agency work at all or from engaging in a particular aspect of such work[3]. Matters specifically relating to the business of estate agency must be taken into account in determining whether a person is unfit to carry on estate agency work[4], and the lead enforcement authority must specify in the order, as the grounds for the order, those matters[5] in relation to which it is satisfied and on which, accordingly, it relies to give it power to make the order[6]. In determining whether to make an order the lead enforcement authority may also take account of whether, in the course of estate agency work or any other business activity, the person in question has engaged in any practice involving a breach of a duty owed by virtue of any enactment, contract or rule of law which is material to his fitness to carry on estate agency work[7].

Failure to comply with a prohibition order is an offence[8].

1   As to the lead enforcement authority see PARA 291.
2   As to the meaning of 'estate agency work' see PARA 255. For activities not amounting to 'estate agency work' for these purposes see PARA 256.
3   Estate Agents Act 1979 s 3(2) (s 3(2), (4), (5), (8) amended by the Enterprise Act 2002 s 278(1), Sch 25 para 9(1), (2)(b)–(d); and SI 2014/631). The lead enforcement authority may, if it considers it appropriate, limit the scope of a prohibition imposed by an order to a particular part of or area within the United Kingdom: Estate Agents Act 1979 s 3(5) (as so amended). For the specified matters to be included in a prohibition order and the procedure to be followed in making the order see s 5, Sch 2 Pt I (amended by the Enterprise Act 2002 s 278(1), Sch 25 para 9(1), (4), (16); and the Consumers, Estate Agents and Redress Act 2007 ss 55(1), (4), 64, Sch 8; the Equality Act 2010 Sch 26 para 5; and SI 2014/631). See also the Consumers, Estate Agents and Redress Act 2007 (Commencement No 4) Order 2008, SI 2008/905.
      Where a prohibition order has the effect of prohibiting a person from holding clients' money the order may contain provision appointing another person as trustee in place of the person to whom the order relates to hold and deal with clients' money held by that person when the order comes into effect, and requiring the expenses and such reasonable remuneration of the new trustee as may be specified in the order to be paid by the person to whom the order relates or, if the order so provides, out of the clients' money: see the Estate Agents Act 1979 s 13(4) (amended by SI 2014/631). However, nothing in the Estate Agents Act 1979 s 13(4) affects the power conferred by the Trustee Act 1925 s 41 (see TRUSTS AND POWERS vol 98 (2013) PARA 289) to appoint a new trustee to hold clients' money: Estate Agents Act 1979 s 13(4). As to the meaning of 'clients' money' see PARA 266.
      Provision is made for the revocation and variation of prohibition orders (see PARA 288) and for the bringing of appeals against such orders (see PARA 289).
4   See the Estate Agents Act 1979 s 3(1)(a)–(d), Sch 1; and PARAS 282–286.
5   Ie the matters falling within the Estate Agents Act 1979 s 3(1)(a)–(d) (see PARAS 282–286).
6   Estate Agents Act 1979 s 3(4) (as amended: see note 3).
7   Estate Agents Act 1979 s 3(2) (as amended: see note 3).
8   A person who fails without reasonable excuse to comply with an order of the lead enforcement authority under the Estate Agents Act 1979 s 3 is liable on conviction on indictment or on summary conviction to a fine which on summary conviction may not exceed the statutory maximum: s 3(8) (as amended: see note 3). As to the powers of magistrates' courts to issue fines on summary conviction see SENTENCING vol 92 (2015) PARA 176. As to offences by bodies corporate see PARA 257. As to defences see PARA 258 note 7.

282. Criminal convictions.

The lead enforcement authority[1] may make an order prohibiting a person from carrying on estate agency work[2] or from engaging in a particular aspect of such work[3] if it is satisfied that that person has committed[4]:

(1)   an offence involving fraud or other dishonesty or violence[5];
(2)   an offence under the Estate Agents Act 1979 (other than an offence involving engaging in estate agency work without having attained the appropriate standards of competence or while bankrupt)[6];
(3)   an offence relating to misleading marketing or unfair commercial practices[7];
(4)   an offence involving the unlawful harassment of debtors[8];

(5)   the offence of pretending to be a licensed conveyancer or recognised body[9];
(6)   an offence involving acting as a company director while disqualified[10];
(7)   specified offences under consumer protection legislation[11];
(8)   specified data protection offences[12];
(9)   a specified offence under the Financial Services Act 1986[13]; or
(10)   an offence involving the sending of malicious communications[14].

Spent convictions are disregarded for these purposes[15].

1   As to the lead enforcement authority see PARA 291.
2   As to the meaning of 'estate agency work' see PARA 255. For activities not amounting to 'estate agency work' for these purposes see PARA 256.
3   As to the power of the lead enforcement authority to make prohibition orders generally see the Estate Agents Act 1979 s 3(2); and PARA 281.
4   Estate Agents Act 1979 s 3(1) (amended by the Enterprise Act 2002 s 278(1), Sch 25 para 9(1), (2); the Consumers, Estate Agents and Redress Act 2007 s 55(1), (2); and SI 2014/631).
5   Estate Agents Act 1979 s 3(1)(a)(i). 'Conviction' for the purposes of s 3(1)(a)(i) includes a conviction before 4 April 1979 (ie the date on which the Estate Agents Act 1979 received Royal Assent) and also includes a conviction outside the United Kingdom (*Antonelli v Secretary of State for Trade and Industry* [1998] QB 948, [1998] 1 All ER 997, CA).
6   Estate Agents Act 1979 s 3(1)(a)(ii). For the offence of engaging in estate agency work without having attained the appropriate standards of competence see s 22(3); and PARA 258. For the offence of engaging in estate agency work while bankrupt see s 23(4); and PARA 259. Offences under s 10(6) (repealed) are also excluded: s 3(1)(a)(ii).
7   Estate Agents Act 1979 s 3(1)(a)(iii); Estate Agents (Specified Offences) (No 2) Order 1991, SI 1991/1091, art 2, Schedule (amended by SI 1992/2833; SI 2008/1277; SI 2013/1575; SI 2013/1881). The offences in question are the Business Protection from Misleading Marketing Regulations 2008, SI 2008/1276, reg 6 (misleading advertising: see COMPETITION vol 18 (2009) PARA 336A; CONSUMER PROTECTION vol 21 (2016) PARA 425) and the Consumer Protection from Unfair Trading Regulations 2008, SI 2008/1277, regs 8–12 (unfair commercial practices: see CONSUMER PROTECTION vol 21 (2016) PARA 423).
     The Estate Agents (Specified Offences) (No 2) Order 1991, SI 1991/1091, is made pursuant to the Estate Agents Act 1979 s 3(6), (7). As to the making of orders and regulations generally see PARA 258 note 2.
8   Estate Agents Act 1979 s 3(1)(a)(iii); Estate Agents (Specified Offences) (No 2) Order 1991, SI 1991/1091, Schedule. For this offence see the Administration of Justice Act 1970 s 40(1)(a); and CRIMINAL LAW vol 25 (2016) PARA 179.
9   Estate Agents Act 1979 s 3(1)(a)(iii); Estate Agents (Specified Offences) (No 2) Order 1991, SI 1991/1091, Schedule (as amended: see note 7). For this offence see the Administration of Justice Act 1985 s 35; and LEGAL PROFESSIONS vol 65 (2015) PARA 433.
10   Estate Agents Act 1979 s 3(1)(a)(iii); Estate Agents (Specified Offences) (No 2) Order 1991, SI 1991/1091, Schedule (as amended: see note 7). The offences in question are those under the Company Directors Disqualification Act 1986 ss 11(1), 12(2), 13 (see COMPANIES vol 14 (2016) PARA 529, COMPANIES vol 15A (2016) PARAS 1780–1781, 1806) and corresponding Northern Irish legislation.
11   Estate Agents Act 1979 s 3(1)(a)(iii); Estate Agents (Specified Offences) (No 2) Order 1991, SI 1991/1091, Schedule (as amended: see note 7). The offences in question are those under the Consumer Credit Act 1974 s 46(1) (repealed), s 154, (see CONSUMER CREDIT vol 21 (2016) PARA 264), s 165(1) (repealed). For current consumer protection law see the Consumer Rights Act 2015; and CONSUMER PROTECTION.
12   Estate Agents Act 1979 s 3(1)(a)(iii); Estate Agents (Specified Offences) (No 2) Order 1991, SI 1991/1091, Schedule (as amended: see note 7). The offences in question are those under the Data Protection Act 1984 ss 5, 6(6), 10(9), 15, all of which have been repealed. For the modern law of data protection see the Data Protection Act 1998; and CONFIDENCE AND INFORMATIONAL PRIVACY.
13   Estate Agents Act 1979 s 3(1)(a)(iii); Estate Agents (Specified Offences) (No 2) Order 1991, SI 1991/1091, Schedule (as amended: see note 7). The offences in question are those under the Financial Services Act 1986 ss 4, 57, 59(5), 105(10), 111(1), 130, 133(1)(b), 199(6), 200(1)–(3),

Sch 6 para 5(3), all of which have been repealed. For the modern law in this area see the Financial Services and Markets Act 2000; and FINANCIAL INSTITUTIONS vol 48 (2015) PARA 1 et seq.

14 Estate Agents Act 1979 s 3(1)(a)(iii); Estate Agents (Specified Offences) (No 2) Order 1991, SI 1991/1091, Schedule (as amended: see note 7). The offence in question is under the Malicious Communications Act 1988 s 1(1)(a)(i), (ii) (see CRIMINAL LAW vol 26 (2016) PARA 829) and the corresponding Northern Irish offence.

15 Estate Agents Act 1979 Sch 1 para 1 (substituted by the Consumers, Estate Agents and Redress Act 2007 s 55(1), (5)). A person is not to be treated for the purposes of the Estate Agents Act 1979 s 3(1)(a) as having committed an offence if he has been convicted of that offence and that conviction is to be treated as spent for the purposes of the Rehabilitation of Offenders Act 1974 or any corresponding Northern Irish enactment: Estate Agents Act 1979 Sch 1 para 1 (as so substituted).

283. Discrimination.

The lead enforcement authority[1] may make an order prohibiting a person from carrying on estate agency work[2] or from engaging in a particular aspect of such work[3] if it is satisfied that that person has committed discrimination in the course of estate agency work[4].

A person commits discrimination for these purposes in the following cases only[5]. The first case is where the person has been found to have contravened a relevant equality provision[6], and no appeal against the finding is pending or can be brought[7]. The second case is where the person has been given an unlawful act notice[8] which specifies a relevant equality provision as the provision by virtue of which the act in question is unlawful, and no appeal against the giving of the notice is pending or can be brought[9]. The third case is where the person is the subject of an injunction, interdict or order under the Equality Act 2006[10], and the unlawful act in question is a contravention of a relevant equality provision[11].

These provisions are subject to a statutory period of limitation[12].

1 As to the lead enforcement authority see PARA 291.
2 As to the meaning of 'estate agency work' see PARA 255. For activities not amounting to 'estate agency work' for these purposes see PARA 256.
3 For the power to make prohibition orders generally see the Estate Agents Act 1979 s 3(2); and PARA 281.
4 Estate Agents Act 1979 s 3(1)(b) (s 3(1) amended by the Enterprise Act 2002 s 278(1), Sch 25 para 9(1), (2); and SI 2014/631).
   It is the duty of the Commission for Equality and Human Rights to furnish to the lead enforcement authority such information relating to any finding, notice, injunction or order falling within the Estate Agents Act 1979 Sch 1 para 2 as is in their possession and appears to them to be relevant to the functions of the lead enforcement authority under the Estate Agents Act 1979: s 9(6) (amended by the Equality Act 2006 ss 40, 91, Sch 3 paras 36, 37, Sch 4; and SI 2014/631).
   As to the law of discrimination see generally DISCRIMINATION vol 33 (2017) PARA 1 et seq.
5 Estate Agents Act 1979 Sch 1 para 2(1) (Sch 1 para 2 substituted by the Equality Act 2010 s 211(1), Sch 26 paras 4, 6(1), (2) (added by SI 2010/2279)).
6 The relevant equality provisions are the Equality Act 2010 Pt 3 (ss 28–31), Pt 4 (ss 32–38) so far as relating to discrimination and victimisation, and s 112 (aiding contraventions) in relation to either of those Parts of that Act so far as relating to discrimination and victimisation: Estate Agents Act 1979 Sch 1 para 2(5) (as substituted: see note 5). See DISCRIMINATION.
7 Estate Agents Act 1979 Sch 1 para 2(2) (as substituted: see note 5).
8 Ie under the Equality Act 2006 s 21: see DISCRIMINATION vol 33 (2017) PARAS 347–348.
9 Estate Agents Act 1979 Sch 1 para 2(3) (as substituted: see note 5).
10 Ie under the Equality Act 2006 s 24: see DISCRIMINATION vol 33 (2017) PARA 346 et seq.
11 Estate Agents Act 1979 Sch 1 para 2(4) (as substituted: see note 5).
12 After the expiry of the period of five years beginning on the day on which any such finding or notice as is referred to in the Estate Agents Act 1979 Sch 1 para 2 became final, no person is to be treated for the purposes of s 3(1)(b) as having committed a contravention of a relevant equality provision by reason only of that finding or notice: Sch 1 para 3 (amended by the Equality Act 2010 Sch 26 paras 4, 6(1), (3) (added by SI 2010/2279)).

284. Dealings with clients and clients' money.

The lead enforcement authority[1] may make an order prohibiting a person from carrying on estate agency work[2] or from engaging in a particular aspect of such work[3] if it is satisfied that that person has failed to comply with any statutory obligation imposed on him[4] with regard to:

(1) accounting for interest on clients' money[5];

(2) the giving of information to clients with respect to remuneration, their prospective liabilities under the agency contract or agreed contractual variations[6]; or

(3) notifying clients with regard to any personal interest he has in a proposed or intended transaction[7].

As from a day to be appointed, the lead enforcement authority may also make such an order if it is satisfied that that person has failed to comply with the statutory obligation[8] imposed on him with regard to the keeping of permanent records[9].

1 As to the lead enforcement authority see PARA 291.

2 As to the meaning of 'estate agency work' see PARA 255. For activities not amounting to 'estate agency work' for these purposes see PARA 256.

3 For the power to make prohibition orders generally see the Estate Agents Act 1979 s 3(2); and PARA 281.

4 Estate Agents Act 1979 s 3(1)(c) (s 3(1) amended by the Enterprise Act 2002 s 278(1), Sch 25 para 9(1), (2); and SI 2014/631). For these purposes, and for the purposes of the provisions described in PARAS 285–286, anything done by a person in the course of his employment is treated as done by his employer as well as by him, whether or not it was done with the employer's knowledge or approval, unless the employer shows that he took such steps as were reasonably practicable to prevent the employee from doing that act, or from doing in the course of his employment acts of that description: Estate Agents Act 1979 s 3(3)(a) (s 3(3) amended by the Consumers, Estate Agents and Redress Act 2007 s 63(1), Sch 7 para 1).

   Anything done by a person as agent for another person with the authority (whether express or implied, and whether precedent or subsequent) of that person is treated as done by that other person as well as by him: Estate Agents Act 1979 s 3(3)(b). Anything done by a business associate of a person is treated as done by that person as well, unless he can show that the act was done without his connivance or consent: s 3(3)(c). As to the meanings of 'associate' and 'business associate' see PARA 257.

5 Ie the obligation imposed under the Estate Agents Act 1979 s 15 (see PARA 269). As to the meaning of 'clients' money' see PARA 266.

6 Ie the obligations imposed under the Estate Agents Act 1979 s 18 (see PARAS 260–262).

7 Ie the obligations imposed under the Estate Agents Act 1979 s 21 (see PARA 264).

8 Ie the obligation imposed by the Estate Agents Act 1979 s 21A (see PARA 265).

9 Estate Agents Act 1979 s 3(1)(c) (prospectively amended by the Consumers, Estate Agents and Redress Act 2007 s 54(2)). At the date at which this volume states the law no day had been appointed for the coming into force of this amendment.

285. Undesirable practices.

The lead enforcement authority[1] may make an order prohibiting a person from carrying on estate agency work[2] or from engaging in a particular aspect of such work[3] if it is satisfied that that person[4] has engaged in an undesirable practice, that is:

(1) a failure to make disclosure of a personal interest[5] promptly[6] and in writing[7];

(2) a failure to disclose to his client[8] promptly and in writing that he himself has, or is seeking to acquire, a beneficial interest in the land or in the proceeds of sale of any interest in the land or he knows that any connected person[9] has, or is seeking to acquire, a beneficial interest in the land or in the proceeds of sale of any interest in the land[10];

(3)   discrimination against a prospective purchaser[11] by an estate agent on the grounds that that purchaser will not be, or is unlikely to be, accepting services[12];

(4)   a failure, following the making of an offer[13], to forward[14] to a client promptly and in writing at all stages before contracts for the disposal of the interest in the land have been exchanged an accurate list of services[15];

(5)   making misrepresentations concerning the existence of an offer[16] or a prospective purchaser[17]; or

(6)   a failure to forward[18] to a client, promptly and in writing, accurate details[19] of any offer the agent has received from a prospective purchaser in respect of an interest in the land[20].

1   As to the lead enforcement authority see PARA 291.
2   As to the meaning of 'estate agency work' see PARA 255. For activities not amounting to 'estate agency work' for these purposes see PARA 256. For these purposes 'estate agent' means any person who in the course of a business (including one in which he is employed) engages in estate agency work and includes cases where he is negotiating on his own behalf: Estate Agents (Undesirable Practices) (No 2) Order 1991, SI 1991/1032, art 1(2).
3   For the power to make prohibition orders generally see the Estate Agents Act 1979 s 3(2); and PARA 281.
4   As to the liability of employees, agents and associates see PARA 284 note 4.
5   Ie as required by the Estate Agents Act 1979 s 21(1) (see PARA 264). 'Interest in land' means any of the interests referred to in s 2 (see PARA 255 note 3) and references to an 'interest in the land' are references to the particular interest in land of which the estate agent is engaged to secure the disposal or acquisition: Estate Agents (Undesirable Practices) (No 2) Order 1991, SI 1991/1032, art 1(2).
6   'Promptly' means within as short a period as is reasonably practicable in the circumstances, from the moment when what is to be done can reasonably be done: Estate Agents (Undesirable Practices) (No 2) Order 1991, SI 1991/1032, art 1(2).
7   Estate Agents Act 1979 s 3(1)(d) (s 3(1) amended by SI 2014/631); Estate Agents (Undesirable Practices) (No 2) Order 1991, SI 1991/1032, art 2(a), Sch 1 para 1. The Estate Agents (Undesirable Practices) (No 2) Order 1991, SI 1991/1032, is made pursuant to the Estate Agents Act 1979 s 3(6). As to the making of orders and regulations generally see PARA 258 note 2.
8   Ie the person on whose behalf the estate agent acts: Estate Agents (Undesirable Practices) (No 2) Order 1991, SI 1991/1032, art 1(2).
9   'Connected person' in relation to an estate agent means his employer or principal, any employee or agent of his or any associate of his or of his employer, principal, employee or agent: Estate Agents (Undesirable Practices) (No 2) Order 1991, SI 1991/1032, art 1(2). As to the meaning of 'associate' see PARA 257.
10 Estate Agents (Undesirable Practices) (No 2) Order 1991, SI 1991/1032, Sch 1 para 2.
11 'Purchaser' means a person to whom an interest in land is transferred or in whose favour it is created: Estate Agents (Undesirable Practices) (No 2) Order 1991, SI 1991/1032, art 1(2). As to the law of discrimination see generally DISCRIMINATION vol 33 (2017) PARA 1 et seq.
12 Estate Agents (Undesirable Practices) (No 2) Order 1991, SI 1991/1032, art 2(b), Sch 2 para 1. 'Services' means any service for consideration provided, or to be provided, to a prospective purchaser by an estate agent or a connected person, or (in a case where the estate agent or connected person would derive a financial benefit from the provision of the service) by another person, and which is such as would ordinarily be made available to a prospective purchaser in connection with his acquisition of an interest in land or his use or enjoyment of it (including the provision to that purchaser of banking and insurance services and financial assistance and securing the disposal for that purchaser of an interest in land if that disposal is one which has to be made in order for him to be able to make the acquisition he is proposing or is one which is a result of that acquisition): art 1(2). 'Financial benefit' includes commission and any performance related bonus: art 1(2).
13 Ie where the estate agent has introduced a prospective purchaser to his client and that purchaser has made an offer: Estate Agents (Undesirable Practices) (No 2) Order 1991, SI 1991/1032, Sch 2 para 2. 'Offer' includes a conditional offer: Sch 2 para 2.

14 'Forward' means despatch to the client by hand, post or fax at the address or to the number given by the client to the agent, which despatch may be made by the person by whom or which the service is being, or is to be, provided: Estate Agents (Undesirable Practices) (No 2) Order 1991, SI 1991/1032, Sch 2 para 2.

15 Estate Agents (Undesirable Practices) (No 2) Order 1991, SI 1991/1032, Sch 2 para 2. This is an undesirable practice for these purposes provided that an application from the prospective purchaser for services has been received by the agent or a connected person or (in a case where the agent or a connected person would derive a financial benefit from the provision of the service) by another person, the agent knows that such application has been received and that it is an application for services, being services in connection with the prospective purchaser's acquisition of the interest in the land or his use or enjoyment of it, or with his disposal of an interest in land which he has to make in order to make that acquisition or which is the result of that acquisition, and that application has not been refused: Sch 2 para 2.

16 'Offer' includes any conditional offer, but does not include offers of a description which the client has indicated in writing to the agent need not be forwarded to him: Estate Agents (Undesirable Practices) (No 2) Order 1991, SI 1991/1032, art 2(c), Sch 3 para 3(b).

17 Estate Agents (Undesirable Practices) (No 2) Order 1991, SI 1991/1032, Sch 3 para 1. It is an undesirable practice for these purposes if the agent knowingly or recklessly, and orally or in writing, makes any misrepresentation as to the existence of, or details relating to, any offer for the interest in the land (Sch 3 para 1(a)) or as to the existence or status of any prospective purchaser of an interest in the land (Sch 3 para 1(b)). A misrepresentation is 'recklessly' made if it is made regardless of whether it is true or false, whether or not the agent had reasons for believing that it might be false: Sch 3 para 3(a). Schedule 3 para 1(a) does not affect the right of an auctioneer to bid at an auction in accordance with the Sale of Land by Auction Act 1867 s 6 (see AUCTION vol 4 (2011) PARA 48) (Estate Agents (Undesirable Practices) (No 2) Order 1991, SI 1991/1032, Sch 3 para 3(c)), and in Sch 3 para 1(b) the 'status of any prospective purchaser' includes the financial standing of that purchaser and his ability to exchange contracts expeditiously or in Scotland conclude a contract expeditiously (Sch 3 para 3(d)).

18 This means despatch to the client by hand, post or fax at the address or to the number given by the client to the agent: Estate Agents (Undesirable Practices) (No 2) Order 1991, SI 1991/1032, Sch 3 para 3(e).

19 Ie excluding details of a description which the client has indicated in writing he does not wish to receive: Estate Agents (Undesirable Practices) (No 2) Order 1991, SI 1991/1032, Sch 3 para 2.

20 Estate Agents (Undesirable Practices) (No 2) Order 1991, SI 1991/1032, Sch 3 para 2. Head (6) in the text does not apply if the estate agent does not forward accurate details of the offer because the estate agent is unable to apply the customer due diligence measures required by the Money Laundering, Terrorist Financing and Transfer of Funds (Information on the Payer) Regulations 2017, SI 2017/692, reg 28, and where relevant regs 33, 35–37, in relation to the offeror: Estate Agents (Undesirable Practices) (No 2) Order 1991, SI 1991/1032, Sch 3 para 2A (added by SI 2017/692).

286. Breach of compliance requirements.

The lead enforcement authority[1] may make an order prohibiting a person from carrying on estate agency work[2] or from engaging in a particular aspect of such work[3] if it is satisfied that that person[4] has:

(1) failed to comply with an enforcement order[5] which was made against him in relation to estate agency work[6];

(2) failed to comply with an undertaking accepted from him[7] in relation to an enforcement order in connection with estate agency work[8];

(3) engaged in estate agency work in relation to residential property[9] in breach of the duty[10] to be a member of an approved redress scheme[11]; or

(4) failed to comply with a requirement[12] to furnish information to the lead enforcement authority[13].

1 As to the lead enforcement authority see PARA 291.

2 As to the meaning of 'estate agency work' see PARA 255. For activities not amounting to 'estate agency work' for these purposes see PARA 256.

3 For the power to make prohibition orders generally see the Estate Agents Act 1979 s 3(2); and PARA 281.

4   Estate Agents Act 1979 s 3(1) (amended by SI 2014/631). As to the liability of employees, agents and associates see PARA 284 note 4.
5   Ie an order under the Enterprise Act 2002 s 217 (see COMPETITION vol 18 (2009) PARA 346).
6   Estate Agents Act 1979 s 3(1)(bb) (s 3(1)(ba), (bb), (ca), (cb) added by the Consumers, Estate Agents and Redress Act 2007 ss 53(2), 55(1), (3), 58(2)).
7   Ie under the Enterprise Act 2002 s 217, s 218 or s 219 (see COMPETITION vol 18 (2009) PARAS 346, 347).
8   Estate Agents Act 1979 s 3(1)(ba) (as added: see note 6).
9   As to the meaning of 'residential property' in connection with redress schemes see PARA 273.
10 Ie the duty imposed by an order under the Estate Agents Act 1979 s 23A(1) (see PARA 273).
11 Estate Agents Act 1979 s 3(1)(ca) (as added: see note 6). As to approved redress schemes see PARA 273 et seq.
12 Ie any requirement imposed by the Consumer Rights Act 2015 Sch 5 para 14 or Sch 5 para 27: see CONSUMER PROTECTION vol 21 (2016) PARAS 711, 722.
13 Estate Agents Act 1979 s 3(1)(cb) (as added (see note 6); amended by the Consumer Rights Act 2015 s 77(2), Sch 6 paras 19, 20).

287. Warning orders.

The lead enforcement authority[1] is empowered to issue warning orders to persons in respect of whom it is minded to make prohibition orders[2]. The lead enforcement authority may give a person a warning order[3] where it is satisfied that, in the course of estate agency work[4] he has done any of the following[5]:

(1)   committed a specified offence under the Estate Agents Act 1979[6];
(2)   committed discrimination[7];
(3)   failed to comply with the specified statutory obligations relating to dealings with clients and clients' money[8];
(4)   acted in relation to residential property[9] in breach of the duty[10] to be a member of an approved redress scheme[11];
(5)   failed to comply with a requirement[12] to furnish information to the lead enforcement authority[13];
(6)   failed to comply with an enforcement order[14] which was made against him in relation to estate agency work[15];
(7)   failed to comply with an undertaking accepted from him[16] in relation to such an order[17]; or
(8)   engaged in an undesirable practice[18],

and that, were he to engage again in any such conduct[19], to fail again to comply with the specified undertaking or order by engaging in the same or similar conduct[20], or to engage again in the specified undesirable practice[21], the lead enforcement authority would consider him unfit and proceed to make a prohibition order[22].

A warning order must state whether, in the opinion of the lead enforcement authority, any further failure or conduct[23] would render the person to whom the order is addressed unfit to carry on estate agency work generally or estate agency work of a description specified in the order[24]. Any further failure or conduct on the part of a person to whom a warning order is addressed[25] is treated as conclusive evidence that that person is unfit to carry on estate agency work as stated in the order, and the lead enforcement authority may proceed to make a prohibition order accordingly[26].

The lead enforcement authority is required to establish and maintain a register of every warning order made by it[27].

1   As to the lead enforcement authority see PARA 291.
2   For the power to make prohibition orders generally see the Estate Agents Act 1979 s 3(2); and PARA 281.

3 See the Estate Agents Act 1979 s 4. The matters to be included in a warning order and the procedure to be followed in making the order are specified in s 5, Sch 2 Pt I (amended by the Enterprise Act 2002 s 278(1), Sch 25 para 9(1), (4), (16); the Consumers, Estate Agents and Redress Act 2007 ss 55(1), (4), 64, Sch 8; the Equality Act 2010 Sch 26 para 5 (added by SI 2010/2279); and by SI 2014/631). Provision is made for the revocation and variation of warning orders (see PARA 288) and for the bringing of appeals (see PARA 289).

4 As to the meaning of 'estate agency work' see PARA 255. For activities not amounting to 'estate agency work' for these purposes see PARA 256.

5 Estate Agents Act 1979 s 4(1) (s 4(1) substituted, and s 4(1A)–(1C), (4) added, and s 4(2), (3) amended, by the Consumers, Estate Agents and Redress Act 2007 s 56; and amended by the Enterprise Act 2002 s 278(1), Sch 25 para 9(1), (3); and SI 2014/631). For the matters to be specified in the order and the procedure to be followed in making the order see the Estate Agents Act 1979 s 5, Sch 2 Pt I; and PARA 281.

6 Ie engaged in conduct falling within the Estate Agents Act 1979 s 3(1)(a) (see PARA 282): s 4(1A)(a) (as added: see note 5).

7 Ie engaged in conduct falling within the Estate Agents Act 1979 s 3(1)(b) (see PARA 283): s 4(1A)(a) (as added: see note 5).

8 Ie failed to comply with any such obligation as is referred to in the Estate Agents Act 1979 s 3(1)(c) (see PARA 284): s 4(1A)(a) (as added: see note 5).

9 As to the meaning of 'residential property' in connection with redress schemes see PARA 273.

10 Ie the duty imposed by an order under the Estate Agents Act 1979 s 23A(1) (see PARA 273).

11 Ie engaged in conduct falling within the Estate Agents Act 1979 s 3(1)(ca) (see PARA 286): s 4(1A)(a) (as added: see note 5).

12 Ie any requirement imposed by the Estate Agents Act 1979.

13 Ie engaged in conduct falling within the Estate Agents Act 1979 s 3(1)(cb) (see PARA 286): s 4(1A)(a) (as added: see note 5).

14 Ie an order under the Enterprise Act 2002 s 217 (see COMPETITION vol 18 (2009) PARA 346).

15 Ie engaged in conduct constituting a failure to comply with an enforcement order mentioned in the Estate Agents Act 1979 s 3(1)(bb) (see PARA 286): s 4(1B)(a)(ii) (as added: see note 5).

16 Ie under the Enterprise Act 2002 s 217, s 218 or s 219 (see COMPETITION vol 18 (2009) PARAS 346, 347).

17 Ie engaged in conduct constituting a failure to comply with an undertaking mentioned in the Estate Agents Act 1979 s 3(1)(ba) (see PARA 286): s 4(1B)(a)(i) (as added: see note 5).

18 See PARA 285.

19 Ie in relation to the matters referred to in the text and notes 11–18.

20 Ie in relation to the matters referred to in the text and notes 29–22.

21 See note 6.

22 Estate Agents Act 1979 s 4(1A)(b), (1B)(b), (1C)(b) (as added: see note 5). 'Prohibition order' means an order under s 3 (see PARA 282): s 4(4) (as so added).

23 Ie any further conduct as mentioned in the Estate Agents Act 1979 s 4(1A)(b) or (1B)(b) or engaging again in the undesirable practice specified in the order, as the case may be: s 4(2), (3) (as amended: see note 5).

24 Estate Agents Act 1979 s 4(2) (as amended: see note 5).

25 See note 29.

26 Estate Agents Act 1979 s 4(3) (as amended: see note 5).

27 See PARA 290.

288. Variation and revocation of orders.

The lead enforcement authority[1] may revoke or vary a prohibition order[2] or a warning order[3] on the application[4] of the person[5] in respect of whom the order was made[6]. The lead enforcement authority may refuse an application for the revocation or variation of a prohibition order if it considers that the applicant remains unfit to carry on any estate agency work[7] at all or, as the case may be, estate agency work of the description which is prohibited by the order[8], and may refuse an application for the revocation or variation of a warning order if it considers that the applicant may repeat the behaviour[9] that occasioned the order[10]. It may, however, vary an order even though it considers that the applicant remains unfit to carry on any estate agency work[11] if the order could, without detriment to the public, be varied in favour of the applicant[12].

The lead enforcement authority is required to establish and maintain a register of every decision made by it on an application for variation or revocation of an order[13].

1 As to the lead enforcement authority see PARA 291.
2 Ie an order under the Estate Agents Act 1979 s 3 (see PARAS 281–286).
3 Ie an order under the Estate Agents Act 1979 s 4 (see PARA 287).
4 An application for variation or revocation must state the reasons why the applicant considers that the order should be revoked or varied, must (in the case of an application for a variation) indicate the variation which the applicant seeks, and must be accompanied by a fee of £2,500: Estate Agents Act 1979 s 6(2); Estate Agents (Fees) Regulations 1982, SI 1982/637, reg 2 (made under the Estate Agents Act 1979 s 33).
5 As to the liability of employees, agents and associates in respect of prohibition orders see PARA 284 note 4.
6 Estate Agents Act 1979 s 6(1) (s 6(1), (3)–(6), Sch 2 Pt II amended by the Enterprise Act 2002 s 278(1), Sch 25 para 9(1), (5), (16); the Consumer Rights Act 2015 Sch 6 para 26(2), (3); and SI 2014/631). The procedure to be followed in making an application for revocation or variation is specified in the Estate Agents Act 1979 s 6(6), Sch 2 Pt II (as so amended). If the lead enforcement authority decides to accede to such an application it must give notice in writing of its decision to the applicant and, upon the giving of that notice, the revocation or, as the case may be, the variation specified in the application must take effect: s 6(3) (as so amended). As to the giving of notices see PARA 270 note 11.
7 As to the meaning of 'estate agency work' see PARA 255. For activities not amounting to 'estate agency work' for these purposes see PARA 256.
8 Estate Agents Act 1979 s 6(4)(a) (as amended: see note 6).
9 This refers to any further conduct as mentioned in the Estate Agents Act 1979 s 4(1A)(b) or (1B)(b) (see PARA 287) or engaging again in the undesirable practice specified in the order, as the case may be: s 6(4)(b) (s 6(4)(b) as amended (see note 6); s 6(4)(b) further amended by the Consumers, Estate Agents and Redress Act 2007 ss 63(1), 64, Sch 7 para 2, Sch 8).
10 Estate Agents Act 1979 s 6(4)(b) (as amended: see notes 6, 9).
11 Ie even if it cannot accede to an application for variation or revocation because it considers that the applicant remains unfit to carry on any estate agency work at all in a particular part of or area within the United Kingdom or remains unfit to carry on estate agency work of a particular description (either throughout the United Kingdom or in a particular part of or area within it), or, as the case may be, remains likely to fail to comply with a relevant statutory obligation or to engage in a particular practice: Estate Agents Act 1979 s 6(5)(a) (as amended: see note 6).
12 Estate Agents Act 1979 s 6(5)(b) (as amended: see note 6).
13 See PARA 290.

289. Appeals against prohibition orders and warning orders.

A person who is notified[1] that the lead enforcement authority[2] has decided to make a prohibition[3] or warning[4] order in respect of him, to refuse an application for the revocation or variation of such an order[5], or to make a limited variation of such an order pursuant to such an application[6], may appeal against the decision to the First-tier Tribunal[7].

1 Ie under the Estate Agents Act 1979 Sch 2 para 9 (amended by the Enterprise Act 2002 s 278(1), Sch 25 para 9(1), (6), (16); and SI 2014/631).
2 As to the lead enforcement authority see PARA 291.
3 Ie an order under the Estate Agents Act 1979 s 3 (see PARAS 281–286).
4 Ie an order under the Estate Agents Act 1979 s 4 (see PARA 287).
5 Ie under the Estate Agents Act 1979 s 6(4) (see PARA 288).
6 Ie under the Estate Agents Act 1979 s 6(5) (see PARA 288).
7 Estate Agents Act 1979 s 7(1) (amended by the Enterprise Act 2002 s 278(1), Sch 25 para 9(1), (6), (16); and SI 2009/1836; SI 2014/631). On such an appeal the First-tier Tribunal may give such directions for disposing of the appeal as it thinks just: Estate Agents Act 1979 s 7(2) (amended by the Enterprise Act 2002 s 278(1), Sch 25 para 9(1), (6), (16); and SI 2009/1836). As to the First-tier Tribunal see COURTS AND TRIBUNALS vol 24 (2010) PARA 874 et seq.

290. Register of orders and decisions.

The lead enforcement authority[1] must establish and maintain a register on which are entered particulars of every prohibition order[2] and warning order[3] and of its decision on any application for revocation or variation[4] of such an order[5]. Provision is made for the rectification of this register by the lead enforcement authority[6] and for the removal of out-of-date particulars[7]. Any person may inspect the register and take copies, and obtain a certified copy of any entry on payment of the prescribed fee[8].

1 As to the lead enforcement authority see PARA 291.
2 Ie an order under the Estate Agents Act 1979 s 3 (see PARAS 281–286).
3 Ie an order under the Estate Agents Act 1979 s 4 (see PARA 287).
4 Ie under the Estate Agents Act 1979 s 6 (see PARA 288).
5 Estate Agents Act 1979 s 8(1) (s 8(1), (3)–(6) amended by the Enterprise Act 2002 s 278(1), Sch 25 para 9(1), (7), (16); SI 2014/631). The particulars must include the terms of the order and of any variation of it and the date on which the order or variation came into operation or is expected to come into operation or, if an appeal against the decision is pending and the order or variation has in consequence not come into operation, a statement to that effect: Estate Agents Act 1979 s 8(2).
6 The lead enforcement authority may, of its own motion or on the application of any person aggrieved, rectify the register by the addition, variation or removal of any particulars: Estate Agents Act 1979 s 8(3) (as amended: see note 5). For provisions relating to applications for rectification see Sch 2 Pt II (amended by the Enterprise Act 2002 s 278(1), Sch 25 para 9(1), (7), (16); the Consumer Rights Act 2015 Sch 6 para 26(2), (3); and SI 2014/631).
7 If it comes to the attention of the lead enforcement authority that any order of which particulars appear in the register is no longer in operation, the lead enforcement authority must remove those particulars from the register: Estate Agents Act 1979 s 8(4) (as amended: see note 5).
8 Any person is entitled, on payment of the fee prescribed in the Estate Agents (Fees) Regulations 1982, SI 1982/637, reg 3, to inspect the register during such office hours as may be specified by a general notice made by the lead enforcement authority (Estate Agents Act 1979 s 8(5)(a) (as amended: see note 5)) and to take copies of any entry, or to obtain from the lead enforcement authority a copy, certified by it to be correct, of any entry in the register (s 8(5)(b) (as so amended)). A certificate given by the lead enforcement authority under s 8(5)(b) is conclusive evidence of the fact that, on the date on which the certificate was given, the particulars contained in the copy to which the certificate relates were entered on the register; and particulars of any matters required to be entered on the register which are so entered are evidence of those matters and are presumed, unless the contrary is proved, to be correct: s 8(6) (as so amended).

(vi) Enforcement and Compliance

291. Enforcement authorities for the purposes of the Estate Agents Act 1979.

The lead enforcement authority[1] and local weights and measures authorities[2] are the 'enforcement authorities' for the purposes of the Estate Agents Act 1979, and are under a duty to enforce the Act's provisions[3]. These enforcement authorities have investigatory powers under the Consumer Rights Act 2015[4].

It is the duty of the lead enforcement authority generally to superintend the working and enforcement of the Estate Agents Act 1979, and where necessary or expedient, itself to take steps to enforce it[5]. The lead enforcement authority is under a duty (so far as appears to it to be practicable and having regard both to the national interest and the interests of persons engaged in estate agency work and of consumers) to keep under review and from time to time advise the Secretary of State about social and commercial developments in the United Kingdom and elsewhere relating to the carrying on of estate agency work and related activities, and the working and enforcement of the Estate Agents Act 1979[6]. It is also required to arrange for the dissemination of such information and advice as it may appear to it expedient to give the public in the United Kingdom about the operation of the Act[7].

1 The 'lead enforcement authority' means the Secretary of State, or a person whom the Secretary of State has arranged to be the lead enforcement authority: see the Estate Agents Act 1979 s 24A(1), (2) (s 24A added by the Housing and Planning Act 2016 s 132(1)). The Secretary of State may make arrangements for either a local weights and measures authority in Great Britain, or the Department of Enterprise, Trade and Investment in Northern Ireland to be the lead enforcement authority for the purposes of the Estate Agents Act 1979 (for the whole of the United Kingdom) instead of the Secretary of State: s 24A(2) (as so added). The arrangements may include provision for payments by the Secretary of State and may include provision about bringing the arrangements to an end: s 24A(3) (as so added). The Secretary of State may by regulations made by statutory instrument make transitional provision for when there is a change in the lead enforcement authority (s 24A(4) (as so added); and the regulations may relate to a specific change in the lead enforcement authority or to changes that might arise from time to time (s 24A(5) (as so added)). At the date at which this volume states the law, no such regulations had been made.

2 As to the local weights and measures authorities see WEIGHTS AND MEASURES vol 99 (2012) PARAS 519–534. Every local weights and measures authority must, whenever the lead enforcement authority requires, report to it in such form and with such particulars as it requires on the exercise of its functions under the Estate Agents Act 1979: s 26(4) (amended by the Enterprise Act 2002 s 278(1), Sch 25 para 9(1), (12), (13); and SI 2014/631).

3 Estate Agents Act 1979 s 26(1)(a), (b) (amended by the Enterprise Act 2002 s 278(1), Sch 25 para 9(1), (12), (13); and SI 2014/631). The Estate Agents Act 1979 ss 25, 26 do not authorise the institution of proceedings in Scotland: s 26(3).

4 Estate Agents Act 1979 s 26(1A) (added by the Consumer Rights Act 2015 s 77(2), Sch 6 paras 19, 24). As to the investigatory powers of enforcers under the Consumer Rights Act 2015 Sch 5 see CONSUMER PROTECTION vol 21 (2016) PARA 686 et seq.

5 Estate Agents Act 1979 s 25(1) (amended by the Enterprise Act 2002 s 278(1), Sch 25 para 9(1), (12); and SI 2014/631).

6 Estate Agents Act 1979 s 25(2) (amended by the Enterprise Act 2002 s 278(1), Sch 25 para 9(1), (12); and SI 2014/631).

7 Estate Agents Act 1979 s 25(3) (amended by the Enterprise Act 2002 s 278(1), Sch 25 para 9(1), (12); and SI 2014/631). The information may be in such form and manner as the lead enforcement authority considers appropriate: see the Estate Agents Act 1979 s 25(3) (as so added).

292. Notice of convictions and judgments.

If a person is convicted of an offence by or before a court in the United Kingdom, or a judgment is given against a person by a court in civil proceedings in the United Kingdom[1], then the court may make arrangements to bring the conviction or judgment to the attention of the lead enforcement authority[2] if it appears to the court that:

(1) having regard to the functions of the lead enforcement authority under the Estate Agents Act 1979 it is expedient for the conviction or judgment to be brought to the attention of the lead enforcement authority[3]; and

(2) without such arrangements the conviction or judgment may not be brought to the attention of the lead enforcement authority[4].

1 Estate Agents Act 1979 s 9A(1)(a), (b) (s 9A added by SI 2014/631).
2 As to the lead enforcement authority see PARA 291.
3 Estate Agents Act 1979 s 9A(2)(a) (as added: see note 1).
4 Estate Agents Act 1979 s 9A(2)(b) (as added: see note 1).

(2) ACCOMMODATION AGENCIES

(i) Scope of Regulation

293. Regulation of letting agencies and property management agencies.
There is currently no statutory regulation of private sector letting or property management agents in England. A system of self-regulation operates through the codes of conduct of trade associations, but there is no legal requirement for agents to be members of such bodies[1]. These professional bodies may operate client money protection schemes which reimburse landlords and tenants in the event of misappropriation of rents or deposits by agents.

However, in recent years important changes to the law have been introduced. Since 1 October 2014[2], private sector letting agents and property managing agents have been required by the Enterprise and Regulatory Reform Act 2013 to belong to an approved government-administered redress scheme[3]. The following year, the Consumer Rights Act 2015 brought in the requirement for letting agents to publish their fee tariffs[4]. Traders offering holiday accommodation contracts must observe the requirements in the Timeshare, Holiday Products, Resale and Exchange Regulations 2010[6].

When the Housing and Planning Act 2016 comes into force, local authorities will be able to seek banning orders against letting agents and property management agents who commit certain offences[5]. The Act will also introduce a database of rogue property agents[7].

1   Trade associations include the Association of Residential Letting Agents ('ARLA') and the UK Association of Letting Agents ('UKALA') (the latter works closely with the National Landlords Association ('NLA')). There is also the National Assured Letting Scheme ('NALS').
2   See the Redress Schemes for Lettings Agency Work and Property Management Work (Requirement to Belong to a Scheme etc) (England) Order 2014, SI 2014/2359, art 1.
3   See the Enterprise and Regulatory Reform Act 2013 ss 83–88; and PARA 294 et seq. At present the three approved schemes are Ombudsman Services Property, Property Redress Scheme and the Property Ombudsman: see *Lettings Agents and Property Managers: which government-approved redress scheme do you belong to?* (October 2014, Department for Communities and Local Government)
4   See the Consumer Rights Act 2015 ss 83–88.
6   See the Timeshare, Holiday Products, Resale and Exchange Contracts Regulations 2010, SI 2010/2960; and CONSUMER PROTECTION vol 21 (2016) PARA 578 et seq. A 'holiday accommodation contract' means a timeshare contract, a long-term holiday product contract, a resale contract, or an exchange contract: see reg 4; and CONSUMER PROTECTION vol 21 (2016) PARA 578.
5   See the Housing and Planning Act 2016 ss 13–27 (not yet in force); and HOUSING vol 56 (2017) PARA 719 et seq.
7   See the Housing and Planning Act 2016 ss 28–39 (not yet in force); and HOUSING vol 56 (2017) PARA 724 et seq.

(ii) Redress Schemes

294. Requirement for lettings agencies and property management agencies to belong to redress schemes.
A person who engages in lettings agency work[1] or in property management work[2] must be a member of an approved or government administered redress scheme[3] for dealing with complaints[4] in connection with that work[5]. Redress

schemes provide for complaints against members to be investigated and determined by an independent person[6].

1   As to the meaning of 'lettings agency work' see PARA 295. References to persons who engage in lettings agency work do not include references to persons who engage in that work in the course of their employment under a contract of employment: Enterprise and Regulatory Reform Act 2013 s 86(1), (2).

2   As to the meaning of 'property management work' see PARA 296. References to persons who engage in property management work do not include references to persons who engage in that work in the course of their employment under a contract of employment: Enterprise and Regulatory Reform Act 2013 s 86(1), (2).

3   The redress scheme must either be one that is approved by the Secretary of State or one designated by the Secretary of State as a government administered redress scheme: Redress Schemes for Lettings Agency Work and Property Management Work (Requirement to Belong to a Scheme etc) Order 2014, SI 2014/2359, arts 3(2), 5(2).
    A 'government administered redress scheme' means a redress scheme which is administered by or on behalf of the Secretary of State, and is designated for the purposes of the order by the Secretary of State: Enterprise and Regulatory Reform Act 2013 ss 83(3), 84(2). The order may provide for this duty to apply only to specified descriptions of persons who engage in lettings agency work, or only in relation to specified descriptions of such work: ss 83(4), 84(3).

4   Ie a complaint made by a person who is or has been a prospective landlord or a prospective tenant: Redress Schemes for Lettings Agency Work and Property Management Work (Requirement to Belong to a Scheme etc) Order 2014, SI 2014/2359, art 3(3).

5   Enterprise and Regulatory Reform Act 2013 ss 83(1), 84(1); Redress Schemes for Lettings Agency Work and Property Management Work (Requirement to Belong to a Scheme etc) Order 2014, SI 2014/2359, arts 3(1), 5(1).
    The Enterprise and Regulatory Reform Act 2013 ss 83(4)–(6), 84(3)–(5) specify what the order may provide and also require the Secretary of State to be satisfied that all persons who are to be subject to the duty will be eligible to join a redress scheme before the duty applies to them.

6   Enterprise and Regulatory Reform Act 2013 ss 83(2), 84(2).
    Nothing in ss 83–87 prevents a redress scheme from providing:
    (1)   for membership to be open to persons who are not subject to the duty to be a member of a scheme (s 88(5)(a));
    (2)   for the investigation and determination of any complaints in relation to which the duty does not apply, where the members concerned have voluntarily accepted the jurisdiction of the scheme over those complaints (s 88(5)(b));
    (3)   for the exclusion from investigation and determination under the scheme of any complaint in such cases or circumstances as may be specified in or determined under the scheme (s 88(5)(c)).

295. Meaning of 'lettings agency work' under the Enterprise and Regulatory Reform Act 2013.

'Lettings agency work' means things done by any person in the course of a business in response to instructions received from:

(1)   a prospective landlord (that is a person seeking to find another person wishing to rent a dwelling-house in England under a domestic tenancy[1] and, having found such a person, to grant such a tenancy)[2];

(2)   a prospective tenant (that is a person seeking to find a dwelling-house in England to rent under a domestic tenancy and, having found such a dwelling-house, to obtain such a tenancy of it)[3].

However, 'lettings agency work' does not include any of the following things when done by a person who does no other things falling within heads (1) and (2) above:

(a)   publishing advertisements or disseminating information[4];

(b)   providing a means by which:

      (i)   a prospective landlord or a prospective tenant can, in response to an advertisement or dissemination of information, make direct contact with a prospective tenant or (as the case may be) prospective landlord;

      (ii)   a prospective landlord and a prospective tenant can continue to communicate directly with each other[5].

'Lettings agency work' also does not include things done by:

(A)   a local authority[6];

(B)   the employer, where the prospective tenant is an employee[7];

(C)   the person for whom the prospective tenant provides work or services, where the prospective tenant is a worker[8];

(D)   the person for whom the prospective tenant provides work or services, where the prospective tenant is:

      (I)   an employee who provides work or services under the contract of employment to a person who is not the prospective tenant's employer; or

      (II)   a worker who provides work or services under the worker's contract to a person who is not a party to that contract[9];

(E)   the hirer, where the prospective tenant is an agency worker[10];

(F)   the person for whom the prospective tenant provides services under a contract for services[11];

(G)   an educational establishment or other body as may be prescribed by order made by the Secretary of State[12];

(H)   an authorised person within the meaning of the Legal Services Act 2007[13].

1   'Domestic tenancy' means:
    (1)   a tenancy which is an assured tenancy for the purposes of the Housing Act 1988 except where the landlord is a private registered provider of social housing (see the Housing and Regeneration Act 2008 s 80; and HOUSING vol 56 (2017) PARA 53); or where the tenancy is a long lease within the meaning given by s 84(10) (Enterprise and Regulatory Reform Act 2013 s 83(10)(a));
    (2)   a tenancy under which a dwelling-house is let as a separate dwelling and which is of a description specified for the purposes of the Enterprise and Regulatory Reform Act 2013 s 83 in an order made by the Secretary of State (s 83(10)(b), (11)).
2   Enterprise and Regulatory Reform Act 2013 s 83(7)(a). A 'dwelling-house' may be a house or part of a house: s 86(1), (3).
3   Enterprise and Regulatory Reform Act 2013 s 83(7)(b).
4   Enterprise and Regulatory Reform Act 2013 s 83(8)(a).
5   Enterprise and Regulatory Reform Act 2013 s 83(8)(b).
6   Enterprise and Regulatory Reform Act 2013 s 83(9)(a). 'Local authority' means a county or district council, a London borough council, the Common Council of the City of London in its capacity as a local authority, and the Council of the Isles of Scilly: s 86(1), (4).
7   Enterprise and Regulatory Reform Act 2013 s 83(9)(b); Redress Schemes for Lettings Agency Work and Property Management Work (Requirement to Belong to a Scheme etc) Order 2014, SI 2014/2359, art 4(1), (2)(a).
8   Enterprise and Regulatory Reform Act 2013 s 83(9)(b); Redress Schemes for Lettings Agency Work and Property Management Work (Requirement to Belong to a Scheme etc) Order 2014, SI 2014/2359, art 4(2)(b).
9   Enterprise and Regulatory Reform Act 2013 s 83(9)(b); Redress Schemes for Lettings Agency Work and Property Management Work (Requirement to Belong to a Scheme etc) Order 2014, SI 2014/2359, art 4(2)(c).
10 Enterprise and Regulatory Reform Act 2013 s 83(9)(b); Redress Schemes for Lettings Agency Work and Property Management Work (Requirement to Belong to a Scheme etc) Order 2014, SI 2014/2359, art 4(2)(d). As to the meaning of 'agency worker' and the rights of such workers see the Agency Workers Regulations 2010, SI 2010/93; and EMPLOYMENT vol 39 (2014) PARA 95 et seq.

11 Enterprise and Regulatory Reform Act 2013 s 83(9)(b); Redress Schemes for Lettings Agency Work and Property Management Work (Requirement to Belong to a Scheme etc) Order 2014, SI 2014/2359, art 4(2)(e).

12 Enterprise and Regulatory Reform Act 2013 s 83(9)(b); Redress Schemes for Lettings Agency Work and Property Management Work (Requirement to Belong to a Scheme etc) Order 2014, SI 2014/2359, art 4(3)(a). Article 4(3)(a) refers to institutions within the meaning of the Local Government Finance Act 1992 Sch 1 para 5: see LOCAL GOVERNMENT FINANCE vol 70 (2012) PARA 322.

13 Enterprise and Regulatory Reform Act 2013 s 83(9)(b); Redress Schemes for Lettings Agency Work and Property Management Work (Requirement to Belong to a Scheme etc) Order 2014, SI 2014/2359, art 4(3)(b). As to persons authorised under the Legal Services Act 2007 s 18 see LEGAL PROFESSIONS vol 65 (2015) PARA 356.

296. Meaning of 'property management work' under the Enterprise and Regulatory Reform Act 2013.

'Property management work' means things done by any person ('A') in the course of a business in response to instructions received from another person ('C') where:

(1) C wishes A to arrange services, repairs, maintenance, improvements or insurance or to deal with any other aspect of the management of premises in England on C's behalf[1]; and

(2) the premises consist of or include a dwelling-house let under a relevant tenancy[2].

However, 'property management work' does not include:

(a) things done by a person who is a social landlord[3];

(b) things done in relation to premises which consist of or include more than one dwelling-house where the land is registered as commonhold land (whether or not there is a relevant tenancy in relation to any of the commonhold units)[4];

(c) things done in relation to premises which are used wholly or mainly for the accommodation of students where certain conditions are met[5];

(d) things done in relation to a dwelling-house occupied by students who have been nominated to occupy the dwelling-house by a certain institution or body[6];

(e) things done in relation to premises where the following conditions are met[7]:

    (i) the first condition is that either of the following applies to the premises:

        (A) it is not operated on a commercial basis and its costs of operation are provided wholly or in part by a government department or agency, by a local authority or by a parish council;

        (B) it is managed by a voluntary organisation or charity[8];

    (ii) the second condition is that the premises are used wholly or mainly for providing accommodation to persons who have been subject to any incident (or pattern of incidents) of controlling, coercive or threatening behaviour, physical violence, abuse of any other description (whether physical or mental in nature) or threats of any such violence or abuse[9];

(f) things done by a person ('A') in the course of a business where the premises are subject to a mortgage and A is the receiver of the income of it, or where A is a specified authority, an RTM company or an authorised person within the meaning of the Legal Services Ac t 2007[10];

(g)   things done by a person ('A') in the course of a business in response to instructions received from a specified authority or a social landlord[11].

1   Enterprise and Regulatory Reform Act 2013 s 84(6)(a).
2   Enterprise and Regulatory Reform Act 2013 s 84(6)(b). As to the meaning of 'dwelling-house' see PARA 295 note 2.
     'Relevant tenancy' means:
     (1)   a tenancy which is an assured tenancy for the purposes of the Housing Act 1988 (see the Enterprise and Regulatory Reform Act 2013 s 84(8)(a));
     (2)   a tenancy which is a regulated tenancy for the purposes of the Rent Act 1977 (see the Enterprise and Regulatory Reform Act 2013 s 84(8)(b));
     (3)   a long lease (as to the meaning of which see below) other than one to which the Landlord and Tenant Act 1954 Pt 2 (ss 23–46) applies (see the Enterprise and Regulatory Reform Act 2013 s 84(8)(c));
     (4)   a tenancy of a description specified for these purposes in an order made by the Secretary of State, (s 84(8)(d) (but such an order may not provide for a tenancy to which the Landlord and Tenant Act 1954 Pt 2 applies to be a relevant tenancy) (s 84(9)).
     As to assured tenancies see LANDLORD AND TENANT vol 63 (2016) PARA 825 et seq. As to regulated tenancies see LANDLORD AND TENANT vol 63 (2016) PARA 692. As to the tenancies to which the Landlord and Tenant Act 1954 Pt 2 applies see LANDLORD AND TENANT vol 64 (2016) PARA 1597. In head (3) above, 'long lease' means a lease which is a long lease for the purposes of the Leasehold Reform, Housing and Urban Development Act 1993 Pt 1 Ch 1 (ss 1–38) or which, in the case of a shared ownership lease, would be such a lease if the tenant's total share (within the meaning given by that section) were 100 per cent: Enterprise and Regulatory Reform Act 2013 s 84(10).
3   Enterprise and Regulatory Reform Act 2013 s 84(7)(a). This refers to a person who is a social landlord for the purposes of the Housing Act 1996 Sch 2: see HOUSING vol 56 (2017) PARAS 51 et seq, 131 et seq.
4   Enterprise and Regulatory Reform Act 2013 s 84(7)(b); Redress Schemes for Lettings Agency Work and Property Management Work (Requirement to Belong to a Scheme etc) Order 2014, SI 2014/2359, art 6(1), (2). 'Commonhold land' has the same meaning as in the Commonhold and Leasehold Reform Act 2002 s 1 (see REAL PROPERTY AND REGISTRATION vol 87 (2017) PARAS 1103–1104); and 'commonhold unit' has the same meaning as in s 11 (see REAL PROPERTY AND REGISTRATION vol 87 (2017) PARA 1131): Redress Schemes for Lettings Agency Work and Property Management Work (Requirement to Belong to a Scheme etc) Order 2014, SI 2014/2359, art 6(13).
5   Enterprise and Regulatory Reform Act 2013 s 84(7)(b); Redress Schemes for Lettings Agency Work and Property Management Work (Requirement to Belong to a Scheme etc) Order 2014, SI 2014/2359, art 6(1), (3). 'Property management work' does not include things done in relation to premises which are used wholly or mainly for the accommodation of students where a condition in heads (1)–(3) is met (see art 6(3)–(6)):
     (1)   The first condition is that the premises are owned or managed by an institution within the meaning of the Local Government Finance Act 1992 Sch 1 para 5 (see LOCAL GOVERNMENT FINANCE vol 70 (2012) PARA 322), or by a body established for charitable purposes only.
     (2)   The second condition is that the premises are a hall of residence.
     (3)   The third condition is that the students have been nominated to occupy the premises by an institution or body of the kind mentioned in head (1).
6   Enterprise and Regulatory Reform Act 2013 s 84(7)(b); Redress Schemes for Lettings Agency Work and Property Management Work (Requirement to Belong to a Scheme etc) Order 2014, SI 2014/2359, art 6(1), (7). This refers to an institution within the meaning of the Local Government Finance Act 1992 Sch 1 para 5 (see LOCAL GOVERNMENT FINANCE vol 70 (2012) PARA 322) or a body established for charitable purposes only: art 6(4), (7).
7   Enterprise and Regulatory Reform Act 2013 s 84(7)(b); Redress Schemes for Lettings Agency Work and Property Management Work (Requirement to Belong to a Scheme etc) Order 2014, SI 2014/2359, art 6(1), (8).
8   Redress Schemes for Lettings Agency Work and Property Management Work (Requirement to Belong to a Scheme etc) Order 2014, SI 2014/2359, art 6(9)(a), (b). 'Government department'

includes any body or authority exercising statutory functions on behalf of the Crown: art 6(13). 'Voluntary organisation' means a body, other than a public or local authority, whose activities are not carried on for profit: art 6(13).

9 Redress Schemes for Lettings Agency Work and Property Management Work (Requirement to Belong to a Scheme etc) Order 2014, SI 2014/2359, art 6(10).

10 Enterprise and Regulatory Reform Act 2013 s 84(7)(b); Redress Schemes for Lettings Agency Work and Property Management Work (Requirement to Belong to a Scheme etc) Order 2014, SI 2014/2359, art 6(1), (11). By art 6(11)(b)(i), (ii), (iii), this applies where A is:

    (1)   an authority to which the Local Government Act 1974 Pt 3 (ss 23–34) (see LOCAL GOVERNMENT vol 69 (2009) PARA 853) applies;

    (2)   an RTM company exercising the right to manage under the Commonhold and Leasehold Reform Act 2002 Pt 2 (ss 71–179) (see LANDLORD AND TENANT vol 63 (2016) PARA 567 et seq);

    (3)   an authorised person within the meaning of the Legal Services Act 2007 s 18 (see LEGAL PROFESSIONS vol 65 (2015) PARA 356).

As to RTM companies (right to manage companies) see the Commonhold and Leasehold Reform Act 2002 ss 71(1), 73; and LANDLORD AND TENANT vol 63 (2016) PARA 567 et seq.

11 Enterprise and Regulatory Reform Act 2013 s 84(7)(b); Redress Schemes for Lettings Agency Work and Property Management Work (Requirement to Belong to a Scheme etc) Order 2014, SI 2014/2359, art 6(1), (12). This refers to an authority to which the Local Government Act 1974 Pt 3 (ss 23–34) applies (see LOCAL GOVERNMENT vol 69 (2009) PARA 853) and to a social landlord for the purposes of the Housing Act 1996 Sch 2 (see HOUSING vol 56 (2017) PARAS 51 et seq, 131 et seq): see the Redress Schemes for Lettings Agency Work and Property Management Work (Requirement to Belong to a Scheme etc) Order 2014, SI 2014/2359, art 6(12)(a), (b).

297. Approval of redress schemes.

The Secretary of State[1] may by order make provision about the approval of redress schemes[2] for those who engage in lettings agency work[3] or in property management work[4].

In exercise of this power, an order has been made in relation to England which sets out the procedure that is to be followed where an application for approval is made[5]. The order specifies the conditions that must be satisfied before the Secretary of State may approve a redress scheme[6] and the conditions that must be satisfied before the Secretary of State may designate a scheme as a government administered redress scheme[7]. For example, redress schemes must make satisfactory provision for the redress which members may be required to provide to complainants, including providing an apology or explanation, paying compensation and taking such other actions in the interests of the complainant as the ombudsman may specify[8].

In deciding whether a redress scheme is satisfactory, the Secretary of State must have regard to the interests of scheme members, prospective landlords and tenants, persons instructing property management agents and any person with a relevant tenancy who occupies a dwelling-house in premises in relation to a client has instructed a person to engage in property management work[9]. The Secretary of State must also have regard to such principles as in his opinion constitute generally accepted principles of best practice in relation to consumer redress schemes[10]. Scheme administrators are required to provide such information as the Secretary of State may reasonably require on the operation of the approved scheme[11].

The order also sets out the procedure that is to be followed where the Secretary of State decides to withdraw the approval of a redress scheme[12] or to revoke the designation of a government administered redress scheme[13].

1 As to the Secretary of State see PARA 240 note 1.
2 As to the meaning of 'redress scheme' see PARA 294.

3   As to the meaning of 'lettings agency work' see PARA **295**.
4   See the Enterprise and Regulatory Reform Act 2013 ss 87(1), (2), 88(1)–(4). As to the meaning of 'property management work' see PARA **296**.
5   See the Redress Schemes for Lettings Agency Work and Property Management Work (Approval and Designation of Schemes) (England) Order 2013, SI 2013/3192, art 3.
6   See the Redress Schemes for Lettings Agency Work and Property Management Work (Approval and Designation of Schemes) (England) Order 2013, SI 2013/3192, art 4.
7   See the Redress Schemes for Lettings Agency Work and Property Management Work (Approval and Designation of Schemes) (England) Order 2013, SI 2013/3192, art 5.
8   See the Redress Schemes for Lettings Agency Work and Property Management Work (Approval and Designation of Schemes) (England) Order 2013, SI 2013/3192, arts 4(1)(f), (2), 5(1)(e), (2). The 'ombudsman' is the independent person mentioned in the Enterprise and Regulatory Reform Act 2013 s 83(2) (see PARA **294**): Redress Schemes for Lettings Agency Work and Property Management Work (Approval and Designation of Schemes) (England) Order 2013, SI 2013/3192, art 2.
9   See the Redress Schemes for Lettings Agency Work and Property Management Work (Approval and Designation of Schemes) (England) Order 2013, SI 2013/3192, art 6.
10 See the Redress Schemes for Lettings Agency Work and Property Management Work (Approval and Designation of Schemes) (England) Order 2013, SI 2013/3192, art 6.
11 See the Redress Schemes for Lettings Agency Work and Property Management Work (Approval and Designation of Schemes) (England) Order 2013, SI 2013/3192, art 7.
12 See the Redress Schemes for Lettings Agency Work and Property Management Work (Approval and Designation of Schemes) (England) Order 2013, SI 2013/3192, art 8.
13 Redress Schemes for Lettings Agency Work and Property Management Work (Approval and Designation of Schemes) (England) Order 2013, SI 2013/3192, art 9.

298. Enforcement of redress scheme orders.

Redress scheme orders under the Enterprise and Regulatory Reform Act 2013[1] may make provision for sanctions to be imposed in respect of a breach of a requirement imposed by the order and for the investigation of suspected breaches of such a requirement[2].

In exercise of this power an order has been made which makes the following provision for the enforcement of redress scheme orders[3]. Every enforcement authority is under a duty to enforce the redress scheme order within its area[4]. Where an enforcement authority is satisfied on the balance of probabilities that a person has failed to comply with the requirement to belong to a redress scheme[5], the authority may by notice require the person to pay the authority a monetary penalty[6].

Where an enforcement authority proposes to impose a monetary penalty on a person, it must serve a notice of intent on that person[7]. The person on whom a notice of intent is served may within 28 days[8] make written representations and objections to the enforcement authority in relation to the proposed imposition of the monetary penalty[9]. After the end of the period for making representations and objections, the enforcement authority must decide whether to impose the monetary penalty, with or without modifications[10]. Where the enforcement authority decides to impose a monetary penalty, the authority must serve a final notice on the person[11]. The enforcement authority may at any time (by giving notice in writing) withdraw a notice of intent or final notice, and reduce the amount specified in the notice of intent or final notice[12].

A person who is served with a final notice imposing a monetary penalty may appeal to the First-tier Tribunal against that notice[13]. The grounds for appeal are that:

(1)   the decision to impose a monetary penalty was based on an error of fact[14];
(2)   the decision was wrong in law[15];
(3)   the amount of the monetary penalty is unreasonable[16];

(4)   the decision was unreasonable for any other reason[17].

Where a person has appealed to the First-tier Tribunal, the final notice is suspended until the appeal is finally determined or withdrawn[18]. The Tribunal may then either quash, confirm or vary the final notice[19].

The enforcement authority may recover the monetary penalty on the order of a court, as if payable under a court order[20].

1   Ie an order under the Enterprise and Regulatory Reform Act 2013 s 83(1) or s 84(1): see PARAS 294, 295. As to the meaning of 'redress scheme' see PARA 294.
2   Enterprise and Regulatory Reform Act 2013 s 85(1). Orders may make provision for the imposition of civil penalties, the making of orders prohibiting a person from engaging in lettings agency work or (as the case may be) property management work or from engaging in a particular description of such work and the creation of criminal offences in respect of such breaches: see s 85(2). Provision made for the imposition of a sanction by way of civil penalty must include provision for appeals to a court or tribunal against the imposition of the sanction, and such other provision as the Secretary of State considers appropriate for safeguarding the interests of persons on whom the sanction may be imposed: s 85(3). Functions may be conferred on a person that exercises functions of a public nature (see s 85(4)) and the Secretary of State may make payments out of money provided by Parliament to a person on whom functions are conferred under these provisions (s 85(5)).
3   See the Redress Schemes for Lettings Agency Work and Property Management Work (Requirement to Belong to a Scheme etc) Order 2014, SI 2014/2359, Pt 4 (arts 7–10).
4   Redress Schemes for Lettings Agency Work and Property Management Work (Requirement to Belong to a Scheme etc) Order 2014, SI 2014/2359, art 7. 'Enforcement authority' means a district council, a London borough council, the Common Council of the City of London in its capacity as a local authority, or the Council of Isles of Scilly: art 2.
5   Ie under the Redress Schemes for Lettings Agency Work and Property Management Work (Requirement to Belong to a Scheme etc) Order 2014, SI 2014/2359, art 3 (lettings agency work) or art 5 (property management work): see PARA 294. As to the meaning of 'lettings agency work' see PARA 295. As to the meaning of 'property management work' see PARA 296.
6   The penalty is of such amount as the authority may determine, (not exceeding £5,000): Redress Schemes for Lettings Agency Work and Property Management Work (Requirement to Belong to a Scheme etc) Order 2014, SI 2014/2359, art 8(1), (2). Sums received by an enforcement authority under a monetary penalty may be used by the authority for any of its functions: art 10(3).
7   See the Redress Schemes for Lettings Agency Work and Property Management Work (Requirement to Belong to a Scheme etc) Order 2014, SI 2014/2359, art 8(3), Schedule para 1(1). The notice of intent must be served within six months of the date on which the enforcement authority is first satisfied that the person has failed to comply with art 3 (requirement to belong to a redress scheme: lettings agency work) or art 5 (requirement to belong to a redress scheme: property management work): Schedule para 1(2). The notice of intent must include the reasons for imposing the monetary penalty, the amount of the penalty and information as to the right to make representations and objections within 28 days beginning with the day after the date on which the notice of intent was sent: Schedule para 1(3).
8   Ie 28 days beginning with the day after the date on which the notice was sent: see Redress Schemes for Lettings Agency Work and Property Management Work (Requirement to Belong to a Scheme etc) Order 2014, SI 2014/2359, Schedule para 2.
9   Redress Schemes for Lettings Agency Work and Property Management Work (Requirement to Belong to a Scheme etc) Order 2014, SI 2014/2359, Schedule para 2.
10 Redress Schemes for Lettings Agency Work and Property Management Work (Requirement to Belong to a Scheme etc) Order 2014, SI 2014/2359, Schedule para 3(1).
11 Redress Schemes for Lettings Agency Work and Property Management Work (Requirement to Belong to a Scheme etc) Order 2014, SI 2014/2359, Schedule para 3(2). The final notice must include:
     (1)   the reasons for imposing the monetary penalty (Schedule para 3(3)(a));
     (2)   information about the amount to be paid (Schedule para 3(3)(b));
     (3)   information about how payment may be paid (Schedule para 3(3)(c));
     (4)   information about the period in which the payment must be made, which must not be less than 28 days (Schedule para 3(3)(d));
     (5)   information about rights of appeal (Schedule para 3(3)(e)); and
     (6)   information about the consequences of failing to comply with the notice (Schedule para 3(3)(f)).

12 Redress Schemes for Lettings Agency Work and Property Management Work (Requirement to Belong to a Scheme etc) Order 2014, SI 2014/2359, Schedule para 4.

13 Redress Schemes for Lettings Agency Work and Property Management Work (Requirement to Belong to a Scheme etc) Order 2014, SI 2014/2359, art 9(1). As to the First-tier Tribunal see COURTS AND TRIBUNALS vol 24 (2010) PARA 874 et seq.

14 Redress Schemes for Lettings Agency Work and Property Management Work (Requirement to Belong to a Scheme etc) Order 2014, SI 2014/2359, art 9(2)(a).

15 Redress Schemes for Lettings Agency Work and Property Management Work (Requirement to Belong to a Scheme etc) Order 2014, SI 2014/2359, art 9(2)(b).

16 Redress Schemes for Lettings Agency Work and Property Management Work (Requirement to Belong to a Scheme etc) Order 2014, SI 2014/2359, art 9(2)(c).

17 Redress Schemes for Lettings Agency Work and Property Management Work (Requirement to Belong to a Scheme etc) Order 2014, SI 2014/2359, art 9(2)(d).

18 Redress Schemes for Lettings Agency Work and Property Management Work (Requirement to Belong to a Scheme etc) Order 2014, SI 2014/2359, art 9(3).

19 Redress Schemes for Lettings Agency Work and Property Management Work (Requirement to Belong to a Scheme etc) Order 2014, SI 2014/2359, art 9(4).

20 Redress Schemes for Lettings Agency Work and Property Management Work (Requirement to Belong to a Scheme etc) Order 2014, SI 2014/2359, art 10(1). In proceedings for the recovery of the amount due, a certificate which is:
      (1)   signed by the enforcement authority's chief finance officer; and
      (2)   states that the amount due has not been received by a date specified in that certificate,
      is conclusive evidence of that fact, and a certificate to that effect and purporting to be signed is to be treated as being signed, unless the contrary is proved: art 10(2).

(iii) Duty to Publicise Fees Etc

299. Duty of letting agents to publicise fees.

A letting agent[1] must publicise details of the agent's relevant fees[2] by:

(1)   displaying a list of the fees at each of the agent's premises at which the agent deals face-to-face with persons using or proposing to use services to which the fees relate, and at a place in each of those premises at which the list is likely to be seen by such persons[3]; and

(2)   publishing a list of the fees on the agent's website (if it has one)[4].

The list of fees must include a description of each fee that is sufficient to enable a person who is liable to pay it to understand the service or cost that is covered by the fee or the purpose for which it is imposed (as the case may be)[5]. The list must also include the amount of each fee inclusive of any applicable tax or, where the amount of a fee cannot reasonably be determined in advance, a description of how that fee is calculated[6]. In the case of a fee which tenants are liable to pay, the list of fees must include an indication of whether the fee relates to each dwelling-house or each tenant under a tenancy of the dwelling-house[7].

1 As to the meaning of 'letting agent' see PARA 301.
2 Consumer Rights Act 2015 s 83(1). 'Relevant fees', in relation to a letting agent, means the fees, charges or penalties (however expressed) payable to the agent by a landlord or tenant:
      (1)   in respect of letting agency work carried on by the agent (s 85(1)(a));
      (2)   in respect of property management work carried on by the agent (s 85(1)(b)); or
      (3)   otherwise in connection with an assured tenancy of a dwelling-house, or a dwelling-house that is, has been or is proposed to be let under an assured tenancy (s 85(1)(c)).
   However, the following are not 'relevant fees':
      (a)   the rent payable to a landlord under a tenancy (s 85(2)(a));
      (b)   any fees, charges or penalties which the letting agent receives from a landlord under a tenancy on behalf of another person (s 85(2)(b));
      (c)   a tenancy deposit within the meaning of the Housing Act 2004 s 212(8) (see LANDLORD AND TENANT vol 63 (2016) PARA 866) (Consumer Rights Act 2015 s 85(2)(b)); or

(d)   any fees, charges or penalties of a description specified in regulations made by the
        appropriate national authority (s 85(2)(c)).
3   Consumer Rights Act 2015 s 83(2)(a), (b).
4   Consumer Rights Act 2015 s 83(3).
5   Consumer Rights Act 2015 s 83(4)(a). References to anything which is payable, or which a person
    is liable to pay, to a letting agent include anything that the letting agent claims a person is liable
    to pay, regardless of whether the person is in fact liable to pay it: s 88(4).
6   Consumer Rights Act 2015 s 83(4)(c).
7   Consumer Rights Act 2015 s 83(4)(b).

300.   Membership of client money protection schemes and redress schemes.

Where a letting agent[1] engages in letting agency or property management work[2]
in relation to dwelling-houses in England, the following requirements apply[3].

If the agent holds money on behalf of persons to whom the agent provides
services as part of that work, he is under a duty to display or publish, with the list
of fees[4], a statement of whether the agent is a member of a client money protection
scheme[5].

If the agent is required to be a member of a redress scheme for dealing with
complaints in connection with that work, the agent is under a duty to display or
publish, with the list of fees, a statement that indicates that the agent is a member
of a redress scheme, and that gives the name of the scheme[6].

The appropriate national authority[7] may by regulations[8] specify other ways in
which a letting agent must publicise details of its fees or (where applicable) a
statement concerning membership of a client money protection scheme or redress
scheme[9].

1   As to the meaning of 'letting agent' see PARA 301.
2   As to the meaning of 'letting agency work' see PARA 301. As to the meaning of 'property
    management work' see PARA 302.
3   Consumer Rights Act 2015 s 83(5).
4   As to the duty to publicise fees see PARA 299.
5   Consumer Rights Act 2015 s 83(6). A 'client money protection scheme' means a scheme which
    enables a person on whose behalf a letting agent holds money to be compensated if all or part of
    that money is not repaid to that person in circumstances where the scheme applies: s 83(9).
6   Consumer Rights Act 2015 s 83(7). 'Redress scheme' means a redress scheme for which provision
    is made by order under the Enterprise and Regulatory Reform Act 2013 s 83 or s 84: Consumer
    Rights Act 2015 s 83(9). As to redress schemes see PARA 294 et seq.
7   Legislation enacted following the establishment of the Welsh Assembly Government which confers
    functions on the Secretary of State and the Welsh Ministers often refers to those bodies collectively
    as 'the appropriate national authority', and that expression is used to cover any situation where the
    function in question is exercised in relation to England by the Secretary of State and in relation to
    Wales by the Welsh Ministers, and also where the functions may be carried out jointly: see the
    National Assembly for Wales (Transfer of Functions) Order 1999, SI 1999/672, art 4; and
    CONSTITUTIONAL LAW vol 20 (2014) PARA 351 et seq. As to the Secretary of State see PARA 240
    note 1.
8   Such regulations are made by statutory instrument: see the Consumer Rights Act 2015 s
    88(5)–(11).
9   See the Consumer Rights Act 2015 s 83(8).

301.   Meaning of 'letting agent' and 'letting agency work' under the
         Consumer Rights Act 2015.

A 'letting agent' is a person who engages in letting agency work (whether or not
that person engages in other work)[1]. A person is not a letting agent if he engages
in letting agency work in the course of his employment under a contract of
employment[2]. Nor is a person a letting agent if he is an authorised person under
the Legal Services Act 2007[3] engaged in legal activity[4] and he does nothing else

that is classified as 'lettings agency work'[5]. Further exclusions may be made by regulations made by the appropriate national authority[6].

'Letting agency work' means things done by a person in the course of a business in response to instructions received from:

(1)   a prospective landlord (that is a person seeking to find another person wishing to rent a dwelling-house under an assured tenancy and, having found such a person, to grant such a tenancy)[7]; or

(2)   a prospective tenant (that is a person seeking to find a dwelling-house to rent under an assured tenancy and, having found such a dwelling-house, to obtain such a tenancy of it)[8].

However, 'letting agency work' does not include any of the following things when done by a person who does no other things falling within heads (1) and (2) above:

(a)   publishing advertisements or disseminating information[9];

(b)   providing a means by which a prospective landlord or a prospective tenant can, in response to an advertisement or dissemination of information, make direct contact with a prospective tenant or a prospective landlord[10];

(c)   providing a means by which a prospective landlord and a prospective tenant can communicate directly with each other[11].

'Letting agency work' also does not include things done by a local authority[12].

1   Consumer Rights Act 2015 s 84(1).
2   Consumer Rights Act 2015 s 84(2).
3   Ie an authorised person under the Legal Services Act 2007 s 18 (see LEGAL PROFESSIONS vol 65 (2015) PARA 356): Duty of Letting Agents to Publicise Fees etc (Exclusion) (England) Regulations 2015, SI 2015/951, reg 2; Duty of Letting Agents to Publicise Fees etc (Exclusion) (Wales) Regulations 2016, SI 2016/178, reg 2.
4   Ie a legal activity as defined in the Legal Services Act 2007 s 12 (see LEGAL PROFESSIONS vol 65 (2015) PARA 352): Duty of Letting Agents to Publicise Fees etc (Exclusion) (England) Regulations 2015, SI 2015/951, reg 2; Duty of Letting Agents to Publicise Fees etc (Exclusion) (Wales) Regulations 2016, SI 2016/178, reg 2.
5   Duty of Letting Agents to Publicise Fees etc (Exclusion) (England) Regulations 2015, SI 2015/951, reg 3; Duty of Letting Agents to Publicise Fees etc (Exclusion) (Wales) Regulations 2016, SI 2016/178, reg 3.
6   See the Consumer Rights Act 2015 s 84(3). As to the making of such regulations see s 88(5)–(11). As to the appropriate national authority see PARA 300 note 7.
7   Consumer Rights Act 2015 s 86(1)(a). 'Landlord' includes a person who proposes to be a landlord under a tenancy and a person who has ceased to be a landlord under a tenancy because the tenancy has come to an end: s 88(1). References to a tenancy include a proposed tenancy and a tenancy that has come to an end: s 88(3).
8   Consumer Rights Act 2015 s 86(1)(b). 'Tenant' includes a person who proposes to be a tenant under a tenancy and a person who has ceased to be a tenant under a tenancy because the tenancy has come to an end: s 88(1).
9   Consumer Rights Act 2015 s 86(2)(a).
10 Consumer Rights Act 2015 s 86(2)(b).
11 Consumer Rights Act 2015 s 86(2)(c).
12 Consumer Rights Act 2015 s 86(3). For these purposes, 'local authority' means a county council, a county borough council, a district council, a London borough council, the Common Council of the City of London in its capacity as local authority, or the Council of the Isles of Scilly: s 88(2).

302.   Meaning of 'property management work' under the Consumer Rights Act 2015.

'Property management work', in relation to a letting agent[1], means things done by the agent in the course of a business in response to instructions received from another person where:

(1)   that person wishes the agent to arrange services, repairs, maintenance, improvements or insurance in respect of, or to deal with any other aspect of the management of, premises on the person's behalf[2]; and

(2)   the premises consist of a dwelling-house let under an assured tenancy[3].

1   As to the meaning of 'letting agent' see PARA 301.
2   Consumer Rights Act 2015 s 86(4)(a).
3   Consumer Rights Act 2015 s 86(4)(b). 'Dwelling-house' may be a house or part of a house: s 88(1). 'Assured tenancy' means a tenancy which is an assured tenancy for the purposes of the Housing Act 1988 (see LANDLORD AND TENANT vol 63 (2016) PARA 825 et seq) except where:
    (1)   the landlord is a private registered provider of social housing, a registered social landlord, or a fully mutual housing association; or
    (2)   the tenancy is a long lease (Consumer Rights Act 2015 s 88(1)).
    'Registered social landlord' means a body registered as a social landlord under the Housing Act 1996 Pt 1 Ch 1 (ss A1–7) (see HOUSING vol 56 (2017) PARA 51 et seq): Consumer Rights Act 2015 s 88(1). 'Fully mutual housing association' has the same meaning as in the Housing Associations Act 1985 Pt 1 (see s 1(1), (2); and HOUSING vol 56 (2017) PARA 13): Consumer Rights Act 2015 s 88(1).
    'Long lease' means a lease which:
    (a)   is a long lease for the purposes of the Leasehold Reform, Housing and Urban Development Act 1993 Pt 1 Ch 1 (see LANDLORD AND TENANT vol 64 (2016) PARA 1331); or
    (b)   in the case of a shared ownership lease (see LANDLORD AND TENANT vol 64 (2016) PARA 1331), would be a lease within head (a) if the tenant's total share were 100% (Consumer Rights Act 2015 s 88(1)).

303. Enforcement of duty to publicise fees etc.

It is the duty of every local weights and measures authority in England and Wales to enforce the provisions of the Consumer Rights Act 2015 relating to letting agents' duty to publicise fees etc[1]. Where a local weights and measures authority in England and Wales is satisfied on the balance of probabilities that a letting agent has breached a duty relating to the publication of fees etc[2], the authority may impose a financial penalty on the agent in respect of that breach[3]. If a letting agent breaches the duty to publish its list of fees etc on its website[4], that breach is taken to have occurred in each area of a local weights and measures authority in England and Wales in which a dwelling-house to which the fees relate is located[5].

A local weights and measures authority in England and Wales may impose a penalty in respect of a breach which occurs in England and Wales but outside that authority's area (as well as in respect of a breach which occurs within that area)[6]. However, a local weights and measures authority in England and Wales may impose a penalty in respect of a breach which occurs outside its area and in the area of a local weights and measures authority in Wales only if it has obtained the consent of that authority[7].

Only one penalty under these provisions may be imposed on the same letting agent in respect of the same breach[8]. The amount of a financial penalty may be such as the authority imposing it determines, but must not exceed £5,000[9].

Before imposing a financial penalty the local weights and measures authority must serve a notice of intent[10]. The letting agent may, within 28 days[11], make written representations to the local weights and measures authority about the proposal to impose a financial penalty[12].

After the end of the period for making representations the local weights and measures authority must decide whether to impose a financial penalty on the letting agent, and if it decides to do so, it must decide the amount of the penalty[13].

If the authority decides to impose a financial penalty on the agent, it must serve a final notice imposing that penalty[14]. The local weights and measures authority may at any time withdraw a notice of intent or final notice, or reduce the amount specified in a notice of intent or final notice[15].

A letting agent on whom a final notice is served by a local weights and measures authority in England may appeal against that notice to the First-tier Tribunal[16]. A letting agent on whom a final notice is served by a local weights and measures authority in Wales, may appeal to the residential property tribunal[17]. The grounds for an appeal are that:

(1) the decision to impose a financial penalty was based on an error of fact[18];

(2) the decision was wrong in law[19];

(3) the amount of the financial penalty is unreasonable[20]; or

(4) the decision was unreasonable for any other reason[21].

If a letting agent appeals, the final notice is suspended until the appeal is finally determined or withdrawn[22]. The First-tier Tribunal or (as the case may be) the residential property tribunal may then either quash, confirm or vary the final notice[23].

If a letting agent does not pay the whole or any part of a financial penalty which it is liable to pay then the local weights and measures authority which imposed the financial penalty may recover the penalty or part on the order of the county court as if it were payable under an order of that court[24].

1 Consumer Rights Act 2015 s 87(1). This refers to the provisions of Pt 3 Ch 3 (ss 83–88): see PARA 299 et seq. As to the meaning of 'letting agent' see PARA 301. As to weights and measures authorities see WEIGHTS AND MEASURES vol 99 (2012) PARA 519.
　　A local weights and measures authority in England must have regard to any guidance issued by the Secretary of State about compliance by letting agents with duties imposed by or under s 83, and about the exercise of its functions under s 87 or Sch 9: s 87(9). Similarly, a local weights and measures authority in Wales must have regard to any guidance issued by the Welsh Ministers about compliance by letting agents with duties imposed by or under s 83, and about the exercise of its functions under s 87 or Sch 9: s 87(10). The Secretary of State and the Welsh Ministers may make regulations amending these provisions: see s 87(11), (12).
2 Ie a duty imposed by or under the Consumer Rights Act 2015 s 83: see PARAS 299–300.
3 Consumer Rights Act 2015 s 87(3).
4 Ie the duty in the Consumer Rights Act 2015 s 83(3): see PARA 299.
5 Consumer Rights Act 2015 s 87(2).
6 Consumer Rights Act 2015 s 87(4).
7 Consumer Rights Act 2015 s 87(5).
8 Consumer Rights Act 2015 s 87(6).
9 Consumer Rights Act 2015 s 87(7). A local weights and measures authority may use the proceeds of a financial penalty for the purposes of any of its functions (whether or not the function is expressed to be a function of a local weights and measures authority): Sch 9 para 6(5).
10 Consumer Rights Act 2015 s 87(8), Sch 9 para 1(1). The notice of intent must be served before the end of the period of six months beginning with the first day on which the authority has sufficient evidence of the agent's breach: Sch 9 para 1(2). However, if the agent is in breach of the duty on that day, and the breach continues beyond the end of that day, the notice of intent may be served at any time when the breach is continuing, or within the period of six months beginning with the last day on which the breach occurs: Sch 9 para 1(3).
　　The notice of intent must set out the amount of the proposed financial penalty, the reasons for proposing to impose the penalty, and information about the right to make representations: Sch 9 para 1(4).
11 Ie within the period of 28 days beginning with the day after that on which the notice of intent was sent: see the Consumer Rights Act 2015 Sch 9 para 2.
12 Consumer Rights Act 2015 Sch 9 para 2.
13 Consumer Rights Act 2015 Sch 9 para 3(1).

14 Consumer Rights Act 2015 Sch 9 para 3(2). The final notice requires the penalty to be paid within the period of 28 days beginning with the day after that on which the notice was sent: Sch 9 para 3(3). The final notice must set out:
    (1)   the amount of the financial penalty (Sch 9 para 3(4)(a));
    (2)   the reasons for imposing the penalty (Sch 9 para 3(4)(b));
    (3)   information about how to pay the penalty (Sch 9 para 3(4)(c));
    (4)   the period for payment of the penalty (Sch 9 para 3(4)(d));
    (5)   information about rights of appeal (Sch 9 para 3(4)(e)); and
    (6)   the consequences of failure to comply with the notice (Sch 9 para 3(4)(f)).
15 Consumer Rights Act 2015 Sch 9 para 4(1). This is done by giving notice in writing to the letting agent on whom the notice was served: Sch 9 para 4(2).
16 Consumer Rights Act 2015 Sch 9 para 5(1)(a). As to the First-tier Tribunal see COURTS AND TRIBUNALS vol 24 (2010) PARA 876 et seq.
17 Consumer Rights Act 2015 Sch 9 para 5(1)(b). An appeal to the residential property tribunal must be brought within the period of 28 days beginning with the day after that on which the final notice was sent: Sch 9 para 5(3). As to residential property tribunals see HOUSING vol 56 (2017) PARAS 34–35.
18 Consumer Rights Act 2015 Sch 9 para 5(2)(a).
19 Consumer Rights Act 2015 Sch 9 para 5(2)(b).
20 Consumer Rights Act 2015 Sch 9 para 5(2)(c).
21 Consumer Rights Act 2015 Sch 9 para 5(2)(d).
22 Consumer Rights Act 2015 Sch 9 para 5(4).
23 Consumer Rights Act 2015 Sch 9 para 5(5). The final notice may not, however, be varied so as to make it impose a financial penalty of more than £5,000: Sch 9 para 5(6).
24 Consumer Rights Act 2015 Sch 9 para 6(1), (2).
    In proceedings before the County Court for the recovery of a financial penalty or part of a financial penalty, a certificate which is signed by the chief finance officer of the local weights and measures authority (see the Local Government and Housing Act 1989 s 5) which imposed the penalty, and which states that the amount due has not been received by a date specified in the certificate, is conclusive evidence of that fact: Sch 9 para 6(3), (6). A certificate to that effect and purporting to be so signed is to be treated as being so signed unless the contrary is proved: Sch 9 para 6(4).

(iv) Offences

304. Illegal commissions and advertisements etc.

A person is guilty of an offence[1] if he:
    (1)   demands or accepts money in consideration of registering, or undertaking to register, the name or requirements of any person seeking the tenancy of a house[2]; or
    (2)   demands or accepts money in consideration of supplying, or undertaking to supply to any person addresses or other particulars of houses to let[3]; or
    (3)   issues any advertisement, list or other document describing any house as being to let without the authority of the owner or his agent[4].

No offence is committed by a person who demands or accepts, from the owner of a house, remuneration payable to him as the owner's agent[5]. Nor is an offence committed by a solicitor or person authorised under the Legal Services Act 2007 who demands or accepts remuneration in respect of business done by him as such[6]. Demanding or accepting payment for the display in a shop, or publication in a newspaper (including any periodical or magazine), of any advertisement or notice, or the display or publication of an advertisement or notice received for the purpose in the ordinary course of business, does not constitute the offence[7].

1 The offence is punishable on summary conviction by a fine not exceeding level 3 on the standard scale or up to three months' imprisonment, or both: Accommodation Agencies Act 1953 s 1(5) (amended by virtue of the Criminal Justice Act 1982 ss 38, 46). As from a day to be appointed, the

offence is punishable only by the fine without the alternative or additional custodial sentence: see the Accommodation Agencies Act 1953 s 1(5) (prospectively amended by the Criminal Justice Act 2003 s 332, Sch 37 Pt 9). At the date at which this volume states the law no day had been appointed. As to the powers of magistrates' courts to issue fines on summary conviction see SENTENCING vol 92 (2015) PARA 176.

2   Accommodation Agencies Act 1953 s 1(1)(a). 'House' includes any part of a building which is occupied or intended to be occupied as a dwelling: s 1(6).

3   Accommodation Agencies Act 1953 s 1(1)(b).

4   Accommodation Agencies Act 1953 s 1(1)(c). 'Owner' means the person having power to grant a lease of the house: s 1(6). The Accommodation Agencies Act 1953 was originally only to operate temporarily (see s 2(4) (repealed)), but was continued from time to time and has now been made permanent: see the Expiring Laws Act 1969 s 1(a).

     A requirement to pay a 'deposit' based on anticipated rent before supplying addresses of accommodation is within the mischief contemplated by these provisions, and an offence is committed although the 'deposit' paid is returnable in cases where the agent is unsuccessful in finding accommodation: *McInnes v Clarke* [1955] 1 All ER 346, [1955] 1 WLR 102, DC. An offence is also committed where in consideration of the supply of particulars of property, a person agrees to pay a percentage of one year's rent in the event of his taking a lease, and it is immaterial that no part of this commission is demanded or paid in advance: *Crouch and Lees v Haridas* [1972] 1 QB 158, [1971] 3 All ER 172, CA. A person who demands or accepts a returnable deposit may be guilty of an offence: *Saunders v Soper* [1975] AC 239, [1974] 3 All ER 1025, HL (distinguishing *McInnes v Clarke*). No offence is committed where an agency accepts payment under an agreement between the agency and the client that a fee will be payable if the agency finds acceptable accommodation and the client takes a tenancy of that accommodation: *Saunders v Soper*. An agreement for the making of a payment which contravenes the Act is illegal and unenforceable: *Crouch and Lees v Haridas*.

5   Accommodation Agencies Act 1953 s 1(2).

6   Accommodation Agencies Act 1953 s 1(3) (amended by the Legal Services Act 2007 s 208(1), Sch 21 para 22(a)). An authorised person is a person (other than a solicitor) who, for the purposes of the Legal Services Act 2007, is an authorised person in relation to an activity which is a reserved legal activity (within the meaning of that Act): Accommodation Agencies Act 1953 s 1(6) (definition added by the Legal Services Act 2007 s 208(1), Sch 21 para 22(b)). As to authorised persons under the Legal Services Act 2007 see s 18; and LEGAL PROFESSIONS vol 65 (2015) PARA 356.

7   Accommodation Agencies Act 1953 s 1(4), (6).

305–400. Discrimination in disposal or management of premises.

It is unlawful to discriminate in the disposal or management of premises against any person on the grounds of any of the protected characteristics listed in the Equality Act 2010[1]. The protected characteristics are age[2], disability[3], marriage and civil partnership[4], pregnancy and maternity[5], race[6], religion or belief[7], sex[8], sexual orientation[9], and gender reassignment[10].

1   See DISCRIMINATION vol 33 (2017) PARA 45.

2   See DISCRIMINATION vol 33 (2017) PARA 46.

3   See DISCRIMINATION vol 33 (2017) PARAS 47–55.

4   See DISCRIMINATION vol 33 (2017) PARA 57.

5   See DISCRIMINATION vol 33 (2017) PARAS 62, 73.

6   See DISCRIMINATION vol 33 (2017) PARA 58.

7   See DISCRIMINATION vol 33 (2017) PARA 59.

8   See DISCRIMINATION vol 33 (2017) PARA 60.

9   See DISCRIMINATION vol 33 (2017) PARA 63.

10   See DISCRIMINATION vol 33 (2017) PARAS 56, 61.

AGRICULTURAL LAND AND ALLOTMENTS

1. FARM BUSINESS TENANCIES

(1) NATURE OF FARM BUSINESS TENANCIES

401. Tenancies beginning on or after 1 September 1995.
The Agricultural Tenancies Act 1995 applies in relation to any tenancy[1] beginning on or after 1 September 1995[2] which fulfils the conditions for farm business tenancies[3], except any tenancy of an agricultural holding[4] which:

(1) is granted by a written contract of tenancy[5] entered into before 1 September 1995[6] and indicating (in whatever terms) that the Agricultural Holdings Act 1986[7] is to apply in relation to the tenancy[8];

(2) is obtained by virtue of a direction under the statutory provisions relating to succession to agricultural tenancies on death or retirement[9];

(3) is granted[10] in specified circumstances[11] where a successful application for succession on death has been made[12];

(4) is granted on an agreed succession[13] by a written contract of tenancy indicating (in whatever terms) that the provisions relating to the death or retirement of an agricultural tenant[14] are to apply in relation to the tenancy[15];

(5) is created by the acceptance of a tenant, in accordance with the provisions as to compensation known as the 'Evesham custom'[16], on the terms and conditions of the previous tenancy[17];

(6) is granted to a person who, immediately before the grant of the tenancy, was the tenant of the holding, or of any agricultural holding which comprised the whole or a substantial part of the land comprised in the holding[18], under a tenancy in relation to which the Agricultural Holdings Act 1986 applied and is so granted because an agreement between the parties (not being an agreement expressed to take effect as a new tenancy between the parties) has effect as an implied surrender followed by the grant of the tenancy[19] (there being a limited exception to this category[20]); or

(7) is granted to a person who, immediately before the grant of the tenancy, was the tenant of the holding, or of any agricultural holding which comprised the whole or a substantial part of the land comprised in the holding, under a tenancy in relation to which the Agricultural Holdings Act 1986 applied, and is so granted by a written contract of tenancy indicating (in whatever terms) that that Act is to apply in relation to the tenancy[21] (there being a limited exception to this category[22]).

The Agricultural Holdings Act 1986 continues to apply to such excluded tenancies and to tenancies granted before 1 September 1995[23].

1 In the Agricultural Tenancies Act 1995 'tenancy' means any tenancy other than a tenancy at will, and includes a sub-tenancy and an agreement for a tenancy or sub-tenancy, and 'tenant' includes a sub-tenant and any person deriving title from the original tenant or sub-tenant: s 38(1). The designation of 'tenant' continues to apply until the conclusion of any proceedings taken under the Agricultural Tenancies Act 1995 in respect of compensation: s 38(5).

2 Ie the date on which the Agricultural Tenancies Act 1995 was brought into force: see s 41(2). For these purposes a tenancy begins on the day on which, under the terms of the tenancy, the tenant is entitled to possession under that tenancy; and references to the 'beginning' of the tenancy are references to that day: s 38(4).

3 See the Agricultural Tenancies Act 1995 s 1; and PARA 402.

4 As to the meaning of 'agricultural holding' for these purposes see the Agricultural Holdings Act 1986 s 1(1); and PARA 423 (definition applied by the Agricultural Tenancies Act 1995 s 4(3)(a) (s

4(1), (2)(a), (e), (f), (3)(a) amended, s 4(2)(b) substituted, s 4(1)(g), (2)(c) (2A)–(2C), (3)(c) added, by SI 2006/2805)).

5 As to the meaning of 'contract of tenancy' for these purposes see the Agricultural Holdings Act 1986 s 1(5); and PARA 425 (definition applied by the Agricultural Tenancies Act 1995 s 4(3)(a)).

6 A tenancy granted pursuant to a contract is taken for the purposes of the Agricultural Tenancies Act 1995 to have been granted when the contract was entered into: s 38(3).

7 As to agricultural tenancies under the Agricultural Holdings Act 1986 see PARA 421 et seq.

8 Agricultural Tenancies Act 1995 s 4(1)(a) (as amended: see note 4).

9 Agricultural Tenancies Act 1995 s 4(1)(b) (amended by SI 2013/1036). For the statutory provisions relating to succession to agricultural tenancies on death or retirement see the Agricultural Holdings Act 1986 ss 39, 53; and PARAS 502, 507.

10 Ie following a direction under the Agricultural Holdings Act 1986 s 39 (see PARA 502).

11 Ie circumstances falling within the Agricultural Holdings Act 1986 s 45(6) (see PARA 504).

12 Agricultural Tenancies Act 1995 s 4(1)(c).

13 For this purpose a tenancy (the 'current tenancy') is granted on an agreed succession if, and only if:

    (1)   the previous tenancy of the holding or a related holding was a tenancy in relation to which the Agricultural Holdings Act 1986 Pt IV (ss 34–59) (see PARAS 497–510) applied (Agricultural Tenancies Act 1995 s 4(2)(a) (as amended: see note 4)); and

    (2)   the current tenancy is granted to a person (alone or jointly with other persons) who, if the tenant under that previous tenancy (the 'previous tenant') had died immediately before the grant, would have been his close relative (Agricultural Tenancies Act 1995 s 4(2)(b) (as so substituted)); and

    (3)   either the current tenancy is granted to a person (alone or jointly with other persons) who was or had become the sole or sole remaining applicant for a direction under the Agricultural Holdings Act 1986 s 39 or 53 for a tenancy (s 4(2)(c), (2A)(a) (as so added; s 4(2A)(a) amended by SI 2013/1036)) and the current tenancy is granted as a result of an agreement between the landlord and the previous tenant (Agricultural Tenancies Act 1995 s 4(2A)(b)(i) (as so added)) and is granted, and begins, before the date of the giving of any retirement notice by the previous tenant, or if no retirement notice is given, before the date of death of the previous tenant (s 4(2A)(b)(ii) (as so added)).

As to the meanings of 'close relative', 'related holding' and 'retirement notice' for these purposes see the Agricultural Holdings Act 1986 ss 35(2), 49(3); and PARAS 498 note 5, 499 note 2 (definitions applied by the Agricultural Tenancies Act 1995 s 4(3)(b), (c) (s 4(3)(c) as added: see note 4)).

14 Ie the Agricultural Holdings Act 1986 Pt IV (ss 34–59) (see PARAS 497–510).

15 Agricultural Tenancies Act 1995 s 4(1)(d).

16 As to the 'Evesham custom' see the Agricultural Holdings Act 1986 s 80(3)–(5); and PARA 563.

17 Agricultural Tenancies Act 1995 s 4(1)(e) (as amended: see note 4).

18 The references in the Agricultural Tenancies Act 1995 s 4(1)(g), (2B) (see the text and notes 20–21) to a 'substantial part of the land comprised in the holding' mean a substantial part determined by reference to either area or value: s 4(2C) (as added: see note 4).

19 Agricultural Tenancies Act 1995 s 4(1)(f) (as amended: see note 4).

20 The Agricultural Holdings Act 1986 will not apply by virtue of the Agricultural Tenancies Act 1995 s 4(1)(f) or s 4(1)(g) (see the text and notes 19, 21) in relation to the tenancy of an agricultural holding (the 'current holding') where:

    (1)   the whole or a substantial part of the land comprised in the current holding (see note 18) was comprised in an agricultural holding (the 'previous holding') which was subject to a tenancy granted after 19 October 2006 in relation to which the Agricultural Holdings Act 1986 applied by virtue of the Agricultural Tenancies Act 1995 s 4(1)(f) or s 4(1)(g) (s 4(2B)(a) (as so added));

    (2)   the whole or a substantial part of the land comprised in the previous holding was comprised in an agricultural holding (the 'original holding') which was at 19 October 2006 subject to a tenancy in relation to which the Agricultural Holdings Act 1986 applied (Agricultural Tenancies Act 1995 s 4(2B)(b) (as so added)); and

    (3)   the land comprised in the original holding does not, on the date of the grant of the tenancy of the current holding, comprise the whole or a substantial part of the land comprised in the current holding (s 4(2B)(c) (as so added)).

21 Agricultural Tenancies Act 1995 s 4(1)(g) (as added: see note 4).

22 See note 20.

23 See the Agricultural Tenancies Act 1995 ss 2, 4(1); and PARA 421 et seq.

402. Conditions for farm business tenancies.

A tenancy[1] is a farm business tenancy[2] if:

(1)   it meets the business conditions[3];

(2)   it meets either the agriculture condition or the notice conditions[4];

(3)   it did not begin before 1 September 1995[5]; and

(4)   it is not a tenancy of an agricultural holding[6] beginning on or after that date with respect to which the Agricultural Holdings Act 1986 applies[7].

The 'business conditions' are that all or part of the land comprised in the tenancy is farmed[8] for the purposes of a trade or business[9] and that, since the beginning of the tenancy[10], all or part of the land so comprised has been so farmed[11]. The 'agriculture condition' is that the character of the tenancy is[12] primarily or wholly agricultural[13].

The 'notice conditions' are that the landlord[14] and the tenant each gave the other a written notice[15] to the effect that the land in question is intended to be held under a farm business tenancy[16] and that the character of the tenancy[17] at the beginning was primarily or wholly agricultural[18]. In the case of successive tenancies there is a limited extension allowing the subsequent tenancy to take the benefit of the notice conditions previously having been met[19].

Any use of land in breach of the terms of the tenancy, any commercial activities carried on in breach of those terms, and any cessation of such activities in breach of those terms, must be disregarded in determining whether at any time the tenancy meets the business conditions or the agriculture condition, unless the landlord or his predecessor in title has consented to or acquiesced in the breach[20].

A farm business tenancy cannot be a secure tenancy[21] or an assured tenancy[22].

1   As to the meaning of 'tenancy' and 'tenant' see PARA **401** note 1.

2   Ie for the purposes of the Agricultural Tenancies Act 1995.

3   Agricultural Tenancies Act 1995 s 1(1)(a).

4   Agricultural Tenancies Act 1995 s 1(1)(a).

5   Agricultural Tenancies Act 1995 ss 1(1)(b), 2(1)(a). 1 September 1995 is the date on which the Agricultural Tenancies Act 1995 was brought into force: see s 41(2).

6   As to the meaning of 'agricultural holding' for these purposes see the Agricultural Holdings Act 1986 s 1(1); and PARA **423** (definition applied by the Agricultural Tenancies Act 1995 s 2(2)).

7   Agricultural Tenancies Act 1995 s 2(1)(b). As to the circumstances in which the Agricultural Holdings Act 1986 will continue to apply to a tenancy after 1 September 1995 see s 4; and PARAS **401, 421.**

8   As to references to the 'farming' of land see PARA **424.**

9   Agricultural Tenancies Act 1995 s 1(2)(a).

10 As to when a tenancy begins for these purposes see PARA **401** note 2. If in any proceedings any question arises as to whether a tenancy was a farm business tenancy at any time and it is proved that all or part of the land comprised in the tenancy was farmed for the purposes of a trade or business at that time, it is presumed, unless the contrary is proved, that all or part of the land so comprised has been so farmed since the beginning of the tenancy: Agricultural Tenancies Act 1995 s 1(7).

11 Agricultural Tenancies Act 1995 s 1(2)(b).

12 Ie having regard to the terms of the tenancy, the use of the land comprised in the tenancy, the nature of any commercial activities carried on on that land and any other relevant circumstances: Agricultural Tenancies Act 1995 s 1(3).

13 Agricultural Tenancies Act 1995 s 1(3).

14 'Landlord' includes any person from time to time deriving title from the original landlord: Agricultural Tenancies Act 1995 s 38(1). The designation of 'landlord' continues to apply until the conclusion of any proceedings taken under the Agricultural Tenancies Act 1995 in respect of compensation: s 38(5).

15 The notice must be given on or before whichever is the earlier of the day on which the parties enter into any instrument creating the tenancy, other than an agreement to enter into a tenancy on a future date and the beginning of the tenancy (Agricultural Tenancies Act 1995 s 1(4), (5)). The notice must not be included in any instrument creating the tenancy: s 1(6).

Any notice or other document required or authorised to be given under the Agricultural Tenancies Act 1995 is duly given to a person if it is delivered to him, it is left at his proper address or it is given to him in a manner authorised by a written agreement made, at any time before the giving of the notice, between him and the person giving the notice; and a notice or other document is not duly given to a person if its text is transmitted to him by facsimile or other electronic means otherwise than by virtue of this provision: s 36(1)–(3). Where a notice or other document is to be given to a body corporate, the notice or document is duly given if it is given to the secretary or clerk of that body: s 36(4). When a notice or other document is to be given to a landlord under a farm business tenancy and either an agent or servant of his is responsible for the control of the management of the holding, or such a document is to be given to a tenant under a farm business tenancy and an agent or servant of his is responsible for the carrying on of a business on the holding, the notice or document is duly given if it is given to that agent or servant: s 36(5).

For these purposes the proper address of any person to whom a notice or other document is to be given is the registered or principal office of a body corporate (in the case of the secretary or clerk of a body corporate) and the last known address of the person in question (in any other case): s 36(6). Unless or until the tenant under a farm business tenancy has received notice that the person who before that time was entitled to receive the rents and profits of the holding (the 'original landlord') has ceased to be so entitled, and notice of the name and address of the person who has become entitled to receive the rents and profits, any notice or other document given to the original landlord by the tenant is deemed for these purposes to have been given to the landlord under the tenancy: s 36(7).

'Holding', in relation to a farm business tenancy, means the aggregate of the land comprised in the tenancy: s 38(1).

16 Agricultural Tenancies Act 1995 s 1(4)(a). The notice must identify (by name or otherwise) the land to be comprised in the tenancy or proposed tenancy (s 1(4)(a)(i)) and must contain a statement to the effect that the person giving the notice intends that the tenancy or proposed tenancy is to be, and remain, a farm business tenancy (s 1(4)(a)(ii)). There is no prescribed form.

17 Ie having regard to the terms of the tenancy and any other relevant circumstances: Agricultural Tenancies Act 1995 s 1(4)(b).

18 Agricultural Tenancies Act 1995 s 1(4)(b).

19 Where:
(1) a tenancy (the 'new tenancy') is granted to a person who, immediately before the grant, was the tenant under a farm business tenancy (the 'old tenancy') which met the notice conditions (Agricultural Tenancies Act 1995 s 3(1)(a));
(2) either the land comprised in the new tenancy is the same as the land comprised in the old tenancy, apart from any changes in area which are small in relation to the size of the holding and do not affect the character of the holding or the old tenancy and the new tenancy are both fixed term tenancies, but the term date (ie, in relation to a fixed term tenancy, the date fixed for the expiry of the term) under the new tenancy is earlier than the term date under the old tenancy (s 3(1)(b), (2), (3), (5)); and
(3) except as respects the matters mentioned under head (2) above and matters consequential on them, the terms of the new tenancy are substantially the same as the terms of the old tenancy (s 3(1)(c)),
the new tenancy is taken for these purposes to meet the notice conditions specified in s 1(4) (s 3(4)). 'Fixed term tenancy' means any tenancy other than a periodic tenancy: s 38(1).

20 Agricultural Tenancies Act 1995 s 1(8). The landlord under a farm business tenancy, whatever his estate or interest in the holding, may, for the purposes of the Agricultural Tenancies Act 1995, give any consent, make any agreement or do or have done to him any other act which he might give, make, do or have done to him if he were owner in fee simple or, if his interest is an interest in a leasehold, were absolutely entitled to that leasehold: s 32.

21 See the Housing Act 1985 Sch 1 para 8; and LANDLORD AND TENANT vol 63 (2016) PARA 1054.

22 See the Housing Act 1988 Sch 1 para 7; and LANDLORD AND TENANT vol 63 (2016) PARA 839.

403. Crown land.

The Agricultural Tenancies Act 1995 applies[1] in relation to land in which there subsists, or has at any material time subsisted, a Crown interest[2] as it applies in relation to land in which no such interest subsists or has ever subsisted[3]. For these purposes[4]:

(1)   where an interest belongs to Her Majesty in right of the Crown and forms part of the Crown Estate, the Crown Estate Commissioners are treated as the owner of the interest[5];

(2)   where an interest belongs to Her Majesty in right of the Crown and does not form part of the Crown Estate, the government department having the management of the land or, if there is no such department, such person as Her Majesty may appoint in writing under the Royal Sign Manual is treated as the owner of the interest[6];

(3)   where an interest belongs to Her Majesty in right of the Duchy of Lancaster, the Chancellor of the Duchy is treated as the owner of the interest[7];

(4)   where an interest belongs to a government department or is held in trust for Her Majesty for the purposes of a government department, that department is treated as the owner of the interest[8]; and

(5)   where an interest belongs to the Duchy of Cornwall, such person as the Duke of Cornwall or the possessor for the time being of the Duchy of Cornwall appoints is treated as the owner of the interest[9].

If any question arises as to who is to be treated as the owner of a Crown interest, that question must be referred to the Treasury, whose decision is final[10].

1   As to the tenancies to which the Agricultural Tenancies Act 1995 applies see PARA 401.
2   Ie an interest which belongs to Her Majesty in right of the Crown or of the Duchy of Lancaster or to the Duchy of Cornwall, or to a government department, or which is held in trust for Her Majesty for the purposes of a government department: Agricultural Tenancies Act 1995 s 37(4).
3   Agricultural Tenancies Act 1995 s 37(1).
4   Ie for the purposes of the Agricultural Tenancies Act 1995.
5   Agricultural Tenancies Act 1995 s 37(2)(a). As to the Crown Estate and the Crown Estate Commissioners see CROWN AND CROWN PROCEEDINGS vol 29 (2014) PARAS 192–213.
6   Agricultural Tenancies Act 1995 s 37(2)(b).
7   Agricultural Tenancies Act 1995 s 37(2)(c). As to the Duchy of Lancaster see CROWN AND CROWN PROCEEDINGS vol 29 (2014) PARAS 214–231.
8   Agricultural Tenancies Act 1995 s 37(2)(d).
9   Agricultural Tenancies Act 1995 s 37(2)(e). As to the Duchy of Cornwall see CROWN AND CROWN PROCEEDINGS vol 29 (2014) PARAS 232–267. If the interest is that of landlord, the appointed person may do any act or thing which a landlord is authorised or required to do under the Agricultural Tenancies Act 1995: s 37(2)(e). As to the meaning of 'landlord' see PARA 402 note 14. For the power of limited owners to give consents, make agreements and enter into transactions see s 32; and PARA 402 note 20.
10 Agricultural Tenancies Act 1995 s 37(3).

(2) TERMINATION OF FARM BUSINESS TENANCIES

404. Termination of the tenancy.

Notwithstanding any agreement to the contrary[1], a farm business tenancy[2] for a term of more than two years will, instead of terminating on the term date[3], continue (as from that date) as a tenancy[4] from year to year, but otherwise on the terms of the original tenancy so far as applicable, unless at least 12 months before the term date a written notice has been given[5] by either party to the other of his intention to terminate the tenancy[6].

Notwithstanding any provision to the contrary in the tenancy[7], where a farm business tenancy is a tenancy from year to year a notice to quit the holding[8] or part of the holding will be invalid unless:

(1)   it is in writing[9];

(2)   it is to take effect at the end of a year of the tenancy[10]; and

(3)   it is given at least 12 months before the date on which it is to take effect[11].

Notwithstanding any provision to the contrary in the tenancy[12], where a farm business tenancy is a tenancy for a term of more than two years, any notice to quit the holding or part of the holding given in pursuance of any provision of the tenancy will be invalid unless it is in writing and is given at least 12 months before the date on which it is to take effect[13].

1   Agricultural Tenancies Act 1995 s 5(4).
2   As to the meaning of 'farm business tenancy' see PARA 402.
3   For these purposes 'term date', in relation to a fixed term tenancy, means the date fixed for the expiry of the term: Agricultural Tenancies Act 1995 s 5(2). 'Fixed term tenancy' means any tenancy other than a periodic tenancy: s 38(1).
4   As to the meaning of 'tenancy' see PARA 401 note 1.
5   As to the giving of notices see PARA 402 note 15.
6   Agricultural Tenancies Act 1995 s 5(1) (ss 5(1), 6(1)(c), 7(1) amended by SI 2006/2805). For the purposes of the Law of Property Act 1925 s 140 (apportionment of conditions on severance of reversion: see PARA 495; and LANDLORD AND TENANT vol 62 (2016) PARA 446), a notice under Agricultural Tenancies Act 1995 s 5(1) is taken to be a notice to quit: s 5(3). There is no prescribed form of notice.
7   The Agricultural Tenancies Act 1995 s 6(1) does not, however, apply in relation to a counter-notice given by the tenant by virtue of the Law of Property Act 1925 s 140(2) (apportionment of conditions on severance of reversion: see PARA 495; and LANDLORD AND TENANT vol 62 (2016) PARA 446): Agricultural Tenancies Act 1995 s 6(3).
8   As to the meaning of 'holding' see PARA 402 note 15.
9   Agricultural Tenancies Act 1995 s 6(1)(a). There is no prescribed form of notice.
10   Agricultural Tenancies Act 1995 s 6(1)(b).
11   Agricultural Tenancies Act 1995 s 6(1)(c) (as amended: see note 6). Where, by virtue of s 5(1) (see the text and notes 1–6), a farm business tenancy for a term of more than two years is to continue (as from the term date as defined in s 5(2) (see note 3)) as a tenancy from year to year, a notice to quit which complies with s 6(1) and which is to take effect on the first anniversary of the term date will not be invalid merely because it is given before the term date: s 6(2).
12   Agricultural Tenancies Act 1995 s 7(1) (see the text and note 13) does not, however, apply in relation to a counter-notice given by the tenant by virtue of the Law of Property Act 1925 s 140(2) (apportionment of conditions on severance of reversion: see PARA 495; and LANDLORD AND TENANT vol 62 (2016) PARA 446) (Agricultural Tenancies Act 1995 s 7(2)) or to a tenancy which, by virtue of the Law of Property Act 1925 s 149(6) (lease for life or lives or for a term determinable with life or lives or on the marriage of, or formation of a civil partnership by, the lessee: see LANDLORD AND TENANT vol 62 (2016) PARA 234), takes effect as such a term of years as is mentioned in s 149(6) (Agricultural Tenancies Act 1995 s 7(3) (amended by the Civil Partnership Act 2004 s 81, Sch 8 para 49)).
13   Agricultural Tenancies Act 1995 s 7(1) (as amended: see note 6).

(3) FIXTURES AND FITTINGS

405. Tenant's right to remove fixtures and buildings.
Any fixture of whatever description acquired or affixed to a holding[1] by a tenant[2] under a farm business tenancy[3], and any building[4] acquired or erected by a tenant on such a holding, may be removed by the tenant at any time during the continuance of the tenancy or at any time after the termination of the tenancy[5] when he remains in possession as tenant (whether or not under a new tenancy)[6]. Such fixture remains the tenant's property so long as he may remove it by virtue of these provisions[7].

These provisions apply notwithstanding any agreement or custom to the contrary[8] but do not apply to:

(1)   a fixture affixed or a building erected in pursuance of some obligation[9];

(2)   a fixture affixed or a building erected instead of some fixture or building belonging to the landlord[10];

(3)   a fixture or building in respect of which the tenant has obtained[11] compensation[12]; or

(4)   a fixture or building in respect of which the landlord has given his consent[13] on condition that the tenant agrees not to remove it and which the tenant has agreed not to remove[14].

1   As to the meaning of 'holding' see PARA 402 note 15.
2   As to the meanings of 'tenant' and 'tenancy' see PARA 401 note 1.
3   As to the meaning of 'farm business tenancy' see PARA 402. These provisions apply whether the fixture was acquired or affixed for the purposes of agriculture or not: Agricultural Tenancies Act 1995 s 8(1)(a). As to the meaning of 'agriculture' see PARA 424.
4   'Building' includes any part of a building: Agricultural Tenancies Act 1995 s 38(1).
5   'Termination', in relation to a tenancy, means the cesser of the tenancy by reason of effluxion of time or from any other cause: Agricultural Tenancies Act 1995 s 38(1).
6   Agricultural Tenancies Act 1995 s 8(1), (5). In the removal of a fixture or building by virtue of these provisions the tenant must not do any avoidable damage to the holding (s 8(3)) and immediately after so removing a fixture or building must make good all damage to the holding that is occasioned by the removal (s 8(4)). No right to remove fixtures that subsists otherwise than by virtue of these provisions is exercisable by the tenant under a farm business tenancy: s 8(7).
7   Agricultural Tenancies Act 1995 s 8(1).
8   Agricultural Tenancies Act 1995 s 8(6); for the limited exception to this see s 8(2)(d); and the text and notes 13–14.
9   Agricultural Tenancies Act 1995 s 8(2)(a).
10   Agricultural Tenancies Act 1995 s 8(2)(b). As to the meaning of 'landlord' see PARA 402 note 14. For the power of limited owners to give consents see s 32; and PARA 402 note 20.
11   Ie under the Agricultural Tenancies Act 1995 s 16 (see PARA 411) or otherwise.
12   Agricultural Tenancies Act 1995 s 8(2)(c).
13   Ie under the Agricultural Tenancies Act 1995 s 17 (see PARA 411).
14   Agricultural Tenancies Act 1995 s 8(2)(d).

(4) RENT REVIEWS

406. Farm business tenancies generally contracted-out.

The provisions of the Agricultural Tenancies Act 1995 governing rent reviews under farm business tenancies[1] do not apply to a tenancy[2] which is created by an instrument which:

(1)   expressly states that the rent is not to be reviewed during the tenancy[3]; or

(2)   provides that the rent is to be varied, at a specified time or times during the tenancy, either by or to a specified amount or in accordance with a specified formula which does not preclude a reduction and which does not require or permit the exercise by any person of any judgment or discretion in relation to the determination of the rent of the holding, but otherwise is to remain fixed[4]; or

(3)   does not contain any provision which precludes a reduction in the rent during the tenancy and either expressly states that Part II of the Act (the rent review provisions) does not apply or makes provision for the reference of rent reviews to an independent expert whose decision is final[5].

Farm business tenancies are, accordingly, capable of being in those specified cases contracted-out of the statutory rent review provisions, although these continue to apply, notwithstanding any agreement to the contrary, in non-contracted-out cases[6].

1   Ie the Agricultural Tenancies Act 1995 Pt II (ss 9–14) (see the text and notes 2–6; and PARAS 407–409). As to the meaning of 'farm business tenancy' see PARA 402.
2   As to the meanings of 'tenant' and 'tenancy' see PARA 401 note 1.
3   Agricultural Tenancies Act 1995 s 9(a) (s 9(a) amended, s 9(c) added, by SI 2006/2805).
4   Agricultural Tenancies Act 1995 s 9(b).
5   Agricultural Tenancies Act 1995 s 9(c) (as added: see note 3). Section 9(c) is not applicable where the provision in the instrument creating the tenancy referred to therein is made before 19 October 2006 (ie the date on which the Regulatory Reform (Agricultural Tenancies) (England and Wales) Order 2006, SI 2006/2805, was brought into force: see art 1(1)(b)): art 14(3).
6   See the Agricultural Tenancies Act 1995 s 9. As to the statutory rent review provisions see ss 10–14; and PARAS 407–409.

407. Rent to be referred to arbitration in statutory rent review cases.

Unless they have exercised their right to contract-out of the statutory rent review provisions[1], the landlord[2] or tenant[3] under a farm business tenancy[4] may by notice in writing given to the other[5] require that the rent to be payable in respect of the holding[6] as from the review date[7] be referred to arbitration[8].

1   As to the statutory rent review provisions see the Agricultural Tenancies Act 1995 ss 10–14; the text and notes 2–8; and PARAS 408–409. For the right to contract-out of these provisions see PARA 406.
2   As to the meaning of 'landlord' see PARA 402 note 14.
3   As to the meanings of 'tenant' and 'tenancy' see PARA 401 note 1.
4   As to the meaning of 'farm business tenancy' see PARA 402.
5   This notice is known as a 'statutory review notice': Agricultural Tenancies Act 1995 ss 10(1), 14. As to the giving of notices see PARA 402 note 15. For the power of limited owners to make agreements and enter into transactions see s 32; and PARA 402 note 20.
6   As to the meaning of 'holding' see PARA 402 note 15.
7   'Review date', in relation to a statutory review notice, means a date which is specified in the notice and which complies with the Agricultural Tenancies Act 1995 s 10(3)–(6) (see PARA 408): ss 10(2), 14.
8   Agricultural Tenancies Act 1995 s 10(1). Where a statutory review notice has been given in relation to a farm business tenancy but no arbitrator has been appointed under an agreement made since the notice was given, and no person has been appointed under such an agreement to determine the question of the rent (otherwise than as arbitrator) on a basis agreed by the parties, either party may, at any time during the period of six months ending with the review date, apply to the President of the Royal Institution of Chartered Surveyors (the 'RICS') for the appointment of an arbitrator by him: s 12. As to the Royal Institution of Chartered Surveyors generally see BUILDING CONTRACTS vol 6 (2011) PARA 490.
    Any matter which is required to be determined by arbitration under the Agricultural Tenancies Act 1995 must be determined by the arbitration of a sole arbitrator: s 30(1). Any application under the Act to the President of the RICS for the appointment of an arbitrator by him must be made in writing and must be accompanied by such reasonable fee as the President may determine in respect of the costs of making the appointment: s 30(2). Where an arbitrator appointed for the purposes of the Act dies or is incapable of acting and no new arbitrator has been appointed by agreement, either party may apply to the President of the RICS for the appointment of a new arbitrator by him: s 30(3). The arbitrator will act under the Arbitration Act 1996: see s 2; and ARBITRATION vol 2 (2017) PARA 509 et seq.

408. The review date.

If the parties to a farm business tenancy[1] have agreed in writing that the rent is to be, or may be, varied as from a specified date or dates, or at specified intervals, the review date for the purposes of a statutory rent review[2] of the tenancy must be a date as from which the rent could be varied under the agreement[3]; and if the parties have agreed in writing that the review date for these purposes is to be a specified date or dates, the review date must be that date or one of those dates[4]. If, however, the parties have not so agreed the review date:

(1) must be an anniversary of the beginning of the tenancy[5] or, where the landlord[6] and the tenant have agreed in writing that the review date for these purposes is to be some other day of the year, that day of the year[7]; and

(2) must not fall before the end of the period of three years beginning with the latest of:

  (a) the beginning of the tenancy[8];

  (b) any date as from which there took effect a previous direction of an arbitrator as to the amount of the rent[9];

  (c) any date as from which there took effect a previous determination as to the amount of the rent made, otherwise than as arbitrator, by a person appointed under an agreement between the landlord and the tenant[10]; and

  (d) any date as from which there took effect a previous agreement in writing between the landlord and the tenant, entered into since the grant of the tenancy, as to the amount of the rent[11].

In any event the review date must be at least 12 months but less than 24 months after the day on which the statutory review notice is given[12].

1 As to the meaning of 'farm business tenancy' see PARA 402. For the power of limited owners to make agreements and enter into transactions see the Agricultural Tenancies Act 1995 s 32; and PARA 402 note 20.

2 As to such reviews see PARA 407. For the power to contract out of statutory rent reviews see PARA 406.

3 Agricultural Tenancies Act 1995 s 10(4).

4 Agricultural Tenancies Act 1995 s 10(5).

5 As to the meanings of 'tenant' and 'tenancy' see PARA 401 note 1. As to when a tenancy begins for these purposes see PARA 401 note 2. If a farm business tenancy (the 'new tenancy') arises between a person who immediately before the date of the beginning of the tenancy was entitled to a severed part of the reversionary estate in the land comprised in a farm business tenancy (the 'original tenancy') in which the land to which the new tenancy relates was then comprised and the person who immediately before that date was the tenant under the original tenancy, and the rent payable under the new tenancy at its beginning represents merely the appropriate portion of the rent payable under the original tenancy immediately before the beginning of the new tenancy, references to the 'beginning of the tenancy' in s 10(6) must be taken to be references to the beginning of the original tenancy and references to 'rent' in s 10(6) must be taken to be references to the rent payable under the original tenancy until the first occasion following the beginning of the new tenancy on which any such direction, determination or agreement with respect to the rent of the new holding as is mentioned in s 10(6) takes effect: s 11.

6 As to the meaning of 'landlord' see PARA 402 note 14.

7 Agricultural Tenancies Act 1995 s 10(6)(a).

8 Agricultural Tenancies Act 1995 s 10(6)(b)(i).

9 Agricultural Tenancies Act 1995 s 10(6)(b)(ii). As to the appointment of an arbitrator for the purposes of a rent review under the Agricultural Tenancies Act 1995 see PARA 407.

10 Agricultural Tenancies Act 1995 s 10(6)(b)(iii).

11 Agricultural Tenancies Act 1995 s 10(6)(b)(iv).

12 Agricultural Tenancies Act 1995 s 10(3). There is no prescribed form. As to the giving of the statutory review notice see PARA 407. As to the giving of notices generally see PARA 402 note 15.

409. Amount of rent.

On any reference made in pursuance of a statutory review notice[1], the arbitrator[2] must determine the rent properly payable in respect of the holding[3] at the review date[4] and accordingly must, with effect from that date, increase or reduce the rent previously payable or direct that it continues unchanged[5]. For these purposes the rent properly payable in respect of a holding is the rent at which the holding might reasonably be expected to be let on the open market by a willing landlord to a willing tenant[6], taking into account all relevant factors[7], subject to the proviso that the arbitrator:

(1)　　must disregard any increase in the rental value of the holding which is due to tenant's improvements[8];

(2)　　must disregard any effect on the rent of the fact that the tenant who is a party to the arbitration is in occupation of the holding[9]; and

(3)　　must not fix the rent at a lower amount by reason of any dilapidation or deterioration of, or damage to, buildings[10] or land caused or permitted by the tenant[11].

1　As to the giving of the statutory review notice see PARA 407.

2　As to the appointment of an arbitrator for the purposes of a rent review under the Agricultural Tenancies Act 1995 see PARA 407.

3　As to the meaning of 'holding' see PARA 402 note 15.

4　As to the review date see PARA 408.

5　Agricultural Tenancies Act 1995 s 13(1). See *Barclays Bank plc v Bean* [2004] 3 EGLR 71, [2005] BPIR 563.

6　Agricultural Tenancies Act 1995 s 13(2).

7　The 'relevant factors' for these purposes include (in every case) the terms of the tenancy (including those which are relevant for the purposes of the Agricultural Tenancies Act 1995 s 10(4)–(6) (see PARA 408), but not those which (apart from s 13) preclude a reduction in the rent during the tenancy): s 13(2) (amended by SI 2006/2805).

8　Agricultural Tenancies Act 1995 s 13(3). 'Tenant's improvement', and references to the provision of such an improvement, have the meanings given by s 15 (see PARA 410): ss 13(5), 34(2). The arbitrator is not required to disregard any increase in the rental value of the holding which is due to:

(1)　　any tenant's improvement provided under an obligation which was imposed on the tenant by the terms of his tenancy or any previous tenancy and which arose on or before the beginning of the tenancy in question (s 13(3)(a));

(2)　　any tenant's improvement to the extent that any allowance or benefit has been made or given by the landlord in consideration of its provision (s 13(3)(b)); and

(3)　　any tenant's improvement to the extent that the tenant has received any compensation from the landlord in respect of it (s 13(3)(c)).

As to compensation for tenant's improvements see PARAS 410–419. As to when a tenancy begins for these purposes see PARA 401 note 2.

In estimating the best rent or reservation in the nature of rent of land comprised in a farm business tenancy for the purposes of a relevant instrument, it is not necessary to take into account against the tenant any increase in the value of that land arising from any tenant's improvements: s 34(1). 'Relevant instrument' means any Act of Parliament, deed or other instrument which authorises a lease to be made on the condition that the best rent or reservation in the nature of rent is reserved: s 34(2). As to the meaning of 'farm business tenancy' see PARA 402.

9　Agricultural Tenancies Act 1995 s 13(4)(a).

10　As to the meaning of 'building' see PARA 405 note 4.

11　Agricultural Tenancies Act 1995 s 13(4)(b).

(5) COMPENSATION FOR IMPROVEMENTS

410. Meaning of 'tenant's improvement'.

For these purposes[1] a 'tenant's improvement', in relation to any farm business tenancy[2], means either:

(1)　　any physical improvement which is made on the holding[3] by the tenant[4] by his own effort or wholly or partly at his own expense[5]; or

(2)   any intangible advantage which is obtained for the holding by the tenant
        by his own effort or wholly or partly at his own expense and becomes
        attached to the holding[6].

For these purposes references to the 'provision' of a tenant's improvement are
references to the making by the tenant of any physical improvement falling within
head (1) above or the obtaining by the tenant of any intangible advantage falling
within head (2) above[7].

1   Ie for the purposes of the Agricultural Tenancies Act 1995 Pt III (ss 15–27) (see the text and notes
    2–7; and PARAS 411–419).
2   As to the meaning of 'farm business tenancy' see PARA 402.
3   As to the meaning of 'holding' see PARA 402 note 15.
4   As to the meanings of 'tenant' and 'tenancy' see PARA 401 note 1.
5   Agricultural Tenancies Act 1995 ss 15(a), 27. The purposes authorised by the Settled Land Act
    1925 s 73 (see SETTLEMENTS vol 91 (2012) PARA 709) or the Universities and College Estates
    Act 1925 s 26 (see EDUCATION vol 36 (2015) PARA 1329) for the application of capital money
    include the payment of expenses incurred by a landlord under a farm business tenancy in, or in
    connection with, the making of any physical improvement on the holding: Agricultural Tenancies
    Act 1995 s 33(1)(a) (amended by the Trusts of Land and Appointment of Trustees Act 1996 s
    25(2), Sch 4). For the power of limited owners to enter into transactions see the Agricultural
    Tenancies Act 1995 s 32; and PARA 402 note 20.
6   Agricultural Tenancies Act 1995 s 15(b).
7   Agricultural Tenancies Act 1995 s 15.

411. Tenant's right to compensation for improvements.
In general[1], the tenant[2] under a farm business tenancy[3] is entitled on the
termination[4] of the tenancy, on quitting the holding[5], to obtain from his landlord[6]
compensation in respect of any tenant's improvement[7]. A tenant's entitlement in
this regard does not, however, extend to any physical improvement which is
removed from the holding or any intangible advantage which does not remain
attached to the holding[8].

A tenant is not entitled to compensation[9] in respect of a tenant's improvement
which consists of planning permission[10] unless:
(1)   the landlord has given his consent in writing[11] to the making of the
        application for planning permission[12];
(2)   that consent is expressed to be given for the purpose of enabling a
        specified physical improvement[13] lawfully to be provided by the tenant
        or of enabling the tenant lawfully to effect a specified change of use[14];
        and
(3)   on the termination of the tenancy, the specified physical improvement
        has not been completed or the specified change of use has not been
        effected[15].

Other than where the tenant's improvement consists of planning permission[16], a
tenant is not entitled to compensation in respect of any tenant's improvement
unless the landlord has given his consent in writing to the provision of the tenant's
improvement[17].

The statutory provisions providing for the payment to outgoing tenants of
compensation for milk quota[18] do not apply in relation to a farm business
tenancy[19].

1   Ie subject to the provisions of the Agricultural Tenancies Act 1995 Pt III (ss 15–27) (see the text
    and notes 2–19; and PARAS 412–419).
2   As to the meanings of 'tenant' and 'tenancy' see PARA 401 note 1.
3   As to the meaning of 'farm business tenancy' see PARA 402.
4   As to the 'termination' of a farm business tenancy see PARA 405 note 5.

5   As to the meaning of 'holding' see PARA 402 note 15.

6   As to the meaning of 'landlord' see PARA 402 note 14. For the power of limited owners to give
    consents, make agreements and enter into transactions see the Agricultural Tenancies Act 1995 s
    32; and PARA 402 note 20.

7   Agricultural Tenancies Act 1995 s 16(1). As to the meaning of 'tenant's improvement' see PARA
    410. As to the amount of compensation payable see PARAS 413–414. The purposes authorised by
    the Settled Land Act 1925 s 73 (see SETTLEMENTS vol 91 (2012) PARA 709) or the Universities
    and College Estates Act 1925 s 26 (see EDUCATION vol 36 (2015) PARA 1329) for the application
    of capital money, and the purposes authorised by the Settled Land Act 1925 s 71 (see SETTLEMENTS
    vol 91 (2012) PARA 750) as purposes for which money may be raised by mortgage, include the
    payment of compensation under the Agricultural Tenancies Act 1995 s 16 (s 33(1)(b), (2) (s 33(1),
    (2), (4) amended by the Trusts of Land and Appointment of Trustees Act 1996 s 25(2), Sch 4)).
        Where the landlord under a farm business tenancy is a tenant for life or in a fiduciary position
    and is liable to pay compensation under the Agricultural Tenancies Act 1995 s 16, he may require
    the sum payable as compensation and any costs, charges and expenses incurred by him in
    connection with the tenant's claim thereunder to be paid out of any capital money held on the same
    trusts as the settled land: s 33(3). For this purpose, 'capital money' includes any personal estate
    held on the same trusts as the land: s 33(4) (as so amended).
        Any compensation payable under s 16 by the Chancellor of the Duchy of Lancaster may be
    raised and paid under the Duchy of Lancaster Act 1817 s 25 (application of monies) as an expense
    incurred in improvement of land belonging to Her Majesty in right of the Duchy: Agricultural
    Tenancies Act 1995 s 37(5). In the case of land belonging to the Duchy of Cornwall, the purposes
    authorised by the Duchy of Cornwall Management Act 1863 s 8 (application of monies: see
    CROWN AND CROWN PROCEEDINGS vol 29 (2014) PARA 253) for the advancement of parts of such
    gross sums as are there mentioned include the payment of compensation under the Agricultural
    Tenancies Act 1995 s 16 (s 37(6)), although nothing in this requirement is to be taken as
    prejudicing the operation of the Duchy of Cornwall Management Act 1982 (Agricultural
    Tenancies Act 1995 s 37(7)). As to the application of the Agricultural Tenancies Act 1995 to
    Crown land see PARA 403. As to the Duchies of Lancaster and Cornwall see CROWN AND CROWN
    PROCEEDINGS vol 29 (2014) PARAS 214–267.
        At common law an agricultural tenant is not entitled to compensation from his landlord for
    improvements or acts of husbandry of which the landlord obtains the benefit when the tenant quits
    the holding, although this rule could be modified by the custom of the country and the parties
    could themselves provide for compensation in their agreement: see *Wigglesworth v Dallison*
    (1779) 1 Doug KB 201. As to the right to compensation in respect of tenancies governed by the
    Agricultural Holdings Act 1986 see PARA 511 et seq.

8   Agricultural Tenancies Act 1995 s 16(2).

9   Ie under the Agricultural Tenancies Act 1995 s 16 (see the text and notes 1–8).

10 As to the meaning of 'planning permission' see the Town and Country Planning Act 1990 s 336(1);
    and PLANNING vol 81 (2010) PARA 54 (definition applied by the Agricultural Tenancies Act
    1995 s 27). Where a physical improvement which has been completed or a change of use which has
    been effected is authorised by any planning permission granted on an application made by the
    tenant, these provisions (ie s 18: see the text and notes 11–15) do not prevent any value
    attributable to the fact that the physical improvement or change of use is so authorised from being
    taken into account under s 20 (see PARA 413) in determining the amount of compensation payable
    in respect of the physical improvement or in respect of any intangible advantage obtained as a
    result of the change of use: s 20(4).

11 Any such consent may be given either unconditionally or on condition that the tenant agrees to a
    specified variation in the terms of the tenancy: Agricultural Tenancies Act 1995 s 18(2). Such
    variation must be related to the physical improvement or change of use in question: s 18(3).

12 Agricultural Tenancies Act 1995 s 18(1)(a).

13 Ie a specified physical improvement falling within the Agricultural Tenancies Act 1995 s 15(a) (see
    PARA 410).

14 Agricultural Tenancies Act 1995 s 18(1)(b).

15 Agricultural Tenancies Act 1995 s 18(1)(c).

16 Agricultural Tenancies Act 1995 s 17(5).

17 Agricultural Tenancies Act 1995 s 17(1). Any such consent may be given in the instrument creating
    the tenancy or elsewhere (s 17(2)) and may be given either unconditionally or on condition that the

tenant agrees to a specified variation in the terms of the tenancy (s 17(3)), provided that any such variation is related to the tenant's improvement in question (s 17(4)).

Provision is made for the resolution by arbitration of disputes arising from a refusal of, a failure to give, or any variation in the terms of a tenancy required by the landlord as a condition of, consent under s 17(1): see s 19; and PARA 412.

18 Ie the Agriculture Act 1986 s 13, Sch 1; PARA 520; and AGRICULTURAL PRODUCTION AND MARKETING vol 1A (2017) PARA 6.
19 Agricultural Tenancies Act 1995 s 16(3).

412. Disputes as to landlord's consent to improvements.

Where in relation to any tenant's improvement[1] the tenant[2] under a farm business tenancy[3] is aggrieved by:

(1)   the refusal of his landlord[4] to give his consent[5] to the provision of the improvement[6];

(2)   the failure of his landlord to give such consent within two months of a written request by the tenant for such consent[7]; or

(3)   any variation in the terms of the tenancy required by the landlord as a condition of giving such consent[8],

the tenant may, unless:

(a)   he has already provided or begun to provide the improvement in question (unless that improvement is a routine improvement)[9];

(b)   the period of two months beginning with the day on which notice of the refusal or variation[10] was given to the tenant has elapsed[11]; or

(c)   the period of four months beginning with the day on which the written request[12] was given to the landlord has elapsed[13],

by notice in writing given to the landlord demand that the question be referred to arbitration[14].

The arbitrator[15] must consider whether, having regard to the terms of the tenancy and any other relevant circumstances (including the circumstances of the tenant and the landlord), it is reasonable for the tenant to provide the tenant's improvement[16]. He may unconditionally approve the provision of the tenant's improvement or may withhold his approval (although he may not give his approval subject to any condition or vary any condition required[17] by the landlord)[18], and if he gives his approval it has effect for these purposes[19] and for the purposes of the terms of the farm business tenancy as if it were the consent of the landlord[20].

1 As to the meaning of 'tenant's improvement' see PARA 410.
2 As to the meanings of 'tenant' and 'tenancy' see PARA 401 note 1.
3 As to the meaning of 'farm business tenancy' see PARA 402.
4 As to the meaning of 'landlord' see PARA 402 note 14.
5 Ie under the Agricultural Tenancies Act 1995 s 17(1) (see PARA 411). For the power of limited owners to give consents see s 32; and PARA 402 note 20.
6 Agricultural Tenancies Act 1995 s 19(1)(a).
7 Agricultural Tenancies Act 1995 s 19(1)(b).
8 Agricultural Tenancies Act 1995 s 19(1)(c).
9 Agricultural Tenancies Act 1995 s 19(2). 'Routine improvement', in relation to a farm business tenancy, means any tenant's improvement which is a physical improvement made in the normal course of farming the holding or any part of the holding and does not consist of fixed equipment or an improvement to fixed equipment, but does not include any improvement whose provision is prohibited by the terms of the tenancy: s 19(10). As to the meaning of 'holding' see PARA 402 note 15. As to the 'farming' of land see PARA 424. 'Fixed equipment' includes any building or structure affixed to land and any works constructed on, in, over or under land, and also includes anything grown on land for a purpose other than use after severance from the land, consumption of the thing grown or its produce, or amenity: s 19(10). As to the meaning of 'building' see PARA 405 note 4.

10 Ie the refusal or variation referred to in the Agricultural Tenancies Act 1995 s 19(1)(a) or (c) (see the text and notes 1–8). As to the giving of notices see PARA 402 note 15.

11 Agricultural Tenancies Act 1995 s 19(3)(a).

12 Ie the request referred to in the Agricultural Tenancies Act 1995 s 19(1)(b) (see the text and note 7).

13 Agricultural Tenancies Act 1995 s 19(3)(b).

14 Agricultural Tenancies Act 1995 s 19(1). 'Arbitration' means arbitration under s 19. For general provisions as to arbitrations under the Agricultural Tenancies Act 1995 see s 30; and PARA 407 note 8. The purposes authorised by the Settled Land Act 1925 s 73 (see SETTLEMENTS vol 91 (2012) PARA 709) or the Universities and College Estates Act 1925 s 26 (see EDUCATION vol 36 (2015) PARA 1329) for the application of capital money include the payment of the costs, charges and expenses incurred by a landlord under a farm business tenancy on a reference to arbitration under these provisions: Agricultural Tenancies Act 1995 s 33(1)(c) (amended by the Trusts of Land and Appointment of Trustees Act 1996 s 25(2), Sch 4).

15 Where the tenant has given notice under the Agricultural Tenancies Act 1995 s 19(1) (see the text and notes 1–14) but no arbitrator has been appointed under an agreement made since the notice was given, the tenant or the landlord may apply to the President of the Royal Institution of Chartered Surveyors (the 'RICS') for the appointment of an arbitrator by him: s 19(4). No such application may, however, be made at any time after giving a notice under s 19(1) in relation to any tenant's improvement which is not a routine improvement where the tenant has begun to provide the improvement (s 19(9)(a)); and where such an application has been made but no arbitrator has been appointed before that time, the application will be ineffective (s 19(9)(b)). As to the Royal Institution of Chartered Surveyors generally see BUILDING CONTRACTS vol 6 (2011) PARA 490.

16 Agricultural Tenancies Act 1995 s 19(5).

17 Ie under the Agricultural Tenancies Act 1995 s 17(3) (see PARA 411). In a case falling within s 19(1)(c) (see the text and note 8) the withholding by the arbitrator of his approval does not affect the validity of the landlord's consent or of the condition subject to which it was given: s 19(8).

18 Agricultural Tenancies Act 1995 s 19(6). Where, at any time after giving a notice under s 19(1) in relation to any tenant's improvement which is not a routine improvement, the tenant begins to provide the improvement, no award may be made by virtue of s 19(6) after that time except as to the costs of the reference and award in a case where the arbitrator was appointed before that time: s 19(9)(c).

19 Ie for the purposes of the Agricultural Tenancies Act 1995 Pt III (ss 15–27).

20 Agricultural Tenancies Act 1995 s 19(7).

413. Amount of compensation for improvements not consisting of planning permission.

The amount of compensation payable to a tenant[1] in respect of any tenant's improvement[2] which does not consist of planning permission[3] is an amount equal to the increase attributable to the improvement in the value of the holding[4] at the termination of the tenancy as land comprised in a tenancy[5]. Where the landlord and the tenant have entered into an agreement in writing whereby any benefit is given or allowed to the tenant in consideration of the provision of a tenant's improvement, the amount of compensation otherwise payable in respect of that improvement is reduced by the proportion which the value of the benefit bears to the amount of the total cost of providing the improvement[6].

Where a grant has been or will be made to the tenant out of public money in respect of a tenant's improvement, the amount of compensation otherwise payable in respect of that improvement is reduced by the proportion which the amount of the grant bears to the amount of the total cost of providing the improvement[7].

Where after 19 October 2006 the landlord and the tenant have agreed in writing to limit the amount of compensation payable in respect of any tenant's improvement[8], that amount must be the lesser of the amount determined in accordance with the statutory provisions relating to the calculation of the amount of compensation payable in respect of tenant's improvements not consisting of planning permission[9] and the compensation limit[10].

1 Ie under the Agricultural Tenancies Act 1995 s 16 (see PARA 411). As to the meanings of 'tenant' and 'tenancy' see PARA 401 note 1.
2 As to the meaning of 'tenant's improvement' see PARA 410.
3 As to the meaning of 'planning permission' see the Town and Country Planning Act 1990 s 336(1); and PLANNING vol 81 (2010) PARA 54 (definition applied by the Agricultural Tenancies Act 1995 s 27). As to the amount of compensation in respect of tenant's improvements which consist of planning permission see PARA 414.
4 As to the meaning of 'holding' see PARA 402 note 15. In any case falling within the Agricultural Tenancies Act 1995 s 24(1)(a) or (b) (compensation for improvements where possession of part of holding is resumed: see PARA 416), these provisions apply on the termination of the tenancy in relation to the land then comprised in the tenancy, as if the references therein to the 'holding' were a reference to the original holding (see PARA 416 note 9), although this is subject to the proviso that where the landlord and the tenant have agreed in writing to limit the amount of compensation payable under the Agricultural Tenancies Act 1995 s 16 (see PARA 411) in respect of any tenant's improvement not consisting of planning permission, that improvement is provided for both the relevant part (ie the part of the holding of which the landlord has resumed possession) and the land comprised in the tenancy after the termination date, the case falls within s 24(1)(a) or (b), the tenant has already received compensation in respect of the improvement determined in accordance with s 24(2) (see PARA 416) and further compensation in respect of the improvement is payable under s 16 on termination of the tenancy, the compensation limit referred to in s 20(4A) (see the text and notes 8–10) must, for the purposes of determining that further compensation, be reduced by an amount equal to the amount of compensation already received by the tenant in respect of the improvement: s 24(1)(a), (4), (4A) (ss 20(1), 24(4) amended, ss 20(4A), (4B), 24(4A) added, by SI 2006/2805). As to the meaning of 'landlord' see PARA 402 note 14. As to the 'termination' of a farm business tenancy see PARA 405 note 5.
5 Agricultural Tenancies Act 1995 s 20(1), (5) (s 20(1) as amended: see note 4).
6 Agricultural Tenancies Act 1995 s 20(2). For the power of limited owners to make agreements see s 32; and PARA 402 note 20.
7 Agricultural Tenancies Act 1995 s 20(3).
8 Ie under the Agricultural Tenancies Act 1995 s 16 (see PARA 411).
9 Ie the Agricultural Tenancies Act 1995 s 20(1)–(4) (see the text and notes 1–7; and PARA 411).
10 Agricultural Tenancies Act 1995 s 20(4A) (as added: see note 4). 'Compensation limit' means either an amount agreed by the parties in writing or, where the parties are unable to agree on an amount, an amount equal to the cost to the tenant of making the improvement: s 20(4B) (as so added). See, however, note 4.

414. Amount of compensation for improvements consisting of planning permission.

The amount of compensation payable to the tenant[1] in respect of a tenant's improvement[2] which consists of planning permission[3] is an amount equal to the increase attributable to the fact that the relevant development[4] is authorised by the planning permission in the value of the holding[5] at the termination of the tenancy as land comprised in a tenancy[6].

Where the landlord and the tenant have entered into an agreement in writing whereby any benefit is given or allowed to the tenant in consideration of the obtaining of planning permission by the tenant, the amount of compensation otherwise payable in respect of that permission is reduced by the proportion which the value of the benefit bears to the amount of the total cost of obtaining the permission[7].

1 Ie under the Agricultural Tenancies Act 1995 s 16 (see PARA 411). As to the meanings of 'tenant' and 'tenancy' see PARA 401 note 1.
2 As to the meaning of 'tenant's improvement' see PARA 410.

3 As to the meaning of 'planning permission' see the Town and Country Planning Act 1990 s 336(1); and PLANNING vol 81 (2010) PARA 54 (definition applied by the Agricultural Tenancies Act 1995 s 27).

4 Ie the physical improvement or change of use specified in the landlord's consent under the Agricultural Tenancies Act 1995 s 18 (see PARA 411) in accordance with s 18(1)(b): s 21(2).

5 As to the meaning of 'holding' see PARA 402 note 15. In any case falling within the Agricultural Tenancies Act 1995 s 24(1)(a) or (b) (compensation for improvements where possession of part of holding is resumed: see PARA 416), these provisions apply on the termination of the tenancy in relation to the land then comprised in the tenancy, as if the references therein to the 'holding' were a reference to the original holding (see PARA 416 note 9), although this is subject to the proviso that where the landlord and the tenant have agreed in writing to limit the amount of compensation payable under the Agricultural Tenancies Act 1995 s 16 (see PARA 411) in respect of any tenant's improvement not consisting of planning permission, that improvement is provided for both the relevant part (ie the part of the holding of which the landlord has resumed possession) and the land comprised in the tenancy after the termination date, the case falls within s 24(1)(a) or (b), the tenant has already received compensation in respect of the improvement determined in accordance with s 24(2) (see PARA 416) and further compensation in respect of the improvement is payable under s 16 on termination of the tenancy, the compensation limit referred to in s 20(4A) (see PARA 412) must, for the purposes of determining that further compensation, be reduced by an amount equal to the amount of compensation already received by the tenant in respect of the improvement: s 24(1)(a), (4), (4A) (s 24(4) amended and s 24(4A) added, by SI 2006/2805). As to the meaning of 'landlord' see PARA 402 note 14. As to the 'termination' of a farm business tenancy see PARA 405 note 5.

6 Agricultural Tenancies Act 1995 s 21(1).

7 Agricultural Tenancies Act 1995 s 21(3). For the power of limited owners to make agreements see s 32; and PARA 402 note 20.

415. Compensation in event of successive tenancies.

Where the tenant[1] under a farm business tenancy[2] has remained in the holding[3] during two or more such tenancies he will not be deprived of his right to compensation[4] by reason only that any tenant's improvement[5] was provided during a tenancy other than the one at the termination[6] of which he quits the holding[7].

The landlord[8] and tenant under a farm business tenancy may agree that the tenant is to be entitled to compensation on the termination of the tenancy even though at that termination the tenant remains in the holding under a new tenancy[9], and where the landlord and the tenant have so agreed in relation to any tenancy (the 'earlier tenancy'), the tenant is not entitled to compensation at the end of any subsequent tenancy in respect of any tenant's improvement provided during the earlier tenancy in relation to the land comprised in the earlier tenancy[10].

1 As to the meanings of 'tenant' and 'tenancy' see PARA 401 note 1.

2 As to the meaning of 'farm business tenancy' see PARA 402.

3 As to the meaning of 'holding' see PARA 402 note 15.

4 Ie under the Agricultural Tenancies Act 1995 s 16 (see PARA 411). As to the amount of compensation in relation to improvements not consisting of planning permission see PARA 413; and as to the amount of compensation in relation to improvements consisting of planning permission see PARA 414.

5 As to the meaning of 'tenant's improvement' see PARA 410.

6 As to the 'termination' of a farm business tenancy see PARA 405 note 5.

7 Agricultural Tenancies Act 1995 s 23(1).

8 As to the meaning of 'landlord' see PARA 402 note 14.

9 Agricultural Tenancies Act 1995 s 23(2). For the power of limited owners to make agreements see s 32; and PARA 402 note 20.

10 Agricultural Tenancies Act 1995 s 23(3).

416. Compensation where possession of part of holding is resumed.

Where the landlord[1] under a farm business tenancy[2] resumes possession of part of the holding[3] in pursuance of any provision of the tenancy[4] or a person entitled to a severed part of the reversionary estate in a holding held under a farm business tenancy resumes possession of part of the holding by virtue of a notice to quit that part given[5] to the tenant[6], the statutory provisions relating to the payment of compensation for tenant's improvements[7] apply to that part of the holding (the 'relevant part') as if it were a separate holding which the tenant had quitted in consequence of a notice to quit and, in the latter case[8], as if the person resuming possession were the landlord of that separate holding[9].

1   As to the meaning of 'landlord' see PARA 402 note 14.
2   As to the meaning of 'farm business tenancy' see PARA 402.
3   As to the meaning of 'holding' see PARA 402 note 15.
4   Agricultural Tenancies Act 1995 s 24(1)(a). As to the meanings of 'tenant' and 'tenancy' see PARA 401 note 1.
5   Ie by virtue of the Law of Property Act 1925 s 140 (apportionment of conditions on severance of reversion: see PARA 495; and LANDLORD AND TENANT vol 62 (2016) PARA 446).
6   Agricultural Tenancies Act 1995 s 24(1)(b).
7   Ie the Agricultural Tenancies Act 1995 Pt III (ss 15–27) (see PARA 410 et seq).
8   Ie in a case falling within the Agricultural Tenancies Act 1995 s 24(1)(b) (see the text and notes 5–6).
9   Agricultural Tenancies Act 1995 s 24(1). This is subject to the proviso that the amount of compensation payable to the tenant under s 16 (see PARA 411) in respect of any tenant's improvement provided for the relevant part by the tenant and not consisting of planning permission must, subject to s 20(2)–(4) (see PARAS 411, 413), be an amount equal to the increase attributable to the tenant's improvement in the value of the original holding on the termination date as land comprised in a tenancy (s 24(2) (s 24(2), (5) amended by SI 2006/2805)) and that the amount of compensation so payable under the Agricultural Tenancies Act 1995 s 16 in respect of any tenant's improvement which consists of planning permission relating to the relevant part must, subject to s 21(3) (see PARA 414), be an amount equal to the increase attributable to the fact that the relevant development is authorised by the planning permission in the value of the original holding on the termination date as land comprised in a tenancy (s 24(3)).

    As to the meaning of 'planning permission' see the Town and Country Planning Act 1990 s 336(1); and PLANNING vol 81 (2010) PARA 54 (definition applied by the Agricultural Tenancies Act 1995 s 27). As to the meaning of 'tenant's improvement' see PARA 410. 'Original holding' means the land comprised in the farm business tenancy on the date when the landlord gave his consent under s 17 or s 18 (see PARA 411) in relation to the tenant's improvement or, where approval in relation to the tenant's improvement was given by an arbitrator, on the date on which that approval was given: s 24(5) (as so amended). 'Relevant development', in relation to any tenant's improvement which consists of planning permission, has the meaning given by the Agricultural Tenancies Act 1995 s 21(2) (see PARA 414): s 24(5) (as so amended). 'Termination date' means the date on which possession of the relevant part was resumed: s 24(5) (as so amended).

417. Compensation where reversionary estate in holding is severed.

Where the reversionary estate in the holding[1] comprised in a farm business tenancy[2] is for the time being vested in more than one person in several parts, the tenant[3] is entitled, on quitting the entire holding, to require that any compensation payable to him[4] is determined as if the reversionary estate were not so severed[5]. Where these provisions apply, the arbitrator[6] must, where necessary, apportion the amount awarded between the persons who for these purposes[7] together constitute the landlord[8] of the holding, and any additional costs of the award caused by the apportionment must be directed by the arbitrator to be paid by those persons in such proportions as he determines[9].

1   As to the meaning of 'holding' see PARA 402 note 15.

2　As to the meaning of 'farm business tenancy' see PARA 402.

3　As to the meanings of 'tenant' and 'tenancy' see PARA 401 note 1.

4　Ie under the Agricultural Tenancies Act 1995 s 16 (see PARA 411). As to the amount of compensation in relation to improvements not consisting of planning permission see PARA 413; and as to the amount of compensation in relation to improvements consisting of planning permission see PARA 414.

5　Agricultural Tenancies Act 1995 s 25(1).

6　For general provisions as to arbitrations under the Agricultural Tenancies Act 1995 see s 30; and PARA 407 note 8.

7　Ie for the purposes of the Agricultural Tenancies Act 1995 Pt III (ss 15–27) (see PARA 410 et seq).

8　As to the meaning of 'landlord' see PARA 402 note 14.

9　Agricultural Tenancies Act 1995 s 25(2).

418.　Settlement of claims for compensation.

No claim by a tenant[1] under a farm business tenancy[2] for compensation for improvements[3] is enforceable unless before the end of the period of two months beginning with the date of the termination of the tenancy[4] the tenant has given notice in writing to his landlord[5] of his intention to make the claim and of the nature of the claim[6], and any such claim by a tenant must[7] be determined by arbitration[8].

Where the landlord and the tenant have not settled the claim by agreement in writing and no arbitrator has been appointed under an agreement made since the notice of claim[9] was given, either party may, after the end of the period of four months beginning with the date of the termination of the tenancy[10], apply[11] for the appointment of an arbitrator[12].

1　As to the meanings of 'tenant' and 'tenancy' see PARA 401 note 1.

2　As to the meaning of 'farm business tenancy' see PARA 402.

3　Ie under the Agricultural Tenancies Act 1995 s 16 (see PARA 411). As to the amount of compensation in relation to improvements not consisting of planning permission see PARA 413; and as to the amount of compensation in relation to improvements consisting of planning permission see PARA 414.

4　As to the 'termination' of a farm business tenancy see PARA 405 note 5. Where a tenant lawfully remains in occupation of part of the holding after the termination of a farm business tenancy, references in the Agricultural Tenancies Act 1995 s 22(2), (3) to the termination of the tenancy must, in the case of a claim relating to that part of the holding, be construed as references to the termination of the occupation: s 22(5). As to the meaning of 'holding' see PARA 402 note 15.

5　As to the meaning of 'landlord' see PARA 402 note 14. As to the giving of notices see PARA 402 note 15.

6　Agricultural Tenancies Act 1995 s 22(2).

7　Ie subject to the provisions of the Agricultural Tenancies Act 1995 s 22 (see the text and notes 8–12).

8　Agricultural Tenancies Act 1995 s 22(1). The arbitration referred to in the text is arbitration under s 22. For general provisions as to arbitrations under the Agricultural Tenancies Act 1995 see s 30; and PARA 407 note 8. The purposes authorised by the Settled Land Act 1925 s 73 (see SETTLEMENTS vol 91 (2012) PARA 709) or the Universities and College Estates Act 1925 s 26 (see EDUCATION vol 36 (2015) PARA 1329) for the application of capital money include the payment of the costs, charges and expenses incurred by a landlord under a farm business tenancy on a reference to arbitration under these provisions: Agricultural Tenancies Act 1995 s 33(1)(c) (amended by the Trusts of Land and Appointment of Trustees Act 1996 s 25(2), Sch 4).

9　Ie the notice under the Agricultural Tenancies Act 1995 s 22(2) (see the text and notes 1–6).

10　See note 4.

11　Ie to the President of the Royal Institution of Chartered Surveyors (the 'RICS'): s 22(3). As to the Royal Institution of Chartered Surveyors generally see BUILDING CONTRACTS vol 6 (2011) PARA 490.

12　Agricultural Tenancies Act 1995 s 22(3). Where an application under s 22(3) relates wholly or partly to compensation in respect of a routine improvement which the tenant has provided or has begun to provide and that application is made at the same time as an application under s 19(4) (see

PARA 412) relating to the provision of that improvement, the President of the RICS must appoint the same arbitrator on both applications and, if both applications are made by the same person, only one fee is payable by virtue of s 30(2) (see PARA 407 note 8): s 22(4). As to the meaning of 'routine improvement' see s 19(10); and PARA 412 note 9 (definition applied by s 22(4)(a)).

419. Contractual provisions on compensation.

A tenant[1] is entitled to compensation in accordance with the statutory provisions governing compensation[2] and not otherwise, and is so entitled notwithstanding any agreement to the contrary[3]. Nothing in those provisions[4] should be construed as disentitling a tenant to compensation in any case for which those provisions do not provide for compensation[5].

1   As to the meanings of 'tenant' and 'tenancy' see PARA 401 note 1.
2   Ie the Agricultural Tenancies Act 1995 Pt III (ss 15–27) (apart from s 26) (see PARAS 410–418).
3   Agricultural Tenancies Act 1995 s 26(1).
4   See note 2.
5   Agricultural Tenancies Act 1995 s 26(2).

(6) DISPUTE RESOLUTION

420. Determination of disputes.

Special provision is made for the determination by arbitration[1] of:

(1)   rent in pursuance of a statutory review notice[2];
(2)   disputes arising from a refusal of, a failure to give, or any variation in the terms of a tenancy[3] required by the landlord[4] as a condition of, consent to the provision of a tenant's improvement[5];
(3)   any claim for compensation for tenant's improvements[6]; or
(4)   any dispute relating to rent review, in any case where the provisions relating to rent reviews[7] are excluded[8].

Any other dispute between the landlord and the tenant under a farm business tenancy[9], under the terms of the tenancy or under any custom, must be determined by arbitration[10] unless:

(a)   the tenancy is created by an instrument which includes provision for disputes to be resolved[11] by any person other than the landlord or the tenant or a third party appointed by either of them without the consent or concurrence of the other[12]; and
(b)   either the landlord and the tenant have jointly referred the dispute to the third party under that provision[13] or the landlord or the tenant has referred the dispute to the third party under that provision and notified the other in writing of the making of the reference[14].

1   For general provisions as to arbitrations under the Agricultural Tenancies Act 1995 see s 30; and PARA 407 note 8.
2   Agricultural Tenancies Act 1995 s 28(5)(a). As to rent reviews see PARAS 406–409. As to the meaning of 'statutory review notice' see s 10(1); and PARA 407 (definition applied by s 28(5)(a)).
3   As to the meanings of 'tenant' and 'tenancy' see PARA 401 note 1.
4   As to the meaning of 'landlord' see PARA 402 note 14.
5   Agricultural Tenancies Act 1995 s 28(5)(b). As to such disputes see s 19(1); and PARA 412. As to the meaning of 'tenant's improvement' see PARA 410.
6   Agricultural Tenancies Act 1995 s 28(5)(c). As to claims for compensation for tenant's improvements see Pt III (ss 15–27); and PARAS 410–419. As to the arbitration provisions see PARA 418.
7   Ie the Agricultural Tenancies Act 1995 Pt II (ss 9–14) (see PARAS 406–409).

8 Agricultural Tenancies Act 1995 s 28(5)(d) (added by SI 2006/2805). As to the exclusion of the
   provisions relating to rent reviews see the Agricultural Tenancies Act 1995 s 9(c)(ii); and PARA
   406. This provision does not apply where the provision in the instrument creating the tenancy
   referred to in s 9(c) is made before 19 October 2006 (ie the date on which the Regulatory Reform
   (Agricultural Tenancies) (England and Wales) Order 2006, SI 2006/2805, was brought into force:
   see art 1(1)(b)): art 14(3).

9 Ie a dispute concerning the rights and obligations of the landlord and the tenant under the
   Agricultural Tenancies Act 1995: s 28(1). As to the meaning of 'farm business tenancy' see PARA
   402.

10 Agricultural Tenancies Act 1995 s 28(1). Where such a dispute has arisen, the landlord or the
   tenant may give notice in writing to the other specifying the dispute and stating that, unless before
   the end of the period of two months beginning with the day on which the notice is given the parties
   have appointed an arbitrator by agreement, he proposes to apply to the President of the Royal
   Institution of Chartered Surveyors (the 'RICS') for the appointment of an arbitrator by him: s
   28(2). Where such a notice has been given, but no arbitrator has been appointed by agreement,
   either party may, after the end of the period of two months referred to in s 28(2), apply to the
   President of the RICS for the appointment of an arbitrator by him: s 28(3). As to the giving of
   notices see PARA 402 note 15. As to the Royal Institution of Chartered Surveyors generally see
   BUILDING CONTRACTS vol 6 (2011) PARA 490.

11 For these purposes a term of the tenancy does not provide for disputes to be 'resolved' by any
   person unless that person (whether or not acting as arbitrator) is enabled under the terms of the
   tenancy to give a decision which is binding in law on both parties: Agricultural Tenancies Act 1995
   s 29(2).

12 Agricultural Tenancies Act 1995 s 29(1)(a). For the power of limited owners to give consents and
   make agreements see s 32; and PARA 402 note 20.

13 Agricultural Tenancies Act 1995 s 29(1)(b)(i).

14 Agricultural Tenancies Act 1995 s 29(1)(b)(ii). This provision applies only if the period of four
   weeks beginning with the date on which the landlord or the tenant was notified as referred to in
   the text has expired and the other has not given a notice under s 28(2) (see note 10) in relation to
   the dispute before the end of that period: s 29(1)(b)(ii).

2. AGRICULTURAL HOLDINGS ACT TENANCIES

(1) TENANCIES TO WHICH THE AGRICULTURAL HOLDINGS ACT 1986 APPLIES

421. Continuing application of the Agricultural Holdings Act 1986.

Notwithstanding the enactment of the Agricultural Tenancies Act 1995, which makes provision governing tenancies of agricultural holdings created on or after 1 September 1995[1], the Agricultural Holdings Act 1986 continues to apply to all agricultural tenancies created before that date[2] and to certain other tenancies (principally, succession tenancies) which although granted after that date, are specifically excluded from the application of the Agricultural Tenancies Act 1995[3]. Subject to this and to other specified provisions[4], the Agricultural Holdings Act 1986 applies in relation to tenancies of agricultural holdings whenever created, agreements whenever made, and other things whenever done[5].

1 Ie the date on which the Agricultural Tenancies Act 1995 was brought into force: see s 41(2). Agricultural tenancies to which the Agricultural Tenancies Act 1995 applies are held as 'farm business tenancies' provided they comply with specified conditions: see PARA 401 et seq.
2 Thus the Agricultural Holdings Act 1986 continues to apply to all existing agricultural tenancies and also to those granted by a written contract of tenancy entered into before 1 September 1995 and indicating (in whatever terms) that the Agricultural Holdings Act 1986 is to apply in relation to the tenancy: see the Agricultural Tenancies Act 1995 s 4(1)(a); and PARA 401.
3 See the Agricultural Tenancies Act 1995 ss 2, 4(1); and PARA 422.
4 Ie subject to the Agricultural Holdings Act 1986 ss 4, 34 (see PARAS 428, 497), Sch 12 (modifications), and any other provision to the contrary: s 98(1).
5 Agricultural Holdings Act 1986 s 98(1). Provision is made for the modification of the Agricultural Holdings Act 1986 in relation to tenancies of agricultural holdings granted or agreed to be granted, agreements made, and things done before certain dates no later than 1 March 1948 (ie the date on which the Agriculture Act 1947 Pt III (repealed), from which these provisions are derived, was brought into force: see s 111(2) (repealed); and the Agriculture Act 1947 (Commencement) (No 1) Order 1948, SI 1948/342): see the Agricultural Holdings Act 1986 s 98(2), Sch 12 paras 1–5, 10. Special provision is also made with respect to compensation for tenant-right matters in relation to tenants of agricultural holdings who entered into occupation before specified dates not later than 31 December 1951 (ie the date on which the Agricultural Holdings Act (Variation of Fourth Schedule) Order 1951, SI 1951/2168 (revoked) came into operation): see the Agricultural Holdings Act 1986 s 98(3), Sch 12 paras 6–9. As to the meaning of 'agricultural holding' see PARA 423.

422. Tenancies which cannot be farm business tenancies.

The only tenancies commencing after 1 September 1995[1] to which the Agricultural Holdings Act 1986 can apply are:
   (1)   tenancies obtained by virtue of a direction under the statutory provisions relating to succession to agricultural tenancies on death or retirement[2];
   (2)   tenancies granted[3] where a successful application for succession on death has been made[4];
   (3)   tenancies granted on an agreed succession by a written contract of tenancy indicating (in whatever terms) that the provisions relating to the death or retirement of an agricultural tenant[5] are to apply in relation to the tenancy[6];
   (4)   tenancies created by the acceptance of a tenant, in accordance with the provisions as to compensation known as the 'Evesham custom'[7], on the terms and conditions of the previous tenancy[8];

(5)   tenancies granted to a person who, immediately before the grant, was the tenant of the holding, or of any agricultural holding[9] which comprised the whole or a substantial part of the land comprised in the holding, under a tenancy in relation to which the Agricultural Holdings Act 1986 applied and which is so granted because an agreement between the parties (not being an agreement expressed to take effect as a new tenancy between the parties) has effect as an implied surrender followed by the grant of the tenancy[10] (there being a limited exception to this category[11]); or

(6)   tenancies granted to a person who, immediately before the grant, was the tenant of the holding, or of any agricultural holding which comprised the whole or a substantial part of the land comprised in the holding, under a tenancy in relation to which the Agricultural Holdings Act 1986 applied, and which is so granted by a written contract of tenancy indicating (in whatever terms) that that Act is to apply in relation to the tenancy[12] (there being a limited exception to this category[13]).

1   Ie the date on which the Agricultural Tenancies Act 1995 was brought into force: see s 41(2). The Agricultural Holdings Act 1986 continues to apply to all existing agricultural tenancies including those agreed to be granted by a written contract of tenancy entered into before 1 September 1995 and indicating (in whatever terms) that the Agricultural Holdings Act 1986 is to apply in relation to the tenancy: see the Agricultural Tenancies Act 1995 s 4(1)(a); and PARAS 401, 421.

2   Agricultural Tenancies Act 1995 ss 2, 4(1)(b) (s 4(1)(b) amended by SI 2013/1036). The statutory provisions relating to succession to agricultural tenancies on death or retirement are the Agricultural Holdings Act 1986 ss 39, 53 (see PARAS 502, 507).

3   Ie following a direction under the Agricultural Holdings Act 1986 s 39 (see PARA 502) in circumstances falling within s 45(6) (see PARA 504).

4   Agricultural Tenancies Act 1995 s 4(1)(c).

5   Ie the Agricultural Holdings Act 1986 Pt IV (ss 34–59) (see PARAS 497–510).

6   Agricultural Tenancies Act 1995 s 4(1)(d). For this purpose, a tenancy (the 'current tenancy') is granted on an agreed succession if, and only if:

(1)   the previous tenancy of the holding or a related holding was a tenancy in relation to which the Agricultural Holdings Act 1986 Pt IV (ss 34–59) (see PARAS 497–510) applied (Agricultural Tenancies Act 1995 s 4(2)(a) (s 4(1)(e), (f), (2)(a) amended, s 4(1)(g), (2)(c), (2A)–(2C), (3)(c) added, s 4(2)(b) substituted, by SI 2006/2805));

(2)   the current tenancy is granted to a person (alone or jointly with other persons) who, if the tenant under that previous tenancy (the 'previous tenant') had died immediately before the grant, would have been his close relative (Agricultural Tenancies Act 1995 s 4(2)(b) (as so substituted)); and

(3)   either the current tenancy is granted to a person (alone or jointly with other persons) who was or had become the sole or sole remaining applicant for a direction under the Agricultural Holdings Act 1986s 39 or 53 for a tenancy (s 4(2)(c), (2A)(a) (as so added; s 4(2A)(a) amended by SI 2013/1036)) or the current tenancy is granted as a result of an agreement between the landlord and the previous tenant (Agricultural Tenancies Act 1995 s 4(2A)(b)(i) (as so added)) and is granted, and begins, before the date of the giving of any retirement notice by the previous tenant, or if no retirement notice is given, before the date of death of the previous tenant (s 4(2A)(b)(ii) (as so added)).

As to the meanings of 'close relative', 'related holding' and 'retirement notice' for these purposes see the Agricultural Holdings Act 1986 ss 35(2), 49(3); and PARAS 498 note 5, 499 note 2 (definitions applied by the Agricultural Tenancies Act 1995 s 4(3)(b), (c) (s 4(3)(c) as so added)). The amendments made by the Regulatory Reform (Agricultural Tenancies) (England and Wales) Order 2006, SI 2006/2805, do not apply to any tenancy granted before the amendments came into force (ie 19 October 2006): see art 1(1)(b), 12(12).

7   As to the 'Evesham custom' see the Agricultural Holdings Act 1986 s 80(3)–(5); and PARA 563.

8   Agricultural Tenancies Act 1995 s 4(1)(e).

9   As to the meaning of 'agricultural holding' see PARA 423.

10 Agricultural Tenancies Act 1995 s 4(1)(f) (as amended: see note 6).

11 The Agricultural Holdings Act 1986 will not apply by virtue of the Agricultural Tenancies Act 1995 s 4(1)(f) or s 4(1)(g) (see the text and notes 10, 12) in relation to the tenancy of an agricultural holding (the 'current holding') where:

(1)   the whole or a substantial part of the land comprised in the current holding was comprised in an agricultural holding (the 'previous holding') which was subject to a tenancy granted after 19 October 2006 in relation to which the Agricultural Holdings Act 1986 applied by virtue of the Agricultural Tenancies Act 1995 s 4(1)(f) or s 4(1)(g) (s 4(2B)(a) (as added: see note 6));

(2)   the whole or a substantial part of the land comprised in the previous holding was comprised in an agricultural holding (the 'original holding') which was at 19 October 2006 subject to a tenancy in relation to which the Agricultural Holdings Act 1986 applied (Agricultural Tenancies Act 1995 s 4(2B)(b) (as so added)); and

(3)   the land comprised in the original holding does not, on the date of the grant of the tenancy of the current holding, comprise the whole or a substantial part of the land comprised in the current holding (s 4(2B)(c) (as so added)).

The references in s 4(1)(g) and s 4(2B) to a 'substantial part of the land comprised in the holding' mean a substantial part determined by reference to either area or value: s 4(2C) (as so added).

12 Agricultural Tenancies Act 1995 s 4(1)(g) (as amended: see note 6).

13 See note 11.

(2) DEFINITION OF AGRICULTURAL HOLDING

423. Meaning of 'agricultural holding'.

An 'agricultural holding' is the aggregate of the land (whether agricultural land[1] or not[2]) comprised in a contract of tenancy[3] which is a contract for an agricultural tenancy[4], not being a contract under which the land is let to the tenant[5] during his continuance in any office, appointment[6] or employment held under the landlord[7]. A contract for an agricultural tenancy relating to any land exists if, having regard to the terms of the tenancy[8], to the actual or contemplated use of the land at the time the contract was concluded and subsequently[9], and to any other relevant circumstances[10], the whole of the land comprised in the contract, subject to such exceptions only as do not substantially affect the character of the tenancy, is let for use as agricultural land[11].

1   As to the meaning of 'agricultural land' see PARA 424.

2   Mixed user (ie both agricultural and non-agricultural) is contemplated by the words 'whether agricultural land or not', and it is the aggregate of land and the land uses thereof that may determine the existence or continued existence of an agricultural holding. There may be a tenancy of an agricultural holding even where the land is partly in non-agricultural use; it is not necessary for every inch of the holding to be used for agriculture or for the purposes of an agricultural trade or business: see *Short v Greeves* [1988] 1 EGLR 1, CA at 2 per Dillon LJ. Even if a non-agricultural use (such as a garden centre) is introduced or expanded on an agricultural holding, the court will not lightly treat a tenancy as having ceased to be within the protection of the Agricultural Holdings Act 1986: *Short v Greeves* (6 acres were let as an agricultural holding, and not as a business tenancy under the provisions of Part II of the Landlord and Tenant Act 1954, notwithstanding presence of a 1.2 acre garden centre, predominantly selling goods not grown on the land (indeed, not plants at all) such as as sheds, with about 60% shop's turnover being from those goods. Neither turnover (nor, similarly, relative profitability) are conclusive, but are only indications which can be used in order to see if the nature of the tenancy has in fact changed: *Short v Greeves*.

The object of the agricultural holdings legislation is to maintain continuity in the conduct of farming and horticultural operations: see *Weatherall v Smith* [1980] 2 All ER 530, [1980] 1 WLR 1290, CA (1 acre paddock let for grazing, subsequently used as a jumping paddock. Remitted for rehearing). A tenancy can in principle cease to be an agricultural holding, where agricultural use is wholly or substantially abandoned, bringing about a change in the character of the tenancy from agricultural to (for example) commercial. But where the tenancy is clearly an agricultural one to start with, strong evidence is needed to show that agricultural user has been abandonment. Any such abandonment must be more than temporary: *Wetherall v Smith* at 1299 per Sir David Cairns; *Hickson & Welch Ltd v Cann* (1977) 40 P & CR 218n, CA. There is no minimum size of agricultural holding: *Stevens v Sedgeman* [1951] 2 KB 434, [1951] 2 All ER 33, CA (0.5 acre); and see *Craddock v Hampshire County Council* [1958] 1 All ER 449, [1958] 1 WLR 202, CA (0.229 acre). A mixed tenancy cannot be severed such that the provisions relating to agricultural holdings apply to the part which is used for agriculture and not to the part which is used for other purposes: *Howkins v Jardine* [1951] 1 KB 614, [1951] 1 All ER 320, CA. The contract of tenancy may restrict the user so that only agricultural activities are permitted: *Jewell v McGowan* [2002] EWCA Civ 145, [2002] 3 EGLR 87.

3	As to the meaning of 'contract of tenancy' see PARA 425.

4	As to the meaning of 'contract for an agricultural tenancy' see the text and notes 8–11.

5	'Tenant' means the holder of land under a contract of tenancy and includes the executors, administrators, assigns or trustee in bankruptcy of a tenant, or other person deriving title from a tenant: Agricultural Holdings Act 1986 s 96(1); Agriculture (Miscellaneous Provisions) Act 1968 s 17(1) (amended by the Agricultural Holdings Act 1986 Sch 14 para 46). It does not include an assignee of farming stock or of a right to statutory compensation (as to which see PARA 515 et seq): *Ecclesiastical Comrs for England v National Provincial Bank Ltd* [1935] 1 KB 566, CA. If a trustee in the tenant's bankruptcy disclaims the tenancy, he loses all benefits under the lease: *Schofield v Hincks* (1888) 58 LJQB 147; *Re Morrish, ex p Sir W Hart-Dyke* (1882) 22 ChD 410, CA; *Re Wadsley, Bettinson's Representative v Trustee* (1925) 94 LJ Ch 215.

   The designation of 'tenant' continues to apply to the parties until the conclusion of any proceedings taken under or in pursuance of the Agricultural Holdings Act 1986 in respect of compensation: s 96(6).

6	A tenancy for a trial period is not an appointment: *Verrall v Farnes* [1966] 2 All ER 808, [1966] 1 WLR 1254.

7	Agricultural Holdings Act 1986 s 1(1); Agriculture (Miscellaneous Provisions) Act 1968 s 17(1) (as amended: see note 5). 'Landlord' means any person entitled for the time being to receive the rents and profits of any land (Agricultural Holdings Act 1986 s 96(1); Agriculture (Miscellaneous Provisions) Act 1968 s 17(1) (as so amended)), and the designation of 'landlord' continues to apply to the parties until the conclusion of any proceedings taken under or in pursuance of the Agricultural Holdings Act 1986 in respect of compensation (Agricultural Holdings Act 1986 s 96(6); Agriculture (Miscellaneous Provisions) Act 1968 s 17(1) (as so amended)). Thus a purchaser may become landlord, though he will not be landlord until entitled either at law or in equity to receive the rents and profits, that is normally until the date fixed for completion of the purchase: *Farrow v Orttewell* [1933] Ch 480 at 484 per Bennett J (decision, but not this particular statement, affd on appeal [1933] Ch 488, CA). Cf *Tombs v Turvey* (1923) 93 LJKB 785, CA (clause in sale agreement disentitling purchaser to rent); *Richards v Pryse* [1927] 2 KB 76, CA (completion held to mean the date of actual completion, not the day fixed for completion). This definition of 'landlord' does not, however, affect the common law rule that only the legal estate owner may serve a notice to quit: *Farrow v Orttewell* at 485.

8	Agricultural Holdings Act 1986 s 1(2)(a).

9	Agricultural Holdings Act 1986 s 1(2)(b). Any subsequent change of use of the land for agriculture contrary to the terms of the tenancy does not make it subject to an agricultural tenancy unless it has been effected with the landlord's permission, consent or acquiescence: s 1(3).

10	Agricultural Holdings Act 1986 s 1(2)(c).

11	Agricultural Holdings Act 1986 s 1(2).

## 424.	'Agriculture', 'agricultural', 'agricultural land' and 'farming'.

For the purposes of the principal legislation relating to agricultural land[1], 'agriculture' is defined as including horticulture, fruit growing, seed growing, dairy farming and livestock[2] breeding and keeping, the use of land as grazing land[3], meadow land, osier land, market gardens and nursery grounds[4], and the use of land for woodlands where that use is ancillary to the farming of the land for other agricultural purposes, and 'agricultural' is construed accordingly[5]. References to the 'farming' of land include references to the carrying on in relation to the land of any agricultural activity[6].

For the purposes of the Agriculture Act 1947, the Agriculture Act 1967, the Agriculture Act 1970 Pt III and the Agricultural Holdings Act 1986 'agricultural land' means land used for agriculture[7] which is so used for the purposes of a trade or business[8], or which is designated[9] by the Secretary of State or the Welsh

Ministers[10], and it includes any land so designated as land which in the opinion of the Secretary of State or the Welsh Ministers ought to be brought into use for agriculture[11].

1   Ie for the purposes of the Agriculture Act 1947, the Agriculture Act 1967, the Agriculture Act 1970 Pt III (ss 37–65), the Agricultural Holdings Act 1986 and the Agricultural Tenancies Act 1995. This definition is also used for the purposes of the Town and Country Planning Act 1990, and in a less exhaustive form for the purposes of the legislation governing allotments and cottage holdings (see note 5).

2   'Livestock' includes any creature kept for the production of food, wool, skins or fur or for the purpose of its use in the farming of land, and in the Agricultural Holdings Act 1986 also includes the carrying on in relation to land of any agricultural activity: Agriculture Act 1947 s 109(3); Agriculture Act 1970 s 37(4); Agricultural Holdings Act 1986 s 96(1); Agricultural Tenancies Act 1995 s 38(1). Hence it will normally exclude horses; and land used for keeping horses rather than grazing by horses is not land used for agriculture: see *Belmont Farm Ltd v Minister of Housing and Local Government* (1962) 60 LGR 319, 13 P & CR 417, DC; *Sykes v Secretary of State for the Environment* (1980) 42 P & CR 19, [1981] 1 EGLR 137, DC; *McClinton v McFall* (1974) 232 Estates Gazette 707. Fish farming is agriculture (*Minister of Agriculture, Fisheries and Food v Appleton* [1970] 1 QB 221, [1969] 3 All ER 1051, DC), as is keeping bees for the production of honey, but keeping pheasants for shooting is not (*Earl of Normanton v Giles* [1980] 1 All ER 106, [1980] 1 WLR 28, HL; *Reeve v Atterby* [1978] CLY 73; *Lord Glendyne v Rapley* [1978] 2 All ER 110, [1978] 1 WLR 601, CA).

3   The grazing need not be by 'livestock' as defined in note 2: see *Rutherford v Maurer* [1962] 1 QB 16, [1961] 2 All ER 775, CA (decided in relation to the identical definition in the Agricultural Holdings Act 1948 s 94(1) (repealed)).

4   There is no definition of 'market gardening' in the Agricultural Holdings Act 1986 or any of the principal legislation relating to agriculture. An experimental bulb farm is not a market garden (*Watters v Hunter* 1927 SC 310 at 317, Ct of Sess), but land used for growing raspberries for jam-making has been held to be (*Grewar v Moncur's Curator Bonis* 1916 SC 764, Ct of Sess) and so has land used as an orchard with rhubarb and other crops grown underneath the trees, the fruit and crops being sold (*Lowther v Clifford* [1927] 1 KB 130, CA). In *Bickerdike v Lucy* [1920] 1 KB 707 (decided under the Corn Production Act 1917 (repealed)) a person employed in a private garden, some of the produce of which was sold, was held not to be employed in a market garden; see also *Re Wallis, ex p Sully* (1885) 14 QBD 950; and cf *Roberts v Wynn* [1950] WN 300, DC (garden run as business within definition). Land covered with glass-houses for the purpose of growing fruit and vegetables for sale was held to be a market garden or nursery ground for the purposes of assessment under the Public Health Act 1875 s 211(1)(b) (repealed): *Purser v Worthing Local Board of Health* (1887) 18 QBD 818, CA; but cf *Smith v Richmond* [1899] AC 448, HL.

5   Agriculture Act 1947 s 109(3); Agriculture Act 1967 s 75(2); Agriculture Act 1970 s 37(4); Agricultural Holdings Act 1986 s 96(1); Agricultural Tenancies Act 1995 s 38(1); Town and Country Planning Act 1990 s 336(1). Less exhaustive versions of this definition have effect for the purposes of the legislation governing allotments and cottage holdings: in the Small Holdings and Allotments Act 1908 and the Agricultural Land (Utilisation) Act 1931 'agriculture' (and 'cultivation') include horticulture and the use of land for any purpose of husbandry, inclusive of the keeping or breeding of livestock, poultry, or bees, and the growth of fruit, vegetables, and the like (Small Holdings and Allotments Act 1908 s 61(1); Agricultural Land (Utilisation) Act 1931 s 20(2)), and 'land' includes any right or easement in or over land (Small Holdings and Allotments Act 1908 s 61(2)); while for the purposes of the Allotments Act 1922 'agriculture' includes forestry, horticulture, and the keeping and breeding of livestock (s 22(1)).

6   Agriculture Act 1947 s 109(5); Agriculture Act 1967 s 75(2); Agriculture Act 1970 s 37(4); Agricultural Holdings Act 1986 s 96(4); Agricultural Tenancies Act 1995 s 38(2).

7   References in the Agriculture Act 1947, the Agriculture Act 1967 and the Agricultural Holdings Act 1986 to 'the use of land for agriculture' include, in relation to land forming part of an agricultural unit, references to any use of the land in connection with the farming of the unit: Agriculture Act 1947 s 109(6); Agriculture Act 1967 s 75(2); Agricultural Holdings Act 1986 s 96(5). A dwelling house may be land 'used for agriculture'; it is a question of fact and degree whether it is so used in any particular case: *Blackmore v Butler* [1954] 2 QB 171, [1954] 2 All ER 403, CA (where a cottage occupied by an agricultural worker, without land other than its site and a garden, was held in the particular circumstances of that case to be 'agricultural land').

     An 'agricultural unit' is land which is occupied as a unit for agricultural purposes, including any dwelling house or other building occupied by the same person for the purpose of farming the land and any other land falling within the definition of 'agricultural land' which is in the occupation of the same person, being land as to which the Secretary of State is or the Welsh Ministers are satisfied that, having regard to its character and situation and other relevant circumstances (which, in relation to an owner or occupier, include all circumstances affecting management or farming other than the personal circumstances of the owner or occupier (Agriculture Act 1947 s 109(3)), it ought in the interests of full and efficient production to be farmed in conjunction with the agricultural unit, and he directs or they direct accordingly (s 109(2); Agriculture Act 1967 s 75(2); Agricultural Holdings Act 1986 s 96(1)). The Secretary of State and the Welsh Ministers must not give such a direction as respects any land unless it is for the time being not in use for any purpose which appears to him or them to be substantial, having regard to the use to which it might be put for agriculture: Agriculture Act 1947 s 109(2) proviso. 'Owner' was defined by s 21 (repealed) and meant, subject to certain exceptions, the person in whom the legal estate in fee simple was vested. In relation to any agricultural activity, the person having the right to carry it on is deemed to be the 'occupier' of the land: s 109(5); Agriculture Act 1970 s 37(4).

8 'Trade or business' is not confined to agricultural trades or businesses: *Rutherford v Maurer* [1962] 1 QB 16, [1961] 2 All ER 775, CA (tenancy of a field let for grazing horses used in association with a riding school business is an agricultural holding, whereas an identical letting for the tenant's personal hunting horses or pets will not be). The use of the land, however, must be agricultural: see *Blackmore v Butler* [1954] 2 QB 171, [1954] 2 All ER 403, CA (see note 7); *Iredell v Brocklehurst* (1950) 155 EG 268, CA. See also *Dow Agrochemicals Ltd v EA Lane (North Lynn) Ltd* (1965) 115 LJo 76, 192 Estates Gazette 737, CCA. An allotment cultivated to produce food for sale as a trade or business falls within this definition, but an allotment garden cultivated by the occupier to produce food for home consumption does not: see *Stevens v Sedgeman* [1951] 2 KB 434, [1951] 2 All ER 33, CA. As to allotment gardens see PARA 649.

9 Ie designated for the purposes of the Agriculture Act 1947 s 109(1) and, by extension, the Agricultural Holdings Act 1986 s 96(1).

10 As to the Secretary of State and the Welsh Ministers see PARA 741.

11 Agriculture Act 1947 s 109(1); Agriculture Act 1967 s 75(2); Agriculture Act 1970 s 37(4); Agricultural Holdings Act 1986 s 1(4). Such designations are not to extend to land used as pleasure grounds, private gardens or allotment gardens, or to land kept or preserved mainly or exclusively for the purposes of sport or recreation, except where the Secretary of State or the Welsh Ministers are satisfied that its use for agriculture would not be inconsistent with its use for those purposes and it is so stated in the designation: Agriculture Act 1947 s 109(1) proviso. 'Allotment garden' means an allotment not exceeding 0.10 hectare in extent which is wholly or mainly cultivated by the occupier for the production of vegetables or fruit for consumption by himself or his family: Allotments Act 1922 s 22(1); Agriculture Act 1947 s 109(3) (amended by SI 1978/446); Allotments Act 1925 s 1; Agriculture Act 1970 s 37(4): this definition is also used for the purposes of the Emergency Laws (Miscellaneous Provisions) Act 1953 (see s 5(4)(a)). The report of the Departmental Committee of Inquiry into Allotments 1969 (Cmnd 4166) recommended that allotment gardens be termed 'leisure gardens' and suggested a definition (see PARAS 672–681 of that report).

425. Contract of tenancy.

A 'contract of tenancy' is a letting of land, or an agreement[1] for letting land, for a term of years[2] or from year to year[3], and a letting or an agreement converted into a letting or agreement for 90 years[4] is deemed to be a letting of, or an agreement for letting, land for a term of years[5]. It does not include an attornment clause in a mortgage[6]. There must be a single contract of tenancy[7].

1 'Agreement' includes an agreement arrived at by means of valuation or otherwise, and 'agreed' has a corresponding meaning: Agricultural Holdings Act 1986 s 96(1).

2 A tenancy for a definite term of more than one year but less than two years is a letting for a term of years for these purposes: *EWP Ltd v Moore* [1992] QB 460, [1992] 1 All ER 880, CA.

3 For the provisions as to land let for an interest less than a tenancy from year to year see PARA 427.

4 Ie by the Law of Property Act 1925 s 149(6) (lease for life or lives or for a term determinable with life or lives or on the marriage of, or formation of a civil partnership by, the lessee: see LANDLORD AND TENANT vol 62 (2016) PARA 234).

5 Agricultural Holdings Act 1986 s 1(5).

6 *Steyning and Littlehampton Building Society v Wilson* [1951] Ch 1018, [1951] 2 All ER 452; *Wyatt v King* (1951) 157 Estates Gazette 124 (followed in *Alliance Building Society v Pinwill*

[1958] Ch 788, [1958] 2 All ER 408). These cases were decided under materially identical provisions in the Agricultural Holdings Act 1948 (repealed).
7 *Darby v Williams* (1974) 232 Estates Gazette 579; *Blackmore v Butler* [1954] 2 QB 171, [1954] 2 All ER 403, CA.

(3) STATUTORY PROTECTION OF AGRICULTURAL TENANTS

426. Protection of annual tenants.
The Agricultural Holdings Act 1986 provides lifetime security of tenure for tenants by imposing restrictions on the operation of a notice to quit; in order that a landlord should not avoid these provisions the Act treats certain agreements as if they were annual tenancies[1]. Tenancies for fixed terms of more than one year but less than two are not protected by these provisions[2].

1 See PARA 427 et seq.
2 *Gladstone v Bower* [1960] 2 QB 384, [1960] 3 All ER 353, CA.

427. Conversion into tenancies of lettings for less than from year to year, and licences.
Subject to certain exceptions[1], where any land is let[2] to a person for use as agricultural land[3] for an interest less than a tenancy from year to year[4] or a person is granted a licence to occupy land for use as agricultural land[5], where the circumstances are such that if his interest were a tenancy from year to year he would in respect of that land be the tenant[6] of an agricultural holding[7], then the agreement takes effect as if it were a tenancy from year to year[8]. A tenancy for one year exactly is converted into a tenancy from year to year[9]. Where the question concerns conversion of a licence, the licence must give exclusive rights of occupation and not involve sharing with the landowner[10]. Gratuitous[11] and non-contractual[12] licences are excluded. A licence of any duration may be converted[13].

The conversion of a letting under these provisions does not apply where:
(1)   the Secretary of State or the Welsh Ministers[14] has or have approved the agreement before it was entered into[15];
(2)   the agreement for the letting of the land or the granting of the licence to occupy the land was made (whether or not it expressly so provided) in contemplation of the use of the land only for grazing or mowing (or both) during some specified period of the year[16];
(3)   the licence or tenancy was granted by a person whose interest in the land was less than a tenancy from year to year[17]; or
(4)   the agreement was made before 1 March 1948[18] and was a periodic tenancy less than from year to year[19].

A prerequisite of conversion is a true relationship of landlord[20] and tenant, and, therefore, conversion is not applicable to an attornment under a mortgage[21].

Grazing or mowing agreements[22] have to be restricted to these purposes in order for the exemption from conversion to apply, and if so restricted will not be converted if the tenant or licensee ploughs[23]. The inclusion of small ancillary buildings will not cause the tenancy or licence to be converted[24]. If a grazier is permitted to remain in occupation on the expiry of a grazing agreement without any express new agreement there is an implication of renewal of the expired agreement rather than the creation of a tenancy from year to year[25]. The agreement has to be restricted to a specified period of a year[26]. There may be successive grazing agreements running for several years but this of itself will not take them outside the exception[27]. A letting of 'six month periods', however, implies a minimum of two such periods and hence a year, and is thus converted into a tenancy from year to year[28].

Any arrangements entered into on or after 1 September 1995[29] where exclusive possession is given will be farm business tenancies to which the provisions of the Agricultural Holdings Act 1986 are inapplicable[30].

1 See the text and notes 14–19.
2 Ie under the Agricultural Holdings Act 1986. New lettings of agricultural land are, in general, covered by the Agricultural Tenancies Act 1995 (see PARA 401 et seq). See also the text and notes 29–30.
3 As to the meanings of 'agricultural' and 'agricultural land' see PARA 424.
4 Agricultural Holdings Act 1986 s 2(2)(a).
5 Agricultural Holdings Act 1986 s 2(2)(b).
6 As to the meaning of 'tenant' see PARA 423 note 5.
7 As to the meaning of 'agricultural holding' see PARA 423.
8 Agricultural Holdings Act 1986 s 2(1). As to the meaning of 'agreement' see PARA 425 note 1. These provisions take effect subject to necessary modifications, such as relating to the date on which the rent falls due; and furthermore the agreement takes effect as a tenancy from year to year as from the date of the original agreement rather than from the expiry date of the original contractual term: see *Calcott v JS Bloor (Measham) Ltd* [1998] 1 WLR 1490, [1998] 3 EGLR 1, CA. See *Davies v Davies* [2002] EWCA Civ 1791, 146 Sol Jo LB 281 (a one-off obligation to re-seed prevented the arrangement from being converted into a yearly tenancy). Any dispute arising as to the operation of the Agricultural Holdings Act 1986 s 2 in relation to any agreement must be determined by arbitration under that Act: s 2(4). But, notwithstanding s 2(4), the parties to the agreement may instead refer for third party determination the dispute that has arisen as to the operation of s 2: s 2(5) (added by the Deregulation Act 2015 Sch 4 para 2).
9 *Bernays v Prosser* [1963] 2 QB 592, [1963] 2 All ER 321, CA.
10 *Harrison-Broadley v Smith* [1964] 1 All ER 867, [1964] 1 WLR 456, CA; *Bahamas International Trust Co Ltd v Threadgold* [1974] 3 All ER 881, [1974] 1 WLR 1514, HL. As to the particular problems of farming through the medium of a limited company see *Troop v Gibson* [1986] 1 EGLR 1, 277 Estates Gazette 1134, CA. See also *McCarthy v Bence* [1990] 1 EGLR 1, [1990] 17 EG 78, CA. See also *Well Barn Farming Ltd v Backhouse* [2005] EWHC 1520 (Ch), [2005] 3 EGLR 109 (predecessor landlord had received consideration for licence as he had been allowed to cut back woodland).
11 *Mitton v Farrow* [1980] 2 EGLR 1, 255 Estates Gazette 449, CA (an agreement to bring the land into good heart may be adequate consideration); and see also *Verrall v Farnes* [1966] 2 All ER 808, [1966] 1 WLR 1254; *Goldsack v Shore* [1950] 1 KB 708, [1950] 1 All ER 276, CA.
12 *Collier v Hollinshead* [1984] 2 EGLR 14, 272 Estates Gazette 941 (family relationship).
13 *Snell v Snell* (1964) 191 Estates Gazette 361, CA.
14 As to the Secretary of State and the Welsh Ministers see PARA 741.
15 Agricultural Holdings Act 1986 s 2(1); and see *Finbow v Air Ministry* [1963] 2 All ER 647, [1963] 1 WLR 697; *Bedfordshire County Council v Clarke* (1974) 230 Estates Gazette 1587; *Epsom and Ewell Borough Council v C Bell (Tadworth) Ltd* [1983] 2 All ER 59, [1983] 1 WLR 379; *Secretary of State for Social Services v Beavington* (1982) 262 Estates Gazette 551.
16 Agricultural Holdings Act 1986 s 2(3)(a). See the text and notes 22–28. See also *Brown v Tiernan* (1992) 65 P & CR 324, [1993] 1 EGLR 11 (agreement restricting grazing of cattle to a specified period of the year, but permitting use of the land for other purposes for the whole of the year is not within the exception in the Agricultural Holdings Act 1986 s 2(3)(a)).
17 Agricultural Holdings Act 1986 s 2(3)(b).
18 Ie the date on which the Agriculture Act 1947 Pt III (repealed), from which these provisions are derived, was brought into force: see s 111(2) (repealed); and the Agriculture Act 1947 (Commencement) (No 1) Order 1948, SI 1948/342.
19 Agricultural Holdings Act 1986 s 98, Sch 12 para 1.
20 As to the meaning of 'landlord' see PARA 423 note 7.
21 *Steyning and Littlehampton Building Society v Wilson* [1951] Ch 1018, [1951] 2 All ER 452.
22 See the text and note 16.
23 *Lory v London Borough of Brent* [1971] 1 All ER 1042, [1971] 1 WLR 823; but see also *Boyce v Rendells* (1983) 268 Estates Gazette 268, CA; and contrast with a contract of agistment (see ANIMALS vol 2 (2017) PARAS 18–20).

24 *Avon County Council v Clothier* (1977) 75 LGR 344, 242 Estates Gazette 1048, CA.

25 *Reid v Dawson* [1955] 1 QB 214, [1954] 3 All ER 498, CA.

26 *Reid v Dawson* [1955] 1 QB 214, [1954] 3 All ER 498, CA; *Chaloner v Bower* [1984] 1 EGLR 4, 269 Estates Gazette 725, CA; *Watts v Yeend* [1987] 1 All ER 744, [1987] 1 WLR 323, CA. Cf *Stone v Whitcombe* (1980) 40 P & CR 296, 257 Estates Gazette 929, CA.

27 *Scene Estates Ltd v Amos* [1957] 2 QB 205, [1957] 2 All ER 325, CA; cf where the parties expressly agreed to renewals, the statutory conversion applied: *Short Bros (Plant) Ltd v Edwards* (1978) 249 Estates Gazette 539; and see *South West Water Authority v Palmer* (1983) 268 Estates Gazette 357, CA.

28 *Rutherford v Maurer* [1962] 1 QB 16, [1961] 2 All ER 775, CA.

29 Ie the date on which the Agricultural Tenancies Act 1995 was brought into force: see PARA 421 note 1; and PARA 401 et seq.

30 See the Agricultural Tenancies Act 1995 ss 1, 4; and PARA 401 et seq.

428. Tenancies for two years or more.

Instead of terminating on the term date[1], a tenancy[2] of an agricultural holding[3] for a term of two years or more continues as a tenancy from year to year unless either party gives written notice[4] of intention to terminate the tenancy not less than one year nor more than two years before the term date[5], or unless the tenant dies before the term date[6]. Such a notice is deemed to be a notice to quit[7]. An agreement[8] purporting to exclude these provisions is ineffective except where, in relation to a tenancy for not less than two nor more than five years, the proposed landlord and tenant so agree and, on a joint written application by them, the Secretary of State or the Welsh Ministers[9] notify them of his or their approval; the tenancy has to be in writing and must indicate, either in itself or by indorsement upon it, that the relevant provisions do not apply[10].

Where a tenancy to which these provisions apply has been granted to any person or persons on or after 12 September 1984[11] and that person (or the survivor) dies before the term date[12], and no notice to terminate the tenancy has been given, then the tenancy is terminable[13]. If the death occurs a year or more before the term date the tenancy terminates on the term date[14]; if the death occurs at any other time the tenancy continues for a further 12 months and expires on the first anniversary of the term date[15]. Termination of the tenancy on death is deemed to be termination by reason of a notice to quit given by the landlord, and the tenant's right to compensation for disturbance[16] is preserved[17].

1 'Termination', in relation to a tenancy, means the cesser of the contract of tenancy by reason of effluxion of time or from any other cause: Agricultural Holdings Act 1986 s 96(1). Where the contract of tenancy is rescinded and occupation abandoned by reason of the failure of one of the parties to perform a necessary condition of the contract, there is no termination of the tenancy within the meaning of this definition: see *Todd v Bowie* (1902) 4 F 435 (decided under the Agricultural Holdings (Scotland) Act 1883). If by the terms of the agreement, or by custom, a tenant is entitled or required to give up possession of different parts of his holding at different times, the termination of the tenancy takes place at the time when the last part of the holding held under the contract of tenancy is given up by the tenant: *Swinburne v Andrews* [1923] 2 KB 483, CA; followed in *Re Arden and Rutter* [1923] 2 KB 865, CA. Cf *Black v Clay* [1894] AC 368, HL; *Morley v Carter* [1898] 1 QB 8, where the tenancy was held to have terminated in respect of each part as it was given up; and see *Re Paul, ex p Earl of Portarlington* (1889) 24 QBD 247, where the tenancy was held to have terminated at the end of a customary period of holding over after notice to quit. As to the meaning of 'contract of tenancy' see PARA 425.

For these purposes 'term date' means, in relation to a tenancy granted for a term of years, the date fixed for the expiry of that term: ss 3(4), 4(4).

2 The provisions described in the text and notes 3–7 do not apply to tenancies falling within the Law of Property Act 1925 s 149(6) (lease for life or lives or for a term determinable with life or lives or on the marriage of, or formation of a civil partnership by, the lessee: see LANDLORD AND TENANT vol 62 (2016) PARA 234): Agricultural Holdings Act 1986 s 3(3).

3 As to the meaning of 'agricultural holding' see PARA 423.

4 Any notice, request, demand or other instrument under the Agricultural Holdings Act 1986 is duly given to or served on the person to or on whom it is to be given or served if it is delivered to him or left at his proper address or sent in a registered letter or by recorded delivery: s 93(1). See *Grimes v Trustee of the Essex Farmers and Union Hunt* [2017] EWCA Civ 361 (no notice given where the landlord served notice at the address given in the contract but had been notified of a change of address). It is duly given to or served on an incorporated company or body if it is given to or served on the secretary or clerk: s 93(2). Where an agent or servant is responsible for the management or farming of the holding, service by or to (as the case may be) that servant or agent is due service: s 93(3). Where a tenant has not received notice of a change of landlord and of the name and address of the new landlord, he makes due service if he serves a notice on the original landlord: s 93(4). Unless or until the tenant of an agricultural holding has received notice that the person who before that time was entitled to receive the rents and profits of the holding (the 'original landlord') has ceased to be so entitled and notice of the name and address of the person who has become entitled to receive the rents and profits, any notice or other document served upon or delivered to the original landlord by the tenant is deemed for the purposes of the Agricultural Holdings Act 1986 to have been served upon or delivered to the landlord of the holding: s 93(5). Service on an erstwhile agent of the original but past landlord is not valid service under s 93(5): see *Lodgepower Ltd v Taylor* [2004] EWCA Civ 1367, [2005] 1 EGLR 1, [2005] 08 EG 192. The 'proper address' of any person is, in the case of the secretary or clerk of an incorporated body, the registered or principal office and, in any other case, the last known address of the person in question: Agricultural Holdings Act 1986 s 93(4). As to the meaning of 'landlord' see PARA 423 note 7. As to the meaning of 'tenant' see PARA 423 note 5.

5 Agricultural Holdings Act 1986 s 3(1)(a).

6 Agricultural Holdings Act 1986 ss 3(1)(b), 4(1). As to the death of a tenant see the text and notes 11–17.

7 Agricultural Holdings Act 1986 s 3(2). Thus s 26 (restriction on operation of notice to quit: see PARA 471) and s 60 (compensation for disturbance: see PARAS 544–545) will apply. As to notices to quit see PARAS 470–496.

8 As to the meaning of 'agreement' see PARA 425 note 1.

9 As to the Secretary of State and the Welsh Ministers see PARA 741.

10 Agricultural Holdings Act 1986 s 5. As to contracting out generally see *Johnson v Moreton* [1980] AC 37, [1978] 3 All ER 37, HL; *Featherstone v Staples* [1986] 2 All ER 461, [1986] 1 WLR 861, CA; *Elsden v Pick* [1980] 3 All ER 235, [1980] 1 WLR 898, CA; *Sparkes v Smart* [1990] 2 EGLR 245. There is no comparable provision in respect of the Agricultural Holdings Act 1986 s 2 (see PARA 427) but given the requirement that the exclusion of s 2 has to be approved by the Secretary of State or the Welsh Ministers, it is likely that it is not possible to contract out therefrom.

11 Ie the date on which the Agricultural Holdings Act 1948 s 3A (repealed), from which the Agricultural Holdings Act 1986 s 4 derives, came into force.

12 As to the term date see note 1.

13 Agricultural Holdings Act 1986 s 4(1), (2).

14 Agricultural Holdings Act 1986 s 4(2)(a).

15 Agricultural Holdings Act 1986 s 4(2)(b).

16 See the Agricultural Holdings Act 1986 s 60; and PARAS 544–545.

17 Agricultural Holdings Act 1986 s 4(3).

429. Sub-tenancies.

There is a power for the Lord Chancellor by order to make supplementary provision to extend the statutory provisions conferring security of tenure on tenants of agricultural holdings so as to protect agricultural sub-tenants against the head landlord should the head tenancy be determined[1].

Whilst the head tenancy endures the sub-tenant enjoys the same security of tenure and benefits and burdens of an agricultural holding as any other tenant; sub-tenants are not protected on the termination of the superior interest of the head tenant by the head landlord[2] even if the head tenant determines his own tenancy, for example by giving notice to quit or surrendering[3].

1 See the Agricultural Holdings Act 1986 s 29, Sch 4 paras 6, 7; and PARA 496. But at the date at which this volume states the law this power had not been exercised. As to the meaning of 'agricultural holding' see PARA 423.

2 *Mellor v Watkins* (1874) LR 9 QB 400; *Brown v Wilson* (1949) 208 LT 144.

3   See *Pennell v Payne* [1995] QB 192, [1995] 2 All ER 592 (overruling *Brown v Wilson* (1949) 208 LT 144). See also the Law of Property Act 1925 s 139; and LANDLORD AND TENANT vol 62 (2016) PARAS 529, 532. In *Barrett v Morgan* [2000] 2 AC 264, [2000] 1 All ER 481, HL, a sub-tenancy was determined when the head tenant did not serve a counter-notice after receipt of a notice to quit from the head landlord even though there had been an agreement by the head tenant with his landlord that no counter-notice would be served. Cf *Gisborne v Burton* [1989] QB 390, [1988] 3 All ER 760, CA, where the court gave protection to the sub-tenant because the sub-tenancy was a sham granted deliberately to avoid the security provisions of the Agricultural Holdings Act 1986.
     As to the service of notices see PARA 428 note 4.

(4) TERMS OF THE AGRICULTURAL TENANCY

(i) Agricultural Holdings Tenancy Agreement: Introduction

430. Right to a written tenancy agreement.
Where in respect of a tenancy of an agricultural holding[1] there is not in force a written agreement[2] embodying all the terms of the tenancy (including any model clauses)[3], or there is such an agreement but it does not make provision for one or more of the matters specified below[4], the landlord[5] or tenant[6] may refer the terms of the tenancy to arbitration or third party determination[7]; it is a condition precedent to such a referral that either party has requested the other to enter into an agreement in writing embodying all the terms of the tenancy and containing provision for all the said specified matters, but no such agreement has been reached[8].

The specified matters are:
(1)   the names of the parties[9];
(2)   particulars of the holding with sufficient description (by reference to a map or plan) of the fields and other parcels of land comprised in the holding to identify its extent[10];
(3)   the term or terms for which the holding or different parts of it is or are agreed to be let[11];
(4)   the rent reserved and the dates on which it is payable[12];
(5)   the incidence of liability for rates (including drainage rates)[13];
(6)   a covenant by the tenant in the event of the destruction by fire of harvested crops grown on the holding for consumption on it to return to the holding the full equivalent manurial value of the crops destroyed, in so far as the return of that value is required for the fulfilment of his responsibilities to farm in accordance with the rules of good husbandry[14];
(7)   a covenant by the tenant to insure against damage by fire all dead stock and harvested crops grown on the holding for consumption on it[15];
(8)   a power for the landlord to re-enter on the holding in the event of the tenant not performing his obligations under the agreement[16]; and
(9)   a covenant by the tenant not to assign, sub-let or part with possession of the holding or any part of it without the landlord's written consent[17].

The role of the arbitrator in his award or, as the case may be, the third party in his determination, is to specify the existing terms of the tenancy subject to any variations agreed between landlord and tenant[18]. In so far as these terms do not make provision for or are inconsistent with the matters specified in heads (1) to (9) above, the arbitrator or third party must include them in his award or determination in a way that appears to the arbitrator or the third party to be reasonable and just between landlord and tenant[19]. He may also include any further provision relating to the tenancy which has been agreed between landlord and tenant[20]. He may also vary the rent if it appears to him that it is equitable to do so by reason of any provision which he is required to include in his award or his determination[21].

Where the arbitrator or, as the case may be, the third party, makes an award or determination, that award or determination takes effect as if the terms and provisions specified therein were contained in a written agreement between landlord and tenant; it has effect as from the date of the award or determination or as from such later date as may be specified in it[22].

1   As to the meaning of 'agricultural holding' see PARA 423.
2   As to the meaning of 'agreement' see PARA 425 note 1. A tenancy of agricultural land may be created orally if it takes effect in possession for a term not exceeding three years and is at the best rent which can reasonably be obtained without taking a fine: see the Law of Property Act 1925 s 54(2); and LANDLORD AND TENANT vol 62 (2016) PARA 95. The fact that a tenancy may last longer than three years, as may, for example, a tenancy from year to year, does not make it a tenancy for a term exceeding three years: *Re Knight, ex p Voisey* (1882) 21 ChD 442, CA; *Kushner v Law Society* [1952] 1 KB 264 at 274, [1952] 1 All ER 404 at 407, DC, per Lord Goodard CJ.
3   Agricultural Holdings Act 1986 s 6(1)(a). As to the model clauses see s 7; and PARA 432.
4   Agricultural Holdings Act 1986 s 6(1)(b).
5   As to the meaning of 'landlord' see PARA 423 note 7.
6   As to the meaning of 'tenant' see PARA 423 note 5.
7   Where the landlord or tenant has the right under the Agricultural Holdings Act 1986 s 6(1) above to refer the terms of the tenancy to arbitration under that Act, the landlord and tenant may instead refer the terms of the tenancy for third party determination under that Act: s 6(1A) (added by the Deregulation Act 2015 Sch 4 para 3(2)). As to arbitration and third party determinations generally see PARA 568 et seq.
8   Agricultural Holdings Act 1986 s 6(1).
9   Agricultural Holdings Act 1986 Sch 1 para 1.
10   Agricultural Holdings Act 1986 Sch 1 para 2.
11   Agricultural Holdings Act 1986 Sch 1 para 3.
12   Agricultural Holdings Act 1986 Sch 1 para 4.
13   Agricultural Holdings Act 1986 Sch 1 para 5.
14   Agricultural Holdings Act 1986 Sch 1 para 6. The Agriculture Act 1947 ss 10, 11 (see AGRICULTURAL PRODUCTION AND MARKETING vol 1A (2017) PARAS 11–913) (which specify the circumstances in which an owner of agricultural land is deemed for the purposes of that Act to fulfil his responsibilities to manage the land in accordance with the rules of good estate management and an occupier of such land is deemed for those purposes to fulfil his responsibilities to farm it in accordance with the rules of good husbandry) apply for the purposes of the Agricultural Holdings Act 1986: s 96(3).
15   Agricultural Holdings Act 1986 Sch 1 para 7. This requirement does not apply where the interest of the tenant is held by a government department or where the tenant has made provision, approved by the Secretary of State or the Welsh Ministers, in lieu of such insurance: Sch 1 para 7. As to the Secretary of State and the Welsh Ministers see PARA 741.
16   Agricultural Holdings Act 1986 Sch 1 para 8. See also *Parry v Million Pigs Ltd* (1980) 260 Estates Gazette 281.
17   Agricultural Holdings Act 1986 Sch 1 para 9. If the terms of the tenancy neither make provision for, not make provision inconsistent with, the matter specified in Sch 1 para 9 and the landlord requests the tenant in writing to enter into an agreement in writing embodying all the terms of the tenancy, then the tenant may not, without the landlord's written consent, assign, sub-let or part with possession of the holding or any part of it during the period while the determiniation of the terms of the tenancy is pending (such period being the period beginning with the date of service of the landlord's request on the tenant and ending with the date on which an agreement is concluded in accordance with that request or (as the case may be) with the date on which the award of an arbitrator or the determination of a third party on a reference under s 6 relating to the tenancy takes effect), and any such transaction in those circumstances is void: s 6(5), (6) (s 6(6) amended by the Deregulation Act 2015 Sch 4 para 3(6)).

18 Agricultural Holdings Act 1986 s 6(2)(a) (amended by the Deregulation Act 2015 Sch 4 para 3(3)(a)).

19 Agricultural Holdings Act 1986 s 6(2)(b) (amended by the Deregulation Act 2015 Sch 4 para 3(3)(b)).

20 Agricultural Holdings Act 1986 s 6(2)(c).

21 Agricultural Holdings Act 1986 s 6(3) (amended by the Deregulation Act 2015 Sch 4 para 3(4)).

22 Agricultural Holdings Act 1986 s 6(4) (amended by the Deregulation Act 2015 Sch 4 para 3(5)).

431. Stipulation for additional rent or penalties.

It was once common in agricultural leases for the tenant to covenant not to do certain acts, with a stipulation that if he did them he would pay an additional rent, or a sum of money[1]. However, the Agricultural Holdings Act 1986 provides that notwithstanding any provision in a contract of tenancy[2] of an agricultural holding[3] making the tenant[4] liable to pay a higher rent or other liquidated damages in the event of any breach or non-fulfilment of a term or condition in the contract, a landlord[5] is not entitled to recover any sum in consequence of any breach or non-fulfilment of any such term or condition in excess of the damage actually suffered by him in consequence of the breach or non-fulfilment[6].

1 See eg *Legh v Lillie* (1860) 6 H & N 165, where there was a covenant not to remove manure except on payment of an increased rent. It was held not to be an answer to a breach of covenant that the tenant had brought on to the premises a quantity of manure larger and better in quality than that removed.

2 As to the meaning of 'contract of tenancy' see PARA 425.

3 As to the meaning of 'agricultural holding' see PARA 423.

4 As to the meaning of 'tenant' see PARA 423 note 5.

5 As to the meaning of 'landlord' see PARA 423 note 7.

6 Agricultural Holdings Act 1986 s 24 (amended by the Tribunals, Courts and Enforcement Act 2007 ss 86, 146, Sch 14 paras 41, 43, Sch 23 Pt 4).

(ii) Fixtures, Fittings and Buildings

432. The model clauses.

The Secretary of State and the Welsh Ministers[1] are both empowered, after consultation with bodies of persons as appear to them to represent the interests of landlords[2] and tenants[3] of agricultural holdings[4], to make regulations[5] prescribing terms as to the maintenance, repair and insurance of fixed equipment[6]; such terms are known as the 'model clauses'[7]. The model clauses are deemed to be incorporated in every contract of tenancy except in so far as they would impose on one of the parties to an agreement in writing a liability which under that agreement is imposed on the other[8]. If the terms of the written agreement release a party from an obligation to maintain, repair or insure under the model clauses without imposing the liability on the other party, the regulations, while being incorporated, are of no effect because the contractual terms prevail over the model clauses[9].

1 As to the Secretary of State and the Welsh Ministers see PARA 741.

2 As to the meaning of 'landlord' see PARA 423 note 7.

3 As to the meaning of 'tenant' see PARA 423 note 5.

4 As to the meaning of 'agricultural holding' see PARA 423.

5 The regulations may provide for the determination by arbitration or third party determination of any matter arising from them: Agricultural Holdings Act 1986 s 7(2) (amended by the Deregulation Act 2015 Sch 4 para 4). The regulations currently in force are the Agriculture (Maintenance, Repair and Insurance of Fixed Equipment) Regulations 1973, SI 1973/1473 (revoked in relation to England but not in relation to Wales) and the Agriculture (Model Clauses

for Fixed Equipment) (England) Regulations 2015, SI 2015/950 (which extend to England and Wales, but which apply in England only); and PARA 433.

Any power to make an order or regulations conferred by any provision of the Agricultural Holdings Act 1986 (except s 85 or s 86 (see PARAS 572–575)) is exercisable by statutory instrument: s 94(1).

6   'Fixed equipment' includes any building or structure affixed to land and any works on, in, over or under land, and also includes anything grown on land for a purpose other than use after severance from the land, consumption of the thing grown or of produce thereof, or amenity: Agricultural Holdings Act 1986 s 96(1). 'Building' includes any part of a building: s 96(1).
7   Agricultural Holdings Act 1986 s 7(1).
8   Agricultural Holdings Act 1986 s 7(3).
9   *Burden v Hannaford* [1956] 1 QB 142, [1955] 3 All ER 401, CA.

433. Obligations for maintenance, repair and insurance of fixed equipment.

Regulations provide for certain terms ('model clauses') as to the maintenance, repair and insurance of fixed equipment to be deemed incorporated in every contract of tenancy of an agricultural holding to which the Agricultural Holdings Act 1986 applies[1]. Responsibility for maintaining and repairing fixed equipment is divided between the landlord and the tenant[2]. Subject to a few exceptions, the landlord has a duty to insure against loss or damage by fire[3].

Provision is made for any matter arising under the regulations, in default of agreement, to be determined by arbitration or third party determination[4].

1   See the Agriculture (Model Clauses for Fixed Equipment) (England) Regulations 2015, SI 2015/950, reg 2(1). The Agriculture (Model Clauses for Fixed Equipment) (England) Regulations 2015, SI 2015/950 extend to England and Wales but apply in England only: reg 1(2). Similar provision is made in relation to Wales by the Agriculture (Maintenance, Repair and Insurance of Fixed Equipment) Regulations 1973, SI 1973/1473 (revoked in relation to England).
2   See the Agriculture (Model Clauses for Fixed Equipment) (England) Regulations 2015, SI 2015/950, Sch 1.
3   See the Agriculture (Model Clauses for Fixed Equipment) (England) Regulations 2015, SI 2015/950, Sch 2 para 2(1). As to landlords to whom this does not apply see reg 2(2).
4   See the Agriculture (Model Clauses for Fixed Equipment) (England) Regulations 2015, SI 2015/950, Sch 1, para 17. As to arbitration and third party determinations see PARA 566 et seq.

434. Variation of written agreement.

Where there is a written tenancy agreement which effects substantial modifications to the model clauses[1], the landlord[2] or the tenant[3] may refer the terms of the tenancy to arbitration or third party determination[4].

It is a condition precedent that the party seeking to vary the terms has previously requested the other party to vary the terms in order to bring them into conformity with the model clauses and no agreement has been reached[5]. On such a reference the arbitrator, or third party, must consider whether, disregarding the rent, the terms are justifiable having regard to the circumstances of the holding and of the landlord and tenant; if he determines that they are not so justifiable, he may vary them as appears just and reasonable between the parties[6]. He may vary the rent if it appears equitable to do so by reason of any provision included in his award or, as the case may be, his determination[7]. An award by the arbitrator or, as the case may be, the determination of a third party, has effect as if the terms and provisions contained in it were contained in a written agreement between the landlord and tenant; it takes effect from the date of the making of the award or determination or, if the award so provides, from such later date as may be specified in it[8].

1   As to the model clauses see PARA 432.
2   As to the meaning of 'landlord' see PARA 423 note 7.
3   As to the meaning of 'tenant' see PARA 423 note 5.

4 Agricultural Holdings Act 1986 s 8(1), (2), (2A) (s 8(2A) added by the Deregulation Act 2015 Sch 4 para 5(2)). As to arbitrations and third party determinations generally see PARA 566 et seq. Where there has been a reference to arbitration or third party determination under the Agricultural Holdings Act 1986 s 8 relating to a tenancy, no subsequent reference to arbitration relating to that tenancy may be made before the expiry of three years from the coming into effect of the award of the arbitrator or, as the case may be, the determination of the third party, on the previous reference: s 8(6) (amended by the Deregulation Act 2015 Sch 4 para 5(6)).
5 Agricultural Holdings Act 1986 s 8(2). As to the meaning of 'agreement' see PARA 425 note 1.
6 Agricultural Holdings Act 1986 s 8(3) (amended by the Deregulation Act 2015 Sch 4 para 5(3)).
7 Agricultural Holdings Act 1986 s 8(4) (amended by the Deregulation Act 2015 Sch 4 para 5(4)). See also the Agricultural Holdings Act 1986 Sch 2 para 4(1)(b), (2)(b), under which the general rule that a reference to arbitration may not be made in respect of an increase or reduction in rent within three years of a previous increase or reduction is excluded in relation to a variation of rent consequent upon an award concerning the model clauses under the provisions described above.
8 Agricultural Holdings Act 1986 s 8(5) (amended by the Deregulation Act 2015 Sch 4 para 5(5)).

435. Compensation and adjustment of rent on transfer of liability for fixed equipment.

Where liability for the maintenance or repair of any item of fixed equipment[1] is transferred from the tenant[2] to the landlord[3], whether by virtue of a written agreement made by an arbitrator or a third party[4] or of an award of an arbitrator or determination of a third party bringing a written agreement into accord with the regulations[5], or by virtue of the operation of the model clauses[6], the landlord may require determination by arbitration and payment by the tenant of the relevant compensation[7]. The landlord and tenant may instead refer for third party determination the question of the amount of any relevant compensation that the tenant is to be required to pay[8].

Where the transfer is from landlord to tenant, any claim by the tenant in respect of the landlord's previous failure to discharge the liability must, if the tenant so requires, be determined by arbitration or by third party determination[9]. In either case the application must be made within one month from the date on which the transfer of liability took effect[10]. Where the terms of a tenancy as to maintenance, repair or insurance of fixed equipment are varied by new regulations made in respect of the model clauses[11], and a reference is made to arbitration or for third party determination regarding a written tenancy agreement[12] within the prescribed period after the coming into force of the new regulations, the arbitrator or third party must disregard the variation for the purposes of the reference[13].

1 As to the meaning of 'fixed equipment' see PARA 432 note 6.
2 As to the meaning of 'tenant' see PARA 423 note 5.
3 As to the meaning of 'landlord' see PARA 423 note 7.
4 As to the securing of written tenancy agreements by reference to arbitration or third party determination see the Agricultural Holdings Act 1986 s 6; and PARA 430.
5 See the Agricultural Holdings Act 1986 s 8; and PARA 434. As to the meaning of 'agreement' see PARA 425 note 1.
6 As to the model clauses see the Agricultural Holdings Act 1986 s 7; and PARA 432.
7 Agricultural Holdings Act 1986 s 9(1). 'Relevant compensation' means compensation which would have been payable in respect of deterioration, dilapidation or damage under s 71 (whether recoverable as a statutory right or under a written contract of tenancy) (see PARAS 553–555), in respect of any previous failure by the tenant to discharge the liability transferred to the landlord under s 9(1), if the tenant had quitted the holding on the termination of his tenancy at the date of transfer: s 9(2) (amended by the Deregulation Act 2015 Sch 4 para 6(3)).
   Outstanding liabilities may be substantial (see *Payne v Haine* (1847) 16 M & W 541; *Proudfoot v Hart* (1890) 25 QBD 42, CA), but to some extent mitigated by the principle in *Evans v Jones* [1955] 2 QB 58, [1955] 2 All ER 118, CA, that in determining whether a tenant had complied with his obligation to repair or maintain any item, regard should be had to its age, character and condition at the beginning of the tenancy, and to the length of the tenancy.

8   Agricultural Holdings Act 1986 s 9(1A) (added by the Deregulation Act 2015 Sch 6 para 6(2)).
9   Agricultural Holdings Act 1986 s 9(3), (3A) (s 9(3A) added by the Deregulation Act 2015 Sch 4 para 6(4)). As to arbitrations and third party determinations generally see PARA 566 et seq.
10 Agriculture (Miscellaneous Time-Limits) Regulations 1959, SI 1959/171, reg 2(2), (3).
11 See PARA 432.
12 See PARA 430.
13 Agricultural Holdings Act 1986 s 9(4) (amended by the Deregulation Act 2015 Sch 4 para 6(5)). The 'prescribed period' for these purposes is a period prescribed on each occasion of the variation by the regulations. The regulations in question are the Agriculture (Model Clauses for Fixed Equipment) (England) Regulations 2015, SI 2015/950 and the Agriculture (Maintenance, Repair and Insurance of Fixed Equipment) Regulations 1973, SI 1973/1473 (see PARA 433).

436. Tenant's right to remove fixtures and buildings.

In general, any engine, machinery, fencing or other fixture affixed to an agricultural holding[1] by the tenant[2], whether for the purposes of agriculture[3] or not[4], and any building[5] erected by him on the holding[6], is removable by him at any time during the continuance of the tenancy or within two months after its termination[7], and remains his property so long as he is entitled to remove it[8]. This applies equally to fixtures and buildings acquired, rather than affixed or erected, by the tenant[9]. The right is exercisable only if the tenant has paid all the rent and has performed or satisfied all his other obligations to the landlord in respect of the holding[10] and at least one month before both the exercise of the right and the termination of the tenancy has given the landlord written notice of his intention to remove the fixture or building[11]. A tenant who removes a fixture without giving notice to the landlord of his intention to remove cannot afterwards claim for expenses or loss suffered through the removal as compensation for disturbance[12]. The landlord may give a counter-notice to the tenant electing to purchase the fixture or building, and in that case the landlord is liable to pay to the tenant the fair value of the fixture or building to an incoming tenant, and the right to remove the fixture or building is thereby extinguished[13]. In exercising a right of removal the tenant must not do any avoidable damage, and must immediately after the removal make good all damage so done which has been occasioned by the removal[14].

To the common law rule that whatever is affixed by the tenant to the freehold becomes the property of the owner of the freehold and cannot be severed by the tenant either during the continuance or after the determination of the term, exceptions have been admitted by the courts in respect of fixtures erected by a tenant for the purposes of mere ornament or convenience or for the purposes of trade[15]. The exception in favour of trade fixtures has not, however, been extended by the courts to fixtures erected for agricultural purposes[16], although it does apply to fixtures of certain trades with a strongly agricultural flavour, such as market gardens or the business of a nurseryman, for example greenhouses, cider mills and even trees and shrubs planted by a nurseryman for sale[17].

The right of an agricultural tenant to remove Dutch barns[18] and barns resting on the soil which have sunk into the soil by their own weight[19], or placed upon staddles[20], has been recognised on the ground that such structures are not fixtures, it being necessary to constitute a fixture that the soil should have been displaced for the purpose of receiving the article, or that the chattel should have been cemented or otherwise fastened to some fabric previously attached to the ground[21].

A market gardener or nurseryman has, however, been held to be entitled to remove greenhouses and hothouses erected for the purposes of his business[22], and shrubs and trees, or such as are likely to become trees, planted with a view to sale[23], but not orchard trees[24].

1   As to the meaning of 'agricultural holding' see PARA 423. Tenants of market gardens are given additional rights in respect of improvements: see the Agricultural Holdings Act 1986 ss 79–81; and PARA 561 et seq. Note the right to require a record to be made under s 22(1)(b): see PARA 446. As to the parties' ability to contract out see *Johnson v Moreton* [1980] AC 37, [1978] 3 All ER 37, HL; and PARA 428.
2   As to the meaning of 'tenant' see PARA 423 note 5.
3   As to the meaning of 'agriculture' see PARA 424.
4   Agricultural Holdings Act 1986 s 10(1)(a).
5   As to the meaning of 'building' see PARA 432 note 6.
6   Agricultural Holdings Act 1986 s 10(1)(b).
7   As to the termination of an agricultural tenancy see PARA 428 note 1.
8   Agricultural Holdings Act 1986 s 10(1). This provision does not apply to:
     (1)   a fixture or building affixed or erected in pursuance of some obligation (s 10(2)(a));
     (2)   a fixture or building affixed or erected instead of some fixture or building belonging to the landlord (s 10(2)(b));
     (3)   a building in respect of which the tenant is entitled to compensation (s 10(2)(c));
     (4)   a fixture or building affixed or erected before 1 January 1884 (s 10(2)(d)); or
     (5)   a fixture or building acquired by the tenant before 1 January 1901 (Sch 12 para 3).
   As to the meaning of 'landlord' see PARA 423 note 7. The dates mentioned above are the dates on which the Agricultural Holdings (England) Act 1883 and the Agricultural Holdings Act 1900, from which these provisions in part derive, were respectively brought into force.
9   Agricultural Holdings Act 1986 s 10(7). No right of removal that subsists otherwise than by virtue of s 10 is prejudiced by the operation thereof: s 10(8).
10 Agricultural Holdings Act 1986 s 10(3)(a).
11 Agricultural Holdings Act 1986 s 10(3)(b). As to the service of notices see PARA 428 note 4.
12 *Re Harvey and Mann* (1920) 89 LJKB 687, CA.
13 Agricultural Holdings Act 1986 s 10(4). Any dispute as to the amount payable by the landlord in this case may be determined by arbitration: s 10(6). But, notwithstanding s 10(6), the landlord and tenant may instead refer for third party determination under the Agricultural Holdings Act 1986 the dispute that has arisen with respect to the amount payable by the landlord under s 10(4): s 10(6A) (added by the Deregulation Act 2015 Sch 4 para 7). As to arbitrations and third party determinations generally see PARA 566 et seq.
14 Agricultural Holdings Act 1986 s 10(5).
15 See further LANDLORD AND TENANT vol 62 (2016) PARA 174.
16 *Elwes v Maw* (1802) 3 East 38.
17 *Penton v Robart* (1801) 2 East 88; *Oakley v Monck* (1866) LR 1 Exch 159; *Mears v Callender* [1901] 2 Ch 388; *Wardell v Usher* (1841) 3 Scott NR 508.
18 *Dean v Allalley* (1799) 3 Esp 11.
19 *Culling v Tufnal* (1694) Bull NP (5th Edn) 34; *Wansbrough v Maton* (1836) 4 Ad & El 884.
20 *Wiltshear v Cottrell* (1853) 1 E & B 674.
21 *Turner v Cameron* (1870) LR 5 QB 306 at 311. The traditional distinction between chattels and fixtures is re-stated in *Elitestone Ltd v Morris* [1997] 2 All ER 513, [1997] 1 WLR 687, HL.
22 *Penton v Robart* (1801) 2 East 88; *Mears v Callender* [1901] 2 Ch 388.
23 *Penton v Robart* (1801) 2 East 88; *Oakley v Monck* (1866) LR 1 Exch 159.
24 *Mears v Callender* [1901] 2 Ch 388.

437. Provision of fixed equipment.

If the Tribunal[1] is satisfied, on the application by the tenant[2] of an agricultural holding[3], as to the matters mentioned below, it may direct the landlord[4] to carry out, within a period specified in the direction, such work for the provision, alteration or repair of fixed equipment[5] as will enable the tenant to comply with requirements imposed by or under any enactment[6].

Before making such a direction the Tribunal must be satisfied that it is reasonable, having regard to the tenant's responsibilities to farm in accordance with the rules of good husbandry[7], that the tenant should carry on on the holding an agricultural[8] activity specified in his application to the extent and in the manner so specified and:

(1)   that, unless fixed equipment is provided on the holding, the tenant in so carrying out that activity will contravene requirements imposed by or under any enactment[9]; or

(2)   that it is reasonable that he should use, for purposes connected with that activity, fixed equipment already provided on the holding, but that, unless that equipment is altered or repaired, he would, in using it for those purposes, contravene those requirements[10].

Where, however, it appears to the Tribunal that an agricultural activity specified in the tenant's application has not been carried on on the holding for a period of at least three years immediately preceding the making of the application, it must not direct the landlord to carry out work in connection with that activity unless it is satisfied that the starting of the activity did not, or, if it has not already been started, will not, constitute or form part of a substantial alteration of the type of farming carried on on the holding[11]. Further, the Tribunal must not so direct the landlord to carry out work unless it is satisfied that it is reasonable to do so having regard to:

(a)   the landlord's responsibilities to manage the land in accordance with the rules of good estate management[12];

(b)   the period for which the holding may be expected to remain separate[13]; and

(c)   any other material consideration[14],

and that the landlord has refused to carry out the work on the tenant's written request or has not agreed to carry it out within a reasonable time after that request[15].

The Tribunal must not in any case make a direction if the contract of tenancy[16] or any other agreement between the landlord and tenant provides for the carrying out of the work by the landlord or tenant, or if the landlord must carry it out in order to comply with a requirement imposed on him by or under any enactment[17]. On a failure by the landlord to comply with the Tribunal's direction, the tenant has the same remedies as if the contract of tenancy had contained an undertaking by the landlord to carry out the work directed within the period specified[18], and notwithstanding any term in the contract of tenancy restricting the carrying out of alterations by the tenant, those remedies include the right to carry out the work himself and recover the reasonable cost from the landlord[19]. The Tribunal may, on the landlord's application, extend or further extend the time for compliance with a direction, if satisfied that such an extension is required to allow sufficient time both for the completion of any necessary or desirable preliminary arrangements (including the determination of any application by the landlord for a grant in respect of the work) and for the carrying out of the work[20]. The landlord may obtain an increase of rent in respect of an improvement carried out in compliance with a direction of the tribunal as if it were carried out at the request of the tenant[21].

1   'The Tribunal' means, where the agricultural holding (or the greater part of the holding) is in England, the First-tier Tribunal and, where the agricultural holding (or the greater part of the holding) is in Wales, the Agricultural Land Tribunal for Wales (see the Agriculture Act 1947 s 73): Agricultural Holdings Act 1986 s 96(1) (definition substituted by SI 2013/1036). As to the First-tier Tribunal and the Agricultural Land Tribuna for Wales see PARAS 767–768.

2   As to the meaning of 'tenant' see PARA 423 note 5.

3   As to the meaning of 'agricultural holding' see PARA 423.

4   As to the meaning of 'landlord' see PARA 423 note 7.
5   As to the meaning of 'fixed equipment' see PARA 432 note 6.
6   Agricultural Holdings Act 1986 s 11(1).
7   As to the rules of good husbandry for the purposes of the Agricultural Holdings Act 1986 see, by virtue of s 96(3) (see PARA 430 note 14), the Agriculture Act 1947 ss 10, 11; and AGRICULTURAL PRODUCTION AND MARKETING vol 1A (2017) PARAS 11–13.
8   As to the meaning of 'agricultural' see PARA 424.
9   Agricultural Holdings Act 1986 s 11(1)(a).
10 Agricultural Holdings Act 1986 s 11(1)(b).
11 Agricultural Holdings Act 1986 s 11(2).
12 Agricultural Holdings Act 1986 s 11(3)(a). As to the rules of good estate management see AGRICULTURAL PRODUCTION AND MARKETING vol 1A (2017) PARAS 11–13.
13 Agricultural Holdings Act 1986 s 11(3)(a).
14 Agricultural Holdings Act 1986 s 11(3)(a).
15 Agricultural Holdings Act 1986 s 11(3)(b).
16 As to the meaning of 'contract of tenancy' see PARA 425.
17 Agricultural Holdings Act 1986 s 11(4).
18 Agricultural Holdings Act 1986 s 11(5).
19 Agricultural Holdings Act 1986 s 11(6). If the tenant receives any grant out of money provided by Parliament in respect of the work, the reasonable cost is reduced by the amount of the grant: s 11(8).
20 Agricultural Holdings Act 1986 s 11(7).
21 See the Agricultural Holdings Act 1986 s 13; and PARA 440.

(iii) Determination of Rent

438. Arbitration or third party determination of rent.

The landlord[1] or tenant[2] of an agricultural holding[3] may by notice in writing served on the other party[4] demand that the rent to be payable for the holding as from the next termination date[5] should be referred to arbitration[6] or third party determination[7]. On a reference the arbitrator or third party must determine what rent should be properly payable in respect of the holding at the next termination date following the date of the demand for arbitration, or as the case may be, for third party determination, and accordingly must, with effect from that next termination date, increase or reduce the rent previously payable or direct that it continue unchanged[8].

A demand for arbitration ceases to be effective on the next termination date following the date of the demand unless before that termination date an arbitrator has been appointed by agreement between the parties[9] or an application has been made to the President of the Royal Institution of Chartered Surveyors[10] for the appointment of an arbitrator by him[11].

For the purpose of such a reference the rent properly payable is that at which, having regard to the terms of the tenancy other than those relating to rent, the holding might reasonably be expected to be let by a prudent and willing landlord to a prudent and willing tenant, taking into account all relevant factors[12], including the terms of the tenancy (including those relating to rent), the character and situation of the holding (including the locality in which it is situated), the productive capacity[13] of the holding and its related earning capacity[14] and the current level of rents for comparable lettings[15]. The rent must be assessed for the holding and such assessment is not restricted to the rent referable to pure agricultural activity[16]. On such a reference the arbitrator, or as the case may be, the third party, must disregard any effect on the rent of the fact that the tenant who is a party to the arbitration or third party determination is in occupation of the holding[17] and any increase in the rental value of the holding which is due to tenant's improvements[18] or fixed equipment[19] other than those executed or provided under an obligation imposed on the tenant by the terms of his contract of tenancy[20]. The arbitrator or, as the case may be, the third party must also disregard any increase in rental value due to improvements executed by the landlord, in so far as the landlord has received or will receive grants out of money provided by Parliament or local government funds[21] in respect thereof[22]. In certain cases, the arbitrator or, as the case may be, the third party must also disregard any increase in the rental value of land which comprises or is part of a holding to which a dairy produce quota is transferred[23]. The arbitrator or, as the case may be, the third party must not fix the rent at a lower amount by reason of any dilapidation or deterioration of, or damage to, buildings or land caused or permitted by the tenant[24].

1   As to the meaning of 'landlord' see PARA 423 note 7. A landlord may serve a notice under these provisions without prejudice to his separate claim that no tenancy actually exists: see *Grammer v Lane* [2000] 2 All ER 245, [2000] 1 EGLR 1, CA.
2   As to the meaning of 'tenant' see PARA 423 note 5.
3   As to the meaning of 'agricultural holding' see PARA 423.
4   As to the service of notices see PARA 428 note 4.
5   The 'next termination date' following the date of the demand or reference is the next day following the date of the demand or reference on which the tenancy of the holding could be determined by notice to quit given at the date of the demand or reference: Agricultural Holdings Act 1986 s 12(4) (amended by the Deregulation Act 2015 Sch 4 para 8(4)).
6   Agricultural Holdings Act 1986 s 12(1). The demand must be worded to accord with this provision: *White v Morley* [1932] EGD 166. As to the determination of claims on termination of tenancy generally see PARA 566 et seq.
7   Agricultural Holdings Act 1986 s 12(1A) (added by the Deregulation Act 2015 Sch 4 para 8(2)).
8   Agricultural Holdings Act 1986 s 12(2) (amended by SI 2006/2805 and the Deregulation Act 2015 Sch 4 para 8(3)). As to the circumstances in which increases in rent may be made on account of improvements see PARA 440. See also *University College, Oxford v Durdy* [1982] Ch 413, [1982] 1 All ER 1108, CA (date of reference to arbitration was date of arbitrator's appointment).
9   Agricultural Holdings Act 1986 s 12(3)(a). As to when an application is deemed to have been made on time see *Thompson v Bradley* (30 November 2006, unreported).
10 As to the Royal Institution of Chartered Surveyors generally see BUILDING CONTRACTS vol 6 (2011) PARA 490.
11 Agricultural Holdings Act 1986 s 12(3)(b). There is no such provision in relation to references for third party determination.
12 Relevant factors include 'marriage value' in relation to the subject holding: *JW Childers Trustees v Anker* (1995) 73 P & CR 458, [1996] 1 EGLR 1, CA.
13 The 'productive capacity' of a holding means the productive capacity of the holding, taking into account fixtures and other available facilities, on the assumption that it is in the occupation of a competent tenant practising a system of farming which is suitable to the holding: Agricultural Holdings Act 1986 s 12(5), Sch 2 para 1(2)(a).
14 'Related earning capacity' means the extent to which, in the light of the productive capacity of a holding (see note 13), a competent tenant practising a suitable system of farming could reasonably be expected to profit from farming the holding: Agricultural Holdings Act 1986 Sch 2 para 1(2)(b).
15 Agricultural Holdings Act 1986 Sch 2 para 1(1). In determining the current level of rents for comparable lettings the arbitrator, or, as the case may be, the third party, must take into account any available evidence as to rents which are, or in the case of rents currently being tendered are likely to become, payable in respect of tenancies of comparable agricultural holdings similar to those of the tenancy under consideration, but must disregard:
    (1)   any element of the rents compared which is due to an appreciable scarcity of comparable holdings (see *99 Bishopsgate Ltd v Prudential Assurance Co Ltd* (1984) 270 Estates Gazette 950, [1985] 1 EGLR 72, 273 Estates Gazette 984, CA (Agricultural Holdings Act 1986 Sch 2 para 1(3)(a));
    (2)   any element which is due to the fact that the tenant of, or a person tendering for, any comparable holding, occupies land in the vicinity of the holding which may conveniently be occupied together with that holding (Sch 2 para 1(3)(b)); and
    (3)   any effect on the rents due to any allowances or reductions made in consideration of the charging of premiums (Sch 2 para 1(3)(c)).

16 See *Tummon v Barclays Bank Trust Co Ltd* (1979) 39 P & CR 300, 250 Estates Gazette 980.
17 Agricultural Holdings Act 1986 Sch 2 para 3(a) (amended by the Deregulation Act 2015 Sch 4 para 25(3), (4)).
18 For these purposes 'tenant's improvements' are improvements executed wholly or partly at the expense of the tenant (whether or not such expense has been or will be reimbursed by a grant out of money provided by Parliament or local government funds), if the landlord has given no equivalent allowance or benefit in consideration of their execution: Agricultural Holdings Act 1986 Sch 2 para 2(2)(a). The continuous adoption by a tenant of a system of farming which is more beneficial to the holding than the system required by the contract of tenancy or, where there is no such requirement, than the system normally practised on comparable holdings, is deemed for this purpose to be an improvement executed at the tenant's expense: Sch 2 para 2(4).
19 As to the meaning of 'fixed equipment' see PARA 432 note 6.
20 Agricultural Holdings Act 1986 Sch 2 para 2(1)(a) (amended by the Deregulation Act 2015 Sch 4 para 25(3)). As to the meaning of 'contract of tenancy' see PARA 425.
21 'Local government funds' means, in relation to any grant in respect of an improvement executed by the landlord or tenant of an agricultural holding, the funds of any body which, under or by virtue of any enactment, has power to make grants in respect of improvements of the description in question within any particular area (whether or not it is a local authority for that area): Agricultural Holdings Act 1986 s 96(1).
22 Agricultural Holdings Act 1986 Sch 2 para 2(1)(b) (as amended: see note 20).
23 Where there is a reference under the Agricultural Holdings Act 1986 s 12 in respect of land which comprises or is part of a holding in relation to which quota is registered under the Dairy Produce Quotas Regulations 2005, SI 2005/465 (see AGRICULTURAL PRODUCTION AND MARKETING vol 1A (2017) PARA 6 et seq) which was transferred to the tenant by virtue of a transaction the cost of which was borne wholly or partly by him, the arbitrator must (subject to any agreement between the landlord and tenant to the contrary) disregard:
    (1)   in a case where the land comprises the holding, any increase in the rental value of the land which is due to that quota (or, as the case may be, the corresponding part of that quota) (Agriculture Act 1986 s 15(1)(a)); or
    (2)   in a case where the land is part of the holding, any increase in that value which is due to so much of that quota (or part) as would fall to be apportioned to the land under the Dairy Produce Quotas Regulations 2005, SI 2005/465 on a change of occupation of the land (Agriculture Act 1986 s 15(1)(b)).
In determining for these purposes whether quota was transferred to a tenant by virtue of a transaction the cost of which was borne wholly or partly by him:
    (a)   any payment made by the tenant in consideration for the grant or assignment to him of the tenancy, or any previous tenancy of any land comprised in the holding, must be disregarded (s 15(2)(a));
    (b)   any person who would be treated under Sch 1 para 2, 3 or 4 (see AGRICULTURAL PRODUCTION AND MARKETING vol 1A (2017) PARA 6) as having had quota transferred to him or having paid the whole or part of the cost of any transaction for the purposes of a claim under Sch 1 must be so treated for these purposes (s 15(2)(b)); and
    (c)   any person who would be so treated under Sch 1 para 4, if a sub-tenancy to which his tenancy is subject had terminated, must be so treated for these purposes (s 15(2)(c)).
As to the meaning of 'tenant' see PARA 423 note 5 (definitions applied by s 15(3)). The Agricultural Holdings Act 1986 s 95 (Crown land: see PARA 581) applies to these provisions as it applies to the provisions of the Agricultural Holdings Act 1986: Agriculture Act 1986 s 15(4).
24 Agricultural Holdings Act 1986 Sch 2 para 3(b) (amended by the Deregulation Act 2015 Sch 4 para 25(4)(a)).

439. Frequency of arbitrations.

Arbitration[1] may not be sought if the next termination date[2] following the date of the demand falls earlier than the end of three years after the commencement of the tenancy[3], the date as from which there took effect a previous increase or reduction of rent[4], or the date as from which there took effect a previous direction of an arbitrator or third party[5] that the rent should continue unchanged[6]. For this purpose, there must be disregarded:

(1)   any increase in rent awarded by an arbitrator or determined by a third party on the drawing up of a written agreement[7] or on an award or determination concerning modifications to the model clauses[8];

(2)   any increase in rent attributable to the landlord's[9] improvements[10], or any reduction of rent agreed between the landlord and tenant in consequence of any change in the fixed equipment[11] provided by the landlord[12]; and

(3)   any reduction of rent on the giving of notice to quit part of a holding[13].

Where the reversionary interest upon the termination[14] of the tenancy has been severed and the rent has been apportioned, the old tenancy is deemed to continue for the purpose of determining the frequency of arbitration or third party determination[15]. If the parties agree to adjust the boundaries of the holding[16] or vary any other terms of the tenancy apart from rent, then unless the parties agree to the contrary this will not result in a new contract of tenancy[17] and any consequent variation in rent is also to be disregarded in determining the frequency of arbitration or third party determination[18].

1   As to arbitrations generally see PARA 566 et seq.
2   As to the meaning of 'next termination date' see PARA 438 note 5.
3   Agricultural Holdings Act 1986 Sch 2 para 4(1)(a). As to termination and regrant see *Jenkin R Lewis & Son Ltd v Kerman* [1971] Ch 477, [1970] 1 All ER 833; on appeal [1971] Ch 477, [1970] 3 All ER 414, CA.
    If:
    (1)   a tenancy of an agricultural holding (the 'new tenancy') is granted to a person who, immediately before the grant of the new tenancy, was the tenant of the holding, or of any agricultural holding which comprised the whole or a substantial part of the land comprised in the holding (ie as determined by reference to either area or value), under a contract of tenancy (the 'previous tenancy') (Agricultural Holdings Act 1986 Sch 2 para 7(1)(a), (2) (Sch 2 para 7 added by SI 2006/2805));
    (2)   the Agricultural Holdings Act 1986 applies in relation to the new tenancy by virtue of the Agricultural Tenancies Act 1995 s 4(1)(g) (see PARAS 401, 421) (Agricultural Holdings Act 1986 Sch 2 para 7(1)(b) (as so added)); and
    (3)   the rent payable under the new tenancy is unchanged from that payable under the previous tenancy, disregarding any increase or reduction in rent solely attributable to an adjustment of the boundaries of the holding (Sch 2 para 7(1)(c) (as so added)),
   the reference in Sch 2 para 4(1)(a) to the commencement of the tenancy is read as referring to the commencement of the previous tenancy until the first occasion following the commencement of the new tenancy on which any such increase or reduction of, or direction with respect to, the rent payable under the new tenancy as is mentioned in Sch 2 para 4(1)(b), (c) (see the text and notes 4–6) takes effect (Sch 2 para 7(3) (as so added)). As to the meaning of 'agricultural holding' see PARA 423. As to the meaning of 'tenant' see PARA 423 note 5. As to the meaning of 'contract of tenancy' see PARA 425.
4   Agricultural Holdings Act 1986 Sch 2 para 4(1)(b). This applies whether or not such increase or reduction was made under s 12 (see PARA 438). In the circumstances set out in note 3 heads (1)–(3), references to 'rent' in Sch 2 para 4(1)(b) and Sch 2 para 4(1)(c) (see the text and note 6) must be read as references to the rent payable under the previous tenancy until the first occasion following the commencement of the new tenancy on which any such increase or reduction of, or direction with respect to, the rent payable under the new tenancy as is mentioned in Sch 2 para 4(1)(b), (c) takes effect: Sch 2 para 7(3) (as added: see note 3).
5   Ie under the Agricultural Holdings Act 1986 s 12 (see PARA 438).
6   Agricultural Holdings Act 1986 Sch 2 para 4(1)(c) (amended by the Deregulation Act 2015 Sch 4 para 25(5)). See note 4.
7   Ie under the Agricultural Holdings Act 1986 s 6(3) (see PARA 430).
8   Agricultural Holdings Act 1986 Sch 2 para 4(2)(a). References concerning modifications to the model clauses are made under s 8(4) (see PARA 434).
9   As to the meaning of 'landlord' see PARA 423 note 7.
10 Ie under the Agricultural Holdings Act 1986 s 13(1), (3) (see PARA 440).
11 As to the meaning of 'fixed equipment' see PARA 432 note 6.

12 Agricultural Holdings Act 1986 Sch 2 para 4(2)(b). The surrender of part of a holding which consists wholly or solely of a building or structure fixed to the land does not amount to a 'change in the fixed equipment provided by the landlord', and such surrender was therefore not disregarded in *Mann v Gardner* (1990) 61 P & CR 1, [1991] 1 EGLR 9, CA (demand for arbitration was ineffective where it was based on such surrender less than three years before the demand). This decision was held to be per incuriam in *Secretary of State for Defence v Spencer* [2002] EWHC 2116 (Ch), [2003] 1 WLR 75 (surrender or addition of land amounts to a variation of other terms of the tenancy (see the text and note 16)).

13 Agricultural Holdings Act 1986 Sch 2 para 4(2)(c). As to the reduction in rent on the giving of notice to quit part of a holding see s 33; and PARA 494.

14 As to the termination of an agricultural tenancy see PARA 428 note 1.

15 See the Agricultural Holdings Act 1986 Sch 2 para 5; and *Jelley v Buckman* [1974] QB 488, [1973] 3 All ER 853, CA. See also the Law of Property Act 1925 s 140 (see PARA 495; and LANDLORD AND TENANT vol 62 (2016) PARA 446); and *Stiles v Farrow* (1977) 241 Estates Gazette 623.

16 Adjustments of boundaries must be distinguished from surrender and regrant: *Jenkin R Lewis & Son Ltd v Kerman* [1971] Ch 477, [1970] 1 All ER 833; on appeal [1971] Ch 477, [1970] 3 All ER 414, CA. An addition (or surrender) of land may be treated as a variation of 'other terms of the tenancy': *Secretary of State for Defence v Spencer* [2002] EWHC 2116 (Ch), [2003] 1 WLR 75.

17 Agricultural Holdings Act 1986 Sch 2 para 6(a).

18 Agricultural Holdings Act 1986 Sch 2 para 6(b).

440. Variation of rent for improvements.

In certain circumstances a landlord[1] may charge an increased rent if he has carried out an improvement[2], and the question whether compensation is provided for the improvement[3] under the Agricultural Holdings Act 1986 is immaterial[4]. This right arises in the case of the following improvements[5]:

(1)   an improvement carried out at the request of, or in agreement with, the tenant[6];

(2)   an improvement carried out in compliance with a direction of the Tribunal[7] to provide, alter or repair fixed equipment[8];

(3)   a long term improvement carried out by the landlord after the Tribunal has given its consent thereto[9] on an application by the tenant[10]; and

(4)   an improvement made in compliance with a direction given by the Secretary of State or the Welsh Ministers[11] under powers conferred by or under any enactment[12].

The landlord must serve notice[13] of increase on the tenant within six months of the completion of the improvement and the increase can be charged from the date of the completion of the improvement[14]. The rent may be increased by an amount equal to the increase in the rental value of the holding attributable to the carrying out of the improvement[15], except where a grant has been made to the landlord in respect of the improvement out of money provided by Parliament or local government funds[16], in which case the increase in rent is to be reduced proportionately[17]. No increase of rent may be made in respect of any improvement under heads (1) and (2) above if within six months from its completion the landlord and tenant agree on any increase of rent or other benefit to the landlord in respect of the improvement[18].

Disputes as to rent increases in respect of landlord's improvements must be determined by arbitration or third party determination[19].

Where work has been carried out by the tenant on the failure of the landlord to comply with a direction of the kind mentioned in head (2) above, the work is treated, for the purposes of these provisions, as if carried out by the landlord and as if any grant made to the tenant in respect thereof out of money provided by

Parliament had been made to the landlord[20]; but no increase may take effect until the tenant has recovered the reasonable cost of the work from the landlord[21].

1   As to the meaning of 'landlord' see PARA 423 note 7.
2   See the Agricultural Holdings Act 1986 s 13(1); and the text and notes 3–21.
3   Ie under the Agricultural Holdings Act 1986 Pt V (ss 60–78) or Pt VI (ss 79–82).
4   Agricultural Holdings Act 1986 s 13(8).
5   As to the application of the Agricultural Holdings Act 1986 s 13 to opencast coal operations see the Opencast Coal Act 1958 s 14; and MINES, MINERALS AND QUARRIES vol 76 (2013) PARA 419.
6   Agricultural Holdings Act 1986 s 13(2)(a). As to the meaning of 'tenant' see PARA 423 note 5.
7   Ie in England, the First-tier Tribunal (see PARA 768) and in Wales, the Agricultural Land Tribunal for Wales (see PARA 767): see PARA 437 note 1.
8   Agricultural Holdings Act 1986 s 13(2)(b). As to the meaning of 'fixed equipment' see PARA 432 note 6. As to the power of the tribunal to give such a direction, and for the position where the tenant carries out work in default of compliance by the landlord, see s 11; and PARA 437.
9   Ie under the Agricultural Holdings Act 1986 s 67(5) (see PARA 536).
10 Agricultural Holdings Act 1986 s 13(2)(c).
11 As to the Secretary of State and the Welsh Ministers see PARA 741.
12 Agricultural Holdings Act 1986 s 13(2)(d).
13 As to the service of notices see PARA 428 note 4.
14 Agricultural Holdings Act 1986 s 13(1).
15 Agricultural Holdings Act 1986 s 13(1).
16 As to the meaning of 'local government funds' see PARA 438 note 21.
17 Agricultural Holdings Act 1986 s 13(4)(a), (b). The reference in the text to money provided out of local government funds does not apply in relation to improvements under head (2) in the text: s 13(4)(a).
18 Agricultural Holdings Act 1986 s 13(3). As to arbitrations and third party determinations generally see PARA 566 et seq.
19 Agricultural Holdings Act 1986 s 13(7), (7A) (s 13(7A) added by the Deregulation Act 2015 Sch 4 para 9).
20 Agricultural Holdings Act 1986 s 13(5).
21 Agricultural Holdings Act 1986 s 13(6). As to compensation for improvements generally see PARA 522 et seq.

(iv) Cultivation of Land and Disposal of Produce

441. Variation of terms as to permanent pasture.
Where a contract of tenancy[1] provides for the maintenance of specified land, or a specified proportion of the holding, as permanent pasture[2] the landlord[3] or the tenant[4] may by written notice served on the other party demand a reference to arbitration or third party determination[5] of the question whether it is expedient in order to secure the full and efficient farming[6] of the holding that the area of land required to be maintained as permanent pasture should be reduced[7]. The arbitrator or third party may by his award or, as the case may be, his determination, direct that the provisions in the contract as to land which is to be maintained as permanent pasture or is to be treated as arable land, and as to cropping, have effect subject to such modifications as may be specified in the direction[8]. If the arbitrator or third party gives a direction reducing the area of land under the contract of tenancy to be maintained as permanent pasture, he may order that the contract of tenancy is to have effect as if it provided that, on quitting the holding on the termination of the tenancy[9], the tenant should leave such area of land as may be specified in the order as permanent pasture[10], or as temporary pasture sown with a seeds mixture of such a kind as may be so specified[11], in addition to the area of land required to be maintained as permanent pasture by the contract of tenancy (as modified by the direction)[12]. The area of land so required to be left must not, however, exceed the area by which the

permanent pasture required to be maintained under the contract has been reduced[13]. No compensation is payable in respect of anything done in pursuance of such an order[14], and where the landlord and tenant agree to a variation of the terms of the tenancy such as could have been made by a direction or order as described above, they may also in that agreement agree to the exclusion of compensation[15].

1   As to the meaning of 'contract of tenancy' see PARA 425.
2   'Pasture' includes meadow: s 96(1). As to what constitutes permanent pasture see PARA 442.
3   As to the meaning of 'landlord' see PARA 423 note 7.
4   As to the meaning of 'tenant' see PARA 423 note 5.
5   As to arbitrations and third party determinations generally see PARA 566 et seq.
6   As to the 'farming' of land see PARA 424.
7   Agricultural Holdings Act 1986 s 14(1), (2), (2A) (s 14(2A) added by the Deregulation Act 2015 Sch 4 para 10(2)). As to the service of notices see PARA 428 note 4.
8   Agricultural Holdings Act 1986 s 14(3) (amended by the Deregulation Act 2015 Sch 4 para 10(3)).
9   As to the termination of an agricultural tenancy see PARA 428 note 1.
10 Agricultural Holdings Act 1986 s 14(4)(a).
11 Agricultural Holdings Act 1986 s 14(4)(b).
12 Agricultural Holdings Act 1986 s 14(4) (amended by the Deregulation Act 2015 Sch 4 para 10(4)).
13 Agricultural Holdings Act 1986 s 14(5).
14 Agricultural Holdings Act 1986 s 76(1)(a).
15 Agricultural Holdings Act 1986 s 78(2).

442.   What constitutes permanent pasture.

Sowing clover with the spring corn does not constitute laying down land in permanent pasture[1], nor does merely sowing common grass seed make land old meadow again[2].

It has been stated that continuance in pasture for 20 years impresses on the land the character of ancient meadow or pasture[3]; and land that has formerly been ploughed may after a sufficient lapse of time become ancient pasture which a tenant will be restrained from ploughing[4].

In regard, however, to modern tenancies, it will often be a question of the construction of the relevant terms of the contract of tenancy whether or not land which is arable at the commencement of the tenancy and is subsequently laid down to grass by the tenant becomes 'pasture land' or 'grass land', the ploughing of which may be restrained by injunction[5].

1   *Birch v Stephenson* (1811) 3 Taunt 469.
2   *Simmons v Norton* (1831) 7 Bing 640.
3   *Morris v Morris* (1825) 1 Hog 238.
4   *Fermier v Maund* (1638) 1 Rep Ch 116.
5   *Rush v Lucas* [1910] 1 Ch 437; *Clarke-Jervoise v Scutt* [1920] 1 Ch 382.

443.   Restriction on ploughing up.

Ploughing up meadow land is prima facie waste, and will be restrained even though there is no express covenant in the lease against it[1]; but if the ploughing is done for the purpose of ameliorating the meadow, and does in fact ameliorate it, the act may be justified[2]. The restriction on ploughing ancient pasture is the same as on meadow[3]. So far as tenancies governed by the Agricultural Holdings Act 1986 are concerned, the statutory right of freedom of cropping extends only to arable land[4].

1   *Drury v Molins* (1801) 6 Ves 328; *Martin v Coggan* (1824) 1 Hog 120; *Simmons v Norton* (1831) 7 Bing 640.
2   *Simmons v Norton* (1831) 7 Bing 640. See also *Altman's Case* (1577) 3 Dyer 361b (digging drainage ditch to improve field was not waste).

3 *Atkins v Temple* (1625) 1 Rep Ch 13.
4 See the Agricultural Holdings Act 1986 s 15(1); and PARA 444. 'Arable land' in that provision does not include land in grass which, by the terms of a contract of tenancy, is to be retained in the same condition throughout the tenancy: s 15(7).

444. Disposal of produce and cropping.

Notwithstanding any custom of the country[1] or the provisions of any contract of tenancy[2] or agreement respecting the method of cropping arable land[3] or the disposal of crops, a tenant[4] of an agricultural holding[5] may dispose of the produce of his holding, other than manure produced thereon[6], and may practise any system of cropping of the arable land on his holding[7]; he may exercise these rights without incurring any penalty, forfeiture or liability[8]. He must, however, before exercising such right, or as soon as possible thereafter, make suitable and adequate provision to return to the holding the full equivalent manurial value of all crops sold off or removed in contravention of the custom, contract or agreement[9], and, in the case of a system of cropping, to protect the holding from injury or deterioration[10].

In the case of a tenancy from year to year these provisions have no application[11] as respects the year before the tenant quits the holding, or any period after he has given or received notice to quit which results in his quitting the holding[12], or, in the case of any other tenancy, as respects the year before the termination thereof[13].

These provisions do not apply to a tenancy of land let as a smallholding by a smallholdings authority[14] or by the Secretary of State or the Welsh Ministers[15] in pursuance of a scheme approved by the Secretary of State or the Welsh Ministers for these purposes which provides for the farming of such holdings on a co-operative basis[16] or for the disposal of the produce of such holdings[17] or provides other centralised services for the tenants of such holdings[18].

Where it appears to the Secretary of State or the Welsh Ministers that any scheme relating to smallholdings, which he has or they have approved for the purposes of these provisions, is not being satisfactorily carried out, he or they may, after giving at least one month's notice to the persons responsible for the management of the scheme[19] and giving those persons an opportunity of making representations[20], withdraw approval to the scheme, and thereupon the statutory right of freedom of cropping and disposal of produce will apply to the tenancies formerly restricted under the scheme[21].

Unless there is written agreement to the contrary, the tenant may not, at any time after he has given or received notice to quit, sell or remove from the holding any manure or compost or any hay, straw or roots[22] grown in the last year of the tenancy without the prior written consent of the landlord[23].

If the tenant exercises these rights of cropping and disposal of produce in a manner that actually results, or is likely to result, in injury to or deterioration of the holding, the landlord has two remedies only and no other: first, should the case so require, he may obtain an injunction restraining the tenant's exercise of such rights[24]; and secondly, in any case, he may, on the tenant quitting the holding, recover damages for any injury or deterioration attributable to the exercise by the tenant of his rights[25].

For the purposes of any proceedings for such an injunction, the question whether a tenant is exercising or has exercised his rights in such a manner as to, or to be likely to, injure or deteriorate the holding is to be determined by arbitration or third party determination[26], and the award or determination is conclusive proof of the facts stated in the award or determination not only for those purposes but also for the purposes of an arbitration at the termination of the tenancy respecting a claim by the landlord for damages for such injury or deterioration[27].

1 As to the customs of the country see PARAS 449–453.
2 As to the meaning of 'contract of tenancy' see PARA 425.
3 As to the meaning of 'arable land' see PARA 443 note 4.
4 As to the meaning of 'tenant' see PARA 423 note 5.
5 As to the meaning of 'agricultural holding' see PARA 423.
6 Agricultural Holdings Act 1986 s 15(1)(a).
7 Agricultural Holdings Act 1986 s 15(1)(b).
8 Agricultural Holdings Act 1986 s 15(1).
9 Agricultural Holdings Act 1986 s 15(4)(a). As to the exclusion of things done in discharge of the obligations imposed by s 15(4) from the categories of improvements for which a tenant may claim compensation see s 76(3); and PARA 519.
10 Agricultural Holdings Act 1986 s 15(4)(b). See note 9.
11 Where the protection does not apply the tenant is liable on his covenants: see *Lord Eldon v Hedley Bros* [1935] 2 KB 1, CA.
12 Agricultural Holdings Act 1986 s 15(2)(a). As to the restriction on the removal from the holding or the sale of manure, or compost, hay, straw or roots grown in the last year of a tenancy, after notice to terminate the tenancy see the text and notes 22–23.
13 Agricultural Holdings Act 1986 s 15(2)(b). As to the termination of an agricultural tenancy see PARA 428 note 1. The fact that it may not be known that the relevant time is within the last year of the tenancy is immaterial: see *Lord Eldon v Hedley Bros* [1935] 2 KB 1, CA.
14 As to smallholdings authorities see PARAS 748–751.
15 As to the Secretary of State and the Welsh Ministers see PARA 741.
16 Agricultural Holdings Act 1986 s 82(1)(a).
17 Agricultural Holdings Act 1986 s 82(1)(b).
18 Agricultural Holdings Act 1986 s 82(1)(c).
19 Agricultural Holdings Act 1986 s 82(3)(a).
20 Agricultural Holdings Act 1986 s 82(3)(b). As to the service of notices see PARA 428 note 4.
21 Agricultural Holdings Act 1986 s 82(2).
22 'Roots' means the produce of any root crop of a kind normally grown for consumption on the holding: Agricultural Holdings Act 1986 s 15(7).
23 Agricultural Holdings Act 1986 s 15(3). As to the meaning of 'landlord' see PARA 423 note 7.
24 Agricultural Holdings Act 1986 s 15(5)(a). The saving in the Agricultural Holdings Act 1986 for customary and other remedies does not affect s 15(5): see s 97. See also *Kent v Conniff* [1953] 1 QB 361, [1953] 1 All ER 155, CA.
25 Agricultural Holdings Act 1986 s 15(5)(b).
26 As to arbitrations and third party determinations generally see PARA 566 et seq.
27 See the Agricultural Holdings Act 1986 s 15(6), (6A), (6B) (s 15(6) amended and s 15(6A), (6B) added by the Deregulation Act 2015 Sch 4 para 11).

445. Good husbandry and good estate management.

At common law there is no implied obligation on a landlord to manage his estate in accordance with the rules of good estate management, whereas there is an implied covenant by the tenant to use and cultivate the land in a good and husbandlike manner according to the custom of the country, and to keep the buildings wind- and water-tight[1]. No sanctions are available to a tenant against a landlord breaching the rules of good estate management. A tenant in breach of the rules of good husbandry is exposed to the grant of a certificate of bad husbandry by the Tribunal[2], and thereafter an incontestable notice to quit[3]. Unless there is an express term of the tenancy the landlord has no right to serve a notice to remedy on the basis of a breach of the rules of good husbandry.

1 *Powley v Walker* (1793) 5 Term Rep 373; *Wedd v Porter* [1916] 2 KB 91. As to custom of the country and district see *Tucker v Linger* (1882) 21 Ch D 18; *Hutton v Warren* (1836) 1 M & W 466. 'Good estate management' is defined by the Agriculture Act 1947 s 10 and 'good husbandry'

by s 11 (see AGRICULTURAL PRODUCTION AND MARKETING vol 1A (2017) PARAS 11–13); ss 10, 11 are applied to agricultural holdings governed by the Agricultural Holdings Act 1986 by s 96(3) (see PARA 430 note 14).

2   Ie in England, the First-tier Tribunal (see PARA 768) and in Wales, the Agricultural Land Tribunal for Wales (see PARA 767): see PARA 437 note 1.

3   See the Agricultural Holdings Act 1986 Sch 3 Pt I Case C, Pt II para 9; and PARA 476. Good husbandry is also relevant for tenant's compensation under s 65(2)(b) (see PARA 539) and compensation due to the landlord under s 71(1) (see PARA 553). As to the service of notices see PARA 428 note 4.

(v) Keeping Records

446. Record of condition of holding.

A landlord[1] or tenant[2] of an agricultural holding[3] may, at any time during the tenancy, require a record to be made of the fixed equipment[4] on the holding and of the general condition of the holding itself (including any parts not under cultivation)[5], and in addition a tenant may require a record to be made of any existing improvements executed by him or for which he, with the written consent of the landlord, paid compensation to an out-going tenant, and of any fixtures or buildings[6] which the tenant is entitled[7] to remove[8]. The record is to be made by a person appointed, in default of agreement between the landlord and tenant, by the President of the Royal Institution of Chartered Surveyors[9], and the person so appointed has power to enter the holding at all reasonable times for the purpose of making such a record[10]. In default of agreement the cost of making any such record is to be borne by the landlord and tenant in equal shares[11].

1   As to the meaning of 'landlord' see PARA 423 note 7.
2   As to the meaning of 'tenant' see PARA 423 note 5.
3   As to the meaning of 'agricultural holding' see PARA 423.
4   As to the meaning of 'fixed equipment' see PARA 432 note 6.
5   Agricultural Holdings Act 1986 s 22(1)(a). The making of such a record is a condition precedent to a claim by a tenant for compensation for the continuous adoption of a special system of farming under s 70: see s 70(2)(b); and PARA 548.
6   As to the meaning of 'building' see PARA 432 note 6.
7   Ie under the Agricultural Holdings Act 1986 s 10 (see PARA 436).
8   Agricultural Holdings Act 1986 s 22(1)(b).
9   As to the Royal Institution of Chartered Surveyors generally see BUILDING CONTRACTS vol 6 (2011) PARA 490. An application to the President for a person to be appointed by him must be accompanied by the prescribed fee: Agricultural Holdings Act 1986 s 22(4). At the date at which this volume states the law that fee is £115: Agricultural Holdings (Fees) Regulations 1996, SI 1996/337, reg 2(a). Any instrument of appointment purporting to be made by the President and to be signed by him or on his behalf is to be taken to be such an instrument unless the contrary is shown: Agricultural Holdings Act 1986 s 22(5).
10   Agricultural Holdings Act 1986 s 22(2).
11   Agricultural Holdings Act 1986 s 22(3).

(vi) Powers of Entry

447. Landlord's power of entry.

The landlord[1] of an agricultural holding[2] or any person authorised by him may at all reasonable times enter on the holding, or any part of it, for the purposes of viewing the state of the holding[3], fulfilling the landlord's responsibilities to manage the holding in accordance with the rules of good estate management[4], or providing or improving fixed equipment[5] on the holding otherwise than in fulfilment of those responsibilities[6]. The landlord also has a power to enter in order to execute repairs[7]. The landlord's covenant of quiet enjoyment means that if he enters the tenant's premises without contractual or statutory authority he is a trespasser[8].

1   As to the meaning of 'landlord' see PARA 423 note 7.
2   As to the meaning of 'agricultural holding' see PARA 423.
3   Agricultural Holdings Act 1986 s 23(1)(a).
4   Agricultural Holdings Act 1986 s 23(1)(b). As to the rules of good estate management see AGRICULTURAL PRODUCTION AND MARKETING vol 1A (2017) PARAS 11–13.
5   As to the meaning of 'fixed equipment' see PARA 432 note 6.
6   Agricultural Holdings Act 1986 s 23(1)(c).
7   See the Agriculture (Maintenance, Repair and Insurance of Fixed Equipment) Regulations 1973, SI 1973/1473, Schedule para 4(2) (revoked in relation to England but not in relation to Wales); and the Agriculture (Model Clauses for Fixed Equipment) (England) Regulations 2015, SI 2015/950, Sch 1 para 5. As to those regulations see PARA 433.
8   *Mint v Good* [1951] 1 KB 517, [1950] 2 All ER 1159, CA; *McGreal v Wake* (1984) 13 HLR 107, [1984] 1 EGLR 42, CA.

(vii) Extension of Tenancies in LiEU of Claims to Emblements

448. Tenancies determined by death or cesser of landlord's estate.
Where the tenancy of any agricultural holding[1] held by a tenant[2] at a rack rent determines by the death or cesser of the estate of any landlord[3] entitled for his life, or for any other uncertain interest, instead of claims to emblements[4] the tenant is entitled to continue in occupation of the holding until the occupation is determined by a 12 months' notice to quit expiring at the end of a year of the tenancy, and then to quit upon the terms of his tenancy in the same manner as if it were then determined by effluxion of time or other lawful means during the continuance of his landlord's estate[5]. The succeeding landlord is entitled to recover from the tenant, in the same manner as his predecessor could have done, a fair proportion of the rent for the period from the date of the death or cesser of the estate of his predecessor to the time of the tenant so quitting[6]. The succeeding landlord and the tenant are, as between themselves and against each other, entitled to all the benefits and advantages, and are subject to the terms, conditions and restrictions to which the preceding landlord and tenant respectively would have been entitled and subject if the tenancy had determined at the expiration of the 12 months' notice to quit[7].

1   As to the meaning of 'agricultural holding' see PARA 423.
2   As to the meaning of 'tenant' see PARA 423 note 5.
3   As to the meaning of 'landlord' see PARA 423 note 7.
4   As to emblements see PARA 466.
5   Agricultural Holdings Act 1986 s 21(1). It has been held that this provision applies to the case of a tenancy of glebe lands, terminating upon the cesser of the lessor's incumbency: see *Stephens v Balls* (1957) 107 LJo 764, County Court. As to the service of notices see PARA 428 note 4.
6   Agricultural Holdings Act 1986 s 21(2).
7   Agricultural Holdings Act 1986 s 21(3).

(viii) Customs of the Country

449. Incorporation of custom in the tenancy.
The custom of the country, whereas once prevalent, is in modern times likely to have been excluded by the terms of the tenancy agreement itself[1] or by statute[2]. In general, a custom, when once proved, is applicable to every agricultural tenancy

in the district however created, whether orally or by writing[3]. It is a contractual term which the law implies in the absence of any particular contract between the parties[4]. The custom of the country does not imply an immemorial or universal usage, but only the prevalent usage of the neighbourhood where the land lies which has subsisted for a reasonable length of time[5]. The custom may vary not only between counties but between different parts of the same county[6].

1   *Wilkins v Wood* (1848) 17 LJQB 319; *Wigglesworth v Dallison* (1779) 1 Doug KB 201; *Senior v Armytage* (1816) Holt NP 197, as explained in *Hutton v Warren* (1836) 1 M & W 466. Custom was excluded by the agreements in *Webb v Plummer* (1819) 2 B & Ald 746; *Richards v Davies* [1921] 1 Ch 90. See PARA 452.

2   The Agricultural Holdings Act 1986 s 97 (see PARA 565) preserves customary rights save in so far as superseded. Customs inconsistent with s 15(5) (disposal of produce, etc: see PARA 444), s 77 (compensation for improvements: see PARA 514) or s 83(1) (arbitration: see PARA 566) are excluded.

3   See note 1.

4   *Boraston v Green* (1812) 16 East 71. As to express covenants to cultivate in a husbandlike manner or according to the custom of the country see PARA 455.

     In the absence of agreement, a custom of the country can determine the commencement and duration of a tenancy as starting from particular quarter-days; such a custom may be incorporated even into a written contract of tenancy: see *Doe d Dagget v Snowdon* (1775) 2 Wm Bl 1224.

5   See *Williams v Lewis* [1915] 3 KB 493 at 494 per Bray J, approving the statement in the text as contained in an earlier edition of this work. See also *Legh v Hewitt* (1803) 4 East 154; *Dalby v Hirst* (1819) 1 Brod & Bing 224; *Tucker v Linger* (1882) 21 ChD 18, CA (affd (1883) 8 App Cas 508, HL); *Dashwood v Magniac* [1891] 3 Ch 306 at 324. The custom that the tenant goes out as he came in has no reference to claims for bad farming, but applies only to valuations of tenant-right: *Williams v Lewis* at 495 per Bray J.

6   A schedule of customs was prepared in 1945 by the sub-committee of the Central Association of Agricultural Valuers. A list of the more important customs prevailing in the different counties at that time may be found in Mustoe and Wood *Agricultural Law and Tenant Right* (4th edn. London, 1949) 389 et seq. An historic compilation collecting and commenting on the custom of the various counties is contained in Sidney Wright *The Law Relating to Landed Estates* (London, 1897). A further resource is the 1926 edition of Lely & Aggs *Agricultural Holdings*. See also *The Agricultural Holdings Act 1883* by James Brooke Little (London, 1884) and Wonnacott, *The History of the Law of Landlord and Tenant in England and Wales* (2011).

450. Proof of custom.

The custom of the country is the custom prevalent throughout the district, and is not proved by showing that it is the usage of a particular estate or of the property, however large, of a particular individual; and such usage will not be imported into the terms of a tenancy where it is not shown that the tenant was aware of it[1]. The custom is to be collected, not from what witnesses say they think the custom is, but from what they depose to having been done publicly throughout the district[2]. Custom must be proved by the party alleging it. Thus a custom to retain part of the holding or to take away-going crops, etc, must be proved by the tenant; and in the absence of proof of such custom the tenant must give up possession of land and crops at the termination of the tenancy[3].

1   *Womersley v Dally* (1857) 26 LJ Ex 219.
2   *Tucker v Linger* (1882) 21 ChD 18 at 34, CA, per Jessel MR; affd (1883) 8 App Cas 508, HL.
3   *Caldecott v Smythies* (1837) 7 C & P 808.

451. Reasonableness of custom.

A custom of the country must be reasonable, otherwise it is void[1]. The reasonableness or unreasonableness of the custom is a question of law for the court, and is not a question of fact[2].

The following customs have been held to be reasonable:

(1)   that the tenant should have the away-going crop after the expiration of the term of the tenancy[3], and crop one-third of the arable for that purpose[4];

(2)   that on a taking from old Lady Day (5 April) the tenant should enter upon the arable at Candlemas (2 February) to prepare for the Lent corn[5];

(3)   that a tenant should be entitled to a portion of the expenses of draining the land, though the drainage be done without the landlord's consent or knowledge[6];

(4)   that if there is no incoming tenant the landlord should pay to the outgoing tenant the valuation for fallows, dressing, etc[7];

(5)   that a tenant may leave his away-going crop in the barn of the farm after he has quitted the premises[8];

(6)   that a tenant should provide work and labour, tillage and sowing, and all materials for cultivation in his away-going year, and that the landlord should make him compensation for the same[9];

(7)   that the tenant should collect flints turned up in the ordinary course of good husbandry and sell them for his own benefit, notwithstanding a reservation in the lease of minerals to the landlord[10]; and

(8)   that the landlord should deduct rent in arrear from the valuation payable to the outgoing tenant[11].

1   *Bradburn v Foley* (1878) 3 CPD 129.
2   *Tyson v Smith* (1838) 9 Ad & El 406 at 421.
3   *Wigglesworth v Dallison* (1779) 1 Doug KB 201.
4   *Griffiths v Tombs* (1833) 7 C & P 810; *Caldecott v Smythies* (1837) 7 C & P 808.
5   *Doe d Dagget v Snowdon* (1775) 2 Wm Bl 1224.
6   *Mousley v Ludlam* (1851) 21 LJQB 64. Compensation for drainage works is also recoverable under the Agricultural Holdings Act 1986: see Sch 7 para 23, Sch 8 para 1, Sch 9 para 16; and PARAS 523, 529. As to compensation for improvements under the Agricultural Holdings Act 1986 generally see PARA 522 et seq.
7   *Dalby v Hirst* (1819) 1 Brod & Bing 224; *Faviell v Gaskoin* (1852) 7 Exch 273.
8   *Beavan v Delahay* (1788) 1 Hy Bl 5; *Lewis v Harris* (1778) 1 Hy Bl 7n.
9   *Senior v Armytage* (1816) Holt NP 197.
10 *Tucker v Linger* (1883) 8 App Cas 508, HL.
11 *Re Wilson, ex p Lord Hastings* (1893) 62 LJQB 628.

452. Exclusion of custom.

Customary compensation for any improvement is excluded by statute, subject to certain exceptions, and accordingly all customs of the country which led to compensation are to this extent nullified[1]. Where the terms of a lease are inconsistent with the custom of the country, the custom is excluded[2]. Thus a custom for an allowance from the incoming tenant for foldage (a mode of manuring) was excluded by the terms of a lease which provided for the tenant keeping a flock of sheep on the farm and in the last year of the term carrying the manure out on to the fallows, the landlord paying on the quitting of the farm for fallowing the land and the cartage of dung, but nothing for the dung itself[3]. Where there was a provision in a lease that the tenant should leave the manure in the fold to be expended by the landlord or incoming tenant, but that provision did not mention any payment for it, a custom for the outgoing tenant to leave the manure and be paid for it was excluded[4]. A covenant in a lease by the tenant, not to underlet or permit any other person to use or occupy any part of the demised premises without the landlord's consent, excluded a custom for the outgoing tenant to sell or let the grass keep in the last year of the tenancy but did not exclude agistment[5].

1 See the Agricultural Holdings Act 1986 s 77; and PARA 514.
2 See the cases cited in PARA 449 note 1.
3 *Webb v Plummer* (1819) 2 B & Ald 746.
4 *Roberts v Barker* (1833) 1 Cr & M 808.
5 *Richards v Davies* [1921] 1 Ch 90. As to contracts of agistment see ANIMALS vol 2 (2017) PARAS 18–20.

453. Custom not excluded.

Where a lease contained no stipulations as to the mode of quitting, the outgoing tenant was held to be entitled to his away-going crop as against the incoming tenant according to the custom of the country, even if the crop had been sown in contravention of the terms of the lease, and that contravention might have entitled the landlord to damages for the removal of the crop[1].

A stipulation in a lease that the tenant would consume three-quarters of the hay and straw on the farm and spread the manure arising therefrom, and leave what was not spread for the use of the landlord on receiving a reasonable price for it, did not exclude a custom of the country by which the tenant was entitled on quitting to receive from the landlord or incoming tenant a reasonable allowance for seeds and labour on the arable during the last year of the tenancy, and was bound to leave the manure for the landlord if he would purchase it[2].

1 *Holding v Pigott* (1831) 7 Bing 465 (landlord was not a party to the action). See also *Martin v Coulman* (1834) 4 LJKB 37; *Re Constable and Cranswick* (1899) 80 LT 164. See, however, *Muncey v Dennis* (1856) 1 H & N 216, where there are dicta to the effect that reliance cannot be placed against anyone on a custom inconsistent with the terms of a lease, the tenant being unable to have any greater right against a stranger than he has against his landlord.
2 *Hutton v Warren* (1836) 1 M & W 466. For a further example see also PARA 451 text and note 9. As to the statutory right of a tenant whose tenancy is governed by the Agricultural Holdings Act 1986 to dispose of produce other than manure see PARA 444; and as to his right to receive compensation for seeds sown and acts of husbandry see PARA 530.

(ix) Express and Implied Terms

454. Obligations that will be implied.

There is no implied covenant or warranty on the part of the landlord that the land leased or let is reasonably fit for cultivation[1], or that no noxious plants are growing on the demised premises[2].

The law implies an undertaking or covenant on the part of an agricultural tenant to cultivate the land in a husbandlike manner according to the custom of the country, whether the land is or is not in good condition at the commencement of his tenancy, unless there is a particular agreement dispensing with that engagement[3].

The custom of the country includes not only special customs regulating particular matters, but also the prevalent course of good husbandry in the district[4]; and the rule will be broken if the tenant does not follow this course of husbandry[5]. The tenant may sell hay or straw off the premises[6], provided this is not contrary to special custom or to the terms of the lease[7], but he is bound to consume on the farm such produce as would be consumed thereon if the farm were treated in a husbandlike manner[8], and not to remove manure[9]; and he must not commit waste[10].

A tenant under a tenancy from year to year of a farm and buildings at a fixed rent, who has not entered into any other express agreement with the landlord than as to the amount of rent, is also under an obligation to use the premises in a husbandlike or tenantlike manner, but is not liable to sustain and uphold the premises[11]. The bare relation of landlord and tenant is a sufficient consideration for the tenant's promise to cultivate the land in a good and husbandlike manner according to the custom of the country[12]. Such an undertaking is, however, implied only where the relation of landlord and tenant actually exists, and for that reason neglect by an incumbent to cultivate glebe land in a husbandlike manner does not render him or his executors liable in an action by a succeeding incumbent, though he or they may be liable for leaving the buildings, hedges and fences in a state of decay[13].

1   *Sutton v Temple* (1843) 12 M & W 52; *Hart v Windsor* (1843) 12 M & W 68.
2   *Erskine v Adeane, Bennett's Claim* (1873) 8 Ch App 756; *Cheater v Cater* [1918] 1 KB 247, CA.
3   *Brown v Crump* (1815) 1 Marsh 567; *Williams v Lewis* [1915] 3 KB 493 at 494 per Bray J, approving the statement in the text as contained in an earlier edition of this work. See also *Onslow v —* (1809) 16 Ves 173; *Hallifax v Chambers* (1839) 4 M & W 662; *Westropp v Elligott* (1884) 9 App Cas 815 at 823–824, HL, per Lord Blackburn; *Wedd v Porter* [1916] 2 KB 91, CA. The erection of needless dwelling houses is a breach of an implied covenant to use the land as an agricultural holding, and may also be waste: *Brooke v Mernagh* (1888) 23 LR Ir 86; *Brooke v Kavanagh* (1888) 23 LR Ir 112. An implied covenant is enforceable by an assignee of the reversion expectant on the determination of a tenancy: *Wedd v Porter*.
4   *Legh v Hewitt* (1803) 4 East 154 at 159, 161; and see PARA 455.
5   Eg if he has half his farm under tillage at the same time, while no other farmer in the neighbourhood tills more than a third: *Legh v Hewitt* (1803) 4 East 154. A tenant is not, however, necessarily bound to have a certain portion of the land every year in a certain tillage or to leave a certain quantity fallow: *Brown v Crump* (1815) 1 Marsh 567. As to the right of a tenant of a holding whose tenancy is governed by the Agricultural Holdings Act 1986 to practise any system of cropping arable land notwithstanding any custom to the contrary see PARA 444.
6   He may not, however, do so after having given or received notice to quit, in relation to such produce grown in the last year of the tenancy: see the Agricultural Holdings Act 1986 s 15(3); and PARA 444. As to the service of notices see PARA 428 note 4.
7   *Gough v Howard* (1801) Peake Add Cas 197. A tenant of a holding under a tenancy governed by the Agricultural Holdings Act 1986 has a statutory right to dispose of the produce of the holding, notwithstanding any custom or agreement to the contrary, within the limits of and subject to the safeguards provided by the statute: see PARA 444.
8   *Onslow v —* (1809) 16 Ves 173; *Brown v Crump* (1815) 1 Marsh 567 at 569. If the tenant exercises his statutory right to dispose of produce, he must return to the holding the full equivalent manurial value of the produce removed from the holding: see PARA 444.
9   *Powley v Walker* (1793) 5 Term Rep 373; *Gough v Howard* (1801) Peake Add Cas 197. The removal of manure is not included in the statutory right of disposal of produce under the Agricultural Holdings Act 1986: see PARA 444.
10 Eg by turning pasture land into arable: *Co Litt* 53b; *Simmons v Norton* (1831) 7 Bing 640 at 647. However, the land must be in pasture at the beginning of the tenancy: *Goring v Goring* (1676) 3 Swan 661; *Rush v Lucas* [1910] 1 Ch 437.
11 *Warren v Keen* [1954] 1 QB 15, [1953] 2 All ER 1118, CA (explaining *Wedd v Porter* [1916] 2 KB 91, CA, and disapproving the use in that case of the expression 'wind and water tight').
12 *Powley v Walker* (1793) 5 Term Rep 373; *Onslow v —* (1809) 16 Ves 173; *Westropp v Elligott* (1884) 9 App Cas 815 at 823–824, HL, per Lord Blackburn.
13 *Bird v Relph* (1833) 4 B & Ad 826; and see ECCLESIASTICAL LAW vol 34 (2011) PARA 946.

455. Express covenants as to management of farm by tenant.

The management of the farm is usually regulated by express covenants, which may prescribe a particular system of tillage[1], or may contain a general covenant to cultivate in a husbandlike manner[2] according to the best rules of husbandry practised in the district. Compliance with a covenant to treat a farm in a good and husbandlike manner is proved by evidence of management in accordance with the custom of the country[3]. A covenant to cultivate on a particular system according to the custom of the country binds the tenant to adopt the system only so far as the custom makes it universally obligatory[4]. Conversion of part of a farm, consisting of arable and pasture land, into a market garden, and the erection of glass-houses, etc, thereon, is not a breach of a covenant to cultivate the farm in a good, proper and husbandlike manner according to the best rules of husbandry practised in the neighbourhood[5]. On the other hand, such a covenant, or the ordinary obligation to cultivate in a husbandlike manner according to the custom of the country, is broken by having in arable tillage half a farm, when it is proved that no other farmers in the neighbourhood put more than one-third in tillage, and some even less[6].

An agreement to manage and leave the farm as it has been managed and left by former tenants does not impose on the tenant without notice the terms on which former tenants have held; he must be guided by the condition and mode of management when he took possession[7].

A covenant not to sow with more than two grain crops during four years applies to any four years of the term however taken, and not to each successive four years from the commencement[8]. A covenant to cultivate on the four-course system according to the custom of the country means cultivating in that manner only so far as is obligatory by the custom[9].

Subject to certain exceptions, a tenant of an agricultural holding governed by the Agricultural Holdings Act 1986 has full right to adopt any system of cropping the arable land on the holding, notwithstanding any covenant or custom to the contrary, without incurring any penalty, forfeiture or liability, provided that he makes suitable and adequate provisions to protect the holding from injury or deterioration[10].

Under a covenant by the tenant to permit the landlord to enter on such part of the land as in the last year of the term is sown with barley or oats, and to sow clover therewith, the tenant is not bound to inform the landlord of an intention to sow barley or oats[11].

1　As to the four-course system see *Rankin v Lay* (1860) 2 De GF & J 65.
2　A covenant to manage pasture in a husbandlike manner forbids the conversion of pasture into arable land: *Drury v Molins* (1801) 6 Ves 328; *Clarke-Jervoise v Scutt* [1920] 1 Ch 382. As to such a covenant in respect of land which is not for the time being built on see *Hills v Rowland* (1853) 4 De GM & G 430.
3　*Legh v Hewitt* (1803) 4 East 154 at 160; *Williams v Lewis* [1915] 3 KB 493 at 494–495.
4　*Newson v Smythies* (1859) 1 F & F 477 at 479.
5　*Meux v Cobley* [1892] 2 Ch 253.
6　*Legh v Hewitt* (1803) 4 East 154 at 159 per Lord Ellenborough CJ: 'I understand the parties to have meant no more than this, that the tenant should conform to the prevalent usage of the country where the lands lie. From the subject matter of the contract it is evident that the word custom, as here used, cannot mean a custom in the strict legal signification of the word; for that must be taken with reference to some defined limit or space'.
7　*Liebenrood v Vines* (1815) 1 Mer 15 at 18; *Viscount Hood v Kendall* (1855) 17 CB 260. As to a covenant to leave 'the turnip or fallow breaks once ploughed for the incoming tenant' see *Hunter v Miller* (1863) 9 LT 159, HL.
8　*Fleming v Snook* (1842) 5 Beav 250.
9　*Newson v Smythies* (1859) 1 F & F 477.
10　See PARA 444.
11　*Hughes v Richman* (1774) 1 Cowp 125.

456.　Covenants to consume or not to remove produce.

The removal of produce which is usually consumed on the farm, such as straw, hay and roots, may be prohibited by express covenant; but the prohibition is usually modified, for example, where it is restricted to the last year of the term[1] or where the removal is permitted on condition of bringing back an equivalent in manure[2]. The tenant of an agricultural holding also has the right by statute, subject to certain exceptions and safeguards, to disregard the provisions of any covenant or agreement restricting his right to dispose of the produce of the holding, other than manure, without incurring any penalty, liability or forfeiture[3].

A lease containing a covenant to consume all hay, straw and clover grown on the farm, and to use the manure on the farm, but silent as to hay, etc, unconsumed on quitting, is not inconsistent with a custom that the tenant be paid for all hay, etc, left unconsumed on his quitting; such a covenant means only that the tenant will not remove any hay, etc, from the farm; it does not compel the tenant to cause all of it to be consumed during the tenancy[4]. A tenant is not liable under a covenant to consume all hay and straw and spread the manure therefrom on the farm after destruction of his stacks of hay and corn by accidental fire[5].

A covenant by the tenant not to sell or remove from the premises during the last year of the term any of the hay, straw and fodder which arises and grows thereon, prohibits him from selling or removing during the last year any hay, straw, etc, grown in previous years[6].

A covenant by a tenant not to sell any hay or straw, etc, off the farm is broken by a sale of straw off the farm by the tenant after the determination of the tenancy[7]. An absolute covenant to consume hay and straw on the farm, being equivalent to a negative covenant not to remove it, may be enforced by injunction[8]. Such a covenant touches and concerns the land, and the benefit of it therefore runs with the reversion[9].

Where a tenant bound by covenant to consume the hay on the farm, or to bring in manure, has sold, on quitting, a rick of hay without informing the purchaser of the obligation to bring in manure, and the hay is injured by lapse of time caused by the refusal of the incoming tenant to permit the taking of the hay until the performance of the covenant to bring in manure, the purchaser is entitled to refuse to take it, and the vendor cannot recover the price of the hay[10].

Where a clause in a farming agreement provides that no hay or straw may be sold off the holding, unless the 'value' of the hay, etc, so sold off is returned in manure on the land, it is not clear whether the tenant, having sold the hay or straw, is bound only to return as much manure as the straw would have produced, or to return in manure the price or market value of the straw[11].

Where the tenant is entitled to be paid by the landlord or incoming tenant at 'a fair price' for the hay, straw, etc, left on the farm, but not for the manure, he is entitled only to a fodder or consuming price of the hay and straw, not to the market price[12]. Where the tenant is entitled to be paid for the hay, straw and manure left on the farm 'at a fair valuation', the valuer is not necessarily bound to value the same either at the market or the consuming price, it being a matter of evidence what is a 'fair valuation'[13].

1   *Gale v Bates* (1864) 3 H & C 84. As to the statutory restriction on the removal of manure, etc, after notice to quit an agricultural holding governed by the Agricultural Holdings Act 1986, see PARA 444.

2   See *Westropp v Elligott* (1884) 9 App Cas 815 at 825, HL. A covenant not to mow meadow land more than once a year without an exception of cases where an equivalent in manure is returned to the land is not so unusual a covenant as to form an objection to the lessee's title on assignment: *Hyde v Warden* (1877) 3 Ex D 72 at 82, CA. The farm is not prejudiced if the tenant returns the 'full equivalent manurial value' of the produce sold off (see the Agricultural Holdings Act 1986 s 15; and PARA 444); but this is not a fixed value, and a stipulation for the return of one-third of the market value avoids the uncertainty. As to extension of the term where the tenant is bound to consume the last year's produce on the premises see *Earl St Germains v Willan* (1823) 2 B & C 216; but more usually the tenant is entitled to be paid for hay and straw, and for manure left on

quitting. A requirement in a lease for the payment of additional rent for each ton of 'hay, straw, or other dry fodder' sold off has been held to include the selling off of hay which was bad and not fit for fodder: see *Fielden v Tattersall* (1863) 1 New Rep 332. A restriction is imposed upon the right of the landlord to require additional rent or other liquidated damages for the breach or non-observance by the tenant of terms of the contract of tenancy: see PARA **431**.

3 As to the right to dispose of produce see PARA **444**.
4 *Muncey v Dennis* (1856) 1 H & N 216.
5 *Re Hull and Lady Meux* [1905] 1 KB 588.
6 *Gale v Bates* (1864) 3 H & C 84; *Meggeson v Groves* [1917] 1 Ch 158.
7 *Massey v Goodall* (1851) 17 QB 310.
8 *Crosse v Duckers* (1873) 27 LT 816.
9 *Chapman v Smith* [1907] 2 Ch 97.
10 *Smith v Chance* (1819) 2 B & Ald 753.
11 *Lowndes v Fountain* (1855) 11 Exch 487. Where produce of a holding is disposed of in exercise of the statutory right, it is the full equivalent manurial value of the crops that is to be returned to the holding: see the Agricultural Holdings Act 1986 s 15(4); and PARA **444**.
12 *Clarke v Westrope* (1856) 18 CB 765.
13 *Cumberland v Bowes* (1854) 15 CB 348.

457. Manuring covenants.

A covenant by a tenant with his landlord to leave the manure made by him on the farm and to sell it to the incoming tenant at a valuation gives the tenant a right of on-stand on the farm for the manure until sold to an incoming tenant, and trespass lies against an incoming tenant for the removal and use of the manure before the valuation[1].

A covenant by a tenant to manure with two sufficient sets of muck within the space of six of the last years of the term, the last set to be laid within three years of the expiration of the term, is satisfied by laying both sets within the last three years of the term[2].

The condition of a bond that the tenant must not sell or convey away any dung, compost or manure from the farm is broken by the removal of manure made by cattle purchased from the tenant and allowed to remain on the farm and fed by the purchaser with provender from his own farm[3].

A covenant by a tenant that he will consume on the farm all the turnips, etc, but that if he shall take or sell off any part thereof, which he is at liberty to do, then for every ton sold he shall bring back and spread a certain quantity of manure, is an alternative covenant, and in order to make the tenant liable for a breach of it, both failure to consume and failure to bring back manure must be proved[4].

1 *Beaty v Gibbons* (1812) 16 East 116.
2 *Pownall v Moores* (1822) 5 B & Ald 416.
3 *Hindle v Pollitt* (1840) 6 M & W 529.
4 *Richards v Bluck* (1848) 6 CB 437.

458. Burning of heather, rough grass, etc.

Where a lease[1] of land contains a covenant, condition or agreement which prohibits or restricts the burning of heather or grass by the tenant[2], the appropriate tribunal[3], on the tenant's application, may, if it appears to it that the covenant, condition or agreement is preventing or impeding the proper use of the land or any of it for agriculture and that in all the circumstances it is expedient to do so, give such directions as it thinks fit for avoiding or relaxing the provision[4]. This power is exercisable in respect of all leases notwithstanding any stipulation to the contrary[5].

1 'Lease' means a lease, under-lease or other tenancy, assignment operating as a lease or under-lease, or an agreement for such lease, under-lease or other tenancy, or assignment: Landlord and Tenant Act 1927 s 25(1); definition applied by the Hill Farming Act 1946 s 21(3).

2   'Tenant' means any person entitled in possession to the holding under any contract of tenancy,
    whether the interest of such tenant was acquired by original contract, assignment, operation of law
    or otherwise: Landlord and Tenant Act 1927 s 25(1); definition applied by the Hill Farming Act
    1946 s 21(3). For the power to regulate the burning of heather and grass see s 20; and
    AGRICULTURAL PRODUCTION AND MARKETING vol 1A (2017) PARAS 362–365.
3   For these purposes 'appropriate tribunal' means, in England, the First-tier Tribunal and, in Wales,
    the Agricultural Land Tribunal for Wales: Hill Farming Act 1946 s 21(1B) (s 21(1) amended and
    s 21(1A), (1B) added by SI 2013/1036). Where the land lies partly in Wales and partly in England,
    for the purposes of anything required or authorised to be done under s 21 by or before an
    appropriate tribunal in relation to that land, the land is deemed to be situated entirely in the place
    where the greater part of the land lies: Hill Farming Act 1946 s 21(1A) (as so added). As to the
    First-tier Tribunal and the Agricultural Land Tribunal for Wales see PARAS 768–767 and see also
    PARA 437 note 1.
4   Hill Farming Act 1946 s 21(1) (substituted by the Agriculture Act 1958 s 8, Sch 1 para 1; and
    amended (see note 3)).
5   Hill Farming Act 1946 s 21(2). See, however, the Heather and Grass etc Burning (England)
    Regulations 2007, SI 2007/2003; the Heather and Grass etc Burning (Wales) Regulations 2008,
    SI 2008/1081; and AGRICULTURAL PRODUCTION AND MARKETING vol 1A (2017)
    PARAS 362–365.

459. Enforcement of custom by injunction.

The general law relating to injunctions applies to agricultural tenancies,
including in relation to custom[1]. A tenant will be restrained by injunction from
committing any act of voluntary waste or from acting contrary to the custom of
the country. Thus a tenant may be restrained from ploughing up ancient pasture
or meadow land[2], from sowing pernicious crops[3], from carrying away manure[4],
hay, straw and turnips[5], and from damaging hedgerows[6], contrary to the custom
of the country[7].

1   See CIVIL PROCEDURE vol 12 (2015) PARA 1114.
2   *Drury v Molins* (1801) 6 Ves 328; *Lord Grey de Wilton v Saxon* (1801) 6 Ves 106; *Pratt v Brett*
    (1817) 2 Madd 62. In *Re Pemberton and Cooper and Cooper* (1912) 107 LT 716, a tenant who
    had been restrained from ploughing up pasture land by interim injunction which was dissolved at
    the hearing of the action was held to be entitled to damages for the loss resulting. See also
    Clarke-Jervoise v Scutt [1920] 1 Ch 382.
3   *Pratt v Brett* (1817) 2 Madd 62.
4   *Pulteney v Shelton* (1799) 5 Ves 260n.
5   *Walton v Johnson* (1848) 15 Sim 352.
6   *Onslow v —* (1809) 16 Ves 173.
7   As to an injunction to restrain a tenant in relation to cropping and the disposal of produce see the
    Agricultural Holdings Act 1986 s 15; and PARA 444.

(x) Rights in Respect of Tillages and Crops on Quitting Holdings

460. Compensation where no right to take crops.

If the tenant of an agricultural holding governed by the Agricultural Holdings
Act 1986 has no right to sell or remove from the holding crops or produce grown
on the holding in the last year of tenancy he may be entitled to claim statutory
compensation for them from his landlord[1].

1   See the Agricultural Holdings Act 1986 s 65(1), Sch 8 para 7; and PARA 530. The property in hay
    and straw, which the tenant is prohibited by s 15 (see PARA 444) from removing or selling after
    notice to terminate the tenancy, passes to the landlord by operation of law on the tenant's quitting
    the holding: *Thomas v National Farmers Union Mutual Insurance Society Ltd* [1961] 1 All ER
    363, [1961] 1 WLR 386.

461.   Tenant-right generally.

'Tenant-right' is a term used to express the right of the tenant to take or receive after the determination of his tenancy the benefit of the labour and capital expended by him in cleaning, tilling and sowing the land during his tenancy, which he would otherwise lose by the determination of the tenancy[1]. In the Agricultural Holdings Act 1986 the expression 'tenant-right matters' is used to describe specified matters[2] for which compensation may be payable under the Act, except in the case of a tenant who entered into occupation of the holding before 1 March 1948[3], and who does not elect that those provisions should apply to him[4]. Such a tenant is excluded from the general prohibition on the payment of compensation by custom where the matter in question is covered by statute[5].

At common law an assignment by an agricultural tenant of all his goods and effects on the holding, and 'all his estate and interest thereon and therein', includes the tenant-right or tillages on the holding[6]; and an assignment by a tenant of all his goods and effects, etc, and 'all his tenant-right and interest yet to come and unexpired in and to the farms and premises', passes the tenant's interest in crops grown in future years, including away-going crops[7].

1   Tenant-right does not usually include permanent improvements as these are not the subject of compensation by the custom of the country with certain exceptions, eg in Lincolnshire. It includes such things as growing or severed crops or produce left on the farm by the outgoing tenant, eg hay, straw, sometimes farmyard manure, and seeds sown, tillages, cultivations or acts of husbandry carried out by the outgoer, the benefit of which would be reaped by his successor.

2   Ie matters specified in the Agricultural Holdings Act 1986 s 65, Sch 8 Pt II. See generally ss 64–69; and PARA 528 et seq. As to compensation see PARA 511 et seq.

3   Ie the date on which the Agriculture Act 1947 Pt III (repealed), from which these provisions are derived, was brought into force: see s 111(2) (repealed); and the Agriculture Act 1947 (Commencement) (No 1) Order 1948, SI 1948/342.

4   See the Agricultural Holdings Act 1986 Sch 12 para 6; and PARA 532. As to election by the tenant see further PARAS 512, 514.

5   See the Agricultural Holdings Act 1986 ss 77, 78(3); and PARAS 512, 514.

6   *Cary v Cary* (1862) 10 WR 669.

7   *Petch v Tutin* (1846) 15 M & W 110 (following *Grantham v Hawley* (1616) Hob 132 on the point that goods to come into existence at a future time are assignable by deed).

462.   Meaning of 'tillages'.

Tillages[1] are the expenses and acts of husbandry in general, such as seeds and labour, fallows and unapplied manure[2]; and if the landlord accepts tillage and manure, an agreement by him to pay for it will be implied[3].

1   Rights of tillage are not prejudiced by the Agricultural Holdings Act 1986, except as therein expressly provided: see s 97; and PARA 565. Tillages are, however, tenant-right matters within s 65, Sch 8 para 8 (see PARA 530), for which compensation is payable under the Act, except in the case of a tenant who entered into occupation before 1 March 1948 and who does not elect that the provisions should apply to him: see PARA 461. The date mentioned above is the date on which the Agriculture Act 1947 Pt III (repealed), from which the Agricultural Holdings Act 1986 is in part derived, was brought into force: see s 111(2) (repealed); and the Agriculture Act 1947 (Commencement) (No 1) Order 1948, SI 1948/342.

2   *Martin v Coulman* (1834) 4 LJKB 37.

3   *Dalby v Hirst* (1819) 1 Brod & Bing 224; *Martin v Coulman* (1834) 4 LJKB 37; *Hutton v Warren* (1836) 1 M & W 466. Where a tenant becomes a yearly tenant on such of the terms of a written agreement as are applicable to a yearly tenancy, these terms will include a stipulation for payment for tillages: *Brocklington v Saunders* (1864) 13 WR 46. An alternative method is for the incoming tenant to enter to plough and sow during the last year of the expiring tenancy: see *Milner v Jordan* (1846) 8 QB 615.

463. Incidence of liability for payment.

Where the landlord is liable to pay an outgoing tenant for tillages, etc, the liability attaches to the landlord's interest in the land, and devolves upon the person who, when the payment becomes due, is then in receipt, or entitled to receipt, of the rent[1].

A vendor who, after the contract for sale but before completion, pays the outgoing tenant's valuation is entitled, in the absence of a stipulation to the contrary, to be reimbursed by the purchaser[2]; and a purchaser of land subject to the terms of an existing tenancy is deemed to have notice of the tenant's claim to compensation under the Agricultural Holdings Act 1986[3]. The 'outgoing tenant's valuation' means such sum as is found to be payable by the landlord to the tenant after balancing any payment due by the tenant to the landlord for dilapidations, and any payment due from the landlord to the tenant in respect of tenant-right and so forth[4].

An alleged custom that the outgoing tenant should look to the incoming tenant, to the exclusion of the landlord's liability, for payment for seeds, tillages, etc, is unreasonable, and cannot be supported[5], but the incoming tenant may become liable to the outgoing tenant by express or tacit agreement[6].

A tenant is not entitled to be paid for tillages, etc, if he quits the holding before the due determination of the tenancy[7]; but, if a contract of tenancy for a term of years is determinable by notice at the expiry of a lesser period, the tenant's rights are preserved on his quitting after due notice at the earlier date[8]. The trustee of a bankrupt tenant who disclaims is not entitled to compensation for tenant-right[9].

1   *Mansel v Norton* (1883) 22 ChD 769, CA; *Faviell v Gaskoin* (1852) 7 Exch 273; *Womersley v Dally* (1857) 26 LJ Ex 219. These cases deal with customary compensation. In cases of compensation under the Agricultural Holdings Act 1986 the same result follows from the definition of 'landlord' in s 96(1) (see PARA 423 note 7).
2   *Bennett v Stone* [1902] 1 Ch 226, CA.
3   *Re Earl of Derby and Fergusson's Contract* [1912] 1 Ch 479. See also *Dale v Hatfield Chase Corpn* [1922] 2 KB 282, CA. These cases were decided under corresponding provisions of the Agricultural Holdings Act 1948. As to the tenant's right, until he has notice of the sale, to continue to serve documents on the vendor, see the Agricultural Holdings Act 1986 s 93(5); and PARA 428 note 4.
4   *Oades v Spafford* [1948] 2 KB 74, [1948] 1 All ER 607, CA (applying *Dalton v Pickard* (1911) [1926] 2 KB 545n, CA).
5   *Bradburn v Foley* (1878) 3 CPD 129.
6   *Bradburn v Foley* (1878) 3 CPD 129; *Codd v Brown* (1867) 15 LT 536; *Stafford v Gardner* (1872) LR 7 CP 242; and see *Sucksmith v Wilson* (1866) 4 F & F 1083. Such an agreement does not, however, affect any existing rights of the landlord: *Petrie v Daniel* (1804) 1 Smith KB 199; *Stafford v Gardner*; *Re Wilson, ex p Lord Hastings* (1893) 62 LJQB 628.
7   *Whittaker v Barker* (1832) 1 Cr & M 113; *England v Shearburn* (1884) 52 LT 22. See also *Marquis of Breadalbane v Stewart* [1904] AC 217, HL.
8   *Bevan v Chambers* (1896) 12 TLR 417.
9   *Re Wadsley, Bettinson's Representative v Trustee* (1925) 94 LJ Ch 215.

464. Rights to away-going crops under custom or agreement.

The tenant may also, either by custom or agreement[1], have the right to the benefit of work which has been done, but has not become productive during the last year of the term; thus he may have the right to sell or take the away-going crops himself[2]. Apart from such custom or agreement, the tenant must at the end of the term give up possession of the farm together with all growing crops[3]. A custom as to any of these matters is excluded by an express agreement which is inconsistent with it[4].

Where a Lady Day tenancy[5] is prematurely determined by a judicial proceeding the custom that the tenant should have an away-going crop has no operation[6].

1 Rights to away-going crops are not prejudiced by the Agricultural Holdings Act 1986 except as therein expressly provided: see s 97; and PARA 565. Crops or produce which the tenant has a right to sell or remove are not the subject of a statutory claim for compensation: see s 65, Sch 8 para 7; and PARAS 530, 465.
2 *Wigglesworth v Dallison* (1779) 1 Doug KB 201.
3 *Caldecott v Smythies* (1837) 7 C & P 808.
4 Thus a custom for the tenant to have away-going crops is excluded by an agreement as to such crops: *Boraston v Green* (1812) 16 East 71. As to custom to pay for manure see *Clarke v Roystone* (1845) 13 M & W 752.
5 As to commencement and time of entry when determined by the custom of the country see PARA 449 note 4.
6 *Thorpe v Eyre* (1834) 1 Ad & El 926; and see *Re Wadsley, Bettinson's Representative v Trustee* (1925) 94 LJ Ch 215 (bankruptcy: disclaimer by trustee).

465. Entry to take away-going crops.

A clause in a tenancy agreement entitling the tenant to take an away-going crop does not entitle the tenant to retain possession of any part of the land against the landlord after the determination of the tenancy, but imports a licence to the tenant to enter the land for the purpose of taking the crop[1]. Where, however, custom applies to the tenancy and the tenant is entitled by custom to the away-going crop and is bound to repair fences, he may be entitled also to actual possession of the land on which the crop is growing until the crop is carried away[2]. By custom, if such a custom applies to the tenancy, a tenant may also be entitled to leave his away-going crop in the barn of the farm after he has quit the premises[3].

Where custom applies to the tenancy, trespass will not lie by the landlord or incoming tenant against the outgoing tenant for taking an away-going crop according to the custom of the country, even if the outgoing tenant has committed a breach of covenant in cropping too much of the land and not manuring it[4].

1 *Strickland v Maxwell* (1834) 2 Cr & M 539.
2 *Griffiths v Puleston* (1844) 13 M & W 358. This does not prevent recovery of possession of the part of the land to which the privilege does not extend: *Doe d Waters v Houghton* (1827) 1 Man & Ry KB 208.
3 *Beavan v Delahay* (1788) 1 Hy Bl 5; *Lewis v Harris* (1778) 1 Hy Bl 7n.
4 *Boraston v Green* (1812) 16 East 71; and see *Griffiths v Tombs* (1833) 7 C & P 810, where, however, the overcropping was on oral permission from the landlord.

466. Emblements.

At common law[1] a tenant holding for an uncertain interest[2], whose interest determines otherwise than by or in consequence of his own act[3], has the right, under the name of emblements, to enter upon the land after determination to cut and carry away those crops[4] that normally repay within the year[5] the labour by which they are produced[6].

1 As to the statutory right to an extended tenancy in place of emblements conferred by the Agricultural Holdings Act 1986 s 21 see PARA 448. Section 97 (see PARA 565) preserves the common law right in cases to which s 21 does not apply.
2 This includes a tenancy from year to year: *Kingsbury v Collins and Elmes* (1827) 4 Bing 202 at 207; *Graves v Weld* (1833) 5 B & Ad 105 at 114.
3 Eg by forfeiture for breach of covenant, or by resignation of a benefice: Com Dig tit 'Biens' G2; *Bulwer v Bulwer* (1819) 2 B & Ald 470; *Oland's Case* (1602) 5 Co Rep 116a; *Nicholas v Simonds* (1625) 2 Roll Rep 468; and see *Davis v Eyton* (1830) 7 Bing 154. No right to emblements arises where a tenancy at will is determined by the tenant: Co Litt 68 cited in *Kingsbury v Collins and Elmes* (1827) 4 Bing 202 at 207.

4   Eg grain crops, roots, clover, potatoes and hops: Co Litt 55b: *Latham v Atwood* (1638) Cro Car 515; *Evans v Roberts* (1826) 5 B & C 829 at 832; *Graves v Weld* (1833) 5 B & Ad 105 at 119; *Haines v Welch and Marriott* (1868) LR 4 CP 91.

5   *Graves v Weld* (1833) 5 B & Ad 105 at 118.

6   Shep Touch 244; 2 Bl Com 123; and see *Hayling v Okey* (1853) 8 Exch 531; *Kingsbury v Collins and Elmes* (1827) 4 Bing 202. The right to emblements is personal property and not an interest in land: Co Litt 55b; *Hallen v Runder* (1834) 1 Cr M & R 266 per Parke B (citing *Mayfield v Wadsley* (1824) 3 B & C 357).

467. Growing crops as chattels.

A sale of growing crops may be a sale either of an interest in land or a sale of chattels, depending on to whether it is a sale of something attached to the soil and growing or a sale of the severed crop[1]. But, even if the sale is of the crop when growing, it may still nonetheless be a sale of chattels if the crop is *fructus industriales* (that is, produced by man's labour), emblements, or if the agreement obliges the buyer to sever the crop prior to sale[2].

A contract for the sale of *fructus industriales* while growing, whether they are in a state of maturity or have still to derive nutriment from the land in order to bring them to that state, is not a contract for the sale of any interest in land, but is merely a contract for the sale of goods[3]. There is likewise no sale of an interest in land when the owner of the soil sells what is on the land, whether natural produce, such as timber, grass or apples, or *fructus industriales*, on terms that he will cut or sever them from the land and deliver them to the purchaser[4].

On these principles, it has been held that the sale of a growing crop of wheat[5], of a crop of growing corn and the eatage of the stubble afterwards, together with some growing potatoes and whatever lay grass was in the fields[6], of a crop of potatoes which had matured[7], and of a crop of growing potatoes[8], were all sales of chattels only.

1   The caselaw on this matter is not entirely consistent but the statement in the text appears to be the principle. 'Emblements', industrial growing crops and things attached to or forming part of the land which are agreed to be severed before sale or under the contract of sale are included in the term 'goods' as defined by the Sale of Goods Act 1979 s 61(1); and SALE OF GOODS AND SUPPLY OF SERVICES vol 91 (2012) PARA 31. As to emblements see PARA 466.

2   The distinction between *fructus industriales* and *fructus naturales* is discussed in *Saunders (Inspector of Taxes) v Pilcher* [1949] 2 All ER 1097 at 1104–1105, CA, per Jenkins LJ, where he described the former as being 'those crops which, broadly speaking, are produced in the year by the labour of the year' and the latter as 'crops such as fruit growing on trees, where the productive act is the planting of the trees, and where the fruit is produced by the trees year after year, primarily as the result of that initial productive act'.

3   *Duppa v Mayo* (1669) 1 Wms Saund 275 at 277; *Marshall v Green* (1875) 1 CPD 35 at 39.

4   *Washbourn v Burrows* (1847) 1 Exch 107. As to sales which are sales of an interest in land see PARA 722.

5   *Mayfield v Wadsley* (1824) 3 B & C 357.

6   *Jones v Flint* (1839) 10 Ad & El 753.

7   *Parker v Staniland* (1809) 11 East 362; *Warwick v Bruce* (1813) 2 M & S 205.

8   *Evans v Roberts* (1826) 5 B & C 829; *Sainsbury v Matthews* (1838) 4 M & W 343.

468. Growing crops as an interest in land.

Notwithstanding the principles previously articulated[1], a sale of growing grass for the purpose of being mown and made into hay by the purchaser, a sale of hops not yet in bine, a sale of growing turnips (no time being stipulated for removing them) and a contract with an incoming tenant to take and pay for growing crops and tillages in consideration of letting him a farm, have all been held to be sales of an interest in land[2].

The initial labour of planting a fruit tree does not render all the fruit that in subsequent years may grow in it the produce of man's labour, and the sale of fruit growing on a tree, without provision for its severance from the tree before the property passes, is accordingly a sale of an interest in land[3]. An unconditional sale of underwood or growing trees to be cut by the purchaser is a sale of an interest in land[4]; but not when it is stipulated that they be removed as soon as possible by the purchaser[5] or when they are sold by cubic measure with a view to immediate felling and removal[6].

1 See PARA 467.
2 See *Crosby v Wadsworth* (1805) 6 East 602; *Carrington v Roots* (1837) 2 M & W 248; *Waddington v Bristow* (1801) 2 Bos & P 452 (although doubted in *Rodwell v Phillips* (1842) 9 M & W 501 at 503); *Emmerson v Heelis* (1809) 2 Taunt 38 (although criticised in *Evans v Roberts* (1826) 5 B & C 829 at 833; and in *Jones v Flint* (1839) 10 Ad & El 753 at 759); *Earl of Falmouth v Thomas* (1832) 1 Cr & M 89. But, in order to be effective, a sale of crops constituting an interest in land and not a sale of chattels will have to comply with the formalities prescribed by the Law of Property (Miscellaneous Provisions) Act 1989: see s 2(1); and CONVEYANCING vol 23 (2016) PARA 27 et seq.
3 See *Saunders (Inspector of Taxes) v Pilcher* [1949] 2 All ER 1097 at 1104, CA, per Jenkins LJ (explaining why fruit on a tree is not *fructus industriales*) (see PARA 467 note 2); *Rodwell v Phillips* (1842) 9 M & W 501.
4 *Scorell v Boxall* (1827) 1 Y & J 396.
5 *Marshall v Green* (1875) 1 CPD 35.
6 *Smith v Surman* (1829) 9 B & C 561.

469. Right to exclusive possession on sale of a growing crop.
Where a crop of growing grass in a close is sold for the purpose of being mown and made into hay by the purchaser, the purchaser acquires a right to the exclusive possession of the close for that purpose, and may maintain an action of trespass against any person entering the close and taking the grass even with the assent of the vendor[1], and the purchaser of a growing crop has exclusive possession and may sue a trespasser notwithstanding that he is bound to consume part of the crop on the land[2].

The grant of fruit growing on a tree implies an undertaking by the grantor not to destroy the tree before the fruit is gathered[3].

1 *Crosby v Wadsworth* (1805) 6 East 602.
2 *Wellaway v Courtier* [1918] 1 KB 200.
3 See *M'Intyre v Belcher* (1863) 14 CBNS 654 at 665 per Willes J.

(5) NOTICES TO QUIT AGRICULTURAL TENANCY

(i) Length of Notice to Quit

470. Requirement of 12 months' notice.
Subject to the exceptions listed below, a notice to quit an agricultural holding[1] or part of a holding is invalid if it purports to terminate the tenancy before the expiry of 12 months from the end of the then current year of the tenancy, notwithstanding any provision to the contrary in the contract of tenancy[2]. This provision does not apply:

(1) where the tenant[3] is insolvent[4];
(2) to a notice given pursuant to a provision in the contract of tenancy authorising the resumption of possession of the holding or some part of it for some specified purpose other than the use of the land for agriculture[5];
(3) to a notice given by a tenant to a sub-tenant[6];

(4)   where the tenancy is one which by virtue of the Law of Property Act 1925[7] takes effect as such a term of years as is mentioned in that Act[8];

(5)   where following a rent review of an agricultural holding[9] the arbitrator or third party awards or determines that the rent payable in respect of the holding must be increased and a notice to quit the holding is given by the tenant at least six months before it purports to take effect (provided that the notice to quit purports to terminate the tenancy at the end of the year of the tenancy beginning with the date as from which the rent increase is effective)[10];

(6)   where the tenancy of an agricultural holding is of a specified category entered into before 25 March 1947[11]; and

(7)   where the arbitrator or third party has specified a date for the termination of the tenancy in the event of the tenant's failure to do work under a notice to remedy or where there has been an extension of time under a notice to remedy[12].

Where the Tribunal[13] has granted a certificate of bad husbandry[14], it may specify in the certificate a minimum period of notice for termination of the tenancy (being not less than two months)[15] and direct the application of that period instead of the period normally required[16].

1   As to the meaning of 'agricultural holding' see PARA 423. As to the service of notices to quit see PARA 428 note 4. The Protection from Eviction Act 1977 s 5 (validity of notices to quit: see LANDLORD AND TENANT vol 62 (2016) PARA 208) will not apply even though a tenancy of an agricultural holding includes a dwelling house: see *National Trust for Places of Historic Interest or Natural Beauty v Knipe* [1997] 4 All ER 627, [1998] 1 WLR 230, CA.

2   Agricultural Holdings Act 1986 s 25(1). As to the meaning of 'contract of tenancy' see PARA 425. This provision applies to a notice exercising an option to determine a fixed term before its normal expiry (*Edell v Dulieu* [1924] AC 38, HL); and also to a notice given by as well as to a tenant (*Flather v Hood* (1928) 44 TLR 698). A notice which is invalid under this provision may still be effective if the tenant actually quits in pursuance of it: *Thomas v National Farmers Union Mutual Insurance Society Ltd* [1961] 1 All ER 363, [1961] 1 WLR 386. A landlord or a tenant served with a notice to quit of less than the statutory length may waive his rights: *Elsden v Pick* [1980] 3 All ER 235, [1980] 1 WLR 898, CA. A notice to quit of the correct length is invalid if served before the commencement of the tenancy: *Lower v Sorrell* [1963] 1 QB 959, [1962] 3 All ER 1074, CA. The addition of a fetter to the statutory length was held to be valid in *Re Midland Rly Co's Agreement, Charles Clay & Sons Ltd v British Railways Board* [1971] Ch 725, [1971] 1 All ER 1007, CA (overruled on other grounds by *Prudential Assurance Co Ltd v London Residuary Body* [1992] 2 AC 386, [1992] 3 All ER 504, HL (a lease, including a periodic tenancy, must be of certain duration)).

3   As to the meaning of 'tenant' see PARA 423 note 5.

4   Agricultural Holdings Act 1986 s 25(2)(a). A tenant is insolvent if:

    (1)   he has been made bankrupt or has made a composition or arrangement with his creditors (s 96(2)(a) (amended by SI 2016/481)); or

    (2)   where the tenant is a body corporate, a winding-up order has been made with respect to it, or a resolution for voluntary winding-up has been passed with respect to it (other than a resolution passed solely for the purpose of its reconstruction or of its amalgamation with another body corporate) (Agricultural Holdings Act 1986 s 96(2)(b)).

5   Agricultural Holdings Act 1986 s 25(2)(b). As to 'agriculture' and the use of the land for agriculture see PARA 424. A provision in the contract authorising the resumption of possession for any non-agricultural purpose is a 'specified purpose': *Paddock Investments Ltd v Lory* [1975] 2 EGLR 5, CA. Such a provision will be invalid if it does not provide sufficient time to enable compensation claims to be made within the time limits specified in the Act: *Re Disraeli's Agreement, Cleasby v Park Estate (Hughenden) Ltd* [1939] Ch 382, [1938] 4 All ER 658; *Parry v Million Pigs Ltd* (1980) 260 Estates Gazette 281.

6   Agricultural Holdings Act 1986 s 25(2)(c).

7   Ie the Law of Property Act 1925 s 149(6) (lease for life or lives or for a term determinable with life or lives or on the marriage of, or formation of a civil partnership by, the lessee: see LANDLORD AND TENANT vol 62 (2016) PARA 234).

8 Agricultural Holdings Act 1986 s 25(2)(d).

9 Ie on a reference under the Agricultural Holdings Act 1986 s 12 (see PARA 438).

10 Agricultural Holdings Act 1986 s 25(3) (amended by the Deregulation Act 2015 Sch 4 para 13). Such a notice to quit is not invalid by virtue of any term of the contract of tenancy requiring a longer period of notice to terminate the tenancy: Agricultural Holdings Act 1986 s 25(5).

11 Agricultural Holdings Act 1986 Sch 12 para 4 (amended by SI 2003/1615; SI 2012/1659). The specified categories are:

    (1)   notice given by or on behalf of the Secretary of State where the land is required for naval, military or air force purposes (Agricultural Holdings Act 1986 Sch 12 para 4(1)(a)); and

    (2)   notice given by a corporation carrying on a railway, dock, canal, water or other undertaking (Sch 12 para 4(1)(b)).

12 See the Agricultural Holdings (Arbitration on Notices) Order 1987, SI 1987/710, arts 7, 15; Agricultural Holdings Act 1986 s 83(1A); and PARAS 486, 490.

13 Ie in England, the First-tier Tribunal (see PARA 768) and in Wales, the Agricultural Land Tribunal for Wales (see PARA 767): see PARA 437 note 1.

14 As to certificates of bad husbandry see PARA 445.

15 Agricultural Holdings Act 1986 s 25(4)(a). Such a notice to quit is not invalid either by virtue of any term of the contract of tenancy requiring a longer period of notice to terminate the tenancy or by reason of the tenancy terminating at a date other than the end of a year of the tenancy: s 25(5).

16 Agricultural Holdings Act 1986 s 25(4)(b).

(ii) Restriction on Operation of Notices to Quit

471. Restriction by counter-notice.

Where a notice to quit the whole or part of an agricultural holding[1] is given to the tenant[2], and he serves a counter-notice in writing on the landlord[3] not later than one month from the giving of the notice to quit[4], then, subject to certain exceptions[5], the notice to quit is ineffective unless the Tribunal[6] consents to its operation[7]. The counter-notice must require that these provisions[8] apply to the notice to quit[9].

1 As to the meaning of 'agricultural holding' see PARA 423. As to notice to quit part of a holding see PARA 492.

2 Agricultural Holdings Act 1986 s 26(1)(a). As to the meaning of 'tenant' see PARA 423 note 5. As to the operation of a notice to quit given to a sub-tenant as a consequence of the service of notice on a tenant see PARA 496.

3 As to the meaning of 'landlord' see PARA 423 note 7.

4 Agricultural Holdings Act 1986 s 26(1)(b). As to the service of notices see PARA 428 note 4.

5 In general the application of this provision is excluded in relation to any of the Cases A–H set out in the Agricultural Holdings Act 1986 s 26(2), Sch 3: see further PARAS 474–481. In addition, s 26(1) does not apply where notice to quit a holding or part of a holding is given to a sub-tenant by a tenant who has himself been given notice to quit that holding or part and the fact that the tenant has been given such notice is stated in the notice given to the sub-tenant (Agricultural Holdings (Arbitration on Notices) Order 1987, SI 1987/710, art 16(1)); in that case the notice given to the sub-tenant is effective only if the notice given to the tenant by the landlord has effect (art 16(2)).

6 Ie in England, the First-tier Tribunal (see PARA 768) and in Wales, the Agricultural Land Tribunal for Wales (see PARA 767): see PARA 437 note 1.

7 Agricultural Holdings Act 1986 s 26(1). As to the giving and withholding of consent to the operation of notices to quit see PARA 472.

8 Ie the provision of the Agricultural Holdings Act 1986 s 26(1).

9 Agricultural Holdings Act 1986 s 26(1)(b). Counter-notices are not to be strictly construed, and one which erroneously referred to the equivalent provision of repealed legislation was held valid in *Ward v Scott* [1950] WN 76. There must, however, be a clear intention to invoke the statute, and a mere threat to 'appeal' is not sufficient; a technical defect which does not mislead will not invalidate the notice: *Mountford v Hodkinson* [1956] 2 All ER 17, [1956] 1 WLR 422, CA; *Frankland v Capstick* [1959] 1 All ER 209, [1959] 1 WLR 205, CA.

472. Giving or withholding of consent by the Tribunal.

The Tribunal[1] must consent to the operation of a notice to quit the whole or part of an agricultural holding[2] if, but only if, it is satisfied as to one or more of the matters listed below specified in the landlord's application[3], unless it appears to it in all the circumstances that a fair and reasonable landlord[4] would not insist on possession, in which case it must withhold consent[5]. The matters as to which the tribunal must be satisfied are:

(1)   that the carrying out of the purpose for which the landlord proposes to terminate the tenancy is desirable in the interests of good husbandry[6] as respects the land to which the notice relates, treated as a separate unit[7];

(2)   that the carrying out of that purpose is desirable in the interests of the sound management of the estate of which the land to which the notice relates forms part or which that land constitutes[8];

(3)   that the carrying out of that purpose is desirable for the purposes of agricultural[9] research, education, experiment or demonstration, or for the purposes of the enactments relating to smallholdings or allotments[10];

(4)   that greater hardship would be caused by the withholding than by the giving of consent[11]; or

(5)   that the landlord proposes to terminate the tenancy for the purpose of a use other than for agriculture[12] not falling within Case B (non-agricultural use)[13].

The Tribunal may attach conditions to its consent to the operation of a notice to quit to ensure that the land is in fact used for the purposes for which the landlord proposes to terminate the tenancy[14], but must vary or revoke any condition, if satisfied on an application by the landlord that by reason of change of circumstances or otherwise the variation or revocation ought to be made[15]. Where such a condition has been imposed and it is proved on application to the Tribunal on behalf of the Crown that the landlord has failed to comply with it within the time allowed or has acted in contravention of it, the Tribunal may by order impose a penalty on the landlord of an amount not exceeding two years' rent of the holding at the rate payable immediately prior to the termination of the tenancy, or, where the notice related to part only of the holding, the proportion of that rent which the tribunal considers to be attributable to that part[16]. In such proceedings the Tribunal may order the payment by any party of such sum as it considers a reasonable contribution towards costs[17]. A penalty imposed by the Tribunal is a debt due to the Crown and, when recovered, must be paid into the Consolidated Fund[18]. Orders made by the Tribunal for the imposition on the landlord of a penalty or for the payment of costs are enforceable in the same manner as a judgment or order of the county court to the like effect[19].

1   Ie in England, the First-tier Tribunal (see PARA 768) and in Wales, the Agricultural Land Tribunal for Wales (see PARA 767): see PARA 437 note 1.

2   As to the meaning of 'agricultural holding' see PARA 423.

3   Agricultural Holdings Act 1986 s 27(1).

4   As to the meaning of 'landlord' see PARA 423 note 7.

5   Agricultural Holdings Act 1986 s 27(2); and see *Evans v Roper* [1960] 2 All ER 507, [1960] 1 WLR 814, DC; *Cooke v Talbot* (1977) 243 Estates Gazette 831.

6   As to the rules of good husbandry for the purposes of the Agricultural Holdings Act 1986 see, by virtue of s 96(3) (see PARA 430 note 14), the Agriculture Act 1947 ss 10, 11; and AGRICULTURAL PRODUCTION AND MARKETING vol 1A (2017) PARAS 11–13.

7   Agricultural Holdings Act 1986 s 27(3)(a). The tribunal is required to make a comparison between the future use of the land proposed by the landlord and the use of the land by the tenant: *Davies v Price* [1958] 1 All ER 671, [1958] 1 WLR 434, CA.

8   Agricultural Holdings Act 1986 s 27(3)(b). In considering what is 'sound management of the
    estate' the whole and every part of the estate must be taken into consideration: *Evans v Roper*
    [1960] 2 All ER 507, [1960] 1 WLR 814, DC. In order to come within this ground, the purpose
    must be one which relates to the physical management of the land, and not one which will merely
    benefit the landlord financially: see *National Coal Board v Naylor* [1972] 1 All ER 1153, [1972]
    1 WLR 908, DC. Cf *Purser v Bailey* [1967] 2 QB 500, sub nom *Bailey v Purser* [1967] 2 All ER
    189, CA (landlord's personal financial position is not relevant under this head).
9   As to the meaning of 'agricultural' see PARA 424.
10 Agricultural Holdings Act 1986 s 27(3)(c), (d). As to the enactments relating to smallholdings and
    allotments see PARA 627 et seq.
11 Agricultural Holdings Act 1986 s 27(3)(e). The financial result for the respective parties estimated
    to flow from the granting or withholding of consent may be the largest single deciding factor but
    is not the only factor: *Purser v Bailey* [1967] 2 QB 500, sub nom *Bailey v Purser* [1967] 2 All ER
    189, CA. The tribunal is entitled to consider hardship to all who may be affected, and to consider
    hardship notwithstanding the fact that it may have other contributory causes. Hardship to third
    parties will be taken into account but only in so far as hardship to those parties is hardship to the
    landlord or tenant: *Harte v Frampton* [1948] 1 KB 73, [1947] 2 All ER 604.
12 As to the meaning of 'agriculture' see PARA 424.
13 Agricultural Holdings Act 1986 s 27(3)(f). As to Case B see PARA 475.
14 Agricultural Holdings Act 1986 s 27(4). A condition requiring the grant to the tenant by the
    landlord of a new lease of part of the land to which the notice to quit relates is not a condition
    which the tribunal has power to attach by virtue of this provision: *R v Agricultural Land Tribunal
    (South-Eastern Area), ex p Boucher* (1952) 159 Estates Gazette 192.
15 Agricultural Holdings Act 1986 s 27(5).
16 Agricultural Holdings Act 1986 s 27(6). This is the only remedy for a breach of a condition and
    the tenant cannot refuse to comply with the notice to quit by reason of such breach: *Martin Smith
    v Smale* [1954] 1 All ER 237, [1954] 1 WLR 247, CA.
17 Agricultural Holdings Act 1986 s 27(7) (amended by SI 2013/1036).
18 Agricultural Holdings Act 1986 s 27(8).
19 Agricultural Holdings Act 1986 s 27(9).

(iii) Notices to Quit where Counter-notice Procedure Unavailable

473. Exclusion of tenant's right to serve a counter-notice.

The provisions enabling a tenant[1] to serve a counter-notice[2] and thereby render
the landlord's[3] notice to quit ineffective without the consent of the Tribunal[4] are
excluded in eight specified Cases[5] and a landlord serving notice in reliance upon
any of the reasons set out in those Cases need only establish the validity of the
reasons stated in the notice, provided that the Case on which he relies is stated in
the notice[6]. There is provision under which the tenant may contest questions
arising under notices to quit in certain of those Cases[7].

1   As to the meaning of 'tenant' see PARA 423 note 5.
2   See PARAS 471–472.
3   As to the meaning of 'landlord' see PARA 423 note 7.
4   Ie in England, the First-tier Tribunal (see PARA 768) and in Wales, the Agricultural Land Tribunal
    for Wales (see PARA 767): see PARA 437 note 1.
5   Agricultural Holdings Act 1986 s 26(2). The eight exceptions are Cases A–H set out in Sch 3 Pt
    I: see PARAS 474–481.
6   *Budge v Hicks* [1951] 2 KB 335, [1951] 2 All ER 245, CA. It must also be clear whether the notice
    relies on one of those Cases or is a notice to which a counter-notice may be served: *Cowan v
    Wrayford* [1953] 2 All ER 1138, [1953] 1 WLR 1340, CA; *Mills v Edwards* [1971] 1 QB 379,
    [1971] 1 All ER 922, CA.
7   See the Agricultural Holdings (Arbitration on Notices) Order 1987, SI 1987/710, arts 9, 10; and
    PARA 488 et seq.

474. Case A: smallholdings.

Case A applies to a holding let on or after 12 September 1984[1] as a smallholding by a smallholdings authority[2], the Secretary of State or the Welsh Ministers[3] in pursuance of statutory provisions relating to smallholdings[4] where:

(1)   the tenant[5] has attained the age of 65[6];

(2)   if the result of the notice to quit taking effect would be to deprive the tenant of living accommodation occupied by him under the tenancy, suitable alternative accommodation is or will be available for him when the notice takes effect[7]; and

(3)   the instrument under which the tenancy was granted contains an acknowledgment signed by the tenant that the tenancy is subject to the provisions of Case A[8],

and it is stated in the notice to quit that it is given for that reason[9]. The reasons stated may be contested by arbitration[10].

A certificate of the housing authority that it will provide suitable alternative accommodation by a specified date is conclusive of that question[11]. In the absence of such a certificate accommodation will be deemed to be suitable if it falls within one of several categories of tenancy providing the tenant with security of tenure[12].

The accommodation must be reasonably suitable to the tenant's family as regards proximity to place of work and either:

(a)   similar as regards rental and extent to dwelling houses[13] provided in the neighbourhood by a housing authority to meet needs similar to those of the tenant and his family[14]; or

(b)   reasonably suitable to the means of the tenant and the needs of him and his family as regards extent and character[15].

Similar furniture to that provided by the landlord[16] or reasonably suitable furniture must be provided in the alternative accommodation[17]. Accommodation is not suitable to the tenant and his family if their occupation of it would result in its being an overcrowded dwelling house[18].

1   Ie the date on which the Agricultural Holdings Act 1984, from which the Agricultural Holdings Act 1986 Sch 3 (see the text and notes 2–18; and PARAS 475–481) derives, came into force: see the Agricultural Holdings Act 1984 s 11(2) (repealed).

2   As to smallholdings authorities see PARAS 748–751.

3   As to the Secretary of State and the Welsh Ministers see PARA 741.

4   Ie the Agriculture Act 1970 Pt III (ss 37–65) (see PARA 627 et seq).

5   As to the meaning of 'tenant' see PARA 423 note 5.

6   Agricultural Holdings Act 1986 s 26(2), Sch 3 Pt I Case A(a).

7   Agricultural Holdings Act 1986 Sch 3 Pt I Case A(b). As to the service of notices see PARA 428 note 4.

8   Agricultural Holdings Act 1986 Sch 3 Pt I Case A(c). Alternatively, the instrument under which the tenancy is granted may contain an acknowledgment signed by the tenant that the tenancy is subject to the provisions of the Agricultural Holdings (Notices to Quit) Act 1977 s 2(3), Case I (repealed), which was the precursor of Case A in the Agricultural Holdings Act 1986.

9   Agricultural Holdings Act 1986 Sch 3 Pt I Case A.

10   See the Agricultural Holdings (Arbitration on Notices) Order 1987, SI 1987/710, art 9; and PARA 488. As to arbitrations generally see PARA 566 et seq.

11   Agricultural Holdings Act 1986 s 26(3), Sch 3 Pt II paras 1, 2. Any document purporting to be a certificate of a housing authority named in it issued for the purposes of Sch 3 and to be signed by the proper officer of the authority, must be received in evidence and, unless the contrary is shown, deemed to be such a certificate without further proof: Sch 3 Pt II para 6.

12   Agricultural Holdings Act 1986 Sch 3 Pt II para 3 (amended by the Housing Act 1988 s 140, Sch 17 para 69).

13   A 'dwelling house' may be a house or part of a house: Agricultural Holdings Act 1986 Sch 3 Pt II para 7(2).

14 Agricultural Holdings Act 1986 Sch 3 Pt II para 4(1)(a). For these purposes a certificate of a housing authority stating the extent of the accommodation afforded by dwelling houses provided by the authority to meet the needs of tenants with families of such number as may be specified in the certificate and the amount of the rent charged by the authority for dwelling houses affording accommodation of that extent is conclusive evidence of the facts so stated: Sch 3 Pt II para 4(2).
15 Agricultural Holdings Act 1986 Sch 3 Pt II para 4(1)(b).
16 As to the meaning of 'landlord' see PARA 423 note 7.
17 Agricultural Holdings Act 1986 Sch 3 Pt II para 4(3).
18 Agricultural Holdings Act 1986 Sch 3 Pt II para 5. An overcrowded dwelling house in this context is one which is overcrowded for the purposes of the Housing Act 1985 (see s 324; and HOUSING vol 56 (2017) PARA 649): Agricultural Holdings Act 1986 Sch 3 Pt II para 5.

475. Case B: non-agricultural use.

Case B applies where the notice to quit[1] is given on the ground that the land is required for a use[2], other than for agriculture[3]:

(1)   for which permission has been granted on an application under the enactments relating to town and country planning (and any enactment amending or replacing any of those Acts)[4];

(2)   for which permission under those enactments is granted by a general development order[5] by reason only of the fact that the use is authorised by a private or local Act[6], an order approved by both Houses of Parliament or by the National Assembly for Wales[7] or an order[8] regarding efficiency, improvement or construction in harbours[9];

(3)   for which any provision contained in an Act[10] not forming part of the town and country planning enactments[11] which deems permission under those enactments to have been granted[12];

(4)   which any such provision deems not to constitute development for the purposes of those enactments[13]; or

(5)   for which permission is not required under those enactments by reason only of Crown immunity[14],

and that fact is stated in the notice[15].

A question arising under a notice to quit falling within Case B may be contested by arbitration[16].

1 As to the service of notices see PARA 428 note 4.
2 The meaning of 'use' in planning legislation should not be imported into Case B. The singular 'use' includes the plural 'uses'. There is no restriction that Case B can only be used if and only if the land is required for a use or uses which are wholly and exclusively non-agricultural. Case B may apply where the landlord requires the land for two or more concurrent or consecutive uses, only one of which is the use of land for agriculture: see *Floyer-Acland v Osmond* (2000) 80 P & CR 229, [2000] 2 EGLR 1, CA (land required for mineral extraction, but subject to a restoration and after-care covenant). The landlord need not establish that the land is required for his own use: *Paddock Investments Ltd v Lory* [1975] 2 EGLR 5, CA. The requirement need not be exclusively by the landlord himself: *Ruby Joint Water Board v Foottit* [1973] AC 202, [1972] 1 All ER 1057, HL. 'Required' involves both a bona fide intention to implement the change of use and a reasonable prospect of carrying it out: *Paddock Investments Ltd v Lory* (approving *Jones v Gates* [1954] 1 All ER 158, [1954] 1 WLR 222, CA, on this point only). Outline planning consent is sufficient: *Paddock Investments Ltd v Lory*; *Rugby Joint Water Board v Foottit*. See also the discussion in *The Trustees of the North Berwick Trust v James B Miller & Co* [2009] CSIH 15 at [22] et seq per Lord Justice Clerk (dealing with materially identical Scottish provisions. In *John v George* (1995) 71 P & CR 375, [1996] 1 EGLR 7, CA, the landlords were estopped from serving a valid Case B notice to quit because of pre-planning permission negotiations with the tenant.
3 As to the meaning of 'agriculture' see PARA 424. A condition that after mineral extraction and workings the land should be restored so that it was suitable for agriculture does not mean that the land is not required for a non-agricultural use: see *Floyer-Acland v Osmond* (2000) 80 P & CR 229, [2000] 2 EGLR 1, CA.
4 Agricultural Holdings Act 1986 Sch 3 Pt I Case B(a) (Case B substituted by the Agricultural Holdings (Amendment) Act 1990 s 1(1), (2)). For these purposes, no account is to be taken of

permission which relates to the working of coal by opencast operations (Agricultural Holdings Act 1986 Sch 3 Pt II para 8(1)(b)) and which was granted subject to a restoration condition and an aftercare condition in which the use specified is agriculture or forestry (Sch 3 Pt II para 8(1)(c)). As to the meaning of 'aftercare condition' see the Town and Country Planning Act 1990 s 336(1), Sch 5 para 2; and PLANNING vol 82 (2010) PARA 908 (definitions applied by the Agricultural Holdings Act 1986 Sch 3 Pt II para 8(2) (amended by the Planning (Consequential Provisions) Act 1990 s 4, Sch 2 para 72)). As to the enactments relating to town and country planning see the Town and Country Planning Act 1990 s 336(1); and PLANNING vol 81 (2010) PARA 2 (definition applied by the Agricultural Holdings Act 1986 Sch 3 Pt II para 8A(1)(b) (Sch 3 Pt II para 8A added by the Agricultural Holdings (Amendment) Act 1990 s 1(3))).

5   'General development order' means an order under the Town and Country Planning Act 1990 s 59 (see PLANNING vol 81 (2010) PARA 387) which is made as a general order: Agricultural Holdings Act 1986 Sch 3 Pt II para 8A(1)(a) (as added: see note 4). In relation to anything done before the commencement of the Town and County Planning Act 1990 Pt III (ss 55–106) (ie before 24 August 1990) see the Agricultural Holdings Act 1986 Sch 3 Pt II para 8A(2) (as so added).

6   Agricultural Holdings Act 1986 Sch 3 Pt I Case B(b)(i) (as substituted: see note 4).

7   Agricultural Holdings Act 1986 Sch 3 Pt I Case B(b)(ii) (as substituted: see note 4). For provisions as to the bringing of subordinate legislation made by the Welsh Ministers before the National Assembly for Wales see the Government of Wales Act 2006 s 162(1), Sch 11 paras 33–35.

8   Ie an order under the Harbours Act 1964 s 14 or s 16 (see PORTS AND HARBOURS vol 85 (2012) PARAS 27–29, 32–33).

9   Agricultural Holdings Act 1986 Sch 3 Pt I Case B(b)(iii) (as substituted: see note 4).

10 Agricultural Holdings Act 1986 Sch 3 Pt I Case B(c)(i) (as substituted: see note 4).

11 Agricultural Holdings Act 1986 Sch 3 Pt I Case B(c)(ii) (as substituted: see note 4).

12 Agricultural Holdings Act 1986 Sch 3 Pt I Case B(c) (as substituted: see note 4).

13 Agricultural Holdings Act 1986 Sch 3 Pt I Case B(d) (as substituted: see note 4).

14 Agricultural Holdings Act 1986 Sch 3 Pt I Case B(e) (as substituted: see note 4).

15 Agricultural Holdings Act 1986 Sch 3 Pt I Case B (as substituted: see note 4).

16 See the Agricultural Holdings (Arbitration on Notices) Order 1987, SI 1987/710, art 9; and PARA 488. As to arbitrations generally see PARA 566 et seq.

476. Case C: certificate of bad husbandry.

Case C applies where, not more than six months before the giving of the notice to quit[1], the Tribunal[2] granted a certificate[3] that the tenant[4] of the holding was not fulfilling his responsibilities to farm[5] in accordance with the rules of good husbandry[6], and that fact is stated in the notice[7].

For these purposes a landlord[8] may apply to the Tribunal for a certificate that the tenant is not fulfilling his responsibilities to farm in accordance with the rules of good husbandry, and if the Tribunal is satisfied that the tenant is not fulfilling those responsibilities it must grant the certificate[9].

In determining whether to grant the certificate the Tribunal must disregard any practice adopted by the tenant in pursuance of any provision of the contract of tenancy[10] or other agreement with the landlord which indicates that the object of the practice is the furtherance of:

(1)   the conservation of flora or fauna or of geological or physiographical features of special interest[11];

(2)   the protection of buildings[12] or other objects of archaeological, architectural or historic interest[13]; or

(3)   the conservation or enhancement of the natural beauty or amenity of the countryside or the promotion of its enjoyment by the public[14].

In granting a certificate the Tribunal may specify a minimum period of notice for termination of the tenancy of not less than two months, in place of the normal statutory period of notice[15].

No compensation for disturbance, whether basic or additional, is payable where the operation of a counter-notice is excluded by Case C[16].

1 As to the service of notices see PARA 428 note 4.
2 Ie in England, the First-tier Tribunal (see PARA 768) and in Wales, the Agricultural Land Tribunal for Wales (see PARA 767): see PARA 437 note 1.
3 Ie a certificate under the Agricultural Holdings Act 1986 s 26(3), Sch 3 Pt II para 9 (see the text and notes 4–15).
4 As to the meaning of 'tenant' see PARA 423 note 5.
5 As to the 'farming' of land see PARA 424.
6 As to the rules of good husbandry for the purposes of the Agricultural Holdings Act 1986 see, by virtue of s 96(3) (see PARA 430 note 14), the Agriculture Act 1947 ss 10, 11; and AGRICULTURAL PRODUCTION AND MARKETING vol 1A (2017) PARAS 11–13.
7 Agricultural Holdings Act 1986 Sch 3 Pt I Case C.
8 As to the meaning of 'landlord' see PARA 423 note 7.
9 Agricultural Holdings Act 1986 Sch 3 Pt II para 9(1).
10 As to the meaning of 'contract of tenancy' see PARA 425.
11 Agricultural Holdings Act 1986 Sch 3 Pt II para 9(2)(a).
12 As to the meaning of 'building' see PARA 432 note 6.
13 Agricultural Holdings Act 1986 Sch 3 Pt II para 9(2)(b).
14 Agricultural Holdings Act 1986 Sch 3 Pt II para 9(2)(c). In determining whether to grant a certificate under Sch 3 para 9 the Tribunal must also disregard any practice adopted by the tenant in compliance with any obligation accepted by or imposed on the tenant under statutory provisions concerning the designation of nitrate sensitive areas: Agricultural Holdings Act 1986 Sch 3 Pt II para 9(3) (added by the Water Act 1989 s 190(1), Sch 25 para 75; and amended by the Water Consolidation (Consequential Provisions) Act 1991 s 2(1), Sch 1 para 43). Provision concerning the designation of nitrate sensitive areas was made by the Water Resources Act 1991 ss 94, 95 which have now been repealed.
15 See the Agricultural Holdings Act 1986 s 25(4), (5); and PARA 470.
16 See the Agricultural Holdings Act 1986 s 61(1); and PARA 544.

477. Case D: non-compliance with notice to pay rent due or notice to remedy a breach of the tenancy.

Case D applies where at the date of the giving of the notice to quit[1] the tenant[2] had failed to comply with a written notice served on him by the landlord[3], being either a notice requiring him within two months of the service of the notice to pay any rent due in respect of the agricultural holding[4] to which the notice to quit relates[5] or a notice requiring him within a reasonable period specified in the notice to remedy[6] any breach by the tenant that was capable of being remedied of any term or condition of his tenancy which was not inconsistent with his responsibilities to farm[7] in accordance with the rules of good husbandry[8], and the notice to quit states that it is given by reason of such matter[9].

Where a notice in the prescribed form[10] requires the doing of any work of repair, maintenance or replacement, any further notice requiring the doing of any such work which is served on the tenant less than 12 months after the earlier notice must be disregarded unless the earlier notice was withdrawn with his agreement in writing[11]. A period of less than six months is not a reasonable period within which work may be done[12]. Any provision of the contract of tenancy[13] or other agreement with the landlord which indicates that the object of the practice is the furtherance of:

    (1)   the conservation of flora or fauna or of geological or physiographical features of special interest[14];

    (2)   the protection of buildings[15] or other objects of archaeological, architectural or historic interest[16]; or

    (3)   the conservation or enhancement of the natural beauty or amenity of the countryside or the promotion of its enjoyment by the public[17],

must be regarded as a term or condition which is not inconsistent with the tenant's responsibilities to farm in accordance with the rules of good husbandry[18].

Where a notice to quit is given under Case D relying on the tenant's failure to comply with a notice to do work[19], and the tenant serves on the landlord a counter-notice within one month of the notice to quit[20], the notice to quit is ineffective unless the Tribunal[21] consents to its operation on an application by the landlord[22]. The tenant may question the validity of the reason stated for the giving of the notice to quit by means of a notice requiring the determination of the question by arbitration[23], and in such a case a prior counter-notice is ineffective[24]; if, apart from this provision, the notice to quit would have effect in consequence of the arbitration, the tenant may serve such a counter-notice within one month of the delivery of the award to him[25].

Questions arising on notices to quit falling within Case D may be determined by arbitration[26].

1 As to the service of notices see PARA 428 note 4.
2 As to the meaning of 'tenant' see PARA 423 note 5.
3 As to the meaning of 'landlord' see PARA 423 note 7.
4 As to the meaning of 'agricultural holding' see PARA 423.
5 Agricultural Holdings Act 1986 Sch 3 Pt I Case D(a). Such notice must be in the prescribed form: see Sch 3 Pt II para 10(1)(a); and the Agricultural Holdings (Forms of Notice to Pay Rent or to Remedy) Regulations 1987, SI 1987/711, reg 3, Form 1. Rent must actually be due at the date of the preliminary notice: *Magdalen College, Oxford v Heritage* [1974] 1 All ER 1065, [1974] 1 WLR 441, CA; *Pickard v Bishop* (1975) 31 P & CR 108; *Urwick v Taylor* (1969) 212 Estates Gazette 1257. Payment of the overdue rent after the expiry of the two months' notice to pay is not compliance with the notice and does not prevent the tenant losing the protection of security of tenure given by the Agricultural Holdings Act 1986 even though the payment is made before the service of the notice to quit: *Stoneman v Brown* [1973] 2 All ER 225, [1973] 1 WLR 459, CA.
6 In order to comply with a notice to remedy, the tenant must remedy the breach completely: *Price v Romilly* [1960] 3 All ER 429, [1960] 1 WLR 1360.
7 As to the 'farming' of land see PARA 424.
8 Agricultural Holdings Act 1986 Sch 3 Pt I Case D(b). As to the rules of good husbandry for the purposes of the Agricultural Holdings Act 1986 see, by virtue of s 96(3) (see PARA 430 note 14), the Agriculture Act 1947 ss 10, 11; and AGRICULTURAL PRODUCTION AND MARKETING vol 1A (2017) PARAS 11–13. For these purposes compliance with any obligation accepted by or imposed on the tenant under the statutory provisions concerning the designation of nitrate sensitive areas (ie under the Water Resources Act 1991 ss 94, 95 (now repealed)) is not capable of constituting a breach by the tenant of the terms or conditions of his tenancy: Agricultural Holdings Act 1986 Sch 3 Pt II para 10(3) (added by the Water Act 1989 s 190(1), Sch 25 para 75; and amended by the Water Consolidation (Consequential Provisions) Act 1991 s 2(1), Sch 1 para 43).
    Notice must be in the prescribed form: see the Agricultural Holdings Act 1986 Sch 3 Pt II para 10(1)(a); and the Agricultural Holdings (Forms of Notice to Pay Rent or to Remedy) Regulations 1987, SI 1987/711, reg 4, Form 2. Different forms may be prescribed for this purpose in relation to different circumstances: Agricultural Holdings Act 1986 Sch 3 Pt II para 10(2).
9 Agricultural Holdings Act 1986 Sch 3 Pt I Case D.
10 See note 8.
11 Agricultural Holdings Act 1986 Sch 3 Pt II para 10(1)(b).
12 Agricultural Holdings Act 1986 Sch 3 Pt II para 10(1)(c).
13 As to the meaning of 'contract of tenancy' see PARA 425.
14 Agricultural Holdings Act 1986 Sch 3 Pt II paras 9(2)(a), 10(1)(d).
15 As to the meaning of 'building' see PARA 432 note 6.
16 Agricultural Holdings Act 1986 Sch 3 Pt II para 9(2)(b).
17 Agricultural Holdings Act 1986 Sch 3 Pt II para 9(2)(c).
18 Agricultural Holdings Act 1986 Sch 3 Pt II para 10(1)(d).
19 Agricultural Holdings Act 1986 s 28(1). 'Notice to do work' means a notice served on a tenant of an agricultural holding for the purposes of Case D(b) (see the text and notes 6–8), being a notice requiring the doing of any work of repair, maintenance or replacement: s 28(6). The fact that the position of a tenant who is served with a notice to remedy requiring him to do work is far stronger

than that of a tenant who is served with a non-work notice to remedy (inasmuch as the former has earlier and easier recourse to statutory arbitration) does not amount to discriminatory treatment in breach of the Convention for the Protection of Human Rights and Fundamental Freedoms (Rome, 4 November 1950; TS 71 (1953); Cmd 8969) art 14 (prohibition on discrimination: see RIGHTS AND FREEDOMS vol 88A (2013) PARA 506): *Lancashire County Council v Taylor* [2005] EWCA Civ 284, [2005] 1 WLR 2668, [2005] 2 EGLR 17.

20 Agricultural Holdings Act 1986 s 28(3).
21 Ie in England, the First-tier Tribunal (see PARA 768) and in Wales, the Agricultural Land Tribunal for Wales (see PARA 767): see PARA 437 note 1.
22 Agricultural Holdings Act 1986 s 28(2). The tribunal must so consent unless it appears to it, having regard to:
(1)   the extent to which the tenant has failed to comply with the notice to do work (s 28(5)(a));
(2)   the consequences of his failure to comply with it in any respect (s 28(5)(b)); and
(3)   the circumstances surrounding any such failure (s 28(5)(c)),
that a fair and reasonable landlord would not insist on possession (s 28(5)).
23 As to arbitrations generally see PARA 566 et seq.
24 Agricultural Holdings Act 1986 s 28(4)(a). In connection with proceedings under these provisions see *William Smith (Wakefield) Ltd v Parisride Ltd* [2005] EWHC 462 (Admin), [2005] 2 EGLR 22, [2005] 24 EG 180 (counter-notice for tribunal proceedings served by tenant under the Agricultural Holdings Act 1986 s 26 was not invalid under s 28(4) where it was served concurrently with notice requiring arbitration).
25 Agricultural Holdings Act 1986 s 28(4)(b).
26 See the Agricultural Holdings (Arbitration on Notices) Order 1987, SI 1987/710, art 9; and PARA 488 et seq.

478. Case E: irremediable breach.

Case E applies where at the date of the giving of the notice to quit[1] the landlord's[2] interest in the holding to which the notice relates had been materially prejudiced by the commission by the tenant[3] of a breach, not capable of being remedied, of any term or condition of the tenancy which was not inconsistent with the tenant's responsibilities to farm[4] in accordance with the rules of good husbandry[5], and it is stated in the notice that it is given for that reason[6].

Where the landlord is a smallholdings authority[7], or is the Secretary of State or the Welsh Ministers[8] and the holding is on land held for the purposes of smallholdings[9], then in considering whether the landlord's interests have been materially prejudiced, regard must be had to the effect of the breach not only on the holding itself but also on the carrying out of the arrangements for the letting and conduct of smallholdings[10].

Any provision of the contract of tenancy[11] or other agreement with the landlord which indicates that the object of the practice is the furtherance of:
(1)   the conservation of flora or fauna or of geological or physiographical features of special interest[12];
(2)   the protection of buildings[13] or other objects of archaeological, architectural or historic interest[14]; or
(3)   the conservation or enhancement of the natural beauty or amenity of the countryside or the promotion of its enjoyment by the public[15],
must be regarded as a term or condition which is not inconsistent with the tenant's responsibilities to farm in accordance with the rules of good husbandry[16].

Questions arising on notices to quit which fall within Case E may be determined by arbitration[17].

1 As to the service of notices see PARA 428 note 4.
2 As to the meaning of 'landlord' see PARA 423 note 7.
3 As to the meaning of 'tenant' see PARA 423 note 5.
4 As to the 'farming' of land see PARA 424.

5   As to the rules of good husbandry for the purposes of the Agricultural Holdings Act 1986 see, by virtue of s 96(3) (see PARA 430 note 14), the Agriculture Act 1947 ss 10, 11; and AGRICULTURAL PRODUCTION AND MARKETING vol 1A (2017) PARAS 11–13.

6   Agricultural Holdings Act 1986 Sch 3 Pt I Case E. For these purposes compliance with any obligation accepted by or imposed on the tenant under the statutory provisions concerning the designation of nitrate sensitive areas (ie under the Water Resources Act 1991 ss 94, 95 (now repealed)) is not capable of constituting a breach by the tenant of the terms or conditions of his tenancy: Agricultural Holdings Act 1986 Sch 3 Pt II para 11(3) (added by the Water Act 1989 s 190(1), Sch 25 para 75; and amended by the Water Consolidation (Consequential Provisions) Act 1991 s 2(1), Sch 1 para 43). A sub-letting in breach of covenant falls within Case E: *Scala House and District Property Co Ltd v Forbes* [1974] QB 575, [1973] 3 All ER 308, CA; *Troop v Gibson* [1986] 1 EGLR 1, (1985) 277 Estates Gazette 1134. In *Pennell v Payne* [1995] QB 192, [1995] 2 All ER 592, there was no material prejudice to the freeholder where the tenant sub-let as the sub-tenant had no security of tenure against the head landlord.

7   Agricultural Holdings Act 1986 Sch 3 Pt II para 11(1)(a). As to smallholdings authorities see PARAS 748–751.

8   As to the Secretary of State and the Welsh Ministers see PARA 741.

9   Agricultural Holdings Act 1986 Sch 3 Pt II para 11(1)(b).

10   Agricultural Holdings Act 1986 Sch 3 Pt II para 11(1).

11   As to the meaning of 'contract of tenancy' see PARA 425.

12   Agricultural Holdings Act 1986 Sch 3 Pt II paras 9(2)(a), 11(2).

13   As to the meaning of 'building' see PARA 432 note 6.

14   Agricultural Holdings Act 1986 Sch 3 Pt II para 9(2)(b).

15   Agricultural Holdings Act 1986 Sch 3 Pt II para 9(2)(c).

16   Agricultural Holdings Act 1986 Sch 3 Pt II para 11(2).

17   See the Agricultural Holdings (Arbitration on Notices) Order 1987, SI 1987/710, art 9; and PARA 488 et seq. As to arbitrations generally see PARA 566 et seq.

479. Case F: insolvency.

Case F applies where at the date of the giving of the notice to quit[1] the tenant[2] was a person who had become insolvent[3] and it is stated in the notice that it is given for that reason[4].

Questions arising on notices to quit which fall within Case F may be determined by arbitration[5].

1   As to the service of notices see PARA 428 note 4.

2   As to the meaning of 'tenant' see PARA 423 note 5.

3   As to when a tenant is 'insolvent' for these purposes see PARA 470 note 4.

4   Agricultural Holdings Act 1986 Sch 3 Pt I Case F.

5   See the Agricultural Holdings (Arbitration on Notices) Order 1987, SI 1987/710; and PARA 482 et seq. As to arbitrations generally see PARA 566 et seq.

480. Case G: death of tenant.

Case G applies where the notice to quit[1] is given following the death of a person who immediately before his death was the sole (or sole surviving) tenant[2] under the contract of tenancy[3], and not later than the end of the period of three months beginning with the date of any relevant notice[4], and it is stated in the notice to quit that it is given by reason of that person's death[5].

1   As to the service of notices see PARA 428 note 4.

2   As to the meaning of 'tenant' see PARA 423 note 5. For these purposes 'tenant' does not include an executor, administrator, trustee in bankruptcy or other person deriving title from a tenant by operation of law: Agricultural Holdings Act 1986 Sch 3 Pt II para 12(a).

3   Agricultural Holdings Act 1986 Sch 3 Pt I Case G(a). As to the meaning of 'contract of tenancy' see PARA 425.

4   Agricultural Holdings Act 1986 Sch 3 Pt I Case G(b). A reference to the date of any relevant notice is to be construed as a reference to the date on which a written notice was served on the landlord by or on behalf of an executor or administrator of the tenant's estate informing the landlord of the tenant's death, or the date on which the landlord was given notice of any succession application

with respect to the holding under s 39 (applications for tenancy of holding: see PARA 502) or s 41 (application to be treated as eligible: see PARA 499) or, where both of these events occur, to the date of whichever of them occurs first: Sch 3 Pt II para 12(b). As to the meaning of 'landlord' see PARA 423 note 7.

The relevant notice must be expressed in terms sufficiently clear to bring home to the ordinary landlord that the executors of the deceased are purporting to exercise the rights given to them under the Agricultural Holdings Act 1986: *Lees v Tatchell* (1990) 60 P & CR 228, [1990] 1 EGLR 10, CA.

5   Agricultural Holdings Act 1986 Sch 3 Pt I Case G.

481. Case H: ministry amalgamations.

Case H applies where the notice to quit[1] is given by the Secretary of State or the Welsh Ministers[2] and the Secretary of State certifies or the Welsh Ministers certify in writing that the notice to quit is given in order to enable him or them to use or dispose of the land for the purpose of any amalgamation[3] or the reshaping of any agricultural unit[4], and the instrument under which the tenancy was granted contains an acknowledgement signed by the tenant[5] that the tenancy is subject to the provisions of Case H, its precursor[6] or the statutory provisions empowering the Secretary of State and the Welsh Ministers to promote amalgamations and boundary adjustments[7].

1   As to the service of notices see PARA 428 note 4.
2   As to the Secretary of State and the Welsh Ministers see PARA 741.
3   For these purposes an 'amalgamation' is an amalgamation within the meaning of the Agriculture Act 1967 s 26(1) (see AGRICULTURAL PRODUCTION AND MARKETING vol 1A (2017) PARA 41): Agricultural Holdings Act 1986 Sch 3 Pt I Case H(a).
4   Agricultural Holdings Act 1986 Sch 3 Pt I Case H(a). As to the meaning of 'agricultural unit' see PARA 424 note 7.
5   As to the meaning of 'tenant' see PARA 423 note 5.
6   The precursor of Case H was the Agricultural Holdings (Notices to Quit) Act 1977 s 2(3) Case H (repealed).
7   Agricultural Holdings Act 1986 Sch 3 Pt I Case H(b). For the statutory provisions empowering the Secretary of State and the Welsh Ministers to promote amalgamations and boundary adjustments see the Agriculture Act 1967 s 29; and AGRICULTURAL PRODUCTION AND MARKETING vol 1A (2017) PARA 420.

(iv) Arbitration on Notices to Do Work

482. Arbitration on notice to remedy.

Where a tenant[1] on whom notice to do work[2] has been served wishes to have determined by arbitration[3]:

(1)   his liability under the terms or conditions of his tenancy to do any of the work specified in the notice[4];
(2)   the deletion from the notice of any item or part of an item of work on the ground that it is unnecessary or unjustified[5]; or
(3)   the substitution, in the case of any item or part of an item of work, of a different method or material for the method or material which the notice would otherwise require to be followed or used[6],

he must do so by service of a notice requiring the question or questions to be determined by arbitration[7]. The tenant's notice must be in writing and must be served on the landlord[8] within one month after the service on the tenant of the notice to do work[9]. The notice must specify, as the case may be, any items in respect of which the tenant denies liability[10], any items or parts of items which the tenant claims to be unnecessary or unjustified[11], and any method or material in respect of which the tenant desires a substitution to be made[12].

1   As to the meaning of 'tenant' see PARA 423 note 5.
2   A 'notice to do work' means a notice to remedy which requires the doing of any work of repair, replacement or maintenance; and a 'notice to remedy' is a notice served on the tenant of an agricultural holding for the purposes of Case D (see PARA 477) requiring him to remedy a breach of a term or condition of his tenancy: Agricultural Holdings (Arbitration on Notices) Order 1987, SI 1987/710, art 2(1). A notice to remedy must be in the prescribed form: see the Agricultural Holdings Act 1986 Sch 3 Pt II para 10(1)(a); and the Agricultural Holdings (Forms of Notice to Pay Rent or to Remedy) Regulations 1987, SI 1987/711, reg 4, Form 2. Different forms may be prescribed for this purpose in relation to different circumstances: Agricultural Holdings Act 1986 Sch 3 Pt II para 10(2). A notice to remedy requiring the doing of any work of repair, maintenance or replacement must be in the form prescribed by the Agricultural Holdings (Forms of Notice to Pay Rent or to Remedy) Regulations 1987, SI 1987/711, Form 2; and any other notice to remedy must be in the form prescribed by Form 3. As to the service of notices see PARA 428 note 4. As to the making of orders generally see PARA 432 note 5.
3   Ie arbitration under the Agricultural Holdings Act 1986: Agricultural Holdings (Arbitration on Notices) Order 1987, SI 1987/710, art 3(1). As to arbitrations generally see PARA 566 et seq.
4   Agricultural Holdings (Arbitration on Notices) Order 1987, SI 1987/710, art 3(1)(a).
5   Agricultural Holdings (Arbitration on Notices) Order 1987, SI 1987/710, art 3(1)(b).
6   Agricultural Holdings (Arbitration on Notices) Order 1987, SI 1987/710, art 3(1)(c).
7   Agricultural Holdings (Arbitration on Notices) Order 1987, SI 1987/710, art 3(1). Any other questions must be raised at the same time: see art 4(1), (2); and PARA 483. A failure by the tenant to comply with the notice in respect of work, liability for which he does not dispute will enable the landlord to serve a notice for non-compliance: see *Ladd's Radio and Television Service Ltd v Docker* (1973) 226 Estates Gazette 1565, CA.
8   As to the meaning of 'landlord' see PARA 423 note 7.
9   Agricultural Holdings (Arbitration on Notices) Order 1987, SI 1987/710, art 3(2). No form is prescribed for the tenant's notice.
10   Agricultural Holdings (Arbitration on Notices) Order 1987, SI 1987/710, art 3(3)(a).
11   Agricultural Holdings (Arbitration on Notices) Order 1987, SI 1987/710, art 3(3)(b).
12   Agricultural Holdings (Arbitration on Notices) Order 1987, SI 1987/710, art 3(3)(c).

483. Notice on additional questions.

Where a tenant[1] on whom a notice to do work[2] has been served wishes to have determined by arbitration[3] any additional question[4], he must do so by serving on the landlord[5], within one month after the service of the notice to do work, a written notice requiring the question to be so determined[6]. Where the tenant on whom a notice to do work has been served does not wish a question[7] to be determined by arbitration, but wishes to have any other question[8] arising under the notice determined by arbitration, he must do so either by serving on the landlord, within one month after the service of the notice to do work, a written notice requiring the question to be so determined[9] or by serving a notice requiring arbitration[10].

1   As to the meaning of 'tenant' see PARA 423 note 5.
2   As to the meaning of 'notice to do work' see PARA 482 note 2. As to the service of notices see PARA 428 note 4.
3   Ie arbitration under the Agricultural Holdings Act 1986: Agricultural Holdings (Arbitration on Notices) Order 1987, SI 1987/710, art 4(1). As to arbitrations generally see PARA 566 et seq.
4   A question in addition to one specified in the Agricultural Holdings (Arbitration on Notices) Order 1987, SI 1987/710, art 3(1) (see PARA 482), but which is not itself such a question: art 4(1).
5   As to the meaning of 'landlord' see PARA 423 note 7.
6   Agricultural Holdings (Arbitration on Notices) Order 1987, SI 1987/710, art 4(1).
7   Ie a question under the Agricultural Holdings (Arbitration on Notices) Order 1987, SI 1987/710, art 3(1) (see PARA 482).
8   Ie a question not within the Agricultural Holdings (Arbitration on Notices) Order 1987, SI 1987/710, art 3(1).

9   Agricultural Holdings (Arbitration on Notices) Order 1987, SI 1987/710, art 4(2)(a).
10 Agricultural Holdings (Arbitration on Notices) Order 1987, SI 1987/710, art 4(2)(b). The notice
    requiring arbitration must be in accordance with art 9 (see PARA 488).

484. Subsequent events making time unreasonable.

A tenant[1] who has required arbitration[2] and who has been found liable to comply with a notice to do work[3] or with any part of it is not precluded from subsequently requiring arbitration[4] on the ground that in consequence of anything happening before the expiration of the time for doing the work, as extended by the arbitrator[5], it would have been unreasonable to require the tenant to do the work within that time[6].

1   As to the meaning of 'tenant' see PARA 423 note 5.
2   Ie arbitration under the Agricultural Holdings Act 1986 by virtue of the Agricultural Holdings
    (Arbitration on Notices) Order 1987, SI 1987/710, art 4(1) (see PARA 483). As to arbitrations
    generally see PARA 566 et seq.
3   As to the meaning of 'notice to do work' see PARA 482 note 2.
4   Ie under the Agricultural Holdings (Arbitration on Notices) Order 1987, SI 1987/710, art 9 (see
    PARA 488).
5   Ie extended under the Agricultural Holdings (Arbitration on Notices) Order 1987, SI 1987/710,
    art 6(2) (see PARA 485).
6   Agricultural Holdings (Arbitration on Notices) Order 1987, SI 1987/710, art 4(3).

485. Modification of notice and extension of time.

In addition to his other powers[1] the arbitrator may, in relation to any question of the deletion from a notice to do work[2] of any item or part of an item on the ground that it is unnecessary or unjustified, modify such a notice by deleting any item or part of an item specified in the notice as to which, having due regard to the interests of good husbandry[3] as respects the agricultural holding[4] to which the notice relates, and of sound management of the estate which consists solely or partly of that holding, the arbitrator is satisfied that it is unnecessary or unjustified[5]. Additionally, in relation to any question arising on a notice to do work as to the substitution, in the case of any item or part of an item, of a different method or material[6], the arbitrator may modify the notice to effect such substitution where, having regard to the purpose which that item or part is intended to achieve, he is satisfied that the method or material which the notice would otherwise require to be used would involve undue difficulty or expense[7], the substituted method or material would be substantially as effective for that purpose[8], and that in all the circumstances the substitution is justified[9].

Where a tenant requires any question to be determined by arbitration[10] the time specified for doing the work which is the subject of the arbitration is extended until the termination[11] of the arbitration[12]. Where the arbitrator finds that the tenant is liable to comply with the notice to do work or with any part of it, he must extend the time for doing that work by such further period as he thinks fit[13].

1   See PARA 486.
2   Ie any question specified in the Agricultural Holdings (Arbitration on Notices) Order 1987,
    SI 1987/710, art 3(1)(b) (see PARA 482). As to the meaning of 'notice to do work' see PARA 482
    note 2.
3   As to the rules of good husbandry for the purposes of the Agricultural Holdings Act 1986 see, by
    virtue of s 96(3) (see PARA 430 note 14), the Agriculture Act 1947 ss 10, 11; and AGRICULTURAL
    PRODUCTION AND MARKETING vol 1A (2017) PARAS 11–13.
4   As to the meaning of 'agricultural holding' see PARA 423.
5   Agricultural Holdings (Arbitration on Notices) Order 1987, SI 1987/710, art 5(a).
6   Ie any question specified in the Agricultural Holdings (Arbitration on Notices) Order 1987,
    SI 1987/710, art 3(1)(c) (see PARA 482).

7 Agricultural Holdings (Arbitration on Notices) Order 1987, SI 1987/710, art 5(b)(i).
8 Agricultural Holdings (Arbitration on Notices) Order 1987, SI 1987/710, art 5(b)(ii).
9 Agricultural Holdings (Arbitration on Notices) Order 1987, SI 1987/710, art 5(b)(iii).
10 Ie under the Agricultural Holdings (Arbitration on Notices) Order 1987, SI 1987/710, art 3 (see PARA 482) or art 4 (see PARAS 483–484).
11 'Termination', in relation to arbitration, means the date on which the arbitrator's award is delivered to the tenant: Agricultural Holdings (Arbitration on Notices) Order 1987, SI 1987/710, art 2(1).
12 Agricultural Holdings (Arbitration on Notices) Order 1987, SI 1987/710, art 6(1).
13 Agricultural Holdings (Arbitration on Notices) Order 1987, SI 1987/710, art 6(2).

486. Date of termination of tenancy on failure to do work.
Where the arbitrator extends the time specified for doing any work[1] he may, either of his own motion or on the application of the landlord[2] made not later than 14 days after the termination[3] of the arbitration, specify a date for the termination of the tenancy by notice to quit in the event of the tenant's failure to do the work within the extended time[4]. The date so specified must not, however, be earlier than whichever is the later of:

(1)   the date on which the tenancy could have been terminated by notice to quit served on the expiration of the time originally specified in the notice to do work[5]; and

(2)   six months after the expiration of the extended time[6].

Where the landlord makes an application for the arbitrator to specify a date, he must, unless the application is made at the arbitration, at the same time give written notice[7] of the application to the tenant[8], and the tenant is entitled to be heard on the application[9]. A notice to quit on a date specified by the arbitrator must be served on the tenant within one month of the expiration of the extended time and, subject to any right of the tenant to contest it, will be valid notwithstanding that it is served less than 12 months before the date on which the tenancy is to be terminated or that that date is not the end of a year of the tenancy[10].

1 Ie under the Agricultural Holdings (Arbitration on Notices) Order 1987, SI 1987/710, art 6(2) (see PARA 485).
2 As to the meaning of 'landlord' see PARA 423 note 7.
3 As to the meaning of 'termination' see PARA 485 note 11.
4 Agricultural Holdings (Arbitration on Notices) Order 1987, SI 1987/710, art 7(1).
5 Agricultural Holdings (Arbitration on Notices) Order 1987, SI 1987/710, art 7(2)(a). As to the meaning of 'notice to do work' see PARA 482 note 2.
6 Agricultural Holdings (Arbitration on Notices) Order 1987, SI 1987/710, art 7(2)(b).
7 As to the service of notices see PARA 428 note 4.
8 As to the meaning of 'tenant' see PARA 423 note 5.
9 Agricultural Holdings (Arbitration on Notices) Order 1987, SI 1987/710, art 7(3).
10 Agricultural Holdings (Arbitration on Notices) Order 1987, SI 1987/710, art 7(4). As to the normal period of notice required on a notice to quit see PARA 470.

487. Recovery of the cost of work.
Where an arbitration relates wholly or partly to a question as to the liability of the tenant[1] to do work specified in the notice to do work[2] and it appears to the arbitrator that the tenant has done work specified in the notice which he was under no obligation to do, the arbitrator must determine the reasonable cost of such work, which is then recoverable from the landlord[3].

1 As to the meaning of 'tenant' see PARA 423 note 5.
2 Ie a question under the Agricultural Holdings (Arbitration on Notices) Order 1987, SI 1987/710, art 3(1)(a) (see PARA 482). As to the meaning of 'notice to do work' see PARA 482 note 2.

3 Agricultural Holdings (Arbitration on Notices) Order 1987, SI 1987/710, art 8. As to the meaning of 'landlord' see PARA 423 note 7. The provisions of the Agricultural Holdings Act 1986 s 85(1) (recovery of a sum as if payable as an order of the county court if the sum is not paid within 14 days of becoming due: see PARA 572) apply to the recovery of this cost from the landlord: Agricultural Holdings (Arbitration on Notices) Order 1987, SI 1987/710, art 8.

(v) Arbitration concerning Notices to Quit

488. Notice requiring arbitration, appointment of arbitrator and service of counter-notice.

Where it is stated in a notice to quit that the notice is given for one or more of the reasons stated in Case A[1], B[2], D[3] or E[4], and the tenant[5] wishes to contest any question arising out of the provisions relating to those Cases[6], he must within one month after the service of the notice[7] serve on the landlord[8] notice in writing requiring the question to be determined by arbitration[9]. This is the only procedure available for the purpose of contesting a reason specified in a notice to quit given under Case A, B, D or E[10]. However, it does not follow that the tenant is precluded from challenging in court a notice to quit on some other ground, eg that it is bad in law or is unclear[11].

A notice requiring arbitration[12] ceases to be effective three months after the date of service unless before the expiry of those three months, for the purposes of the arbitration either:

(1) an arbitrator has been appointed by agreement between the parties[13]; or

(2) an application has been made[14] for the appointment of an arbitrator[15].

Where arbitration is required in respect of a notice to quit which is capable of taking effect either as a notice the operation of which can be restricted by the service of a counter-notice[16] or as a notice the operation of which cannot be so restricted[17], and in consequence of the arbitration the notice takes effect as a notice the operation of which can be restricted by the service of a counter-notice[18], the time within which a counter-notice may be served by the tenant on the landlord is one month from the termination of the arbitration[19].

1 See PARA 474.
2 See PARA 475.
3 See PARA 477.
4 See PARA 478.
5 As to the meaning of 'tenant' see PARA 423 note 5.
6 Ie arising out of the Agricultural Holdings Act 1986 s 26(2), Sch 3 (see PARAS 474–481).
7 As to the service of notices see PARA 428 note 4.
8 As to the meaning of 'landlord' see PARA 423 note 7.
9 Agricultural Holdings (Arbitration on Notices) Order 1987, SI 1987/710, art 9. 'Arbitration' means arbitration under the Agricultural Holdings Act 1986: Agricultural Holdings (Arbitration on Notices) Order 1987, SI 1987/710, art 9. As to arbitrations generally see PARA 566 et seq.
10 *Ladd's Radio and Television Service Ltd v Docker* (1973) 226 Estates Gazette 1565, CA; *Crown Estates Comrs v Allingham* (1973) 226 Estates Gazette 2153, CA; *A-G for the Duchy of Lancaster v Simcock* [1966] Ch 1, [1965] 2 All ER 32; *Magdalen College, Oxford v Heritage* [1974] 1 All ER 1065, [1974] 1 WLR 441, CA; *Harding v Marshall* (1983) 267 Estates Gazette 161, CA; *Parrish v Kinsey* [1983] 2 EGLR 13, 268 Estates Gazette 1113, CA.
11 *Rous v Mitchell* [1991] 1 All ER 676, [1991] 1 WLR 469, CA (court retained jurisdiction on failure of tenant to serve demand for arbitration where notice to quit was fraudulent)). In the case of a serviceman (see PARA 491 note 8) the tenant's failure to serve a notice under the Agricultural Holdings (Arbitration on Notices) Order 1987, SI 1987/710, art 9 does not affect his right to contest a question in proceedings consequent upon the service of a counter-notice or in any arbitration which the Tribunal has required for the purpose of determining such question: see art

17(3). The Tribunal in England is the First-tier Tribunal (see PARA 768) and in Wales, the Agricultural Land Tribunal for Wales (see PARA 767): see PARA 437 note 1.

12 Ie under Agricultural Holdings (Arbitration on Notices) Order 1987, SI 1987/710, art 9 (see the text and notes 1–9).

13 Agricultural Holdings (Arbitration on Notices) Order 1987, SI 1987/710, art 10(a).

14 Ie under the Agricultural Holdings Act 1986 s 84(2) (see PARA 567).

15 Agricultural Holdings (Arbitration on Notices) Order 1987, SI 1987/710, art 10(b) (amended by SI 2006/2805).

16 Ie a notice to which the Agricultural Holdings Act 1986 s 26(1) (see PARA 471) applies. See *Rous v Mitchell* [1991] 1 All ER 676, [1991] 1 WLR 469, CA (failure to serve demand for arbitration where notice to quit was fraudulent).

17 Ie a notice to which the Agricultural Holdings Act 1986 s 26(2) (see PARA 473) applies.

18 See note 14.

19 Agricultural Holdings (Arbitration on Notices) Order 1987, SI 1987/710, art 11. As to the meaning of 'termination' in relation to arbitration see PARA 485 note 11. As to the disapplication of art 11 in relation to servicemen see art 17(4). As to a serviceman as tenant on whom a notice to quit is served see PARA 491.

489. Postponement of operation of notice to quit.

Where a tenant[1] requires the determination by arbitration of a question arising out of a notice to quit[2], the operation of the notice is suspended until the expiry of the time fixed[3] for appointing or making an application for the appointment of an arbitrator[4], or, where such appointment or application has already been made, until the termination of the arbitration[5].

Where, in consequence of an arbitration, a notice to quit takes effect or the Tribunal[6] has consented to its operation[7], and the notice would otherwise come into operation on or within six months after the termination of the arbitration or the giving of the consent[8], the arbitrator or the Tribunal may, either of his or its own motion or on the application of the tenant made not later than 14 days after the termination of the arbitration or the giving of the consent, postpone the termination of the tenancy for a period not exceeding 12 months[9]. Where the tenant makes such an application he must, unless it is made at the hearing or before the Tribunal, at the same time give the landlord[10] written notice[11] of the application, and the landlord is entitled to be heard on the application[12].

1 As to the meaning of 'tenant' see PARA 423 note 5.

2 Ie by virtue of the Agricultural Holdings (Arbitration on Notices) Order 1987, SI 1987/710, art 9 (see PARA 488), under the Agricultural Holdings Act 1986. As to arbitrations generally see PARA 566 et seq.

3 Ie under the Agricultural Holdings (Arbitration on Notices) Order 1987, SI 1987/710, art 10 (see PARA 488).

4 Agricultural Holdings (Arbitration on Notices) Order 1987, SI 1987/710, art 12(a) (amended by SI 2006/2805).

5 Agricultural Holdings (Arbitration on Notices) Order 1987, SI 1987/710, art 12(b). As to the meaning of 'termination' in relation to arbitrations see PARA 485 note 11.

6 Ie in England, the First-tier Tribunal (see PARA 768) and in Wales, the Agricultural Land Tribunal for Wales (see PARA 767): see PARA 437 note 1.

7 Agricultural Holdings (Arbitration on Notices) Order 1987, SI 1987/710, art 13(1)(a). The reference in the text to a tribunal consenting to the operation of a notice to quit is a reference to the tribunal having so consented under the Agricultural Holdings Act 1986 s 26(1) (see PARA 471) or s 28(2) (see PARA 477).

8 Agricultural Holdings (Arbitration on Notices) Order 1987, SI 1987/710, art 13(1)(b).

9 Agricultural Holdings (Arbitration on Notices) Order 1987, SI 1987/710, art 13(1).

10 As to the meaning of 'landlord' see PARA 423 note 7.

11 As to the service of notices see PARA 428 note 4.

12 Agricultural Holdings (Arbitration on Notices) Order 1987, SI 1987/710, art 13(2).

490. Extension of time under notice to remedy after notice to quit.

Where a notice to quit is stated to be by reason of the tenant's[1] failure to remedy a breach of any term or condition of his tenancy within the time specified in the notice to remedy[2] or within that time as extended[3], and it appears to the arbitrator[4] that, notwithstanding that the time originally specified was reasonable, it would have been unreasonable to require the tenant to remedy the breach within that time[5], then the arbitrator may treat the time as having been extended or further extended and may make his award as if the time had not expired[6].

Where the time specified for doing any work is so extended[7], the arbitrator may, of his own motion or on the application of the landlord made not later than 14 days after the termination of the arbitration[8], specify a date for the termination of the tenancy by a subsequent notice to quit in the event of the tenant's failure to do the work in the extended time[9]. That date must not be earlier than whichever is the later of the date on which the tenancy could have been terminated by the original notice to quit[10] or six months after the expiration of the extended time[11]. Where the landlord applies to the arbitrator to specify such a date, he must, unless the application is made at the arbitration, at the same time give the tenant written notice of the application, and the tenant is entitled to be heard on the application[12]. A notice to quit on a date so specified must be served on the tenant within one month after the expiration of the extended time and is valid notwithstanding that it is served less than 12 months before the date on which the tenancy is terminated or that that date is not the end of the year of the tenancy[13]. Where a subsequent notice to quit is given on a date specified, in a case where the original notice to quit included a statement in accordance with Case D to the effect that it was given by reason of the tenant's failure to comply with a notice to do work[14], if the tenant serves a written counter-notice on the landlord within one month of that subsequent notice (or, if the date specified in that notice for the determination is earlier, before that date) the subsequent notice is ineffective without the consent of the Tribunal[15]. On such an application made by the landlord the Tribunal must consent to the operation of the notice to quit unless it appears to it, having regard to the extent to which the tenant has failed to comply with the notice to do work[16], to the consequences of his failure to comply with it in any respect[17], and to the circumstances surrounding any such failure[18], that a fair and reasonable landlord would not insist on possession[19].

1 As to the meaning of 'tenant' see PARA 423 note 5.
2 Agricultural Holdings (Arbitration on Notices) Order 1987, SI 1987/710, art 14(a)(i). See Case D(b); and PARA 477. As to the meaning of 'notice to remedy' see PARA 482 note 2.
3 Agricultural Holdings (Arbitration on Notices) Order 1987, SI 1987/710, art 14(a)(ii). The reference in the text to the time as extended is a reference to its extension either by the landlord or in pursuance of art 6 (see PARA 485). As to the meaning of 'landlord' see PARA 423 note 7.
4 Ie on an arbitration under the Agricultural Holdings (Arbitration on Notices) Order 1987, SI 1987/710, art 9 (see PARA 488).
5 Agricultural Holdings (Arbitration on Notices) Order 1987, SI 1987/710, art 14(b).
6 Agricultural Holdings (Arbitration on Notices) Order 1987, SI 1987/710, art 14. The arbitrator may extend the time by such period as he considers reasonable having regard to the length of time which has elapsed since the service of the notice to remedy: art 14. As to the service of notices see PARA 428 note 4.
7 Ie under the Agricultural Holdings (Arbitration on Notices) Order 1987, SI 1987/710, art 14 (see the text and notes 1–6).
8 As to the meaning of 'termination' in relation to arbitrations see PARA 485 note 11.
9 Agricultural Holdings (Arbitration on Notices) Order 1987, SI 1987/710, art 15(1).
10 Agricultural Holdings (Arbitration on Notices) Order 1987, SI 1987/710, art 15(2)(a). The notice referred to in the text is the notice which was the subject of the arbitration.
11 Agricultural Holdings (Arbitration on Notices) Order 1987, SI 1987/710, art 15(2)(b).

12 Agricultural Holdings (Arbitration on Notices) Order 1987, SI 1987/710, art 15(3).
13 Agricultural Holdings (Arbitration on Notices) Order 1987, SI 1987/710, art 15(4).
14 As to the meaning of 'notice to do work' see PARA 482 note 2.
15 Agricultural Holdings (Arbitration on Notices) Order 1987, SI 1987/710, art 15(5). In England the Tribunal is the First-tier Tribunal (see PARA 768) and in Wales it is the Agricultural Land Tribunal for Wales (see PARA 767): see PARA 437 note 1.
16 Agricultural Holdings (Arbitration on Notices) Order 1987, SI 1987/710, art 15(6)(a).
17 Agricultural Holdings (Arbitration on Notices) Order 1987, SI 1987/710, art 15(6)(b).
18 Agricultural Holdings (Arbitration on Notices) Order 1987, SI 1987/710, art 15(6)(c).
19 Agricultural Holdings (Arbitration on Notices) Order 1987, SI 1987/710, art 15(6).

491. Notice to quit where tenant is a serviceman.

Where a serviceman[1] who is the tenant of an agricultural holding[2] which comprises a dwelling house occupied by the person responsible for the control (whether as tenant or as servant or agent of the tenant) of the farming[3] of the holding[4] is given notice[5] to quit the holding[6] or part thereof being a part which consists of or comprises such a dwelling house[7], and the notice is given during the tenant's period of residence protection[8], he may serve a counter-notice[9] on the landlord[10], rendering the notice to quit ineffective without the consent of the Tribunal[11], notwithstanding that the circumstances fall within any of Cases B to G[12]. If the Tribunal is satisfied that any of the circumstances do fall within those Cases, it is not obliged to withhold consent by reason only of its not being satisfied of the existence of circumstances which are normally prerequisite to consent[13].

In determining whether to give or withhold its consent the Tribunal, if it is satisfied that the circumstances fall within any of Cases B to G, or that circumstances exist of which it must normally be satisfied before giving consent[14], must consider to what extent, if at all, the existence of those circumstances is directly or indirectly attributable to the serviceman's performing or having performed the period of relevant service[15]. Furthermore, the Tribunal must in any event consider to what extent, if at all, the giving of consent at a time during the period of protection would cause special hardship in view of circumstances directly or indirectly due to the serviceman's performing or having performed the period of relevant service[16], and must withhold consent unless in all the circumstances it considers it reasonable to give it[17].

When a serviceman is serving abroad[18], counter-notice may be authorised by the Tribunal to be served on his behalf; subsequent necessary acts may be done and proceedings conducted by a person deemed duly authorised so to do by the Tribunal[19].

Where, on an application by the landlord for the Tribunal's consent to a notice to quit, it appears to the Tribunal that the reason or reasons fall within Case B, Case D or Case E and that it is expedient that any question arising in relation to such reasons should be determined by arbitration, it may require the determination of the question before considering whether to grant or withhold consent[20].

1 See note 8.
2 As to the meaning of 'tenant' see PARA 423 note 5. As to the meaning of 'agricultural holding' see PARA 423.
3 As to the 'farming' of land see PARA 424.
4 Ie a dwelling house within the Rent Act 1977 s 10 (see LANDLORD AND TENANT vol 63 (2016) PARA 713) or the Housing Act 1988 Sch 1 para 7 (see LANDLORD AND TENANT vol 63 (2016) PARA 839): Agricultural Holdings Act 1986 s 30, Sch 5 para 2(2)(a) (amended by the Housing Act 1988 s 140(1), Sch 17 para 70).
5 As to the service of notices see PARA 428 note 4.

6 Agricultural Holdings Act 1986 Sch 5 para 2(1)(b)(i).
7 Agricultural Holdings Act 1986 Sch 5 para 2(1)(b)(ii), (2)(b).
8 Agricultural Holdings Act 1986 Sch 5 para 2(1)(a). 'Period of residence protection' means, in the case of a serviceman who performs a period of relevant service other than a short period of training, the period comprising that period of service and the four months immediately following the date on which it ends; a 'serviceman' is a man or woman who performs a period of relevant service; and 'relevant service' and 'short period of training' have the meanings given by the Reserve and Auxiliary Forces (Protection of Civil Interests) Act 1951 s 64(1) (see ARMED FORCES vol 3 (2011) PARA 357): Agricultural Holdings Act 1986 Sch 5 para 1.
   As to where notice to quit is served before the period of residence protection see note 17.
9 Ie a notice within the Agricultural Holdings Act 1986 s 26(1) (see PARA 471).
10 As to the meaning of 'landlord' see PARA 423 note 7.
11 Ie in England, the First-tier Tribunal (see PARA 768) and in Wales, the Agricultural Land Tribunal for Wales (see PARA 767): see PARA 437 note 1. See also the Reserve and Auxiliary Forces (Agricultural Tenants) Regulations 1959, SI 1959/84, reg 3 (amended by SI 2013/1036).
12 Agricultural Holdings Act 1986 Sch 5 para 3(1). For Cases B–G see PARAS 475–480.
13 Agricultural Holdings Act 1986 Sch 5 para 3(1). The circumstances normally prerequisite to consent are those contained in s 27(3)(a)–(f) (see PARA 472).
14 See note 13.
15 Agricultural Holdings Act 1986 Sch 5 para 3(2)(a). See also note 17.
16 Agricultural Holdings Act 1986 Sch 5 para 3(2)(b). See also note 17.
17 Agricultural Holdings Act 1986 Sch 5 para 3(2). The provisions of Sch 5 para 3(2) apply, mutatis mutandis, to a serviceman to whom notice was given before his period of residence protection began, who subsequently served a counter-notice, where the Tribunal has not by the beginning of that period decided whether to give or withhold consent to the operation of the notice: Sch 5 para 4.
18 Ie when he is performing a period of relevant service and is outside the United Kingdom: Agricultural Holdings Act 1986 Sch 5 para 6(2). 'United Kingdom' means Great Britain and Northern Ireland: Interpretation Act 1978 s 5, Sch 1. 'Great Britain' means England, Scotland and Wales: Union with Scotland Act 1706, preamble art I; Interpretation Act 1978 s 22(1), Sch 2 para 5(a). Neither the Isle of Man nor the Channel Islands are within the United Kingdom. See further CONSTITUTIONAL AND ADMINISTRATIVE LAW vol 20 (2014) PARA 3.
19 See the Reserve and Auxiliary Forces (Agricultural Tenancies) Regulations 1959, SI 1959/84, regs 5, 6 (made under the Reserve and Auxiliary Forces (Protection of Civil Interests) Act 1951 s 22(4); and amended by SI 2013/1036). Application is to be made in writing to the secretary of the tribunal for the area in which the holding is wholly or in greater part situate (Reserve and Auxiliary Forces (Agricultural Tenancies) Regulations 1959, SI 1959/84, reg 7); and authority is given by the chairman (regs 5, 6).
20 Agricultural Holdings (Arbitration on Notices) 1959 1987, SI 1987/710, art 17(1).

492. Notice to quit part under section 31.
A notice to quit part of an agricultural holding[1] would be bad at common law in the absence of a contractual provision authorising the giving of such notice[2]. But, a notice to quit part of an agricultural holding held on a tenancy from year to year given by the landlord[3] of the holding is not invalid on the ground that it relates to part only of the holding if it is given either for the purpose of adjusting the boundaries between agricultural units[4] or amalgamating agricultural units or parts of such units[5], or with a view to the use of the land[6] to which the notice relates for the purpose of any of the objects listed below[7], and the notice states that it is given for that purpose or with a view to any such use object, as the case may be[8].

The objects mentioned above are:
(1) the erection of cottages or other houses for farm labourers whether with or without gardens[9];
(2) the provision of gardens for cottages or other houses for farm labourers[10];
(3) the provision of allotments[11];

(4)   the letting of land (with or without other land) as a smallholding[12];

(5)   the planting of trees[13];

(6)   the opening or working of a deposit of coal, ironstone, limestone, brick-earth, or other mineral, or a stone quarry, or a clay, sand or gravel pit, or the construction of any works or buildings to be used in connection therewith[14];

(7)   the making of a watercourse or reservoir[15]; or

(8)   the making of a road, railway, tramroad, siding, canal or basin, or a wharf, pier or other work connected therewith[16].

1   As to the meaning of 'agricultural holding' see PARA 423.
2   *Re Bebington's Tenancy, Bebington v Wildman* [1921] 1 Ch 559; *Woodward v Earl of Dudley* [1954] Ch 283, [1954] 1 All ER 559. The landlord's notice to quit part of the premises must be in writing: cf *Moyle v Jenkins* (1881) 8 QBD 116, DC; *R v Shurmer* (1886) 17 QBD 323; *R v Harris* (1918) 82 JP 196.
3   As to the meaning of 'landlord' see PARA 423 note 7.
4   As to the meaning of 'agricultural unit' see PARA 424 note 7.
5   Agricultural Holdings Act 1986 s 31(1)(a).
6   As to the use of land for agriculture see PARA 424 note 7.
7   Agricultural Holdings Act 1986 s 31(1)(b).
8   Agricultural Holdings Act 1986 s 31(1).
9   Agricultural Holdings Act 1986 s 31(2)(a).
10 Agricultural Holdings Act 1986 s 31(2)(b).
11 Agricultural Holdings Act 1986 s 31(2)(c).
12 Agricultural Holdings Act 1986 s 31(2)(d). For this purpose, a 'smallholding' is a smallholding under the Agriculture Act 1970 Pt III (ss 37–65) (see PARA 627 et seq).
13 Agricultural Holdings Act 1986 s 31(2)(e).
14 Agricultural Holdings Act 1986 s 31(2)(f).
15 Agricultural Holdings Act 1986 s 31(2)(g).
16 Agricultural Holdings Act 1986 s 31(2)(h).

493. Notice to quit part under other means.

The contract of tenancy[1] may expressly provide for notice to quit part only of the holding; additionally, on severance by conveyance, surrender or otherwise of the reversionary estate in any land comprised in a lease (which includes an underlease or other tenancy) every condition or right of re-entry (which includes the right to determine the lease by notice to quit or otherwise) is apportioned and remains annexed to the several parts of the reversionary estate as severed[2].

1   As to the meaning of 'contract of tenancy' see PARA 425.
2   Law of Property Act 1925 s 140(1).

494. Rent reduction following notice to quit part.

Where the landlord[1] resumes possession of part of the holding, whether such resumption is by virtue of the Agricultural Holdings Act 1986 or in pursuance of a provision in that behalf contained in the contract of tenancy[2] the tenant is entitled to a proportionate reduction of rent in respect of that part of the holding, and in respect of any depreciation of the value to him of the residue of the holding caused by the severance or by the use to be made of the part severed[3]. In default of agreement the amount of that reduction must be determined by arbitration[4] or notwithstanding this provision, the landlord and tenant may instead refer for third party determination the question of the amount of rent to which the tenant is entitled[5]. Where it falls to the arbitrator or, as the case may be, the third party, to assess the amount of reduction in a case where the landlord's resumption of possession of part of the holding is pursuant to a provision in the contract of tenancy[6], the arbitrator must take into consideration any benefit or relief allowed to the tenant under the contract of tenancy[7].

1   As to the meaning of 'landlord' see PARA 423 note 7.
2   Agricultural Holdings Act 1986 ss 31(1) (see PARA 492), 33(1). As to the meaning of 'contract of tenancy' see PARA 425.
3   Agricultural Holdings Act 1986 s 33(1).
4   Agricultural Holdings Act 1986 s 33(2). As to arbitrations generally see PARA 566 et seq.
5   Agricultural Holdings Act 1986 s 33(2A) (added by the Deregulation Act 2015 Sch 4 para 14(2)). As to third party determinations see PARA 568.
6   As to the meaning of 'contract of tenancy' see PARA 425.
7   Agricultural Holdings Act 1986 s 33(3) (amended by the Deregulation Act 2015 Sch 4 para 14(3)).

495.   Notice to quit part treated as notice to quit entire holding.

Where a notice to quit is served by a person entitled to a severed part of the reversion so that it extends to part only of the land demised, the lessee may within one month determine the lease in regard to the rest of the land by giving to the owner of the reversionary estate therein a counter-notice expiring at the same time as the original notice[1]. Where a notice to quit part of an agricultural holding[2] is given to a tenant[3] and that notice either has been rendered valid[4] or is a notice given by a person entitled to a severed part of the reversionary estate in the holding[5], then if within 28 days after the giving of the notice[6] or, where the operation of the notice depends on proceedings under statute[7], within 28 days after the time at which it is determined that the notice has effect[8], the tenant gives to the landlord[9] (or the person entitled under the severance) written counter-notice that he accepts the notice to quit as a notice to quit the entire holding, the notice to quit takes such effect[10].

1   Law of Property Act 1925 ss 140(1), (2), 154 (s 140(2) amended by the Agricultural Holdings Act 1948 s 98, Sch 8). See also LANDLORD AND TENANT vol 62 (2016) PARA 446.
2   As to the meaning of 'agricultural holding' see PARA 423.
3   As to the meaning of 'tenant' see PARA 423 note 5. As to the service of notices see PARA 428 note 4.
4   Agricultural Holdings Act 1986 s 32(1)(a). The reference in the text to a notice having been rendered valid is a reference to its being so rendered by virtue of s 31 (see PARA 492).
5   Agricultural Holdings Act 1986 s 32(1)(b).
6   Agricultural Holdings Act 1986 s 32(2)(a).
7   Ie proceedings under the Agricultural Holdings Act 1986 Pt III (ss 25–33).
8   Agricultural Holdings Act 1986 s 32(2)(b).
9   As to the meaning of 'landlord' see PARA 423 note 7.
10   Agricultural Holdings Act 1986 s 32(2). Severance of the freehold reversion does not operate to create two or more tenancies, whether or not accompanied by a legal apportionment of the rent: *Jelley v Buckman* [1974] QB 488, [1973] 3 All ER 853, CA; *Stiles v Farrow* (1977) 241 Estates Gazette 623. If the landlord of the newly created severed part is a mere nominee of the landlord of the remaining part and if that fact is clear on the face of the documents, even though the estate may have been severed the equitable interest will remain whole and undivided and the nominee landlord of the severed part will not be able to implement the provisions of the Law of Property Act 1925 s 140 (see the text and note 1): *Persey v Bazeley* (1984) 47 P & CR 37, CA. Cf also *John v George* (1995) 71 P & CR 375, [1996] 1 EGLR 7, CA (landlords conveyed part of reversion to trustees on trust for daughter; trustees notice to quit part upheld). For the position relating to compensation see the Agricultural Holdings Act 1986 s 60(1)(b); and PARA 544.

496.   Operation of notices to quit against sub-tenants.

The right of a tenant[1] to restrict the operation of a notice to quit by means of a counter-notice does not apply where notice to quit a holding or part of a holding is given to a sub-tenant[2] by a tenant who has himself been given notice to quit[3] that holding or that part and the fact that the tenant has been given such notice is stated in the notice given to the sub-tenant[4]; but the notice given to the sub-tenant will not have effect if that given to the tenant does not have effect[5]. A notice to quit part of a holding which is accepted by the tenant[6] as a notice to quit the entire holding is deemed for the purpose of these provisions to be a notice to quit the entire holding given by the landlord to his tenant[7]. If the notice to quit served by the landlord on the tenant is a valid notice to quit which puts an end to the tenancy of the whole of the property at the expiry of the notice, any sub-tenancy created during the existence of the tenancy is also ended by the ordinary application of common law[8].

1 Ie under the Agricultural Holdings Act 1986 s 26(1) (see PARA 471). As to the meaning of 'tenant' see PARA 423 note 5.
2 There is power to provide:
   (1)   for excluding sub-tenants from the right to give counter-notices to notices to quit (Agricultural Holdings Act 1986 s 29, Sch 4 para 6); and
   (2)   for safeguarding the interests of sub-tenants by such provision as appears expedient, including provision enabling the Tribunal, where the interest of a tenant is terminated by notice to quit, to secure that a sub-tenant will hold from the landlord on the like terms as he held from the tenant (Sch 4 para 7).
The provisions cited in the text were made under the first limb of this power. At the date at which this volume states the law, the power had not been exercised as respects the second limb. In England, the Tribunal is the First-tier Tribunal (see PARA 768) and in Wales it is the Agricultural Land Tribunal for Wales (see PARA 767): see PARA 437 note 1. As to the meaning of 'landlord' see PARA 423 note 7.
3 As to the service of notices see PARA 428 note 4.
4 Agricultural Holdings (Arbitration on Notices) Order 1987, SI 1987/710, art 16(1).
5 Agricultural Holdings (Arbitration on Notices) Order 1987, SI 1987/710, art 16(2).
6 Ie under the Agricultural Holdings Act 1986 s 32 (see PARA 495).
7 Agricultural Holdings (Arbitration on Notices) Order 1987, SI 1987/710, art 16(3).
8 *Sherwood v Moody* [1952] 1 All ER 389, [1952] 1 TLR 450. In considering a series of transactions involving the grant of a tenancy and sub-tenancy which taken together constituted a composite scheme intended to avoid the security of tenure provisions, the court refused to apply this principle and held that the sub-tenant was entitled to statutory protection: *Gisborne v Burton* [1989] QB 390, [1988] 3 All ER 760, CA. Cf *Barrett v Morgan* [2000] 2 AC 264, [2000] 1 All ER 481, where a collusive agreement by the tenant with the landlord not to serve a counter-notice did not prevent the sub-tenancy from being determined.

(6) SUCCESSION ON DEATH OR RETIREMENT

(i) Tenancies with and without Succession Rights

497.   Tenancies with succession rights.
     In relation to certain tenancies of agricultural holdings[1] provision is made by the Agricultural Holdings Act 1986[2] governing the succession to such tenancies on the death of a sole or sole surviving tenant[3] or on the retirement of the tenant or tenants[4]. In order for those provisions to apply the tenancy must either have been granted before 12 July 1984[5] or have been granted after that date in any of the following circumstances:
   (1)   the tenancy is already a succession tenancy, that is a tenancy granted by virtue of a direction of the Tribunal[6] on the death or retirement of the previous tenant[7];
   (2)   the tenancy was granted after such a direction of the Tribunal following the death of the previous tenant but before that direction took effect[8];

(3)   the tenancy was granted by a written contract of tenancy[9] indicating (in whatever terms) that the relevant statutory provisions[10] would apply to it[11]; or

(4)   the tenancy is a re-grant to a person who, immediately before 12 July 1984, was a tenant of the holding or of any agricultural holding which comprised the whole or a substantial part of the land in the holding in question[12].

1   As to the meaning of 'agricultural holding' see PARA 423.
2   The relevant provisions of the Agricultural Holdings Act 1986 are contained in Pt IV (ss 34–59) (see the text and notes 3–12; and PARAS 498–510).
3   See the Agricultural Holdings Act 1986 ss 35–48; and PARAS 502–505. For these purposes 'tenant' does not include an executor, administrator, trustee in bankruptcy or other person deriving title from a tenant by operation of law: ss 34(2), 37(9), 49(2). As to the meaning of 'tenant' generally see PARA 423 note 5.
4   See the Agricultural Holdings Act 1986 ss 49–58; and PARAS 506–509.
5   Agricultural Holdings Act 1986 s 34(1)(a). The date mentioned in the text is the date on which the Agricultural Holdings Act 1984, from which these provisions in part derive, was passed (ie received the Royal Assent).
6   Ie in England, the First-tier Tribunal (see PARA 768) and in Wales, the Agricultural Land Tribunal for Wales (see PARA 767): see PARA 437 note 1.
7   Agricultural Holdings Act 1986 s 34(1)(b)(i). Such directions are made under s 39 (death of previous tenant: see PARA 502) or s 53 (retirement of previous tenant: see PARA 507).
8   Agricultural Holdings Act 1986 s 34(1)(b)(ii). Such directions are made under s 39 in the circumstances set out in s 45(6) (see PARA 504).
9   As to the meaning of 'contract of tenancy' see PARA 425.
10 Ie the Agricultural Holdings Act 1986 Pt IV.
11 Agricultural Holdings Act 1986 s 34(1)(b)(iii).
12 Agricultural Holdings Act 1986 s 34(1)(b)(iv). Where the Agricultural Holdings Act 1986 applies in relation to a tenancy by virtue of the Agricultural Tenancies Act 1995 s 4(1)(g) (see PARAS 401, 421), the reference in the Agricultural Holdings Act 1986 s 34(1)(b)(iv) to a 'substantial part of the land comprised in the holding' means a substantial part determined by reference to either area or value: s 34(3) (added by SI 2006/2805).

498.   Tenancies without succession rights.

The following forms of tenancy do not carry with them succession rights[1]:

(1)   tenancies for a fixed term of years of which more than 27 months remain unexpired[2];

(2)   former fixed term tenancies for more than one but less than two years[3];

(3)   tenancies where on the previous two occasions of the death of the sole or sole surviving tenant[4] of the holding or a related holding[5], a succession tenancy was granted by virtue of a direction[6] of the Tribunal[7] or such a direction had been made but had not taken effect[8], or such a tenancy was granted by the landlord to a close relative[9] who was the sole remaining potential applicant for such a direction[10];

(4)   tenancies subject to a notice to quit before death or retirement, where if it was available to the tenant to serve a counter-notice[11] he had not done so before the expiry of the period of one month allowed for so doing[12] or the Tribunal had consented before the death of the tenant to the operation of the notice to quit[13];

(5)   tenancies subject to a valid notice to quit which falls within Case C[14] or Case F[15];

(6)   tenancies subject to a valid notice to quit which falls within Case B[16], Case D[17] or Case E[18], where:

(a)   the time for requiring arbitration[19] had expired before the death without such requirement being made[20];

(b)   the time for serving a counter-notice on the upholding of the notice on arbitration had expired before the death without such counter-notice being served[21]; or

(c)   the Tribunal had before the death consented to the operation of the notice[22];

(7)   where the holding consists of land held by a smallholdings authority[23] or by the Secretary of State or the Welsh Ministers[24] for the purposes of smallholdings[25]; and

(8)   tenancies granted by trustees in whom the land is vested on charitable trusts the sole or principal object of which is the settlement or employment in agriculture[26] of persons who have served in the armed forces[27].

1   Ie the right to apply for a direction under the Agricultural Holdings Act 1986 s 39 (see PARA 502) or s 53 (see PARA 507).

2   Agricultural Holdings Act 1986 s 36(1), (2)(a). This does not apply in relation to succession on the retirement of the previous tenant: most of the exclusions relating to death are applied by s 51(1) (see PARA 506) to retirement, but s 51(1) does not refer to s 36(2).

3   Agricultural Holdings Act 1986 s 36(2)(b); and see note 2. Tenancies of this kind were wholly excluded from security of tenure: *Gladstone v Bower* [1960] 2 QB 384, [1960] 3 All ER 353, CA. Such tenancies can no longer exist: any tenancies of between one and two years will now be farm business tenancies under the Agricultural Tenancies Act 1995 (see PARA 401 et seq).

4   As to the meaning of 'tenant' see PARA 497 note 3.

5   A 'related holding', in relation to the holding in question, means any agricultural holding comprising the whole or a substantial part of the land comprised in the holding: Agricultural Holdings Act 1986 ss 35(2), 49(3). Where the Agricultural Holdings Act 1986 applies in relation to a tenancy by virtue of the Agricultural Tenancies Act 1995 s 4(1)(g) (see PARAS 401, 421) the reference in the Agricultural Holdings Act 1986 ss 35(2), 49(3) to a 'substantial part of the land comprised in the holding' means a substantial part determined by reference to either area or value: ss 35(3), 49(4) (added by SI 2006/2805).

6   Ie a direction under the Agricultural Holdings Act 1986 s 39 (death of previous tenant: see PARA 502).

7   Ie in England, the First-tier Tribunal (see PARA 768) and in Wales, the Agricultural Land Tribunal for Wales (see PARA 767): see PARA 437 note 1.

8   Agricultural Holdings Act 1986 s 37(1)(a). See s 45(6); and PARA 504.

9   As to the meaning of 'close relative' see PARA 499.

10   Agricultural Holdings Act 1986 s 37(1)(b). This applies equally where, by agreement with the landlord before the death, the holding became let under a tenancy granted by the landlord or under an assignment of the existing tenancy to a person who, had the deceased tenant died before such grant or assignment, would have been the deceased tenant's close relative: s 37(2). For further provisions as to exclusion where two successions have already occurred see s 37(3)–(8). As to the meaning of 'landlord' see PARA 423 note 7.

    This exclusion from succession rights on the death of a tenant applies, mutatis mutandis, in relation to the retirement of a tenant: see s 51(1); and PARA 506.

11   Ie a counter-notice under the Agricultural Holdings Act 1986 s 26(1) (see PARA 471).

12   Agricultural Holdings Act 1986 s 38(1)(a).

13   Agricultural Holdings Act 1986 s 38(1)(b). As to the granting or withholding of such consent by the tribunal see PARA 472. This exclusion from succession rights on the death of a tenant applies, mutatis mutandis, in relation to the retirement of a tenant: sees 51(1); and PARA 506.

14   See PARA 476.

15   Agricultural Holdings Act 1986 s 38(2). For Case F see PARA 479.

16   See PARA 475.

17   See PARA 477.

18   See PARA 478.

19   As to such arbitration see PARA 482 et seq.

20   Agricultural Holdings Act 1986 s 38(3)(a).

21   Agricultural Holdings Act 1986 s 38(3)(b).

22   Agricultural Holdings Act 1986 s 38(3)(c).

23 As to smallholdings authorities see PARAS 748–751.

24 As to the Secretary of State and the Welsh Ministers see PARA 741.

25 Agricultural Holdings Act 1986 s 38(4). For this purpose, a 'smallholding' is a smallholding under the Agriculture Act 1970 Pt III (ss 37–65) (see PARA 627 et seq).

26 As to the meaning of 'agriculture' see PARA 424.

27 Agricultural Holdings Act 1986 s 38(5).

499. Eligible persons.

For the purposes of the provisions relating to succession on death or retirement[1] 'eligible person' means any surviving close relative (in the case of death) of the deceased tenant[2] or (in the case of retirement) the nominated successor[3] of the retiring tenant[4] whom:

(1)　in the seven years ending with the date of the death or retirement[5] derived his only or principal source of livelihood for a continuous period of at least five years, or for two or more discontinuous periods together amounting to at least five years, from his agricultural work[6] on the holding or on an agricultural unit[7] of which the holding forms part (the 'livelihood condition')[8]; and

(2)　is not the occupier of a commercial unit of agricultural land (the 'occupancy condition')[9].

A 'close relative' of a deceased or retiring tenant is the deceased or retiring tenant's wife, husband or civil partner, brother, sister or child, or other person treated as a child of the family in relation to the relevant marriage or civil partnership[10].

1 Ie the Agricultural Holdings Act 1986 ss 36–48 (death: see PARAS 502–505) or ss 49–58 (retirement: see PARAS 506–509).

2 Agricultural Holdings Act 1986 s 35(2). 'Holding' (except where the context otherwise requires) means the agricultural holding mentioned in s 35(1) (ie the holding held under a tenancy which falls within s 34(1)(a) or (b) (see PARA 497) (s 35(2)) or the holding in respect of which the retirement notice (see note 2) is given (s 49(3)).

3 'Nominated successor' means the eligible person named in the retirement notice: Agricultural Holdings Act 1986 s 49(3).

4 Agricultural Holdings Act 1986 s 50(4), Sch 6 para 13. The 'retiring tenant' is the tenant by whom the retirement notice was given, or, where it was given by joint tenants (and the context so permits), any one of those tenants, and the 'retiring tenants' accordingly means those tenants: Agricultural Holdings Act 1986 s 49(3). 'Retirement notice' means the notice mentioned in s 49(1) (see PARA 506): s 49(3).

5 'Retirement date' means the date specified in the retirement notice as the date as from which the proposed succession is to take place: Agricultural Holdings Act 1986 s 49(3).

6 As to the meaning of 'agricultural', and as to the meaning of 'agricultural land', see PARA 424. In the case of the deceased's wife or the wife of the retiring tenant the reference in the Agricultural Holdings Act 1986 ss 36(3)(a), 50(2)(a) to the relative's agricultural work is to be read as a reference to agricultural work carried out by either the wife or the deceased (or, as the case may be, retiring tenant) (or both of them) (ss 36(4), 50(3)); and in the case of the deceased's or retiring tenant's civil partner such reference is to be read as a reference to agricultural work carried out by either the civil partner or the deceased (or, as the case may be, retiring tenant) (or both of them) (ss 36(4A), 50(3A) (as added: see note 2)).

7 As to the meaning of 'agricultural unit' see PARA 424 note 7.

8 Agricultural Holdings Act 1986 ss 36(3)(a), (5), 50(2)(a), Sch 6 paras 1(1), 11, 12. For these purposes any period (not exceeding three years in all) within the stated period of seven years during which a close relative of the deceased or the nominated successor was attending a full-time course at a university, college or other establishment of higher or further education, is to be treated as a period during which his only or principal source of livelihood was his work on the holding: Sch 6 para 2 (amended by the Education Reform Act 1988 s 237(1), Sch 12 para 96).

The reference in the Agricultural Holdings Act 1986 ss 36(3)(a), 50(2)(a) to agricultural work carried out by a person on the holding or on an agricultural unit of which the holding forms part includes agricultural work carried out by him from the holding or an agricultural unit of which the holding forms part (ss 36(6)(a), 50(5)(a) (ss 36(6), 50(5) added by SI 2006/2805, art 5(1), (3))) and other work carried out by him on or from the holding or an agricultural unit of which the holding forms part (Agricultural Holdings Act 1986 ss 36(6)(b), 50(5)(b) (as so added)) which is of a description approved in writing by the landlord after 19 October 2006 (ie the date on which this amendment was brought into force) (Agricultural Holdings Act 1986 ss 36(6), 50(5) (as so added)).

The nominated successor is required to satisfy the livelihood condition in s 50(2)(a) by reference only to the seven years ending with the date of the giving of the retirement notice, rather than the seven years ending with the date of the tribunal hearing: see *Trustees of the Shirley Children's Settlement v Crabtree* [2007] EWHC 1532 (Admin), [2007] All ER (D) 332 (Jun). The guidance given by the Court of Appeal in that case specifically discourages 'a legalistic approach' to livelihood: see *Bailey v Lockitt* (2016) ALT/11/2016 (Upper Tribunal).

In connection with the requirement that the applicant for a tenancy establishes his economic dependence on the holding see *Welby v Casswell* (1995) 71 P & CR 137, [1995] 42 EG 134, CA.

For an example of a case in which an applicant satisfied neither the livelihood condition nor the alternative 'suitable person' test under s 41(1)(b) (see PARA 501) see *Thomson v Church Comrs for England* [2006] EWHC 1773 (Admin), [2006] All ER (D) 162 (Jul).

9 Agricultural Holdings Act 1986 ss 36(3)(b), 50(2)(b), Sch 6 para 1(1). For this purpose, a 'commercial unit of agricultural land' is a unit capable, when farmed under competent management, of producing a net annual income of an amount not less than the aggregate of the average annual earnings of two full-time male agricultural workers aged 20 or over: Sch 6 para 3(1). The Secretary of State and the Welsh Ministers may produce statements as to the net annual income which, in his or their view, the land is capable of producing for the purpose of the definition of 'commercial unit': see Sch 6 paras 5, 14 (Sch 6 para 5 amended by SI 2013/1036). As to the 'farming' of land see PARA 424. As to the Secretary of State and the Welsh Ministers see PARA 741. The Secretary of State's and the Welsh Ministers' prescribed figures as to units of production must be applied for these purposes: Sch 6 para 3(2). As to those prescribed figures see Sch 6 para 4; the Agricultural Holdings (Units of Production) (England) Order 2017, SI 2017/977; the Agricultural Holdings (Units of Production) (Wales) (No 2) Order 2015, SI 2015/1642; the Agricultural Holdings (Units of Production) (Wales) (No 3) Order 2015, SI 2015/1975; and the Agricultural Holdings (Units of Production) (Wales) Order 2016, SI 2016/1082.

10 Agricultural Holdings Act 1986 ss 35(2), 49(3) (ss 35(2), 49(3) amended, and ss 36(4A), 50(3A) added, by the Civil Partnership Act 2004 s 81, Sch 8 paras 36–38).

500. Special provisions regarding the occupancy condition.

For the purposes of the occupancy condition[1]:

(1)   there must generally be disregarded certain types of occupation, namely occupation:

(a)   under a tenancy approved[2] by the Secretary of State and the Welsh Ministers[3];

(b)   under a tenancy for more than one but less than two years[4];

(c)   under a tenancy not within head (a) or (b) above and not having effect as a contract of tenancy[5];

(d)   under a tenancy the conversion of which into a tenancy from year to year has been excluded[6];

(e)   under a farm business tenancy[7] for less than five years (including a farm business tenancy which is a periodic tenancy)[8];

(f)   as a licensee[9]; and

(g)   as an executor, administrator, trustee in bankruptcy or other person deriving title by operation of law[10],

although in all but the last case[11] such disregards do not apply in the case of a tenancy or licence granted to a close relative[12] of the deceased or the nominated successor[13] by his spouse[14] or civil partner[15] or by a body corporate controlled by him[16];

(2)   where any agricultural land[17] is jointly occupied[18] by a close relative of the deceased or the nominated successor and one or more other persons as beneficial joint tenants[19], tenants in common[20], joint tenants under a tenancy[21] or joint licensees[22], the relative is treated for the purposes of the occupancy condition as occupying the whole of the land[23];

(3)   where a close relative of the deceased (in the case of a succession on death) is, by virtue of a direction of the Tribunal[24], for the time being entitled (whether or not with any other person) to a tenancy of the whole or part of any agricultural holding[25] held by the deceased at the date of death other than the holding, he must be deemed to be in occupation of the land comprised in that holding or (as the case may be) in that part of that holding[26];

(4)   where the nominated successor (in the case of a succession on retirement) is, by virtue of a direction of the Tribunal[27], for the time being entitled to a tenancy of any agricultural holding held by the retiring tenant other than the holding he must be deemed to be in occupation of that holding[28];

(5)   occupation by the spouse or civil partner of a close relative of the deceased or the nominated successor[29], or by a body corporate controlled by a close relative of the deceased or the nominated successor[30], is treated as occupation by the relative[31]; and

(6)   where any agricultural land is occupied by any person under certain types of limited tenancies[32] or as a licensee[33] and that tenancy or licence was granted by a close relative of the deceased or the nominated successor or a connected person[34] (or both), being at the time it was granted a person or persons entitled to occupy the land otherwise than under a tenancy, or in a capacity, falling within certain restrictions[35], the close relative must be deemed to be in occupation of the whole of the land[36].

1   As to the occupancy condition see PARA 499.
2   Ie approved under the Agricultural Holdings Act 1986 s 2(1) (see PARA 427). This also applies to a tenancy falling within s 2(3)(a) (see PARA 427). 'Tenancy' means the tenancy of the holding: ss 35(2), 49(3).
3   Agricultural Holdings Act 1986 Sch 6 para 6(1)(a). As to the Secretary of State and the Welsh Ministers see PARA 741.
4   Agricultural Holdings Act 1986 Sch 6 para 6(1)(b).
5   Agricultural Holdings Act 1986 Sch 6 para 6(1)(c). As to the meaning of 'contract of tenancy' see PARA 425.
6   Agricultural Holdings Act 1986 Sch 6 para 6(1)(d). This is a tenancy to which s 3 does not apply by virtue of s 5 (see PARA 428).
7   Ie within the meaning of the Agricultural Tenancies Act 1995 (see PARA 402): Agricultural Holdings Act 1986 Sch 6 para 6(1)(dd) (added by the Agricultural Tenancies Act 1995 s 40, Schedule para 32).
8   Agricultural Holdings Act 1986 Sch 6 para 6(1)(dd) (as added: see note 7).
9   Agricultural Holdings Act 1986 Sch 6 para 6(1)(e).
10   Agricultural Holdings Act 1986 Sch 6 para 6(1)(f).
11   Ie the case specified under the Agricultural Holdings Act 1986 Sch 6 para 6(1)(f) (see head (g) in the text).
12   As to the meaning of 'close relative' see PARA 499.
13   As to the meaning of 'nominated successor' see PARA 499 note 3.
14   Any reference in the Agricultural Holdings Act 1986 Sch 6 to the 'spouse' of a close relative of the deceased or the nominated successor does not apply in relation to any time when the relative's marriage is the subject of a decree of judicial separation or a decree nisi of divorce or of nullity of marriage: Sch 6 para 1(3).

15 Any reference in the Agricultural Holdings Act 1986 Sch 6 to the civil partner of a close relative of the deceased or the nominated successor does not apply in relation to any time when the relative's civil partnership is subject to a separation order under the Civil Partnership Act 2004 Pt 2 Ch 2 (ss 37–64) (Agricultural Holdings Act 1986 Sch 6 para 1(4)(a) (Sch 6 paras 1(2), 6(2), 9(1)(a), (2), 10(3)(a) amended, Sch 6 para 1(4) added, by the Civil Partnership Act 2004 Sch 8 para 39)) or a dissolution order, nullity order or presumption of death order that is a conditional order under the Civil Partnership Act 2004 Pt 2 Ch 2 (Agricultural Holdings Act 1986 Sch 6 para 1(4)(b) (as so added)).

16 Agricultural Holdings Act 1986 Sch 6 para 6(2) (as amended: see note 15). For these purposes a body corporate is controlled by a close relative of the deceased or the nominated successor if he or his spouse or his civil partner, or he and his spouse together or he and his civil partner together, have the power to secure, either by means of the holding of shares or the possession of voting power in or in relation to that or any other body corporate or by virtue of any powers conferred by the articles of association or other document regulating that or any other body corporate, that the affairs of that body corporate are conducted in accordance with his, her or their wishes, respectively: Sch 6 para 1(2) (as so amended).

17 As to the meaning of 'agricultural', and as to the meaning of 'agricultural land', see PARA 424.

18 References in the Agricultural Holdings Act 1986 Sch 6 paras 7–10 (see the text and notes 19–36) to the occupation of land by any person do not include occupation under a tenancy, or in a capacity, falling within Sch 6 para 6(1)(a)–(f) (see heads (a)–(g) in the text): Sch 6 para 6(3).

19 Agricultural Holdings Act 1986 Sch 6 para 7(1)(a). See note 31.

20 Agricultural Holdings Act 1986 Sch 6 para 7(1)(b). See note 31.

21 Agricultural Holdings Act 1986 Sch 6 para 7(1)(c). See note 31.

22 Agricultural Holdings Act 1986 Sch 6 para 7(1)(d). See note 31.

23 Agricultural Holdings Act 1986 Sch 6 para 7(1). If, however, the Tribunal in proceedings under s 39 (see PARA 502) or, as the case may be, s 53 (see PARA 507) determines on the application of the close relative or the nominated successor that his appropriate share of the net annual income which the land is, or was at any time, capable of producing for the purposes of Sch 6 para 3 (see PARA 499) is or was then less than the aggregate of the earnings referred to therein, then, for the purpose of determining whether the occupancy condition is or was then satisfied in his case, the net annual income which the land is, or (as the case may be) was, capable of so producing must be treated as limited to his appropriate share: Sch 6 paras 7(2), 15. For this purpose the appropriate share of the close relative or the nominated successor must be ascertained:
    (1)   where he is a beneficial or other joint tenant or a joint licensee, by dividing the net annual income which the land is or was at the time in question capable of producing for the purposes of Sch 6 para 3 by the total number of joint tenants or joint licensees for the time being (Sch 6 para 7(3)(a)); and
    (2)   where he is a tenant in common, by dividing the said net annual income in such a way as to attribute to him and to the other tenant or tenants in common shares of the income proportionate to the extent for the time being of their respective undivided shares in the land (Sch 6 para 7(3)(b)).
In England the Tribunal is the First-tier Tribunal (see PARA 768) and in Wales it is the Agricultural Land Tribunal for Wales (see PARA 767): see PARA 437 note 1.

24 Ie under the Agricultural Holdings Act 1986 s 39 (see PARA 502).

25 As to the meaning of 'agricultural holding' see PARA 423.

26 Agricultural Holdings Act 1986 Sch 6 para 8(1). Where by virtue of this provision any land is deemed to be occupied by each of two or more close relatives of the deceased as a result of a direction entitling them to a joint tenancy of the land, the provisions of Sch 6 para 7 (see the text and notes 17–23) apply to each of the relatives as if the land were jointly occupied by him and the other relative or relatives as joint tenants under that tenancy: Sch 6 para 8(2).

27 Ie under the Agricultural Holdings Act 1986 s 53(7) (see PARA 507).

28 Agricultural Holdings Act 1986 Sch 6 para 16.

29 Agricultural Holdings Act 1986 Sch 6 para 9(1)(a) (as amended: see note 15).

30 Agricultural Holdings Act 1986 Sch 6 para 9(1)(b).

31 Agricultural Holdings Act 1986 Sch 6 para 9(1). Schedule 6 para 9(1) also applies to Sch 6 para 7 (see the text and notes 17–23) (Sch 6 para 9(1)(a) (as amended: see note 15)), and where Sch 6 para 7 applies to a close relative of the deceased or the nominated successor in relation to any time by virtue of the joint occupation of land by his spouse or civil partner or a body corporate and any other person or persons, Sch 6 para 7(2), (3) applies to the relative or successor as if he were the holder of the interest in the land for the time being held by his spouse or civil partner, or the body corporate, as the case may be (Sch 6 para 9(2) (as so amended)).

32 Ie such a tenancy as is mentioned in the Agricultural Holdings Act 1986 Sch 6 para 6(1)(a)–(d) (see heads (a)–(d) in the text).

33 Agricultural Holdings Act 1986 Sch 6 para 10(1)(a).

34 For this purpose 'connected person', in relation to a close relative of the deceased or the nominated successor, means the relative's or successor's spouse or civil partner (Agricultural Holdings Act 1986 Sch 6 para 10(3)(a) (as amended: see note 15)) or a body corporate controlled by the relative or successor (Sch 6 para 10(3)(b)).

35 Agricultural Holdings Act 1986 Sch 6 para 10(1)(b). The restrictions referred to in the text are those mentioned in Sch 6 para 6(1)(a)–(f) (see heads (a)–(g) in the text).

36 Agricultural Holdings Act 1986 Sch 6 para 10(1). This is the case unless the tenancy or licence was granted by the person or persons referred to in Sch 6 para 10(1) (see the text and notes 32–35) and one or more other persons who were at the time it was granted entitled to occupy the land as mentioned in Sch 6 para 10(1)(b), in which case the provisions of Sch 6 para 7(2), (3) (see note 23) apply to the close relative or the nominated successor as if the land were jointly occupied by him and the said other person or persons as holders of their respective interests for the time being in the land: Sch 6 para 10(2). For the purposes of Sch 6 para 10(2) (and of Sch 6 para 7(2), (3)) any interest in the land for the time being held by a connected person by whom the tenancy or licence was granted must be attributed to the relative or successor: Sch 6 para 10(3).

501. Special provisions regarding the livelihood condition.

In the case of an application to succeed on death (but not in the case of an application to succeed on retirement) provision is made for a person who does not fully satisfy the livelihood condition[1] still to be treated as an eligible person for the purposes of an application to succeed to the tenancy[2]. Any surviving close relative[3] of the deceased who for some part of the seven years ending with the date of death engaged (whether full-time or part-time) in agricultural work on the holding[4], who satisfies the occupancy condition[5] but who does not fully satisfy the livelihood condition, but who does satisfy it to a material extent[6], may within the period of three months beginning with the day after the date of death apply to the Tribunal[7] for a determination that he is to be treated as an eligible person for the purposes of the provisions relating to succession on death[8], and if on such an application the Tribunal is satisfied that the applicant satisfies the occupancy condition and satisfies the livelihood condition to a material extent[9], and it appears to the Tribunal that in all the circumstances it would be fair and reasonable for the applicant to be able to apply[10] for a direction entitling him to a tenancy of the holding[11], the Tribunal must determine that he is to be treated as an eligible person for the purposes of the provisions relating to succession on death, but must otherwise dismiss the application[12].

1 As to the livelihood condition see PARA 499.

2 See the Agricultural Holdings Act 1986 s 41; and the text and notes 3–12.

3 As to the meaning of 'close relative' see PARA 499.

4 The references in the Agricultural Holdings Act 1986 s 41(1) and s 41(6) to agricultural work carried out by a person on the holding include agricultural work carried out by him from the holding and other work carried out by him on or from the holding which is of a description approved in writing by the landlord after 19 October 2006: s 41(7) (added by SI 2006/2805, art 5(2)). 19 October 2006 is the date on which this amendment came into force: see art 1(1)(b).

5 Agricultural Holdings Act 1986 s 41(1)(a). As to the occupancy condition see PARA 499.

6 Agricultural Holdings Act 1986 s 41(1)(b). Without prejudice to the generality of this provision, cases where the livelihood condition might be less than fully satisfied include cases where the close relative's agricultural work on the holding fell short of providing him with his principal source of livelihood because the holding was too small: s 41(6). See *Thomson v Church Comrs for England* [2006] EWHC 1773 (Admin), [2006] All ER (D) 162 (Jul).

7 Ie in England, the First-tier Tribunal (see PARA 768) and in Wales, the Agricultural Land Tribunal for Wales (see PARA 767): see PARA 437 note 1.

8 Agricultural Holdings Act 1986 s 41(2). As to the provisions relating to succession on death see PARAS 502–505 (death).

9 Agricultural Holdings Act 1986 s 41(3)(a).

10 Ie under the Agricultural Holdings Act 1986 s 39 (see PARA 502).
11 Agricultural Holdings Act 1986 s 41(3)(b).
12 Agricultural Holdings Act 1986 s 41(3). In relation to a person in respect of whom the Tribunal
    has determined as mentioned in s 41(3), ss 36–48 apply as if he were an eligible person: s 41(4).
    A person to whom these provisions apply may make an application under s 39 (see PARA 502) as
    well as an application under s 41; and if the Tribunal determines that a person who has made an
    application under s 39 is to be treated as an eligible person for these purposes, the application
    under s 39 must (without prejudice to s 41(4)) be treated as made by an eligible person: s 41(5).

(ii) Succession on Death

502. Application for succession.

Any eligible person[1] may apply to the Tribunal[2] for a direction entitling him to
the tenancy[3] of a holding[4] on the death of the previous tenant[5]. Any such
application must be made within three months beginning with the day after the
date of death[6]. Where only one application is made, the Tribunal must satisfy itself
that the applicant was an eligible person at the date of death[7] and that he has not
subsequently ceased to be so[8], and, having determined eligibility, must then go on
to determine whether he is in their opinion a suitable person to become the tenant
of the holding[9].

In determining whether the applicant is a suitable person to be granted the
tenancy, the Tribunal must have regard to all relevant matters, including the
extent to which the applicant has been trained in or has had practical experience
of agriculture, his age, physical health and financial standing, and the views (if
any) stated by the landlord on the applicant's suitability[10]. The landlord must be
given an opportunity to state his views[11].

If there is more than one applicant, the Tribunal must follow that procedure in
relation to each as if he were the only applicant[12]. Where only one is suitable, the
Tribunal must give a direction that that applicant is entitled to the tenancy[13].
Where more than one is suitable the Tribunal must determine which is the most
suitable[14] and give a direction accordingly[15]. In that case the Tribunal has an
alternative power, with the landlord's consent, to direct a joint tenancy of the
holding between up to four specified applicants[16], and in any case an applicant or
applicants may agree to a direction specifying a tenancy or joint tenancy of part
of the holding[17]. If the applicants include a person validly designated[18] by the
deceased in his will[19] as the person he wished to succeed him as tenant of the
holding, the Tribunal must first determine the suitability of that applicant, and
must proceed to the other applicants only if that applicant is unsuitable[20].

Special provision is made as to the order of hearing of applications where the
deceased was tenant of more than one holding[21].

1 As to the meaning of 'eligible person' see PARA 499.
2 Ie in England, the First-tier Tribunal (see PARA 768) and in Wales, the Agricultural Land Tribunal
   of Wales (see PARA 767): see PARA 437 note 1.
3 As to the meaning of 'tenancy' see PARA 500 note 2.
4 As to the meaning of 'holding' see PARA 499 note 3.
5 Agricultural Holdings Act 1986 s 36(1). As to the meaning of 'tenant' see PARA 423 note 5. As to
   the making of orders generally see PARA 432 note 5. See also *Kellett v Alexander* (1980) 257
   Estates Gazette 494.
6 Agricultural Holdings Act 1986 s 39(1). 'Date of death' means the date of death of the deceased:
   s 35(2). As to applications made to the First-tier Tribunal under s 39 see the Tribunal Procedure
   (First-tier Tribunal) (Property Chamber) Rules 2013, SI 2013/1169, rr 41–43.
7 Agricultural Holdings Act 1986 s 39(2)(a).
8 Agricultural Holdings Act 1986 s 39(2)(b).
9 Agricultural Holdings Act 1986 s 39(2).

10 Agricultural Holdings Act 1986 s 39(8). As to the meaning of 'agriculture' see PARA 424. As to the meaning of 'landlord' see PARA 423 note 7.
11 Agricultural Holdings Act 1986 s 39(7).
12 Agricultural Holdings Act 1986 s 39(3). See, however, the text and notes 16–18.
13 Agricultural Holdings Act 1986 s 39(5).
14 Agricultural Holdings Act 1986 s 39(6)(a).
15 Agricultural Holdings Act 1986 s 39(6)(b).
16 Agricultural Holdings Act 1986 s 39(9).
17 Agricultural Holdings Act 1986 s 39(10).
18 A person is to be taken to be validly designated as the person the deceased wishes to succeed him as tenant only if the will contains an effective bequest of the tenancy to that person or, not containing such bequest, specifically mentions the holding and exclusively designates that person as the person the deceased wishes to succeed him as tenant: Agricultural Holdings Act 1986 s 40(1). See further s 40(2)–(4).
19 'Will' includes codicil: Agricultural Holdings Act 1986 s 40(1).
20 Agricultural Holdings Act 1986 s 39(4).
21 See the Agricultural Holdings Act 1986 s 42 (substituted by SI 2013/1036).

503. Notice to quit by landlord.

Where the landlord[1] has given notice to quit[2] which falls within Case G[3], that notice is effective provided no application to succeed to the tenancy[4] has been made within the required time[5] or, such application having been made, either no applicant is found by the Tribunal[6] to be suitable[7], or alternatively the tribunal has consented[8] to the operation of the notice to quit[9].

Before giving a direction entitling any person to succeed to a tenancy in a case falling within Case G the Tribunal must afford the landlord opportunity to apply for consent to the operation of the notice to quit[10].

Where the Tribunal consents to the operation of a notice to quit it must dismiss any application for succession in relation to the holding or part to which the notice to quit relates[11]. Where on an application for succession the applicant has agreed to accept a direction entitling him to a tenancy of part only of the holding[12] in question[13], the Tribunal must give consent to the operation of the notice to quit in relation to that part of the holding excluded from the direction[14].

In certain circumstances the operation of the notice to quit may be postponed[15].

1 As to the meaning of 'landlord' see PARA 423 note 7.
2 As to the service of notices see PARA 428 note 4.
3 See PARA 480.
4 As to the meaning of 'tenancy' see PARA 500 note 2.
5 Agricultural Holdings Act 1986 s 43(1)(a). As to the required time see s 39(1); and PARA 502.
6 Ie in England, the First-tier Tribunal (see PARA 768) and in Wales, the Agricultural Land Tribunal for Wales (see PARA 767): see PARA 437 note 1.
7 Agricultural Holdings Act 1986 s 43(1)(b)(i). As to the suitability of an applicant see PARA 499.
8 Ie under the Agricultural Holdings Act 1986 s 44 (see the text and notes 10–15).
9 Agricultural Holdings Act 1986 s 43(1)(b)(ii). Such consent may validly take effect in relation to part only of a holding: s 43(2).
10 Agricultural Holdings Act 1986 s 44(1). The Tribunal must not entertain an application for consent to which s 43(1) (see the text and notes 1–9) applies except in pursuance of s 44(1): s 44(3). The grounds for the granting of consent are those contained in s 27 (see PARA 472): s 44(2).
11 Agricultural Holdings Act 1986 s 44(4). This is subject to s 44(5) (as to which see the text and notes 12–14).
12 As to the meaning of 'holding' see PARA 499 note 2.
13 Ie under the Agricultural Holdings Act 1986 s 39(10) (see PARA 502).
14 Agricultural Holdings Act 1986 s 44(5).
15 See Agricultural Holdings Act 1986 s 44(6), (7).

504. Effect of direction entitling applicant to a tenancy.

A direction by the Tribunal[1] entitling the applicant or applicants to a tenancy[2] of the holding[3] entitles him or them to a tenancy or joint tenancy as from the relevant time[4], on the same terms as those on which the holding was let immediately before it ceased to be let under the contract of tenancy[5] under which it was let at the date of death[6].

If on the date of death, the holding was held by the deceased for a fixed term of years and the holding is subject to a direction of entitlement to succession, the tenancy takes effect with the terms on which it was let prior to the death, except that it is treated as if before the date of the death it had become a tenancy from year to year[7].

The terms of any tenancy which is the subject of a succession direction are deemed to include, if they do not do so already, a covenant by the tenant not to assign, sub-let or part with possession of the holding or any part of it without the landlord's written consent[8]. Any tenancy of the holding inconsistent with the tenancy which is the subject of the succession direction must, if it would not otherwise cease at the relevant time, cease at that time as though it had been terminated at that time by a valid notice to quit given by the tenant[9]. A direction ceases to have effect if the person or persons whom it entitles to a tenancy becomes or become tenant of the holding before the relevant time under a tenancy granted by the landlord and accepted by the person or persons concerned[10]. The rights conferred on any person by a direction (as distinct from rights acquired after he has become tenant) are not capable of assignment[11]. Relevant provisions of the Agricultural Holdings Act 1986[12] are applied where the person entitled to a tenancy under a direction following the death of the previous tenant himself dies before the relevant time[13].

1   Ie in England, the First-tier Tribunal (see PARA 768) and in Wales, the Agricultural Land Tribunal for Wales (see PARA 767): see PARA 437 note 1.
2   As to the meaning of 'tenancy' see PARA 500 note 2.
3   As to the meaning of 'holding' see PARA 499 note 2.
4   The 'relevant time' is the end of the 12 months immediately following the end of the year of tenancy in which the deceased died, except where a notice to quit falling within Case G (see PARA 480) was given to the tenant which would have terminated the tenancy at a time after the end of those 12 months, in which case it means that time: Agricultural Holdings Act 1986 s 46(1). See further s 46(2). As to the meaning of 'tenant' see PARA 423 note 5.
5   As to the meaning of 'contract of tenancy' see PARA 425.
6   Agricultural Holdings Act 1986 ss 45(1), 47(1). As to the meaning of 'date of death' see PARA 502 note 6. Such tenancy is deemed to be granted at that time by the landlord and accepted by the person or persons entitled: s 45(1). Where a supervening interest has been created by the landlord, the entitlement to the tenancy is deemed to have been granted by the person entitled to that interest: see s 45(2)–(4). As to the meaning of 'landlord' see PARA 423 note 7.
7   Agricultural Holdings Act 1986 s 47(2).
8   Agricultural Holdings Act 1986 s 47(3).
9   Agricultural Holdings Act 1986 s 45(5). As to the service of notices see PARA 428 note 4.
10 Agricultural Holdings Act 1986 s 45(6). In such a case the provisions of s 48 as to arbitration (see PARA 505) do not apply. As to the relevant time see note 4.
11 Agricultural Holdings Act 1986 s 45(7).
12 Ie the Agricultural Holdings Act 1986 ss 34–48 (see PARA 497 et seq).
13 See the Agricultural Holdings Act 1986 s 45(8); and the Agriculture (Miscellaneous Provisions) Act 1976 (Application of Provisions) Regulations 1977, SI 1977/1215 (which have effect as if made under the Agricultural Holdings Act 1986 s 45(8)).

505. Arbitration or third party determination on terms of new tenancy.

Where the Tribunal[1] gives a direction entitling an applicant to a tenancy[2], the provisions described below apply[3].

The landlord[4] or tenant[5] may by notice in writing served[6] on the other within the prescribed period[7] demand a reference to arbitration or for third party determination[8] in respect of one or both of the following questions[9]:

(1)   what variations in the terms of the tenancy are justifiable having regard to the circumstances of the holding and the length of time since the holding was first let on those terms (question (a))[10]; and

(2)   what rent should be or have been properly payable at the relevant time (question (b))[11].

Where question (a) is referred to arbitration or third party determination, with or without question (b), the arbitrator or, as the case may be, the third party, must determine what variations are justifiable[12] and include in his award or, as the case may be, his determination, any provisions necessary to entitle the landlord or tenant to recover compensation paid or payable[13], and with effect from the relevant time, he must vary the terms or direct that they are to remain unchanged[14]. Where, in a reference on question (a) but not question (b), the arbitrator or, as the case may be, the third party, includes a provision in the terms of the tenancy (not being a provision as to compensation), and it appears to him that by reason thereof it would be equitable to vary the rent accordingly, he may do so with effect from the relevant time[15]. Where question (b) is referred to arbitration or third party determination, with or without question (a), the arbitrator or, as the case may be, the third party, must determine what rent should be or have been properly payable[16] in respect of the holding at the relevant time, and must accordingly increase or reduce the rent or direct that it is to remain unchanged[17].

On any reference the arbitrator may include in his award or, as the case may be, the third party may include in his determination, any further provisions relating to the tenancy to which the tenant is entitled or which he has obtained under a direction, as may be agreed between the landlord and tenant[18]. If the date of the award or, as the case may be, the determination, is before the relevant time, the provisions as to the effect of a direction entitling an applicant to the tenancy[19] will have effect subject to and in accordance with the award or determination[20]. If the award or, as the case may be, the determination, is made after the relevant time it will have effect as if its terms were contained in an agreement in writing between the landlord and the tenant and having effect as from the relevant time[21].

1   Ie in England, the First-tier Tribunal (see PARA 768) and in Wales, the Agricultural Land Tribunal for Wales (see PARA 767): see PARA 437 note 1.

2   As to the giving of such directions see the Agricultural Holdings Act 1986 s 39; and PARA 502.

3   Agricultural Holdings Act 1986 s 48(1). The provisions of s 48(3)–(12) (see the text and notes 4–21) apply, mutatis mutandis, to succession on the retirement of the previous tenant as they apply in relation to the death of the previous tenant: see s 56(3), (4); and PARA 508.

4   For these purposes 'landlord' means the landlord of the holding: Agricultural Holdings Act 1986 s 48(2). As to the meaning of 'landlord' generally see PARA 423 note 7. As to the meaning of 'holding' see PARA 499 note 2.

5   For these purposes 'tenant' means the person or persons entitled to a tenancy or joint tenancy of the holding by virtue of the direction: Agricultural Holdings Act 1986 s 48(2). As to the meaning of 'tenant' generally see PARA 423 note 5. Where in accordance with s 39(10) (see PARA 502) the tenancy to which a direction under s 39 entitles the person or persons concerned is a tenancy of part of the deceased's holding, references in ss 45, 48 to 'holding' must be read as references to the whole of the deceased's holding or to the part of that holding to which the direction relates, as the context requires: ss 46(3), 48(2). As to the meaning of 'tenancy' see PARA 500 note 2.

6   As to the service of notices see PARA 428 note 4.
7   The 'prescribed period' is the period between the giving of the direction and the end of the three months immediately following the relevant time, or the end of the three months immediately following the date of the direction, whichever last occurs: Agricultural Holdings Act 1986 s 48(2). As to the meaning of the 'relevant time' see PARA 504 note 4.
8   As to arbitrations and third party determinations generally see PARA 566 et seq.
9   Agricultural Holdings Act 1986 s 48(3) (substituted by the Deregulation Act 2015 Sch 4 para 16(2)).
10 Agricultural Holdings Act 1986 s 48(4)(a).
11 Agricultural Holdings Act 1986 s 48(4)(b). In this context, the rent properly payable is the rent at which the holding might reasonably be expected to be let by a prudent and willing landlord to a prudent and willing tenant, taking into account all relevant factors including the terms of the tenancy or prospective tenancy (including terms as to rent) and other matters specified in Sch 2 para 1(1) (see PARA 438): s 48(9).
12 Agricultural Holdings Act 1986 s 48(5)(a) (s 48(5) amended by the Deregulation Act 2015 Sch 4 para 16(3)).
13 Agricultural Holdings Act 1986 s 48(5)(b) (as amended: see note 12). This compensation is: (1) paid or payable by the landlord, whether under the Agricultural Holdings Act 1986 or by agreement or custom, on the termination of the deceased's tenancy (s 48(8)(a)); or (2) paid or payable to the landlord, whether under the Act or by agreement, on that termination, in respect of any dilapidation or deterioration of, or damage to, any part of the holding or anything in or on the holding which the tenant is or will be liable to make good under the terms of his tenancy (s 48(8)(b)). As to the termination of an agricultural tenancy see PARA 428 note 1.
14 Agricultural Holdings Act 1986 s 48(5).
15 Agricultural Holdings Act 1986 s 48(6) (amended by the Deregulation Act 2015 Sch 4 para 16(4)).
16 As to the rent properly payable see note 11.
17 Agricultural Holdings Act 1986 s 48(7) (amended by the Deregulation Act 2015 Sch 4 para 16(5)).
18 Agricultural Holdings Act 1986 s 48(10) (amended by the Deregulation Act 2015 Sch 4 para 16(6)).
19 Ie the provisions of the Agricultural Holdings Act 1986 s 47(1) (see PARA 504).
20 Agricultural Holdings Act 1986 s 48(11) (amended by the Deregulation Act 2015 Sch 4 para 16(7)).
21 Agricultural Holdings Act 1986 s 48(12) (amended by the Deregulation Act 2015 Sch 4 para 16(8)).

(iii) Succession on Retirement

506. Right to succeed on retirement.
The tenant[1], or all the tenants in the case of a joint tenancy, may serve on the landlord[2] a notice (the 'retirement notice')[3] indicating, in whatever terms, his or their wish that a single eligible person[4] named in the notice succeed him or them as from the date specified in the notice[5]. In addition to being a tenancy to which the general provisions as to succession apply[6], it must be a tenancy from year to year[7].

The provisions excluding the right to succeed to a tenancy on the death of a tenant[8] apply also in respect of the retirement of a tenant[9], with additional exclusions where:

(1)   the retiring tenant[10] has at any time given any other retirement notice in respect of the holding[11] or a related holding[12] and an application to become tenant has been made by any nominated successor[13] in respect of that notice[14];

(2)   at the retirement date[15] the retiring tenant is under 65, unless at that date he will by reason of bodily or mental infirmity, which is likely to be permanent[16], be incapable of conducting the farming of the holding[17] in

such a way as to secure fulfilment of the responsibilities to farm in accordance with the rules of good husbandry[18], and that fact is stated in the notice[19];

(3)   the holding was already subject to a notice to quit[20] falling within Case B[21], Case D[22] or Case E[23], unless it is determined by arbitration[24] that the notice to quit is ineffective or if, on the service of a counter-notice[25], the Tribunal[26] withholds consent to the operation of the notice to quit[27] or the time for applying for such consent has expired without such application having been made[28].

1   As to the meaning of 'tenant' see PARA 497 note 3.
2   As to the meaning of 'landlord' see PARA 423 note 7.
3   Agricultural Holdings Act 1986 s 49(1)(b), (3). As to the meaning of 'retirement notice' see PARA 499 note 4.
4   As to the meaning of 'eligible person' see PARA 499.
5   Agricultural Holdings Act 1986 s 49(1)(b). The date so specified must be a date on which the tenancy could have been lawfully terminated by a notice to quit given at the date of the retirement notice; it must fall not less than one year but not more than two years after the date of the notice: s 49(1)(b). As to the meaning of 'tenancy' see PARA 500 note 2.
6   As to those provisions see PARA 497.
7   Agricultural Holdings Act 1986 s 49(1)(a).
8   See the Agricultural Holdings Act 1986 ss 37, 38; and PARA 498.
9   Agricultural Holdings Act 1986 s 51(1), which also contains modifications to ss 37, 38 necessary in the case of retirement.
10   As to the meaning of 'retiring tenant' see PARA 499 note 4.
11   As to the meaning of 'holding' see PARA 499 note 2.
12   As to the meaning of 'related holding' see PARA 498 note 5.
13   As to the meaning of 'nominated successor' see PARA 499 note 3.
14   Agricultural Holdings Act 1986 s 51(2). Applications to become successor are made under s 53 (see PARA 507). An application which is invalidated by virtue of s 52(1), (2) (see note 28), or which is withdrawn or abandoned, is treated as if it were never made: ss 52(5), 53(10).
15   As to the meaning of 'retirement date' see PARA 499 note 5.
16   Agricultural Holdings Act 1986 s 51(3)(b).
17   As to the 'farming' of land see PARA 424.
18   As to the rules of good husbandry for the purposes of the Agricultural Holdings Act 1986 see, by virtue of s 96(3) (see PARA 430 note 14), the Agriculture Act 1947 ss 10, 11; and AGRICULTURAL PRODUCTION AND MARKETING vol 1A (2017) PARAS 11–13.
19   Agricultural Holdings Act 1986 s 51(3)(a).
20   As to the service of notices see PARA 428 note 4.
21   See PARA 475.
22   See PARA 477.
23   See PARA 478.
24   As to arbitrations generally see PARA 566 et seq.
25   As to a counter-notice to a notice to quit see PARA 471.
26   Ie in England, the First-tier Tribunal (see PARA 768) and in Wales, the Agricultural Land Tribunal for Wales (see PARA 767): see PARA 437 note 1.
27   As to the giving or withholding of consent to a notice to quit by the tribunal see PARA 472.
28   Agricultural Holdings Act 1986 s 51(4), (5). Where the tenancy becomes subject to a valid notice to quit given after the date of the retirement notice but before the hearing of any application for succession by the nominated successor, and the notice:
    (1)   falls within Case C (see PARA 476), in relation to Sch 3 Pt II para 9 or within Case F (see PARA 479) (s 52(1)); or
    (2)   includes a statement that it is founded on a reason within Case B or Case D (s 52(2)),
then the retirement notice is ineffective and no further proceedings may be taken in respect of it; unless, in the case of head (2), the tribunal determines that the notice to quit is ineffective, or on the service of a counter-notice the tribunal withholds consent to the operation of the notice to quit, or the time for applying for such consent has expired without such application having been made (s 52(3)).

Notices to quit not falling within ss 51, 52 do not have effect during the relevant period (ie one month beginning with the day after the date of the retirement notice) or, where an application for succession (see PARA 507) has been made within that period, before the disposal of the application, or, in any event, where a direction of entitlement to succession has been given: see s 54.

507. Application to succeed on retirement.

The nominated successor[1] of a retiring tenant[2] may apply to the Tribunal[3] for a direction entitling him to a tenancy[4] of the holding[5]. That application must be made within the relevant period[6]. It must be accompanied by a copy of the retirement notice[7] and be signed by both the nominated successor and the retiring tenant (or tenants where the retirement notice was given by joint tenants)[8]. If the retirement notice includes a statement that it is given on the ground of bodily or mental infirmity[9], the Tribunal must, before proceeding with the application, satisfy itself that the retiring tenant will thereby be incapable of conducting the farming of the holding[10] in such a way as to secure fulfilment of the responsibilities to farm in accordance with the rules of good husbandry[11], and that such incapacity is likely to be permanent[12]. If the Tribunal is satisfied that the nominated successor was an eligible person[13] at the date of the giving of the retirement notice[14] and has not ceased to be so since that date[15], then it must then go on to determine whether he is in their opinion a suitable person to become the tenant of the holding[16]. Before the Tribunal makes such a determination the landlord[17] must be given an opportunity to state his views on the suitability of the nominated successor, and in making the determination the Tribunal must have regard to all relevant matters, including the nominated successor's training in or practical experience of agriculture[18], his age, physical health and financial standing[19], and the views stated by the landlord on his suitability[20]. If the nominated person is determined by the Tribunal to be a suitable person, the Tribunal must give a direction entitling him to a tenancy of the holding[21], unless it appears, on an application by the landlord, that greater hardship would be caused by giving the direction than by refusing the nominated successor's application[22]. If the Tribunal does not give the direction on the application, then the retirement notice is ineffective[23]. If the application by the nominated successor is abandoned or withdrawn it is treated as never having been made[24].

1   As to the meaning of 'nominated successor' see PARA 499 note 3.
2   As to the meaning of 'retiring tenant' see PARA 499 note 4.
3   Ie in England, the First-tier Tribunal (see PARA 768) and in Wales, the Agricultural Land Tribunal for Wales (see PARA 767): see PARA 437 note 1.
4   As to the meaning of 'tenancy' see PARA 500 note 2.
5   Agricultural Holdings Act 1986 s 50(1). As to the meaning of 'holding' see PARA 499 note 2. This right is subject to s 57(2) (death of retiring tenant: see PARA 509), and is excluded in the circumstances described in PARA 506. As to the making of orders generally see PARA 432 note 5. See also *Kellett v Alexander* (1980) 257 Estates Gazette 494.
6   Agricultural Holdings Act 1986 s 53(1). For these purposes the 'relevant period' is generally the period of one month beginning with the day after the date of the giving of the retirement notice: s 53(2). Provision must be made by Tribunal Procedure Rules and by order under the Agriculture Act 1947 s 73(3) (procedure of Agricultural Land Tribunal for Wales: see PARA 767) for requiring any person making an application to the Tribunal for a direction under the Agricultural Holdings Act 1986 s 53 to give notice of the application to the landlord of the agricultural holding to which the application relates: s 53(11) (substituted by SI 2013/1036). As to applications made to the First-tier Tribunal under the Agricultural Holdings Act 1986 s 53 see the Tribunal Procedure (First-tier Tribunal) (Property Chamber) Rules 2013, SI 2013/1169, r 41.
7   Agricultural Holdings Act 1986 s 53(3)(a). As to the meaning of 'retirement notice' see PARA 499 note 4.
8   Agricultural Holdings Act 1986 s 53(3)(b).
9   Ie under the Agricultural Holdings Act 1986 s 51(3) (see PARA 506).

10 As to the meaning of 'holding' see PARA 499 note 2. As to the 'farming' of land see PARA 424.
11 Agricultural Holdings Act 1986 s 53(4)(a). As to the rules of good husbandry for the purposes of the Agricultural Holdings Act 1986 see, by virtue of s 96(3) (see PARA 430 note 14), the Agriculture Act 1947 ss 10, 11; and AGRICULTURAL PRODUCTION AND MARKETING vol 1A (2017) PARAS 11–13.
12 Agricultural Holdings Act 1986 s 53(4)(b).
13 As to the meaning of 'eligible person' see PARA 499. It is to be noted in particular that no application under s 42 to be treated as eligible (see PARA 502) is possible in the case of retirement succession.
14 Agricultural Holdings Act 1986 s 53(5)(a).
15 Agricultural Holdings Act 1986 s 53(5)(b).
16 Agricultural Holdings Act 1986 s 53(5).
17 As to the meaning of 'landlord' see PARA 423 note 7.
18 Agricultural Holdings Act 1986 s 53(6)(a).
19 Agricultural Holdings Act 1986 s 53(6)(b). As to the meaning of 'agriculture' see PARA 424.
20 Agricultural Holdings Act 1986 s 53(6)(c).
21 Agricultural Holdings Act 1986 s 53(7).
22 Agricultural Holdings Act 1986 s 53(8).
23 Agricultural Holdings Act 1986 s 53(9).
24 Agricultural Holdings Act 1986 s 53(10).

508. Effect of direction for succession on retirement.

A direction[1] by the Tribunal[2] entitling the nominated successor to a tenancy[3] of the holding[4] so entitles that successor with effect from the relevant time[5] and on the same terms as those upon which the holding was let immediately before it ceased to be let under the contract of tenancy[6] under which it was let at the date of the giving of the retirement notice[7]. Such a tenancy is accordingly deemed to have been granted at that time by the landlord and accepted by the nominated successor[8]. Any tenancy of the holding inconsistent with the tenancy which is the subject of the succession direction must, if it would not otherwise cease at the relevant time, cease at that time as though it had been terminated at that time by a valid notice to quit given by the tenant[9]. The rights conferred on any person by a direction (as distinct from rights acquired after he has become tenant[10]) are not capable of assignment[11]. Provision may be made by regulations for the application of the statutory provisions[12] to cases where the nominated successor dies before the relevant time[13].

The terms of any tenancy which is the subject of a succession direction are deemed to include, if they do not do so already, a covenant by the tenant not to assign, sub-let or part with possession of the holding or any part of it without the landlord's written consent[14].

There is provision for the referral to arbitration or third party determination[15] of certain questions arising on the giving of a direction of entitlement to succession[16].

1 Ie a direction under the Agricultural Holdings Act 1986 s 53 (see PARA 507).
2 Ie in England, the First-tier Tribunal (see PARA 768) and in Wales, the Agricultural Land Tribunal for Wales (see PARA 767): see PARA 437 note 1.
3 As to the meaning of 'nominated successor' see PARA 499 note 3. As to the meaning of 'tenancy' see PARA 500 note 2.
4 As to the meaning of 'holding' see PARA 499 note 2.
5 'Relevant time' means the retirement date, except that in certain circumstances the tribunal is empowered to alter it to either three months after the retirement date or three months after the giving of the direction: Agricultural Holdings Act 1986 s 55(8). As to the meaning of 'retirement date' see PARA 499 note 5.
6 As to the meaning of 'contract of tenancy' see PARA 425.

7   Agricultural Holdings Act 1986 ss 55(1), 56(1). As to the meaning of 'retirement notice' see PARA 499 note 4.

8   Agricultural Holdings Act 1986 s 55(1). Where a supervening interest has been created by the landlord, the entitlement to the tenancy is deemed to have been granted by the person entitled to that interest: see s 55(2)–(4). As to the meaning of 'landlord' see PARA 423 note 7.

9   Agricultural Holdings Act 1986 s 55(5). As to the service of notices see PARA 428 note 4.

10 As to the meaning of 'tenant' see PARA 423 note 5.

11 Agricultural Holdings Act 1986 s 55(6).

12 Ie the Agricultural Holdings Act 1986 ss 37(6), 50–58 (see PARA 497 et seq).

13 Agricultural Holdings Act 1986 s 55(7). At the date at which this volume states the law no such regulations had been made. As to the making of regulations generally see PARA 432 note 5.

14 Agricultural Holdings Act 1986 s 56(2).

15 As to arbitrations and third party determinations generally see PARA 566 et seq.

16 See the Agricultural Holdings Act 1986 s 56(3), (4), applying, with modifications relating to third party determination effected by the Deregulation Act 2015 Sch 4, the provisions of s 48(3)–(12) (as to which see PARA 505) to succession on retirement.

509. Death of retiring tenant.

Where the retiring tenant[1] dies after giving his retirement notice[2] but when no application by a nominated successor[3] has been made or before the final disposal of such application, the retirement notice is ineffective and no further proceedings may be taken with regard to it; the succession provisions normally applicable on the death of a tenant[4] apply in such a case[5].

If the retiring tenant dies when the Tribunal[6] has already given a direction that the nominated successor is entitled to the tenancy[7] but before the retirement date, that direction stands[8].

If the Tribunal has disposed of the application other than by the giving of a direction, the provisions as to succession on the death of the tenant apply[9]. The death of only one of joint retiring tenants does not affect the rights of the nominated successor[10].

Where the retiring tenant, being the sole or sole surviving tenant, dies[11] and the nominated successor is entitled under a direction to become the tenant of the holding[12], then for the purpose of determining whether, in relation to any other agricultural holding[13] held by the retiring tenant at the date of his death[14], the nominated successor is a person in whose case the occupancy condition[15] is satisfied, the nominated successor is deemed to be in occupation of the holding[16].

1   As to the meaning of 'retiring tenant' see PARA 499 note 4.

2   Agricultural Holdings Act 1986 s 57(1). As to the meaning of 'retirement notice' see PARA 499 note 4.

3   As to the meaning of 'nominated successor' see PARA 499 note 3.

4   As to the meaning of 'tenant' see PARA 423 note 5.

5   Agricultural Holdings Act 1986 s 57(2).

6   Ie in England, the First-tier Tribunal (see PARA 768) and in Wales, the Agricultural Land Tribunal for Wales (see PARA 767): see PARA 437 note 1.

7   As to the meaning of 'tenancy' see PARA 500 note 2.

8   Agricultural Holdings Act 1986 s 57(3).

9   Agricultural Holdings Act 1986 s 57(4).

10 Agricultural Holdings Act 1986 s 57(5).

11 Agricultural Holdings Act 1986 s 58(a).

12 Agricultural Holdings Act 1986 s 58(b). As to the meaning of 'holding' see PARA 499 note 2.

13 As to the meaning of 'agricultural holding' see PARA 423.

14 As to the meaning of 'date of death' see PARA 502 note 6.

15 Ie the condition set out in the Agricultural Holdings Act 1986 s 36(3)(b) (see PARA 499).

16 Agricultural Holdings Act 1986 s 58.

(iv) Succession without Application to the Tribunal

510. Inter vivos agreements.

A succession may take place by agreement where the landlord[1] and tenant[2] agree that the tenant should retire and a new tenancy be granted[3], or the existing tenancy assigned[4], to a person who at that time would have been a close relative[5] had the tenant died immediately before the relevant grant or assignment[6]. There is no requirement that the tenant should have reached retirement age and the close relative does not have to satisfy the other tests for eligibility or suitability: this arrangement is deemed for the purposes of the two succession rule[7] to be an occasion on which a tenancy was obtained on the death of the tenant by virtue of a direction from the Tribunal[8].

1 As to the meaning of 'landlord' see PARA 423 note 7.
2 As to the meaning of 'tenant' see PARA 423 note 5.
3 Agricultural Holdings Act 1986 s 37(2)(a).
4 Agricultural Holdings Act 1986 s 37(2)(b).
5 As to the meaning of 'close relative' see PARA 499.
6 See the Agricultural Holdings Act 1986 s 37(2); and PARA 498.
7 As to the two succession rule see PARA 498 head (3). In the case of certain historic transactions, the two succession rule is modified to reflect the legal provisions applicable at the time of that transaction: see the Agricultural Holdings Act 1986 s 37(7), (8); and PARA 498.
8 Agricultural Holdings Act 1986 s 37(2). In England, the Tribunal is the First-tier Tribunal (see PARA 768) and in Wales, it is the Agricultural Land Tribunal for Wales (see PARA 767): see PARA 437 note 1.

(7) COMPENSATION UNDER THE AGRICULTURAL HOLDINGS ACT 1986

(i) Compensation: Introduction

511. Source of right to compensation.

At common law an agricultural tenant is not entitled to compensation[1] from his landlord for improvements or acts of husbandry of which the landlord obtains the benefit when the tenant quits the holding[2]. This rule may be modified by the custom of the country[3], and the parties may themselves provide for compensation in their agreement. The right to compensation is, however, now almost wholly regulated by statute to the exclusion of both custom and agreement, though a written agreement may entitle a claimant to compensation where he has no right to it under statute[4].

1 As to compensation for damage by game see PARA 521.
2 *Wigglesworth v Dallison* (1779) 1 Doug KB 201.
3 *Wigglesworth v Dallison* (1779) 1 Doug KB 201.
4 As to the right to compensation in respect of tenancies governed by the Agricultural Holdings Act 1986 see PARA 512 et seq.

512. Effect of agreements as to compensation.

Where the Agricultural Holdings Act 1986 provides for compensation[1], a landlord[2] or tenant[3] is entitled to compensation in accordance with the statutory provisions and not otherwise[4], save as expressly provided by the Act, and is so entitled notwithstanding any agreement to the contrary[5].

Where the landlord and tenant enter into an agreement in writing for any such variation of the terms of the contract of tenancy[6] as could be made by the direction or order of an arbitrator or determination by a third party[7] in connection with the amount of land to be maintained as permanent pasture[8], the agreement may provide for the exclusion of compensation[9].

In the case of long term improvements begun on or after 1 March 1948[10] for which compensation is payable, the landlord and tenant may agree in writing to substitute a different measure of compensation from that laid down in the Act[11].

In the case of tenant-right matters[12], the parties may in a written contract of tenancy substitute for the measure of compensation contained in the Act an alternative method of calculation for the compensation[13].

Where the Act makes no provision for compensation, nothing therein is to be construed as disentitling a tenant or a landlord to compensation, but no claim for compensation in such a case is enforceable except under an agreement in writing, other than a claim by a tenant in respect of a tenant-right matter[14] where the tenant entered into occupation of the holding before 1 March 1948 and does not give notice electing that the relevant statutory provision[15] is to apply to him[16].

A provision in an agreement which shortens the time within which a claim for compensation for improvements is to be made[17], or which allows for the giving of a notice of such a short period as to prevent the tenant from giving the requisite statutory notices in respect of any claims for compensation[18], or which permits re-entry without notice[19], is void. An agreement which expressly states that a holding is not to be treated as a market garden so as to exclude a claim for compensation for fruit trees and bushes[20] is not avoided by the Act, as the right to claim compensation does not arise[21].

1 For the statutory provisions as to compensation see PARA 515 et seq.
2 As to the meaning of 'landlord' see PARA 423 note 7.
3 As to the meaning of 'tenant' see PARA 423 note 5.
4 Cf *Dean v Secretary of State for War* [1950] 1 All ER 344, CA, where a claim for compensation for disturbance under the Agricultural Holdings Act 1923 s 12(6) (repealed) was held to be recoverable under the terms of an agreement in excess of the statutory limits.
5 Agricultural Holdings Act 1986 s 78(1). See *Mears v Callender* [1901] 2 Ch 388.
6 As to the meaning of 'contract of tenancy' see PARA 425.
7 As to arbitrations and third party determinations generally see PARA 566 et seq.
8 Ie under the Agricultural Holdings Act 1986 s 14 (see PARA 441).
9 Agricultural Holdings Act 1986 s 78(2).
10 Ie the date on which the Agriculture Act 1947 Pt III (repealed), from which these provisions are derived, was brought into force: see s 111(2) (repealed); and the Agriculture Act 1947 (Commencement) (No 1) Order 1948, SI 1948/342.
11 Agricultural Holdings Act 1986 s 67(2). Long term improvements are specified in s 64, Sch 7: see further PARA 529.
12 Ie the matters specified in the Agricultural Holdings Act 1986 s 65, Sch 8 Pt II (see PARA 530).
13 Agricultural Holdings Act 1986 s 66(4).
14 Ie one specified in the Agricultural Holdings Act 1986 Sch 8 paras 7–10 (see PARA 530).
15 Ie the Agricultural Holdings Act 1986 s 65(1).
16 Agricultural Holdings Act 1986 s 78(3). See Sch 12 paras 6–8; and PARA 532.
17 *Cathcart v Chalmers* [1911] AC 246, HL.
18 *Re Disraeli Agreement, Cleasby v Park Estate (Hughenden) Ltd* [1939] Ch 382, [1938] 4 All ER 658.
19 *Coates v Diment* [1951] 1 All ER 890; *Parry v Million Pigs Ltd* (1980) 260 Estates Gazette 281.
20 Ie under the Agricultural Holdings Act 1986 s 79(1), Sch 12 para 10 (see PARA 565).
21 *Re Masters and Duveen* [1923] 2 KB 729, CA.

513. Exclusion of compensation for pasture provided in pursuance of order.

No compensation is payable to a tenant[1] under statute, custom or agreement in respect of anything done in pursuance of an order[2] made consequent on a direction by an arbitrator or third party[3] reducing the area of land which under the contract of tenancy[4] is to be maintained as permanent pasture[5].

1 As to the meaning of 'tenant' see PARA 423 note 5.
2 Ie under the Agricultural Holdings Act 1986 s 14(4) (see PARA 441).
3 As to arbitrations and third party determinations generally see PARA 566 et seq.
4 As to the meaning of 'contract of tenancy' see PARA 425.
5 Agricultural Holdings Act 1986 s 76(1), (2).

514. Exclusion of compensation for improvements under custom.

A landlord[1] or tenant[2] of an agricultural holding[3] is not entitled under custom to any compensation from his tenant or landlord for any improvement, whether or not the improvement is one which qualifies for statutory compensation, or for any tenant-right matters specified in the Agricultural Holdings Act 1986[4] or otherwise[5]. This provision does not apply to compensation for long term improvements[6] or short term improvements for which no consent is required[7], begun before 1 March 1948[8], or to compensation for the specified tenant-right matters, where the tenant entered into occupation of his holding before that date and does not elect[9] that the Act should apply to him as regards those matters[10].

1 As to the meaning of 'landlord' see PARA 423 note 7.
2 As to the meaning of 'tenant' see PARA 423 note 5.
3 As to the meaning of 'agricultural holding' see PARA 423.
4 Ie in the Agricultural Holdings Act 1986 Sch 8 Pt II: see PARA 530. See also Sch 12 para 8; the text and notes 6–10; and PARA 539.
5 Agricultural Holdings Act 1986 s 77(1).
6 Ie improvements of a kind specified in the Agricultural Holdings Act 1986 Sch 7 (see PARA 529).
7 Ie improvements of a kind specified in the Agricultural Holdings Act 1986 Sch 8 Pt I (see PARA 529).
8 The date mentioned in the text is the date on which the Agriculture Act 1947 Pt III (repealed), from which these provisions are derived, was brought into force: see the Agriculture Act 1947 s 111(2) (repealed); and the Agriculture Act 1947 (Commencement) (No 1) Order 1948, SI 1948/342.
9 As to the time within which election is to be made see PARA 532.
10 Agricultural Holdings Act 1986 s 77(2).

(ii) Statutory Right to Compensation on Quitting Holding

515. Scope of statutory compensation.

Compensation under the Agricultural Holdings Act 1986 is payable to tenants[1] on quitting their holdings[2] for disturbance[3], for the continuous adoption of a special system of farming[4], for the making of specified improvements and for certain tenant-right matters[5]. Where compensation is payable for disturbance, additional compensation to assist in the reorganisation of the tenant's affairs is also generally payable[6]. A right to compensation is also given to landlords[7] for deterioration or dilapidation of the holding due to the tenant's failure to farm in accordance with the rules of good husbandry[8]. There is a right to compensation payable to the tenant on quitting the holding in respect of milk quota registered to him in relation to the holding[9], and provision is also made as to the compulsory acquisition of tenanted land[10].

1 As to the meaning of 'tenant' see PARA 423 note 5.
2 As to the meaning of 'agricultural holding' see PARA 423.

3   See PARA 544.
4   See PARAS 548–549.
5   See PARA 522 et seq.
6   See PARA 544.
7   As to the meaning of 'landlord' see PARA 423 note 7.
8   See PARA 553 et seq. As to the rules of good husbandry for the purposes of the Agricultural
    Holdings Act 1986 see, by virtue of s 96(3) (see PARA 430 note 14), the Agriculture Act 1947 ss
    10, 11; and AGRICULTURAL PRODUCTION AND MARKETING vol 1A (2017) PARAS 11–13.
9   See PARA 520.
10 See PARA 591 et seq.

516. Application to parts of a holding.

Where the landlord[1] resumes possession of a part of an agricultural holding[2], whether in pursuance of a provision contained in the contract of tenancy[3] or under statute[4], the statutory compensation provisions apply to the part as if it were a separate holding which the tenant[5] had quit in consequence of a notice to quit[6]. Where such possession is taken under a provision in the contract of tenancy the arbitrator or, as the case may be, the third party[7], in assessing the amount of compensation payable to the tenant[8], must take into consideration any benefit or relief allowed to the tenant under the contract of tenancy in respect of the land repossessed by the landlord[9].

1   As to the meaning of 'landlord' see PARA 423 note 7.
2   As to the meaning of 'agricultural holding' see PARA 423.
3   As to the meaning of 'contract of tenancy' see PARA 425.
4   This may be:
    (1)   by virtue of the right conferred by the Agricultural Holdings Act 1986 s 31 (see PARA
          492) to serve a notice to quit part of a holding (s 74(1));
    (2)   by virtue of consent given by the Tribunal consequent on a notice to quit given by reason
          of the death of the tenant (see s 43(2); and PARA 503) (s 74(1)); or
    (3)   where a person entitled to a severed part of the reversionary estate in an agricultural
          holding resumes possession of part of the holding by virtue of a notice to quit that part
          given to the tenant by virtue of the Law of Property Act 1925 s 140 (see PARA 495; and
          LANDLORD AND TENANT vol 62 (2016) PARA 446) (Agricultural Holdings Act 1986 s
          74(3)).
    In England, the Tribunal is the First-tier Tribunal (see PARA 768) and in Wales it is the Agricultural
    Land Tribunal for Wales (see PARA 767): see PARA 437 note 1.
5   As to the meaning of 'tenant' see PARA 423 note 5.
6   Agricultural Holdings Act 1986 s 74(1), (2).
7   Ie the third party appointed under the Agricultural Holdings Act 1986 s 84A (see PARA 568). As
    to the determination of claims generally see PARA 566 et seq.
8   Ie except the amount of compensation under the Agricultural Holdings Act 1986 s 60(2)(b) (ie
    additional compensation: see PARA 545): s 74(2)(b).
9   Agricultural Holdings Act 1986 s 74(2)(b) (amended by the Deregulation Act 2015 Sch 4 para 17).

517. Compensation where reversion divided.

Where the reversionary estate in an agricultural holding[1] has become vested in more than one person in several parts, the tenant[2] is entitled to require any statutory compensation[3] payable to him to be determined as if the holding had not been so severed[4]. In such cases the arbitrator, or as the case may be, the third party[5] must, where necessary, apportion the amount awarded between the persons who for the purposes of the Agricultural Holdings Act 1986 constitute the landlord[6], and any additional cost of the award caused by the apportionment must be directed by the arbitrator or the third party, to be paid by those persons in such proportions as he determines[7].

1   As to the meaning of 'agricultural holding' see PARA 423.
2   As to the meaning of 'tenant' see PARA 423 note 5.
3   Ie compensation payable to him under the Agricultural Holdings Act 1986.
4   Agricultural Holdings Act 1986 s 75(1).
5   As to arbitrations and third party determinations generally see PARA 566 et seq.
6   As to the meaning of 'landlord' see PARA 423 note 7.
7   Agricultural Holdings Act 1986 s 75(2) (amended by the Deregulation Act 2015 Sch 4 para 18).

518. Compensation from mortgagee.

The statutory power[1] of a mortgagor in possession to create a lease of agricultural land binding on the mortgagee is exercisable in the case of mortgages of agricultural land[2] to which the Agricultural Holdings Act 1986 applies notwithstanding any contrary intention expressed in the mortgage deed or otherwise in writing[3].

Formerly[4], where the contract of tenancy was not binding on the mortgagee, a mortgagee of an agricultural holding was not personally liable to pay any sums due to the occupier of the holding by way of compensation or costs[5], but such sums could be set off against rent or other sums due from the occupier in respect of the holding, and if the sum was not so set off the occupier was entitled to obtain from the Secretary of State[6] an order charging the holding with the sum due[7]. These provisions have some continuing relevance, since it is provided that a charge on an agricultural holding created thereunder takes priority over any other charge[8], however and whenever created or arising[9].

1   Ie under the Law of Property Act 1925 s 99: see MORTGAGE vol 77 (2016) PARAS 349–353.
2   As to the meaning of 'agricultural land' see the Agriculture Act 1947 s 109(1); and PARA 424 (definition applied by the Law of Property Act 1925 s 99(13B) (s 99(13) amended, and s 99(13A), (13B) added, by the Agricultural Tenancies Act 1995 s 31(1)–(3))).
3   See the Law of Property Act 1925 s 99(13), (13A), (13B) (s 99(13) as amended, and s 99(13A), (13B) as added: see note 2). See also MORTGAGE vol 77 (2016) PARA 350. See further *Barclays Bank plc v Bean* [2004] 3 EGLR 71, [2005] BPIR 563. Note that by virtue of the Law of Property Act 1925 s 99(13), (13A), (13B) the statutory power to grant leases can be excluded if the mortgage is granted in relation to a lease which would be a farm business tenancy under the Agricultural Tenancies Act 1995 (see PARA 401 et seq).
4   Ie under the Agricultural Holdings Act 1948 s 74 (repealed). See the text and notes 8, 9.
5   Ie under the Agricultural Holdings Act 1948 s 66 (repealed). See the text and notes 8, 9.
6   As to the Secretary of State see PARA 741.
7   Agricultural Holdings Act 1948 s 74 (repealed). See the text and notes 8, 9.
8   Ie except a charge created or arising under the Agricultural Holdings Act 1986 s 85 (see PARAS 572–574).
9   Agricultural Holdings Act 1986 s 87(6). As between themselves, such charges rank in order of creation: s 87(6).

519. Exclusion of compensation for things done in compliance with statute.

No compensation is payable to a tenant[1] under the Agricultural Holdings Act 1986, or under any custom or agreement, in respect of anything done in pursuance of an award of an arbitrator or, as the case may be, a third party determination,[2] varying the provisions of a contract of tenancy[3] as to the maintenance of permanent pasture[4]. In assessing compensation to an outgoing tenant of an agricultural holding[5] where land has been ploughed up in pursuance of such a direction by an arbitrator or third party, the value per hectare of any tenant's pasture[6] comprised in the holding is to be taken not to exceed the average value per hectare of the whole of the tenant's pasture comprised in the holding on the termination of the tenancy[7].

A tenant of an agricultural holding is not entitled to any compensation for a relevant short term improvement for which consent is not required[8] or, save in certain circumstances[9], for any tenant-right matter[10] if it is an improvement or matter made or effected in compliance with the tenant's obligation[11] to make suitable and adequate provision to return to the holding the full equivalent manurial value of all crops sold off or removed from the holding in contravention of the custom, contract or agreement or, in the case of an exercise of the right by the tenant to practise any system of cropping, to protect the holding from injury or deterioration[12].

1   As to the meaning of 'tenant' see PARA 423 note 5.
2   Ie an order under the Agricultural Holdings Act 1986 s 14(4) (see PARA 441). As to arbitrations and third party determinations generally see PARA 566 et seq.
3   As to the meaning of 'contract of tenancy' see PARA 425.
4   Agricultural Holdings Act 1986 s 76(1)(a).
5   As to the meaning of 'agricultural holding' see PARA 423.
6   'Tenant's pasture' means pasture laid down at the expense of the tenant or paid for by the tenant on entering on the holding: Agricultural Holdings Act 1986 s 76(2).
7   Agricultural Holdings Act 1986 s 76(1)(b). As to the termination of an agricultural tenancy see PARA 428 note 1.
8   Ie short term improvements begun on or after 1 March 1948, and other matters, specified in the Agricultural Holdings Act 1986 Sch 8 Pt I (see PARA 529).
9   Ie subject to the Agricultural Holdings Act 1986 Sch 12 para 8, under which the tenant must elect for compensation on the statutory basis in accordance with Sch 8 Pt II (see PARA 530).
10 Ie a matter specified in the Agricultural Holdings Act 1986 Sch 8 Pt II (see PARA 530).
11 Ie an obligation under the Agricultural Holdings Act 1986 s 15(4) (see PARA 444).
12 Agricultural Holdings Act 1986 s 76(3). As to the right to dispose of produce and to practise any system of cropping see s 15; and PARA 444.

520.   Compensation for milk quota.

Compensation may be payable where on the termination of a tenancy under the Agricultural Holdings Act 1986 the tenant has milk quota registered as his in relation to a holding consisting of or including that land[1].

1   See the Agriculture Act 1986 s 13, Sch 1; and AGRICULTURAL PRODUCTION AND MARKETING vol 1A (2017) PARA 6.

(iii) Compensation for Damage by Game

521.   Tenant's rights to compensation under statute.

Where the tenant[1] of an agricultural holding[2] under the Agricultural Holdings Act 1986 sustains damage to his crops from any wild animals or birds, the common law right to kill[3] and to take which is vested in the landlord[4] or anyone claiming under him[5], being animals or birds which the tenant does not have permission in writing to kill, he is entitled to compensation from his landlord subject to certain requirements[6]. Those requirements are that the tenant must give his landlord:

(1)   notice in writing[7] within one month after the tenant first became, or ought reasonably to have become, aware of the occurrence of the damage[8];

(2)   a reasonable opportunity[9] to inspect the damage, in the case of damage to a growing crop[10], before the crop is begun to be reaped, raised or consumed[11], and in the case of damage to a crop which has been reaped or raised, before the crop has begun to be removed from the land[12]; and

(3)   notice in writing of the claim, together with particulars of it, within one month after the expiry of the year[13] in respect of which the claim is made[14].

In default of agreement made after the damage has been suffered, the amount of compensation to which the tenant is entitled must be determined by arbitration[15] or[16] third party determination[17]. A tenant can obtain a charge on the holding for game damage compensation[18].

The landlord is liable to the tenant where the right to kill and take the animals or birds which caused the damage has been granted to some other person but the landlord is entitled to an indemnity from that other person, and any dispute in respect of such indemnity must be determined by arbitration[19] or[20] third party determination[21]. The landlord's liability extends beyond his own land to game from a neighbouring estate[22], subject to any indemnity from his neighbour[23]. It is not possible for the landlord to contract out of his liability to the tenant[24]. Permission in writing to the tenant to kill any particular kind of game excludes compensation for damage caused by that species[25].

1 As to the meaning of 'tenant' see PARA 423 note 5.
2 As to the meaning of 'agricultural holding' see PARA 423.
3 At common law the tenant has the exclusive right to the game on land in his occupation unless the right is reserved to the landlord: *Moore v Earl of Plymouth* (1817) 7 Taunt 614. Common law also gives a right to compensation, but there is no liability where damage occurs through the natural increase in game already on the land: *Farrer v Nelson* (1885) 15 QBD 258. By statute an occupier of land has the right, as an incident of his occupation, to kill hares and rabbits, and any agreement or condition which seeks to exclude the right is void: see the Ground Game Act 1880 ss 1, 3; and ANIMALS vol 2 (2017) PARA 73. Further, the Secretary of State and the Welsh Ministers may require any person having the right to do so to destroy or take rabbits, hares and other rodents, deer, foxes and moles, and certain unprotected wild birds, for the prevention of damage to crops, pasture, animal or human foodstuffs, livestock, trees, hedges, banks or works on land, and may also serve a notice on the occupier of any land requiring him to take steps to prevent the escape of any animals from land: see the Agriculture Act 1947 ss 98–100; and AGRICULTURAL PRODUCTION AND MARKETING vol 1A (2017) PARAS 116–118. As to the Secretary of State and the Welsh Ministers see PARA 741.
4 As to the meaning of 'landlord' see PARA 423 note 7.
5 Ie other than the tenant himself: Agricultural Holdings Act 1986 s 20(1).
6 Agricultural Holdings Act 1986 s 20(1).
7 As to the service of notices see PARA 428 note 4.
8 Agricultural Holdings Act 1986 s 20(2)(a).
9 As to what constitutes reasonable opportunity see *Dale v Hatfield Chase Corpn* [1922] 2 KB 282, CA; *Barbour v M'Douall* 1914 SC 844, Ct of Sess.
10 Seed once sown is treated as a growing crop whether or not it has germinated: Agricultural Holdings Act 1986 s 20(3)(a).
11 Agricultural Holdings Act 1986 s 20(2)(b)(i).
12 Agricultural Holdings Act 1986 s 20(2)(b)(ii).
13 'Year' means any period of 12 months ending, in any year, with 29 September or with such other date as may by agreement between the landlord and tenant be substituted for that date: Agricultural Holdings Act 1986 s 20(3)(b).
14 Agricultural Holdings Act 1986 s 20(3)(c).
15 Agricultural Holdings Act 1986 s 20(4).
16 Ie under the Agricultural Holdings Act 1986.
17 See the Agricultural Holdings Act 1986 s 20(4A) (added by the Deregulation Act 2015 Sch 4 para 12(2)). As to third party determinations see PARA 568.
18 See the Agricultural Holdings Act 1986 s 85(2); and PARA 573.

19 Agricultural Holdings Act 1986 s 20(5).
20 Ie under the Agricultural Holdings Act 1986.
21 Agricultural Holdings Act 1986 s 20(4A) (added by the Deregulation Act 2015 Sch 4 para 12(3)).
22 *Thomson v Earl of Galloway* 1919 SC 611, Ct of Sess.
23 *Farrer v Nelson* (1885) 15 QBD 258.
24 See the Agricultural Holdings Act 1986 s 78(1); and PARA 512.
25 *Ross v Watson* 1943 SC 406, Ct of Sess.

(iv) Compensation for Old Improvements

522. Right to compensation for old improvements.

A tenant[1] under the Agricultural Holdings Act 1986 has a statutory right[2] on the termination of his tenancy[3] and upon quitting the holding[4] to obtain from his landlord[5] compensation for specified improvements[6] carried out on the holding and begun before 1 March 1948[7]. Such improvements are termed 'old improvements'[8].

The tenant does not have a right to compensation in respect of old improvements where the contract of tenancy[9] was made before 1 January 1921[10] and the improvement was one which he was required to carry out by the terms of his tenancy[11]. Further, the old improvement must have been one made on land which, at the time when the improvement was begun, was either a holding within the meaning of the Agricultural Holdings Act 1923 as originally enacted[12], or fell to be treated as such[13].

In lieu of statutory compensation, a tenant may claim compensation under custom, agreement or otherwise, if he is so entitled[14].

1   As to the meaning of 'tenant' see PARA 423 note 5.
2   This right is subject to the conditions described in PARA 525 et seq.
3   As to the termination of an agricultural tenancy see PARA 428 note 1.
4   As to the meaning of 'agricultural holding' see PARA 423.
5   As to the meaning of 'landlord' see PARA 423 note 7.
6   Ie specified in the Agricultural Holdings Act 1986 Sch 9. As to those improvements see PARA 523.
7   Agricultural Holdings Act 1986 Sch 9 Pt I para 1(1). See also Sch 12 para 5. The date mentioned in the text is the date on which the Agriculture Act 1947 Pt III (repealed), from which these provisions are derived, was brought into force: see s 111(2) (repealed); and the Agriculture Act 1947 (Commencement) (No 1) Order 1948, SI 1948/342.
8   Agricultural Holdings Act 1986 Sch 9 Pt I para 1(2). It should be noted that some of the items formerly contained in the Agricultural Holdings Act 1948 Sch 2 (repealed) are no longer included (eg protecting young fruit trees).
9   As to the meaning of 'contract of tenancy' see PARA 425.
10   Ie the date on which the Agriculture Act 1920, from which these provisions in part derive, was brought into force: see s 36(1) (repealed).
11   Agricultural Holdings Act 1986 Sch 9 Pt I para 1(3); and see *Huckell v Saintey* [1923] 1 KB 150, CA.
12   A 'holding' for the purposes of the Agricultural Holdings Act 1923 as originally enacted was any parcel of land held by a tenant which was either wholly agricultural or wholly pastoral, or in part agricultural and as to the residue pastoral, or in whole or in part cultivated as a market garden, and was let or agreed to be let for a term of years, or for lives, or for lives and years, or from year to year, and not let to a tenant during his continuance in any office, appointment, or employment held under the landlord, but it did not include any allotment garden or any land cultivated as a garden unless it was cultivated wholly or mainly for the purposes of the trade or business of market gardening: Agricultural Holdings Act 1923 s 57(1) (repealed). In *Re Lancaster and Macnamara* [1918] 2 KB 472, CA, the demise of a farm with an inn was held not to constitute an agricultural holding. In *Howatson v M'Clymont* 1914 51 Sc LR 153, parkland without buildings tenanted by a dairy keeper was used solely for grazing purposes and was held to be an agricultural holding. In *Re Russell and Harding* (1922) 128 LT 476, CA, the land remained an agricultural holding although the farmhouse had been sub-let as a boarding house. In *Re Joel's Lease, Berwick v Baird* [1930] 2 Ch 359, a stud farm for breeding racehorses was held not to be an agricultural holding.

A letting for successive periods of 364 days was not within the definition: see *Land Settlement Association Ltd v Carr* [1944] KB 657, [1944] 2 All ER 126, CA.
13 Agricultural Holdings Act 1986 Sch 9 Pt I para 1(5). 'Fell to be treated as such' means treated as such by virtue of the Agricultural Holdings Act 1923 s 33 (repealed), which provided that where land comprised in a contract of tenancy was not a holding within the meaning of the Act by reason only of the fact that the land so comprised included land (called 'non-statutory land'), which, owing to the nature of the buildings thereon or the use to which it was put, would not, if it had been separately let, be a holding within the meaning of the Act, the provisions of the Act relating to compensation for improvements and disturbance should, unless otherwise agreed in writing, apply to the part of the land exclusive of the non-statutory land as if that part were a separate holding. This did not apply to contracts of tenancy made before 1 January 1921.
14 Agricultural Holdings Act 1986 Sch 9 Pt I para 1(4).

523. The nature of old improvements.

The old improvements[1] for which compensation is payable are:
(1)   erection, alteration or enlargement of buildings[2];
(2)   formation of silos[3];
(3)   making and planting of osier beds[4];
(4)   making of water meadows or works of irrigation[5];
(5)   making of gardens[6];
(6)   making or improvement of roads or bridges[7];
(7)   making or improvement of watercourses, ponds, wells or reservoirs or of works for the application of water power or for the supply of water for agricultural[8] or domestic purposes[9];
(8)   making or removal of permanent fences[10];
(9)   planting of hops[11];
(10)   planting of orchards or fruit bushes[12];
(11)   reclaiming of waste land[13];
(12)   warping or weiring of land[14];
(13)   embankments and sluices against floods[15];
(14)   erection of wirework in hop gardens[16];
(15)   provision of permanent sheep-dipping accommodation[17]; and
(16)   drainage[18].

Until the Agricultural Holdings Act 1984 was enacted[19], there was a category of improvements for which no notice or consent was required for a claim for compensation[20].

1   As to the meaning of 'old improvements' see PARA 522.
2   Agricultural Holdings Act 1986 Sch 9 Pt II para 1. As to the meaning of 'building' see PARA 432 note 6.
3   Agricultural Holdings Act 1986 Sch 9 Pt II para 2.
4   Agricultural Holdings Act 1986 Sch 9 Pt II para 3.
5   Agricultural Holdings Act 1986 Sch 9 Pt II para 4.
6   Agricultural Holdings Act 1986 Sch 9 Pt II para 5.
7   Agricultural Holdings Act 1986 Sch 9 Pt II para 6.
8   As to the meaning of 'agricultural' see PARA 424.
9   Agricultural Holdings Act 1986 Sch 9 Pt II para 7.
10 Agricultural Holdings Act 1986 Sch 9 Pt II para 8.
11 Agricultural Holdings Act 1986 Sch 9 Pt II para 9.
12 Agricultural Holdings Act 1986 Sch 9 Pt II para 10.
13 Agricultural Holdings Act 1986 Sch 9 Pt II para 11.
14 Agricultural Holdings Act 1986 Sch 9 Pt II para 12.
15 Agricultural Holdings Act 1986 Sch 9 Pt II para 13.
16 Agricultural Holdings Act 1986 Sch 9 Pt II para 14.
17 Agricultural Holdings Act 1986 Sch 9 Pt II para 15.
18 Agricultural Holdings Act 1986 Sch 9 Pt II para 16.
19 The Agricultural Holdings Act 1984 received Royal Assent on 12 July 1984 and came into force on 12 September 1984 (s 11(2) (repealed)).

20 Ie improvements specified in the Agricultural Holdings Act 1948 Sch 2 Pt III (repealed). These improvements were chalking of land; clay-burning; claying of land or spreading blaes upon the land; liming of land; marling of land; application to land of purchased artificial or other purchased manure; consumption on the holding by cattle, sheep, pigs or by horses other than those regularly employed on the holding of corn, cake, or other feeding-stuff not produced on the holding; consumption in the same manner of corn proved to have been produced and consumed on the holding; laying down temporary pasture with clover, grass, lucerne, sainfoin, or other seeds, sown more than two years prior to the termination of the tenancy, in so far as the value of the temporary pasture on the holding at the time of quitting exceeds the value of the temporary pasture on the holding at the commencement of the tenancy for which the tenant did not pay compensation; repairs to buildings, being buildings necessary for the proper cultivation or working of the holding, other than repairs which the tenant was himself under an obligation to execute. This provision was repealed as spent by the Agricultural Holdings Act 1984 Sch 3 para 27(a).

524. Amount of compensation for old improvements.

The measure of statutory compensation for old improvements[1] is an amount equal to the increase attributable to the improvement in the value of the agricultural holding[2] having regard to the holding's character and situation and the average requirements of tenants reasonably skilled in husbandry[3].

In ascertaining the amount of statutory compensation to be paid to a tenant[4] in respect of old improvements, any benefit which the landlord[5] has given or allowed to the tenant in consideration of the tenant's executing the improvement, whether expressly stated in the contract of tenancy[6] to be so given or allowed or not, is to be taken into account[7].

1   As to the meaning of 'old improvements' see PARA 522. As to the nature of old improvements see PARA 523.
2   As to the meaning of 'agricultural holding' see PARA 423.
3   Agricultural Holdings Act 1986 Sch 9 Pt I para 2(1).
4   As to the meaning of 'tenant' see PARA 423 note 5.
5   As to the meaning of 'landlord' see PARA 423 note 7.
6   As to the meaning of 'contract of tenancy' see PARA 425.
7   Agricultural Holdings Act 1986 Sch 9 Pt I para 2(2).

525. Consent to permanent old improvements.

Compensation is not payable for a specified old improvement[1], unless before the execution of the improvement the landlord[2] consented in writing[3] to the making of the improvement[4]. Such consent could be unconditional, or upon such terms as to compensation or otherwise as was agreed[5]. Where the consent was given upon agreed terms as to compensation, compensation payable under the agreement is substituted for compensation payable under the Agricultural Holdings Act 1986[6].

1   Ie an improvement specified by the Agricultural Holdings Act 1986 Sch 9 Pt II. As to the meaning of 'old improvements' see PARA 522. As to the nature of old improvements see PARA 523.
2   As to the meaning of 'landlord' see PARA 423 note 7.
3   The consent may be given in the lease. A lease providing that the tenant may at his own cost convert meadow into orchard is such a consent (*Mears v Callender* [1901] 2 Ch 388) but not the mere recognition in a lease of the tenant's right to plant fruit trees (*Re Morse and Dixon* (1917) 87 LJKB 1, CA).
4   Agricultural Holdings Act 1986 Sch 9 Pt I para 3(1).
5   Agricultural Holdings Act 1986 Sch 9 Pt I para 3(1). As to whether the landlord can impose a condition that no compensation is to be payable see *Mears v Callender* [1901] 2 Ch 388; cf *Turnbull v Millar* 1942 SC 521, Ct of Sess. See also the comments of Lord Hailsham of St Marylebone LC in *Johnson v Moreton* [1980] AC 37 at 58, [1978] 3 All ER 37 at 47–48, HL.
6   Agricultural Holdings Act 1986 Sch 9 Pt I para 3(2).

526. Compensation for drainage as an old improvement.

Compensation is payable for drainage[1] provided the tenant[2] had, not more than three nor less than two months before beginning the work, given notice[3] of his intention to execute the improvement and of the manner in which he proposed to execute it[4]. The landlord[5] and tenant must have agreed upon the terms on which the improvement was to be executed[6]. In a case where no agreement was reached, and the tenant did not withdraw the notice, the landlord must have failed to exercise within a reasonable time the right conferred on him[7] to do it himself[8]. These provisions, requiring notice to be given as a prerequisite to entitlement to compensation, have no application if the parties agree by the contract of tenancy[9] or otherwise to dispense with notice[10]. An agreement to dispense with notice need not be in writing[11]. If the parties agreed, whether after notice was given or by agreement to dispense with notice, upon terms as to compensation upon which the improvement was to be executed, compensation payable under the agreement is substituted for the compensation under the Agricultural Holdings Act 1986[12].

1 Drainage is item 16 in the Agricultural Holdings Act 1986 Sch 9 Pt II (see PARA 523).
2 As to the meaning of 'tenant' see PARA 423 note 5.
3 As to the service of notices see PARA 428 note 4.
4 Agricultural Holdings Act 1986 Sch 9 Pt I para 4(1).
5 As to the meaning of 'landlord' see PARA 423 note 7.
6 Agricultural Holdings Act 1986 Sch 9 Pt I para 4(1)(a).
7 Ie by the Agricultural Holdings Act 1923 s 3 (repealed).
8 Agricultural Holdings Act 1986 Sch 9 Pt I para 4(1)(b).
9 As to the meaning of 'contract of tenancy' see PARA 425.
10 Agricultural Holdings Act 1986 Sch 9 Pt I para 4(2).
11 *Hamilton Ogilvy v Elliot* (1904) 7 F 1115.
12 Agricultural Holdings Act 1986 Sch 9 Pt I para 4(3).

527. Change of tenancy or tenant where old improvements claimed.

A tenant[1] who has remained in his agricultural holding[2], or in any agricultural holding which comprised the whole or a substantial part of the land comprised in the holding, during two or more tenancies is not deprived of his right to compensation for old improvements[3] by reason only that the improvements were not made during the tenancy at the termination[4] of which he quits the holding[5].

Where, on entering into occupation of an agricultural holding, the tenant, with the consent in writing of his landlord[6], paid to an outgoing tenant any statutory compensation[7] in respect of the whole or part of an improvement, he is entitled, on quitting the holding, to claim compensation for the improvement or part in the same manner, if at all, as the outgoing tenant would have been entitled if the outgoing tenant had remained tenant of the holding and quitted it at the time at which the tenant quits it[8].

If the incoming tenant agrees to pay on entry such sum as is found to be due as compensation from the landlord, the liability to pay arises at and the period of limitation runs from the date at which the amount due has been ascertained[9]. An agreement between the incoming tenant and the outgoing tenant relating to compensation for old improvements does not affect the landlord's rights if he is not a party to the agreement[10]. An agreement between the landlord and the outgoing tenant that the landlord will only seek compensation against the incoming tenant for old improvements will be void[11].

1 As to the meaning of 'tenant' see PARA 423 note 5.
2 As to the meaning of 'agricultural holding' see PARA 423.
3 As to the meaning of 'old improvements' see PARA 522. As to the nature of old improvements see PARA 523.

4 As to the termination of an agricultural tenancy see PARA 428 note 1.
5 Agricultural Holdings Act 1986 Sch 9 Pt I para 5(1) (Sch 9 Pt I para 5(1) amended, and Sch 9 Pt I para 5(1A) added, by SI 2006/2805). Where the Agricultural Holdings Act 1986 applies in relation to a tenancy by virtue of the Agricultural Tenancies Act 1995 s 4(1)(g) (see PARAS 401, 421), the reference in the Agricultural Holdings Act 1986 Sch 9 Pt I para 5(1) to a 'substantial part of the land comprised in the holding' means a substantial part determined by reference to either area or value: Sch 9 Pt I para 5(1A) (as so added).
  The amendments made by the Regulatory Reform (Agricultural Tenancies) (England and Wales) Order 2006, SI 2006/2805, do not apply in relation to compensation payable on the termination of a tenancy where that tenancy was granted before 19 October 2006 (ie the date on which art 6 was brought into force: see art 1(1)(b)): see art 6(8).
6 As to the meaning of 'landlord' see PARA 423 note 7.
7 Ie compensation for old improvements payable under the Agricultural Holdings Act 1986 Sch 9, or under the Agricultural Holdings Act 1923 or the Agricultural Holdings Act 1948 (both of which are now repealed).
8 Agricultural Holdings Act 1986 Sch 9 Pt I para 5(2).
9 *Cheshire County Council v Hopley* (1923) 130 LT 123.
10 *Petrie v Daniel* (1804) 1 Smith KB 199.
11 This is by virtue of the Agricultural Holdings Act 1986 s 78 (see PARA 512). Cf *Greenshields v Roger* 1922 SC 140, HL.

(v) Compensation for Relevant Improvements and Tenant-right

A. ENTITLEMENT

528. Right to compensation.

A tenant[1] of an agricultural holding[2] is entitled, subject to certain exceptions[3], on quitting the holding on the termination of the tenancy[4], to obtain from his landlord[5] compensation for relevant improvements carried out by the tenant and for tenant-right matters[6]. Relevant improvements are those specified in the Agricultural Holdings Act 1986[7] and begun on or after 1 March 1948[8]. It is immaterial with regard to the tenant's right to compensation for relevant improvements that he entered into occupation before 1 March 1948: the test is whether the improvements were commenced on or after that date[9].

The Secretary of State and the Welsh Ministers[10] have power to vary by order the provisions which specify relevant improvements and tenant-right matters[11] after consultation with such bodies as appear to them to represent the interests of landlords and tenants of agricultural holdings[12].

1 As to the meaning of 'tenant' see PARA 423 note 5.
2 As to the meaning of 'agricultural holding' see PARA 423.
3 See PARAS 540–543.
4 As to the termination of an agricultural tenancy see PARA 428 note 1.
5 As to the meaning of 'landlord' see PARA 423 note 7.
6 Agricultural Holdings Act 1986 ss 64(1), (2), 65(1). As to the nature of statutory tenant-right see PARA 530; and as to the tenant's right to elect for statutory compensation see PARA 532.
7 Ie in the Agricultural Holdings Act 1986 Sch 7 or Sch 8 Pt I (see PARA 529).
8 Agricultural Holdings Act 1986 s 64(1), (2). As to the nature of 'relevant improvements' see PARA 529. The date mentioned in the text is the date on which the Agriculture Act 1947 Pt III (repealed), from which these provisions are derived, was brought into force: see s 111(2) (repealed); and the Agriculture Act 1947 (Commencement) (No 1) Order 1948, SI 1948/342.
9 Agricultural Holdings Act 1986 s 64(3).
10 As to the Secretary of State and the Welsh Ministers see PARA 741.
11 Ie the provisions of the Agricultural Holdings Act 1986 Schs 7, 8.
12 Agricultural Holdings Act 1986 s 91(1). Such an order may make such provision as to the operation of the Agricultural Holdings Act 1986 in relation to tenancies current when the order takes effect as appears to the Secretary of State or the Welsh Ministers to be just having regard to

the variation of the Schedules affected by the order: s 91(2). The power to vary extends beyond Schs 7, 8 to Sch 10 (market garden improvements): see PARA 561 et seq. As to the making of orders generally see PARA 432 note 5.

529. The nature of relevant improvements.

Relevant improvements for which compensation is payable[1] are either long term improvements[2] or short term improvements for which no consent is required[3] carried out on the holding by the tenant on or after 1 March 1948[4].

Long term improvements are divided into two categories, namely improvements to which the consent of the landlord is required[5] and improvements to which the consent of the landlord or the approval of the Tribunal[6] is required[7].

The improvements to which the consent of the landlord is required are:

(1) making or planting of osier beds[8];
(2) making of water meadows[9];
(3) making of watercress beds[10];
(4) planting of hops[11];
(5) planting of orchards or fruit bushes[12];
(6) warping or weiring of land[13];
(7) making of gardens[14]; and
(8) provision of underground tanks[15].

The improvements to which the consent of the landlord or the approval of the Tribunal is required are:

(a) erection, alteration or enlargement of buildings[16], and making or improvement of permanent yards[17];
(b) carrying out works in compliance with an improvement notice served, or an undertaking accepted, under certain housing legislation[18];
(c) erection or construction of loading platforms, ramps, hard standings for vehicles or other similar facilities[19];
(d) construction of silos[20];
(e) claying of land[21];
(f) marling of land[22];
(g) making or improvement of roads or bridges[23];
(h) making or improvement of water courses, culverts, ponds, wells or reservoirs, or of works for the application of water power for agricultural[24] or domestic purposes or of works for the supply, distribution or use of water for such purposes (including the erection or installation of any structure or equipment which forms part of or is to be used for or in connection with operating any such works)[25];
(i) making or removal of permanent fences[26];
(j) reclaiming of waste land[27];
(k) making or improvement of embankments or sluices[28];
(l) erection of wirework for hop gardens[29];
(m) provision of permanent sheep-dipping accommodation[30];
(n) removal of bracken, gorse, tree roots, boulders or other like obstructions to cultivation[31];
(o) land drainage (other than improvements relating to mole drainage)[32];
(p) provision or laying-on of electric light or power[33];
(q) provision of facilities for the storage or disposal of sewage or farm waste[34];
(r) repairs to fixed equipment[35], being equipment reasonably required for the proper farming of the holding[36], other than repairs which the tenant is under an obligation to carry out[37];

(s)   the grubbing up of orchards or fruit bushes[38]; and

(t)   planting trees otherwise than as an orchard and bushes other than fruit bushes[39].

Short term improvements (to which no consent is required) begun on or after 1 March 1948 for which compensation is payable are:

(i)   mole drainage and works carried out to secure its efficient functioning[40];

(ii)   protection of fruit trees against animals[41];

(iii) clay burning[42];

(iv)   liming (including chalking) of land[43];

(v)   application to land in Wales of purchased manure and fertiliser, whether organic or inorganic[44];

(vi)   in relation to Wales, consumption on the holding of corn (whether produced on the holding or not), or of cake or other feeding stuff not produced on the holding, by horses, cattle, sheep, pigs or poultry[45];

(vii) application to land in England of manure, fertiliser, soil improvers and digestate[46]; and

(viii) in relation to England, production of manure arising from the consumption on the holding of relevant feedingstuff[47] by livestock and equidae where the manure is held in storage on the holding[48].

1 As to the right to compensation, and as to the meaning of 'relevant improvement', see PARA 528.

2 Ie those specified by the Agricultural Holdings Act 1986 Sch 7 (see heads (1)–(8), (a)–(t) in the text).

3 Ie those specified by the Agricultural Holdings Act 1986 Sch 8 paras 1–6 (see heads (i)–(vi) in the text).

4 Agricultural Holdings Act 1986 s 64(1), (2). As to the meaning of 'tenant' see PARA 423 note 5. The date mentioned in the text is the date on which the Agriculture Act 1947 Pt III (repealed), from which these provisions are derived, was brought into force: see s 111(2) (repealed); and the Agriculture Act 1947 (Commencement) (No 1) Order 1948, SI 1948/342.

5 See heads (1)–(8) in the text. As to the meaning of 'landlord' see PARA 423 note 7.

6 Ie in England, the First-tier Tribunal (see PARA 768) and in Wales, the Agricultural Land Tribunal for Wales (see PARA 767): see PARA 437 note 1.

7 See heads (a)–(t) in the text.

8 Agricultural Holdings Act 1986 Sch 7 para 1.

9 Agricultural Holdings Act 1986 Sch 7 para 2.

10 Agricultural Holdings Act 1986 Sch 7 para 3.

11 Agricultural Holdings Act 1986 Sch 7 para 4.

12 Agricultural Holdings Act 1986 Sch 7 para 5.

13 Agricultural Holdings Act 1986 Sch 7 para 6.

14 Agricultural Holdings Act 1986 Sch 7 para 7.

15 Agricultural Holdings Act 1986 Sch 7 para 8.

16 As to the meaning of 'building' see PARA 432 note 6.

17 Agricultural Holdings Act 1986 Sch 7 para 9.

18 Agricultural Holdings Act 1986 Sch 7 para 10. The housing legislation referred to in the text is the Housing Act 1985 Pt VII (repealed) or the Housing Act 1974 Pt VIII (repealed).

19 Agricultural Holdings Act 1986 Sch 7 para 11.

20 Agricultural Holdings Act 1986 Sch 7 para 12.

21 Agricultural Holdings Act 1986 Sch 7 para 13.

22 Agricultural Holdings Act 1986 Sch 7 para 14.

23 Agricultural Holdings Act 1986 Sch 7 para 15.

24 As to the meaning of 'agricultural' see PARA 424.

25 Agricultural Holdings Act 1986 Sch 7 para 16.

26 Agricultural Holdings Act 1986 Sch 7 para 17.

27 Agricultural Holdings Act 1986 Sch 7 para 18.

28 Agricultural Holdings Act 1986 Sch 7 para 19.

29 Agricultural Holdings Act 1986 Sch 7 para 20.

30 Agricultural Holdings Act 1986 Sch 7 para 21.

31 Agricultural Holdings Act 1986 Sch 7 para 22.

32   Agricultural Holdings Act 1986 Sch 7 para 23. Improvements relating to mole drainage are those
     falling within Sch 8 para 1 (see head (i) in the text).
33   Agricultural Holdings Act 1986 Sch 7 para 24.
34   Agricultural Holdings Act 1986 Sch 7 para 25.
35   As to the meaning of 'fixed equipment' see PARA 432 note 6.
36   As to the 'farming' of land see PARA 424.
37   Agricultural Holdings Act 1986 Sch 7 para 26.
38   Agricultural Holdings Act 1986 Sch 7 para 27.
39   Agricultural Holdings Act 1986 Sch 7 para 28.
40   Agricultural Holdings Act 1986 Sch 8 para 1.
41   Agricultural Holdings Act 1986 Sch 8 para 2.
42   Agricultural Holdings Act 1986 Sch 8 para 3.
43   Agricultural Holdings Act 1986 Sch 8 para 4.
44   Agricultural Holdings Act 1986 Sch 8 para 5 (amended by SI 2015/2082).
45   Agricultural Holdings Act 1986 Sch 8 para 6 (amended by SI 2015/2082).
46   Agricultural Holdings Act 1986 Sch 8 para 4A (added by SI 2015/2082).
47   For these purposes 'relevant feedingstuff' means corn (whether produced on the holding or not) or
     cake or other feedingstuff not produced on the holding: Agricultural Holdings Act 1986 Sch 8 para
     5A(2) (added by SI 2015/2082)
48   Agricultural Holdings Act 1986 Sch 8 para 5A(1) (as added: see note 47).

530.   The nature of statutory tenant-right.

Statutory tenant-right matters are:

(1)   growing crops and severed or harvested crops and produce, being in
      either case crops or produce grown on the holding in the last year of
      tenancy, but not including crops or produce which the tenant[1] has a
      right to sell or remove from the holding[2];

(2)   seeds sown and cultivations, fallows and acts of husbandry performed
      on the holding at the expense of the tenant (including the growing of
      herbage crops for commercial seed production)[3];

(3)   pasture laid down with clover, grass, lucerne, sainfoin or other seeds,
      being either pasture laid down at the expense of the tenant otherwise
      than in compliance with an obligation imposed on him by an agreement
      in writing to lay it down to replace temporary pasture comprised in the
      holding when the tenant entered on the holding which was not paid for
      by him[4] or pasture paid for by the tenant on entering on the holding[5];

(4)   acclimatisation, hefting or settlement of hill sheep[6] on hill land[7]; and

(5)   in areas of the country where arable crops can be grown[8] in an unbroken
      series of not less than six years and it is reasonable that they should be
      grown on the holding or part of it, the residual fertility value of the sod
      of the excess qualifying leys[9] on the holding, if any[10].

1   As to the meaning of 'tenant' see PARA 423 note 5.
2   Agricultural Holdings Act 1986 Sch 8 para 7.
3   Agricultural Holdings Act 1986 Sch 8 para 8.
4   Agricultural Holdings Act 1986 Sch 8 para 9(a).
5   Agricultural Holdings Act 1986 Sch 8 para 9(b).
6   'Hill sheep' means sheep which:
    (1)   have been reared and managed on a particular hill or mountain (Agricultural Holdings
          Act 1986 Sch 8 para 10(2)(a));
    (2)   have developed an instinct not to stray from the hill or mountain (Sch 8 para 10(2)(b));
    (3)   are able to withstand the climatic conditions typical of the hill or mountain (Sch 8 para
          10(2)(c)); and
    (4)   have developed resistance to diseases which are likely to occur in the area in which the
          hill or mountain is situated (Sch 8 para 10(2)(d)).
7   Agricultural Holdings Act 1986 Sch 8 para 10(1). 'Hill land' means any hill or mountain where
    only hill sheep are likely to thrive throughout the year: Sch 8 para 10(2).
8   For these purposes:

(1)   the growing of an arable crop includes the growing of clover, grass, lucerne, sainfoin or other seeds grown for a period of less than one year but does not include the laying down of a ley continuously maintained as such for more than one year (Agricultural Holdings Act 1986 Sch 8 para 11(2)(a));

(2)   the qualifying leys comprising the excess qualifying leys are those indicated to be such by the tenant (Sch 8 para 11(2)(b)); and

(3)   qualifying leys laid down at the expense of the landlord without reimbursement by the tenant or any previous tenant of the holding or laid down by and at the expense of the tenant pursuant to agreement by him with the landlord for the establishment of a specified area of leys on the holding as a condition of the landlord giving consent to the ploughing or other destruction of permanent pasture or pursuant to a direction given by an arbitrator on a reference under s 14(2) (see PARA 441), are not included in the excess qualifying leys (Sch 8 para 11(2)(c)).

As to the meaning of 'landlord' see PARA 423 note 7. As to leys see note 9.

9   'Leys' means land laid down with clover, grass, lucerne, sainfoin or other seeds, but does not include permanent pasture; 'qualifying leys' means leys continuously maintained as such for a period of three or more growing seasons since being laid down, and arable land which within the three growing seasons immediately preceding the termination of the tenancy was ley continuously maintained before being destroyed by ploughing or some other means for the production of a tillage crop or crops; 'excess qualifying leys' means the area of qualifying leys on the holding at the termination of the tenancy which is equal to the area (if any) by which one-third of the aggregate of the areas of leys on the holding at the termination of the tenancy, on the date one year prior to such termination, and on the date two years prior to such termination, exceeds the accepted proportion at the termination of the tenancy; and 'accepted proportion' means the area which represents the proportion which the total area of the leys on the holding would, taking into account the capability of the holding, be expected to bear to the area of the holding, excluding the permanent pasture on the holding, or, if a greater proportion is provided for by or under the terms of the tenancy, that proportion: Agricultural Holdings Act 1986 Sch 8 para 11(3). As to the termination of an agricultural tenancy see PARA 428 note 1.

10   Agricultural Holdings Act 1986 Sch 8 para 11(1).

531. Change of tenancy or tenant where relevant improvements claimed.

Where the tenant[1] of an agricultural holding[2] has remained in the holding, or in any agricultural holding which comprised the whole or a substantial part of the land comprised in the holding, during two or more tenancies, he must not be deprived of his right to compensation under the Agricultural Holdings Act 1986 in respect of relevant improvements[3] by reason only that the improvements were made during a tenancy other than the one at the termination of which[4] he quits the holding[5].

Where, on entering into occupation of an agricultural holding, the tenant with the consent in writing of his landlord[6] paid to an outgoing tenant any compensation payable by the landlord[7] in respect of the whole or part of a relevant improvement[8], or has paid to the landlord himself the amount of any such compensation payable to an outgoing tenant[9], he is entitled, on quitting the holding, to claim compensation in respect thereof in the same manner, if at all[10], as the outgoing tenant would have been entitled if the outgoing tenant had remained tenant of the holding and quitted it at the same time as the tenant himself quits it[11]. In cases not falling within the above provision, a tenant who, on entering into occupation of the holding, paid to his landlord any amount in respect of the whole or part of a relevant improvement is entitled on quitting the holding, subject to any written agreement between himself and the landlord, to claim compensation in respect thereof in the same manner, if at all, as he would have been entitled if he had been the tenant of the holding at the time when the improvement was carried out and the improvement or part had been carried out by him[12].

1   As to the meaning of 'tenant' see PARA 423 note 5.

2 As to the meaning of 'agricultural holding' see PARA 423.

3 As to the right to compensation, and as to the meaning of 'relevant improvement', see PARA 528.

4 As to the termination of an agricultural tenancy see PARA 428 note 1.

5 Agricultural Holdings Act 1986 s 69(1) (s 69(1) amended, and s 69(1A) added, by SI 2006/2805). Where the Agricultural Holdings Act 1986 applies in relation to a tenancy by virtue of the Agricultural Tenancies Act 1995 s 4(1)(g) (see PARA 401), the reference in the Agricultural Holdings Act 1986 s 69(1) to a 'substantial part of the land comprised in the holding' means a substantial part determined by reference to either area or value: s 69(1A) (as so added).

The amendments made by the Regulatory Reform (Agricultural Tenancies) (England and Wales) Order 2006, SI 2006/2805, do not apply in relation to compensation payable on termination of a tenancy where that tenancy was granted before 19 October 2006 (ie the date on which art 6 was brought into force: see art 1(1)(b)): see art 6(8).

6 As to the meaning of 'landlord' see PARA 423 note 7. The consent may be contained in the contract of tenancy. An alleged custom that the outgoing tenant should seek payment from the incoming tenant rather than the landlord for compensation has been held bad: see *Bradburn v Foley* (1878) 3 CPD 129.

7 Ie under the Agricultural Holdings Act 1986, or under the Agricultural Holdings Act 1948 or the Agriculture Act 1947 Pt III (ss 22–46) (repealed).

8 Agricultural Holdings Act 1986 s 69(2)(a).

9 Agricultural Holdings Act 1986 s 69(2)(b).

10 The tenant only has rights commensurate with those of his predecessor. As to the enforcement of an agreement by the incoming tenant to pay compensation to the outgoing tenant see *Cheshire County Council v Hopley* (1923) 130 LT 123.

11 Agricultural Holdings Act 1986 s 69(2).

12 Agricultural Holdings Act 1986 s 69(3).

532. Election on tenant-right matters where entry prior to 1 March 1948.

Where the tenant[1] entered into occupation of the agricultural holding[2] before 1 March 1948[3] he is not entitled to statutory compensation in respect of the tenant-right matters[4] unless, before the termination of the tenancy[5], he gives written notice[6] to the landlord[7] stating that he elects that the statutory compensation provision[8] is to apply to him in respect of those matters[9]. Otherwise compensation will be payable under the custom of the district and the provisions (if any) of the tenancy agreement[10].

Where the tenancy terminates by reason of a notice to quit and during the currency of the notice the landlord gives notice in writing requiring the tenant so to elect, the tenant cannot do so later than one month from receiving the landlord's notice[11] or one month from the termination of any proceedings[12] on which the operation of the notice to quit depends[13].

Special rules apply in respect of acclimatising, hefting or settlement of hill sheep on hill land[14]. A tenant who entered into occupation before 1 March 1948 and who has already elected prior to 31 December 1951[15] that statutory compensation should apply must make another specific election in regard to acclimatisation; and a tenant who entered into occupation on or after 1 March 1948, but before 31 December 1951, must make the same specific election[16]. However, any tenant who has entered into occupation on or after 31 December 1951 enjoys an automatic right to the statutory basis of compensation[17].

1 As to the meaning of 'tenant' see PARA 423 note 5.

2 As to the meaning of 'agricultural holding' see PARA 423.

3 Ie the date on which the Agriculture Act 1947 Pt III (repealed), from which these provisions are derived, was brought into force: see s 111(2) (repealed); and the Agriculture Act 1947 (Commencement) (No 1) Order 1948, SI 1948/342.

4 See PARA 530.

5 As to the termination of an agricultural tenancy see PARA 428 note 1.

6 As to the service of notices see PARA 428 note 4.

7 As to the meaning of 'landlord' see PARA 423 note 7.

8   Ie the Agricultural Holdings Act 1986 s 65(1) (see PARA 528).
9   Agricultural Holdings Act 1986 Sch 12 para 6(1).
10 It is provided that as a general rule no claim can be made for compensation for improvements or
    tenant-right matters under custom; but tenant-right claims in the case of tenants who went into
    occupation before 1 March 1948 are an exception to this rule: see the Agricultural Holdings Act
    1986 Sch 12 para 8(1)(b).
11 Agricultural Holdings Act 1986 Sch 12 para 6(2)(a).
12 Ie under the Agricultural Holdings Act 1986 ss 26, 27 (including any proceedings under Sch 3). See
    PARAS 471–472.
13 Agricultural Holdings Act 1986 Sch 12 para 6(2)(b).
14 See the Agricultural Holdings Act 1986 Sch 8 para 10; and PARA 530.
15 Ie the date on which the Agricultural Holdings Act (Variation of Fourth Schedule) Order 1951,
    SI 1951/2168 (revoked) came into operation.
16 Agricultural Holdings Act 1986 Sch 12 para 7.
17 Agricultural Holdings Act 1986 Sch 12 para 7.

B. CONSENTS

533. Long term improvements begun on or after 1 March 1948.

Generally, a tenant[1] under the Agricultural Holdings Act 1986 is not entitled to
compensation for long term improvements[2] unless the landlord[3] consented to
them in writing[4]. Such consent may be given unconditionally or on such terms as
to compensation or otherwise as may be agreed in writing between the parties[5]. If
an agreement as to compensation is made, the measure of compensation laid
down has effect subject to the provisions of that agreement[6].

Where the tenant of a holding has carried out a long term improvement[7] in
accordance with the provision of a hill farming land improvement scheme[8] for the
making of the improvement and for the tenant's being responsible for doing the
work, being a provision included at the instance or with the consent of the
landlord, the landlord is deemed to have consented thereto for the purposes of the
compensation provisions[9], and any agreement between the landlord and tenant as
to compensation or otherwise in relation to the improvement has effect as an
agreement mentioned in those provisions[10].

1   As to the meaning of 'tenant' see PARA 423 note 5.
2   As to long term improvements see the Agricultural Holdings Act 1986 Sch 7; and PARA 529.
3   As to the meaning of 'landlord' see PARA 423 note 7.
4   Agricultural Holdings Act 1986 s 67(1).
5   Agricultural Holdings Act 1986 s 67(2). The agreement may be in the contract of tenancy itself:
    Gardner v Beck [1947] EGD 169.
6   Agricultural Holdings Act 1986 s 67(2). As to the statutory measure of compensation see PARA
    538.
7   Ie as specified in the Agricultural Holdings Act 1986 Sch 7. See PARA 529.
8   Ie approved under the Hill Farming Act 1946 s 1. See also AGRICULTURAL PRODUCTION AND
    MARKETING vol 1A (2017) PARAS 413–414.
9   Agricultural Holdings Act 1986 s 68(3)(a). The 'compensation provisions' are those of s 67(1) (see
    the text and notes 1–4).
10 Agricultural Holdings Act 1986 s 68(3)(b).

534. Short term improvements begun on or after 1 March 1948 and tenant-right.

The landlord's[1] consent or approval is not a prerequisite to a tenant's[2] claim for
statutory compensation in respect of short term improvements[3], nor in respect of
tenant-right matters[4].

1   As to the meaning of 'landlord' see PARA 423 note 7.
2   As to the meaning of 'tenant' see PARA 423 note 5.

3   Ie as specified in the Agricultural Holdings Act 1986 Sch 8 paras 1–6 (see PARA 529).
4   Ie as specified in the Agricultural Holdings Act 1986 Sch 8 paras 7–11 (see PARA 530).

535.   Notice of mole drainage.

A tenant[1] is not entitled to statutory compensation for mole drainage and works carried out to secure its efficient functioning[2], unless, not later than one month before the improvement was begun, he gave notice in writing[3] to the landlord[4] of his intention to carry out the improvement[5].

1   As to the meaning of 'tenant' see PARA 423 note 5.
2   Ie the improvements specified in the Agricultural Holdings Act 1986 Sch 8 para 1 (see PARA 529).
3   As to the service of notices see PARA 428 note 4.
4   As to the meaning of 'landlord' see PARA 423 note 7.
5   Agricultural Holdings Act 1986 s 68(1).

C. APPROVALS AND DIRECTIONS

536.   Approval of the Tribunal.

In the case of specified[1] long term improvements, a tenant[2] who is aggrieved by the refusal of his landlord[3] to consent to an improvement, or as to the conditions which the landlord seeks to impose as a prerequisite to his consent, may apply to the Tribunal[4] for approval of the carrying out of the improvement[5]. The Tribunal may approve the carrying out of the improvement, either unconditionally or upon such terms as to reduce the compensation, or as to other matters, as may seem just, or may withhold its approval[6]. It is a prerequisite of a tenant's application to the Tribunal that he must first have sought the landlord's consent. If approval is granted, the landlord may serve notice in writing on the Tribunal, and on the tenant, that he himself proposes to carry out the improvement[7]. If the landlord does not serve such notice[8], or if there was such a notice but the tribunal, on an application by the tenant, decides that the landlord has failed to carry out the improvement within a reasonable time[9], the Tribunal's approval takes effect as if it were the consent of the landlord, and any terms on which it was given take effect as if contained in a written agreement between the landlord and the tenant[10]. If the landlord does carry out the improvement he will be entitled to claim an increase in rent[11].

1   Ie specified in the Agricultural Holdings Act 1986 Sch 7 paras 9–28 (see PARA 529).
2   As to the meaning of 'tenant' see PARA 423 note 5.
3   As to the meaning of 'landlord' see PARA 423 note 7.
4   Ie in England, the First-tier Tribunal (see PARA 768) and in Wales, the Agricultural Land Tribunal for Wales (see PARA 767): see PARA 437 note 1.
5   Agricultural Holdings Act 1986 s 67(3).
6   Agricultural Holdings Act 1986 s 67(4).
7   Agricultural Holdings Act 1986 s 67(5). As to the service of notices see PARA 428 note 4.
8   Agricultural Holdings Act 1986 s 67(6)(a).
9   Agricultural Holdings Act 1986 s 67(6)(b).
10 Agricultural Holdings Act 1986 s 67(6).
11 Ie under the Agricultural Holdings Act 1986 s 13 (see PARA 440).

537.   Compensation to mesne landlord where fixed equipment provided under direction.

Where, on the application of a sub-tenant, the Tribunal[1] has directed his immediate landlord[2] to do work for the provision, alteration or repair of fixed equipment[3] and that work constitutes a long term improvement[4], the immediate landlord is entitled to claim compensation as respects that work against his superior landlord notwithstanding that the superior landlord has not consented to the carrying out of the work[5]. If, on the failure of the immediate landlord to comply with the direction, the sub-tenant has himself carried out the work, the compensation provisions[6] have effect for the purposes of a claim by the immediate landlord against his superior landlord as if the work had been carried out by the immediate landlord and as if any grant made to the sub-tenant in respect of the work out of money provided by Parliament had been made to the immediate landlord[7].

1 Ie in England, the First-tier Tribunal (see PARA 768) and in Wales, the Agricultural Land Tribunal for Wales (see PARA 767): see PARA 437 note 1.
2 As to the meaning of 'landlord' see PARA 423 note 7.
3 As to the meaning of 'fixed equipment' see PARA 432 note 6. As to the power to give such a direction see the Agricultural Holdings Act 1986 s 11; and PARA 437.
4 Ie an improvement specified in the Agricultural Holdings Act 1986 Sch 7 (see PARA 529).
5 Agricultural Holdings Act 1986 s 68(2)(a).
6 Ie the Agricultural Holdings Act 1986 ss 64, 66 (see PARAS 528–529, 538–539).
7 Agricultural Holdings Act 1986 s 68(2)(b).

D. MEASURE OF COMPENSATION

538. Long term improvements begun on or after 1 March 1948.

The amount of compensation payable for long term improvements[1] is an amount equal to the increase attributable to the improvement in the value of the agricultural holding[2] as a holding, having regard to the character and situation of the holding and the average requirements of tenants[3] reasonably skilled in husbandry[4].

1 Ie those specified by the Agricultural Holdings Act 1986 Sch 7 (see PARA 529). Where an agricultural holding governed by the Agricultural Holdings Act 1986 on which long term improvements have been made or a special system of farming has been adopted becomes subject to a compulsory rights order for the purposes of opencast mining and at the end of the period of occupation the tenant's land has lost the benefit of the improvements or special system, the provisions of the Agricultural Holdings Act 1986 as to compensation for long term improvements and as to compensation for a special system of farming apply subject to the provisions of the Opencast Coal Act 1958 s 24(3)–(8): see s 24(1), (2); and MINES, MINERALS AND QUARRIES vol 76 (2013) PARA 472. For this purpose, 'long term improvements' are those of a description specified in the Agricultural Holdings Act 1986 Sch 7 whether begun before or after 1 March 1948: see the Opencast Coal Act 1958 s 24(9); and MINES, MINERALS AND QUARRIES vol 76 (2013) PARA 472. The date mentioned above is the date on which the Agriculture Act 1947 Pt III (repealed), from which these provisions are in part derived, was brought into force: see s 111(2) (repealed); and the Agriculture Act 1947 (Commencement) (No 1) Order 1948, SI 1948/342.
2 As to the meaning of 'agricultural holding' see PARA 423.
3 As to the meaning of 'tenant' see PARA 423 note 5.
4 Agricultural Holdings Act 1986 s 66(1). It should be noted that, unlike the position in respect of improvements under Sch 8 (see PARAS 528–530), the method for calculation is not prescribed in respect of improvements contained in Sch 7.

539. Short term improvements begun on or after 1 March 1948 and tenant-right matters.

The measure of statutory compensation and method of calculation for short term improvements[1] begun on or after 1 March 1948[2] and tenant-right matters[3] is the value of the improvements or matters to an incoming tenant[4] calculated in accordance with such method, if any, as may be prescribed by regulations[5].

In the case of tenant-right matters[6] no compensation is payable for crops or produce grown, seeds sown, cultivations, fallows or acts of husbandry performed or pastures laid down in contravention of the terms of a written tenancy agreement, unless this was reasonably necessary in consequence of the giving of a direction under the Agriculture Act 1947[7] or the tenant shows that the term of the contract contravened or was inconsistent with the fulfilment of his responsibilities to farm the holding[8] in accordance with the rules of good husbandry[9].

Whilst a landlord[10] and tenant may substitute the method for calculating tenant-right matters in a written contract of tenancy[11], in the case of short term improvements it is not possible to contract outside the Agricultural Holdings Act 1986[12], though consideration must be given in respect of short term improvements to any benefit[13] given or allowed to the tenant by the landlord in an agreement in writing[14]. Further, where a grant out of money provided by Parliament or local government funds[15] has been or will be made to the tenant in respect of a short term improvement the grant must be taken into account when assessing compensation[16].

A landlord and tenant may, however, agree in writing for compensation to be paid in cases not covered by the Agricultural Holdings Act 1986[17].

1   See the Agricultural Holdings Act 1986 Sch 8 paras 1–6; and PARA 529.
2   Ie the date on which the Agriculture Act 1947 Pt III (repealed), from which these provisions are derived, was brought into force: see s 111(2) (repealed); and the Agriculture Act 1947 (Commencement) (No 1) Order 1948, SI 1948/342.
3   See the Agricultural Holdings Act 1986 Sch 8 paras 7–11; and PARA 530.
4   As to the meaning of 'tenant' see PARA 423 note 5.
5   Agricultural Holdings Act 1986 s 66(2). The Agriculture (Calculation of Value for Compensation) Regulations 1978, SI 1978/809 (amended by SI 1980/751; SI 1981/822; SI 1983/1475) are currently in force in relation to Wales but have been revoked in relation to England by SI 2015/327 with effect from 1 October 2015. At the date at which this volume states the law no successor regulations were in force in relation to England.
6   See note 3.
7   Agricultural Holdings Act 1986 s 65(2)(a). Provision for the giving of directions was made under the Agriculture Act 1947 s 95 (repealed).
8   As to the 'farming' of land see PARA 424.
9   Agricultural Holdings Act 1986 s 65(2)(b). As to the rules of good husbandry for the purposes of the Agricultural Holdings Act 1986 see, by virtue of s 96(3) (see PARA 430 note 14), the Agriculture Act 1947 ss 10, 11; and AGRICULTURAL PRODUCTION AND MARKETING vol 1A (2017) PARAS 11–13.
10 As to the meaning of 'landlord' see PARA 423 note 7.
11 See the Agricultural Holdings Act 1986 s 66(4); and PARA 512. As to the meaning of 'contract of tenancy' see PARA 425.
12 See the Agricultural Holdings Act 1986 s 78(1); and PARA 512.
13 The benefit may be a reduction in rent: *M'Quarter v Fergusson* 1911 SC 640, Ct of Sess. As to other benefits see *Earl of Galloway v M'Clelland* 1915 SC 1062, Ct of Sess (temporary pasture at commencement of lease held a benefit); *Findlay v Munro* 1917 SC 419, Ct of Sess (right to take two white crops not a benefit); *Mackenzie v Macgillivray* 1921 SC 722, Ct of Sess (landlord's abstention from terminating tenancy not a benefit).
14 Agricultural Holdings Act 1986 s 66(3).
15 As to the meaning of 'local government funds' see PARA 438 note 21.
16 Agricultural Holdings Act 1986 s 66(5).
17 See the Agricultural Holdings Act 1986 s 78(3); and PARA 512. That provision is subject to Sch 12 para 8, whereby if a tenant who entered into occupation of the holding prior to 1 March 1948 has not elected for tenant-right compensation on a statutory basis, either as a whole or in relation to acclimatisation, hefting or settlement of hill sheep on hill land, his customary rights are preferred.

E. LIMITATIONS ON COMPENSATION

540. Compensation limitation for tenancy made before 1 January 1921.

A tenant[1] of an agricultural holding[2] is not entitled to statutory compensation for a relevant improvement[3] which he was required to carry out by the terms of his tenancy in the case of a contract of tenancy[4] made before 1 January 1921[5].

1   As to the meaning of 'tenant' see PARA 423 note 5.
2   As to the meaning of 'agricultural holding' see PARA 423.
3   As to the right to compensation, and as to the meaning of 'relevant improvement', see PARAS 528–529.
4   As to the meaning of 'contract of tenancy' see PARA 425.
5   Agricultural Holdings Act 1986 Sch 12 para 5. The date mentioned in the text is the date on which the Agriculture Act 1920, from which these provisions in part derive, was brought into force: see s 36(1) (repealed). In respect of contracts made on or after 1 January 1921 the landlord cannot require the tenant to contract out of his right to compensation: see s 78(1); and PARA 512.

541. Compensation limitation by adjustment in respect of grants.

Where a grant out of money provided by Parliament or local government funds[1] has been or will be made to the tenant[2] of an agricultural holding[3] in respect of a relevant improvement[4], the grant must be taken into account[5] in assessing compensation under the Agricultural Holdings Act 1986 for the improvement[6].

Where a person other than the tenant claiming compensation has contributed to the cost of carrying out works in compliance with an improvement notice[7], or with an undertaking to improve housing accepted[8] by a local authority, compensation in respect of the works as relevant improvements must be reduced proportionately[9].

1   As to the meaning of 'local government funds' see PARA 438 note 21.
2   As to the meaning of 'tenant' see PARA 423 note 5.
3   As to the meaning of 'agricultural holding' see PARA 423.
4   As to the right to compensation, and as to the meaning of 'relevant improvement', see PARAS 528–529.
5   The parties cannot contract out of the statutory prescribed measure for the improvements specified in the Agricultural Holdings Act 1986 Sch 8 paras 1–6 (see PARA 529) (in contrast with the position as to tenant-right matters contained in Sch 8 paras 7–11 (see PARA 530)), but in both cases the benefits may be taken into account.
6   Agricultural Holdings Act 1986 s 66(5).
7   Ie a notice under the Housing Act 1985 Pt VII (repealed). As to improvement notices see HOUSING vol 56 (2017) PARA 571 et seq.
8   Ie under the Housing Act 1985 s 211 (repealed).
9   Agricultural Holdings Act 1986 s 68(5)(b).

542. Compensation limitation by reason of breach of covenant of the tenancy.

No compensation is payable to a tenant[1] for crops or produce grown, seeds sown, cultivations, fallows or acts of husbandry performed, or pasture laid down, in breach of the terms of a written contract of tenancy[2], unless the growing of the crops or produce, the sowing of the seeds, the performance of the cultivations, the fallows or acts of husbandry, or the laying down of the pasture was reasonably necessary in consequence of the giving of a direction under the Agriculture Act 1947[3], or the tenant shows that the term of the contract contravened was inconsistent with the fulfilment of his responsibilities to farm the holding[4] in accordance with the rules of good husbandry[5].

1   As to the meaning of 'tenant' see PARA 423 note 5.

2 As to the meaning of 'contract of tenancy' see PARA 425.
3 Agricultural Holdings Act 1986 s 65(2)(a). Provision for the giving of directions was made under the Agriculture Act 1947 s 95 (repealed).
4 As to the 'farming' of land see PARA 424.
5 Agricultural Holdings Act 1986 s 65(2)(b). As to the rules of good husbandry for the purposes of the Agricultural Holdings Act 1986 see, by virtue of s 96(3) (see PARA 430 note 14), the Agriculture Act 1947 ss 10, 11; and AGRICULTURAL PRODUCTION AND MARKETING vol 1A (2017) PARAS 11–13.

543. Compensation limitation by reason of improvement grant under the Hill Farming Act 1946.

In assessing the amount of any compensation payable under custom or agreement to the tenant[1] of an agricultural holding[2] under the Agricultural Holdings Act 1986, if it is shown to the satisfaction of the person assessing the compensation that the cultivations in respect of which the compensation is claimed were wholly or in part the result of or incidental to work in respect of the cost of which an improvement grant for livestock rearing land has been paid[3], the amount of the grant must be taken into account as if it had been a benefit allowed to the tenant in consideration of his executing the cultivations, and the compensation will be reduced to such extent as that person considers appropriate[4].

1 As to the meaning of 'tenant' see PARA 423 note 5.
2 As to the meaning of 'agricultural holding' see PARA 423.
3 Ie under the Hill Farming Act 1946 s 1 (see AGRICULTURAL PRODUCTION AND MARKETING vol 1A (2017) PARAS 413–414).
4 Agricultural Holdings Act 1986 s 68(4).

(vi) Compensation for Disturbance

544. Entitlement to compensation for disturbance.

Under the Agricultural Holdings Act 1986 the tenant's[1] entitlement to compensation for disturbance may arise:

(1)   in certain limited circumstances where the tenancy terminates[2] in consequence of a notice to quit given by the landlord[3] or of a counter-notice given by the tenant, enlarging the landlord's notice to quit part of the holding[4], and the tenant quits the holding in consequence of the notice or counter-notice[5]; or

(2)   where the tenant's interest is compulsorily acquired[6].

The Agricultural Holdings Act 1986 grants the tenant the right to receive basic compensation[7] and in certain circumstances both basic and additional compensation[8].

The rules governing the tenant's entitlement differ in the case of basic and additional compensation[9]. However, in all cases no compensation is payable if the landlord's notice to quit is given for one of the reasons stated in Case C (bad husbandry)[10], Case D (failure to comply with a notice to pay rent due or to remedy a breach of a term or condition of the tenancy)[11], Case E (commission of any irremediable breach of a term or condition of the tenancy)[12], Case F (insolvency of the tenant)[13] or Case G (death of sole or sole surviving tenant)[14]. Further, the tenant should in any event show a causal link between the notice to quit and his departure[15]. However, where he holds over after the expiration of the notice and subsequently vacates the land after a judgment for possession or on being ejected, it is a question to be decided on the facts of the case whether or not he quit in consequence of the notice to quit[16]. A tenant who quits in consequence of a notice to quit, which is in fact invalid, but which he accepts as valid, is entitled to claim compensation for disturbance[17].

Where the tenant has sub-let the holding and in consequence of a notice to quit given by his landlord has become liable to pay statutory compensation for disturbance to his sub-tenant, the tenant is not debarred from himself recovering such compensation from his landlord by reason only that, not being in occupation of the holding, he does not quit the holding on termination of his tenancy[18].

The right to additional, but not basic, compensation is excluded in two further cases:

(a)   where the notice to quit is given for one of the reasons stated in Case A (smallholdings)[19] or Case H (notice to quit by the Secretary of State or the Welsh Ministers for the purpose of the amalgamation or the reshaping of agricultural units)[20];

(b)   where the notice to quit contains a statement either that the carrying out of the purpose for which the landlord proposes to terminate the tenancy is desirable on any of certain statutory grounds[21] or that the landlord will suffer hardship unless the notice has effect[22].

If the landlord makes an application for consent to the operation of the notice to quit to the Tribunal[23], then it is a further condition of the exclusion that the Tribunal should consent to its operation, stating in the reasons for its decision that it is satisfied as to any of the matters specified[24]. Accordingly, the additional compensation is not excluded where upon receipt of a notice to quit stating any of the grounds mentioned above, the tenant fails to serve a counter-notice[25]; nor where the Tribunal consents to the operation of the notice for reasons connected with the purposes of enactments relating to smallholdings[26]; further, the additional compensation is payable where the Tribunal gives more than one reason for consenting to the operation of the notice to quit and the reasons include a non-agricultural use[27] not falling within Case B[28], and also where the landlord applies on the ground of sound management and the reasons given by the Tribunal (whilst being satisfied on that ground) include a statement it would have also been satisfied on the ground of non-agricultural use not falling within Case B had that been specified in the notice[29].

A point to note is that if a landlord serves a notice to quit without stating any reason he will be liable for basic and additional compensation[30]. In many cases, however, additional compensation becomes payable pursuant to a Case B notice to quit when the landlord has planning permission for non-agricultural development, and is viewed by the landlord as an acceptable price for recovery of the property.

It is not possible to contract out of entitlement to statutory compensation for disturbance under the Agricultural Holdings Act 1986[31].

1   As to the meaning of 'tenant' see PARA 423 note 5.
2   As to the termination of an agricultural tenancy see PARA 428 note 1.
3   Agricultural Holdings Act 1986 s 60(1)(a). As to the meaning of 'landlord' see PARA 423 note 7.
4   Agricultural Holdings Act 1986 s 60(1)(b).
5   Agricultural Holdings Act 1986 s 60(1). See PARA 550.
6   See, in particular, the Land Compensation Act 1973 s 48; and PARA 593. See also PARAS 591–592.
7   See the Agricultural Holdings Act 1986 s 60(2), (3); and PARA 545.
8   See the Agricultural Holdings Act 1986 s 60(4); and PARA 545.
9   Basic compensation entitlement is governed by the Agricultural Holdings Act 1986 s 60(2)(a) and additional compensation by s 60(2)(b) (see PARA 545).
10 See PARA 476.

11 See PARA 477.

12 See PARA 478.

13 See PARA 479.

14 Agricultural Holdings Act 1986 s 61(1). As to Case G see PARA 480.

15 This may also be of considerable importance for tax purposes. Provided a tenant can show that the amount paid to him pursuant to the Agricultural Holdings Act 1986 s 60 is on a true analysis a statutory sum to compensate him for loss or expense which is incurred, accordingly representing no element of gain, it would seem that no capital gains tax is payable on the receipt: *Davis v Powell* [1977] 1 All ER 471, [1977] 1 WLR 258; followed in *Drummond (Inspector of Taxes) v Austin Brown* [1983] STC 506 (a case under the provisions of the Landlord and Tenant Act 1954). Further, statutory compensation under these provisions is not to be seen as a capital sum derived from the disposal of an asset (the tenancy) nor as a capital sum received for the surrender of rights: *Davis v Powell*. However, if there is any element of 'bargain', such as termination on short notice rather than strict compliance with the statutory requirements, the capital gains tax exemption may be prejudiced.

16 *Preston v Norfolk County Council* [1947] KB 775, [1947] 2 All ER 124, CA (following *Mills v Rose* (1923) 68 Sol Jo 420, CA; distinguishing *Cave v Page* (1923) 67 Sol Jo 659, CA (a case under the Agricultural Holdings Act 1908 s 11 (repealed), disagreeing with *Hendry v Walker* 1927 SLT 333, Ct of Sess)). Cf also *Gulliver v Catt* [1952] 2 QB 308, [1952] 1 All ER 929, CA.

As to the meaning of 'landlord' for these purposes see PARA 423 note 7. The right subsists even where there is a change of landlord between the date of the notice and the date of quitting: *Dale v Hatfield Chase Corpn* [1922] 2 KB 282, CA.

17 *Westlake v Page* [1926] 1 KB 299, CA; *Kestell v Langmaid* [1950] 1 KB 233, [1949] 2 All ER 749, CA. The notice must, however, be given by the landlord (within the definition in the Agricultural Holdings Act 1986: see PARA 423 note 7); and accordingly an equitable owner has no locus standi: *Bradshaw v Bird* [1920] 3 KB 144, CA; *Farrow v Orttewell* [1933] Ch 480.

18 Agricultural Holdings Act 1986 s 63(2).

19 See PARA 474.

20 Agricultural Holdings Act 1986 s 61(2). As to Case H see PARA 481.

21 Ie the grounds contained in the Agricultural Holdings Act 1986 s 27(3)(a)–(c) (see PARA 472).

22 Agricultural Holdings Act 1986 s 61(3)(a).

23 Ie in England, the First-tier Tribunal (see PARA 768) and in Wales, the Agricultural Land Tribunal for Wales (see PARA 767): see PARA 437 note 1.

24 Agricultural Holdings Act 1986 s 61(3)(b). In this provision the matters specified are those contained in s 27(3)(a)–(c), (e) (see PARA 472).

25 Ie under the Agricultural Holdings Act 1986 s 26(1)(b) (see PARA 471). As to the service of notices see PARA 428 note 4.

26 Ie the Agricultural Holdings Act 1986 s 27(3)(d) (see PARA 472). As to the enactments relating to smallholdings see PARA 627 et seq.

27 As to the meaning of 'agricultural' see PARA 424. As to the use of land for agriculture see PARA 424 note 7.

28 Agricultural Holdings Act 1986 s 61(4). As to non-agricultural use not falling within Case B see s 27(3)(f); and PARA 472.

29 Agricultural Holdings Act 1986 s 61(5).

30 It is open, however, to the tenant to serve a counter-notice under the Agricultural Holdings Act 1986 s 26(1) (see PARA 471).

31 See the Agricultural Holdings Act 1986 s 78(1); and PARA 512.

545. Measure of compensation for disturbance.

In the case of basic compensation[1] the amount payable is:

(1)   an amount equal to one year's rent for the holding at the rate at which rent was payable immediately before the termination of the tenancy[2]; or

(2)   an amount equal to either the amount of the tenant's[3] actual loss or two years' rent for the holding, whichever is the smaller[4].

The 'amount of the tenant's actual loss' means the amount of the loss or expense directly attributable[5] to the quitting of the holding which is unavoidably incurred by the tenant upon or in connection with the sale or removal of his household goods, implements of husbandry, fixtures, farm produce or farm stock in or used in connection with the holding, and includes any expenses reasonably incurred by him in the preparation of his claim for basic compensation (not being costs of an arbitration to determine the right to or the amount of the compensation for disturbance)[6]. Accordingly, the tenant may claim an amount equal to one year's rent for the holding at the rate at which rent was payable immediately before the termination of the tenancy without proof of loss or expense; but he cannot claim more without substantiating actual loss of the kind mentioned above, at the same time complying with two statutory requirements, the first being that not less than one month[7] before the termination of the tenancy he should give his landlord[8] notice in writing[9] of his intention to make such a claim[10] and the second being that before their sale he should give the landlord a reasonable opportunity[11] to make a valuation of any of such goods, implements, fixtures, produce or stock as may be comprised in the tenant's claim for actual loss[12].

It would seem that notice in such circumstances by one joint tenant (the one who suffered loss) would be sufficient to substantiate a claim[13]; but caution would dictate that all be parties to the document.

The scope of the tenant's claim for actual loss is wide and has included loss due to the deterioration of stock on a sale[14] and the loss attributable to sheep not tied to the holding being sold at 'breakup' instead of 'going concern' value[15]. However, loss suffered on crops owing to an error in valuation by agreed arbitrators is not sufficiently attributable to the tenant's quitting the holding[16].

Should the tenant substantiate a claim for additional compensation, the measure is a further four years' rent over and above any sums payable as basic compensation[17]. The maximum therefore to which a tenant may be entitled is six years' rent of the holding at the rate at which rent was payable immediately before the termination of the tenancy.

Compensation for disturbance is in addition to any compensation to which the tenant may be otherwise entitled[18].

1 As to the entitlement to compensation for disturbance under the Agricultural Holdings Act 1986 see PARA 544.
2 Agricultural Holdings Act 1986 s 60(2)(a), (3)(a). As to the termination of an agricultural tenancy see PARA 428 note 1.
3 As to the meaning of 'tenant' see PARA 423 note 5.
4 Agricultural Holdings Act 1986 s 60(3)(b).
5 The scope of the words 'loss or expense directly attributable' has been considered in *Re Evans and Glamorgan County Council* (1912) 76 JP 468; *Barbour v M'Douall* 1914 SC 844, Ct of Sess; *Keswick v Wright* 1924 SC 766, Ct of Sess.
6 Agricultural Holdings Act 1986 s 60(5).
7 A resumption clause in a tenancy agreement is void if it does not permit the tenant sufficient time to give this notice: *Re Disraeli Agreement, Cleasby v Park Estate (Hughenden) Ltd* [1939] Ch 382, [1938] 4 All ER 658; *Coates v Diment* [1951] 1 All ER 890; *Parry v Million Pigs Ltd* (1980) 260 Estates Gazette 281.
8 As to the meaning of 'landlord' see PARA 423 note 7.
9 As to the service of notices see PARA 428 note 4.
10 Agricultural Holdings Act 1986 s 60(6)(a).
11 Whether a reasonable opportunity has been given is a question of fact for the arbitrator; merely giving notice of intention to claim compensation is not necessarily the giving of a reasonable opportunity, nor does the mere absence of a notice of sale prevent a reasonable opportunity being given: *Dale v Hatfield Chase Corpn* [1922] 2 KB 282, CA. See also *Barbour v M'Douall* 1914 SC 844, Ct of Sess.
12 Agricultural Holdings Act 1986 s 60(6)(b).
13 *Howson v Buxton* (1928) 97 LJKB 749, CA (doubted in *Jacobs v Chaudhuri* [1968] 2 QB 470, [1968] 2 All ER 124, CA (a case on the Landlord and Tenant Act 1954 s 24(1))). See also *Newman v Keedwell* (1977) 35 P & CR 393, 244 Estates Gazette 469; *Lloyd v Sadler* [1978] QB 774, [1978] 2 All ER 529, CA; *Featherstone v Staples* [1986] 2 All ER 461, [1986] 1 WLR 861, CA.

14 *Barbour v M'Douall* 1914 SC 844, Ct of Sess.
15 *Keswick v Wright* 1924 SC 766, Ct of Sess.
16 *Macgregor v Board of Agriculture for Scotland* 1925 SC 613, Ct of Sess.
17 Agricultural Holdings Act 1986 s 60(2)(b), (4).
18 Agricultural Holdings Act 1986 s 60(7).

546. Procedure for claiming compensation for disturbance.

Apart from the preliminary notice required where a claim is made for basic compensation[1] of an amount greater than one year's rent of the holding[2], compensation for disturbance is subject to the general rule that notice be given within two months after the date of termination[3].

1　As to the entitlement to compensation for disturbance under the Agricultural Holdings Act 1986 see PARAS 544–545.
2　See the Agricultural Holdings Act 1986 s 60(6)(a); and PARA 545.
3　Agricultural Holdings Act 1986 s 83(2). It is unclear whether one notice satisfies s 60(6)(a) and s 83(2): *Lady Hallinan v Jones* [1984] 2 EGLR 20, 272 Estates Gazette 1081.

547. Compensation for disturbance and sub-tenancies.

Where the tenant[1] of an agricultural holding[2] has sub-let the holding[3] and the sub-tenancy terminates[4] by operation of law in consequence of the termination of the tenancy by reason of a notice to quit or counter-notice[5], the sub-tenant is entitled to compensation for disturbance as if he were a tenant quitting in consequence of such a notice or counter-notice[6]. Further, the tenant is not debarred from recovering such compensation by reason only that, owing to not being in occupation of the holding, on the termination of his tenancy he does not quit the holding[7].

1　As to the meaning of 'tenant' see PARA 423 note 5.
2　As to the meaning of 'agricultural holding' see PARA 423.
3　Agricultural Holdings Act 1986 s 63(1)(a).
4　As to the termination of an agricultural tenancy see PARA 428 note 1.
5　Agricultural Holdings Act 1986 s 63(1)(b). See also s 60(1); and PARA 544.
6　Agricultural Holdings Act 1986 s 63(1). As to notices to quit given to sub-tenants see PARA 496.
7　See the Agricultural Holdings Act 1986 s 63(2); and PARA 544.

(vii) Compensation for Adopting a Special System of Farming

548. Entitlement to compensation for high farming.

Where the tenant[1] of an agricultural holding[2] governed by the Agricultural Holdings Act 1986 shows that, by the continuous adoption of a system of farming[3] which has been more beneficial to the holding either than the system of farming required by the contract of tenancy[4] or, in so far as no system of farming is so required, than the system of farming normally practised on comparable agricultural holdings[5], and shows that the value of the holding as such has been increased during the tenancy, having regard to the character and situation of the holding and the average requirements of tenants reasonably skilled in husbandry, he is entitled, on quitting the holding on the termination of his tenancy[6], to obtain compensation for such 'high farming' from his landlord[7]. Payment of such compensation is subject to three provisos:

 (1) it is not payable unless the tenant has, not later than one month before the termination of the tenancy, given to the landlord[8] notice in writing[9] of his intention to make such a claim[10];

 (2) a record of condition of the fixed equipment[11] in the holding and of the general condition of the holding must have been made[12]; and

(3)   compensation is not payable in respect of any matter arising before the date of the record so made, or if more than one record has been made, before the first of them[13].

1   As to the meaning of 'tenant' see PARA 423 note 5.
2   As to the meaning of 'agricultural holding' see PARA 423.
3   As to the 'farming' of land see PARA 424.
4   Agricultural Holdings Act 1986 s 70(1)(a). As to the meaning of 'contract of tenancy' see PARA 425.
5   Agricultural Holdings Act 1986 s 70(1)(b).
6   As to the termination of an agricultural tenancy see PARA 428 note 1.
7   See the Agricultural Holdings Act 1986 s 70(1).
8   As to the meaning of 'landlord' see PARA 423 note 7.
9   As to the service of notices see PARA 428 note 4.
10 Agricultural Holdings Act 1986 s 70(2)(a).
11 As to the meaning of 'fixed equipment' see PARA 432 note 6.
12 Agricultural Holdings Act 1986 s 70(2)(b). The record of condition is to be made under s 22 (see PARA 446).
13 Agricultural Holdings Act 1986 s 70(3).

549.   Amount of compensation for high farming.

The amount of compensation for adopting a special system of farming[1] is the sum equivalent to the increase in the value of the agricultural holding[2], this being an objective test which does not countenance other than the average requirements of a reasonably skilled tenant farmer. In assessing the value of the holding for these purposes due allowance is to be made for any compensation agreed or awarded to be paid to the tenant[3] for old[4] and relevant[5] improvements or, where the tenant is entitled to statutory compensation for tenant-right matters[6], to any such specified matter, if those improvements or matters have caused or contributed to the benefit[7].

These provisions do not entitle a tenant to any compensation which he would not otherwise be entitled to recover for old or relevant improvements or for improvements in respect of which the statutory provisions relating to market gardens[8] apply or, where the tenant is within the statutory provisions relating to compensation for specified tenant-right matters[9], for those tenant-right matters[10]. Accordingly, for example, a tenant could not employ a 'high farming' claim to obtain compensation for a long term improvement[11] in respect of which he had failed to obtain the landlord's consent.

It is notoriously difficult to substantiate a claim for compensation in respect of 'high farming'. Few tenants, for example, would put in train a record of condition at a suitably early stage in their tenancy[12].

1   As to entitlement to compensation for these purposes see PARA 548.
2   See the Agricultural Holdings Act 1986 s 70(1); and PARA 548. As to the meaning of 'agricultural holding' see PARA 423.
3   As to the meaning of 'tenant' see PARA 423 note 5.
4   As to the meaning of 'old improvement' see PARA 522.
5   As to the meaning of 'relevant improvement', see PARA 528.
6   As to such entitlement see the Agricultural Holdings Act 1986 Sch 8 paras 7–11; and PARA 530.
7   Agricultural Holdings Act 1986 s 70(4).
8   As to improvements in respect of market gardens see the Agricultural Holdings Act 1986 ss 79–81; and PARAS 561–565.
9   Ie under the Agricultural Holdings Act 1986 Sch 8 paras 7–11 (see PARA 530).
10 Agricultural Holdings Act 1986 s 70(5).
11 Ie under the Agricultural Holdings Act 1986 Sch 7 paras 1–8 (see PARA 529).

12 The claim for 'high farming' is generally seen as a 'dead letter'. There are also considerable difficulties in separating those improvements subject to a claim for 'high farming' from those subject to other claims.

(viii) General Supplementary Provisions regarding Compensation

550. Compensation for quitting part of a holding.

A tenant[1] may be given notice[2] to quit part of a holding in four circumstances:

(1)   where such a notice is valid in specified cases[3];

(2)   in the case of a notice to quit within Case G (death of the tenant)[4] where the Tribunal[5] gives consent in relation to only part of the holding[6];

(3)   under a clause in the contract of tenancy[7]; and

(4)   by the owner of a severed part of the reversion[8].

Only in the first and last mentioned cases may he enlarge the landlord's[9] notice into a notice to quit the whole[10].

Should the tenant quit part only, in the first three cases the compensation provisions are applicable as if the part of the holding were a separate holding[11] provided only that in the case of resumption of possession of part pursuant to a clause in the contract of tenancy the arbitrator or, as the case may be, the third party, in assessing compensation (except additional compensation[12]) must take into consideration any benefit or relief allowed to the tenant under the contract of tenancy in respect of the land resumed by the landlord[13]. In the last mentioned case the compensation provisions are applicable to the part of the holding as if it were a separate holding which the tenant had quitted in consequence of the notice to quit and the person resuming possession were the landlord of that separate holding[14].

If, in a case in which the tenant accepts a notice to quit part of his holding as a notice to quit the entire holding, the part of the holding affected by the notice given by the landlord, together with any other part of the holding affected by a previous notice given by the landlord to the tenant, is less than one-fourth part of the original holding, and the holding as proposed to be diminished is reasonably capable of being cultivated as a separate holding, statutory compensation for disturbance is not payable except in respect of the part of the holding to which the notice to quit related[15]. However, the enlarged notice to quit still terminates the tenancy of the whole.

1   As to the meaning of 'tenant' see PARA 423 note 5.
2   As to the service of notices see PARA 428 note 4.
3   See the Agricultural Holdings Act 1986 s 74(1); and PARA 516. See also s 31(1), (2); and PARA 492.
4   See PARA 480.
5   Ie in England, the First-tier Tribunal (see PARA 768) and in Wales, the Agricultural Land Tribunal for Wales (see PARA 767): see PARA 437 note 1.
6   See the Agricultural Holdings Act 1986 s 74(1); and PARA 516. As to the restriction on the operation of a notice to quit given by reason of death of the tenant see s 43(1), (2); and PARA 503.
7   See the Agricultural Holdings Act 1986 s 74(2); and PARA 516. As to the meaning of 'contract of tenancy' see PARA 425.
8   See the Agricultural Holdings Act 1986 s 74(3); and PARA 516.
9   As to the meaning of 'landlord' see PARA 423 note 7.
10 See the Agricultural Holdings Act 1986 s 32; and PARA 495.
11 See the Agricultural Holdings Act 1986 s 74(1), (2); and PARA 516.
12 Ie under the Agricultural Holdings Act 1986 s 60(2)(b) (see PARA 545).
13 See the Agricultural Holdings Act 1986 s 74(2)(b); and PARA 516.

14 See the Agricultural Holdings Act 1986 s 74(3); and PARA 516.
15 Agricultural Holdings Act 1986 s 63(3).

551. Compensation for termination of a tenancy under an early resumption clause.

Where the tenancy of an agricultural holding[1] or part of it terminates[2] by reason of a notice to quit under a provision authorising the resumption of possession for some specified purpose other than the use of the land for agriculture[3] and the tenant[4] quits the holding or part in consequence[5], compensation, additional to any other compensation, is payable by the landlord[6] to the tenant of an amount equal to the value of the additional benefit, if any, which would have accrued to the tenant if the tenancy had been terminated by the notice to quit on the expiration of 12 months from the end of the year of tenancy current when the notice was given[7]. In the case of a tenancy for two years or upwards, the current year for this purpose is that beginning with such day in the 12 months ending with the date on which the notice to quit was served as corresponds to the day on which the term would expire by effluxion of time[8].

1 As to the meaning of 'agricultural holding' see PARA 423.
2 As to the termination of an agricultural tenancy see PARA 428 note 1.
3 Agricultural Holdings Act 1986 s 62(1)(a). As to the meaning of 'agriculture' see PARA 424. As to the use of land for agriculture see PARA 424 note 7. The clause authorising early resumption is held void if it does not permit the tenant sufficient time to give all requisite notices: see PARA 470.
4 As to the meaning of 'tenant' see PARA 423 note 5.
5 Agricultural Holdings Act 1986 s 62(1)(b).
6 As to the meaning of 'landlord' see PARA 423 note 7.
7 Agricultural Holdings Act 1986 s 62(2). The sums payable may be substantial, for example where the tenant loses vital buildings on short notice. The tenant need only serve notice of his claim within two months after the date of termination: s 83(2). Contracting out of these provisions is not possible: see s 78(1); and PARA 512.
8 Agricultural Holdings Act 1986 s 62(3).

552. Additional compensation on compulsory acquisition.

Additional compensation may be payable where an interest in an agricultural holding governed by the Agricultural Holdings Act 1986 is acquired in pursuance of any enactment providing for the acquiring or taking of possession of land compulsorily[1].

1 See the Agriculture (Miscellaneous Provisions) Act 1968 ss 12, 13; and PARAS 591–592.

(ix) Landlord's Compensation for Deterioration of Holding

553. Landlord's compensation under the Agricultural Holdings Act 1986 for particular deterioration.

A landlord[1] of an agricultural holding[2] governed by the Agricultural Holdings Act 1986 is entitled to recover from a tenant[3], when that tenant quits the holding on the termination[4] of his tenancy[5], compensation in respect of the dilapidation or deterioration of, or damage to, any part[6] of the holding or anything in or on the holding caused by the non-fulfilment by the tenant of his responsibilities to farm[7] in accordance with the rules of good husbandry[8]. But there is no rule that a tenant is required to leave the land as he found it. He must simply leave it in the condition required to discharge his responsibilities to farm in accordance with the rules of good husbandry[9].

1 As to the meaning of 'landlord' see PARA 423 note 7.

2   As to the meaning of 'agricultural holding' see PARA 423.
3   As to the meaning of 'tenant' see PARA 423 note 5.
4   As to the termination of an agricultural tenancy see PARA 428 note 1.
5   A statutory claim for dilapidations cannot be pursued during the currency of the tenancy except
    where the Opencast Coal Act 1958 s 25 (see MINES, MINERALS AND QUARRIES vol 76 (2013)
    PARA 473) or the Agricultural Holdings Act 1986 s 9 (transitional arrangements where liability
    in respect of fixed equipment is transferred: see PARA 435) applies.
6   These provisions specifically relate to dilapidations or deterioration affecting part of a holding or
    anything in or on the holding. Accordingly, for example, in *Evans v Jones* [1955] 2 QB 58, [1955]
    2 All ER 118, CA, it was held that the deterioration of particular fields due to a failure to apply
    fertiliser gave rise to a claim under the statutory predecessor to the Agricultural Holdings Act 1986
    s 71(1) (ie the Agricultural Holdings Act 1948 s 57 (repealed)).
7   As to the 'farming' of land see PARA 424.
8   Agricultural Holdings Act 1986 s 71(1). As to the rules of good husbandry for the purposes of the
    Agricultural Holdings Act 1986 see, by virtue of s 96(3) (see PARA 430 note 14), the Agriculture
    Act 1947 ss 10, 11; and AGRICULTURAL PRODUCTION AND MARKETING vol 1A (2017)
    PARAS 11–13.
9   See *Williams v Lewis* [1915] 3 KB 493; *Evans v Jones* [1955] 2 QB 58, [1955] 2 All ER 118, CA; cf
    Proudfoot v Hart (1890) 25 QBD 42.

554. Measure of landlord's compensation under the Agricultural Holdings Act 1986 for particular deterioration.

The amount of compensation for particular deterioration payable under the Agricultural Holdings Act 1986[1] is the cost, as at the date of the tenant's[2] quitting the holding, of making good the dilapidation, deterioration or damage[3], subject to a limitation that the costs must not exceed the amount (if any) by which the value of the landlord's[4] reversion in the holding is diminished[5] owing to the specific dilapidation, deterioration or damage[6].

1   See the Agricultural Holdings Act 1986 s 71(1); and PARA 553.
2   As to the meaning of 'tenant' see PARA 423 note 5.
3   Agricultural Holdings Act 1986 s 71(2). In *Barrow Green Estate Co v Walker's Executors* [1954]
    1 All ER 204, [1954] 1 WLR 231, CA, it was held that in determining a claim under the
    predecessor to the Agricultural Holdings Act 1986 s 71 (ie the Agricultural Holdings Act 1948 s
    57 (repealed)), the arbitrator was bound to take into account the terms of the contract of tenancy
    together with the terms of any other agreement affecting the holding and the statutory regulations
    as to repair.
4   As to the meaning of 'landlord' see PARA 423 note 7.
5   There is no rule that a tenant is required to leave the land as he found it. He must leave it in the
    condition required to discharge his responsibilities to farm in accordance with the rules of good
    husbandry: see *Williams v Lewis* [1915] 3 KB 493; *Evans v Jones* [1955] 2 QB 58, [1955] 2 All
    ER 118, CA; cf *Proudfoot v Hart* (1890) 25 QBD 42.
6   Agricultural Holdings Act 1986 s 71(5). As to the rules of good husbandry for the purposes of the
    Agricultural Holdings Act 1986 see, by virtue of s 96(3) (see PARA 430 note 14), the Agriculture
    Act 1947 ss 10, 11; and AGRICULTURAL PRODUCTION AND MARKETING vol 1A (2017)
    PARAS 11–13.

555. Landlord's contractual compensation for particular deterioration.

If a written contract of tenancy[1] provides for compensation in respect of matters otherwise falling within the statutory provision as to deterioration[2], the landlord[3] may, in lieu of claiming compensation under that provision, claim compensation in reliance upon the contractual provisions[4].

A landlord may not claim compensation both under the relevant statutory provisions[5] and under the contract of tenancy[6]. Where the landlord elects to rely upon his contractual claims, any claim by the landlord against the tenant[7] in respect of any liability for the maintenance or repair of any item of fixed equipment[8] transferred from the tenant to the landlord[9] must be disregarded[10].

1   As to the meaning of 'contract of tenancy' see PARA 425.
2   See the Agricultural Holdings Act 1986 s 71(1); and PARA 553.
3   As to the meaning of 'landlord' see PARA 423 note 7.
4   Agricultural Holdings Act 1986 s 71(3). Save in respect of the transitional exceptions in s 9 (see PARA 435), the contractual claim only arises at the termination of the tenancy: s 71(4)(a). However, in *Kent v Conniff* [1953] 1 QB 361, [1953] 1 All ER 155, CA, it was held that a landlord may bring a common law action for damages during the currency of a tenancy. Cf the Agriculture (Maintenance, Repair and Insurance of Fixed Equipment) Regulations 1973, SI 1973/1473; the Agriculture (Model Clauses for Fixed Equipment) (England) Regulations 2015, SI 2015/950; and PARA 433. Note also the landlord's ability to obtain an injunction to restrain a tenant in the exercise of his rights relating to the disposal of produce and cropping where injury or deterioration is likely to be caused to the holding: see the Agricultural Holdings Act 1986 s 15(5); and PARA 444. As to the termination of an agricultural tenancy see PARA 428 note 1.
5   Ie the Agricultural Holdings Act 1986 s 71(1) (see PARA 553).
6   Agricultural Holdings Act 1986 s 71(4)(b). However, this does not preclude the landlord from claiming in the alternative provided he later abandons one head of claim: see *Boyd v Wilton* [1957] 2 QB 277, [1957] 2 All ER 102, CA.
7   As to the meaning of 'tenant' see PARA 423 note 5.
8   As to the meaning of 'fixed equipment' see PARA 432 note 6.
9   See the Agricultural Holdings Act 1986 ss 6–9; and PARAS 432–435.
10 Agricultural Holdings Act 1986 s 71(4).

556. Notices and disputes regarding landlord's compensation for particular deterioration.

Any dispute in respect of the landlord's claim for compensation, whether in reliance upon the statutory provision[1] or the contract of tenancy[2], is to be determined by arbitration or third party determination[3]. For the landlord's claims to be enforceable, it is a prerequisite that notice be given within two months of the termination of the tenancy[4] of an intention to make such a claim[5].

1   Ie the Agricultural Holdings Act 1986 s 71(1) (see PARA 553).
2   See PARA 555.
3   As to arbitrations and third party determinations generally see PARA 566 et seq.
4   As to the termination of an agricultural tenancy see PARA 428 note 1.
5   Agricultural Holdings Act 1986 s 83(1A), (2) (s 83(1A) added by the Deregulation Act 2015 Sch 4 para 20).

557. Landlord's compensation for general deterioration.

Where, on the quitting of an agricultural holding[1] by the tenant[2] on the termination[3] of the tenancy, the landlord[4] shows that the value of the holding generally has been reduced by reason of any of the specified kinds of dilapidation, deterioration or damage[5] or by the tenant's non-fulfilment of his responsibilities to farm[6] in accordance with the rules of good husbandry[7], the landlord, in so far as he is not compensated under statute or pursuant to the provisions of a written contract of tenancy[8], is entitled to a sum in compensation for general deterioration of the holding[9].

1   As to the meaning of 'agricultural holding' see PARA 423.
2   As to the meaning of 'tenant' see PARA 423 note 5.
3   As to the termination of an agricultural tenancy see PARA 428 note 1.
4   As to the meaning of 'landlord' see PARA 423 note 7.
5   Ie as specified in the Agricultural Holdings Act 1986 s 71(1) (see PARA 553).
6   As to the 'farming' of land see PARA 424.

7   Agricultural Holdings Act 1986 s 72(1). As to the rules of good husbandry for the purposes of the
    Agricultural Holdings Act 1986 see, by virtue of s 96(3) (see PARA 430 note 14), the Agriculture
    Act 1947 ss 10, 11; and AGRICULTURAL PRODUCTION AND MARKETING vol 1A (2017)
    PARAS 11–13.
8   As to the meaning of 'contract of tenancy' see PARA 425.
9   Agricultural Holdings Act 1986 s 72(2). A claim under s 72 may be made in conjunction with a
    claim under s 71, or as a separate claim; however, the landlord cannot recover compensation
    twice, ie once under each provision: see *Evans v Jones* [1955] 2 QB 58, [1955] 2 All ER 118, CA.

558.   Measure of landlord's compensation for general deterioration.

The amount of compensation payable in respect of general deterioration of the
holding[1] is equal to the decrease attributable to the matter in question in the value
of the holding as a holding, having regard to the character and situation of the
holding and the average requirements of tenants reasonably skilled in husbandry[2].

1   Ie under the Agricultural Holdings Act 1986 s 72(1) (see PARA 557).
2   Agricultural Holdings Act 1986 s 72(3).

559.   Notices and disputes regarding landlord's compensation for general deterioration.

The landlord[1] must have given written notice[2] to the tenant[3], not later than one
month before the termination of the tenancy[4], of his intention to claim
compensation for general deterioration[5]. Any dispute in respect of the landlord's
claim for such compensation is to be determined by arbitration or third party
determination[6].

1   As to the meaning of 'landlord' see PARA 423 note 7.
2   As to the service of notices see PARA 428 note 4.
3   As to the meaning of 'tenant' see PARA 423 note 5.
4   As to the termination of an agricultural tenancy see PARA 428 note 1.
5   Agricultural Holdings Act 1986 s 72(4). As to whether such a notice dispenses with the need for
    a notice under s 83(1) (see PARA 566) see *Lady Hallinan v Jones* [1984] 2 EGLR 20, 272 Estates
    Gazette 1081.
6   As to arbitrations and third party determinations generally see PARA 566 et seq.

560.   Landlord's compensation claim for deterioration may survive successive tenancies.

Where the tenant[1] of an agricultural holding[2] has remained on the holding, or
on any agricultural holding which comprised the whole or a substantial part of the
land comprised in the holding, during two or more tenancies, his landlord[3] does
not lose his right to compensation in respect of any dilapidation, deterioration or
damage to the holding[4] by reason only that the tenancy during which any act or
omission occurred which caused the dilapidation, deterioration or damage to the
holding was a tenancy other than the tenancy which was in existence when the
tenant quits the holding[5].

1   As to the meaning of 'tenant' see PARA 423 note 5.
2   As to the meaning of 'agricultural holding' see PARA 423.
3   As to the meaning of 'landlord' see PARA 423 note 7.
4   Ie under the Agricultural Holdings Act 1986 ss 71, 72 (see PARAS 553–559).
5   Agricultural Holdings Act 1986 s 73(1) (s 73(1) amended, and s 73(2) added, by SI 2006/2805).
    Where the Agricultural Holdings Act 1986 applies in relation to a tenancy by virtue of the
    Agricultural Tenancies Act 1995 s 4(1)(g) (see PARAS 401, 421), the reference in the Agricultural
    Holdings Act 1986 s 73(1) to a 'substantial part of the land comprised in the holding' means a
    substantial part determined by reference to either area or value: s 73(2) (as so added)).
        The amendments made by the Regulatory Reform (Agricultural Tenancies) (England and
    Wales) Order 2006, SI 2006/2805, do not apply in relation to compensation payable on

termination of a tenancy where that tenancy was granted before 19 October 2006 (ie the date on which art 6 was brought into force: see art 1(1)(b)): see art 6(8).

Note that any substantial change in the identity of the landlord or tenant would prevent s 73 being applicable: see *Jenkin R Lewis & Son Ltd v Kerman* [1971] Ch 477, [1970] 3 All ER 414, CA; cf *Trustees of Saunders v Ralph* (1993) 66 P & CR 335, [1993] 2 EGLR 1 (where the addition of a new tenant did not amount to the surrender of the old tenancy).

(x) Market Gardens

561. Compensation for improvements to market gardens.

The statutory rights to compensation under the Agricultural Holdings Act 1986 payable to a tenant[1] of an agricultural holding[2] apply to market gardens[3] which fall into one of the following categories:

(1)   where it has been agreed in writing[4] on or after 1 January 1896[5] that the holding[6] should be let or treated[7] as a market garden[8];

(2)   where the tenancy was current on 1 January 1896 and the holding[9] was at that date in use for cultivation as a market garden with the knowledge of the landlord[10], and the tenant had then executed on the holding, without having received before the execution a written notice of dissent by the landlord, a 'market garden improvement' (other than one consisting of such an alteration of a building[11] as did not constitute an enlargement of it)[12]; or

(3)   where an agricultural holding, or part of it, is directed to be treated as a market garden by the Tribunal[13].

Further, in addition to the extended rights conferred in respect of such market gardens for the removal of fixtures and buildings[14], the following special provisions apply with regard to compensation for improvements:

(a)   in the case of improvements begun on or after 1 March 1948[15] (irrespective of landlord's consent), market garden improvements[16] qualify for compensation as if they were short term improvements[17] begun on or after that date[18]; and

(b)   in the case of improvements begun before that date, those consisting of the erection or enlargement of, but not alteration to, buildings qualify for compensation as if they were old improvements[19].

1   As to the meaning of 'tenant' see PARA 423 note 5.
2   As to the meaning of 'agricultural holding' see PARA 423.
3   As to the meaning of 'market garden' see PARA 424 note 4.
4   The agreement may be contained in the original contract of tenancy or otherwise.
5   Agricultural Holdings Act 1986 s 98(2), Sch 12 para 10(1). The date mentioned in the text is referable to the commencement of the Market Gardeners Compensation Act 1895.
6   Where the land to which the agreement relates consists of part of a holding only, the provisions apply as if that part were a separate holding: Agricultural Holdings Act 1986 s 79(1).
7   The word 'treated' does not mean simply that the holding must be in use or cultivation as a market garden, but that it must be let as a market garden by one person as landlord and occupied by the other as tenant. This provision has been held not to apply to a holding in fact used and cultivated as a market garden where the tenancy agreement contained a proviso that 'nothing herein contained shall be deemed to be an agreement by the landlord that the premises hereby demised or any part thereof shall be let or treated as a market garden': *Re Masters and Duveen* [1923] 2 KB 729, CA. 'Let as a market garden' means 'let for the purpose of' a market garden and therefore includes a permissive right to cultivate as a market garden: *Saunders-Jacobs v Yates* [1933] 1 KB 392; affd [1933] 2 KB 240, CA.
8   Agricultural Holdings Act 1986 s 79(1).
9   Where the land is part of an agricultural holding only, it is treated as a separate holding: Agricultural Holdings Act 1986 Sch 12 para 10(4).
10 As to the meaning of 'landlord' see PARA 423 note 7.

11 As to the meaning of 'building' see PARA 432 note 6.

12 Agricultural Holdings Act 1986 Sch 12 para 10(2). A 'market garden improvement' is an improvement of a kind specified in Sch 10 (see note 16).

13 See the Agricultural Holdings Act 1986 s 80; and PARA 562. In England, the Tribunal is the First-tier Tribunal (see PARA 768) and in Wales, the Agricultural Land Tribunal for Wales (see PARA 767): see PARA 437 note 1.

14 See PARA 565.

15 Ie the date on which the Agriculture Act 1947 Pt III (repealed), from which these provisions are derived, was brought into force: see s 111(2) (repealed); and the Agriculture Act 1947 (Commencement) (No 1) Order 1948, SI 1948/342.

16 Ie:
    (1)   planting of standard or other fruit trees permanently set out (Agricultural Holdings Act 1986 Sch 10 para 1);
    (2)   planting of fruit bushes permanently set out (Sch 10 para 2);
    (3)   planting of strawberry plants (Sch 10 para 3);
    (4)   planting of asparagus, rhubarb and other vegetable crops which continue productive for two or more years (Sch 10 para 4); and
    (5)   erection, alteration or enlargement of buildings for the purpose of the trade or business of a market gardener (Sch 10 para 5).

17 For short term improvements see the Agricultural Holdings Act 1986 Sch 8 paras 1–6; and PARA 529.

18 Agricultural Holdings Act 1986 s 79(2).

19 Agricultural Holdings Act 1986 s 79(2). The 'old improvements' referred to in the text are those included in Sch 9 Pt II (see PARA 523).

562. Direction by a Tribunal as to market gardens.

In order to obtain a direction from the Tribunal[1] that an agricultural holding[2], or part of it, is to be treated as a market garden[3], the tenant[4] must first establish that the landlord[5] refused, or failed within a reasonable time, to agree in writing that the holding or that part of it, as the case may be, is to be treated as a market garden[6]. On an application by the tenant for such a direction the Tribunal may, after being satisfied that the holding or part is suitable for the purposes of market gardening, direct that the special compensation provisions[7] apply to the holding or part of it in relation to all the market garden improvements[8] or to some only[9].

Where such a direction is given by the Tribunal, then, if the tenancy is terminated by notice to quit given by the tenant or by reason of the tenant becoming insolvent[10], the tenant is not entitled to compensation in respect of the improvements specified in the direction unless two conditions are satisfied[11]. The first of these is that the tenant, not later than one month after the date on which the notice to quit is given[12] or the date of the insolvency[13], as the case may be, or such later date as may be agreed, produces to the landlord an offer in writing by a substantial or otherwise suitable person (being an offer which is to hold good for a period of three months from the date on which it is produced):

    (1)   to accept a tenancy of the holding from the termination of the existing tenancy[14], and on the terms and conditions of that tenancy so far as applicable[15]; and

    (2)   subject to the following provisions, to pay to the outgoing tenant all compensation payable under the Agricultural Holdings Act 1986 or under the contract of tenancy[16].

The second is that the landlord fails to accept the offer within three months after it has been produced[17].

If the landlord accepts any such offer, the incoming tenant must pay to the landlord on demand all sums payable to him by the outgoing tenant on the termination of the tenancy in respect of the rent or breach of contract or otherwise in respect of the holding, and any amount so paid may, subject to any agreement between the outgoing tenant and the incoming tenant, be deducted by the incoming tenant from any compensation payable by him to the outgoing tenant[18].

Any direction given by the Tribunal that an agricultural holding, or part of it, is to be treated as a market garden, may be given subject to such conditions (if any) for the protection of the landlord as the Tribunal thinks fit[19]. Without prejudice to the generality of this provision, where a direction relates to part only of an agricultural holding, it may, on the application of the landlord, be given subject to the condition that it is to become operative only in the event of the tenant's consenting to the division of the holding into two parts, of which one must be that to which the direction relates, to be held at rents settled, in default of agreement, by arbitration under the Agricultural Holdings Act 1986[20], but otherwise on the same terms and conditions (so far as applicable) as those on which the holding is held[21]. Notwithstanding provision for rents to be settled by arbitration, the landlord and tenant may instead refer those rents to be settled by third party determination under the Agricultural Holdings Act 1986[22].

A new tenancy created by the acceptance of a tenant in accordance with these provisions on the terms and conditions of the existing tenancy is deemed for the purposes of the supplementary provisions in respect of arbitration as to rent[23] not to be a new tenancy[24].

1   Ie in England, the First-tier Tribunal (see PARA 768) and in Wales, the Agricultural Land Tribunal for Wales (see PARA 767): see PARA 437 note 1.
2   As to the meaning of 'agricultural holding' see PARA 423.
3   As to the meaning of 'market garden' see PARA 424 note 4.
4   As to the meaning of 'tenant' see PARA 423 note 5.
5   As to the meaning of 'landlord' see PARA 423 note 7.
6   Agricultural Holdings Act 1986 s 80(1).
7   Ie the Agricultural Holdings Act 1986 s 79(2)–(5) (see PARAS 561–565).
8   Ie the improvements specified in the Agricultural Holdings Act 1986 Sch 10 (see PARA 561 note 16).
9   Agricultural Holdings Act 1986 s 80(2).
10 As to when a tenant is 'insolvent' see PARA 470 note 4; definition applied by the Agricultural Holdings Act 1986 s 80(9).
11 Agricultural Holdings Act 1986 s 80(3). The provisions contained in s 80(3)–(5) are known as the 'Evesham custom': see further PARA 563.
12 As to the service of notices see PARA 428 note 4.
13 The reference to the date of the insolvency is a reference to the date of the occurrence of the event in question: Agricultural Holdings Act 1986 s 80(9).
14 As to the termination of an agricultural tenancy see PARA 428 note 1.
15 Agricultural Holdings Act 1986 s 80(4)(a)(i).
16 Agricultural Holdings Act 1986 s 80(4)(a)(ii). As to the meaning of 'contract of tenancy' see PARA 425.
17 Agricultural Holdings Act 1986 s 80(4)(b).
18 Agricultural Holdings Act 1986 s 80(5).
19 Agricultural Holdings Act 1986 s 80(6).
20 As to arbitrations generally see PARA 566 et seq.
21 Agricultural Holdings Act 1986 s 80(7).
22 Agricultural Holdings Act 1986 s 80(7A) (added by the Deregulation Act 2015 Sch 4 para 19). As to third party determinations generally see PARA 568.
23 Ie the provisions of the Agricultural Holdings Act 1986 Sch 2, supplementary to s 12 (see PARA 438).
24 Agricultural Holdings Act 1986 s 80(8).

563. Substituted compensation by agreement: Evesham custom.

A landlord[1] and tenant[2] may agree in writing to substitute the statutory compensation payable in respect of market garden improvements[3] for agreed compensation provided it is fair and reasonable[4] having regard to the circumstances existing when the agreement was entered into by the parties[5]. Where the landlord and tenant of an agricultural holding[6] have agreed that the holding be let or treated as a market garden[7] they may by agreement in writing substitute for the provisions as to compensation which would otherwise be applicable to the holding the provisions as to compensation known as the 'Evesham custom'[8].

1   As to the meaning of 'landlord' see PARA **423** note 7.
2   As to the meaning of 'tenant' see PARA **423** note 5.
3   As to the right to compensation for improvements to market gardens see PARA **561**.
4   In *Bell v Graham* 1908 SC 1060, Ct of Sess, it was held that 'if parties of full age sign an agreement the presumption of fact is very strong that it is fair and reasonable'.
5   Agricultural Holdings Act 1986 s 81(1).
6   As to the meaning of 'agricultural holding' see PARA **423**.
7   As to the meaning of 'market garden' see PARA **424** note 4.
8   Agricultural Holdings Act 1986 s 81(2). The Evesham custom for compensation was abolished by the Agriculture Act 1947 s 27 but its provisions have been enacted by statute (see the Agricultural Holdings Act 1986 s 80(3)–(5); and PARA **562**). Section 81(2) overrides in these circumstances the provisions of s 77 (see PARA **514**) providing that there is to be no compensation under custom for any improvement or tenant-right matter. For the custom to apply, the tenancy must be terminated either by the tenant's notice to quit or by reason of the tenant's insolvency: see s 80(3); and PARA **562**.

564.   Measure of compensation for market garden improvements.

The measure of compensation for market garden improvements[1] is the value to the incoming tenant[2].

1   Ie the improvements specified in the Agricultural Holdings Act 1986 Sch 10 (see PARA **561** note 16). As to the meaning of 'market garden' see PARA **424** note 4.
2   This is implied by the provision in the Agricultural Holdings Act 1986 s 79(2) (see PARA **561**) that the Act is to apply as if improvements in Sch 10 were included among those in Sch 8 paras 1–6 (see s 66(2); and PARAS **529**, **539**).

565.   Removal of fixtures from market gardens.

The statutory right of removal[1] applies to every fixture or building[2] affixed or erected by the tenant[3] to or upon a holding or acquired by him after 1 January 1901[4] for the purposes of a trade or business as a market gardener[5], either:

(1)   when it has been agreed in writing on or after 1 January 1896[6], that the holding[7] should be let or treated[8] as a market garden[9]; or

(2)   where the tenancy was current on 1 January 1896 and the holding[10] was at that date in use or cultivation as a market garden with the knowledge of the landlord[11], and the tenant had then executed on the holding, without having received before the execution a written notice[12] of dissent by the landlord, a market garden improvement[13].

The general restriction on the removal of buildings where the tenant is entitled to compensation[14] does not apply to any building erected by the tenant on the holding or acquired by him for the purposes of his trade or business as a market gardener[15], and the restriction on the removal of fixtures or buildings affixed or erected before 1 January 1884[16] does not apply to any building acquired by him for those purposes, whenever erected[17]. Further, in such cases the tenant may also remove all fruit trees and fruit bushes planted by him on the holding and not permanently set out, but, if he does not remove them before the termination of his tenancy[18], they remain the property of the landlord, and the tenant is not entitled to any compensation in respect of them[19].

The above provisions as to fixtures and buildings may be excluded by agreement between the landlord and tenant[20]; and, if a tenant is entitled by the custom of the country to remove machinery or fixtures, that right is preserved to him, and may be exercised by him according to the custom without any statutory restrictions[21].

1   As to the statutory right to remove fixtures generally see the Agricultural Holdings Act 1986 s 10; and PARA 436.

2   As to the meaning of 'building' see PARA 432 note 6.

3   As to the meaning of 'tenant' see PARA 423 note 5.

4   Ie the date on which the Agricultural Holdings Act 1900 s 4 (repealed), which first extended the rights in question to fixtures acquired by the tenant as opposed to those affixed or erected by him, was brought into force. The time limit is only referable to the acquisition of fixtures and buildings: Agricultural Holdings Act 1986 Sch 12 para 3.

5   See PARA 561 et seq. As to the meaning of 'market garden' see PARA 424 note 4.

6   Agricultural Holdings Act 1986 Sch 12 para 10(1). The date mentioned in the text is referable to the commencement of the Market Gardeners Compensation Act 1895.

7   Where the land to which the agreement relates consists of part of a holding only, the provisions apply as if that part were a separate holding: Agricultural Holdings Act 1986 s 79(1).

8   'Treated' means treated as between landlord and tenant for the purposes of their rights in respect of the holding, rather than 'used' or 'cultivated': *Re Masters and Duveen* [1923] 2 KB 729, CA.

9   Agricultural Holdings Act 1986 s 79(1).

10 Where the use or cultivation takes place on part only of an agricultural holding, these provisions apply as if that part were a separate holding: Agricultural Holdings Act 1986 Sch 12 para 10(4).

11 As to the meaning of 'landlord' see PARA 423 note 7.

12 As to the service of notices see PARA 428 note 4.

13 Agricultural Holdings Act 1986 Sch 12 para 10(2), (3). The improvements referred to are those specified in the Agricultural Holdings Act 1986 Sch 10 (see PARA 561 note 16). Improvements consisting of such alterations of buildings as do not constitute enlargements of them are excepted: Sch 12 para 10(2)(b).

14 Ie the restriction made by the Agricultural Holdings Act 1986 s 10(2)(c) (see PARA 436).

15 Agricultural Holdings Act 1986 s 79(3)(a).

16 Ie the restriction made by the Agricultural Holdings Act 1986 s 10(2)(d) (see PARA 436). The date mentioned in the text is the date on which the Agricultural Holdings (England) Act 1883, from which these provisions in part derive, was brought into force: see s 53 (repealed).

17 Agricultural Holdings Act 1986 s 79(3)(b).

18 As to the termination of an agricultural tenancy see PARA 428 note 1. Removal after termination may lead to a liability in damages: see *Barff v Probyn* (1895) 64 LJQB 557.

19 Agricultural Holdings Act 1986 s 79(4). See also s 79(2), Sch 10; and PARA 561.

20 *Mears v Callender* [1901] 2 Ch 388; *Premier Dairies Ltd v Garlick* [1920] 2 Ch 17; *Re Masters and Duveen* [1923] 2 KB 729, CA.

21 Agricultural Holdings Act 1986 s 97.

(8) DETERMINATION OF CLAIMS

(i) Methods of Determination

566. Arbitration and third party determination.

Any matter which by or by virtue of the Agricultural Holdings Act 1986 or regulations made under it is required to be determined by arbitration under that Act must, notwithstanding any agreement (under a contract of tenancy or otherwise) providing for a different method of arbitration, be determined by the arbitration of a single arbitrator[1] or by third party determination[2].

1   Agricultural Holdings Act 1986 s 84(1) (amended by SI 2006/2805). Arbitrations under the Agricultural Holdings Act 1986 were previously governed by specific arbitration provisions contained therein; however, following the amendments made by the Regulatory Reform

(Agricultural Tenancies) (England and Wales) Order 2006, SI 2006/2805, arts 7, 18, Sch 2 (in particular, the repeal of the Agricultural Holdings Act 1986 Sch 11, which contained the mechanisms governing arbitrations under that Act), the Agricultural Holdings Act 1986 no longer makes specific provision for arbitrations thereunder and the Arbitration Act 1996 Pt I (ss 1–84) (see ARBITRATION vol 2 (2017) PARA 509 et seq), which governs all arbitrations for which specific provision is not made, accordingly applies. Where by virtue of the Agricultural Holdings Act 1986 compensation under an agreement is to be substituted for compensation under the Agricultural Holdings Act 1986 for improvements or for any such matters as are specified in Sch 8 paras 7–11 (compensation for tenant-right matters: see PARA 530) the arbitrator must award compensation in accordance with the agreement instead of in accordance with the Agricultural Holdings Act 1986: s 84(5) (as so substituted).

2   See the Agricultural Holdings Act 1986 s 84A(1) (added by the Deregulation Act 2015 Sch 4 para 21). Provision is made throughout the Agricultural Holdings Act 1986 for claims that may be referred to arbitration to be referred for third party determination instead: see PARA 568.

567. Appointment of arbitrator.

The arbitrator must be a person appointed by agreement between the parties or, in default of agreement, a person appointed on the application of either of the parties by the President of the Royal Institution of Chartered Surveyors (the 'RICS')[1]. If the arbitrator dies, or is incapable of acting, a new arbitrator may be appointed as if no arbitrator had been appointed[2].

If the parties fail to reach an agreement in writing as to any claims arising under the Agricultural Holdings Act 1986 within eight months, the claim must be determined by arbitration[3].

In the case of rent review pursuant to a demand for arbitration the arbitrator must be appointed before the date when the new rent will come into effect if the appointment is made by agreement[4]. If an appointment is not agreed between the parties, the application for the appointment of the arbitrator must be made before the date from which the new rent will come into effect[5]. In the case of a notice to quit given for one of the specified Cases the arbitrator must be appointed within three months of the date of the demand for arbitration, otherwise the demand is rendered ineffective and the notice to quit takes effect regardless of whether or not the landlord could have established the ground referred to in the notice[6].

In all other cases there are no such time limits, although regard must be had to the equitable doctrines of waiver, estoppel and laches.

1   Agricultural Holdings Act 1986 s 84(2), (6) (s 84(2)–(4) substituted, and s 84(6) added, by SI 2006/2805). As to the Royal Institution of Chartered Surveyors generally see BUILDING CONTRACTS vol 6 (2011) PARA 490. No application may be made to the President of the RICS for an arbitrator to be appointed by him under the Agricultural Holdings Act 1986 s 84 unless the application is accompanied by such fee as may be prescribed as the fee for such an application; but once the fee has been paid in connection with any such application no further fee is payable in connection with any subsequent application for the appointment by him of a new arbitrator in relation to that arbitration: s 84(4) (as so substituted). At the date at which this volume states the law the fee is £115: Agricultural Holdings (Fees) Regulations 1996, SI 1996/337, reg 2(b) (amended by SI 2006/2805).

2   Agricultural Holdings Act 1986 s 84(3) (as so substituted).

3   See the Agricultural Holdings Act 1986 s 83(4), (5); and PARA 570.

4   See the Agricultural Holdings Act 1986 s 12, Sch 2; and PARA 438.

5   See the Agricultural Holdings Act 1986 s 12(3); and PARA 438.

6   See the Agricultural Holdings (Arbitration on Notices) (Variation) Order 1987, SI 1987/710, art 10; and PARA 488.

568. Third party determinations.

Parties who wish to refer a matter for third party determination[1] under the Agricultural Holdings Act 1986 must jointly appoint a third party to determine the matter[2]. However, they may not jointly appoint a third party to determine a matter once an arbitrator has been appointed[3] either by agreement between them or by the president of the Royal Institution of Chartered Surveyors[4].

Any matter which by or by virtue of the Agricultural Holdings Act 1986 or regulations made under it may be determined by third party determination under the Agricultural Holdings Act 1986 is to be treated as having been referred for third party determination under it once an appointment has been so made[5].

If a third party appointed under these provisions to determine a matter dies, or is incapable of acting, the parties may (instead of appointing a replacement) agree to proceed as if they had not referred the matter for third party determination under the Agricultural Holdings Act 1986[6].

Where by virtue of the Agricultural Holdings Act 1986 compensation under an agreement is to be substituted for compensation under it for improvements or for certain other matters for which compensation is payable[7], the third party must award compensation in accordance with the agreement instead of in accordance with the Agricultural Holdings Act 1986[8].

1   References to 'third party determination' are to the determination of a matter by the third party appointed under the Agricultural Holdings Act 1986 s 84A(1) or a replacement third party jointly appointed by the parties on a termination of the earlier appointment; and references to a 'third party', in the context of such a determination, are to the third party so appointed: AHA 1986 s 84A(4) (s 84A added by the Deregulation Act 2015 Sch 4 para 21).
2   Agricultural Holdings Act 1986 s 84A(1) (as added: see note 1).
3   Ie appointed under the Agricultural Holdings Act 1986 s 84(2) (see PARA 567).
4   See the Agricultural Holdings Act 1986 s 84A(2) (as added: see note 1). As to the Royal Institution of Chartered Surveyors generally see BUILDING CONTRACTS vol 6 (2011) PARA 490. See however note 6.
5   See the Agricultural Holdings Act 1986 s 84A(3) (as added: see note 1).
6   Agricultural Holdings Act 1986 s 84A(5) (as added: see note 1). A matter that has been referred for third party determination under the Agricultural Holdings Act 1986 may not be determined by arbitration under it except by virtue of s 84A(5): s 84A(6) (as so added).
7   Ie any such matters as are specified in the Agricultural Holdings Act 1986 Sch 8 Pt 2 (see PARA 530).
8   Agricultural Holdings Act 1986 s 84A(7) (as added: see note 1).

569.   Settlement on termination of tenancy.

Any claim arising on the termination[1] of a tenancy of an agricultural holding[2] protected by the Agricultural Holdings Act 1986 may, and generally will, be settled by agreement between the parties or their respective agents; if, however, disputes which cannot be settled by agreement arise, they will be settled by arbitration or by third party determination under the Agricultural Holdings Act 1986[3].

1   As to the termination of an agricultural tenancy see PARA 428 note 1.
2   As to the meaning of 'agricultural holding' see PARA 423.
3   See the Agricultural Holdings Act 1986 ss 83(1), (1A) 84(1) (s 84(1) amended, and s 84(5) substituted, by SI 2006/2805; and the Agricultural Holdings Act 1986 s 83(1A) added by the Deregulation Act 2015 Sch 4 para 20(2)). As to arbitration and third party determinations see PARAS 566–568.

570.   Notice of arbitration claims.

Any claim for compensation under the Agricultural Holdings Act 1986 by the landlord[1] or the tenant[2] must be made before the expiration of two months from the termination of the tenancy[3] or the termination of occupation where a tenant lawfully remains in occupation[4] of part of a holding after the termination of the tenancy and the claim relates to that part[5]. This provision does not refer to cases where, under the contract of tenancy itself, for example in an express holdover clause, possession of one part of the holding must be given up at a different date from the rest; in such a case, the tenancy does not terminate until the later date[6].

The claim must be made by notice in writing[7]. Failure to serve the notice within the two month period will be fatal to the claim[8]. A condition in a tenancy agreement which reduces the time within which a claim must be made to some lesser period is void[9]. An indication of an intention to serve a notice is not sufficient[10].

1   As to the meaning of 'landlord' see PARA **423** note 7.
2   As to the meaning of 'tenant' see PARA **423** note 5.
3   As to the termination of an agricultural tenancy see PARA **428** note 1.
4   A mere right of access for the purpose of tending and removing a crop is not a continued occupation: *Coutts v Barclay-Harvey* 1956 SLT (Sh Ct) 54.
5   Agricultural Holdings Act 1986 s 83(2), (6). An arbitrator may not be appointed under s 84(2) (see PARA **567**) to determine a claim which has become enforceable by virtue of the service of a notice under s 83(2) above before the expiry of eight months from the termination of the tenancy: s 83(4) (substituted by the Deregulation Act 2015 Sch 4 para 20(3)). Although there is no provision for extending the eight month period by agreement, following the principles adopted by the House of Lords in *Kammins Ballroom Co Ltd v Zenith Investments (Torquay) Ltd* [1971] AC 850, [1970] 2 All ER 871, HL, it is submitted that the parties may agree to waive the eight month time limit.
6   The Agricultural Holdings Act 1986 s 83(6) refers to the continuation of occupation, a term to be used in contrast with legal possession. In *Swinburne v Andrews* [1923] 2 KB 483, CA, Bankes LJ expressed the opinion that the provision applied to the case where, after the termination of the tenancy, the tenant is allowed to remain in possession of part for a time. See also *Re Arden and Rutter* [1923] 2 KB 865, CA; *Coutts v Barclay-Harvey* 1956 SLT (Sh Ct) 54. Any holdover must be lawful; the Agricultural Holdings Act 1986 s 83(6) does not apply where the tenant has refused to vacate after the expiration of a notice to quit or the termination of the tenancy by other means.
7   Agricultural Holdings Act 1986 s 83(2). As to the service of notices see PARA **428** note 4.
8   Agricultural Holdings Act 1986 s 83(2).
9   *Cathcart v Chalmers* [1911] AC 246, HL.
10 *Lady Hallinan v Jones* [1984] 2 EGLR 20, 272 Estates Gazette 1081, County Court. In that case it was held that a notice served under the provision in the Agricultural Holdings Act 1948 now contained in the Agricultural Holdings Act 1986 s 72 (see PARAS **557–559**) that a claim for compensation for general deterioration of a holding must be given not later than one month before the termination of the tenancy satisfied the requirements of s 72(4) and s 83(2) so that there was no need to serve a separate notice under s 83(2) once the tenancy had actually terminated.

571. Contents of notice of claim.

The notice of an arbitration claim[1] must specify the nature of the claim being made by the landlord[2] or the tenant[3], although it is sufficient if the notice refers to the statutory provision, custom or term of an agreement under which the claim is made[4]. It is not, however, necessary to employ that method: the purpose of the notice of claim is to enable the party receiving it to know, in general terms, the nature of the claim[5]. Notices are not therefore to be construed with great strictness and are not invalidated by errors other than those calculated to mislead[6]. A notice may be framed in the alternative, leaving the claimant to elect at a later stage which of two mutually inconsistent claims he will pursue[7].

1   See PARA **570**.
2   As to the meaning of 'landlord' see PARA **423** note 7.
3   Agricultural Holdings Act 1986 s 83(3). As to the meaning of 'tenant' see PARA **423** note 5.
4   Agricultural Holdings Act 1986 s 83(3).
5   In *Lord Newborough v Davies* (1966) 116 NLJ 1291, a landlord served a written notice of claim headed 'Notice under Section 70 of the Agricultural Holdings Act 1948', which was supported by a schedule of details of the work necessary and the cost involved; it was held that the notice sufficiently specified the nature of the claim since it referred to the Agricultural Holdings Act 1948 s 70 (repealed) and the schedule obviously gave effect to s 70(2) (now the Agricultural Holdings Act 1986 s 83). See also *Re Hewetson and Pennington-Ramsden's Arbitration* (1966) 116 NLJ

613, County Court. For a comparison between the preliminary notice of intention to claim under the Agricultural Holdings Act 1986 s 83(2) and the subsequent statement of case to be delivered to the arbitrator see *ED & AD Cooke Bourne (Farms) Ltd v Mellows* [1983] QB 104, [1982] 2 All ER 208, CA.

6   *Frankland v Capstick* [1959] 1 All ER 209, [1959] 1 WLR 205, CA. As to the construction of notices generally see *Mannai Investment Co Ltd v Eagle Star Life Assurance Co Ltd* [1997] AC 749, [1997] 3 All ER 352, HL.

7   *Boyd v Wilton* [1957] 2 QB 277, [1957] 2 All ER 102, CA. The Agricultural Holdings Act 1923 s 16(2) (repealed) required 'particulars' of the claim to be given by the party claiming. In cases under that provision notices have been held to satisfy the requirement or not according to whether they gave the party against whom the claim was made fair notice of the claim against him: see *Spreckley v Leicestershire County Council* [1934] 1 KB 366; *Re O'Connor and Brewin's Arbitration* [1933] 1 KB 20. It has been suggested, by reference to the Scottish cases in particular, that a mere reference to the number of a clause in a tenancy agreement may be insufficient for specifying the nature of the claim: see *Simpson v Henderson* 1944 SC 365, Ct of Sess; *Adam v Smythe* 1948 SC 445, Ct of Sess; *Edinburgh Corpn v Gray* 1948 SC 538, Ct of Sess.

(ii) Recovery of Sum Due

572. Recovery by action.

Any sum agreed, awarded or determined by third party determination under the Agricultural Holdings Act 1986 to be paid by way of compensation, costs or otherwise by a landlord[1] or a tenant[2], if not paid within 14 days after the payment becomes due, may be recovered, except as otherwise provided[3], upon an order made by the County Court as if it were payable under an order of that court[4].

1   As to the meaning of 'landlord' see PARA 423 note 7.
2   As to the meaning of 'tenant' see PARA 423 note 5.
3   See the Agricultural Holdings Act 1986 s 85(3) (sums not recoverable against a trustee landlord personally); and PARA 574.
4   Agricultural Holdings Act 1986 s 85(1) (amended by the Deregulation Act 2015 Sch 4 para 22). The correctness of the decision in *Horrell v Lord St John of Bletso* [1928] 2 KB 616, that the similar provision in the Agricultural Holdings Act 1923 s 19 (repealed) did not preclude recovery in the High Court where the sum involved was in excess of that ordinarily recovered in the county court, was doubted in *Jones v Pembrokeshire County Council* [1967] 1 QB 181, [1966] 1 All ER 1027 (applying *Re Jones and Carter's Arbitration* [1922] 2 Ch 599, CA). As to the satisfaction of county court judgments see the County Courts Act 1984 s 71; and CIVIL PROCEDURE vol 12A (2015) PARA 1272.

573. Tenant's charge for compensation.

Where a sum becomes due to a tenant[1] as compensation[2] from the landlord[3] and the landlord fails to discharge his liability within one month from the date on which the sum becomes due, the tenant is entitled to obtain from the Secretary of State or the Welsh Ministers[4] an order charging the holding with payment of the amount due[5].

1   As to the meaning of 'tenant' see PARA 423 note 5.
2   The provision does not extend to 'costs or otherwise', the phrase used in the Agricultural Holdings Act 1986 s 85(1) (see PARA 572) or 'any sum agreed or awarded' under the Act, the phrase used in s 85(3)(a) (see PARA 574).
3   As to the meaning of 'landlord' see PARA 423 note 7.
4   As to the Secretary of State and the Welsh Ministers see PARA 741.
5   Agricultural Holdings Act 1986 s 85(2).

574. Recovery where landlord not beneficial owner.

Where a landlord[1] of an agricultural holding[2] is entitled to receive the rents and profits otherwise than for his own benefit, whether as trustee or otherwise, he is not liable to pay any sum agreed or awarded under the Agricultural Holdings Act

1986 to be paid to the tenant[3] or awarded under that Act to be paid by the landlord, and it is not recoverable from him personally[4]. If such a landlord fails to pay any sum agreed or awarded under the Agricultural Holdings Act 1986 payable by the landlord to the tenant within one month after the payment becomes due, the tenant may obtain from the Secretary of State or the Welsh Ministers[5] an order charging the holding with payment of the sum due[6]. Where a landlord entitled so to receive the rents and profits proposes to pay or pays to the tenant the sum due, he is himself entitled, either before or after making a payment, to obtain from the Secretary of State or the Welsh Ministers an order charging the holding with the repayment of that sum[7].

1 As to the meaning of 'landlord' see PARA 423 note 7.
2 As to the meaning of 'agricultural holding' see PARA 423.
3 As to the meaning of 'tenant' see PARA 423 note 5.
4 Agricultural Holdings Act 1986 s 85(3)(a).
5 As to the Secretary of State and the Welsh Ministers see PARA 741.
6 Agricultural Holdings Act 1986 s 85(3)(b).
7 Agricultural Holdings Act 1986 s 86(3) (amended by the Deregulation Act 2015 Sch 4 para 23(3)).

575. Landlord's charge for repayment.

Where a landlord[1] of an agricultural holding[2] governed by the Agricultural Holdings Act 1986 has paid to the tenant[3] the amount due to him, whether under the Agricultural Holdings Act 1986, custom, agreement or otherwise, in respect of compensation for an improvement[4] or for specified tenant-right matters[5] or for disturbance[6], or where the landlord has defrayed the costs of executing a long term improvement[7], having elected to do so[8] following a tenant's application to Tribunal[9] for approval[10], he may obtain an order from the Secretary of State or the Welsh Ministers[11] charging the holding or any part of it with repayment of the amount of compensation or cost[12].

1 As to the meaning of 'landlord' see PARA 423 note 7.
2 As to the meaning of 'agricultural holding' see PARA 423.
3 As to the meaning of 'tenant' see PARA 423 note 5.
4 Ie an improvement falling within the Agricultural Holdings Act 1986 s 64(1) (see PARAS 528–529) or Sch 9 Pt I para 1 (see PARA 522).
5 Ie the matters specified in the Agricultural Holdings Act 1986 Sch 8 paras 7–11 (see PARA 530).
6 Agricultural Holdings Act 1986 s 86(1)(a).
7 Ie of a kind specified in the Agricultural Holdings Act 1986 Sch 7 paras 9–28 (see PARA 529).
8 Ie under the Agricultural Holdings Act 1986 s 67(5) (see PARA 536).
9 Ie in England, the First-tier Tribunal (see PARA 768) and in Wales, the Agricultural Land Tribunal for Wales (see PARA 767): see PARA 437 note 1.
10 Agricultural Holdings Act 1986 s 86(1)(b).
11 As to the Secretary of State and the Welsh Ministers see PARA 741.
12 Agricultural Holdings Act 1986 s 86(1). As to the right of a landlord entitled to receive rents and profits as trustee or otherwise to obtain a charge for sums paid to the tenant see PARA 574. As to the charging of church and charity lands see PARA 582.

576. Exclusion of liability for tenancy determination where charge made.

Notwithstanding anything in any deed, will or other instrument to the contrary, where the estate or interest in an agricultural holding[1] of the landlord[2] is determinable or liable to forfeiture by reason of his creating or suffering any charge on it, that estate or interest will not be determined or forfeited by reason that the tenant[3] obtains a charge on the holding for payment of compensation due[4] or that the landlord obtains a charge[5] on the holding for the repayment of compensation paid by him to the tenant or of the cost of improvements which he has the right to carry out in place of the tenant[6].

1 As to the meaning of 'agricultural holding' see PARA 423.
2 As to the meaning of 'landlord' see PARA 423 note 7.
3 As to the meaning of 'tenant' see PARA 423 note 5.
4 Ie under the Agricultural Holdings Act 1986 s 85(2) (see PARA 573).
5 Ie under the Agricultural Holdings Act 1986 s 86(1) (see PARA 575).
6 Agricultural Holdings Act 1986 s 87(5).

577. Matters included in charging orders.

An order made by the Secretary of State or the Welsh Ministers[1] charging an agricultural holding[2] or part of it with payment or repayment of a sum must also charge it with payment of all costs properly incurred in obtaining the charge[3]. Such an order must be made in favour of the person obtaining the charge and his executors, administrators and assigns, and must make such provision for the payment of interest and for the payment of the sum charged by instalments, and contain such directions for giving effect to the charge, as the Secretary of State or the Welsh Ministers may think fit[4].

1 As to the Secretary of State and the Welsh Ministers see PARA 741.
2 As to the meaning of 'agricultural holding' see PARA 423.
3 Agricultural Holdings Act 1986 s 87(1).
4 Agricultural Holdings Act 1986 s 87(2).

578. Payment and extent of charge.

In the case of a charge in favour of the landlord[1], where he is not the absolute owner for his own benefit, no instalment or interest may be made payable after the time when the improvement will, in the opinion of the Secretary of State or the Welsh Ministers[2], have become exhausted[3]. A charge for the repayment of compensation paid by him to the tenant[4], or for the cost of improvements which he has the right to carry out in place of the tenant[5], will bind not only the landlord, but all successors in title; however, if the landlord himself has a leasehold interest, the charge will not extend beyond the interest of the landlord, his executors, administrators and assigns[6].

1 As to the meaning of 'landlord' see PARA 423 note 7.
2 As to the Secretary of State and the Welsh Ministers see PARA 741.
3 Agricultural Holdings Act 1986 s 87(4).
4 As to the meaning of 'tenant' see PARA 423 note 5.
5 Ie under the Agricultural Holdings Act 1986 s 86 (see PARAS 574–575).
6 Agricultural Holdings Act 1986 s 87(3).

579. Registration and priority of charges.

A charge made by the Secretary of State or the Welsh Ministers[1] under the enforcement provisions of the Agricultural Holdings Act 1986[2] is registrable[3]. If not registered before the completion of a purchase it will be void against a purchaser for value of the land charged[4]. A tenant's[5] charge for compensation due from the landlord[6], a tenant's charge in respect of sums agreed or awarded to be paid where the landlord receives the rent and profits otherwise than for his own benefit[7], and an occupier's charge for compensation or for costs connected therewith where the contract of tenancy is not binding on the mortgagee[8], rank in priority to any other charge however and whenever created or arising, and, as between themselves, rank in the order of their creation and not in the order of their registration under the Land Charges Act 1972[9]. These provisions bind the Crown[10].

1   As to the Secretary of State and the Welsh Ministers see PARA 741.
2   Ie the Agricultural Holdings Act 1986 ss 85, 86 (see PARAS 572–575).
3   In the case of unregistered land it is registrable as a land charge Class A: Land Charges Act 1972 s 2(1), (2)(b), Sch 2 paras 1(g), (i), 3 (amended by the Agricultural Holdings Act 1986 Sch 14 para 51, Sch 15 Pt I). See REAL PROPERTY AND REGISTRATION vol 87 (2017) PARA 664. As to registration of a land charge in the case of registered land see REAL PROPERTY AND REGISTRATION vol 87 (2017) PARA 641 et seq.
4   Land Charges Act 1972 s 4(2).
5   As to the meaning of 'tenant' see PARA 423 note 5.
6   Ie a charge under the Agricultural Holdings Act 1986 s 85(2) (see PARA 573). As to the meaning of 'landlord' see PARA 423 note 7.
7   Ie a charge under the Agricultural Holdings Act 1986 s 85(3) (see PARA 574).
8   Ie under the Agricultural Holdings Act 1948 ss 66, 74 (repealed).
9   Agricultural Holdings Act 1986 s 87(6).
10 Agricultural Holdings Act 1986 s 87(8).

580.   Assignment of charge.

Any company incorporated by Parliament, and having power to advance money for the improvement of land[1], may take an assignment of any charge obtained by a tenant[2] for compensation due from his landlord[3] or by a landlord for compensation paid or expenses in executing improvements[4], upon any terms that may be agreed between the parties, and may also assign any charge so acquired by it[5].

1   See PARA 600 et seq.
2   As to the meaning of 'tenant' see PARA 423 note 5.
3   Ie a charge under the Agricultural Holdings Act 1986 s 85(2) (see PARA 573). As to the meaning of 'landlord' see PARA 423 note 7.
4   Ie under the Agricultural Holdings Act 1986 s 86(1) (see PARA 575).
5   Agricultural Holdings Act 1986 s 87(7).

(9) SPECIAL CATEGORIES OF LAND OR LANDLORD

581.   Crown and Duchy land.

With one exception[1], the Agricultural Holdings Act 1986 applies to land belonging to the Crown[2] and the Duchies of Lancaster and Cornwall[3] and also to land where the landlord[4] or tenant[5] is a government department holding on behalf of the Crown, subject to such modifications as may be prescribed[6].

Compensation payable by the Chancellor of the Duchy of Lancaster for long term improvements[7] must be raised and paid as an expense incurred in improvement of land belonging to Her Majesty in right of the Duchy[8], whereas additional compensation for disturbance[9] or compensation on termination of a tenancy[10] through early resumption[11] may be so paid[12]. Compensation payable for short term improvements and tenant-right matters[13] must be paid out of the annual revenues of the Duchy. Special provisions also apply in relation to compensation payable by the Duke of Cornwall or other possessor for the time being of the Duchy of Cornwall. Compensation for long term improvements must, and additional compensation for disturbance and compensation on termination through early resumption[14] may, be paid and advances made for this purpose, subject to the provisions[15] with respect to land improvement in the Duchy of Cornwall[16].

1   Ie the Agricultural Holdings Act 1986 s 11 (see PARA 437) which relates to the provision of fixed equipment necessary to comply with statutory requirements.
2   As to the Crown Estate see CROWN AND CROWN PROCEEDINGS vol 29 (2014) PARA 192 et seq.
3   As to the Duchies of Lancaster and Cornwall see CROWN AND CROWN PROCEEDINGS vol 29 (2014) PARAS 214–267. As to officers who represent the Crown or the Duchy as landlords see the Agricultural Holdings Act 1986 s 95(2).
4   As to the meaning of 'landlord' see PARA 423 note 7.
5   As to the meaning of 'tenant' see PARA 423 note 5.
6   Agricultural Holdings Act 1986 s 95(1), (3). Modifications may be prescribed by regulations. At the date at which this volume states the law no modifications had been prescribed. As to the making of regulations generally see PARA 432 note 5.
7   Ie relevant improvements specified in the Agricultural Holdings Act 1986 Sch 7 (see PARA 529), improvements falling within Sch 9 Pt I para 1 (see PARA 522) and improvements specified in Sch 10 (see PARA 561): s 95(7).
8   Ie within the Duchy of Lancaster Act 1817 s 25.
9   Ie under the Agricultural Holdings Act 1986 s 60(2)(b) (see PARA 545).
10   As to the termination of an agricultural tenancy see PARA 428 note 1.
11   Ie under the Agricultural Holdings Act 1986 s 62 (see PARA 551).
12   Agricultural Holdings Act 1986 s 95(4).
13   Ie relevant improvements specified in the Agricultural Holdings Act 1986 Sch 8 paras 1–6 (see PARA 529) and such matters as are specified in Sch 8 paras 7–11 (see PARA 530): s 95(7).
14   See the text and notes 10, 11.
15   Ie the Duchy of Cornwall Management Act 1863 s 8.
16   Agricultural Holdings Act 1986 s 95(5). This is without prejudice to the operation of the Duchy of Cornwall Management Act 1982: Agricultural Holdings Act 1986 s 95(6).

582. Church and charity land.

The rights of a landlord[1] of an agricultural holding[2] to obtain an order charging land[3] may not be exercised by trustees for ecclesiastical or charitable purposes except with the approval in writing of the Charity Commission[4].

1   As to the meaning of 'landlord' see PARA 423 note 7.
2   As to the meaning of 'agricultural holding' see PARA 423.
3   See PARA 575.
4   Agricultural Holdings Act 1986 s 86(4) (amended by the Charities Act 2006 Sch 8 para 79).

583. Landlord with limited interest.

The landlord[1] of an agricultural holding[2] may give any consent or enter into any agreement which he could have done as a freeholder, or, where his interest is an interest in a leasehold, as if he were entitled to the leasehold, even though he has a more limited interest in the land[3].

Specified improvements[4] are deemed to be improvements authorised by the Settled Land Act 1925[5], and where capital money is applied for such improvements, the money so expended will not have to be repaid out of income[6].

Capital money may also be applied in some circumstances for repairs of fixed equipment without the need to repay out of income where the trustees are satisfied, after taking professional advice, that there is a legal obligation to carry out the works and that they are properly executed at a reasonable cost[7]. The tenant for life cannot be repaid out of capital money sums paid to tenants of agricultural holdings upon the termination of their tenancies[8]. The tenant for life can obtain a charge for compensation paid by him to the tenant[9] of an agricultural holding for improvements, tenant-right or disturbance[10].

Whether a charge obtained by a landlord[11] may be redeemed or discharged out of capital money will depend upon whether it comes within the relevant provisions of the Settled Land Act 1925: it must be an improvement created on a holding under the Agricultural Holdings Act 1986 or any similar previous enactment[12]. The word 'improvement' would cover long term and short term improvements begun on or after 1 March 1948[13] for which compensation is payable[14], and market garden improvements[15], but not tenant-right matters[16] or disturbance[17].

1   As to the meaning of 'landlord' see PARA 423 note 7.
2   As to the meaning of 'agricultural holding' see PARA 423.
3   Agricultural Holdings Act 1986 s 88.
4   Ie long term improvements begun on or after 1 March 1948 for which compensation is payable (see the Agricultural Holdings Act 1986 Sch 7; and PARA 529).
5   Ie authorised by the Settled Land Act 1925 Sch 3 Pt I (see SETTLEMENTS vol 91 (2012) PARA 717).
6   Agricultural Holdings Act 1986 s 89(1) (amended by the Trusts of Land and Appointment of Trustees Act 1996 Sch 4); Settled Land Act 1925 s 73(1)(iv) (amended by the Agricultural Holdings Act 1986 Sch 14 para 11).
7   *Re Duke of Northumberland, Halifax v Northumberland* [1951] Ch 202, [1950] 2 All ER 1181; *Re Sutherland's Settlement Trusts* [1953] Ch 792, [1953] 2 All ER 27; *Re Lord Brougham and Vaux's Settled Estates* [1954] Ch 24, [1953] 2 All ER 655; *Re Wynn, Public Trustee v Newborough* [1955] 2 All ER 865, [1955] 1 WLR 940; *Re Boston's Will Trusts, Inglis v Boston* [1956] Ch 395, [1956] 1 All ER 593; *Re Pelly, Ransome v Pelly* [1957] Ch 1, [1956] 2 All ER 326, CA.
8   *Re Duke of Wellington's Parliamentary Estates* [1972] Ch 374, [1971] 2 All ER 1140.
9   As to the meaning of 'tenant' see PARA 423 note 5.
10 See the Agricultural Holdings Act 1986 s 83; and PARAS 566–571. See also *Re Duke of Wellington's Parliamentary Estates* [1972] Ch 374, [1971] 2 All ER 1140.
11 See PARA 573.
12 Settled Land Act 1925 s 73(1)(ii) (amended by the Finance Act 1963 Sch 11 Pt VI; and the Agricultural Holdings Act 1986 Sch 14 para 11).
13 The date mentioned in the text is the date on which the Agriculture Act 1947 Pt III (repealed), from which these provisions are derived, was brought into force: see s 111(2) (repealed); and the Agriculture Act 1947 (Commencement) (No 1) Order 1948, SI 1948/342.
14 Ie improvements specified in the Agricultural Holdings Act 1986 Sch 7, Sch 8 paras 1–6 (see PARA 529).
15 Ie the improvements specified in the Agricultural Holdings Act 1986 Sch 10 (see PARA 561 note 16). As to the meaning of 'market garden' see PARA 424 note 4.
16 Ie the matters specified in the Agricultural Holdings Act 1986 Sch 8 paras 7–11 (see PARA 530).
17 See PARA 544.

584. Leases required to be at best rent.

Limited owners, such as a tenant for life, are sometimes required by an Act[1], deed or other instrument authorising a tenancy to be made, to ensure that they obtain the best rent. In the case of an agricultural holding[2] let under the provisions of the Agricultural Holdings Act 1986, in establishing rent, or a reservation in the nature of a rent, it is not necessary to take into account against the tenant[3] any increase in the value of the holding arising from any improvements made or paid for by him[4].

1   See eg the Settled Land Act 1925 s 42 (leases by tenant for life: see SETTLEMENTS vol 91 (2012) PARA 740).
2   As to the meaning of 'agricultural holding' see PARA 423.
3   As to the meaning of 'tenant' see PARA 423 note 5.
4   Agricultural Holdings Act 1986 s 90.

585. Mortgagor landlord.

A mortgagor in possession may grant agricultural or occupation leases for any term not exceeding 50 years subject to any contrary intention expressed in the mortgage deed or by a separate document in writing[1]. However, any power to grant such leases cannot be excluded or restricted in any mortgage of agricultural land made after 1 March 1948[2] but before 1 September 1995[3] nor where a mortgage is made on or after 1 September 1995 but[4] the lease is governed by the Agricultural Holdings Act 1986[5].

1   See the Law of Property Act 1925 s 99(1), (13); and MORTGAGE vol 77 (2016) PARA 348 et seq.
2   Ie the date on which the Agriculture Act 1947 Pt III (repealed) was brought into force: see s 111(2) (repealed); and the Agriculture Act 1947 (Commencement) (No 1) Order 1948, SI 1948/342.
3   Ie the date on which the Agricultural Tenancies Act 1995 was brought into force: see s 41(2); and PARA 401.
4   Ie by virtue of the Agricultural Tenancies Act 1995 s 4 (see PARAS 421–422).
5   See the Law of Property Act 1925 s 99(13A); and MORTGAGE vol 77 (2016) PARA 350.

(10) BANKRUPTCY OF TENANT

586. Continued farming by trustee in bankruptcy of agricultural tenant.

Where the trustee in bankruptcy[1] of a yearly tenant of an agricultural holding carries on the farming for the benefit of the creditors, and at the determination of the tenancy claims compensation from the landlord due under the Agricultural Holdings Act 1986, or under custom or agreement, the landlord may not set off against the amount of such compensation rent which was due from the tenant before the bankruptcy[2]. However, if a custom of the country is proved for the landlord to deduct from the tenant's claims for compensation all arrears of rent, the custom will prevail notwithstanding the bankruptcy of the tenant[3].

1   See generally BANKRUPTCY AND INDIVIDUAL INSOLVENCY vol 5 (2013) PARA 314 et seq. As to the disentitlement of a tenant of an agricultural holding to serve a counter-notice on the landlord after receiving a notice to quit given on the grounds of the tenant's bankruptcy or compounding with his creditors see PARA 479. As to the right of a tenant of a holding let or treated as a market garden to compensation for improvement under the Evesham custom where notice to quit is given on those grounds see PARA 563.
2   *Alloway v Steere* (1882) 10 QBD 22, DC.
3   *Re Wilson, ex p Lord Hastings* (1893) 62 LJQB 628.

587. Forfeiture on tenant's bankruptcy: effect on covenant to consume fodder.

Where there is an absolute covenant by a tenant for a term of years not to sell or remove the hay and straw, but to consume the same on the holding, and also to leave on the holding unconsumed all fodder grown in the last year of the term, on being paid for the same by valuation, then if the tenancy is forfeited on the bankruptcy of the tenant for breach of condition, and the landlord re-enters and forfeits the tenancy, the landlord is not bound by the stipulation to pay for the unconsumed hay and straw[1].

1   *Silcock v Farmer* (1882) 46 LT 404, CA; but see *Re Morrish, ex p Hart Dyke* (1882) 22 Ch D 410, CA.

588. Disclaimer by tenant's trustee in bankruptcy.

The trustee in bankruptcy of a tenant has power to disclaim the tenancy[1]. If a trustee in bankruptcy of a tenant sells hay, etc, off the holding without returning manure as required by the custom of the country or by the terms of the contract of tenancy, and then disclaims the tenancy, he becomes personally liable to the landlord for his wrongful act[2].

In the absence of any order of the court dealing with such matter, when the trustee in bankruptcy of a tenant disclaims the tenancy he is not entitled to be paid for fallows, etc[3], or entitled to the benefit of any of the provisions in the tenancy which were to come into effect upon the expiration or sooner determination of the tenancy[4], nor, in such cases, may he claim compensation for unexhausted improvements under custom or statute[5].

If a trustee in bankruptcy of a tenant disclaims the tenancy, the court may make such orders with respect to fixtures, tenant's improvements and other matters arising out of the tenancy as the court thinks just[6].

1 See the Insolvency Act 1986 s 315; and BANKRUPTCY AND INDIVIDUAL INSOLVENCY vol 5 (2013) PARA 490 et seq.
2 *Schofield v Hincks* (1888) 58 LJQB 147.
3 See PARA 451.
4 *Re Morrish, ex p Hart Dyke* (1882) 22 Ch D 410, CA.
5 *Schofield v Hincks* (1888) 58 LJQB 147; *Re Wadsley, Bettinson's Representative v Trustee* (1925) 94 LJ Ch 215.
6 See the Insolvency Act 1986 s 317(2) (which provides for the court to make the orders where the court gives a direction that the disclaimer is to take effect); and BANKRUPTCY AND INDIVIDUAL INSOLVENCY vol 5 (2013) PARA 499.

589. Concept of reputed ownership abolished.

The doctrine of reputed ownership has been abolished by the omission of the words 'goods in the reputed ownership of the bankrupt'[1] from the definition of the bankrupt's estate in the Insolvency Act 1986[2].

1 See eg the Bankruptcy Act 1914 s 38(c) (repealed).
2 See the Insolvency Act 1986 s 283; and BANKRUPTCY AND INDIVIDUAL INSOLVENCY vol 5 (2013) PARA 211.

3. COMPULSORY ACQUISITION OF AGRICULTURAL LAND

(1) TENANCIES GOVERNED BY THE AGRICULTURAL TENANCIES ACT 1995

590. Compensation for displacement payable by acquiring authority.

Where land[1] is used for the purposes of agriculture and is so used by way of a trade or business, or is not so used but is comprised in a farm business tenancy[2] and used for the purposes of a trade or business, and the person carrying on the trade or business is displaced from the land because an interest in it is compulsorily acquired or sold by agreement to an authority possessing compulsory purchase powers[3], the acquiring authority[4] may pay to that person such reasonable allowance as it thinks fit towards his removal expenses and the loss which, in its opinion[5], he will sustain by reason of the resulting disturbance of his trade or business[6].

1   As to the meaning of 'land' see the Land Compensation Act 1961 s 39(1); and COMPULSORY ACQUISITION OF LAND vol 18 (2009) PARA 516; definition applied by the Agriculture (Miscellaneous Provisions) Act 1963 s 22(4).
2   As to the meaning of 'farm business tenancy' see PARA 402.
3   As to the meaning of 'authority possessing compulsory purchase powers' see the Land Compensation Act 1961 s 39(1); and COMPULSORY ACQUISITION OF LAND vol 18 (2009) PARA 763; definition applied by the Agriculture (Miscellaneous Provisions) Act 1963 s 22(4).
4   As to the meaning of 'acquiring authority' see the Land Compensation Act 1961 s 39(1); and COMPULSORY ACQUISITION OF LAND vol 18 (2009) PARA 622; definition applied by the Agriculture (Miscellaneous Provisions) Act 1963 s 22(5).
5   In estimating the loss the authority must have regard to the period for which the land might reasonably have been expected to be available for the purpose of the trade or business, and to the availability of other land suitable for that purpose: Agriculture (Miscellaneous Provisions) Act 1963 s 22(2).
6   Agriculture (Miscellaneous Provisions) Act 1963 s 22(1) (amended by the Agricultural Tenancies Act 1995 Schedule para 21(2)). These provisions have effect without prejudice to the operation of any other enactment authorising the making of payments to persons displaced from any land: Agriculture (Miscellaneous Provisions) Act 1963 s 22(3).

(2) TENANCIES GOVERNED BY THE AGRICULTURAL HOLDINGS ACT 1986

591. Additional payments in consequence of compulsory acquisition of agricultural holdings governed by the Agricultural Holdings Act 1986.

Where in pursuance of any enactment providing for the acquiring or taking of possession[1] of land compulsorily an acquiring authority[2] acquires from the tenant[3] the interest in an agricultural holding[4] or any part of an agricultural holding governed by the Agricultural Holdings Act 1986[5], or takes possession of the holding or any part of it, additional compensation[6] is payable, subject to specified limitations[7], as if the acquiring authority were the landlord[8] and compensation for disturbance had become payable[9], subject to supplementary provisions relating to assessment and payment of compensation[10].

Compensation payable to a tenant under the Land Compensation Act 1973 is to be assessed without regard to the right of the landlord to give notice to quit or any notice to quit already served by the landlord on the ground of the acquiring authority's intention to use the land[11]. It is provided that in any event compensation must be reduced by any amount received as additional payment on compulsory acquisition[12], but must not be less than the sums to which the tenant would be so entitled[13]. If the acquiring authority serves notice to treat or notice of entry on part of the holding there is power for the tenant to serve a counter-notice enlarging the acquiring authority's notice[14].

Where a tenant receives notice to quit from his landlord whose interest is being compulsorily acquired and the notice is given on the ground that the land is no longer required for agricultural use, the tenant may elect to claim compensation from the acquiring authority as if no notice to quit had been served (instead of claiming against the landlord)[15].

Occupier's loss payment may also be available[16].

1 'Possession' means actual possession: Agriculture (Miscellaneous Provisions) Act 1968 s 17(1).
2 An 'acquiring authority' is any person authorised by any enactment to acquire or take possession of land compulsorily: Agriculture (Miscellaneous Provisions) Act 1968 ss 12(1), 17(1).
3 As to the meaning of 'tenant' see PARA 423 note 5. For these purposes a tenant of an agricultural holding is treated as not being a tenant of it in so far as, immediately before the acquiring of the interest or the taking of possession, he was neither in possession nor entitled to take possession of any land comprised in the holding; and, in determining whether a tenant was so entitled, any agreement under the Agricultural Holdings Act 1986 s 2(2) (see PARA 427) which relates to the land and has not taken effect as an agreement for a tenancy from year to year must be disregarded: Agriculture (Miscellaneous Provisions) Act 1968 s 13(1) (amended by the Agricultural Holdings Act 1986 Sch 14 para 45). Accordingly, neither a tenant who has sub-let nor a tenant under a grazing agreement or a consent tenancy pursuant to the Agricultural Holdings Act 1986 s 2 (see PARA 427) would be so entitled.
4 As to the meaning of 'agricultural holding' see PARA 423.
5 No sum is payable by virtue of these provisions in respect of any land comprised in a farm business tenancy under the Agricultural Tenancies Act 1995 (see PARA 401 et seq): Agriculture (Miscellaneous Provisions) Act 1968 s 12(1A) (added by the Agricultural Tenancies Act 1995 Schedule para 23). As to compensation for displacement in respect of a farm business tenancy see PARA 590.
6 Ie compensation under the Agricultural Holdings Act 1986 s 60(2)(b), (4) (see PARA 545).
7 See the text and notes 11–16; and PARA 592.
8 As to the meaning of 'landlord' see PARA 423 note 7.
9 Agriculture (Miscellaneous Provisions) Act 1968 s 12(1) (amended by the Agricultural Holdings Act 1986 Sch 14 para 44).
10 See the Agriculture (Miscellaneous Provisions) Act 1968 Sch 3 (amended by the Agricultural Holdings Act 1986 Sch 13 para 3, Sch 14 para 48; and the Housing and Planning Act 2016 Sch 16 para 8). Disputes as to compensation are to be referred to and are determinable by the Upper Tribunal: Agriculture (Miscellaneous Provisions) Act 1968 Sch 3 para 1. The Agricultural Holdings Act 1986 refers to the Lands Tribunal but this tribunal has been abolished and its functions have been transferred to the Upper Tribunal see COMPULSORY ACQUISITION OF LAND vol 18 (2009) PARA 720 et seq. Where the sum to be paid as additional compensation by the acquiring authority could otherwise fall to be ascertained by reference to a rent at a rate which was not determined by arbitration and the authority considers it to be unduly high, it may apply to the Upper Tribunal to have the rent considered: Sch 3 para 2 (as so amended). Where, on such an application, the tribunal is satisfied that the rent is not substantially higher than the rent which would be determined for the holding on an arbitration under the Agricultural Holdings Act 1986 s 12 (see PARA 438) at the date of the application or, if it is substantially higher, it was not fixed by the parties to the tenancy contract with a view to increasing any compensation or additional sum payable on compulsory acquisition or the taking of possession of any land included in the holding, it must dismiss the application: Agriculture (Miscellaneous Provisions) Act 1968 Sch 3 para 3 (as so amended). The provisions of the Land Compensation Act 1961 Pt I (ss 1–4) and s 32, the Compulsory Purchase Act 1965 ss 6, 9, 11, 12, 20(4), (5), 22(1)–(3), (5), 26, Sch 1 paras 6–8, 10, Sch 2, and of the Lands Clauses Acts or other enactments corresponding to those provisions of the Compulsory Purchase Act 1965 apply with necessary modifications and adaptations to the

acquisition of the interest or the taking of possession under these provisions: Agriculture (Miscellaneous Provisions) Act 1968 Sch 3 paras 4, 5 (as so amended). See COMPULSORY ACQUISITION OF LAND.

11 See the Land Compensation Act 1973 s 48(3); and COMPULSORY ACQUISITION OF LAND vol 18 (2009) PARA 807. This effectively reverses the decision in *Rugby Joint Water Board v Foottit* [1973] AC 202, [1972] 1 All ER 1057, HL, a case in which it was held that, where a landlord was entitled to serve (under what is now the Agricultural Holdings Act 1986 Sch 3, Case B (see PARA 475)) notice to quit in respect of land acquired either by the landlord or by the authority with compulsory purchase powers, the compensation was to be assessed on the basis that the tenancy was unprotected and the landlord was entitled to obtain vacant possession on the expiration of the notice to quit.

12 Ie under the Agriculture (Miscellaneous Provisions) Act 1968 s 12.

13 See the Land Compensation Act 1973 s 48(5), (6); and COMPULSORY ACQUISITION OF LAND vol 18 (2009) PARA 807.

14 See the Land Compensation Act 1973 ss 53, 55; and COMPULSORY ACQUISITION OF LAND vol 18 (2009) PARAS 622, 703.

15 See the Land Compensation Act 1973 s 59; and COMPULSORY ACQUISITION OF LAND vol 18 (2009) PARA 824. This covers the position where the tenant has received notice to quit from a landlord whose interest is being compulsorily acquired and the notice is given on the ground that the land is required for non-agricultural use. Whereas before the enactment of s 59 the tenant could only proceed against the landlord for compensation under the Agricultural Holdings Act 1948 and the Agriculture (Miscellaneous Provisions) Act 1968, it is now open to him to elect to claim compensation from the acquiring authority as if no notice to quit had been served. If such an election is made, no claim can be made against the landlord.

16 See the Land Compensation Act 1973 ss 33A–33K; PARA 594; and COMPULSORY ACQUISITION OF LAND.

592. Exceptions where no additional payment is made in consequence of compulsory acquisition of agricultural holdings governed by the Agricultural Holdings Act 1986.

The provisions for additional payments in consequence of the compulsory acquisition or taking of possession of agricultural holdings governed by the Agricultural Holdings Act 1986[1] do not apply in respect of an agricultural holding[2] held on a tenancy for a term of two years or upwards[3]. By way of exception, these provisions do apply in a case where the amount of compensation payable to the tenant[4] of the holding by the acquiring authority[5] in consequence of the acquisition or taking of possession[6] in question is exceeded by the aggregate of the amounts which, if the tenancy had been from year to year, would have been so payable by way of compensation and by virtue of those provisions[7]. In any such case the sum payable by virtue of those provisions in consequence of the acquisition or taking of possession in question is, subject to a contrary determination by the Upper Tribunal[8], to be an amount equal to the excess[9].

No sum is payable[10] to the tenant of an agricultural holding in consequence of an acquiring of an interest or taking of possession unless the date on which the acquisition or taking of possession occurs is later than 3 July 1968[11] and:

(1)   in the case of such an acquisition, unless the date on which notice to treat in respect of the interest to be acquired is served or treated as served on the tenant by the acquiring authority after the initial date[12]; and

(2)   where in the case of such a taking of possession prior notice of the taking of possession is by virtue of any enactment required to be served on the tenant by the acquiring authority, unless the date on which the notice is so served is after the initial date[13].

In addition, the compensation provisions[14] do not apply where the acquiring authority requires the land comprised in the agricultural holding or part in question for the purposes of agricultural research or experiment or of demonstrating agricultural methods or for the purposes of the enactments relating to smallholdings[15]; however, where an acquiring authority exercises in relation to any land any power to acquire or take possession of land compulsorily which is conferred on the authority for certain purposes[16], the authority is deemed not to require the land for any of the purposes mentioned above[17].

If a person is entitled in respect of the same interest in land to a payment both by virtue of the compensation provisions[18] and under the statutory provisions concerned with additional loss payments for agricultural land[19], only one payment may be made[20].

1 Ie the provisions of the Agriculture (Miscellaneous Provisions) Act 1968 s 12(1) (see PARA **591**). No sum is payable by virtue of those provisions in respect of any land comprised in a farm business tenancy under the Agricultural Tenancies Act 1995: see PARA **591** note 5.
2 As to the meaning of 'agricultural holding' see PARA **423**.
3 Agriculture (Miscellaneous Provisions) Act 1968 s 12(2).
4 As to the meaning of 'tenant' see PARA **423** note 5.
5 As to the meaning of 'acquiring authority' see PARA **591** note 2.
6 As to the meaning of 'possession' see PARA **591** note 1.
7 Agriculture (Miscellaneous Provisions) Act 1968 s 12(2).
8 Ie a determination under the Agriculture (Miscellaneous Provisions) Act 1968 Sch 3 (see PARA **591**). Schedule 3 refers to the Lands Tribunal but this tribunal has been abolished and its functions transferred to the Upper Tribunal see COMPULSORY ACQUISITION OF LAND vol 18 (2009) PARA **720** et seq.
9 Agriculture (Miscellaneous Provisions) Act 1968 s 12(2).
10 Ie by virtue of the Agriculture (Miscellaneous Provisions) Act 1968 s 12(1) (see PARA **591**).
11 Ie the date on which the Agriculture (Miscellaneous Provisions) Act 1968 received Royal Assent.
12 Agriculture (Miscellaneous Provisions) Act 1968 s 12(3)(a). The 'initial date' is 1 November 1967: s 17(1).
13 Agriculture (Miscellaneous Provisions) Act 1968 s 12(3)(b).
14 See note 1.
15 As to the enactments relating to smallholdings see PARAS **627–648**.
16 Ie conferred by virtue of the Town and Country Planning Act 1990 s 226 or s 230 (see PLANNING vol 83 (2010) PARAS **1112–1113, 1116**) or the New Towns Act 1981 s 10 (see PLANNING vol 83 (2010) PARAS **1504, 1506**).
17 Agriculture (Miscellaneous Provisions) Act 1968 s 13(2) (amended by the New Towns Act 1981 Sch 12 para 4; and the Planning (Consequential Provisions) Act 1990 Sch 2 para 19).
18 See note 1.
19 Ie the Land Compensation Act 1973 s 33B (see COMPULSORY ACQUISITION OF LAND).
20 Agriculture (Miscellaneous Provisions) Act 1968 s 12(4) (added by the Planning and Compulsory Purchase Act 2004 Sch 7 para 4). See further the Land Compensation Act 1973 s 33H; PARA **594**; and COMPULSORY ACQUISITION OF LAND.

593. Compensation payable by acquiring authority in respect of agricultural holdings.

Special rules apply to the assessment of compensation where in pursuance of any enactment providing for the acquisition or taking of possession compulsorily an acquiring authority[1] either acquires the interest of the landlord[2] in an agricultural holding[3] to which the Agricultural Holdings Act 1986 applies, or any part of it[4], or acquires the interest of the tenant[5] in, or takes possession of, an agricultural holding or any part of it[6].

In the case of a payment by the acquiring authority to the landlord, in assessing the compensation, there must be disregarded any right of the landlord to serve a notice to quit[7], and any notice to quit already served by the landlord, which would not be or would not have been effective if:

(1) in Case B[8] the reference to the land being required did not include a reference to its being required by an acquiring authority[9]; and

(2) the reference in the Agricultural Holdings Act 1986[10] in relation to the landlord's proposal to terminate the tenancy for use other than agriculture, not falling within Case B, did not include a reference to its being used by an acquiring authority[11].

If the tenant has quit the holding or any part of it by reason of a notice to quit which is to be so disregarded, it must be assumed that he has not done so[12].

In the case of a payment by an acquiring authority to a tenant, in assessing the tenant's compensation, there must be disregarded any right of the landlord to serve a notice to quit, and any notice to quit already served by the landlord, which would not be or would not have been effective if Case B and the related reference[13] were construed as above[14]. The tenant's compensation must be reduced by an amount equal to any payment which the acquiring authority is liable to make to him, in respect of the acquisition or taking of possession in question, under the provisions relating to additional payments[15]. If the tenant's compensation, so calculated, is less than it would have been had these provisions not been enacted, it must be increased to the amount of the deficiency[16]. Further, in assessing the tenant's compensation no account is to be taken of any benefit which might accrue to the tenant by virtue of the additional compensation provisions contained in the Agricultural Holdings Act 1986[17].

1 As to the meaning of 'acquiring authority' see the Land Compensation Act 1961 s 39(1); and COMPULSORY ACQUISITION OF LAND vol 18 (2009) PARA 622; definition applied by the Land Compensation Act 1973 s 87(1).

2 As to the meaning of 'landlord' see PARA 423 note 7; definition applied by the Land Compensation Act 1973 s 87(1).

3 As to the meaning of 'agricultural holding' see PARA 423; definition applied by the Land Compensation Act 1973 s 87(1) (amended by the Agricultural Holdings Act 1986 Sch 14 para 56).

4 Land Compensation Act 1973 s 48(1)(a) (s 48(1) amended, and s 48(1A) added, by the Agricultural Tenancies Act 1995 Schedule para 24). The provisions of the Land Compensation Act 1973 s 48 do not have effect where the tenancy of the agricultural holding is a tenancy to which, by virtue of the Agricultural Tenancies Act 1995 s 4 (see PARAS 401, 421) the Agricultural Holdings Act 1986 does not apply: Land Compensation Act 1973 s 48(1A) (as so added). As to compensation for displacement in respect of a tenancy governed by the Agricultural Tenancies Act 1995 see PARA 590.

5 As to the meaning of 'tenant' see PARA 423 note 5; definition applied by the Land Compensation Act 1973 s 87(1).

6 Land Compensation Act 1973 s 48(1)(b) (as amended: see note 4).

7 As to the meaning of 'notice to quit' see PARA 428; definition applied by the Land Compensation Act 1973 s 87(1).

8 Ie Case B in the Agricultural Holdings Act 1986 s 26(2), Sch 3 Pt I (see PARA 475).

9 Land Compensation Act 1973 s 48(2)(a)(i) (s 48(2) amended by the Agricultural Holdings Act 1986 Sch 14 para 53(1), (2)).

10 Ie the reference in the Agricultural Holdings Act 1986 s 27(3)(f) (see PARA 472). This is one of the matters as to which the First-tier tribunal (in England) or the Agricultural Land Tribunal for Wales (in Wales) must be satisfied before giving consent to a notice to quit.

11 Land Compensation Act 1973 s 48(2)(a)(ii) (as amended: see note 9).

12 Land Compensation Act 1973 s 48(2) (as amended: see note 9).

13 See the text and notes 8, 10.

14 Land Compensation Act 1973 s 48(3) (amended by the Agricultural Holdings Act 1986 Sch 14 para 53(3)).

15 Land Compensation Act 1973 s 48(5). The provisions relating to additional payments on compulsory acquisition or taking of possession are contained in the Agriculture (Miscellaneous Provisions) Act 1968 s 12 (see PARAS 591–592).

16 Land Compensation Act 1973 s 48(6).
17 Land Compensation Act 1973 s 48(6A) (added by the Agricultural Holdings Act 1986 Sch 14 para
    53(4)). In this context 'additional compensation provisions' means the Agricultural Holdings Act
    1986 s 60(2)(b) (see PARA 545), but not including that provision as applied by the Agriculture
    (Miscellaneous Provisions) Act 1968 s 12 (see PARAS 591–592): Land Compensation Act 1973 s
    48(6A) (as so added).

(3) COMPENSATION GENERALLY

594. Entitlement to payment by acquiring authority of occupier's loss payment.

A person who has a qualifying interest in agricultural land[1] which is acquired
compulsorily[2] is entitled, provided he has occupied the land for the specified
period[3], to a payment of a specified amount[4] which in respect of an interest in land
may not exceed £25,000[5]. Such payment must be made by the acquiring
authority[6]. A payment of an equal amount may be made in respect of the
acquisition of such an interest by an acquiring authority by agreement[7]. No
payment will, however, be made where specified statutory improvement or repair
notices or orders relating to hazards have effect or are operative in relation to the
land in question[8], and payments may also be affected by the prior initiation of
insolvency proceedings[9] or the death of the entitled person[10]. If a person is entitled
in respect of the same interest in agricultural land to a payment both under these
provisions[11] and by virtue of statutory entitlement to additional payments in
consequence of the compulsory acquisition of an agricultural holding[12], payment
may be made in respect of only one entitlement[13].

1 Land Compensation Act 1973 s 33B(1)(a), (b) (ss 33A, 33B, 33D, 33H, 33K added by the Planning
   and Compulsory Purchase Act 2004 ss 106(1), (2), 107(1), (2), 109). An interest in land is a
   qualifying interest if it is a freehold interest or an interest as tenant and (in either case) it subsists
   for a period of not less than one year ending with whichever is the earliest of:
   (1)   the date on which the acquiring authority takes possession of the land under the
          Compulsory Purchase Act 1965 s 11 (entry to take possession of land: see COMPULSORY
          ACQUISITION OF LAND vol 18 (2009) PARA 645) (Land Compensation Act 1973 s
          33A(4)(a) (as so added));
   (2)   the vesting date (within the meaning of the Compulsory Purchase (Vesting Declarations)
          Act 1981: see COMPULSORY ACQUISITION OF LAND vol 18 (2009) PARA 687) if a
          declaration is made under s 4 (general vesting declaration: see COMPULSORY ACQUISITION
          OF LAND vol 18 (2009) PARA 687) (Land Compensation Act 1973 s 33A(4)(c) (as so
          added));
   (3)   the date on which compensation is agreed between the person and the acquiring
          authority (s 33A(4)(d) (as so added)); and
   (4)   the date on which the amount of compensation is determined by the Upper Tribunal (s
          33A(4)(e) (as so added; amended by SI 2009/1307)).
   As to the meaning of 'acquiring authority' see the Land Compensation Act 1961 s 39(1); and
   COMPULSORY ACQUISITION OF LAND vol 18 (2009) PARA 622; definition applied by the Land
   Compensation Act 1973 s 87(1). As to the meaning of 'agricultural land' see PARA 424; definition
   applied by the Land Compensation Act 1973 s 87(1). As to the Upper Tribunal see COMPULSORY
   ACQUISITION OF LAND vol 18 (2009) PARA 720 et seq.
2 Land Compensation Act 1973 s 33B(1)(c) (as added: see note 1). The compulsory acquisition of
   an interest in land includes acquisition of the interest in consequence of the service of a purchase
   notice under the Town and Country Planning Act 1990 s 137 (right to require purchase of certain
   interests: see PLANNING vol 83 (2010) PARA 1142) (Land Compensation Act 1973 s 33A(5)(a)
   (as so added)) and a notice under the Town and Country Planning Act 1990 s 150 (purchase of
   blighted land: see PLANNING vol 83 (2010) PARA 1168) (Land Compensation Act 1973 s
   33A(5)(b) (as so added)).

3   Land Compensation Act 1973 s 33B(1)(d) (as added: see note 1). The 'specified period' is that specified in s 33A(4) (see note 1).
4   Land Compensation Act 1973 s 33B(2) (as added: see note 1). The payment to which the person is entitled is whichever is the greatest of 2.5% of the value of his interest (s 33B(2)(a) (as so added)), the 'land amount' (s 33B(2)(b) (as so added)), and the 'buildings amount' (s 33B(2)(c) (as so added)). The value of an interest is its value for the purpose of deciding the amount of compensation payable in respect of the acquisition (s 33B(5) (as so added)), subject to the following:
    (1)   if an interest consists partly of a dwelling in respect of which the person is entitled to a home loss payment, the value of the interest is the value of the whole interest less the value of so much of the interest as is represented by the dwelling (s 33B(6) (as so added)); and
    (2)   if the Land Compensation Act 1961 s 5 r (5) (equivalent reinstatement: see COMPULSORY ACQUISITION OF LAND vol 18 (2009) PARA 754) applies for the purpose of assessing the amount of compensation, the value of the interest is nil (Land Compensation Act 1973 s 33B(7) (as so added)).
The 'land amount' is the greater of £300 and:
    (a)   where the area of the land does not exceed 100 hectares, £100 per hectare or part thereof (s 33B(8) (as so added)); or
    (b)   where the area of the land exceeds 100 hectares, £100 per hectare for the first 100 hectares and £50 per hectare for the next 300 hectares or part thereof: s 33B(8) (s 33B(8) as so added).
The 'buildings amount' is £25 per square metre (or part of a square metre) of the gross floor space (measured externally) of any buildings on the land: s 33B(9), (10) (as so added). As to the meaning of 'dwelling' for these purposes see the Land Compensation Act 1973 s 87(1); and COMPULSORY ACQUISITION OF LAND vol 18 (2009) PARA 802.
    The Secretary of State and the Welsh Ministers may by regulations substitute for any amount or percentage figure specified in ss 33A–33K such other amount or percentage figure (as the case may be) as they think fit: s 33K(1), (2) (as so added). At the date at which this volume states the law no such regulations had been made. As to the Secretary of State and the Welsh Ministers see PARA 741.
5   Land Compensation Act 1973 s 33B(3) (as added: see note 1).
6   Land Compensation Act 1973 s 33B(4) (as added: see note 1). A claim for payment must be made in writing to the acquiring authority (s 33E(1), (2) (as so added)), giving such particulars as the authority may reasonably require for the purpose of deciding whether a payment is to be made (s 33E(3)(a) (as so added)) and the amount of any such payment (s 33E(3)(b) (as so added)). For the purposes of the Limitation Act 1980 (see LIMITATION PERIODS) a person's right of action to recover such a payment must be taken to have accrued on the date of his displacement from the land: s 33E(4)(b) (as so added). Provision is made for the resolution of disputes as to payment by the Upper Tribunal: see s 33I; and COMPULSORY ACQUISITION OF LAND vol 18 (2009) PARA 836.
7   See the Land Compensation Act 1973 s 33J; and COMPULSORY ACQUISITION OF LAND vol 18 (2009) PARA 837.
8   See the Land Compensation Act 1973 s 33D; and COMPULSORY ACQUISITION OF LAND vol 18 (2009) PARA 832.
9   See the Land Compensation Act 1973 s 33F; and COMPULSORY ACQUISITION OF LAND vol 18 (2009) PARA 834.
10 See the Land Compensation Act 1973 s 33G; and COMPULSORY ACQUISITION OF LAND vol 18 (2009) PARA 835.
11 Land Compensation Act 1973 s 33H(1)(a) (as added: see note 1).
12 Land Compensation Act 1973 s 33H(1)(b) (as added: see note 1). As to this entitlement see the Agriculture (Miscellaneous Provisions) Act 1968 s 12(1); and PARAS 591–592.
13 Land Compensation Act 1973 s 33H(2) (as added: see note 1). If the person makes a claim under both provisions he must be paid in respect of the entitlement which produces the greater amount: s 33H(3) (as so added).

595.   Notice to treat by acquiring authority in respect of part of agricultural land.

Where an acquiring authority[1] serves notice to treat in respect of any agricultural land[2] on a person, whether in occupation or not, who has a greater interest in the land than as tenant[3] for a year or from year to year, and that person has such an interest in other agricultural land comprised in the same agricultural unit[4], that person (the 'claimant') may, within two months beginning on the date of service of the notice to treat, serve a counter-notice[5] on the authority claiming that the other land is not reasonably capable of being farmed, either by itself or in conjunction with other relevant land[6], as a separate agricultural unit[7], and requiring the authority to purchase his interest in the whole of the other land[8].

If within two months beginning with the date of service of the counter-notice, the authority does not agree in writing to accept the counter-notice as valid, the claimant or the authority may in the two months after that period refer it to the Upper Tribunal[9]. The Tribunal must determine whether the claim in the counter-notice is justified and declare it to be valid or invalid accordingly[10]. Where the counter-notice is accepted or declared valid, the authority is deemed to be authorised to acquire compulsorily the land to which the claim relates, and to have served a notice to treat in respect thereof on the date of the original notice to treat[11]. A counter-notice may be withdrawn by the claimant at any time before the Tribunal has determined compensation or during the six weeks beginning with the date of such determination[12]. The compensation payable in pursuance of a notice to treat which is deemed to have been served by the authority must be assessed on certain statutory assumptions relating to planning permission[13].

Where, in consequence of a counter-notice requiring an authority to purchase the whole of a claimant's interest in land[14], the authority becomes entitled to a lease of any land, but not to the interest of the lessor, the authority must offer to surrender the lease to the lessor on such terms as the authority considers reasonable[15]. If the lessor refuses to accept any sum payable under these terms, or refuses or fails to make out his title to the authority's satisfaction, the authority may pay into court any sum payable to the lessor[16]. Where an authority which becomes entitled to the lease of any land as described above is a body incorporated by or under any enactment, the corporate powers of the authority include, if they would not otherwise do so, power to farm the land[17].

1 As to the meaning of 'acquiring authority' see the Land Compensation Act 1961 s 39(1); and COMPULSORY ACQUISITION OF LAND vol 18 (2009) PARA 622; definition applied by the Land Compensation Act 1973 s 87(1).

2 As to the meanings of 'agricultural' and 'agricultural land' see PARA 424; definition applied by the Land Compensation Act 1973 s 87(1).

3 As to the meaning of 'tenant' see PARA 423 note 5; definition applied by the Land Compensation Act 1973 s 87(1).

4 As to the meaning of 'agricultural unit' see PARA 424 note 7; definition applied by the Land Compensation Act 1973 s 87(1).

5 Where a counter-notice is served, the claimant must, within the same period of two months, serve a copy on any other person who has an interest in the land to which the requirement in the counter-notice relates; failure to do so, however, does not invalidate the counter-notice: Land Compensation Act 1973 s 53(2).

6 'Other relevant land' means:
   (1) land comprised in the same agricultural unit as the land to which the notice to treat relates, being land in which the claimant does not have an interest greater than as tenant for a year or from year to year (Land Compensation Act 1973 s 53(3)(a)); and
   (2) land comprised in any other agricultural unit occupied by him on the date of service of the notice to treat, being land in respect of which he is then entitled to a greater interest than as tenant for a year or from year to year (s 53(3)(b)).

   Where an acquiring authority has served a notice to treat in respect of land in the holding other than that to which the notice relates, or in respect of other relevant land, or such a notice is deemed to have been served by virtue of the Town and Country Planning Act 1990 ss 137–144 (purchase notices: see PLANNING vol 83 (2010) PARA 1142 et seq), then, unless and until the notice to treat is withdrawn, the provisions of the Land Compensation Act 1973 ss 53, 54 have effect as if that land did not form part of the other agricultural land in the holding or did not constitute other relevant land: s 53(4) (amended by the Planning (Consequential Provisions) Act 1990 Sch 2 para 29(9)).

7   Land Compensation Act 1973 s 53(1)(a). This also applies where a notice is deemed to have been served under the Compulsory Purchase (Vesting Declarations) Act 1981 Pt III (ss 7–9) (see COMPULSORY ACQUISITION OF LAND vol 18 (2009) PARAS 689, 693–694): Land Compensation Act 1973 s 53(5) (amended by the Compulsory Purchase (Vesting Declarations) Act 1981 Sch 3; and the Planning (Consequential Provisions) Act 1990 Sch 2 para 29(9)).

8   Land Compensation Act 1973 s 53(1)(b). See note 7.

9   Land Compensation Act 1973 s 54(1) (amended by SI 2009/1307). As to the Upper Tribunal see COMPULSORY ACQUISITION OF LAND vol 18 (2009) PARA 720 et seq.

10 Land Compensation Act 1973 s 54(1).

11 Land Compensation Act 1973 s 54(2).

12 Land Compensation Act 1973 s 54(3) (amended by SI 2009/1307). Where a counter-notice is so withdrawn, any notice to treat deemed to have been served in consequence of the counter-notice is also deemed to have been withdrawn: Land Compensation Act 1973 s 54(3). Without prejudice to that provision, the general power to withdraw a notice to treat conferred by the Land Compensation Act 1961 s 31 (see COMPULSORY ACQUISITION OF LAND vol 18 (2009) PARA 636) is not exercisable in the case of a notice to treat which is deemed to have been served in consequence of a counter-notice under the Land Compensation Act 1973 s 54: s 54(4).

13 Land Compensation Act 1973 s 54(5). The statutory assumptions referred to in the text are those contained in s 5(2)–(4) (see COMPULSORY ACQUISITION OF LAND vol 18 (2009) PARA 896).

14 Ie a counter-notice under the Land Compensation Act 1973 ss 53, 54 (see the text and notes 1–13).

15 Land Compensation Act 1973 s 54(6)(a). The question of what terms are reasonable may be referred by the authority or the lessor to the Upper Tribunal, and must be so referred if at the end of three months after the offer of surrender the question has not been resolved; on a reference the lessor will be deemed to have accepted the surrender at the expiration of one month after the date of the determination or on such other date as the Tribunal directs, and to have agreed such terms as the Tribunal has held to be reasonable: s 54(6)(b), (c) (s 54(6)(b) amended by SI 2009/1307).

16 Land Compensation Act 1973 s 54(7). The Compulsory Purchase Act 1965 s 9(2), (5) (deposit of compensation in cases of refusal to convey: see COMPULSORY ACQUISITION OF LAND vol 18 (2009) PARAS 661, 664) applies with the necessary modifications to that sum: Land Compensation Act 1973 s 54(7).

17 Land Compensation Act 1973 s 54(8). As to the 'farming' of land see PARA 424; definition applied by s 87(1).

596. Compensation where compulsory rights for opencast coal mining acquired.

Where the Coal Authority[1] compulsorily acquires temporary rights of occupation and use of agricultural land for the purposes of opencast coal mining by means of a compulsory rights order[2], the occupier is entitled to receive from the Authority annual compensation based on the annual value of the land, adjusted by reference to expected profit or loss, and also compensation for the costs of removal and in respect of forced sales of property[3].

On the termination of the occupation by the Authority, the occupier is entitled to compensation by way of payment of the cost of works for restoring the land and compensation for diminution in the value of the holding; there may be additional compensation payable on re-occupation[4]. Where the land subject to the compulsory rights order consists of or includes land which constitutes or forms part of an agricultural holding, provision is made for modifying the right of the tenant to receive compensation from his landlord in respect of long term improvements and the adoption of a special farming system[5]. Compensation is payable by the Authority to a tenant in respect of short term improvements and tenant-right matters and in respect of market garden improvements[6].

1 Formerly the National Coal Board, and then the British Coal Corporation: see the Coal Industry Act 1987 s 1; the Coal Industry Act 1994 s 1; and MINES, MINERALS AND QUARRIES vol 76 (2013) PARA 51 et seq.

2 Ie a compulsory rights order made under the Opencast Coal Act 1958 Pt I (ss 1–16) (see MINES, MINERALS AND QUARRIES vol 76 (2013) PARA 422 et seq).

3 See the Opencast Coal Act 1958 ss 17, 18, 27, Sch 3; and MINES, MINERALS AND QUARRIES vol 76 (2013) PARA 463 et seq.

4 See the Opencast Coal Act 1958 ss 21–23, 23A; and MINES, MINERALS AND QUARRIES vol 76 (2013) PARA 466 et seq.

5 See the Opencast Coal Act 1958 ss 24, 25, 37, Sch 7 Pt I; and MINES, MINERALS AND QUARRIES vol 76 (2013) PARAS 472–473.

6 See the Opencast Coal Act 1958 ss 26, 28, Sch 4; and MINES, MINERALS AND QUARRIES vol 76 (2013) PARAS 474, 477. 'Market garden improvements' are the improvements specified in the Agricultural Holdings Act 1986 Sch 10 (see PARA 561 note 16). As to the meaning of 'market garden' see PARA 424 note 4.

4. USE AND IMPROVEMENT OF AGRICULTURAL LAND

(1) AGRICULTURAL LAND IMPROVEMENT

(i) Agricultural Land Improvement: Introduction

597. Meaning of 'improvement' and controls on making improvements.

There is no precise statutory definition of 'improvement' and statutes using the word interpret it non-exhaustively by listing particular matters to be included in the meaning[1]. It has been judicially decided that 'improvement' in relation to land consists of the execution of works on the land which are something more than ordinary repairs and which, by implication, must give increased value to the land[2].

In the present context, 'land' is to be taken to mean not only bare land but also any buildings, including any dwelling house.

All land, whether vested in absolute or limited owners or in trustees, is subject to planning legislation[3]. Owners desiring to carry out development work, which may include in some instances works of improvement, have to obtain planning permission. In addition to planning controls imposed by public statutes, the land may be subject to restrictive covenants which bind the land in the hands of successive owners and may limit the landowner's right to execute improvements on it[4]. A tenant may by the terms of his lease be subject to additional restrictions on the execution of improvements, and a substantial alteration of premises may be treated as waste[5]. Whereas, on the one hand, a landowner's right to execute improvements on his land may be limited, he may, on the other hand, be obliged by statute to execute works of improvement on his land[6].

1   See the Improvement of Land Act 1864 s 9; the Limited Owners Residences Act (1870) Amendment Act 1871 s 3; the Settled Land Act 1882 s 30; and PARAS 599 et seq, 604. Works for the supply of sewage to land for agricultural purposes are also deemed 'improvements' (see the Public Health Act 1936 s 33; and SETTLEMENTS vol 91 (2012) PARA 717). A landowner assessed for public works or improvements is authorised to obtain an absolute charging order on the inheritance of the lands improved: see the Improvement of Land Act 1864 s 57; and PARA 615.
2   *Re Lindsay's Settlement (No 2)* [1941] Ch 119 at 125, [1941] 1 All ER 143.
3   See the Town and Country Planning Act 1990 s 57; and PLANNING vol 81 (2010) PARAS 313–314.
4   As to restrictive covenants see REAL PROPERTY AND REGISTRATION vol 87 (2017) PARA 1005 et seq.
5   As to liability for waste see SETTLEMENTS vol 91 (2012) PARA 887. As to the nature of waste generally see LANDLORD AND TENANT vol 62 (2016) PARA 324.
6   See PARA 599 text and note 6.

598. Limited owners: powers to make improvements.

Limited owners are free to execute improvements if there is no restriction imposed by law on their execution[1]. Some improvements have been considered to be waste for which a remainderman or reversioner could impeach the life tenant[2]. Apart from statute[3] and the express terms of the settlement or trust instrument from which the limited owner derives his estate or interest, a limited owner has no claim against the capital of the funds for the cost of buildings erected or improvements made by him[4].

1   See PARA 583.

2   As to ameliorating waste see LANDLORD AND TENANT vol 62 (2016) PARA 325. As to the
     protection against liability for waste of a tenant for life carrying out authorised improvements see
     PARA 614; and SETTLEMENTS vol 91 (2012) PARA 887.
3   See PARA 599.
4   *Bostock v Blakeney* (1789) 2 Bro CC 653; *Caldecott v Brown* (1842) 2 Hare 144; *Mathias v
     Mathias* (1858) 3 Sm & G 552; *Rowley v Ginnever* [1897] 2 Ch 503.

599. Financing of improvement to land.

Statutes concerned with the improvement of land may be grouped in five main
classes, namely:

(1)   statutes enabling landowners, including limited owners, to charge on
       the inheritance, or to pay out of capital, or to raise capital for, the cost
       of improvements[1];

(2)   statutes enabling tenants to cause their landlords to bear the whole or
       part of the cost of improvements[2], or landlords to obtain some
       recoupment of the cost of improvements effected by them[3];

(3)   statutes enabling landowners to obtain financial assistance from public
       funds towards the cost of improvements[4];

(4)   statutes enabling public authorities to effect necessary or expedient
       works together with powers for the recovery of the cost thereof from
       owners[5]; and

(5)   statutes enabling public authorities to compel owners to execute works
       of improvement on their land[6].

There is also a series of private Acts constituting improvement companies which
advance money for the execution of improvements[7]; and there are enactments
under which certain universities and colleges may raise money on the security of
land for the purpose of making improvements[8].

1   See the Improvement of Land Act 1864; and PARA 603 et seq. As to the application of capital
     money arising under the Settled Land Act 1925 in payment for improvements see SETTLEMENTS vol
     91 (2012) PARA 716. It should be noted, in particular, that such capital money may be applied
     in discharge of any charge in respect of an improvement created on a holding under the
     Agricultural Holdings Act 1986, or in payment for an improvement authorised by the Settled Land
     Act 1925 of any money expended and costs incurred by a landlord under the Agricultural Holdings
     Act 1986, or under custom or agreement or otherwise, in or about the execution of any
     improvement comprised in Sch 7 (see PARA 529): see the Settled Land Act 1925 s 73(1)(ii), (iv);
     and SETTLEMENTS vol 91 (2012) PARA 709.
         The improvements authorised by the Settled Land Act 1925 are divided into improvements the
     costs of which are not liable to be replaced by instalments (Sch 3 Pt I), those the costs of which the
     trustees or the court may require to be replaced by instalments (Sch 3 Pt II) and those the costs of
     which the trustees and the court must require to be so replaced (Sch 3 Pt III). Improvements of
     certain kinds have in effect been added to Sch 3, in particular:
     (1)   certain operations set out in the Hill Farming Improvements (Settled Land and Trusts for
            Sale) Regulations 1951, SI 1951/1816 (made under the Hill Farming Act 1946 s 11 (see
            PARA 604)) are added to the Settled Land Act 1925 Sch 3 Pt I; and
     (2)   improvements specified in the Agricultural Holdings Act 1986 Sch 7 (see PARA 529) are
            added to the Settled Land Act 1925 Sch 3 Pt I (Agricultural Holdings Act 1986 s 89(1)
            (amended by the Trusts of Land and Appointment of Trustees Act 1996 Sch 4)),
     but a tenant for life paying compensation to a farm tenant at the end of the tenancy for
     improvements carried out by that tenant during the tenancy cannot be reimbursed directly by the
     trustees of the settlement out of capital money which is subject to the trusts of the settlement
     (similarly this is so for tenant-right and disturbance) (*Re Duke of Wellington's Parliamentary
     Estates* [1972] Ch 374, [1971] 2 All ER 1140). Even if a tenant for life can obtain a charge under
     the Agricultural Holdings Act 1986 s 86(1) (see PARA 575) it is uncertain whether he can require
     the trustees of the settlement to make a payment out of capital money under the Settled Land Act

1925 s 73(1)(ii) and even if the tenant for life could require the trustees of the settlement to do so, the tenant for life may still be liable to the remainderman: *Re Duke of Manchester's Settlement* [1910] 1 Ch 106.

  In addition, matters in respect of which expenditure may be approved for grant under a scheme under the Agriculture Act 1970 s 29 (promotion of amalgamations and boundary adjustments by the Secretary of State and the Welsh Ministers: see AGRICULTURAL PRODUCTION AND MARKETING vol 1A (2017) PARA 420), may be added to any of the parts of the Settled Land Act 1925 Sch 3 by regulations made under the Agriculture Act 1970 s 30(1) (supplementary provisions as to capital grants: see AGRICULTURAL PRODUCTION AND MARKETING vol 1A (2017) PARA 426), but no such regulations were in force at the date at which this volume states the law.

2 Examples are the Agricultural Holdings Act 1986 ss 64–69, 94(1), (2), Sch 12 paras 5, 6(1), (2) (see PARA 522 et seq); and the Landlord and Tenant Act 1927 ss 1–3 and the Landlord and Tenant Act 1954 Pt III (ss 47–50) (see LANDLORD AND TENANT vol 64 (2016) PARA 1679 et seq).

3 Under the Agricultural Holdings Act 1986, a landlord who has carried out certain improvements may be entitled to charge an increased rent: see ss 13, 98(1); and PARA 440.

4 Examples are the various financial aids for improvements considered in PARA 604.

5 See eg the Public Health Act 1936 ss 291, 293, 294; and ENVIRONMENTAL QUALITY AND PUBLIC HEALTH vol 45 (2010) PARA 123.

6 Examples are provisions of the land drainage legislation such as the Land Drainage Act 1991 ss 28–31 (see WATER AND WATERWAYS vol 101 (2009) PARA 588) which relate to the restoration and improvement of ditches.

7 See PARAS 600–602.

8 See the Universities and College Estates Act 1925 s 30, Sch 1; and EDUCATION vol 36 (2015) PARA 1329. Where, under powers conferred by the Universities and College Estates Act 1925, capital money is applied in payment for any improvement specified in the Agricultural Holdings Act 1986 (see PARA 604) no provision is in general to be made for replacing the money out of income: s 89(2).

(ii) Companies Empowered to Make Advances

600. The origin of the improvement companies.

The Private Money Drainage Act 1849[1] enabled landowners to charge by way of terminable rentcharge, upon the inheritance of the lands improved, money borrowed from other persons or advanced by themselves for the drainage of their lands[2]. Almost simultaneously several companies were incorporated by private Acts of Parliament for the purpose of executing improvements of land and making advances to landowners for the expenses of improvements on the security of terminable rentcharges arising out of the lands so improved. In 1864 the law relating to the improvement of land was amended and consolidated by the Improvement of Land Act 1864[3].

1 The Private Money Drainage Act 1849 was repealed and replaced by the Improvement of Land Act 1864. The former Act was passed after the whole of the advances authorised by prior legislation (ie the Public Money Drainage Acts 1846, 1847 and 1848 (all repealed)), had been made, and the object of the Act was to enable money to be advanced in future from private sources.

2 As to rentcharges in general see REAL PROPERTY AND REGISTRATION vol 87 (2017) PARA 1033 et seq.

3 See PARA 603 et seq.

601. Private improvement companies Acts.

All the private Acts incorporating improvement companies[1] are in practically the same form as the Improvement of Land Act 1864, and contain substantially identical provisions as to:

  (1) the persons who, as landowners[2], may obtain advances;

(2)   the proceedings leading to a provisional order, and ultimately to an absolute order charging the land with a rentcharge payable for a term of years[3]; and

(3)   the priority of the rentcharge, and the remedies for recovering it, and other minor matters[4].

1   See PARA 600.
2   See PARA 603.
3   See PARAS 608–615.
4   See PARAS 616–620. Private Acts incorporating improvement companies (see PARA 600) generally provide that a charge is to have priority over every other charge, whether existing at the time or made afterwards. Where two land improvement companies obtained charges under their respective Acts, each of which conferred priority in such terms, the charges were held to rank in order of date: *Pollock v Lands Improvement Co* (1888) 37 ChD 661. An improvement company's charge overrides encumbrances prior in date, although there has been no investigation of title: *General Land Drainage and Improvement Co v United Counties Bank Ltd* (1910) 103 LT 418. The charge must be registered as a land charge Class A or, in the case of registered land, protected by an entry on the register: see PARA 616.

602.   The Agricultural Mortgage Corporation.

Pursuant to the Agricultural Credits Act 1928, a company limited by shares[1] was incorporated, called the Agricultural Mortgage Corporation Limited, and having for its principal objects the making of loans on mortgages of agricultural land and the making of loans under the Improvement of Land Acts 1864 and 1899[2], for agricultural purposes[3]. Whilst all legislation relating to the establishment and operation of the Corporation has been repealed[4].

1   See the Agricultural Credits Act 1928 s 2(1) (repealed).
2   See PARA 603 et seq.
3   See the Agricultural Credits Act 1928 s 1 (repealed).
4   Such repeals do not, however, affect any mortgages or debentures subsisting on 25 September 1991: Agriculture and Forestry (Financial Provisions) Act 1991 s 1(3).

(iii)   By Whom Powers Are Exercised

603.   Meaning of 'landowner' within the Improvement Acts.

For the purpose of the Improvements Acts[1] the landowner is, in effect, the person[2] who is in actual possession or receipt of the rents and profits of the land, whatever his tenure[3] and without regard to the real amount of his interest, unless such person is a tenant under a lease or agreement which is not renewable and which has less than 25 years unexpired[4]. The purpose of the Improvement Acts is to enable owners, including limited owners, to raise money for improvements by means of rentcharges on the land[5], and the object of the foregoing definition of landowner is to obviate the necessity of inquiring into the title of the landowner in connection with rentcharges. Provided that he is the landowner, as so defined, the rentcharge is valid, notwithstanding that his title is defective or that he has no title[6].

As the landowner for the time being is bound to keep down the rentcharge[7], the result is that, if the person who originated the terminable charge continues to be the landowner during the whole period of its existence, he will, although he is a limited owner, bear the whole cost of an improvement effected under these Acts, unless, under the powers of the Settled Land Act 1925, the rentcharge is redeemed out of capital money[8].

1   The term 'Improvement Acts' is used to describe the Improvement of Land Act 1864 and the Acts which are construed as one with it (namely the Limited Owners Residences Act 1870 (see s 2), the

Limited Owners Residences Act (1870) Amendment Act 1871 (see s 4), and the District Councils (Water Supply Facilities) Act 1897 (see s 7)), together with the Settled Land Act 1882 s 30 and the Improvement of Land Act 1899. There is no official collective title for these Acts (which are discussed generally in PARA 604 et seq), but the first and last Acts mentioned above may be cited together as the Improvement of Land Acts 1864 and 1899: see the Improvement of Land Act 1899 s 9(2).

2   'Person' includes a company or other corporation: Improvement of Land Act 1864 s 10.

3   Persons holding under a lease or an agreement for a lease for a term of years not renewable, of which less than 25 years remain unexpired at the time of the making of an application to the Secretary of State or the Welsh Ministers for improvements to be sanctioned, are excepted from the definition of 'landowner' and in that case the person who for the time being is in the actual receipt of the rent payable by the person so excepted (unless he is himself within the exception) is deemed, jointly with the person liable for its payment, to be the owner of such lands: see the Improvement of Land Act 1864 s 8. As to the Secretary of State and the Welsh Ministers see PARA 741.

4   See the Improvement of Land Act 1864 s 8. A tenant for life is a landowner within this definition, as is also the representative of a person who, but for a disability, would be a landowner as defined: see ss 8, 24 (amended by the Mental Treatment Act 1930 s 20(5); and the Mental Health Act 1983 Sch 5 para 29). 'Landowner' is similarly defined in the private Acts under which improvement companies make advances for improvements. As to these Acts see PARAS 600–601.

5   As to rentcharges see PARA 616 et seq.

6   *General Land Drainage and Improvement Co v United Counties Bank Ltd* (1910) 103 LT 418 (a case decided under a private Act). The landowner must, however, be a person capable of contracting for the execution of improvements on the land; thus a charge on the land of a limited company, the borrowings of which for the purpose of the improvements were in excess of the powers conferred on it by Act of Parliament, was invalid: *Baroness Wenlock v River Dee Co* (1888) 38 ChD 534, CA.

7   See the Improvement of Land Act 1864 s 66; and PARA 617.

8   See the Settled Land Act 1925 s 73(1)(xiii); PARA 599 note 1; and SETTLEMENTS vol 91 (2012) PARA 709.

(iv) Improvements Authorised

604. Description of improvements authorised under the Improvement Acts.
Improvements which may be carried out under the Improvement of Land Act 1864 were originally confined to improvements of an agricultural nature therein specified[1], and proved to the satisfaction of the appropriate body, originally the Inclosure Commissioners and now the Secretary of State or the Welsh Ministers, to add to the permanent value of the lands to be charged to an extent equal to the expense thereof[2]. The improvements specified have been extended by subsequent Acts, and the improvements which may now be carried out may be summarised as follows:

(1)   all improvements authorised by the Improvement of Land Act 1864[3] and the Settled Land Act 1925[4];

(2)   the making of works for the supply of sewage to lands for agricultural purposes[5];

(3)   the erection, completion or improvement of a mansion house with the usual and necessary outbuildings and appurtenances[6].

1   See the Improvement of Land Act 1864 s 9. The improvements specified in that provision are: the drainage of land and the straightening, widening, deepening or otherwise improving of the drains, streams and watercourses of any land; the irrigation and warping of land; the embanking and weiring of land from the sea or tidal waters, or from lakes, rivers or streams, in a permanent manner; the inclosing of lands and the straightening of fences and redivision of fields; the reclamation of land, including all operations necessary thereto; the making of permanent farm roads and permanent tramways and railways and navigable canals for all purposes connected with the improvement of the estate; the clearing of land; the erection of labourers' cottages, farmhouses and other buildings required for farm purposes, and the improvement of and addition to labourers' cottages, farmhouses and other buildings for farm purposes already erected, such improvement or

additions being of a permanent nature; planting for shelter; the construction or erection of any engine-houses, water-wheels, saw and other mills, kilns, shafts, wells, ponds, tanks, reservoirs, dams, leads, pipes, conduits, watercourses, bridges, weirs, sluices, flood-gates or hatches, which will increase the value of any lands for agricultural purposes; the construction or improvement of jetties or landing places on the sea coast, or on the banks of navigable rivers or lakes, for the transport of cattle, sheep and other agricultural stock and produce, and of lime, manure and other articles, and things for agricultural purposes, provided that the Secretary of State or the Welsh Ministers must be satisfied that such works will add to the permanent value of the lands to be charged to an extent equal to the expense thereof; and the execution of all such works as may be necessary for carrying into effect or deriving the full benefit of any matter mentioned above. The Settled Land Act 1882 s 30 extends to all improvements authorised by that Act the enumeration of improvements in the Improvement of Land Act 1864 s 9, and will now comprise, by virtue of the Interpretation Act 1978 ss 16(1), 17(2)(a), Sch 2 para 3, all improvements authorised by the Settled Land Act 1925 s 83, Sch 3: see note 5. As to the Secretary of State and the Welsh Ministers see PARA 741.

2   To this requirement (arising from the Improvement of Land Act 1864 ss 15, 25, 50) there are a few exceptions: see PARA 613 note 2.

3   See note 1.

4   See the Settled Land Act 1925 s 83, Sch 3 (see PARA 599); the Hill Farming Act 1946 s 11 (amended by the Livestock Rearing Act 1951 s 1(2)(b); and the Trusts of Land and Appointment of Trustees Act 1996 Sch 4); the Agriculture Act 1970 s 30 (see AGRICULTURAL PRODUCTION AND MARKETING vol 1A (2017) PARA 426); the Agricultural Holdings Act 1986 Sch 7 (see PARA 529); and the Hill Farming Improvements (Settled Land and Trusts for Sale) Regulations 1951, SI 1951/1816.

5   See the Public Health Act 1936 s 33; the Settled Land Act 1925 Sch 3 Pt I para (iv); and SETTLEMENTS vol 91 (2012) PARA 717.

6   Ie under the Limited Owners Residences Act 1870 and the Limited Owners Residences Act (1870) Amendment Act 1871. The amount to be charged on any estate must not exceed two years' rental after certain deductions: Limited Owners Residences Act 1870 s 4 (but see PARA 532 note 3). The charge, which does not take priority over any incumbrance affecting the land charged at the time when the charge is created (s 9), may be upon the whole of the landowner's estate, that is, not only on the particular land upon which the improvement is executed, but also on any other lands, in the same neighbourhood, settled on the same trusts: see the Limited Owners Residences Act (1870) Amendment Act 1871 s 3. The improvement, if suitable, may be allowed by the Secretary of State or the Welsh Ministers, even though no increase of the permanent value of the lands in excess of the yearly charge is thereby effected: Limited Owners Residences Act 1870 s 7. As to the calculation of yearly value see s 5; and as to insurance see s 8. Cf the Settled Land Act 1925 Sch 3 Pt I para (xxv); and SETTLEMENTS vol 91 (2012) PARA 717.

605. Powers of landowner regarding contributions made to district councils in respect of water supply.

With the sanction of the Secretary of State or the Welsh Ministers[1], contributions made by a landowner[2] towards the expenses incurred by a district council[3] for the purpose of supplying water to any of his lands may be charged on the land in the same manner and with the like effect as in the case of a charge under the Improvement of Land Act 1864[4]. Where the contribution is by agreement to be payable by half-yearly instalments, the charge may be made in favour of the district council, to secure the payment to it of the contribution[5]. If the supply is beneficial to residents or labourers on the estate, the charge may be sanctioned even though it is not shown that the supply will effect the increase usually required in the value of the land[6]. The requirements of the Improvement of Land Act 1864, with respect to matters and proceedings previous to the execution of a charge[7], may be dispensed with in cases where the annual amount payable under the proposed charge does not exceed the rate or rent payable for water supply at the date of its execution[8].

1   As to the Secretary of State and the Welsh Ministers see PARA 741.

2   As to the meaning of 'landowner' see PARA 603.

3 As to the district councils in England and Wales see LOCAL GOVERNMENT vol 69 (2009) PARA 22 et seq.
4 District Councils (Water Supply Facilities) Act 1897 s 1. As to charges under the Improvement of Land Act 1864 see PARA 608 et seq.
5 District Councils (Water Supply Facilities) Act 1897 s 2.
6 District Councils (Water Supply Facilities) Act 1897 s 4.
7 As to those requirements see PARA 608 et seq.
8 District Councils (Water Supply Facilities) Act 1897 s 5.

606. Extent of power to charge settled land in respect of improvements.

All improvements on which capital money arising under the Settled Land Act 1925 may be expended may be treated as improvements authorised by the Improvement of Land Act 1864 and their cost may be secured by way of terminable charges in accordance with the procedure provided by that Act[1]. Except by the adoption of this procedure, there is no jurisdiction to charge the inheritance of settled land with the cost of improvements the costs of which are not liable to be replaced by instalments[2]. Rentcharges may be created out of the settled land to repay the cost of improvements the costs of which may or must be required to be replaced by instalments[3].

1 Settled Land Act 1882 s 30 (amended by the Statute Law (Repeals) Act 1993). For the procedure see PARA 608 et seq.
2 *Standing v Gray* [1903] 1 IR 49. The improvements the costs of which are not liable to be replaced by instalments are those specified in the Settled Land Act 1925 Sch 3 Pt I (see PARA 599 note 1).
3 See the Settled Land Act 1925 ss 84, 85; and SETTLEMENTS vol 91 (2012) PARA 710 et seq. Such rentcharges, however, take effect only as though limited by the settlement, and may be overreached; but they cannot be redeemed out of capital money: s 85(3). Power to pay for improvements out of capital is, however, not available to trustees holding under a trust for sale: *Re Wynn* [1955] 2 All ER 865, [1955] 1 WLR 940; *Re Boston's Will Trusts* [1956] Ch 395, [1956] 1 All ER 593. The improvements the costs of which may or must be required to be replaced by instalments are those specified in the Settled Land Act 1925 Sch 3 Pts II, III respectively (see PARA 599 note 1).

607. Improvements authorised for land improvement companies.

Improvement companies[1] are authorised, by resolution passed by three-quarters of the shareholders present at an extraordinary meeting specially summoned for the purpose, to adopt, as improvements authorised by their own Acts, all or any of the improvements which are authorised by the Improvement of Land Act 1864, or by the enactments amending and extending the scope of that statute[2]. The principal improvements specified in these private Acts are agricultural drainage, irrigation, embanking, inclosing and reclaiming, the making of farm roads, farm buildings and mills and waterworks for farm purposes, and planting[3].

1 Ie companies authorised by any Act of Parliament to execute or advance money for the execution of improvements of land: see the Improvement of Land Act 1899 s 7.
2 Improvement of Land Act 1899 s 1(3). For the improvements in question see PARA 604. Where a private company has so adopted the improvements authorised by the Limited Owners Residences Act 1870 and the Limited Owners Residences Act (1870) Amendment Act 1871, it may execute or advance money for the execution of them as though such improvements were authorised by its special improvement Act; it would seem therefore that the limitations imposed by the Limited Owners Residences Act 1870 and the Limited Owners Residences Act (1870) Amendment Act 1871 on the amount of money which may be expended and on the priority of the charge given will not apply in such cases. This conclusion seems to follow from the fact that the Improvement of Land Act 1899 s 1(3) proviso was repealed by the Improvement of Land Act (1899) Amendment Act 1925.
3 See the Acts cited in PARA 600.

(v) Procedure for Obtaining Land Improvement Charge

A. APPLICATION AND INVESTIGATION

608. Application for obtaining land improvement charge.
An application to the Secretary of State or the Welsh Ministers[1] for the purpose of obtaining a charge for improvements under the Improvement of Land Act 1864, or the Acts amending or extending it[2], may be made by any landowner[3].

In the case of persons under a disability, such as minors, the application may be made by their guardians or other representatives[4]. Where the land to which the application relates is held in right of an ecclesiastical benefice, the Secretary of State or the Welsh Ministers must not sanction the improvement until the patron of the benefice and the bishop of the diocese have signified, by writing, their consents to the application[5]. Joint applications may be made by several landowners[6].

The application must be made in the prescribed form, but it may be withdrawn or altered until the proposed improvements have been sanctioned by the Secretary of State or the Welsh Ministers[7].

1   As to the Secretary of State and the Welsh Ministers see PARA 741.
2   As to those Acts see PARA 603.
3   See the Improvement of Land Act 1864 s 11. As to the meaning of 'landowner' see PARA 603.
4   See the Improvement of Land Act 1864 s 24. As to judicial functions and powers with respect to the property and affairs of a person lacking capacity see MENTAL HEALTH AND CAPACITY vol 75 (2013) PARA 597 et seq.
5   Improvement of Land Act 1864 s 20.
6   See the Improvement of Land Act 1864 s 12. Adjoining lands or easements, or conveniences over them, may be acquired, for the purposes of the execution of improvements, from persons enabled to sell or dispose of any such adjoining lands etc under the Lands Clauses Consolidation Act 1845: Improvement of Land Act 1864 s 32. As to such persons see the Lands Clauses Consolidation Act 1845 ss 6, 7; and COMPULSORY ACQUISITION OF LAND vol 18 (2009) PARA 550 et seq. The amount of the purchase money may be added to the charge: Improvement of Land Act 1864 s 49.
7   Improvement of Land Act 1864 s 11. The forms may be issued by the Secretary of State or the Welsh Ministers from time to time: s 13.

609. Investigation by the Secretary of State or the Welsh Ministers into application for land improvement charge.
If the Secretary of State sees or the Welsh Ministers[1] see fit to entertain the application, he or they may appoint an inspector, who is to report, except where the proposed outlay is to be made in respect of planting only, on whether proposed improvements will effect a permanent increase of the yearly value of the land exceeding the yearly amount proposed to be charged thereon in respect of the improvements applied for[2]. The applicant may also be required to give security for the expenses of such investigation[3], and any alterations in the proposed improvements may be required where considered expedient[4].

1   As to the Secretary of State and the Welsh Ministers see PARA 741.
2   Improvement of Land Act 1864 s 15. As to improvements under the Limited Owners Residences Act 1870 and the Limited Owners Residences Act (1870) Amendment Act 1871 see PARA 604 note 6.
3   Improvement of Land Act 1864 s 14 (amended by the Statute Law (Repeals) Act 1993).
4   Improvement of Land Act 1864 s 16.

610. Interference by proposed improvement with rivers and canals.
If in the opinion of the Secretary of State or the Welsh Ministers[1] any proposed improvement will interfere with any navigable river or canal, the landowner must

give notice[2] in writing to the body having the management or control of that river or canal, and, in the event of the body dissenting, an order of the court must be obtained authorising the Secretary of State or the Welsh Ministers to sanction the improvement[3].

Provision is also made for works to be carried out in accordance with plans deposited with the river or canal authority, and under the supervision of its engineer, and for saving the rights of such authorities[4].

1   As to the Secretary of State and the Welsh Ministers see PARA 741.
2   Notices under the Improvement of Land Act 1864 may be served by registered post or recorded delivery; if the person to be served has no residence or place of business in this country or it cannot be ascertained notices may be served in such manner as the Secretary of State or the Welsh Ministers may direct or approve: see s 7 (amended by SI 2001/1149 and the Postal Services Act 2011 Sch 12 para 72); and the Recorded Delivery Service Act 1962 s 1(1).
3   Improvement of Land Act 1864 ss 19, 21 (amended by the Settled Land Act 1882 s 64, Schedule; the Statute Law Revision Act 1893; and the Statute Law (Repeals) Act 1974). The costs of such application, which is made by summons to a judge of the Business and Property Courts of England and Wales, are in the discretion of the judge, and if he so directs may be deemed to be part of the expenses of the application for the proposed improvements: Improvement of Land Act 1864 ss 21, 23 (amended by the Settled Land Act 1882 s 64, Schedule; the Administration of Justice Act 1965 s 34, Sch 2; and the Statute Law (Repeals) Act 1974).
4   See the Improvement of Land Act 1864 s 47.

611.   Rights and powers of drainage and other authorities to remain unaffected by Improvement Acts.

The rights, privileges, powers and authorities vested in or to be discharged by any drainage authority are not lessened or altered by the Improvement of Land Act 1864, and no work in connection with improvements may be done to interfere in any way with any sewers, drains or watercourses under the control of any drainage authority: new sewers, drains, watercourses or works of drainage may not be made within the district and jurisdiction of any drainage authority unless previously approved by that authority; and, if and when they are made, they are to be and remain subject in all respects to that jurisdiction[1]. Similar protection is accorded to the interests of the Environment Agency in relation to the river Thames[2], and more generally to the London borough councils or Environment Agency[3] and water companies[4]. Special consents are also required in cases affecting Crown land[5], the rights of certain government departments[6], harbours, tidal and navigable waters, and the foreshore[7].

1   Improvement of Land Act 1864 s 43. This provision refers to commissioners of sewers, but these were replaced by catchment boards and drainage boards constituted (or, in the case of certain drainage boards, continued) under the Land Drainage Act 1930 ss 1–3, 17, 18, 83(2), (3) (repealed). The catchment boards so constituted were succeeded by river boards constituted under the River Boards Act 1948 (repealed); by river authorities constituted under the Water Resources Act 1963 s 3 (repealed); by water authorities under the Water Act 1972 Sch 1 (repealed); by the National Rivers Authority under the Water Act 1989 Sch 1; and now by the Environment Agency under the Environment Act 1995 (see ENVIRONMENTAL QUALITY AND PUBLIC HEALTH vol 45 (2010) PARA 68 et seq) or, in relation to Welsh devolved functions of the Environment Agency, the Natural Resources Body for Wales (see FORESTRY vol 52 (2014) PARA 38). Drainage boards were continued under the Land Drainage Act 1976 s 6 (repealed), and further continued as internal drainage boards within the areas of regional flood defence committees first under the Water Act 1989 s 140 (repealed) and now under the Land Drainage Act 1991 (see WATER AND WATERWAYS vol 101 (2009) PARA 569 et seq).

    As to the provisions of the Land Drainage Act 1991 ss 22, 30, which provide for work to be done on land for drainage purposes, see WATER AND WATERWAYS vol 101 (2009) PARAS 587–588.

2   See the Improvement of Land Act 1864 s 44. This provision refers to the Conservators of the river Thames; they were abolished by the Water Act 1973 s 33(d) (repealed) and their powers made exercisable by the Thames Water Authority, subsequently by the National Rivers Authority, and now by the Environment Agency (see note 1).

3   Improvement of Land Act 1864 s 45. That provision refers to the Metropolitan Board of Works, whose powers, duties and liabilities were transferred to the London County Council by the Local Government Act 1888 s 40(8) (repealed). By the Local Law (Greater London Council and Inner London Boroughs) Order 1965, SI 1965/540, the functions of that council were transferred to the Greater London Council, which in turn was abolished by the Local Government Act 1985 s 2 and its functions under the Land Drainage Act 1976 were transferred to the Thames Water Authority, the London borough councils and the Common Council of the City of London under the Local Government Act 1985 Sch 7 (repealed), to the National Rivers Authority or water companies by the Water Act 1989 s 4 (repealed), s 136, Sch 2, Sch 15 (repealed), and then to the Environment Agency by the Environment Act 1995 s 2 (see ENVIRONMENTAL QUALITY AND PUBLIC HEALTH vol 45 (2010) PARA 70; WATER AND WATERWAYS vol 100 (2009) PARA 12). As to administrative areas and authorities in London see LONDON GOVERNMENT vol 71 (2013) PARA 14 et seq. As to the Common Council of the City of London see LONDON GOVERNMENT vol 71 (2013) PARAS 34–38.

4   Improvement of Land Act 1864 s 46.

5   Improvement of Land Act 1864 ss 35, 37, 38 (dealing also with land of the Duchies of Cornwall and Lancaster).

6   Improvement of Land Act 1864 ss 36, 39, 42.

7   See the Improvement of Land Act 1864 ss 40, 41.

612.   Delivery of specifications of improvements under Improvement Acts.

Before the commencement of any sanctioned improvements, detailed specifications and, in the case of buildings and in any other case if required, detailed plans or drawings, must be delivered to and approved by the Secretary of State or the Welsh Ministers[1], whose officers may visit the site and report on the proposals[2]. The Secretary of State and the Welsh Ministers also have the power to inspect the improvements while in progress[3].

1   As to the Secretary of State and the Welsh Ministers see PARA 741.

2   Improvement of Land Act 1864 ss 30, 31.

3   Improvement of Land Act 1864 s 48.

B. PROVISIONAL AND ABSOLUTE ORDER

613.   Provisional order for charge of sanctioned improvements under Improvement Acts.

The Secretary of State or the Welsh Ministers[1], if satisfied as to the permanent value[2] of proposed improvements, may sanction the improvements by an order called a provisional order[3]. The provisional order must name the landowner to whom it is issued, express the greatest sum to be charged and the rate of interest and term of years for the repayment thereof (the interest rate to be such as the Secretary of State or the Welsh Ministers may from time to time authorise[4], and the term not to exceed 40 years[5]), specify the lands on which such repayment is to be charged[6], and express, or refer to some contract or other document expressing, the general scheme of the improvements to be executed[7].

1   As to the Secretary of State and the Welsh Ministers see PARA 741.

2   The improvements must effect a permanent increase in the yearly value of the land exceeding the yearly amount proposed to be charged thereon: see the Improvement of Land Act 1864 s 25. This rule does not apply in the following cases: planting (see s 15 proviso; and PARA 609); erection of a mansion house under the Limited Owners Residences Act 1870 if the discretion under s 7 (see PARA 604 note 6) is exercised; erection of a farmhouse or cottage for occupation by a person

cultivating lands to be charged, if the Secretary of State or the Welsh Ministers are satisfied that such erection is required for the proper cultivation of the land (Agricultural Credits Act 1923 s 3(3)).

3 See the Improvement of Land Act 1864 ss 25, 27 (s 25 amended by the Statute Law (Repeals) Act 1993). The form of order is set out in the Improvement of Land Act 1864 Sch (A).

4 Agricultural Credits Act 1923 s 3(1).

5 Improvement of Land Act 1899 s 1(1).

6 The lands charged may include not only the lands improved, but any other lands shown by statutory declaration to the satisfaction of the Secretary of State or the Welsh Ministers to be held for the same estates and interests free from incumbrances or subject to the same incumbrances: Improvement of Land Act 1899 s 1(2).

7 Improvement of Land Act 1864 s 26. Section 26 also provides for provisional orders to be drawn up, at the landowner's request, so as to take effect under the private Act of a company with which the landowner has contracted for a loan or for the improvements: s 26.

614. Effect of provisional order regarding sanctioned improvements within Improvement Acts.

A provisional order creates in favour of the landowner named in it a title to an absolute charge, on the completion of the improvements, which he may assign by indorsement to any other person, either absolutely or by way of security[1]. Modifications of or alterations in any matter contained in the order may be sanctioned by the Secretary of State or the Welsh Ministers[2] with the consent of every person interested, provided that no modification or alteration increases the sum to be charged or extends or curtails the term of repayment[3].

A provisional order authorises the landowner, his successors, representatives, employees or contractors to enter the land and carry out the improvements, and is a complete protection from impeachment of waste[4].

1 See the Improvement of Land Act 1864 s 27.

2 As to the Secretary of State and the Welsh Ministers see PARA 741.

3 See the Improvement of Land Act 1864 s 29. Although there is no express power so to modify a provisional order, an absolute order may be modified under the Improvement of Land Act 1899 so as to extend the term of repayment in respect of the planting of woods or trees: s 1(4) (amended by the Statute Law (Repeals) Act 1993).

4 See the Improvement of Land Act 1864 s 34. As to liability for waste see SETTLEMENTS vol 91 (2012) PARA 887. As to the nature of waste generally see LANDLORD AND TENANT vol 62 (2016) PARA 324.

615. Absolute order for charge following execution of sanctioned improvements within Improvement Acts.

After the improvements sanctioned have been satisfactorily executed, the Secretary of State or the Welsh Ministers[1] execute under seal a charge upon the fee simple of the lands comprised in the provisional order for the sum expressed to be chargeable by that order in respect of the improvements[2], with interest thereon[3]. This charge is called an absolute order[4]. Its execution is conclusive evidence of the validity of the charge[5], but not of the capacity of the landowner to contract[6]. Copies of absolute orders are kept by the Secretary of State or the Welsh Ministers, and any copy authenticated by seal is evidence of the contents of the absolute order[7]. In the event of the death of any landowner, or the determination of his interest, between the date of the provisional order and the completion of the improvements, then if his successor completes the work, absolute orders will be made in favour of both the predecessor, or his representatives, and the successor in proportion to the amounts expended[8]. If the successor does not proceed with the works within three months, his predecessor, or his representatives, may complete the works and entitle themselves to the absolute order[9].

1 As to the Secretary of State and the Welsh Ministers see PARA 741.

2   The expenses of the application to the Secretary of State or the Welsh Ministers and of contracts relating to the execution of the improvements or the advance of money relating to their execution, may be included in the charge: Improvement of Land Act 1864 s 50 (amended by the Statute Law (Repeals) Act 1993).

3   See the Improvement of Land Act 1864 s 49. The absolute order may be made after part of the improvements has been completed, for a proportional part of the sum involved: s 49. See also ss 57, 58 for the right of a landowner to require a similar charge to be executed in respect of costs incurred by him for public or general works of drainage or other improvements required to be made and authorised to be charged on the inheritance under other Acts, royal charters, commission under the great seal or the seal of the Duchy of Lancaster; but note that there do not appear to be any modern powers which could bring these provisions into operation. For the power to create the charge in such form as to take effect under the private Act of an improvement company see s 53. The charges are to be in the form in Sch (B): see s 52.

4   Improvement of Land Act 1864 s 51.

5   Improvement of Land Act 1864 s 55.

6   See *Baroness Wenlock v River Dee Co* (1888) 38 ChD 534, CA; and PARA 603 note 6.

7   Improvement of Land Act 1864 s 51.

8   See the Improvement of Land Act 1864 s 28. Section 28 also makes provision as to the right of the successor to terminate the proceedings upon certain conditions and for the right of the predecessor's assignee to complete the improvements.

9   Improvement of Land Act 1864 s 25.

C. EFFECT, REGISTRATION AND ENFORCEMENT

616.   Effect of charge created by absolute order within Improvement Acts.
The charge created by an absolute order takes effect by way of rentcharge payable by half-yearly instalments, which include both principal and interest, for the term of years fixed by the provisional order[1]. It creates a charge on the lands for the amount from time to time remaining undischarged, with priority over all existing and future incumbrances affecting the lands, whether created under the powers of any Act of Parliament or otherwise, except charges created under the Improvement of Land Act 1864 or charges of prior date under other Acts existing in 1864 and authorising the charging of lands with the expenses of improvements[2]. Absolute orders affecting unregistered land may be entered in the register of land charges as Class A land charges, and if not so registered before the completion of the purchase are void against a purchaser of the land charged or of any interest in that land[3].

1   Improvement of Land Act 1864 s 51. As to the term of years see PARA 613. Terminable rentcharges of this nature can only be redeemed before the expiration of the term by agreement (*Re Knatchbull's Settled Estate* (1885) 29 ChD 588 at 592, 595, CA; *Re Lord Egmont's Settled Estates* (1890) 45 ChD 395 at 400, CA). In *Re Earl of Strafford and Maples* [1896] 1 Ch 235, CA, a part of lands charged was released by agreement between the tenant for life and the owner of the charge.

2   Improvement of Land Act 1864 s 59. This provision also mentions certain obsolete exceptions to the rule of priority, namely charges under Acts authorising advances of public money for the improvement of land, tithe commutation rentcharges, quit rents, Crown rents, chief rents and other charges incidental to tenure. These incidents of tenure were extinguished by the Law of Property Act 1922 ss 138, 139 (repealed): see CUSTOM AND USAGE vol 32 (2012) PARA 41 et seq. Tithe rentcharges were extinguished by the Tithe Act 1936 s 1 (repealed): see ECCLESIASTICAL LAW vol 34 (2011) PARA 979.

   Where part only of the land charged is subject to a mortgage or other incumbrance, the charge created under the Improvement of Land Act 1864 has priority only to the extent of a due proportion of the charge as soon as it has been ascertained: s 59 proviso. As to apportionment see s 68; and PARA 618. As to rentcharges created under the Limited Owners Residences Act 1870 and the Limited Owners Residences Act (1870) Amendment Act 1871 see PARA 604 note 6. As to rentcharges under the private Acts of land improvement companies see PARA 601; and *Pollock v Lands Improvement Co* (1888) 37 ChD 661.

3   See the Land Charges Act 1972 ss 2(1), (2), 4(2), 17(1); and REAL PROPERTY AND REGISTRATION vol 87 (2017) PARAS 662, 664, 682. Land improvement charges for securing money, if registered before 1970, take effect as if created by a deed of charge by way of legal mortgage, but without prejudice to the priority of the charge; but they do not have that effect if registered after that date: see s 4(1); and REAL PROPERTY AND REGISTRATION vol 87 (2017) PARA 666. If the charge was registered before 1 January 1970, any body corporate which, but for the charge, would have power to advance money on the security of the estate or interest affected by it, has that power notwithstanding the charge: see s 4(4); and REAL PROPERTY AND REGISTRATION vol 87 (2017) PARA 666.

617.   Enforcement of charge within Improvement Acts.

Provision is made for the charging and payment of interest where charges fall into arrears[1]. If these statutory remedies are unavailing, a sale[2] or mortgage for the purpose of raising the charge may be ordered by the High Court, under its equitable jurisdiction[3], but there is no remedy against the landowner personally[4]. Charges are assignable[5], and must be kept down by the tenant for life as between him and the remainderman[6]. If the charge is paid by a tenant or occupier at a rent, he may, except when he has joined in the application or duly consented to be charged, deduct the amount from the rent payable to the landowner[7].

1   See the Improvement of Land Act 1864 s 64. The arrears are not to bear interest for a longer period than six months, but interest at the rate of 5% for any period not exceeding six months is recoverable in the same manner as the sum in arrear. If at the expiration of six months from the time of a payment falling into arrear there is not upon the land charged goods that would be sufficient to pay the amount outstanding under the Tribunals, Courts and Enforcement Act 2007 Sch 12, interest for six months and the cost of the distress, the arrears continue to bear interest at the rate of 5% per annum until payment: Improvement of Land Act 1864 s 64 (amended by the Tribunals, Courts and Enforcement Act 2007 Sch 14 para 17).
2   In the case of a charge registered as a land charge of Class A before 1 January 1970, the charge takes effect as if it had been created by deed of charge by way of legal mortgage, and consequently the chargee will have the statutory powers of sale under the Law of Property Act 1925 s 101: see MORTGAGE vol 77 (2016) PARA 446 et seq.
3   *Scottish Widows' Fund v Craig* (1882) 20 ChD 208.
4   *Scottish Drainage and Improvement Co v Campbell* (1889) 14 App Cas 139, HL. This was a case of a Scottish land improvement company, but the decision would seem to be applicable to all charges, whether created under the Improvement of Land Act 1864 or under the private Act of an English improvement company.
5   See the Improvement of Land Act 1864 s 65. The assignment is by deed duly stamped, and notice of the assignment should be sent to the Secretary of State or the Welsh Ministers: s 65. For the form of assignment see Sch (C). As to the Secretary of State and the Welsh Ministers see PARA 741.
6   Improvement of Land Act 1864 s 66.
7   Improvement of Land Act 1864 s 67.

D. APPORTIONMENT, RELEASE AND REDEMPTION

618.   Apportionment and release of charges within Improvement Acts.

Charges created under the Improvement of Land Act 1864, or any other Act authorising the creation of improvement charges by the Secretary of State and the Welsh Ministers[1], may, with the consent of the landowner or separate owners and with due notice to any assignee or his representative, be apportioned by the Secretary of State or the Welsh Ministers among the lands charged, or part of the land may be released, but no apportioned charge can be less than £1 for each half-yearly payment[2]. The apportioned charge is recoverable out of the lands charged by the order of apportionment[3]. An apportionment or release is made by order under seal of the Secretary of State or the Welsh Ministers, and the order may comprise all or any number of rentcharges existing by virtue of previous absolute orders[4], any copy authenticated by the seal of the Secretary of State or the

Welsh Ministers being conclusive evidence of the contents of the order for apportionment or release[5]. Provisions relating to the registration of charges created by absolute orders[6] apply also to the separate charges created by an order of apportionment[7].

1	As to the Secretary of State and the Welsh Ministers see PARA 741.
2	See the Improvement of Land Act 1864 s 68 (amended by the Improvement of Land Act 1899 Sch 2; the Mental Health Act 1959 Sch 7 Pt I; the Mental Capacity Act 2005 Sch 6 para 2; and by virtue of the Decimal Currency Act 1969 s 10(1)).
3	Improvement of Land Act 1864 s 70.
4	Improvement of Land Act 1864 s 71.
5	Improvement of Land Act 1864 s 69 (amended by the Improvement of Land Act 1899 Sch 2; and the Statute Law (Repeals) Act 1974). The form of order is set out in the Improvement of Land Act 1864 Schs (D), (E).
6	See PARA 616.
7	This follows because the apportionment creates separate and distinct charges: see the Improvement of Land Act 1864 s 68 (as amended: see note 2).

### 619.	Exoneration and redemption within Improvement Acts in the case of settled estates.

Provision is made for limited owners to exonerate one part of a settled estate from a charge by charging it upon another part[1], and for the redemption of improvement rentcharges out of capital money[2].

1	See the Settled Land Act 1925 ss 69, 82; and SETTLEMENTS vol 91 (2012) PARAS 752, 754.
2	See the Settled Land Act 1925 s 73(1)(xiii); but see PARA 599 note 1; and see also SETTLEMENTS vol 91 (2012) PARA 709.

### 620.	Loans by Agricultural Mortgage Corporation.

Where a loan has been made by the Agricultural Mortgage Corporation Limited[1], for defraying the expenses of an improvement of any specified kind[2], and the loan is, under the terms of the mortgage securing the loan, repayable by instalments, the repayment secured by the mortgage is deemed to constitute an improvement rentcharge which may be redeemed out of capital money, and when it is so redeemed the tenant for life must maintain and insure the improvement[3].

1	See PARA 602.
2	Ie of a kind authorised by the Settled Land Act 1925 Sch 3 Pt I.
3	See the Settled Land Act 1925 ss 73(1)(xiii), 88, Sch 3 Pt I; and SETTLEMENTS vol 91 (2012) PARAS 709, 717, 865. The reference to 'redemption' includes a reference to discharging, as it falls due, so much of any periodical payment as represents repayment of capital: Agriculture Act 1967 s 68.

### (vi)	Maintenance and Repair of Improvements

### 621.	Maintenance and repair of improvements within Improvement Acts.

During the continuance of a charge, the person bound to make the periodical payments of such charge is liable to maintain the works in respect of which the charge is made, and he may, if necessary, enter on adjoining lands for that purpose[1]. If required, he must certify to the Secretary of State or the Welsh Ministers[2] the state of the improvements[3]. He is also bound to keep insured against fire all improvements susceptible of damage by fire; if he fails to insure, the person entitled to the charge may effect the insurance at the expense of the person liable to insure[4]. If the person bound to make the periodical payments neglects to maintain improvements, he will be liable to an action by a remainderman for damage[5], and, in addition, the Secretary of State or the Welsh Ministers may inspect the improvements and cause the necessary works to be executed, the expense being recoverable as if it had been part of the charge[6]. If an improvement consisting of an embankment or work constructed in, under or across any tidal water or navigable river is abandoned or falls into decay, the nuisance may be abated by the Secretary of State or the Welsh Ministers at the cost of the landowner[7]. If, however, the maintenance of any improvements becomes unnecessary, the person bound to make the periodical payments may be relieved from liability for maintenance on a certificate of the Secretary of State or the Welsh Ministers given after inspection and notice to interested parties[8].

1   See the Improvement of Land Act 1864 ss 72, 73 (both amended by the Statute Law (Repeals) Act 1993).
2   As to the Secretary of State and the Welsh Ministers see PARA **741**.
3   Improvement of Land Act 1864 s 72 (as amended: see note 1).
4   Improvement of Land Act 1864 s 74.
5   Improvement of Land Act 1864 s 72 (as amended: see note 1).
6   Improvement of Land Act 1864 s 75. As to recovery of a charge see PARA **618**.
7   Improvement of Land Act 1864 s 77 (amended by the Statute Law (Repeals) Act 1993).
8   Improvement of Land Act 1864 s 76.

(2) RESTRUCTURING OF HOLDINGS AND USE OF UNCULTIVATED LAND

622.   Projects subject to environmental impact assessment.
Provision is made for the subjection of projects[1] for the restructuring of rural land holdings, and projects to increase the productivity for agriculture[2] of uncultivated land[3] or semi-natural areas, to environmental impact assessments[4]. Those provisions, which were made pursuant to the powers of the Secretary of State and the Welsh Ministers to legislate in relation to the requirement for an assessment of the impact on the environment of projects likely to have significant effects on the environment and the conservation of natural habitats and of wild flora and fauna[5], apply to any such projects other than those specifically exempted by the regulations[6]. These provisions are also enforced pursuant to the operation of the common agricultural policy[7].

1   'Project' means the execution of construction works or other installations or schemes or other interventions in the natural surroundings and landscape: Environmental Impact Assessment (Agriculture) (England) (No 2) Regulations 2006, SI 2006/2522, reg 2(1); Environmental Impact Assessment (Agriculture) (Wales) Regulations 2017, SI 2017/565, reg 2(1).
2   As to the meanings of 'agriculture' and 'agricultural' see PARA **424** (definition applied by the Environmental Impact Assessment (Agriculture) (England) (No 2) Regulations 2006, SI 2006/2522, reg 2(1); Environmental Impact Assessment (Agriculture) (Wales) Regulations 2017, SI 2017/565, reg 2(1)).
3   In England, 'uncultivated land' means land which has not been cultivated in the previous 15 years 'cultivated' means cultivated by physical means (including ploughing and harrowing) or chemical means (including the application of fertilisers) and 'uncultivated land project' means a project to increase the productivity for agriculture of uncultivated land or a semi-natural area (including projects to increase the productivity for agriculture of such land to below the norm): Environmental Impact Assessment (Agriculture) (England) (No 2) Regulations 2006, SI 2006/2522, reg 2(1). Those expressions are not defined for the purposes of the Environmental Impact Assessment (Agriculture) (Wales) Regulations 2017, SI 2017/565. For an example of where land does not come within the description of uncultivated land or a semi-natural area see *R (on the application of Wye Valley Action Association Ltd) v Herefordshire Council* [2011] EWCA Civ 20, [2011] PTSR 1011, [2011] All ER (D) 188 (Jan).

4   See the Environmental Impact Assessment (Agriculture) (England) (No 2) Regulations 2006,
    SI 2006/2522; the Environmental Impact Assessment (Agriculture) (Wales) Regulations 2017,
    SI 2017/565; and PARA 623 et seq.
5   Environmental Impact Assessment (Agriculture) (England) (No 2) Regulations 2006,
    SI 2006/2522, preamble; Environmental Impact Assessment (Agriculture) (Wales) Regulations
    2017, SI 2017/565, preamble. As to the Secretary of State and the Welsh Ministers see PARA 741.
    The regulations were made under the European Communities Act 1972 s 2(2) and implement
    European Parliament and Council Directive (EU) 2011/92 (OJ L26, 28.1.2012, p 1) on the
    assessment of the effects of certain public and private projects on the environment), and Council
    Directive (EC) 92/43 (OJ L206, 22.7.92, p 7) on the conservation of natural habitats and of wild
    fauna and flora (the 'Habitats Directive') in so far as applicable to such projects, and unless it is
    otherwise provided, expressions used both in the Environmental Impact Assessment (Agriculture)
    (England) (No 2) Regulations 2006, SI 2006/2522, or the Environmental Impact Assessment
    (Agriculture) (Wales) Regulations 2017, SI 2017/535, and in the EIA Directive or in the Habitats
    Directive have the same meaning in those regulations as they have in those directives:
    Environmental Impact Assessment (Agriculture) (England) (No 2) Regulations 2006,
    SI 2006/2522, reg 2(1), (2) (amended by SI 2017/593); Environmental Impact Assessment
    (Agriculture) (Wales) Regulations 2017, SI 2017/535, reg 2(1), (2).
6   Environmental Impact Assessment (Agriculture) (England) (No 2) Regulations 2006,
    SI 2006/2522, reg 3(1) (amended by SI 2017/593); Environmental Impact Assessment
    (Agriculture) (Wales) Regulations 2017, SI 2017/565, reg 3(1). As to when a project is exempt see
    the Environmental Impact Assessment (Agriculture) (England) (No 2) Regulations 2006,
    SI 2006/2522, reg 3(2)(a)–(e), 3A–3C (reg 3 amended and regs 3A–3C added by SI 2017/593) and
    the Environmental Impact Assessment (Agriculture) (Wales) Regulations 2017, SI 2017/565, reg
    3(2)(a)–(f), (3)–(5).
7   See the Common Agricultural Policy (Control and Enforcement, Cross-Compliance, Scrutiny of
    Transactions and Appeals) Regulations 2014, SI 2014/3263, reg 18(1), Sch 2 para 2; the Common
    Agricultural Policy (Integrated Administration and Control System and Enforcement and Cross
    Compliance) (Wales) Regulations 2014, SI 2014/3223, reg 13(1), Sch 1 para 10; and
    AGRICULTURAL PRODUCTION AND MARKETING vol 1A (2017) PARA 3.

623. Screening of potentially significant projects by Natural England or Welsh Ministers.

A person must not begin or carry out an uncultivated land project in England[1]
or a restructuring project[2] in England or Wales of an extent which is equal to or
exceeds the threshold applicable to it[3] (or in relation to which Natural England[4]
has excluded the operation of such thresholds[5]), or a project on semi-natural
and/or uncultivated land in Wales, unless he has first obtained a screening
decision[6] permitting the project to proceed[7].

An application for a screening decision must be made to Natural England or
the Welsh Ministers[8] who must decide whether or not a project is likely to have
significant effects on the environment[9], in which case it is a 'significant project'[10].
If Natural England or the Welsh Ministers fails or fail to make or notify a
screening decision[11] the applicant may notify Natural England or the Welsh
Ministers that he intends to treat that failure as a decision that the project is a
significant project[12]. A screening decision, whether made or deemed, has effect for
three years[13].

1   As to the meanings of 'project' and (in England) 'uncultivated land project' and 'uncultivated land'
    see PARA 622 note 3.
2   'Restructuring project' means a project for the restructuring of rural land holdings: Environmental
    Impact Assessment (Agriculture) (England) (No 2) Regulations 2006, SI 2006/2522, reg 2(1);
    Environmental Impact Assessment (Agriculture) (Wales) Regulations 2017, SI 2017/565, reg 2(1).
3   The applicable threshold (which relates to the area of land likely to be affected by the project) is
    calculated in accordance with the Environmental Impact Assessment (Agriculture) (England) (No
    2) Regulations 2006, SI 2006/2522, reg 5, Sch 1 and the Environmental Impact Assessment
    (Agriculture) (Wales) Regulations 2017, SI 2017/565, reg 5, Sch 1.
4   As to Natural England see the Natural Environment and Rural Communities Act 2006 Pt 1 Ch 1
    (ss 1–16); and OPEN SPACES AND COUNTRYSIDE vol 78 (2010) PARA 523.

5 If Natural England believes that a project which is likely to fall below the threshold at which a screening decision is required would nonetheless be likely to have significant effects on the environment it may issue a 'screening notice' providing that the thresholds do not apply to the area of land in question (see the Environmental Impact Assessment (Agriculture) (England) (No 2) Regulations 2006, SI 2006/2522, reg 6, Sch 2 (Sch 2 substituted by SI 2017/593)), and a person must not begin or carry out any uncultivated land project or restructuring project on land to which a relevant screening notice (ie a screening notice which states that it applies to the type of project which is to be carried out (reg 4(3))) applies unless he has first obtained a screening decision (see note 6) permitting the project to proceed (reg 4(2)). There is a right of appeal in England against the service of a screening notice, but not in Wales: see PARA 626.

6 'Screening decision' means a decision made by Natural England or the Welsh Ministers under the Environmental Impact Assessment (Agriculture) (England) (No 2) Regulations 2006, SI 2006/2522, reg 8(1) or the Environmental Impact Assessment (Agriculture) (Wales) Regulations 2017, SI 2017/565, reg 7(1) (see the text and note 9) or a decision deemed to be made by Natural England or the Welsh Ministers under the Environmental Impact Assessment (Agriculture) (England) (No 2) Regulations 2006, SI 2006/2522, reg 8(7) or the Environmental Impact Assessment (Agriculture) (Wales) Regulations 2017, SI 2017/565, reg 7(7) (see note 12): Environmental Impact Assessment (Agriculture) (England) (No 2) Regulations 2006, SI 2006/2522, reg 2(1); Environmental Impact Assessment (Agriculture) (Wales) Regulations 2017, SI 2017/565, reg 2(1). As to the Welsh Ministers see PARA 741.

7 Environmental Impact Assessment (Agriculture) (England) (No 2) Regulations 2006, SI 2006/2522, reg 4(1); Environmental Impact Assessment (Agriculture) (Wales) Regulations 2017, SI 2017/565, reg 4. A person who is in breach of the requirement for a screening decision is guilty of an offence, and may be served with a stop notice or a remediation notice: see PARA 625.

8 Environmental Impact Assessment (Agriculture) (England) (No 2) Regulations 2006, SI 2006/2522, reg 7(1)(a); Environmental Impact Assessment (Agriculture) (Wales) Regulations 2017, SI 2017/565, reg 6(1)(a). As to the information to be included in the application: see the Environmental Impact Assessment (Agriculture) (England) (No 2) Regulations 2006, SI 2006/2522, reg 7(1)(b), (1A), (2), Sch 2 (reg 7 amended and Sch 2 added by SI 2017/593); and the Environmental Impact Assessment (Agriculture) (Wales) Regulations 2017, SI 2017/565, reg 6(1)(b)–(d), (2).

9 Environmental Impact Assessment (Agriculture) (England) (No 2) Regulations 2006, SI 2006/2522, reg 8(1); Environmental Impact Assessment (Agriculture) (Wales) Regulations 2017, SI 2017/565, reg 7(1). As to the selection criteria to be considered see the Environmental Impact Assessment (Agriculture) (England) (No 2) Regulations 2006, SI 2006/2522, Sch 2 (substituted by SI 2017/593); and the Environmental Impact Assessment (Agriculture) (Wales) Regulations 2017, SI 2017/565, Sch 2. Natural England is required to take into account the results of any relevant EU environmental assessment which are reasonably available to it: Environmental Impact Assessment (Agriculture) (England) (No 2) Regulations 2006, SI 2006/2522, reg 8(1A) (added by SI 2017/593). 'EU environmental assessment' means:

   (1)   an assessment carried out under an obligation to which the European Communities Act 1972 s 2(1) applies (other than the European Parliament and Council Directive (EU) 2011/92 (OJ L26, 28.1.2012, p 1) on the assessment of the effects of certain public and private projects on the environment ('the EIA Directive'); or

   (2)   under the law of any part of the United Kingdom implementing an EU obligation other than an obligation arising under the EIA Directive;

   (3)   of the effect of anything on the environment: Environmental Impact Assessment (Agriculture) (England) (No 2) Regulations 2006, SI 2006/2522, reg 2(1) (definition added by SI 2017/593).

Before making a screening decision, Natural England and the Welsh Ministers are required to consult certain bodies: see the Environmental Impact Assessment (Agriculture) (England) (No 2) Regulations 2006, SI 2006/2522, regs 2(1), 8(3) (reg 2(1) amended by SI 2017/593); and the Environmental Impact Assessment (Agriculture) (Wales) Regulations 2017, SI 2017/565, regs 2(1), 7(3). There is a 35 day period in which Natural England or as appropriate, the Welsh Ministers, must make and notify the applicant of, a screening decision within 35 days, which may be extended in England under exceptions circumstances: see the Environmental Impact Assessment (Agriculture) (England) (No 2) Regulations 2006, SI 2006/2522, reg 8(4), (5), (5A) (reg 8(4), (5) amended and (5A) added by SI 2017, SI 2017/593); and the Environmental Impact Assessment (Agriculture) (Wales) Regulations 2017, SI 2017/565, reg 7(4), (5). If Natural England decides or the Welsh Ministers decide that a project is likely to have a significant effect on a European site (either alone or in combination with other projects), and the project is not directly connected with or necessary for the management of the site, the project must be treated as being likely to have significant effects on the environment: Environmental Impact Assessment (Agriculture) (England) (No 2) Regulations 2006, SI 2006/2522, reg 8(2); Environmental Impact Assessment (Agriculture) (Wales) Regulations 2017, SI 2017/565, reg 7(2). There is a right of appeal against a screening decision: see PARA 626.

As to the Secretary of State see PARA 741. In relation to England, 'European site' means those sites described in the Conservation of Habitats and Species Regulations 2010, SI 2010/490, reg 8(1) (see OPEN SPACES AND COUNTRYSIDE vol 78 (2010) PARA 729), and relation to Wales, described in reg 8(1)(a), (b), (d) or (e): Environmental Impact Assessment (Agriculture) (England) (No 2) Regulations 2006, SI 2006/2522, reg 2(1) (amended by SI 2017/593); Environmental Impact Assessment (Agriculture) (Wales) Regulations 2017, SI 2017/565, reg 2(1).

10 Environmental Impact Assessment (Agriculture) (England) (No 2) Regulations 2006, SI 2006/2522, reg 2(1); Environmental Impact Assessment (Agriculture) (Wales) Regulations 2017, SI 2017/565, reg 7(1) (a 'significant project' in England is an uncultivated land project or a restructuring project which Natural England has decided under the Environmental Impact Assessment (Agriculture) (England) (No 2) Regulations 2006, SI 2006/2522, reg 8(1) (see the text and note 9), or is deemed to have decided under reg 8(7) (see note 12), is likely to have significant effects on the environment (reg 2(1); and in Wales, is a project on semi-natural and/or uncultivated land or a restructuring project which the Welsh Ministers have decided or are deemed to have decided is likely to have significant effects on the environment in accordance with the Environmental Impact Assessment (Agriculture) (Wales) Regulations 2017, SI 2017/565, reg 7(1) or (7): (reg 2(1)).

If, after Natural England or the Welsh Ministers has or have made, or is or are deemed to have made, a decision that the project is a significant project, they receive further information or representations and as a result of that further information or those representations decide that the project is not a significant project, they must take all the steps in the Environmental Impact Assessment (Agriculture) (England) (No 2) Regulations 2006, SI 2006/2522, reg 8(4) or the Environmental Impact Assessment (Agriculture) (Wales) Regulations 2017, SI 2017/565, reg 7(6) (see note 9) in respect of that new decision: Environmental Impact Assessment (Agriculture) (England) (No 2) Regulations 2006, SI 2006/2522, reg 8(8); Environmental Impact Assessment (Agriculture) (Wales) Regulations 2017, SI 2017/565, reg 7(9). A decision that a project is not a significant project may also be reviewed if the site subsequently becomes a European site: see the Environmental Impact Assessment (Agriculture) (England) (No 2) Regulations 2006, SI 2006/2522, reg 21(a), Sch 4; and the Environmental Impact Assessment (Agriculture) (Wales) Regulations 2017, SI 2017/565, reg 20, Sch 4.

A person aggrieved by a decision of Natural England or the Welsh Ministers that a project is not a significant project may apply to the High Court for an order quashing the decision: see PARA 626.

11 Ie within the period referred to in the Environmental Impact Assessment (Agriculture) (England) (No 2) Regulations 2006, SI 2006/2522, reg 8(5) or the Environmental Impact Assessment (Agriculture) (Wales) Regulations 2017, SI 2017/565, reg 7(4) (see note 9).

12 Environmental Impact Assessment (Agriculture) (England) (No 2) Regulations 2006, SI 2006/2522, reg 8(6); Environmental Impact Assessment (Agriculture) (Wales) Regulations 2017, SI 2017/565, reg 7(7). Where the applicant has so notified Natural England or the Welsh Ministers, Natural England or the Welsh Ministers is or are deemed to have decided on the date of that notification that the project is a significant project: Environmental Impact Assessment (Agriculture) (England) (No 2) Regulations 2006, SI 2006/2522, reg 8(7); Environmental Impact Assessment (Agriculture) (Wales) Regulations 2017, SI 2017/565, reg 7(8).

13 If the project to which a screening decision relates is not begun within a period of three years beginning with the date the screening decision is either notified to the applicant or deemed to have been taken under the Environmental Impact Assessment (Agriculture) (England) (No 2) Regulations 2006, SI 2006/2522, reg 8(7) or the Environmental Impact Assessment (Agriculture) (Wales) Regulations 2017, SI 2017, reg 7(7) (see note 12), the screening decision ceases to have effect: see the Environmental Impact Assessment (Agriculture) (England) (No 2) Regulations 2006, SI 2006/2522, reg 8(9); and the Environmental Impact Assessment (Agriculture) (Wales) Regulations 2017, SI 2017/565, reg 7(10).

624. Significant projects requiring consent of Natural England or Welsh Ministers.

A person must not begin or carry out a significant project[1] unless he has first obtained consent from Natural England or, as the case may be, the Welsh Ministers[2], and in order to obtain consent an 'environmental statement' must be included in the application[3]. If the project may affect another EEA state[4], Natural England or, as the case may be, the Welsh Ministers must inform that state of the application and invite it to participate in the screening procedure[5].

In relation to England, Natural England must consider (ensuring that in doing so it has, or has access to, any expertise it considers necessary):

(1)   the environmental statement;

(2)   any additional environmental information;

(3)   any representations or opinions it receives under certain provisions[6];

(4)   any features of the significant project or measures to avoid, prevent, reduce or offset any likely significant adverse effects of the significant project on the environment[7].

Following that consideration, Natural England must reach a conclusion about the likely significant effects (including the expected effects deriving from the vulnerability of the significant project to risks of major accidents or disasters) of the significant project on:

(a)   population and human health;

(b)   biodiversity, with particular attention to species and habitats protected under the Habitats Directive and the Wild Birds Directive[8];

(c)   land, soil, water, air and climate;

(d)   material assets, cultural heritage and the landscape;

(e)   the interaction between the factors referred to in heads (a) to (d)[9].

Natural England must consider:

(i)   the conclusion reached in respect of the significant project and the reasons for that conclusion;

(ii)   whether it is appropriate to require the applicant to monitor the significant adverse effects of the significant project on the environment, and if so whether consent should be given subject to conditions to ensure that the applicant is under such a duty and whether consent should be given subject to conditions to require remedial action to be taken in circumstances described in the conditions;

(iii)   whether, having regard to the likely significant environmental effects of the significant project, consent should be given subject to any other conditions;

(iv)   any social or economic impacts which might result from a decision to refuse consent for the significant project[10].

Following that consideration, Natural England must, subject to compliance with the statutory provisions as to the conservation of habitats[11], grant, or refuse to grant, consent for a significant project[12].

Similarly, after considering the environmental statement, any additional environmental information, any representations received pursuant to the consultation process[13] and any social or economic impacts which might result from a decision to refuse consent for the project[14], the Welsh Ministers may, subject to compliance with the statutory provisions as to the conservation of habitats[15], grant, or refuse to grant, consent[16].

Consents may be conditional[17].

1   See PARA 623. As to the meaning of 'project' see PARA 622 note 1; and as to the meaning of 'significant project' see PARA 623 note 10.

2   Environmental Impact Assessment (Agriculture) (England) (No 2) Regulations 2006, SI 2006/2522, reg 9; Environmental Impact Assessment (Agriculture) (Wales) Regulations 2017, SI 2017/565, reg 8. As to Natural England see the Natural Environment and Rural Communities Act 2006 Pt 1 Ch 1 (ss 1–16); and OPEN SPACES AND COUNTRYSIDE vol 78 (2010) PARA 523. As

to the Welsh Ministers see PARA **741**. A person who is in breach of the requirement for consent is guilty of an offence, and may be served with a stop notice or a remediation notice: see PARA **625**.

3 See the Environmental Impact Assessment (Agriculture) (England) (No 2) Regulations 2006, SI 2006/2522, reg 12(1) (substituted by SI 2017/593); and the Environmental Impact Assessment (Agriculture) (Wales) Regulations 2017, SI 2017/565, reg 11(1). An environmental statement must include certain information: see the Environmental Impact Assessment (Agriculture) (England) (No 2) Regulations 2006, SI 2006/2522, reg 9(1), (1A), Sch 3 (reg 9(1), Sch 3 substituted and reg 9(1A) added by SI 2017, SI 2017/593); and the Environmental Impact Assessment (Agriculture) (Wales) Regulations 2017, SI 2017/565, reg 11(2), (3), Sch 3. After receiving a screening decision that a project is a significant project, but before applying for consent for the project from Natural England or the Welsh Ministers, the applicant may ask Natural England or the Welsh Ministers to provide a 'scoping opinion': Environmental Impact Assessment (Agriculture) (England) (No 2) Regulations 2006, SI 2006/2522, reg 10(1); Environmental Impact Assessment (Agriculture) (Wales) Regulations 2017, SI 2017/565, reg 9(1). In relation to Wales, a scoping opinion is the opinion of the Welsh Ministers on what information should be provided in the environmental statement: Environmental Impact Assessment (Agriculture) (Wales) Regulations 2017, SI 2017/565, reg 9(1). In relation to England, the scoping opinion is the opinion of the Secretary of State as to the scope and level of detail of information which is required and a request for such information must include certain information: see the Environmental Impact Assessment (Agriculture) (England) (No 2) Regulations 2006, SI 2006/2522, reg 10(1), (1A) (reg 10(1) amended and reg 10(1A) added by SI 2017/593). As to consultation and the giving of the opinion see the Environmental Impact Assessment (Agriculture) (England) (No 2) Regulations 2006, SI 2006/2522, regs 10(2)–(4), 11; and the Environmental Impact Assessment (Agriculture) (Wales) Regulations 2017, SI 2017/565, regs 9(2)–(4), 10. As to the meaning of 'screening decision' see PARA **623** note 6. As to the administration of the consent application see the Environmental Impact Assessment (Agriculture) (England) (No 2) Regulations 2006, SI 2006/2522, regs 12(2)–(6), 13 (reg 12(5) amended by SI 2017/593); and the Environmental Impact Assessment (Agriculture) (Wales) Regulations 2017, SI 2017/565, regs 11(4), 12. It is an offence to procure a decision on an application by making false representations: see PARA **625**.

4 'EEA state' means a member state, Norway, Iceland or Liechtenstein: Environmental Impact Assessment (Agriculture) (England) (No 2) Regulations 2006, SI 2006/2522, reg 2(1); Environmental Impact Assessment (Agriculture) (Wales) Regulations 2017, SI 2017/565, reg 2(1).

5 See the Environmental Impact Assessment (Agriculture) (England) (No 2) Regulations 2006, SI 2006/2522, reg 14; and the Environmental Impact Assessment (Agriculture) (Wales) Regulations 2017, SI 2017/565, reg 13. For the procedure where a significant project in another member state may affect England see the Environmental Impact Assessment (Agriculture) (England) (No 2) Regulations 2006, SI 2006/2522, reg 15; and for the procedure where a significant project in another member state may affect Wales see the Environmental Impact Assessment (Agriculture) (Wales) Regulations 2017, SI 2017/565, reg 14. Special provision is also made for transborder projects (ie projects where the relevant land is situated partly in England and partly in Wales or partly in England or Wales and partly in Scotland): see the Environmental Impact Assessment (Agriculture) (England) (No 2) Regulations 2006, SI 2006/2522, reg 20; and the Environmental Impact Assessment (Agriculture) (Wales) Regulations 2017, SI 2017/565, reg 19.

6 Ie any representations or opinions it receives under the Environmental Impact Assessment (Agriculture) (England) (No 2) Regulations 2006, SI 2006/2522, regs 12(4)(b), (5)(c), 13(2)(b), (3)(d) and reg 14(5)(b).

7 Environmental Impact Assessment (Agriculture) (England) (No 2) Regulations 2006, SI 2006/2522, reg 15A(1) (added by SI 2017/593).

8 Ie Council Directive (EC) 1992/43 (OJ L206, 22.7.92, p 7) on the conservation of natural habitats and of wild fauna and flora (the 'Habitats Directive') and European Parliament and Council Directive (EC) 2009/147 on the conservation of wild birds (the 'Wild Birds Directive'): Environmental Impact Assessment (Agriculture) (England) (No 2) Regulations 2006, SI 2006/2522, reg 2(1) (definition of Wild Birds Directive added by SI 2017/593).

9 Environmental Impact Assessment (Agriculture) (England) (No 2) Regulations 2006, SI 2006/2522, reg 15A(2) (as added: see note 5).

10 Environmental Impact Assessment (Agriculture) (England) (No 2) Regulations 2006, SI 2006/2522, reg 16(1) (substituted by SI 2017/593).

11 Ie the Conservation of Habitats and Species Regulations 2010, SI 2010, SI 2010/490, regs 41, 43 or 45 (see OPEN SPACES AND COUNTRYSIDE vol 78 (2010) PARA 728 et seq) but that does not

include anything for which a licence has been granted under reg 53): see the Environmental Impact Assessment (Agriculture) (England) (No 2) Regulations 2006, SI 2006/2522, reg 17 (amended by SI 2017/593).

12 Environmental Impact Assessment (Agriculture) (England) (No 2) Regulations 2006, SI 2006/2522, reg 16(2) (as substituted: see note 10). Natural England may make a decision under reg 16(2) only if satisfied that the conclusion reached under reg 15A(2) in respect of the significant project and the reasons for it address the likely significant environmental effects of the significant project: reg 16(3) (as so substituted). Natural England must not make a decision under reg 16(2) before the expiry of the period in the notice under reg 12(5)(c), the expiry of the period of 28 days after the date on which any additional environmental information was sent to the consultation bodies, or the date notice of the additional environmental information was published under reg 13(3), or the expiry of any period agreed with another EEA State under reg 14(6)(b): reg 16(4) (as so substituted). Natural England must reach its decision under reg 16(2) within a reasonable period of time beginning with the date on which it is given all the information it is required to consider in accordance with regulation 15A(1) taking into account the nature and complexity of the application and significant project: reg 16(5) (as so substituted). As to the procedure following a consent decision see reg 19 (substituted by SI 2017/593). A consent decision may be reviewed if the site subsequently becomes a European site: see reg 21(b), Sch 4. As to the meaning of 'European site' see PARA 622 note 9. There is a right of appeal against a refusal of consent and a right to apply to the High Court against a decision to grant consent: see PARA 626.

13 Ie received under the Environmental Impact Assessment (Agriculture) (Wales) Regulations 2017, SI 2017/565, reg 11(4)(a), reg 12(2(b), (3)(d) or reg 13(4)(b).

14 See the Environmental Impact Assessment (Agriculture) (Wales) Regulations 2017, SI 2017/565, reg 15.

15 Ie the Conservation of Habitats and Species Regulations 2010, SI 2010, SI 2010/490, regs 41, 43 or 45 (see OPEN SPACES AND COUNTRYSIDE vol 78 (2010) PARA 728 et seq) but that does not include anything for which a licence has been granted under reg 53): see the Environmental Impact Assessment (Agriculture) (Wales) Regulations 2017, SI 2017/565, reg 16.

16 As to the procedure following a consent decision see the Environmental Impact Assessment (Agriculture) (Wales) Regulations 2017, SI 2017/565, reg 18. A consent decision may be reviewed if the site subsequently becomes a European site: see reg 20(b), Sch 4.

17 See the Environmental Impact Assessment (Agriculture) (England) (No 2) Regulations 2006, SI 2006/2522, reg 18 (amended by SI 2017/593); and the Environmental Impact Assessment (Agriculture) (Wales) Regulations 2017, SI 2017/565, reg 17. It is an offence to carry out work in contravention of a condition of a consent: see PARA 625. There is a right of appeal against a conditional consent: see PARA 626.

625. Punishment and enforcement where procedures not complied with.

Any person who begins or carries out an uncultivated land project (or in Wales, a project on semi-natural and/or uncultivated land)[1] or a restructuring project[2] in breach of the requirement for a screening decision[3] or the requirement for consent[4] is guilty of an offence[5], and may be served with a stop notice[6] or a remediation notice[7], contravention of which is also an offence[8]. It is also an offence to carry out work in contravention of a condition of a consent[9] or to procure a decision on an application by making false representations[10]. There are powers of entry and powers to act in default of any notices issued pursuant to these provisions[11], and provisions as to the time limits within which proceedings must be brought[12].

1 As to the meanings of 'project', 'uncultivated land project' and 'uncultivated land' see PARA 622 note 3.

2 As to the meaning of 'restructuring project' see PARA 623 note 2.

3 Ie in breach of the Environmental Impact Assessment (Agriculture) (England) (No 2) Regulations 2006, SI 2006/2522, reg 4 or the Environmental Impact Assessment (Agriculture) (Wales) Regulations 2017, SI 2017/565, reg 4 (see PARA 623). As to the meaning of 'screening decision' see PARA 623 note 6.

4 Ie in breach of the Environmental Impact Assessment (Agriculture) (England) (No 2) Regulations 2006, SI 2006/2522, reg 9 or the Environmental Impact Assessment (Agriculture) (Wales) Regulations 2017, SI 2017/565, reg 8 (see PARA 624).

5   See the Environmental Impact Assessment (Agriculture) (England) (No 2) Regulations 2006, SI 2006/2522, reg 22; and the Environmental Impact Assessment (Agriculture) (Wales) Regulations 2017, SI 2017/565, reg 21. A person guilty of such an offence is liable on summary conviction to a fine: Environmental Impact Assessment (Agriculture) (England) (No 2) Regulations 2006, SI 2006/2522, reg 22(1); Environmental Impact Assessment (Agriculture) (Wales) Regulations 2017, SI 2017/565, reg 21(1). As to the powers of Magistrates' courts to issue fines on summary conviction see SENTENCING vol 92 (2015) PARA 176. In relation to certain offences in England, Natural England may impose a fixed monetary penalty, or variable monetary penalty, or accept an enforcement undertaking: see the Environmental Impact Assessment (Agriculture) (England) (No 2) Regulations 2006, SI 2006/2522, reg 30A (added by SI 2010/1159). As to Natural England see the Natural Environment and Rural Communities Act 2006 Pt 1 Ch 1 (ss 1–16); and OPEN SPACES AND COUNTRYSIDE vol 78 (2010) PARA 523. As to the Welsh Ministers see PARA 741. There is a right of appeal against the service of a stop notice: see PARA 626.

6   See the Environmental Impact Assessment (Agriculture) (England) (No 2) Regulations 2006, SI 2006/2522, reg 25; and the Environmental Impact Assessment (Agriculture) (Wales) Regulations 2017, SI 2017/565, reg 24. Stop notices are served by Natural England or, where applicable, the Welsh Ministers: Environmental Impact Assessment (Agriculture) (England) (No 2) Regulations 2006, SI 2006/2522, reg 25(1); Environmental Impact Assessment (Agriculture) (Wales) Regulations 2017, SI 2017/565, reg 24(1).

7   See the Environmental Impact Assessment (Agriculture) (England) (No 2) Regulations 2006, SI 2006/2522, reg 27; and the Environmental Impact Assessment (Agriculture) (Wales) Regulations 2017, SI 2017/565, reg 26. Remediation notices are served by Natural England or, where applicable, the Welsh Ministers: Environmental Impact Assessment (Agriculture) (England) (No 2) Regulations 2006, SI 2006/2522, reg 27(1); Environmental Impact Assessment (Agriculture) (Wales) Regulations 2017, SI 2017/565, reg 26(1). There is a right of appeal against the service of a remediation notice: see PARA 626.

8   See the Environmental Impact Assessment (Agriculture) (England) (No 2) Regulations 2006, SI 2006/2522, regs 26, 28; and the Environmental Impact Assessment (Agriculture) (Wales) Regulations 2017, SI 2017/565, regs 25, 27. A person guilty of contravening a stop notice is liable on summary conviction to a fine not exceeding the statutory maximum and on conviction on indictment to a fine (Environmental Impact Assessment (Agriculture) (England) (No 2) Regulations 2006, SI 2006/2522, reg 26(4); Environmental Impact Assessment (Agriculture) (Wales) Regulations 2017, SI 2017/565, reg 25(2)); and a person guilty of contravening a remediation notice is liable on summary conviction to a fine and, if the failure is continued after conviction, to a further fine not exceeding £100 for every day the failure continues (Environmental Impact Assessment (Agriculture) (England) (No 2) Regulations 2006, SI 2006/2522, reg 28; Environmental Impact Assessment (Agriculture) (Wales) Regulations 2017, SI 2017/565, reg 27).

9   See the Environmental Impact Assessment (Agriculture) (England) (No 2) Regulations 2006, SI 2006/2522, reg 23; and the Environmental Impact Assessment (Agriculture) (Wales) Regulations 2017, SI 2017/565, reg 22(1). A person guilty of such an offence is liable on summary conviction to a fine: Environmental Impact Assessment (Agriculture) (England) (No 2) Regulations 2006, SI 2006/2522, reg 23; Environmental Impact Assessment (Agriculture) (Wales) Regulations 2017, SI 2017/565, reg 22(2).

10 See the Environmental Impact Assessment (Agriculture) (England) (No 2) Regulations 2006, SI 2006/2522, reg 24; and the Environmental Impact Assessment (Agriculture) (Wales) Regulations 2017, SI 2017/565, reg 23. A person guilty of this offence is liable on summary conviction to a fine not exceeding the statutory maximum and on conviction on indictment to a fine: Environmental Impact Assessment (Agriculture) (England) (No 2) Regulations 2006, SI 2006/2522, reg 24(2); Environmental Impact Assessment (Agriculture) (Wales) Regulations 2017, SI 2017/565, reg 23(2).

11 See the Environmental Impact Assessment (Agriculture) (England) (No 2) Regulations 2006, SI 2006/2522, reg 30; and the Environmental Impact Assessment (Agriculture) (Wales) Regulations 2017, SI 2017/565, reg 29.

12 See the Environmental Impact Assessment (Agriculture) (England) (No 2) Regulations 2006, SI 2006/2522, reg 29; and the Environmental Impact Assessment (Agriculture) (Wales) Regulations 2017, SI 2017/565, reg 28.

626. Appeals generally in connection with environmental impact assessments.

A person may appeal to the Secretary of State or, as the case may be, the Welsh Ministers[1] against a stop notice[2] or a remediation notice[3], and a person may appeal to the Secretary of State against a screening notice[4], on the grounds that

Natural England[5] or (as the case may be) the Welsh Ministers did not have power to serve the notice or include a particular requirement in it, that there has been some material irregularity, defect or error in, or in connection with, the notice, or that any of the requirements of the notice are unreasonable[6]. On appeal the Secretary of State or the Welsh Ministers may affirm, vary or revoke the notice[7].

Applicants for screening decisions[8] in respect of significant projects[9], and applicants for consent for significant projects whose applications have either been refused or granted conditionally[10], may appeal against those decisions to the Secretary of State or the Welsh Ministers[11]. The Secretary of State and the Welsh Ministers may allow or dismiss the appeal, or reverse any part of the relevant decision, and may consider the appeal as if he or they were making a decision on the matter in question for the first time[12].

Provision is made for the administration of appeals against notices and decisions[13], which may be determined either by written representation[14] or by a hearing or local inquiry[15].

A person aggrieved by a decision of Natural England or the Welsh Ministers that a project is not a significant project or by a decision to grant consent for a significant project may make an application to the High Court for an order quashing the decision[16], and the court may quash the decision if it is satisfied that the decision was not lawfully made[17] or the interests of the person who has applied to the court have been substantially prejudiced by a failure to comply with any relevant statutory requirement[18]. Provision is made for the administration of such applications[19].

1   As to the Secretary of State and the Welsh Ministers see PARA 741.
2   As to the issue of stop notices see PARA 625.
3   As to the issue of remediation notices see PARA 625.
4   As to the meaning of 'screening notice' see PARA 623 note 5.
5   As to Natural England see the Natural Environment and Rural Communities Act 2006 Pt 1 Ch 1 (ss 1–16); and OPEN SPACES AND COUNTRYSIDE vol 78 (2010) PARA 523.
6   Environmental Impact Assessment (Agriculture) (England) (No 2) Regulations 2006, SI 2006/2522, reg 31(1)(a)–(c), (2); Environmental Impact Assessment (Agriculture) (Wales) Regulations 2017, SI 2017/565, reg 30(1)(a), (2), (7). An appeal also lies against a notice under the Environmental Impact Assessment (Agriculture) (England) (No 2) Regulations 2006, SI 2006/2522, Sch 4 para 5 or the Environmental Impact Assessment (Agriculture) (Wales) Regulations 2017, SI 2017/565, Sch 4 para 5 (see PARAS 623–624): Environmental Impact Assessment (Agriculture) (England) (No 2) Regulations 2006, SI 2006/2522, reg 31(1)(d); Environmental Impact Assessment (Agriculture) (Wales) Regulations 2017, SI 2017/565, reg 30(1)(a), (7).
7   Environmental Impact Assessment (Agriculture) (England) (No 2) Regulations 2006, SI 2006/2522, reg 31(7)(a); Environmental Impact Assessment (Agriculture) (Wales) Regulations 2017, SI 2017/565, reg 31(7)(a).
8   As to the meaning of 'screening decision' see PARA 623 note 6.
9   As to the meaning of 'significant project' see PARA 623 note 10.
10 As to the granting of applications and the imposition of conditions see PARA 624.
11 Environmental Impact Assessment (Agriculture) (England) (No 2) Regulations 2006, SI 2006/2522, reg 32(1), (2)(a), (b); Environmental Impact Assessment (Agriculture) (Wales) Regulations 2017, SI 2017/565, reg 30(1)(b), (3)(a), (b), (7). An appeal also lies against a notification of a further decision under the Environmental Impact Assessment (Agriculture) (England) (No 2) Regulations 2006, SI 2006/2522, Sch 4 para 3 or the Environmental Impact Assessment (Agriculture) (Wales) Regulations 2017, SI 2017/565, Sch 4 para 3 (see PARAS 623–624): Environmental Impact Assessment (Agriculture) (England) (No 2) Regulations 2006, SI 2006/2522, reg 32(2)(c); Environmental Impact Assessment (Agriculture) (Wales) Regulations 2017, SI 2017/565, reg 30(3)(c).
12 Environmental Impact Assessment (Agriculture) (England) (No 2) Regulations 2006, SI 2006/2522, reg 32(10); Environmental Impact Assessment (Agriculture) (Wales) Regulations 2017, SI 2017/565, reg 31(7).

13 See the Environmental Impact Assessment (Agriculture) (England) (No 2) Regulations 2006, SI 2006/2522, regs 31(3)–(6), (7)(b), (8)–(11), 32(3)–(9), (11)–(16), 36; and the Environmental Impact Assessment (Agriculture) (Wales) Regulations 2017, SI 2017/565, regs 30(3)–(6), 31, 33.

14 See the Environmental Impact Assessment (Agriculture) (England) (No 2) Regulations 2006, SI 2006/2522, reg 33; and the Environmental Impact Assessment (Agriculture) (Wales) Regulations 2017, SI 2017/535, reg 30(5)(a).

15 See the Environmental Impact Assessment (Agriculture) (England) (No 2) Regulations 2006, SI 2006/2522, reg 34; and the Environmental Impact Assessment (Agriculture) (Wales) Regulations 2017, SI 2017/535, reg 30(5)(b), (c).

16 Environmental Impact Assessment (Agriculture) (England) (No 2) Regulations 2006, SI 2006/2522, reg 35(1); Environmental Impact Assessment (Agriculture) (Wales) Regulations 2017, SI 2017/535, reg 33(1).

17 Environmental Impact Assessment (Agriculture) (England) (No 2) Regulations 2006, SI 2006/2522, reg 35(2)(a); Environmental Impact Assessment (Agriculture) (Wales) Regulations 2017, SI 2017/535, reg 33(2)(a).

18 Environmental Impact Assessment (Agriculture) (England) (No 2) Regulations 2006, SI 2006/2522, reg 35(2)(b); Environmental Impact Assessment (Agriculture) (Wales) Regulations 2017, SI 2017/535, reg 33(2)(b). 'Any relevant statutory requirement' means any requirement of the Environmental Impact Assessment (Agriculture) (England) (No 2) Regulations 2006, SI 2006/2522, or the Environmental Impact Assessment (Agriculture) (Wales) Regulations 2017, SI 2017/535: Environmental Impact Assessment (Agriculture) (England) (No 2) Regulations 2006, SI 2006/2522, reg 35(2)(b); Environmental Impact Assessment (Agriculture) (Wales) Regulations 2017, SI 2017/535, reg 34(2)(b).

19 See the Environmental Impact Assessment (Agriculture) (England) (No 2) Regulations 2006, SI 2006/2522, reg 35(3), (4); and the Environmental Impact Assessment (Agriculture) (Wales) Regulations 2017, SI 2017/535, reg 33(3), (4).

5. SMALLHOLDINGS

(1) SMALLHOLDINGS: INTRODUCTION

627. Meaning of 'smallholding'.

In general terms a 'smallholding' may be said to be a unit of land let by a smallholdings authority[1], the Secretary of State or the Welsh Ministers[2] as a smallholding for cultivation by the occupier, with or without limited additional help. There is no definition of 'smallholding' in the Agriculture Act 1970, which reorganised the smallholdings system, but for the purposes of the Small Holdings and Allotments Acts 1908 to 1931[3] 'small holding'[4] means an agricultural holding which exceeds 1 acre and either does not exceed 50 acres or, if exceeding 50 acres, is at the date of sale or letting of an annual value for income tax purposes not exceeding £100[5].

For the purposes of the repealed smallholdings provisions of the Agriculture Act 1947[6] 'smallholding' meant a holding, other than a holding provided, or such as apart from that Act could be provided, under any enactment relating to the provision of cottage holdings[7], used or intended to be used for agriculture[8], being a holding exceeding 1 acre but not exceeding 50 acres[9]. As originally enacted this provision extended to include holdings of between 50 and 75 acres of which the annual full fair rent[10] did not exceed £150[11].

Useful reference may also be made to the statutory provisions setting out the powers of smallholdings authorities. These provide for the letting of holdings which are capable, when farmed under reasonably skilled management, of providing full-time employment for not more than two persons with or without additional part-time employment for another person[12], and such holdings may accordingly be considered 'smallholdings' for these purposes. In the principal statutory provisions relating to smallholdings, now embodied in the Agriculture Act 1970 Part III[13], 'existing smallholding' means a unit of land which, being held for the purposes of smallholdings[14] by a smallholdings authority[15] (or, as the case may be, by the Secretary of State or the Welsh Ministers[16]), is for the time being let as a smallholding[17] or, if it is not for the time being in use, was so let when it was last in use[18].

1   As to smallholdings authorities see PARAS 748–751.
2   As to the Secretary of State and the Welsh Ministers see PARA 741.
3   Ie in effect the Small Holdings and Allotments Act 1908, the Land Settlement (Facilities) Act 1919, the Small Holdings and Allotments Act 1926 and the Agricultural Land (Utilisation) Act 1931 Pt II (ss 12, 17, 20): Land Settlement (Facilities) Act 1919 s 34; Small Holdings and Allotments Act 1926 s 23(1); Agricultural Land (Utilisation) Act 1931 s 25(1). These Acts replaced various earlier Acts, but the position as regards smallholdings sold and leased under repealed Acts was preserved by the Small Holdings and Allotments Act 1908 s 62 (repealed), the Land Settlement (Facilities) Act 1919 s 32(2), and the Small Holdings and Allotments Act 1926 s 15 (repealed in relation to smallholdings). The provisions of these Acts relating to smallholdings were almost wholly repealed, subject to savings, by the Agriculture Act 1947 Sch 8 Pt II, and subsequent amendments were made to the surviving provisions by the Agriculture Act 1970 Sch 4.
4   Note that in the Small Holdings and Allotments Acts 1908 to 1931 'small holding' was spelt as two words, but there is no material difference between that usage and the modern expression 'smallholding'.
5   Small Holdings and Allotments Act 1908 s 61(1) (amended by the Small Holdings and Allotments Act 1926 s 16).
6   Ie the Agriculture Act 1947 Pt IV (ss 47–67), largely repealed by the Agriculture Act 1970 (see Sch 5 Pt III) and replaced by the Agriculture Act 1970 Pt III (ss 37–65).
7   As to cottage holdings see PARAS 730–740.
8   As to the meaning of 'agriculture' for the purposes of the Agriculture Act 1947 see PARA 424.

9 See the Agriculture Act 1947 s 66 (repealed); and the Agriculture (Miscellaneous Provisions) Act 1954 s 3(1), Sch 3 (repealed).

10 Ie such rent as a tenant might reasonably be expected to pay for the holding if let as such on the terms, other than the terms as to rent, on which it was in fact let: Agriculture Act 1947 s 52(2) (repealed).

11 This extended meaning operated until 4 June 1954 (ie the date on which the Agriculture (Miscellaneous Provisions) Act 1954 was passed), but any holding used or intended to be used for agriculture which before that date was provided as a smallholding for the purposes of the Small Holdings and Allotments Acts 1908 to 1931, or the Agriculture Act 1947 Pt IV, and any holding provided by virtue of the Agriculture (Miscellaneous Provisions) Act 1954 s 3(2) (repealed), was to be treated as a smallholding for the purposes of the Agriculture Act 1947 Pt IV: Agriculture (Miscellaneous Provisions) Act 1954 s 3(1) (repealed).

12 See the Agriculture Act 1970 s 39; and PARAS 633–634.

13 Ie the Agriculture Act 1970 Pt III (ss 37–65).

14 'The purposes of smallholdings' includes the purposes which were the purposes of smallholdings in accordance with the Agriculture Act 1947 Pt IV: Agriculture Act 1970 s 37(2)(c). Under the Agriculture Act 1947 it was the duty of specified local authorities to provide smallholdings for the purpose of affording to persons with agricultural experience an opportunity of becoming farmers on their own account: s 47(1) (repealed).

15 Any reference in the Agriculture Act 1970 Pt III to land held by a smallholdings authority for the purposes of smallholdings is construed as including a reference to any land in which an interest is so held by the authority, other than a right to take possession arising under the Small Holdings and Allotments Acts 1908 to 1931: Agriculture Act 1970 s 37(2)(a).

16 As to land held by the Secretary of State or the Welsh Ministers for smallholdings purposes see PARA 744.

17 Ie let under the Agriculture Act 1970 or under the previous enactments relating to smallholdings (as to which see note 3).

18 Agriculture Act 1970 s 37(1).

628. The smallholdings system.

Smallholdings, unlimited in size but, if above 50 acres, limited in value, could be provided under the Small Holdings and Allotments Acts 1908 to 1931[1], by specified local authorities for persons desiring to buy or lease them and able themselves to cultivate them properly[2], the primary aim being to relieve unemployment and assist re-settling ex-servicemen.

The Agriculture Act 1947 repealed the smallholdings provisions of the earlier Acts and introduced a new smallholdings code[3], whereby specified local authorities were under a duty to provide smallholdings, limited in size, to persons with agricultural experience seeking the opportunity of becoming farmers on their own account, to the extent that a demand existed for smallholdings, suitable land could be obtained for the purpose, and the smallholdings could be provided without detriment to the general interests of agriculture[4].

Provision was made by the Agriculture Act 1970, which repealed most of the relevant provisions of the Agriculture Act 1947, for the reorganisation of smallholdings authorities'[5] smallholdings estates[6], having regard to the general interests of agriculture and of good estate management, with a view to providing opportunities for persons to be farmers on their own account by letting holdings to persons qualified, or likely shortly to become qualified, by reason of agricultural experience, to farm them on their own account[7], and a new smallholdings code[8] was introduced.

1 As to the Small Holdings and Allotments Acts 1908 to 1931 see PARA 627 note 3.

2 See the Small Holdings and Allotments Act 1926 s 1 (repealed). For a history of smallholdings legislation see the Northfield Committee of Inquiry into the Acquisition and Occupancy of Agricultural Land (1979) (Cmnd 7599).

3 See the Agriculture Act 1947 Pt IV (ss 47–67) (largely repealed).

4 See the Agriculture Act 1947 s 47 (repealed).

5 As to smallholdings authorities see PARAS 748–751.

6   See the Agriculture Act 1970 ss 40–43; and PARAS 640–643.
7   See the Agriculture Act 1970 ss 39, 44; and PARAS 631, 634–635, 748.
8   See the Agriculture Act 1970 Pt III (ss 37–65); and PARA 629 et seq.

(2) PROVISION OF LAND FOR SMALLHOLDINGS

(i) Acquisition, Appropriation and Disposal

629. Acquisition of land for smallholdings.
A smallholdings authority[1] cannot acquire land compulsorily for the purposes
of smallholdings[2], but is empowered to acquire land by agreement[3]. The Secretary
of State and the Welsh Ministers[4] may acquire by agreement any land which in his
or their opinion is required for the purposes of smallholdings[5], and may designate
any land vested in them as being land held for those purposes[6].

A smallholdings authority, the Secretary of State or the Welsh Ministers may
take on lease for the purposes of smallholdings, for a term not exceeding 35 years
and with or without a right of renewal for a further similar term, land forming
part of the possessions of the Duchy of Cornwall[7], certain glebe land[8], and any
other land in relation to which a statutory power to lease land for agricultural
purposes for a specified maximum term may be exercised[9].

1   As to smallholdings authorities see PARAS 748–751.
2   Agriculture Act 1970 s 48(2). As to the purposes of smallholdings see PARA 627 note 14. As to the
    meaning of 'smallholding' see PARA 627. An authority was formerly able to acquire land by
    compulsory hiring or purchase but the relevant statutory provision (the Agriculture Act 1947 s
    48(1)) has been repealed.
3   See the Local Government Act 1972 ss 120, 124; and LOCAL GOVERNMENT vol 69 (2009)
    PARAS 509, 516. Where an authority proposes, in the exercise of its power to acquire land by
    agreement, to acquire land outside its area for the purposes of smallholdings, it must consult the
    council of the county or (in Wales) county or county borough in whose area the land is situated:
    Agriculture Act 1970 s 48(1) (amended by the Local Government Act 1972 s 272(1), Sch 30; and
    the Local Government (Wales) Act 1994 s 66(6), Sch 16 para 38(2)). As to the counties and county
    boroughs and their councils see LOCAL GOVERNMENT vol 69 (2009) PARAS 24 et seq, 37 et seq.
    Where an authority proposes to acquire land by agreement the acquisition is governed by the
    Compulsory Purchase Act 1965 Pt I (ss 1–32) (see COMPULSORY ACQUISITION OF LAND): Local
    Government Act 1972 s 120(3).
4   As to the Secretary of State and the Welsh Ministers see PARA 741.
5   Agriculture Act 1970 s 55. This is an application of the general power under the Agriculture Act
    1947 s 82 to acquire land by agreement (as to which see PARA 742).
6   Agriculture Act 1970 s 54(7).
7   Agriculture Act 1970 s 61(1), (2)(b). As to the Duchies of Lancaster and Cornwall see CROWN AND
    CROWN PROCEEDINGS vol 29 (2014) PARAS 214–267.
8   See the Agriculture Act 1970 s 61(3) (amended by the Church of England (Miscellaneous
    Provisions) Measure 2006 Sch 5 para 17).
9   See the Agriculture Act 1970 s 61(6).

**630. Appropriation or disposal of surplus land held for smallholdings
purposes.**
Smallholdings authorities[1] may appropriate for some other approved purpose,
or may dispose of, smallholdings[2] land belonging to them and not required for the
purposes of smallholdings[3]. An authority, the Secretary of State and the Welsh
Ministers[4] may also let land[5] held by them the purposes of smallholdings[6] which
is not for the time being required for use for those purposes, for such period and

for such purpose as they think fit, at the best rent which appears to be obtainable for the land for that purpose, and on such other terms as they may determine[7]. Smallholdings authorities may let land acquired or appropriated for smallholdings[8] for cultivation[9] as an allotment[10], although this does not authorise a council to let any land held by it under a contract of tenancy or the use of any land so held in contravention of any term or condition of the contract[11].

1 As to smallholdings authorities see PARAS 748–751.
2 As to the meaning of 'smallholding' see PARA 627.
3 See the Local Government Act 1972 ss 122, 123, 126, 127; and LOCAL GOVERNMENT vol 69 (2009) PARAS 513, 515, 518, 520. As to land held by a smallholdings authority for the purposes of smallholdings see PARA 627 text and notes 14, 15.
4 As to the Secretary of State and the Welsh Ministers see PARA 741.
5 For this purpose 'letting land' includes granting (in the case of a smallholdings authority, with the approval of the Secretary of State and the Welsh Ministers), a licence to a person to occupy the land for use as agricultural land, and granting a licence to a person to occupy the land where it is to be used only for grazing or mowing during a specified part of the year: Agriculture Act 1970 ss 49(2), 54(1), (2). As to 'agricultural land' and the 'occupier' of land for this purpose see PARA 424. Any letting in pursuance of this power made after 1 September 1995 will be a farm business tenancy within the meaning of the Agricultural Tenancies Act 1995: see s 4; and PARA 401 et seq.
6 As to land held by the Secretary of State or the Welsh Ministers for smallholdings purposes see PARA 744.
7 Agriculture Act 1970 s 49(1). In relation to a smallholdings authority this power is without prejudice to its general power to appropriate or dispose of smallholdings land (see the text and notes 1–3) (s 49(4)), but the general power of an authority to let land does not enable it to let land for the time being held by it for the purposes of smallholdings otherwise than in accordance with s 49(1) or in accordance with the specific provisions as to the letting of smallholdings (ie the Agriculture Act 1970 s 44 (PARA 631) (s 49(3)).
    As to the appropriation or disposal of land acquired or appropriated for planning purposes see the Town and Country Planning Act 1990 ss 232, 233; and PLANNING vol 83 (2010) PARA 1122 et seq.
8 As to the acquisition of land for smallholdings see PARA 629.
9 As to the meaning of 'cultivation' for these purposes see PARA 424 note 5.
10 As to allotments see PARAS 649–729.
11 Allotments Act 1922 s 15.

(ii) Letting as a Smallholding

631. General provisions as to smallholdings lettings.

Any land held for the purposes of smallholdings by a smallholdings authority, the Secretary of State or the Welsh Ministers may be let by that body as a smallholding[1]. No such landholder may, however, let a holding resulting from an enlargement or amalgamation of existing smallholdings[2] or create any new smallholding where the enlargement, amalgamation or creation is not in accordance with approved reorganisation proposals[3] for the time being in force[4], unless the letting or creation is effected with the written consent of the Secretary of State or the Welsh Ministers (or their statutory predecessors) given before reorganisation proposals[5] have been submitted or before proposals so submitted have been approved[6].

1 Agriculture Act 1970 ss 44(1), 54(1), (2). As to the meaning of 'smallholding' see PARA 627. As to land held by a smallholdings authority for the purposes of smallholdings see PARA 627 text and notes 14, 15. As to smallholdings authorities see PARAS 748–751. As to land held by the Secretary of State or the Welsh Ministers for smallholdings purposes see PARA 744. As to the Secretary of State and the Welsh Ministers see PARA 741.
    For the persons to whom the land may be let see PARA 635.

2 Ie under the Agriculture Act 1970 s 40(2)(a); see PARA 640. As to the meaning of 'existing smallholding' see PARA 627.
3 Ie under the Agriculture Act 1970 ss 40–43; see PARAS 640–643.
4 Agriculture Act 1970 s 44(4).
5 Ie under the Agriculture Act 1970 s 40, s 42 or s 43; see PARAS 640–643.
6 Agriculture Act 1970 s 44(4).

632. Advertisement of vacant smallholdings.

Every smallholdings authority[1], the Secretary of State and the Welsh Ministers[2] must, once in any year[3] during which any smallholding[4] on a smallholdings estate[5] becomes available for letting[6], cause a notice to be published[7] stating that they provide smallholdings for letting, describing the location and types of smallholdings on the estate or available for letting, and setting out the requirements to be fulfilled by tenants[8].

1 As to smallholdings authorities see PARAS 748–751.
2 As to the Secretary of State and the Welsh Ministers see PARA 741.
3 'Year' means a 12 month period ending on 31 March: Smallholdings (Selection of Tenants) Regulations 1970, SI 1970/1049, reg 4(2).
4 As to the meaning of 'smallholding' see PARA 627.
5 'Smallholdings estate', in relation to anything falling to be done by a smallholdings authority, means the aggregate of the land which is for the time being held by the authority for the purposes of smallholdings: Agriculture Act 1970 s 37(1). As to land held by a smallholdings authority for the purposes of smallholdings see PARA 627 text and notes 14, 15.
6 Ie under the Agriculture Act 1970 s 44 (see PARA 631).
7 In the context of smallholdings being made available for lettings by smallholdings authorities such a notice must be caused to be published in at least one newspaper circulating substantially outside the authority's area: Smallholdings (Selection of Tenants) Regulations 1970, SI 1970/1049, reg 4(1). No specific provision is made as to the publications in which the Secretary of State and the Welsh Ministers are required to publish such notices.
8 Smallholdings (Selection of Tenants) Regulations 1970, SI 1970/1049, reg 4(1). As to the selection of tenants see PARA 635.

633. Extent of smallholdings.

Holdings let by smallholdings authorities[1] must either fall within what is known as the upper limit for a smallholding[2], or must be let in accordance with the authority's reorganisation proposals[3], approved by the Secretary of State or the Welsh Ministers[4], notwithstanding that it appears to the Secretary of State or the Welsh Ministers that in the case of one or more holdings the upper limit would be exceeded, if it is represented by the authority, and the Secretary of State or the Welsh Ministers is or are satisfied, that the holdings are to be let as smallholdings[5] and that, by reason of the nature or extent of fixed equipment[6] on the holding or holdings, or of the special qualities of the soil, or other exceptional circumstances, it is necessary or expedient for them to exceed that limit[7].

1 As to smallholdings authorities see PARAS 748–751.
2 As to the upper limit for a smallholding see PARA 634. As to the meaning of 'smallholding' see PARA 627.
3 Ie under the Agriculture Act 1970 s 41 (see PARA 640).
4 As to the Secretary of State and the Welsh Ministers see PARA 741.
5 Ie under the Agriculture Act 1970 s 44 (see PARA 631).
6 'Fixed equipment' includes any building or structure affixed to land and any works on, in, over or under land, and also includes anything grown on land for a purpose other than use after severance from the land, consumption of the thing grown or of produce thereof, or amenity, and references to fixed equipment on land are construed accordingly: Agriculture Act 1947 s 109(3); Agriculture Act 1970 s 37(4).
7 Agriculture Act 1970 ss 39(1), 41(4).

634. The upper limit for a smallholding.

A holding is treated as falling within the upper limit for a smallholding[1] if in the opinion of the Secretary of State or the Welsh Ministers[2] it is capable, when farmed[3] under reasonably skilled management, of providing full-time employment for not more than two persons, including the tenant, with or without additional part-time employment for another person[4]. The holding is treated as being so capable if its standard labour requirements are less than 900 standard person-days in aggregate in a year on average[5]. In any other case the holding is treated as exceeding the upper limit for a smallholding[6].

In estimating the number of persons for whom a holding is capable of providing full-time employment it must be assumed that the system of husbandry suitable for the district is followed, and that the greater part of the feeding stuffs required by any livestock[7] kept on the holding is grown there[8]. In the case of an existing smallholding[9] the number of standard man-days is estimated by multiplying a prescribed number[10] per hectare, based on the type of crop[11], or a prescribed number[12] per head, based on the type of livestock[13], by the number of hectares or average number of head of livestock shown to the satisfaction of the Secretary of State or the Welsh Ministers to be comprised in the agricultural operations carried on on the holding in an average year, adding the crop and livestock results together, and increasing the total by 15 per cent[14]. In the case of a proposed smallholding[15] the number of standard man-days is estimated by making a similar calculation in respect of the hectarage and average number of head of livestock shown to the satisfaction of the Secretary of State or the Welsh Ministers to be capable of being comprised in the agricultural operations carried on on the holding when farmed under reasonably skilled management[16].

1   As to the meaning of 'smallholding' see PARA 627.
2   As to the Secretary of State and the Welsh Ministers see PARA 741.
3   As to the farming of land see PARA 424.
4   Agriculture Act 1970 s 39(2).
5   Smallholdings (Full-Time Employment) Regulations 1970, SI 1970/1050, reg 3(2).
6   Agriculture Act 1970 s 39(2).
7   As to the meaning of 'livestock' see PARA 424 note 2.
8   Smallholdings (Full-Time Employment) Regulations 1970, SI 1970/1050, reg 3(1).
9   In this context 'existing smallholding' means a holding held by a smallholdings authority for the purposes of smallholdings and let as a smallholding at a time when the authority submits proposals to the Secretary of State or the Welsh Ministers under the Agriculture Act 1970 s 40, s 42 or s 43, in which that holding is included (see PARAS 640–643), or, if the holding is not at that time let as a smallholding and is not being used for any purpose, is a holding which, when last let, was let as a smallholding: Smallholdings (Full-Time Employment) Regulations 1970, SI 1970/1050, Schedule. As to land held by a smallholdings authority for the purposes of smallholdings see PARA 627 text and notes 14, 15.
10 See the Smallholdings (Full-Time Employment) Regulations 1970, SI 1970/1050, Schedule, Table (amended by SI 1992/2816).
11 Where double cropping is practised the area of both crops is included: Smallholdings (Full-Time Employment) Regulations 1970, SI 1970/1050, Schedule para 3.
12 See the Smallholdings (Full-Time Employment) Regulations 1970, SI 1970/1050, Schedule, Table.
13 Baby animals are not counted: see the Smallholdings (Full-Time Employment) Regulations 1970, SI 1970/1050, Schedule para 6.
14 Smallholdings (Full-Time Employment) Regulations 1970, SI 1970/1050, Schedule para 1.
15 'Proposed smallholding' means a holding which a smallholdings authority, in any proposals of the kind referred to in note 9 submitted by it to the Secretary of State or the Welsh Ministers, proposes to form by enlarging or amalgamating existing smallholdings or by creating new smallholdings: Smallholdings (Full-Time Employment) Regulations 1970, SI 1970/1050, Schedule.
16 Smallholdings (Full-Time Employment) Regulations 1970, SI 1970/1050, Schedule para 2.

635. Selection of smallholdings tenants.

A smallholdings authority[1], the Secretary of State and the Welsh Ministers[2] may not let land as a smallholding[3] except to a person who is to farm[4] the holding and who either is regarded by the authority as being qualified by reason of his agricultural[5] experience to farm the holding on his own account or is a person in respect of whom it is satisfied that within a reasonably short time he will become eligible to be so regarded[6]. Notwithstanding this, a smallholdings authority, the Secretary of State or the Welsh Ministers may let land as a smallholding, or as part of a group of two or more smallholdings, to two or more persons proposing to farm the land together on a co-operative system if, having regard to their aggregate agricultural experience, the authority, the Secretary of State or the Welsh Ministers is or are satisfied that they are, or will within a reasonably short time become, qualified to farm the land together on such a system on their own account[7].

The Secretary of State and the Welsh Ministers may by regulations make provision as to the selection of tenants to whom land may be let for smallholdings[8]. In pursuance of this power it has been provided that no person may be selected as a tenant to whom a smallholding may be let unless he shows to the satisfaction of the smallholdings authority, the Secretary of State or the Welsh Ministers that for a period of not less than five years (whether continuous or not)[9] he has been occupied in full-time practical farm work[10]. Where a smallholdings authority, the Secretary of State or the Welsh Ministers intends or intend to re-let a smallholding after the death of a tenant, it, him or they must first consider applications from specified close relations of the deceased[11].

1   As to smallholdings authorities see PARAS 748–751.
2   As to the Secretary of State and the Welsh Ministers see PARA 741.
3   As to the meaning of 'smallholding' see PARA 627.
4   As to the farming of land see PARA 424.
5   As to the meaning of 'agricultural' see PARA 424.
6   Agriculture Act 1970 ss 44(2), 54(1), (2).
7   Agriculture Act 1970 s 44(3).
8   Agriculture Act 1970 s 44(6).
9   Any period during which a person was attending a full-time course in agriculture at a university, college or other establishment of further education is, up to a maximum of three years, deemed to be a period during which he was occupied in full-time practical farm work: Smallholdings (Selection of Tenants) Regulations 1970, SI 1970/1049, reg 3(1).
10   Smallholdings (Selection of Tenants) Regulations 1970, SI 1970/1049, reg 3(1). This does not apply to the surviving spouse or civil partner of a deceased tenant of a smallholding in relation to the first letting of that smallholding after the death of the tenant if he or she is residing on the smallholding when that letting is under consideration by the smallholdings authority, the Secretary of State or the Welsh Ministers: reg 3(2) (amended by SI 2005/2114).
11   Smallholdings (Selection of Tenants) Regulations 1970, SI 1970/1049, reg 3(1) (reg 3(3), (4) added by SI 1976/2001). A smallholdings authority, the Secretary of State or the Welsh Ministers may not consider an application for the first letting of a smallholding after the death of the tenant by a person who is not a spouse, civil partner, brother, sister or child of the deceased tenant, or any person not being a brother, sister or child who, in case of any marriage or civil partnership to which the deceased tenant was at any time a party, was treated by the deceased tenant as a child of the family in relation to that marriage or civil partnership, unless every application from such a person has been considered and refused: Smallholdings (Selection of Tenants) Regulations 1970, SI 1970/1049, reg 3(3), (4) (as so added; reg 3(4) amended by SI 2005/2114).

636. Rent for a smallholding.

In determining the rent at which it is to let land as a smallholding[1], a smallholdings authority[2], the Secretary of State and the Welsh Ministers[3] must have regard to the rent which, in their opinion, might reasonably be expected to be determined to be the proper rent if the land were already let as an agricultural holding[4], if the terms of that letting, other than the terms as to rent, were those on which the authority proposes to let the land[5], and if the matter of what rent should be payable had been referred to arbitration[6].

These provisions also apply[7] in relation to a revision by agreement of the rent at which land has been let by a smallholdings authority, the Secretary of State or the Welsh Ministers as a smallholding, including land so let under the previous enactments relating to smallholdings[8].

1 As to the meaning of 'smallholding' see PARA 627.
2 As to smallholdings authorities see PARAS 748–751.
3 As to the Secretary of State and the Welsh Ministers see PARA 741.
4 Agriculture Act 1970 ss 45(1)(a), 54(1), (2). Section 45(1)(a) refers to land let as an 'agricultural holding'. That term is used in connection with tenancies governed by the Agricultural Holdings Act 1986 (see PARA 423), but not in connection with tenancies governed by the Agricultural Tenancies Act 1995, which are known as 'farm business tenancies' (see ss 2, 4; PARA 401; and see further PARA 638); it is thought, however, that farm business tenancies should be taken to be 'agricultural holdings' for the present purposes. As to statutory rent reviews under the Agricultural Holdings Act 1986 see PARAS 438–440; and as to statutory rent reviews under the Agricultural Tenancies Act 1995 see PARAS 406–409.
5 Agriculture Act 1970 s 45(1)(b).
6 Agriculture Act 1970 s 45(1)(c). The arbitration would be under the Arbitration Act 1996 (as to which see ARBITRATION vol 2 (2017) PARA 509 et seq): see the Agriculture Act 1970 s 45(1)(c); the Agricultural Holdings Act 1986 s 12; the Agricultural Tenancies Act 1995 s 10; and PARAS 407, 438. For the purposes of such arbitration it is assumed that there would be no improvements (including matters treated as equivalent to improvements), dilapidations, deterioration under the enactments relating to agricultural holdings which are for the time being in force or damage of which special account, by way of reducing or increasing the rent, would fall to be taken in determining the rent payable: Agriculture Act 1970 s 45(2). As to increases of rent for certain improvements to agricultural holdings under the Agricultural Holdings Act 1986 see s 13; and PARA 440.
7 Excluding the assumption set out in note 4.
8 Agriculture Act 1970 s 45(3). 'The previous enactments relating to smallholdings' means the Small Holdings and Allotments Acts 1908 to 1931 and the Agriculture Act 1947 Pt IV (ss 47–67) (largely repealed): Agriculture Act 1970 s 37(1).

637. Lettings and sales under earlier smallholdings legislation.

Where smallholdings were sold or let before 1 October 1949[1] the statutory provisions then applicable as to payments for sales by terminable annuities[2], as to the conditions affecting the holdings sold or let[3], and as to the recovery of possession on breach of those conditions[4], continue to apply subject to certain modifications[5].

Any land held by a smallholdings authority immediately before 1 August 1970[6] for the purposes of smallholdings[7] continues to be held by it for those purposes, subject to any power exercisable by it by virtue of any enactment to appropriate or dispose of the land for other purposes[8], and the repeal of the smallholdings provisions of earlier legislation[9] does not affect the validity of any letting effected before 1 August 1970[10].

1 Ie the date on which the Agriculture Act 1947 Pt IV (ss 47–67) came into operation: Agriculture Act 1947 (Commencement) Order 1949, SI 1949/1201.
2 See the Small Holdings and Allotments Act 1926 s 5 (repealed in relation to smallholdings).
3 See the Small Holdings and Allotments Act 1926 s 6 (repealed in relation to smallholdings).
4 See the Small Holdings and Allotments Act 1926 s 7 (repealed in relation to smallholdings) (amended by the Statute Law (Repeals) Act 1993).
5 Agriculture Act 1947 s 67(2)(a), Sch 8 Pt II (Sch 8 Pt II amended by the Agriculture Act 1970 Sch 4; and the Statute Law (Repeals) Act 2004). The provisions referred to in notes 2–4 continue to apply except in so far as they provide for the sale or other disposition of smallholdings not authorised

by the Agriculture Act 1970 Pt III (ss 37–65), and except in so far as the Small Holdings and Allotments Act 1926 s 6(1) renders the consent of the Secretary of State or the Welsh Ministers unnecessary where no contribution is payable by them, and the requirement of s 6(1)(c) as to good husbandry must be construed as requiring the owner or occupier to fulfil his responsibilities to farm the holding in accordance with the rules of good husbandry. As to the Secretary of State and the Welsh Ministers see PARA 741. As to the rules of good husbandry see AGRICULTURAL PRODUCTION AND MARKETING vol 1A (2017) PARAS 11–13.

6   Ie the date on which the Agriculture Act 1970 Pt III (ss 37–65) came into operation: Agriculture Act 1970 (Commencement No 2) Order 1970, SI 1970/1048.
7   As to smallholdings authorities see PARAS 748–751. As to land held by smallholdings authorities for the purposes of smallholdings see PARA 627 text and notes 14, 15.
8   Agriculture Act 1970 Sch 3 para 2. As to such dealings see PARA 630.
9   See the Agriculture Act 1970 Sch 5 Pt III (repealed), which repealed, inter alia, much of the Agriculture Act 1947 Pt IV (ss 47–67).
10 Agriculture Act 1970 Sch 3 para 3; Agriculture Act 1970 (Commencement No 2) Order 1970, SI 1970/1048.

638. Application to smallholdings of legislation relating to agricultural holdings and farm business tenancies.

A smallholding[1] which comprises land which is used for agriculture[2] and which is so used for the purposes of trade or business, or land which is designated by the Secretary of State or the Welsh Ministers[3] as agricultural land for the purposes of the Agriculture Act 1947, is subject to the provisions of that Act, which are principally concerned with securing efficiencies in estate management, husbandry and production[4].

A smallholding which is, or which is comprised in land the aggregate of which (whether agricultural land[5] or not) is, comprised in a contract of tenancy[6] entered into before 1 September 1995[7] which is a contract for an agricultural tenancy[8], not being a contract under which the land is let to the tenant during his continuance in an office, appointment or employment held under the landlord, is an 'agricultural holding' for the purposes of the Agricultural Holdings Act 1986 and is accordingly subject to the provisions of that Act, which are principally concerned with the regulation of tenancy agreements concerning agricultural land[9].

A smallholding which is comprised in a tenancy which begins on or after 1 September 1995 and which complies with certain conditions[10] will in general be subject to the provisions of the Agricultural Tenancies Act 1995 relating to farm business tenancies[11].

1   As to the meaning of 'smallholding' see PARA 627.
2   As to the meaning of 'agriculture' for these purposes, and as to land being 'used' for agriculture, see PARA 424.
3   As to the Secretary of State and the Welsh Ministers see PARA 741.
4   See the Agriculture Act 1947 s 109(1); and PARA 424. Any land so designated which in the opinion of the Secretary of State or the Welsh Ministers ought to be brought into use for agriculture is included: see s 109(1); and PARA 424.
5   As to 'agricultural land' for these purposes see PARA 424.
6   As to a 'contract of tenancy' for these purposes see PARA 425.
7   Such a tenancy entered into on or after 1 September 1995 (ie the date on which the Agricultural Tenancies Act 1995 came into force: see s 41(2); and PARA 401) will in general be subject to the provisions of the Agricultural Tenancies Act 1995 relating to farm business tenancies (see the text and notes 11–13) and not to the provisions of the Agricultural Holdings Act 1986 concerned with the regulation of tenancy agreements concerning agricultural land: see the Agricultural Tenancies Act 1995 ss 1, 2; and PARA 401 et seq.
8   As to when a contract of tenancy is a contract for an agricultural tenancy under the Agricultural Holdings Act 1986 see s 1(2); and PARA 423.
9   See the Agricultural Holdings Act 1986 s 1(1); and PARA 423 et seq.

10 Ie the business conditions together with either the agriculture or notice conditions: see the Agricultural Tenancies Act 1995 s 1; and PARA **402**.

11 See the Agricultural Tenancies Act 1995 ss 1(1), 2(1); and PARA **401** et seq. As to the tenancies beginning on or after 1 September 1995 which are not subject to the provisions relating to farm business tenancies (ie certain tenancies arising pursuant to contracts which indicated that the Agricultural Holdings Act 1986 was to apply; certain succession tenancies; tenancies granted under the Evesham custom; and certain variations of existing tenancies), and which are instead subject to the Agricultural Holdings Act 1986 (see the text and notes 4–9), see the Agricultural Tenancies Act 1995 ss 1(1)(b), 2(1)(b), 4; and PARA **401**.

639. Application to smallholdings of legislation relating to planning permission, rating and non-agricultural usage.

Planning permission is not required for the development of smallholdings[1], since cultivation of a smallholding amounts to agricultural use for the purposes of the Town and Country Planning Act 1990[2] and the use of land for the purposes of agriculture does not amount to development of the land for the purposes of that Act[3]. Hereditaments consisting of agricultural land are generally exempt from non-domestic rating[4].

Smallholdings are usually let for cultivation and may have restrictions that they should not be used for any trade or business. If a smallholding is subsequently used for a trade or business which is not agriculture the letting may be governed by the provisions of the Landlord and Tenant Act 1954 relating to security of tenure for business tenants[5]. Protection is given to a tenant where the property comprised in the tenancy is or includes premises which are occupied by the tenant and are so occupied for the purposes of a business carried on by him or for those and other purposes; however, a tenant will not be protected where the business is carried on in breach of a covenant unless the landlord has waived the breach[6].

1 As to the meaning of 'smallholding' see PARA **627**.
2 See PARA **424**.
3 See the Town and Country Planning Act 1990 s 55(2)(e); and PLANNING vol 81 (2010) PARA **298**.
4 See the Local Government Finance Act 1988 Sch 5 paras 1(a), 2(1)(d); and LOCAL GOVERNMENT FINANCE vol 70 (2012) PARAS **92–93**.
5 See the Landlord and Tenant Act 1954 Pt II (ss 23–46); and LANDLORD AND TENANT vol 64 (2016) PARA **1592** et seq. For the tenancies excluded from the protections of Pt II, which include tenancies of agricultural holdings subject to the provisions of the Agricultural Holdings Act 1986 and farm business tenancies subject to the Agricultural Tenancies Act 1995 (see PARA **638**), see the Landlord and Tenant Act 1954 s 43; and LANDLORD AND TENANT vol 64 (2016) PARA **1599**.
6 See the Landlord and Tenant Act 1954 s 23(1), (4); and LANDLORD AND TENANT vol 64 (2016) PARA **1597**.

(iii) Reorganisation of Smallholdings

640. Compulsory reviews of smallholdings estates.

The Secretary of State and the Welsh Ministers[1] may direct[2] a smallholdings authority[3] to carry out a review of its smallholdings estate[4] and to submit proposals for its future management[5]. Such proposals must comply with any directions of the Secretary of State or the Welsh Ministers as to form and content[6], and in formulating them, the authority must, in particular, consider to what extent, if any, with a view to giving effect to the general aim of statutory smallholdings[7] and having regard to the general interests of agriculture[8] and of good estate management, that estate should be reorganised:

(1)   by enlarging existing smallholdings[9], or by amalgamating them or part of them with other land, with or without improvements[10];

(2)   by improving existing smallholdings without any enlargement or amalgamation[11]; or

(3)   by creating new smallholdings, with or without improvements[12].

Any proposals so submitted must also indicate how far the authority's previous proposals[13] are intended to remain unaltered and how far they are to be amended or superseded[14]. The Secretary of State and the Welsh Ministers may approve or reject any proposals submitted in pursuance of these provisions[15], and may also direct subsequent reviews at intervals of not less than five years after the previous proposals have been approved[16].

1   As to the Secretary of State and the Welsh Ministers see PARA 741.
2   Any such direction must be complied with within such period as may be specified in the direction or such extended period as the Secretary of State or the Welsh Ministers may allow: Agriculture Act 1970 s 42(2).
3   As to smallholdings authorities see PARAS 748–751.
4   As to the meaning of 'smallholdings estate' see PARA 632 note 5.
5   Agriculture Act 1970 s 42(1). The power to direct the carrying out of a review may be exercised at any time after the end of five years after the approval by the Secretary of State or the Welsh Ministers of proposals for the reorganisation of a smallholdings authority's smallholdings estate under the Agriculture Act 1970 s 40, which required every smallholdings authority which immediately before 1 August 1970 held any land for the purposes of smallholdings to review its estate and submit proposals with respect to its future management (see s 40; and the Agriculture Act 1970 (Commencement No 2) Order 1970, SI 1970/1048). Such proposals were then approved or rejected as set out in PARA 641: Agriculture Act 1970 s 41(1).
      A smallholdings authority could apply for an exemption from a requirement under s 40 (see s 40(4)), whereupon the authority was required to carry out a review and submit proposals within five years of said revocation; an authority whose exemption from s 40 has never been revoked can therefore not be required to carry out a review and submit proposals under s 42, since by virtue of s 42(1) the requirements of that section only operate where an authority has previously submitted proposals under s 40 (see above), but it may be required to submit proposals if it elects to make changes to its smallholdings estate (see PARA 643).
      Provision is made for the payment of grants under the Agriculture Act 1967 Pt II (ss 26–40) so as to enable smallholdings authorities to give effect to proposals under the Agriculture Act 1970 ss 40–43, provided the grant was applied for before the end of 1975: see s 50 (amended by the Agriculture (Miscellaneous Provisions) Act 1972 ss 9(7), 26(3), (4), Sch 6). As to the payment of grants under the Agriculture Act 1967 Pt II see AGRICULTURAL PRODUCTION AND MARKETING vol 1A (2017) PARAS 416–422.
6   Agriculture Act 1970 ss 40(3), 42(3).
7   See PARA 748.
8   As to the meaning of 'agriculture' see PARA 424.
9   As to the meaning of 'existing smallholding' see PARA 627.
10 Agriculture Act 1970 s 40(2)(a). It is immaterial whether or not the other land is or forms part of an existing smallholding or is otherwise comprised in the authority's smallholdings estate: s 40(2)(a).
11 Agriculture Act 1970 s 40(2)(b).
12 Agriculture Act 1970 s 40(2)(c). References in Pt III (ss 37–65) to the creation of a new smallholding must be construed as references to any letting of land by a smallholdings authority, the Secretary of State or the Welsh Ministers where:
      (1)   the land is held for the purposes of smallholdings and the letting is a letting of the land as a smallholding (s 37(3)(a));
      (2)   immediately before the letting the land or part of it is being used (or, if not then in use, is land which was last used) otherwise than as land held and let as mentioned in head (1) (s 37(3)(b)); and
      (3)   the land so let is not a holding resulting from an enlargement or amalgamation as in the text to notes 9–11, or from a similar enlargement or amalgamation by the Secretary of State or the Welsh Ministers (s 37(3)(c)).

As to land held by a smallholdings authority for the purposes of smallholdings see PARA 627 text and notes 14, 15. As to land held by the Secretary of State or the Welsh Ministers for smallholdings purposes see PARA 744.

13 As to the previous requirement for making proposals see note 5.
14 Agriculture Act 1970 s 42(2).
15 See PARA 641.
16 Agriculture Act 1970 s 42(4). Where different parts of proposals were approved on different dates the period of five years runs from the latest such date: s 42(7). Section 41 applies for the approval or rejection of proposals submitted following subsequent reviews: see PARA 641.

641. Approval or rejection of proposals for smallholdings reorganisation.

The Secretary of State and the Welsh Ministers[1] may either approve proposals for the reorganisation of a smallholdings estate[2] submitted by a smallholdings authority[3], or may reject them and direct the authority to submit new proposals within a time specified in the direction[4]. In determining whether to approve the proposals the Secretary of State and the Welsh Ministers must have regard to the considerations to which the authority was required to have regard in making the proposals[5], and must not approve proposals in so far as it appears that any resulting smallholding[6] would exceed the upper limit for a smallholding[7]. Nevertheless, the Secretary of State and the Welsh Ministers may approve proposals notwithstanding that any resulting smallholding would exceed this limit if the holdings are to be let as smallholdings[8] or if it is otherwise considered expedient to exceed it[9].

The Secretary of State and the Welsh Ministers may approve any proposals either as submitted or with appropriate modifications, and may approve them, with or without modifications, either conditionally or unconditionally[10], and thereupon, until the proposals are amended or superseded, the smallholdings authority has a duty both to perform its statutory functions[11] in such a way as to give effect to the proposals as so approved[12] and to comply with any conditions subject to which the approval is given[13].

1 As to the Secretary of State and the Welsh Ministers see PARA 741.
2 As to the meaning of 'smallholdings estate' see PARA 632 note 5.
3 Ie in pursuance of the Agriculture Act 1970 s 42 (see PARA 640) or s 43 (see PARAS 642, 643). As to smallholdings authorities see PARAS 748–751.
4 Agriculture Act 1970 ss 41(1), 42(3).
5 Agriculture Act 1970 s 41(5). As to these considerations see s 40(2); and PARA 640.
6 As to the meaning of 'smallholding' see PARA 627.
7 Agriculture Act 1970 s 41(3). As to the upper limit for smallholdings see PARA 634.
8 Agriculture Act 1970 s 41(4)(a). As to the letting of smallholdings see s 44; and PARA 631.
9 Agriculture Act 1970 s 41(4)(b). It may be considered expedient to exceed the upper limit for smallholdings for reasons relating to the nature or extent of fixed equipment on the holding or holdings, or the special qualities of the soil, or where other exceptional circumstances prevail: s 41(4)(b). As to the meaning of 'fixed equipment' see PARA 633 note 6.
10 Agriculture Act 1970 s 41(2).
11 Ie its functions under the Agriculture Act 1970 Pt III (ss 37–65). 'Functions' includes powers and duties: Agriculture Act 1947 s 109(1); Agriculture Act 1970 s 37(4).
12 Agriculture Act 1970 ss 41(6)(a), 42(5)(a).
13 Agriculture Act 1970 ss 41(6)(b), 42(5)(b).

642. Other smallholdings proposals requiring approval.

Where a smallholdings authority[1], other than an exempt smallholdings authority[2], proposes to enlarge, amalgamate or improve existing smallholdings or to create new smallholdings[3], it must submit its proposals to the Secretary of State or the Welsh Ministers[4] if:

(1)   the transaction would be inconsistent with any previously approved reorganisation proposals for the time being in force and has not been provided for by previously approved proposals not being the initial or review proposals[5]; and

(2)   the transaction is intended to be carried out at a time when no review of the smallholdings estate[6] is required by a direction of the Secretary of State or the Welsh Ministers to be carried out[7].

Such proposals must be submitted by way of amending the authority's previously approved proposals submitted on a review for the time being in force[8], must comply with any directions of the Secretary of State or the Welsh Ministers as to form and content[9], and are then subject to approval or rejection by the Secretary of State or the Welsh Ministers[10]. Where the proposals are approved it is the authority's duty to perform its smallholdings functions under the Agriculture Act 1970[11] in such a way as to give effect to the approved proposals for the time being in force, and to comply with any conditions subject to which the approval was given[12].

1   As to smallholdings authorities see PARAS 748–751.
2   As to exempt authorities see PARA 640 note 5.
3   Ie under the Agriculture Act 1970 s 40(2)(a), (b) or (c): see PARA 640. As to the meanings of 'smallholding' and 'existing smallholding' see PARA 627.
4   As to the Secretary of State and the Welsh Ministers see PARA 741.
5   Agriculture Act 1970 s 43(1)(a). As to the initial and review proposals see PARA 640.
6   As to the meaning of 'smallholdings estate' see PARA 632 note 5.
7   Agriculture Act 1970 s 43(1)(b).
8   Agriculture Act 1970 s 43(2).
9   Agriculture Act 1970 ss 40(3), 43(5).
10 The procedure for approval or rejection is set out in PARA 641.
11 Ie functions under the Agriculture Act 1970 Pt III (ss 37–65). As to the meaning of 'functions' see PARA 641 note 11.
12 Agriculture Act 1970 ss 42(5), 43(6).

643. Submission of proposals by exempt smallholdings authorities.

Where an exempt smallholdings authority[1] proposes to enlarge a smallholding[2] or to amalgamate the whole or part of one or more existing smallholdings[3] with other land or to create new smallholdings[4], and that transaction has not been included in previously approved proposals[5], it must submit to the Secretary of State or the Welsh Ministers[6] proposals for carrying out that transaction[7]. Such proposals must comply with any directions of the Secretary of State or the Welsh Ministers as to form and content[8], and are then subject to approval or rejection by the Secretary of State or the Welsh Ministers[9]. If an exempt authority proposes to improve an existing smallholding[10] it may, for the purpose of obtaining an increased capital grant[11], submit to the Secretary of State or the Welsh Ministers proposals for carrying out the improvement[12]. Where the proposals are approved the authority has a duty both to perform its smallholdings functions under the Agriculture Act 1970[13] in such a way as to give effect to the proposals as so approved and also to comply with any conditions subject to which the approval was given[14].

1   For the purposes of the Agriculture Act 1970 s 43 'exempt smallholdings authority' means a smallholdings authority in respect of which a direction under s 40(4) (see PARA 640 note 5) has been made: s 43(8). As to smallholdings authorities generally see PARAS 748–751.
2   As to the meaning of 'smallholding' see PARA 627.
3   As to the meaning of 'existing smallholding' see PARA 627.
4   Ie under the Agriculture Act 1970 s 40(2)(a) or (c): see PARA 640.

5 Ie proposals under the Agriculture Act 1970 s 43 (see PARA **642**).
6 As to the Secretary of State and the Welsh Ministers see PARA **741**.
7 Agriculture Act 1970 s 43(3).
8 Agriculture Act 1970 ss 40(3), 43(5).
9 The procedure for approval or rejection is set out in PARA **641**.
10 Ie under the Agriculture Act 1970 s 40(2)(b) (see PARA **640**).
11 Ie under the Agriculture Act 1970 s 51: see PARA **648**.
12 Agriculture Act 1970 s 43(4).
13 Ie functions under the Agriculture Act 1970 Pt III (ss 37–65). As to the meaning of 'functions' see PARA **641** note 11.
14 Agriculture Act 1970 ss 41(6), 43(7).

(3) PROVISION OF SERVICES FOR SMALLHOLDINGS

644. Managing smallholdings.

The powers of a smallholdings authority[1], the Secretary of State and the Welsh Ministers[2], in relation to land held for the purposes of smallholdings[3] include, in general, all powers required for the management of land so held[4]. In particular, an authority, the Secretary of State and the Welsh Ministers have the following powers:

(1) for the benefit of the occupiers of smallholdings provided by them, to further the formation of corporate or unincorporated bodies of persons having for their object or one of their objects the promotion of efficiency in the conduct of smallholdings through co-operative methods, including the co-operative purchase and hiring of requisites for, or the co-operative sale, marketing or preparation for marketing of the produce of, the smallholdings, and to assist the activities of such bodies[5];

(2) to assist or promote co-operative schemes for the conduct of smallholdings provided by the authority, the Secretary of State or the Welsh Ministers, by purchasing or hiring, and by selling or letting machinery and other equipment, live[6] or dead stock, seeds, fertilisers or other requisites, and by the provision of services[7];

(3) to carry out arrangements made by them for the disposal by them of the produce of smallholdings which they have provided[8];

(4) to provide, improve, maintain or repair fixed equipment[9] or to carry out other improvements for the benefit of the land held by them for the purposes of smallholdings[10].

In general, the provision of buildings or the making of any material change in the use of buildings on land acquired for smallholdings requires planning permission, but certain development is permitted, as in the case of land used for allotments, without permission[11].

1 As to smallholdings authorities see PARAS **748–751**. The powers given to smallholdings authorities which are considered in this paragraph relate only to their capacity as corporations, and nothing in those provisions may be construed as authorising any act or omission on the part of a smallholdings authority which, apart from these provisions, would be actionable at the suit of any persons on any grounds other than a limitation imposed by law on their capacity as corporations: Agriculture Act 1970 s 37(5). As to the capacity of corporations and the operation of the doctrine of ultra vires see CORPORATIONS vol 24 (2010) PARA 424 et seq.
2 As to the Secretary of State and the Welsh Ministers see PARA **741**.
3 As to the meaning of 'smallholding' see PARA **627**. As to land held by a smallholdings authority for the purposes of smallholdings see PARA **627** text and notes 14, 15. As to land held by the Secretary of State or the Welsh Ministers for smallholdings purposes see PARA **744**.
4 Agriculture Act 1970 ss 47(1), 54(1), (2).

5   See the Agriculture Act 1970 s 47(2); and PARA 750.

6   As to the meaning of 'livestock' see PARA 424 note 2.

7   Agriculture Act 1970 s 47(3). Where for the purpose of assisting the conduct of smallholdings on land held for the purposes of smallholdings the Secretary of State or the Welsh Ministers have acquired by purchase or hiring machinery or other equipment, live or dead stock, seeds, fertilisers or other requisites, or provide any services, the powers of the Secretary of State and the Welsh Ministers under s 47(3) (as applied by s 54(2)) include power to sell or let them to, or (as the case may be) to provide the services for, any persons, whether they are tenants of smallholdings or not: s 54(3).

8   Agriculture Act 1970 s 47(4). Where any arrangements are made by the Secretary of State or the Welsh Ministers under s 47(4) (as applied by s 54(2)), and it appears to the Secretary of State or the Welsh Ministers that any facilities provided in accordance with the arrangements are not required to be reserved exclusively for disposing of the produce of smallholdings on land held for the purposes of smallholdings, the arrangements may include provision for the use of those facilities for disposing of the produce of other agricultural holdings: s 54(4).

9   As to the meaning of 'fixed equipment' see PARA 633 note 6.

10   Agriculture Act 1970 s 46(1). See PARA 645.

11   See PARA 722.

645. Equipment of smallholdings.

In addition to their powers to provide, improve, maintain and repair fixed equipment[1] on land held by them for the purposes of smallholdings[2], to carry out any other improvement on or for the benefit of any such land[3], a smallholdings authority, the Secretary of State and the Welsh Ministers may enter into an agreement with a tenant of any such land for the provision, improvement, maintenance or repair by them of fixed equipment on the land, or the carrying out by them of other improvements on it or for its benefit, on terms specified in the agreement[4].

1   As to the meaning of 'fixed equipment' see PARA 633 note 6.

2   As to the purposes of smallholdings, and as to land held by a smallholdings authority for those purposes, see PARA 627 notes 14, 15. As to land held by the Secretary of State or the Welsh Ministers for smallholdings purposes see PARA 744. As to the meaning of 'smallholding' see PARA 627. As to smallholdings authorities see PARAS 748–751. As to the Secretary of State and the Welsh Ministers see PARA 741.

3   See the Agriculture Act 1970 ss 46(1), 54(1), (2); and PARA 644.

4   Agriculture Act 1970 ss 46(2), 54(1), (2).

646. Power of smallholdings authorities to make loans and guarantees.

A smallholdings authority[1] may make loans for the purpose of providing working capital[2] for a tenant of a smallholding provided by it[3], or for an intending tenant, or may guarantee the repayment of and the payment of interest on any loan made for that purpose by another person[4], but no such loan or guarantee[5] may exceed three-quarters of the aggregate working capital which, in the authority's opinion, is required for the proper working of the holding[6], and no loan may be made or guaranteed save under a written agreement specifying the maximum period of the loan or guarantee and the rate of interest[7].

1   As to smallholdings authorities see PARAS 748–751.

2   'Working capital' includes any sum paid or payable by an incoming tenant, whether to the landlord or to the outgoing tenant, in respect of compensation paid or payable to an outgoing tenant: Agriculture Act 1970 s 37(1).

3   'Smallholding provided by a smallholdings authority' means any land for the time being held by the authority for the purposes of smallholdings and let as a smallholding either under the Agriculture Act 1970 Pt III (ss 37–65) or under the previous enactments relating to smallholdings: s 37(2)(b). As to the meaning of 'smallholding', the purposes of smallholdings, and land held by a smallholdings authority for those purposes, see PARA 627. As to the previous enactments relating to smallholdings see PARA 636 note 8.

4   Agriculture Act 1970 s 53(1). For a similar power of the Secretary of State and the Welsh Ministers in respect of loans (but not guarantees) see PARA 647. As to the Secretary of State and the Welsh Ministers generally see PARA 741.

5   If two or more loans are made or guaranteed this restriction is applicable to the aggregate amount of those loans: Agriculture Act 1970 s 53(2).

6   Agriculture Act 1970 s 53(2).

7   Agriculture Act 1970 s 53(7). The loan must bear interest at one-half of one per cent above the rate which, on the date of the agreement, is the rate determined by the Treasury under the National Loans Act 1968 s 5 in respect of local loans then made on the security of local rates (as defined in s 6(2)) for the same period or, where two or more rates are so determined, such of those rates as the Treasury specifies for the purpose and publishes in the London Gazette: Agriculture Act 1970 s 53(3)–(5), (8). The authority may not guarantee a loan which bears a higher rate of interest than would be chargeable had the authority made the loan: s 53(6). As to the National Loans Act 1968 ss 5, 6 see CONSTITUTIONAL AND ADMINISTRATIVE LAW vol 20 (2014) PARA 509; and FINANCIAL INSTRUMENTS AND TRANSACTIONS vol 49 (2015) PARA 169. As to the Treasury see CONSTITUTIONAL AND ADMINISTRATIVE LAW vol 20 (2014) PARA 263 et seq.

647. Power of Secretary of State and Welsh Ministers to make loans in connection with smallholdings.

The Secretary of State and the Welsh Ministers[1] may, in accordance with arrangements made by him or them with Treasury approval[2], make loans to provide working capital[3] for a smallholdings tenant on land held by the Secretary of State or the Welsh Ministers for smallholdings purposes[4], or for an intending tenant[5], but the loan, or, if two or more loans are so made, the aggregate amount of the loans, must not exceed three-quarters of the aggregate working capital which in the opinion of the Secretary of State or the Welsh Ministers is required for the proper working of the smallholding[6].

1   As to the Secretary of State and the Welsh Ministers see PARA 741.

2   As to the Treasury see CONSTITUTIONAL AND ADMINISTRATIVE LAW vol 20 (2014) PARA 263 et seq.

3   As to the meaning of 'working capital' see PARA 646 note 2.

4   As to the meaning of 'smallholding' and the purposes of smallholdings see PARA 627. As to land held by the Secretary of State or the Welsh Ministers for smallholdings purposes see PARA 744.

5   Agriculture Act 1970 s 54(5).

6   Agriculture Act 1970 s 54(6).

648. Increase of farm capital grants to smallholdings authority.

Where a farm capital grant[1] was made to a smallholdings authority[2] in respect of expenditure:

(1)   incurred or to be incurred in respect of certain works or facilities required to give effect to approved reorganisation proposals[3]; and

(2)   qualified under the scheme for consideration for the grant within five years beginning with 1 January 1971[4],

the Secretary of State or, as the case may be, the Welsh Ministers[5] may increase the grant by one-tenth of the relevant expenditure[6]. No increase can, however, be granted if the land on which the works are to be carried out or the facilities provided is or forms part of a holding which, in the opinion of the Secretary of State or the Welsh Ministers, would without those works or facilities be a commercial unit[7].

Application for an increase may be made at any time after the smallholdings authority has submitted relevant proposals[8], and where the relevant proposals are comprised in reorganisation proposals submitted on an initial review[9] the increase may be granted when the Secretary of State or the Welsh Ministers, as the case may be, has or have approved so much of those proposals as consist of the relevant proposals[10].

1 Ie a grant made under a scheme made under the Agriculture Act 1970 s 29 (see AGRICULTURAL PRODUCTION AND MARKETING vol 1A (2017) PARAS 423–427).
2 As to smallholdings authorities see PARAS 748–751.
3 Agriculture Act 1970 s 51(1)(a). The reference in the text to approved reorganisation proposals is a reference to proposals approved under s 41 or s 43: see PARA 640 et seq.
4 Agriculture Act 1970 s 51(1)(b). 1 January 1971 is the date when the first such scheme (ie the Farm Capital Grant Scheme 1970, SI 1970/1759 (revoked)) providing for grants to smallholdings authorities came into operation.
5 As to the Secretary of State and the Welsh Ministers see PARA 741.
6 Agriculture Act 1970 s 51(1).
7 Agriculture Act 1970 s 51(1). As to the meaning of 'commercial unit' see the Agriculture Act 1967 s 40(2)(a); and AGRICULTURAL PRODUCTION AND MARKETING vol 1A (2017) PARA 416 note 5.
8 Ie under the Agriculture Act 1970 s 40 or s 43 (see PARA 640 et seq). 'Relevant proposals' means the proposals in connection with which the smallholdings authority claims that the works or facilities are required: s 51(2)(a).
9 Ie under the Agriculture Act 1970 s 40; see PARA 640 et seq.
10 Agriculture Act 1970 s 51(2).

6. ALLOTMENTS

(1) ALLOTMENTS: INTRODUCTION

649. Meaning of 'allotment'.

The term 'allotment' is used in this title mainly as referring to lands which are held by local authorities[1] under the Allotments Acts 1908 to 1950[2] for the purpose of providing persons resident in their areas with small plots of land for cultivation[3]. Whilst there is no comprehensive statutory definition of 'allotment' for the purposes of those Acts, a field garden[4] and an allotment garden[5] are generally allotments[6]. Although there are no general statutory limits on the size of an allotment or requirements as to its use, definitions for the purposes of particular enactments sometimes prescribe these; for example, 'allotment' in the Allotments Act 1925 means an allotment garden or any parcel of land not more than five acres in extent cultivated or intended to be cultivated as a garden or farm or partly as a garden and partly as a farm[7]; and for the purpose of certain provisions relating to compensation on the termination of a tenancy[8], 'allotment' means any parcel of land, whether attached to a cottage or not, of not more than two acres in extent, held by a tenant under a landlord[9] otherwise than under a farm business tenancy[10] and cultivated as a farm or a garden or partly as a garden and partly as a farm[11].

1 Local authorities' obligations to provide allotments are now confined to providing allotment gardens: see PARA 659; and as to the meaning of 'allotment garden' see note 5.
2 The Allotments Acts 1908 to 1950 are: so much of the Small Holdings and Allotments Act 1908 as relates to allotments; so much of the Land Settlement (Facilities) Act 1919 as amends the Small Holdings and Allotments Act 1908; the Allotments Act 1922; the Allotments Act 1925; the Small Holdings and Allotments Act 1926; so much of the Agricultural Land (Utilisation) Act 1931 Pt II (ss 12, 17, 20) as relates to allotments; and the Allotments Act 1950: Land Settlement (Facilities) Act 1919 s 34; Allotments Act 1922 s 23(1); Allotments Act 1925 s 14(1); Small Holdings and Allotments Act 1926 s 23(1); Agricultural Land (Utilisation) Act 1931 s 25(1); Allotments Act 1950 s 15(1).
3 As to the meaning of 'cultivation' see PARA 424 note 5.
4 A field garden is an allotment for the labouring poor: see the Commons Act 1876, preamble (repealed). As to field garden allotments see PARA 651.
5 As to the meaning of 'allotment garden' see PARA 424 note 11.
6 See the Small Holdings and Allotments Act 1908 s 61(1) and the Allotments Act 1925 s 1.
7 Allotments Act 1925 s 1. The definition is subject to any contrary requirement of the context: s 1.
8 See the Allotments Act 1922 s 3; and PARA 717.
9 In the Allotments Act 1922 and the Allotments Act 1950 the expression 'landlord' means in relation to any land the person for the time being entitled to receive the rents and profits of the land; and the designations of 'landlord' and 'tenant' continue to apply to the parties until the conclusion of any proceedings taken under the Act in respect of compensation and include the legal personal representative of either party: Allotments Act 1922 s 22(1); Allotments Act 1950 s 14(1).
10 Ie a farm business tenancy within the meaning of the Agricultural Tenancies Act 1995; see ss 1, 2; and PARA 401 et seq.
11 Allotments Act 1922 s 3(7) (amended by the Agricultural Tenancies Act 1995 Schedule para 3). Such an allotment does not include a plot occupied by a seedsman for business purposes, but is a plot cultivated for food or pleasure: *Cooper v Pearse* [1896] 1 QB 562.

650. Parochial and other allotments.

During the nineteenth century allotments[1] were provided for cultivation by poor and industrious parishioners and as recreation grounds for the parishioners[2] under certain Poor Law and Inclosure Acts and by appropriation of parochial charity lands for that purpose. The allotments here considered are field garden allotments[3] and allotments for fuel and certain other public purposes[4]. Provision was also formerly made for the acquisition and administration of poor allotments[5].

Allotments vested in the overseers[6], or churchwardens and overseers, of a rural parish were transferred to the parish council when that council came into being[7] or, where there was no parish council, to the parish meeting[8]. Trustees holding any property for the purposes of allotments for the benefit of the inhabitants of a parish or community council may, with the approval of the Charity Commission[9] and with the consent of that council, transfer the property to the council or to persons appointed by it, to be held on the same trusts and subject to the same conditions as when it was held by the trustees[10]. The Local Government Board had power to confer on municipal, county borough and urban district councils the powers, duties and liabilities of parish councils[11], and in 1933 all remaining functions and liabilities of vestries and churchwardens not relating to the church or charities were transferred to the borough or urban district council[12].

Allotment wardens, who managed allotments and field gardens for the labouring poor[13], could transfer the management to the appropriate council[14], and the powers and duties of wardens, committees and managers of allotments in rural parishes were transferred to the parish or community council or, where there was no such council, persons appointed by the parish or community meeting[15].

Allotments held by overseers or churchwardens of urban parishes were transferred to county borough and urban district councils and are now vested in district and London borough councils or, in Wales, county or county borough councils[16].

Thus, with the exception of allotments which have not been transferred to the local authority by the trustees in whom they are vested, any such allotment, together with the powers and duties respecting it, is now vested in or under the control of the London borough, district, parish, or, in Wales, county, county borough or community council, and is managed by it as one unit with lands acquired under the Allotments Acts[17].

1   As to the meaning of 'allotment' see PARA 649.
2   As to allotments for recreation see OPEN SPACES AND COUNTRYSIDE vol 78 (2010) PARA 537.
3   See PARAS 651, 658, 669, 695, 701.
4   See PARAS 652–654, 658, 746.
5   Poor allotments were parish lands possessed or acquired by poor law authorities under the Poor Relief Act 1819, or by the inclosure of waste or common land under the Poor Relief Act 1831, or by the inclosure under the Crown Lands Allotments Act 1831 of forest or waste Crown land, for the employment of poor persons or for letting to poor persons for cultivation on their own account: Poor Relief Act 1819 ss 12, 13; Poor Relief Act 1831 ss 1, 2; Crown Lands Allotments Act 1831. Those Acts were repealed by the Poor Law Act 1927, itself repealed by the Poor Law Act 1930, repealed in turn by the National Assistance Act 1948 Sch 7 (repealed). Land inclosed in the exercise of those powers or otherwise appropriated for the general benefit of the poor of any parish was subsequently authorised to be let to industrious cottagers living in or near the parish where the land was situated for the purpose of cultivation (see the Allotments Act 1832 ss 1, 11 (repealed)), and the rents derived from those lettings were to be applied, after the deduction of all proper charges, in aid of the poor rate of the parish (see the Poor Allotments Management Act 1873 s 14 (repealed)).
       In this title 'inclosure' is used as referring to a legal process involving the extinction of common rights, as opposed to the 'enclosure' of land with fences or walls: see the Report of the Royal Commission on Common Land 1955–1958 (Cmnd 462) App III para 29.
6   Overseers were abolished and their functions transferred to rating authorities by the Rating and Valuation Act 1925 s 62(1) (repealed), (3).
7   Local Government Act 1894 s 6(1)(c)(iii).
8   See the Local Government Act 1894 s 19 (amended by the Statute Law Revision Act 1908; the Local Government Act 1933 ss 307, 308, Sch 11 Pt IV; the Charities Act 1960 Sch 7 Pt I; and

SI 1979/1123); and the Overseers Order 1927, SR & O 1927/55, arts 4(2), 7 (now lapsed). The effect of subsequent legislation has been that statutory references to parishes and parish councils, so far as relating to Wales, should be read as references to communities and community councils: see PARA 659 note 2.

9   As to the Charity Commission see CHARITIES vol 8 (2015) PARAS 543–578.
10 See the Charities Act 2011 s 298(1), (2); and CHARITIES vol 8 (2015) PARA 266.
11 Local Government Act 1894 s 33 (repealed).
12 Local Government Act 1933 s 269(1) (repealed). Those functions and liabilities are now vested in district and London borough councils or, in Wales, county or county borough councils: see PARA 659 notes 1–5.
13 See the Inclosure Act 1845 s 108 (amended by the Statute Law Revision Act 1891).
14 See the Small Holdings and Allotments Act 1908 s 33(1); and PARA 695.
15 Small Holdings and Allotments Act 1908 s 33(3).
16 See the Overseers Order 1927, SR & O 1927/55, arts 4, 5 (lapsed); and PARA 659 notes 1–5.
17 Small Holdings and Allotments Act 1908 s 33(4).

651.   Field garden allotments.

Field gardens are allotments for the labouring poor[1], and comprise lands appropriated as such upon the inclosure[2] of lands or the regulation of commons[3]. Their management was formerly the responsibility of allotment wardens[4] but is now the responsibility of local authorities (generally parish or community councils)[5].

1   See the Commons Act 1876, preamble (repealed). The term 'allotment' in the Small Holdings and Allotments Act 1908 includes a field garden: see s 61(1); and PARA 649. 'Field garden allotment' in the Acquisition of Land Act 1981 and the Town and Country Planning Act 1990 means any allotment set out as a field garden allotment under an Inclosure Act: see the Acquisition of Land Act 1981 s 19(4); the Town and Country Planning Act 1990 s 336; COMPULSORY ACQUISITION OF LAND vol 18 (2009) PARA 531; PLANNING vol 83 (2010) PARA 1112.
2   As to the meaning of 'inclosure' see PARA 650 note 5.
3   See the Inclosure Act 1845 ss 31 (repealed), 73; the Inclosure Act 1846 s 4 (repealed); the Commons Act 1876 ss 21–23 (repealed); the Commonable Rights Compensation Act 1882 s 3; and OPEN SPACES AND COUNTRYSIDE vol 78 (2010) PARA 554.
4   See the Inclosure Act 1845 s 108 (amended by the Statute Law Revision Act 1891).
5   As to the transfer of the allotment wardens' management functions see PARA 650; and see further PARA 701.

652.   Fuel allotments.

A fuel allotment has been defined as an allotment set out as a fuel allotment under an Inclosure Act[1], or as land which by any enactment relating to inclosure or any instrument having effect under such an enactment is vested in trustees upon trust that the land or the rents and profits of the land be used for the purpose of providing poor persons with fuel[2]. Fuel allotments were frequently set out both under private Inclosure Acts and in the early days of the Inclosure Commissioners in the north of England and other hilly regions where there were turbary rights and peat or turf which could be used as fuel[3]. They were often of considerable extent, and, coming as they did within the definition of land subject to be inclosed[4], when no longer suitable for the purposes for which they were set out or not required, were the subject of subsequent inclosure or regulation[5].

1   See the Acquisition of Land Act 1981 s 19(4); the Town and Country Planning Act 1990 s 336(1); COMPULSORY ACQUISITION OF LAND vol 18 (2009) PARA 531; PLANNING vol 83 (2010) PARA 1112.
2   See the Charities Act 2011 s 68(6), Sch 5 para 1(c); and CHARITIES vol 8 (2015) PARA 185. As to the meaning of 'inclosure' see PARA 650 note 5. Allotments for the supply of fuel for the labouring poor were among the principal matters for which allotments could be made and continued in use under parochial or other management: see the Inclosure Act 1845 s 34 (repealed).

As to the vesting of fuel allotments see PARA 654; as to exchange, appropriation and change of use see PARAS 727–729, 746. As to the establishment of charitable fuel allotments see PARA 658.

The Charity Commission or the High Court may, notwithstanding the restriction on diverting fuel allotments from the purposes declared by the Act authorising their inclosure (see the Commons Act 1876 s 19; and OPEN SPACES AND COUNTRYSIDE vol 78 (2010) PARA 552), establish schemes for the administration of charitable fuel allotments, which may provide for the sale or letting of an allotment or any part of it, for the discharge of the land sold or let from restrictions on its use imposed by or under any enactment relating to inclosure, and for the application of the purchase money or rent received by the trustees, for the exchange of an allotment or part of it for other land and for the application of money payable to the trustees for equality of exchange, and for the use of an allotment or any part of it for any purposes specified in the scheme (see the Charities Act 2011 ss 68, 69, Sch 5 paras 1(c), 2; and CHARITIES vol 8 (2015) PARAS 185, 189). The scheme may modify or supersede in relation to the fuel allotment the provision made by the Inclosure Act or instrument thereunder setting up the allotment as if that provision had been made by a scheme (see the Charities Act 2011 s 68(6); and CHARITIES vol 8 (2015) PARA 185). As to the Charity Commission see CHARITIES vol 8 (2015) PARA 543 et seq.

3   As to rights of common of turbary (ie the right to dig turf or peat in another man's ground for fuel) see COMMONS vol 13 (2017) PARAS 356, 357. Because rights in fuel allotments are vested in a fluctuating body of persons they cannot be registered as commons. In practice, many areas of land formerly set aside as fuel allotments are now to all intents and purposes public open land.

4   See the Inclosure Act 1845 s 11; and COMMONS vol 13 (2017) PARA 319.

5   Eg the fuel allotment which was the subject of dispute in *A-G v Meyrick* [1893] AC 1, HL; and Harrow Weald Common, which was an old gravel allotment and was the subject of a scheme under the Metropolitan Commons Acts (as to which see LONDON GOVERNMENT vol 71 (2013) PARA 301).

    Where fuel allotments provided under local Inclosure Acts before 1845 became useless and unproductive, the trustees, together with the churchwardens and overseers of the parish, were required to let them to industrious cottagers living in or near the parish for the purposes of cultivation, and the rents received from the lettings were to be applied for the purchase of fuel for distribution to poor parishioners: see the Allotments Act 1832 s 8 (repealed).

653. Allotments for other public purposes.

Allotments may be made to highway authorities for obtaining stone, gravel and other materials for road repairs, and the grass and herbage of such allotments may be awarded to other persons or let by the authority[1]. A highway authority may by ceasing to use such allotments and obtaining its materials elsewhere lose its right to extract such materials, and an adverse title may be acquired against the authority by other persons[2].

1   See the Inclosure Act 1845 s 72; and HIGHWAYS, STREETS AND BRIDGES vol 55 (2012) PARA 80. The terms of the Act and the award must be strictly adhered to: where an allotment was made under the Inclosure Acts for obtaining stone, gravel and other materials for repairing highways and public and private roads for the use of the inhabitants of the parish, it was held that such allotments were for road repairs only, and that a user by inhabitants for private purposes was not authorised: *Rylatt v Marfleet* (1845) 14 M & W 233. As to the vesting of allotments for public purposes see PARA 654; as to exchange, appropriation and change of use see PARAS 727–729, 648.

2   *Thew v Wingate* (1862) 10 B & S 714; *Smith v Stocks* (1869) 10 B & S 701 at 713.

654. Vesting of fuel and other allotments.

Fuel allotments[1] and other allotments for public purposes[2] might be allotted to such persons and subject to such directions as the valuer should direct, or if the valuer should not think it necessary or proper to direct it to be otherwise made, the allotment was to be made to the churchwardens and overseers of the parish[3]. Such allotments were frequently vested in the lord of the manor as trustee for the labouring poor of the parish or other persons entitled, or they may have been set out for this purpose, but not allotted to any specific persons by name or office. In such cases questions have arisen as to the ownership of the soil. Where the allotment was not made to any person by name or office, the lord's interest in the soil remained, if there was nothing in the Act or award to transfer it, and he consequently had power to refuse his consent to, and to prevent, a subsequent inclosure[4]. If the allotment was made to the lord as trustee, and the trust as declared in the award did not exhaust the beneficial interest in the land, the lord was entitled to the unexhausted benefit[5]. Where, however, the allotment was made to the churchwardens and overseers for the purposes of a fuel allotment, the legal estate in the land was vested in them[6], and presumably the lord would be excluded from any benefit if he received an allotment in respect of his right and interest in the soil, and there was no reservation of rights from which a reservation of the soil of the fuel allotment might be implied[7].

1   As to fuel allotments see PARA 652.
2   As to other allotments for public purposes see PARA 653.
3   See the Inclosure Act 1845 s 73; and OPEN SPACES AND COUNTRYSIDE vol 78 (2010) PARA 549. Overseers have been abolished, and fuel allotments are vested in parish, district, county, county borough or community councils: see PARA 650.
4   See *R v Inclosure Comrs for England and Wales* (1871) 23 LT 778, where a large fuel allotment had been set out under an early inclosure on Chobham Common. As to the meaning of 'inclosure' see PARA 650 note 5.
5   *A-G v Meyrick* [1893] AC 1, HL.
6   *Simcoe v Pethick* [1898] 2 QB 555, CA. See, however, note 3.
7   See *A-G v Meyrick* [1893] AC 1, HL.

655. Privately let allotments.

Land privately owned may be let for use as allotments free from local authority control; and whilst the statutory provisions relating to the determination of tenancies and compensation[1] apply to such land it is otherwise governed by the general law relating to the letting of land, and is not further discussed in this title.

1   See PARA 702 et seq.

656. Application to allotments of legislation relating to agricultural holdings and farm business tenancies.

An allotment which comprises land which is used or ought to be brought into use for agriculture[1] and which is so used for the purposes of trade or business, or land which is designated by the Secretary of State or the Welsh Ministers[2] as agricultural land for the purposes of the Agriculture Act 1947[3], is subject to the provisions of that Act, which are principally concerned with securing efficiencies in estate management, husbandry and production[4].

An allotment which is, or which is comprised in land the aggregate of which (whether agricultural land[5] or not) is, comprised in a contract of tenancy[6] entered into before 1 September 1995[7] which is a contract for an agricultural tenancy[8], not being a contract under which the land is let to the tenant during his continuance in an office, appointment or employment held under the landlord[9], is an 'agricultural holding' for the purposes of the Agricultural Holdings Act 1986 and is accordingly subject to the provisions of that Act, which are principally concerned with the regulation of tenancy agreements concerning agricultural land[10].

An allotment which is comprised in a tenancy which begins on or after 1 September 1995 and which complies with certain conditions[11] will in general be subject to the provisions of the Agricultural Tenancies Act 1995 relating to farm business tenancies[12]. An allotment garden cannot be subject to the provisions relating to farm business tenancies as, by definition, it cannot be land used for the purposes of trade or business[13]. Nor may a cottage holding be so subject, since no new cottage holding could be granted after 1970[14].

1   As to the meaning of 'agriculture' for these purposes see PARA 424.
2   As to the Secretary of State and the Welsh Ministers see PARA 741. Note that no such designation may extend to land used as allotment gardens: see the Agriculture Act 1947 s 109(1) (proviso); and PARA 424.
3   As to the meaning of 'agricultural land' for these purposes see PARA 424.
4   See the Agriculture Act 1947 s 109(1); and PARA 424.
5   See note 3.
6   As to the meaning of 'contract of tenancy' for these purposes see PARA 425.
7   Such a tenancy entered into on or after 1 September 1995 (ie the date on which the Agricultural Tenancies Act 1995 came into force: see s 41(2)) will in general be subject to the provisions of the Agricultural Tenancies Act 1995 relating to farm business tenancies (see the text and notes 11–12) and not to the provisions of the Agricultural Holdings Act 1986 concerned with the regulation of tenancy agreements concerning agricultural land: see the Agricultural Tenancies Act 1995 ss 1, 2; and PARA 401 et seq.
8   As to a 'contract for an agricultural tenancy' for these purposes see PARA 423.
9   See *Stevens v Sedgman* [1951] 2 KB 434, [1951] 2 All ER 33, CA, where an allotment of under half an acre used by the tenant to produce vegetables was held to be an agricultural holding.
10 See the Agricultural Holdings Act 1986 s 1(1); and PARA 423. Note that an allotment garden cannot be an agricultural holding as, by definition (see PARA 424 note 11), it cannot be land used for the purposes of trade or business.
11 Ie the business conditions together with either the agriculture or notice conditions: see the Agricultural Tenancies Act 1995 s 1; and PARA 402.
12 See the Agricultural Tenancies Act 1995 ss 1(1), 2(1); and PARA 401 et seq. As to the tenancies beginning on or after 1 September 1995 which are not subject to the provisions relating to farm business tenancies (ie certain tenancies arising pursuant to contracts which indicated that the Agricultural Holdings Act 1986 was to apply; certain succession tenancies; tenancies granted under the Evesham custom; and certain variations of existing tenancies), and which are instead subject to the Agricultural Holdings Act 1986 (see the text and notes 5–10), see the Agricultural Tenancies Act 1995 ss 1(1)(b), 2(1)(b), 4; and PARA 401.
13 See PARA 424 note 11.
14 See PARAS 730–731.

657. Application to allotments of legislation relating to rating, planning permission and non-agricultural usage.

Allotments, including allotment gardens[1], are 'agricultural land' for the purposes of the exemption from non-domestic rating applicable to hereditaments consisting of agricultural land[2]. Planning permission is not required for the development of allotments, since cultivation of an allotment amounts to agricultural use for the purposes of the Town and Country Planning Act 1990[3] and the use of land for the purposes of agriculture does not amount to development of the land for the purposes of that Act[4].

Allotments are usually let for cultivation and may have restrictions that they should not be used for any trade or business. If an allotment is subsequently used for a trade or business without sufficient agricultural use the letting may be governed by the provisions of the Landlord and Tenant Act 1954 relating to security of tenure for business tenants[5]. Protection is given to a tenant where the property comprised in the tenancy is or includes premises which are occupied by the tenant and are so occupied for the purposes of a business carried on by him or for those and other purposes; however, a tenant will not be protected where the business is carried on in breach of a covenant unless the landlord has waived the breach[6].

1   Ie within the meaning of the Allotments Act 1922 (see PARA 424 note 11).

2   See the Local Government Finance Act 1988 Sch 5 paras 1(a), 2(1)(d); and LOCAL GOVERNMENT FINANCE vol 70 (2012) PARAS 92–93.
3   As to the meaning of 'agriculture' for the purposes of the Town and Country Planning Act 1990 see PARA 424.
4   See the Town and Country Planning Act 1990 s 55(2)(e); and PLANNING vol 81 (2010) PARA 298.
5   See the Landlord and Tenant Act 1954 Pt II (ss 23–46); and LANDLORD AND TENANT vol 64 (2016) PARA 1592 et seq. For the tenancies excluded from the protections of Pt II, which include tenancies of agricultural holdings subject to the provisions of the Agricultural Holdings Act 1986 and farm business tenancies subject to the Agricultural Tenancies Act 1995 (see PARA 656), see the Landlord and Tenant Act 1954 s 43; and LANDLORD AND TENANT vol 64 (2016) PARA 1599.
6   See the Landlord and Tenant Act 1954 s 23(1), (4); and LANDLORD AND TENANT vol 64 (2016) PARA 1597.

658. Administration of charitable allotments.

Any provisions with respect to allotments for recreation grounds, field gardens or other public or parochial purposes contained in any Act relating to inclosure or in any award or order made under it, and any provisions as to the management of any such allotments contained in any such Act, award or order, may, on the application of any district or parish council interested in the allotment, be dealt with by a scheme of the Charity Commission in the exercise of their ordinary jurisdiction as if those provisions had been established by the founder in the case of a charity having a founder[1].

1   Commons Act 1899 s 18 (amended by the Charities Act 2006 Sch 8 para 10).

(2) PROVISION OF ALLOTMENT LAND

(i) Local Authorities to Provide Land for Allotments

659. Local authorities' duty to provide allotments.

A general duty is placed on any district[1], parish[2], or London borough council[3], or, in Wales, any community[4], county or county borough council[5], if it is of opinion that there is a demand for allotments[6] in its area, to provide a sufficient number of allotments, and to let them to persons resident there and desiring to take the same[7]. Where the population of the relevant district, parish, London borough, community, county or county borough, according to the last published census, is under 10,000, the council's duty is limited to the provision of allotment gardens[8]. Where the population is 10,000 or higher, the council's obligation is limited to the provision of allotment gardens not exceeding one-eighth of an acre[9].

Any land which on 31 July 1953[10] was let by a local authority[11] as an allotment garden under the Defence (General) Regulations 1939[12] or was appropriated for letting thereunder, may be let for use by tenants as allotment gardens or to a society having as its object the cultivation of vacant land for the purpose of subletting for such use[13], but once any such land is returned to use as a park or open space or is otherwise appropriated for use for any purpose other than letting for allotment gardens it may not again be so let[14].

1   The Small Holdings and Allotments Act 1908 s 23(1) refers to an 'urban district' but in practice this is a reference to a district in England, since the English urban districts (and their councils) were abolished on 1 April 1974 and statutory references thereto were replaced with references to districts (and their councils), and the Welsh districts (and their councils) were abolished on 1 April 1996 and statutory references thereto (or their councils) were replaced with references to counties

or county boroughs (or their councils): see the Local Government Act 1972 ss 1(10), 20(6), (7), 179(1), (3) and the Local Government (Wales) Act 1994 s 17(1), (2), (4), (5); and as to the districts and counties in England and the counties and county boroughs in Wales see LOCAL GOVERNMENT vol 69 (2009) PARA 22 et seq.

2 As respects England, 'parish' is generally construed as a reference to a rural parish continued under the name of a parish by the Local Government Act 1972 s 1(6), urban parishes having been abolished on 1 April 1974 (ss 1(10), 20(6), 179(1), (4)). As respects Wales, 'parish' is construed as a reference to a community established under s 20(4), Sch 4 (as originally enacted) and continued by s 20(1): see s 179(1), (4); and as to parishes and communities generally see LOCAL GOVERNMENT vol 69 (2009) PARA 22 et seq. In rural parishes or communities having no parish or community council the authority is the parish or community meeting: Small Holdings and Allotments Act 1908 s 61(4); Allotments Act 1922 s 22(1); Local Government Act 1972 s 179(1), (4); Allotments Act 1950 s 10(3).

3 The Small Holdings and Allotments Act 1908 s 23(1) refers to a 'borough' but in practice this is a reference only to London boroughs since all other English boroughs were abolished on 1 April 1974 (Local Government Act 1972 ss 1(9), (10), 26), and since 'borough' in any Act passed before 1 April 1974 cannot apply to county boroughs in Wales (Local Government (Wales) Act 1994 s 64(2)). As to the London boroughs and their councils see LONDON GOVERNMENT vol 71 (2013) PARA 20 et seq. Note that in the case of an inner London borough the power to provide allotments is permissive not mandatory and the provisions relating to the making of representations on the need for allotments by residents (see note 6) do not apply: Small Holdings and Allotments Act 1908 s 23(1) (amended by the Land Settlement (Facilities) Act 1919 s 25, Schs 2, 3); London Government Act 1963 s 55(4).

4 As to the establishment and role of communities and their councils see note 2.

5 As to the establishment and role in Wales of counties and county boroughs and their councils see note 1.

6 As to the meaning of 'allotment' see PARA 649. Representations in writing may be made to the local authority on the need for allotments by any six resident registered parliamentary electors or persons who are liable to pay an amount in respect of council tax, and the local authority must take such representation into consideration: Small Holdings and Allotments Act 1908 s 23(2) (amended by the Local Government Finance Act 1992 Sch 13 para 4). As to the registration of parliamentary electors see ELECTIONS AND REFERENDUMS vol 37 (2013) PARA 113 et seq. As to liability for council tax see LOCAL GOVERNMENT FINANCE vol 70 (2012) PARA 298 et seq. See also note 3.

7 Small Holdings and Allotments Act 1908 s 23(1) (as amended: see note 3).

8 Allotments Act 1950 s 9(a). As to the meaning of 'allotment garden' see PARA 424 note 11.

9 Allotments Act 1950 s 9(b). Section 9(b) as drafted refers to 'twenty poles': however, the pole (30¼ square yards) is no longer recognised as a unit of area and the area 'one-eighth of an acre' has accordingly been substituted.

10 Ie the date on which the Emergency Laws (Miscellaneous Provisions) Act 1953 was passed.

11 In the Emergency Laws (Miscellaneous Provisions) Act 1953 s 5 as originally enacted 'local authority' meant the Common Council of the City of London, the council of a metropolitan borough or the council of a county, county borough or county district: s 5(4)(b). As to the Common Council of the City of London see LONDON GOVERNMENT vol 71 (2013) PARA 34 et seq. As to the effect of successive local government reorganisations on the other local authorities referred to in s 5(4)(b) see notes 1–3; and LOCAL GOVERNMENT vol 69 (2009) PARA 22 et seq.

12 See the Defence (General) Regulations 1939, SR & O 1939/927, reg 62A (added by SR & O 1939/1838; and amended by SR & O 1940/1611; SR & O 1941/456) (now revoked), which authorised a local authority to let, to tenants for use as an allotment garden or to an allotment society, land occupied by the authority, unoccupied land to the possession of which it was entitled, and land forming part of a park or open space under its management or control.

13 Emergency Laws (Miscellaneous Provisions) Act 1953 s 5(1) (amended by the Statute Law (Repeals) Act 1976). A tenancy of land which, on 31 July 1953, was subsisting under the Defence (General) Regulations 1939, SR & O 1939/927, reg 62A (as added: see note 12), continues in force as if it had been granted under the Emergency Laws (Miscellaneous Provisions) Act 1953 s 5(1): s 5(5).

14 Emergency Laws (Miscellaneous Provisions) Act 1953 s 5(2).

660. Acquisition of land for allotments.

The necessary land for allotments[1] may be acquired by a local authority[2] by hiring by agreement[3], by compulsory hiring[4], by purchase by agreement[5], by compulsory purchase[6], and by the appropriation of land held for other purposes[7]. Certain local authorities may enter on unoccupied land for the purpose of providing allotment gardens[8]. Land may also be acquired by transfer from allotment wardens and trustees[9]. Acquisitions and disposals of land for the purposes of the provision of allotments generally require the approval of the Secretary of State or the Welsh Ministers[10].

1   As to the meaning of 'allotment' see PARA 649.
2   As to the local authorities which may be concerned with the provision of allotments generally see PARA 659.
3   See PARAS 665–669.
4   See PARAS 673–690.
5   See PARAS 662–664.
6   See PARAS 670–672, 546–551.
7   See PARA 691.
8   See PARA 692. As to the meaning of 'allotment garden' see PARA 424 note 11.
9   See PARA 695.
10 See the Small Holdings and Allotments Regulations 1919, SR & O 1919/1197, reg 1(1)(1). As to the Secretary of State and the Welsh Ministers see PARA 741.

661. Acquisition of land for future allotments.

A district or London borough council, or, in Wales, a county or county borough council[1], may acquire land for allotments[2], notwithstanding that the land or any part of it cannot immediately be let in allotments, if the Secretary of State or the Welsh Ministers[3] is or are satisfied that there is a reasonable expectation that the land will eventually be required for allotments[4].

1   The Allotments Act 1925 s 5 refers to 'the council of a borough or an urban district' but should be construed as referring to the authorities mentioned in the text: see PARA 659 notes 1–5. As to the powers of local authorities in connection with the provision of allotments generally see PARA 659.
2   As to the meaning of 'allotment' see PARA 649.
3   As to the Secretary of State and the Welsh Ministers see PARA 741.
4   Allotments Act 1925 s 5 (amended by the Statute Law (Repeals) Act 1993). Acquisitions and disposals of land for the purposes of the provision of allotments generally require the approval of the Secretary of State or the Welsh Ministers: see the Small Holdings and Allotments Regulations 1919, SI 1919/1197, reg 1(1)(1).

(ii) Acquisition of Land for Allotments by Agreement

A. PURCHASE

662. Purchase by agreement of land for allotments.

The council of any district, parish, or London borough, or, in Wales, community, county or county borough[1] may, for the purpose of providing allotments[2], by agreement purchase land[3] situated either within or without its area[4]. Land in the Duchy of Lancaster[5] may be sold to local authorities for the purpose of allotments[6]. A tenant for life may make a grant in fee simple or absolutely of any part of the settled land for a nominal price, or for less than the best price obtainable, or gratuitously[7].

1   The Small Holdings and Allotments Act 1908 s 25(1) refers to 'the council of a borough, urban district or parish' but should be construed as referring to the authorities mentioned in the text: see

PARA 659 notes 1–5. As to the powers of local authorities in connection with the provision of allotments generally see PARA 659.

2   As to the meaning of 'allotment' see PARA 649.

3   As to the meaning of 'land' see PARA 424 note 5.

4   Small Holdings and Allotments Act 1908 s 25(1). For procedure and powers of entry where land is purchased by agreement see PARAS 663–664. Acquisitions and disposals of land for the purposes of the provision of allotments generally require the approval of the Secretary of State or the Welsh Ministers: see the Small Holdings and Allotments Regulations 1919, SI 1919/1197, reg 1(1)(1). As to the Secretary of State and the Welsh Ministers see PARA 741.

5   As to the Duchies of Lancaster and Cornwall see CROWN AND CROWN PROCEEDINGS vol 29 (2014) PARAS 214–267.

6   See the Local Government Act 1972 s 130; and LOCAL GOVERNMENT vol 69 (2009) PARA 534.

7   See the Settled Land Act 1925 s 57(2); and SETTLEMENTS vol 91 (2012) PARA 732. The amount which may be granted is restricted, as in the case of leases: see PARA 666.

663. Procedure for purchasing land for allotments by agreement.

The procedure for the non-compulsory purchase[1] of land[2] by councils[3] for the purpose of providing allotments is in general that provided for by the Compulsory Purchase Act 1965[4]. Provision is made as to the persons empowered to sell their interests[5], the payment of compensation where the title to the land is in doubt[6], powers of entry[7], the purchase or redemption of special interests in the land such as mortgages[8], the release of the land from rentcharges and, in the case of divided land, the apportionment of rents[9], the compensation of tenants at will[10], compensation for the purchase of common land[11], the purchase of, or payment of compensation for, land inadvertently omitted from the purchase[12], conveyancing costs[13], and the service of notices[14].

1   Ie purchase by agreement: see PARA 662.

2   As to the meaning of 'land' see PARA 424 note 5.

3   The local authorities empowered to purchase land for the purpose of providing allotments are district, parish, or London borough councils, or, in Wales, community, county or county borough councils: see PARA 662; and as to the local authorities which may be concerned with the provision of allotments generally, see PARA 659. As to the meaning of 'allotment' see PARA 649.

4   Small Holdings and Allotments Act 1908 s 38 (amended by the Compulsory Purchase Act 1965 s 38(1), Sch 6; and the Statute Law (Repeals) Act 1993). For the relevant provisions of the Compulsory Purchase Act 1965 see Pt I (ss 1–32) (excluding ss 4–8 (which make provision as to time limits, the payment of compensation and the sale of divided land), s 10 (compensation for injurious affection), s 23(1)–(5) (conveyancing costs), and s 31 (ecclesiastical property)); and COMPULSORY ACQUISITION OF LAND vol 18 (2009) PARA 549 et seq.

5   See the Compulsory Purchase Act 1965 ss 2, 3, Sch 1; and COMPULSORY ACQUISITION OF LAND vol 18 (2009) PARA 553.

6   See the Compulsory Purchase Act 1965 ss 9, 25, 26, 28; and COMPULSORY ACQUISITION OF LAND vol 18 (2009) PARA 661 et seq.

7   See the Compulsory Purchase Act 1965 ss 11–13; PARA 664; and COMPULSORY ACQUISITION OF LAND vol 18 (2009) PARA 638 et seq.

8   See the Compulsory Purchase Act 1965 ss 14–17; and COMPULSORY ACQUISITION OF LAND vol 18 (2009) PARAS 712–714. Any expenses incurred by a council in the purchase or redemption of any quit rent, chief rent, tithe, or other rentcharge, or other perpetual annual sum issuing out of acquired land, is deemed to have been incurred in the purchase of the land: Small Holdings and Allotments Act 1908 s 61(3) (amended by the Statute Law (Repeals) Act 1964; and the Statute Law (Repeals) Act 1993).

9   See the Compulsory Purchase Act 1965 ss 18–19; note 8; and COMPULSORY ACQUISITION OF LAND vol 18 (2009) PARAS 707–710.

10 See the Compulsory Purchase Act 1965 s 20; and COMPULSORY ACQUISITION OF LAND vol 18 (2009) PARA 699.

11 See the Compulsory Purchase Act 1965 Sch 4; and COMMONS vol 13 (2017) PARAS 648–650.

12 See the Compulsory Purchase Act 1965 s 22; and COMPULSORY ACQUISITION OF LAND vol 18 (2009) PARAS 648–650.
13 See the Compulsory Purchase Act 1965 Sch 5; and COMPULSORY ACQUISITION OF LAND vol 18 (2009) PARA 658.
14 See the Compulsory Purchase Act 1965 s 30; and COMPULSORY ACQUISITION OF LAND vol 18 (2009) PARA 618.

664. Entry on land for allotments purchased by agreement.

A council[1] which has agreed[2] to purchase land[3] for the provision of allotments may in general enter on and take possession of the land in accordance with the provisions of the Compulsory Purchase Act 1965[4]. However, a council which has agreed to purchase land subject to the interest of a yearly tenant[5] may, at any time after such agreement has been made and after giving not less than 14 days' notice to the person in possession, enter on and take possession of the land or such part thereof as is specified in the notice to treat, without previous consent[6]. The exercise of this power is subject to the payment of compensation to the person in possession of the land[7]. If the notice of entry relates to land on which there is a dwelling house, and the length of notice is less than three calendar months, the occupier of the dwelling house may, by notice served on the council within ten days after the service on him of the notice of entry, appeal to an arbitrator against the notice, and the council will not be entitled to enter on the land except on such date and on such conditions as the arbitrator may award[8].

1　The local authorities empowered to purchase land for the purpose of providing allotments are district, parish, or London borough councils, or, in Wales, community, county or county borough councils: see PARA 662; and as to the local authorities which may be concerned with the provision of allotments generally, see PARA 659. As to the meaning of 'allotment' see PARA 649.
2　Ie for the purposes of the Small Holdings and Allotments Act 1908.
3　See PARA 662. As to the meaning of 'land' see PARA 424 note 5.
4　Small Holdings and Allotments Act 1908 s 38 (amended by the Compulsory Purchase Act 1965 s 38(1), Sch 6; and the Statute Law (Repeals) Act 1993); see PARA 663. The relevant provisions are the Compulsory Purchase Act 1965 ss 11–13; see COMPULSORY ACQUISITION OF LAND vol 18 (2009) PARA 638 et seq.
5　Ie a person in possession of the land whose interest is not greater than that of a tenant for a year, or from year to year.
6　Land Settlement (Facilities) Act 1919 s 2(2).
7　Land Settlement (Facilities) Act 1919 s 2(2). The compensation payable is such amount, with interest, as would have been payable if the council had been authorised to purchase the land compulsorily and the person in possession had, in pursuance of such a power, been required to quit possession before the expiration of his term or interest in the land (but without the necessity of compliance with the Lands Clauses Consolidation Act 1845 ss 84–90 (see COMPULSORY ACQUISITION OF LAND vol 18 (2009) PARAS 638–644)): Land Settlement (Facilities) Act 1919 s 2(2).
8　Land Settlement (Facilities) Act 1919 s 2(3). Any such appeal is determinable by an arbitrator under and in accordance with the Agricultural Holdings Act 1986, except that, in default of agreement, the arbitrator must be appointed by the President of the Royal Institution of Chartered Surveyors: Land Settlement (Facilities) Act 1919 s 2(3) (amended by the Agricultural Holdings Act 1986 Sch 14). As to arbitration under the Agricultural Holdings Act 1986 see PARA 566 et seq. As to the Royal Institution of Chartered Surveyors generally see BUILDING CONTRACTS vol 6 (2011) PARA 490.

B. LEASE OR HIRE

665. Local authorities' power to take land for allotments on lease.

The council of any district, parish, or London borough, or, in Wales, any community, county or county borough[1], may, for the purpose of providing allotments[2], by agreement take on lease land[3], whether situated within or without its area[4].

1   The Small Holdings and Allotments Act 1908 s 25(1) refers to 'the council of a borough, urban district or parish' but should be construed as referring to the authorities mentioned in the text: see PARA 659 notes 1–5. As to the powers of local authorities in connection with the provision of allotments generally see PARA 659.

2   As to the meaning of 'allotment' see PARA 649.

3   As to the meaning of 'land' see PARA 424 note 5.

4   Small Holdings and Allotments Act 1908 s 25(1). For the power of entry onto land agreed to be hired see PARA 668. As to compensation for improvements at the determination of the tenancy see PARAS 719, 720. Acquisitions of land for the purposes of the provision of allotments generally require the approval of the Secretary of State or the Welsh Ministers: see the Small Holdings and Allotments Regulations 1919, SI 1919/1197, reg 1(1)(1); and as to the Secretary of State and the Welsh Ministers see PARA 741. Local authorities may also take on lease for allotments land held by county councils for the purposes of smallholdings: see PARA 630.

666. Leases for allotments purposes by limited owners.

Any person having power to lease land[1] for agricultural[2] purposes for a limited term[3], whether subject to any consent or conditions or not, may, subject to the like consent and conditions (if any), lease land to the council of any district, parish, or London borough, or, in Wales, community, county or county borough[4] for the purposes of allotments[5] for a term not exceeding 35 years, either with or without such rights of renewal as are conferred[6] in the case of land hired compulsorily for those purposes[7]. A tenant for life may make a lease of settled land for any term of years absolute for a nominal rent, or for less than the best rent obtainable, or gratuitously, for the purposes of the Small Holdings and Allotments Acts 1908 to 1931[8], but, except under a court order, not more than two acres in a district, or ten acres in a parish may be leased unless full consideration is paid or reserved for the excess[9].

1   As to the meaning of 'land' see PARA 424 note 5.

2   As to the meaning of 'agriculture' for these purposes see PARA 424 note 5.

3   Eg a mortgagor or mortgagee in possession (see the Law of Property Act 1925 s 99(1), (2), (3)(i); and MORTGAGE vol 77 (2016) PARA 349 et seq) or a tenant of settled land (see the Settled Land Act 1925 ss 41–43, 57; and SETTLEMENTS vol 91 (2012) PARAS 738–742).

4   The Small Holdings and Allotments Act 1908 refers here to 'a council', but this should be construed as a reference to the authorities referred to in the text (ie the local authorities empowered to acquire land for the purposes of that Act). As to the local authorities which may be concerned with the provision of allotments generally see PARA 659.

5   As to the meaning of 'allotment' see PARA 649.

6   Ie by the Small Holdings and Allotments Act 1908 (see PARA 682).

7   Small Holdings and Allotments Act 1908 s 40(1) (amended by the Agriculture Act 1970 Sch 5 Pt III). The provisions of the Law of Property Act 1922 providing for the conversion of perpetually renewable leases into long terms (see s 145, Sch 15 para 1; and LANDLORD AND TENANT vol 62 (2016) PARA 435) do not affect the power conferred by the Small Holdings and Allotments Act 1908 s 40 to grant leases with a similar right of renewal: Law of Property Act 1922 Sch 15 para 9. Acquisitions of land for the purposes of the provision of allotments generally require the approval of the Secretary of State or the Welsh Ministers: see the Small Holdings and Allotments Regulations 1919, SI 1919/1197, reg 1(1).

8   See the Settled Land Act 1925 s 57(2); and SETTLEMENTS vol 91 (2012) PARA 732. As to the Small Holdings and Allotments Acts 1908 to 1931 see PARA 627 note 3.

9   Settled Land Act 1925 s 57(2) proviso.

667. Leases for allotments purposes of Duchy of Cornwall land.

The like powers of leasing as may be exercised by limited owners[1] may be exercised, in the case of land[2] forming part of the possessions of the Duchy of

Cornwall[3], by the Duke of Cornwall or other persons for the time being empowered to dispose of land belonging to that Duchy[4].

1   See PARA 666.
2   As to the meaning of 'land' see PARA 424 note 5.
3   As to the Duchies of Lancaster and Cornwall see CROWN AND CROWN PROCEEDINGS vol 29 (2014) PARAS 214–267.
4   Small Holdings and Allotments Act 1908 s 40(2) (amended by the Crown Estate Act 1961 Sch 3 Pt II; and the Duchy of Lancaster Act 1988 Schedule). Similar provisions relating to the Duchy of Lancaster and to glebe land have been repealed (although note that land in the Duchy of Lancaster may still be sold for the purpose of allotments (see PARA 662), but may not in general be compulsorily acquired (see PARA 685)).

668. Entry on land for allotments hired by agreement.

Where an agreement for the hiring of land[1] has been made[2], the council entitled to hire the land[3] may, at any time and on giving not less than 14 days' notice to each owner, lessee and occupier of the land, enter on and take possession of the land or such part thereof as is specified in the agreement without previous consent or compliance with the statutory provisions relating to entry on land compulsorily acquired[4]. The exercise of this power is subject to the payment of compensation[5]. Where a council has agreed to hire land subject to the interest of a yearly tenant[6] it may, at any time after such agreement has been made and after giving not less than 14 days' notice to the person in possession, enter on and take possession of the land or such part thereof as is specified in the agreement, without previous consent[7]. The exercise of this power is also subject to the payment of compensation to the person in possession of the land[8].

If the notice of entry relates to land on which there is a dwelling house, and the length of notice is less than three calendar months, the occupier of the dwelling house may, by notice served on the council within ten days after the service on him of the notice of entry, appeal to an arbitrator against the notice, and the council will not be entitled to enter on the land except on such date and on such conditions as the arbitrator may award[9].

1   As to the meaning of 'land' see PARA 424 note 5.
2   Ie under the Small Holdings and Allotments Act 1908 (see PARA 665 et seq).
3   Ie a district, parish, or London borough council, or, in Wales, a community, county or county borough council: see PARA 665. As to the local authorities under a duty to provide allotments: see PARA 659.
4   Land Settlement (Facilities) Act 1919 s 2(2), (4); Small Holdings and Allotments (Compulsory Hiring) Regulations 1936, SR & O 1936/196, reg 25(1)(a). The statutory provisions relating to entry on land compulsorily acquired are the Lands Clauses (Consolidation) Act 1845 ss 84–90 (see COMPULSORY ACQUISITION OF LAND vol 18 (2009) PARAS 638–644).
5   Land Settlement (Facilities) Act 1919 s 2(2). The compensation payable is such amount, with interest, as would have been payable if the Lands Clauses (Consolidation) Act 1845 ss 84–90 (see COMPULSORY ACQUISITION OF LAND vol 18 (2009) PARAS 638–644) had been complied with, and must include such compensation by way of rent or otherwise, together with interest on such part of the compensation as is not paid by way of rent at the rate of 5% per annum from the time of entry on the land until such compensation is paid, as would have been payable if the council had at the date of entry hired the land of which possession is taken and extinguished the interest therein of any existing tenant: Small Holdings and Allotments (Compulsory Hiring) Regulations 1936, SR & O 1936/196, reg 25(2). In this context 'existing tenant', in relation to any land proposed or authorised to be hired, means a tenant thereof under a lease for a term no greater than the term for which the land is proposed or authorised to be hired; and 'lease' includes an agreement for a lease: reg 27.
6   Ie a person in possession of the land whose interest is not greater than that of a tenant for a year, or from year to year.

7   Land Settlement (Facilities) Act 1919 s 2(2), (4).
8   Land Settlement (Facilities) Act 1919 s 2(2), (4). The compensation payable is such amount, with interest, as would have been payable if the council had been authorised to hire the land compulsorily and the person in possession had, in pursuance of such a power, been required to quit possession before the expiration of his term or interest in the land (but without the necessity of compliance with the Lands Clauses Consolidation Act 1845 ss 84–90): Land Settlement (Facilities) Act 1919 s 2(2), (4); Small Holdings and Allotments (Compulsory Hiring) Regulations 1936, SR & O 1936/196, reg 25(1)(a).
9   Land Settlement (Facilities) Act 1919 s 2(3) (as originally enacted), (4). Any such appeal is determinable by an arbitrator under and in accordance with the Agricultural Holdings Act 1986, except that, in default of agreement, the arbitrator must be appointed by the President of the Royal Institution of Chartered Surveyors: Land Settlement (Facilities) Act 1919 s 2(3) (amended by the Agricultural Holdings Act 1986 Sch 14). As to arbitration under the Agricultural Holdings Act 1986 see PARA 566 et seq. As to the Royal Institution of Chartered Surveyors generally see BUILDING CONTRACTS vol 6 (2011) PARA 490.

669. Acquisition of land for field garden allotments.

The council of any district, parish, or London borough, or, in Wales, community, county or county borough[1], may, for the purpose of providing field gardens[2], by agreement take on lease land[3], whether situated within or without its area, or may purchase such land compulsorily[4].

1   The Small Holdings and Allotments Act 1908 s 25(1) refers to 'the council of a borough, urban district or parish' but should be construed as referring to the authorities mentioned in the text: see PARA 659 notes 1–5. As to the powers of local authorities in connection with the provision of allotments generally see PARA 659.
2   As to field garden allotments see PARA 651.
3   As to the meaning of 'land' see PARA 424 note 5. As to the hiring of land by agreement see PARAS 665–668.
4   Small Holdings and Allotments Act 1908 s 25(1) (amended by the Acquisition of Land (Authorisation Procedure) Act 1946 Sch 4; and the Acquisition of Land Act 1981 s 34; and by virtue of the Local Government Act 1972 s 179). Any purchase so made must be in accordance with the provisions of the Small Holdings and Allotments Act 1908, the Compulsory Purchase Act 1965 Pt I (ss 1–32) and the Acquisition of Land Act 1981: Small Holdings and Allotments Act 1908 ss 25(1) (as so amended); Compulsory Purchase Act 1965 s 1(1) (substituted by the Acquisition of Land Act 1981 Sch 4 para 14(1), (2)). As to compulsory purchase see PARAS 670–672; and COMPULSORY ACQUISITION OF LAND.

(iii) Compulsory Acquisition of Land to Provide Allotments

A. PURCHASE

670. Compulsory purchase for allotments generally.

The council of any district, parish, or London borough, or, in Wales, any community, county or county borough[1] may compulsorily purchase land[2], whether situated within or without its area, for the purposes of providing allotments[3]. Where such an authority proposes to purchase land compulsorily it may be authorised to do so by the Secretary of State or the Welsh Ministers[4].

Any question of disputed compensation is determinable by the Upper Tribunal[5]. In determining the amount of any disputed compensation no additional allowance may be made on account of the purchase being compulsory[6].

1   The Small Holdings and Allotments Act 1908 s 25(1) refers to 'the council of a borough, urban district or parish' but should be construed as referring to the authorities mentioned in the text: see PARA 659 notes 1–5. As to the powers of local authorities in connection with the provision of allotments generally see PARA 659.
2   As to the meaning of 'land' see PARA 424 note 5. As to the procedure for compulsory purchase see PARA 671. As to the land which may and may not be compulsorily acquired see PARA 685. As to

the matters influencing decisions on the making of compulsory acquisition orders see PARA **686**. As to the continuation or creation of easements over land compulsorily acquired see PARA **687**.

3   Small Holdings and Allotments Act 1908 s 25(1). As to the meaning of 'allotment' see PARA **649**. As to the time limits within which notices to treat for the purposes of compulsory purchase must be served, and the circumstances in which notices may be withdrawn, see PARA **688**. As to powers of entry on land proposed to be compulsorily acquired see PARA **672**.

4   Small Holdings and Allotments Act 1908 s 39(1) (amended by the Acquisition of Land (Authorisation Procedure) Act 1946; and SI 1955/554); Small Holdings and Allotments Regulations 1919, SI 1919/1197, reg 1(1)(1). The Small Holdings and Allotments Act 1908 s 39(1) refers to 'a council' but this should be construed as a reference to the local authorities empowered to acquire land compulsorily, that is to say, those referred to in the text. As to the Secretary of State and the Welsh Ministers see PARA **741**.

5   See the Land Compensation Act 1961 s 1; and COMPULSORY ACQUISITION OF LAND vol 18 (2009) PARA **718**.

6   Small Holdings and Allotments Act 1908 s 39(5). See further the Land Compensation Act 1961 s 5(1); and COMPULSORY ACQUISITION OF LAND vol 18 (2009) PARA **754**.

671. Procedure for compulsory purchase for allotments purposes.

The procedure for the compulsory purchase of land for the purposes of allotments[1] is principally governed by the Compulsory Purchase Act 1965[2] and the Acquisition of Land Act 1981[3]. The relevant provisions of the Compulsory Purchase Act 1965[4] make provision as to the persons empowered to sell their interests[5], the time limits within which powers of compulsory purchase must be exercised[6], the service of notices to treat[7], the payment of compensation for severance or division or injurious affection[8], the payment of compensation where the title to the land is in doubt[9], powers of entry[10], the purchase or redemption of special interests in the land such as mortgages[11], the release of the land from rentcharges and, in the case of divided land, the apportionment of rents[12], the compensation of tenants at will[13], compensation for the purchase of common land[14], the purchase of, or payment of compensation for, land inadvertently omitted from the purchase[15], conveyancing costs[16], the service of notices[17], and the payment of compensation for the purchase of, or damage to, ecclesiastical property[18]. The Acquisition of Land Act 1981 makes provision for the issue, notification, timetables, advertisement and confirmation of compulsory purchase orders[19], the administration of such orders in relation to certain land acquired by statutory undertakers, National Trust land, and land forming part of a common or open space[20], the questioning of the validity of compulsory purchase orders[21], the compulsory acquisition of rights over certain land (generally land which has been acquired by statutory undertakers) by way of the creation of new rights[22], the extinguishment of certain public rights of way[23], the exception of tunnels[24] and minerals from purchases[25], and general provisions as to compensation, information, inquiries and the service of documents[26].

A compulsory purchase must also be in accordance with the relevant provisions of the Small Holdings and Allotments Act 1908[27].

1   As to the compulsory purchase of land for the purposes of allotments see PARA **670**. As to the meaning of 'land' see PARA **424** note 5. As to the meaning of 'allotment' see PARA **649**.

2   Compulsory Purchase Act 1965 s 1(1) (substituted by the Acquisition of Land Act 1981 Sch 4 para 14(1), (2)).

3   Small Holdings and Allotments Act 1908 s 25(1) (amended by the Acquisition of Land (Authorisation Procedure) Act 1946 Sch 4; and by the Acquisition of Land Act 1981 s 34); Acquisition of Land Act 1981 s 1(1)(b), (2).

4   Ie the Compulsory Purchase Act 1965 Pt I (ss 1–32).

5   See the Compulsory Purchase Act 1965 ss 2, 3, Sch 1; and COMPULSORY ACQUISITION OF LAND vol 18 (2009) PARA **553**.

6 See the Compulsory Purchase Act 1965 s 4; and COMPULSORY ACQUISITION OF LAND vol 18 (2009) PARA 617.

7 See the Compulsory Purchase Act 1965 ss 5–6; and COMPULSORY ACQUISITION OF LAND vol 18 (2009) PARA 616.

8 See the Compulsory Purchase Act 1965 ss 7–8, 10; and COMPULSORY ACQUISITION OF LAND vol 18 (2009) PARAS 628–630, 718.

9 See the Compulsory Purchase Act 1965 ss 9, 25, 26, 28; and COMPULSORY ACQUISITION OF LAND vol 18 (2009) PARA 661 et seq.

10 See the Compulsory Purchase Act 1965 ss 11–13; PARA 672; and COMPULSORY ACQUISITION OF LAND vol 18 (2009) PARA 638 et seq.

11 See the Compulsory Purchase Act 1965 ss 14–17; and COMPULSORY ACQUISITION OF LAND vol 18 (2009) PARAS 711–714. Any expenses incurred by a council in the purchase or redemption of any quit rent, chief rent, tithe, or other rentcharge, or other perpetual annual sum issuing out of acquired land, is deemed to have been incurred in the purchase of the land: Small Holdings and Allotments Act 1908 s 61(3) (amended by the Statute Law (Repeals) Act 1964; and the Statute Law (Repeals) Act 1993).

12 See the Compulsory Purchase Act 1965 ss 18–19; note 11; and COMPULSORY ACQUISITION OF LAND vol 18 (2009) PARA 707 et seq.

13 See the Compulsory Purchase Act 1965 s 20; and COMPULSORY ACQUISITION OF LAND vol 18 (2009) PARA 700.

14 See the Compulsory Purchase Act 1965 s 21, Sch 4; and COMMONS vol 13 (2017) PARA 384 et seq.

15 See the Compulsory Purchase Act 1965 s 22; and COMPULSORY ACQUISITION OF LAND vol 18 (2009) PARA 648 et seq.

16 See the Compulsory Purchase Act 1965 s 23, Sch 5; and COMPULSORY ACQUISITION OF LAND vol 18 (2009) PARA 658.

17 See the Compulsory Purchase Act 1965 s 30; and COMPULSORY ACQUISITION OF LAND vol 18 (2009) PARA 618.

18 See the Compulsory Purchase Act 1965 s 31; and COMPULSORY ACQUISITION OF LAND vol 18 (2009) PARA 668.

19 See the Acquisition of Land Act 1981 ss 2, 10–15; and COMPULSORY ACQUISITION OF LAND vol 18 (2009) PARA 557 et seq.

20 See the Acquisition of Land Act 1981 Pt III (ss 16–22); and COMPULSORY ACQUISITION OF LAND.

21 See the Acquisition of Land Act 1981 Pt IV (ss 23–27); and COMPULSORY ACQUISITION OF LAND vol 18 (2009) PARA 612 et seq.

22 See the Acquisition of Land Act 1981 Pt V (ss 28–31); and COMPULSORY ACQUISITION OF LAND vol 18 (2009) PARA 606 et seq.

23 See the Acquisition of Land Act 1981 Pt VI (ss 32–33); and HIGHWAYS, STREETS AND BRIDGES vol 55 (2012) PARA 836.

24 See the Acquisition of Land Act 1981 s 2A; and COMPULSORY ACQUISITION OF LAND.

25 See the Acquisition of Land Act 1981 s 3, Sch 2; and MINES, MINERALS AND QUARRIES vol 76 (2013) PARA 138 et seq.

26 See the Acquisition of Land Act 1981 ss 4–6; and COMPULSORY ACQUISITION OF LAND.

27 Small Holdings and Allotments Act 1908 s 25(1) (as amended: see note 3). The provisions referred to in the text are ss 39, 41–43, 45 (see PARAS 670, 674 et seq).

672. Entry on land compulsorily purchased for allotments.

A district, parish, or London borough council, or, in Wales, a community, county or county borough council[1] which has agreed[2] to purchase land[3] compulsorily for the provision of allotments may in general enter on and take possession of the land in accordance with the provisions of the Compulsory Purchase Act 1965[4]. Where, however, a council has agreed to purchase land compulsorily subject to the interest of a yearly tenant[5] it may, at any time after such agreement has been made and after giving not less than 14 days' notice to the person in possession, enter on and take possession of the land or such part thereof as is specified in the notice to treat without previous consent[6]. The exercise of this power is subject to the payment of compensation to the person in possession of the land[7] together with interest at the rate currently prescribed[8].

If a notice of entry relates to land on which there is a dwelling house, and the length of notice is less than three calendar months, the occupier of the dwelling house may, by notice served on the council within ten days after the service on him of the notice of entry, appeal to an arbitrator against the notice, and the council will not be entitled to enter on the land except on such date and on such conditions as the arbitrator may award[9].

1 Ie the local authorities empowered to purchase land compulsorily for the purpose of providing allotments: see PARAS 670–671. As to the local authorities which may be concerned with the provision of allotments generally see PARA 659. As to the meaning of 'allotment' see PARA 649.
2 Ie for the purposes of the Small Holdings and Allotments Act 1908.
3 As to the meaning of 'land' see PARA 424 note 5.
4 Compulsory Purchase Act 1965 s 1(1) (substituted by the Acquisition of Land Act 1981 Sch 4 para 14(1), (2)). The relevant provisions are the Compulsory Purchase Act 1965 ss 11–13; see COMPULSORY ACQUISITION OF LAND vol 18 (2009) PARA 638 et seq. A council which has entered on the land by virtue of s 11(1) is not entitled to withdraw the notice to treat in accordance with the Small Holdings and Allotments Act 1908 s 39(8): Land Settlement (Facilities) Act 1919 s 2(1) (amended by the Acquisition of Land (Authorisation Procedure) Act 1946 Sch 4, and by the Acquisition of Land Act 1981 Sch 4 para 2).
5 Ie a person in possession of the land whose interest is not greater than that of a tenant for a year, or from year to year.
6 Land Settlement (Facilities) Act 1919 s 2(2).
7 Land Settlement (Facilities) Act 1919 s 2(2). The compensation payable is such amount, with interest, as would have been payable if the council had been authorised to purchase the land compulsorily and the person in possession had, in pursuance of such a power, been required to quit possession before the expiration of his term or interest in the land (but without the necessity of compliance with the Lands Clauses Consolidation Act 1845 ss 84–90 (as to which see COMPULSORY ACQUISITION OF LAND vol 18 (2009) PARAS 638–644)): Land Settlement (Facilities) Act 1919 s 2(2).
8 See the Land Compensation Act 1961 s 32(1); the Acquisition of Land (Rate of Interest after Entry) Regulations 1995, SI 1995/2262; and COMPULSORY ACQUISITION OF LAND vol 18 (2009) PARA 641.
9 Land Settlement (Facilities) Act 1919 s 2(3) (amended by the Acquisition of Land (Authorisation Procedure) Act 1946 Sch 4). Any such appeal is determinable by an arbitrator under and in accordance with the Agricultural Holdings Act 1986, except that, in default of agreement, the arbitrator must be appointed by the President of the Royal Institution of Chartered Surveyors: Land Settlement (Facilities) Act 1919 s 2(3) (amended by the Agricultural Holdings Act 1986 Sch 14). As to arbitration under the Agricultural Holdings Act 1986 see PARA 566 et seq. As to the Royal Institution of Chartered Surveyors generally see BUILDING CONTRACTS vol 6 (2011) PARA 490.

B. LEASE OR HIRE

673. Compulsory hiring of land for allotments.

The only remaining circumstances under which land may be compulsorily hired for allotments[1] are where a district council or, in Wales, a county or county borough council[2], proposes to hire land compulsorily for the purpose of leasing it to a parish or community council for allotments[3].

1 As to the meaning of 'land' see PARA 424 note 5. As to the meaning of 'allotment' see PARA 649. As to the land which may and may not be compulsorily acquired see PARA 685. As to the continuation or creation of easements over land compulsorily acquired see PARA 687.

2 Ie the local authorities empowered to hire land compulsorily on behalf of parishes or communities, that is to say, those referred to in the Land Settlement (Facilities) Act 1919 s 17: see note 3; and PARA 659 notes 1–5. As to the powers of local authorities in connection with the provision of allotments generally see PARA 659.

3 Ie under the Land Settlement (Facilities) Act 1919 s 17: see PARA 689. By virtue of the amendments effected to the Small Holdings and Allotments Act 1908 s 25 by the Acquisition of Land (Authorisation Procedure) Act 1946 and the Acquisition of Land Act 1981, a local authority has no power of compulsory hiring for the purpose of allotments under the Small Holdings and Allotments Act 1908, and the provisions as to compulsory hiring in that Act accordingly apply only to district, county or county borough councils acquiring land for letting to parish or community councils for allotments under the Land Settlement (Facilities) Act 1919 s 17 (see PARA 689). As to parish and community councils see PARA 659 notes 2, 4. Acquisitions of land for the purposes of the provision of allotments generally require the approval of the Secretary of State or the Welsh Ministers: see the Small Holdings and Allotments Regulations 1919, SI 1919/1197, reg 1(1)(1). As to the Secretary of State and the Welsh Ministers see PARA 741.

674. Compulsory hiring orders for allotments purposes.

When a council[1] proposes to hire land[2] compulsorily[3] it may submit to the Secretary of State or the National Assembly for Wales[4] an order for the compulsory hiring of the land specified in the order for a period of not less than 14 and not more than 35 years[5].

1 In practice this refers to a district council (in England) or a county or county borough council (in Wales), which are the only councils empowered to hire land compulsorily for allotments: see PARA 673. As to the meaning of 'allotment' see PARA 649. As to the powers of local authorities in connection with the provision of allotments generally see PARA 659.

2 As to the meaning of 'land' see PARA 424 note 5. As to the land which may and may not be compulsorily acquired see PARA 685. As to the matters influencing decisions on the making of compulsory acquisition orders see PARA 686. As to the continuation or creation of easements over land compulsorily acquired see PARA 687.

3 Ie for the purpose of leasing it to a parish or community council for allotments under the Land Settlement (Facilities) Act 1919 s 17 (see PARA 689).

4 As to the Secretary of State and the Welsh Ministers see PARA 741.

5 Small Holdings and Allotments Act 1908 s 39(2). As to the time limits within which notices to treat for the purposes of compulsory purchase must be served, and the circumstances in which notices may be withdrawn, see PARA 688.

675. Form and content of compulsory hiring orders for allotments purposes.

A compulsory hiring order[1] must be in the prescribed form, or to the like effect[2], and must incorporate such provisions as the Secretary of State or the Welsh Ministers[3] may prescribe for the purpose of carrying it into effect and of protecting the council[4] and the persons interested in the land[5]. The order must also incorporate any regulations made by the Secretary of State or the Welsh Ministers[6] and must determine the terms and conditions of the hiring other than the rent[7]. The order must be published and advertised by the council, and notice of it must be given to parties affected[8]. Subsequently the order will be confirmed[9] unless an objection[10] to the order is lodged and persisted in, in which event the Secretary of State or the Welsh Ministers must hold a public inquiry in the locality[11].

1 Ie an order for the compulsory hiring of land for allotments: see PARA 674.

2 Small Holdings and Allotments Act 1908 Sch 1 Pt I(1); Small Holdings and Allotments (Compulsory Hiring) Regulations 1936, SR & O 1936/196, reg 1. The form itself is set out in the Appendix.

3 As to the Secretary of State and the Welsh Ministers see PARA 741.

4 In practice this is a reference to a district council (in England) or a county or county borough council (in Wales), which are the only councils empowered to hire land compulsorily for allotments: see PARA 673. As to the meaning of 'allotment' see PARA 649.

5   Small Holdings and Allotments Act 1908 Sch 1 Pt I(1). As to the meaning of 'land' see PARA 424 note 5; note that for the purposes of the Small Holdings and Allotments (Compulsory Hiring) Regulations 1936, SR & O 1936/196, 'land' includes stints and other alienable common rights of grazing (reg 27). As to the acquisition of common rights see COMPULSORY ACQUISITION OF LAND vol 18 (2009) PARA 609. As to stinted pasture see COMMONS vol 13 (2017) PARA 609. As to the land which may and may not be compulsorily acquired for allotments see PARA 685. As to the matters influencing decisions on the making of compulsory acquisition orders see PARA 686. As to the continuation or creation of easements over land compulsorily acquired see PARA 687.

6   Small Holdings and Allotments Act 1908 Sch 1 Pt II(1); Small Holdings and Allotments (Compulsory Hiring) Regulations 1936, SR & O 1936/196, reg 28. By way of such incorporation the order may also incorporate in adapted form certain provisions of the Lands Clauses Acts and the Railways Clauses Consolidation Act 1845 ss 77–85: see the Small Holdings and Allotments Act 1908 Sch 1 Pt I(1), Pt II(1); Small Holdings and Allotments (Compulsory Hiring) Regulations 1936, SR & O 1936/196, reg 28. 'The Lands Clauses Acts' means the Lands Clauses Consolidation Act 1845, the Lands Clauses Consolidation Acts Amendment Act 1850, and any other Act for the time being in force amending those Acts: Interpretation Act 1978 s 5, Sch 1. As to the Lands Clauses Acts see COMPULSORY ACQUISITION OF LAND. As to the Railways Clauses Consolidation Act 1845 ss 77–85 see MINES, MINERALS AND QUARRIES vol 76 (2013) PARA 145 et seq.

7   Small Holdings and Allotments Act 1908 Sch 1 Pt II(2). In particular, the order must provide for the insertion in the lease of covenants by the council to cultivate the land in a proper manner, and to pay to the landlord, at the determination of the tenancy on the council quitting the land, compensation for depreciation, and, unless otherwise agreed, to keep the buildings and premises in repair: Sch 1 Pt II(2)(a). Where land is compulsorily hired, the council must be allowed a reasonable time in which to remedy breaches of covenant: *Hopley v Tarvin Parish Council* (1910) 74 JP 209. The order must not authorise the breaking up of pasture unless this can be done without depreciating the value of the land or the circumstances are such that allotments cannot otherwise be successfully cultivated: Small Holdings and Allotments Act 1908 Sch 1 Pt II(2)(b) (amended by the Land Settlement (Facilities) Act 1919 s 25(1), Sch 2) (although see, in connection with allotment gardens, PARA 676 text and notes 5–7). The order must not, except with the landlord's consent, confer on the council any right to fell or cut timber or trees, or any right to take, sell or carry away any minerals, gravel, sand or clay, except so far as may be necessary or convenient for the purpose of erecting buildings on the land or otherwise adapting the land for allotments, and except upon payment of compensation for minerals, gravel, sand or clay so used: Small Holdings and Allotments Act 1908 Sch 1 Pt II(2)(c). The order may provide for the continuance or creation of easements over the land authorised to be acquired: see PARA 687. As to the payment of compensation and rent on compulsory hiring see PARA 679. As to the meaning of 'cultivation' see PARA 424 note 5. 'Landlord' in relation to land compulsorily hired means the person for the time being entitled to receive the rent from the council: s 61(1). Provision is made for the construction of any enactment incorporated with an order: see Sch 1 Pt I(7). Provision is also made in connection with the acquisition of ecclesiastical lands: see Sch 1 Pt I(8) (substituted by the Church of England (Miscellaneous Provisions) Measure 2006 Sch 5 para 1); the Endowments and Glebe Measure 1976 ss 15, 20; the Church Commissioners Measure 1947 ss 1, 2; the Ecclesiastical Leasing Act 1858 s 2; and ECCLESIASTICAL LAW.

8   See the Small Holdings and Allotments Act 1908 Sch 1 Pt I(2); and the Small Holdings and Allotments (Compulsory Hiring) Regulations 1936, SR & O 1936/196, regs 2, 3, 17, 24. Any notice required by the Small Holdings and Allotments Act 1908 to be given may be sent by registered post: s 61(5). An order may, on the application of any interested party, make provision to secure the interest of any party other than the owner or existing tenant in any compensation payable in respect of the compulsory hiring: Small Holdings and Allotments (Compulsory Hiring) Regulations 1936, SR & O 1936/196, reg 5(2). In this context 'owner', in relation to any land proposed or authorised to be hired, means the person who by himself or his agent is in actual possession, or receipt of the rents and profits, of the land (except a tenant thereof under a lease for a term no greater than the term for which the land is proposed or authorised to be hired) and that without regard to the real amount of interest of such person: reg 27. As to the meaning of 'existing tenant' and 'lease' see PARA 668 note 5.

9   As to confirmation see PARA 677.

10   Objections must be presented to the Secretary of State or the Welsh Ministers and, if required by the notice, a copy sent to the clerk to the council, within one calendar month from the date on

which the notice was sent to the objector or, if no notice was sent to him, from the date of the latest advertisement: Small Holdings and Allotments (Compulsory Hiring) Regulations 1936 SR & O 1936/196, regs 2(3), 4.

11   Small Holdings and Allotments Act 1908 Sch 1 Pt I(3), (4). As to inquiries see PARA 747.

676. Compulsory hiring of pasture land in connection with allotments.

No order may be made authorising the compulsory hiring for the purpose of allotments[1] of land[2] which at the date of the order is pasture land, if it is proved to the satisfaction of the Secretary of State or the Welsh Ministers[3] that arable land which is equally suitable for the purpose is reasonably available for hiring by the council[4]. An order authorising the compulsory hiring of land for the provision of allotment gardens[5] may authorise the breaking up of pasture[6], but in other cases the order may not authorise the breaking up of pasture unless the Secretary of State or the Welsh Ministers is or are satisfied that it can be broken up without depreciating the value of the land, or that the circumstances are such that allotments cannot otherwise be successfully cultivated[7].

1   Ie the compulsory hiring by district councils (in England) or county or county borough councils (in Wales) for letting to parish or community councils under the Land Settlement (Facilities) Act 1919 s 17: see PARA 689. As to the meaning of 'allotment' see PARA 649.

2   As to the meaning of 'land' see PARA 424 note 5. As to the land which may and may not be compulsorily acquired see PARA 685. As to the matters influencing decisions on the making of compulsory acquisition orders see PARA 686. As to the continuation or creation of easements over land compulsorily acquired see PARA 687.

3   As to the Secretary of State and the Welsh Ministers see PARA 741.

4   Allotments Act 1922 s 8(4).

5   As to the meaning of 'allotment garden' see PARA 424 note 11.

6   See the Allotments Act 1922 s 8(5), which provides that the Small Holdings and Allotments Act 1908 Sch 1 Pt II(2)(b) (which restricts the breaking up of pasture compulsorily hired: see the text and note 7), does not apply to land compulsorily hired for the provision of allotment gardens.

7   Small Holdings and Allotments Act 1908 Sch 1 Pt II(2)(b) (amended by the Land Settlement (Facilities) Act 1919 Sch 2). As to the meaning of 'cultivation' see PARA 424 note 5. The meaning of 'successfully cultivated' was discussed in *Knowles v Salford Corpn* [1922] 1 Ch 328 at 344, CA, per Warrington LJ.

677. Confirmation of compulsory hiring order for allotments purposes.

A compulsory hiring order[1] is not effective unless and until it is confirmed by the Secretary of State or the Welsh Ministers[2], who may confirm it with or without modifications[3]. Confirmation is conclusive evidence that applicable legislative requirements have been complied with and that the order has been duly made and is within the hiring authority's statutory powers[4]. Notice of confirmation of the order must be given to each owner, occupier and lessee[5].

In confirming an order, the Secretary of State or the Welsh Ministers must have regard to the same considerations regarding the effect of the order on existing holdings and the affected area generally as a council[6] making an order is required to have regard[7].

1   Ie an order under the Small Holdings and Allotments Act 1908 s 39(2), as to which see PARA 674. As to the compulsory hiring of land for the purposes of allotments generally see PARA 673. As to the meaning of 'land' see PARAS 424 note 5, 675 note 5. As to the land which may and may not be compulsorily acquired see PARA 685. As to the continuation or creation of easements over land compulsorily acquired see PARA 687. As to the meaning of 'allotment' see PARA 649.

2   As to the Secretary of State and the Welsh Ministers see PARA 741.

3   See the Small Holdings and Allotments Act 1908 s 39(3) (amended by the Acquisition of Land (Authorisation Procedure) Act 1946 Sch 4; and the Statute Law (Repeals) Act 1986). Notices to

treat must be served within three months of the confirmation of the order: see PARA **688**. Confirmation of the order enables a council to enter on and take possession of the land proposed to be compulsorily hired: see PARA **684**.

4   Small Holdings and Allotments Act 1908 s 39(3) (as amended: see note 3). The validity of a confirmed order cannot be challenged: see *Ex p Ringer* (1909) 73 JP 436; but see *Minister of Health v R, ex p Yaffe* [1931] AC 494, HL, where it was held that a scheme unauthorised by the Housing Act 1925 (repealed) could not be made law by an order of the minister which, under that Act, was to have statutory effect. See also the general principle laid down in *Frewin v Lewis* (1838) 4 My & Cr 249 at 254 per Lord Cottenham LC. Where a council neglected to comply with the condition precedent of endeavouring to obtain suitable land by agreement before making an order (see the Compulsory Purchase Act 1965 s 5; and COMPULSORY ACQUISITION OF LAND vol 18 (2009) PARA 616), an injunction restraining it from proceeding was refused while an inquiry was pending: *Reddaway v Lancashire County Council* (1925) 41 TLR 422.

5   Small Holdings and Allotments (Compulsory Hiring) Regulations 1936, SR & O 1936/196, reg 5(1). Provision is made for the service of notices: see reg 24. As to the meaning of 'owner' see PARA 675 note 8.

6   In practice this refers to a district council (in England) or a county or county borough council (in Wales), which are the only councils empowered to hire land compulsorily for allotments: see PARA 673.

7   See the Small Holdings and Allotments Act 1908 s 41(2); and PARA **686**.

678. Enforcement of compulsory hiring order for allotments purposes.

A council[1] requiring to hire compulsorily[2] any land[3] authorised to be hired by a compulsory hiring order[4] must, within three calendar months after the date on which the order is confirmed[5], give notice to that effect[6] to the owner[7] of such land, and to any existing tenant[8] thereof, or to such of those parties as may, after diligent inquiry, be known to the council, demanding from those parties the particulars of their estate and interest in the land, in so far as such particulars are required in order to ascertain the owner thereof and the interests of the existing tenants (if any)[9]. On receipt of the particulars of the interest of an existing tenant, the council must, within 21 days, give notice to the tenant stating whether the council desires to extinguish his interest[10] or to hire the land subject to it[11]. If the council fails to give such notice it is deemed to desire to extinguish the interest[12].

1   In practice this refers to a district council (in England) or a county or county borough council (in Wales), which are the only councils empowered to hire land compulsorily for allotments: see PARA 673. As to the meaning of 'allotment' see PARA 649.

2   Ie by way of an order under the Small Holdings and Allotments Act 1908 s 39(2), as to which see PARA **674**.

3   As to the meaning of 'land' see PARAS **424** note 5, 675 note 5. As to the land which may and may not be compulsorily acquired see PARA **685**. As to the continuation or creation of easements over land compulsorily acquired see PARA **687**.

4   Ie an order under the Small Holdings and Allotments Act 1908 s 39(2).

5   Small Holdings and Allotments (Compulsory Hiring) Regulations 1936, SR & O 1936/196, reg 6(3). As to confirmation of a compulsory hiring order see PARA 677.

6   The council must state in every such notice the particulars of the land required to be hired; the term for which the council is authorised to hire it; the council's willingness to treat for the hiring; and a date consistent with the terms of the order on which it requires the tenancy to commence: Small Holdings and Allotments (Compulsory Hiring) Regulations 1936, SR & O 1936/196, reg 6(1). Provision is made for the service of notices: see reg 24.

7   As to the meaning of 'owner' see PARA 675 note 8. Where the owner is a tenant the council must also give notice, within three calendar months after the date on which the order is confirmed, to the person in receipt of the rent reserved under the lease under which the owner holds as tenant that it requires to hire compulsorily the lands specified in the notice: Small Holdings and Allotments (Compulsory Hiring) Regulations 1936, SR & O 1936/196, reg 6(2), (3). As to the meaning of 'lease' see PARA 668 note 5.

8   As to the meaning of 'existing tenant' see PARA **668** note 5.

9   Small Holdings and Allotments (Compulsory Hiring) Regulations 1936, SR & O 1936/196, reg 6(1). Special provision is made for the determination of the rent, compensation, and other matters where the council cannot after diligent inquiry ascertain the owner or existing tenant, or where the owner or tenant fails to state the particulars demanded by the notice to treat or fails to treat with the council in respect of his interest: see reg 11; and as to the determination of rent and compensation see PARA 679. Costs reasonably incurred by an owner or existing tenant in furnishing any particulars of his estate or interest must be paid by the council: reg 17(1). In the event of disagreement as to costs, the council must pay such costs as may be authorised: see reg 17(2).

10 Any interest of an existing tenant which is extinguished under the powers conferred by a compulsory order is extinguished upon, and by reason of, the commencement of the tenancy of the council: Small Holdings and Allotments (Compulsory Hiring) Regulations 1936, SR & O 1936/196, reg 7. Provision is made for the calculation and payment of compensation to an existing tenant whose interest is extinguished, subject to the provision of proof of such an interest: see regs 8, 10, 21. 'Compulsory order' means an order under the Small Holdings and Allotments Acts 1908 to 1931 and the Allotments Acts 1922 and 1925 which authorises land to be compulsorily hired: Small Holdings and Allotments (Compulsory Hiring) Regulations 1936, SR & O 1936/196, reg 27.

11 Small Holdings and Allotments (Compulsory Hiring) Regulations 1936, SR & O 1936/196, reg 7. Provision is made for the service of notices: see reg 24.

12 Small Holdings and Allotments (Compulsory Hiring) Regulations 1936, SR & O 1936/196, reg 7.

679.   Determination of compensation or rent payable on compulsory hiring for allotments purposes.

In default of agreement:

(1)   the amount of rent to be paid by a council[1] for land[2] compulsorily hired[3];

(2)   the amount of any other compensation to be paid by a council to any person entitled to compensation in respect of the land or any interest in it or in respect of improvements executed on it or otherwise[4]; and

(3)   where part only of a holding held for an unexpired term is hired, the rent to be paid for the residue of the holding during the remainder of the term[5],

must be determined by a single valuer[6] appointed by the Secretary of State or the Welsh Ministers[7]. In assessing the value of the hired land the existence of mines and minerals[8] should be disregarded, and only the surface value should be taken into consideration[9].

Any person interested in the valuation must give the valuer all the assistance, information and explanations he requires and produce to him or give him access to relevant documents, at the council's expense[10].

1   In practice this refers to a district council (in England) or a county or county borough council (in Wales), which are the only councils empowered to hire land compulsorily for allotments: see PARA 673. As to the meaning of 'allotment' see PARA 649.

2   As to the meaning of 'land' see PARAS 424 note 5, 675 note 5. As to the land which may and may not be compulsorily acquired see PARA 685. As to the continuation or creation of easements over land compulsorily acquired see PARA 687.

3   Small Holdings and Allotments Act 1908 Sch 1 Pt II(3)(a). The reference in the text to land compulsorily hired is a reference to land compulsorily hired by way of an order under s 39(2), as to which see PARA 674. As to the compulsory hiring of land for the purposes of allotments generally see PARA 673.

    In fixing the rent to be paid for the land compulsorily hired the valuer must take into consideration any rent (if any) at which the land has been let and the annual value of the land for the purposes of income tax or rating, any loss (if any) caused to the owner by severance, the terms and conditions of the hiring (including any reservation of sporting or fishing rights) and all other circumstances connected with the land, but must not make any allowance in respect of any use to which the owner might otherwise have put the land, being a use in respect of which he might resume possession: Sch 1 Pt II(4). As to resuming possession see PARA 683. In fixing the rent the valuer must also take into consideration the interest of any existing tenant and the existence of any reservation, exception or easement affecting the land, which must be valued subject to such interest, reservation, exception or easement (Small Holdings and Allotments (Compulsory Hiring) Regulations 1936, SR & O 1936/196, reg 13), and must have regard not only to the value of the land but also to any damage to be sustained by the owner of the land by its severance from other land of his, or by reason of other land of his being otherwise injuriously affected (see reg 14(1)). The valuer must, within one month of his appointment (or such extended period as the Secretary of State or the Welsh Ministers may allow), make and sign a determination of all relevant matters determinable at that date and must within one month of the commencement of the council's tenancy (see PARA 680) (or such extended period as the Secretary of State or the Welsh Ministers may allow), make and sign a determination of all outstanding matters: see reg 19. Every such determination must be duly stamped and sent to the council, the owner and any existing tenant affected by it: reg 20. Provision is made for the determination of the rent to be paid by the council in circumstances where the owner of the land would be unable, except under powers conferred by the Small Holdings and Allotments (Compulsory Hiring) Regulations 1936, SR & O 1936/196, to lease the land: see reg 9.

As to the meaning of 'lease' see PARA 668 note 5. As to the meaning of 'owner' see PARA 675 note 8. As to the meaning of 'existing tenant' see PARA 668 note 5. As to the designation 'tenant' see PARA 649 note 9. As to the Secretary of State and the Welsh Ministers see PARA 741.

4   Small Holdings and Allotments Act 1908 Sch 1 Pt II(3)(b). Provision as to the payment of compensation is made by the Small Holdings and Allotments (Compulsory Hiring) Regulations 1936, SR & O 1936/196, reg 21.

5   Small Holdings and Allotments Act 1908 Sch 1 Pt II(3)(c). Any compensation awarded to a tenant in respect of the depreciation of the value to him of the residue of his holding caused by the withdrawal from the holding of the hired land must so far as possible be provided for by taking that compensation into account in fixing the rent to be paid for the residue of the holding during the remainder of the term: Sch 1 Pt II(5). Every existing tenant is entitled to compensation from the council for the damage done to him in his tenancy by the severance of the hired land from unhired land held by him: Small Holdings and Allotments (Compulsory Hiring) Regulations 1936, SR & O 1936/196, reg 14(2). See also reg 21.

6   The Acquisition of Land (Assessment of Compensation) Act 1919 s 7(2) (repealed) provided that any matter required by the Small Holdings and Allotments Act 1908 to be determined by a single valuer should be determined by an official arbitration under the Acquisition of Land (Assessment of Compensation) Act 1919 (now repealed). The Lands Tribunal Act 1949 s 1(3)(a)(i) subsequently provided that any question directed to be determined by an official arbitrator was to be referred to and determined by the Lands Tribunal (now replaced by the Upper Tribunal: see COMPULSORY ACQUISITION OF LAND vol 18 (2009) PARA 721). However, by the date on which s 1 came into force (1 January 1950: see the Lands Tribunal Act (Appointed Day) Order 1949, SI 1949/2335), the Acquisition of Land (Assessment of Compensation) Act 1919 s 7(2) had been repealed (by the Agriculture Act 1947 s 110, Sch 13) and there was therefore no provision in force requiring reference to an official arbitrator through which the Lands Tribunal could acquire jurisdiction under the Lands Tribunal Act 1949 s 1(3)(a); it is accordingly submitted that the detailed provisions in the text continue to apply. It should however be noted that the Land Compensation Act 1961 s 1 and the Compulsory Purchase Act 1965 s 6 (see COMPULSORY ACQUISITION OF LAND) give the Upper Tribunal general power to assess compensation, and the Lands Tribunal Act 1949 s 1(5) (see COMPULSORY ACQUISITION OF LAND vol 18 (2009) PARA 721) empowers it to act as arbitrator with the parties' consent.

7   Small Holdings and Allotments Act 1908 Sch 1 Pt II(3). A tenant in occupation may, however, by written notice served on the council before the determination of his tenancy, require that any claim by him against the council referable to arbitration under the Agricultural Holdings Act 1986 (see PARA 566 et seq) must be so referred, in which case the claims in question must be determined by arbitration under the Agricultural Holdings Act 1986 and not by valuation under the Small Holdings and Allotments Act 1908: Sch 1 Pt II(3) (proviso) (amended by the Agricultural Holdings Act 1986 Sch 14 para 3). Additionally, if an owner or existing tenant does not agree with the council as to any matter which under the Small Holdings and Allotments Act 1908 Sch 1 Pt II(3) is in default of such agreement to be determined by a single valuer, the council may require that the rent, compensation or other matter to be determined must be determined in manner provided by the Small Holdings and Allotments Acts 1908 to 1931, and the Allotments Acts 1922 to 1950: Small Holdings and Allotments (Compulsory Hiring) Regulations 1936, SR & O 1936/196, reg 11. As to the Small Holdings and Allotments Acts 1908 to 1931 see PARA 627 note 3; as to the

Allotments Acts 1922 to 1950 see PARA 649 note 2; and as to the provisions of that legislation concerned with compensation see PARAS 705–720. Any notice required by the Small Holdings and Allotments Act 1908 to be served may be sent by registered post: s 61(5).

In assessing compensation, the valuer is required to act on his own knowledge and experience, but must also hear any authorities or parties authorised to appear, and witnesses, but must not, except in such cases as the Secretary of State or the Welsh Ministers otherwise direct, hear counsel or expert witnesses: Small Holdings and Allotments Act 1908 Sch 1 Pt I(5) (amended by the Lands Tribunal Act 1949 Sch 2); Allotments Act 1922 s 8(3); Small Holdings and Allotments Act 1926 s 17(3)(b).

8 Subject to any provision in the compulsory hiring order mines and minerals are, unless the owner and council otherwise agree, reserved out of the lease: see the Small Holdings and Allotments (Compulsory Hiring) Regulations 1936, SR & O 1936/196, reg 22.

9 *Earl of Carlisle v Northumberland County Council* (1911) 105 LT 797.

10 See the Small Holdings and Allotments Act 1908 Sch 1 Pt II(6) (amended by the Land Settlement (Facilities) Act 1919 Sch 2).

680. Execution of lease and commencement of tenancy on compulsory hiring for allotments purposes.

The owner[1] of land proposed to be compulsorily hired[2] must, on the application of the council[3], execute a lease of the land in accordance with the compulsory hiring order[4]. If the owner refuses or fails within one month of notification by the council to execute the lease, or if the owner cannot after diligent inquiry be ascertained by the council, the council must execute the lease in duplicate and forward one copy to the owner, if he can be found[5]. A lease so executed by the owner or the council is binding on and enures for the benefit of all persons interested in the hired land, and cannot cause any forfeiture of the land or of any land held with it or create any right of entry on any such land, or any right of action for breach of a covenant not to assign, or like covenant[6], and takes effect as from the date specified by the council in the notice to treat given by the council to the owner of the land[7].

1 As to the meaning of 'owner' see PARA 675 note 8.

2 As to the meaning of 'land' see PARAS 424 note 5, 675 note 5. The reference in the text to land compulsorily hired is a reference to land compulsorily hired by way of an order under the Small Holdings and Allotments Act 1908 s 39(2), as to which see PARA 674. As to the compulsory hiring of land for the purposes of allotments generally see PARA 673. As to the land which may and may not be compulsorily acquired see PARA 685. As to the continuation or creation of easements over land compulsorily acquired see PARA 687. As to the meaning of 'allotment' see PARA 649.

3 In practice this refers to a district council (in England) or a county or county borough council (in Wales), which are the only councils empowered to hire land compulsorily for allotments: see PARA 673.

4 Small Holdings and Allotments (Compulsory Hiring) Regulations 1936, SR & O 1936/196, reg 15(1). A compulsory hiring order is an order under the Small Holdings and Allotments Act 1908 s 39(2). As to the meaning of 'lease' see PARA 668 note 5. A lease must be executed as soon as the amount of the rent to be paid by the council for the land proposed to be compulsorily hired, and the amount of any other compensation to be paid by the council to any person entitled thereto in respect of the land or any interest therein, or in respect of improvements executed on the land or otherwise, have been determined (so far as such matters can be determined before the tenancy of the council commences), and is subject to the interest of any existing tenant which the council has notified that it does not desire to extinguish, and to any reservation, exception, or easement subject to which the land is to be hired: reg 15(1). As to the determination of compensation or rent payable on compulsory hiring see PARA 679. As to the meaning of 'existing tenant' see PARA 668 note 5.

Costs reasonably incurred by an owner of land in connection with the preparation and execution of the lease and any counterpart must be paid by the council: reg 17(1). In the event of disagreement as to the amount of such costs, the council must pay such costs as may be authorised: see reg 17(2).

As to leases of compulsorily hired land subject to a mortgage see PARA 681.

5   Small Holdings and Allotments (Compulsory Hiring) Regulations 1936, SR & O 1936/196, reg
    15(1). A lease so executed takes effect as if it had been duly executed by the owner. Provision is
    made for the service of notices: see reg 24.
6   Small Holdings and Allotments (Compulsory Hiring) Regulations 1936, SR & O 1936/196, reg
    15(2).
7   Small Holdings and Allotments (Compulsory Hiring) Regulations 1936, SR & O 1936/196, reg
    16. This is subject to the power of the council under the Small Holdings and Allotments Act 1908
    s 39(8) (see PARA 688) to withdraw such a notice to treat: Small Holdings and Allotments
    (Compulsory Hiring) Regulations 1936, SR & O 1936/196, reg 16 (proviso).

681. Effect of leases of land subject to mortgage compulsorily hired for allotments purposes.

Where land[1] authorised to be compulsorily hired for allotments[2] is subject to a
mortgage, any lease made in pursuance of the order by the mortgagor or
mortgagee in possession will have effect as if it were a lease authorised under the
statutory power[3] to be made by the mortgagor or mortgagee in possession[4].

1   As to the meaning of 'land' see PARA 424 note 5. As to the land which may and may not be
    compulsorily acquired see PARA 685.
2   Ie in pursuance of an order under the Small Holdings and Allotments Act 1908 s 39(2), as to which
    see PARA 674 et seq. As to the compulsory hiring of land for the purposes of allotments generally
    see PARA 673. As to the meaning of 'allotment' see PARA 649.
3   Ie under the Law of Property Act 1925 s 99 (see MORTGAGE vol 77 (2016) PARA 348 et seq).
4   Small Holdings and Allotments Act 1908 s 39(6).

682. Renewal of tenancy after compulsory hiring for allotments purposes.

Where land[1] has been hired compulsorily[2] for allotments, the council[3] may, by
giving to the landlord[4] written notice[5] not more than two years nor less than one
year before the expiration of the tenancy, renew the tenancy for such term, not
being less than 14 nor more than 35 years, as may be specified in the notice, and
at such rent as, in default of agreement, may be determined by valuation by a
valuer[6] appointed by the Secretary of State or the Welsh Ministers[7], but otherwise
on the same terms and conditions as the original lease, and so from time to time[8].
If, however, on any such notice being given, the landlord proves to the satisfaction
of the Secretary of State or the Assembly that any land included in the tenancy is
required for the amenity or convenience of any dwelling house, that land must be
excluded from the renewed tenancy[9].

1   As to the meaning of 'land' see PARA 424 note 5. As to the land which may and may not be
    compulsorily acquired see PARA 685. As to the continuation or creation of easements over land
    compulsorily acquired see PARA 687.
2   Ie hired by way of an order under the Small Holdings and Allotments Act 1908 s 39(2), as to which
    see PARA 674. As to the compulsory hiring of land for the purposes of allotments generally see
    PARA 673. As to the meaning of 'allotment' see PARA 649.
3   In practice this refers to a district council (in England) or a county or county borough council (in
    Wales), which are the only councils empowered to hire land compulsorily for allotments: see PARA
    673.
4   As to the meaning of 'landlord' see PARA 675 note 7.
5   Any notice required by the Small Holdings and Allotments Act 1908 to be given may be sent by
    registered post: s 61(5). Where in pursuance of s 44 a council has given notice to the landlord of
    land compulsorily hired by it to renew the tenancy, it is lawful for the council to withdraw the
    notice at any time not less than three months before the expiration of the tenancy if it appears to
    it that the rent assessed in pursuance of s 44 is such as would involve loss to it, but in any such case
    the landlord is entitled to obtain from the council compensation for any loss or expenses which he
    may have sustained or incurred by reason or in consequence of the notice to renew and of the
    notice to withdraw, such compensation to be determined in like manner as the compensation for
    withdrawal of notice to treat under s 39(8) (see PARA 688): Small Holdings and Allotments Act
    1926 s 18(1).

6 See PARA 679 note 6.
7 As to the Secretary of State and the Welsh Ministers see PARA 741.
8 Small Holdings and Allotments Act 1908 s 44(1). In assessing the rent to be paid under s 44, the valuer must not take into account any increase in the value of the holding:

    (1)   due to improvements in respect of which the council would have been entitled to compensation, if instead of renewing the tenancy the council had quitted the land on the determination of the tenancy (s 44(2)(a));

    (2)   due to any use to which the land might otherwise be put during the renewed term, being a use in respect of which the landlord is entitled to resume possession of the land under the Act (s 44(2)(b)); or

    (3)   due to the establishment by the council of other smallholdings or allotments in the neighbourhood (s 44(2)(c)).

As to the resumption of possession see PARA 683. The valuer must also not take into account any depreciation in the value of the land in respect of which the landlord would have been entitled to compensation if the council had quitted the land on the determination of the tenancy: s 44(2).

The provisions of the Law of Property Act 1922 providing for the conversion of perpetually renewable leases into long terms (see s 145, Sch 15 para 1; and LANDLORD AND TENANT vol 62 (2016) PARA 435) do not affect any right of renewal conferred by the Small Holdings and Allotments Act 1908 s 44: Law of Property Act 1922 Sch 15 para 9.
9 Small Holdings and Allotments Act 1908 s 44(1) proviso.

683. Resumption of possession by landlord after compulsory hiring for allotments purposes.

Where land[1] has been hired compulsorily[2] for allotments, and the land or any part of it at any time during the council's[3] tenancy is shown to the satisfaction of the Secretary of State or the Welsh Ministers[4] to be required by the landlord[5] to be used for building, mining, or other industrial purposes, or for roads necessary therefor, the landlord may resume possession of the land or part of it[6] upon giving the council 12 months' previous written notice of his intention, or such shorter notice as may be required by the compulsory hiring order[7].

The notice will not be valid if given before the Secretary of State or the Welsh Ministers is or are satisfied as to the purpose for which the land is required, and where an applicant has failed to satisfy the Secretary of State or the Welsh Ministers that any land is required for such a purpose, no further application with a view to resuming possession of the same land or any part of it for the same purpose can be entertained within two years after the previous application[8].

On the determination of any tenancy created by compulsory hiring any questions as to the amount due by the council for depreciation is in default of agreement to be determined by arbitration[9].

1 As to the meaning of 'land' see PARA 424 note 5. As to the land which may and may not be compulsorily acquired see PARA 685. As to the continuation or creation of easements over land compulsorily acquired see PARA 687.
2 Ie hired by way of an order under the Small Holdings and Allotments Act 1908 s 39(2), as to which see PARA 674. As to the compulsory hiring of land for the purposes of allotments generally see PARA 673. As to the meaning of 'allotment' see PARA 649.
3 In practice this refers to a district council (in England) or a county or county borough council (in Wales), which are the only councils empowered to hire land compulsorily for allotments: see PARA 673.
4 As to the Secretary of State and the Welsh Ministers see PARA 741.
5 As to the meaning of 'landlord' see PARA 675 note 7.
6 If a part only of the land is resumed, the rent payable by the council (see PARA 679) will as from the date of resumption be reduced by such sum as in default of agreement may be determined by a valuer appointed by the Secretary of State or the Welsh Ministers: Small Holdings and Allotments Act 1908 s 46(1). As to the valuer see PARA 679 note 6.

7 Small Holdings and Allotments Act 1908 s 46(1) (amended by the Land Settlement (Facilities) Act 1919 Sch 2). Any notice required by the Small Holdings and Allotments Act 1908 to be given may be sent by registered post: s 61(5).
8 Small Holdings and Allotments Act 1926 s 18(2). For the council's right to compensation see PARA 720.
9 Small Holdings and Allotments Act 1908 Sch 1 Pt II(7).

684. Entry on land compulsorily hired for allotments purposes.

Where an order for the compulsory hiring of land[1] has been made[2], and where necessary confirmed[3], the council[4] entitled to hire the land under the order may, at any time after a notice to treat has been served[5], and on giving not less than 14 days' notice to each owner[6], lessee and occupier of the land, enter on and take possession of the land or such part thereof as is specified in the notice without previous consent or compliance with the statutory provisions relating to entry on land compulsorily acquired[7]. The exercise of this power is subject to the payment of compensation[8]. Where the land to be compulsorily hired is subject to the interest of a yearly tenant[9], the council is entitled, subject to the payment of compensation to the person in possession, to enter on and take possession of the land or such part thereof as is specified in the agreement, without previous consent[10].

If a notice of entry relates to land on which there is a dwelling house, and the length of notice is less than three calendar months, the occupier of the dwelling house may, by notice served on the council within ten days after the service on him of the notice of entry, appeal to an arbitrator against the notice, and the council will not be entitled to enter on the land except on such date and on such conditions as the arbitrator may award[11].

Where a council has entered on land in accordance with the foregoing provisions it is not entitled to withdraw the notice to treat[12].

1 See PARA 674 et seq. As to the meaning of 'land' see PARA 424 note 5.
2 Ie under the Small Holdings and Allotments Act 1908.
3 As to confirmation of compulsory hiring orders see PARA 677.
4 This is a reference to a district council or, in Wales, a county or county borough council: see PARA 673. As to the local authorities which may be concerned with the provision of allotments generally see PARA 659.
5 As to notices to treat see PARA 688. A notice under the Small Holdings and Allotments (Compulsory Hiring) Regulations 1936, SR & O 1936/196, reg 6 (see PARA 678) is deemed for these purposes to be a notice to treat: reg 25(1)(b).
6 As to the meaning of 'owner' see PARA 675 note 8.
7 Land Settlement (Facilities) Act 1919 s 2(1) (as originally enacted), (4) (s 2(1) amended by the Acquisition of Land (Authorisation Procedure) Act 1946 s 6, Sch 4); Small Holdings and Allotments (Compulsory Hiring) Regulations 1936, SR & O 1936/196, reg 25(1)(a). The statutory provisions relating to entry on land compulsorily acquired are the Lands Clauses (Consolidation) Act 1845 ss 84–90 (see COMPULSORY ACQUISITION OF LAND vol 18 (2009) PARA 638 et seq). Where a lease to an acquiring council has been executed in accordance with the Small Holdings and Allotments (Compulsory Hiring) Regulations 1936, SR & O 1936/196 (see regs 15, 16; and PARA 680), the council may, subject to the interest of any existing tenant which is not to be extinguished by the hiring, enter on the land as from the date specified by the council in the notice to treat (see PARA 688): reg 16. As to the meaning of 'existing tenant' see PARA 668 note 5.

   If in any case a council is authorised by a compulsory hiring order and the Small Holdings and Allotments (Compulsory Hiring) Regulations 1936, SR & O 1936/196, to enter upon and hold any land authorised to be compulsorily hired, and the owner or occupier of any such lands or any other person refuses to give up the possession thereof, or hinders the council from entering upon the land, a court of summary jurisdiction, on complaint made by the council, may require the owner or occupier of such land or other person to deliver possession to the council or permit it to enter thereon, and any such order may be enforced as provided by the Magistrates' Courts Act

1980 s 63 (see MAGISTRATES vol 71 (2013) PARA 626; SENTENCING vol 92 (2015) PARA 2): Small Holdings and Allotments (Compulsory Hiring) Regulations 1936, SR & O 1936/196, reg 18.
8　Land Settlement (Facilities) Act 1919 s 2(1) (as originally enacted), (4) (amended by the Acquisition of Land (Authorisation Procedure) Act 1946 s 6, Sch 4). The compensation payable is such amount, with interest, as would have been payable if the Lands Clauses (Consolidation) Act 1845 ss 84–90 (see COMPULSORY ACQUISITION OF LAND vol 18 (2009) PARA 638 et seq) had been complied with, and must include such compensation by way of rent or otherwise, together with interest on such part of the compensation as is not paid by way of rent at the rate of 5% per annum from the time of entry on the land until such compensation is paid, as would have been payable if the council had at the date of entry hired the land of which possession is taken and extinguished the interest therein of any existing tenant: Small Holdings and Allotments (Compulsory Hiring) Regulations 1936, SR & O 1936/196, reg 25(2).
9　Ie a person in possession of the land whose interest is not greater than that of a tenant for a year, or from year to year.
10　See the Land Settlement (Facilities) Act 1919 s 2(2), (4); and the Small Holdings and Allotments (Compulsory Hiring) Regulations 1936, SR & O 1936/196, reg 25(1)(a).
11　Land Settlement (Facilities) Act 1919 s 2(3) (as originally enacted), (4) (s 2(3) amended by the Acquisition of Land (Authorisation Procedure) Act 1946 s 6, Sch 4). Any such appeal is determinable by an arbitrator under and in accordance with the Agricultural Holdings Act 1986, except that, in default of agreement, the arbitrator must be appointed by the President of the Royal Institution of Chartered Surveyors: Land Settlement (Facilities) Act 1919 s 2(3) (amended by the Agricultural Holdings Act 1986 Sch 14). As to arbitration under the Agricultural Holdings Act 1986 see PARA 566 et seq. As to the Royal Institution of Chartered Surveyors generally see BUILDING CONTRACTS vol 6 (2011) PARA 490.
12　Land Settlement (Facilities) Act 1919 s 2(1) (as originally enacted), (4); Acquisition of Land (Authorisation Procedure) Act 1946 s 6, Sch 4. The reference in the text to a council not being entitled to withdraw the notice to treat is a reference to its not being entitled to exercise the powers conferred by the Small Holdings and Allotments Act 1908 s 39(8) (as to which see PARA 688).

C. COMPULSORY ACQUISITION GENERALLY

685.   General restrictions on compulsory acquisition for allotments purposes.
No land[1] may be authorised by order[2] to be compulsorily acquired for allotments[3], either by purchase[4] or hiring[5], which at the date of the order:

(1)　　forms part of any park[6], garden, or pleasure ground[7];
(2)　　forms part of the home farm attached to or usually occupied with a mansion house[8];
(3)　　is otherwise required for the amenity or convenience of any dwelling house[9]; or
(4)　　is woodland not wholly surrounded by or adjacent to land acquired[10] by a council[11],

unless the order authorises the compulsory acquisition of a holding of 50 acres or less in extent or any part of such a holding[12].

Land which is part of the property of the National Trust[13] may also not be compulsorily acquired[14] for the purposes of allotments[15]. Land which is or forms part of a metropolitan common[16], or which is subject to regulation under an order or scheme made in pursuance of the Inclosure Acts 1845 to 1899 or under any local Act or otherwise, or which is or forms part of any town or village green or of any area appointed as a public park, garden or pleasure ground or for use for the purposes of public recreation, may only be compulsorily acquired for allotments where the order for compulsory purchase is confirmed by Parliament or the National Assembly for Wales[17]. Certain Crown lands, including those belonging to the Duchies of Cornwall and Lancaster, and any land subject to rights of common, may not be compulsorily hired for allotments[18].

Statutory considerations to which local authorities, the Secretary of State or the Welsh Ministers must have regard in making or confirming compulsory acquisition orders may further restrict the land available for compulsory acquisition[19].

1　As to the meaning of 'land' see PARA 424 note 5.

2　Ie under the Small Holdings and Allotments Act 1908 (see PARAS 670, 674).

3　As to the meaning of 'allotment' see PARA 649.

4　See PARA 670 et seq.

5　See PARA 673 et seq.

6　'Park' means an ordinary, not an ancient legal park: *Pease v Courtney* [1904] 2 Ch 503. See note 8.

7　Small Holdings and Allotments Act 1908 s 41(1) (amended by the Acquisition of Land (Authorisation Procedure) Act 1946 s 6, Sch 4).

8　Small Holdings and Allotments Act 1908 s 41(1) (as amended: see note 7). Land forming part of any park or of any home farm attached to and usually occupied with a mansion house may, however, be compulsorily acquired if not required for the amenity or convenience of the mansion house (Land Settlement (Facilities) Act 1919 s 16(1)(a)), except that such a holding may not in whole or part be compulsorily acquired by a council (see note 11) where it is shown to the satisfaction of the council that the holding is the principal means of livelihood of the occupier thereof, unless the occupier is a tenant and consents to the acquisition (s 16(3) (amended by the Small Holdings and Allotments Act 1926 Schs 1, 2)). Where it is proposed to acquire any such land, the order authorising the acquisition of the land will not be valid unless confirmed or made by the Secretary of State or the Welsh Ministers: Land Settlement (Facilities) Act 1919 s 16(2). As to the Secretary of State and the Welsh Ministers see PARA 741. As to what is a 'mansion house' cf the Settled Land Act 1925 s 65(2); and SETTLEMENTS vol 91 (2012) PARA 690.

9　Small Holdings and Allotments Act 1908 s 41(1) (as amended: see note 7).

10　Ie under the Small Holdings and Allotments Act 1908 (see PARAS 670, 674).

11　Small Holdings and Allotments Act 1908 s 41(1) (as amended: see note 7). The reference in the text to a council is, in connection with land compulsorily purchased, a reference to a district, parish, or London borough council, or, in Wales, a community, county or county borough council (see PARA 670), or, in connection with land compulsorily hired, a reference to a district council or, in Wales, a county or county borough council (see PARA 673). As to the local authorities which may be concerned with the provision of allotments generally see PARA 659.

12　Land Settlement (Facilities) Act 1919 s 16(1)(b).

13　Ie land which forms part of the trust property to which the National Trust Act 1907 applies, as to which see NATIONAL CULTURAL HERITAGE vol 77 (2016) PARA 973 et seq.

14　Ie under the Small Holdings and Allotments Act 1908 (see PARAS 670, 674).

15　Land Settlement (Facilities) Act 1919 s 28(4).

16　Ie within the meaning of the Metropolitan Commons Act 1866 ss 3, 4 (see LONDON GOVERNMENT vol 71 (2013) PARA 301). Note, however, that land which is or which forms part of non-metropolitan commons may be appropriated under the Land Settlement (Facilities) Act 1919: see PARA 691 notes 7, 8.

17　Land Settlement (Facilities) Act 1919 s 28(1). In confirming such an order, regard must be had to the same considerations, and the same inquiries held, as are directed by the Commons Act 1876 to be taken into consideration and held in the forming of an opinion as to whether an application under the Inclosure Acts should be acceded to or not (see ss 7, 10, 11; and COMMONS vol 13 (2017) PARA 319): Land Settlement (Facilities) Act 1919 s 28(2). As to the Inclosure Acts see COMMONS vol 13 (2017) PARA 319 et seq. Procedural provision is also made: see the Land Settlement (Facilities) Act 1919 s 28(2). Where an order for compulsory purchase provides for giving other land in exchange for the common or open space to be purchased, the order may vest the land given in exchange in the persons in whom the common or open space purchased was vested subject to the same rights, trusts and incidents as attached to the common or open space and discharge the purchased land from all rights, trusts and incidents to which it was previously subject: s 28(3). Exchanges of land generally require the approval of the Secretary of State or the Welsh Ministers: see the Small Holdings and Allotments Regulations 1919, SR & O 1919/1197, reg 1(1)(1).

18　See the Small Holdings and Allotments (Compulsorily Hiring) Regulations 1936, SR & O 1936/196, reg 30. As to the Crown Estate see CROWN AND CROWN PROCEEDINGS vol 29 (2014)

PARA 192 et seq. As to the Duchies of Lancaster and Cornwall see CROWN AND CROWN PROCEEDINGS vol 29 (2014) PARAS 214–267. As to restriction on the compulsory acquisition of common land see COMMONS vol 13 (2017) PARA 379 et seq.

19 See the Small Holdings and Allotments Act 1908 s 41(2); and PARA 686.

686. Matters influencing decisions on compulsory acquisition for allotments purposes.

In making an order[1] for the compulsory acquisition of land[2] for allotments[3], either by purchase[4] or hiring[5], a council[6] must:

(1)   have regard to the extent of land held or occupied in the locality by any owner or tenant and to the convenience of other property belonging to or occupied by the same owner or tenant[7];

(2)   so far as is practicable avoid taking an undue or inconvenient quantity of land from any one owner or tenant[8]; and

(3)   so far as practicable avoid displacing any considerable number of agricultural labourers or others employed on or about the land[9].

1 Ie under the Small Holdings and Allotments Act 1908 (see PARAS 670, 674).
2 As to the meaning of 'land' see PARA 424 note 5. As to the land which may and may not be compulsorily acquired see PARA 685.
3 As to the meaning of 'allotment' see PARA 649. As to the powers of local authorities in connection with the provision of allotments generally see PARA 659.
4 See PARA 670 et seq.
5 See PARA 673 et seq.
6 See PARA 685 note 11.
7 Small Holdings and Allotments Act 1908 s 41(2). As to the time limits within which notices to treat for the purposes of compulsory purchase must be served, and the circumstances in which notices may be withdrawn, see PARA 688.
8 Small Holdings and Allotments Act 1908 s 41(2).
9 Small Holdings and Allotments Act 1908 s 41(2). For this purpose, where part only of a holding is taken, the Secretary of State or the Welsh Ministers must take into consideration the size and character of the existing agricultural buildings not proposed to be taken which were used in connection with the holding, and the quantity and nature of the land available for occupation therewith: s 41(2). As to the Secretary of State and the Welsh Ministers see PARA 741.

687. Creation of easements for allotments purposes.

An order[1] for the compulsory purchase[2] or hiring[3] of land[4] for allotments[5] may provide for the continuance of any existing easement or the creation of any new easement over the land authorised to be acquired[6]. If the owner of the land to be acquired so requires, every such order must provide for the creation of such new easements as are reasonably necessary to secure the continued use and enjoyment by the owner and his tenants of all means of access, drainage, water supply, and other similar conveniences used or enjoyed by them over the land to be acquired[7]. However, no new easement created by or in pursuance of the order over land hired by a district council (in England) or a county or county borough council (in Wales)[8] continues beyond the determination of the hiring[9].

1 Ie under the Small Holdings and Allotments Act 1908 (see PARAS 670, 674).
2 See PARA 670 et seq.
3 See PARA 673 et seq.
4 As to the meaning of 'land' see PARA 424 note 5.
5 As to the meaning of 'allotment' see PARA 649.
6 Small Holdings and Allotments Act 1908 s 39(4) (amended by the Acquisition of Land (Authorisation Procedure) Act 1946 s 6, Sch 4).
7 Small Holdings and Allotments Act 1908 s 39(4) proviso.

8   Ie the councils empowered to hire land compulsorily for allotments: see PARA 673. As to these
    councils generally see PARA 659.
9   Small Holdings and Allotments Act 1908 s 39(4).

688. Notice to treat following compulsory acquisition for allotments purposes.

Where an order has been made for the compulsory acquisition[1] of any land[2] for allotments[3], notice to treat must be served within three calendar months after the date of the order, or the date of the confirmation of the order, failing which the order, so far as relating to the land in respect of which notice to treat has not been served, will become null and void[4]; and no further order authorising the compulsory acquisition of that land or any part of it, if made within three years after the expiration of those three calendar months, will be valid unless confirmed by the Secretary of State or the Welsh Ministers[5], nor may such further order be confirmed unless it is proved to the satisfaction of the Secretary of State or the Welsh Ministers that there are special reasons justifying the failure to exercise the powers under the original order and the making of the order submitted for confirmation[6].

If, after the amount of the compensation (including, in the case of land compulsorily hired, the rent) to be paid has been determined[7], it appears to the council[8] that the land cannot be let for allotments at such rent as will secure the council from loss, the council may, at any time within six weeks after the determination of the amount, by written notice withdraw the relevant notice to treat[9]. This power may not, however, be exercised where the council has entered on the land[10].

1   Ie by purchase (see PARA 670 et seq) or hiring (see PARA 673 et seq).
2   As to the meaning of 'land' see PARA 424 note 5.
3   As to the meaning of 'allotment' see PARA 649.
4   Allotments Act 1922 s 12(1).
5   As to the Secretary of State and the Welsh Ministers see PARA 741.
6   Allotments Act 1922 s 12(2).
7   As to the determination of compensation and rent in relation to land compulsorily hired see PARA 679. As to the determination of compensation in relation to land compulsorily purchased see PARAS 670, 671.
8   See PARA 685 note 11.
9   Small Holdings and Allotments Act 1908 s 39(8). Any person on whom notice of withdrawal has been served is entitled to obtain from the council compensation for any loss or expenses which he may have sustained or incurred by reason or in consequence of the notice to treat and of the notice of withdrawal: s 39(8). The amount of compensation is, in default of agreement, determinable by a single arbitrator in accordance with the Agricultural Holdings Act 1986 and not under the Land Compensation Act 1961: Small Holdings and Allotments Act 1908 s 58(1) (amended by the Agricultural Holdings Act 1986 Sch 14 para 2); Small Holdings and Allotments Act 1926 s 17(3)(a); Land Compensation Act 1961 s 40(2)(a). The remuneration of an arbitrator so appointed is fixed by the Secretary of State or the Welsh Ministers: Small Holdings and Allotments Act 1908 s 58(3). As to arbitration under the Agricultural Holdings Act 1986 see PARA 566 et seq.
10 Land Settlement (Facilities) Act 1919 s 2(1) (amended by the Acquisition of Land (Authorisation Procedure) Act 1946 s 6, Sch 4; and the Acquisition of Land Act 1981 Sch 4 para 2). The reference in the text to entry on the land is a reference to entry by virtue of the Compulsory Purchase Act 1965 s 11(1) (see COMPULSORY ACQUISITION OF LAND vol 18 (2009) PARA 645). As to entry on land compulsorily purchased see PARA 672. As to entry on land compulsorily hired see PARA 684.

689. Acquisition of land for allotments on behalf of parishes and communities.

A parish or (in Wales) community council[1] which proposes to acquire land[2] compulsorily, whether by purchase[3] or hiring[4], must, instead of itself making or submitting a compulsory hiring order[5] to the Secretary of State or the Welsh Ministers[6], make a representation to the district or (in Wales) county or county borough council[7], which may, on behalf of the parish or community council, exercise the statutory powers of compulsory acquisition[8]. The order will be carried into effect by the district, county or county borough council but the land acquired will be assured or demised to the parish or community council, which will pay all expenses[9]. If the district, county or county borough council refuses to proceed on the representation the parish or community council may petition the Secretary of State or the Welsh Ministers, who may, after appropriate inquiry, make such an order as the district, county or county borough council might have made[10]. A district, county or county borough council may also acquire land for leasing to a parish or community council within the district, county or county borough for the provision of allotments[11].

1 The Small Holdings and Allotments Act 1908 s 39(7) and the Land Settlement (Facilities) Act 1919 s 17 refer to a parish council only but this should be read in relation to Wales as a reference to a community council: see PARA 659 note 2.

2 As to the meaning of 'land' see PARA 424 note 5. As to the land which may and may not be compulsorily acquired for allotments see PARA 685. As to the matters influencing decisions on the making of compulsory acquisition orders see PARA 686. As to the continuation or creation of easements over land compulsorily acquired see PARA 687. As to the meaning of 'allotment' see PARA 649.

3 See PARA 670.

4 See PARA 673.

5 As to compulsory hiring orders see PARA 674.

6 As to the Secretary of State and the Welsh Ministers see PARA 741.

7 The Small Holdings and Allotments Act 1908 s 39(7) and the Land Settlement (Facilities) Act 1919 s 17 refer to a district council only but this should be read in relation to Wales as a reference to a county or county borough council: see PARA 659 note 1.

8 Small Holdings and Allotments Act 1908 s 39(7) (amended by the Local Government Act 1972 Sch 29 Pt II para 9(4)). The reference in the text to the statutory powers of compulsory acquisition is a reference to the powers of compulsory acquisition under the Small Holdings and Allotments Act 1908.

9 Small Holdings and Allotments Act 1908 s 39(7) (as amended: see note 7).

10 Small Holdings and Allotments Act 1908 s 39(7) proviso (as amended: see note 7).

11 Land Settlement (Facilities) Act 1919 s 17 (amended by the Local Government Act 1972 Sch 29 Pt II para 10).

690. Expenses on compulsory acquisition for allotments purposes.

The expenses of a district, county or county borough council[1] incurred in respect of the compulsory acquisition of lands for allotments[2] on behalf of a parish or community council[3] must be paid by the parish or community council[4].

1 The Small Holdings and Allotments Act 1908 s 39(7) refers to a district council but this should be construed as a reference to the authorities mentioned in the text: see PARA 659 note 1. As to the local authorities which may be concerned with the provision of allotments generally see PARA 659.

2 As to the meaning of 'allotment' see PARA 649. As to the meaning of 'land' see PARA 424 note 5. As to the compulsory acquisition of land for allotments see PARA 670 et seq.

3 The Small Holdings and Allotments Act 1908 s 39(7) refers to a parish council but this should be construed as a reference to the authorities mentioned in the text: see PARA 659 note 2.

4 Small Holdings and Allotments Act 1908 s 39(7) (amended by the Local Government Act 1972 Sch 29 Pt II para 9(4)).

(iv) Acquisitions other than by Agreement or Compulsory Acquisition

691. Powers of local authorities to appropriate land for allotments.

The council of any district, parish, London borough or, in Wales, county, county borough or community[1] may, where no power of appropriation is otherwise provided, appropriate for the purpose of allotments[2] any land[3] held by it for its other purposes[4]. A district council or, in Wales, a county or county borough council[5] may, where it considers it is necessary or expedient to do so for the better carrying into effect of the applicable legislation[6] and where no power of appropriation is otherwise provided, appropriate for any purpose for which it is authorised to acquire land under that legislation any land held by it for any of its other purposes[7]. However, land which is or forms part of a metropolitan common[8], or which is subject to regulation under an order or scheme made in pursuance of the Inclosure Acts 1845 to 1899 or under any local Act or otherwise, or which is or forms part of any town or village green or of any area appointed as a public park, garden or pleasure ground or for use for the purposes of public recreation, may not be so appropriated[9].

1 The Land Settlement (Facilities) Act 1919 s 22(1) refers to 'the council of a borough, urban district or parish' but this should be construed as a reference to the councils referred to in the text: see PARA 659 notes 1–5. As to the local authorities which may be concerned with the provision of allotments generally see PARA 659.

2 As to the meaning of 'allotment' see PARA 649.

3 As to the meaning of 'land' see PARA 424 note 5.

4 Land Settlement (Facilities) Act 1919 s 22(1)(a) (amended by the Local Government, Planning and Land Act 1980 Sch 5 para 3, Sch 34 Pt V).

5 The Land Settlement (Facilities) Act 1919 s 12(1) refers to a 'district council' but this should be construed as a reference to the councils referred to in the text: see PARA 659 notes 1–5.

6 Ie the Allotments Acts 1908 to 1950, as to which see PARA 649 note 2.

7 Land Settlement (Facilities) Act 1919 s 12(1)(c)(i) (amended by the Local Government Act 1972 Sch 29 Pt II para 10). The exercise of this power is subject to the consent of the Secretary of State or the Welsh Ministers (Land Settlement (Facilities) Act 1919 s 12(1)(c)(i) (as so amended); Small Holdings and Allotments Regulations 1919, SR & O 1919/1197, reg 1(1)(2), (8)), unless the power is being exercised by a county council in respect of land acquired under the Small Holdings and Allotments Act 1926 Pt I (ss 1–15) (acquisition of land for smallholdings; as to which see PARA 629 et seq) (s 20(1)). As to the Secretary of State and the Welsh Ministers see PARA 741.

    Where the land to be appropriated forms part of any common, then in giving or withholding consent to the appropriation the Secretary of State or the Welsh Ministers must have regard to the same considerations, and hold the same inquiries, as are directed by the Commons Act 1876 to be taken into consideration and held in the forming of an opinion as to whether an application under the Inclosure Acts should be acceded to or not (see ss 7, 10, 11; and COMMONS vol 13 (2017) PARA 319): Land Settlement (Facilities) Act 1919 s 28(2). As to the Inclosure Acts see COMMONS vol 13 (2017) PARA 319 et seq. Procedural provision is also made: see the Land Settlement (Facilities) Act 1919 s 28(2). Where a consent by the Secretary of State or the Welsh Ministers to the appropriation of land provides for giving other land in exchange for the common or open space to be appropriated, any order made by the Secretary of State or the Welsh Ministers in relation to the consent may vest the land given in exchange in the persons in whom the common or open space appropriated was vested subject to the same rights, trusts and incidents as attached to the common or open space and discharge the appropriated land from all rights, trusts and incidents to which it was previously subject: Land Settlement Facilities Act 1919 s 28(3). Exchanges of land generally require the approval of the Secretary of State or the Welsh Ministers: see the Small Holdings and Allotments Regulations 1919, SI 1919/1197, reg 1(1)(1).

    The exercise of the power under the Land Settlement (Facilities) Act 1919 s 12(1)(c)(i) is also subject to such conditions as to the repayment of any loan made for the purpose of the acquisition of the land or otherwise as the Secretary of State or the Welsh Ministers may impose: s 12(1)(c)(i) (as so amended).

8 Ie within the meaning of the Metropolitan Commons Act 1866 ss 3, 4 (see LONDON GOVERNMENT vol 71 (2013) PARA 301). Note, however, that land which is or which forms part of non-metropolitan commons may be appropriated under the Land Settlement (Facilities) Act 1919 (see note 7).

9 Land Settlement (Facilities) Act 1919 s 28(1). Note, however, the effect of s 28(2) (see note 7); and the Town and Country Planning Act 1990 s 229(1) (see PLANNING vol 83 (2010) PARA 1124).

692. Power of local authority to enter on unoccupied land for purpose of providing allotment gardens.

The council of a London borough or district or, in Wales, a county or county borough[1] may, for the purpose of providing allotment gardens[2], enter on any land[3], other than agricultural land[4] and certain public land or land held for the purposes of public undertakings[5], which is not the subject of a rateable occupation[6]. The council may adapt the land for use for that purpose[7] and let it either to tenants or to any association[8] for the purpose of sub-letting for such use[9].

The council's right of occupation may be terminated by the council on six months' written notice[10], or by the owner on three months' (where the land is required for any purpose other than agriculture, sport or recreation), or six months'[11] (where the land is required for use for sport or recreation) written notice[12]. The owner's notice must tell the council the purpose for which the resumption is required[13], and the council may, by counter-notice served within 21 days of the receipt of that notice, demand that the question whether the resumption is required in good faith for the purpose specified be determined by arbitration[14]. Possession of the land may not be resumed until after the period for demanding arbitration has elapsed or, where arbitration is demanded, until after the arbitration[15]. On the termination of the occupation the council may remove any erection or work of adaptation, making good any injury to the land caused by the removal[16].

Any person interested in any land entered upon in pursuance of these powers who suffers any loss thereby is entitled, on making a claim not later than one year after the termination of the right of occupation, to be paid by the council by way of compensation such periodical or other payments as may represent the loss[17]. Any tenant[18] to whom land is let by a council in pursuance of these powers and whose tenancy is terminated by the termination of the right of occupation of the council is, unless otherwise agreed in the contract of tenancy, entitled to recover from the council such compensation (if any) as would have been recoverable if his tenancy had been terminated by notice to quit given by the council, and has the same right to remove his crops as if the tenancy had been so terminated[19].

1 The Allotments Act 1922 s 10(1) refers to 'the council of a borough or urban district' but this should be construed as a reference to the councils referred to in the text: see PARA 659 notes 1–4. As to the local authorities which may be concerned with the provision of allotments generally see PARA 659.

2 As to the meaning of 'allotment garden' see PARA 424 note 11.

3 As to the meaning of 'land' see PARA 424 note 5. Before entry the council must give not less than 14 days' notice in writing to the owner of the land in the manner set out in the Small Holdings and Allotments (Compulsory Hiring) Regulations 1936, SR & O 1936/196, reg 24 (as to which see PARA 677): Allotments Act 1922 s 10(2). 'Owner' includes the person who, but for the council's occupation, would be entitled to possession of the land: s 10(7).

4 Ie land which is 'agricultural land' for the purposes of the Local Government Act 1929 Pt V (largely repealed): such land is excluded from the purview of the Allotments Act 1922 s 10 by the Local Government Act 1929 Sch 10 para 16. The reference is to agricultural land within the meaning of Pt V (ss 67–84), which provided for the exclusion of such land for rating purposes, and should now be read as a reference to agricultural land as defined by the Local Government Finance Act 1988 Sch 5 para 2 (see LOCAL GOVERNMENT FINANCE vol 70 (2012) PARA 93).

5 Land being the property of a local authority, land which has been acquired by any corporation or company for the purposes of a railway, dock, canal, water, or other public undertaking, land forming part of any metropolitan common within the meaning of the Metropolitan Commons Act 1866 (see ss 3, 4; and LONDON GOVERNMENT vol 71 (2013) PARA 301), land which is subject, or might be made subject, to regulation under an order or scheme made in pursuance of the Inclosure Acts 1845 to 1899 (see COMMONS vol 13 (2017) PARA 319 et seq) or under any local Act or otherwise, land which is or forms part of any town or village green, or any area dedicated or appropriated as a public park, garden, or pleasure ground or for use for the purposes of public recreation, and land forming part of the New Forest (as defined in the New Forest Act 1877) or of the trust property to which the National Trust Act 1907 applies (see NATIONAL CULTURAL HERITAGE vol 77 (2016) PARA 973 et seq), is excepted from the powers of entry conferred by the Allotments Act 1922 s 10: s 10(6).

6 Allotments Act 1922 s 10(1)(a), (6)(a). 'Rateable occupation' is defined as such occupation as would involve liability to payment of the poor rate or any rate leviable in the like manner as the poor rate: s 10(7). All rates (including the poor rate) were consolidated to form the 'general rate' by the General Rate Act 1967 s 2 (repealed). The non-domestic element of the general rate was replaced by a new form of non-domestic rating by the Local Government Finance Act 1988 Pt III (ss 41–67) (as to which see LOCAL GOVERNMENT FINANCE), and it is conceived that it is to this form of non-domestic rating that this definition of 'rateable occupation' should be taken to refer.

7 Allotments Act 1922 s 10(1)(b).

8 Ie an association to which land may be let by the council under the Small Holdings and Allotments Acts 1908 to 1931. As to the Small Holdings and Allotments Acts 1908 to 1931 see PARA 627 note 3. As to consent to lettings see the Small Holdings and Allotments Regulations 1919, SR & O 1919/1197, reg 1(1), (3).

9 Allotments Act 1922 s 10(1)(c). Any tenancy created must terminate when the council's right of occupation terminates: s 10(1)(c).

10 Allotments Act 1922 s 10(1)(c), (3)(a). The notice must expire on or before 6 April or on or after 29 September in any year: s 10(3)(a).

11 The notice must expire on or before 6 April or on or after 29 September in any year: Allotments Act 1922 s 10(3)(b).

12 Allotments Act 1922 s 10(1)(c), (3)(b) (substituted by the Allotments Act 1925 s 6).

13 Allotments Act 1922 s 11(1).

14 Allotments Act 1922 s 11(2) (amended by the Allotments Act 1925 s 9; and the Agricultural Holdings Act 1986 Sch 14 para 10). Arbitration is under the Agricultural Holdings Act 1986, as to which see PARA 566 et seq.

15 Allotments Act 1922 s 11(3) (amended by the Allotments Act 1925 s 9).

16 Allotments Act 1922 s 10(1)(d).

17 Allotments Act 1922 s 10(5). In default of agreement such payments will be determined by valuation made by a person appointed, in default of agreement, by the Secretary of State or the Welsh Ministers: s 10(5). As to the Secretary of State and the Welsh Ministers see PARA 741. Any periodical payment of compensation in the nature of rent must not exceed the rental value of the land (ie the annual rent which a tenant might reasonably be expected to pay for the land if the land had continued in the same condition as at the date of entry or, as the case may be, as at the date when possession was first taken): s 10(5), (7). As to the designation 'tenant' see PARA 649 note 9.

18 See note 17.

19 Allotments Act 1922 s 10(4).

693. Sale or lease of allotment land.

A county council in England[1], or a county or county borough council in Wales[2], may sell or let to any district, parish, or London borough council, or, in Wales, any community council[3], for the purpose of allotments[4], any land[5] acquired by it for smallholdings[6] or cottage holdings[7]. The exercise of this power is subject to the consent of the Secretary of State or the Welsh Ministers[8]. A district, parish or London borough council[9] could formerly[10] sell or let to the county or county borough council, for the purpose of cottage holdings, any land acquired by it for allotments[11].

A district council or, in Wales, a county or county borough council[12] may, where it considers it is necessary or expedient to do so for the better carrying into effect of the Small Holdings and Allotments Acts 1908 to 1931[13], sell, mortgage, exchange or let any land acquired by it under that Act, or any interest in any such land[14].

1 As to the English counties and their councils see LOCAL GOVERNMENT vol 69 (2009) PARA 24 et seq.
2 As to county and county borough councils in Wales see LOCAL GOVERNMENT vol 69 (2009) PARA 37 et seq.
3 The Small Holdings and Allotments Act 1908 s 45 confers power on a county council to sell or let to a borough, urban district or parish council but should be construed as referring to the authorities mentioned in the text: see PARA 659 notes 1–5. As to the powers of local authorities in connection with the provision of allotments generally see PARA 659.
4 As to the meaning of 'allotment' see PARA 649.
5 As to the meaning of 'land' see PARA 424 note 5.
6 As to the meaning of 'smallholding' see PARA 627. As to the acquisition of land for smallholdings see PARA 629.
7 Small Holdings and Allotments Act 1908 s 45 (amended by the Acquisition of Land (Authorisation Procedure) Act 1946 Schs 4, 6); Agricultural Land (Utilisation) Act 1931 s 12(1). Land can no longer be acquired for, or provided as, cottage holdings: see PARA 730 et seq.
8 Small Holdings and Allotments Regulations 1919, SR & O 1919/1197, reg 1(1)(1), (3). As to the Secretary of State and the Welsh Ministers see PARA 741.
9 Owing to the cessation of the powers to sell cottage holdings in 1970 (see PARA 731), this is in effect a reference to the district and parish councils in England and Wales as they were constituted prior to the reorganisation of local authorities effected by the Local Government Act 1972 (see PARA 659 notes 1, 2), or the London borough councils.
10 Ie until 1970: see PARA 731.
11 Small Holdings and Allotments Act 1908 s 45 (as amended: see note 7); Agricultural Land (Utilisation) Act 1931 s 12(1). Note that land may no longer be sold or let for cottage holdings: see PARA 731.
12 The Land Settlement (Facilities) Act 1919 s 12(1) refers to a 'district council' but this should be construed as a reference to the councils referred to in the text: see PARA 659 notes 1, 5.
13 As to the Small Holdings and Allotments Act 1908 to 1931 see PARA 627 note 3.
14 Land Settlement (Facilities) Act 1919 s 12(1)(b) (amended by the Local Government Act 1972 Sch 29 Pt II para 10). The exercise of the power of sale, mortgage or exchange is subject to the consent of the Secretary of State or the Welsh Ministers (Land Settlement (Facilities) Act 1919 s 12(1)(b) (as so amended); Small Holdings and Allotments Regulations 1919, SR & O 1919/1197, reg 1(1)(1), (3), (8)), unless the power is being exercised by a county council in respect of land acquired under the Small Holdings and Allotments Act 1926 Pt I (ss 1–15) (acquisition of land for smallholdings; as to which see PARA 629 et seq) (s 20(1)).

694. Letting of New Forest land for allotment gardens.

The Secretary of State[1] has a continuing power to let[2] to a local authority[3], for any term, land in the New Forest[4] for use as allotment gardens[5], and may let such further land in the Forest, not exceeding 60 acres, as he may agree with the verderers of the Forest[6]. While so let, the land is free from rights of common and similar rights except the right of the public to use any highway on the land[7].

1 Powers in relation to land in the New Forest were originally vested in the Commissioners of Woods, who were retitled the Commissioners of Crown Lands (ultimately the Crown Estate Commissioners) by the Forestry (Title of Commissioner of Woods) Order 1924, SR & O 1924/1370. The estate and powers of the Crown and the Commissioners of Crown Lands in or in connection with lands situated in the New Forest were transferred to the Forestry Commissioners by the combined effect of the Forestry (Transfer of Woods) Act 1923 s 1 (repealed) and the Forestry (Transfer of Woods) Order 1924, SR & O 1924/386 (amended by SR & O 1926/677). All land vested in the Forestry Commissioners was subsequently transferred to the Minister of Agriculture and Fisheries (now the Secretary of State: see PARA 741) by the Forestry Act 1945 s 4(5) (repealed). A reservation was made in s 4(5), (6) (repealed; but continued by the Forestry Act 1967 Sch 6 para 4(2)) under which former Commission land was deemed to have been placed at the disposal of the Commissioners for the purposes of the exercise of their functions under the

Forestry Acts 1919 to 1945, but this did not expressly extend to the Commissioners' functions under the Allotments Act 1922, and it is accordingly submitted that the powers under s 21 are exercisable by the Secretary of State. As to the Forestry Commission and the Commissioners generally see FORESTRY vol 52 (2014) PARA 37 et seq.

2   Ie under the provisions of the Small Holdings and Allotments Acts 1908 to 1919 which relate to allotments: Allotments Act 1922 ss 21(1), 22(1). As to the meaning of 'allotment' see PARA 649.

3   The Allotments Act 1922 s 21(1) refers to 'a local authority under the Allotments Acts'. As to the local authorities empowered to take land on lease for the purposes of allotments see PARA 665. As to the powers of local authorities in connection with the provision of allotments generally see PARA 659.

4   Ie any land in the New Forest as defined in the New Forest Act 1877 which is vested in the Secretary of State (see note 1) and was on 5 April 1922 being used for the provision of allotment gardens. As to the meaning of 'land' see PARA 424 note 5.

5   See the Allotments Act 1922 s 21(1). If the land is used for any other purpose, the lease will become void: s 21(1) (proviso).

6   Allotments Act 1922 s 21(1). As to the verderers of the New Forest see FORESTRY vol 52 (2014) PARA 9.

7   Allotments Act 1922 s 21(2). Rent received by the Secretary of State is divisible between him and the verderers of the Forest in such proportions as may be agreed or, in default of agreement, determined by the arbitration of a single arbitrator: see s 21(3) (amended by the Arbitration Act 1996 Sch 4).

695.   Sale, exchange, transfer and use of field garden allotments.

Allotment wardens (or their successors)[1] may, with the approval of the Secretary of State or the Welsh Ministers[2], sell all or any part of a field garden[3] and purchase other suitable land for the same purpose[4]. The Secretary of State and the Welsh Ministers may also authorise the exchange of inconveniently placed or unsuitable field gardens for other land[5].

Allotment wardens or their successors may, by agreement with the council of the London borough, district, parish, or, in Wales, county, county borough or community in which the field garden is wholly or partly situated, transfer the management of the land[6] to the council upon such terms as may be agreed subject to the sanction, as regards the wardens, of the Secretary of State or the Assembly, and thereupon the land vests in the council[7].

Any land forming part of a field garden allotment which has been compulsorily acquired[8] by a minister, local authority or statutory undertakers, or appropriated by a local authority for planning purposes, may, notwithstanding anything in any enactment relating to such allotments or by which the land is specially regulated, be used either, if acquired by a minister, in any manner for any purpose for which he acquired it or, in any other case, by any person in any manner in accordance with planning permission[9].

1   As to the allotment wardens and (where relevant) their successors see PARAS 650, 651.

2   As to the Secretary of State and the Welsh Ministers see PARA 741.

3   As to field garden allotments see PARA 651.

4   See the Commons Act 1876 s 27; and OPEN SPACES AND COUNTRYSIDE vol 78 (2010) PARA 551. Approval would not be given unless it was proved that more suitable land could and would be forthwith purchased: see s 27.

5   See the Inclosure Act 1845 s 149; and OPEN SPACES AND COUNTRYSIDE vol 78 (2010) PARA 551.

6   As to the meaning of 'land' see PARA 424 note 5.

7   Small Holdings and Allotments Act 1908 s 33(1). Section 33 refers to 'the council of the borough, urban district or parish' but this should be construed as a reference to the authorities mentioned in the text: see PARA 659 notes 1–5.

8   As to the acquisition of land for field garden allotments see PARA 669.

9   See the Town and Country Planning Act 1990 s 241(1); and PLANNING vol 83 (2010) PARA 1140. It was formerly unlawful to use any field garden for any purpose other than that

declared by the Act and award under which it was set out, notwithstanding anything in any other Act: see the Commons Act 1876 s 19; and OPEN SPACES AND COUNTRYSIDE vol 78 (2010) PARA 552.

(3) LETTING OF ALLOTMENTS

(i) Terms and Conditions

696. Regulation of lettings of allotments.

A district, parish, London borough, or, in Wales, a community, county or county borough council[1] may make such rules[2] as appear to be necessary or proper for regulating the letting of allotments[3], for preventing any undue preference in such letting, and generally for giving effect to the statutory requirements relating to the provision of allotments[4]. The rules may define the persons eligible to be tenants[5], the notices to be given[6] for the letting of allotments, the size of the allotments, the conditions under which they are to be cultivated, and the rent to be paid for them[7], and must provide for reasonable notice[8] to be given to determine the tenancy[9]. Sub-letting of an allotment is forbidden, except with the consent of the council[10].

1 The Small Holdings and Allotments Act 1908 s 28 refers to 'a borough, urban district or parish council' but should be construed as referring to the authorities mentioned in the text: see PARA 659 notes 1–5. As to the powers of local authorities in connection with the provision of allotments generally see PARA 659.
2 Rules for the time being in force under the Small Holdings and Allotments Act 1908 s 28 are binding on all persons, and the council must cause them to be from time to time made known, in such manner as the council thinks fit, to all persons interested, and must cause a copy of them to be given gratis to any inhabitant of the council's area who demands it: s 28(4).
3 Ie under the Allotments Acts 1908 to 1950 (see PARA 649 note 2). As to the meaning of 'allotment' see PARA 649.
4 Small Holdings and Allotments Act 1908 s 28(1). The reference in the text to the statutory requirements relating to the provision of allotments is a reference to Pt II (ss 23–35). Unless otherwise provided, the rules apply to an allotment held under a tenancy made before they come into operation: Land Settlement (Facilities) Act 1919 s 21(3).
5 Such persons must in any case be resident in the council's area: see the Small Holdings and Allotments Act 1908 s 23(1); and PARA 659.
6 Any notice required by the Small Holdings and Allotments Act 1908 to be given may be sent by registered post: s 61(5).
7 Small Holdings and Allotments Act 1908 s 28(2).
8 For the length of notice in the case of an allotment which is an agricultural holding see the Agricultural Holdings Act 1986 s 25; and PARA 470. In the case of an allotment garden see the Allotments Act 1922 s 1(1)(a); and PARA 703.
9 Small Holdings and Allotments Act 1908 s 28(3) (amended by the Local Government, Planning and Land Act 1980 Sch 5 para 1(a), Sch 34 Pt V).
10 Small Holdings and Allotments Act 1908 s 27(4) (amended by the Land Settlement (Facilities) Act 1919 Sch 2).

697. Rent of allotments.

Land[1] let[2] by a district, parish, London borough, or, in Wales, a community, county or county borough council[3] for use as an allotment must be let at such a rent as a tenant[4] may reasonably be expected to pay for the land if let for such use on the terms (other than terms as to rent) on which it is in fact let[5], although the council may let such land at a lesser rent if it is satisfied that there exist special circumstances affecting the person to whom it is to be let which render it proper for it to let the land to him at the lesser rent[6]. Unless the yearly rent for land let by a council for allotments is £1.25 or less, not more than one quarter's rent may be required to be paid in advance[7].

1 As to the meaning of 'land' see PARA 424 note 5.
2 Ie under the Allotments Acts 1908 to 1950; as to which see PARA 649 note 2.
3 The Allotments Act 1950 s 10(6) refers only to 'a council' but should be construed as referring to the authorities empowered to let land for allotments: see PARA 659. As to the meaning of 'allotment' see PARA 649.
4 As to the designation 'tenant' see PARA 649 note 19.
5 Allotments Act 1950 s 10(1). As to the recovery of rent see PARA 698. 'Reasonable rent' was considered in *Harwood v Borough of Reigate and Banstead* (1981) 43 P & CR 336, 80 LGR 660. The deputy judge held that the council should not discriminate between charges made for allotments and those made for other recreational activities provided by the council. The report of the Departmental Committee of Inquiry into Allotments 1969 (Cmnd 4166) had recommended that 'allotment gardening should in future be considered primarily as a recreation'.
6 Allotments Act 1950 s 10(1) proviso.
7 Allotments Act 1950 s 10(2) (amended by virtue of the Decimal Currency Act 1969 s 10(1)).

698. Recovery of rent and possession in the case of allotments.

Rent[1] for an allotment[2] let by a district, parish, London borough, or, in Wales, a community, county or county borough council[3], and the possession of any allotment after notice to quit or failure to deliver up possession as required by law, may be recovered by the council as landlord[4]. The court directing recovery of possession of an allotment from any tenant may stay delivery of possession until the payment of any compensation[5] due to the outgoing tenant has been made or secured to the court's satisfaction[6].

1 As to the levying and payment of rent see PARA 697.
2 As to the meaning of 'allotment' see PARA 649.
3 The Small Holdings and Allotments Act 1908 s 30(1) refers only to 'a council' but should be construed as referring to the authorities empowered to let land for allotments: see PARA 659.
4 Small Holdings and Allotments Act 1908 s 30(1). As to the recovery of rent see LANDLORD AND TENANT vol 62 (2016) PARA 277 et seq; as to distress for rent see LANDLORD AND TENANT vol 62 (2016) PARA 282 et seq.
5 As to compensation see PARA 705 et seq.
6 Small Holdings and Allotments Act 1908 s 30(3). The tenant of an agricultural holding is entitled to a charge on the holding in respect of compensation due from the landlord: see the Agricultural Holdings Act 1986 s 85(2); and PARA 573.

699. Keeping hens and rabbits in the case of allotments.

An occupier of land[1] may keep hens or rabbits, otherwise than by way of trade or business, in any place on the land, and erect or place and maintain structures reasonably necessary for that purpose, notwithstanding any provision of a lease or tenancy to the contrary or any covenant, contract or undertaking relating to the use of the land[2]. This provision does not authorise the keeping of hens or rabbits in a place or manner so as to be prejudicial to health or a nuisance, nor does it affect the operation of any enactment[3].

1 As to the meaning of 'land' see PARA 424 note 5.
2 Allotments Act 1950 s 12(1).
3 Allotments Act 1950 s 12(1) proviso.

700. Unlet allotments.

An allotment[1] which cannot be let for allotments[2] may be let to any person whatever at the best annual rent which can be obtained, without premium, and on such terms as may enable the council to resume possession within a period not exceeding 12 months if it should at any time be required for letting for allotments[3].

1   As to the meaning of 'allotment' see PARA 649.
2   Ie let in accordance with the provisions of the Allotments Acts 1908 to 1950 and the rules made thereunder. As to the making of rules see PARA 696.
3   Small Holdings and Allotments Act 1908 s 27(5) (amended by the Statute Law (Repeals) Act 1993).

701. Letting and management of field garden allotments.

Allotment wardens (or their successors)[1] may let field garden allotments[2] not exceeding one quarter of an acre to poor inhabitants of the parish or community[3] for one year or on a tenancy from year to year at the full yearly agricultural value free of all rentcharge and other rates, but if any land cannot be let in quarter acre plots they can let field gardens not exceeding one acre in size at a fair agricultural rent[4]. Surplus rents are available for the maintenance and improvement of field gardens or of recreation grounds, and can also be used for drainage, fencing or the hiring or purchasing of additional land for field gardens or recreation grounds[5].

No building may be erected for or used as a dwelling house on a field garden allotment[6]. The tenancy of a field garden allotment is determinable by one month's notice in the event of the occupier being 40 days in arrears with his rent, or failing to observe the terms and conditions of his tenancy, or going to reside more than one mile outside the parish or community[7]. Possession can be recovered by county court proceedings, and rent can be recovered by distress or otherwise by the wardens or their successors as if the legal estate were vested in them[8].

1   As to the allotment wardens and (where relevant) their successors see PARAS 650, 651.
2   As to field garden allotments see PARA 651.
3   The Inclosure Act 1845 s 109 refers to a parish but this should be construed as a reference to the authorities mentioned in the text: see PARA 659 note 2.
4   See the Inclosure Act 1845 s 109 (amended by the Statute Law Revision Act 1891); and the Commons Act 1876 s 26 (amended by the Statute Law Revision Act 1894).
5   See the Commons Act 1876 s 27; the Commons Act 1879 s 2; the Commons Act 1899 s 16; and OPEN SPACES AND COUNTRYSIDE vol 78 (2010) PARAS 550, 551.
6   Inclosure Act 1845 s 109 (as amended: see note 4).
7   Inclosure Act 1845 s 110 (amended by the Statute Law Revision Act 1891; and the Allotments Act 1922 s 23(2), Schedule). The provision there made for the determination of field garden tenancies is similar to that made by the Small Holdings and Allotments Act 1908 s 30(2) in respect of allotments let by councils, and the special statutory provisions applicable to the determination of tenancies of allotments which are allotment gardens or agricultural holdings (as to which see PARAS 702, 703) apply equally to field gardens in either of those categories.
8   Inclosure Act 1845 ss 111, 112 (s 111 amended by the Rent Act 1965 s 51, Sch 6 para 1).

(ii) Determination of Lettings

702. Provisions applicable to determination of allotment tenancies.

The provisions applicable to the determination of the tenancy of an allotment[1] differ according to whether the allotment concerned is an allotment garden[2], an agricultural holding[3], or a farm business tenancy[4], or is in none of those categories. If the allotment is an allotment garden it cannot also be an agricultural holding or a farm business tenancy[5], and special provisions apply to the determination of its letting[6]. If the allotment is an agricultural holding the tenancy may be determined only in accordance with the provisions of the Agricultural Holdings Act 1986[7]. If the allotment is let on a farm business tenancy, the tenancy must be determined in accordance with the Agricultural Tenancies Act 1995[8]. If, however, the allotment falls within none of these categories there are no statutory provisions specifically applicable to the determination of a tenancy of it, except where it is let by a district, parish, London borough, or, in Wales, a community, county or county borough council[9], in which case, if the rent is in arrear for 40 days, or if it appears to the council that a tenant, not less than three months after the commencement of the tenancy, has not observed the rules affecting the allotment[10], or is resident more than a mile out of the district, parish, borough, community, county or county borough for which the allotments are provided, the council may give him one month's notice determining the tenancy[11].

Special provision is made for the determination of an allotment tenancy and compensation therefor where allotment land is comprised in a compulsory rights order under the Opencast Coal Act 1958[12].

1   As to the meaning of 'allotment' see PARA 649.
2   As to the meaning of 'allotment garden' see PARA 424 note 11.
3   Ie within the meaning of the Agricultural Holdings Act 1986 s 1(1) (see PARA 423).
4   Ie within the meaning of the Agricultural Tenancies Act 1995 s 1 (see PARA 402).
5   See PARA 649.
6   See PARA 703.
7   See *Stevens v Sedgman* [1951] 2 KB 434, [1951] 2 All ER 33, CA. As to the termination of tenancies under the Agricultural Holdings Act 1986 see PARA 428.
8   As to the termination of tenancies under the Agricultural Tenancies Act 1995 see ss 5–7; and PARA 404.
9   The Small Holdings and Allotments Act 1908 s 30 refers only to 'a council' but should be construed as referring to the authorities empowered to let land for allotments: see PARA 659.
10 Ie rules made by or in pursuance of the Small Holdings and Allotments Act 1908 (see PARA 696).
11 Small Holdings and Allotments Act 1908 s 30(2) (amended by the Allotments Act 1922 Schedule). Notice is given by serving it on the tenant or, if he resides out of the council's area, by leaving it at his last known place of abode in the area, or by fixing it in some conspicuous manner on the allotment: Small Holdings and Allotments Act 1908 s 30(2).
12 See the Opencast Coal Act 1958 Sch 8; and MINES, MINERALS AND QUARRIES vol 76 (2013) PARAS 451, 491–492.

703. Determination of tenancies of allotment gardens.

Where land[1] is let on a tenancy for use by the tenant as an allotment garden[2], or is let to a council of any district, parish, or London borough, or, in Wales, community, county or county borough[3], or an association[4], for subletting for that use[5], the tenancy or any part thereof cannot be terminated by the landlord[6] by notice to quit or re-entry, notwithstanding any agreement to the contrary[7], except[8]:

(1)   by 12 months'[9] or longer notice to quit expiring on or before 6 April or on or after 29 September[10];

(2)   by re-entry after three months' previous written notice to the tenant under a power of re-entry contained in or affecting the contract of tenancy, on account of the land being required for building, mining or other industrial purpose[11], or for roads or sewers necessary in connection with those purposes[12];

(3)   by re-entry under a power contained in or affecting the contract of tenancy in the case of land let by a corporation or company being the owners or lessees of a railway, dock, canal, water or other public undertaking on account of the land being required for any non-agricultural purpose for which the land was acquired or held by it

or has been appropriated by it under statutory provision, but so that, except in a case of emergency, the tenant must be given three months' written notice of the intended re-entry[13];

(4)   by re-entry under a power contained in or affecting the contract of tenancy in the case of land let by a council, after three months' previous written notice to the tenant on account of the land being required by the council for a non-agricultural purpose for which it was acquired, or has been appropriated under any statutory provision[14]; or

(5)   by re-entry for non-payment of rent, breach of any term or condition of the tenancy, bankruptcy of the tenant, the tenant compounding with creditors, or, in the case of an association, its liquidation[15].

These provisions do not apply to land held by or on behalf of the Secretary of State[16] and let for use as an allotment garden when possession of the land is required for naval, military or air force purposes or the purposes of the Secretary of State[17]. These provisions also do not apply to land attached to a cottage[18] or to land forming part of a Royal Park[19].

1   As to the meaning of 'land' see PARA 424 note 5.
2   As to the meaning of 'allotment garden' see PARA 424 note 11. As to the determination by notice of an allotment tenancy by a council see PARA 702.
3   The Allotments Act 1922 s 1(1) refers to 'a local authority' but this should be construed as a reference to the authorities mentioned in the text, ie those empowered to take land on lease for the purposes of allotments. As to those authorities see PARA 665. As to the powers of local authorities in connection with the provision of allotments generally see PARA 659.
4   Local authorities were empowered to provide allotments to co-operative societies and allotment associations under the Small Holdings and Allotments Act 1926 s 3(b) (repealed) (extended by the Small Holdings and Allotments Act 1908 s 27(6)). See also the Allotments Act 1922 s 15; and PARA 630.
5   Where land is used by the tenant as an allotment garden, then, for these purposes, unless the contrary is proved, the land is deemed to have been let to him to be used as an allotment garden and, where the land has been sublet to him by a council which holds the land under a contract of tenancy, the land is deemed to have been let to that council for the purpose of being sublet for such use: Allotments Act 1922 s 22(4); Allotments Act 1950 s 7.
6   As to the meaning of 'landlord' see PARA 649 note 9. Note also, as to the meaning of 'landlord' in connection with land compulsorily hired, PARA 536 note 7.
7   See *Wombwell UDC v Burke* [1966] 2 QB 149, [1966] 1 All ER 911, CA, where a notice expiring in accordance with the Allotments Act 1922 but not with the agreement was upheld.
8   Allotments Act 1922 s 1(1).
9   The Allotments Act 1922 s 1(1)(a) (as originally enacted) prescribed a period of six months, which still applies in the case of land let under the Defence (General) Regulations 1939, SR & O 1939/927, reg 62A (revoked), or the Emergency Laws (Miscellaneous Provisions) Act 1953 s 5: s 5(3); Allotments Act 1950 s 6.
10   Allotments Act 1922 s 1(1)(a) (amended by the Allotments Act 1950 s 1).
11   'Industrial purpose' does not include use for agriculture or sport: Allotments Act 1922 s 22(1). As to the meaning of 'agriculture' see PARA 424 note 5.
12   Allotments Act 1922 s 1(1)(b).
13   Allotments Act 1922 s 1(1)(c).
14   Allotments Act 1922 s 1(1)(d) (amended by the Statute Law (Repeals) Act 1993).
15   Allotments Act 1922 s 1(1)(e).
16   As to the Secretary of State see PARA 741.
17   Allotments Act 1922 s 1(4) (amended by the Allotments Act 1950 s 8; and by SI 1964/488). The Allotments Act 1922 s 1(4) refers to the Minister of Supply, the land, functions etc formerly vested in whom became vested in the Secretary of State for Trade and Industry, by the following process: the functions of the Minister of Supply in connection with radioactive substances and atomic energy were transferred to the Lord President of the Council (see the Transfer of Functions (Atomic Energy and Radioactive Substances) Order 1953, SI 1953/1673), then to the Prime Minister (see the Transfer of Functions (Atomic Energy and Radioactive Substances) Order 1957, SI 1957/561), the Secretary of State for Education and Science (see the Secretary of State for Education and Science Order 1964, SI 1964/490), the Minister of Technology (see the Minister of Technology

Order 1964, SI 1964/2048), and finally to the Secretary of State for Trade and Industry (see the Secretary of State for Trade and Industry Order 1970, SI 1970/1537; the Secretary of State (New Departments) Order 1974, SI 1974/692; and the Transfer of Functions (Trade and Industry) Order 1983, SI 1983/1127). Other land and functions of the Minister of Supply continued to reside with him on his redesignation as the Minister of Aviation (see the Minister of Aviation Order 1959, SI 1959/1768), the relevant functions of whom were then transferred to the Board of Trade (see the Transfer of Functions (Civil Aviation) Order 1966, SI 1966/741), and then to the Secretary of State for Trade and Industry (see the Secretary of State for Trade and Industry Order 1970, SI 1970/1537; the Secretary of State (New Departments) Order 1974, SI 1974/692; and the Transfer of Functions (Trade and Industry) Order 1983, SI 1983/1127). No order was made transferring to either the Secretary of State for Wales, the National Assembly for Wales or the Welsh Ministers any of the relevant functions so far as exercisable in relation to Wales. The Secretary of State for Trade and Industry has been redesignated the Secretary of State for Business, Enterprise and Regulatory Reform which has also been redesignated as the Secretary of State for Business, Innovation and Skills.

18 Allotments Act 1922 s 3(1); Allotments Act 1950 s 6.
19 Allotments Act 1922 s 7 (amended by the Statute Law (Repeals) Act 1993). Otherwise, however, these provisions do apply to land vested in Her Majesty in right of the Crown or the Duchy of Cornwall and, except as before provided (see text and notes 16, 17), to land vested in any government department for public purposes: Allotments Act 1922 s 7. As to the management of the Royal Parks see CROWN AND CROWN PROCEEDINGS vol 29 (2014) PARA 281; OPEN SPACES AND COUNTRYSIDE vol 78 (2010) PARA 560 et seq. As to the Crown Estate see CROWN AND CROWN PROCEEDINGS vol 29 (2014) PARA 192 et seq. As to the Duchies of Lancaster and Cornwall see CROWN AND CROWN PROCEEDINGS vol 29 (2014) PARAS 214–267.

704. Resumption of possession by superior owner where land held by authority for allotments purposes.

Where land[1] has been let to a district, parish, London borough, or, in Wales, a community, county or county borough council[2], or an association[3], for the purpose of being sublet for use as allotment gardens[4], or is occupied by a council under its power to enter unoccupied land[5], and the landlord[6], or the person who, but for such occupation, would be entitled to possession, proposes to resume possession for any particular purpose, written notice of that purpose must be given to the council or association[7].

The council may by counter-notice served within 21 days after receipt of the notice on the person requiring possession demand that the question whether possession is required in good faith for the specified purpose be determined by arbitration[8]. Possession must not be resumed until after the period of 21 days or the determination of the question[9].

1 As to the meaning of 'land' see PARA 424 note 5.
2 The Allotments Act 1922 s 11(1) refers to 'a local authority' but this should be construed as a reference to the authorities mentioned in the text, ie those empowered to take land on lease for the purposes of allotments. As to those authorities see PARA 665. As to the powers of local authorities in connection with the provision of allotments generally see PARA 659.
3 Local authorities were empowered to provide allotments to co-operative societies and allotment associations under the Small Holdings and Allotments Act 1926 s 3(b) (repealed) (extended by the Small Holdings and Allotments Act 1908 s 27(6)). See also the Allotments Act 1922 s 15; and PARA 630.
4 As to the meaning of 'allotment garden' see PARA 424 note 11.
5 See the Allotments Act 1922 s 10; and PARA 692.
6 As to the meaning of 'landlord' see PARA 649 note 9.
7 Allotments Act 1922 s 11(1). Note that s 11 does not apply where possession is required by a corporation or company as owners or lessees of a railway, dock, canal, water or other public undertaking: s 11(4).

8   Allotments Act 1922 s 11(2) (amended by the Allotments Act 1925 s 9). Arbitration is under the Agricultural Holdings Act 1986 (as to which see PARA 566 et seq): Allotments Act 1922 s 11(2) (amended by the Agricultural Holdings Act 1986 Sch 14 para 10).
9   Allotments Act 1922 s 11(3) (amended by the Allotments Act 1925 s 9).

(iii) Compensation at End of Tenancies

A. RIGHT TO COMPENSATION

705.   Rights on expiration of tenancy of allotment.

On the expiration of his tenancy of an allotment[1], a tenant may be entitled to compensation for improvements, for disturbance and other matters, and a landlord may be entitled to compensation for deterioration to the allotment[2]. The tenant may alternatively have the right to remove fixtures, fruit trees and bushes and like matters. The rights of the landlord and tenant may arise under custom[3] or agreement, or under statute. The statutory provisions applicable differ, as in the case of determination of tenancies[4], according to whether the allotment is an allotment garden[5], an agricultural holding[6], a farm business tenancy[7] or an allotment not in any of those groups[8]. Special provision for compensation is made where an allotment tenancy terminates in pursuance of a compulsory rights order under the Opencast Coal Act 1958[9].

1   As to the meaning of 'allotment' see PARA 649.
2   As to the meaning of 'landlord', and the designations 'landlord' and 'tenant', see PARA 649 note 9.
3   Customary rights are considered in relation to agricultural tenancies under the Agricultural Holdings Act 1986: see PARA 449–453.
4   See PARAS 702–703.
5   As to the meaning of 'allotment garden' see PARA 424 note 11. For provisions as to compensation see PARAS 706–714.
6   Ie under the Agricultural Holdings Act 1986. As to compensation for allotments which are agricultural holdings see PARA 715.
7   As to compensation for allotments which are farm business tenancies see PARA 716.
8   For general provision as to compensation see PARAS 717–720.
9   See the Opencast Coal Act 1958 Sch 8; and MINES, MINERALS AND QUARRIES vol 76 (2013) PARAS 451, 491–492.

B. ALLOTMENT GARDENS

706.   Compensation for improvements on quitting allotment gardens.

The tenant[1] of an allotment garden[2] which is not a parcel of land[3] attached to a cottage[4], is entitled, notwithstanding any agreement to the contrary, on quitting the land or part of the land on the termination of the tenancy of the whole or that part of it, to obtain from the landlord[5] compensation[6] for ordinary growing crops[7] and for manure applied to the land[8] based on their value to an incoming tenant[9], but the compensation is recoverable only if the tenancy was terminated by the landlord by statutory re-entry[10] or by notice to quit[11]. A tenant whose tenancy is determined by the termination of his landlord's tenancy can recover compensation from his landlord as if notice to quit had been given by his landlord[12]. Compensation is similarly recoverable by a district, parish, London borough, or, in Wales, a community, county or county borough council[13], or an association[14], where it has sublet land for allotment gardens[15]. Save as above or as provided by the contract of tenancy the tenant of an allotment garden is not entitled to compensation for improvements[16], although compensation for disturbance[17] may be recoverable[18].

1 As to the designation 'tenant' see PARA 649 note 9.
2 As to the meaning of 'allotment garden' see PARA 424 note 11. These provisions do not apply to land forming part of a Royal Park; otherwise, they apply to land vested in Her Majesty in right of the Crown or the Duchy of Lancaster, and to land forming part of the possessions of the Duchy of Cornwall, and, except as before provided, to land vested in any government department for public purposes: Allotments Act 1922 s 7 (amended by the Statute Law (Repeals) Act 1993); Allotments Act 1950 s 7. As to the management of the Royal Parks see CROWN AND CROWN PROCEEDINGS vol 29 (2014) PARA 281; OPEN SPACES AND COUNTRYSIDE vol 78 (2010) PARA 560 et seq. As to the Crown Estate see CROWN AND CROWN PROCEEDINGS vol 29 (2014) PARA 192 et seq. As to the Duchies of Lancaster and Cornwall see CROWN AND CROWN PROCEEDINGS vol 29 (2014) PARAS 214–267.
3 As to the meaning of 'land' see PARA 424 note 5.
4 Allotments Act 1922 s 3(1); Allotments Act 1950 s 6.
5 As to the meaning of 'landlord' see PARA 649 note 9.
6 Allotments Act 1922 s 2(1), (7). As to compensation in respect of certain smaller allotments see PARA 717.
7 If the tenancy terminates between 29 September and 11 October, inclusive, by notice to quit or termination of the landlord's tenancy, the tenant is entitled to remove growing crops within 21 days after the tenancy terminates: Allotments Act 1922 s 2(9).
8 Allotments Act 1922 s 2(3).
9 Allotments Act 1922 s 22(3).
10 Ie under the Allotments Act 1922 s 1(1)(b), (c) or (d) (see PARA 703).
11 Allotments Act 1922 s 2(2) (substituted by the Allotments Act 1950 s 2(1)). This provision applies also to land let under the Emergency Laws (Miscellaneous Provisions) Act 1953 s 5: s 5(3).
12 Allotments Act 1922 s 2(4).
13 The Allotments Act 1922 s 2(6) refers to 'a local authority' but this should be construed as referring to the authorities empowered to let land for allotments: see PARA 659.
14 Local authorities were empowered to provide allotments to co-operative societies and allotment associations under the Small Holdings and Allotments Act 1926 s 3(b) (repealed) (extended by the Small Holdings and Allotments Act 1908 s 27(6)). See also the Allotments Act 1922 s 15; and PARA 630.
15 See the Allotments Act 1922 s 2(6); and PARA 719.
16 Allotments Act 1922 s 2(8).
17 See PARA 707.
18 Allotments Act 1950 s 3(3).

707. Compensation for disturbance of allotment garden.

Where land[1] is let for use by a tenant[2] as an allotment garden[3], or to a district, parish, London borough, or, in Wales, a community, county or county borough council[4], or an association[5], for the purpose of being sublet for such use, and the tenancy is terminated, as to the whole or any part of the land comprised in it, by statutory re-entry[6], by the termination of the landlord's[7] tenancy[8], or, where the landlord is a local authority which has let land previously unoccupied[9], by the termination of its right of occupation[10], the tenant is entitled, notwithstanding any agreement to the contrary, on quitting the land or that part of it, to recover from the landlord compensation for disturbance[11], in addition to any compensation to which a tenant may be entitled for growing crops and manure[12]. The amount of compensation for disturbance is one year's rent at the rate payable immediately before the termination of the tenancy where the whole tenancy is terminated[13] or, where the tenancy of only part of the land is terminated, an amount bearing to one year's rent the same proportion that the area of that part bears to the area of the whole[14].

1 As to the meaning of 'land' see PARA 424 note 5.

2   As to the designation 'tenant' see PARA 649 note 9.
3   As to the meaning of 'allotment garden' see PARA 424 note 11.
4   The Allotments Act 1950 s 3(1) refers to 'a local authority' but this should be construed as referring to the authorities empowered to lease and let land for allotments: see PARA 659.
5   Local authorities were empowered to provide allotments to co-operative societies and allotment associations under the Small Holdings and Allotments Act 1926 s 3(b) (repealed) (extended by the Small Holdings and Allotments Act 1908 s 27(6)). See also the Allotments Act 1922 s 15; and PARA 630.
6   Allotments Act 1950 s 3(1)(a). The reference in the text to 'statutory re-entry' is a reference to re-entry under the Allotments Act 1922 s 1(1)(b), (c) or (d) (see PARA 703).
    The Allotments Act 1950 s 3 applies whether the land was let before or after 26 October 1950 (ie the date on which the Allotments Act 1950 was passed) (s 3(1)), but does not apply to any parcel of land attached to a cottage or let under the Defence (General) Regulations 1939, SR & O 1939/927, reg 62A (revoked) or under the Emergency Laws (Miscellaneous Provisions) Act 1953 s 5 (s 5(3); Allotments Act 1950 s 6). These provisions do not apply to land forming part of a Royal Park; otherwise, they apply to land vested in Her Majesty in right of the Crown or the Duchy of Lancaster, and to land forming part of the possessions of the Duchy of Cornwall, and, except as before provided, to land vested in any government department for public purposes: Allotments Act 1922 s 7 (amended by the Statute Law (Repeals) Act 1993); Allotments Act 1950 s 7. As to the management of the Royal Parks see CROWN AND CROWN PROCEEDINGS vol 29 (2014) PARA 281; OPEN SPACES AND COUNTRYSIDE vol 78 (2010) PARA 560 et seq. As to the Crown Estate see CROWN AND CROWN PROCEEDINGS vol 29 (2014) PARA 192 et seq. As to the Duchies of Lancaster and Cornwall see CROWN AND CROWN PROCEEDINGS vol 29 (2014) PARAS 214–267.
7   As to the meaning of 'landlord' see PARA 649 note 9.
8   Allotments Act 1950 s 3(1)(b). See note 6.
9   Ie under the Allotments Act 1922 s 10 (see PARA 692).
10 Allotments Act 1950 s 3(1)(c). See note 6.
11 Allotments Act 1950 s 3(1). See note 6.
12 Allotments Act 1950 s 3(3). As to such compensation see PARA 706.
13 Allotments Act 1950 s 3(2)(a).
14 Allotments Act 1950 s 3(2)(b).

708.   Landlord's compensation for deterioration of allotment.

Where the tenant[1] of land[2] let for use as an allotment garden[3] quits the land on the termination of his tenancy, the landlord[4] is entitled, notwithstanding any agreement to the contrary, to recover from the tenant compensation in respect of any deterioration of the land caused by the tenant's failure to maintain it clean and in a good state of cultivation and fertility[5]. The amount of any such compensation is the cost, as at the date of the tenant's quitting the land, of making good the deterioration[6].

Where the tenant has remained on the land during two or more tenancies the landlord is not deprived of his right to compensation for deterioration by reason only that the tenancy during which part or all of the deterioration occurred was a tenancy other than that at the termination of which the tenant quitted the land[7].

1   As to the designation 'tenant' see PARA 649 note 9.
2   As to the meaning of 'land' see PARA 424 note 5.
3   As to the meaning of 'allotment garden' see PARA 424 note 11.
4   As to the meaning of 'landlord' see PARA 649 note 9.
5   Allotments Act 1950 s 4(1). Section 4 is applied and disapplied in the circumstances in which s 3 is applied and disapplied: see PARA 707 note 6.
6   Allotments Act 1950 s 4(2).
7   Allotments Act 1950 s 4(3).

709.   Compensation payable by mortgagee to dispossessed allotment tenant.

Where a contract of tenancy, not being a farm business tenancy[1], in respect of an allotment[2] or allotment garden[3] is made with a mortgagor but is not binding on the mortgagee, the tenant[4] is entitled, if deprived of possession by the mortgagee, to recover compensation[5], including compensation for disturbance[6], from him as if he were the landlord[7] and had terminated the tenancy, but subject to the deduction from the compensation of rent or other sums due from the tenant in respect of the land[8].

1   Ie within the meaning of the Agricultural Tenancies Act 1995 s 1 (see PARAS 402, 656).
2   As to the meaning of 'allotment' in this context see the Allotments Act 1922 s 3(7); and PARA 649.
3   As to the meaning of 'allotment garden' see PARA 424 note 11.
4   As to the designation 'tenant' see PARA 649 note 9.
5   Ie under the Allotments Act 1922 ss 2, 3 (see PARAS 706, 717).
6   Ie under the Allotments Act 1950 s 3 (see PARA 707): s 3(4).
7   As to the meaning of 'landlord' see PARA 649 note 9.
8   Allotments Act 1922 s 4(2). These provisions do not apply to land forming part of a Royal Park; otherwise, they apply to land vested in Her Majesty in right of the Crown or the Duchy of Lancaster, and to land forming part of the possessions of the Duchy of Cornwall, and, except as before provided, to land vested in any government department for public purposes: s 7 (amended by the Statute Law (Repeals) Act 1993). As to the management of the Royal Parks see CROWN AND CROWN PROCEEDINGS vol 29 (2014) PARA 281; OPEN SPACES AND COUNTRYSIDE vol 78 (2010) PARA 560 et seq. As to the Crown Estate see CROWN AND CROWN PROCEEDINGS vol 29 (2014) PARA 192 et seq. As to the Duchies of Lancaster and Cornwall see CROWN AND CROWN PROCEEDINGS vol 29 (2014) PARAS 214–267.

710. Compensation to allotment tenant for fruit trees, bushes or other improvements.

A tenant[1] of an allotment[2] who has paid compensation to an outgoing tenant for fruit trees or bushes or other improvements has the same rights as to compensation or removal as he would have had if the trees or bushes had been provided and planted or the improvement made by him and at his expense[3].

1   As to the designation 'tenant' see PARA 649 note 9.
2   As to the meaning of 'allotment' see PARA 649.
3   Allotments Act 1922 s 5. These provisions do not apply to land forming part of a Royal Park; otherwise, they apply to land vested in Her Majesty in right of the Crown or the Duchy of Lancaster, and to land forming part of the possessions of the Duchy of Cornwall, and, except as before provided, to land vested in any government department for public purposes: s 7 (amended by the Statute Law (Repeals) Act 1993). As to the management of the Royal Parks see CROWN AND CROWN PROCEEDINGS vol 29 (2014) PARA 281; OPEN SPACES AND COUNTRYSIDE vol 78 (2010) PARA 560 et seq. As to the Crown Estate see CROWN AND CROWN PROCEEDINGS vol 29 (2014) PARA 192 et seq. As to the Duchies of Lancaster and Cornwall see CROWN AND CROWN PROCEEDINGS vol 29 (2014) PARAS 214–267.

711. Adjustment of tenancy compensation in case of allotment gardens.

Out of any money payable to the tenant[1] of an allotment garden[2] by way of statutory compensation[3] or compensation for disturbance[4], the landlord[5] is entitled to deduct any sum due to him from the tenant under or in respect of the tenancy, including compensation[6] for deterioration[7]. Similarly, out of any money due to the landlord in respect of the tenancy, including compensation for deterioration, the tenant is entitled to deduct any money due to him from the landlord by way of compensation for crops or manure or for disturbance[8].

1   As to the designation 'tenant' see PARA 649 note 9.
2   As to the meaning of 'allotment garden' see PARA 424 note 11.
3   Ie compensation under the Allotments Act 1922 s 2 (see PARA 706).
4   Ie under the Allotments Act 1950 s 3 (see PARA 707).
5   As to the meaning of 'landlord' see PARA 649 note 9.

6   Ie under the Allotments Act 1950 s 4 (see PARA 708).
7   Allotments Act 1950 s 5(1). These provisions do not apply to land forming part of a Royal Park; otherwise, they apply to land vested in Her Majesty in right of the Crown or the Duchy of Lancaster, and to land forming part of the possessions of the Duchy of Cornwall, and, except as before provided, to land vested in any government department for public purposes: Allotments Act 1922 s 7 (amended by the Statute Law (Repeals) Act 1993); Allotments Act 1950 s 7. As to the management of the Royal Parks see CROWN AND CROWN PROCEEDINGS vol 29 (2014) PARA 281; OPEN SPACES AND COUNTRYSIDE vol 78 (2010) PARA 560 et seq. As to the Crown Estate see CROWN AND CROWN PROCEEDINGS vol 29 (2014) PARA 192 et seq. As to the Duchies of Lancaster and Cornwall see CROWN AND CROWN PROCEEDINGS vol 29 (2014) PARAS 214–267.
8   Allotments Act 1950 s 5(2).

712. Removal of improvements made by tenant of allotments and allotment gardens.

Fruit trees and bushes provided and planted by a tenant of land[1] held under a contract of tenancy of an allotment garden[2] or certain allotments[3], and any erection, fencing or other improvement erected or made by him and at his expense or in respect of which he has paid compensation to an outgoing tenant[4] may be removed by him before the expiration of the tenancy, provided he makes good any injury caused by the removal[5]. The tenant of an allotment, who is not a tenant under a farm business tenancy[6], may also, before the expiration of his tenancy, remove any fruit and other trees and bushes planted or acquired by him, and any tool-house, shed or greenhouse built or acquired by him, for which he has no claim for compensation[7].

1   As to the meaning of 'land' see PARA 424 note 5.
2   As to the meaning of 'allotment garden' see PARA 424 note 11.
3   Ie under the Allotments Act 1922 ss 1–3 (see PARAS 703, 706). As to the meaning of 'allotment' see PARA 649.
4   As to the designation 'tenant' see PARA 649 note 9.
5   Allotments Act 1922 ss 4(1), 5. These provisions do not apply to land forming part of a Royal Park; otherwise, they apply to land vested in Her Majesty in right of the Crown or the Duchy of Lancaster, and to land forming part of the possessions of the Duchy of Cornwall, and, except as before provided, to land vested in any government department for public purposes: s 7 (amended by the Statute Law (Repeals) Act 1993). As to the management of the Royal Parks see CROWN AND CROWN PROCEEDINGS vol 29 (2014) PARA 281; OPEN SPACES AND COUNTRYSIDE vol 78 (2010) PARA 560 et seq. As to the Crown Estate see CROWN AND CROWN PROCEEDINGS vol 29 (2014) PARA 192 et seq. As to the Duchies of Lancaster and Cornwall see CROWN AND CROWN PROCEEDINGS vol 29 (2014) PARAS 214–267.
6   Ie within the meaning of the Agricultural Tenancies Act 1995 s 1 (see PARAS 402, 656): see the Small Holdings and Allotments Act 1908 s 47(5) (s 47(4) amended, s 47(5) added, by the Agricultural Tenancies Act 1995 Schedule para 1(1), (5), (6)).
7   Small Holdings and Allotments Act 1908 s 47(4) (as amended: see note 6).

713. Assessment and recovery of compensation in case of allotments.

In default of agreement, the compensation[1] under a contract of a tenancy, not being a farm business tenancy[2], must be assessed by the valuation of a person whom, unless agreed upon by the landlord and tenant[3], must be appointed by the County Court[4]. If the amount agreed or determined is not paid within 14 days, it may be recovered upon order made by the County Court as money ordered to be paid by the County Court under its ordinary jurisdiction is recoverable[5].

The valuer's proper charges are borne by the landlord and tenant in such proportion as the valuer directs, but he may recover them from either party, and any amount paid by one party in excess of the amount the valuer directs to be borne by that party is recoverable from the other party or can be deducted from the compensation payable[6].

1   Ie compensation under the Allotments Act 1922 or under the Allotments Act 1950, and such further compensation, if any, as is recoverable under the contract of tenancy.
2   Ie within the meaning of the Agricultural Tenancies Act 1995 s 1 (see PARAS **402, 656**).
3   As to the meaning of 'landlord', and the designations 'landlord' and 'tenant', see PARA **649** note 9.
4   Allotments Act 1922 s 6(1) (amended by the Agricultural Tenancies Act 1995 Schedule para 4 and the Crime and Courts Act 2013 Sch 9 para 59); Allotments Act 1950 s 7. An application in writing is required to be made for this purpose by the landlord or the tenant: Allotments Act 1922 s 6(1). These provisions do not apply to land forming part of a Royal Park; otherwise, they apply to land vested in Her Majesty in right of the Crown or the Duchy of Lancaster, and to land forming part of the possessions of the Duchy of Cornwall, and, except as before provided, to land vested in any government department for public purposes: s 7 (amended by the Statute Law (Repeals) Act 1993). As to the management of the Royal Parks see CROWN AND CROWN PROCEEDINGS vol 29 (2014) PARA 281; OPEN SPACES AND COUNTRYSIDE vol 78 (2010) PARA 560 et seq. As to the Crown Estate see CROWN AND CROWN PROCEEDINGS vol 29 (2014) PARA 192 et seq. As to the Duchies of Lancaster and Cornwall see CROWN AND CROWN PROCEEDINGS vol 29 (2014) PARAS 214–267.
5   Allotments Act 1922 s 6(1) (as amended: see note 4).
6   Allotments Act 1922 s 6(2).

714.   Compensation to allotment tenant at end of council's occupation.

Unless the contract of tenancy otherwise provides, a tenant[1] to whom land[2] has been let by a London borough or district or, in Wales, a county or county borough council[3] under its power in relation to unoccupied land[4] and whose tenancy is terminated by the termination of the council's right of occupation, is entitled to recover from the council such compensation, if any, as would have been recoverable if his tenancy had been terminated by notice to quit given by the council, and has the same right to remove his crops as if the tenancy had been so terminated[5]. If, however, the rent payable by the tenant exceeds 1p per quarter acre[6] the tenant is entitled to claim compensation notwithstanding any agreement in the contract of tenancy to the contrary[7]. Compensation for disturbance also may be claimed by the tenant notwithstanding any such agreement[8].

1   As to the designation 'tenant' see PARA **649** note 9.
2   As to the meaning of 'land' see PARA **424** note 5.
3   The Allotments Act 1922 s 10 refers to 'the council of a borough or urban district' but this should be construed as a reference to the authorities empowered thereunder to enter on unoccupied land for the purposes of providing allotments: see PARAS **659, 692**. As to the meaning of 'allotment' see PARA **649**.
4   Ie under the Allotments Act 1922 s 10 (see PARA **692**).
5   Allotments Act 1922 s 10(4). As to compensation and the removal of crops see PARA **705** et seq.
6   The Allotments Act 1925 s 7 as drafted refers to '1p per pole'. However, the pole (30¼ square yards) is no longer recognised as a unit of area and an area of one quarter of an acre has accordingly been substituted.
7   Allotments Act 1925 s 7 (amended by virtue of the Decimal Currency Act 1969 s 10(1) and the Statute Law (Repeals) Act 1993).
8   See the Allotments Act 1950 s 3(1)(c); and PARA **707**.

C. OTHER ALLOTMENTS

715.   Compensation for allotments that are agricultural holdings.

Where an allotment[1] is an agricultural holding[2] the tenant may claim compensation for improvements and tenant-right matters, for disturbance and for the continuous adoption of a special system of farming in accordance with the provisions of the Agricultural Holdings Act 1986 in that behalf[3], and has the rights of removing fixtures conferred on tenants of such holdings[4]. He is liable to pay compensation to his landlord for deterioration to the holding[5].

In the case of certain allotments of not more than two acres[6] which are also agricultural holdings, the tenant[7] may alternatively claim compensation in accordance with the provisions of the Allotments Act 1922[8].

1 As to the meaning of 'allotment' see PARA 649.
2 Ie within the meaning of the Agricultural Holdings Act 1986 s 1(1) (see PARA 423). These provisions do not apply to allotments held under farm business tenancies, for which special provision is made: see PARA 716.
3 See PARAS 548–549.
4 See PARA 436.
5 See PARAS 553–560.
6 Ie 'allotments' as defined in the Allotments Act 1922 s 3(7) (see PARAS 649, 717).
7 As to the designation 'tenant' see PARA 649 note 9.
8 Allotments Act 1922 s 3(5) (amended by the Agricultural Holdings Act 1986 Sch 14 para 9). As to these provisions see PARA 706 et seq. The tenant of an allotment let by a district, parish, London borough, or, in Wales, a community, county or county borough council may claim compensation for certain improvements as if the allotment were a market garden within the Agricultural Holdings Act 1986 s 79 (see PARA 561) or alternatively under the Allotments Act 1922 s 3, even if the allotment exceeds two acres: see the Small Holdings and Allotments Act 1908 s 47(1), (3); and PARA 718. The Small Holdings and Allotments Act 1908 s 47(3) refers to 'a council' but this should be construed as meaning the authorities referred to above, ie those empowered to let land for allotments: see PARA 659.

716. Compensation for allotments that are farm business tenancies.

Where allotments[1] are let under a farm business tenancy[2], any compensation payable to the tenant will be in accordance with the statutory provisions as to compensation on the termination of such tenancies[3] and not under the Allotments Acts[4]. The tenant is entitled to compensation for improvements which add to the letting value of the holding on the determination of the tenancy[5]. No compensation will be payable unless the landlord, or for improvements other than planning permission[6] the landlord or arbitrator, has given consent to the improvements[7]. There are no special provisions for market gardens.

1 As to the meaning of 'allotment' see PARA 649.
2 Ie within the meaning of the Agricultural Tenancies Act 1995 s 1 (see PARAS 402, 656).
3 Ie the Agricultural Tenancies Act 1995 Pt III (ss 15–27) (see PARAS 410–419).
4 Small Holdings and Allotments Act 1908 s 47(1), (5) (s 47(1) amended, s 47(5) added, by the Agricultural Tenancies Act 1995 Schedule para 1(1), (2), (6)); Allotments Act 1922 s 3(7) (amended by the Agricultural Tenancies Act 1995 Schedule para 3).
5 See the Agricultural Tenancies Act 1995 ss 16, 20, 21; and PARAS 411, 413–414.
6 Improvements are defined to include physical improvements and intangible improvements such as planning permission: see the Agricultural Tenancies Act 1995 s 15; and PARA 410.
7 See the Agricultural Tenancies Act 1995 s 17; and PARA 411.

717. Compensation for allotments not exceeding two acres.

The tenant[1] of an allotment[2] of not more than two acres in extent, whether attached to a cottage or not, but not being an allotment garden[3], and which is cultivated as a farm or a garden, or partly as a garden and partly as a farm[4], is entitled, on the termination of his tenancy by effluxion of time or from any other cause, and notwithstanding any agreement to the contrary, to obtain from the landlord[5] compensation for:

(1) crops, including fruit, growing on the land in the ordinary course of cultivation, and for labour expended on and manure applied to the land[6]; and

(2) fruit trees or bushes provided and planted by the tenant with the landlord's previous written consent, and drains, outbuildings, pigsties, fowlhouses or other structural improvements made or erected by the tenant and at his expense with such consent[7].

The compensation is based on the value to an incoming tenant of the crops and other subjects of compensation[8].

Any sum due to the landlord from the tenant in respect of rent, any breach of the contract of tenancy, or wilful or negligent damage committed or permitted by the tenant, must be deducted from the compensation[9], and, in default of agreement, the amount of compensation is determined and recovered as in the case of allotment gardens[10].

The tenant has the same right to remove fruit trees, bushes and fixtures, and to compensation where deprived of possession by a mortgagee or where he has paid compensation to an outgoing tenant, as has the tenant of an allotment garden[11].

Where the allotment is an agricultural holding[12] a claim for compensation may alternatively (but not additionally) be made under the Agricultural Holdings Act 1986[13].

1 As to the designation 'tenant' see PARA 649 note 9.

2 As to the meaning of 'allotment' see PARA 649. These provisions do not apply to allotments held under farm business tenancies, for which special provision is made; see the Small Holdings and Allotments Act 1908 s 47(1); and PARA 716. These provisions also do not apply to land forming part of a Royal Park; otherwise, they apply to land vested in Her Majesty in right of the Crown or the Duchy of Lancaster, and to land forming part of the possessions of the Duchy of Cornwall, and, except as before provided, to land vested in any government department for public purposes: Allotments Act 1922 s 7 (amended by the Statute Law (Repeals) Act 1993). As to the management of the Royal Parks see CROWN AND CROWN PROCEEDINGS vol 29 (2014) PARA 281; OPEN SPACES AND COUNTRYSIDE vol 78 (2010) PARA 560 et seq. As to the Crown Estate see CROWN AND CROWN PROCEEDINGS vol 29 (2014) PARA 192 et seq. As to the Duchies of Lancaster and Cornwall see CROWN AND CROWN PROCEEDINGS vol 29 (2014) PARAS 214–267.

3 As to the meaning of 'allotment garden' see PARA 424 note 11.

4 Allotments Act 1922 s 3(7) (amended by the Agricultural Tenancies Act 1995 Schedule para 3).

5 As to the meaning of 'landlord' see PARA 649 note 9.

6 Allotments Act 1922 s 3(2)(a). Compensation under this provision in respect of allotments exceeding two acres and let by a district, parish, London borough, or, in Wales, a community, county or county borough council may also be claimed at the tenant's election under the Small Holdings and Allotments Act 1908 s 47(3) (see PARA 718).

7 Allotments Act 1922 s 3(2)(b). See note 6.

8 Allotments Act 1922 s 22(3).

9 Allotments Act 1922 s 3(3).

10 Allotments Act 1922 s 3(4). As to compensation for allotment gardens see PARA 706.

11 See the Allotments Act 1922 ss 4, 5; and PARAS 710, 712.

12 Ie within the meaning of the Agricultural Holdings Act 1986 s 1(1) (see PARA 423).

13 See the Allotments Act 1922 s 3(5) (amended by the Agricultural Holdings Act 1986 Sch 14 para 9). It would appear that where such an application is made, the whole of the Agricultural Holdings Act 1986, including the provisions as to the measure and recovery of compensation, will apply: see *Stevens v Sedgman* [1951] 2 KB 434 at 440, [1951] 2 All ER 33 at 35, CA, per Somervell LJ.

718. Compensation for allotments let by council.

The tenant of an allotment[1] let to him by a district, parish, London borough, or, in Wales, a community, county or county borough council[2] has, as against the council, the same rights with respect to compensation for improvements effected by planting standard or other fruit trees or fruit bushes permanently set out, and planting strawberry plants and asparagus, rhubarb and other vegetable crops which continue productive for two or more years, as if it had been agreed in writing that the allotment should be let under the Agricultural Holdings Act 1986 as a market garden[3]. The tenant is not, however, entitled to compensation for such improvements if executed contrary to an express written prohibition by the council[4].

The tenant of an allotment provided by a council[5] may, if he so elects, claim compensation for improvements under the provisions applicable to allotments not exceeding two acres[6], instead of claiming as if the allotment were let as a market garden, notwithstanding that the allotment exceeds two acres[7].

1   As to the meaning of 'allotment' see PARA 649. These provisions do not apply to allotments held under farm business tenancies, for which special provision is made (see PARA 716).
2   The Small Holdings and Allotments Act 1908 s 47 refers to 'a council' but this should be construed as referring to the authorities empowered to let land for allotments, ie those referred to in the text: see PARA 649.
3   Small Holdings and Allotments Act 1908 s 47(1), Sch 2 Pt I (s 47(1) amended by the Agricultural Tenancies Act 1995 Schedule para 1(1), (2)); Agricultural Holdings Act 1986 s 79. As to compensation for market gardens see PARAS 561–565.
4   Small Holdings and Allotments Act 1908 s 47(1) proviso (amended by the Local Government, Planning and Land Act 1980 Sch 5 para 1(c), Sch 34 Pt VI).
5   Ie an allotment to which the Small Holdings and Allotments Act 1908 Pt II (ss 23–35) applies.
6   Ie an allotment as defined in the Allotments Act 1922 s 3(7) (see PARA 717).
7   Small Holdings and Allotments Act 1908 s 47(3) (amended by the Agricultural Tenancies Act 1995 Schedule para 1(1), (4); and by the Statute Law (Repeals) Act 1993).

D. COMPENSATION TO COUNCILS OR ASSOCIATIONS AS TENANTS

719. Compensation for land let for allotment gardens.

Where land[1] is let to a district, parish, London borough, or, in Wales, a community, county or county borough council[2], or an association[3], under a contract of tenancy made after 4 August 1922[4] for the purpose of being sublet for use by the tenants[5] as allotment gardens[6], the council or association may claim compensation for improvements in the same manner as may individual tenants of allotment gardens[7], notwithstanding that the crops have been grown and the manure applied by the subtenants[8]. The council or association may also claim compensation for disturbance in respect of land let to it for subletting as allotment gardens[9].

1   As to the meaning of 'land' see PARA 424 note 5. These provisions do not apply to land forming part of a Royal Park; otherwise, they apply to land vested in Her Majesty in right of the Crown or the Duchy of Lancaster, and to land forming part of the possessions of the Duchy of Cornwall, and, except as before provided, to land vested in any government department for public purposes: Allotments Act 1922 s 7 (amended by the Statute Law (Repeals) Act 1993). As to the management of the Royal Parks see CROWN AND CROWN PROCEEDINGS vol 29 (2014) PARA 281; OPEN SPACES AND COUNTRYSIDE vol 78 (2010) PARA 560 et seq. As to the Crown Estate see CROWN AND CROWN PROCEEDINGS vol 29 (2014) PARA 192 et seq. As to the Duchies of Lancaster and Cornwall see CROWN AND CROWN PROCEEDINGS vol 29 (2014) PARAS 214–267.
2   The Allotments Act 1922 s 2(6) refers to 'a local authority' but this should be construed as referring to the authorities empowered to lease and let land for allotments, ie those referred to in the text: see PARA 659.
3   Local authorities were empowered to provide allotments to co-operative societies and allotment associations under the Small Holdings and Allotments Act 1926 s 3(b) (repealed) (extended by the Small Holdings and Allotments Act 1908 s 27(6)). See also the Allotments Act 1922 s 15; and PARA 630.
4   Ie the date on which the Allotments Act 1922 was passed.
5   As to the designation 'tenant' see PARA 649 note 9.

6　As to the meaning of 'allotment garden' see PARA 424 note 11.
7　See PARA 706.
8　Allotments Act 1922 s 2(6).
9　See the Allotments Act 1950 s 3(1); and PARA 707.

720. Compensation for land let for allotments.

Where land[1] is let for the provision of allotments[2], other than allotment gardens[3], to a district, parish, London borough, or, in Wales, a community, county or county borough council[4], or to an allotments association[5], the right of the council or association to claim compensation from the landlord[6] on the determination of the tenancy is subject to the terms of the contract of tenancy, notwithstanding the provisions of any Act to the contrary[7].

On the determination of a tenancy of land[8] hired by a council[9], whether compulsorily[10] or by agreement[11], the council, on quitting the land, is entitled, subject to any provision to the contrary in the agreement or order for hiring, to compensation under the Agricultural Holdings Act 1986[12] for any improvement in respect of[13]:

(1)　　the planting of standard or other fruit trees or fruit bushes permanently set out, or the planting of strawberry plants or of asparagus, rhubarb and other vegetable crops which continue productive for two or more years[14]; and

(2)　　any of:
　　(a)　the erection, alteration, or enlargement of buildings[15];
　　(b)　the formation of silos[16];
　　(c)　the laying down of permanent pasture[17];
　　(d)　the making and planting of osier beds[18];
　　(e)　the making of water meadows or works of irrigation[19];
　　(f)　the making of gardens[20];
　　(g)　the making or improvement of roads or bridges[21];
　　(h)　the making or improvement of watercourses, ponds, wells, or reservoirs, or of works for the application of water power or for supply of water for agricultural or domestic purposes[22];
　　(i)　the making or removal of permanent fences[23];
　　(j)　the planting of hops[24];
　　(k)　the planting of orchards or fruit bushes[25];
　　(l)　the protection of young fruit trees[26];
　　(m)　the reclamation of waste land[27];
　　(n)　the warping or weiring of land[28];
　　(o)　the making of embankments and sluices against floods[29];
　　(p)　the erection of wirework in hop gardens[30];
　　(q)　drainage[31];
　　(r)　the provision of permanent sheep-dipping accommodation[32]; and
　　(s)　in the case of arable land, the removal of bracken, gorse, tree roots, boulders, and other like obstructions to cultivation[33],

where such improvement was necessary and proper to adapt the land for allotments[34].

1　As to the meaning of 'land' see PARA 424 note 5.
2　As to the meaning of 'allotment' see PARA 649.
3　As to the meaning of 'allotment garden' see PARA 424 note 11.
4　Ie under the Small Holdings and Allotments Act 1908: see s 25; and PARA 665. The Allotments Act 1922 s 2(6) refers to 'a local authority' but this should be construed as referring to the authorities empowered to lease and let land for allotments, ie those referred to in the text: see PARA 659.

5   Local authorities were empowered to provide allotments to co-operative societies and allotment associations under the Small Holdings and Allotments Act 1926 s 3(b) (repealed) (extended by the Small Holdings and Allotments Act 1908 s 27(6)). See also the Allotments Act 1922 s 15; and PARA 630.

6   As to the meaning of 'landlord' see PARA 649 note 9.

7   Land Settlement (Facilities) Act 1919 s 23; Allotments Act 1922 s 2(6). This provision does not prejudice or affect the tenant's right to claim compensation from the council on the determination of his tenancy (as to which see PARA 718): Land Settlement (Facilities) Act 1919 s 23 proviso.

8   These provisions do not apply to allotments held under farm business tenancies, for which special provision is made (see PARA 716).

9   The Small Holdings and Allotments Act 1908 s 47(2) refers to 'a council' but this should be construed as referring to the authorities empowered to hire land for allotments: see the text and note 4; and PARA 659.

10   As to the compulsory hiring of land see PARA 673 et seq. In the case of land hired compulsorily the compensation is such sum as fairly represents the increase, if any, in the value to the landlord and his successors in title of the land due to such improvements: Small Holdings and Allotments Act 1908 s 47(2) proviso.

11   As to the hiring of land for allotments by agreement see PARA 665 et seq.

12   Compensation may be claimed under the Agricultural Holdings Act 1986 as if the land were a holding which it was agreed in writing under s 79 should be let as a market garden and as if the improvements specified in the text were comprised in Schs 8, 10: Small Holdings and Allotments Act 1908 s 47(2) (amended by the Agricultural Holdings Act 1986 Sch 14). As to compensation for market gardens see PARAS 561–565.

13   Small Holdings and Allotments Act 1908 s 47(2) (amended by the Land Settlement (Facilities) Act 1919 Sch 2; the Agricultural Holdings Act 1986 Sch 14 para 1; and the Agricultural Tenancies Act 1995 Schedule para 1(1), (3)).

14   Small Holdings and Allotments Act 1908 Sch 2 Pt I.

15   Small Holdings and Allotments Act 1908 Sch 2 Pt II(1).

16   Small Holdings and Allotments Act 1908 Sch 2 Pt II(2).

17   Small Holdings and Allotments Act 1908 Sch 2 Pt II(3).

18   Small Holdings and Allotments Act 1908 Sch 2 Pt II(4).

19   Small Holdings and Allotments Act 1908 Sch 2 Pt II(5).

20   Small Holdings and Allotments Act 1908 Sch 2 Pt II(6).

21   Small Holdings and Allotments Act 1908 Sch 2 Pt II(7).

22   Small Holdings and Allotments Act 1908 Sch 2 Pt II(8).

23   Small Holdings and Allotments Act 1908 Sch 2 Pt II(9).

24   Small Holdings and Allotments Act 1908 Sch 2 Pt II(10).

25   Small Holdings and Allotments Act 1908 Sch 2 Pt II(11).

26   Small Holdings and Allotments Act 1908 Sch 2 Pt II(12).

27   Small Holdings and Allotments Act 1908 Sch 2 Pt II(13).

28   Small Holdings and Allotments Act 1908 Sch 2 Pt II(14).

29   Small Holdings and Allotments Act 1908 Sch 2 Pt II(15).

30   Small Holdings and Allotments Act 1908 Sch 2 Pt II(16).

31   Small Holdings and Allotments Act 1908 Sch 2 Pt II(17).

32   Small Holdings and Allotments Act 1908 Sch 2 Pt II(18) (Sch 2 Pt II(18), (19) added by the Small Holdings and Allotments Act 1926 Sch 1).

33   Small Holdings and Allotments Act 1908 Sch 2 Pt II(19) (as added: see note 32).

34   Small Holdings and Allotments Act 1908 s 47(2) (as amended: see note 13).

(4) PROVISION OF ALLOTMENT SERVICES AND IMPROVEMENTS

721. General powers of management of allotment land.

A district council or, in Wales, a county or county borough council[1] may, where it considers it is necessary or expedient to do so for better carrying into effect the Small Holdings and Allotments Acts 1908 to 1931[2], manage any land acquired by the council under that legislation[3]. Further, the authority has power to execute improvements[4], sell, mortgage, let or exchange such land[5], appropriate allotment land for other purposes, and appropriate other land for use as allotments[6].

1   The Land Settlement (Facilities) Act 1919 s 12(1) refers to a 'district council' but this should be construed as a reference to the councils referred to in the text: see PARA 659 notes 1, 5.
2   As to the Small Holdings and Allotments Act 1908 to 1931 see PARA 627 note 3.
3   Land Settlement (Facilities) Act 1919 s 12(1)(d) (amended by the Local Government Act 1972 Sch 29 Pt II para 10). The exercise of this power is subject to the consent of the Secretary of State or the Welsh Ministers (Land Settlement (Facilities) Act 1919 s 12(1); Small Holdings and Allotments Regulations 1919, SR & O 1919/1197, reg 1(1)(1), (4), (8)), unless the power is being exercised by a county council in respect of land acquired under the Small Holdings and Allotments Act 1926 Pt I (ss 1–15) (acquisition of land for smallholdings: see PARA 629 et seq) (s 20(1)). As to the Secretary of State and the Welsh Ministers see PARA 741.
4   See the Land Settlement (Facilities) Act 1919 s 12(1)(a); and PARA 722.
5   See the Land Settlement (Facilities) Act 1919 s 12(1)(b); and PARA 693.
6   See the Land Settlement (Facilities) Act 1919 s 12(1)(c); and PARA 691.

722.   Improvement and adaptation of allotment land.

A district council or, in Wales, a county or county borough council[1] may, where it considers it is necessary or expedient to do so for the better carrying into effect of the Small Holdings and Allotments Acts 1908 to 1931[2], erect, repair or improve dwelling houses and other buildings on any land[3] acquired by it for the purposes of allotments[4], or execute any other improvement on or in connection with and for the benefit of any such land, or arrange with the tenant of any such land for the execution of any such improvement on such terms as may be agreed[5].

A district, parish, London borough or, in Wales, a community, county or county borough council[6] may improve any land acquired by it for allotments and adapt it for letting in allotments, by draining, fencing and dividing the land, acquiring approaches, making roads, and otherwise as it thinks fit[7]. Such a council may also from time to time do such things as may be necessary for maintaining such drains, fences, approaches and roads, or otherwise for maintaining the allotments in a proper condition[8]. It may also adapt the land for allotments by erecting buildings and adapting existing buildings, although not more than one dwelling house may be erected for occupation with any one allotment, and no dwelling house may be erected for occupation with an allotment of less than one acre[9].

1   The Land Settlement (Facilities) Act 1919 s 12(1) refers to a 'district council' but this should be construed as a reference to the councils referred to in the text: see PARA 659 notes 1, 5. As to the powers of local authorities in connection with the provision of allotments generally see PARA 659.
2   As to the Small Holdings and Allotments Act 1908 to 1931 see PARA 627 note 3.
3   As to the meaning of 'land' see PARA 424 note 5.
4   As to the acquisition of land for allotments see PARA 660 et seq. As to the meaning of 'allotment' see PARA 649.
5   Land Settlement (Facilities) Act 1919 s 12(1)(a) (amended by the Local Government Act 1972 Sch 29 Pt II para 10). The exercise of this power is subject to the consent of the Secretary of State or the Welsh Ministers (Land Settlement (Facilities) Act 1919 s 12(1); Small Holdings and Allotments Regulations 1919, SR & O 1919/1197, reg 1(1)(1), (4), (8)), unless the power is being exercised by a county council in respect of land acquired under the Small Holdings and Allotments Act 1926 Pt I (ss 1–15) (acquisition of land for smallholdings: see PARA 629 et seq) (s 20(1)). As to the Secretary of State and the Welsh Ministers see PARA 741.
6   The Small Holdings and Allotments Act 1908 s 26 refers to 'the council of any borough, urban district or parish' but should be construed as referring to the authorities mentioned in the text: see PARA 659 notes 1–5.
7   Small Holdings and Allotments Act 1908 s 26(1).
8   Small Holdings and Allotments Act 1908 s 26(1).

9   Small Holdings and Allotments Act 1908 s 26(2). The building power is permissive, and the
    council may validly enter into restrictive covenants preventing its exercising the power: *Stourcliffe
    Estate Co Ltd v Bournemouth Corpn* [1910] 2 Ch 12, CA. The exercise of a council's power to
    erect, repair or improve dwelling houses or other buildings may be subject to the consent of the
    Secretary of State or the Welsh Ministers: Small Holdings and Allotments Regulations 1919,
    SI 1919/1197, reg 1(1)(4).
        In general the provision of buildings or the making of any material change in the use of
    buildings on agricultural land requires planning permission (see the Town and Country Planning
    Act 1990 s 57; and PLANNING vol 81 (2010) PARAS 313–314), but certain development is
    allowed without any application for permission being made (see the Town and Country Planning
    (General Permitted Development) Order 1995, SI 1995/418, art 3, Sch 2 Pt 2 (Minor Operations),
    Pt 4 (Temporary Buildings and Uses), Pt 6 (Agricultural Buildings and Operations); and the Town
    and Country Planning (General Permitted Development) (England) Order2015, SI 2015/596, art
    3, Sch 2 Pt 2 (Minor Operations), Pt 4 (Temporary Buildings and Uses), Pt 6 (Agricultural and
    Forestry)); and PLANNING).

723. Power of authorities to provide common pasture and grazing rights.

Where it appears to the council of any London borough, district or parish or,
in Wales, any county, county borough or community[1] that, as regards its area,
land[2] can be acquired for affording common pasture at such price or rent that all
expenses incurred by the council in acquiring the land and otherwise in relation to
the land when acquired may reasonably be expected to be recouped out of charges
paid in respect of the land, and that the acquisition of such land is desirable in
view of the wants and circumstances of the population, the council may prepare
and carry into effect a scheme for providing such common pasture[3]. Rules may be
made regulating the turning out of animals and fixing the charges to be made for
each animal[4].

The council of any London borough, district or parish or, in Wales, any county,
county borough or community[5] may also[6] acquire land for the purpose of letting
to tenants of allotments grazing and other similar rights over the land acquired for
the allotments, and may acquire for that purpose stints and other alienable
common rights of grazing[7].

1   The Small Holdings and Allotments Act 1908 s 34 refers to 'the council of any borough, urban
    district or parish' but should be construed as referring to the authorities mentioned in the text: see
    PARA 659 notes 1–5. As to the powers of local authorities in connection with the provision of
    allotments generally see PARA 659.
2   As to the meaning of 'land' see PARA 424 note 5.
3   Small Holdings and Allotments Act 1908 s 34(1) (amended by the Land Settlement (Facilities) Act
    1919 Schs 2, 3; and the Local Government Act 1972 Sch 29 Pt II para 9(2)). Upon such a scheme
    being carried into effect the provisions of the Small Holdings and Allotments Act 1908 relating to
    allotments will, with the necessary modifications, apply in like manner as if 'allotments' in those
    provisions included common pasture, and 'rent' included a charge for turning out an animal: s
    34(2) (amended by the Local Government Act 1972 Sch 29 Pt II para 9(2)).
4   Small Holdings and Allotments Act 1908 s 34(2) (proviso).
5   The Small Holdings and Allotments Act 1908 s 42 refers initially only to 'a council', but in view
    of the subsequent reference to the powers to acquire land for the purposes of allotments this should
    be read as a reference to the councils empowered to acquire land for the purposes of that Act, that
    is to say, the councils referred to in the text.
6   Ie in pursuance of its powers to acquire land for allotments.
7   Small Holdings and Allotments Act 1908 s 42(1) (s 42(1), (2) amended by the Land Settlement
    (Facilities) Act 1919 Sch 2); Agriculture Act 1947 s 67(2). Any rights created or acquired by the
    council under the Small Holdings and Allotments Act 1908 s 42 are to be let to tenants of
    allotments in such manner and subject to such regulations as the council thinks expedient: s 42(2)
    (as so amended). As to the acquisition of common rights see COMPULSORY ACQUISITION OF LAND vol
    18 (2009) PARA 609. As to stinted pasture see COMMONS vol 13 (2017) PARA 317.

724. Provision by authorities of plants, fertilisers and implements.

Where in the opinion of a London borough, district, parish, or, in Wales, county, county borough or community council[1] there are inadequate facilities for the purchase or hire from a society on a co-operative basis of fruit trees, seeds, plants, fertilisers or implements required for the purposes of allotments[2] cultivated as gardens, whether provided by the council or otherwise, the council may purchase any of those articles and sell them to the cultivators or, in the case of implements, allow their use, at a price or charge sufficient to cover the cost of purchase[3].

1 The Land Settlement (Facilities) Act 1919 s 21(1) refers to 'the council of any borough, urban district or parish' but this should be construed as a reference to the councils referred to in the text: see PARA 659 notes 1–5. As to the local authorities which may be concerned with the provision of allotments generally see PARA 659.
2 As to the meaning of 'allotment' see PARA 649.
3 Land Settlement (Facilities) Act 1919 s 21(1), (2).

725. Use of schoolroom in connection with allotments.

Provision is made for certain schoolrooms, except while being used for educational purposes, to be used free of charge for the purposes of the Allotments Acts or, with the consent of any two managers or, as the case may be, governors, to be used for public meetings to discuss any question relating to allotments[1], subject to expenses and any damage being paid for by the council or persons calling the meeting[2].

Before any public meeting may be so held not less than six days' notice, signed by not less than six resident registered parliamentary electors[3] or council tax payers[4], must be given to the clerk of the local education authority or, in the case of a voluntary school, to one of the managers or governors[5]. If the room is not then available the clerk, manager or governor must write to one of the signatories, naming some other day when the room will be available[6].

1 As to the meaning of 'allotment' see PARA 649.
2 Small Holdings and Allotments Act 1908 s 35(1) (amended by the Local Government Act 1972 Sch 30). The Small Holdings and Allotments Act 1908 s 35(1) provides that any room in a county or voluntary primary or secondary school in respect of which a grant is made out of money provided by Parliament may be used for the purposes referred to in the text, and for references to governors to be substituted for references to managers where appropriate: s 35(1) (as so amended); Education Act 1944 ss 9, 120(1)(a), (c) (repealed). Provision for county and voluntary schools (voluntary schools being categorised as either controlled, aided or special agreement schools) continued to be made under the Education Act 1996 Pt II (ss 31–182) (see in particular ss 31, 32) until the repeal of those provisions by the School Standards and Framework Act 1998 s 140(3), Sch 31, and the introduction of a new framework for maintained schools under Pt II (ss 20–83), under which county schools were recategorised as community schools and voluntary schools were recategorised as voluntary controlled schools (if they were formerly controlled schools) or voluntary aided schools (if they were formerly aided or special agreement schools): see s 20, Sch 2 para 1; and EDUCATION vol 35 (2015) PARA 106 et seq. Provision was also made for the redesignation of grant-maintained schools which had formerly been county or voluntary schools: see Sch 2 para 3; and EDUCATION vol 35 (2015) PARA 106.
3 As to the registration of electors see ELECTIONS AND REFERENDUMS vol 37 (2013) PARA 112 et seq.
4 As to liability to council tax see LOCAL GOVERNMENT FINANCE vol 70 (2012) PARA 302 et seq.
5 Small Holdings and Allotments Act 1908 ss 23(2), 35(2)(a) (s 23(2) amended by the Local Government Finance Act 1992 Sch 13 para 4); Education Act 1944 ss 6, 120(1)(c), Sch 1 (repealed); and see note 2. Any notice required by the Small Holdings and Allotments Act 1908 to be given may be sent by registered post: s 61(5).
6 Small Holdings and Allotments Act 1908 s 35(2)(b).

726. Borrowing powers of authorities in connection with allotments.

The council of a London borough, district, parish, or, in Wales, county, county borough or community[1] may borrow for the purposes of acquiring, improving and adapting land[2] for allotments[3]. District, London borough, county and county borough councils[4] may borrow for the purposes of making grants to co-operative societies[5]. The Public Works Loan Commissioners may lend money to any local authority for any purpose for which the authority has power to borrow[6].

1   The Small Holdings and Allotments Act 1908 s 53(4) here refers to 'the council of a borough, urban district or parish' but this should be construed as a reference to the councils referred to in the text: see PARA 659 notes 1–5. As to the local authorities which may be concerned with the provision of allotments generally see PARA 659.

2   As to the meaning of 'land' see PARA 424 note 5.

3   Small Holdings and Allotments Act 1908 s 53(4) (amended by the Land Settlement (Facilities) Act 1919 Sch 2; and the London Government Order 1970, Schedule). As to the meaning of 'allotment' see PARA 649. As to local authority borrowing powers generally see the Local Government Act 2003 Pt 1 (ss 1–24); and LOCAL GOVERNMENT vol 69 (2009) PARA 1 et seq.

4   The Small Holdings and Allotments Act 1908 s 52(1) refers only to county councils, and s 53(4) refers to 'the council of a borough or urban district', but these should be construed as references to the councils referred to in the text: see PARA 659 notes 1–5.

5   Small Holdings and Allotments Act 1908 ss 52(1), 53(4) (s 52(1) amended by the Local Government Act 1929 Sch 12 Pt V; and the Local Government Act 1933 Sch 11 Pt IV; and repealed in its application to Greater London by the London Government Order 1970, SI 1970/211; Small Holdings and Allotments Act 1908 s 53(4) as amended (see note 3)). As to grants and advances to co-operative societies see PARA 755. The exercise of a council's powers to determine the period within which any money borrowed by it is to be repaid is subject to the consent of the Secretary of State or the Welsh Ministers: see the Small Holdings and Allotments Regulations 1919, SI 1919/1197, reg 1(1)(6).

6   See the National Loans Act 1968 s 3(11), Sch 4; and FINANCIAL INSTRUMENTS AND TRANSACTIONS vol 49 (2015) PARA 167 et seq.

(5) DISPOSAL AND CHANGE OF USE OF ALLOTMENT LAND

727. Appropriation by authorities of allotment land for other purposes.

A London borough, district, parish, or, in Wales, county, county borough or community council[1] may, where no power of appropriation is otherwise provided, appropriate for its other purposes land[2] acquired by it for allotments[3]. A district council or, in Wales, a county or county borough council[4] may, where it considers it is necessary or expedient to do so for the better carrying into effect of the applicable legislation[5] and where no power of appropriation is otherwise provided, appropriate for any of its other purposes land acquired by it under that legislation[6].

Certain local authorities[7] may be authorised, by order made by the authority and confirmed by the Secretary of State or the Welsh Ministers, to appropriate, for any purpose for which it can be authorised to acquire land[8] under any enactment[9], any land which is or forms part of a common, open space or fuel or field garden allotment[10] and is for the time being held by the council for other purposes[11]. Land so appropriated may be used in any manner in accordance with planning permission notwithstanding anything in any enactment relating to land of that kind[12].

1   The Land Settlement (Facilities) Act 1919 s 22(1) refers to 'the council of a borough, urban district or parish' but this should be construed as a reference to the councils referred to in the text: see

PARA 659 notes 1–5. As to the local authorities which may be concerned with the provision of allotments generally see PARA 659.

2   As to the meaning of 'land' see PARA 424 note 5.

3   Land Settlement (Facilities) Act 1919 s 22(1)(b) (amended by the Local Government, Planning and Land Act 1980 Sch 5 para 3, Sch 34 Pt V). As to the meaning of 'allotment' see PARA 649.

4   The Land Settlement (Facilities) Act 1919 s 12(1) refers to a 'district council' but this should be construed as a reference to the councils referred to in the text: see PARA 659 notes 1–5.

5   Ie the Allotments Acts 1908 to 1950, as to which see PARA 649 note 2.

6   Land Settlement (Facilities) Act 1919 s 12(1)(c)(ii) (amended by the Local Government Act 1972 Sch 29 Pt II para 10). The exercise of this power is subject to the consent of the Secretary of State or the Welsh Ministers (Land Settlement (Facilities) Act 1919 s 12(1) (as so amended); Small Holdings and Allotments Regulations 1919, SR & O 1919/1197, reg 1(1)(2), (8)), unless the power is being exercised by a county council in respect of land acquired under the Small Holdings and Allotments Act 1926 Pt I (ss 1–15) (acquisition of land for smallholdings: see PARA 629 et seq) (s 20(1)). The exercise of the power is also subject to such conditions as to the repayment of any loan made for the purpose of the acquisition of the land or otherwise as the Secretary of State or the Welsh Ministers may impose (Land Settlement (Facilities) Act 1919 s 12(1)(c) (as so amended)). As to the Secretary of State and the Welsh Ministers see PARA 741.

7   Ie the authorities which are local authorities for the purposes of the Town and Country Planning Act 1990: see s 336(1); and PLANNING vol 81 (2010) PARA 3.

8   For these purposes 'land' includes any corporeal hereditament, including a building, and, in relation to any acquisition of land under the Town and Country Planning Act 1990 Pt IX (ss 226–246) (see PLANNING vol 83 (2010) PARA 1112 et seq), includes any interest in or right over land: s 336(1).

9   'Enactment' includes an enactment in any local or private Act of Parliament, and an order, rule, regulation, byelaw or scheme made under an Act of Parliament: Town and Country Planning Act 1990 s 336(1).

10   'Fuel or field garden allotment' means any allotment set out as a fuel or field garden allotment under an Inclosure Act: Town and Country Planning Act 1990 s 336(1). The land which may come within this definition for these purposes includes any such land which is specially regulated by any enactment, whether public general or local or private, but not land which is Green Belt land within the meaning of the Green Belt (London and Home Counties) Act 1938: Town and Country Planning Act 1990 s 229(2). The Inclosure Acts are the Inclosure Acts 1845 to 1882, as to which see COMMONS vol 13 (2017) PARA 319 et seq. As to field garden allotments and fuel allotments generally see PARAS 651–652. As to the meaning of 'Green Belt land' for the purposes of the Green Belt (London and Home Counties) Act 1938 see s 2(1); and PLANNING vol 81 (2010) PARA 317.

11   Town and Country Planning Act 1990 s 229(1), (2); and see further PLANNING vol 83 (2010) PARA 1124. Where the appropriation is under the general statutory provisions relating to the appropriation of land by local authorities (ie the Local Government Act 1972 ss 122, 126), the total amount of land appropriated in any particular common, fuel or field garden allotment must not exceed in aggregate 250 square yards, notice of the proposed appropriation must be advertised and objections considered, and the appropriation will be subject to the rights of other persons in, over and in respect of the land: see ss 122(1), (2), (2A), 126(3), (4), (4A); and LOCAL GOVERNMENT vol 69 (2009) PARAS 513, 518.

12   See the Town and Country Planning Act 1990 ss 241(1)(b), 246(3); and PLANNING vol 83 (2010) PARA 1140.

728.   Sale or exchange by authorities of surplus allotment land.

Where a district, parish, London borough or, in Wales, a community, county or county borough council[1] is of the opinion that any land[2] acquired by it for allotments[3], or any part of any such land, is not needed for the purpose of allotments, or that more suitable land is available, it may sell[4] or let[5] the land[6], or exchange the land for more suitable land, and may pay or receive money for equality of exchange[7].

Where, however, a district, parish, London borough, community, county or county borough council[8] has purchased or appropriated land for allotments[9], it must not sell, appropriate, use or dispose of the land for any purpose other than for allotments without the consent of the Secretary of State or the Welsh Ministers[10].

1   The Small Holdings and Allotments Act 1908 s 32 refers to 'the council of any borough, urban district or parish' but should be construed as referring to the authorities mentioned in the text: see PARA 659 notes 1–5. As to the powers of local authorities in connection with the provision of allotments generally see PARA 659.

2   As to the meaning of 'land' see PARA 424 note 5.

3   As to the acquisition of land for allotments see PARA 660 et seq. As to the meaning of 'allotment' see PARA 649.

4   The proceeds of a sale of land acquired for allotments, and any money received by the council on any exchange by way of equality of exchange, must be applied in discharging, either by way of a sinking fund or otherwise, the debts and liabilities of the council in respect of the land acquired by it for allotments, or in acquiring, adapting, and improving other land for allotments, and any surplus remaining may be applied for any purpose for which capital money may be applied, and the interest thereon (if any) may be applied in acquiring other land for allotments, or must be applied in like manner as receipts from allotments under the Allotments Acts 1908 to 1950 are applicable: Small Holdings and Allotments Act 1908 s 32(2) (amended by the Local Government, Planning and Land Act 1980 Sch 5 para 1(b), Sch 34 Pt V). As to the Allotments Acts 1908 to 1950 see PARA 649 note 2.

5   Any money received from the letting of the land may be applied in acquiring other land for allotments, or must be applied in like manner as receipts from allotments under the Allotments Acts 1908 to 1950 are applicable: Small Holdings and Allotments Act 1908 s 32(2) (as amended: see note 4).

6   Ie otherwise than under the provisions of the Allotments Acts 1908 to 1950.

7   Small Holdings and Allotments Act 1908 s 32(1) (amended by the Local Government Act 1972 Sch 30). As to the application of the proceeds of an exchange see note 4. Acquisitions and disposals of land for the purposes of the provision of allotments generally require the approval of the Secretary of State or the Welsh Ministers: see the Small Holdings and Allotments Regulations 1919, SI 1919/1197, reg 1(1)(1). As to the Secretary of State and the Welsh Ministers see PARA 741. The power of sale under the Small Holdings and Allotments Act 1908 s 32 is of general application, and is not qualified by the narrower power to sell allotments under the Commons Act 1876 s 27 (see OPEN SPACES AND COUNTRYSIDE vol 78 (2010) PARA 551): *Snelling v Burstow Parish Council* [2013] EWCA Civ 1411, [2014] 1 WLR 2388, [2013] All ER (D) 126 (Nov).

8   The Allotments Act 1925 s 8 refers here to 'a local authority' but this should be construed as referring to the authorities empowered to purchase or appropriate land for use as allotments, ie those mentioned in the text: see PARA 659.

9   For the power to purchase or appropriate land for allotments see PARAS 662, 670, 691.

10 Allotments Act 1925 s 8 (amended by the Agricultural Land (Utilisation) Act 1931 Sch 2; the Statute Law (Repeals) Act 1993; and SI 1955/554). See also the Small Holdings and Allotments Regulations 1919, SI 1919/1197, reg 1(1)(1). Consent may be given unconditionally or subject to such conditions as the Secretary of State or the Welsh Ministers think fit, but may not be given unless the Secretary of State or the Welsh Ministers is or are satisfied that adequate provision will be made for allotment holders displaced by the action of the council or that such provision is unnecessary or not reasonably practicable: Allotments Act 1925 s 8 (as so amended). The matter of the making or otherwise of 'adequate provision' is determinable with reference to the reasonable needs of the displaced allotment holders and not to the standard of provision previously enjoyed: *R v Secretary of State for the Environment, ex p Gosforth Allotments and Gardens Association* (1996) 74 P & CR 93, [1996] 2 EGLR 117, CA.

729. Appropriation by authorities of field garden allotments for development or other planning purposes.

A district, London borough, or, in Wales, county or county borough council may, in the exercise of its powers to acquire land compulsorily for development or other planning purposes[1], appropriate, for any purpose for which it can be authorised to acquire land under any enactment, any land held by it for other purposes, being land which is or forms part of a field garden allotment[2]. In so far as a compulsory purchase or appropriation order authorises the purchase or appropriation of land forming part of a field garden allotment the order is subject to special parliamentary procedure[3] unless the Secretary of State or the Welsh Ministers[4] is or are satisfied that equivalent land has been or will be given in exchange, vested in the same persons and subject to the same rights, trusts and incidents, or that the land is required for the widening of an existing highway and that it is unnecessary to give other land in exchange, and certifies accordingly[5].

1 Ie under the Town and Country Planning Act 1990 s 226(1) (see PLANNING vol 83 (2010) PARA 1112).

2 See the Town and Country Planning Act 1990 s 226(1), (3); and PLANNING vol 83 (2010) PARA 1112. As to field garden allotments see PARA 651.

3 As to special parliamentary procedure see COMPULSORY ACQUISITION OF LAND vol 18 (2009) PARA 605.

4 As to the Secretary of State and the Welsh Ministers see PARA 741.

5 See the Acquisition of Land Act 1981 s 19; Town and Country Planning Act 1990 s 229(3); COMPULSORY ACQUISITION OF LAND vol 18 (2009) PARA 531; PLANNING vol 83 (2010) PARA 1124. Exchanges of land generally require the approval of the Secretary of State or the Welsh Ministers: see the Small Holdings and Allotments Regulations 1919, SI 1919/1197, reg 1(1)(1).

7. COTTAGE HOLDINGS

(1) COTTAGE HOLDINGS: INTRODUCTION

730. Meaning of 'cottage holding'.

'Cottage holding' means a holding comprising a dwelling house, together with not less than a quarter of an acre[1] and not more than one acre of agricultural[2] land which can be cultivated by the occupier of the dwelling house and his family[3].

1   The Agricultural Land (Utilisation) Act 1931 refers to 'forty perches'; however, the perch (30¼ square yards) is no longer recognised as a unit of area and the area 'one quarter of an acre' has accordingly been substituted.
2   As to the meaning of 'agriculture' see PARA 424 note 5.
3   Agricultural Land (Utilisation) Act 1931 s 20(1).

731. Cottage holdings before and after 1970.

Until 1 August 1970[1] cottage holdings could be acquired, bought, sold and let by county councils, county borough councils[2] and the Greater London Council[3], acting as cottage holding authorities[4]. Cottage holdings could be provided for sale or letting to any person who in the council's opinion was suitable and who satisfied the council that he would reside permanently in the dwelling house comprised in the holding, and that he had the intention, knowledge and capital to cultivate satisfactorily the land forming part of the holding[5], and detailed statutory provisions governed their disposition, management and use[6].

Since 1 August 1970 councils[7] have no longer been empowered to sell or let land as a cottage holding or acquire land for the purpose of being sold or let as a cottage holding[8]. The policy has accordingly been to allow existing cottage holdings, which are few in number, to run down and ultimately disappear, experience having shown that the cottage holding is not a viable agricultural unit and that in practice there has been a tendency for them to be confused, by local authorities as well as by occupiers, with smallholdings[9]. Accordingly, in this title the law relating to cottage holdings is treated in detail only where it remains of importance[10].

1   Ie the day on which the provisions of the Agriculture Act 1970 relating to cottage holdings (ie Pt III (ss 37–65)) were brought into force by the Agriculture Act 1970 (Commencement No 2) Order 1970, SI 1970/1048.
2   Owing to the cessation of the powers to provide cottage holdings in 1970 (see PARA 737), this is in effect a reference to the counties and county boroughs in England and Wales, and their councils, as they were constituted prior to the reorganisation of local authorities effected by the Local Government Act 1972. A county or county borough council had power to delegate its powers in this regard to a district council: Small Holdings and Allotments Act 1926 s 9 (amended by the Local Government Act 1972 Sch 30; and the Statute Law (Repeals) Act 1993); Agricultural Land (Utilisation) Act 1931 s 12(1) (amended by the Agriculture Act 1970 Sch 4).
3   The Greater London Council was abolished by the Local Government Act 1985 s 1; see LONDON GOVERNMENT vol 71 (2013) PARAS 5, 18.
4   See the Small Holdings and Allotments Act 1926 s 4 (repealed), and the Agricultural Land (Utilisation) Act 1931 s 12(1) (as amended: see note 2). A seller of land to a council for cottage holdings could sell the land to the council in consideration of a perpetual annuity payable by the council: see the Land Settlement (Facilities) Act 1919 s 9, Sch 1 (both as amended); and the Land Settlement (Annuities) Regulations 1919, SR & O 1919/1961 (as modified by SI 2003/1633).
5   See the Small Holdings and Allotments Act 1926 s 1 (repealed); and the Agricultural Land (Utilisation) Act 1931 s 12(1) (as amended: see note 2). As in the case of smallholdings, councils could make advances towards the purchase price of a cottage holding: Small Holdings and Allotments Act 1926 s 13(1) (amended by the Agricultural Land (Utilisation) Act 1931 Sch 2). The Small Holdings and Allotments Act 1926 s 5 (see PARA 732) and s 6 (see PARA 734) applied to a terminable annuity so charged on a holding so purchased as if the advance was the purchase

money: Small Holdings and Allotments Act 1926 s 13(2). Councils were also required to maintain a list of owners and occupiers of cottage holdings sold or let by them, and a map or plan showing the size, boundaries and situation of each holding (Small Holdings and Allotments Act 1926 s 10): to the extent that this requirement continues to have effect the councils likely to be affected by it are the successor bodies of the councils which were formerly empowered to provide cottage holdings, as to which see note 7.

6   These provisions were the Small Holdings and Allotments Acts 1908 to 1931 (as to which see PARA 627 note 3) as at the applicable time enacted. The provisions of the Small Holdings and Allotments Act 1908 to 1931 applicable to smallholdings before 1 October 1949 (ie the date on which the Agriculture Act 1947 Pt IV (ss 47–67) (which did not apply to cottage holdings (s 66(1) (repealed)) was brought into force by the Agriculture Act 1947 (Commencement) Order 1949, SI 1949/1201) apply to cottage holdings, with the further requirement that the owner or occupier should reside in the dwelling house: Agricultural Land (Utilisation) Act 1931 s 12(1) (as amended: see note 2), which has effect subject to the Agriculture Act 1970 s 60 (see PARA 737): Agricultural Land (Utilisation) Act 1931 s 12(1) (as so amended). Cottage holdings existing on 1 August 1970 continue to be subject to the specified statutory provisions.

7   The Agriculture Act 1970 s 60 refers to a county council, a county borough council or the Greater London Council, although in practice this should be read as a reference to the successor bodies of the councils referred to in the text (see the text and notes 2–3). The successor bodies of the English county and county borough councils are the English county councils, as to which see LOCAL GOVERNMENT vol 69 (2009) PARA 24 et seq. The successor bodies of the Welsh county and county borough councils are the newly constituted Welsh county and county borough councils, as to which see LOCAL GOVERNMENT vol 69 (2009) PARA 37 et seq. The principal successor bodies of the Greater London Council are the London boroughs and the Common Council of the City of London; see LONDON GOVERNMENT vol 71 (2013) PARAS 5, 18, 20 et seq, 34 et seq.

A county council in England may make arrangements with the council of any district in the county for the exercise, as agents for the county council, of any of its powers for the adaptation and management of cottage holdings for the district, and the district council may undertake to pay the whole or any part of the loss, if any, incurred in connection with such cottage holdings: Small Holdings and Allotments Act 1926 s 9 (amended by the Local Government Act 1972 Sch 30; and the Statute Law (Repeals) Act 1993). These arrangements did not authorise the exercise on behalf of a county council of the power of submitting proposals and estimates for the purpose of obtaining contributions: Small Holdings and Allotments Act 1926 s 9 (proviso). Although s 9 does not specifically limit its application to England, since district councils in Wales have been abolished (see the Local Government (Wales) Act 1994 s 20(6), (7) (as originally enacted)) and statutory references thereto replaced with references to county or county borough councils (s 17(1), (2), (4), (5)), there are now no authorities in Wales at the district council level to which the Welsh counties and county boroughs could delegate in pursuance of these powers; note also that although the successor bodies of the Greater London Council (ie, principally, the London boroughs and the Common Council of the City of London) have powers in relation to the management of cottage holdings they cannot enjoy the delegated powers set out in the text.

8   See the Agriculture Act 1970 s 60(1) (amended by the Local Government Act 1972 Sch 30; and the Local Government (Wales) Act 1994 s 66(6), Sch 16 para 38(3)); and PARA 737.

9   See the First Report of Wise Committee of Inquiry into Statutory Smallholdings (Cmnd 2936) paras 132, 133, 481, 482.

10   See PARAS 732–740.

(2) PROVISION AND OPERATION OF COTTAGE HOLDINGS

732. Consideration for sale of cottage holdings.

Where a council sold a cottage holding[1] the consideration had to be a terminable annuity equal to the full fair rent[2] of the holding for 60 years or, at the purchaser's option, a terminable annuity for a less period of an equivalent capital value[3]. The annuity is paid in equal half-yearly instalments, secured by a charge on the holding[4]. The council may postpone payment of all or part of the annuity for up to five years on account of capital expenditure by the purchaser which in the council's opinion increases the holding's value, but must do so on such terms as will, in its opinion, prevent the council from incurring any loss or increased loss[5].

1   As to the meaning of 'cottage holding' see PARA 730. As to the councils who could provide cottage holdings, and the successor bodies required to manage such holdings as continue to exist, see PARA 731.
2   Questions as to what was a full fair rent or as to the amount of the annuity were to be determined by the council: Small Holdings and Allotments Act 1926 s 5(5). As to the application of the Small Holdings and Allotments Act 1926 to cottage holdings see PARA 731 note 6.
3   Small Holdings and Allotments Act 1926 s 5(1). The Rentcharges Act 1977 ss 8–10 (see REAL PROPERTY AND REGISTRATION vol 87 (2017) PARAS 1097–1098), relating to the redemption of rentcharges, would apply to a terminable annuity under the Small Holdings and Allotments Act 1926 s 5(1) when charged on the holding.
4   Small Holdings and Allotments Act 1926 s 5(2).
5   Small Holdings and Allotments Act 1926 s 5(3).

733. Advances for maintenance of cottage holdings.

Councils may advance money to owners of cottage holdings[1] provided by them or purchased with their assistance[2] for the purpose of constructing, altering or adapting houses or farm buildings on the holding, and may guarantee advances, including interest, made for those purposes by a building, industrial or provident society to owners who are members of that society[3]. The council must be satisfied that the houses will be in all respects fit for human habitation, and that the houses and buildings will be necessary for the requirements of the cottage holdings[4]. The advance, which must be made after a valuation[5], must be secured by a mortgage not exceeding 90 per cent of the mortgagor's interest, and must provide for repayment by instalments or by an annuity, or, in the event of non-compliance with conditions, on demand[6]. It may be made by instalments during construction of up to 50 per cent of the value of the work done[7].

1   As to the meaning of 'cottage holding' see PARA 730. As to the councils who could provide cottage holdings, and the successor bodies required to manage such holdings as continue to exist, see PARA 731.
2   Councils could formerly provide assistance towards the purchase of cottage holdings: see the Small Holdings and Allotments Act 1926 s 13(1); and PARA 731 note 5.
3   Small Holdings and Allotments Act 1926 s 14(1) (amended by the Agricultural Land (Utilisation) Act 1931 Sch 2). As to the application of the Small Holdings and Allotments Act 1926 to cottage holdings see PARA 731 note 6. The making of advances and the fulfilling of guarantees (except of interest) are purposes for which the council may borrow: Small Holdings and Allotments Act 1926 s 14(4) (amended by the Local Government Act 1933 Sch 11 Pt IV; and SI 1970/211). Note that the exercise of a council's powers to determine the period within which any money borrowed by the council is to be repaid is subject to the consent of the Secretary of State or the Welsh Ministers: see the Small Holdings and Allotments Regulations 1919, SI 1919/1197, reg 1(1)(6). As to the Secretary of State and the Welsh Ministers see PARA 741.
4   Small Holdings and Allotments Act 1926 s 14(2).
5   Small Holdings and Allotments Act 1926 s 14(3)(c).
6   Small Holdings and Allotments Act 1926 s 14(3)(a).
7   Small Holdings and Allotments Act 1926 s 14(3)(b).

734. Conditions affecting cottage holdings sold by councils.

Land sold by a council for cottage holdings[1] was required to be sold, except where the relevant minister[2] otherwise directed, subject to a reservation of all minerals vested in the council[3]. Any cottage holding so sold was required to be held for a term of 40 years from the date of the sale and for so long thereafter as the holding remained charged with the terminable annuity, and had to be so held subject to the following conditions[4]:

(1)   that periodical payments under the annuity be duly made[5];

(2)   that the holding be not divided[6], sold, assigned, let or sublet without the council's consent[7];

(3)   that the holding be cultivated by the owner or occupier in accordance with the rules of good husbandry[8] and used for the purpose of agriculture only[9];

(4)   that not more than one dwelling house be erected on the holding[10] and the owner or occupier reside permanently in it[11];

(5)   that any dwelling house erected on the holding comply with council requirements as to health and overcrowding[12];

(6)   that any dwelling house or other building on the holding be kept in repair and insured against fire, with premium receipts to be produced to the council when required[13]; and

(7)   that no dwelling house or building on the holding be used for the sale of intoxicating liquors[14].

The council could relax or dispense with any of these conditions[15]. If any condition was broken the council could, after giving an opportunity of remedying the breach, take possession or order the sale of the holding without taking possession[16].

1   As to the meaning of 'cottage holding' see PARA 730. As to the councils who could provide cottage holdings, and the successor bodies required to manage such holdings as continue to exist, see PARA 731.

2   As to the various transfers of ministerial powers relating to cottage holdings and agricultural land generally see PARA 741.

3   Land Settlement (Facilities) Act 1919 s 11(1) (repealed). As to the application of the Land Settlement (Facilities) Act 1919 and the Small Holdings and Allotments Act 1926 to cottage holdings see PARA 731 note 6.

4   Small Holdings and Allotments Act 1926 s 6(1).

5   Small Holdings and Allotments Act 1926 s 6(1)(a).

6   If the holding, while subject to these conditions, would on the owner's decease become subdivided by reason of any devise, bequest, intestacy or otherwise, the council could require it to be sold within 12 months of the decease to some one person, and if default was made in so selling it, could either take possession, or order a sale without taking possession: Small Holdings and Allotments Act 1926 s 6(3).

7   Small Holdings and Allotments Act 1926 s 6(1)(b).

8   Ie as defined in the Agricultural Holdings Act 1923 s 57 (repealed); see now the Agriculture Act 1947 s 11; and AGRICULTURAL PRODUCTION AND MARKETING vol 1A (2017) PARA 12.

9   Small Holdings and Allotments Act 1926 s 6(1)(c).

10 Unless, in the opinion of the council, additional accommodation is required for the proper cultivation of the holding: Small Holdings and Allotments Act 1926 s 6(1)(d).

11 Agricultural Land (Utilisation) Act 1931 s 12(1)(a).

12 Small Holdings and Allotments Act 1926 s 6(1)(e).

13 Small Holdings and Allotments Act 1926 s 6(1)(f).

14 Small Holdings and Allotments Act 1926 s 6(1)(g).

15 Small Holdings and Allotments Act 1926 s 6(1) proviso. Where a contribution is payable by the minister he could consent to any relaxation or dispensation and, in giving consent, could impose terms as to the consideration to be charged and its application in satisfaction of his contributions: s 6(1) proviso.

16 Small Holdings and Allotments Act 1926 s 6(2). As to sales without taking possession see PARA 739.

735. Assistance to cottage holdings.

Councils providing cottage holdings[1] have all the powers of promoting and assisting co-operative associations that they formerly possessed in respect of smallholdings[2].

1 As to the meaning of 'cottage holding' see PARA 730. As to the councils who could provide cottage holdings, and the successor bodies required to manage such holdings as continue to exist, see PARA 731.
2 See the Agricultural Land (Utilisation) Act 1931 s 12(1) (amended by the Agriculture Act 1970 Sch 4). As to these powers (expressed as exercised in relation to allotments) see the Small Holdings and Allotments Act 1908 s 49; and PARA 755.

(3) SUBSEQUENT TRANSACTIONS INVOLVING COTTAGE HOLDINGS LAND

736. Letting of cottage holdings land.

Because a cottage holding let by a council[1] is generally held subject to the same conditions under which it would be held if it were sold[2], and because these conditions are consistent only with the use of the land as a cottage holding, land used for cottage holdings cannot be let for any purpose, although a council may appropriate the land for some purpose other than cottage holdings[3], and then let the land.

1 As to the meaning of 'cottage holding' see PARA 730. As to the councils who could provide cottage holdings, and the successor bodies required to manage such holdings as continue to exist, see PARA 731. No land could be let as a cottage holding by a letting effected by a council after 1 August 1970, whether the land was previously so let or not (although land let by a council as a cottage holding before that date continues to be so let): Agriculture Act 1970 s 60(1)(a), (b) (as originally enacted).
2 Small Holdings and Allotments Act 1926 s 6(4). As to the application of the Small Holdings and Allotments Act 1926 to cottage holdings see PARA 731 note 6. As to the conditions of letting see PARA 734.
3 See the Local Government Act 1972 ss 122, 126; and LOCAL GOVERNMENT vol 69 (2009) PARAS 513, 518.

737. Sale of cottage holding land.

Although it has not been permitted since 1 August 1970 for land to be sold by a council as a cottage holding[1] this does not mean that cottage holdings land[2] cannot be sold; any such sale must, however, be for some purpose other than the use of the land for cottage holdings.

Where any cottage holdings land is sold, exchanged or appropriated for other purposes by a council[3] to which contributions are payable in respect of cottage holdings land[4], the council must forthwith after completion of the sale, exchange or appropriation furnish particulars thereof to the Secretary of State or the Welsh Ministers[5] in a prescribed form of statement[6] signed by the treasurer, accountant or other authorised council officer[7]. The Secretary of State or the Welsh Ministers may adjust, in such manner as he or they think fit having regard to any such particulars, the amount or aggregate amount of any contributions payable to the council in relation to cottage holdings land in a case where the land sold, exchanged or appropriated is land which has been, or formed part of, land in respect of which contributions have been made or undertaken to be made[8] in connection with proposals and estimates relating to that land[9]. The council must also furnish any other particulars which the Secretary of State or the Welsh

Ministers may require at any time for the purpose of satisfying him or it that contributions payable to it should continue to be paid[10].

If a council does not comply with the statutory requirements[11] in relation to land held by it for the purpose of cottage holdings the Secretary of State or the Welsh Ministers may determine that contributions which would otherwise be payable to him or them should be withheld or reduced, whereupon the Secretary of State or the Welsh Ministers must withhold or reduce them accordingly[12]. Any person authorised by the Secretary of State or the Welsh Ministers may at all reasonable times inspect the council's books and other documents relating to transactions in connection with which any contributions are payable to the council[13].

1   See PARA 731. As to the meaning of 'cottage holding' see PARA 730.
2   'Cottage holdings land' means land held by a county or county borough council or the Greater London Council immediately before 1 August 1970 for the purposes of cottage holdings: Smallholdings (Contributions Towards Losses) Regulations 1970, SI 1970/1051, reg 2(2) (amended by SI 1974/396); Agriculture Act 1970 (Commencement No 2) Order 1970, SI 1970/1048. The Smallholdings (Contributions Towards Losses) Regulations 1970, SI 1970/1051, are applied in relation to cottage holdings by the Agriculture Act 1970 s 60(2)–(4) (s 60(2) amended by SI 1974/396).
3   As to this power see the Local Government Act 1972 ss 122, 126; and LOCAL GOVERNMENT vol 69 (2009) PARAS 513, 518.
4   The Smallholdings (Contributions Towards Losses) Regulations 1970, SI 1970/1051, regs 4–8 do not apply to a council to which no contributions are payable in respect of cottage holdings land, and cease to apply to it when contributions cease to be payable to it: reg 9.
5   As to the Secretary of State and the Welsh Ministers see PARA 741.
6   See the Smallholdings (Contributions Towards Losses) Regulations 1970, SI 1970/1051, reg 5, Sch 2; and see notes 2, 4.
7   Smallholdings (Contributions Towards Losses) Regulations 1970, SI 1970/1051, reg 5(1); and see note 4.
8   Ie under the Small Holdings and Allotments Act 1926 s 2, as applied to cottage holdings by s 12 (repealed) or by the Agricultural Land (Utilisation) Act 1931 s 12: Smallholdings (Contributions Towards Losses) Regulations 1970, SI 1970/1051, regs 3(2), 5(2)(b). See also note 4.
9   Smallholdings (Contributions Towards Losses) Regulations 1970, SI 1970/1051, reg 5(1); and see note 4.
10   Smallholdings (Contributions Towards Losses) Regulations 1970, SI 1970/1051, reg 6; and see note 4.
11   Ie the requirements of the Agriculture Act 1970 Pt III (ss 37–65).
12   Smallholdings (Contributions Towards Losses) Regulations 1970, SI 1970/1051, reg 7; and see note 4.
13   Smallholdings (Contributions Towards Losses) Regulations 1970, SI 1970/1051, reg 8; and see note 4.

738.   Council taking possession of a cottage holding.

Where a council[1], either on breach of any condition[2] or on the decease of an owner[3], takes possession of a cottage holding, it vests in the council, which may either retain it under the council's own management or sell or otherwise dispose of it[4]. However, where it takes possession, the council must pay the owner either an agreed sum[5] or the value[6] of the interest in the holding less the redemption value of the annuity[7] and any arrears of annuity then due[8]. The costs incidental to taking possession or disposing of the holding[9] are deducted from the sum payable to the owners[10]. If the value of the holding, ascertained as mentioned above, proves to be less than the redemption value together with any arrears of the annuity, the council may recover the deficiency summarily from the owner as a civil debt[11].

1 As to the councils who could provide cottage holdings, and the successor bodies required to manage such holdings as continue to exist, see PARA 731. As to the meaning of 'cottage holding' see PARA 730.
2 See PARA 734.
3 See PARA 734 note 6.
4 Small Holdings and Allotments Act 1926 s 7(1). As to the application of the Small Holdings and Allotments Act 1926 to cottage holdings see PARA 731 note 6. As to the procedure on sale without taking possession see PARA 739; as to sales generally see PARA 737.
5 Small Holdings and Allotments Act 1926 s 7(2)(a).
6 In the absence of sale and in default of agreement the value must be settled by an arbitrator under the arbitration provisions of the Agricultural Holdings Act 1986 (see PARA 566 et seq): Small Holdings and Allotments Act 1926 s 7(2)(b).
7 Ie the amount at which the annuity may be redeemed under the Law of Property Act 1925 s 191 (repealed: see now the Rentcharges Act 1977 ss 8–10; and REAL PROPERTY AND REGISTRATION vol 87 (2017) PARAS 1097–1098).
8 Small Holdings and Allotments Act 1926 s 7(2)(b).
9 These include the costs of any arbitration: see note 6.
10 Small Holdings and Allotments Act 1926 s 7(4). The sum payable carries interest at 5% per annum from the date of taking possession if not paid within three months after that date: Small Holdings and Allotments Act 1926 s 7(3).
11 Small Holdings and Allotments Act 1926 s 7(6). As to the recovery of civil debts see the Magistrates' Courts Act 1980 s 58; and MAGISTRATES vol 71 (2013) PARA 625.

739. Council ordering sale without taking possession of a cottage holding.

Where a council orders the sale of a cottage holding without taking possession[1] it must cause the holding to be put up for auction[2]. The sale by auction may be made either subject to the charge in respect of the terminable annuity[3], or free, wholly or partly, from that charge[4]. In either case, the purchase money to be paid by the purchaser on the auction is subject to the same provisions as purchase money payable on the first sale of a holding[5]. The council must retain out of the proceeds of sale a sum equal to the redemption value of any annuity charged on the holding, unless the holding is sold subject to the terminable annuity, together with any arrears of the annuity and all costs, the balance being paid to the owner[6]. If, however, the council is unable to sell the holding for such sum as will reimburse it for the aforementioned amounts, it may take possession without being liable to pay the owner anything, and with the right to recover summarily from him, as a civil debt, the amount of the deficiency[7].

1 As to the meaning of 'cottage holding' see PARA 730. As to the councils who could provide cottage holdings, and the successor bodies required to manage such holdings as continue to exist, see PARA 731. The council cannot sell the land as a cottage holding and it must therefore be sold for other purposes: see PARA 737.
2 Small Holdings and Allotments Act 1926 s 8(1). As to the application of the Small Holdings and Allotments Act 1926 to cottage holdings see PARA 731 note 6.
3 As to the terminable annuity see PARA 732.
4 Small Holdings and Allotments Act 1926 s 8(3).
5 Small Holdings and Allotments Act 1926 s 8(3). As to the provisions referred to see PARA 732.
6 Small Holdings and Allotments Act 1926 s 8(1).
7 Small Holdings and Allotments Act 1926 s 8(2). As to the recovery of civil debts see the Magistrates' Courts Act 1980 s 58; and MAGISTRATES vol 71 (2013) PARA 625.

740. Compensation for improvements and right of removal of fixtures in case of cottage holdings.

A tenant to whom a cottage holding[1] has been let[2] has against the council[3] the same right to compensation for specified improvements[4] as he would have had if the holding had been a market garden[5]. He is not, however, entitled to compensation for improvements executed contrary to an express written prohibition by the council[6]. If the tenant feels aggrieved by such a prohibition he may appeal to the Secretary of State or the Welsh Ministers[7], who may confirm, vary or annul the prohibition: in this respect the Secretary of State's or the Welsh Ministers' decision is final[8].

A tenant may, before the expiration of his tenancy, remove any fruit and other trees and bushes planted or acquired by him for which he has no claim for compensation, and may remove any toolshed, greenhouse, fowlhouse or pigsty built or acquired by him for which he has no such claim[9].

If the cottage holding is an agricultural holding[10] he may claim compensation for improvements and remove buildings and fixtures in accordance with the Agricultural Holdings Act 1986[11].

1   As to the meaning of 'cottage holding' see PARA 730.
2   Land can no longer be let as a cottage holding, although existing lettings may continue in effect: see PARAS 731, 736.
3   As to the councils who could provide cottage holdings, and the successor bodies required to manage such holdings as continue to exist, see PARA 731.
4   Ie the planting of standard or other fruit trees permanently set out, fruit bushes permanently set out, strawberry plants, and asparagus, rhubarb and other vegetable crops which continue productive for two or more years: Small Holdings and Allotments Act 1908 s 47, Sch 2 Pt I. As to the application of the Small Holdings and Allotments Act 1908, the Small Holdings and Allotments Act 1926 and the Agricultural Land (Utilisation) Act 1931 to cottage holdings see PARA 731 note 6. It should be noted that the amendments made to the cited provisions by the Agricultural Tenancies Act 1995, under which farm business tenancies are created, are not relevant to cottage holdings: new cottage holdings could not be granted after 1970, whereas farm business tenancies could not be created before 1995.
5   Small Holdings and Allotments Act 1908 s 47(1). For a market garden tenant's right to compensation for improvements see PARAS 561–565.
6   Small Holdings and Allotments Act 1908 s 47(1) proviso (amended by the Local Government, Planning and Land Act 1980 Sch 5 para 1(c)).
7   As to the Secretary of State and the Welsh Ministers see PARA 741.
8   Agricultural Land (Utilisation) Act 1931 s 12(1A) (added by the Local Government, Planning and Land Act 1980 Sch 33 para 2).
9   Small Holdings and Allotments Act 1908 s 47(4).
10 Ie within the meaning of the Agricultural Holdings Act 1986 (as to which see PARA 423).
11 See PARAS 436, 561–565.

8. ADMINISTRATION AND AUTHORITIES

(1) THE SECRETARY OF STATE AND THE WELSH MINISTERS

741. Ministerial powers and functions in respect of agricultural land.

Powers and functions in respect of agricultural land in England (including smallholdings, allotments and, to the extent that they still exist, cottage holdings) are exercised primarily by the Secretary of State[1] or, in Wales, by the Welsh Ministers[2].

1 In any enactment, 'Secretary of State' means one of Her Majesty's principal secretaries of state: see the Interpretation Act 1978 s 5, Sch 1.
2 Statutory functions relating to agricultural land so far as exercisable in relation to Wales, are now almost exclusively the responsibility of the Welsh Ministers following the establishment of the Welsh Assembly Government under the Government of Wales Act 2006. The Welsh Assembly Government was renamed the Welsh Government / Llywodraeth Cymru by the Wales Act 2014.

742. Acquisition and management of agricultural land by Secretary of State and Welsh Ministers.

The Secretary of State and the Welsh Ministers[1] have power to acquire by agreement[2]:

(1)   any land used for agriculture[3];

(2)   any other agricultural land[4];

(3)   where any such land is offered to the Secretary of State or the Welsh Ministers for acquisition on the condition that he or they also acquire other land not falling within the above categories, that other land[5]; and

(4)   any land as respects which compulsory purchase powers are by the Agriculture Act 1947 vested in the Secretary of State or the Welsh Ministers[6].

The general powers of the Secretary of State and the Welsh Ministers to acquire and manage land[7] include power to acquire, hold or dispose of land for the purpose of effecting amalgamations[8] of agricultural land and reshaping of agricultural units[9], and for those purposes to enter into transactions involving loss[10]. The Secretary of State and the Welsh Ministers also have power to acquire by agreement any land which in their opinion is required for the purposes of smallholdings[11]. Certain authorities may enter into management arrangements with persons having interests in land which may, inter alia, restrict agricultural operations on the land[12].

Land acquired by the Secretary of State and the Welsh Ministers may be managed, farmed, sold, let or otherwise disposed of by them either in such manner as they consider expedient for the purpose for which the land was acquired[13] or, if they are satisfied that the land ought to be devoted to some other purpose, then in such manner as they consider expedient for that purpose[14]. The powers of the Secretary of State and the Welsh Ministers are subject to any statutory restriction, and no such land may be sold unless, having regard to the use proposed for the land, it appears to the Secretary of State or the Welsh Ministers expedient that it should be sold[15]. In managing the land the Secretary of State and the Welsh Ministers may provide for the welfare of tenants or others employed in agriculture on the land[16].

1 As to the Secretary of State and the Welsh Ministers see PARA 741.

2 When in pursuance of the powers conferred by the Agriculture Act 1947 s 82 (see the text and notes 3–6) the Secretary of State or the Welsh Ministers purchase land in pursuance of the powers under the Ecclesiastical Leasing Acts, the consent of the patron is not required: s 82(2). The 'Ecclesiastical Leasing Acts' are the Ecclesiastical Leasing Acts 1842 and 1858 (which, by the Endowments and Glebe Measure 1976 s 47(3), Sch 7, no longer apply to incumbents). As to the provisions of the Ecclesiastical Leasing Act 1858 s 1 regarding sales with the consent of the patron see ECCLESIASTICAL LAW vol 34 (2011) PARAS 927, 929.

3 Agriculture Act 1947 s 82(1)(a). As to the meaning of 'agriculture' see PARA 424.

4 Agriculture Act 1947 s 82(1)(b). As to the meaning of 'agricultural land' see PARA 424.

5 Agriculture Act 1947 s 82(1)(c).

6 Agriculture Act 1947 s 82(1)(d). As to the compulsory acquisition of agricultural land generally see PARAS 590–596.

7 Ie the powers of the Secretary of State and the Welsh Ministers under the Agriculture Act 1947 ss 82, 90 (see the text and notes 1–6, 8–16).

8 As to amalgamations see AGRICULTURAL PRODUCTION AND MARKETING vol 1A (2017) PARA 416 et seq.

9 As to the meaning of 'agricultural unit' see PARA 424 note 7.

10 See the Agriculture Act 1967 s 29(1), (2); and AGRICULTURAL PRODUCTION AND MARKETING vol 1A (2017) PARA 420.

11 See the Agriculture Act 1970 s 55; and PARA 629.

12 See the Wildlife and Countryside Act 1981 s 39; and OPEN SPACES AND COUNTRYSIDE vol 78 (2010) PARA 763.

13 Agriculture Act 1947 s 90(1)(a).

14 Agriculture Act 1947 s 90(1)(b).

15 Agriculture Act 1947 s 90(1) proviso.

16 Agriculture Act 1947 s 90(2).

743. Powers of entry and inspection for purposes of acquisition and management available to Secretary of State and Welsh Ministers.

For the purpose of determining whether the powers to acquire and manage land conferred by the Agriculture Act 1947[1] are to be exercised in relation to land, or whether any direction given under any such power has been complied with, any person authorised by the Secretary of State or the Welsh Ministers[2] has power at all reasonable times to enter on and inspect any land[3]. In the case of land which the Secretary of State or the Welsh Ministers may consider acquiring[4], or which is used for residential purposes, 24 hours' notice must be given to the occupier[5]. In all other cases notice must be given to the occupier that it is proposed to enter during a specified period, not exceeding 14 days and beginning at least 24 hours after the giving of the notice, and the entry must take place during that period[6]. The authorised person may be required to produce documentary proof of his authority[7]. Obstructing the exercise of these powers is an offence[8].

1 The powers relevant to this title are the powers under the Agriculture Act 1947 ss 82, 90 (see PARA 742).

2 As to the Secretary of State and the Welsh Ministers see PARA 741.

3 Agriculture Act 1947 s 106(1).

4 The only extant powers of acquisition to which these provisions apply are those in the Agriculture Act 1947 s 82 (see PARA 742).

5 Agriculture Act 1947 s 106(3). For these purposes, 'occupier' in relation to unoccupied land means the person entitled to occupy it: Pests Act 1954 s 1(13).

6 Agriculture Act 1947 s 106(4) (amended by the Agriculture Act 1958 Sch 2 Pt I). Any notice or other document required or authorised by or under the Agriculture Act 1947 to be given to or served on any person is duly given or served if it is delivered to him, or left at his proper address, or sent to him by post in a registered letter, and any such document required or authorised to be given to or served on an incorporated company or body is duly given or served if given to or served on the secretary or clerk of the company or body: s 107(1), (2). For these purposes the proper address of any person to or on whom any such document is to be given or served is, in the case of the secretary or clerk of any incorporated company or body, that of the registered or principal

office of the company or body, and in any other case is the last known address of the person in question: s 107(3). Where any document is to be given to or served on a person as being the person having any interest in land, and it is not practicable after reasonable inquiry to ascertain his name or address, the document may be given or served by addressing it to him by the description of the person having that interest in the land (naming it), and delivering the document to some responsible person on the land or by affixing it, or a copy of it, to some conspicuous object on the land: s 107(4). Where any such document or notice is to be given or served on any person as being the owner of the land and the land is vested in the incumbent of a benefice of the Church of England, a copy must be served on the Diocesan Board of Finance for the diocese in which the land is situated (s 107(5) (amended by the Church of England (Miscellaneous Provisions) Measure 2006 s 14, Sch 5 para 2)).

7   Agriculture Act 1947 s 106(2) (amended by the Agriculture Act 1970 Sch 5 Pt III).
8   See the Agriculture Act 1947 s 106(7) (amended by the Pests Act 1954 s 5(1), SI 2013/1035). The penalty on summary conviction is a fine not exceeding level 2 on the standard scale: Agriculture Act 1947 s 106(7) (amended by virtue of the Criminal Justice Act 1982 ss 35, 46). As to the standard scale and the powers of magistrates' courts to issue fines on summary conviction see SENTENCING vol 92 (2015) PARA 176.

744. Powers of Secretary of State and Welsh Ministers concerning smallholdings land.

The Secretary of State and the Welsh Ministers[1] may designate any land vested in them as being land held for the purposes of smallholdings[2], and may at any time revoke such a designation[3]. In relation to land held by them for the purposes of smallholdings, the Secretary of State and the Welsh Ministers have powers and duties with regard to the letting, equipping and managing of smallholdings, and the letting of surplus land, corresponding to those of smallholdings authorities[4].

The Secretary of State and the Welsh Ministers also have power to:

(1)   approve reorganisation proposals[5];
(2)   acquire smallholdings land[6];
(3)   make regulations for any purpose for which regulations are authorised or required to be made relating to smallholdings[7];
(4)   exercise control over the selection of tenants by making regulations[8];
(5)   make loans in respect of smallholdings[9];
(6)   increase the amount of certain capital grants[10];
(7)   act in default of smallholdings authorities[11],

and must make an annual report[12].

1   As to the Secretary of State and the Welsh Ministers see PARA 741.
2   As to the meaning of 'smallholding' and the purposes of smallholdings see PARA 627.
3   See the Agriculture Act 1970 s 54(7); and PARA 629.
4   Agriculture Act 1970 s 54(1), (2). As to these powers and duties see ss 44–47, 49(1), (2). As to smallholdings authorities see PARAS 748–751.
5   See the Agriculture Act 1970 ss 41–43; and PARA 640 et seq.
6   See the Agriculture Act 1970 s 55; and PARA 629.
7   Agriculture Act 1970 s 63.
8   See the Agriculture Act 1970 s 44(6); and PARA 635.
9   See the Agriculture Act 1970 s 54(5), (6); and PARA 647.
10 See the Agriculture Act 1970 s 51; and PARA 648.
11 See the Agriculture Act 1970 s 56; and PARA 745.
12 Agriculture Act 1970 s 59(2).

745. Default powers of Secretary of State and Welsh Ministers over smallholdings authorities.

Where the Secretary of State or the Welsh Ministers[1] is or are satisfied that a smallholdings authority[2] is not satisfactorily exercising its functions[3] they may:

(1)   direct the authority to exercise its functions in such manner as is specified in the direction[4]; or

(2)   by order transfer all or any of its functions to the Secretary of State or the Welsh Ministers[5].

Where any functions of a smallholdings authority have been transferred to the Secretary of State or the Welsh Ministers[6], and any property has been acquired or any liabilities have been incurred in the performance of those functions while so transferred, any order varying or revoking that order[7] may contain such provisions with respect to the transfer, vesting or discharge of any such property or liabilities as appear to the Secretary of State or the Welsh Ministers to be expedient in the circumstances[8].

1   As to the Secretary of State and the Welsh Ministers see PARA 741.
2   As to smallholdings authorities see PARAS 748–751.
3   As to the meaning of 'functions' see PARA 641 note 11.
4   Agriculture Act 1970 s 56(1)(a). This power is without prejudice to any other power to give directions under Pt III (ss 37–65): s 56(6).
5   Agriculture Act 1970 s 56(1)(b), (2). Before the Secretary of State or the Welsh Ministers make an order under s 56(1)(b) they must give the authority an opportunity of making representations, which they must consider, and if the authority so requires must afford it the opportunity of being heard by a person appointed for the purpose: s 56(3)(a).
      The performance by the Secretary of State or the Welsh Ministers of functions so transferred has effect as if the Secretary of State or the Welsh Ministers were the authority's duly authorised agent, except that any expenses incurred by the Secretary of State or the Welsh Ministers in the performance of those functions must be defrayed in the first instance by them: s 56(4)(a). The Secretary of State or the Welsh Ministers must certify, in respect of such successive periods as they may determine, the amount of the expenses so incurred in each such period and the amount of any receipts in each such period from the performance of those functions, and the difference between those amounts, as certified by the Secretary of State or the Welsh Ministers, is recoverable by them from the smallholdings authority or payable by them to the authority, as the case may require: s 56(4)(b).
6   Ie by an order in accordance with the Agriculture Act 1970 s 56(1)(b) (see note 5).
7   Power to make such an order may be inferred from the Agriculture Act 1970 s 56(5); the Act contains no such explicit power.
8   Agriculture Act 1970 s 56(5). Before coming to a decision on an application by a smallholdings authority to revoke an order transferring its functions, being an application made no earlier than 12 months after the making of the order or of any previous application, the Secretary of State or the Welsh Ministers must give the authority an opportunity of making representations to them, which they must consider, and if the authority so requires must afford it the opportunity of being heard by a person appointed for the purpose: s 56(3)(b).

746. Powers of Secretary of State and Welsh Ministers concerning allotments land.

The Secretary of State and the Welsh Ministers[1] may, on the application of the trustees, or other persons interested, authorise the exchange of allotments held for the benefit of poor inhabitants, or for any other public or parochial purpose, for other more suitable lands[2]. A fuel allotment[3], notwithstanding the restriction on user otherwise than in accordance with the Act or award under which it was set out, may in certain circumstances be otherwise used[4] and may be the subject of compulsory acquisition and appropriation in the same way as field garden allotments[5]. The Secretary of State and the Welsh Ministers may also authorise a local authority to purchase land compulsorily for allotments[6] and may make grants to allotment societies[7].

1   As to the Secretary of State and the Welsh Ministers see PARA 741.
2   See the Inclosure Act 1845 s 149; PARA 695; and OPEN SPACES AND COUNTRYSIDE vol 78 (2010) PARA 551.
3   As to the meaning of 'fuel or field garden allotment' see PARA 727 note 10.
4   See the Town and Country Planning Act 1990 s 241(1); PARA 695; PLANNING vol 83 (2010) PARA 1140.

5   See the Town and Country Planning Act 1990 ss 226(3), (8), 229(1)–(3); and PLANNING vol 83 (2010) PARAS 1112, 1124.

6   See the Small Holdings and Allotments Act 1908 s 39(1); and PARA 670.

7   See the Small Holdings and Allotments Act 1908 s 49(4); and PARA 755.

747. Inquiries by Secretary of State and Welsh Ministers concerning allotments.

The Secretary of State and the Welsh Ministers[1], and their officers, have the same powers for the purposes of an inquiry under the Allotments Acts[2] as they have for the purposes of an inquiry under the Public Health Acts[3]. Notices of the inquiries must be given and published in accordance with such general or special directions as the Secretary of State or the Welsh Ministers may give[4].

1   As to the Secretary of State and the Welsh Ministers see PARA 741.

2   Ie the Allotments Acts 1908 to 1950: see PARA 649 note 2.

3   Small Holdings and Allotments Act 1908 s 57(1) (amended by the Small Holdings and Allotments Act 1926 Sch 2). As to the Public Health Acts see ENVIRONMENTAL QUALITY AND PUBLIC HEALTH vol 45 (2010) PARAS 1–2.

4   Small Holdings and Allotments Act 1908 s 57(2).

(2) SMALLHOLDINGS AUTHORITIES

748. Designation and aim of smallholdings authorities.

County councils in England, and county or county borough councils in Wales, are the smallholdings authorities[1]. Smallholdings authorities must make it their general aim, having regard to the general interests of agriculture[2] and of good estate management[3], to provide opportunities for persons to be farmers on their own account by letting holdings limited in size so as to provide full-time employment for not more than the occupier and one other person, to persons satisfying certain requirements[4].

1   Agriculture Act 1970 s 38(b), (bb) (s 38(b) amended, s 38(bb) added, by the Local Government (Wales) Act 1994 Sch 16 para 38(1), Sch 18). As to the English counties and their councils see LOCAL GOVERNMENT vol 69 (2009) PARA 24 et seq; as to the counties and county boroughs in Wales and their councils see LOCAL GOVERNMENT vol 69 (2009) PARA 37 et seq. As to the meaning of 'smallholding' see PARA 627.

2   As to the meaning of 'agriculture' see PARA 424.

3   As to the principles of good estate management see PARA 445; and AGRICULTURAL PRODUCTION AND MARKETING vol 1A (2017) PARAS 11, 13.

4   Agriculture Act 1970 ss 39(1), (2), 41(4); see further PARAS 633–635.

749. Records and plans of smallholdings.

Every smallholdings authority[1] must compile and keep, and, if so required by a person authorised by the Secretary of State or the Welsh Ministers[2], as the case may be, must produce to him a record of all land which is or has at any time been held by the authority for the purposes of smallholdings[3], of the occupiers[4] of such of the land as is let by it as smallholdings and of the rents, and of the purchasers of so much of the land as it has sold[5], and a map or plan showing the size, boundaries and situation of each smallholding it provides[6].

1   As to smallholdings authorities see PARAS 748–751.

2   As to the Secretary of State and the Welsh Ministers see PARA 741.

3   As to the meaning of 'smallholding' and the purposes of smallholdings see PARA 627.

4   As to the 'occupier of land' for these purposes see PARA 424 note 7.

5   Agriculture Act 1970 s 58(2)(a).
6   Agriculture Act 1970 s 58(2)(b). As to the meaning of 'smallholding provided by a smallholdings authority' see PARA 646 note 3.

750.   Promotion of smallholdings societies.

A smallholdings authority[1] may, for the benefit of the occupiers[2] of smallholdings provided by them, further the formation of smallholdings societies and assist their carrying on and the extension of their activities[3]. Smallholdings societies[4] are bodies of persons, whether corporate or unincorporate, having for their object or one of their objects the promotion of efficiency in the conduct of smallholdings through co-operative methods, and in particular through the co-operative purchase and hiring of requisites or the co-operative sale, marketing or preparation for marketing of produce[5].

1   As to smallholdings authorities see PARAS 748–751.
2   As to the 'occupier of land' for these purposes see PARA 424 note 7.
3   Agriculture Act 1970 s 47(2). As to the meaning of 'smallholding provided by a smallholdings authority' see PARA 646 note 3. As to the meaning of 'smallholding' see PARA 627. Note that these powers are also exercisable by the Secretary of State and the Welsh Ministers: see s 54(1), (2); and PARA 744. As to the Secretary of State and the Welsh Ministers see PARA 741.
4   The term 'smallholdings society' is not a statutory term.
5   Agriculture Act 1970 ss 47(2). 'Produce' includes anything, whether live or dead, produced in the course of agriculture: Agriculture Act 1947 s 109(3); Agriculture Act 1970 s 37(4).

751.   Public accountability in relation to smallholdings.

Every smallholdings authority[1] must, before such date each year as the Secretary of State or the Welsh Ministers[2] direct, send to him or them a report, relating to such matters as he or they direct, of its proceedings during the previous financial year[3]. There must then be laid before Parliament or the National Assembly for Wales, in each financial year, a report summarising the annual reports so submitted by the smallholdings authorities and of the Secretary of State's or the Welsh Ministers' own proceedings in relation to smallholdings[4].

A smallholdings authority must keep a separate account of its receipts and expenses, including capital receipts and expenses, with respect to smallholdings[5].

1   As to smallholdings authorities see PARAS 748–751.
2   As to the Secretary of State and the Welsh Ministers see PARA 741.
3   Agriculture Act 1970 s 59(1).
4   Agriculture Act 1970 s 59(2). As to the meaning of 'smallholding' see PARA 627.
5   Agriculture Act 1970 s 58(1).

(3) ALLOTMENTS AUTHORITIES

752.   Designation of allotments authorities.

The local authorities primarily responsible for the provision and management of allotments are the councils of London boroughs, districts, and parishes, and, in Wales, counties, county boroughs and communities[1], although inner London boroughs are not obliged to provide allotments[2]. In the case of parishes not having parish councils the authority responsible is the parish meeting[3].

1   See PARA 659.
2   See the London Government Act 1963 s 55(4)(a), which operates so as to modify the Small Holdings and Allotments Act 1908 s 23 (duty of councils to provide allotments: see PARA 659) in respect of inner London boroughs.
3   See the Small Holdings and Allotments Act 1908 s 61(4); and PARA 659.

753. Powers of entry of allotments authorities to ascertain suitability of land.

Allotments authorities[1] may, with a view to ascertaining whether any land is suitable for any purpose for which it has power to acquire land[2], authorise in writing[3] any person to enter and inspect the land specified, and anyone who obstructs or impedes any person acting under and in accordance with such authority commits an offence[4].

1   As to the allotments authorities see PARA 752. The Land Settlement (Facilities) Act 1919 s 19 refers initially only to 'a council', but in view of the subsequent reference to the powers to acquire land under the Small Holdings and Allotments Act 1908 (see the text and note 2) it is clear that this should be construed as a reference to the councils empowered to acquire land for the purposes of that Act, that is to say, the councils referred to in PARA 752: see PARA 659 notes 1–5.
2   Ie under the Small Holdings and Allotments Act 1908 (the 'principal Act', by virtue of the Land Settlement (Facilities) Act 1919 s 1 (repealed)).
3   A person exercising a power of entry and inspection under the Land Settlement (Facilities) Act 1919 s 19 may be required to produce his authority.
4   Land Settlement (Facilities) Act 1919 s 19 (amended by virtue of the Criminal Justice Act 1982 s 46). The offence is punishable on summary conviction by a fine not exceeding level 2 on the standard scale: Land Settlement (Facilities) Act 1919 s 19 (as so amended). As to the standard scale and the powers of magistrates' courts to issue fines on summary conviction see SENTENCING vol 92 (2015) PARA 176.

754. Power of allotments authorities to appoint and remove allotment managers.

Allotments authorities[1] may appoint and remove managers of land acquired by them for allotments[2]. These managers must consist either partly of council members and partly of other persons who are residents and are liable to pay to the council in whose area the land is situated an amount in respect of council tax, or wholly of such other persons[3], with such powers, including the power of incurring expenses, as the council determines[4].

1   As to the allotments authorities see PARA 752. The Small Holdings and Allotments Act 1908 s 29(1) refers to 'the council of a borough, urban district, or parish' but this should be construed as a reference to the councils referred to in PARA 752: see PARA 659 notes 1–5.
2   Small Holdings and Allotments Act 1908 s 29(1). As to the meaning of 'allotment' see PARA 649. As to the acquisition of land for allotments see PARA 660.
3   Small Holdings and Allotments Act 1908 s 29(1) (amended by the Local Government Finance Act 1992 Sch 13 para 5). As to liability for council tax see LOCAL GOVERNMENT FINANCE vol 70 (2012) PARA 298 et seq.
4   See the Small Holdings and Allotments Act 1908 s 29(2).

755. Promotion and assistance of allotments societies.

Allotments authorities[1] may promote the formation or extension of allotments societies[2], may assist such societies financially by making grants or advances, or by guaranteeing advances, upon such terms and conditions as to rate of interest and repayment or otherwise, and on such security, as the authority thinks fit[3]. For this purpose, authorities may borrow money[4] and the Public Works Loan Commissioners may lend it to them[5]. Those authorities may also let to a society accommodation for the sale or storage of goods[6], and may employ as their agents any other society having as one of its objects the promotion of co-operation in connection with the cultivation of allotments[7].

1   As to the allotments authorities see PARA 752. The Small Holdings and Allotments Act 1908 s 49(1), (2) refers to 'a county or borough or urban district council' but this should be construed as a reference to the authorities referred to in PARA 752: see PARA 659 notes 1–5.
2   Small Holdings and Allotments Act 1908 s 49(1) (amended by the Land Settlement (Facilities) Act 1919 Sch 2). 'Allotments societies' are societies on a co-operative basis having for their object, or

one of their objects, the provision or profitable working of allotments, whether in relation to the purchase of requisites, the sale of produce, credit banking, insurance or otherwise: Small Holdings and Allotments Act 1908 s 49(1). 'Society' includes any body of persons, whether incorporated or unincorporated: Agricultural Land (Utilisation) Act 1931 s 20(1). As to the distribution of the proceeds of sale of land owned by an allotments society see *Re St Andrews' Allotment Association's Trusts, Sarjeant v Probert* [1969] 1 All ER 147, [1969] 1 WLR 229.

3   Small Holdings and Allotments Act 1908 s 49(2) (amended by the Land Settlement (Facilities) Act 1919 Sch 2; and the Local Government, Planning and Land Act 1980 Sch 5 para 1). The consent of the Secretary of State or the Welsh Ministers is required for the exercise by a county or county borough council of its powers to incur expenditure under the Small Holdings and Allotments Act 1908 s 49: Small Holdings and Allotments Regulations 1919, SI 1919/1197, reg 1(1)(7). As to the Secretary of State and the Welsh Ministers see PARA 741.

4   See the Small Holdings and Allotments Act 1908 ss 52(1), 53(4); and PARA 726. The exercise of an authority's powers to determine the period within which any money borrowed by the authority is to be repaid is subject to the consent of the Secretary of State or the Welsh Ministers: see the Small Holdings and Allotments Regulations 1919, SI 1919/1197, reg 1(1)(6).

5   See the National Loans Act 1968 s 3(11), Sch 4 para 1; and FINANCIAL INSTRUMENTS AND TRANSACTIONS vol 49 (2015) PARA 167 et seq.

6   Small Holdings and Allotments Act 1908 s 49(2) (amended by the Small Holdings and Allotments Act 1926 Sch 1).

7   Small Holdings and Allotments Act 1908 s 49(1), (4) (s 49(4) amended by the Statute Law (Repeals) Act 1993). With Treasury consent the Secretary of State and the Welsh Ministers may make grants to any other society out of money provided by Parliament: Small Holdings and Allotments Act 1908 s 49(4) (as so amended). As to the Treasury see CONSTITUTIONAL AND ADMINISTRATIVE LAW vol 20 (2014) PARA 263.

756.   Sales or lettings by allotments authorities to co-operative societies.
Allotments authorities[1] may let one or more allotments[2] to persons working on a co-operative system, and may, with the consent of the Secretary of State or the Welsh Ministers[3], sell one or more allotments to any association formed for the purposes of creating or promoting the creation of allotments[4].

1   As to the allotments authorities see PARA 752. The Small Holdings and Allotments Act 1908 s 27(6) refers only to 'a council' but should be construed as referring to the authorities empowered to sell or let land for allotments: see PARAS 752, 659 notes 1–5.

2   As to the meaning of 'allotment' see PARA 649.

3   As to the Secretary of State and the Welsh Ministers see PARA 741.

4   Small Holdings and Allotments Act 1908 s 27(6) (amended by the Land Settlement (Facilities) Act 1919 Sch 2). As to allotment societies generally see PARA 755. As to letting land to an association see also the Allotments Act 1922 s 15; and PARA 630. As to consent to lettings and sales see the Small Holdings and Allotments Regulations 1919, SR & O 1919/1197, reg 1(1)(1), (3).

(4) RURAL DEVELOPMENT BOARDS

(i) Establishment and Functions

757.   Purposes and functions of Rural Development Boards.
In areas of hills and uplands where special problems of development and special needs exist, the Secretary of State and the Welsh Ministers[1] are empowered to establish[2] Rural Development Boards[3]. These boards are subject to the directions[4] of the Secretary of State and the Welsh Ministers, and must submit annual reports and accounts[5]. The special problems and needs include special difficulties in the formation of commercial agricultural units[6], the need for an overall programme for guidance in making decisions as to the complementary use

of land for agriculture[7] and forestry[8], the need for improved public services, and the need for preserving and taking full advantage of amenities[9] and scenery[10].

The functions of a board are to keep under review all means of meeting such problems and needs, and to draw up in consultation with local authorities and other bodies, and take measures to implement, a programme to meet these problems and needs[11]; a board and the appropriate forestry authority[12] must consult together and act in concert[13]. Any expenditure involved in implementing such a programme is subject to the approval of the Secretary of State or the Welsh Ministers[14]. Subject to the approval of the Secretary of State or the Welsh Ministers and the Treasury[15], a board may make grants or loans[16] towards the undertaking of measures to implement any such programme[17]. On making a grant or loan a board may impose such conditions as it thinks fit[18].

1   As to the Secretary of State and the Welsh Ministers see PARA 741.
2   As to the procedure for establishing a board see PARA 758. The provisions of the Agriculture Act 1967 Pt III (ss 41–57) controlling afforestation and sales of land are, as respects the area of a Rural Development Board, a local land charge: s 45(6) (substituted by the Local Land Charges Act 1975 Sch 1).
3   See the Agriculture Act 1967 s 45(1).
4   See the Agriculture Act 1967 s 54.
5   See the Agriculture Act 1967 s 53.
6   As to the meaning of 'agricultural unit' see PARA 424 note 7.
7   As to the meaning of 'agriculture' see PARA 424.
8   Such overall programme is one having regard, among other things, to the special economic considerations and long term nature of forestry: Agriculture Act 1967 s 45(3).
9   For examples of amenities to be considered see the Agriculture Act 1967 s 45(4).
10 Agriculture Act 1967 s 45(2).
11 See the Agriculture Act 1967 s 46(1).
12 'The appropriate forestry authority' means the Forestry Commission in relation to England and the Natural Resources Body for Wales in relation to Wales: Agriculture Act 1967 s 57(1) (added by SI 2013/755). As to the Commission and the Forestry Commissioners generally see FORESTRY vol 52 (2014) PARA 37 et seq. As to the Natural Resources Body for Wales generally see FORESTRY vol 52 (2014) PARA 38.
13 Agriculture Act 1967 s 46(3) (amended by SI 2013/755). Any disputes between them are determined by the Secretary of State or the Welsh Ministers: Agriculture Act 1967 s 46(3).
14 See the Agriculture Act 1967 s 46(2).
15 As to the Treasury see CONSTITUTIONAL AND ADMINISTRATIVE LAW vol 20 (2014) PARA 263.
16 Or payments partly by way of grant and partly by way of loan: see the Agriculture Act 1967 s 47(1).
17 Agriculture Act 1967 s 47(1). For particular objects of financial assistance see s 47(1)(a)–(c). As to offences see AGRICULTURAL PRODUCTION AND MARKETING vol 1A (2017) PARA 422.
18 Agriculture Act 1967 s 47(2).

758. Establishment and dissolution of Rural Development Boards.

Rural Development Boards are established by order of the Secretary of State or the Welsh Ministers[1], fixing the date of establishment and the boundaries of the board's area[2]. Notice of the proposal to establish a board must be given in local newspapers and a period of at least 28 days allowed for objections[3]. Objectors may propose on a variety of grounds that the area of the board be either increased or decreased[4]. Objections, unless withdrawn, must be dealt with either through a public local inquiry or a hearing by a person appointed by the Secretary of State or the Welsh Ministers for the purpose[5]. The proposals may be modified after objections have been considered and fresh opportunity must be given for objections to the modified proposals unless the Secretary of State is or the Welsh Ministers are satisfied that all interested persons have already had a sufficient opportunity[6].

Boards may be dissolved, or their areas varied, by order of the Secretary of State or the Welsh Ministers[7]; in the case of variation, the procedure described above must again be followed[8].

1　As to the Secretary of State and the Welsh Ministers see PARA **741**.
2　See the Agriculture Act 1967 Sch 5 Pt I para 1. The order must specify the board's area by reference to a map: Sch 5 Pt I para 1(2). For provisions as to the way in which the area is to be delineated see Sch 5 Pt I para 1(3), (4). When made, the order must be published in local newspapers and is open to inspection, with the map: Sch 5 Pt I para 5. Provisions as to the setting aside of orders by the High Court under the Acquisition of Land Act 1981 Pt IV (ss 23–27) (see COMPULSORY ACQUISITION OF LAND vol 18 (2009) PARAS 612, 614) apply to such an order: see the Agriculture Act 1967 Sch 5 Pt I para 6A(1) (Sch 5 Pt I para 6A added by the Acquisition of Land Act 1981 Sch 4 para 15(3)). As to the constitution and procedure of Rural Development Boards see the Agriculture Act 1967 Sch 6 Pt 2 (amended by SI 2012/2404).
　　Orders establishing or dissolving Rural Development Boards, being local in nature, are not recorded in this work.
3　See the Agriculture Act 1967 Sch 5 Pt I para 2. The Secretary of State and the Welsh Ministers must first consult with local authorities and interested public bodies: see Sch 5 Pt I para 2(1).
4　See the Agriculture Act 1967 Sch 5 Pt I para 3.
5　See the Agriculture Act 1967 Sch 5 Pt I para 4(2). Provisions as to evidence and costs under the Local Government Act 1972 s 250(2)–(5) (see LOCAL GOVERNMENT vol 69 (2009) PARA 105) apply to such a public local inquiry or hearing: Agriculture Act 1967 Sch 5 Pt I para 6A(3) (as added: see note 2).
6　See the Agriculture Act 1967 Sch 5 Pt I para 4(4), (5).
7　See the Agriculture Act 1967 Sch 5 Pt I para 6.
8　Agriculture Act 1967 Sch 5 Pt I para 6(2). Dissolution orders may contain consequential and transitional provisions: Sch 5 Pt I para 6(3). Orders establishing or dissolving Rural Development Boards, being local in nature, are not recorded in this work.

(ii) Acquisition of Land, Control of Transfers and Related Powers

759. Acquisition and use of land by Rural Development Boards.

In the discharge of its functions, a Rural Development Board may acquire land[1] by agreement, and manage, improve, farm, sell, let[2], develop or build on its land, acquire farming businesses and stock, and provide equipment for its tenants engaged in agriculture or forestry[3].

1　'Land' includes any estate or interest in land: Agriculture Act 1967 s 75(2).
2　A board may sell or let any land subject to any depreciatory conditions imposed in the interests of the community or for any purpose connected with the board's functions: Agriculture Act 1967 s 46(4)(b).
3　See the Agriculture Act 1967 s 46(4). As to the acquisition of land for the purpose of effecting amalgamations see PARA 765.

760. Control by Rural Development Boards of transfers of land.

Subject to a number of exceptions[1], any transfer[2] of land within the area of a Rural Development Board[3] requires the board's written consent[4]. For these purposes, 'land' means agricultural land[5], woodland[6], unenclosed mountain, hill or heath land, or common or waste land[7]. An application for consent must be in such form as the board directs; and the board may refuse or grant the consent applied for[8]. The board may not refuse consent unless it is satisfied that the land, if acquired by it:

(1)　can suitably be used or disposed of by it to effect amalgamations[9] or to promote the co-ordination of the use of the land for forestry and agriculture[10];

(2)   is land which in the opinion of the board and the appropriate forestry authority[11] ought to be planted by the appropriate forestry authority[12]; or

(3)   can suitably be used or disposed of by it for some purpose ancillary to the use of other land for agriculture or forestry[13],

or unless it is satisfied that refusal of its consent will prevent the creation of an uncommercial unit of agricultural land[14].

Within two months of receipt of an application for consent, the board must notify the applicant of its decision; unless consent is granted, the notice must give the reasons for the decision[15]. If the board refuses consent, the applicant may appeal to the Secretary of State or the Welsh Ministers[16] within two months of receipt of the notice withholding consent[17].

1   See PARA 761.
2   'Transfer of land' includes the grant of a lease for a term exceeding ten years, and assignment of a lease with an unexpired term exceeding ten years: Agriculture Act 1967 s 49(13).
3   As to the establishment and functions of Rural Development Boards see PARAS 757–758.
4   Agriculture Act 1967 s 49(1).
5   As to the meaning of 'agricultural land' see PARA 424.
6   'Woodland' includes all land used primarily for the growing of trees: Agriculture Act 1967 s 57(1).
7   Agriculture Act 1967 s 50(1).
8   Agriculture Act 1967 s 49(2). As to service of the application see s 49(10).
9   Agriculture Act 1967 s 49(3)(a). As to amalgamations of agricultural land and reshaping agricultural units see PARA 765.
10   See the Agriculture Act 1967 s 49(3)(b).
11   As to the meaning of 'appropriate forestry authority' see PARA 757 note 12.
12   See the Agriculture Act 1967 s 49(3)(c) (amended by SI 2013/755).
13   See the Agriculture Act 1967 s 49(3)(d).
14   See the Agriculture Act 1967 s 49(3).
15   Agriculture Act 1967 s 49(4). In the event of non-compliance, the applicant may give the board 14 days' notice to remedy its default and upon expiry of that period, if the board has not notified him of its decision, it will be obliged to give its consent: s 49(10), (11).
16   As to the Secretary of State and the Welsh Ministers see PARA 741.
17   See the Agriculture Act 1967 s 49(5). The ground of appeal is 'that the application for consent ought to be granted', which would seem to allow any question of fact or law to be raised: see s 49(5). The Secretary of State or the Welsh Ministers must afford the appellant and the board, if either so desires, an opportunity of appearing before and being heard by a person appointed for the purpose: s 49(5). A further appeal lies to the High Court and the Court of Appeal on a question of law or a case stated: s 49(5) (amended by the Planning (Consequential Provisions) Act 1990 Sch 2 para 15(1)). This provision applies the provisions of the Town and Country Planning Act 1990 s 289 (see PLANNING) as to appeals against enforcement notices.

761. Exemptions from control of Rural Development Boards.

The consent of a Rural Development Board[1] is not required in the following cases: transfers to or from a local authority[2], the Environment Agency[3], a national park authority[4], the National Trust[5], and certain other specified bodies[6]; transfers by an individual to a member of his family[7] or to the trustees of a settlement exclusively for the benefit of members of his family[8]; transfers effected in pursuance of a contract of sale concluded before the land came to be in the area of a board[9]; transfers giving effect to the devolution of the land on death or bankruptcy, or under the terms of a settlement[10]; and transfers by a mortgagee or chargee under a mortgage or charge created before the land came into the board's area[11].

1   As to the requirement for consent see PARA 760. As to the establishment and functions of Rural Development Boards see PARAS 757–758.
2   In the Agriculture Act 1967 'local authority' means (in England) the council of a county or a London borough, the Common Council of the City of London and a district council, and (in

Wales) the council of a county or county borough: s 75(1) (amended by the Local Government Act 1972 Sch 30 and the Local Government (Wales) Act 1994 Sch 16 para 30, Sch 18).

3   As to the Environment Agency see ENVIRONMENTAL QUALITY AND PUBLIC HEALTH vol 45 (2010) PARA 68 et seq.

4   As to the national park authorities see OPEN SPACES AND COUNTRYSIDE vol 78 (2010) PARA 526 et seq.

5   As to the National Trust see NATIONAL CULTURAL HERITAGE vol 77 (2016) PARA 973 et seq.

6   Agriculture Act 1967 s 50(3) (amended by the Agriculture (Miscellaneous Provisions) Act 1968 s 47; the Water Act 1989 Sch 25 para 34; the Planning (Consequential Provisions) Act 1990 Sch 2 para 15(2); the Environment Act 1995 Sch 10 para 6, Sch 24; and SI 2013/755). The other bodies are: statutory undertakers within the meaning of the Town and Country Planning Act 1990 ss 262, 336(1) (see PLANNING vol 83 (2010) PARA 1186 et seq), corporations carrying on nationalised industries, the Natural Environment Research Council (see NATIONAL CULTURAL HERITAGE vol 77 (2016) PARA 966), water undertakers (see WATER AND WATERWAYS vol 100 (2009) PARA 134 et seq), sewerage undertakers (see ENVIRONMENTAL QUALITY AND PUBLIC HEALTH vol 46 (2010) PARA 999 et seq), Natural Resources Body for Wales and internal drainage boards (see WATER AND WATERWAYS vol 101 (2009) PARA 569 et seq): see the Agriculture Act 1967 s 50(3) (as so amended).

7   'Family' means spouse, lineal descendant or ancestor, brother and sister and their children; and an adopted child is treated as a child, and a relationship of the half blood as of the whole blood: see the Agriculture Act 1967 s 50(4).

8   See the Agriculture Act 1967 s 50(4).

9   Or up to three months after the establishment of the board, if the establishing order so provides: Agriculture Act 1967 s 50(5).

10   See the Agriculture Act 1967 s 50(6)(a).

11   See the Agriculture Act 1967 s 50(6)(b).

762.   Acquisition by Rural Development Board where its consent refused.

Within three months of the date of receipt of a notice withholding consent to the transfer of land[1], the applicant may serve on a Rural Development Board[2] a notice requiring the board to purchase the estate or interest proposed to be transferred[3]. If the applicant's estate or interest in the land is greater than that which is proposed to be transferred, the board may, by notice given within two months of receipt of the purchase notice, require that the purchase notice apply to all the estate or interest of the applicant in the land[4]. Upon service of a purchase notice, a board is authorised to acquire compulsorily the estate or interest, and is deemed to have served a notice to treat[5]. The applicant may withdraw the purchase notice within six weeks from the final determination of compensation by the Upper tribunal[6], or, if there has been no final determination, at any time before the acceptance in writing by the applicant of an unconditional offer[7] by the board[8].

1   As to such notice see PARA 760. In the case where an appeal has been brought (see PARA 760 text and notes 16–17) and is unsuccessful, the period of three months runs from the final determination of the appeal: Agriculture Act 1967 s 49(6).

2   As to the establishment and functions of Rural Development Boards see PARAS 757–758.

3   Agriculture Act 1967 s 49(6). Where the proposed transfer is by way of the grant of a lease for a term exceeding ten years, 'estate or interest' means the proposed transferor's estate and interest both in the reversion and the lease: s 49(13).
    The Secretary of State or the Welsh Ministers may give directions for the inclusion of other land in a purchase notice, on the ground that the applicant wishes to dispose of land falling partly outside the board's jurisdiction, and would be substantially prejudiced if he were unable to dispose of all the land in one transaction: see s 50(2). As to the Secretary of State and the Welsh Ministers see PARA 741.

4   See the Agriculture Act 1967 s 49(9). See also note 3.

5   See the Agriculture Act 1967 s 49(7). This provision applies the provisions as to compulsory purchase orders (see the Compulsory Purchase Act 1965 Pt I (ss 1–32); and COMPULSORY

ACQUISITION OF LAND vol 18 (2009) PARA 513 et seq), excluding the power of entry (see s 11(1); and COMPULSORY ACQUISITION OF LAND vol 18 (2009) PARA 645), and excluding the right to withdraw the notice to treat (see the Land Compensation Act 1961 s 31; and COMPULSORY ACQUISITION OF LAND vol 18 (2009) PARA 636).

6   A claim is not deemed to be fully determined so long as, in relation to a decision of the Upper Tribunal, the time for applying for permission to appeal to the Court of Appeal, or for applying for permission to appeal from the decision of the Court of Appeal on such an appeal, has not expired: Agriculture Act 1967 s 49(8A) (added by SI 2009/1307). As to determination of compensation see COMPULSORY ACQUISITION OF LAND vol 18 (2009) PARA 753 et seq. In the assessment of compensation, no account is to be taken of any depreciation of the value of the relevant interest attributable to the provisions of the Agriculture Act 1967 ss 49, 50: s 50(8).

7   Ie an offer in writing of a sum of compensation payable pursuant to the purchase notice: see the Agriculture Act 1967 s 49(8).

8   See the Agriculture Act 1967 s 49(8) (amended by SI 2009/1307).

763. Contravention of control giving rise to compulsory purchase.

Failure to obtain a Rural Development Board's consent[1] to any transaction does not invalidate the transaction[2], but the board has power to acquire by a compulsory purchase order[3] all the estate and interest of the transferor in land transferred in contravention of the control provisions[4].

1   As to the requirement of such consent see PARAS 760–761. As to the establishment and functions of Rural Development Boards see PARAS 757–758.

2   See the Agriculture Act 1967 s 50(9).

3   Ie an order to which the Compulsory Purchase Act 1965 Pt I (ss 1–32) (see COMPULSORY ACQUISITION OF LAND vol 18 (2009) PARA 513 et seq) applies: see the Agriculture Act 1967 ss 49(7), 50(7). The Acquisition of Land Act 1981 Pt IV (ss 23–27) (see COMPULSORY ACQUISITION OF LAND vol 18 (2009) PARAS 612, 614) applies to any notice to treat served in pursuance of the Agriculture Act 1967 s 50(7): see s 50(7) (amended by the Acquisition of Land Act 1981 Sch 4 PARA 15(2)). As to compulsory purchase orders and notices to treat see COMPULSORY ACQUISITION OF LAND vol 18 (2009) PARA 556 et seq.

4   See the Agriculture Act 1967 s 50(7). Notice to treat must be served within six years from the date of transfer: s 50(7).

764. Other powers of Rural Development Boards.

A Rural Development Board may carry out or commission the carrying out of inquiries, investigations and researches in connection with its functions[1]. It may in writing authorise a person to enter[2] on any land in the board's area[3] to determine whether, and in what way, the functions of the board should be exercised[4]; on leaving the land such person must leave it as effectively secured against trespassers as he found it[5]. A board may by notice require a landowner or occupier in its area to furnish such information as it may reasonably require to discharge its functions[6]; any information so obtained is, with certain exceptions, confidential[7]. No person may plant trees on land in a board's area without a licence granted by that board, but no licence is required, inter alia, for planting by the appropriate forestry authority[8].

1   See the Agriculture Act 1967 s 46(4)(f). As to the establishment and functions of Rural Development Boards see PARAS 757–758.

2   Entry may be at any reasonable time but may not be demanded as of right without 48 hours' notice, or seven days in the case of residential property; and documentary authority must be produced if required: Agriculture Act 1967 s 55(1).

3   As to a board's area see PARA 758.

4   See the Agriculture Act 1967 s 55(1). Wilful obstruction of a person exercising this power is punishable on summary conviction by a fine not exceeding level 1 on the standard scale: s 55(1)

(amended by virtue of the Criminal Justice Act 1982 ss 38, 46). As to the standard scale and the powers of magistrates' courts to issue fines on summary conviction see SENTENCING vol 92 (2015) PARA 176.

5   See the Agriculture Act 1967 s 55(2).

6   See the Agriculture Act 1967 s 55(3). Failure without reasonable cause to furnish the required information within three months is punishable on summary conviction by a fine not exceeding level 3 on the standard scale: s 55(3) (amended by virtue of the Criminal Justice Act 1982 ss 38, 46).

7   Disclosure may be made with consent or to a member, officer, servant or agent of the board, the Secretary of State or the Welsh Ministers or an officer, servant or agent of the Secretary of State or the Welsh Ministers; or for the purpose of proceedings under the Agriculture Act 1967 Pt III (ss 41–57) or any criminal proceedings: s 55(4). Unauthorised disclosure is punishable on summary conviction by a fine not exceeding the prescribed sum, imprisonment not exceeding three months, or both, or on conviction on indictment by an unlimited fine, imprisonment not exceeding two years, or both: s 55(4) (amended by virtue of the Magistrates' Courts Act 1980 s 32(2)).

8   See the Agriculture Act 1967 s 52; and FORESTRY vol 52 (2014) PARA 57. As to the meaning of 'appropriate forestry authority' see PARA 757 note 12.

(iii) Promotion of Amalgamations and Boundary Adjustments

765. Exercise of powers of acquisition and disposal by Rural Development Boards.

A Rural Development Board[1] may exercise its powers to acquire, hold and dispose of land[2] in such a way as to effect amalgamations of agricultural land[3] and to reshape agricultural units[4]. A board may enter into transactions involving loss, including amalgamating holdings of land in a way which renders less valuable, or useless, any buildings or equipment on any of the land, allowing the occupier of an uncommercial unit[5] to retain occupation of a dwelling house on the land when the remainder of the unit is acquired by the board for the purposes of amalgamation, and selling land subject to depreciatory conditions ensuring continued single ownership and occupation for agricultural purposes[6]. A deed by which a board conveys land may apply statutory conditions[7] to any of that land, and to any other land, but only if all the persons who will have an estate or interest in the land to which such conditions are applied have executed the deed[8]. Certain special provisions apply to land in respect of which these powers have been exercised[9].

1   As to the establishment and functions of Rural Development Boards see PARAS 757–758.

2   As to those powers see PARA 759.

3   As to the meaning of 'agricultural land' see PARA 424. As to 'amalgamation' see the Agriculture Act 1967 s 26(1); and AGRICULTURAL PRODUCTION AND MARKETING vol 1A (2017) PARA 416 (definition applied by the Agriculture Act 1967 s 57(1)).

4   Agriculture Act 1967 s 48(1). As to the meaning of 'agricultural unit' see PARA 424 note 7.

5   As to the meanings of 'commercial unit' and 'uncommercial unit' see the Agriculture Act 1967 s 26(1); and AGRICULTURAL PRODUCTION AND MARKETING vol 1A (2017) PARA 416 (definition applied by the Agriculture Act 1967 s 57(1)).

6   Agriculture Act 1967 s 48(1).

7   Ie the conditions in the Agriculture Act 1967 ss 26, 28, 29, 48, Sch 3 (see AGRICULTURAL PRODUCTION AND MARKETING vol 1A (2017) PARA 416 et seq).

8   See the Agriculture Act 1967 s 48(2) (amended by the Agriculture Act 1970 s 33(2)). In the case of land comprised in a settlement or subject to a trust of land, the person having the powers of a tenant for life and the trustees for land may execute the deed on behalf of all other persons who are or may become entitled to benefit under the settlement or trust, as well as on his own behalf: Agriculture Act 1970 s 33(2) (amended by the Trusts of Land and Appointment of Trustees Act 1996 Sch 3 para 11).

9   The provisions of the Agriculture Act 1967 s 27 (see AGRICULTURAL PRODUCTION AND MARKETING vol 1A (2017) PARA 418) as to grants to outgoers are applicable: see s 27(1)(b). The provisions of the Agricultural Holdings Act 1986 Sch 3 Pt I Case H (see PARA 481) relating to notices to quit are also applicable: see the Agriculture Act 1967 s 48(4) (substituted by the Agricultural Holdings Act 1986 Sch 14 para 41). If the board certifies that a tenancy is granted by it in connection with transactions for amalgamations and the reshaping of agricultural units, the exclusion of the application of the Rent Act 1977 under s 14 (see LANDLORD AND TENANT vol 63 (2016) PARA 706) applies as if the board were a local authority: Agriculture Act 1967 s 48(5).

766. Schemes by Rural Development Boards for co-ordinated amalgamation and reshaping.

If it appears to a Rural Development Board that in any part of its area[1] there is a need, for the benefit of the community and for the mutual advantage of those owning and occupying the agricultural land[2], of a co-ordinated scheme of amalgamations, reshaping of agricultural units[3] and afforestation[4], to be effected by transfers and exchanges of land and grants, surrenders, renunciations and variations of tenancies, the board may proceed to make such a scheme[5]. The scheme must be based on a comprehensive plan for the uses of the land, including afforestation[6]. The scheme must be published and made available for inspection, and the board must invite submissions to it on any aspect of the scheme[7]. The board is required to submit the scheme, and the submissions made thereon, to the Secretary of State or the Welsh Ministers[8], who may direct a public inquiry to be held[9]. After considering the reports of the board and the public inquiry, if any, the Secretary of State or the Welsh Ministers must either reject or approve the scheme, with or without modifications[10]; notice of approval must be published[11]. If the scheme is approved, the Secretary of State or the Welsh Ministers will direct the board to enter into negotiations to implement the scheme, and the board must endeavour to arrive at proposals for the scheme which all concerned will be willing to implement[12]. If the Secretary of State is, or the Welsh Ministers are, satisfied that the board has entered into binding agreements to carry out the transactions necessary to implement the scheme except with respect to an area of outstanding land small in comparison with the total and that the terms of the scheme in relation to the acquisition of the outstanding land are equitable, he or they may authorise the board to acquire the outstanding land compulsorily[13].

1   As to the establishment and functions of Rural Development Boards see PARAS 757–758. As to a board's area see PARA 758.
2   As to the meaning of 'agricultural land' see PARA 424.
3   As to the meaning of 'agricultural unit' see PARA 424 note 7.
4   As to the board's functions in connection with afforestation see the Agriculture Act 1967 s sch52; and FORESTRY vol 52 (2014) PARA 57.
5   See the Agriculture Act 1967 s 51(1).
6   Agriculture Act 1967 s 51(2)(a).
7   Agriculture Act 1967 s 51(2)(b). The means of publication are at the discretion of the board: s 51(2)(b).
8   As to the Secretary of State and the Welsh Ministers see PARA 741.
9   See the Agriculture Act 1967 s 51(3).
10 Agriculture Act 1967 s 51(4).
11 Ie in such manner as appears appropriate to the Secretary of State or the Welsh Ministers: see the Agriculture Act 1967 s 51(5).
12 See the Agriculture Act 1967 s 51(5), (6).
13 See the Agriculture Act 1967 s 51(7) (amended by SI 1978/244). The Acquisition of Land Act 1981 (see COMPULSORY ACQUISITION OF LAND) applies as if the board were a local authority: see the Agriculture Act 1967 s 51(7) (amended by the Acquisition of Land Act 1981 Sch 4 para 1, Sch 6 Pt I).

(5) TRIBUNALS

767. The Tribunal in Wales.

For Wales[1], the Agricultural Land Tribunal for Wales[2] hears and determines references and applications made to it under any enactment[3]. Applications to and proceedings of the Agricultural Land Tribunal are regulated by rules[4].

Where it appears to the Agricultural Land Tribunal for Wales that any person concerned in a reference or application has acted frivolously, vexatiously or oppressively in applying for the reference or application or in connection with them, the Tribunal may order him to pay to any other party either a specified sum in respect of his costs or the assessed amount of those costs, and it may do so whether or not the reference or application proceeds to a hearing[5]. Provision is made for the assessment in the County Court of any costs so required to be assessed[6] and for the recovery of sums assessed to be payable[7].

An appeal on any point of law from a decision of the Agricultural Land Tribunal for Wales may be made to the Upper Tribunal[8]. Where the Agricultural Land Tribunal for Wales is notified of an appeal to the Upper Tribunal under these provisions, effect is not given to the Tribunal's decision unless and until the Tribunal otherwise orders after the appeal and any appeal arising from that appeal have been concluded (or the right to take or continue such an appeal has lapsed); and, in a case relating to a notice to quit, the Tribunal may postpone (or further postpone) the date at which the tenancy is to be terminated by the notice, if it has effect[9].

At the date at which this volume states the law the operation of the Agricultural Land Tribunal for Wales is governed by relevant provisions of the Agriculture Act 1947 and related subordinate legislation[10]; however, functions of the Agricultural Land Tribunal for Wales may be transferred by order to the Upper Tribunal established under the Tribunals, Courts and Enforcement Act 2007[11].

1 Where any land lies partly in Wales and partly in England, for the purposes of anything required or authorised to be done by or before the appropriate tribunal in relation to that land, the land is deemed to be situated entirely in the place where the greater part of the land lies: Agriculture Act 1947 s 75(1) (s 75 substituted by SI 2013/1036). Tribunal Procedure Rules may make provision for the transfer of proceedings to or from the First-tier Tribunal where, after the making of the application, of the Agricultural Holdings Act 1986 s 42 (procedure where deceased held more than one holding: see PARA 502) applies to the determination of associated applications: Agriculture Act 1947 s 75(2) (as so substituted). For these purposes 'appropriate tribunal' means, where the land (or the greater part of the land) is in England, the First-tier Tribunal and, where the land (or the greater part of the land) is in Wales, the Agricultural Land Tribunal for Wales: s 75(3) (as so substituted).

2 The Agricultural Land Tribunal for Wales is referred to in the Government of Wales Act 2006 (see Sch 9A), the Wales Act 2017 (see s 59) and the Welsh Language (Wales) Measure 2011 (Sch 6) as 'Tribiwnlys Tir Amaethyddol Cymru'. However, it is submitted that this is incorrect and the correct translation should be 'Tribiwnlys Tir Amaethyddol yng Nghymru'. As to the constitution of the Agricultural Land Tribunal for Wales see the Agriculture Act 1947 Sch 9 paras 13–24.

3 Agriculture Act 1947 s 73(1) (substituted by SI 2013/1036); Agricultural Land Tribunals (Areas) Order 1982, SI 1982/97, art 2(1). The Lord Chancellor must consult the chairman of the Agricultural Land Tribunals before making such an order: Agriculture Act 1947 s 73(1) (as so amended).

4 See the Agriculture Act 1947 s 73(3), (4) (amended by the Agriculture Act 1958 Sch 1 para 3, Sch 3 Pt I; the Agricultural Holdings Act 1986 Sch 14 para 18; SI 2013/1036); and the Agricultural Land Tribunals (Rules) Order 2007, SI 2007/3105.

5 Agriculture (Miscellaneous Provisions) Act 1954 s 5(1) (amended by the Agriculture Act 1958 Sch 1 para 26; SI 2013/1036). As to the assessment of costs see CIVIL PROCEDURE vol 12A (2015) PARAS 1704, 1749 et seq.

6 See the Agriculture (Miscellaneous Provisions) Act 1954 s 5(2) (amended by the Crime and Courts Act 2013 Sch 9 para 58(a)).

7   See the Agriculture (Miscellaneous Provisions) Act 1954 s 5(3) (amended by the Tribunals, Courts and Enforcement Act 2007 Sch 13 para 25; Crime and Courts Act 2013 Sch 9 para 58).

8   Agriculture (Miscellaneous Provisions) Act 1954 s 6(1) (s 6(1), (5), (6) substituted by SI 2013/1036). As to the Upper Tribunal see COURTS AND TRIBUNALS vol 24 (2010) PARA 874 et seq.

9   Agriculture (Miscellaneous Provisions) Act 1954 s 6(5) (as substituted: see note 7). An order made under the Agriculture Act 1947 s 73(3) must make such provision as necessary or expedient for enabling the chairman of the Upper Tribunal to exercise all or any of the tribunal's powers under the Agriculture (Miscellaneous Provisions) Act 1954 s 6(5), and for regulating any proceedings before the tribunal consequent on notification of the appeal or on the decision on such an appeal, and enabling any such proceedings to be dealt with by a tribunal constituted for that purpose, where they cannot conveniently be dealt with by the tribunal originally constituted for the purposes of the proceedings: s 6(6) (as so substituted). As to which see the Agricultural Land Tribunals (Rules) Order 2007, SI 2007/3105, Schedule Pt 5, r 38(1) (amended by SI 2013/1036).

10   See the Agriculture Act 1947 s 73, Sch 9.

11   See the Tribunals, Courts and Enforcement Act 2007 s 32, Sch 6 Pt 7; and COURTS AND TRIBUNALS vol 24 (2010) PARA 874 et seq. At the date at which this volume states the law no such order had been made in relation to Wales. As to orders made in relation to England see PARA 768.

768. Tribunals in England.

In relation to England[1], Agricultural Land Tribunals have been abolished and their functions transferred to the First-tier Tribunal[2]. Application to and proceedings of the First-tier Tribunal are regulated by rules[3].

Where, after the First-tier Tribunal has made a decision for the purposes of certain enactments[4], a party seeks permission to appeal, effect must not be given to the decision unless and until the Tribunal otherwise orders following the conclusion of the appeal; and the Tribunal may, in a case relating to a notice to quit, postpone (or further postpone) the date at which the tenancy is to be terminated by the notice, if it has effect[5].

1   As to the situation where land lies partly in Wales and partly in England see the Agriculture Act 1947 s 75(1); and PARA 767 note 1. As to the power to transfer functions from the Agricultural Land Tribunals for areas in England to the First-tier Tribunal or the Upper Tribunal see the Tribunals, Courts and Enforcement Act 2007 s 30, Sch 6 Pt 1; and COURTS AND TRIBUNALS vol 24 (2010) PARA 874 et seq.

2   See the Transfer of Tribunal Functions Order 2013, SI 2013/1036, art 3.

3   See the Tribunal Procedure (First-tier Tribunal) (Property Chamber) Rules 2013, SI 2013/1169.

4   Ie:
    (1)   the Agriculture (Miscellaneous Provisions) Act 1954;
    (2)   the Agriculture Act 1947;
    (3)   the Opencast Coal Act 1958;
    (4)   the Forestry Act 1967;
    (5)   the Land Compensation Act 1973 s 59 or 61;
    (6)   the Agricultural Holdings Act 1986 and regulations made under that Act;
    (7)   the Agriculture Act 1986;
    (8)   the Land Drainage Act 1991;
    (9)   the Agricultural Tenancies Act 1995;
    (10)   schemes under the Farm Land and Rural Development Act 1988 s 2;
    (11)   regulations under the European Communities Act 1972 s 2(2) in relation to Set-Aside of agricultural land: Agriculture (Miscellaneous Provisions) Act 1954 s 6A(2) (added by SI 2013/1036).

5   Agriculture (Miscellaneous Provisions) Act 1954 s 6A(1) (as added: see note 3).

INDEX

Agency

References are to paragraph numbers; superior figures refer to notes

References are to paragraph numbers; superior figures refer to notes

References are to paragraph numbers; superior figures refer to notes

References are to paragraph numbers; superior figures refer to notes

Agricultural Land and Allotments

References are to paragraph numbers; superior figures refer to notes

References are to paragraph numbers; superior figures refer to notes

References are to paragraph numbers; superior figures refer to notes

References are to paragraph numbers; superior figures refer to notes

References are to paragraph numbers; superior figures refer to notes